# DATABASE SYSTEM CONCEPTS

# McGraw-Hill Series in Computer Science

**Senior Consulting Editor**

*C.L. Liu, University of Illinois at Urbana-Champaign*

**Consulting Editor**

*Allen B. Tucker, Bowdoin College*

*Fundamentals of Computing and Programing*
*Computer Organization and Architecture*
*Computers in Society/Ethics*
*Systems and Languages*
*Theoretical Foundations*
*Software Engineering and Database*
*Artificial Intelligence*
*Networks, Parallel and Distributed Computing*
*Graphics and Visualization*
*The MIT Electrical and Computer Science Series*

## Software Engineering and Database

**Cohen:** *Ada as a Second Language*
**Fairley:** *Software Engineering Concepts*
**Silberschatz, Korth, and Sudarshan:** *Database System Concepts*
**Musa, Iannino, and Okumoto:** *Software Reliability*
**Pressman:** *Software Engineering: A Beginner's Guide*
**Pressman:** *Software Engineering: A Practitioner's Approach*
**Wiederhold:** *Database Design*

# DATABASE SYSTEM CONCEPTS
## Third Edition

**Abraham Silberschatz**

*Bell Laboratories*

**Henry F. Korth**

*Bell Laboratories*

**S. Sudarshan**

*Indian Institute of Technology, Bombay*

Boston, Massachusetts   Burr Ridge, Illinois   Dubuque, Iowa
Madison, Wisconsin   New York, New York   San Francisco, California   St. Louis, Missouri

# WCB/McGraw-Hill
## A Division of the *McGraw-Hill* Companies

DATABASE SYSTEM CONCEPTS, THIRD EDITION, THIRD PRINTING

This book is printed on acid-free paper.

4 5 6 7 8 9 0 DOC/DOC 1 0 9

ISBN 0-07-031086-6

The editor was Elizabeth A. Jones.
The production supervisor was Scott Hamilton.
The cover was designed by Christopher Brady.
R. R. Donnelley & Sons was printer and binder.

**Library of Congress Cataloging-in-Publication Data**
Silberschatz, Abraham.
     Database system concepts / Abraham Silberschatz, Henry F. Korth,
S. Sudarshan. – 3rd ed.
         p . cm. – (McGraw-Hill series in computer science)
     ISBN 0-07-031086-6 (acid-free paper)
     Includes bibliographical references and index.
     1. Database management. I. Korth, Henry F. II. Sudarshan, S.
III. Title. IV. Series
QA76.9.D3 S5637   1998
005.74—dc21                                                    98-13188

http://www.mhhe.com

*In memory of my father Joseph Silberschatz,*
*and my grandparents Stepha and Aaron Rosenblum*

*Avi Silberschatz*


*In memory of my grandparents:*
*Giuseppa and Anthony Affatigato and Gertrude and Frank Korth*

*Hank Korth*


*In memory of my grandfather, S. Mahalingam*

*S. Sudarshan*

# CONTENTS

# PREFACE

Database management has evolved from a specialized computer application to a central component of a modern computing environment. As such, knowledge about database systems has become an essential part of an education in computer science. Our purpose in this text is to present the fundamental concepts of database management. These concepts include aspects of database design, database languages, and database-system implementation.

This text is intended for a first course in databases at the junior or senior undergraduate, or first-year graduate, level. In addition to basic material for a first course, the text also contains advanced material that can be used for course supplements, or as introductory material for an advanced course.

We assume only a familiarity with basic data structures, computer organization, and a high-level (Pascal-like) programming language. Concepts are presented using intuitive descriptions, many of which are based on our running example of a bank enterprise. Important theoretical results are covered, but formal proofs are omitted. The bibliographic notes contain pointers to research papers in which results were first presented and proved, as well as references to material for further reading. In place of proofs, figures and examples are used to suggest why we should expect the result in question to be true.

The fundamental concepts and algorithms covered in the book are often based on those used in existing commercial or experimental database systems. Our aim is to present these concepts and algorithms in a general setting that is not tied to one particular database system.

In this third edition of *Database System Concepts*, we have retained the overall style of the first and second editions, while addressing the evolution of database management. Every chapter has been edited, and most have been modified extensively. We shall describe the changes in detail shortly.

# Organization

The text is organized in eight major parts, plus two appendices:

- **Overview** (Chapters 1 and 2). Chapter 1 provides a general overview of the nature and purpose of database systems. We explain how the concept of a database system has developed, what the common features of database systems are, what a database system does for the user, and how a database system interfaces with operating systems. We also introduce an example database application: a banking enterprise consisting of multiple bank branches. This example is used as a running example throughout the book. This chapter is motivational, historical, and explanatory in nature. Chapter 2 presents the entity–relationship model. This model provides a high-level view of the issues in database design, and of the problems that we encounter in capturing the semantics of realistic applications within the constraints of a data model.
- **Relational model** (Chapters 3 through 5). Chapter 3 focuses on the relational data model, covering the relevant relational algebra and relational calculus. Chapter 4 focuses on the most influential of the user-oriented relational languages: SQL. Chapter 5 covers other relational languages. These three chapters describe data manipulation: queries, updates, insertions, and deletions. Algorithms and design issues are deferred to later chapters. Thus, these chapters are suitable for those individuals or lower-level classes who want to learn what a database system is, without getting into the details of what the internal algorithms and structure are.
- **Database constraints** (Chapters 6 and 7). Chapter 6 presents constraints from the standpoint of database integrity; Chapter 7 shows how constraints can be used in the design of a relational database. Functional dependencies and referential integrity are presented in Chapter 6, as are mechanisms for integrity maintenance, such as triggers and assertions. The theme of this chapter is the protection of the database from accidental damage. Chapter 7 introduces the theory of relational database design. Such topics as normalization and data dependencies are covered, with emphasis on the motivation for each normal form and on the intuitive meaning of each type of data dependency.
- **Object-based systems** (Chapters 8 and 9). Chapter 8 covers object-oriented databases. It introduces the concepts of object-oriented programming, and shows how these concepts form the basis for a data model. No prior knowledge of object-oriented languages is assumed. Chapter 9 covers object-relational databases, and shows how we can extend the relational data model to include object-oriented features, such as inheritance and complex types.
- **Data storage and retrieval** (Chapters 10 through 12). Chapter 10 deals with disk, file, and file-system structure, and with the mapping of relational and object data to a file system. A variety of data-access techniques are presented in Chapter 11, including hashing, $B^+$-tree indices, and grid file indices. Chapter 12 addresses query-evaluation algorithms, and query optimization based on equivalence-preserving query transformations. These chapters are targeted

at people who want to gain an understanding of the internals of the storage and retrieval components of a database.

- **Transaction management** (Chapters 13 through 15). Chapter 13 focuses on the fundamentals of a transaction-processing system, including transaction atomicity, consistency, isolation, and durability, as well as the notion of serializability. It is suitable for those individuals or classes that need an introduction to the issues of transaction management, yet do not require the details of concurrency-control and recovery protocols. In Chapter 14, we focus on concurrency control, and present several techniques for ensuring serializability, including locking, timestamping, and optimistic (validation) techniques. Deadlock issues are also covered in that chapter. Chapter 15 covers the primary techniques for ensuring correct transaction execution despite system crashes and disk failures. These techniques include logs, shadow pages, checkpoints, and database dumps.

- **Parallel and distributed systems** (Chapters 16 through 18). Chapter 16 covers computer-system architecture, and describes the influence of the underlying computer system on the database system. We discuss centralized systems, client–server systems, parallel and distributed architectures, and network types. In Chapter 17, on parallel databases, we explore a variety of parallelizing techniques, including I/O parallelism, interquery and intraquery parallelism, and interoperation and intraoperation parallelism. We also discuss cost estimation, query optimization, and parallel-system design. Chapter 18 revisits issues of database design, transaction management, and query evaluation and optimization, in the context of a distributed database system.

- **Advanced topics** (Chapters 19 through 21). Chapter 19 covers numerous special topics, including security and integrity, standardization, performance benchmarks and performance tuning, time in databases, user interfaces, and active databases. Chapter 20 deals with advanced transaction processing. We discuss transaction-processing monitors, high-performance transaction systems, real-time transaction systems, and transactional workflows. In Chapter 21, we introduce numerous new applications for database systems. First, we discuss decision-support systems, including data-analysis, data-mining, and data-warehousing applications. We then examine spatial and geographic databases, multimedia databases, and mobile and personal databases. Finally, we investigate information-retrieval systems for textual data, and distributed information systems, including the World Wide Web.

- **Appendices**. Although most new database applications use either the relational model or the object-oriented model, the network and hierarchical data models are still in use. As we did in the second edition, we have covered systems based on the network and hierarchical models in Appendices A and B, respectively. However, due to a decline in interest in teaching these older models, the full text of these appendices has been moved to the internet, with only a summary appearing in the printed text. The full version of the appendices is available on the web (http://www.bell-labs.com/topic/books/db-book) or via anonymous FTP from ftp.research.bell-labs.com in directory dist/db-book.

# The Third Edition

Many comments and suggestions were forwarded to us concerning the first and second editions. These inputs — coupled with our own observations while teaching at the University of Texas, IIT Bombay, and IBM, and with our analysis of the directions in which database technology is evolving — have prodded us to produce this third edition, and have guided us in its production. Our basic procedure was to rewrite the material in each chapter, bringing the older material up to date, adding discussions on recent developments in database technology, improving the exercises, and adding new references. We have also restructured the organization of parts of the book. For the benefit of those readers familiar with the second edition, we explain the main changes here.

- **Entity–Relationship model**. We have improved our coverage of the entity–relationship (E-R) model. Chapter 2 in the third edition is similar to the previous Chapter 2; however, we have expanded coverage of issues in E-R database design. Design issues are discussed throughout the chapter, and are addressed in particular in two new sections, 2.2 and 2.8. Extended E-R features are discussed in more detail than in the second edition, as is reduction of an E-R schema to tables (Sections 2.7 and 2.9, respectively).

- **Relational databases**. In the second edition, we expanded our coverage of the relational model. In the third edition, we again devote Chapter 3 to the relational model and to the formal relational languages: the relational algebra and the relational calculus. In Section 3.5, we have added discussions of the generalized projection, outer-join operations, and aggregation. Chapter 4 now covers SQL exclusively. Our coverage of SQL has been significantly expanded to include features of the SQL-92 standard, in addition to the existing coverage based on the SQL-89. Some SQL implementations may support only SQL-89 and not SQL-92; we explicitly identify those features of SQL-92 that are not supported in SQL-89. We now cover QBE, and Quel, in Chapter 5. The research language Datalog, which had been presented in the second edition in Chapter 14, is included now in Chapter 5, and receives a more detailed discussion. Chapter 6 covers integrity constraints; Chapter 7 covers database-design issues and normal forms. These chapters were Chapters 5 and 6, respectively, in the second edition.

- **Object-based databases**. Expansions to our coverage of the object-oriented data model appear in Chapters 8, 9, and 10. In Chapter 8, we augment the material from Chapter 13 in the second edition with a discussion of object-oriented programming languages. Chapter 9 is a new chapter in which we present object-relational data models. These models extend the relational data model by providing a richer type system, including object orientation, and add constructs to relational query languages, such as SQL, to deal with the added data types. Chapter 10 now includes a section on the storage structures for object-oriented databases (Section 10.9).

- **Query processing**. Our treatment of query processing has been greatly expanded from the second edition. In Chapter 12, we now present detailed explanations of what different ways we have for implementing various relational operations, and of how to estimate their execution costs. We have also expanded our coverage of query transformations that preserve equivalence of the query results, and have incorporated new material on query optimization. Chapter 17 now has expanded coverage of parallel query processing.

- **Transaction processing**. As we did for the second edition, we have reorganized and slightly expanded our coverage of transaction processing (Chapters 13 through 15). Some of the advanced material on transaction processing from Chapter 12 in the second edition is now organized in a new chapter on advanced transaction processing: Chapter 20 (see the note on advanced topics that follows). Chapter 13 introduces issues in all aspects of transaction management, with details deferred to later chapters. This organization allows instructors to choose between just introducing transaction-processing concepts (by covering only Chapter 13), or offering detailed coverage (based on Chapters 13 through 15).

- **Computer architectures and parallel systems**. Chapter 16 is a new chapter that covers computer-system architecture and the influence of the underlying computer system on the database system. We discuss centralized systems, client–server systems, and network types. We also present parallel and distributed architectures; we cover these systems in detail in Chapters 17 and 18, respectively. Chapter 17 is also a new chapter; it covers parallel databases. We explore a variety of parallelizing techniques, including I/O parallelism, interquery and intraquery parallelism, and interoperation and intraoperation parallelism. We also discuss cost evaluation, query optimization, and parallel-system design. New material on disk organization based on the RAID architectures is included in Chapter 10.

- **Advanced topics**. Although we have modified and updated the entire text, we concentrate our presentation of material pertaining to ongoing database research and new database applications in three new chapters.

    We present numerous special topics in Chapter 19. Chapter 16 in the second edition on security and integrity, now appears as Section 19.1. The remaining sections are new material pertaining to standardization projects, performance benchmarks, performance tuning, time in databases, user interfaces, and active databases.

    Some of the material on transaction processing in Chapter 20 appeared previously in Chapter 12 in the second edition; Section 20.1 on transaction processing monitors, Section 20.2 on high-performance transaction systems, Section 20.4 on real-time transaction systems, and Section 20.6 on transactional workflows are all new.

    In Chapter 21, we introduce several new applications for database systems; the material in this chapter is all new. First, we discuss decision-support systems, including data-analysis, data-mining, and data-warehousing applications. We then discuss spatial and geographic databases, multimedia databases, and mobile and personal databases. Finally, we discuss information-retrieval systems for textual data, and distributed information systems, including the World Wide Web.

## Instructor's Note

The book contains both basic and advanced material, which might not be covered in a single semester. It is possible to design courses using various subsets of the chapters. We outline possibilities here:

- Chapter 5 can be omitted if students will not be using QBE, Quel, or Datalog as part of the course.
- Chapter 7 contains a series of normal forms, in decreasing order of practical importance. Later sections (Section 7.4 on) may be omitted, if desired.
- If object-orientation is to be covered in a separate advanced course, Chapters 8 and 9, and Section 10.9, can be omitted. Alternatively, they could constitute the foundation of an advanced course in object databases.
- Chapters 11 and 12 contain some material that may be more suitable for an advanced course. You might choose to omit some or all of Sections 11.6, 11.9, 12.7, 12.8, and 12.10.
- Both our coverage of transaction processing (Chapters 13 through 15) and our coverage of database-system architecture (Chapters 16 through 18) consist of an overview chapter (Chapters 13 and 16, respectively), followed by chapters with details. You might choose to use Chapters 13 and 16, while omitting Chapters 14, 15, 17, and 18, if you defer these latter chapters to an advanced course.
- The sections of the final three chapters (Chapters 19 through 21) are largely independent. Based on instructor or student interest, a custom-tailored set of subsections may be chosen as end-of-semester enrichment material. Those chapters as a whole are suitable for an advanced topics course.

Model course syllabi, based on the text, can be found on the World Wide Web home page of the book (see following section).

## Supplements and Mailing List

For information about the teaching supplements that complement this book, send electronic mail to wcbcomp@mcgraw-hill.com. In the United States, you may call 800-338-3987. The McGraw-Hill web page for Computer Science texts is http://www.mhhe.com/engcs/compsci.

We also now provide an environment in which users can communicate among themselves and with us. We have created a mailing list consisting of users of our book with the electronic mail address db-book@research.bell-labs.com. If you wish to be on the list, please send a message to db-book@research.bell-labs.com, include your name, affiliation, title, and electronic mail address.

# Home Page

A World Wide Web home page for the book is available with the URL:

http://www.bell-labs.com/topic/books/db-book

The home page contains information about the book, such as up-to-date errata, model course syllabi, and information about teaching supplements.

# Errata

We have endeavored to eliminate typos, bugs, and the like from the text. But, as in new releases of software, bugs probably remain. We would appreciate it if you would notify us of any errors or omissions in the book. An updated errata page will be accessible from the book's WWW home page. Also, if you would like to suggest improvements or to contribute exercises, we would be glad to hear from you. Any correspondence should be sent to Avi Silberschatz, Bell Laboratories, Lucent Technologies Inc., 700 Mountain Avenue, Murray Hill, NJ 07974, USA. Internet electronic mail should be addressed to db-book@research.bell-labs.com.

# Acknowledgments

This edition is based on the two previous editions, so we thank once again the many people who helped us with the first and second editions, including Don Batory, Haran Boral, Robert Brazile, Sara Strandtman, Won Kim, Anil Nigam, Bruce Porter, Carol Kroll, Jim Peterson, Fletcher Mattox, Ron Hitchens, Alberto Mendelzon, Alan Fekete, Hyoung-Joo Kim, Keith Marzullo, Mark Roth, Greg Speegle, and Henry Korth (father of Henry F.)

Greg Speegle and Dawn Bezviner helped us to prepare the instructor's manual for the first edition. Their work served as the basis for the new instructor's manual for the third edition, which was prepared with the help of K. V. Raghavan.

This edition has benefited from the many useful comments provided to us by the numerous students who have used the second edition in our classes at the University of Texas and at IBM, or have used drafts of the third edition at IIT Bombay. In addition, numerous people have written or spoken to us about the book, and have offered suggestions and comments. Although we cannot mention all these people here, we especially thank R. B. Abhyankar, Paul Bourgeois, Michael Carey, J. Edwards, Christos Faloutsos, Homma Farian, Shashi Gadia, Jim Gray, Le Gruenwald, Yannis Ioannidis, Gary Lindstrom, Dave Maier, Hector Garcia-Molina, Ami Motro, Cyril Orji, K. V. Raghavan, Marek Rusinkiewicz, S. Seshadri, Shashi Shekhar, Amit Sheth, Nandit Soparkar, and Marianne Winslett.

Lyn Dupré copyedited the book. Sara Strandtman edited our text into the LATEXformat, and helped us prepare the revised text for this edition. Sara also edited the instructor's manual and transparencies.

The new cover—an evolution of the covers of the first two editions—was drawn by Chris Brady of McGraw-Hill. Marilyn Turnamian created an early draft of the cover design. The idea of using ships as part of the cover concept was originally suggested to us by Bruce Stephan. We would also like to thank our editor, Eric Munson, for his wisdom and patience.

Finally, Sudarshan would like to acknowledge his brother, Mohan, and mother, Indira, for their support. Hank would like to acknowledge his wife, Joan, and his children, Abby and Joe, for their love and understanding. Avi would like to acknowledge his mother for her love and support.

A. S.

H. F. K.

S. S.

# CHAPTER

# 1

# INTRODUCTION

A *database-management system* (DBMS) consists of a collection of interrelated data and a set of programs to access those data. The collection of data, usually referred to as the *database*, contains information about one particular enterprise. The primary goal of a DBMS is to provide an environment that is both *convenient* and *efficient* to use in retrieving and storing database information.

Database systems are designed to manage large bodies of information. The management of data involves both the definition of structures for the storage of information and the provision of mechanisms for the manipulation of information. In addition, the database system must provide for the safety of the information stored, despite system crashes or attempts at unauthorized access. If data are to be shared among several users, the system must avoid possible anomalous results.

The importance of information in most organizations—which determines the value of the database—has led to the development of a large body of concepts and techniques for the efficient management of data. In this chapter, we present a brief introduction to the principles of database systems.

## 1.1 Purpose of Database Systems

Consider part of a savings-bank enterprise that keeps information about all customers and savings accounts. One way to keep the information on a computer is to store it in permanent system files. To allow users to manipulate the information, the system has a number of application programs that manipulate the files, including

- A program to debit or credit an account
- A program to add a new account

1

- A program to find the balance of an account
- A program to generate monthly statements

These application programs have been written by system programmers in response to the needs of the bank organization.

New application programs are added to the system as the need arises. For example, suppose that new government regulations allow the savings bank to offer checking accounts. As a result, new permanent files are created that contain information about all the checking accounts maintained in the bank, and new application programs may need to be written to deal with situations that do not arise in savings accounts, such as handling overdrafts. Thus, as time goes by, more files and more application programs are added to the system.

The typical *file-processing system* just described is supported by a conventional operating system. Permanent records are stored in various files, and different application programs are written to extract records from, and to add records to, the appropriate files. Before the advent of DBMSs, organizations typically stored information using such systems.

Keeping organizational information in a file-processing system has a number of major disadvantages

- **Data redundancy and inconsistency**. Since the files and application programs are created by different programmers over a long period, the various files are likely to have different formats and the programs may be written in several programming languages. Moreover, the same information may be duplicated in several places (files). For example, the address and telephone number of a particular customer may appear in a file that consists of savings-account records and in a file that consists of checking-account records. This redundancy leads to higher storage and access cost. In addition, it may lead to *data inconsistency*; that is, the various copies of the same data may no longer agree. For example, a changed customer address may be reflected in savings-account records but not elsewhere in the system.
- **Difficulty in accessing data**. Suppose that one of the bank officers needs to find out the names of all customers who live within the city's 78733 zip code. The officer asks the data-processing department to generate such a list. Because this request was not anticipated when the original system was designed, there is no application program on hand to meet it. There is, however, an application program to generate the list of *all* customers. The bank officer has now two choices: Either obtain the list of all customers and have the needed information extracted manually, or ask the data-processing department to have a system programmer write the necessary application program. Both alternatives are obviously unsatisfactory. Suppose that such a program is written, and that, several days later, the same officer needs to trim that list to include only those customers who have an account balance of $10,000 or more. As expected, a program to generate such a list does not exist. Again, the officer has the preceding two options, neither of which is satisfactory.

The point here is that conventional file-processing environments do not allow needed data to be retrieved in a convenient and efficient manner. More responsive data-retrieval systems must be developed for general use.

- **Data isolation**. Because data are scattered in various files, and files may be in different formats, it is difficult to write new application programs to retrieve the appropriate data.

- **Integrity problems**. The data values stored in the database must satisfy certain types of *consistency constraints*. For example, the balance of a bank account may never fall below a prescribed amount (say, $25). Developers enforce these constraints in the system by adding appropriate code in the various application programs. However, when new constraints are added, it is difficult to change the programs to enforce them. The problem is compounded when constraints involve several data items from different files.

- **Atomicity problems**. A computer system, like any other mechanical or electrical device, is subject to failure. In many applications, it is crucial to ensure that, once a failure has occurred and has been detected, the data are restored to the consistent state that existed prior to the failure. Consider a program to transfer $50 from account $A$ to $B$. If a system failure occurs during the execution of the program, it is possible that the $50 was removed from account $A$ but was not credited to account $B$, resulting in an inconsistent database state. Clearly, it is essential to database consistency that either both the credit and debit occur, or that neither occur. That is, the funds transfer must be *atomic*— it must happen in its entirety or not at all. It is difficult to ensure this property in a conventional file-processing system.

- **Concurrent-access anomalies**. So that the overall performance of the system is improved and a faster response time is possible, many systems allow multiple users to update the data simultaneously. In such an environment, interaction of concurrent updates may result in inconsistent data. Consider bank account $A$, containing $500. If two customers withdraw funds (say $50 and $100 respectively) from account $A$ at about the same time, the result of the concurrent executions may leave the account in an incorrect (or inconsistent) state. Suppose that the programs executing on behalf of each withdrawal read the old balance, reduce that value by the amount being withdrawn, and write the result back. If the two programs run concurrently, they may both read the value $500, and write back $450 and $400, respectively. Depending on which one writes the value last, the account may contain either $450 or $400, rather than the correct value of $350. To guard against this possibility, the system must maintain some form of supervision. Because data may be accessed by many different application programs that have not been coordinated previously, however, supervision is difficult to provide.

- **Security problems**. Not every user of the database system should be able to access all the data. For example, in a banking system, payroll personnel need to see only that part of the database that has information about the various bank employees. They do not need access to information about customer accounts. Since application programs are added to the system in an ad hoc manner, it is difficult to enforce such security constraints.

These difficulties, among others, have prompted the development of DBMSs. In what follows, we shall see the concepts and algorithms that have been developed for database systems to solve the problems mentioned. In most of this book, we use a bank enterprise as a running example of a typical data-processing application found in a corporation. A typical data-processing application stores a large number of records, each of which is fairly simple and small.

In Chapters 8 and 9, we consider different classes of database applications, such as interactive design applications. Applications in these categories typically deal with more complex and larger records, such as a complete building design, but there are fewer records. There is a substantial amount of research and development work underway to provide database systems that are both sufficiently powerful and sufficiently flexible to manage these applications.

## 1.2   View of Data

A DBMS is a collection of interrelated files and a set of programs that allow users to access and modify these files. A major purpose of a database system is to provide users with an *abstract* view of the data. That is, the system hides certain details of how the data are stored and maintained.

### 1.2.1   Data Abstraction

For the system to be usable, it must retrieve data efficiently. This concern has led to the design of complex data structures for the representation of data in the database. Since many database-systems users are not computer trained, developers hide the complexity from users through several levels of abstraction, to simplify users' interactions with the system:

- **Physical level**. The lowest level of abstraction describes *how* the data are actually stored. At the physical level, complex low-level data structures are described in detail.

- **Logical level**. The next-higher level of abstraction describes *what* data are stored in the database, and what relationships exist among those data. The entire database is thus described in terms of a small number of relatively simple structures. Although implementation of the simple structures at the logical level may involve complex physical-level structures, the user of the logical level does not need to be aware of this complexity. The logical level of abstraction is used by database administrators, who must decide what information is to be kept in the database.

- **View level**. The highest level of abstraction describes only part of the entire database. Despite the use of simpler structures at the logical level, some complexity remains, because of the large size of the database. Many users of the database system will not be concerned with all this information. Instead, such

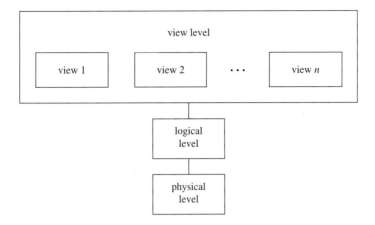

Figure 1.1 The three levels of data abstraction.

users need to access only a part of the database. So that their interaction with the system is simplified, the view level of abstraction is defined. The system may provide many views for the same database.

The interrelationship among these three levels of abstraction is illustrated in Figure 1.1.

An analogy to the concept of data types in programming languages may clarify the distinction among levels of abstraction. Most high-level programming languages support the notion of a record type. For example, in a Pascal-like language, we may declare a record as follows:

**type** *customer* = **record**
     *customer-name* : string;
     *social-security* : string;
     *customer-street* : string;
     *customer-city* : string;
   **end**;

This code defines a new record called *customer* with four fields. Each field has a name and a type associated with it. A banking enterprise may have several such record types, including

- *account*, with fields *account-number* and *balance*
- *employee*, with fields *employee-name* and *salary*

At the physical level, a *customer*, *account*, or *employee* record can be described as a block of consecutive storage locations (for example, words or bytes). The language compiler hides this level of detail from programmers. Similarly, the database system hides many of the lowest-level storage details from database programmers. Database administrators may be aware of certain details of the physical organization of the data.

At the logical level, each such record is described by a type definition, as illustrated in the previous code segment, and the interrelationship among these record types is defined. Programmers using a programming language work at this level of abstraction. Similarly, database administrators usually work at this level of abstraction.

Finally, at the view level, computer users see a set of application programs that hide details of the data types. Similarly, at the view level, several views of the database are defined, and database users see these views. In addition to hiding details of the logical level of the database, the views also provide a security mechanism to prevent users from accessing parts of the database. For example, tellers in a bank see only that part of the database that has information on customer accounts; they cannot access information concerning salaries of employees.

## 1.2.2    Instances and Schemas

Databases change over time as information is inserted and deleted. The collection of information stored in the database at a particular moment is called an *instance* of the database. The overall design of the database is called the database *schema*. Schemas are changed infrequently, if at all.

Analogies to the concepts of data types, variables, and values in programming languages is useful here. Returning to the *customer*-record type definition, note that, in declaring the type *customer*, we have *not* declared any variables. To declare such variables in a Pascal-like language, we write

$$\textbf{var } customer1 : customer;$$

Variable *customer*1 now corresponds to an area of storage containing a *customer* type record.

A database schema corresponds to the programming-language type definition. A variable of a given type has a particular value at a given instant. Thus, the value of a variable in programming languages corresponds to an *instance* of a database schema.

Database systems have several schemas, partitioned according to the levels of abstraction that we discussed. At the lowest level is the *physical schema*; at the intermediate level is the *logical schema*; and at the highest level is a *subschema*. In general, database systems support one physical schema, one logical schema, and several subschemas.

## 1.2.3    Data Independence

The ability to modify a schema definition in one level without affecting a schema definition in the next higher level is called *data independence*. There are two levels of data independence:

1. **Physical data independence** is the ability to modify the physical schema without causing application programs to be rewritten. Modifications at the physical level are occasionally necessary to improve performance.

2. **Logical data independence** is the ability to modify the logical schema without causing application programs to be rewritten. Modifications at the logical level are necessary whenever the logical structure of the database is altered (for example, when money-market accounts are added to a banking system).

Logical data independence is more difficult to achieve than is physical data independence, since application programs are heavily dependent on the logical structure of the data that they access.

The concept of data independence is similar in many respects to the concept of *abstract data types* in modern programming languages. Both hide implementation details from the users, to allow users to concentrate on the general structure, rather than on low-level implementation details.

# 1.3    Data Models

Underlying the structure of a database is the *data model*: a collection of conceptual tools for describing data, data relationships, data semantics, and consistency constraints. The various data models that have been proposed fall into three different groups: object-based logical models, record-based logical models, and physical models.

## 1.3.1    Object-Based Logical Models

Object-based logical models are used in describing data at the logical and view levels. They are characterized by the fact that they provide fairly flexible structuring capabilities and allow data constraints to be specified explicitly. There are many different models, and more are likely to come. Several of the more widely known ones are

- The entity–relationship model
- The object-oriented model
- The semantic data model
- The functional data model

In this book, we examine the *entity–relationship model* and the *object-oriented model* as representatives of the class of the object-based logical models. The entity–relationship model, explored in Chapter 2, has gained acceptance in database design and is widely used in practice. The object-oriented model, examined in Chapter 8, includes many of the concepts of the entity–relationship model, but represents executable code as well as data. It is rapidly gaining acceptance in practice. We shall give brief descriptions of both models next.

### 1.3.1.1    The Entity–Relationship Model

The entity–relationship (E-R) data model is based on a perception of a real world that consists of a collection of basic objects, called *entities*, and of *relationships*

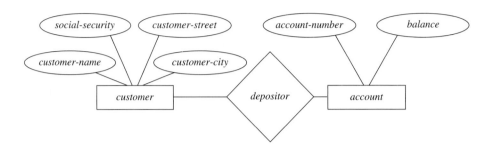

Figure 1.2    A sample E-R diagram.

among these objects. An entity is a "thing" or "object" in the real world that is distinguishable from other objects. For example, each person is an entity, and bank accounts can be considered to be entities. Entities are described in a database by a set of *attributes*. For example, the attributes *account-number* and *balance* describe one particular account in a bank. A *relationship* is an association among several entities. For example, a *Depositor* relationship associates a customer with each account that she has. The set of all entities of the same type, and the set of all relationships of the same type, are termed an *entity set* and *relationship set*, respectively.

In addition to entities and relationships, the E-R model represents certain constraints to which the contents of a database must conform. One important constraint is *mapping cardinalities*, which express the number of entities to which another entity can be associated via a relationship set.

The overall logical structure of a database can be expressed graphically by an *E-R diagram*, which is built up from the following components:

- **Rectangles**, which represent entity sets
- **Ellipses**, which represent attributes
- **Diamonds**, which represent relationships among entity sets
- **Lines**, which link attributes to entity sets and entity sets to relationships

Each component is labeled with the entity or relationship that it represents.

As an illustration, consider part of a database banking system consisting of customers and of the accounts that these customers have. The corresponding E-R diagram is shown in Figure 1.2. This example is extended in Chapter 2.

### 1.3.1.2    The Object-Oriented Model

Like the E-R model, the object-oriented model is based on a collection of objects. An object contains values stored in *instance variables* within the object. An object also contains bodies of code that operate on the object. These bodies of code are called *methods*.

Objects that contain the same types of values and the same methods are grouped together into *classes*. A class may be viewed as a type definition for objects. This combination of data and methods comprising a type definition is similar to a programming-language abstract data type.

The only way in which one object can access the data of another object is by invoking a method of that other object. This action is called *sending a message* to the object. Thus, the call interface of the methods of an object defines that object's externally visible part. The internal part of the object—the instance variables and method code—are not visible externally. The result is two levels of data abstraction.

To illustrate the concept, let us consider an object representing a bank account. Such an object contains instance variables *account-number* and *balance*. It contains a method *pay-interest*, which adds interest to the balance. Assume that the bank had been paying 6-percent interest on all accounts, but now is changing its policy to pay 5 percent if the balance is less than $1000 or 6 percent if the balance is $1000 or greater. Under most data models, making this adjustment would involve changing code in one or more application programs. Under the object-oriented model, the only change is made within the *pay-interest* method. The external interface to the objects remains unchanged.

Unlike entities in the E-R model, each object has its own unique identity, independent of the values that it contains. Thus, two objects containing the same values are nevertheless distinct. The distinction among individual objects is maintained in the physical level through the assignment of distinct object identifiers.

## 1.3.2   Record-Based Logical Models

Record-based logical models are used in describing data at the logical and view levels. In contrast to object-based data models, they are used both to specify the overall logical structure of the database and to provide a higher-level description of the implementation.

Record-based models are so named because the database is structured in fixed-format records of several types. Each record type defines a fixed number of fields, or attributes, and each field is usually of a fixed length. As we shall see in Chapter 10, the use of fixed-length records simplifies the physical-level implementation of the database. This simplicity is in contrast to many of the object-based models, whose richer structure often leads to variable-length records at the physical level.

The three most widely accepted record-based data models are the relational, network, and hierarchical models. The relational model, which has gained favor over the other two in recent years, is examined in detail in Chapters 3 through 7. The network and hierarchical models, still used in a large number of older databases, are described in the appendices. Here, we present a brief overview of each model.

### 1.3.2.1   Relational Model

The relational model uses a collection of tables to represent both data and the relationships among those data. Each table has multiple columns, and each column has a unique name. Figure 1.3 presents a sample relational database comprising of two tables: one shows bank customers, and the other shows the accounts that belong to those customers. It shows, for example, that customer Johnson, with

| customer-name | social-security | customer-street | customer-city | account-number |
|:---:|:---:|:---:|:---:|:---:|
| Johnson | 192-83-7465 | Alma | Palo Alto | A-101 |
| Smith | 019-28-3746 | North | Rye | A-215 |
| Hayes | 677-89-9011 | Main | Harrison | A-102 |
| Turner | 182-73-6091 | Putnam | Stamford | A-305 |
| Johnson | 192-83-7465 | Alma | Palo Alto | A-201 |
| Jones | 321-12-3123 | Main | Harrison | A-217 |
| Lindsay | 336-66-9999 | Park | Pittsfield | A-222 |
| Smith | 019-28-3746 | North | Rye | A-201 |

| account-number | balance |
|:---:|:---:|
| A-101 | 500 |
| A-215 | 700 |
| A-102 | 400 |
| A-305 | 350 |
| A-201 | 900 |
| A-217 | 750 |
| A-222 | 700 |

Figure 1.3    A sample relational database.

social-security number 192-83-7465, lives on Alma in Palo Alto, and has two accounts: A-101, with a balance of $500, and A-201, with a balance of $900. Note that customers Johnson and Smith share account number A-201 (they may share a business venture).

### 1.3.2.2   Network Model

Data in the network model are represented by collections of *records* (in the Pascal sense), and relationships among data are represented by *links*, which can be viewed as pointers. The records in the database are organized as collections of arbitrary graphs. Figure 1.4 presents a sample network database using the same information as in Figure 1.3.

### 1.3.2.3   Hierarchical Model

The hierarchical model is similar to the network model in the sense that data and relationships among data are represented by records and links, respectively. It differs from the network model in that the records are organized as collections of trees rather than arbitrary graphs. Figure 1.5 presents a sample hierarchical database with the same information as in Figure 1.4.

### 1.3.2.4   Differences Among the Models

The relational model differs from the network and hierarchical models in that it does not use pointers or links. Instead, the relational model relates records by the

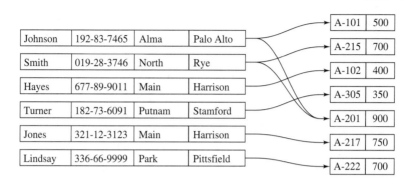

Figure 1.4    A sample network database.

values that they contain. This freedom from the use of pointers allows a formal mathematical foundation to be defined.

### 1.3.3    Physical Data Models

Physical data models are used to describe data at the lowest level. In contrast to logical data models, there are few physical data models in use. Two of the widely known ones are the *unifying model* and the *frame-memory model*.

Physical data models capture aspects of database-system implementation that are not covered in this book.

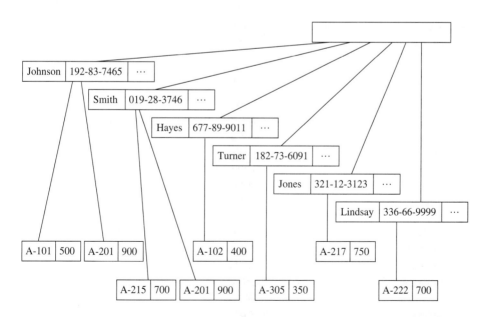

Figure 1.5    A sample hierarchical database.

# 1.4    Database Languages

A database system provides two different types of languages: one to specify the database schema, and the other to express database queries and updates.

## 1.4.1    Data-Definition Language

A database schema is specified by a set of definitions expressed by a special language called a *data-definition language* (DDL). The result of compilation of DDL statements is a set of tables that is stored in a special file called *data dictionary*, or *data directory*.

A data dictionary is a file that contains *metadata*—that is, data about data. This file is consulted before actual data are read or modified in the database system.

The storage structure and access methods used by the database system are specified by a set of definitions in a special type of DDL called a *data storage and definition* language. The result of compilation of these definitions is a set of instructions to specify the implementation details of the database schemas—details are usually hidden from the users.

## 1.4.2    Data-Manipulation Language

The levels of abstraction that we discussed in Section 1.2 apply not only to the definition or structuring of data, but also to the manipulation of data. By *data manipulation*, we mean

- The retrieval of information stored in the database
- The insertion of new information into the database
- The deletion of information from the database
- The modification of information stored in the database

At the physical level, we must define algorithms that allow efficient access to data. At higher levels of abstraction, we emphasize ease of use. The goal is to provide efficient human interaction with the system.

A *data-manipulation language* (DML) is a language that enables users to access or manipulate data as organized by the appropriate data model. There are basically two types:

- **Procedural DMLs** require a user to specify *what* data are needed and *how* to get those data.
- **Nonprocedural DMLs** require a user to specify *what* data are needed *without* specifying how to get those data.

Nonprocedural DMLs are usually easier to learn and use than are procedural DMLs. However, since a user does not have to specify how to get the data, these languages may generate code that is not as efficient as that produced by procedural languages. We can remedy this difficulty through various optimization techniques, several of which we discuss in Chapter 12.

A *query* is a statement requesting the retrieval of information. The portion of a DML that involves information retrieval is called a *query language*. Although technically incorrect, it is common practice to use the terms *query language* and *data-manipulation language* synonymously.

## 1.5  Transaction Management

Often, several operations on the database form a single logical unit of work. An example that we saw earlier is a funds transfer, in which one account (say *A*) is debited and another account (say *B*) is credited. Clearly, it is essential that either both the credit and debit occur, or that neither occur. That is, the funds transfer must happen in its entirety or not at all. This all-or-none requirement is called *atomicity*. In addition, it is essential that the execution of the fund transfer preserve the consistency of the database. That is, the value of the sum $A + B$ must be preserved. This correctness requirement is called *consistency*. Finally, after the successful execution of a funds transfer, the new values of accounts *A* and *B* must persist, despite the possibility of system failure. This persistency requirement is called *durability*.

A *transaction* is a collection of operations that performs a single logical function in a database application. Each transaction is a unit of both atomicity and consistency. Thus, we require that transactions do not violate any database-consistency constraints. That is, if the database was consistent when a transaction started, the database must be consistent when the transaction successfully termi- nates. However, during the execution of a transaction, it may be necessary tem- porarily to allow inconsistency. This temporary inconsistency, although necessary, may lead to difficulty if a failure occurs.

It is the responsibility of the programmer to define properly the various transactions, such that each preserves the consistency of the database. For exam- ple, the transaction to transfer funds from account *A* to account *B* could be defined to be composed of two separate programs: one that debits account *A*, and another that credits account *B*. The execution of these two programs one after the other will indeed preserve consistency. However, each program by itself does not trans- form the database from a consistent state to a new consistent state. Thus, those programs are not transactions.

Ensuring the atomicity and durability properties is the responsibility of the database system itself—specifically, of the *transaction-management component*. In the absence of failures, all transactions complete successfully, and atomicity is achieved easily. However, due to various types of failure, a transaction may not always complete its execution successfully. If we are to ensure the atomicity property, a failed transaction must have no effect on the state of the database. Thus, the database must be restored to the state in which it was before the transaction in question started executing. It is the responsibility of the database system to detect system failures and to restore the database to a state that existed prior to the occurrence of the failure.

Finally, when several transactions update the database concurrently, the consistency of data may no longer be preserved, even though each individual transaction is correct. It is the responsibility of the *concurrency-control manager* to control the interaction among the concurrent transactions, to ensure the consistency of the database.

Database systems designed for use on small personal computers may not have all the features noted. For example, many small systems impose the restriction of only one user being allowed to access the database at a time. Others leave the tasks of backup and recovery to the user. This setup allows for a smaller data manager, with fewer requirements for physical resources—especially main memory. Although such a low-cost, low-feature approach is sufficient for small personal databases, it is inadequate to meet the needs of a medium- to large-scale enterprise.

## 1.6    Storage Management

Databases typically require a large amount of storage space. Corporate databases are usually measured in terms of *gigabytes* or, for the largest databases, *terabytes* of data. A gigabyte is 1000 megabytes (1 billion bytes), and a terabyte is 1 million megabytes (1 trillion bytes). Since the main memory of computers cannot store this much information, the information is stored on disks. Data are moved between disk storage and main memory as needed. Since the movement of data to and from disk is slow relative to the speed of the central processing unit, it is imperative that the database system structure the data so as to minimize the need to move data between disk and main memory.

The goal of a database system is to simplify and facilitate access to data. High-level views help to achieve this goal. Users of the system should not be burdened unnecessarily with the physical details of the implementation of the system. Nevertheless, a major factor in a user's satisfaction or lack thereof with a database system is that system's performance. If the response time for a request is too long, the value of the system is diminished. The performance of a system depends on what the efficiency is of the data structures used to represent the data in the database, and on how efficiently the system is able to operate on these data structures. As is the case elsewhere in computer systems, a tradeoff must be made not only between space and time, but also between the efficiency of one kind of operation and that of another.

A *storage manager* is a program module that provides the interface between the low-level data stored in the database and the application programs and queries submitted to the system. The storage manager is responsible for the interaction with the file manager. The raw data are stored on the disk using the file system, which is usually provided by a conventional operating system. The storage manager translates the various DML statements into low-level file-system commands. Thus, the storage manager is responsible for storing, retrieving, and updating of data in the database.

## 1.7   Database Administrator

One of the main reasons for using DBMSs is to have central control of both the data and the programs that access those data. The person who has such central control over the system is called the *database administrator* (DBA). The functions of the DBA include the following:

- **Schema definition**. The DBA creates the original database schema by writing a set of definitions that is translated by the DDL compiler to a set of tables that is stored permanently in the *data dictionary*.

- **Storage structure and access-method definition**. The DBA creates appropriate storage structures and access methods by writing a set of definitions, which is translated by the data-storage and data-definition–language compiler.

- **Schema and physical-organization modification**. Programmers accomplish the relatively rare modifications either to the database schema or to the description of the physical storage organization by writing a set of definitions that is used by either the DDL compiler or the data-storage and data-definition–language compiler to generate modifications to the appropriate internal system tables (for example, the data dictionary).

- **Granting of authorization for data access**. The granting of different types of authorization allows the database administrator to regulate which parts of the database various users can access. The authorization information is kept in a special system structure that is consulted by the database system whenever access to the data is attempted in the system.

- **Integrity-constraint specification**. The data values stored in the database must satisfy certain consistency constraints. For example, perhaps the number of hours an employee may work in 1 week may not exceed a specified limit (say, 80 hours). Such a constraint must be specified explicitly by the database administrator. The integrity constraints are kept in a special system structure that is consulted by the database system whenever an update takes place in the system.

## 1.8   Database Users

A primary goal of a database system is to provide an environment for retrieving information from and storing new information into the database. There are four different types of database-system users, differentiated by the way that they expect to interact with the system.

- **Application programmers** are computer professionals who interact with the system through DML calls, which are embedded in a program written in a *host* language (for example, Cobol, PL/I, Pascal, C). These programs are commonly referred to as *application programs*. Examples in a banking system include programs that generate payroll checks, that debit accounts, that credit accounts, or that transfer funds between accounts.

Since the DML syntax is usually markedly different from the host language syntax, DML calls are usually prefaced by a special character so that the appropriate code can be generated. A special preprocessor, called the *DML precompiler*, converts the DML statements to normal procedure calls in the host language. The resulting program is then run through the host-language compiler, which generates appropriate object code.

There are special types of programming languages that combine control structures of Pascal-like languages with control structures for the manipulation of a database object (for example, relations). These languages, sometimes called *fourth-generation languages*, often include special features to facilitate the generation of forms and the display of data on the screen. Most major commercial database systems include a fourth-generation language.

- **Sophisticated users** interact with the system without writing programs. Instead, they form their requests in a database query language. Each such query is submitted to a *query processor* whose function is to break down DML statement into instructions that the storage manager understands. Analysts who submit queries to explore data in the database fall in this category.

- **Specialized users** are sophisticated users who write specialized database applications that do not fit into the traditional data-processing framework. Among these applications are computer-aided design systems, knowledge-base and expert systems, systems that store data with complex data types (for example, graphics data and audio data), and environment-modeling systems. Several of these applications are covered in Chapters 8 and 9.

- **Naive users** are unsophisticated users who interact with the system by invoking one of the permanent application programs that have been written previously. For example, a bank teller who needs to transfer $50 from account *A* to account *B* invokes a program called *transfer*. This program asks the teller for the amount of money to be transferred, the account from which the money is to be transferred, and the account to which the money is to be transferred.

## 1.9   Overall System Structure

A database system is partitioned into modules that deal with each of the responsibilities of the overall system. Some of the functions of the database system may be provided by the computer's operating system. In most cases, the computer's operating system provides only the most basic services, and the database system must build on that base. Thus, the design of a database system must include consideration of the interface between the database system and the operating system.

The functional components of a database system can be broadly divided into the query processor components and the storage manager components.   The query processor components include

- **DML compiler**, which translates DML statements in a query language into low-level instructions that the query evaluation engine understands. In addition, the DML compiler attempts to transform a user's request into an equivalent but more efficient form, thus finding a good strategy for executing the query.
- **Embedded DML precompiler**, which converts DML statements embedded in an application program to normal procedure calls in the host language. The precompiler must interact with the DML compiler to generate the appropriate code.
- **DDL interpreter**, which interprets DDL statements and records them in a set of tables containing *metadata*.
- **Query evaluation engine**, which executes low-level instructions generated by the DML compiler.

The storage manager components provides the interface between the low-level data stored in the database and the application programs and queries submitted to the system. The storage manager components include

- **Authorization and integrity manager**, which tests for the satisfaction of integrity constraints and checks the authority of users to access data.
- **Transaction manager**, which ensures that the database remains in a consistent (correct) state despite system failures, and that concurrent transaction executions proceed without conflicting.
- **File manager**, which manages the allocation of space on disk storage and the data structures used to represent information stored on disk.
- **Buffer manager**, which is responsible for fetching data from disk storage into main memory, and deciding what data to cache in memory.

In addition, several data structures are required as part of the physical system implementation:

- **Data files**, which store the database itself.
- **Data dictionary**, which stores metadata about the structure of the database. The data dictionary is used heavily. Therefore, great emphasis should be placed on developing a good design and efficient implementation of the dictionary.
- **Indices**, which provide fast access to data items that hold particular values.
- **Statistical data**, which store statistical information about the data in the database. This information is used by the query processor to select efficient ways to execute a query.

Figure 1.6 shows these components and the connections among them.

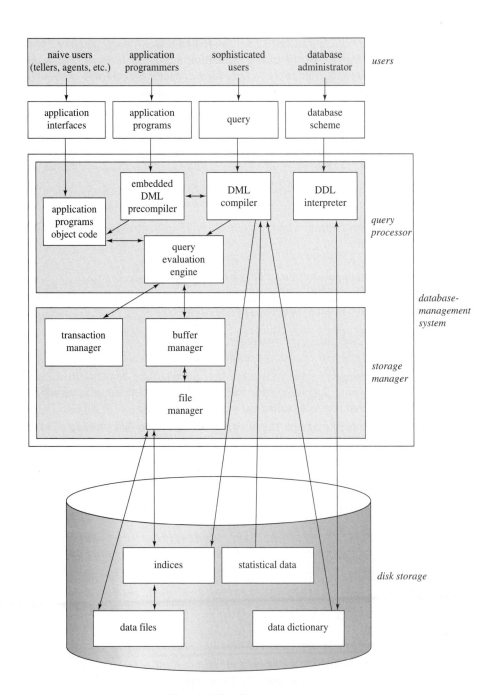

Figure 1.6    System structure.

# 1.10   Summary

A *database-management system* (DBMS) consists of a collection of interrelated data and a collection of programs to access that data. The data describe one particular enterprise. The primary goal of a DBMS is to provide an environment that is both *convenient* and *efficient* for people to use in retrieving and storing information.

Database systems are designed to store large bodies of information. The management of data involves both the definition of structures for the storage of information and the provision of mechanisms for the manipulation of information. In addition, the database system must provide for the safety of the information stored, in the face of system crashes or attempts at unauthorized access. If data are to be shared among several users, the system must avoid possible anomalous results.

A major purpose of a database system is to provide users with an abstract view of the data. That is, the system hides certain details of how the data are stored and maintained. It does so by defining three levels of abstraction at which it may be viewed: the *physical level*, the *logical level*, and the *view level*.

Underlying the structure of a database is the *data model*: a collection of conceptual tools for describing data, data relationships, data semantics, and data constraints. The various data models that have been proposed fall into three different groups: *object-based logical models*, *record-based logical models*, and *physical data models*.

Databases change over time as information is inserted and deleted. The collection of information stored in the database at a particular moment is called an *instance* of the database. The overall design of the database is called the database *schema*. The ability to modify a schema definition in one level without affecting a schema definition in the next-higher level is called *data independence*. There are two levels of data independence: *physical* data independence and *logical* data independence.

A database schema is specified by a set of definitions that are expressed by a *data-definition language* (DDL). DDL statements are compiled into a set of tables that is stored in a special file called the *data dictionary*; the data dictionary thus contains *metadata*.

A *data-manipulation language* (DML) is a language that enables users to access or manipulate data. There are basically two types: procedural DMLs, which require a user to specify what data are needed and how to get those data, and nonprocedural DMLs, which require a user to specify what data are needed without specifying how to get those data.

The *transaction manager* is responsible for ensuring that the database remains in a consistent (correct) state despite system failures. The transaction manager also ensures that concurrent transaction executions proceed without conflicting.

A *storage manager* is a program module that provides the interface between the low-level data stored in the database and the application programs and queries submitted to the system. The storage manager is responsible for interaction with the data stored on disk.

# Exercises

**1.1.** What are four main differences between a file-processing system and a DBMS?

**1.2.** This chapter has described several major advantages of a database system. What are two disadvantages?

**1.3.** Explain the difference between physical and logical data independence.

**1.4.** List five responsibilities of the database manager. For each responsibility, explain the problems that would arise if the responsibility were not discharged.

**1.5.** What are five main functions of a database administrator?

**1.6.** List seven programming languages that are procedural, and two that are nonprocedural. Which group is easier to learn and use? Explain your answer.

**1.7.** List six major steps that you would take in setting up a database for a particular enterprise.

**1.8.** Consider a two-dimensional integer array of size $n \times m$ that is to be used in your favorite programming language. Using the array as an example, illustrate the difference (a) between the three levels of data abstraction, and (b) between a schema and instances.

# Bibliographical Notes

Discussions concerning the evolution of DBMSs and the development of database technology are offered by Fry and Sibley [1976] and by Sibley [1976].

The three levels of data abstraction were introduced in the CODASYL DBTG report [CODASYL 1971]. A similar proposal was put forward in the ANSI/SPARC report, in which these levels were termed *internal*, *conceptual*, and *external* [ANSI 1975].

The entity–relationship, object-oriented, relational, network, and hierarchical models are covered in other chapters of this book. More extensive bibliographic references are provided in later chapters of this book.

Semantic data models are based on data models that were initially developed in connection with research in artificial intelligence. Discussion concerning the various models can be found in Roussopoulos and Mylopoulos [1975], Wong and Mylopoulos [1977], and Hammer and McLeod [1981]. Surveys of semantic data models are provided by Hull and King [1987] and by Peckham and Maryanski [1988].

The functional data model was proposed by Sibley and Kerschberg [1977], and has been extended by Shipman [1981]. Several functional query languages have been proposed, including FQL [Buneman and Frankel 1979] and DAPLEX [Shipman 1981].

The unifying model was introduced by Batory and Gotlieb [1982]. The frame memory structure was introduced by March et al. [1981].

Database-administration issues are covered in Weldon [1981]. Other textbooks covering database systems include Abiteboul et al. [1995], Date [1995], Elmasri and Navathe [1994], O'Neil [1994], and Ullman [1988].

Several books contain collections of research papers on database management. Among these are Bancilhon and Buneman [1990], Date [1986, 1990], Kim et al. [1985], Kim [1995], and Stonebraker [1994]. A review of accomplishments in database management and an assessment of future research challenges appears in Silberschatz et al. [1990, 1996].

# CHAPTER
# 2

## ENTITY–RELATIONSHIP MODEL

The entity–relationship (E-R) data model is based on a perception of a real world that consists of a set of basic objects called *entities*, and of *relationships* among these objects. It was developed to facilitate database design by allowing the specification of an *enterprise schema*, which represents the overall logical structure of a database. The E-R data model is one of several semantic data models; the semantic aspect of the model lies in the attempt to represent the meaning of the data. The E-R model is extremely useful in mapping the meanings and interactions of real-world enterprises onto a conceptual schema. Because of this utility, many database-design tools draw on concepts from the E-R model.

## 2.1 Basic Concepts

There are three basic notions that the E-R data model employs: entity sets, relationship sets, and attributes.

### 2.1.1 Entity Sets

An *entity* is a "thing" or "object" in the real world that is distinguishable from all other objects. For example, each person in an enterprise is an entity. An entity has a set of properties, and the values for some set of properties may uniquely identify an entity. For example, the social-security number 677-89-9011 uniquely identifies one particular person in the enterprise.[†] Similarly, loans can be thought

---

[†]In the United States, the government assigns to each person in the country a unique number, called a social-security number, to identify them uniquely. Each person is supposed to have only one social-security number, and no two people are supposed to have the same social-security number.

| | | | |
|---|---|---|---|
| Jones | 321-12-3123 | Main | Harrison |
| Smith | 019-28-3746 | North | Rye |
| Hayes | 677-89-9011 | Main | Harrison |
| Jackson | 555-55-5555 | Dupont | Woodside |
| Curry | 244-66-8800 | North | Rye |
| Williams | 963-96-3963 | Nassau | Princeton |
| Adams | 335-57-7991 | Spring | Pittsfield |

| | |
|---|---|
| L-17 | 1000 |
| L-23 | 2000 |
| L-15 | 1500 |
| L-14 | 1500 |
| L-93 | 500 |
| L-11 | 900 |
| L-16 | 1300 |

*customer*                              *loan*

**Figure 2.1    Entity sets *customer* and *loan*.**

of as entities, and loan number L-15 at the Perryridge branch uniquely identifies a loan entity. An entity may be concrete, such as a person or a book, or it may be abstract, such as a loan, or a holiday or a concept. In this text, we assume for simplicity that the enterprises with which we are dealing are located in the United States, and that all the person entities with which we deal have social-security numbers. We address the problem of choosing unique identifiers in Section 2.4.1.

An *entity set* is a set of entities of the same type that share the same properties, or attributes. The set of all persons who are customers at a given bank, for example, can be defined as the entity set *customer*. Similarly, the entity set *loan* might represent the set of all loans awarded by a particular bank. The individual entities that constitute a set are said to be the *extension* of the entity set. Thus, all the individual bank customers are the extension of the entity set *customer*.

Entity sets do not need to be disjoint. For example, it is possible to define the entity set of all employees of a bank (*employee*) and the entity set of all customers of the bank (*customer*). A *person* entity may be an *employee* entity, a *customer* entity, both, or neither.

An entity is represented by a set of *attributes*. Attributes are descriptive properties possessed by each member of an entity set. The designation of an attribute for an entity set expresses that the database stores similar information concerning each entity in the entity set; however, each entity may have its own value for each attribute. Possible attributes of the *customer* entity set are *customer-name*, *social-security*, *customer-street*, and *customer-city*. Possible attributes of the *loan* entity set are *loan-number* and *amount*. For each attribute, there is a set of permitted values, called the *domain*, or *value set*, of that attribute. The domain of attribute *customer-name* might be the set of all text strings of a certain length. Similarly, the domain of attribute *loan-number* might be the set of all positive integers.

A database thus includes a collection of entity sets each of which contains any number of entities of the same type. Figure 2.1 shows part of a bank database which consists of two entity sets: *customer* and *loan*.

Formally, an attribute of an entity set is a function that maps from the entity set into a domain. Since an entity set may have several attributes, each entity can be described by a set of (attribute, data value) pairs, one pair for each attribute of the entity set. For example, a particular *customer* entity may be described by the set {(*name*, Hayes), (*social-security*, 677-89-9011), (*customer-street*, Main), (*customer-city*, Harrison)}, meaning that the entity describes a person named Hayes who holds social-security number 677-89-9011, and resides at Main Street in Harrison. We can see, at this point, an integration of the abstract schema with the actual enterprise being modeled. The attribute values describing an entity will constitute a significant portion of the data stored in the database.

An attribute, as used in the E-R model, can be characterized by the following attribute types.

- **Simple** and **composite** attributes. In our examples thus far, the attributes have been simple; that is, they are not divided into subparts. Composite attributes, on the other hand, can be divided into subparts (that is, other attributes). For example, *customer-name* could be structured as a composite attribute consisting of *first-name*, *middle-initial*, and *last-name*. Using composite attributes in a design schema is a good choice if a user will wish to refer to an entire attribute on some occasions, and to only a component of the attribute on other occasions. Suppose we were to substitute for the *customer* entity-set attributes *customer-street* and *customer-city*, the composite attribute *customer-address* with the attributes *street*, *city*, *state*, and *zip-code*.[†] Composite attributes help us to group together related attributes, making the modeling cleaner.

  Note also that a composite attribute may appear as a hierarchy. Returning to our example composite attribute of *customer-address*, its component attribute *street* can be further divided into *street-number*, *street-name*, and *apt-number*. These examples of composite attributes, for the *customer* entity set, are depicted in Figure 2.2.

- **Single-valued** and **multivalued** attributes. The attributes that we have specified in our examples all have a single value for a particular entity. For instance, the *loan-number* attribute for a specific loan entity refers to only one loan number. Such attributes are said to be *single valued*. There may be instances where an attribute has a set of values for a specific entity. Consider an *employee* entity set with the attribute *dependent-name*. Any particular employee may have zero, one, or more dependents; therefore, different employee entities within the entity set will have different numbers of values for the *dependent-name* attribute. This type of attribute is said to be *multivalued*. Where appropriate, upper and lower bounds may be placed on the number of values in a multivalued attribute. For example, a bank may limit the number of addresses recorded for a single customer to two. Placing bounds in this

---

[†]We assume the *customer-street* and address format used in the United States, which includes a numeric postal code called a "zip code."

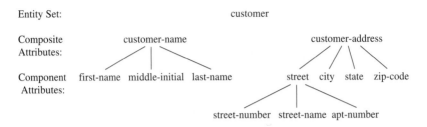

Figure 2.2   Composite attributes *customer-name* and *customer-address*.

case expresses that the *customer-address* attribute of the *customer* entity set
may have between zero and two values.

- **Null** attributes. A *null* value is used when an entity does not have a value for
  an attribute. As an illustration, if a particular employee has no dependents,
  the *dependent-name* value for that employee will be *null*, and will have the
  meaning of "not applicable." *Null* can also designate that an attribute value
  is unknown. An unknown value may be either *missing* (the value does exist,
  but we do not have that information) or *not known* (we do not know whether
  or not the value actually exists). For instance, if the *social-security* value
  for a particular customer is *null*, we assume that the value is missing, since
  it is required for tax reporting. A null value for the *apt-number* attribute
  could mean that the address does not include an apartment number, that an
  apartment number exists but we do not know what it is, or that we do not
  know whether or not an apartment number is part of the customer's address.

- **Derived** attribute. The value for this type of attribute can be derived from the
  values of other related attributes or entities. For instance, let us say that the
  *customer* entity set has an attribute *loans-held*, which represents how many
  loans a customer has from the bank. we can derive the value for this attribute
  by counting the number of *loan* entities associated with that customer. As another example, consider that the *employee* entity set has the related attributes
  *start-date* and *employment-length*, which represent the first day an employee
  began working for the bank and the total length of time an employee has
  worked for the bank, respectively. The value for *employment-length* can be
  derived from the value for *start-date* and the current date. In this case, *start-
  date* may be referred to as a *base* attribute, or a *stored* attribute.

A database for a banking enterprise may include a number of different entity
sets. For example, in addition to keeping track of customers and loans, the bank
also provides accounts, which are represented by the entity set *account* with attributes *account-number* and *balance*. Also, if the bank has a number of different
branches, then we may keep information about all the branches of the bank. Each
*branch* entity set may be described by the attributes *branch-name*, *branch-city*,
and *assets*.

In this chapter, we shall be dealing with various different entity sets. To
avoid confusion, unique attribute names are used. We shall define the new entity
sets as the occasion arises.

## 2.1.2 Relationship Sets

A *relationship* is an association among several entities. For example, we can define a relationship that associates customer Hayes with loan L-15. This relationship specifies that Hayes is a customer with loan number L-15.

A *relationship set* is a set of relationships of the same type. Formally, it is a mathematical relation on $n \geq 2$ (possibly nondistinct) entity sets. If $E_1, E_2, \ldots, E_n$ are entity sets, then a relationship set $R$ is a subset of

$$\{(e_1, e_2, \ldots, e_n) \mid e_1 \in E_1, e_2 \in E_2, \ldots, e_n \in E_n\}$$

where $(e_1, e_2, \ldots, e_n)$ is a relationship.

Consider the two entity sets *customer* and *loan* in Figure 2.1. We define the relationship set *borrower* to denote the association between customers and the bank loans that the customers have. This association is depicted in Figure 2.3.

As another example, consider the two entity sets *loan* and *branch*. We can define the relationship set *loan-branch* to denote the association between a bank loan and the branch in which that loan is maintained.

The association between entity sets is referred to as *participation*; that is, the entity sets $E_1, E_2, \ldots, E_n$ *participate* in relationship set $R$. A relationship instance in an E-R schema represents that an association exists between the named entities in the real-world enterprise that is being modeled. As an illustration, the individual *customer* entity Hayes, who has social-security number 677-89-9011, and the *loan* entity L-15 participate in a relationship instance of *borrower*. This relationship instance represents that, in the real-world enterprise, the person called Hayes who holds social-security number 677-89-9011 has taken the loan that is numbered L-15.

The function that an entity plays in a relationship is called that entity's *role*. Since entity sets participating in a relationship set are generally distinct, roles are implicit and are not usually specified. However, they are useful when the meaning of a relationship needs clarification. Such is the case when the entity sets

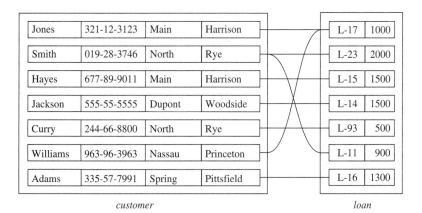

*customer*        *loan*

Figure 2.3   Relationship set *borrower*.

of a relationship set are not distinct; that is, the same entity set participates in a relationship set more than once, in different roles. In this type of relationship set, which is sometimes called a *recursive* relationship set, explicit role names are necessary to specify how an entity participates in a relationship instance. For example, consider an entity set *employee* that records information about all the employees of the bank. We may have a relationship set *works-for* that is modeled by ordered pairs of *employee* entities. The first employee of a pair takes the role of manager, whereas the second takes the role of worker. In this way, all relationships of *works-for* are characterized by (manager, worker) pairs; (worker, manager) pairs are excluded.

A relationship may also have *descriptive attributes*. Consider a relationship set *depositor* with entity sets *customer* and *account*. We could associate the attribute *access-date* to that relation to specify the most recent date on which a customer accessed an account. The *depositor* relationship among the entities corresponding to customer Jones and account A-217 is described by {(*access-date*, 23 May 1996)}, which means that the most recent time that Jones accessed account A-217 was on 23 May 1996.

The relationship sets *borrower* and *loan-branch* provide an example of a *binary* relationship set—that is, one that involves two entity sets. Most of the relationship sets in a database system are binary. Occasionally, however, relationship sets involve more than two entity sets. As an example, we could combine the *borrower* and *loan-branch* relationship sets to form a ternary relationship set *CLB* involving the entity sets *customer*, *loan*, and *branch*. Thus, the ternary relationship among the entities corresponding to customer Hayes, loan L-15, and the Perryridge branch specifies that customer Hayes has loan L-15 at the Perryridge branch.

The number of entity sets that participate in a relationship set is also the *degree* of the relationship set. A binary relationship set is of degree 2; a ternary relationship set is of degree 3.

## 2.2    Design Issues

The notions of an entity set and a relationship set are not precise, and it is possible to define a set of entities and the relationships among them in a number of different ways. In this section, we examine basic issues in the design of an E-R database schema. The design process is covered in further detail in Section 2.7.4.

### 2.2.1    Use of Entity Sets or Attributes

Consider the entity set *employee* with attributes *employee-name* and *telephone-number*. It can easily be argued that a telephone is an entity in its own right with attributes *telephone-number* and *location* (the office where the telephone is located). If we take this point of view, the *employee* entity set must be redefined as follows:

- The *employee* entity set with attribute *employee-name*

- The *telephone* entity set with attributes *telephone-number* and *location*
- The relationship set *emp-telephone*, which denotes the association between employees and the telephones that they have

What, then, is the main difference between these two definitions of an employee? In the first case, the definition implies that every employee has precisely one telephone number associated with him. In the second case, however, the definition states that employees may have several telephone numbers (including zero) associated with them. Thus, the second definition is more general than the first one, and may more accurately reflect the real-world situation.

Even if we are given that each employee has precisely one telephone number associated with him, the second definition may still be more appropriate if the telephone is shared among several employees.

It would not be appropriate, however, to apply the same technique to the attribute *employee-name*; it is difficult to argue that *employee-name* is an entity in its own right (in contrast to the telephone). Thus, it is appropriate to have *employee-name* as an attribute of the *employee* entity set.

Two natural questions thus arise: What constitutes an attribute, and what constitutes an entity set? Unfortunately, there are no simple answers. The distinctions mainly depend on the structure of the real-world enterprise being modeled, and on the semantics associated with the attribute in question.

## 2.2.2 Use of Entity Sets or Relationship Sets

It is not always clear whether an object is best expressed by an entity set or a relationship set. In Section 2.1.1, we assumed that a bank loan is modeled as an entity. An alternative is to model a loan not as an entity, but rather as a relationship between customers and branches, with *loan-number* and *amount* as descriptive attributes. Each loan is represented by a relationship between a customer and a branch.

If every loan is held by exactly one customer and is associated with exactly one branch, we may find satisfactory the design where a loan is represented as a relationship. However, with this design, we cannot represent conveniently a situation in which several customers hold a loan jointly. We must define a separate relationship for each holder of the joint loan. Then, we must replicate the values for the descriptive attributes *loan-number* and *amount* in each such relationship. Each such relationship must, of course, have the same value for the descriptive attributes *loan-number* and *amount*. Two problems arise as a result of the replication: (1) the data are stored multiple times, wasting storage space; and (2) updates potentially leave the data in an inconsistent state, where the values differ in two relationships for attributes that are supposed to have the same value. The issue of how to avoid such replication is treated formally by *normalization theory*, discussed in Chapter 7. The problem of replication of the attributes *loan-number* and *amount* is absent in the original design of Section 2.1.1, because there *loan* is an entity set.

One possible guideline in determining whether to use an entity set or a relationship set is to designate a relationship set to describe an action that occurs between entities. This approach can also be useful in deciding whether certain attributes may be more appropriately expressed as relationships.

### 2.2.3   Binary Versus n-ary Relationship Sets

It is always possible to replace a nonbinary ($n$-ary, for $n > 2$) relationship set by a number of distinct binary relationship sets. For simplicity, consider the abstract ternary ($n = 3$) relationship set $R$, relating entity sets $A$, $B$, and $C$. We replace the relationship set $R$ by an entity set $E$, and create three relationship sets:

- $R_A$, relating $E$ and $A$
- $R_B$, relating $E$ and $B$
- $R_C$, relating $E$ and $C$

If the relationship set $R$ had any attributes, these are assigned to entity set $E$; otherwise, a special identifying attribute is created for $E$ (since every entity set must have at least one attribute to distinguish members of the set). For each relationship $(a_i, b_i, c_i)$ in the relationship set $R$, we create a new entity $e_i$ in the entity set $E$. Then, in each of the three new relationship sets, we insert a relationship as follows:

- $(e_i, a_i)$ in $R_A$
- $(e_i, b_i)$ in $R_B$
- $(e_i, c_i)$ in $R_C$

We can generalize this process in a straightforward manner to $n$-ary relationship sets. Thus, conceptually, we can restrict the E-R model to include only binary relationship sets. However, this restriction is not always desirable.

- An identifying attribute may have to be created for the entity set created to represent the relationship set. This attribute, along with the extra relationship sets required, increase the complexity of the design and (as we shall see in Section 2.9) overall storage requirements.
- A $n$-ary relationship set shows more clearly that several entities participate in a single relationship. In the corresponding design using binary relationships, it is more difficult to enforce this participation constraint.

## 2.3   Mapping Constraints

An E-R enterprise schema may define certain constraints to which the contents of a database must conform. In this section, we examine mapping cardinalities and existence dependencies—two of the most important types of constraints.

### 2.3.1 Mapping Cardinalities

*Mapping cardinalities*, or cardinality ratios, express the number of entities to which another entity can be associated via a relationship set.

Mapping cardinalities are most useful in describing binary relationship sets, although occasionally they contribute to the description of relationship sets that involve more than two entity sets. In this section, we shall concentrate on only binary relationship sets.

For a binary relationship set $R$ between entity sets $A$ and $B$, the mapping cardinality must be one of the following:

- **One to one**. An entity in $A$ is associated with at most one entity in $B$, and an entity in $B$ is associated with at most one entity in $A$. (See Figure 2.4a.)
- **One to many**. An entity in $A$ is associated with any number of entities in $B$. An entity in $B$, however, can be associated with at most one entity in $A$. (See Figure 2.4b.)
- **Many to one**. An entity in $A$ is associated with at most one entity in $B$. An entity in $B$, however, can be associated with any number of entities in $A$. (See Figure 2.5a.)
- **Many to many**. An entity in $A$ is associated with any number of entities in $B$, and an entity in $B$ is associated with any number of entities in $A$. (See Figure 2.5b.)

The appropriate mapping cardinality for a particular relationship set is obviously dependent on the real-world situation that is being modeled by the relationship set.

As an illustration, consider the *borrower* relationship set. If, in a particular bank, a loan can belong to only one customer, and a customer can have several loans, then the relationship set from *customer* to *loan* is one to many. This type of relationship is depicted in Figure 2.3. If a loan can belong to several customers (as can loans taken jointly by several business partners), the relationship set is many to many.

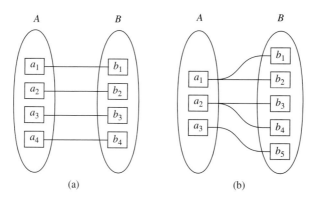

Figure 2.4   Mapping cardinalities. (a) One to one. (b) One to many.

The cardinality ratio of a relationship can affect the placement of relationship attributes. Attributes of one-to-one or one-to-many relationship sets can be associated with one of the participating entity sets, rather than with the relationship set. For instance, let us specify that *depositor* is a one-to-many relationship set such that one customer may have several accounts, but each account is held by only one customer. In this case, the attribute *access-date* could be associated with the *account* entity set, as depicted in Figure 2.6; to keep the figure simple, only some of the attributes of the two entity sets are shown. Since each *account* entity participates in a relationship with at most one instance of *customer*, making this attribute designation would have the same meaning as would placing *access-date* with the *depositor* relationship set. Attributes of a one-to-many relationship set can be repositioned to only the entity set on the "many" side of the relationship. For one-to-one relationship sets, the relationship attribute can be associated with either one of the participating entities.

The design decision of where to place descriptive attributes in such cases— as a relationship or entity attribute—should reflect the characteristics of the enterprise being modeled. The designer may choose to retain *access-date* as an attribute of *depositor* to express explicitly that an access occurs at the point of interaction between the *customer* and *account* entity sets.

The choice of attribute placement is more clearcut for many-to-many relationship sets. Returning to our example, let us specify the perhaps more realistic case that *depositor* is a many-to-many relationship set expressing that a customer may have one or more accounts, and that an account can be held by one or more customers. If we are to express the date on which a specific customer last accessed a specific account, *access-date* must be an attribute of the *depositor* relationship set, rather than either one of the participating entities. If *access-date* were an attribute of *account*, for instance, we could not determine which customer made the most recent access to a joint account. When an attribute is determined by the combination of participating entity sets, rather than by either entity separately, that attribute must be associated with the many-to-many relationship set. The place-

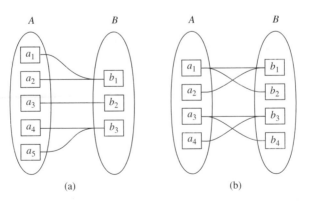

(a)                                   (b)

Figure 2.5    Mapping cardinalities. (a) Many to one. (b) Many to many.

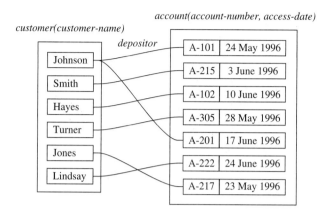

Figure 2.6    *Access-date* as attribute of the *account* entity set.

ment of *access-date* as a relationship attribute is depicted in Figure 2.7; again, to
keep the figure simple, only some of the attributes of the two entity sets are shown.

## 2.3.2    Existence Dependencies

Another important class of constraints is *existence dependencies*. Specifically, if
the existence of entity *x* depends on the existence of entity *y*, then *x* is said to be

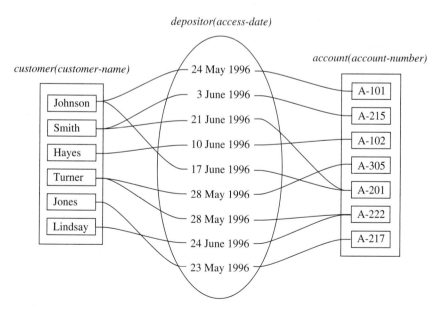

Figure 2.7    *Access-date* as attribute of the *depositor* relationship set.

*existence dependent* on *y*. Operationally, if *y* is deleted, so is *x*. Entity *y* is said to be a *dominant entity*, and *x* is said to be a *subordinate entity*.

As an illustration, consider the entity set *loan* and the entity set *payment* that keeps information about all the payments that were made in connection to a particular loan. The *payment* entity set is described by the attributes *payment-number*, *payment-date*, and *payment-amount*. We form a relationship set *loan-payment* between these two entity sets, which is one-to-many from *loan* to *payment*. Every *payment* entity must be associated with a *loan* entity. If a *loan* entity is deleted, then all its associated *payment* entities must be deleted also. In contrast, *payment* entities can be deleted from the database without affecting any *loan*. The entity set *loan*, therefore, is dominant, and *payment* is subordinate, in the *loan-payment* relationship set.

The participation of an entity set *E* in a relationship set *R* is said to be *total* if every entity in *E* participates in at least one relationship in *R*. If only some entities in *E* participate in relationships in *R*, the participation of entity set *E* in relationship *R* is said to be *partial*. Total participation is closely related to existence dependency. For example, since every payment entity must be related to some loan entity by the *loan-payment* relationship, the participation of *payment* in the relationship set *loan-payment* is total. In contrast, an individual can be a bank customer whether or not she has a loan with the bank. Hence, it is possible that only a partial set of the *customer* entities relate to the *loan* entity set, and the participation of *customer* in the *borrower* relationship set is therefore partial.

## 2.4  Keys

It is important to be able to specify how entities within a given entity set and relationships within a given relationship set are distinguished. Conceptually, individual entities and relationships are distinct; from a database perspective, however, the difference among them must be expressed in terms of their attributes. The concept of a *key* allows us to make such distinctions.

### 2.4.1  Entity Sets

A *superkey* is a set of one or more attributes that, taken collectively, allows us to identify uniquely an entity in the entity set. For example, the *social-security* attribute of the entity set *customer* is sufficient to distinguish one *customer* entity from another. Thus, *social-security* is a superkey. Similarly, the combination of *customer-name* and *social-security* is a superkey for the entity set *customer*. The *customer-name* attribute of *customer* is not a superkey, because several people might have the same name.

The concept of a superkey is not sufficient for our purposes, since, as we saw, a superkey may contain extraneous attributes. If *K* is a superkey, then so is any superset of *K*. We are often interested in superkeys for which no proper subset is a superkey. Such minimal superkeys are called *candidate keys*.

It is possible that several distinct sets of attributes could serve as a candidate key. Suppose that a combination of *customer-name* and *customer-street* is sufficient to distinguish among members of the *customer* entity set. Then, both {*social-security*} and {*customer-name*, *customer-street*} are candidate keys. Although the attributes *social-security* and *customer-name* together can distinguish *customer* entities, their combination does not form a candidate key, since the attribute *social-security* alone is a candidate key.

Candidate keys must be designated with care. As we noted, the name of a person is obviously not sufficient, because there may be many people with the same name. In the U. S., the social-security number may be a candidate key. Since non-U.S. residents usually do not have social-security numbers, enterprises may generate their own unique identifiers, such as customer numbers or student-id numbers, or may use some unique combination of other attributes as a key. One that is often used is the combination of name, date of birth, and address, since it is extremely unlikely that two people will have the same values for all these attributes.

We shall use the term *primary key* to denote a candidate key that is chosen by the database designer as the principal means of identifying entities within an entity set. A key (primary, candidate, and super) is a property of the entity set, rather than of the individual entities. Any two individual entities in the set are prohibited from having the same value on the key attributes at the same time. The designation of a key represents a constraint in the real-world enterprise being modeled.

## 2.4.2 Relationship Sets

The primary key of an entity set allows us to distinguish among the various entities of the set. We need a similar mechanism to distinguish among the various relationships of a relationship set.

Let $R$ be a relationship set involving entity sets $E_1, E_2, \ldots, E_n$. Let *primary-key*$(E_i)$ denote the set of attributes that forms the primary key for entity set $E_i$. Assume that the attribute names of all primary keys are unique (if they are not, use an appropriate renaming scheme). The composition of the primary key for a relationship set depends on the structure of the attributes associated with the relationship set $R$.

If the relationship set $R$ has no attributes associated with it, then the set of attributes

$$primary\text{-}key(E_1) \cup primary\text{-}key(E_2) \cup \ldots \cup primary\text{-}key(E_n)$$

describes an individual relationship in set $R$.

If the relationship set $R$ has attributes $a_1, a_2, \ldots, a_m$ associated with it, then the set of attributes

$$primary\text{-}key(E_1) \cup primary\text{-}key(E_2) \cup \ldots \cup primary\text{-}key(E_n) \cup \{a_1, a_2, \ldots, a_m\}$$

describes an individual relationship in set $R$.

In both of the above cases, the set of attributes

$$primary\text{-}key(E_1) \cup primary\text{-}key(E_2) \cup \ldots \cup primary\text{-}key(E_n)$$

form a superkey for the relationship set.

The structure of the primary key for the relationship set depends on the mapping cardinality of the relationship set. As an illustration, consider the entity sets *customer* and *employee*, and a relationship set *cust-banker* that represents an association between a customer and her banker (an employee entity). Suppose that the relationship set is many to many, and also suppose that the relationship set has the attribute *type* associated with it, representing the nature of the relationship (such as loan officer or personal banker). Then the primary key of *cust-banker* consists of the union of the primary keys of *customer* and *employee*. However, if a customer can have only one banker—that is, if the *cust-banker* relationship is many to one—then the primary key of *cust-banker* is simply the primary key of *customer*. For one-to-one relationships either primary key can be used.

The designation of primary keys is more complicated for non-binary relationships. We consider the issue in more detail in Chapter 7.

## 2.5    Entity–Relationship Diagram

As we saw briefly in Section 1.3, the overall logical structure of a database can be expressed graphically by an *E-R diagram*. The relative simplicity and pictorial clarity of this diagramming technique may well account in large part for the widespread use of the E-R model. Such a diagram consists of the following major components:

- **Rectangles**, which represent entity sets
- **Ellipses**, which represent attributes
- **Diamonds**, which represent relationship sets
- **Lines**, which link attributes to entity sets and entity sets to relationship sets
- **Double ellipses**, which represent multivalued attributes
- **Dashed ellipses**, which denote derived attributes
- **Double Lines**, which indicate total participation of an entity in a relationship set

As depicted in Figure 2.8, attributes of an entity set that are members of the primary key are underlined.

Consider the entity-relationship diagram in Figure 2.8, which consists of two entity sets, *customer* and *loan*, related through a binary relationship set *borrower*. The attributes associated with *customer* are *customer-name*, *social-security*, *customer-street*, and *customer-city*. The attributes associated with *loan* are *loan-number* and *amount*.

The relationship set *borrower* may be many-to-many, one-to-many, many-to-one, or one-to-one. To distinguish among these types, we draw either a directed line ($\rightarrow$) or an undirected line (—) between the relationship set and the entity set in question.

- A directed line from the relationship set *borrower* to the entity set *loan* specifies that *borrower* is either a one-to-one, or many-to-one relationship set, from

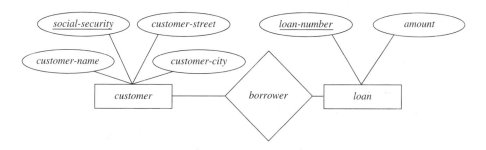

Figure 2.8    E-R diagram corresponding to customers and loans.

*customer* to *loan*; *borrower* cannot be a many-to-many or a one-to-many relationship set, from *customer* to *loan*.

- An undirected line from the relationship set *borrower* to the entity set *loan*
  specifies that *borrower* is either a many-to-many, or one-to-many relationship
  set, from *customer* to *loan*.

Returning to the E-R diagram of Figure 2.8, we see that the relationship
set *borrower* is many to many. If the relationship set *borrower* were one to many,
from *customer* to *loan*, then the line from *borrower* to *customer* would be directed,
with an arrow pointing to the *customer* entity set (Figure 2.9a). Similarly, if the
relationship set *borrower* were many to one from *customer* to *loan*, then the
line from *borrower* to *loan* would have an arrow pointing to the *loan* entity set
(Figure 2.9b). Finally, if the relationship set *borrower* were one to one, then both
lines from *borrower* would have arrows: one pointing to the *loan* entity set, and
one pointing to the *customer* entity set (Figure 2.10).

If a relationship set has also some attributes associated with it, then we
link these attributes to that relationship set. For example, in Figure 2.11, we have
the *access-date* descriptive attribute attached to the relationship set *depositor* to
specify the most recent date on which a customer accessed that account.

We indicate roles in E-R diagrams by labeling the lines that connect diamonds to rectangles. Figure 2.12 shows the role indicators *manager* and *worker*
between the *employee* entity set and the *works-for* relationship set.

Nonbinary relationship sets can be specified easily in an E-R diagram. Figure 2.13 consists of the three entity sets *customer*, *loan*, and *branch*, related
through the relationship set *CLB*. This diagram specifies that a customer may have
several loans, and that loan may belong to several different customers. Further, the
arrow pointing to *branch* indicates that each customer–loan pair is associated with
a specific bank branch. If the diagram had an arrow pointing to *customer*, in addition to the arrow pointing to *branch*, the diagram would specify that each loan
is associated with a specific customer and a specific bank branch.

## 2.6    Weak Entity Sets

An entity set may not have sufficient attributes to form a primary key. Such an
entity set is termed a *weak entity set*. An entity set that has a primary key is termed

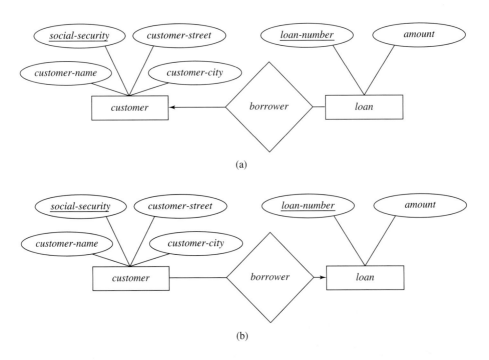

(a)

(b)

Figure 2.9    Relationships. (a) One to many. (b) Many to one.

a *strong entity set*. As an illustration, consider the entity set *payment*, which has the three attributes: *payment-number*, *payment-date*, and *payment-amount*. Although each *payment* entity is distinct, payments for different loans may share the same payment number. Thus, this entity set does not have a primary key; it is a weak entity set. For a weak entity set to be meaningful, it must be part of a one-to-many relationship set. This relationship set should have no descriptive attributes, since any required attributes can be associated with the weak entity set (see the discussion of moving relationship-set attributes to participating entity sets in Section 2.3.1).

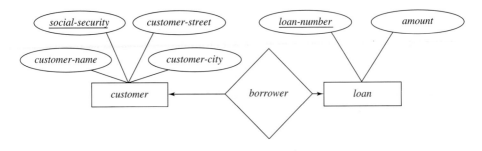

Figure 2.10    One-to-one relationship.

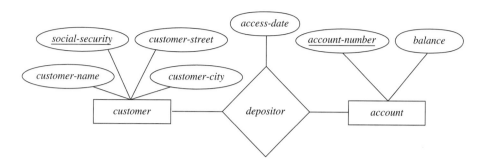

Figure 2.11    E-R diagram with an attribute attached to a relationship set.

The concepts of strong and weak entity sets are related to the existence dependencies introduced in Section 2.3.2. A member of a strong entity set is by definition a dominant entity, whereas a member of a weak entity set is a subordinate entity.

Although a weak entity set does not have a primary key, we nevertheless need a means of distinguishing among all those entities in the entity set that depend on one particular strong entity. The *discriminator* of a weak entity set is a set of attributes that allows this distinction to be made. For example, the discriminator of the weak entity set *payment* is the attribute *payment-number*, since, for each loan, a payment number uniquely identifies one single payment for that loan. The discriminator of a weak entity set is also called the *partial key* of the entity set.

The primary key of a weak entity set is formed by the primary key of the strong entity set on which the weak entity set is existence dependent, plus the weak entity set's discriminator. In the case of the entity set *payment*, its primary key is {*loan-number, payment-number*}, where *loan-number* identifies the dominant entity of a *payment*, and *payment-number* distinguishes *payment* entities within the same loan.

The identifying dominant entity set is said to *own* the weak entity set that it identifies. The relationship that associates the weak entity set with an owner

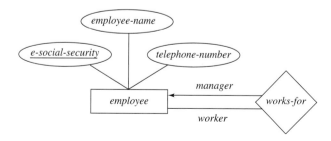

Figure 2.12    E-R diagram with role indicators.

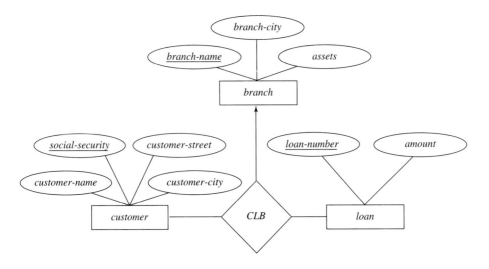

Figure 2.13    E-R diagram with a ternary relationship.

is the *identifying relationship*. In our example, *loan-payment* is the identifying relationship for *payment*.

A weak entity set is indicated in E-R diagrams by a doubly outlined box, and the corresponding identifying relationship by a doubly outlined diamond. In Figure 2.14, the weak entity set *payment* is dependent on the strong entity set *loan* via the relationship set *loan-payment*. The figure also illustrates the use of double lines to indicate *total participation*—the participation of the (weak) entity set *payment* in the relationship *loan-payment* is total, meaning that every payment must be related via *loan-payment* to some account. Finally, the arrow from *loan-payment* to *loan* indicates that each payment is for a single loan. The discriminator of a weak entity set also is underlined, but with a dashed, rather than a solid, line.

A weak entity set may participate as owner in an identifying relationship with another weak entity set. Even though a weak entity set is always existence

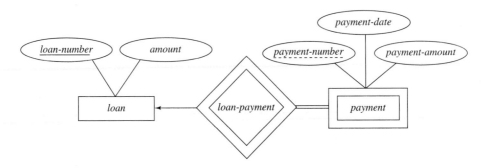

Figure 2.14    E-R diagram with a weak entity set.

dependent on a dominant entity, an existence dependency does not necessarily result in a weak entity set; that is, the subordinate entity set may have a primary key.

In some cases, the database designer may choose to express a weak entity set as a multivalued, composite attribute of the owner entity set. In our example, this alternative would require that the entity set *loan* have a multivalued, composite attribute *payment*, consisting of *payment-number*, *payment-date*, and *payment-amount*. A weak entity set may be more appropriately modeled as an attribute if it participates in only the identifying relationship, and if it has few attributes. Conversely, a weak-entity-set representation will more aptly model a situation where the set participates in relationships other than the identifying relationship, and where the weak entity set has several attributes.

## 2.7   Extended E-R Features

Although the basic E-R concepts can model most database features, some aspects of a database may be more aptly expressed by certain extensions to the basic E-R model. In this section, we discuss the extended E-R features of specialization, generalization, higher- and lower-level entity sets, attribute inheritance, and aggregation.

### 2.7.1   Specialization

An entity set may include subgroupings of entities that are distinct in some way from other entities in the set. For instance, a subset of entities within an entity set may have attributes that are not shared by all the entities in the entity set. The E-R model provides a means for representing these distinctive entity groupings.

Consider the entity set *account* with attributes *account-number* and *balance*. An account is further classified as being one of the following:

- *savings-account*
- *checking-account*

Each of these account types is described by a set of attributes that includes all the attributes of entity set *account* plus additional attributes. For example, *savings-account* entities are described further by the attribute *interest-rate*, whereas *checking-account* entities are described further by the attribute *overdraft-amount*. The process of designating subgroupings within an entity set is *specialization*. The specialization of *account* allows us to distinguish among accounts based on the type of account.

An entity set may be specialized by more than one distinguishing feature. In our example, the distinguishing feature among account entities is the type of account. Another, coexistent, specialization could be based on the type of account ownership, and would result in the entity sets *commercial-account* and *personal-account*. When more than one specialization is formed on an entity set, a particular entity may belong to multiple specializations. For instance, a given account may be both a personal account and a checking account.

We can apply specialization repeatedly to refine the design scheme. For instance, the bank may offer the following three types of checking accounts.

1. A *standard* checking account with a $3.00 monthly service charge and 25 free checks each month. For these accounts, the bank keeps track of the number of checks written from an account each month.

2. A *gold* checking account that requires a $1000.00 minimum balance, pays 2-percent interest, and offers unlimited free check writing. In this case, the bank monitors the minimum balance and the interest paid for each month.

3. A *senior* checking account for customers aged 65 years or older that has no monthly service charge, and that allows unlimited free check writing each month. A record of the customer's date of birth is associated with this type of account.

The specialization of *checking-account* by account type yields the following entity sets.

1. *standard*, with attribute *num-checks*
2. *gold*, with attributes *min-balance* and *interest-payment*
3. *senior*, with attribute *date-of-birth*

In terms of an E-R diagram, specialization is depicted by a *triangle* component labeled ISA, as shown in Figure 2.15. The label ISA stands for "is a" and represents, for example, that a savings account "is an" account. The ISA relationship may also be referred to as a superclass–subclass relationship. Higher- and lower-level entity sets are depicted as regular entity sets—that is, as rectangles containing the name of the entity set.

## 2.7.2  Generalization

The refinement from an initial entity set into successive levels of entity subgroupings represents a *top-down* design process in which distinctions are made explicit. The design process may also proceed in a *bottom-up* manner, in which multiple entity sets are synthesized into a higher-level entity set based on common features. The database designer may have first identified a *checking-account* entity set with the attributes *account-number*, *balance*, and *overdraft-amount*, and a *savings-account* entity set with the attributes *account-number*, *balance*, and *interest-rate*.

There are similarities between the *checking-account* entity set and the *savings-account* entity set in the sense that they have several attributes in common. This commonality can be expressed by *generalization*, which is a containment relationship that exists between a *higher-level* entity set and one or more *lower-level* entity sets. In our example, *account* is the higher-level entity set and *savings-account* and *checking-account* are lower-level entity sets. Higher- and lower-level entity sets also may be designated by the terms *superclass* and *sub-*

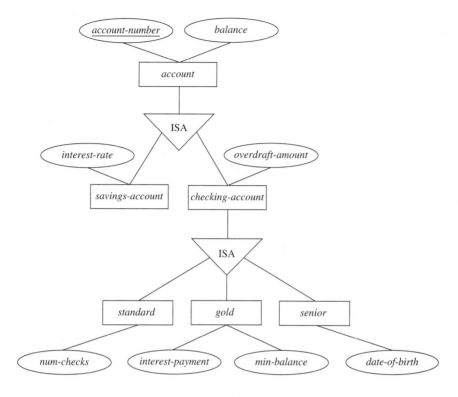

Figure 2.15    Specialization and generalization.

*class*, respectively. The *account* entity set is the superclass of the *savings-account* and *checking-account* subclasses.

For all practical purposes, generalization is a simple inversion of specialization. We will apply both processes, in combination, in the course of designing the E-R schema for an enterprise. In terms of the E-R diagram itself, we do not distinguish between specialization and generalization. New levels of entity representation will be distinguished (specialization) or synthesized (generalization) as the design schema comes to express fully the database application and the user requirements of the database. Differences in the two approaches may be characterized by their starting point and overall goal.

Specialization stems from a single entity set; it emphasizes differences among entities within the set by creating distinct lower level entity sets. These lower-level entity sets may have attributes, or may participate in relationships, that do not apply to all the entities in the higher-level entity set. Indeed, the reason a designer applies specialization is to represent such distinctive features. If *savings-account* and *checking-account* did not each have unique attributes, there would be no need to specialize the *account* entity set.

Generalization proceeds from the recognition that a number of entity sets share some common features (namely, they are described by the same attributes and participate in the same relationship sets). Based on their commonalities, generalization synthesizes these entity sets into a single, higher-level entity set. Generalization is used to emphasize the similarities among lower-level entity sets and to hide the differences; it also permits an economy of representation in that shared attributes are not repeated.

### 2.7.3   Attribute Inheritance

A crucial property of the higher- and lower-level entities created by specialization and generalization is *attribute inheritance*. The attributes of the higher-level entity sets are said to be *inherited* by the lower-level entity sets. For example, *savings-account* and *checking-account* inherit the attributes of *account*. Thus, *savings-account* is described by its *account-number*, *balance*, and *interest-rate* attributes; *checking-account* is described by its *account-number*, *balance*, and *overdraft-amount* attributes. A lower-level entity set (or subclass) also inherits participation in the relationship sets in which its higher-level entity (or superclass) participates. Both the *savings-account* and *checking-account* entity sets participate in the *depositor* relationship set. Attribute inheritance applies through all tiers of lower-level entity sets. The *standard*, *gold*, and *senior* lower-level entity sets inherit the attributes and relationship participation of both *checking-account* and *account*.

Whether a given portion of an E-R model was arrived at by specialization or generalization, the outcome is basically the same:

- A higher-level entity set with attributes and relationships that apply to all of its lower-level entity sets
- Lower-level entity sets with distinctive features that apply only within a particular lower-level entity set

In what follows, although we often refer to only generalization, the properties that we discuss belong fully to both processes.

Figure 2.15 depicts a *hierarchy* of entity sets. In the figure, *checking-account* is a lower-level entity set of *account* and a higher-level entity set of the *standard, gold*, and *senior* entity sets. In a hierarchy, a given entity set may be involved as a lower-level entity set in only one ISA relationship. If an entity set is a lower-level entity set in more than one ISA relationship, the resulting structure is said to be a *lattice*.

### 2.7.4   Design Constraints

To model an enterprise more accurately, the database designer may choose to place certain constraints on a particular generalization. One type of constraint involves determining which entities can be members of a given lower-level entity set. Such membership may be one of the following:

- **Condition-defined**. In condition-defined lower-level entity sets, membership is evaluated on the basis of whether or not an entity satisfies an explicit condition or predicate. For example, assume that the higher-level entity set *account* has the attribute *account-type*. All *account* entities are evaluated on the defining *account-type* attribute. Only those entities that satisfy the condition *account-type* = "savingsaccount" are allowed to belong to the lower-level entity set *savings-account*. All entities that satisfy the condition *account-type* = "checkingaccount" are included in *checking account*. Since all the lower-level entities are evaluated on the basis of the same attribute (in this case, on *account-type*), this type of generalization is said to be *attribute-defined*.

- **User-defined**. User-defined lower-level entity sets are not constrained by a membership condition; rather, entities are assigned to a given entity set by the database user. For instance, let us assume that, after 3 months of employment, bank employees are assigned to one of four work teams. The teams are represented as four lower-level entity sets of the higher-level *employee* entity set. The specific team entity set to which a given employee is assigned is not evaluated automatically based on an explicit defining condition. Instead, team assignment is made on an individual basis by the user in charge of this decision, and is implemented by an operation that adds an entity to an entity set.

A second type of constraint relates to whether or not entities may belong to more than one lower-level entity set within a single generalization. The lower-level entity sets may be one of the following:

- **Disjoint**. A disjointness constraint requires that an entity belong to no more than one lower-level entity set. In our example, an *account* entity can satisfy only one condition for the *account-type* attribute; an entity can be either a savings account or a checking account, but cannot be both.
- **Overlapping**. In overlapping generalizations, the same entity may belong to more than one lower-level entity set within a single generalization. For an illustration, let us return to the employee workteam example, and assume that certain managers participate in more than one workteam. A given employee may therefore appear in more than one of the team entity sets.

Lower-level entity overlap is the default case; a disjointness constraint must be placed explicitly on a generalization (or specialization).

A final constraint, the *completeness constraint* on a generalization, specifies whether or not an entity in the higher-level entity set must belong to at least one of the lower-level entity sets within a generalization. This constraint may be one of the following:

- **Total**. Each higher-level entity must belong to a lower-level entity set.
- **Partial**. Some higher-level entities may not belong to any lower-level entity set.

The *account* generalization is total: All account entities must be either a savings account or a checking account. Because the higher-level entity set arrived at through generalization is generally composed of only those entities in the lower-level entity sets, the completeness constraint for a generalized higher-level entity set is usually total. When the constraint is partial, a higher-level entity is not constrained to appear in a lower-level entity set. The workteam entity sets illustrate a partial specialization. Since employees are assigned to a team only after 3 months on the job, some *employee* entities may not be members of any of the lower-level team entity sets.

We may characterize the team entity sets more fully as a partial, overlapping specialization of *employee*. The generalization of *checking-account* and *savings-account* into *account* is a total, disjoint generalization. The completeness and disjointness constraints, however, are not dependent on each other. Constraint patterns may also be partial–disjoint and total–overlapping.

We can see that certain insertion and deletion requirements follow from the constraints that apply to a given generalization or specialization. For instance, when a total completeness constraint is in place, an entity inserted in a higher-level entity set must also be inserted in at least one of the lower-level entity sets. With a condition-defined constraint, all higher-level entities that satisfy the condition must be inserted in that lower-level entity set. Finally, an entity that is deleted from a higher-level entity set also is deleted from all the associated lower-level entity sets to which it belongs.

## 2.7.5    Aggregation

One limitation of the E-R model is that it is not possible to express relationships among relationships. To illustrate the need for such a construct, we consider again a database describing information about customers and their loans. Suppose that each customer–loan pair may have a bank employee who is the loan officer for that particular pair. Using our basic E-R modeling constructs, we obtain the E-R diagram of Figure 2.16. It appears that the relationship sets *borrower* and *loan-officer* can be combined into one single relationship set. Nevertheless, we should not combine them, because doing so would obscure the logical structure of this schema. For example, if we combine the *borrower* and *loan-officer* relationship sets, then this combination specifies that a loan officer must be assigned to every customer–loan pair, which is not true. The separation into two different relationship sets solves this problem.

There is redundant information in the resultant figure, however, since every customer-loan pair in *loan-officer* is also in *borrower*. If the loan officer were a value rather than an *employee* entity, we could instead make *loan-officer* a multivalued attribute of the relationship *borrower*. But doing so makes it more difficult (logically as well as in execution cost) to find, for example, customer–loan pairs for which an employee is responsible. Since the loan officer is an *employee* entity, this alternative is ruled out in any case.

The best way to model a situation such as the one just described is to use aggregation. *Aggregation* is an abstraction through which relationships are treated

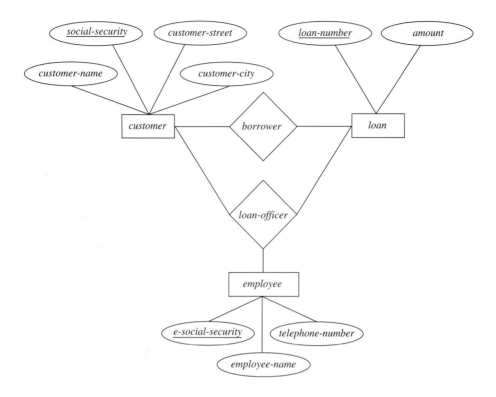

Figure 2.16    E-R diagram with redundant relationships.

as higher-level entities. Thus, for our example, we regard the relationship set *borrower* and the entity sets *customer* and *loan* as a higher-level entity set called *borrower*. Such an entity set is treated in the same manner as is any other entity set. A common notation for aggregation is shown in Figure 2.17.

## 2.8    Design of an E-R Database Schema

The E-R data model gives us substantial flexibility in designing a database schema to model a given enterprise. In this section, we consider how a database designer may select from the wide range of alternatives. Among the decisions to be made are the following:

- Whether to use an attribute or an entity set to represent an object (discussed earlier in Section 2.2.1)
- Whether a real-world concept is expressed most accurately by an entity set or by a relationship set (Section 2.2.2)
- Whether to use a ternary relationship or a pair of binary relationships (Section 2.2.3)

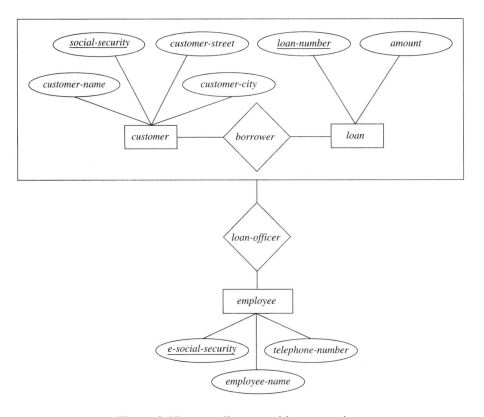

Figure 2.17    E-R diagram with aggregation.

- Whether to use a strong or a weak entity set (Section 2.6); a strong entity set and its dependent weak entity sets may be regarded as a single "object" in the database, since weak entities are existence dependent on a strong entity
- Whether using generalization (Section 2.7.2) is appropriate; generalization, or a hierarchy of ISA relationships, contributes to modularity by allowing common attributes of similar entity sets to be represented in one place in an E-R diagram
- Whether using aggregation (Section 2.7.5) is appropriate; aggregation groups a part of an E-R diagram into a single entity set, allowing us to treat the aggregate entity set as a single unit without concern for the details of its internal structure.

We shall see that the database designer needs a good understanding of the enterprise being modeled to make these decisions.

## 2.8.1    Design Phases

A high-level data model serves the database designer by providing a conceptual framework in which to specify, in a systematic fashion, what the data requirements of the database users are, and how the database will be structured to fulfill these requirements. The initial phase of database design, then, is to characterize fully the data needs of the prospective database users. The outcome of this phase is a *specification of user requirements*.

Next, the designer chooses a data model, and by applying the concepts of the chosen data model, translates these requirements into a conceptual schema of the database. The schema developed at this *conceptual-design* phase provides a detailed overview of the enterprise. Since we have studied only the E-R model so far, we shall use it to develop the conceptual schema. Stated in terms of the E-R model, the schema specifies all entity sets, relationship sets, attributes, and mapping constraints. The designer reviews the schema to confirm that all data requirements are indeed satisfied and are not in conflict with one another. She can also examine the design to remove any redundant features. Her focus at this point is describing the data and their relationships, rather than on specifying physical storage details.

A fully developed conceptual schema will also indicate the functional re-quirements of the enterprise. In a *specification of functional requirements*, users describe the kinds of operations (or transactions) that will be performed on the data. Example operations include modifying or updating data, searching for and retrieving specific data, and deleting data. A review of the schema for meeting functional requirements can be made at this stage of conceptual design.

The process of moving from an abstract data model to the implementation of the database proceeds in two final design phases. In the *logical-design* phase, the high-level conceptual schema is mapped onto the implementation data model of the DBMS that will be used. The resulting DBMS-specific database schema is used in the subsequent *physical-design* phase, in which the physical features of the database are specified. These features include the form of file organization and the internal storage structures; they are discussed in Chapter 10.

In this chapter, we cover only the concepts of the E-R model as used in the conceptual-schema-design phase. We have presented a brief overview of the database-design process to provide a context for the discussion of the E-R data model. Database design receives a full treatment in Chapter 7.

In Sections 2.8.2 and 2.8.3, we apply the two initial database-design phases to our banking-enterprise example. We employ the E-R data model to translate user requirements into a conceptual design schema that is depicted as an E-R diagram.

## 2.8.2   Data Requirements for Banking Enterprise

The initial specification of user requirements may be based on interviews with the database users, and on the designer's own analysis of the enterprise. The description that arises from this design phase serves as the basis for specifying the conceptual structure of the database. The following list itemizes the major requirements for the banking enterprise.

- The bank is organized into branches. Each branch is located in a particular city and is identified by a unique name. The bank monitors the assets of each branch.

- Bank customers are identified by their social-security numbers. The bank stores each customer's name, and the street and city where the customer lives. Customers may have accounts, and can take out loans. A customer may be associated with a particular banker, who may act as a loan officer or personal banker for that customer.

- Bank employees are also identified by their social-security numbers. The bank administration stores the name and telephone number of each employee, the names of the employee's dependents, and the social-security number of the employee's manager. The bank also keeps track of the employee's start date and, thus, length of employment.

- The bank offers two types of accounts—savings and checking accounts. Accounts can be held by more than one customer, and a customer can have more than one account. Each account is assigned a unique account number. The bank maintains a record of each account's balance, and the most recent date on which the account was accessed by each customer holding the account. In addition, each savings account has an interest rate, and overdrafts are recorded for each checking account.

- A loan originates at a particular branch and can be held by one or more customers. A loan is identified by a unique loan number. For each loan, the bank keeps track of the loan amount and the loan payments. Although a loan-payment number does not uniquely identify a particular payment among those for all the bank's loans, a payment number does identify a particular payment for a specific loan. The date and amount are recorded for each payment.

In a real banking enterprise, the bank would keep track of deposits and withdrawals from savings and checking accounts, just as it keeps track of payments to loan accounts. Since the modeling requirements for that tracking are similar, and we would like to keep our example application small, we do not keep track of such deposits and withdrawals in our model.

### 2.8.3   Entity-Sets Designation of Banking Enterprise

Our specification of data requirements serves as the starting point for constructing a conceptual schema for the database. From the specifications listed in Section 2.8.2, we begin to identify entity sets and their attributes.

- The *branch* entity set, with attributes *branch-name*, *branch-city*, and *assets*
- The *customer* entity set, with attributes:
    *customer-name*, *social-security*, *customer-street*; and *customer-city*
  A possible additional attribute is *banker-name*
- The *employee* entity set, with attributes:
    *e-social-security*, *employee-name*, *telephone-number*, *salary*, and *manager*

Additional descriptive features are the multivalued attribute *dependent-name*, the base attribute *start-date*, and the derived attribute *employment-length*

- Two account entity sets—*savings-account* and *checking-account*—with the common attributes of *account-number* and *balance*; in addition, *savings-account* has the attribute *interest-rate*, and *checking-account* has the attribute *overdraft-amount*

- The *loan* entity set, with the attributes:
      *loan-number*, *amount*, and *originating-branch*
  A possible additional attribute is the multivalued composite attribute *loan-payment*, with component attributes:
      *payment-number*, *payment-date*, and *payment-amount*

## 2.8.4   Relationship Sets Designation of Banking Enterprise

We now return to the rudimentary design scheme of Section 2.8.3 and specify the following relationship sets and mapping cardinalities.

- *borrower*, a many-to-many relationship set between *customer* and *loan*

- *loan-branch*, a many-to-one relationship set that indicates in which branch a loan originated

- *loan-payment*, a one-to-many relationship from *loan* to *payment*, which documents that a payment is made on a loan

- *depositor*, with relationship attribute *access-date*, a many-to-many relationship set between *customer* and *account*, indicating that a customer owns an account

- *cust-banker*, with relationship attribute *type*, a many-to-one relationship set expressing that a customer can be advised by a bank employee, and that a bank employee can advise one or more customers

- *works-for*, a relationship set between *employee* entities with role indicators *manager* and *worker*; the mapping cardinalities express that an employee works for only one manager, and that a manager supervises one or more employees

Note that we have replaced the *banker-name* attribute of the *customer* entity set by the *cust-banker* relationship set, and the *manager* attribute of the *employee* entity set by the *works-for* relationship set. We have chosen to retain *loan* as an entity set. The relationship sets *loan-branch* and *loan-payment* have replaced, respectively, the *originating-branch* and *loan-payment* attributes of the *loan* entity set.

## 2.8.5   E-R Diagram for Banking Enterprise

Drawing on the discussions presented in Section 2.8.4, we now present the completed E-R diagram for our example banking enterprise. Figure 2.18 depicts the full representation of a conceptual model of a bank, expressed in terms of E-R concepts. The diagram includes the entity sets, attributes, relationship sets, and

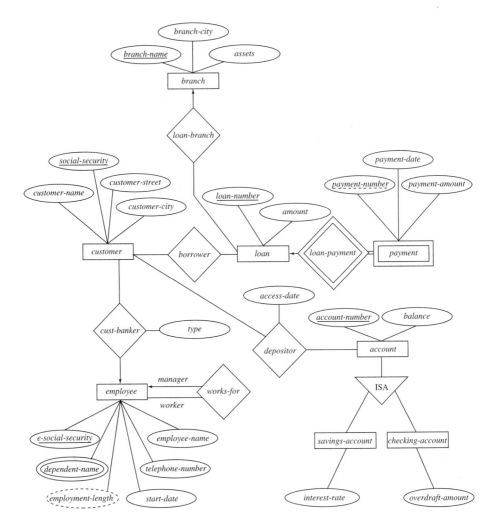

Figure 2.18    E-R diagram for banking enterprise.

mapping cardinalities arrived at through the design processes of Sections 2.8.2 and 2.8.3, and refined in Section 2.8.4.

## 2.9    Reduction of an E-R Schema to Tables

A database that conforms to an E-R database schema can be represented by a collection of tables. For each entity set and for each relationship set in the database, there is a unique table that is assigned the name of the corresponding entity set or relationship set. Each table has multiple columns, each of which has a unique name.

Both the E-R model and the relational-database model are abstract, logical representations of real-world enterprises. Because the two models employ similar design principles, we can convert an E-R design into a relational design. Converting a database representation from an E-R diagram to a table format is the basis for deriving a relational-database design from an E-R diagram. Although important differences exist between a relation and a table, informally, a relation can be considered to be a table of values. In this section, we describe how an E-R schema can be represented by tables; and in Chapter 3, we show how to generate a relational-database schema from an E-R schema.

## 2.9.1  Tabular Representation of Strong Entity Sets

Let $E$ be a strong entity set with descriptive attributes $a_1, a_2, \ldots, a_n$. We represent this entity by a table called $E$ with $n$ distinct columns, each of which corresponds to one of the attributes of $E$. Each row in this table corresponds to one entity of the entity set $E$.

As an illustration, consider the entity set *loan* of the E-R diagram shown in Figure 2.8. This entity set has two attributes: *loan-number* and *amount*. We represent this entity set by a table called *loan*, with two columns, as shown in Figure 2.19. The row

$$(\text{L-17, 1000})$$

in the *loan* table means that loan number L-17 has a loan amount of $1000. We can add a new entity to the database by inserting a row into a table. We can also delete or modify rows.

Let $D_1$ denote the set of all loan numbers, and let $D_2$ denote the set of all balances. Any row of the *loan* table must consist of a 2-tuple $(v_1, v_2)$, where $v_1$ is a loan (that is, $v_1$ is in set $D_1$) and $v_2$ is an amount (that is, $v_2$ is in set $D_2$). In general, the *loan* table will contain only a subset of the set of all possible rows. We refer to the set of all possible rows of *loan* as the *Cartesian product* of $D_1$ and $D_2$, denoted by

$$D_1 \times D_2$$

In general, if we have a table of $n$ columns, we denote the Cartesian product of $D_1, D_2, \ldots, D_n$ by

$$D_1 \times D_2 \times \ldots \times D_{n-1} \times D_n$$

| loan-number | amount |
|:-----------:|:------:|
| L-17 | 1000 |
| L-23 | 2000 |
| L-15 | 1500 |
| L-14 | 1500 |
| L-93 | 500 |
| L-11 | 900 |
| L-16 | 1300 |

Figure 2.19   The *loan* table.

| customer-name | social-security | customer-street | customer-city |
|:---:|:---:|:---:|:---:|
| Jones | 321-12-3123 | Main | Harrison |
| Smith | 019-28-3746 | North | Rye |
| Hayes | 677-89-9011 | Main | Harrison |
| Curry | 244-66-8800 | North | Rye |
| Lindsay | 336-66-9999 | Park | Pittsfield |
| Turner | 182-73-6091 | Putnam | Stamford |
| Williams | 963-96-3963 | Nassau | Princeton |
| Adams | 335-57-7991 | Spring | Pittsfield |
| Johnson | 192-83-7465 | Alma | Palo Alto |

Figure 2.20    The *customer* table.

As another example, consider the entity set *customer* of the E-R diagram shown in Figure 2.8. This entity set has the attributes *customer-name*, *social-security*, *customer-street*, and *customer-city*. The table corresponding to *customer* has four columns, as shown in Figure 2.20.

## 2.9.2  Tabular Representation of Weak Entity Sets

Let $A$ be a weak entity set with attributes $a_1, a_2, \ldots, a_m$. Let $B$ be the strong entity set on which $A$ is dependent. Let the primary key of $B$ consist of attributes $b_1, b_2, \ldots, b_n$. We represent the entity set $A$ by a table called $A$ with one column for each attribute of the set:

$$\{a_1, a_2, \ldots, a_m\} \cup \{b_1, b_2, \ldots, b_n\}$$

As an illustration, consider the entity set *payment* shown in the E-R diagram of Figure 2.14. This entity set has three attributes: *payment-number*, *payment-date*, and *payment-amount*. The primary key of the *loan* entity set, on which *payment* is dependent, is *loan-number*. Thus, *payment* is represented by a table with four columns labeled *loan-number*, *payment-number*, *payment-date*, and *payment-amount*, as depicted in Figure 2.21.

## 2.9.3  Tabular Representation of Relationship Sets

Let $R$ be a relationship set, let $a_1, a_2, \ldots, a_m$ be the set of attributes formed by the union of the primary keys of each of the entity sets participating in $R$, and let the descriptive attributes (if any) of $R$ be $b_1, b_2, \ldots, b_n$. We represent this relationship set by a table called $R$ with one column for each attribute of the set:

$$\{a_1, a_2, \ldots, a_m\} \cup \{b_1, b_2, \ldots, b_n\}$$

| loan-number | payment-number | payment-date | payment-amount |
|:-----------:|:--------------:|:------------:|:--------------:|
| L-17 | 5 | 10 May 1996 | 50 |
| L-23 | 11 | 17 May 1996 | 75 |
| L-15 | 22 | 23 May 1996 | 300 |
| L-14 | 69 | 28 May 1996 | 500 |
| L-93 | 103 | 3 June 1996 | 900 |
| L-17 | 6 | 7 June 1996 | 50 |
| L-11 | 53 | 7 June 1996 | 125 |
| L-93 | 104 | 13 June 1996 | 200 |
| L-17 | 7 | 17 June 1996 | 100 |
| L-16 | 58 | 18 June 1996 | 135 |

Figure 2.21 The *payment* table.

As an illustration, consider the relationship set *borrower* in the E-R diagram of Figure 2.8. This relationship set involves the following two entity sets:

- *customer*, with the primary key *social-security*
- *loan*, with the primary key *loan-number*

Since the relationship set has no attributes, the *borrower* table has two columns labeled *social-security* and *loan-number*, as shown in Figure 2.22.

### 2.9.3.1 Redundancy of Tables

The case of a relationship set linking a weak entity set to the corresponding strong entity set is special. As we noted earlier, these relationships are many to one and have no descriptive attributes. Furthermore, the primary key of a weak entity set includes the primary key of the strong entity set. In the E-R diagram of Figure 2.14, the weak entity set *payment* is dependent on the strong entity set *loan* via the relationship set *loan-payment*. The primary key of *payment* is {*loan-number*, *payment-number*}, and the primary key of *loan* is {*loan-number*}. Since *loan-payment* has no descriptive attributes, the table for *loan-payment* would

| social-security | loan-number |
|:---------------:|:-----------:|
| 321-12-3123 | L-17 |
| 019-28-3746 | L-23 |
| 677-89-9011 | L-15 |
| 555-55-5555 | L-14 |
| 244-66-8800 | L-93 |
| 019-28-3746 | L-11 |
| 963-96-3963 | L-17 |
| 335-57-7991 | L-16 |

Figure 2.22 The *borrower* table.

have two columns, *loan-number* and *payment-number*. The table for the entity set *payment* has four columns, *loan-number*, *payment-number*, *payment-date*, and *payment-amount*. Thus, the *loan-payment* table is redundant. In general, the table for the relationship set linking a weak entity set to its corresponding strong entity set is redundant and does not need to be present in a tabular representation of an E-R diagram.

### 2.9.3.2  Combination of Tables

Consider a many-to-one relationship set *AB* from entity set *A* to entity set *B*. Using our table-construction scheme outlined previously, we get three tables: *A*, *B*, and *AB*. However, if there is an existence dependency of *A* on *B* (that is, for each entity *a* in *A*, the existence of *a* depends on the existence of some entity *b* in *B*), then we can combine the tables *A* and *AB* to form a single table consisting of the union of columns of both tables.

As an illustration, consider the E-R diagram of Figure 2.23. The relationship set *account-branch* is many to one from *account* to *branch*. Further, the double line in the E-R diagram indicates that the participation of *account* in the *account-branch* is total. Hence, an account cannot exist without being associated with a particular branch. Therefore, we require only the following two tables:

- *account*, with attributes *account-number*, *balance*, and *branch-name*
- *branch*, with attributes *branch-name*, *branch-city*, and *assets*

### 2.9.4  Multivalued Attributes

We have seen that attributes in an E-R diagram generally map directly into columns for the appropriate tables. Multivalued attributes, however, are an exception; new tables are created for these attributes.

For a multivalued attribute *M*, we create a table *T* with a column *C* that corresponds to *M* and columns corresponding to the primary key of the entity set or relationship set of which *M* is an attribute. As an illustration, consider the E-R diagram depicted in Figure 2.18. The diagram includes the multivalued attribute *dependent-name*. For this multivalued attribute, we create a table *dependent-name*,

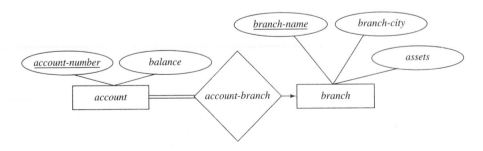

Figure 2.23    E-R diagram.

with columns *dname*, referring to the *dependent-name* attribute of *employee*, and *e-social-security*, representing the primary key of the entity set *employee*. Each dependent of an employee is represented as a unique row in the table.

### 2.9.5  Tabular Representation of Generalization

There are two different methods for transforming to a tabular form an E-R diagram that includes generalization. Although we refer to the generalization depicted in Figure 2.15, we have chosen to simplify this discussion by including only the first tier of lower-level entity sets—that is, *savings-account* and *checking-account*.

1. Create a table for the higher-level entity set. For each lower-level entity set, create a table that includes a column for each of the attributes of that entity set plus a column for each attribute of the primary key of the higher-level entity set. Thus, for the E-R diagram of Figure 2.15, we have three tables:
   - *account*, with attributes *account-number* and *balance*
   - *savings-account*, with attributes *account-number* and *interest-rate*
   - *checking-account*, with attributes *account-number* and *overdraft-amount*

2. If the generalization is disjoint and complete—that is, if no entity is a member of two lower-level entity sets directly below a higher-level entity set, and if every entity in the higher level entity set is also a member of one of the lower-level entity sets—then an alternative representation is possible. Here, create no table for the higher-level entity set. Instead, for each lower-level entity set, create a table that includes a column for each of the attributes of that entity set plus a column for *each* attribute of the higher-level entity set. Then, for the E-R diagram of Figure 2.15, we have two tables.
   - *savings-account*, with attributes *account-number*, *balance*, and *interest-rate*
   - *checking-account*, with attributes *account-number*, *balance*, and *overdraft-amount*

   The *savings-account* and *checking-account* relations corresponding to these tables both have *account-number* as the primary key.

If the second method were used for an overlapping generalization, some values such as *balance* would be stored twice unnecessarily. Similarly, if the generalization were not complete—that is, if some accounts were neither savings nor checking accounts—then such accounts could not be represented with the second method.

### 2.9.6  Tabular Representation of Aggregation

Transforming to a tabular form an E-R diagram which includes aggregation is straightforward. Consider the diagram of Figure 2.17. The table for the relationship set *loan-officer* includes a column for each attribute in the primary key of the entity set *employee* and the relationship set *borrower*. It would also include a column for any descriptive attributes, if they existed, of the relationship set *loan-officer*. Using the same procedure as before for the rest of the diagram, we create the following tables:

- *customer*, with attributes *customer-name*, *social-security*, *customer-street*, and *customer-city*
- *loan*, with attributes *loan-number* and *amount*
- *borrower*, with attributes *social-security* and *loan-number*
- *employee*, with attributes *e-social-security*, *employee-name*, and *telephone-number*
- *loan-officer*, with attributes *social-security*, *loan-number*, and *e-social-security*.

## 2.10   Summary

The entity–relationship (E-R) data model is based on a perception of a real world that consists of a set of basic objects called *entities*, and of *relationships* among these objects. The model is intended primarily for the database-design process. It was developed to facilitate database design by allowing the specification of an *enterprise schema*. Such a schema represents the overall logical structure of the database. This overall structure can be expressed graphically by an *E-R diagram*.

An *entity* is an object that exists and is distinguishable from other objects. We accomplish the distinction by associating with each entity a set of attributes that describes the object. A *relationship* is an association among several entities. The collection of all entities of the same type is an *entity set*, and the collection of all relationships of the same type is a *relationship set*.

*Mapping cardinalities* express the number of entities to which another entity can be associated via a relationship set. Another form of constraint is *existence dependency*, which specifies that the existence of entity $x$ depends on the existence of entity $y$.

An important task in database modeling is to specify how entities and relationships are distinguished. Conceptually, individual entities and relationships are distinct; from a database perspective, however, their difference must be expressed in terms of their attributes. To make such distinctions, we assign a *primary key* to each entity set. The primary key is a set of one or more attributes that, taken collectively, allows us to identify uniquely an entity in the entity set and a relationship in a relationship set. An entity set that does not have sufficient attributes to form a primary key is termed a *weak entity set*. An entity set that has a primary key is termed a *strong entity set*.

*Specialization* and *generalization* define a containment relationship between a higher-level entity set and one or more lower-level entity sets. Specialization is the result of taking a subset of a higher-level entity set to form a lower-level entity set. Generalization is the result of taking the union of two or more disjoint (lower-level) entity sets to produce a higher-level entity set. The attributes of higher-level entity sets are inherited by lower-level entity sets.

One limitation of the E-R model is that it cannot express relationships among relationships. The solution is to use *aggregation*; an abstraction in which relationship sets are treated as higher-level entity sets. Thus, a relationship set and its associated entity sets can be viewed as a higher-level entity that is treated in the same manner as any other entity.

The various features of the E-R model offer the database designer numerous choices in how best to represent the enterprise being modeled. Concepts and objects may, in certain cases, be represented by entities, relationships, or attributes. Aspects of the overall structure of the enterprise may be best described using weak entity sets, generalization, specialization, or aggregation. Often, the designer must weigh the merits of a simple, compact model versus those of a more precise, but more complex, one.

A database that conforms to an E-R diagram can be represented by a collection of tables. For each entity set and for each relationship set in the database, there is a unique table that is assigned the name of the corresponding entity set or relationship set. Each table has a number of columns, each of which, has a unique name. Converting of database representation from an E-R diagram to a table format is the basis for deriving a relational-database design from an E-R diagram.

## Exercises

**2.1.** Explain the distinctions among the terms primary key, candidate key, and superkey.

**2.2.** Construct an E-R diagram for a university registrar's office. The office maintains data about each class, including the instructor, the enrollment, and the time and place of the class meetings. For each student–class pair, a grade is recorded. Document all assumptions that you make about the mapping constraints.

**2.3.** Construct an E-R diagram for a car-insurance company that has a set of customers, each of whom owns one or more cars. Each car has associated with it zero to any number of recorded accidents.

**2.4.** Construct an E-R diagram for a hospital with a set of patients and a set of medical doctors. Associate with each patient a log of the various tests and examinations conducted.

**2.5.** Construct appropriate tables for each of the E-R diagrams in Exercises 2 to 4.

**2.6.** Explain the difference between a weak and a strong entity set.

**2.7.** We can convert any weak entity set to a strong entity set by simply adding appropriate attributes. Why, then, do we have weak entity sets?

**2.8.** Define the concept of aggregation. Give two examples of where this concept is useful.

**2.9.** Consider an E-R diagram in which the same entity set appears several times. Why is allowing this redundancy a bad practice that one should avoid whenever possible?

**2.10.** Consider a university database for the scheduling of classrooms for final exams. This database could be modeled as the single entity set *exam*, with attributes *course-name*, *section-number*, *room-number*, and *time*. Alternatively, one or more additional entity sets could be defined, along with relationship sets to replace some of the attributes of the *exam* entity set, as

- *course* with attributes *name*, *department*, and *c-number*
- *section* with attributes *s-number* and *enrollment*, and dependent as a weak entity set on *course*
- *room* with attributes *r-number*, *capacity*, and *building*

(*a*) Show an E-R diagram illustrating the use of all three additional entity sets listed.

(*b*) Explain what application characteristics would influence a decision to include or not to include each of the additional entity sets.

**2.11.** When designing an E-R diagram for a particular enterprise, you have several alternatives from which to choose.

(*a*) What criteria should you consider in making the appropriate choice?

(*b*) Design three alternative E-R diagrams to represent the university registrar's office of Exercise 2.2. List the merits of each. Argue in favor of one of the alternatives.

**2.12.** An E-R diagram can be viewed as a graph. What do the following mean in terms of the structure of an enterprise schema?

(*a*) The graph is disconnected.

(*b*) The graph is acyclic.

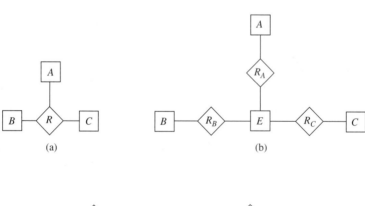

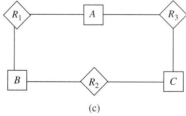

Figure 2.24     E-R diagram for Exercise 2.13. (attributes not shown)

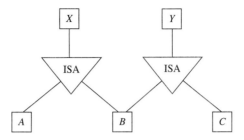

Figure 2.25   E-R diagram for Exercise 2.18 (attributes not shown).

**2.13.** In Section 2.2.3, we represented a ternary relationship (Figure 2.24a) using binary relationships, as shown in Figure 2.24b. Consider the alternative
shown in Figure 2.24c. Discuss the relative merits of these two alternative
representations of a ternary relationship by binary relationships.

**2.14.** Design a generalization–specialization hierarchy for a motor-vehicle sales
company. The company sells motorcycles, passenger cars, vans, and buses.
Justify your placement of attributes at each level of the hierarchy. Explain
why they should not be placed at a higher or lower level.

**2.15.** Explain the distinction between condition-defined and user-defined design
constraints. Which of these constraints can the system check automatically?
Explain your answer.

**2.16.** Explain the distinction between disjoint and overlapping design constraints.

**2.17.** Explain the distinction between total and partial design constraints.

**2.18.** Figure 2.25 shows a lattice structure of generalization and specialization.
For entity sets $A$, $B$, and $C$, explain how attributes are inherited from the
higher-level entity sets $X$ and $Y$. Discuss how to handle a case where an
attribute of $X$ has the same name as some attribute of $Y$.

**2.19.** Consider two separate banks that decide to merge. Assume that both banks
use exactly the same E-R database schema—the one in Figure 2.18. (This
assumption is, of course, highly unrealistic; we consider the more realistic
case in Section 18.9.) If the merged bank is to have a single database, there
are several potential problems:
- The possibility that the two original banks have branches with the same
name
- The possibility that some customers are customers of both original
banks
- The possibility that some loan or account numbers were used at both
original banks (for different loans or accounts, of course)

For each of these potential problems, describe why there is indeed a potential for difficulties. Propose a solution to the problem. For your solution,
explain any changes that would have to be made, and describe what their
affect would be on the schema and the data.

**2.20.** Reconsider the situation described for Exercise 2.19 under the assumption
that one bank is in the U.S., and the other is in Canada. As before, the

banks use the schema of Figure 2.18, except that the Canadian bank uses the *social-insurance* number assigned by the Canadian government, whereas the U.S. bank uses the social-security number, as we have been assuming throughout this chapter. What problems (beyond those identified in Exercise 2.19) might occur in this multinational case? How would you resolve them? Be sure to consider both the scheme and the actual data values in constructing your answer.

# Bibliographical Notes

The E-R data model was introduced by Chen [1976]. A logical design methodology for relational databases using the extended E-R model is presented by Teorey et al. [1986]. Mapping from extended E-R models to the relational model is discussed by Lyngbaek and Vianu [1987], and by Markowitz and Shoshani [1992].

Various data-manipulation languages for the E-R model have been proposed: GERM [Benneworth et al. 1981], GORDAS [ElMasri and Wiederhold 1981], and ERROL [Markowitz and Raz 1983]. A graphical query language for the E-R database was proposed by Zhang and Mendelzon [1983], and by ElMasri and Larson [1985]. An algebra for a general E-R model is presented by Parent and Spaccapietra [1985]. Campbell et al. [1985] present a language for the E-R model that is equivalent in expressive power to the relation algebra and calculus (see Chapter 3). An E-R language with formal mathematical semantics is given in Gogolla and Hohenstein [1991].

The concepts of generalization, specialization, and aggregation were introduced by Smith and Smith [1977], and were expanded in Hammer and McLeod [1981]. Lenzerini and Santucci [1983] have used these concepts in defining cardinality constraints in the E-R model. Logic-based semantics for a variant of the E-R model is given by Di Battista and Lenzerini [1989].

Basic textbook discussions are offered by Batini et al. [1992], and ElMasri and Navathe [1994].

# CHAPTER
# 3

# RELATIONAL
# MODEL

The relational model has established itself as the primary data model for commercial data-processing applications. The first database systems were based on either the network model (see Appendix A) or the hierarchical model (see Appendix B). Those two older models are tied more closely to the underlying implementation of the database than is the relational model.

A substantial theory exists for relational databases. This theory assists in the design of relational databases and in the efficient processing of user requests for information from the database. We shall examine this theory in Chapters 6 and 7.

The relational model is now being used in numerous applications outside the domain of traditional data processing. We shall consider extensions to the relational model required to handle these newer applications in Chapter 9.

## 3.1 Structure of Relational Databases

A relational database consists of a collection of *tables*, each of which is assigned a unique name. Each table has a structure similar to that presented in Chapter 2, where we represented E-R databases by tables. A row in a table represents a *relationship* among a set of values. Since a table is a collection of such relationships, there is a close correspondence between the concept of *table* and the mathematical concept of *relation*, from which the relational data model takes its name. In what follows, we introduce the concept of relation.

In this chapter, we shall be using a number of different relations to illustrate the various concepts underlying the relational data model. These relations represent part of a banking enterprise. They differ slightly from the tables that were used in Chapter 2, so that we can simplify our presentation. We shall discuss criteria for the appropriateness of relational structures in great detail in Chapter 7.

### 3.1.1   Basic Structure

Consider the *account* table of Figure 3.1. It has three column headers: *branch-name*, *account-number*, and *balance*. Following the terminology of the relational model, we refer to these headers as attributes (as we did for the E-R model in Chapter 2). For each attribute, there is a set of permitted values, called the *domain* of that attribute. For the attribute *branch-name*, for example, the domain is the set of all branch names. Let $D_1$ denote this set, $D_2$ denote the set of all account numbers, and $D_3$ the set of all balances. As we saw in Chapter 2, any row of *account* must consist of a 3-tuple $(v_1, v_2, v_3)$, where $v_1$ is a branch name (that is, $v_1$ is in domain $D_1$), $v_2$ is an account number (that is, $v_2$ is in domain $D_2$), and $v_3$ is a balance (that is, $v_3$ is in domain $D_3$). In general, *account* will contain only a subset of the set of all possible rows. Therefore, *account* is a subset of

$$D_1 \times D_2 \times D_3$$

In general, a table of *n* attributes must be a subset of

$$D_1 \times D_2 \times \ldots \times D_{n-1} \times D_n$$

Mathematicians define a relation to be a subset of a Cartesian product of a list of domains. This definition corresponds almost exactly with our definition of *table*. The only difference is that we have assigned names to attributes, whereas mathematicians rely on numeric "names," using the integer 1 to denote the attribute whose domain appears first in the list of domains, 2 for the attribute whose domain appears second, and so on. Because tables are essentially relations, we shall use the mathematical terms *relation* and *tuple* in place of the terms *table* and *row*.

In the *account* relation of Figure 3.1, there are seven tuples. Let the *tuple variable t* refer to the first tuple of the relation. We use the notation $t[branch\text{-}name]$ to denote the value of $t$ on the *branch-name* attribute. Thus, $t[branch\text{-}name]$

| branch-name | account-number | balance |
|---|---|---|
| Downtown | A-101 | 500 |
| Mianus | A-215 | 700 |
| Perryridge | A-102 | 400 |
| Round Hill | A-305 | 350 |
| Brighton | A-201 | 900 |
| Redwood | A-222 | 700 |
| Brighton | A-217 | 750 |

Figure 3.1   The *account* relation.

= "Downtown," and $t[balance] = 500$. Alternatively, we may write $t[1]$ to denote the value of tuple $t$ on the first attribute (*branch-name*), $t[2]$ to denote *account-number*, and so on. Since a relation is a set of tuples, we use the mathematical notation of $t \in r$ to denote that tuple $t$ is in relation $r$.

We shall require that, for all relations $r$, the domains of all attributes of $r$ be atomic. A domain is *atomic* if elements of the domain are considered to be indivisible units. For example, the set of integers is an atomic domain, but the set of all sets of integers is a nonatomic domain. The distinction is that we do not normally consider integers to have subparts, but we consider sets of integers to have subparts—namely, the integers comprising the set. The important issue is not what the domain itself is, but rather how we use domain elements in our database. The domain of all integers would be nonatomic if we considered each integer to be an ordered list of digits. In all our examples, we shall assume atomic domains. In Chapter 9, we shall discuss the *nested relational* data model, which allows nonatomic domains.

It is possible for several attributes to have the same domain. For example, suppose that we have a relation *customer* that has the three attributes *customer-name*, *customer-street*, and *customer-city*, and a relation *employee* that includes the attribute *employee-name*. It is possible that the attributes *customer-name* and *employee-name* will have the same domain: the set of all person names. The domains of *balance* and *branch-name*, on the other hand, certainly ought to be distinct. It is perhaps less clear whether *customer-name* and *branch-name* should have the same domain. At the physical level, both customer names and branch names are character strings. However, at the logical level, we may want *customer-name* and *branch-name* to have distinct domains.

One domain value that is a member of any possible domain is the *null* value, which signifies that the value is unknown or does not exist. For example, suppose that we include the attribute *telephone-number* in the *customer* relation. It may be that a customer does not have a telephone number, or that the telephone number is unlisted. We would then have to resort to null values to signify that the value is unknown or does not exist. We shall see later that null values cause a number of difficulties when we access or update the database, and thus should be eliminated if at all possible.

## 3.1.2  Database Schema

When we talk about a database, we must differentiate between the *database schema*, or the logical design of the database, and a *database instance*, which is a snapshot of the data in the database at a given instant in time.

The concept of a relation corresponds to the programming-language notion of a variable. The concept of a *relation schema* corresponds to the programming-language notion of type definition.

It is convenient to give a name to a relation schema, just as we give names to type definitions in programming languages. We adopt the convention of using lowercase names for relations, and names beginning with an uppercase letter for

| branch-name | branch-city | assets |
|-------------|-------------|--------|
| Downtown    | Brooklyn    | 9000000 |
| Redwood     | Palo Alto   | 2100000 |
| Perryridge  | Horseneck   | 1700000 |
| Mianus      | Horseneck   | 400000 |
| Round Hill  | Horseneck   | 8000000 |
| Pownal      | Bennington  | 300000 |
| North Town  | Rye         | 3700000 |
| Brighton    | Brooklyn    | 7100000 |

Figure 3.2    The *branch* relation.

relation schemas. Following this notation, we use *Account-schema* to denote the relation schema for relation *account*. Thus,

$$Account\text{-}schema = (branch\text{-}name, account\text{-}number, balance)$$

We denote the fact that *account* is a relation on *Account-schema* by

$$account(Account\text{-}schema)$$

In general, a relation schema comprises a list of attributes and their corresponding domains. We shall not be concerned about the precise definition of the domain of each attribute until we discuss the SQL language in Chapter 4.

The concept of a *relation instance* corresponds to the programming language notion of a value of a variable. The value of a given variable may change with time; similarly the contents of a relation instance may change with time as the relation is updated. However, we often simply say "relation" when we actually mean "relation instance."

As an example of a relation instance, consider the *branch* relation of Figure 3.2. The schema for that relation is

$$Branch\text{-}schema = (branch\text{-}name, branch\text{-}city, assets)$$

Note that the attribute *branch-name* appears in both *Branch-schema* and *Account-schema*. This duplication is not a coincidence. Rather, using common attributes in relation schemas is one way of relating tuples of distinct relations. For example, suppose we wish to find the information about all of the accounts maintained in branches located in Brooklyn. We look first at the *branch* relation to find the names of all the branches located in Brooklyn. Then, for each such branch, we would look in the *account* relation to find the information about the accounts maintained at that branch. Using the terminology of the E-R model, we say that the attribute *branch-name* represents the same entity set in both relations.

Let's continue our banking example. We need a relation to describe information about customers. The relation schema is

$$Customer\text{-}schema = (customer\text{-}name, customer\text{-}street, customer\text{-}city)$$

A sample relation *customer* (*Customer-schema*) is shown in Figure 3.3.

| customer-name | customer-street | customer-city |
|---|---|---|
| Jones | Main | Harrison |
| Smith | North | Rye |
| Hayes | Main | Harrison |
| Curry | North | Rye |
| Lindsay | Park | Pittsfield |
| Turner | Putnam | Stamford |
| Williams | Nassau | Princeton |
| Adams | Spring | Pittsfield |
| Johnson | Alma | Palo Alto |
| Glenn | Sand Hill | Woodside |
| Brooks | Senator | Brooklyn |
| Green | Walnut | Stamford |

Figure 3.3    The *customer* relation.

We also need a relation to describe the association between customers and accounts. The relation schema to describe this association is

*Depositor-schema* = (*customer-name, account-number*)

A sample relation *depositor* (*Depositor-schema*) is shown in Figure 3.4.

It would appear that, for our banking example, we could have just one relation schema, rather than several. That is, it may be easier for a user to think in terms of one relation schema, rather than in terms of several. Suppose that we used only one relation for our example, with schema

(*branch-name, branch-city, assets, customer-name, customer-street
customer-city, account-number, balance*)

Observe that, if a customer has several accounts, we must list her address once for each account. That is, we must repeat certain information several times. This repetition is wasteful and is avoided by the use of several relations, as in our example.

In addition, if a branch has no accounts (a newly created branch, say, that has no customers yet), we cannot construct a complete tuple on the preceding

| customer-name | account-number |
|---|---|
| Johnson | A-101 |
| Smith | A-215 |
| Hayes | A-102 |
| Turner | A-305 |
| Johnson | A-201 |
| Jones | A-217 |
| Lindsay | A-222 |

Figure 3.4    The *depositor* relation.

| branch-name | loan-number | amount |
|-------------|-------------|--------|
| Downtown | L-17 | 1000 |
| Redwood | L-23 | 2000 |
| Perryridge | L-15 | 1500 |
| Downtown | L-14 | 1500 |
| Mianus | L-93 | 500 |
| Round Hill | L-11 | 900 |
| Perryridge | L-16 | 1300 |

Figure 3.5    The *loan* relation.

single relation, because no data concerning *customer* and *account* are available yet. To represent incomplete tuples, we must use *null* values that signify that the value is unknown or does not exist. Thus, in our example, the values for *customer-name*, *customer-street*, and so on must be null. By using several relations, we can represent the branch Information for a bank with no customers without using null values. We simply use a tuple on *Branch-schema* to represent the information about the branch, and create tuples on the other schemas only when the appropriate information becomes available.

In Chapter 7, we shall study criteria to help us decide when one set of relation schemas is more appropriate than another, in terms of information repetition and the existence of null values. For now, we shall assume that the relation schemas are given.

We include two additional relations to describe data about loans maintained in the various branches in the bank:

$$Loan\text{-}schema = (branch\text{-}name, loan\text{-}number, amount)$$
$$Borrower\text{-}schema = (customer\text{-}name, loan\text{-}number)$$

The sample relations *loan* (*Loan-schema*) and *borrower* (*Borrower-schema*) are shown in Figures 3.5 and 3.6, respectively.

The banking enterprise that we have described is derived from the E-R diagram shown in Figure 3.7. The relation schemas correspond to the set of tables

| customer-name | loan-number |
|---------------|-------------|
| Jones | L-17 |
| Smith | L-23 |
| Hayes | L-15 |
| Jackson | L-14 |
| Curry | L-93 |
| Smith | L-11 |
| Williams | L-17 |
| Adams | L-16 |

Figure 3.6    The *borrower* relation.

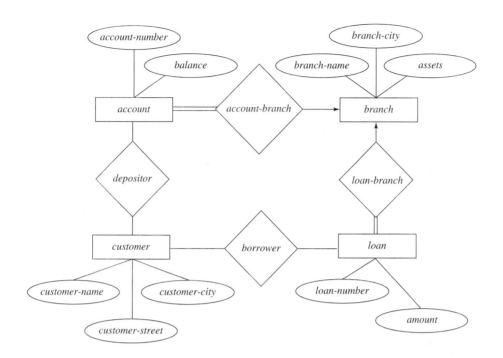

Figure 3.7    E-R diagram for the banking enterprise.

that we might generate using the method outlined in Section 2.9. We assume that the primary key for the *branch* entity set is *branch-name*. The primary key for *Customer-schema* is *customer-name*. We are not using the *social-security* attribute, as we did in Chapter 2, because now we want to have smaller relation schemas in our running example of a bank database. We expect that, in a real-world database, the *social-security* attribute would serve as a primary key. The primary keys for the *account* entity set and the *loan* entity set are *account-number* and *loan-number*, respectively. Note that the tables for *account-branch* and *loan-branch* have been combined into the tables for *account* and *loan* respectively. This can be done since the relationships are many-to-one, and the participation of entity sets *account* and *loan* in the relationships is total, that is, every account or loan must have an associated branch.

Finally, we note that the *customer* relation may contain information about customers who have neither an account nor a loan at the bank.

The banking enterprise described here will serve as our primary example in this chapter and in subsequent ones. On occasion, we shall need to introduce additional relation schemas to illustrate particular points.

### 3.1.3   Keys

The notions of *superkey*, *candidate key*, and *primary key*, as discussed in Chapter 2, are also applicable to the relational model. For example, in *Branch-schema*, {*branch-name*} and {*branch-name, branch-city*} are both superkeys. {*branch-*

*name, branch-city*} is not a candidate key, because {*branch-name*} is a subset
of {*branch-name, branch-city*} and {*branch-name*} itself is a superkey. However,
{*branch-name*} *is* a candidate key, and for our purpose also will serve as a primary
key. The attribute *branch-city* is not a superkey, since two branches in the same
city may have different names (and different asset figures).

Let $R$ be a relation schema. If we say that a subset $K$ of $R$ is a *superkey*
for $R$, we are restricting consideration to relations $r(R)$ in which no two distinct
tuples have the same values on all attributes in $K$. That is, if $t_1$ *and* $t_2$ are in $r$ and
$t_1 \neq t_2$, then $t_1[K] \neq t_2[K]$.

If a relational database schema is based on tables derived from an E-R
schema, it is possible to determine the primary key for a relation schema from
the primary keys of the entity or relationship sets from which the schema is
derived:

- **Strong entity set.** The primary key of the entity set becomes the primary key
  of the relation.
- **Weak entity set.** The table, and thus the relation, corresponding to a weak
  entity set includes
  - The attributes of the weak entity set
  - The primary key of the strong entity set on which the weak entity set
    depends

  The primary key of the relation consists of the union of the primary key of
  the strong entity set and the discriminator of the weak entity set.
- **Relationship set.** The union of the primary keys of the related entity sets
  becomes a superkey of the relation. If the relationship is many-to-many, this
  superkey is also the primary key. Section 2.4.2 describes how to determine
  the primary keys in other cases. Recall from Section 2.9.3 that no table is
  generated for relationship sets linking a weak entity set to the corresponding
  strong entity set.
- **Combined tables.** Recall from Section 2.9.3 that a binary many-to-one relationship set from $A$ to $B$ can be represented by a table consisting of the
  attributes of $A$ and attributes (if any exist) of the relationship set. The primary
  key of the "many" entity set becomes the primary key of the relation (that is,
  if the relationship set is many to one from $A$ to $B$, the primary key of $A$ is the
  primary key of the relation). For one-to-one relationship sets, the relation is
  constructed like that for a many-to-one relationship set. However, either entity
  set's primary key can be chosen as the primary key of the relation, since both
  are candidate keys.
- **Multivalued attributes.** Recall from Section 2.9.4 that a multivalued attribute
  $M$ is represented by a table consisting of the primary key of the entity set or
  relationship set of which $M$ is an attribute plus a column $C$ holding an individual value of $M$. The primary key of the entity or relationship set together
  with the attribute $C$ becomes the primary key for the relation.

From the preceding list, we see that a relation schema may include among
its attributes the primary key of another schema. This key is is called a *foreign*

*key*. For example, the attribute *branch-name* in *Account-schema* is a foreign key, since *branch-name* is the primary key of *Branch-schema*.

### 3.1.4   Query Languages

A *query language* is a language in which a user requests information from the database. These languages are typically of a level higher than that of a standard programming language. Query languages can be categorized as being either procedural or nonprocedural. In a *procedural language*, the user instructs the system to perform a sequence of operations on the database to compute the desired result. In a *nonprocedural language*, the user describes the information desired without giving a specific procedure for obtaining that information.

Most commercial relational-database systems offer a query language that includes elements of both the procedural and the nonprocedural approaches. We shall study several commercial languages in Chapters 4 and 5. In this chapter, we examine "pure" languages: The relational algebra is procedural, whereas the tuple relational calculus and the domain relational calculus are nonprocedural. These query languages are terse and formal, lacking the "syntactic sugar" of commercial languages, but they illustrate the fundamental techniques for extracting data from the database.

Initially, we shall be concerned with only queries. A complete data-manipulation language includes not only a query language, but also a language for database modification. Such languages include commands to insert and delete tuples, as well as commands to modify parts of existing tuples. We shall examine database modification after we complete our discussion of "pure" query languages.

## 3.2   The Relational Algebra

The relational algebra is a *procedural* query language. It consists of a set of operations that take one or two relations as input and produce a new relation as their result. The fundamental operations in the relational algebra are *select, project, union, set difference, Cartesian product,* and *rename*. In addition to the fundamental operations, there are several other operations—namely, set intersection, natural join, division, and assignment. These operations will be defined in terms of the fundamental operations.

### 3.2.1   Fundamental Operations

The select, project, and rename operations are called *unary* operations, because they operate on one relation. The other three operations operate on pairs of relations and are, therefore, called *binary* operations.

#### 3.2.1.1   The Select Operation

The *select* operation selects tuples that satisfy a given predicate. We use the lowercase Greek letter sigma ($\sigma$) to denote selection. The predicate appears as

| branch-name | loan-number | amount |
|-------------|-------------|--------|
| Perryridge  | L-15        | 1500   |
| Perryridge  | L-16        | 1300   |

Figure 3.8    Result of $\sigma_{branch\text{-}name\,=\,\text{"Perryridge"}}$ (*loan*).

a subscript to $\sigma$. The argument relation is given in parentheses following the $\sigma$. Thus, to select those tuples of the *loan* relation where the branch is "Perryridge," we write

$$\sigma_{branch\text{-}name\,=\,\text{"Perryridge"}} \ (loan)$$

If the *loan* relation is as shown in Figure 3.5, then the relation that results from the preceding query is as shown in Figure 3.8.

We can find all tuples in which the amount lent is more than $1200 by writing

$$\sigma_{amount>1200} \ (loan)$$

In general, we allow comparisons using $=, \neq, <, \leq, >, \geq$ in the selection predicate. Furthermore, we can combine several predicates into a larger predicate using the connectives *and* ($\wedge$) and *or* ($\vee$). Thus, to find those tuples pertaining to loans of more than $1200 made by the Perryridge branch, we write

$$\sigma_{branch\text{-}name\,=\,\text{"Perryridge"} \,\wedge\, amount>1200} \ (loan)$$

The selection predicate may include comparisons between two attributes. To illustrate, consider the relation *loan-officer* that consists of three attributes: *customer-name*, *banker-name*, and *loan-number*, which specifies that a particular banker is the loan officer for a loan that belong to some customer. To find all customers who have the same name as their loan officer, we can write

$$\sigma_{customer\text{-}name\,=\,banker\text{-}name}(loan\text{-}officer)$$

Since the special value *null* indicates "value unknown or non-existent," any comparisons involving a null value evaluate to **false**.

### 3.2.1.2   The Project Operation

Suppose we want to list all loan numbers and the amount of the loans, but do not care about the branch name. The *project* operation allows us to produce this relation. The project operation is a unary operation that returns its argument relation, with certain attributes left out. Since a relation is a set, any duplicate rows are eliminated. Projection is denoted by the Greek letter pi ($\Pi$). We list those attributes that we wish to appear in the result as a subscript to $\Pi$. The argument relation follows in parentheses. Thus, the query to list all loan numbers and the amount of the loan can be written as

$$\Pi_{loan\text{-}number,\ amount} \ (loan)$$

The relation that results from this query is shown in Figure 3.9.

| loan-number | amount |
|:-----------:|:------:|
| L-17        | 1000   |
| L-23        | 2000   |
| L-15        | 1500   |
| L-14        | 1500   |
| L-93        | 500    |
| L-11        | 900    |
| L-16        | 1300   |

Figure 3.9   Loan number and the amount of the loan.

### 3.2.1.3   Composition of Relational Operations

The fact that the result of a relational operation is itself a relation is important. Let us consider the more complicated query "Find those customers who live in "Harrison." We write:

$$\Pi_{customer\text{-}name} \left(\sigma_{customer\text{-}city\,=\,\text{"Harrison"}} \left(customer\right)\right)$$

Notice that, instead of giving the name of a relation as the argument of the projection operation, we give an expression that evaluates to a relation.

In general, since the result of a relational-algebra operation is of the same type (relation) as its inputs, relational-algebra operations can be composed together into a *relational-algebra expression*. Composing relational-algebra operations into relational-algebra expressions is just like composing arithmetic operations (such as $+$, $-$, $*$ and $\div$) into arithmetic expressions. We study the formal definition of relational-algebra expressions in Section 3.2.2.

### 3.2.1.4   The Union Operation

Consider a query to find the names of all bank customers who have either an account or a loan or both. Note that the *customer* relation does not contain the information, since a customer does not need to have either an account or a loan at the bank. To answer this query, we need the information in the *depositor* relation (Figure 3.4) and in the *borrower* relation (Figure 3.6). We know how to find the names of all customers with a loan in the bank:

$$\Pi_{customer\text{-}name} \left(borrower\right)$$

We also know how to find the names of all customers with an account in the bank:

$$\Pi_{customer\text{-}name} \left(depositor\right)$$

To answer the query, we need the *union* of these two sets; that is, we need all customer names that appear in either or both of the two relations. We find these data by the binary operation union, denoted, as in set theory, by $\cup$. So the

| customer-name |
|---|
| Johnson |
| Smith |
| Hayes |
| Turner |
| Jones |
| Lindsay |
| Jackson |
| Curry |
| Williams |
| Adams |

Figure 3.10    Names of all customers who have either a loan or an account.

expression needed is

$$\Pi_{customer\text{-}name} \; (borrower) \; \cup \; \Pi_{customer\text{-}name} \; (depositor)$$

The result relation for this query appears in Figure 3.10. Notice that there are 10 tuples in the result, even though there are seven distinct borrowers and six depositors. This apparent discrepancy occurs because Smith, Jones, and Hayes are borrowers as well as depositors. Since relations are sets, duplicate values are eliminated.

Observe that, in our example, we took the union of two sets, both of which consisted of *customer-name* values. In general, we must ensure that unions are taken between *compatible* relations. For example, it would not make sense to take the union of the *loan* relation and the *borrower* relation. The former is a relation of three attributes; the latter is a relation of two. Furthermore, consider a union of a set of customer names and a set of cities. Such a union would not make sense in most situations. Therefore, for a union operation $r \cup s$ to be valid, we require that two conditions hold:

1. The relations $r$ and $s$ must be of the same arity. That is, they must have the same number of attributes.
2. The domains of the $i$th attribute of $r$ and the $i$th attribute of $s$ must be the same, for all $i$.

Note that $r$ and $s$ can be, in general, temporary relations that are the result of relational-algebra expressions.

### 3.2.1.5    The Set Difference Operation

The *set-difference* operation, denoted by $-$, allows us to find tuples that are in one relation but are not in another. The expression $r - s$ results in a relation containing those tuples in $r$ but not in $s$.

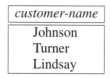

| customer-name |
|---|
| Johnson |
| Turner |
| Lindsay |

Figure 3.11    Customers with an account but no loan.

We can find all customers of the bank who have an account but not a loan by writing

$$\Pi_{customer\text{-}name} \ (depositor) - \Pi_{customer\text{-}name} \ (borrower)$$

The result relation for this query appears in Figure 3.11.

As was the case with the union operation, we must ensure that set differences are taken between *compatible* relations. Therefore, for a set difference operation $r - s$ to be valid, we require that the relations $r$ and $s$ be of the same arity, and that the domains of the $i$th attribute of $r$ and the $i$th attribute of $s$ be the same.

### 3.2.1.6   The Cartesian-Product Operation

The *Cartesian-product* operation, denoted by a cross ($\times$), allows us to combine information from any two relations. We write the Cartesian product of relations $r_1$ and $r_2$ as $r_1 \times r_2$.

Recall that a relation is defined to be a subset of a Cartesian product of a set of domains. From that definition, we should already have an intuition about the definition of the Cartesian-product operation. However, since the same attribute name may appear in both $r_1$ and $r_2$, we need to devise a naming schema to distinguish between these attributes. We do so here by attaching to an attribute the name of the relation from which the attribute originally came. For example, the relation schema for $r = borrower \times loan$ is

(*borrower.customer-name, borrower.loan-number, loan.branch-name,
loan.loan-number, loan.amount*)

With this schema, we can distinguish *borrower.loan-number* from *loan.loan-number*. For those attributes that appear in only one of the two schemas, we shall usually drop the relation-name prefix. This simplification does not lead to any ambiguity. We can then write the relation schema for $r$ as

(*customer-name, borrower.loan-number, branch-name,
loan.loan-number, amount*)

This above naming convention *requires* that the relations that are the arguments of the Cartesian-product operation have distinct names. This requirement causes problems in some cases, such as if the Cartesian product of a relation with itself is desired. A similar problem arises if we use the result of a relational-algebra expression in a Cartesian product, since we will need a name for the relation so that we can refer to ther relation's attributes. In Section 3.2.1.7, we see how to avoid these problems by using a rename operation.

Now that we know the relation schema for $r = borrower \times loan$, what tuples appear in $r$? As you may have suspected, we construct a tuple of $r$ out of each possible pair of tuples: one from the *borrower* relation and one from the *loan* relation. Thus, $r$ is a large relation, as you can see from Figure 3.12, where we included only a portion of the tuples that comprise $r$.

Assume that we have $n_1$ tuples in *borrower* and $n_2$ tuples in *loan*. Then, there are $n_1 * n_2$ ways of choosing a pair of tuples—one tuple from each relation; so there are $n_1 * n_2$ tuples in $r$. In particular, note that for some tuples $t$ in $r$, it may be that $t[borrower.loan\text{-}number] \neq t[loan.loan\text{-}number]$.

In general, if we have relations $r_1(R_1)$ and $r_2(R_2)$, then $r_1 \times r_2$ is a relation whose schema is the concatenation of $R_1$ and $R_2$. Relation $R$ contains all tuples $t$ for which there is a tuple $t_1$ in $r_1$, and $t_2$ in $r_2$ for which $t[R_1] = t_1[R_1]$ and $t[R_2] = t_2[R_2]$.

Suppose that we want to find the names of all customers who have a loan at the Perryridge branch. We need the information in both the *loan* relation and the *borrower* relation to do so. If we write

$$\sigma_{branch\text{-}name = \text{``Perryridge''}}(borrower \times loan)$$

then the result is the relation shown in Figure 3.13. We have a relation that pertains to only the Perryridge branch. However, the *customer-name* column may contain customers who do not have a loan at the Perryridge branch. (If you do not see why that is true, recall that the Cartesian product takes all possible pairings of one tuple from *borrower* with one tuple of *loan*.)

Since the Cartesian-product operation associates *every* tuple of *loan* with every tuple of *borrower*, we know that, if a customer has a loan in the Perryridge branch, then there is some tuple in *borrower* × *loan* that contains his name, and *borrower.loan-number* = *loan.loan-number*. So, if we write

$$\sigma_{borrower.loan\text{-}number = loan.loan\text{-}number}$$
$$(\sigma_{branch\text{-}name = \text{``Perryridge''}}(borrower \times loan))$$

we get only those tuples of *borrower* × *loan* that pertain to customers that have a loan at the Perryridge branch.

Finally, since we want only *customer-name*, we do a projection:

$$\Pi_{customer\text{-}name} (\sigma_{borrower.loan\text{-}number = loan.loan\text{-}number}$$
$$(\sigma_{branch\text{-}name = \text{``Perryridge''}} (borrower \times loan)))$$

The result of this expression is shown in Figure 3.14 and is the correct answer to our query.

### 3.2.1.7   The Rename Operation

Unlike relations in the database, the results of relational-algebra expressions do not have a name that we can use to refer to them. It is useful to be able to give

| customer-name | borrower. loan-number | branch-name | loan. loan-number | amount |
|:---:|:---:|:---:|:---:|:---:|
| Jones | L-17 | Downtown | L-17 | 1000 |
| Jones | L-17 | Redwood | L-23 | 2000 |
| Jones | L-17 | Perryridge | L-15 | 1500 |
| Jones | L-17 | Downtown | L-14 | 1500 |
| Jones | L-17 | Mianus | L-93 | 500 |
| Jones | L-17 | Round Hill | L-11 | 900 |
| Jones | L-17 | Perryridge | L-16 | 1300 |
| Smith | L-23 | Downtown | L-17 | 1000 |
| Smith | L-23 | Redwood | L-23 | 2000 |
| Smith | L-23 | Perryridge | L-15 | 1500 |
| Smith | L-23 | Downtown | L-14 | 1500 |
| Smith | L-23 | Mianus | L-93 | 500 |
| Smith | L-23 | Round Hill | L-11 | 900 |
| Smith | L-23 | Perryridge | L-16 | 1300 |
| Hayes | L-15 | Downtown | L-17 | 1000 |
| Hayes | L-15 | Redwood | L-23 | 2000 |
| Hayes | L-15 | Perryridge | L-15 | 1500 |
| Hayes | L-15 | Downtown | L-14 | 1500 |
| Hayes | L-15 | Mianus | L-93 | 500 |
| Hayes | L-15 | Round Hill | L-11 | 900 |
| Hayes | L-15 | Perryridge | L-16 | 1300 |
| ... | ... | ... | ... | ... |
| ... | ... | ... | ... | ... |
| ... | ... | ... | ... | ... |
| Williams | L-17 | Downtown | L-17 | 1000 |
| Williams | L-17 | Redwood | L-23 | 2000 |
| Williams | L-17 | Perryridge | L-15 | 1500 |
| Williams | L-17 | Downtown | L-14 | 1500 |
| Williams | L-17 | Mianus | L-93 | 500 |
| Williams | L-17 | Round Hill | L-11 | 900 |
| Williams | L-17 | Perryridge | L-16 | 1300 |
| Adams | L-16 | Downtown | L-17 | 1000 |
| Adams | L-16 | Redwood | L-23 | 2000 |
| Adams | L-16 | Perryridge | L-15 | 1500 |
| Adams | L-16 | Downtown | L-14 | 1500 |
| Adams | L 16 | Mianus | L-93 | 500 |
| Adams | L-16 | Round Hill | L-11 | 900 |
| Adams | L-16 | Perryridge | L-16 | 1300 |

Figure 3.12    Result of *borrower* × *loan*.

| customer-name | loan-number | branch-name | loan-number | amount |
|---------------|-------------|-------------|-------------|--------|
| Jones | L-17 | Perryridge | L-15 | 1500 |
| Jones | L-17 | Perryridge | L-16 | 1300 |
| Smith | L-23 | Perryridge | L-15 | 1500 |
| Smith | L-23 | Perryridge | L-16 | 1300 |
| Hayes | L-15 | Perryridge | L-15 | 1500 |
| Hayes | L-15 | Perryridge | L-16 | 1300 |
| Jackson | L-14 | Perryridge | L-15 | 1500 |
| Jackson | L-14 | Perryridge | L-16 | 1300 |
| Curry | L-93 | Perryridge | L-15 | 1500 |
| Curry | L-93 | Perryridge | L-16 | 1300 |
| Smith | L-11 | Perryridge | L-15 | 1500 |
| Smith | L-11 | Perryridge | L-16 | 1300 |
| Williams | L-17 | Perryridge | L-15 | 1500 |
| Williams | L-17 | Perryridge | L-16 | 1300 |
| Adams | L-16 | Perryridge | L-15 | 1500 |
| Adams | L-16 | Perryridge | L-16 | 1300 |

Figure 3.13    Result of $\sigma_{branch\text{-}name\,=\,\text{``Perryridge''}}$ $(borrower \times loan)$.

them names; the *rename* operator, denoted by the lower-case Greek letter rho ($\rho$), lets us perform this task. Given a relational-algebra expression $E$, the expression

$$\rho_x\,(E)$$

returns the result of expression $E$ under the name $x$.

A relation $r$ by itself is considered to be a (trivial) relational-algebra expression. Thus, we can also apply the rename operation to a relation $r$ to get the same relation under a new name.

A second form of the rename operation is as follows. Assume that a relational-algebra expression $E$ has arity $n$. Then, the expression

$$\rho_{x(A_1,A_2,...,A_n)}\,(E)$$

returns the result of expression $E$ under the name $x$, and with the attributes renamed to $A_1, A_2, \ldots, A_n$.

To illustrate the use of renaming a relation, we consider the query "Find the largest account balance in the bank." Our strategy is to compute first a temporary

| customer-name |
|---------------|
| Hayes |
| Adams |

Figure 3.14    Result of

$\Pi_{customer\text{-}name}\,(\sigma_{borrower.loan\text{-}number\,=\,loan.loan\text{-}number}$

$(\sigma_{branch\text{-}name\,=\,\text{``Perryridge''}}\,(borrower \times loan)))$.

relation consisting of those balances that are *not* the largest, and then to take the set difference between the relation $\Pi_{balance}$ (*account*) and the temporary relation just computed, to obtain the result. To compute the temporary relation, we need to compare the values of all account balances. We can do this comparison by computing the Cartesian product *account* × *account* and forming a selection to compare the value of any two balances appearing in one tuple. First, we need to devise a mechanism to distinguish between the two *balance* attributes. We shall use the rename operation to rename one reference to the account relation; thus we can reference the relation twice without ambiguity.

The temporary relation that consists of the balances that are not the largest can now be written as

$$\Pi_{account.balance} \ (\sigma_{account.balance \ < \ d.balance} \ (account \ \times \ \rho_d \ (account)))$$

This expression gives those balances in the *account* relation for which a larger balance appears somewhere in the *account* relation (renamed as *d*). The result contains all balances *except* the largest one. This relation is shown in Figure 3.15. The query to find the largest account balance in the bank can be written as follows:

$$\Pi_{balance} \ (account) \ -$$
$$\Pi_{account.balance} \ (\sigma_{account.balance \ < \ d.balance} \ (account \ \times \ \rho_d \ (account)))$$

Figure 3.16 shows the result of this query.

Let us present one more example to illustrate the rename operation. Consider the query "Find the names of all customers who live on the same street and in the same city as Smith." We can obtain the street and city of Smith by writing

$$\Pi_{customer\text{-}street, \ customer\text{-}city} \ (\sigma_{customer\text{-}name \ = \ \text{“Smith”}} \ (customer))$$

However, in order to find other customers with this street and city, we must reference the *customer* relation a second time. In the following query, we use the rename operation on the preceding expression to give its result the name *smith-addr*, and to rename its attributes to *street* and *city*, instead of *customer-street* and

| balance |
|---------|
| 500 |
| 700 |
| 400 |
| 350 |
| 750 |

Figure 3.15    Result of subexpression

$$\Pi_{account.balance} \ (\sigma_{account.balance \ < \ d.balance} \ (account \ \times \ \rho_d \ (account))).$$

| balance |
|---------|
| 900 |

Figure 3.16    Largest account balance in the bank.

*customer-city*:

$\Pi_{customer.customer-name}$
$(\sigma_{customer.customer-street=smith-addr.street \land customer.customer-city=smith-addr.city}$
$(customer \times \rho_{smith-addr(street,city)}$
$(\Pi_{customer-street, customer-city} (\sigma_{customer-name = \text{"Smith"}}(customer)))))$

The result of this query, when we apply it to the *customer* relation of Figure 3.3, is shown in Figure 3.17.

The rename operation is not strictly required, since it is possible to use a positional notation for attributes. We can name attributes of a relation implicitly using a positional notation, where $1, $2, ... refer to the first attribute, the second attribute, and so on. The positional notation also applies to results of relational-algebra operations. The following relational-algebra expression illustrates the use of positional notation with the unary operator $\sigma$:

$$\sigma_{\$2=\$3}(R \times R)$$

If a binary operation needs to distinguish between its two operand relations, a similar positional notation can be used for relation names as well. For example, $R1 could refer to the first operand, and $R2 could refer to the second operand. However, the positional notation is inconvenient for humans, since the position of the attribute is a number, rather than an easy-to-remember attribute name. Hence, we do not use the positional notation in this textbook.

### 3.2.2    Formal Definition of the Relational Algebra

The operations that we saw in Section 3.2.1 allow us to give a complete definition of an expression in the relational algebra. A basic expression in the relational algebra consists of either one of the following:

- A relation in the database
- A constant relation

A general expression in the relational algebra is constructed out of smaller subexpressions. Let $E_1$ and $E_2$ be relational-algebra expressions. Then, the following

| customer-name |
|---------------|
| Smith |
| Curry |

Figure 3.17    Customers who live on the same street and in the same city as Smith.

are all relational-algebra expressions:

- $E_1 \cup E_2$
- $E_1 - E_2$
- $E_1 \times E_2$
- $\sigma_P(E_1)$, where $P$ is a predicate on attributes in $E_1$
- $\Pi_S(E_1)$, where $S$ is a list consisting of some of the attributes in $E_1$
- $\rho_x(E_1)$, where $x$ is the new name for the result of $E_1$

### 3.2.3 Additional Operations

The fundamental operations of the relational algebra are sufficient to express any relational-algebra query.[†] However, if we restrict ourselves to just the fundamental operations, certain common queries are lengthy to express. Therefore, we define additional operations that do not add any power to the algebra, but that simplify common queries. For each new operation, we give an equivalent expression using only the fundamental operations.

#### 3.2.3.1 The Set-Intersection Operation

The first additional-relational algebra operation that we shall define is *set intersection* ($\cap$). Suppose that we wish to find all customers who have both a loan and an account. Using set intersection, we can write

$$\Pi_{customer\text{-}name}(borrower) \cap \Pi_{customer\text{-}name}(depositor)$$

The result relation for this query appears in Figure 3.18.

Note that we can rewrite any relational algebra expression using set intersection by replacing the intersection operation with a pair of set-difference operations as follows:

$$r \cap s = r - (r - s)$$

Thus, set intersection is not a fundamental operation and does not add any power to the relational algebra. It is simply more convenient to write $r \cap s$ than to write $r - (r - s)$.

| customer-name |
|:---:|
| Hayes |
| Jones |
| Smith |

Figure 3.18   Customers with both an account and a loan at the bank.

---

[†] In Section 3.5, we introduce operations that extend the power of the relational algebra to handle null and aggregate values.

### 3.2.3.2   The Natural-Join Operation

It is often desirable to simplify certain queries that require a Cartesian product. Typically, a query that involves a Cartesian product includes a selection operation on the result of the Cartesian product. Consider the query "Find the names of all customers who have a loan at the bank, and find the amount of the loan." We first form the Cartesian product of the *borrower* and *loan* relations. Then, we select those tuples that pertain to only the same *loan-number*, followed by the projection of the resulting *customer-name*, *loan-number*, and *amount*:

$$\Pi_{customer\text{-}name,\ loan.loan\text{-}number,\ amount}$$
$$(\sigma_{borrower.loan\text{-}number\,=\,loan.loan\text{-}number}\ (borrower\ \times\ loan))$$

The *natural join* is a binary operation that allows us to combine certain selections and a Cartesian product into one operation. It is denoted by the "join" symbol $\bowtie$. The natural-join operation forms a Cartesian product of its two arguments, performs a selection forcing equality on those attributes that appear in both relation schemas, and finally removes duplicate attributes.

Although the definition of natural join is complicated, the operation is easy to apply. As an illustration, let us consider again the example "Find the names of all customers who have a loan at the bank, and find the amount of the loan." This query can be expressed using the natural join as follows:

$$\Pi_{customer\text{-}name,\ loan\text{-}number,\ amount}\ (borrower\ \bowtie\ loan)$$

Since the schemas for *borrower* and *loan* (that is, *Borrower-schema* and *Loan-schema*) have the attribute *loan-number* in common, the natural-join operation considers only pairs of tuples that have the same value on *loan-number*. It combines each such pair of tuples into a single tuple on the union of the two schemas (that is, *customer-name, branch-name, loan-number, amount*). After performing the projection, we obtain the relation shown in Figure 3.19.

Consider two relation schemas $R$ and $S$—which are, of course, lists of attribute names. If we consider the schemas to be *sets*, rather than lists, we can denote those attribute names that appear in both $R$ and $S$ by $R \cap S$, and denote those attribute names that appear in $R$, in $S$, or in both by $R \cup S$. Similarly, those

| customer-name | loan-number | amount |
|:---:|:---:|:---:|
| Jones | L-17 | 1000 |
| Smith | L-23 | 2000 |
| Hayes | L-15 | 1500 |
| Jackson | L-14 | 1500 |
| Curry | L-93 | 500 |
| Smith | L-11 | 900 |
| Williams | L-17 | 1000 |
| Adams | L-16 | 1300 |

**Figure 3.19**   Result of $\Pi_{customer\text{-}name,\ loan\text{-}number,\ amount}\ (borrower\ \bowtie\ loan)$.

| branch-name |
|-------------|
| Brighton    |
| Perryridge  |

Figure 3.20    Result of
$\Pi_{branch\text{-}name}(\sigma_{customer\text{-}city=\text{"Harrison"}} (customer \bowtie account \bowtie depositor))$.

attribute names that appear in $R$ but not $S$ are denoted by $R - S$, whereas $S - R$ denotes those attribute names that appear in $S$ but not in $R$. Note that the union, intersection, and difference operations here are on sets of attributes, rather than on relations.

We are now ready for a formal definition of the natural join. Consider two relations $r(R)$ and $s(S)$. The *natural join* of $r$ and $s$, denoted by $r \bowtie s$ is a relation on schema $R \cup S$ formally defined as follows:

$$r \bowtie s = \Pi_{R \cup S} (\sigma_{r.A_1 = s.A_1 \wedge r.A_2 = s.A_2 \wedge ... \wedge r.A_n = s.A_n} r \times s)$$

where $R \cap S = \{A_1, A_2, \ldots, A_n\}$.

Because the natural join is central to much of relational-database theory and practice, we give several examples of its use.

- Find the names of all branches with customers who have an account in the bank and who live in Harrison.

$$\Pi_{branch\text{-}name}$$
$$(\sigma_{customer\text{-}city=\text{"Harrison"}} (customer \bowtie account \bowtie depositor))$$

The result relation for this query appears in Figure 3.20.

Notice that we wrote *customer* $\bowtie$ *account* $\bowtie$ *depositor* without inserting parentheses to specify the order in which the natural-join operations on the three relations be executed. In the preceding case, there are two possibilities:
  ○ (*customer* $\bowtie$ *account*) $\bowtie$ *depositor*
  ○ *customer* $\bowtie$ (*account* $\bowtie$ *depositor*)
We did not specify which expression we intended, because the two are equivalent. That is, the natural join is *associative*.

- Find all customers who have *both* a loan and an account at the bank.

$$\Pi_{customer\text{-}name} (borrower \bowtie depositor)$$

Note that in Section 3.2.3.1, we wrote an expression for this query using set intersection. We repeat this expression here.

$$\Pi_{customer\text{-}name} (borrower) \cap \Pi_{customer\text{-}name} (depositor)$$

The result relation for this query was shown earlier in Figure 3.18. This example illustrates a general fact about the relational algebra: It is possible to write several equivalent relational-algebra expressions that are quite different from one another.

| branch-name |
|-------------|
| Brighton    |
| Downtown    |

Figure 3.21    Result of $\Pi_{branch\text{-}name}$ $(\sigma_{branch\text{-}city\,=\,\text{"Brooklyn"}}$ $(branch))$.

- Let $r(R)$ and $s(S)$ be relations without any attributes in common; that is, $R \cap S = \emptyset$. ($\emptyset$ denotes the empty set.) Then, $r \bowtie s = r \times s$.

The theta join operation is an extension to the natural-join operation that allows us to combine a selection and a Cartesian product into a single operation. Consider relations $r(R)$ and $s(S)$, and let $\theta$ be a predicate on attributes in the schema $R \cup S$, The *theta join* operation $r \bowtie_\theta s$, is defined as follows:

$$r \bowtie_\theta s = \sigma_\theta(r \times s)$$

### 3.2.3.3   The Division Operation

The *division* operation, denoted by $\div$, is suited to queries that include the phrase "for all." Suppose that we wish to find all customers who have an account at *all* the branches located in Brooklyn. We can obtain all branches in Brooklyn by the expression

$$r_1 = \Pi_{branch\text{-}name} (\sigma_{branch\text{-}city\,=\,\text{"Brooklyn"}} (branch))$$

The result relation for this expression appears in Figure 3.21.

We can find all (*customer-name, branch-name*) pairs for which the customer has an account at a branch by writing

$$r_2 = \Pi_{customer\text{-}name,\ branch\text{-}name} (depositor \bowtie account)$$

Figure 3.22 shows the result relation for this expression.

Now, we need to find customers who appear in $r_2$ with *every* branch name in $r_1$. The operation that provides exactly those customers is the divide operation.

| customer-name | branch-name |
|---------------|-------------|
| Johnson       | Downtown    |
| Smith         | Mianus      |
| Hayes         | Perryridge  |
| Turner        | Round Hill  |
| Lindsay       | Redwood     |
| Johnson       | Brighton    |
| Jones         | Brighton    |

Figure 3.22    Result of $\Pi_{customer\text{-}name,\ branch\text{-}name}$ $(depositor \bowtie account)$.

We formulate the query by writing

$$\Pi_{customer\text{-}name,\ branch\text{-}name}\ (depositor \bowtie account)$$
$$\div\ \Pi_{branch\text{-}name}\ (\sigma_{branch\text{-}city\ =\ \text{``Brooklyn''}}\ (branch))$$

The result of this expression is a relation that has the schema (*customer-name*) and that contains the tuple (Johnson).

Formally, let $r(R)$ and $s(S)$ be relations, and let $S \subseteq R$; that is every attribute of schema $S$ is also in schema $R$. The relation $r \div s$ is a relation on schema $R - S$—that is, on the schema containing all attributes of schema $R$ that are not in schema $S$. A tuple $t$ is in $r \div s$ if and only if both of two conditions hold:

1. $t$ is in $\Pi_{R-S}(r)$
2. For every tuple $t_s$ in $s$, there is a tuple $t_r$ in $r$ satisfying both of the following:
   a. $t_r[S] = t_s[S]$
   b. $t_r[R - S] = t$

It may surprise you to discover that, given a division operation and the schemas of the relations, we can, in fact, define the division operation in terms of the fundamental operations. Let $r(R)$ and $s(S)$ be given, with $S \subseteq R$:

$$r \div s = \Pi_{R-S}\ (r) - \Pi_{R-S}\ (\ (\Pi_{R-S}\ (r) \times s) - \Pi_{R-S,S}(r))$$

To see that this expression is true, we observe that $\Pi_{R-S}\ (r)$ gives us all tuples $t$ that satisfy the first condition of the definition of division. The expression on the right side of the set difference operator,

$$\Pi_{R-S}\ (\ (\Pi_{R-S}\ (r) \times s) - \Pi_{R-S,S}(r)),$$

serves to eliminate those tuples that fail to satisfy the second condition of the definition of division. Let us see how it does so. Consider $\Pi_{R-S}\ (r) \times s$. This relation is on schema $R$, and pairs every tuple in $\Pi_{R-S}\ (r)$ with every tuple in $s$. The expression $\Pi_{R-S,S}(r)$ merely reorders the attributes of $r$.

Thus, $(\Pi_{R-S}\ (r) \times s) - \Pi_{R-S,S}(r)$ gives us those pairs of tuples from $\Pi_{R-S}\ (r)$ and $s$ that do not appear in $r$. If a tuple $t_j$ is in

$$\Pi_{R-S}\ (\ (\Pi_{R-S}\ (r) \times s) - \Pi_{R-S,S}(r)),$$

then there is some tuple $t_s$ in $s$ that does not combine with tuple $t_j$ to form a tuple in $r$. Thus, $t_j$ holds a value for attributes $R - S$ that does not appear in $r \div s$. It is these values that we eliminate from $\Pi_{R-S}\ (r)$.

### 3.2.3.4   The Assignment Operation

It is convenient at times to write a relational-algebra expression in parts using assignment to a temporary relation variable. The *assignment* operation denoted by $\leftarrow$, works in a manner similar to assignment in a programming language. To illustrate this operation, we consider the definition of division given in Section 3.2.3.3.

We could write $r \div s$ as

$$temp1 \leftarrow \Pi_{R-S}(r)$$
$$temp2 \leftarrow \Pi_{R-S}((temp1 \times s) - r)$$
$$result = temp1 - temp2$$

The evaluation of an assignment does not result in any relation being displayed to the user. Rather, the result of the expression to the right of the $\leftarrow$ is assigned to the relation variable on the left of the $\leftarrow$. This relation variable may be used in subsequent expressions.

With the assignment operation, a query can be written as a sequential program consisting of a series of assignments followed by an expression whose value is displayed as the result of the query. For relational-algebra queries, assignment must always be made to a temporary relation variable. Assignments to permanent relations constitute a database modification. We discuss this issue in Section 3.6. Note that the assignment operation does not provide any additional power to the algebra. It is, however, a convenient way to express complex queries.

## 3.3   The Tuple Relational Calculus

When we write a relational-algebra expression, we provide a sequence of procedures that generates the answer to our query. The tuple relational calculus, by contrast, is a *nonprocedural* query language. It describes the desired information without giving a specific procedure for obtaining that information.

A query in the tuple relational calculus is expressed as

$$\{t \mid P(t)\}$$

that is, it is the set of all tuples $t$ such that predicate $P$ is true for $t$. Following our earlier notation, we use $t[A]$ to denote the value of tuple $t$ on attribute $A$, and we use $t \in r$ to denote that tuple $t$ is in relation $r$.

Before we give a formal definition of the tuple relational calculus, we return to some of the queries for which we wrote relational-algebra expressions in Section 3.2.

### 3.3.1   Example Queries

Say that we want to find the *branch-name*, *loan-number*, and *amount* for loans of over \$1200:

$$\{t \mid t \in loan \wedge t[amount] > 1200\}$$

Suppose that we want only the *loan-number* attribute, rather than all attributes of the *loan* relation. To write this query in the tuple relational calculus, we need to write an expression for a relation on the schema (*loan-number*). We need those tuples on (*loan-number*) such that there is a tuple in *loan* with the *amount* attribute > 1200. To express this request, we need the construct "there exists" from mathematical logic. The notation

$$\exists\, t \in r\; (Q(t))$$

means "there exists a tuple $t$ in relation $r$ such that predicate $Q(t)$ is true."

Using this notation, we can write the query "Find the loan number for each loan of an amount greater than \$1200" as

$$\{t \mid \exists\, s \in loan\; (t[loan\text{-}number] = s[loan\text{-}number] \\ \land\; s[amount] > 1200)\}$$

In English, we read the preceding expression as "the set of all tuples $t$ such that there exists a tuple $s$ in relation *loan* for which the values of $t$ and $s$ for the *loan-number* attribute are equal, and the value of $s$ for the *amount* attribute is greater than \$1200."

Tuple variable $t$ is defined on only the *loan-number* attribute, since that is the only attribute for which a condition is specified for $t$. Thus, the result is a relation on (*loan-number*).

Consider the query "Find the names of all customers who have a loan from the Perryridge branch." This query is slightly more complex than the previous queries, since it involves two relations: *borrower* and *loan*. As we shall see, however, all it requires is that we have two "there exists" clauses in our tuple-relational-calculus expression, connected by *and* ($\land$). We write the query as follows:

$$\{t \mid \exists\, s \in borrower\; (t[customer\text{-}name] = s[customer\text{-}name] \\ \land\; \exists\, u \in loan\; (u[loan\text{-}number] = s[loan\text{-}number] \\ \land\; u[branch\text{-}name] = \text{``Perryridge''}))\}$$

In English, this expression is "the set of all (*customer-name*) tuples for which the customer has a loan that is at the Perryridge branch." Tuple variable $u$ ensures that the customer is a borrower at the Perryridge branch. Tuple variable $s$ is restricted to pertain to the same loan number as $s$. The result of this query is shown in Figure 3.23.

To find all customers who have a loan, an account, or both at the bank, we used the union operation in the relational algebra. In the tuple relational calculus, we shall need two "there exists" clauses, connected by *or* ($\lor$):

$$\{t \mid \exists\, s \in borrower\; (t[customer\text{-}name] = s[customer\text{-}name]) \\ \lor\; \exists\, u \in depositor\; (t[customer\text{-}name] = u[customer\text{-}name])\}$$

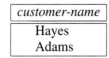

| customer-name |
|---------------|
| Hayes |
| Adams |

Figure 3.23   Names of all customers who have a loan at the Perryridge branch.

This expression gives us the set of all *customer-name* tuples such that at least one of the following holds:

- The *customer-name* appears in some tuple of the *borrower* relation as a borrower from the bank.
- The *customer-name* appears in some tuple of the *depositor* relation as a depositor of the bank.

If some customer has both a loan and an account at the bank, that customer appears only once in the result, because the mathematical definition of a set does not allow duplicate members. The result of this query was shown earlier in Figure 3.10.

If we now want *only* those customers that have *both* an account and a loan at the bank, all we need to do is to change the *or* ($\vee$) to *and* ($\wedge$) in the preceding expression.

$$\{t \mid \exists s \in borrower \ (t[customer\text{-}name] = s[customer\text{-}name])$$
$$\wedge \ \exists u \in depositor \ (t[customer\text{-}name] = u[customer\text{-}name])\}$$

The result of this query was shown in Figure 3.18.

Now consider the query "Find all customers who have an account at the bank but do not have a loan from the bank." The tuple-relational-calculus expression for this query is similar to the expressions that we have just seen, except for the use of the *not* ($\neg$) symbol:

$$\{t \mid \exists u \in depositor \ (t[customer\text{-}name] = u[customer\text{-}name])$$
$$\wedge \ \neg \ \exists s \in borrower \ (t[customer\text{-}name] = s[customer\text{-}name])\}$$

The preceding tuple-relational-calculus expression uses the $\exists u \in depositor \ (\ldots)$ clause to require that the customer have an account at the bank, and it uses the $\neg \ \exists s \in borrower \ (\ldots)$ clause to eliminate those customers who appear in some tuple of the *borrower* relation as having a loan from the bank. The result of this query appeared in Figure 3.11.

The query that we shall consider next uses implication, denoted by $\Rightarrow$. The formula $P \Rightarrow Q$ means "*P* implies *Q*;" that is, "if *P* is true, then *Q* must be true." Note that $P \Rightarrow Q$ is logically equivalent to $\neg P \vee Q$. The use of implication rather than *not* and *or* often suggests a more intuitive interpretation of a query in English.

Consider the query that we used in Section 3.2.3 to illustrate the division operation: "Find all customers who have an account at all branches located in Brooklyn." To write this query in the tuple relational calculus, we introduce the "for all" construct, denoted by $\forall$. The notation

$$\forall t \in r \ (Q(t))$$

means "*Q* is true for all tuples *t* in relation *r*."

We write the expression for our query as follows:

$\{t \mid \forall u \in branch \ (u[branch\text{-}city] = \text{``Brooklyn''} \Rightarrow$
$\quad \exists s \in depositor \ (t[customer\text{-}name] = s[customer\text{-}name]$
$\quad\quad \land \exists w \in account \ (w[account\text{-}number] = s[account\text{-}number]$
$\quad\quad \land w[branch\text{-}name] = u[branch\text{-}name])))\}$

In English, we interpret this expression as "the set of all customers, (that is, (*customer-name*) tuples *t*) such that, for *all* tuples *u* in the *branch* relation, if the value of *u* on attribute *branch-city* is Brooklyn, then the customer has an account at the branch whose name appears in the *branch-name* attribute of *u*."

### 3.3.2 Formal Definition

We are now ready for a formal definition. A tuple-relational-calculus expression is of the form

$$\{t \mid P(t)\}$$

where *P* is a *formula*. Several tuple variables may appear in a formula. A tuple variable is said to be a *free variable* unless it is quantified by a $\exists$ or $\forall$. Thus, in

$\quad t \in loan \ \land \ \exists s \in customer(t[branch\text{-}name] = s[branch\text{-}name])$

*t* is a free variable. Tuple variable *s* is said to be a *bound* variable.

A tuple-relational-calculus formula is built up out of *atoms*. An atom has one of the following forms:

- $s \in r$, where *s* is a tuple variable and *r* is a relation (we do not allow use of the $\notin$ operator)
- $s[x] \ \Theta \ u[y]$, where *s* and *u* are tuple variables, *x* is an attribute on which *s* is defined, *y* is an attribute on which *u* is defined, and $\Theta$ is a comparison operator ($<, \leq, =, \neq, >, \geq$); we require that attributes *x* and *y* have domains whose members can be compared by $\Theta$
- $s[x] \ \Theta \ c$, where *s* is a tuple variable, *x* is an attribute on which *s* is defined, $\Theta$ is a comparison operator, and *c* is a constant in the domain of attribute *x*

We build up formulae from atoms using the following rules:

- An atom is a formula.
- If $P_1$ is a formula, then so are $\neg P_1$ and $(P_1)$.
- If $P_1$ and $P_2$ are formulae, then so are $P_1 \ \lor \ P_2$, $P_1 \ \land \ P_2$, and $P_1 \Rightarrow P_2$.
- If $P_1(s)$ is a formula containing a free tuple variable *s*, and *r* is a relation, then
$$\exists s \in r \ (P_1(s)) \quad and \quad \forall s \in r \ (P_1(s))$$
are also formulae.

As we could for the relational algebra, we can write equivalent expressions that are not identical in appearance. In the tuple relational calculus, these equivalences include the following three rules:

1. $P_1 \wedge P_2$ is equivalent to $\neg \, (\neg P_1 \vee \neg P_2)$.
2. $\forall \, t \, \in \, r \, (P_1(t))$ is equivalent to $\neg \, \exists \, t \, \in \, r \, (\neg P_1(t))$.
3. $P_1 \Rightarrow P_2$ is equivalent to $\neg P_1 \vee P_2$.

### 3.3.3   Safety of Expressions

There is one final issue to be addressed. A tuple-relational-calculus expression may generate an infinite relation. Suppose that we wrote the expression

$$\{t \mid \neg \, (t \, \in \, loan)\}$$

There are infinitely many tuples that are not in *loan*. Most of these tuples contain values that do not even appear in the database! Clearly, we do not wish to allow such expressions.

To assist us in defining a restriction of the tuple relational calculus, we introduce the concept of the *domain* of a tuple relational formula, *P*. Intuitively, the domain of *P*, denoted $dom(P)$, is the set of all values referenced by *P*. These include values mentioned in *P* itself, as well as values that appear in a tuple of a relation mentioned in *P*. Thus, the domain of *P* is the set of all values that appear explicitly in *P* or that appear in one or more relations whose names appear in *P*. For example, $dom(t \, \in \, loan \, \wedge \, t[amount] \, > \, 1200)$ is the set containing 1200 as well as the set of all values appearing in *loan*. Also, $dom(\neg \, (t \, \in \, loan))$ is the set of all values appearing in *loan*, since the relation *loan* is mentioned in the expression.

We say that an expression $\{t \mid P(t)\}$ is *safe* if all values that appear in the result are values from $dom(P)$. The expression $\{t \mid \neg \, (t \, \in \, loan)\}$ is not safe. Note that $dom(\neg \, (t \, \in \, loan))$ is the set of all values appearing in *loan*. However, it is possible to have a tuple *t* not in *loan* that contains values that do not appear in *loan*. The other examples of tuple-relational-calculus expressions that we have written in this section are safe.

### 3.3.4   Expressive Power of Languages

The tuple relational calculus restricted to safe expressions is equivalent in expressive power to the relational algebra. Thus, for every relational-algebra expression, there is an equivalent expression in the tuple relational calculus, and for every tuple-relational-calculus expression, there is an equivalent relational-algebra expression. We will not prove this assertion here; the bibliographic notes contain references to the proof. Some parts of the proof are included in the exercises.

## 3.4   The Domain Relational Calculus

There is a second form of relational calculus called *domain relational calculus*. This form uses *domain* variables that take on values from an attribute's domain, rather than values for an entire tuple. The domain relational calculus, however, is closely related to the tuple relational calculus.

## 3.4.1 Formal Definition

An expression in the domain relational calculus is of the form

$$\{< x_1, \; x_2, \ldots, x_n > \; | \; P(x_1, \; x_2, \ldots, x_n)\}$$

where $x_1, \; x_2, \ldots, x_n$ represent domain variables. $P$ represents a formula composed of atoms, as was the case in the tuple relational calculus. An atom in the domain relational calculus has one of the following forms:

- $< x_1, \; x_2, \ldots, x_n > \in r$, where $r$ is a relation on $n$ attributes and $x_1, \; x_2, \ldots, x_n$ are domain variables or domain constants.
- $x \; \Theta \; y$, where $x$ and $y$ are domain variables and $\Theta$ is a comparison operator $(<, \leq, =, \neq, >, \geq)$. We require that attributes $x$ and $y$ have domains that can be compared by $\Theta$.
- $x \; \Theta \; c$, where $x$ is a domain variable, $\Theta$ is a comparison operator, and $c$ is a constant in the domain of the attribute for which $x$ is a domain variable.

We build up formulae from atoms using the following rules:

- An atom is a formula.
- If $P_1$ is a formula, then so are $\neg P_1$ and $(P_1)$.
- If $P_1$ and $P_2$ are formulae, then so are $P_1 \vee P_2$, $P_1 \wedge P_2$, and $P_1 \Rightarrow P_2$.
- If $P_1(x)$ is a formula in $x$, where $x$ is a domain variable, then

$$\exists \, x \; (P_1(x)) \; \text{and} \; \forall \, x \; (P_1(x))$$

are also formulae.

As a notational shorthand, we write

$$\exists \, a, b, c \; (P(a, b, c))$$

for

$$\exists \, a \; (\exists \, b \; (\exists \, c \; (P(a, b, c))))$$

## 3.4.2 Example Queries

We now give domain-relational-calculus queries for the examples that we considered earlier. Note the similarity of these expressions and the corresponding tuple-relational-calculus expressions

- Find the branch name, loan number, and amount for loans of over $1200:

$$\{< b, l, a > \; | \; < b, l, a > \in \; loan \wedge a > 1200\}$$

- Find all loan numbers for loans with an amount greater than \$1200:

$$\{<l> \;|\; \exists\, b, a\,(<b, l, a> \;\in\; loan \;\wedge\; a \;>\; 1200)\}$$

Although the second query appears similar to the one that we wrote for the tuple relational calculus, there is an important difference. In the tuple calculus, when we write $\exists\, s$ for some tuple variable $s$, we bind it immediately to a relation by writing $\exists\, s \;\in\; r$. However, when we write $\exists\, b$ in the domain calculus, $b$ refers not to a tuple, but rather to a domain value. Thus, the domain of variable $b$ is unconstrained until the subformula $b, l, a \;\in\; loan$ constrains $b$ to branch names that appear in the *loan* relation.

- Find the names of all customers who have a loan from the Perryridge branch and find the loan amount:

$$\{<c, a> \;|\; \exists\, l\,(<c, l> \;\in\; borrower$$
$$\wedge\, \exists\, b\,(<b, l, a> \;\in\; loan \;\wedge\; b \;=\; \text{``Perryridge''}))\}$$

- Find the names of all customers who have a loan, an account, or both at the Perryridge branch:

$$\{<c> \;|\; \exists\, l\,(<c, l> \;\in\; borrower$$
$$\wedge\, \exists\, b, a\,(<b, l, a> \;\in\; loan \;\wedge\; b \;=\; \text{``Perryridge''}))$$
$$\vee\, \exists\, a\,(<c, a> \;\in\; depositor$$
$$\wedge\, \exists\, b, n\,(<b, a, n> \;\in\; account \;\wedge\; b \;=\; \text{``Perryridge''}))\}$$

- Find the names of all customers who have an account at all the branches located in Brooklyn:

$$\{<c> \;|\; \forall\, x, y, z\,(<x, y, z> \;\in\; branch) \;\wedge\; y \;=\; \text{``Brooklyn''} \;\Rightarrow$$
$$\exists\, a, b\,(<x, a, b> \;\in\; account \;\wedge\; <c, a> \;\in\; depositor)\}$$

In English, we interpret the preceding expression as "the set of all (*customer-name*) tuples $c$ such that, for all (*branch-name, branch-city, assets*) tuples, $x, y, z$, if the branch city is Brooklyn, then the following is true":
- There exists a tuple in the relation *account* with account number $a$ and branch name $x$
- There exists a tuple in the relation *depositor* with customer $c$ and account number $a$

## 3.4.3   Safety of Expressions

We noted that, in the tuple relational calculus, it is possible to write expressions that may generate an infinite relation. That led us to define *safety* for tuple-relational-calculus expressions. A similar situation arises for the domain relational calculus. An expression such as

$$\{< b, l, a > \ | \ \neg (< b, l, a > \ \in \ loan)\}$$

is unsafe, because it allows values in the result that are not in the domain of the expression.

For the domain relational calculus, we must be concerned also about the form of formulae within "there exists" and "for all" clauses. Consider the expression

$$\{< x > \ | \ \exists \ y \ (< x, \ y > \in \ r) \ \wedge \ \exists \ z \ (\neg (< x, \ z > \in \ r) \ \wedge \ P(x, z))\}$$

where $P$ is some formula involving $x$ and $z$. We can test the first part of the formula, $\exists \ y \ (< x, \ y > \ \in \ r)$, by considering only the values in $r$. However, to test the second part of the formula, $\exists \ z \ (\neg \ (< x, \ z > \ \in \ r) \ \wedge \ P(x, z))$, we must consider values for $z$ that do not appear in $r$. Since all relations are finite, an infinite number of values do not appear in $r$. Thus, it is not possible, in general, to test the second part of the formula, without considering an infinite number of potential values for $z$. Instead, we add restrictions to prohibit expressions such as the preceding one.

In the tuple relational calculus, we restricted any existentially quantified variable to range over a specific relation. Since we did not do so in the domain calculus, we add rules to the definition of safety to deal with cases like our example. We say that an expression

$$\{< x_1, \ x_2, \ldots, x_n > \ | \ P \ (x_1, \ x_2, \ldots, x_n)\}$$

is safe if all of the following hold:

1. All values that appear in tuples of the expression are values from $dom(P)$.
2. For every "there exists" subformula of the form $\exists \ x \ (P_1(x))$, the subformula is true if and only if there is a value $x$ in $dom(P_1)$ such that $P_1(x)$ is true.
3. For every "for all" subformula of the form $\forall x \ (P_1(x))$, the subformula is true if and only if $P_1(x)$ is true for all values $x$ from $dom(P_1)$.

The purpose of the additional rules is to ensure that we can test "for all" and "there exists" subformulae without having to test infinitely many possibilities. Consider the second rule in the definition of safety. For $\exists \ x \ (P_1(x))$ to be true, we need to find only one $x$ for which $P_1(x)$ is true. In general, there would be infinitely many values to test. However, if the expression is safe, we know that we can restrict our attention to values from $dom(P_1)$. This restriction reduces to a finite number the tuples we must consider.

The situation for subformulae of the form $\forall x \ (P_1(x))$ is similar. To assert that $\forall x \ (P_1(x))$ is true, we must, in general, test all possible values, so we must examine infinitely many values. As before, if we know that the expression is safe, it is sufficient for us to test $P_1(x)$ for those values taken from $dom(P_1)$.

All the domain-relational-calculus expressions that we have written in the example queries of this section are safe.

### 3.4.4   Expressive Power of Languages

When the domain relational calculus is restricted to safe expressions, it is equivalent in expressive power to the tuple relational calculus restricted to safe expressions. Since we noted earlier that the restricted tuple relational calculus is equivalent to the relational algebra, all three of the following are equivalent:

- The relational algebra
- The tuple relational calculus restricted to safe expressions
- The domain relational calculus restricted to safe expressions

## 3.5   Extended Relational-Algebra Operations

The basic relational algebra operations have been extended in several ways. A simple extension is to allow arithmetic operations as part of projection. An important extension is to allow *aggregate operations*, such as computing the sum of the elements of a set, or their average. Another important extension is the *outer-join* operation, which allows relational-algebra expressions to deal with null values, which model missing information.

### 3.5.1   Generalized Projection

The *generalized-projection* operation extends the projection operation by allowing arithmetic functions to be used in the projection list. The generalized projection operation has the form

$$\Pi_{F_1, F_2, \ldots, F_n}(E)$$

where $E$ is any relational-algebra expression, and each of $F_1, F_2, \ldots, F_n$ are arithmetic expressions involving constants and attributes in the schema of $E$. As a special case, the arithmetic expression may be simply an attribute or a constant.

The following example demonstrates the basis for the use of the generalized projection operation. Suppose we have a relation *credit-info*, as depicted in Figure 3.24, which lists the credit limit and expenses so far (the *credit-balance* on the account). If we want to find how much more each person can spend, we can write the following expression:

$$\Pi_{customer\text{-}name,\ limit\ -\ credit\text{-}balance}(credit\text{-}info)$$

| customer-name | limit | credit-balance |
|---------------|-------|----------------|
| Jones         | 6000  | 700            |
| Smith         | 2000  | 400            |
| Hayes         | 1500  | 1500           |
| Curry         | 2000  | 1750           |

Figure 3.24   The *credit-info* relation.

| customer-name | limit − credit-balance |
|---|---|
| Jones | 5300 |
| Smith | 1600 |
| Hayes | 0 |
| Curry | 250 |

Figure 3.25    The result of $\Pi_{customer\text{-}name,\ limit\ -\ credit\text{-}balance}$ (*credit-info*).

Figure 3.25 shows the result of applying this expression to the relation in Figure 3.24.

## 3.5.2  Outer Join

The *outer-join* operation is an extension of the join operation to deal with missing information. Suppose that we have the relations with the following schemas, which contain data on full-time employees:

> *employee (employee-name, street, city)*
> *ft-works (employee-name, branch-name, salary)*

Let us consider the *employee* and *ft-works* relations shown in Figure 3.26. Suppose that we want to generate a single relation with all the information (street, city, branch name, and salary) about full-time employees. A possible approach would be to use the natural-join operation as follows:

> *employee* ⋈ *ft-works*

The result of this expression is shown in Figure 3.27. Notice that we have lost the street and city information about Smith, since the tuple describing Smith is absent from the *ft-works* relation; similarly, we have lost the branch name and salary information about Gates, since the tuple describing Gates is absent from the *employee* relation.

| employee-name | street | city |
|---|---|---|
| Coyote | Toon | Hollywood |
| Rabbit | Tunnel | Carrotville |
| Smith | Revolver | Death Valley |
| Williams | Seaview | Seattle |

| employee-name | branch-name | salary |
|---|---|---|
| Coyote | Mesa | 1500 |
| Rabbit | Mesa | 1300 |
| Gates | Redmond | 5300 |
| Williams | Redmond | 1500 |

Figure 3.26    The *employee* and *ft-works* relations.

| employee-name | street | city | branch-name | salary |
|---|---|---|---|---|
| Coyote | Toon | Hollywood | Mesa | 1500 |
| Rabbit | Tunnel | Carrotville | Mesa | 1300 |
| Williams | Seaview | Seattle | Redmond | 1500 |

Figure 3.27    The result of *employee* ⋈ *ft-works*.

We can use the *outer-join* operation to avoid this loss of information. There are actually three forms of the operation: *left outer join*, denoted ⟕; *right outer join*, denoted ⟖; and *full outer join*, denoted ⟗. All three forms of outer join compute the join, and add extra tuples to the result of the join. The results of the expressions *employee* ⟕ *ft-works*, *employee* ⟖ *ft-works* and *employee* ⟗ *ft-works* are shown in Figures 3.28, 3.29, and 3.30, respectively.

The left outer join takes all tuples in the left relation that did not match with any tuple in the right relation, pads the tuples with null values for all other attributes from the right relation, and adds them to the result of the natural join. In Figure 3.28, tuple (Smith, Revolver, Death Valley, *null*, *null*) is such a tuple. All information from the left relation is present in the result of the left outer join.

The right outer join is symmetric with the left outer join: Tuples from the right relation that did not match any from the left relation are padded with nulls and added to the result of the natural join. In Figure 3.29, tuple (Gates, *null*, *null*, Redmond, 5300) is such a tuple. Thus, all information from the right relation is present in the result of the right outer join.

The full outer join does both of those operations, padding tuples from left relation that did not match any from the right relation, as well as tuples from the right relation that did not match any from the left relation, and adding them to the result of the join. Figure 3.30 shows the result of a full outer join.

### 3.5.3    Aggregate Functions

*Aggregate* functions are functions that take a collection of values and return a single value as a result. For example, the aggregate function **sum** takes a collection of values and returns the sum of the values. Thus, the function **sum** applied on the collection

$$\{1, 1, 3, 4, 4, 11\}$$

| employee-name | street | city | branch-name | salary |
|---|---|---|---|---|
| Coyote | Toon | Hollywood | Mesa | 1500 |
| Rabbit | Tunnel | Carrotville | Mesa | 1300 |
| Williams | Seaview | Seattle | Redmond | 1500 |
| Smith | Revolver | Death Valley | *null* | *null* |

Figure 3.28    Result of *employee* ⟕ *ft-works*.

| employee-name | street | city | branch-name | salary |
|---|---|---|---|---|
| Coyote | Toon | Hollywood | Mesa | 1500 |
| Rabbit | Tunnel | Carrotville | Mesa | 1300 |
| Williams | Seaview | Seattle | Redmond | 1500 |
| Gates | null | null | Redmond | 5300 |

Figure 3.29    Result of *employee* ⋈ *ft-works*.

returns the value 24. The aggregate function **avg** returns the average of the values. When applied to the preceding collection, it returns the value 4. The aggregate function **count** returns the number of the elements in the collection, and would return 6 on the preceding collection. Other common aggregate functions include **min** and **max**, which return the minimum and maximum values in a collection; they return 1 and 11, respectively on the preceding collection.

The collections on which aggregate functions are used can have multiple occurrences of a value; the order in which the values appear is not relevant. Such collections are called *multisets*. Sets are a special case of multisets, where there is only one copy of each element.

To illustrate the concept of aggregation, we shall use the *pt-works* relation depicted in Figure 3.31, showing part-time employees. Suppose that we wanted to find out the total sum of salaries of all the part-time employees in the bank. The relational-algebra expression for this query is:

$$\mathbf{sum} \; _{salary}(pt\text{-}works)$$

The result of this query is a relation with a single attribute, containing a single row with a numerical value corresponding to the sum of all the salaries of all employees working part-time in the bank.

There are cases where we must eliminate multiple occurrences of a value prior to computing an aggregate function. If we do want to eliminate duplicates, we use the same function names as before, with the addition of the hyphenated string "**distinct**" appended to the end of the function name (for example, **count-distinct**). An example arises in the query "Find the number of branches appearing

| employee-name | street | city | branch-name | salary |
|---|---|---|---|---|
| Coyote | Toon | Hollywood | Mesa | 1500 |
| Rabbit | Tunnel | Carrotville | Mesa | 1300 |
| Williams | Seaview | Seattle | Redmond | 1500 |
| Smith | Revolver | Death Valley | null | null |
| Gates | null | null | Redmond | 5300 |

Figure 3.30    Result of *employee* ⟕ *ft-works*

| employee-name | branch-name | salary |
|---|---|---|
| Johnson | Downtown | 1500 |
| Loreena | Downtown | 1300 |
| Peterson | Downtown | 2500 |
| Sato | Austin | 1600 |
| Rao | Austin | 1500 |
| Gopal | Perryridge | 5300 |
| Adams | Perryridge | 1500 |
| Brown | Perryridge | 1300 |

**Figure 3.31**    The *pt-works* relation.

in the *pt-works* relation." In this case, a branch name counts only once, regardless of the number of employees working that branch. We write this query as follows:

$$\textbf{count-distinct }_{branch\text{-}name}(pt\text{-}works)$$

For the relation shown in Figure 3.31, the result of this query is the value 3.

There are circumstances where we would like to apply the aggregate function not only to a single set of tuples, but also to several groups, where each group is a set of tuples; we do so by using an operation called *grouping*. For example, we may want to find the total salary sum of all part-time employees at each branch of the bank individually, rather than in the entire bank. To do so, we need to partition the relation *pt-works* into *groups* based on the branch, and to apply the aggregate function on each group.

The following expression using the aggregation operator $\mathcal{G}$ achieves the desired result:

$$_{branch\text{-}name}\mathcal{G}\textbf{sum }_{salary}(pt\text{-}works)$$

The meaning of the expression is as follows. The attribute *branch-name* to the

| employee-name | branch-name | salary |
|---|---|---|
| Johnson | Downtown | 1500 |
| Loreena | Downtown | 1300 |
| Peterson | Downtown | 2500 |
| Sato | Austin | 1600 |
| Rao | Austin | 1500 |
| Gopal | Perryridge | 5300 |
| Adams | Perryridge | 1500 |
| Brown | Perryridge | 1300 |

**Figure 3.32**    The *pt-works* relation after grouping.

| branch-name | sum of salary |
|-------------|---------------|
| Downtown    | 5300          |
| Austin      | 3100          |
| Perryridge  | 8100          |

**Figure 3.33** Result of $_{branch\text{-}name}\mathcal{G}_{\textbf{sum } salary}$ (*pt-works*).

left of the $\mathcal{G}$ indicates that the input relation *pt-works* must be divided into groups based on the value of *branch-name*. The resulting groups are shown in Figure 3.32. The expression **sum** $_{salary}$(*pt-works*) to the right of the $\mathcal{G}$ indicates that, for each group of tuples (that is, each branch), the aggregation function **sum** must be applied on the collection of values of the *salary* attribute. The output relation consists of tuples with the branch name, and the sum of the salaries for the branch; it is shown in Figure 3.33.

The general form of the *aggregation operation* $\mathcal{G}$ is as follows:

$$_{G_1, G_2, ..., G_n}\mathcal{G}_{F_1\ A_1,\ F_2\ A_2, ...,\ F_m\ A_m}(E)$$

where $E$ is any relational-algebra expression, $G_1, G_2, \ldots, G_n$ constitute a list of attributes on which to group, each $F_i$ is an aggregate function, and each $A_i$ is an attribute name. The meaning of the operation is defined as follows. The tuples in result of expression $E$ are partitioned into groups such that

1. All tuples in a group have the same values for $G_1, G_2, \ldots, G_n$.
2. Tuples in different groups have different values for $G_1, G_2, \ldots, G_n$.

Thus, the groups can be identified by the values of attributes $G_1, G_2, \ldots, G_n$. For each group $(g_1, g_2, \ldots, g_n)$, the result has a tuple $(g_1, g_2, \ldots, g_n, a_1, a_2, \ldots, a_m)$ where, for each $i$, $a_i$ is the result of applying the aggregate function $F_i$ on the multiset of values for attribute $A_i$ in the group.

Going back to our earlier example, if we wanted to find the maximum salary for part-time employees at each branch, in addition to the sum of the salaries, we would write the expression

$$_{branch\text{-}name}\mathcal{G}_{\textbf{sum } salary, \textbf{max } salary}(pt\text{-}works)$$

The result of the expression is shown in Figure 3.34.

| branch-name | sum of salary | max of salary |
|-------------|---------------|---------------|
| Downtown    | 5300          | 2500          |
| Austin      | 3100          | 1600          |
| Perryridge  | 8100          | 5300          |

**Figure 3.34** Result of $_{branch\text{-}name}\mathcal{G}_{\textbf{sum } salary, \textbf{max } salary}(pt\text{-}works)$.

# 3.6    Modification of the Database

We have limited our attention until now to the extraction of information from the database. In this section, we address how to add, remove, or change information in the database.

We express database modifications using the assignment operation. We make assignments to actual database relations using the same notation as that described in Section 3.2.3 for assignment.

## 3.6.1    Deletion

A delete request is expressed in much the same way as a query. However, instead of displaying tuples to the user, we remove the selected tuples from the database. We can delete only whole tuples; we cannot delete values on only particular attributes. In relational algebra, a deletion is expressed by

$$r \leftarrow r - E$$

where $r$ is a relation and $E$ is a relational-algebra query.

Here are several examples of relational-algebra delete requests:

- Delete all of Smith's *depositor* records.

$$depositor \leftarrow depositor - \sigma_{customer\text{-}name = \text{``Smith''}} (depositor)$$

- Delete all loans with amount in the range 0 to 50.

$$loan \leftarrow loan - \sigma_{amount \geq 0 \text{ and } amount \leq 50} (loan)$$

- Delete all accounts at branches located in Needham.

$$r_1 \leftarrow \sigma_{branch\text{-}city = \text{``Needham''}} (account \bowtie branch)$$
$$r_2 \leftarrow \Pi_{branch\text{-}name, \; account\text{-}number, \; balance} (r_1)$$
$$account \leftarrow account - r_2$$

Note that, in the final example, we simplified our expression by using assignment to temporary relations ($r_1$ and $r_2$).

## 3.6.2    Insertion

To insert data into a relation, we either specify a tuple to be inserted or write a query whose result is a set of tuples to be inserted. Obviously, the attribute values for inserted tuples must be members of the attribute's domain. Similarly, tuples inserted must be of the correct arity. In relational algebra, an insertion is expressed by

$$r \leftarrow r \cup E$$

where $r$ is a relation and $E$ is a relational-algebra expression. We express the insertion of a single tuple by letting $E$ be a constant relation containing one tuple.

Suppose that we wish to insert the fact that Smith has $1200 in account A-973 at the Perryridge branch. We write

$$account \leftarrow account \cup \{(\text{"Perryridge"}, \text{A-973}, 1200)\}$$
$$depositor \leftarrow depositor \cup \{(\text{"Smith"}, \text{A-973})\}$$

More generally, we might want to insert tuples based on the result of a query. Suppose that we want to provide as a gift for all loan customers of the Perryridge branch, a new \$200 savings account. Let the loan number serve as the account number for this savings account. We write

$$r_1 \leftarrow (\sigma_{branch\text{-}name\,=\,\text{"Perryridge"}} (borrower \bowtie loan))$$
$$r_2 \leftarrow \Pi_{branch\text{-}name,\ loan\text{-}number} (r_1)$$
$$account \leftarrow account \cup (r_2 \times \{(200)\})$$
$$depositor \leftarrow depositor \cup \Pi_{customer\text{-}name,\ loan\text{-}number} (r_1)$$

Instead of specifying a tuple as we did earlier, we specify a set of tuples that is inserted into both the *account* and *depositor* relation. Each tuple in the *account* relation has the *branch-name* (Perryridge), a *account-number* (which is the same as the loan number), and the initial balance of the new account (\$200). Each tuple in the *depositor* relation has as *customer-name* the name of the loan customer who is being given the new account and the same account number as the corresponding *account* tuple.

### 3.6.3   Updating

In certain situations, we may wish to change a value in a tuple without changing *all* values in the tuple. We can use the generalized projection operator to do this task:

$$r \leftarrow \Pi_{F_1, F_2, \ldots, F_n} (r)$$

where each $F_i$ is either the $i$th attribute of $r$, if the $i$th attribute is not updated, or, if the attribute is to be updated, $F_i$ is an expression, involving only constants and the attributes of $r$, which gives the new value for the attribute.

If we want to select some tuples from $r$ and to update only them, we can use the following expression; here, $P$ denotes the selection condition that chooses which tuples to update:

$$r \leftarrow \Pi_{F_1, F_2, \ldots, F_n} (\sigma_P(r)) \cup (r - \sigma_P(r))$$

To illustrate the use of the update operation, we suppose that interest payments are being made, and that all balances are to be increased by 5 percent. We write

$$account \leftarrow \Pi_{branch\text{-}name,\ account\text{-}number,\ balance\ \leftarrow\ balance\ *1.05} (account)$$

Let us now suppose that accounts with balances over \$10,000 receive 6-percent interest, whereas all others receive 5 percent. We write

$$account \leftarrow \Pi_{BN, AN, balance\ \leftarrow\ balance\ *1.06} (\sigma_{balance > 10000} (account))$$
$$\cup\ \Pi_{BN,\ AN,\ balance\ \leftarrow\ balance\ *1.05} (\sigma_{balance \leq 10000} (account))$$

where the abbreviations $BN$ and $AN$ stand for *branch-name* and *account-number*, respectively.

# 3.7   Views

In our examples up to this point, we have operated at the logical-model level. That is, we have assumed that the collection of relations we are given are the actual relations stored in the database.

It is not desirable for all users to see the entire logical model. Security considerations may require that certain data be hidden from users. Consider a person who needs to know a customer's loan number but has no need to see the loan amount. This person should see a relation described, in the relational algebra, by

$$\Pi_{customer\text{-}name,\ loan\text{-}number}\ (borrower \bowtie loan)$$

Aside from security concerns, we may wish to create a personalized collection of relations that is better matched to a certain user's intuition than is the logical model. An employee in the advertising department, for example, might like to see a relation consisting of the customers who have either an account or a loan at the bank, and the branches with which they do business. The relation that we would create for that employee is

$$\Pi_{branch\text{-}name,\ customer\text{-}name}\ (depositor \bowtie account)$$
$$\cup\ \Pi_{branch\text{-}name,\ customer\text{-}name}\ (borrower \bowtie loan)$$

Any relation that is not part of the logical model but is made visible to a user as a virtual relation, is called a *view*. It is possible to support a large number of views on top of any given set of actual relations.

## 3.7.1   View Definition

We define a view using the **create view** statement. To define a view, we must give the view a name, and must state the query that computes the view. The form of the **create view** statement is

**create view** *v* **as** <query expression>

where <query expression> is any legal relational-algebra query expression. The view name is represented by *v*.

As an example, consider the view consisting of branches and their customers. Assume that we wish this view to be called *all-customer*. We define this view as follows:

**create view** *all-customer* **as**
$$\Pi_{branch\text{-}name,\ customer\text{-}name}\ (depositor \bowtie account)$$
$$\cup\ \Pi_{branch\text{-}name,\ customer\text{-}name}\ (borrower \bowtie loan)$$

Once we have defined a view, we can use the view name to refer to the virtual relation that the view generates. Using the view *all-customer*, we can find all customers of the Perryridge branch by writing

$$\Pi_{customer\text{-}name}\ (\sigma_{branch\text{-}name\,=\,\text{"Perryridge"}}\ (all\text{-}customer))$$

Recall that we wrote the same query in Section 3.2.1 without using views.

View names may appear in any place that a relation name may appear, so long as no update operations are executed on the views. We study the issue of update operations on views in Section 3.7.2.

View definition differs from the relational-algebra assignment operation. Suppose that we define relation $r1$ as follows:

$$r1 \leftarrow \Pi_{branch\text{-}name,\ customer\text{-}name}\ (depositor \bowtie account)$$
$$\cup\ \Pi_{branch\text{-}name,\ customer\text{-}name}(borrower \bowtie loan)$$

The assignment operation is evaluated once, and $r1$ does not change when the relations *depositor, account, loan* or *borrower* are updated. In contrast, if there is any modification to these relations, the set of tuples in the view *all-customer* changes as well. Intuitively, at any given time, the set of tuples in the view relation is defined as the result of evaluation of the query expression that defines the view at that time.

Thus, if a view relation is computed and stored, it may become out of date if the relations used to define it are modified. Instead, views are typically implemented as follows. When a view is defined, the database system stores the definition of the view itself, rather than the result of evaluation of the relational-algebra expression that defines the view. Wherever a view relation is used in a query, it is replaced by the stored query expression. Thus, whenever the query is evaluated, the view relation is recomputed.

Certain database systems allow view relations to be stored, but they make sure that, if the actual relations used in the view definition change, the view is kept up to date. Such views are called *materialized views*. Applications in which a view is used frequently benefit from the use of materialized views, as do applications in which response time to certain view-based queries is of utmost importance. The benefits to queries from the materialization of a view must be weighed against the storage costs and the added overhead for updates.

## 3.7.2 Updates Through Views and Null Values

Although views are a useful tool for queries, they present significant problems if updates, insertions, or deletions are expressed with them. The difficulty is that a modification to the database expressed in terms of a view must be translated to a modification to the actual relations in the logical model of the database.

To illustrate the problem, we consider a clerk who needs to see all loan data in the *loan* relation, except *loan-amount*. Let *branch-loan* be the view given to the clerk. We define this view as

**create view** *branch-loan* **as**
$$\Pi_{branch\text{-}name,\ loan\text{-}number}\ (loan)$$

Since we allow a view name to appear wherever a relation name is allowed, the clerk can write:

$$branch\text{-}loan \leftarrow branch\text{-}loan \cup \{(\text{"Perryridge"}, \text{L-37})\}$$

This insertion must be represented by an insertion into the relation *loan*, since *loan* is the actual relation from which the view *branch-loan* is constructed. However, to insert a tuple into *loan*, we must have some value for *amount*. There are two reasonable approaches to dealing with this insertion:

- Reject the insertion, and return an error message to the user.
- Insert a tuple ("Perryridge", L-37, *null*) into the *loan* relation.

Let us illustrate another problem resulting from modification of the database through views:

**create view** *loan-info* **as**

$$\Pi_{customer\text{-}name,\ amount}(borrower \bowtie loan)$$

This view lists the loan amount for each loan that any customer of the bank has. Consider the following insertion through this view:

$$loan\text{-}info \leftarrow loan\text{-}info \cup \{(\text{"Johnson"}, 1900)\}$$

The only possible method of inserting tuples into the *borrower* and *loan* relations is to insert ("Johnson", *null*) into *borrower* and (*null*, *null*, 1900) into *loan*. Then, we obtain the relations shown in Figure 3.35. However, this update does not have the desired effect, since the view relation *loan-info* still does *not* include the tuple ("Johnson", 1900). (Recall that all comparisons involving *null* are defined to be **false**, so the natural join of *borrower* and *loan* does not contain the required tuple.) Thus, there is no way to update the relations *borrower* and *loan* using nulls to get the desired update on *loan-info*. borrower

| branch-name | loan-number | amount |
|---|---|---|
| Downtown | L-17 | 1000 |
| Redwood | L-23 | 2000 |
| Perryridge | L-15 | 1500 |
| Downtown | L-14 | 1500 |
| Mianus | L-93 | 500 |
| Round Hill | L-11 | 900 |
| Perryridge | L-16 | 1300 |
| null | null | 1900 |

| customer-name | loan-number |
|---|---|
| Jones | L-17 |
| Smith | L-23 |
| Hayes | L-15 |
| Jackson | L-14 |
| Curry | L-93 |
| Smith | L-11 |
| Williams | L-17 |
| Adams | L-16 |
| Johnson | null |

Figure 3.35    Tuples inserted into *loan* and *borrower*.

Due to problems such as these, modifications are generally not permitted on view relations, except in limited cases. The general problem of database modification through views has been the subject of substantial research. The bibliographic notes mention recent works on this subject.

### 3.7.3  Views Defined Using Other Views

In Section 3.7.1, we mentioned that view relations may appear in any place that a relation name may appear, except for restrictions on the use of views in update expressions. Thus, one view may be used in the expression defining another view. For example, we can define the view *perryridge-customer* as follows:

> **create view** *perryridge-customer* **as**
> $$\Pi_{customer\text{-}name} \, (\sigma_{branch\text{-}name = \text{“Perryridge”}} \, (all\text{-}customer))$$

where *all-customer* is itself a view relation.

A view relation $v_1$ is said to *depend directly on* a view relation $v_2$ if $v_2$ is used in the expression defining $v_1$. An example of view dependency is shown pictorially in Figure 3.36. The figure indicates that the view *all-customer* depends directly on the relations *borrower* and *loan*, since the expression defining *all-customer* uses the other two views. Similarly the view *perryridge-customer* depends on the view *all-customer*. A graph such as the one shown in the figure is called a *dependency graph*; it has a node for each view, and a directed edge from view $v_2$ to view $v_1$ if $v_1$ depends directly on $v_2$.

A view relation $v_1$ is said to *depend on* view relation $v_2$ if and only if there is a path in the dependency graph from $v_2$ to $v_1$. In other words, view $v_1$ depends on view $v_2$ if either $v_1$ depends directly on $v_2$, or there is a sequence of view relations $r_1, r_2, \ldots, r_{n-1}, r_n$ such that $v_1$ depends directly on $r_1$, $r_1$ depends directly on $r_2$, and so on, until $r_{n-1}$ depends directly on $r_n$, and $r_n$ depends directly on $v_2$.

A view relation $v$ is said to be *recursive* if it depends on itself. Pictorially, the dependency graph would have a cycle involving $v$ if and only if $v$ is recursive. In Chapter 5, we consider the meaning of recursive views; for now, we simply require that view definitions not be recursive.

*View expansion* is one way to define the meaning of views defined in terms of other views. Let view $v_1$ be defined by an expression $e_1$ that may itself contain uses of view relations. A view relation stands for the expression defining the view, and therefore a view relation can be replaced by the expression that defines it. If we modify an expression by replacing a view relation by the latter's definition, the

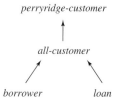

Figure 3.36    Dependency of views.

resultant expression may still contain other view relations. Hence, view expansion
of an expression repeats the replacement step as follows:

> **repeat**
>> Find any view relation $v_i$ in $e_1$
>> Replace the view relation $v_i$ by the expression defining $v_i$
> **until** no more view relations are present in $e_1$

As long as the view definitions are not recursive, this loop will terminate. Thus,
an expression $e$ containing view relations can be understood as the expression
resulting from view expansion of $e$, which does not contain any view relations.
We illustrate view expansion using the following expression:

$$\sigma_{customer\text{-}name=\text{"John"}}(perryridge\text{-}customer)$$

The view-expansion procedure initially generates

$$\sigma_{customer\text{-}name=\text{"John"}}(\Pi_{customer\text{-}name}(\sigma_{branch\text{-}name=\text{"Perryridge"}}(all\text{-}customer)))$$

it then generates

$$\sigma_{customer\text{-}name=\text{"John"}}(\Pi_{customer\text{-}name}(\sigma_{branch\text{-}name=\text{"Perryridge"}}(\Pi_{branch\text{-}name,\ customer\text{-}name}(depositor \bowtie account) \cup \Pi_{branch\text{-}name,\ customer\text{-}name}(borrower \bowtie loan))))$$

There are no more uses of view relations, and view expansion terminates.

## 3.8   Summary

The relational data model is based on a collection of tables. The user of the
database system may query these tables, insert new tuples, delete tuples, and update (modify) tuples. There are several languages for expressing these operations.
The tuple relational calculus and the domain relational calculus are nonprocedural
languages that represent the basic power required in a relational query language.
The relational algebra is a procedural language that is equivalent in power to both
forms of the relational calculus when they are restricted to safe expressions. The
algebra defines the basic operations used within relational query languages.
The relational algebra and the relational calculi are terse, formal languages
that are inappropriate for casual users of a database system. Commercial database
systems, therefore, use languages with more "syntactic sugar." In Chapters 4 and
5, we shall consider the three most influential of the commercial languages: SQL,
QBE, and Quel, as well as the research language, Datalog.
Databases can be modified by insertion, deletion, or update of tuples. We
used the relational algebra with the assignment operator to express these modifications.
Different users of a shared database may benefit from individualized views
of the database. Views are "virtual relations" defined by a query expression. We
used relational algebra as an example to show how such views can be defined

and used. We evaluate queries involving views by replacing the view with the expression that defines the view. Views are useful mechanisms for simplifying database queries, but modification of the database through views may have potentially disadvantageous consequences. Therefore, database systems severely restrict updates through views. For reasons of query-processing efficiency, a view may be materialized—that is, stored physically. Updates that affect materialized views incur additional overhead.

## Exercises

**3.1.** Design a relational database for a university registrar's office. The office maintains data about each class, including the instructor, the number of students enrolled, and the time and place of the class meetings. For each student–class pair, a grade is recorded.

**3.2.** Describe the differences in meaning between the terms *relation* and *relation schema*. Illustrate your answer by referring to your solution to Exercise 3.1

**3.3.** Design a relational database corresponding to the E-R diagram of Figure 3.37.

**3.4.** In Chapter 2, we showed how to represent many-to-many, many-to-one, one-to-many, and one-to-one relationship sets. Explain how primary keys help us to represent such relationship sets in the relational model.

**3.5.** Consider the relational database of Figure 3.38. For each of the following queries, give an expression in the relational algebra, the tuple relational calculus, and the domain relational calculus:

    (*a*) Find the names of all employees who work for First Bank Corporation.

    (*b*) Find the names and cities of residence of all employees who work for First Bank Corporation.

    (*c*) Find the names, street address, and cities of residence of all employees who work for First Bank Corporation and earn more than $10,000 per annum.

    (*d*) Find the names of all employees in this database who live in the same city as the company for which they work.

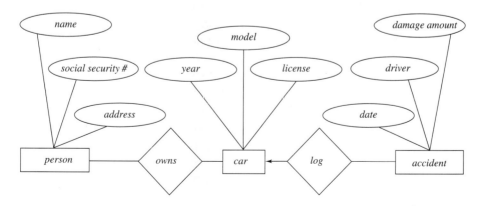

Figure 3.37    E-R diagram.

*employee (employee-name, street, city)*
*works (employee-name, company-name, salary)*
*company (company-name, city)*
*manages (employee-name, manager-name)*

Figure 3.38    Relational database for Exercises 3.5 and 3.12.

(e) Find the names of all employees who live in the same city and on the same street as do their managers.
(f) Find the names of all employees in this database who do not work for First Bank Corporation.
(g) Find the names of all employees who earn more than every employee of Small Bank Corporation.
(h) Assume the companies may be located in several cities. Find all companies located in every city in which Small Bank Corporation is located.

**3.6.** Let the following relation schemas be given:

$$R = (A, B, C)$$
$$S = (D, E, F)$$

Let relations $r(R)$ and $s(S)$ be given. Give an expression in the tuple relational calculus that is equivalent to each of the following:
(a) $\Pi_A(r)$
(b) $\sigma_{B=17}(r)$
(c) $r \times s$
(d) $\Pi_{A,F}(\sigma_{C=D}(r \times s))$

**3.7.** Let $R = (A, B, C)$, and let $r_1$ and $r_2$ both be relations on schema $R$. Give an expression in the domain relational calculus that is equivalent to each of the following:
(a) $\Pi_A(r_1)$
(b) $\sigma_{B=17}(r_1)$
(c) $r_1 \cup r_2$
(d) $r_1 \cap r_2$
(e) $r_1 - r_2$
(f) $\Pi_{A,B}(r_1) \bowtie \Pi_{B,C}(r_2)$

**3.8.** Let $R = (A, B)$ and $S = (A, C)$, and let $r(R)$ and $s(S)$ be relations. Write relational-algebra expressions equivalent to the following domain-relational-calculus expressions:
(a) $\{<a> \mid \exists b (<a, b> \in r \land b = 17)\}$
(b) $\{<a, b, c> \mid <a, b> \in r \land <a, c> \in s\}$
(c) $\{<a> \mid \exists b (<a, b> \in r) \lor \forall c (\exists d (<d, c> \in s) \Rightarrow <a, c> \in s)\}$
(d) $\{<a> \mid \exists c (<a, c> \in s \land \exists b_1, b_2 (<a, b_1> \in r \land <c, b_2> \in r \land b_1 > b_2))\}$

**3.9.** Let $R = (A, B)$ and $S = (A, C)$, and let $r(R)$ and $s(S)$ be relations. Using the special constant *null*, write tuple-relational-calculus expressions equivalent to each of the following:

(a) $r \bowtie s$

(b) $r \bowtie s$

(c) $r \bowtie s$

**3.10.** Consider the relation of Figure 3.19, which shows the result of the query "Find the names of all customers who have a loan at the bank." Rewrite the query to include not only the name, but also the city of residence for each customer. Observe that now customer Jackson no longer appears in the result, even though Jackson does in fact have a loan from the bank.

(a) Explain why Jackson does not appear in the result.

(b) Suppose that you want Jackson to appear in the result. How would you modify the database to achieve this effect?

(c) Again, suppose that you want Jackson to appear in the result. Write a query using an outer join that accomplishes this desire without your having to modify the database.

**3.11.** The outer-join operations extend the natural-join operation so that tuples from the participating relations are not lost in the result of the join. Describe how the theta join operation can be extended so that tuples from the left, right, or both relations are not lost from the result of a theta join.

**3.12.** Consider the relational database of Figure 3.38. Give an expression in the relational algebra for each request:

(a) Modify the database such that Jones now lives in Newtown.

(b) Give all employees of First Bank Corporation a 10-percent salary raise.

(c) Give all managers in this database a 10-percent salary raise.

(d) Give all managers in this database a 10-percent salary raise, unless the salary would be greater than $100,000. In such cases, give only a 3-percent raise.

(e) Delete all tuples in the *works* relation for employees of Small Bank Corporation.

**3.13.** List two reasons why null values might be introduced into the database.

**3.14.** Certain systems allow *marked* nulls. A marked null $\perp_i$ is equal to itself, but if $i \neq j$, then $\perp_i \neq \perp_j$. One application of marked nulls is to allow certain updates through views. Consider the view *loan-info* (Section 3.7). Show how you can use marked nulls to allow the insertion of the tuple ("Johnson", 1900) through *loan-info*.

**3.15.** Using the bank example, write relational-algebra queries to find the accounts held by more than two customers in the following ways:

(a) using an aggregate function.

(b) without using any aggregate functions.

**3.16.** Consider the relational database of Figure 3.38. Give a relational-algebra expression for each of the following queries:

(a) Find the company with the most employees.

(b) Find the company with the smallest payroll.

(c) Find those companies whose employees earn a higher salary, on average, than the average salary at First Bank Corporation.

**3.17.** List two reasons why we may choose to define a view.

**3.18.** List two major problems with processing update operations expressed in
terms of views.

# Bibliographical Notes

The relational model was proposed by E. F. Codd of the IBM Research Laboratory
in the late 1960s [Codd 1970]. This work led to Codd's receipt of the prestigious
ACM Turing Award in 1981 (Codd [1982]). Following Codd's original paper,
several research projects were formed with the goal of constructing practical relational database systems, including System R at the IBM San Jose Research
Laboratory, Ingres at the University of California at Berkeley, Query-by-Example
at the IBM T. J. Watson Research Center, and the Peterlee Relational Test Vehicle
(PRTV) at the IBM Scientific Center in Peterlee, United Kingdom. System R is
discussed in Astrahan et al. [1976, 1979], and Chamberlin et al. [1981]. Ingres is
discussed in Stonebraker [1980, 1986b] and Stonebraker et al. [1976]. Query-by-
example is described in Zloof [1977]. PRTV is described in Todd [1976].

Numerous relational-database products are now commercially available.
These include IBM's DB2, Ingres, Oracle, Sybase, Informix, Microsoft SQL
Server. Database products for personal computers include Microsoft Access, dBase,
and FoxPro. Information about the products can be found in their respective manuals. Textbooks devoted to specific commercial systems include Malamud [1989]
and Date [1987], covering Ingres; Martin et al. [1989] and Date and White [1993],
covering IBM's DB2 product; Date and White [1989] covering SQL/DS; and Corrigan and Gurry [1993] and Koch and Loney [1995], covering Oracle.

General discussion of the relational data model appears in most database
texts. Gardarin and Valduriez [1989], Valduriez and Gardarin [1989], Atzeni and
De Antonellis [1993], and Maier [1983] are texts devoted exclusively to the relational data model.

The original definition of relational algebra is given in Codd [1970]; that of
tuple relational calculus is given in Codd [1972b]. A formal proof of the equivalence of tuple relational calculus and relational algebra was given in Codd [1972b].
Several extensions to the relational calculus have been proposed. Klug [1982] and
Escobar-Molano et al. [1993] describe extensions to scalar aggregate functions.
Extensions to the relational model and discussions concerning incorporation of
null values in the relational algebra (the RM/T model), as well as outer joins, are
presented in Codd [1979]. Codd [1990] is a compendium of E. F. Codd's papers
on the relational model. Outer joins are also discussed in Date [1983b].

The problem of updating relational databases through views is addressed by
Barsalou et al. [1991], Bancilhon and Spyratos [1981], Cosmadakis and Papadimitriou [1984], Dayal and Bernstein [1978, 1982], Keller [1985], and Langerak
[1990].

Blakeley et al. [1986, 1989] and Griffin and Libkin [1995] describe techniques for maintenance of materialized views. Gupta and Mumick [1995] provide
a recent survey of materialized view maintenance.

# CHAPTER
# 4

## SQL

The formal languages described in Chapter 3 provide a concise notation for representing queries. However, commercial database systems require a query language that is more user-friendly. In this chapter, we study the most influential commercially marketed product language, SQL. SQL uses a combination of relational-algebra and relational-calculus constructs.

Although we refer to the SQL language as a "query language," it contains many other capabilities besides querying a database. It includes features for defining the structure of the data, for modifying data in the database, and for specifying security constraints.

It is not our intention to provide a complete users' guide for SQL. Rather, we present SQL's fundamental constructs and concepts. Individual implementations of SQL may differ in details, or may support only a subset of the full language.

In Chapter 5, we present two other influential commercial languages, QBE and Quel, and a language used in research systems, Datalog. These languages represent a variety of styles. QBE is based on the domain relational calculus, Quel is based on the tuple relational calculus, and Datalog is based on the logic-programming language Prolog. All three languages have been influential in research database systems; the first two have also been influential in commercially marketed systems.

## 4.1 Background

SQL has clearly established itself as *the* standard relational-database language. There are numerous versions of SQL. The original version was developed at IBM's San Jose Research Laboratory (now the Almaden Research Center). This language, originally called Sequel, was implemented as part of the System R project in the early 1970s. The Sequel language has evolved since then, and its name has changed to SQL (Structured Query Language). Numerous products now support the SQL language.

In 1986, the American National Standards Institute (ANSI) and the International Standards Organization (ISO) published an SQL standard, called SQL-86. IBM published its own corporate SQL standard, the Systems Application Architecture Database Interface (SAA-SQL) in 1987. An extended standard for SQL, SQL-89, was published in 1989, and database systems today typically support at least the features of SQL-89. The current version of the ANSI/ISO SQL standard is the SQL-92 standard. The bibliographic notes provide references to these standards, as well as to ongoing standardization work on the SQL-3 standard.

In this section, we present a survey of SQL, based on the SQL-89 and SQL-92 standards. You should be aware that some SQL implementations may support only SQL-89, and thus will not support SQL-92. Features of SQL-92 that are not supported in SQL-89 are identified explicitly as SQL-92 features, for the benefit of those people who use database systems that do not fully support SQL-92.

The SQL language has several parts:

- **Data-definition language** (DDL). The SQL DDL provides commands for defining relation schemas, deleting relations, creating indices, and modifying relation schemas.

- **Interactive data-manipulation language** (DML). The SQL DML includes a query language based on both the relational algebra and the tuple relational calculus. It includes also commands to insert tuples into, delete tuples from, and to modify tuples in the database.

- **Embedded DML**. The embedded form of SQL is designed for use within general-purpose programming languages, such as PL/I, Cobol, Pascal, Fortran, and C.

- **View definition**. The SQL DDL includes commands for defining views.

- **Authorization**. The SQL DDL includes commands for specifying access rights to relations and views.

- **Integrity**. The SQL DDL includes commands for specifying integrity constraints that the data stored in the database must satisfy. Updates that violate integrity constraints are disallowed.

- **Transaction control**. SQL includes commands for specifying the beginning and ending of transactions. Several implementations also allow explicit locking of data for concurrency control.

In this chapter, we cover the interactive DML and the basic DDL feature of SQL.

The enterprise that we use in the examples in this chapter, as well as in Chapter 5, is the banking enterprise, with the following relation schemas:

*Branch-schema* = (*branch-name, branch-city, assets*)
*Customer-schema* = (*customer-name, customer-street, customer-city*)
*Loan-schema* = (*branch-name, loan-number, amount*)
*Borrower-schema* = (*customer-name, loan-number*)
*Account-schema* = (*branch-name, account-number, balance*)
*Depositor-schema* = (*customer-name, account-number*)

In Chapter 6, we discuss SQL's features regarding integrity. Transactions are covered in Chapters 13 and 14. Security and authorization are discussed in Chapter 19. In this chapter, as elsewhere in the text, we use hyphenated names for schema, relations, and attributes for ease of reading. In actual SQL systems, however, the underscore ("_") must be used instead.

## 4.2    Basic Structure

A relational database consists of a collection of relations, each of which is assigned a unique name. Each relation has a structure similar to that presented in Chapter 3. SQL allows the use of null values to indicate that the value either is unknown or does not exist. Provisions are made to allow a user to specify which attributes cannot be assigned null values, as we shall discuss in Section 4.11.

The basic structure of an SQL expression consists of three clauses: **select**, **from**, and **where**.

- The **select** clause corresponds to the projection operation of the relational algebra. It is used to list the attributes desired in the result of a query.
- The **from** clause corresponds to the Cartesian-product operation of the relational algebra. It lists the relations to be scanned in the evaluation of the expression.
- The **where** clause corresponds to the selection predicate of the relational algebra. It consists of a predicate involving attributes of the relations that appear in the **from** clause.

That the term *select* has different meaning in SQL and in the relational algebra is an unfortunate historical fact. We emphasize the different interpretations here to minimize potential confusion.

A typical SQL query has the form

**select** $A_1, A_2, \ldots, A_n$
**from** $r_1, r_2, \ldots, r_m$
**where** $P$

Each $A_i$ represents an attribute, and each $r_i$ a relation. $P$ is a predicate. The query is equivalent to the relational-algebra expression

$$\Pi_{A_1, A_2, \ldots, A_n}(\sigma_P (r_1 \times r_2 \times \ldots \times r_m))$$

If the **where** clause is omitted, the predicate *P* is **true**. However, unlike that of a relational-algebra expression, the result of the SQL query may contain multiple copies of some tuples; we return to this issue in Section 4.2.8.

SQL forms the Cartesian product of the relations named in the **from** clause, performs a relational-algebra selection using the **where** clause predicate, and then projects the result onto the attributes of the **select** clause. In practice, SQL may convert the expression into an equivalent form that can be processed more efficiently. However, we shall defer concerns about efficiency to Chapter 12.

## 4.2.1    The select Clause

The result of an SQL query is, of course, a relation. Let us consider a simple query using our banking example, "Find the names of all branches in the *loan* relation":

**select** *branch-name*
**from** *loan*

The result is a relation consisting of a single attribute with the heading *branch-name*.

Formal query languages are based on the mathematical notion of a relation being a set. Thus, duplicate tuples never appear in relations. In practice, duplicate elimination is relatively time consuming. Therefore, SQL (like most other commercial query languages) allows duplicates in relations as well as in the results of SQL expressions. Thus, the preceding query will list each *branch-name* once for every tuple in which it appears in the *loan* relation.

In those cases where we want to force the elimination of duplicates, we insert the keyword **distinct** after **select**. We can rewrite the preceding query as

**select distinct** *branch-name*
**from** *loan*

if we want duplicates removed.

Note that SQL allows us to use the keyword **all** to specify explicitly that duplicates are not removed:

**select all** *branch-name*
**from** *loan*

Since duplicate retention is the default, we will not use **all** in our examples. To ensure the elimination of duplicates in the results of our example queries, we will use **distinct** whenever it is necessary. In most queries where **distinct** is not used, the exact number of duplicate copies of each tuple present in the query result is not important. However, the number is important in certain applications; we return to this issue in Section 4.2.8.

The asterisk symbol "*" can be used to denote "all attributes." Thus, the use of *loan*.* in the preceding **select** clause would indicate that all attributes of *loan* should be selected. A select clause of the form **select** * indicates that all attributes of all relations appearing in the **from** clause must be selected.

The **select** clause can also contain arithmetic expressions involving the operators, $+$, $-$, $*$, and $/$, and operating on constants or attributes of tuples. For example, the query

> **select** *branch-name, loan-number, amount* $*$ 100
> **from** *loan*

will return a relation that is the same as the *loan* relation, except that the attribute *amount* is multiplied by 100.

SQL-92 also provides special data types, such as various forms of the *date* type, and allows several arithmetic functions to operate on these types.

## 4.2.2   The where Clause

Let us illustrate the use of the **where** clause in SQL. Consider the query "Find all loan numbers for loans made at the Perryridge branch with loan amounts greater that $1200." This query can be written in SQL as:

> **select** *loan-number*
> **from** *loan*
> **where** *branch-name* $=$ "Perryridge" **and** *amount* $>$ 1200

SQL uses the logical connectives **and**, **or**, and **not**—rather than the mathematical symbols $\wedge$, $\vee$, and $\neg$—in the **where** clause. The operands of the logical connectives can be expressions involving the comparison operators $<$, $<=$, $>$, $>=$, $=$, and $<>$. SQL allows us to use the comparison operators to compare strings and arithmetic expressions, as well as special types, such as date types.

SQL includes a **between** comparison operator to simplify **where** clauses that specify that a value be less than or equal to some value and greater than or equal to some other value. If we wish to find the loan number of those loans with loan amounts between $90,000 and $100,000, we can use the **between** comparison to write

> **select** *loan-number*
> **from** *loan*
> **where** *amount* **between** 90000 **and** 100000

instead of

> **select** *loan-number*
> **from** *loan*
> **where** *amount* $<=$ 100000 **and** *amount* $>=$ 90000

Similarly, we can use the **not between** comparison operator.

## 4.2.3   The from Clause

Finally, let us discuss the use of the **from** clause. The **from** clause by itself defines a Cartesian product of the relations in the clause. Since the natural join is defined in terms of a Cartesian product, a selection, and a projection, it is a relatively simple matter to write an SQL expression for the natural join.

We write the relational-algebra expression

$$\Pi_{customer\text{-}name,\, loan\text{-}number} \,(borrower \,\bowtie\, loan)$$

for the query "For all customers who have a loan from the bank, find their names and loan numbers." In SQL, this query can be written as

> **select distinct** *customer-name, borrower.loan-number*
> **from** *borrower, loan*
> **where** *borrower.loan-number = loan.loan-number*

Notice that SQL uses the notation *relation-name.attribute-name*, as does the relational algebra, to avoid ambiguity in cases where an attribute appears in the schema of more than one relation. We could have written *borrower.customer-name* instead of *customer-name* in the **select** clause. However, since the attribute *customer-name* appears in only one of the relations named in the **from** clause, there is no ambiguity when we write *customer-name*.

Let us extend the preceding query, and consider a more complicated case in which we require also that customers have a loan from the Perryridge branch: "Find the names and loan numbers of all customers who have a loan at the Perryridge branch." To write this query, we shall need to state two constraints in the **where** clause, connected by the logical connective **and**:

> **select distinct** *customer-name, borrower.loan-number*
> **from** *borrower, loan*
> **where** *borrower.loan-number = loan.loan-number* **and**
>     *branch-name =* "Perryridge"

SQL-92 includes extensions to perform natural joins, and outer joins in the **from** clause. We discuss these extensions in Section 4.10.

## 4.2.4   The Rename Operation

SQL provides a mechanism for renaming both relations and attributes. It uses the **as** clause, taking the form:

> *old-name* **as** *new-name*

The **as** clause can appear in both the **select** and **from** clauses.

Consider again the query that we used earlier:

> **select distinct** *customer-name, borrower.loan-number*
> **from** *borrower, loan*
> **where** *borrower.loan-number = loan.loan-number* **and**
>     *branch-name =* "Perryridge"

The result of this query is a relation with the following two attributes:

*customer-name, loan-number.*

The names of the attributes in the result are derived from the names of the attributes in the relations in the **from** clause.

We cannot, however, always derive names in this way. First, two relations in the **from** clause may have attributes with the same name, in which case a attribute name is duplicated in the result. Second, if we used an arithmetic expression in the **select** clause, the resultant attribute does not have a name. Third, even if a attribute name can be derived from the base relations as in the preceding example, we may want to change the attribute name in the result. Hence, SQL provides a way of renaming the attributes of a result relation.

For example, if we want the attribute name *loan-number* to be replaced with the name *loan-id*, we can rewrite the preceding query as

> **select distinct** *customer-name, borrower.loan-number* **as** *loan-id*
> **from** *borrower, loan*
> **where** *borrower.loan-number = loan.loan-number* **and**
>     *branch-name =* "Perryridge"

## 4.2.5   Tuple Variables

The **as** clause is particularly useful in defining the notion of tuple variables, as is done in the tuple relational calculus. A tuple variable in SQL must be associated with a particular relation. Tuple variables are defined in the **from** clause via the use of the **as** clause. To illustrate, we rewrite the query "For all customers who have a loan from the bank, find their names and loan numbers" as

> **select distinct** *customer-name, T.loan-number*
> **from** *borrower* **as** *T, loan* **as** *S*
> **where** *T.loan-number = S.loan-number*

Note that we define a tuple variable in the **from** clause by placing it after the name of the relation with which it is associated, with the keyword **as** in between (the keyword **as** is optional). When we write expressions of the form *relation-name.attribute-name*, the relation name is, in effect, an implicitly defined tuple variable.

Tuple variables are most useful for comparing two tuples in the same relation. Recall that, in such cases, we could use the rename operation in the relational algebra. Suppose that we want the query "Find the names of all branches that have assets greater than at least one branch located in Brooklyn." We can write the SQL expression

> **select distinct** *T.branch-name*
> **from** *branch* **as** *T, branch* **as** *S*
> **where** *T.assets > S.assets* **and** *S.branch-city =* "Brooklyn"

Observe that we could not use the notation *branch.asset*, since it would not be clear which reference to *branch* is intended.

SQL-92 permits us to use the notation $(v_1, v_2, \ldots, v_n)$ to denote a tuple of arity $n$ containing values $v_1, v_2, \ldots, v_n$. The comparison operators can be used on tuples, and the ordering is defined lexicographically. For example, $(a_1, a_2) <= (b_1, b_2)$ is true if $a_1 < b_1$, or $(a_1 = b_1) \wedge (a_2 <= b_2)$; similarly, the two tuples are equal if all their attributes are equal.

## 4.2.6  String Operations

The most commonly used operation on strings is pattern matching using the operator **like**. We describe patterns using two special characters:

- Percent (%): The % character matches any substring.
- Underscore ( _ ): The _ character matches any character.

Patterns are case sensitive; that is, uppercase characters do not match lowercase characters, or vice versa. To illustrate pattern matching, we consider the following examples:

- "Perry%" matches any string beginning with "Perry".
- "%idge%" matches any string containing "idge" as a substring, for example, "Perryridge", "Rock Ridge", "Mianus Bridge", and "Ridgeway".
- "_ _ _" matches any string of exactly three characters.
- "_ _ _%" matches any string of at least three characters.

Patterns are expressed in SQL using the **like** comparison operator. Consider the query "Find the names of all customers whose street address includes the substring 'Main'." This query can be written as

> **select** *customer-name*
> **from** *customer*
> **where** *customer-street* **like** "%Main%"

For patterns to include the special pattern characters (that is, %, and _ ), SQL allows the specification of an escape character. The escape character is used immediately before a special pattern character to indicate that the special pattern character is to be treated like a normal character. We define the escape character for a **like** comparison using the **escape** keyword. To illustrate, consider the following patterns, which use a backslash (\) as the escape character:

- **like** "ab\%cd%" **escape** "\" matches all strings beginning with "ab%cd".
- **like** "ab\\cd%" **escape** "\" matches all strings beginning with "ab\cd".

SQL allows us to search for mismatches instead of matches by using the **not like** comparison operator.

SQL also permits a variety of functions on character strings, such as concatenating (using "∥"), extracting substrings, finding the length of strings, converting between uppercase and lowercase, and so on.

### 4.2.7   Ordering the Display of Tuples

SQL offers the user some control over the order in which tuples in a relation are displayed. The **order by** clause causes the tuples in the result of a query to appear in sorted order. To list in alphabetic order all customers who have a loan at the Perryridge branch, we write

> **select distinct** *customer-name*
> **from** *borrower, loan*
> **where** *borrower.loan-number* = *loan.loan-number* **and**
>         *branch-name* = "Perryridge"
> **order by** *customer-name*

By default, the **order by** clause lists items in ascending order. To specify the sort order, we may specify **desc** for descending order or **asc** for ascending order. Furthermore, ordering can be performed on multiple attributes. Suppose that we wish to list the entire *loan* relation in descending order of *amount*. If several loans have the same amount, we order them in ascending order by loan number. We express this query in SQL as follows:

> **select** *
> **from** *loan*
> **order by** *amount* **desc**, *loan-number* **asc**

To fulfill an **order by** request, SQL must perform a sort. Since sorting a large number of tuples may be costly, it is desirable to sort only when necessary.

### 4.2.8   Duplicates

The use of relations with duplicates has proved useful in several situations. SQL formally defines not only what tuples are in the result of a query, but also how many copies of each of those tuples appears in the result. We can define the duplicate semantics of an SQL query using *multiset* versions of the relational operators. We define the multiset versions of several of the relational-algebra operators here. Given multiset relations $r_1$ and $r_2$,

1. If there are $c_1$ copies of tuple $t_1$ in $r_1$, and $t_1$ satisfies selection $\sigma_\theta$, then there are $c_1$ copies of $t_1$ in $\sigma_\theta(r_1)$.
2. For each copy of tuple $t_1$ in $r_1$, there is a copy of tuple $\Pi_A(t_1)$ in $\Pi_A(r_1)$, where $\Pi_A(t_1)$ denotes the projection of the single tuple $t_1$.
3. If there are $c_1$ copies of tuple $t_1$ in $r_1$ and $c_2$ copies of tuple $t_2$ in $r_2$, there are $c_1 * c_2$ copies of the tuple $t_1.t_2$ in $r_1 \times r_2$.

For example, suppose that relations $r_1$ with schema $(A, B)$ and $r_2$ with schema $(C)$ are the following multisets:

$$r_1 = \{(1, a), (2, a)\} \qquad r_2 = \{(2), (3), (3)\}$$

Then, $\Pi_B(r_1)$ would be $\{(a), (a)\}$, whereas $\Pi_B(r_1) \times r_2$ would be

$$\{(a, 2), (a, 2), (a, 3), (a, 3), (a, 3), (a, 3)\}$$

We can now define the how many copies of each tuple occur in the result of an SQL query. An SQL query of the form

> **select** $A_1, A_2, \ldots, A_n$
> **from** $r_1, r_2, \ldots, r_m$
> **where** $P$

is equivalent to the relational-algebra expression

$$\Pi_{A_1, A_2, \ldots, A_n}(\sigma_P(r_1 \times r_2 \times \ldots \times r_m))$$

using the multiset versions of the relational operators $\sigma$, $\Pi$, and $\times$.

## 4.3    Set Operations

The SQL-92 operations **union**, **intersect**, and **except** operate on relations and correspond to the relational-algebra operations $\cup$, $\cap$, and $-$. Like union, intersection, and set difference in relational algebra, the relations participating in the operations must be *compatible*; that is, they must have the same set of attributes. SQL-89 has several restrictions on the use of the **union**, **intersect**, and **except** operations, and certain products do not support these operations.

Let us demonstrate how several of the example queries that we considered in Chapter 3 can be written in SQL. We will construct queries involving the **union**, **intersect**, and **except** operations of two sets: the set of all customers who have an account at the bank, which can be derived by

> **select** *customer-name*
> **from** *depositor*

and the set of customers who have a loan at the bank, which can be derived by

> **select** *customer-name*
> **from** *borrower*

We shall refer to the relations obtained as the result of the preceding queries as $d$ and $b$, respectively.

### 4.3.1    The Union Operation

To find all customers having a loan, an account, or both at the bank, we write

> (**select** *customer-name*
>   **from** *depositor*)
> **union**
> (**select** *customer-name*
>   **from** *borrower*)

The **union** operation automatically eliminates duplicates, unlike the **select** clause. Thus, in the preceding query, if a customer—say, Jones—has several accounts or loans (or both) at the bank, then Jones will appear only once in the result.

If we want to retain all duplicates, we must write **union all** in place of **union**:

> (**select** *customer-name*
>   **from** *depositor*)
> **union all**
> (**select** *customer-name*
>   **from** *borrower*)

The number of duplicate tuples in the result is equal to the total number of duplicates that appear in both *d* and *b*. Thus, if Jones has three accounts and two loans at the bank, then there will be five tuples with the name Jones in the result.

## 4.3.2  The Intersect Operation

To find all customers who have both a loan and an account at the bank, we write

> (**select distinct** *customer-name*
>   **from** *depositor*)
> **intersect**
> (**select distinct** *customer-name*
>   **from** *borrower*)

The **intersect** operation automatically eliminates duplicates. Thus, in the preceding query, if a customer—say, Jones—has several accounts and loans at the bank, then Jones will appear only once in the result.

If we want to retain all duplicates, we must write **intersect all** in place of **intersect**:

> (**select** *customer-name*
>   **from** *depositor*)
> **intersect all**
> (**select** *customer-name*
>   **from** *borrower*)

The number of duplicate tuples that appear in the result is equal to the minimum number of duplicates in both *d* and *b*. Thus, if Jones has three accounts and two loans at the bank, then there will be two tuples with the name Jones in the result.

## 4.3.3  The Except Operation

To find all customers who have an account but no loan at the bank, we write

> (**select distinct** *customer-name*
>   **from** *depositor*)
> **except**
> (**select** *customer-name*
>   **from** *borrower*)

The **except** operation automatically eliminates duplicates. Thus, in the preceding query, a tuple with customer name Jones will appear (exactly once) in the result only if Jones has an account at the bank, but has no loan at the bank.

If we want to retain all duplicates, we must write **except all** in place of **except**:

> (**select** *customer-name*
>  **from** *depositor*)
> **except all**
> (**select** *customer-name*
>  **from** *borrower*)

The number of duplicate copies of a tuple in the result is equal to the number of duplicate copies of the tuple in *d* minus the number of duplicate copies of the tuple in *b*, provided that the difference is positive. Thus, if Jones has three accounts and one loan at the bank, then there will be two tuples with the name Jones in the result. If, instead, this customer has two accounts and three loans at the bank, there will be no tuple with the name Jones in the result.

## 4.4   Aggregate Functions

*Aggregate functions* are functions that take a collection (a set or multiset) of values as input and return a single value. SQL offers five built-in aggregate functions:

- Average: **avg**
- Minimum: **min**
- Maximum: **max**
- Total: **sum**
- Count: **count**

The input to **sum** and **avg** must be a collection of numbers, but the other operators can operate on collections of nonnumeric data types, such as strings, as well.

As an illustration, consider the query "Find the average account balance at the Perryridge branch." We write this query as follows:

> **select avg** (*balance*)
> **from** *account*
> **where** *branch-name* = "Perryridge"

The result of this query is a relation with a single attribute, containing a single row with a numerical value corresponding to the average balance at the Perryridge branch. We can optionally give a name to the attribute of the result relation using the **as** clause.

There are circumstances where we would like to apply the aggregate function not only to a single set of tuples, but also to a group of sets of tuples; we specify this wish in SQL using the **group by** clause. The attribute or attributes given in the **group by** clause are used to form groups. Tuples with the same value on all attributes in the **group by** clause are placed in one group.

As an illustration, consider the query "Find the average account balance at each branch." We write this query as follows:

> **select** *branch-name*, **avg** (*balance*)
> **from** *account*
> **group by** *branch-name*

Retaining of duplicates is important in computing an average. Suppose that the account balances at the (small) Brighton branch are $1000, $3000, $2000, and $1000. The average balance is $7000/4 = $1750.00. If duplicates were eliminated, we would obtain the wrong answer ($6000/3 = $2000).

There are cases where we must eliminate duplicates prior to computing an aggregate function. If we do want to eliminate duplicates, we use the keyword **distinct** in the aggregate expression. An example arises in the query "Find the number of depositors for each branch." In this case, a depositor counts only once, regardless of the number of accounts that depositor may have. We write this query as follows:

> **select** *branch-name*, **count** (**distinct** *customer-name*)
> **from** *depositor, account*
> **where** *depositor.account-number* = *account.account-number*
> **group by** *branch-name*

At times, it is useful to state a condition that applies to groups rather than to tuples. For example, we might be interested in only those branches where the average account balance is more than $1200. This condition does not apply to a single tuple; rather, it applies to each group constructed by the **group by** clause. To express such a query, we use the **having** clause of SQL. Predicates in the **having** clause are applied after the formation of groups, so aggregate functions may be used. We express this query in SQL as follows:

> **select** *branch-name*, **avg** (*balance*)
> **from** *account*
> **group by** *branch-name*
> **having avg** (*balance*) > 1200

At times, we wish to treat the entire relation as a single group. In such cases, we do not use a **group by** clause. Consider the query "Find the average balance for all accounts." We write this query as follows:

> **select avg** (*balance*)
> **from** *account*

We use the aggregate function **count** frequently to count the number of tuples in a relation. The notation for this function in SQL is **count** (*). Thus, to find the number of tuples in the *customer* relation, we write

> **select count** (*)
> **from** *customer*

SQL does not allow the use of **distinct** with **count**(*). It is legal to use **distinct** with **max** and **min**, even though the result does not change. We can use the keyword **all** in place of **distinct** to specify duplicate retention, but, since **all** is the default, there is no need to do so.

If a **where** clause and a **having** clause appear in the same query, the predicate in the **where** clause is applied first. Tuples satisfying the **where** predicate are then placed into groups by the **group by** clause. The **having** clause, if it is present, is then applied to each group; the groups that do not satisfy the **having** clause predicate are removed. The remaining groups are used by the **select** clause to generate tuples of the result of the query.

To illustrate the use of both a **having** clause and a **where** clause in the same query, we consider the query "Find the average balance for each customer who lives in Harrison and has at least three accounts."

> **select** *depositor.customer-name*, **avg** (*balance*)
> **from** *depositor, account, customer*
> **where** *depositor.account-number* = *account.account-number* **and**
>             *depositor.customer-name* = *customer.customer-name* **and**
>             *customer-city* = "Harrison"
> **group by** *depositor.customer-name*
> **having count** (**distinct** *depositor.account-number*) >= 3

## 4.5    Null Values

As we indicated earlier, SQL allows the use of *null* values to indicate absence of information about the value of an attribute.

We can use the special keyword **null** in a predicate to test for a null value. Thus, to find all loan numbers that appear in the *loan* relation with null values for *amount*, we write

> **select** *loan-number*
> **from** *loan*
> **where** *amount* **is null**

The predicate **is not null** tests for the absence of a null value.

The use of a *null* value in arithmetic and comparison operations causes several complications. The result of an arithmetic expressions (involving, for example +, −, ∗ or /) is null if any of the input values is null. The result of any comparison involving a *null* value can be thought of as being **false**. More precisely, SQL-92 treats the result of such comparisons as **unknown**, which is neither **true** nor **false**. SQL-92 also allows us to test whether the result of a comparison is unknown, rather than being true or false. In almost all other cases, however, **unknown** is treated just like **false**. Details are provided in references cited in the bibliographic notes.

The existence of null values also complicates the processing of aggregate operators. Assume that some tuples in the *loan* relation have a null value for *amount*. Consider the following query to total all loan amounts:

> **select sum** (*amount*)
> **from** *loan*

The values to be summed in the preceding query include null values, since some tuples have a null value for *amount*. Rather than say that the overall sum is itself *null*, the SQL standard says that the **sum** operator should ignore *null* values in its input.

In general, aggregate functions treat nulls using the following rule: All aggregate functions except **count(\*)** ignore null values in their input collection. As a result of null values being ignored, the collection of values may be empty. The **count** of an empty collection is defined to be 0, and all other aggregate operations return a value of null when applied on an empty collection. The effect of null values on some of the more complicated SQL constructs can be subtle.

# 4.6   Nested Subqueries

SQL provides a mechanism for the nesting of subqueries. A subquery is a **select-from-where** expression that is nested within another query. A common use of subqueries is to perform tests for set membership, set comparisons, and set cardinality. We study these uses in subsequent sections.

## 4.6.1   Set Membership

SQL draws on the relational calculus for operations that allow testing tuples for membership in a relation. The **in** connective tests for set membership, where the set is a collection of values produced by a **select** clause. The **not in** connective tests for the absence of set membership. As an illustration, reconsider the query "Find all customers who have both a loan and an account at the bank." Earlier, we wrote such a query by intersecting two sets: the set of depositors at the bank, and the set of borrowers from the bank. We can take the alternative approach of finding all account holders at the bank who are members of the set of borrowers from the bank. Clearly, this formulation generates the same results as did the previous one, but it leads us to write our query using the **in** connective of SQL. We begin by finding all account holders, and we write the subquery

> (**select** *customer-name*
> **from** *depositor*)

We then need to find those customers who are borrowers from the bank and who appear in the list of account holders obtained in the subquery. We do so by nesting the subquery in an outer **select**. The resulting query is

> **select distinct** *customer-name*
> **from** *borrower*
> **where** *customer-name* **in** (**select** *customer-name*
> **from** *depositor*)

This example shows that it is possible to write the same query several ways in SQL. This flexibility is beneficial, since it allows a user to think about the query in the way that appears most natural. We shall see that there is a substantial amount of redundancy in SQL.

In the preceding example, we tested membership in a one-attribute relation. It is also possible to test for membership in an arbitrary relation in SQL-92. We can thus write the query "Find all customers who have both an account and a loan at the Perryridge branch," which we saw earlier, in yet another way:

**select distinct** *customer-name*
**from** *borrower, loan*
**where** *borrower.loan-number* = *loan.loan-number* **and**
        *branch-name* = "Perryridge" **and**
        (*branch-name, customer-name*) **in**
                (**select** *branch-name, customer-name*
                 **from** *depositor, account*
                 **where** *depositor.account-number* = *account.account-number*)

We now illustrate the use of the **not in** construct. To find all customers who do have a loan at the bank, but do not have an account at the bank, we can write

> **select distinct** *customer-name*
> **from** *borrower*
> **where** *customer-name* **not in** (**select** *customer-name*
>                          **from** *depositor*)

The **in** and **not in** operators can also be used on enumerated sets. The following query selects the names of customers who have a loan at the bank, and whose names are neither "Smith" nor "Jones".

> **select distinct** *customer-name*
> **from** *borrower*
> **where** *customer-name* **not in** ("Smith", "Jones")

### 4.6.2   Set Comparison

Consider the query "Find the names of all branches that have assets greater than those of at least one branch located in Brooklyn." In Section 4.2.5, we wrote this query as follows:

> **select distinct** *T.branch-name*
> **from** *branch* **as** *T, branch* **as** *S*
> **where** *T.assets* > *S.assets* **and** *S.branch-city* = "Brooklyn"

SQL does, however, offer an alternative style for writing the preceding query. The phrase "greater than at least one" is represented in SQL by > **some**. This construct allows us to rewrite the query in a form that resembles closely our formulation of the query in English.

> **select** *branch-name*
> **from** *branch*
> **where** *assets* > **some** (**select** *assets*
>                         **from** *branch*
>                         **where** *branch-city* = "Brooklyn")

The subquery

> (**select** *assets*
> **from** *branch*
> **where** *branch-city* = "Brooklyn")

generates the set of all asset values for all branches in Brooklyn. The > **some** comparison in the **where** clause of the outer **select** is true if the *assets* value of the tuple is greater than at least one member of the set of all asset values for branches in Brooklyn.

SQL also allows < **some**, <= **some**, >= **some**, = **some**, and <> **some** comparisons. As an exercise, verify that = **some** is identical to **in**, whereas <> **some** is *not* the same as **not in**. The keyword **any** is synonymous to **some** in SQL. Early versions of SQL allowed only **any**. Later versions added the alternative **some** to avoid the linguistic ambiguity of the word *any* in English.

Now let us modify our query slightly. Let us find the names of all branches that have assets greater than that of each branch in Brooklyn. The construct > **all** corresponds to the phrase "greater than all." Using this construct, we write the query as follows:

> **select** *branch-name*
> **from** *branch*
> **where** *assets* > **all** (**select** *assets*
>                         **from** *branch*
>                         **where** *branch-city* = "Brooklyn")

As it does for **some**, SQL also allows < **all**, <= **all**, >= **all**, = **all**, and <> **all** comparisons. As an exercise, verify that <> **all** is identical to **not in**.

As another example of set comparisons, consider the query "Find the branch that has the highest average balance." Aggregate functions cannot be composed in SQL. Thus, use of **max** (**avg** (...)) is not allowed. Instead, our strategy is as follows. We begin by writing a query to find all average balances, and then nest it as a subquery of a larger query that finds those branches for which the average balance is greater than or equal to all average balances:

> **select** *branch-name*
> **from** *account*
> **group by** *branch-name*
> **having avg** (*balance*) >= **all** (**select avg** (*balance*)
>                                 **from** *account*
>                                 **group by** *branch-name*)

### 4.6.3    Test for Empty Relations

SQL includes a feature for testing whether a subquery has any tuples in its result. The **exists** construct returns the value **true** if the argument subquery is nonempty. Using the **exists** construct, we can write the query "Find all customers who have both an account and a loan at the bank" in still another way:

**select** *customer-name*
**from** *borrower*
**where exists** (**select** *
    **from** *depositor*
    **where** *depositor.customer-name* = *borrower.customer-name*)

We can test the nonexistence of tuples in a subquery by using the **not exists** construct. We can use the **not exists** construct to simulate the set containment (that is, superset) operation: We can write "relation *A* contains relation *B*" as "**not exists** (B **except** A)". Although it is not part of the SQL-92 standard, the **contains** operator was present in some early relational systems. To illustrate the **not exists** operator, let us consider again the query "Find all customers who have an account at all the branches located in Brooklyn." For each customer, we need to see whether the set of all branches at which that customer has an account contains the set of all branches in Brooklyn. Using the **except** construct, we can write the query as follows:

**select distinct** *S.customer-name*
**from** *depositor* **as** *S*
**where not exists** ((**select** *branch-name*
     **from** *branch*
     **where** *branch-city* = "Brooklyn")
    **except**
    (**select** *R.branch-name*
     **from** *depositor* **as** *T, account* **as** *R*
     **where** *T.account-number* = *R.account-number* **and**
      *S.customer-name* = *T.customer-name*))

Here, the subquery

    (**select** *branch-name*
    **from** *branch*
    **where** *branch-city* = "Brooklyn")

finds all the branches in Brooklyn. The subquery

    (**select** *R.branch-name*
    **from** *depositor* **as** *T, account* **as** *R*
    **where** *T.account-number* = *R.account-number* **and**
     *S.customer-name* = *T.customer-name*)

finds all the branches at which customer *S.customer-name* has an account. Thus, the outer **select** takes each customer and tests whether the set of all branches at which that customer has an account contains the set of all branches located in Brooklyn.

In queries that contain subqueries, a scoping rule applies for tuple variables. In a subquery, it is legal to use only tuple variables defined in the subquery itself or in any query that contains the subquery. If a tuple variable is defined both locally in a subquery and globally in a containing query, the local definition applies. This rule is analogous to the usual scoping rules used for variables in programming languages.

### 4.6.4 Test for the Absence of Duplicate Tuples

SQL includes a feature for testing whether a subquery has any duplicate tuples in its result. The **unique** construct returns the value **true** if the argument subquery contains no duplicate tuples. Using the **unique** construct, we can write the query "Find all customers who have only one account at the Perryridge branch," as follows:

> **select** *T.customer-name*
> **from** *depositor* **as** *T*
> **where unique** (**select** *R.customer-name*
>                      **from** *account, depositor* **as** *R*
>                      **where** *T.customer-name* = *R.customer-name* **and**
>                              *R.account-number* = *account.account-number* **and**
>                              *account.branch-name* = "Perryridge")

We can test for the existence of duplicate tuples in a subquery by using the **not unique** construct. To illustrate this construct, consider the query "Find all customers who have at least two accounts at the Perryridge branch," which we write as

> **select distinct** *T.customer-name*
> **from** *depositor T*
> **where not unique** (**select** *R.customer-name*
>                          **from** *account, depositor* **as** *R*
>                          **where** *T.customer-name* = *R.customer-name* **and**
>                                  *R.account-number* = *account.account-number* **and**
>                                  *account.branch-name* = "Perryridge")

Formally, the **unique** test on a relation is defined to fail if and only if the relation contains two tuples $t_1$ and $t_2$ such that $t_1 = t_2$. Since the test $t_1 = t_2$ fails if any of the fields of $t_1$ or $t_2$ are null, it is possible for **unique** to be true even if there are multiple copies of a tuple, as long as at least one of the attributes of the tuple is null.

## 4.7 Derived Relations

SQL-92 allows a subquery expression to be used in the **from** clause. If such an expression is used, then the result relation must be given a name, and the attributes can be renamed. We accomplish this renaming by using the **as** clause. For example, consider the subquery

> (**select** *branch-name*, **avg** (*balance*)
>  **from** *account*
>  **group by** *branch-name*)
>  **as** *result* (*branch-name, avg-balance*)

This subquery generates a relation consisting of the names of all branches and their corresponding average account balances. This temporary relation is named *result*, with the attributes *branch-name* and *avg-balance*.

Let us illustrate the use of a subquery expression in the **from** clause by considering the query "Find the average account balance of those branches where the average account balance is greater than \$1200." We wrote this query in Section 4.4 using the **having** clause. We can now rewrite this query, without using the **having** clause, as follows:

> **select**  *branch-name, avg-balance*
> **from** (**select** *branch-name*, **avg** (*balance*)
>     **from** *account*
>     **group by** *branch-name*)
>     **as** *result* (*branch-name, avg-balance*)
> **where** *avg-balance* > 1200

Note that we do not need to use the **having** clause, since we compute in the **from** clause the temporary relation *result*, and the attributes of *result* can be used directly in the **where** clause.

## 4.8   Views

We define a view in SQL using the **create view** command. To define a view, we must give the view a name, and must state the query that computes the view. The form of the **create view** command is

> **create view** *v* **as** <query expression>

where <query expression> is any legal query expression. The view name is represented by *v*. Observe that the notation that we used for view definition in the relational algebra (see Chapter 3) is based on that of SQL.

As an example, consider the view consisting of branch names and the names of customers who have either an account or a loan at that branch. Assume that we want this view to be called *all-customer*. We define this view as follows:

> **create view** *all-customer* **as**
>     (**select** *branch-name, customer-name*
>      **from** *depositor, account*
>      **where** *depositor.account-number = account.account-number*)
> **union**
>     (**select** *branch-name, customer-name*
>      **from** *borrower, loan*
>      **where** *borrower.loan-number = loan.loan-number*)

The attribute names of a view can be specified explicitly as follows:

> **create view** *branch-total-loan(branch-name, total-loan)* **as**
> **select** *branch-name*, **sum**(*amount*)
> **from** *loan*
> **groupby** *branch-name*

The preceding view gives for each branch the sum of the amounts of all the loans at the branch. Since the expression **sum**(*amount*) does not have a name, the attribute name is specified explicitly in the view definition.

View names may appear in any place that a relation name may appear. Using the view *all-customer*, we can find all customers of the Perryridge branch by writing

> **select** *customer-name*
> **from** *all-customer*
> **where** *branch-name* = "Perryridge"

Complex queries are much easier to write and to understand if we structure them by breaking them into smaller views that we then combine, just as we structure programs by breaking their task into procedures. However, unlike a procedure definition, a **create view** clause creates a view definition in the database, and the view definition stays in the database until a command **drop view** *view-name* is executed. The SQL-3 standard, which is currently being developed, includes a proposal to support temporary views, which are not stored in the database.

## 4.9 Modification of the Database

We have restricted our attention until now to the extraction of information from the database. We show now how to add, remove, or change information using SQL.

### 4.9.1 Deletion

A delete request is expressed in much the same way as a query. We can delete only whole tuples; we cannot delete values on only particular attributes. In SQL, a deletion is expressed by

> **delete from** *r*
> **where** *P*

where *P* represents a predicate and *r* represents a relation. The **delete** statement first finds all tuples *t* in *r* for which *P*(*t*) is true, and then deletes them from *r*. The **where** clause can be omitted, in which case all tuples in *P* are deleted.

We note that a **delete** command operates on only one relation. If we want to delete tuples from several relations, we must use one **delete** command for each relation. The predicate in the **where** clause may be as complex as a **select** command's **where** clause. At the other extreme, we can have an empty **where** clause. The request

> **delete from** *loan*

deletes all tuples from the *loan* relation. (Well-designed systems will seek confirmation from the user before executing such a devastating request.)

Here are examples of SQL delete requests.

- Delete all account tuples in the Perryridge branch.

> **delete from** *account*
> **where** *branch-name* = "Perryridge"

- Delete all loans with loan amounts between $1300 and $1500.

> **delete from** *loan*
> **where** *amount* **between** 1300 **and** 1500

- Delete all account tuples at every branch located in Needham.

> **delete from** *account*
> **where** *branch-name* **in** (**select** *branch-name*
>                       **from** *branch*
>                       **where** *branch-city* = "Needham")

The preceding **delete** request first finds all branches in Needham, and then deletes all *account* tuples pertaining to those branches.

Note that, although we may delete tuples from only one relation at a time, we may reference any number of relations in a **select-from-where** nested in the **where** clause of a **delete**. The **delete** request can contain a nested **select** that references the relation from which tuples are to be deleted. For example, suppose that we want to delete the records of all accounts with balances below the average at the bank. We could write

> **delete from** *account*
> **where** *balance* < (**select avg** (*balance*)
>                       **from** *account*)

The **delete** statement first tests each tuple in the relation *accounts* to check whether the account has a balance less than the average at the bank. Then, all tuples that fail the test are deleted. Performing all the tests before performing any deletion is important—if some tuples were deleted before other tuples were tested, the average balance could have changed, and the final result of the **delete** would depend on the order in which the tuples were processed!

## 4.9.2   Insertion

To insert data into a relation, we either specify a tuple to be inserted or write a query whose result is a set of tuples to be inserted. Obviously, the attribute values for inserted tuples must be members of the attribute's domain. Similarly, tuples inserted must be of the correct arity.

The simplest **insert** statement is a request to insert one tuple. Suppose that we wish to insert the fact that there is an account A-9732 at the Perryridge branch and that is has a balance of $1200. We write

> **insert into** *account*
>     **values** ("Perryridge", "A-9732", 1200)

In the preceding example, the values are specified in the order in which the corresponding attributes are listed in the relation schema. For the benefit of users who may not remember the order of the attributes, SQL allows the attributes to be specified as part of the **insert** statement. The following are SQL **insert** statements identical in function to the preceding one

> **insert into** *account* (*branch-name, account-number, balance*)
>     **values** ("Perryridge", "A-9732", 1200)

> **insert into** *account* (*account-number, branch-name, balance*)
>     **values** ("A-9732", "Perryridge", 1200)

More generally, we might want to insert tuples based on the result of a query. Suppose that we want to provide as a gift for all loan customers of the Perryridge branch, a new $200 savings account for each loan account they have. Let the loan number serve as the account number for the savings account. We write

> **insert into** *account*
>     **select** *branch-name, loan-number*, 200
>     **from** *loan*
>     **where** *branch-name* = "Perryridge"

Instead of specifying a tuple as we did earlier in this section, we use a **select** to specify a set of tuples. The **select** statement is evaluated first, giving a set of tuples that is then inserted into the *account* relation. Each tuple has the *branch-name* (Perryridge), a *loan-number* (which serves as the account number for the new account), and an initial balance of the new account ($200).

We also need to add tuples to the *depositor* relation; we do so by writing

> **insert into** *depositor*
>     **select** *customer-name, loan-number*
>     **from** *borrower, loan*
>     **where** *borrower.loan-number* = *loan.loan-number* **and**
>         *branch-name* = "Perryridge"

The preceding query inserts a tuple (*customer-name, loan-number*) into the *depositor* relation for each *customer-name* who has a loan in the Perryridge branch with loan number *loan-number*.

It is important that we evaluate the **select** statement fully before we carry out any insertions. If some insertions were carried out even as the **select** statement were being evaluated, a request such as

> **insert into** *account*
>     **select** *
>     **from** *account*

might insert an infinite number of tuples! The first tuple in *account* would be inserted again into *account*, creating a second copy of the tuple. Since this second copy is part of *account* now, the **select** statement may find it, and a third copy will be inserted into *account*. This third copy may then be found by the **select** statement, and a fourth copy inserted, and so on, forever. Evaluating the **select** statement completely before performing insertions avoids such problems.

Our discussion of the **insert** statement considered only examples in which a value is given for every attribute in inserted tuples. It is possible, as we saw in Chapter 3, for inserted tuples to be given values on only some attributes of the schema. The remaining attributes are assigned a null value denoted by *null*. Consider the request

> **insert into** *account*
>     **values** (*null*, "A-401", 1200)

We know that account A-401 has $1200, but the branch name is not known. Consider the query

> **select** *account-number*
>     **from** *account*
>     **where** *branch-name* = "Perryridge"

Since the branch at which account A-401 is maintained is not known, we cannot determine whether it is equal to "Perryridge".

We can prohibit the insertion of null values using the SQL DDL, which we discuss in Section 4.11.

## 4.9.3   Updates

In certain situations, we may wish to change a value in a tuple without changing *all* values in the tuple. For this purpose, the **update** statement can be used. As we could for **insert** and **delete**, we can choose the tuples to be updated using a query.

Suppose that annual interest payments are being made, and all balances are to be increased by 5 percent. We write

> **update** *account*
> **set** *balance* = *balance* * 1.05

The preceding statement is applied once to each tuple in *account*.

Let us now suppose that accounts with balances over \$10,000 receive 6 percent interest, whereas all others receive 5 percent. We write two **update** statements:

> **update** *account*
> **set** *balance* = *balance* * 1.06
> **where** *balance* > 10000

> **update** *account*
> **set** *balance* = *balance* * 1.05
> **where** *balance* <= 10000

Note that, as we saw in Chapter 3, the order in which the two **update** statements are written is important. If we changed the order of the two statements, an account with a balance just under \$10,000 would receive 11.3 percent interest. SQL-92 offers a **case** construct, which we can use to perform both the preceding updates in a single **update** statement; see Exercise 4.11.

In general, the **where** clause of the **update** statement may contain any construct legal in the **where** clause of the **select** statement (including nested **selects**). As with **insert** and **delete**, a nested **select** within an **update** statement may reference the relation that is being updated. As before, all tuples in the relation are first tested to see whether they should be updated, and the updates are carried out afterward. For example, the request "Pay 5 percent interest on accounts whose balance is greater than average" can be written as follows:

> **update** *account*
> **set** *balance* = *balance* * 1.05
> **where** *balance* > **select avg** (*balance*)
>                 **from** *account*

## 4.9.4 Update of a View

The view-update anomaly that we discussed in Chapter 3 exists also in SQL. As an illustration, consider the following view definition:

> **create view** *branch-loan* **as**
>      **select** *branch-name, loan-number*
>      **from** *loan*

Since SQL allows a view name to appear wherever a relation name is allowed, we can write

**insert into** *branch-loan*
**values** ("Perryridge", "L-307")

This insertion is represented by an insertion into the relation *loan*, since *loan* is the actual relation from which the view *branch-loan* is constructed. We must, therefore, have some value for *amount*. This value is a null value. Thus, the preceding **insert** results in the insertion of the tuple

("Perryridge", "L-307", *null*)

into the *loan* relation.

As we saw in Chapter 3, the view-update anomaly becomes more difficult to handle when a view is defined in terms of several relations. As a result, many SQL-based database systems impose the following constraint on modifications allowed through views:

- A modification is permitted through a view only if the view in question is defined in terms of one relation of the actual relational database—that is, of the logical-level database.

Under this constraint, the **update**, **insert**, and **delete** operations would be forbidden on the example view *all-customer* that we defined previously.

## 4.10   Joined Relations

In addition to providing the basic Cartesian-product mechanism for joining tuples of relations provided by earlier versions of SQL, SQL-92 also provides various other mechanisms for joining relations, including condition joins, and natural joins, as well as various forms of outer joins. These additional operations are typically used as subquery expressions in the **from** clause.

### 4.10.1   Examples

We illustrate the various join operations using the relations *loan* and *borrower* in Figure 4.1. We start with a simple example of inner joins. Figure 4.2 shows the

| branch-name | loan-number | amount |
|-------------|-------------|--------|
| Downtown    | L-170       | 3000   |
| Redwood     | L-230       | 4000   |
| Perryridge  | L-260       | 1700   |

loan

| customer-name | loan-number |
|---------------|-------------|
| Jones         | L-170       |
| Smith         | L-230       |
| Hayes         | L-155       |

borrower

Figure 4.1    The loan and borrower relations.

| branch-name | loan-number | amount | customer-name | loan-number |
|-------------|-------------|--------|---------------|-------------|
| Downtown    | L-170       | 3000   | Jones         | L-170       |
| Redwood     | L-230       | 4000   | Smith         | L-230       |

Figure 4.2    Result of *loan* **inner join** *borrower* **on**
*loan.loan-number = borrower.loan-number.*

result of the expression

> *loan* **inner join** *borrower* **on** *loan.loan-number  =  borrower.loan-number*

The expression computes the theta join of the *loan* and the *borrower* relations, with the join condition being *loan.loan-number = borrower.loan-number.* The attributes of the result consist of the attributes of the left-hand-side relation followed by the attributes of the right-hand-side relation. Note that the attribute *loan-number* appears twice in the figure—the first occurrence is from *loan*, and the second is from *borrower.*

We rename the result relation of a join and the attributes of the result relation using an **as** clause, as illustrated here:

> *loan* **inner join** *borrower* **on** *loan.loan-number = borrower.loan-number*
> **as** *lb(branch, loan-number, amount, cust, cust-loan-num)*

The second occurrence of *loan-number* has been renamed to *cust-loan-num.* The ordering of the attributes in the result of the join is important for the renaming.

Next, we consider an example of the use of the **left outer join** operation:

> *loan* **left outer join** *borrower* **on** *loan.loan-number = borrower.loan-number*

The left outer join is computed as follows. First, the result of the inner join is computed as before. Then, for every tuple *t* in the left-hand-side relation *loan* that did not match any tuple in the right-hand-side relation *borrower* in the inner join, a tuple *r* is added to the result of the join as follows. The attributes of tuple *r* that are derived from the left-hand-side relation are filled in with the values from tuple *t*, and the remaining attributes of *r* are filled with null values. The resultant relation is shown in Figure 4.3. The tuples (Downtown, L-170, 3000) and (Redwood, L-230, 4000) are joined with tuples from *borrower* and appear in the result of the inner join, and hence in the result of the left outer join. On the other hand, the tuple (Perryridge, L-260, 1700) did not match any tuple from

| branch-name | loan-number | amount | customer-name | loan-number |
|-------------|-------------|--------|---------------|-------------|
| Downtown    | L-170       | 3000   | Jones         | L-170       |
| Redwood     | L-230       | 4000   | Smith         | L-230       |
| Perryridge  | L-260       | 1700   | *null*        | *null*      |

Figure 4.3    Result of *loan* **left outer join** *borrower* **on**
*loan.loan-number  =  borrower.loan-number.*

| branch-name | loan-number | amount | customer-name |
|-------------|-------------|--------|---------------|
| Downtown    | L-170       | 3000   | Jones         |
| Redwood     | L-230       | 4000   | Smith         |

Figure 4.4    Result of *loan* **natural inner join** *borrower*.

*borrower* in the inner join, and hence a tuple (Perryridge, L-260, 1700, null, null) is present in the result of the left outer join.

Finally, we consider an example of the use of the **natural join** operation.

*loan* **natural inner join** *borrower*

This expression computes the natural join of the two relations. The only attribute name common to *loan* and *borrower* is *loan-number*. The result of the expression is shown in Figure 4.4. The result is similar to the result of the inner join with the **on** condition shown in Figure 4.2, since they have, in effect, the same join condition. However, the attribute *loan-number* appears only once in the result of the natural join, whereas it appears twice in the result of the join with the **on** condition.

## 4.10.2    Join Types and Conditions

In Section 4.10.1, we saw examples of the join operations permitted in SQL-92. Join operations take two relations and return as a result another relation. Although outer-join expressions are typically used in the **from** clause, they can be used anywhere that a relation can be used.

Each of the variants of the join operations in SQL-92 consists of a *join type* and a *join condition*. The join condition defines which tuples in the two relations match, and what attributes are present in the result of the join. The join type defines how tuples in each relation that do not match any tuple in the other relation (based on the join condition) are treated. Figure 4.5 shows some of the allowed join types and join conditions. The first join type is the inner join, and the other three are the three types of outer joins. The three join conditions are the **natural** join and the **on** condition, which we have seen before, and the **using** condition, which we discuss later.

The use of a join condition is mandatory for outer joins, but is optional for inner joins (if it is omitted, a Cartesian product results). Syntactically, the

| Join types | Join Conditions |
|------------|-----------------|
| **inner join** | **natural** |
| **left outer join** | **on** <predicate> |
| **right outer join** | **using** $(A_1, A_2, \ldots, A_n)$ |
| **full outer join** | |

Figure 4.5    Join types and join conditions.

keyword **natural** appears before the join type, as illustrated earlier, whereas the **on** and **using** conditions appear at the end of the join expression. The keywords **inner** and **outer** are optional, since the rest of the join type enables us to deduce whether the join is an inner join or an outer join.

The meaning of the join condition **natural**, in terms of which tuples from the two relations match, is straightforward. The ordering of the attributes in the result of a natural join is as follows. The join attributes (that is, the attributes common to both relations) appear first, in the order in which they appear in the left-hand-side relation. Next come all nonjoin attributes of the left-hand-side relation, and finally all nonjoin attributes of the right-hand-side relation.

The **right outer join** join type is symmetric to the **left outer join**. Tuples from the right-hand-side relation that do not match any tuple in the left-hand-side relation are padded with nulls and are added to the result of the right outer join.

The following expression is an example of combining the natural join condition with the right outer join type.

*loan* **natural right outer join** *borrower*

The result of the expression is shown in Figure 4.6. The attributes of the result are defined by the join type, which is a natural join; hence, *loan-number* appears only once. The first two tuples in the result are from the inner natural join of *loan* and *borrower*. The tuple (Hayes, L-155) from the right-hand-side relation does not match any tuple from the left-hand-side relation *loan* in the natural inner join. Hence, the tuple (null, L-155, Hayes) appears in the join result.

The join condition **using**$(A_1, A_2, \ldots, A_n)$ is similar to the natural join condition, except that the join attributes are the attributes $A_1, A_2, \ldots, A_n$, rather than all attributes that are common to both relations. The attributes $A_1, A_2, \ldots, A_n$ must consist of only attributes that are common to both relations, and they appear only once in the result of the join.

The **full outer join** join type is a combination of the left and right outer-join types. After the result of the inner join is computed, tuples from the left-hand-side relation that did not match with any from the right-hand-side are extended with nulls and are added to the result. Similarly, tuples from the right-hand-side relation that did not match with any tuples from the left-hand-side relation are also extended with nulls, and are added to the result.

For example, the result of the expression

*loan* **full outer join** *borrower* **using** (loan-number)

is shown in Figure 4.7.

| branch-name | loan-number | amount | customer-name |
|---|---|---|---|
| Downtown | L-170 | 3000 | Jones |
| Redwood | L-230 | 4000 | Smith |
| null | L-155 | null | Hayes |

Figure 4.6   Result of *loan* **natural right outer join** *borrower*

| branch-name | loan-number | amount | customer-name |
|-------------|-------------|--------|---------------|
| Downtown | L-170 | 3000 | Jones |
| Redwood | L-230 | 4000 | Smith |
| Perryridge | L-260 | 1700 | *null* |
| null | L-155 | null | Hayes |

Figure 4.7    Result of *loan* **full outer join** *borrower* **using**(*loan-number*)

As another example of the use of the outer-join operation, the query "Find all customers who have an account but no loan at the bank," can be written as

> **select** *d-CN*
> **from** (*depositor* **left outer join** *borrower*
>     **on** *depositor.customer-name* = *borrower.customer-name*)
>     **as** *db*1 (*d-CN, account-number, b-CN, loan-number*)
> **where** *b-CN* **is** *null*

Similarly, the query "Find all customers who have either an account or a loan (but not both) at the bank," can be written using natural full outer joins as:

> **select** *customer-name*
> **from** (*depositor* **natural full outer join** *borrower*)
> **where** *account-number* **is** *null* **or** *loan-number* **is** *null*

SQL-92 also provides two other join types, called **cross join** and **union join**. The first is equivalent to an inner join without a join condition; the second is equivalent to a full outer join on the "false" condition—that is, where the inner join is empty.

## 4.11   Data-Definition Language

In most of our discussions concerning SQL and relational databases, we have accepted a set of relations as given. Of course, the set of relations in a database must be specified to the system by means of a data definition language (DDL).

The SQL DDL allows the specification of not only a set of relations, but also information about each relation, including

- The schema for each relation
- The domain of values associated with each attribute
- The integrity constraints
- The set of indices to be maintained for each relation
- The security and authorization information for each relation
- The physical storage structure of each relation on disk

We shall discuss here schema definition and domain values; we defer discussion of the other SQL DDL features to Chapter 6.

## 4.11.1   Domain Types in SQL

The SQL-92 standard supports a variety of built-in domain types, including the following:

- **char**($n$) is a fixed-length character string, with user-specified length $n$. The full form, **character**, can be used instead.

- **varchar**($n$) is a variable-length character string, with user-specified maximum length $n$. The full form, **character varying**, is equivalent.

- **int** is an integer (a finite subset of the integers that is machine-dependent). The full form, **integer**, is equivalent.

- **smallint** is a small integer (a machine-dependent subset of the integer domain type).

- **numeric**($p, d$) is a fixed-point number, with user-specified precision. The number consists of $p$ digits (plus a sign), and $d$ of the $p$ digits are to the right of the decimal point. Thus, **numeric**(3,1) allows 44.5 to be stored exactly, but neither 444.5 or 0.32 can be stored exactly in a field of this type.

- **real, double precision** are floating-point and double-precision floating-point numbers, with machine-dependent precision.

- **float**($n$) is a floating-point number, with user-specified precision of at least $n$ digits.

- **date** is a calendar date, containing a (four digit) year, month, and day of the month.

- **time** is the time of day, in hours, minutes, and seconds.

Varying-length character strings, date, and time were not part of the SQL-89 standard.

SQL allows arithmetic and comparison operations on the various numeric domains, and comparison operations on all the domains listed here. SQL also provides a data type called **interval**, and allows computations based on dates and times, and on intervals. For example, if $x$ and $y$ are of type **date**, then $x - y$ is an interval whose value is the number of days from date $x$ to date $y$. Similarly, adding or subtracting an interval to a date or time gives back a date or time, respectively.

It is often useful to be able to compare values from *compatible* domains. For example, since every small integer is an integer, a comparison $x < y$, where $x$ is a small integer and $y$ is an integer (or vice versa), makes sense. We make such a comparison by casting small integer $x$ as an integer. A transformation of this sort is called a *type coercion*. Type coercion is used routinely in common programming languages, as well as in database systems.

As an illustration, suppose that the domain of *customer-name* is a character string of length 20, and the domain of *branch-name* is a character string of length 15. We see that, although the string lengths might differ, standard SQL will consider the two domains compatible.

As we discussed in Chapter 3, the *null* value is a member of all domains. For certain attributes, however, null values may be inappropriate. Consider a tuple in the *customer* relation where *customer-name* is null. Such a tuple gives a street and city for an anonymous customer; thus, it does not contain useful information. In cases such as this, we wish to forbid null values, by restricting the domain of *customer-name* to exclude null values.

SQL allows the domain declaration of an attribute to include the specification **not null**, and thus prohibits the insertion of a null value for this attribute. Any database modification that would cause a null to be inserted in a **not null** domain generates an error diagnostic. There are many situations where the prohibition of null values is desirable. A particular case where it is essential to prohibit null values is in the primary key of a relation schema. Thus, in our bank example, in the *customer* relation, we must prohibit a null value for the attribute *customer-name*, which is the primary key for *customer*.

The SQL-92 allows us to define domains using a **create domain** clause, as shown in the following example:

$$\text{\textbf{create domain } } person\text{-}name \text{ \textbf{char}}(20)$$

We can then use the domain name *person-name* to define the type of an attribute, just like a built-in domain.

## 4.11.2   Schema Definition in SQL

We define an SQL relation using the **create table** command:

$$\text{\textbf{create table } } r(A_1 D_1, A_2 D_2, \ldots, A_n D_n,$$
$$\langle \text{integrity-constraint}_1 \rangle,$$
$$\ldots,$$
$$\langle \text{integrity-constraint}_k \rangle)$$

where $r$ is the name of the relation, each $A_i$ is the name of an attribute in the schema of relation $r$, and $D_i$ is the domain type of values in the domain of attribute $A_i$. The allowed integrity constraints include

$$\text{\textbf{primary key } } (A_{j_1}, A_{j_2}, \ldots, A_{j_m})$$

and

$$\text{\textbf{check}}(P)$$

The **primary key** specification says that attributes $A_{j_1}, A_{j_2}, \ldots, A_{j_m}$ form the primary key for the relation. Although the primary key specification is optional, it is generally a good idea to specify a primary key for each relation. The **check** clause specifies a predicate $P$ that must be satisfied by every tuple in the relation; it

```
create table customer
    (customer-name    char(20) not null,
     customer-street  char(30),
     customer-city    char(30),
     primary key (customer-name))

create table branch
    (branch-name      char(15) not null,
     branch-city      char(30),
     assets           integer,
     primary key (branch-name),
     check (assets >= 0))

create table account
    (account-number   char(10) not null,
     branch-name      char(15),
     balance          integer,
     primary key (account-number),
     check (balance >= 0))

create table depositor
    (customer-name    char(20) not null,
     account-number   char(10) not null,
     primary key (customer-name, account-number))
```

Figure 4.8    SQL data definition for part of the bank database.

was introduced in SQL-92. The **create table** command also includes other integrity constraints, which we shall discuss in Chapter 6.

Figure 4.8 presents a partial SQL DDL definition of our bank database. Recall that **null** is a legal value for every type in SQL, unless the type is specifically stated to be **not null**, as shown in the figure.

The attributes of a relation that are declared to be a primary key are required to be *nonnull* and *unique*; that is, no two tuples in the relation can be equal on all the primary-key attributes. If a newly inserted or modified tuple in a relation has null values for any primary-key attribute, or if the tuple has the same value on the primary-key attributes as does another tuple in the relation, an error is flagged, and the update is prevented. Similarly, an error is flagged, and the update prevented, if the **check** condition on the tuple fails. Note that the **not null** declarations that are shown in Figure 4.8 are redundant in SQL-92, since they are specified on attributes that are also part of the primary keys. However, in SQL-89, primary-key attributes were required to be declared **not null** explicitly in the manner shown in the figure.

A common use of the **check** clause is to ensure that attribute values satisfy specified conditions, in effect creating a powerful type system. For instance, the **check** clause in the **create table** command for relation *branch* checks that the value of **assets** is nonnegative. As another example, consider the following:

> **create table** *student*
>   (*name*     **char**(15) **not null**,
>   *student-id*   **char**(10) **not null**,
>   *degree-level*   **char**(15) **not null**,
>   **primary key** (*student-id*),
>   **check** (*degree-level* **in** ("Bachelors", "Masters", "Doctorate")))

Here, we use the **check** clause to simulate an enumerated type, by specifying that *degree-level* must be one of "Bachelors", "Masters", or "Doctorate".

The preceding **check** conditions can be tested quite easily, when a tuple is inserted or modified. However, in general, the **check** conditions can be more complex (and harder to check), since subqueries that refer to other relations are permitted in the **check** condition. For example, the following **check** condition could be specified on the relation *deposit*:

> **check** (*branch-name* **in** (**select** *branch-name* **from** *branch*))

The preceding **check** condition verifies that the *branch-name* in each tuple in the *deposit* relation is actually the name of a branch in the *branch* relation. Thus, the preceding **check** has to be checked not only when a tuple is inserted or modified in *deposit*, but also when the relation *branch* changes (in this case, when a tuple is deleted or modified in relation *branch*). The preceding condition is an example of a class of conditions called *foreign-key* constraints, which we discuss in Chapter 6. Complex **check** conditions, such as the preceding one, can be useful when we want to ensure integrity of data, but we should use them with care, since they may be costly to test.

A newly created relation is empty initially. We can use the **insert** command to load data into the relation. Many relational-database products have special bulk loader utilities to load an initial set of tuples into a relation.

To remove a relation from an SQL database, we use the **drop table** command. The **drop table** command deletes all information about the dropped relation from the database. The command

> **drop table** *r*

is a more drastic action than

> **delete from** *r*

The latter retains relation *r*, but deletes all tuples in *r*. The former deletes not only all tuples of *r*, but also the schema for *r*. After *r* is dropped, no tuples can be inserted into *r* unless it is recreated with the **create table** command.

We use the **alter table** command in SQL-92 to add attributes to an existing relation. All tuples in the relation are assigned *null* as the value for the new attribute. The form of the **alter table** command is

> **alter table** *r* **add** *A  D*

where *r* is the name of an existing relation, *A* is the name of the attribute to be added, and $D$ is the domain of the added attribute. We can drop attributes from a relation using a command

**alter table** $r$ **drop** $A$

where $r$ is the name of an existing relation, and $A$ is the name of an attribute of the relation.

## 4.12   Embedded SQL

SQL provides a powerful declarative query language. Writing queries in SQL is typically much easier than is coding the same queries in a general-purpose programming language. However, access to a database from a general-purpose programming language is required for at least two reasons:

**1.** Not all queries can be expressed in SQL, since SQL does not provide the full expressive power of a general-purpose language. That is, there exist queries that can be expressed in a language such as Pascal, C, Cobol, or Fortran that cannot be expressed in SQL. To write such queries, we can embed SQL within a more powerful language.

   SQL is designed such that queries written in it can be optimized automatically and executed efficiently—and providing the full power of a programming language makes automatic optimization exceedingly difficult.

**2.** Nondeclarative actions—such as printing a report, interacting with a user, or sending the results of a query to a graphical user interface—cannot be done from within SQL. Applications typically have several components, and querying or updating data is only one component; other components are written in general-purpose programming languages. For an integrated application, the programs written in the programming language must be able to access the database.

   The SQL standard defines embeddings of SQL in a variety of programming languages, such as Pascal, PL/I, Fortran, C, and Cobol. A language in which SQL queries are embedded is referred to as a *host* language, and the SQL structures permitted in the host language constitute *embedded* SQL.

   Programs written in the host language can use the embedded SQL syntax to access and update data stored in a database. This embedded form of SQL extends the programmer's ability to manipulate the database even further. In embedded SQL, all query processing is performed by the database system. The result of the query is then made available to the program one tuple (record) at a time.

   An embedded SQL program must be processed by a special preprocessor prior to compilation. Embedded SQL requests are replaced with host-language declarations and procedure calls that allow run-time execution of the database accesses. Then, the resulting program is compiled by the host-language compiler. To identify embedded SQL requests to the preprocessor, we use the EXEC SQL statement; it has the form:

EXEC SQL <embedded SQL statement > END-EXEC

The exact syntax for embedded SQL requests depends on the language in which SQL is embedded. For instance, a semi-colon is used instead of END-EXEC when SQL is embedded in C or Pascal.

We place the statement SQL INCLUDE in the program to identify the place where the preprocessor should insert the special variables used for communication between the program and the database system. Variables of the host language can be used within embedded SQL statements, but they must be preceded by a colon (:) to distinguish them from SQL variables.

Embedded SQL statements are of a form similar to the SQL statements that we described in this chapter. There are, however, several important differences, as we note here.

To write a relational query, we use the **declare cursor** statement. The result of the query is not yet computed. Rather, the program must use the **open** and **fetch** commands (discussed later in this section) to obtain the result tuples.

Consider the banking schema that we have used in this chapter. Assume that we have a host-language variable *amount*, and that we wish to find the names and cities of residence of customers who have more than *amount* dollars in any account. We can write this query as follows:

EXEC SQL
> **declare** *c* **cursor for**
> **select** *customer-name, customer-city*
> **from** *depositor, customer, account*
> **where** *depositor.customer-name = customer.customer-name* **and**
>     *account.account-number = depositor.account-number* **and**
>     *account.balance > :amount*

END-EXEC

The variable *c* in the preceding expression is called a *cursor* for the query. We use this variable to identify the query in the **open** statement, which causes the query to be evaluated, and in the **fetch** statement, which causes the values of one tuple to be placed in host-language variables.

The **open** statement for our sample query is as follows:

EXEC SQL **open** *c*  END-EXEC

This statement causes the database system to execute the query and to save the results within a temporary relation. If the SQL query results in an error, the database system stores an error diagnostic in the SQL communication-area (SQLCA) variables, whose declarations are inserted by the SQL INCLUDE statement.

A series of **fetch** statements is executed to make tuples of the result available to the program. The **fetch** statement requires one host-language variable for each attribute of the result relation. For our example query, we need one variable to hold the *customer-name* value, and another to hold the *customer-city* value. Suppose that those variables are *cn* and *cc*, respectively. A tuple of the result relation is obtained by the statement:

$$\text{EXEC SQL } \textbf{fetch } c \textbf{ into } :cn, :cc \text{ END-EXEC}$$

The program can then manipulate the variables *cn* and *cc* using the features of the host programming language.

A single **fetch** request returns only one tuple. If we are to obtain all tuples of the result, the program must contain a loop to iterate over all tuples. Embedded SQL assists the programmer in managing this iteration. Although a relation is conceptually a set, the tuples of the result of a query are in some fixed physical order. When an **open** statement is executed, the cursor is set to point to the first tuple of the result. When a **fetch** statement is executed, the cursor is updated to point to the next tuple of the result. A variable in the SQLCA is set to indicate that no further tuples remain to be processed. Thus, we can use a **while** loop (or the equivalent, depending on the host language) to process each tuple of the result.

The **close** statement must be used to tell the database system to delete the temporary relation that held the result of the query. For our example, this statement takes the form

$$\text{EXEC SQL } \textbf{close } c \text{ END-EXEC}$$

Embedded SQL expressions for database modification (**update**, **insert**, and **delete**) do not return a result. Thus, they are somewhat simpler to express. A database-modification request takes the form

$$\text{EXEC SQL} < \text{any valid } \textbf{update, insert, or delete} > \text{ END-EXEC}$$

Host-language variables, preceded by a colon, may appear in the SQL database-modification expression. If an error condition arises in the execution of the statement, a diagnostic is set in the SQLCA.

The *dynamic SQL* component of SQL-92 allows programs to construct and submit SQL queries at run time. In contrast, embedded SQL statements must be completely present at compile time, and are compiled by the embedded SQL preprocessor. Using dynamic SQL, programs can create SQL queries as strings at run time (perhaps based on input from the user), and can either have them executed immediately, or have them *prepared* for subsequent use. Preparing a dynamic SQL statement compiles it, and subsequent uses of the prepared statement use the compiled version. The following is an example of the use of dynamic SQL from within a C program:

```
char * sqlprog = "update account set balance = balance *1.05
          where account-number = ?"
EXEC SQL prepare dynprog from :sqlprog;
char account[10] = "A-101";
EXEC SQL execute dynprog using :account;
```

The dynamic SQL program contains a ?, which is a place holder for a value that is provided when the SQL program is executed.

SQL-92 also contains a *module* language, which allows procedures to be defined in SQL. A module typically contains multiple SQL procedures. Each procedure has a name, optional arguments, and a single SQL statement. The procedures can be called directly from an external language without any special syntax.

## 4.13   Other SQL Features

Embedded SQL allows a host-language program to access the database, but it provides no assistance in presenting results to the user or in generating reports. Most commercial database products include a special language to assist application programmers in creating templates on the screen for a user interface, and in formatting data for report generation. These special languages are called *fourth-generation languages*.

Some fourth-generation languages also include high-level constructs to allow iteration over relations to be expressed directly, without forcing programmers to deal with the details of cursor management. However, unlike for SQL and embedded SQL, no single accepted standard currently exists for fourth-generation languages. Rather, each product provides its own proprietary language.

The SQL-92 standard defines the concepts of SQL sessions and SQL environments. SQL sessions provide the abstraction of a client and a server (which could possibly be remote). The client *connects* to an SQL server, establishing a session, executes a series of statements, and finally *disconnects* the session. In addition to the normal SQL commands, a session can also contain commands to *commit* the work carried out in the session, or to *rollback* the work carried out in the session.

An SQL environment contains several components, including a user identifier, and a *schema*. The presence of multiple schemas allows different applications and different users to work independently. All the usual SQL statements, including the DDL and DML statements, operate in the context of a schema. Schemas can be created and dropped by means of **create schema** and **drop schema** statements. If a schema is not set explicitly, a default schema associated with the user identifier is used, so different users see their own schemas. Another use of schemas is to allow multiple versions of an application—one a production version, and others versions being tested—to run on the same database system.

## 4.14   Summary

Commercial database systems do not use the terse, formal query languages of Chapter 3. Instead, they use languages based on the formal languages, but including much "syntactic sugar." Commercial database languages include constructs for update, insertion, and deletion of information, as well as for queries to the database. We have discussed the language SQL which has gained wide acceptance in commercial products.

We saw how to express queries and to modify the database in SQL. Modifications to the database may lead to the generation of null values in tuples. We discussed how nulls can be introduced, and how the SQL query language handles queries on relations containing null values. We showed how to define relations and create views. Further details on the SQL DDL appear in Chapters 6 and 19.

person (*ss#*, name, address)
car (*license*, year, model)
accident (*date*, *driver*, damage-amount)
owns (*ss#*, *license*)
log (*license*, *date*, *driver*)

Figure 4.9    Insurance database.

# Exercises

**4.1.** Consider the insurance database of Figure 4.9, where the primary keys are underlined. Construct the following SQL queries for this relational database.
   (*a*) Find the total number of people whose cars were involved in accidents in 1989.
   (*b*) Find the number of accidents in which the cars belonging to "John Smith" were involved.
   (*c*) Add a new customer to the database.
   (*d*) Delete the Mazda belonging to "John Smith."
   (*e*) Add a new accident record for the Toyota belonging to "Jones."

**4.2.** Consider the employee database of Figure 4.10. Give an expression in SQL for each of the following queries.
   (*a*) Find the names of all employees who work for First Bank Corporation.
   (*b*) Find the names and cities of residence of all employees who work for First Bank Corporation.
   (*c*) Find the names, street address, and cities of residence of all employees who work for First Bank Corporation and earn more than $10,000.
   (*d*) Find all employees in the database who live in the same cities as the companies for which they work.
   (*e*) Find all employees in the database who live in the same cities and on the same streets as do their managers.
   (*f*) Find all employees in the database who do not work for First Bank Corporation.
   (*g*) Find all employees in the database who earn more than every employee of Small Bank Corporation.
   (*h*) Assume that the companies may be located in several cities. Find all companies located in every city in which Small Bank Corporation is located.

employee (*employee-name*, street, city)
works (*employee-name*, company-name, salary)
company (*company-name*, city)
manages (*employee-name*, manager-name)

Figure 4.10    Employee database.

(i) Find all employees who earn more than the average salary of all employees of their company.

(j) Find the company that has the most employees.

(k) Find the company that has the smallest payroll.

(l) Find those companies whose employees earn a higher salary, on average, than the average salary at First Bank Corporation.

**4.3.** Consider the relational database of Figure 4.10. Give an expression in SQL
for each of the following queries.

(a) Modify the database so that Jones now lives in Newtown.

(b) Give all employees of First Bank Corporation a 10-percent raise.

(c) Give all managers of First Bank Corporation a 10-percent raise.

(d) Give all managers of First Bank Corporation a 10-percent raise unless
the salary becomes greater than $100,000; in such cases, give only a
3-percent raise.

(e) Delete all tuples in the *works* relation for employees of Small Bank
Corporation.

**4.4.** Let the following relation schemas be given:

$$R = (A, B, C)$$
$$S = (D, E, F)$$

Let relations $r(R)$ and $s(S)$ be given. Give an expression in SQL that is
equivalent to each of the following queries.

(a) $\Pi_A(r)$

(b) $\sigma_{B=17}(r)$

(c) $r \times s$

(d) $\Pi_{A,F}(\sigma_{C=D}(r \times s))$

**4.5.** Let $R = (A, B, C)$, and let $r_1$ and $r_2$ both be relations on schema $R$. Give
an expression in SQL that is equivalent to each of the following queries.

(a) $r_1 \cup r_2$

(b) $r_1 \cap r_2$

(c) $r_1 - r_2$

(d) $\Pi_{AB}(r_1) \bowtie \Pi_{BC}(r_2)$

**4.6.** Let $R = (A, B)$ and $S = (A, C)$, and let $r(R)$ and $s(S)$ be relations.
Write an expression in SQL for each of the queries below:

(a) $\{< a > \mid \exists b \, (< a, b > \in r \wedge b = 17)\}$

(b) $\{< a, b, c > \mid \ < a, b > \in r \wedge \ < a, c > \in s\}$

(c) $\{< a > \mid \exists c \, (< a, c > \in s \ \wedge \ \exists b_1, b_2 \, (< a, b_1 > \in r \wedge \ < c, b_2 > \\ \in r \wedge b_1 > b_2))\}$

**4.7.** Show that, in SQL, <> **all** is identical to **not in**.

**4.8.** Consider the relational database of Figure 4.10. Using SQL, define a view
consisting of *manager-name* and the average salary of all employees who

work for that manager. Explain why the database system should not allow updates to be expressed in terms of this view.

**4.9.** Consider the SQL query

> **select** $p.a1$
> **from** $p, r1, r2$
> **where** $p.a1 = r1.a1$ **or** $p.a1 = r2.a1$

Under what conditions does the preceding query select values of $p.a1$ that are either in $r1$ or in $r2$? Examine carefully the cases where one of $r1$ or $r2$ may be empty.

**4.10.** SQL-92 provides an operation called **case**, which is defined as follows:

> **case**
> > **when** $pred_1$ **then** $result_1$
> > **when** $pred_2$ **then** $result_2$
> >
> > $\ldots$
> >
> > **when** $pred_n$ **then** $result_n$
> > **else** $result_0$
> **end**

The operation returns $result_i$, where $i$ is the first of $pred_1, pred_2, \ldots,$ $pred_n$ that is satisfied; if none of the predicates is satisfied, the operation returns $result_0$.

Suppose that we have a relation *marks(student-id, score)* and we wish to assign grades to students based on the score as follows: grade $F$ if $score < 40$, grade $C$ if $40 \le score < 60$, grade $B$ if $60 \le score < 80$, and grade $A$ if $80 \le score$. Write queries to do the following:

(*a*) Display the grade for each student, based on the *marks* relation.

(*b*) Find the number of students with each grade.

**4.11.** Use the **case** operation described in Exercise 4.10 to perform, in a single update statement, the following update to each tuple in the *account* relation: "Add 6-percent to *balance* if *balance* > 10000; add 5-percent if *balance* $\le$ 10000."

**4.12.** SQL-92 provides an $n$-ary operation called **coalesce**, which is defined as follows: **coalesce**$(A_1, A_2, \ldots, A_n)$ returns the first nonnull $A_i$ in the list $A_1, A_2, \ldots, A_n$, and returns null if all of $A_1, A_2, \ldots, A_n$ are null. Show how to express the **coalesce** operation using the **case** operation.

**4.13.** Let $a$ and $b$ be relations with the schemas $A(name, address, title)$ and $B(name, address, salary)$, respectively. Show how to express $a$ **natural full outer join** $b$ using the **full outer join** operation with an **on** condition and the **coalesce** operation. Make sure that the result relation does not contain two copies of the attributes *name* and *address*, and that the solution is correct even if some tuples in $a$ and $b$ have null values for attributes *name* or *address*.

**4.14.** Give an SQL schema definition for the employee database of Figure 4.10. Choose an appropriate domain for each attribute and an appropriate primary key for each relation schema.

**4.15.** Write **check** conditions for the schema you defined in Exercise 4.14 to ensure that:

(*a*) Every employee works for a company located in the same city as the city in which the employee lives.

(*b*) No employee earns a salary higher than that of his manager.

**4.16.** Describe the circumstances in which you would choose to use embedded SQL rather than using SQL alone or using only a general-purpose programming language.

## Bibliographical Notes

The original version of SQL, called Sequel 2, is described by Chamberlin et al. [1976]. Sequel 2 was derived from the languages Square [Boyce et al. 1975] and Sequel [Chamberlin and Boyce 1974]. The American National Standard SQL-86 is described in ANSI [1986]. The IBM Systems Application Architecture definition of SQL is defined by IBM [1987]. The official standards for SQL-89 and SQL-92 are available as ANSI [1989] and ANSI [1992], respectively. SQL92 is also described in U. S. Dept. of Commerce [1992], and in X/Open [1992, 1993]. The next version of the SQL standard, tentatively called SQL-3, is currently under development.

Cannan and Otten [1993] is a text devoted to SQL. Textbook descriptions of the SQL-92 language include Date and Darwen [1993] and Melton and Simon [1993]. Date and Darwen [1993] and Date [1993] include a critique of SQL-92. SQL-3 is discussed in Melton [1993] and Melton [1996].

Many database products support SQL features beyond those specified in the standards. More information on these features may be found in the SQL user manuals of the respective products. Date and White [1993] and Martin et al. [1989] cover SQL as implemented in DB2. Several relational database systems are surveyed in Valduriez and Gardarin [1989].

The processing of SQL queries, including algorithms and performance issues, is discussed in Chapter 12. Bibliographic references on these matters appear in that chapter as well.

CHAPTER

5

OTHER
RELATIONAL
LANGUAGES

In Chapter 4, we have described SQL—the most influential commercially marketed relational-database language. In this chapter, we study three additional languages: QBE, Quel and Datalog. We have chosen these languages because they represent a variety of styles. QBE is based on the domain relational calculus; Quel is based on the tuple relational calculus. These two languages have been influential not only in research database systems, but also in commercially marketed systems. Datalog has a syntax modeled after the Prolog language. Although not used commercially at present, Datalog has been used in several research database systems.

Like SQL, QBE and Quel contain many other capabilities besides querying a database. They include features for defining the structure of the data, for modifying data in the database, and for specifying security constraints.

It is not our intention to provide a complete users' guide for these languages. Rather, we present fundamental constructs and concepts. Individual implementations of a language may differ in details, or may support only a subset of the full language.

## 5.1 Query-by-Example

*Query-by-Example* (*QBE*) is the name of both a data-manipulation language and the database system that included this language. The QBE database system was developed at IBM's T. J. Watson Research Center in the early 1970s. The QBE data-manipulation language was later used in IBM's Query Management Facility (QMF). Today, some database systems for personal computers support variants of QBE language. In this section, we consider only the data-manipulation language. It has two distinctive features:

1. Unlike most query languages and programming languages, QBE has a *two-dimensional* syntax: Queries *look* like tables. A query in a one-dimensional language (for example, SQL) *can* be written in one (possibly long) line. A two-dimensional language *requires* two dimensions for its expression. (There is a one-dimensional version of QBE, but we shall not consider it in our discussion).

2. QBE queries are expressed "by example." Instead of giving a procedure for obtaining the desired answer, the user gives an example of what is desired. The system generalizes this example to compute the answer to the query.

Despite these unusual features, there is a close correspondence between QBE and the domain relational calculus.

We express queries in QBE using *skeleton tables*. These tables show the relation schema, as presented in Figure 5.1. Rather than clutter the display with all skeletons, the user selects those skeletons needed for a given query and fills in the skeletons with *example rows*. An example row consists of constants and *example elements*, which are domain variables. To avoid confusion, in QBE domain variables are preceded by an underscore character (_), as in _x, and constants appear without any qualification. This convention is in contrast to those in most other languages, in which constants are quoted and variables appear without any qualification.

### 5.1.1   Queries on One Relation

Returning to our ongoing bank example, to find all loan numbers at the Perryridge branch, we bring up the skeleton for the *loan* relation, and fill it in as follows:

| loan | branch-name | loan-number | amount |
|------|-------------|-------------|--------|
|      | Perryridge  | P._x        |        |

The preceding query causes the system to look for tuples in *loan* that have "Perryridge" as the value for the *branch-name* attribute. For each such tuple, the value of the *loan-number* attribute is assigned to the variable $x$. The value of the variable $x$ is "printed" (actually, displayed), because the command P. appears in the *loan-number* column next to the variable $x$. Observe that this result is similar to what would be done to answer the domain-relational calculus query

$$\{\langle x \rangle \mid \exists\, b, a(\langle b, x, a \rangle \in loan \land b = \text{``Perryridge''})\}$$

QBE assumes that a blank position in a row contains a unique variable. As a result, if a variable does not appear more than once in a query, it may be omitted.

| branch | branch-name | branch-city | assets |
|--------|-------------|-------------|--------|
|        |             |             |        |

| customer | customer-name | customer-street | customer-city |
|----------|---------------|-----------------|---------------|
|          |               |                 |               |

| loan | branch-name | loan-number | amount |
|------|-------------|-------------|--------|
|      |             |             |        |

| borrower | customer-name | loan-number |
|----------|---------------|-------------|
|          |               |             |

| account | branch-name | account-number | balance |
|---------|-------------|----------------|---------|
|         |             |                |         |

| depositor | customer-name | account-number |
|-----------|---------------|----------------|
|           |               |                |

Figure 5.1    QBE skeleton tables for the bank example.

Our previous query could thus be rewritten as

| loan | branch-name | loan-number | amount |
|------|-------------|-------------|--------|
|      | Perryridge  | P.          |        |

QBE (unlike SQL) performs duplicate elimination automatically. To suppress duplicate elimination, we insert the command ALL. after the P. command:

| loan | branch-name | loan-number | amount |
|------|-------------|-------------|--------|
|      | Perryridge  | P.ALL.      |        |

To display the entire *loan* relation, we can create a single row consisting of P. in every field. Alternatively, we can use a shorthand notation by placing a single P. in the column headed by the relation name:

| loan | branch-name | loan-number | amount |
|------|-------------|-------------|--------|
| P.   |             |             |        |

QBE allows queries that involve arithmetic comparisons (for example, >), rather than an equality comparison, as in "Find the loan numbers of all loans with a loan amount of more than $700":

| loan | branch-name | loan-number | amount |
|------|-------------|-------------|--------|
|      |             | P.          | >700   |

Comparisons can involve only one arithmetic expression on the right-hand side of the comparison operation (for example, $> (\_x +\_y - 20)$). The expression can include both variables and constants. The space on the left-hand side of the comparison operation must be blank. The arithmetic operations that QBE supports are $=$, $<$, $\leq$, $>$, $\geq$, and $\neg$.

Note that restricting the right-hand side to a single arithmetic expression implies that we cannot compare two distinct named variables. We shall deal with this difficulty shortly.

As another example, consider the query "Find the names of all branches that are not located in Brooklyn." This query can be written as follows:

| branch | branch-name | branch-city | assets |
|--------|-------------|-------------|--------|
|        | P.          | ¬ Brooklyn  |        |

The primary purpose of variables in QBE is to force values of certain tuples to have the same value on certain attributes. Consider the query "Find the loan numbers of all loans made jointly to Smith and Jones":

| borrower | customer-name | loan-number |
|----------|---------------|-------------|
|          | "Smith"       | P._x        |
|          | "Jones"       | _x          |

To execute the preceding query, the system finds all pairs of tuples in *borrower* that agree on the *loan-number* attribute, where the value for the *customer-name* attribute is "Smith" for one tuple and "Jones" for the other. The value of the *loan-number* attribute is then displayed.

Contrast the preceding query with "Find the loan numbers of all loans made to Smith, to Jones, or to both jointly," which can be written as

| borrower | customer-name | loan-number |
|----------|---------------|-------------|
|          | "Smith"       | P._x        |
|          | "Jones"       | P._y        |

The critical distinction between these two queries lies in the use of the same domain variable ($x$) for both rows in the former query, but of distinct domain variables ($x$ and $y$) in the latter query. Note that, in the domain relational calculus, the former query would be written as

$$\{\langle l \rangle \mid \exists\, x\, (\langle x, l \rangle \in borrower \land x = \text{"Smith"})$$

$$\land \exists\, x\, (\langle x, l \rangle \in borrower \land x = \text{"Jones"})\}$$

whereas the latter query would be written as

$$\{\langle l \rangle \mid \exists\, x\ (\langle x, l \rangle \in\ borrower\ \wedge\ x\ =\ \text{"Smith"})$$

$$\vee\ \exists\, x\ (\langle x, l \rangle \in\ borrower\ \wedge\ x\ =\ \text{"Jones"})\}$$

As another example, consider the query "Find all customers who live in the same city as Jones":

| customer | customer-name | customer-street | customer-city |
|----------|---------------|-----------------|---------------|
|          | P.\_x         |                 | \_y           |
|          | Jones         |                 | \_y           |

## 5.1.2  Queries on Several Relations

QBE allows queries that span several different relations (analogous to Cartesian product or natural join in the relational algebra). The connections among the various relations are achieved through variables that force certain tuples to have the same value on certain attributes. As an illustration, suppose that we want to find the names of all customers who have a loan from the Perryridge branch. This query can be written as

| loan | branch-name | loan-number | amount |
|------|-------------|-------------|--------|
|      | Perryridge  | \_x         |        |

| borrower | customer-name | loan-number |
|----------|---------------|-------------|
|          | P.\_y         | \_x         |

To evaluate the preceding query, the system finds tuples in *loan* with "Perryridge" as the value for the *branch-name* attribute. For each such tuple, the system finds tuples in *borrower* with the same value for the *loan-number* attribute as the *loan* tuple. The values for the *customer-name* attribute are displayed.

We can use a technique similar to the preceding one to write the query "Find the names of all customers who have both an account and a loan at the bank":

| depositor | customer-name | account-number |
|-----------|---------------|----------------|
|           | P.\_x         |                |

| borrower | customer-name | loan-number |
|----------|---------------|-------------|
|          | \_x           |             |

Let us now consider the query "Find the names of all customers who have an account at the bank, but who do not have a loan from the bank." We express queries that involve negation in QBE by placing a **not** sign (¬) under the relation name and next to an example row:

| depositor | customer-name | account-number |
|-----------|---------------|----------------|
|           | P._x          |                |

| borrower | customer-name | loan-number |
|----------|---------------|-------------|
| ¬        | _x            |             |

Compare the preceding query with our earlier query "Find the names of all customers who have both an account and a loan at the bank." The only difference is the ¬ appearing next to the example row in the *borrower* skeleton. This difference, however, has a major effect on the processing of the query. QBE finds all $x$ values for which

1. There is a tuple in the *depositor* relation whose *customer-name* is the domain variable $x$.
2. There is no tuple in the *borrower* relation whose *customer-name* is the same as in the domain variable $x$.

The ¬ can be read as "there does not exist."

The fact that we placed the ¬ under the relation name, rather than under an attribute name, is important. A ¬ under an attribute name is a shorthand for $\neq$. Thus, to find all customers who have at least two accounts, we write

| depositor | customer-name | account-number |
|-----------|---------------|----------------|
|           | P._x          | _y             |
|           | _x            | ¬ _y           |

In English, the preceding query reads "Display all *customer-name* values that appear in at least two tuples, with the second tuple having an *account-number* different from the first."

## 5.1.3   The Condition Box

At times, it is either inconvenient or impossible to express all the constraints on the domain variables within the skeleton tables. To overcome this difficulty, QBE includes a *condition box* feature that allows the expression of general constraints over any of the domain variables. Suppose that we modify the final query in Section 5.1.2 to be "Find all customers who are not named 'Jones' and who have at least two accounts." We want to include an "$x \neq$ Jones" constraint in this query. We do that by bringing up the condition box and entering the constraint "$x \neg =$ Jones":

| conditions |
|------------|
| $x \neg =$ Jones |

Turning to another example, to find all account numbers with a balance between \$1300 and \$1500, we write

| account | branch-name | account-number | balance |
|---------|-------------|----------------|---------|
|         |             | P.             | _x      |

| conditions |
|------------|
| _x ≥ 1300  |
| _x ≤ 1500  |

As another example, consider the query "Find all branches that have assets greater than those of at least one branch located in Brooklyn." This query can be written as

| branch | branch-name | branch-city | assets |
|--------|-------------|-------------|--------|
|        | P._x        |             | _y     |
|        |             | Brooklyn    | _z     |

| conditions |
|------------|
| _y > _z    |

QBE allows complex arithmetic expressions to appear in a condition box. We can write the query "Find all branches that have assets that are at least twice as large as the assets of one of the branches located in Brooklyn" much as we did in the preceding query, by modifying the condition box to

| conditions   |
|--------------|
| _y ≥ 2 * _z  |

QBE also allows logical expressions to appear in a condition box. The logical operators are the words **and** and **or**, or the symbols "&" and "|". To find all account numbers of account with a balance between \$1300 and \$2000, but not exactly \$1500, we write

| account | branch-name | account-number | balance |
|---------|-------------|----------------|---------|
|         |             | P.             | _x      |

| conditions |
|------------|
| _x = (≥ 1300 **and** ≤ 2000 **and** ¬1500) |

QBE includes an unconventional use of the **or** construct to allow comparison with a set of constant values. To find all branches that are located in either Brooklyn or Queens, we write

| branch | branch-name | branch-city | assets |
|--------|-------------|-------------|--------|
|        | P.          | _x          |        |

| conditions |
|------------|
| _x = (Brooklyn **or** Queens) |

### 5.1.4    The Result Relation

The queries that we have written thus far have one characteristic in common: The results to be displayed appear in a single relation schema. If the result of a query includes attributes from several relation schemas, we need a mechanism to display the desired result in a single table. For this purpose, we can declare a temporary *result* relation that includes all the attributes of the result of the query. We print the desired result by including the command P. in only the *result* skeleton table.

As an illustration, consider the query "Find the *customer-name*, *account-number*, and *balance* for all accounts at the Perryridge branch." In relational algebra, we would accomplish this query as follows:

1. Join *depositor* and *account*.
2. Project *customer-name*, *account-number*, and *balance*.

To accomplish this query in QBE, we proceed as follows:

1. Create a skeleton table, called *result*, with attributes *customer-name*, *account-number*, and *balance*. The name of the newly created skeleton table (that is, *result*) must be different from any of the previously existing database relation names.
2. Write the query.

The resulting query is

| account | branch-name | account-number | balance |
|---------|-------------|----------------|---------|
|         | Perryridge  | _y             | _z      |

| depositor | customer-name | account-number |
|-----------|---------------|----------------|
|           | _x            | _y             |

| result | customer-name | account-number | balance |
|--------|---------------|----------------|---------|
| P.     | _x            | _y             | _z      |

### 5.1.5    Ordering of the Display of Tuples

QBE offers the user some control over the order in which tuples in a relation are displayed. We gain this control by inserting either the command AO. (ascending order) or the command DO. (descending order) in the appropriate column. Thus, to list in ascending alphabetic order all customers who have an account at the bank, we write

| depositor | customer-name | account-number |
|-----------|---------------|----------------|
|           | P.AO.         |                |

QBE provides a mechanism for sorting and displaying data in multiple columns. We specify the order in which the sorting should be carried out by including, with each sort operator (AO or DO), an integer surrounded by parentheses. Thus, to list all account numbers at the Perryridge branch in ascending alphabetic order with their respective account balances in descending order, we write

| account | branch-name | account-number | balance |
|---------|-------------|----------------|---------|
|         | Perryridge  | P.AO(1).       | P.DO(2). |

The command P.AO(1). specifies that the account number should be sorted first; the command P.DO(2). specifies that the balances for each account should then be sorted.

## 5.1.6    Aggregate Operations

QBE includes the aggregate operators AVG, MAX, MIN, SUM, and CNT. We must postfix these operators with ALL. to create a multiset on which the aggregate operation is evaluated. The ALL. operator ensures that duplicates are not eliminated. Thus, to find the total balance of all the accounts maintained at the Perryridge branch, we write

| account | branch-name | account-number | balance |
|---------|-------------|----------------|---------|
|         | Perryridge  |                | P.SUM.ALL. |

Suppose that we wish to eliminate duplicates when an aggregate operator is used. Since all aggregate operators must be postfixed with ALL, we must add a new operator, UNQ, to specify that we want duplicates eliminated. Thus, to find the total number of customers who have an account at the bank, we write

| depositor | customer-name | account-number |
|-----------|---------------|----------------|
|           | P.CNT.UNQ.ALL. |               |

QBE also offers the ability to compute functions on groups of tuples using the G. operator, which is analogous to SQL's **group by** construct. Thus, to find the average balance at each branch, we can write

| account | branch-name | account-number | balance |
|---------|-------------|----------------|---------|
|         | P.G.        |                | P.AVG.ALL._x |

The average balance is computed on a branch-by-branch basis. The ALL. in the P.AVG.ALL. entry in the *balance* column ensures that all the balances are considered. If we wish to display the branch names in ascending order, we replace P.G. by P.AO.G.

To find the average account balance at only those branches where the average account balance is more than $1200, we add the following condition box:

| conditions |
|------------|
| AVG.ALL._x > 1200 |

To find the name, street and city of all customers who have more than one account at the bank, we write

| customer | customer-name | customer-street | customer-city |
|----------|---------------|-----------------|---------------|
| P. | _x | | |

| depositor | customer-name | account-number |
|-----------|---------------|----------------|
| | G._x | CNT.ALL._y |

| conditions |
|------------|
| CNT.ALL._y > 1 |

The approach is to count the number of *depositor* tuples pertaining to each customer of the bank. The condition box selects the names of the desired customers and the join with *customer* gives the required information.

As a final example, consider the query "Find all customers who have accounts at each of the branches located in Brooklyn":

| depositor | customer-name | account-number |
|-----------|---------------|----------------|
| | P.G._x | _y |

| account | branch-name | account-number | balance |
|---------|-------------|----------------|---------|
| | CNT.UNQ.ALL._z | _y | |

| branch | branch-name | branch-city | assets |
|--------|-------------|-------------|--------|
| | _z | Brooklyn | |
| | _w | Brooklyn | |

| conditions |
|------------|
| CNT.UNQ.ALL._z = |
| CNT.UNQ.ALL._w |

The domain variable $w$ can hold the value of names of branches located in Brooklyn. Thus, CNT.UNQ.ALL._w is the number of distinct branches in Brooklyn. The domain variable $z$ can hold the value of branches such that both of the following hold:

- The branch is located in Brooklyn.
- The customer whose name is $x$ has an account at the branch.

Thus, CNT.UNQ.ALL._z is the number of distinct branches in Brooklyn at which customer $x$ has an account. If CNT.UNQ.ALL._z = CNT.UNQ.ALL._w, then customer $x$ must have an account at all of the branches located in Brooklyn. In such a case, $x$ is included in the displayed result (because of the P.).

### 5.1.7   Modification of the Database

In this section, we show how to add, remove, or change information using QBE.

#### 5.1.7.1   Deletion

Deletion of tuples from a relation is expressed in much the same way as a query. The major difference is the use of D. in place of P. In QBE (unlike in SQL), we can delete whole tuples, as well as values in selected columns. When we delete information in only some of the columns, null values, specified by −, are inserted.

   We note that a D. command operates on only one relation. If we want to delete tuples from several relations, we must use one D. operator for each relation.

   Here are some examples of QBE delete requests:

- Delete customer Smith.

| customer | customer-name | customer-street | customer-city |
|----------|---------------|-----------------|---------------|
| D.       | Smith         |                 |               |

- Delete the *branch-city* value of the branch whose name is "Perryridge."

| branch | branch-name | branch-city | assets |
|--------|-------------|-------------|--------|
|        | Perryridge  | D.          |        |

Thus, if before the delete operation the *branch* relation contains the tuple (Perryridge, Brooklyn, 50000), the delete results in the replacement of the preceding tuple with the tuple (Perryridge, −, 50000).

- Delete all loans with a loan amount between $1300 and $1500.

| loan | branch-name | loan-number | amount |
|------|-------------|-------------|--------|
| D.   |             | _y          | _x     |

| borrower | customer-name | loan-number |
|----------|---------------|-------------|
| D.       |               | _y          |

| conditions |
|------------|
| _x = (≥ 1300 **and** ≤ 1500) |

Note that, to delete loans we must delete tuples from both the *loan* and *borrower* relations.

• Delete all accounts at all branches located in Brooklyn.

| account | branch-name | account-number | balance |
|---------|-------------|----------------|---------|
| D.      | _x          | _y             |         |

| depositor | customer-name | account-number |
|-----------|---------------|----------------|
| D.        |               | _y             |

| branch | branch-name | branch-city | assets |
|--------|-------------|-------------|--------|
|        | _x          | Brooklyn    |        |

Note that, in expressing a deletion, we can reference relations other than those from which we are deleting information.

## 5.1.7.2   Insertion

To insert data into a relation, we either specify a tuple to be inserted or write a query the result of which is a set of tuples to be inserted. We do the insertion by placing the I. operator in the query expression. Obviously, the attribute values for inserted tuples must be members of the attribute's domain.

The simplest insert is a request to insert one tuple. Suppose that we wish to insert that account A-9732 at the Perryridge branch has a balance of $700. We write

| account | branch-name | account-number | balance |
|---------|-------------|----------------|---------|
| I.      | Perryridge  | A-9732         | 700     |

We can also insert a tuple that contains only partial information. To insert into the *branch* relation information about a new branch with name "Capital" and city "Queens," but with a null asset value, we write

| branch | branch-name | branch-city | assets |
|--------|-------------|-------------|--------|
| I.     | Capital     | Queens      |        |

More generally, we might want to insert tuples based on the result of a query. Let us consider again the situation where we want to provide as a gift for all loan customers of the Perryridge branch, a new $200 savings account for every loan account that they have, with the loan number serving as the account number for the savings account. We write

| account | branch-name | account-number | balance |
|---------|-------------|----------------|---------|
| I.      | Perryridge  | _x             | 200     |

| depositor | customer-name | account-number |
|-----------|---------------|----------------|
| I.        | _y            | _x             |

| loan | branch-name | loan-number | amount |
|------|-------------|-------------|--------|
|      | Perryridge  | _x          |        |

| borrower | customer-name | loan-number |
|----------|---------------|-------------|
|          | _y            | _x          |

To execute the preceding insertion request, the system must get the appropriate information from the *borrower* relation, then must use that information to insert the appropriate new tuple in the *depositor* and *account* relations.

### 5.1.7.3  Updates

There are situations in which we wish to change one value in a tuple without changing *all* values in the tuple. For this purpose, we use the U. operator. As we could for insert and delete, we can choose the tuples to be updated using a query. QBE, however, does not allow users to update the primary key fields.

Suppose that we want to update the asset value of the of the Perryridge branch to $10,000,000. This update is expressed as

| branch | branch-name | branch-city | assets |
|--------|-------------|-------------|--------|
|        | Perryridge  |             | U.10000000 |

The blank field of attribute *branch-city* implies that no updating of that value is required.

The preceding query updates the assets of the Perryridge branch to $10,000,000, regardless of the old value. There are circumstances, however, where we need to update a value using the previous value. We must express such a request using two rows: one specifying the old tuples that need to be updated, and the other indicating the new updated tuples to be inserted in the database.

Suppose that interest payments are being made, and all balances are to be increased by 5 percent. We write

| account | branch-name | account-number | balance |
|---------|-------------|----------------|---------|
| U.      |             |                | _x * 1.05 |
|         |             |                | _x |

This query specifies that we retrieve one tuple at a time from the *account* relation, determine the balance x, and update that balance to x * 1.05.

## 5.2  Quel

*Quel* was introduced as the query language for the Ingres database system, developed at the University of California, Berkeley. The basic structure of Quel closely parallels that of the tuple relational calculus. We express most Quel queries using three types of clauses: **range of**, **retrieve**, and **where**.

- Each tuple variable is declared in a **range of** clause. We write

$$\textbf{range of } t \textbf{ is } r$$

  to declare $t$ to be a tuple variable restricted to take on values of tuples in relation $r$.
- The **retrieve** clause is similar in function to the **select** clause of SQL.
- The **where** clause contains the selection predicate.

A typical Quel query is of the form

$$\textbf{range of } t_1 \textbf{ is } r_1$$
$$\textbf{range of } t_2 \textbf{ is } r_2$$

.

.

.

$$\textbf{range of } t_m \textbf{ is } r_m$$
$$\textbf{retrieve } (t_{i_1}.A_{j_1},\ t_{i_2}.A_{j_2}, \ldots, t_{i_n}.A_{j_n})$$
$$\textbf{where } P$$

Each $t_i$ is a tuple variable, each is a $r_i$ relation, and each $A_{j_k}$ is an attribute. Quel, like SQL, uses the notation

$$t.A$$

to denote the value of tuple variable $t$ on attribute $A$. This expressions has the same meaning as $t[A]$ in the tuple relational calculus.

Quel does not include relational algebra operations such as **intersect, union**, and **minus**. Furthermore, Quel (unlike SQL), does not allow nested subqueries. That is, we *cannot* have a nested **retrieve-where** clause inside a **where** clause. These limitations do not reduce the expressive power of Quel, although they may sometimes make writing a query more complicated.

## 5.2.1    Simple Queries

Let us return to our bank example, and write several of our earlier queries using Quel. First, we find the names of all customers who have a loan at the bank:

$$\textbf{range of } t \textbf{ is } borrower$$
$$\textbf{retrieve } (t.customer\text{-}name)$$

The preceding query does not eliminate duplicates. Thus, the name of a customer who has several loans from the bank will appear several times. To remove duplicates, we must add the keyword **unique** to the **retrieve** clause:

$$\textbf{range of } t \textbf{ is } borrower$$
$$\textbf{retrieve unique } (t.customer\text{-}name)$$

Although duplicate elimination imposes additional overhead in query processing, we shall specify duplicate elimination when necessary in our examples.

Let us consider a more complicated example to find all loan numbers for loans made at the Perryridge branch that have loan amounts greater than $700. This query can be written in Quel as

> **range of** *t* **is** *loan*
> **retrieve** (*t.loan-number*)
> **where** *t.branch-name* = "Perryridge" **and** *t.amount* > 700

To show a Quel query involving more than one relation, let us consider the query "Find the names of all customers who have a loan at the Perryridge branch."

> **range of** *t* **is** *borrower*
> **range of** *s* **is** *loan*
> **retrieve unique** (*t.customer-name*)
> **where** *s.branch-name* = "Perryridge" **and**
>     *t.loan-number* = *s.loan-number*

Note that Quel, like SQL, uses the logical connectives **and**, **or**, and **not**, rather than the mathematical symbols $\land$, $\lor$, and $\lnot$, as are used in the tuple relational calculus. We need to express the join predicate explicitly. Quel does not have a special notation for natural join. Like SQL, it includes pattern-matching comparisons, but we shall not cover them here.

As another example involving two relations, consider the query "Find the names of all customers who have both a loan and an account at the bank":

> **range of** *s* **is** *borrower*
> **range of** *t* **is** *depositor*
> **retrieve unique** (*s.customer-name*)
> **where** *t.customer-name* = *s.customer-name*

In SQL, we had the option of writing such a query by using the relational-algebra operation **intersect**. As we noted, Quel does not include this operation.

## 5.2.2 Tuple Variables

For certain queries, we need to have two distinct tuple variables ranging over the same relation. Consider the query "Find the names of all customers who live in the same city as Jones does." We write this query as follows:

> **range of** *s* **is** *customer*
> **range of** *t* **is** *customer*
> **retrieve unique** (*s.customer-name*)
> **where** *t.customer-name* = "Jones" **and**
>     *s.customer-city* = *t.customer-city*

Since the preceding query requires us to compare tuples pertaining to Jones with every *customer* tuple, we need two distinct tuple variables ranging over *customer*. However, a query often requires only one tuple variable ranging over a relation. In such cases, we may omit the **range of** statement for that relation, and use the relation name itself as an implicitly declared tuple variable. Following this convention, we rewrite the query "Find the names of all customers who have both a loan and an account at the bank" as follows:

> **retrieve unique** (*borrower.customer-name*)
> **where** *depositor.customer-name* = *borrower.customer-name*

The original academic Quel does not allow the use of implicitly declared tuple variables.

## 5.2.3   Aggregate Functions

Aggregate functions in Quel compute functions on groups of tuples. However, they take a form different from that of SQL. In SQL, a **group by** clause is part of the query itself, resulting in a single grouping of tuples for all aggregate functions in the query. In Quel, grouping is specified as part of each aggregate expression.

Quel aggregate expressions can take the following forms:

> *aggregate function* (*t.A*)
> *aggregate function* (*t.A* **where** *P*)
> *aggregate function* (*t.A* **by** $s.B_1$, $s.B_2$, ..., $s.B_n$ **where** *P*)

where

- *aggregate function* is one of **count, sum, avg, max, min, countu, sumu, avgu,** or **any**.
- *t* and *s* are tuple variables.
- $A, B_1, B_2, \ldots, B_n$ are attributes.
- *P* is a predicate similar to the **where** clause in a **retrieve**.

An aggregate expression can appear anywhere a constant can appear. The intuitive meaning of **count, sum, avg, max,** and **min** should be clear. We shall explain **any** later in this section. The functions **countu, sumu,** and **avgu** are identical to **count, sum,** and **avg,** respectively, except that they remove duplicates from their operands.

To find the average account balance for all accounts at the Perryridge branch, we write

> **range of** *t* **is** *account*
> **retrieve avg** (*t.balance*
>> **where** *t.branch-name* = "Perryridge")

Aggregates can appear in the **where** clause. Suppose that we wish to find all accounts that have a balance higher than the average of all balances at the bank. We write

> **range of** *u* **is** *account*
> **range of** *t* **is** *account*
> **retrieve** (*t.account-number*)
> **where** *t.balance* > **avg** (*u.balance*)

The preceding **avg** (. . .) expression computes the average balance of all accounts at the bank.

Let us now consider a modification to the preceding query. Instead of using the average balance at the bank, we consider only the Perryridge branch. Thus, we are finding all accounts whose balance is higher than the average balance of Perryridge-branch accounts. We write this query as follows:

> **range of** *u* **is** *account*
> **range of** *t* **is** *account*
> **retrieve** (*t.account-number*)
> **where** *t.balance* > **avg** (*u.balance*
>             **where** *u.branch-name* = "Perryridge")

Let us modify our query further. We now wish to find all accounts whose balance is higher than the average balance at the branch where the account is held. In this case, we need to compute, for each tuple *t* in *account*, the average balance at branch *t.branch-name*. To form these groups of tuples, we need to use the **by** construct in our aggregate expression:

> **range of** *u* **is** *account*
> **range of** *t* **is** *account*
> **retrieve** (*t.account-number*)
> **where** *t.balance* > **avg** (*u.balance* **by** *t.branch-name*
>             **where** *u.branch-name* = *t.branch-name*)

The effect of the **by** construct in Quel differs from that of the **group by** clause in SQL. The primary source of this distinction is the role of tuple variables. The tuple variable *t* used in **by** is the same one that is used in the rest of the query. However, all other tuple variables are local to the aggregate expression even if a variable with the same name appears elsewhere in the query. Thus, in the preceding Quel query, if we removed "**by** *t.branch-name*" from the expression, we would turn tuple variable *t* into a local variable of the aggregate expression that is not bound to the tuple variable *t* of the outer query.

Let us consider the query "Find the names of all customers who have an account at the bank, but who do not have a loan from the bank." In the relational algebra, we wrote this query using the set difference operation. We can write this query in Quel using the **count** aggregate operation if we think of the query as "Find the names of all customers who have an account at the bank, and for whom the count of the number of loans from the bank is zero."

> **range of** *t* **is** *depositor*
> **range of** *u* **is** *borrower*
> **retrieve unique** (*t.customer-name*)
> **where count** (*u.loan-number* **by** *t.customer-name*
>             **where** *u.customer-name* = *t.customer-name*) = 0

Quel offers another aggregate function that is applicable to this example, called **any**. If we replace **count** in the preceding query with **any**, we obtain 1 if the count is greater than 0; otherwise, we obtain 0. The **any** function allows faster execution of the query, in that processing can stop as soon as one tuple is found. The use of a comparison with **any** is analogous to the "there exists" quantifier of the relational calculus. Thus, we can rewrite our query as

> **range of** *t* **is** *depositor*
> **range of** *u* **is** *borrower*
> **retrieve unique** (*t.customer-name*)
> **where any** (*u.loan-number* **by** *t.customer-name*
>           **where** *u.customer-name* = *t.customer-name*) = 0

As a more complicated example, consider the query "Find the names of all customers who have accounts at each of the branches located in Brooklyn." Our strategy for expressing this query in Quel is as follows: First find out how many branches there are in Brooklyn. Then, compare this number with the number of distinct branches in Brooklyn at which each customer has an account. The **count** aggregate function that we used earlier counts duplicates. Therefore, we use the **countu** function, which counts unique values.

> **range of** *t* **is** *depositor*
> **range of** *u* **is** *account*
> **range of** *s* **is** *branch*
> **range of** *w* **is** *branch*
> **retrieve unique** (*t.customer-name*)
> **where countu** (*s.branch-name* **by** *t.customer-name*
>           **where** *u.account-number* = *t.account-number*
>           **and** *u.branch-name* = *s.branch-name*
>           **and** *s.branch-city* = "Brooklyn") =
>   **countu** (*w.branch-name* **where** *w.branch-city* = "Brooklyn")

We use **by** in the first **countu** expression, since we must restrict consideration to a single customer at a time. However, we do not use **by** in the latter **countu** expression, since we are interested in counting all branches in Brooklyn independent of the bindings of tuple variables external to this **countu** expression.

### 5.2.4   Modification of the Database

Database modification in Quel is similar to modification in SQL, although the syntax differs slightly.

#### 5.2.4.1   Deletion

The form of a Quel deletion is

> **range of** *t* **is** *r*
> **delete** *t*
> **where** *P*

The tuple variable *t* can be defined implicitly. The predicate *P* can be any valid Quel predicate. If the **where** clause is omitted, all tuples in the relation are deleted.

Here are examples of Quel delete requests.

- Delete all tuples in the *loan* relation:

> **range of** *t* **is** *loan*
> **delete** *t*

- Delete all Smith's account records:

> **range of** *t* **is** *depositor*
> **delete** *t*
> **where** *t.customer-name* = "Smith"

- Delete all accounts at branches located in Needham:

> **range of** *t* **is** *account*
> **range of** *u* **is** *branch*
> **delete** *t*
> **where** *t.branch-name* = *u.branch-name*
> **and** *u.branch-city* = "Needham"

### 5.2.4.2   Insertion

Insertion in Quel takes two general forms: insertion of a single tuple, and insertion of a set of tuples. Quel uses the keyword **append** for insertion. Here are examples of Quel insert requests:

- Insert that account A-9732 at the Perryridge branch has a balance of $700:

> **append to** *account* (*branch-name* = "Perryridge",
> *account-number* = A-9732,
> *balance* = 700)

- Provide as a gift for all loan customers of the Perryridge branch, a new $200 savings account for every loan account that they have. Let the loan numbers serve as the account numbers for the new savings accounts.

**range of** *t* **is** *loan*
**range of** *s* **is** *borrower*
**append to** *account* (*branch-name* = *t.branch-name*,
*account-number* = *t.loan-number*,
*balance* = 200)
**where** *t.branch-name* = "Perryridge"
**append to** *depositor* (*customer-name* = *s.customer-name*,
*account-number* = *s.loan-number*)
**where** *t.branch-name* = "Perryridge" **and** *t.loan-number* = *s.loan-number*

Note that we need two **append** to statements to record information on the new account in both the *account* and *depositor* relations.

### 5.2.4.3   Updates

We express updates in Quel using the **replace** command. Examples of Quel update requests follow:

- Pay 5-percent interest (increase all account balances by 5 percent):

$$\textbf{range of } t \textbf{ is } account$$
$$\textbf{replace } t\,(balance = 1.05 * t.balance)$$

- Pay 6-percent interest on accounts that have balances over \$10,000, and 5 percent on all other accounts:

$$\textbf{range of } t \textbf{ is } account$$
$$\textbf{replace } t\,(balance = 1.06 * balance)$$
$$\textbf{where } t.balance > 10000$$
$$\textbf{replace } t\,(balance = 1.05 * balance)$$
$$\textbf{where } t.balance \le 10000$$

Recall that the order of these two interest payments matters for amounts with a balance just under \$10,000.

## 5.2.5   Set Operations

Let us consider a query for which we used the **union** operation in SQL: "Find the names of all customers who have an account, a loan, or both at the bank." Since we do not have a **union** operation in Quel, and we know that Quel is based on the tuple relational calculus, we might be guided by our tuple-relational-calculus expression for this query:

$$\{t \mid \exists\, s \,\in\, borrower\ (t[customer\text{-}name] = s[customer\text{-}name])$$
$$\lor \exists\, u \,\in\, depositor\ (t[customer\text{-}name] = u[customer\text{-}name])\}$$

Unfortunately, the preceding expression does not lead us to a Quel query. The problem is that, in the tuple-relational-calculus query, we obtain customers from *both* tuple variable *s* (whose range is *borrower*) and tuple variable *u* (whose range is *depositor*). In Quel, our **retrieve** clause must be one of the following:

- **retrieve** *s.customer-name*
- **retrieve** *u.customer-name*

If we choose the former, we exclude those depositors who are not borrowers. If we choose the latter, we exclude those borrowers who are not depositors.

To write this query in Quel, we must create a new relation, and must insert tuples into this new relation. Let us call this new relation *temp*. We obtain all depositors of the bank by writing

> **range of** *u* **is** *depositor*
> **retrieve into** *temp* **unique** (*u.customer-name*)

The **into** *temp* clause causes a new relation, *temp*, to be created to hold the result of this query. Now, we can find all borrowers of the bank, and can insert them in the newly created relation *temp*. We do so using the **append** command:

> **range of** *s* **is** *borrower*
> **append to** *temp* **unique** (*s.customer-name*)

We now have a relation *temp* that contains all customers who have an account, a loan, or both at the bank. Our use of the keyword **unique** in both the **retrieve** and **append** requests ensures that any duplicates have been removed.

The relation *temp* contains the desired list of customers. We thus can now write

> **range of** *t* **is** *temp*
> **retrieve unique** (*t.customer-name*)

to complete our query.

The strategy of using **append** allows us to perform unions in Quel. To perform a set difference *r* − *s* (**minus** in SQL), we create a temporary relation representing *r*, and delete tuples of this temporary relation that are also in *s*. To illustrate this strategy, let us consider the query, "Find the names of all customers who have an account at the bank, but who do not have a loan from the bank." We begin by writing the following to create the temporary relation:

> **range of** *u* **is** *depositor*
> **retrieve into** *temp* (*u.customer-name*)

At this point, *temp* contains all customers who have an account at the bank, including those who possibly have a loan from the bank. We now delete those customers who do have a loan.

> **range of** *s* **is** *borrower*
> **range of** *t* **is** *temp*
> **delete** *t*
> **where** *t.customer-name* = *s.customer-name*

The relation *temp* now contains the desired list of customers. We thus can now write

> **range of** *t* **is** *temp*
> **retrieve unique** (*t.customer-name*)

to complete our query.

### 5.2.6    Quel and the Tuple Relational Calculus

To see more clearly the relationship between Quel and the tuple relational calculus, we consider the following Quel query

> **range of** $t_1$ **is** $r_1$
> **range of** $t_2$ **is** $r_2$
>
> .
>
> .
>
> .
>
> **range of** $t_m$ **is** $r_m$
> **retrieve unique** $(t_{i_1}.A_{j_1}, \; t_{i_2}.A_{j_2}, \ldots, t_{i_n}.A_{j_n})$
> **where** $P$

The preceding Quel query would be expressed in the tuple relational calculus as

$$\{t \mid \exists \, t_1 \in r_1, \; t_2 \in r_2, \ldots, t_m \in r_m \; ($$

$$t[r_{i_1}.A_{j_1}] \; = \; t_{i_1}[A_{j_1}] \; \wedge \; t[r_{i_2}.A_{j_2}] \; = \; t_{i_2}[A_{j_2}] \; \wedge \ldots \wedge$$

$$t[r_{i_n}.A_{j_n}] \; = \; t_{i_n}[A_{j_n}] \; \wedge \; P(t_1, \; t_2, \ldots, t_m))\}$$

We can understand this expression by looking at the formula within the "there exists" formula in three parts:

- $t_1 \in r_1 \wedge t_2 \in r_2 \wedge \ldots \wedge t_m \in r_m$. This part constrains each tuple in $t_1, t_2, \ldots, t_m$ to take on values of tuples in the relation over which it ranges.
- $t[r_{i_1}.A_{j_1}] = t_{i_1}[A_{j_1}] \wedge t_{i_2}[A_{j_2}] = t[r_{i_2}.A_{j_2}] \wedge \ldots \wedge t[r_{i_n}.A_{j_n}] = t_{i_n}[A_{j_n}]$. This part corresponds to the **retrieve** clause of the Quel query. We need to ensure that the $k$th attribute in tuple $t$ corresponds to the $k$th entry in the **retrieve** clause. Consider the first entry: $t_{i_1}.A_{j_1}$. This entry is the value of some tuple of $r_{i_1}$ (since the range of $t_{i_1}$ is $r_{i_1}$) on attribute $A_{j_1}$. Thus, we need $t[A_{j_1}] = t_{i_1}[A_{j_1}]$. We used the more cumbersome notation $t[r_{i_1}.A_{j_1}] = t_{i_1}[A_{j_1}]$ to deal with the possibility that the same attribute name appears in more than one relation.
- $P(t_1, t_2, \ldots, t_m)$. This part expresses the constraint on acceptable values for $t_1, t_2, \ldots, t_m$ imposed by the **where** clause in the Quel query.

There are no representations of "for all" and of "there does not exist" in the relational-calculus formulation for the preceding Quel query. Quel achieves the power of the relational algebra by means of the **any** aggregate function and by the use of insertion and deletion on temporary relations.

## 5.3    Datalog

Datalog is a nonprocedural query language that is based on the logic-programming language Prolog. As she does in the relational calculus, a user describes the information desired without giving a specific procedure for obtaining that information. The syntax of Datalog resembles that of Prolog. However, the meaning of Datalog

programs is defined in a purely declarative manner, unlike the more procedural semantics of Prolog, so Datalog simplifies writing simple queries and makes query
optimization easier.

## 5.3.1 Basic Structure

A Datalog program consists of a set of *rules*. Before presenting a formal definition
of Datalog rules and their formal meaning, we consider examples. The following
is an example of a Datalog rule to define a view relation $v1$ containing account
numbers and balances for accounts at the Perryridge branch with a balance of over
$700:

$$v1(A, B) \ :- account(\text{``Perryridge''}, A, B), B > 700$$

Datalog rules define views; the preceding rule *uses* the relation *account*,
and *defines* the view relation $v1$. The symbol :– is read as "if," and the comma
separating the "*account*("Perryridge", $A$, $B$)" from "$B > 700$" is read as "and."
Intuitively, the rule is understood as follows:

> **for all** $A$, $B$
> **if**      ("Perryridge", $A$, $B$) $\in$ *account* **and** $B > 700$
> **then**    $(A, B) \in v1$

Suppose that the relation *account* is as shown in Figure 5.2. Then, the view
relation $v1$ contains the tuples shown in Figure 5.3.

To retrieve the balance of account number A-217 in the view relation $v1$, we
can write the following query:

$$? \ v1(\text{``A-217''}, B)$$

The answer to the query is

$$(\text{A-217, 750})$$

To get the account number and balance of all accounts in relation $v1$, where the
balance is greater than 800, we can write

$$? \ v1(A, B), B > 800$$

| branch-name | account-number | balance |
|-------------|----------------|---------|
| Downtown    | A-101          | 500     |
| Mianus      | A-215          | 700     |
| Perryridge  | A-102          | 400     |
| Round Hill  | A-305          | 350     |
| Perryridge  | A-201          | 900     |
| Redwood     | A-222          | 700     |
| Perryridge  | A-217          | 750     |

Figure 5.2   The *account* relation.

| account-number | balance |
|:--------------:|:-------:|
| A-201          | 900     |
| A-217          | 750     |

Figure 5.3    The *v1* relation.

The answer to this query is

(A-201, 900)

In general, we may need more than one rule to define a view relation. Each rule defines a set of tuples that the view relation must contain. The set of tuples in the view relation is then defined as the union of all these sets of tuples. The following Datalog program specifies the interest rates for accounts. The program has two rules defining a view relation *interest-rate*, whose attributes are the account number and the interest rate. The rules say that, if the balance is less that \$2000, then the interest rate is 0; if the balance is greater than or equal to \$2000, the interest rate is 5 percent.

$$interest\text{-}rate(A, 0) \; :\!- \; account(N, A, B), \; B < 2000$$
$$interest\text{-}rate(A, 5) \; :\!- \; account(N, A, B), \; B >= 2000$$

Datalog rules can also use negation. The following rules define a view relation *c* that contains the names of all customers who have a deposit, but have no loan, at the bank:

$$c(N) \; :\!- \; depositor(N,A), \textbf{ not } is\text{-}borrower(N)$$
$$is\text{-}borrower(N) \; :\!- \; borrower(N, L),$$

In Prolog and in most Datalog implementations, attributes of a relation are recognized by position, and attribute names are omitted. Thus, Datalog rules are compact, compared to SQL queries. However, when relations have a large number of attributes, or the order or number of attributes of relations may change, the positional notation can be cumbersome and error prone. It is not hard to create a variant of Datalog syntax using named attributes, rather than positional attributes. In such a system, the Datalog rule defining *v1* can be written as

$$v1(account\text{-}number \; A, \; balance \; B) \; :\!-$$
$$account(branch\text{-}name \; \text{``Perryridge''}, \; account\text{-}number \; A, \; balance \; B),$$
$$B > 700$$

Translation between the two forms can be done without significant effort, given the relation schema.

## 5.3.2   Syntax of Datalog Rules

Now that we have informally explained rules and queries, let us formally define their syntax; we discuss their meaning in Section 5.3.3. We use the same conventions as in the relational algebra for denoting relation names, attribute names, constants (such as numbers or quoted strings), and variable names. Examples of constants are 4, which is a number, and "John," which is a string; $X$ and *Name* are variables. A *positive literal* has the form

$$p(t_1, t_2, \ldots, t_n)$$

where $p$ is the name of a relation with $n$ attributes, and $t_1, t_2, \ldots, t_n$ are either constants or variables. A *negative literal* has the form

$$\textbf{not } p(t_1, t_2, \ldots, t_n)$$

where relation $p$ has $n$ attributes. The following is an example of a literal:

$$account(\text{"Perryridge"}, A, B)$$

Literals involving arithmetic operations are treated specially. For example, the literal $B > 700$, although not in the syntax just described, can be conceptually understood to stand for $> (B, 700)$, which *is* in the required syntax, and where $>$ is a relation.

But what does this notation mean for arithmetic operations such as ">"? The relation $>$ (conceptually) contains tuples of the form $(x, y)$ for every possible pair of values $x, y$ such that $x > y$. Thus, $(2, 1)$ and $(5, -33)$ are both tuples in $>$. Clearly, the (conceptual) relation $>$ is infinite. Other arithmetic operations (such as $>, =, +$ or $-$) are also treated conceptually as relations. For example, A $=$ B $+$ C stands conceptually for $+(B, C, A)$, where the relation $+$ contains every tuple $(x, y, z)$ such that $z = x + y$.

A *fact* is written in the form

$$p(v_1, v_2, \ldots, v_n).$$

and denotes that the tuple $(v_1, v_2, \ldots, v_n)$ is in relation $p$. A set of facts for a relation can also be written in the usual tabular notation. A *set of facts* for the relations in a database schema is equivalent to an instance of the database schema. *Rules* are built out of literals and have the form

$$p(t_1, t_2, \ldots, t_n) :- L_1, L_2, \ldots, L_n$$

where each $L_i$ is a (positive or negative) literal. The literal $p(t_1, t_2, \ldots, t_n)$ is referred to as the *head* of the rule, and the rest of the literals in the rule constitute the *body* of the rule.

A Datalog *program* consists of a set of rules; the order in which the rules are written has no significance. As mentioned earlier, there may be several rules defining a relation.

Figure 5.4 shows an example of a relatively complex Datalog program, which defines the interest on each account in the Perryridge branch. The first rule of the program defines a view relation *interest*, whose attributes are the account number and the interest earned on the account. The view relations *interest-rate* and *perryridge-account* are used in the rule. The second rule defines the view

$$interest(A, I) \ :- \ perryridge\text{-}account(A, B),$$
$$interest\text{-}rate(A, R), I = B * R/100.$$
$$perryridge\text{-}account(A, B) \ :- \ account(\text{``Perryridge''}, A, B).$$
$$interest\text{-}rate(A, 0) \ :- \ account(N, A, B), B < 2000.$$
$$interest\text{-}rate(A, 5) \ :- \ account(N, A, B), B >= 2000.$$

Figure 5.4    Datalog program that defines interest on Perryridge accounts.

relation *perryridge-account*, using the database relation *account*. The final two rules of the program are rules that we saw earlier.

In Section 3.7.3, we defined when a view *depends on* another view, and when a view is *recursive*. Although the syntax for view definitions in Datalog differs from the syntax used for view definition in Section 3.7.3, the definitions depends-on and recursive views are applicable to Datalog views. For example, in the program in Figure 5.4, relation *interest* depends (directly) on relations *interest-rate* and *perryridge-account*. Relation *interest-rate* in turn depends directly on *account*, as does *perryridge-account*. Since we have a chain of dependencies from *interest* to *interest-rate* to *account*, relation *interest* depends (indirectly) on *account*.

The program in Figure 5.4 is nonrecursive. However, the program in Figure 5.5 is recursive, since *empl* depends on itself (due to the second rule).

### 5.3.3    Semantics of Nonrecursive Datalog

We consider the formal semantics of Datalog programs. For now, we consider only programs that are nonrecursive. The semantics of recursive programs is somewhat more complicated; it is discussed in Section 5.3.6. We define the semantics of a program by starting with the semantics of a single rule.

#### 5.3.3.1    Semantics of a Rule

A *ground instantiation of a rule* is the result of replacing each variable in the rule by some constant. If a variable occurs multiple times in a rule, all occurrences of the variable must be replaced by the same constant. Ground instantiations are often simply called *instantiations*.

Our example rule defining *v1*, and an instantiation of the rule, are shown here:

$$v1(A, B) \ :- \ account(\text{``Perryridge''}, A, B), B > 700$$
$$v1(\text{``A-217''}, 750) \ :- \ account(\text{``Perryridge''}, \text{``A-217''}, 750), 750 > 700$$

Here, variable $A$ was replaced by "A-217," and variable $B$ by 750.

$$empl(X, Y) \ :- \ manager(X, Y).$$
$$empl(X, Y) \ :- \ manager(X, Z), empl(Z, Y).$$

Figure 5.5    Recursive Datalog program.

A rule typically has many possible instantiations. These instantiations correspond to the various ways of assigning values to each variable in the rule.

Suppose that we are given a rule $R$,

$$p(t_1, t_2, \ldots, t_n) :- L_1, L_2, \ldots, L_n$$

and a set of facts $I$ for the relations used in the rule ($I$ can also be thought of as a database instance). Consider any instantiation $R'$ of rule $R$:

$$p(v_1, v_2, \ldots, v_n) :- l_1, l_2, \ldots, l_n$$

where each literal $l_i$ is either of the form $q_i(v_{i,1}, v_{1,2}, \ldots, v_{i,n_i})$ or of the form **not** $q_i(v_{i,1}, v_{1,2}, \ldots, v_{i,n_i})$, and where each $v_i$ and each $v_{i,j}$ is a constant.

We say that the body of rule instantiation $R'$ is *satisfied* in $I$ if

1. For each positive literal $q_i(v_{i,1}, \ldots, v_{i,n_i})$ in the body of $R'$, the set of facts $I$ contains the fact $q(v_{i,1}, \ldots, v_{i,n_i})$.
2. For each negative literal **not** $q_j(v_{j,1}, \ldots, v_{j,n_j})$ in the body of $R'$, the set of facts $I$ does not contain the fact $q_j(v_{j,1}, \ldots, v_{j,n_j})$.

We define the set of facts that can be *inferred* from a given set of facts $I$ using rule $R$ as

$$infer(R, I) = \{p(t_1, \ldots, t_{n_i}) \mid \text{there is an instantiation } R' \text{ of } R,$$
$$\text{where } p(t_1, \ldots, t_{n_i}) \text{ is the head of } R', \text{ and}$$
$$\text{the body of } R' \text{ is satisfied in } I\}.$$

Given a set of rules $\mathcal{R} = \{R_1, R_2, \ldots, R_n\}$, we define

$$infer(\mathcal{R}, I) = infer(R_1, I) \cup infer(R_2, I) \cup \ldots \cup infer(R_n, I)$$

Suppose that we are given a set of facts $I$ containing the tuples for relation *account* shown in Figure 5.2. One possible instantiation of our running-example rule $R$ is

$$v1(\text{``A-217''}, 750) :- account(\text{``Perryridge''}, \text{``A-217''}, 750), 750 > 700.$$

The fact *account*("Perryridge", "A-217", 750) is in the set of facts $I$. Further, 750 is greater than 700, and hence conceptually (750, 700) is in the relation ">". Hence, the body of the rule instantiation is satisfied in $I$. There are other possible instantiations of $R$, and using them we find that $infer(R, I)$ has exactly the set of facts for $v1$ that is shown in Figure 5.6.

| account-number | balance |
|:--------------:|:-------:|
| A-201 | 900 |
| A-217 | 750 |

**Figure 5.6**   Result of *infer*($R, I$).

### 5.3.3.2  Semantics of a Program

When a view relation is defined in terms of another view relation, the set of facts in the first view depends on the set of facts in the second one. We have assumed, in this section, that the definition is nonrecursive; that is, no view relation depends (directly or indirectly) on itself. Hence, we can layer the view relations as follows, and can use the layering to define the semantics of the program:

- A relation is in layer 1 if all relations used in the bodies of rules defining it are stored in the database.
- A relation is in layer 2 if all relations used in the bodies of rules defining it either are stored in the database, or are in layer 1.
- In general, a relation $p$ is in layer $i + 1$ if (1) it is not in layers $1, 2, \ldots, i$, and (2) all relations used in the bodies of rules defining $p$ either are stored in the database, or are in layers $1, 2, \ldots, i$.

Consider the program in Figure 5.4. The layering of view relations in the program is shown in Figure 5.7. The relation *account* is in the database. Relation *interest-rate* is in level 1, since all the relations used in the two rules defining it are in the database. Relation *perryridge-account* is similarly in layer 1. Finally, relation *interest* is in layer 2, since it is not in layer 1 and all the relations used in the rule defining it are in the database or in layers less than 2.

We can now define the semantics of a Datalog program in terms of the layering of view relations. Let the layers in a given program be $1, 2, \ldots, n$. Let $\mathcal{R}_i$ denote the set of all rules defining view relations in layer $i$.

- We define $I_0$ to be the set of facts stored in the database, and define $I_1$ as

$$I_1 = I_0 \cup infer(\mathcal{R}_1, I_0)$$

- We proceed in a similar fashion, defining $I_2$ in terms of $I_1$ and $\mathcal{R}_2$, and so on, using the following definition:

$$I_{i+1} = I_i \cup infer(\mathcal{R}_{i+1}, I_i)$$

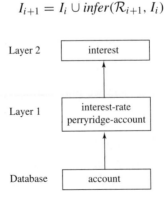

**Figure 5.7    Layering of view relations.**

- Finally, the set of facts in the view relations defined by the program (also called the *semantics of the program*) is given by the set of facts $I_n$ corresponding to the highest layer $n$.

For the program in Figure 5.4, $I_0$ is the set of facts in the database, and $I_1$ is the set of facts in the database along with all facts that we can infer from $I_0$ using the rules for relations *interest-rate* and *perryridge-account*. Finally, $I_2$ contains the facts in $I_1$ along with the facts for relation *interest* that we can infer from the facts in $I_1$ using the rule defining *interest*. The semantics of the program—that is, the set of those facts that are in each of the view relations—is defined as the set of facts $I_2$.

Recall that, in Section 3.7.3, we saw how to define the meaning of nonrecursive relational-algebra views using a technique known as view expansion. View expansion, can be used with nonrecursive Datalog views as well; conversely, the layering technique described here can also be used with relational-algebra views. However, the layering technique can be used with certain extensions of Datalog, where view expansion cannot be used.

### 5.3.4  Safety

It is possible to write rules that generate an infinite number of answers. Consider the rule

$$gt(X, Y) :\!- X > Y$$

Since the relation defining $>$ is infinite, this rule would generate an infinite number of facts for the relation *gt*, which calculation would, correspondingly, take an infinite amount of time and space.

The use of negation can also cause similar problems. Consider the following rule:

$$not\text{-}in\text{-}loan(B, L) :\!- \textbf{not } loan(B, L)$$

The idea is that a tuple *(branch, loan-number)* is in view relation *not-in-loan* if the tuple is not present in the *loan* relation. However, if the set of possible branch names or account numbers is infinite, the relation *not-in-loan* may be infinite as well.

Finally, if we have a variable in the head that does not appear in the body, we may get an infinite number of facts where the variable is instantiated to different values.

So that these possibilities are avoided, Datalog rules are required to satisfy the following *safety* conditions:

1. Every variable that appears in the head of the rule also appears in a nonarithmetic positive literal in the body of the rule.
2. Every variable appearing in a negative literal in the body of the rule also appears in some positive literal in the body of the rule.

If all the rules in a nonrecursive Datalog program satisfy the preceding safety conditions, then all the view relations defined in the program can be shown to be finite, as long as all the database relations are finite. The conditions can be weakened somewhat to allow variables in the head to appear only in an arithmetic literal in the body in some cases. For example, in the rule

$$p(A) :- q(B), A = B + 1$$

we can see that if relation $q$ is finite, then so is $p$, based on the properties of addition, even though variable A appears in only an arithmetic literal.

## 5.3.5 Relational Operations in Datalog

Nonrecursive Datalog expressions without arithmetic operations are equivalent in expressive power to expressions using the basic operations in relational algebra (excluding the modification operations). We shall not formally prove this assertion here. Rather, we shall show through examples how the various relational-algebra operations can be expressed in Datalog. In all cases, we define a view relation called *query* to illustrate the operations.

We have already seen how to do selection using Datalog rules. We perform projections simply by using only the required attributes in the head of the rule. To project out attribute *account-name* from account, we use

$$query(A) :- account(N, A, B)$$

We can obtain the Cartesian product of two relations $r_1$ and $r_2$ in Datalog as follows:

$$query(X_1, X_2, \ldots, X_n, Y_1, Y_2, \ldots, Y_m) :- r_1(X_1, X_2, \ldots, X_n), r_2(Y_1, Y_2, \ldots, Y_m)$$

where $r_1$ is of arity $n$, and $r_2$ is of arity $m$, and the $X_1, X_2, \ldots, X_n, Y_1, Y_2, \ldots, Y_m$ are all distinct variable names.

The union of two relations $r_1$ and $r_2$ (both of arity $n$) is formed as follows:

$$query(X_1, X_2, \ldots, X_n) :- r_1(X_1, X_2, \ldots, X_n)$$
$$query(X_1, X_2, \ldots, X_n) :- r_2(X_1, X_2, \ldots, X_n)$$

Finally, the set difference of two relations $r_1$ and $r_2$ is formed as follows:

$$query(X_1, X_2, \ldots, X_n) :- r_1(X_1, X_2, \ldots, X_n), \textbf{not } r_2(X_1, X_2, \ldots, X_n)$$

It is possible to show that we can express any nonrecursive Datalog query without arithmetic using the relational-algebra operations. We leave this demonstration as an exercise for you to carry out. You can thus establish the equivalence of the basic operations of relational algebra and nonrecursive Datalog without arithmetic operations.

The extended relational update operations of insertion, deletion, and update are supported in certain extensions to Datalog. The syntax for such operations varies from implementation to implementation. Some systems allow the use of $+$

or − in rule heads to denote relational insertion and deletion. For example,

$$+ \ account(\text{``Johnstown''}, \ A, \ B) \ :- account(\text{``Perryridge''}, \ A, \ B)$$

inserts all Perryridge accounts into the set of Johnstown accounts. The aggregation operation of extended relational algebra is supported in some implementations of Datalog. Again, there is no standard syntax for this operation.

## 5.3.6    Recursion in Datalog

Several database applications deal with structures that are similar to tree data structures. For example, consider employees in an organization. Some of the employees are managers. Each manager manages a set of people who report to him or her. But each of these people may in turn be managers, and they in turn may have other people who report to them. Thus employees may be organized in a structure similar to a tree.

Suppose that we have a relation schema

$$\textit{Manager-schema} \ = \ (\textit{employee-name}, \textit{manager-name})$$

Let *manager* be a relation on the preceding schema.

Suppose now, that we want to find out which employees are supervised, directly or indirectly by a given manager—say, Jones. Thus, if the manager of Alon is Barinsky, and the manager of Barinsky is Estovar, and the manager of Estovar is Jones, then Alon, Barinsky, and Estovar are the employees controlled by Jones. People often write programs to manipulate tree data structures using recursion. Using the idea of recursion, we can define the set of people controlled by Jones as follows. The people supervised by Jones are (1) people whose manager is Jones, and (2) people whose manager is supervised by Jones. Note that case (2) is recursive.

We can encode the preceding recursive definition as a recursive Datalog view, called *empl-jones*, as follows.

$$empl\text{-}jones(X) \ :- manager(X, \text{``Jones''} )$$
$$empl\text{-}jones(X) \ :- manager(X, \ Y), \ empl\text{-}jones(Y)$$

The first rule corresponds to case (1); the second rule corresponds to case (2). The view *empl-jones* depends on itself due to the second rule; hence, the preceding Datalog program is recursive. We *assume* that recursive Datalog programs contain no rules with negative literals. The reason will become clear later. The bibliographic notes refer to papers that describe where negation can be used in recursive Datalog programs.

The view relations of a recursive program that contains a set of rules $\mathcal{R}$ are defined to contain exactly the set of facts $I$ computed by the iterative procedure Datalog-Fixpoint shown in Figure 5.8. The recursion in the Datalog program has been turned into an iteration in the procedure. At the end of the procedure, $infer(\mathcal{R}, I) = I$, and $I$ is called a *fixed point* of the program.

Consider the program defining *empl-jones*, with the relation *manager*, as shown in Figure 5.9. The set of facts computed for the view relation *empl-jones*

**procedure** Datalog-Fixpoint
$I$ = set of facts in the database
**repeat**
$Old\_I = I$
$I = I \cup infer(\mathcal{R}, I)$
**until** $I = Old\_I$

Figure 5.8 Datalog-Fixpoint procedure.

in each iteration is shown in Figure 5.10. In each iteration, one more level of employees under Jones is computed, and is added to the set *empl-jones*. The procedure is terminated when there is no change to the set *empl-jones*, which the system detects by finding $I = Old\_I$. Such a termination point must be reached, since the set of managers and employees is finite. On the given *manager* relation, the procedure Datalog-Fixpoint terminates after iteration 4, when it detects that no new facts have been inferred.

You should verify that, at the end of the iteration, the view relation *empl-jones* contains exactly those employees who work under Jones. To print out the names of the employees supervised by Jones defined by the view, you can use the following query:

$$? \ empl\text{-}jones(N)$$

To understand procedure Datalog-Fixpoint, we recall that a rule infers new facts from a given set of facts. Iteration starts with a set of facts $I_0$ set to the facts in the database. These facts are all known to be true, but there may be other facts that are true as well.[†] Next, the set of rules $\mathcal{R}$ in the given Datalog program is used to infer what facts are true, given that facts in $I_0$ are true. We can show that, as long as no rule in the program contains a negative literal, any facts in $infer(\mathcal{R}, I_0)$ also will be present in $infer(\mathcal{R}, J)$ for any set of facts $J$ that contain

| employee-name | manager-name |
|---|---|
| Alon | Barinsky |
| Barinsky | Estovar |
| Corbin | Duarte |
| Duarte | Jones |
| Estovar | Jones |
| Jones | Klinger |
| Rensal | Klinger |

Figure 5.9 The *manager* relation.

---

[†]The word "fact" is used in a technical sense to note membership of a tuple in a relation. Thus, in the Datalog sense of "fact," a fact may be true (the tuple is indeed in the relation) or false (the tuple is not in the relation).

| Iteration number | Tuples in *empl-jones* |
|:---:|:---|
| 0 | |
| 1 | (Duarte), (Estovar) |
| 2 | (Duarte), (Estovar), (Barinsky), (Corbin) |
| 3 | (Duarte), (Estovar), (Barinsky), (Corbin), (Alon) |
| 4 | (Duarte), (Estovar), (Barinsky), (Corbin), (Alon) |

Figure 5.10    Employees of Jones in iterations of procedure Datalog-Fixpoint.

$I_0$. From this assertion, it follows that every fact in $infer(\mathcal{R}, I_0)$ is true, regardless of what other facts also are inferred to be true later.

Let $I_1 = I_0 \cup infer(\mathcal{R}, I_0)$; based on the preceding argument, all facts in $I_1$ are known to be true. Now, $I_1$ corresponds to the value of $I$ in the fixed-point procedure at the end of the first iteration; hence, all the facts inferred by the end of first iteration of the fixed-point procedure are true.

Since facts in $I_1$ are all true, we can deduce that all the facts in $I_2 = I_1 \cup infer(\mathcal{R}, I_1)$ also are true. In general, let

$$I_{i+1} = I_i \cup infer(\mathcal{R}, I_i)$$

The set of facts $I_i$ corresponds to the value of $I$ in the fixed-point procedure, at the end of the $i$th iteration. At each iteration $i$, we can infer that, all facts in $I_i$ are true. Further, it is clear that $I_{i+1} \supseteq I_i$, that is, the set of facts known to be true increases in successive iterations.

For safe Datalog programs, we can show that there will be some point where no more new facts can be derived; that is, for some $k$, $I_{k+1} = I_k$. At this point, then, we have the final set of true facts. Further, given a Datalog program and a database, the fixed-point procedure infers all the facts that can be inferred to be true.

Since procedure Datalog-Fixpoint computes only true facts, so long as no rule in the program has a negative literal, it is said to be *sound* for such programs. Further, it can be shown that the procedure computes all true facts that can be inferred from the given database and Datalog program; hence, procedure Datalog-Fixpoint is also said to be *complete*.

Instead of creating a view for the employees supervised by a specific manager Jones, we can create a more general view relation *empl* that contains every tuple $(X, Y)$ such that $X$ is directly or indirectly managed by $Y$, using the following program (also shown in Figure 5.5):

$$empl(X, Y) \ :- \ manager(X, Y)$$
$$empl(X, Y) \ :- \ manager(X, Z), empl(Z, Y)$$

To find the direct and indirect subordinates of Jones, we simply use the query

$$?\ empl(X, \text{"Jones"})$$

which gives the same set of values for $X$ as the view *empl-jones*. Most Datalog implementations have sophisticated query optimizers and evaluation engines that can run the preceding query at about the same speed as they could evaluate the view *empl-jones*.

The view *empl* defined previously is called the *transitive closure* of the relation *manager*. If the relation *manager* were replaced by any other binary relation $R$, the preceding program would define the transitive closure of $R$.

## 5.3.7    The Power of Recursion

Datalog with recursion has more expressive power than Datalog without recursion. In other words, there are queries on the database that we can answer using recursion, but cannot answer without using it. For example, we cannot express transitive closure in Datalog without using recursion (or for that matter, SQL, QBE or Quel without recursion). Consider the transitive closure of the relation *manager*. Intuitively, a fixed number of joins can find only those employees that are some (other) fixed number of levels down from any manager (we will not attempt to prove this result here). Since any given nonrecursive query has a fixed number of joins, there is a limit on how many levels of employees the query can find. If the number of level of employees in the *manager* relation is more than the limit of the query, the query will miss some levels of employees. Thus, a nonrecursive Datalog program cannot express transitive closure.

An alternative to recursion is to use an external mechanism, such as embedded SQL, to iterate on a nonrecursive query. The iteration in effect implements the fixed-point loop of Figure 5.8. In fact, that is how such queries are implemented on database systems that do not support recursion. However, writing such queries using iteration is more complicated than using recursion, and evaluation using recursion can be optimized to run faster than evaluation using iteration.

The expressive power provided by recursion must be used with care. It is relatively easy to write recursive programs that will generate an infinite number of facts, as the following program illustrates:

$$number(0)$$
$$number(A) \ :- number(B), \ A = B + 1$$

The program generates *number*$(n)$ for all positive $n$, which is clearly infinite, and will not terminate. The second rule of the program does not satisfy the safety condition described in Section 5.3.4. Programs that satisfy the safety condition will terminate, even if they are recursive, provided that all database relations are finite. For such programs, tuples in view relations can contain only constants from the database, and hence the view relations must be finite. The converse is not true; that is, there are programs that do not satisfy the safety conditions, but that do terminate.

The procedure Datalog-Fixpoint iteratively uses the function *infer*$(\mathcal{R}, I)$ to compute what facts are true. Although we considered only the case of Datalog programs without negative literals, the procedure can also be used on views defined using other languages, such as relational algebra, provided that the views satisfy the conditions described next. Regardless of the language used to define a view $V$, the view can be thought of as being defined by an expression $E_V$ that given a set of facts $I$ returns a set of facts $E_V(I)$ for the view relation $V$. Given a set of view definitions $\mathcal{R}$ (in any language), we can define a function $infer(\mathcal{R}, I)$ that returns $I \cup \bigcup_{V \in \mathcal{R}} E_V(I)$. The preceding function is of the same form as the *infer* function for Datalog.

A view $V$ is said to be *monotonic* if, given any two sets of facts $I_1$ and $I_2$ such that $I_1 \subseteq I_2$, then $E_V(I_1) \subseteq E_V(I_2)$, where $E_V$ is the expression used to define $V$. Similarly, the function *infer* is said to be monotonic if

$$I_1 \subseteq I_2 \Rightarrow infer(\mathcal{R}, I_1) \subseteq infer(\mathcal{R}, I_2)$$

Thus, if *infer* is monotonic, given a set of facts $I_0$ that is a subset of the true facts, we can be sure that all facts in $infer(\mathcal{R}, I_0)$ are also true. Using the same reasoning as in Section 5.3.6, we can then show that procedure Datalog-Fixpoint is sound (that is, it computes only true facts) provided that the function *infer* is monotonic.

Relational-algebra expressions that use only the operators $\Pi, \sigma, \times, \bowtie, \cup, \cap$, or $\rho$ are monotonic. Recursive views can be defined using such expressions.

However, relational expressions that use the operator $-$ are not monotonic. For example, let $manager_1$ and $manager_2$ be relations with the same schema as the *manager* relation. Let

$$I_1 = \{ manager_1(\text{``Alon''}, \text{``Barinsky''}), manager_1(\text{``Barinsky''}, \text{``Estovar''}),$$
$$manager_2(\text{``Alon''}, \text{``Barinsky''}) \}$$

and let

$$I_2 = \{ manager_1(\text{``Alon''}, \text{``Barinsky''}), manager_1(\text{``Barinsky''}, \text{``Estovar''}),$$
$$manager_2(\text{``Alon''}, \text{``Barinsky''}), manager_2(\text{``Barinsky''}, \text{``Estovar''}) \}$$

Consider the expression $manager_1 - manager_2$. Now the result of the preceding expression on $I_1$ is (``Barinsky'', ``Estovar''), whereas the result of the expression on $I_2$ is the empty relation. But $I_1 \subseteq I_2$; hence, the expression is not monotonic. Expressions using the grouping operation of extended relational algebra are also nonmonotonic.

The fixed-point technique does not work on recursive views defined with nonmonotonic expressions. However, there are instances where such views are useful, particularly for defining aggregates on part–subpart relationships. Such relationships define of what subparts each part is composed. Subparts themselves may have further subparts, and so on; hence, the relationships, like the manager relationship, have a natural recursive structure. The bibliographic notes provide references to research on defining such views.

It is possible to define some kinds of recursive queries without using views. For example, extended relational operations have been proposed to define transitive closure, and extensions to the SQL syntax to specify (generalized) transitive closure have been proposed. However, recursive view definitions provide more expressive power than do the other forms of recursive queries.

# 5.4  Summary

We have considered three query languages: QBE, Quel, and Datalog. QBE is based on a visual paradigm: The queries look much like tables. QBE and its variants have become popular with nonexpert database users due to the intuitive simplicity of the visual paradigm. Quel is based on the tuple relational calculus, and is similar in many respects to SQL, but avoids much of the latter's complexity. Datalog is derived from Prolog, but unlike Prolog, it has a declarative semantics, making simple queries easier to write and query evaluation easier to optimize. Defining views is particularly easy in Datalog, and the recursive views that Datalog supports makes it possible to write queries, such as transitive-closure queries, that cannot be written without recursion or iteration. However, no accepted standards exist for important features, such as grouping and aggregation, in Datalog. Datalog remains mainly a research language.

# Exercises

**5.1.** Consider the insurance database of Figure 5.11, where the primary keys are specified with leading capital letters. Construct the following QBE queries for this relational-database system.
(*a*) Find the total number of people whose car was involved in an accident in 1989.
(*b*) Find the number of accidents in which at least one car belonging to "John Smith" were involved.
(*c*) Add a new policy holder to the database.
(*d*) Delete the car "Mazda" that belongs to "John Smith."
(*e*) Add a new accident record for the Toyota that belongs to "Williams."

**5.2.** Consider the employee database of Figure 5.12. Give expressions in QBE, Quel, and Datalog for each of the following queries:
(*a*) Find the names of all employees who work for First Bank Corporation.
(*b*) Find the names and cities of residence of all employees who work for First Bank Corporation.
(*c*) Find the names, street addresses, and cities of residence of all employees who work for First Bank Corporation and earn more than $10,000 per annum.
(*d*) Find all employees who live in the city where the company for which they work is located.

*person* (*SS#, name, address*)
*car* (*License, year, model*)
*accident* (*Date, Driver, damage-amount*)
*owns* (*SS#, License*)
*log* (*License, Date, Driver*)

Figure 5.11   Insurance database.

*employee (person-name, street, city)*
*works (person-name, company-name, salary)*
*company (company-name, city)*
*manages (person-name, manager-name)*

Figure 5.12    Employee database.

(e) Find all employees who live in the same city and on the same street as their managers.

(f) Find all employees in the database who do not work for First Bank Corporation.

(g) Find all employees who earn more than every employee of Small Bank Corporation.

(h) Assume that the companies may be located in several cities. Find all companies located in every city in which Small Bank Corporation is located.

**5.3.** Consider the relational database of Figure 5.12. Give expressions in QBE and Quel for each of the following queries:

(a) Find all employees who earn more than the average salary of all employees of their company.

(b) Find the company that has the most employees.

(c) Find the company that has the smallest payroll.

(d) Find those companies whose employees earn a higher salary, on average, than the average salary at First Bank Corporation.

**5.4.** Consider the relational database of Figure 5.12. Give expressions in QBE and Quel for each of the following queries:

(a) Modify the database so that Jones now lives in Newtown.

(b) Give all employees of First Bank Corporation a 10-percent raise.

(c) Give all managers in the database a 10-percent raise.

(d) Give all managers in the database a 10-percent raise, unless the salary would be greater than $100,000. In such cases, give only a 3-percent raise.

(e) Delete all tuples in the *works* relation for employees of Small Bank Corporation.

**5.5.** Let the following relation schemas be given:

$$R = (A, B, C)$$
$$S = (D, E, F)$$

Let relations $r(R)$ and $s(S)$ be given. Give expressions in QBE, Quel, and Datalog equivalent to each of the following queries:

(a) $\Pi_A(r)$

(b) $\sigma_{B = 17}(r)$

(c) $r \times s$

(d) $\Pi_{A,F}(\sigma_{C = D}(r \times s))$

**5.6.** Let $R = (A, B, C)$, and let $r_1$ and $r_2$ both be relations on schema $R$. Give expressions in QBE, Quel, and Datalog equivalent to each of the following queries:

(a) $r_1 \cup r_2$

(b) $r_1 \cap r_2$

(c) $r_1 - r_2$

(d) $\Pi_{AB}(r_1) \bowtie \Pi_{BC}(r_2)$

**5.7.** Let $R = (A, B)$ and $S = (A, C)$, and let $r(R)$ and $s(S)$ be relations. Write expressions in QBE, Quel, and Datalog for each of the following queries:

(a) $\{<a> \mid \exists b (<a, b> \in r \wedge b = 17)\}$

(b) $\{<a, b, c> \mid <a, b> \in r \wedge <a, c> \in s\}$

(c) $\{<a> \mid \exists c (<a, c> \in s \wedge \exists b_1, b_2 (<a, b_1> \in r \wedge <c, b_2> \in r \wedge b_1 > b_2))\}$

**5.8.** In Section 5.2.3, on page 169, we wrote a Quel expression to find all accounts whose balance is higher than the average balance at the branch where the account is held. That query included a use of **by**. Explain what would be retrieved if "**by** *t.branch-name*" were not included in the statement of the query.

**5.9.** Consider the relational database of Figure 5.12. Write a Datalog program for each of the following queries:

(a) Find all employees who work (directly or indirectly) under the manager "Jones".

(b) Find all cities of residence of all employees who work (directly or indirectly) under the manager "Jones".

(c) Find all pairs of employees who have a (direct or indirect) manager in common.

(d) Find all pairs of employees who have a (direct or indirect) manager in common, and are at the same number of levels of supervision below the common manager.

**5.10.** Write an extended relational-algebra view equivalent to the Datalog rule

$$p(A, C, D) :\!- q1(A, B), \ q2(B, C), \ q3(4, B), \ D = B + 1 \, .$$

**5.11.** Describe how an arbitrary Datalog rule can be expressed as an extended relational-algebra view.

## Bibliographical Notes

The experimental version of Query-by-Example is described in Zloof [1977]; the commercial version is described in IBM [1978b]. Numerous database systems— in particular, database systems that run on personal computers—implement QBE or variants. Quel is defined by Stonebraker et al. [1976]. Stonebraker [1986b] provides a collection of research and survey papers related to the Ingres system. Ingres is now owned by Computer Associates.

Implementations of Datalog include LDL system (described in Tsur and Zaniolo [1986] and Naqvi and Tsur [1988]), Nail! (described in Derr et al. [1993]), and Coral (described in Ramakrishnan et al. [1992a, 1993]). Early discussions concerning logic databases were presented in Gallaire and Minker [1978] and in Gallaire et al. [1984]. A collection of selected papers on this subject is given in Minker [1988]. Ullman [1988, 1989] provides extensive textbook discussions of logic query languages and implementation techniques; these are the sources of the Datalog syntax we have used. Ramakrishnan and Ullman [1995] provide a more recent survey on deductive databases. Further coverage of query-processing techniques for Datalog is given by Bancilhon and Ramakrishnan [1986], Beeri and Ramakrishnan [1991], Ramakrishnan et al. [1992b], Srivastava et al. [1995], and Mumick et al. [1996]. Datalog programs that have both recursion and negation can be assigned a simple semantics if the negation is "stratified"—that is, if there is no recursion through negation. Stratified negation is discussed by Chandra and Harel [1982], and by Apt and Pugin [1987]. An important extension, called the *modular-stratification semantics*, which handles a class of recursive programs with negative literals, is discussed in Ross [1990]; an evaluation technique for such programs is described by Ramakrishnan et al. [1992c].

# CHAPTER 6

# INTEGRITY CONSTRAINTS

Integrity constraints provide a means of ensuring that changes made to the database by authorized users do not result in a loss of data consistency. Thus, integrity constraints guard against accidental damage to the database.

We have already seen a form of integrity constraint for the E-R model in Chapter 2. These constraints were in the following forms:

- **Key declarations**—the stipulation that certain attributes form a candidate key for a given entity set. The set of legal insertions and updates is constrained to those that do not create two entities with the same value on a candidate key.
- **Form of a relationship**—many to many, one to many, one to one. A one-to-one or one-to-many relationship restricts the set of legal relationships among entities of a collection of entity sets.

In general, an integrity constraint can be an arbitrary predicate pertaining to the database. However, arbitrary predicates may be costly to test. Thus, we usually limit ourselves to integrity constraints that can be tested with minimal overhead.

## 6.1 Domain Constraints

We have seen that a domain of possible values must be associated with every attribute. In Chapter 4, we saw how such constraints are specified in the SQL DDL. Domain constraints are the most elementary form of integrity constraint. They are tested easily by the system whenever a new data item is entered into the database.

It is possible for several attributes to have the same domain. For example, the attributes *customer-name* and *employee-name* might have the same domain: the set of all person names. However, the domains of *balance* and *branch-name* certainly ought to be distinct. It is perhaps less clear whether *customer-name* and *branch-name* should have the same domain. At the implementation level, both customer names and branch names are character strings. However, we would normally not consider the query "Find all customers who have the same name as a branch" to be a meaningful query. Thus, if we view the database at the conceptual, rather than the physical, level, *customer-name* and *branch-name* should have distinct domains.

From the previous discussion, we can see that a proper definition of domain constraints not only allows us to test values inserted in the database, but also permits us to test queries to ensure that the comparisons made make sense.

The principle behind attribute domains is similar to that behind typing of variables in programming languages. Strongly typed programming languages allow the compiler to check the program in greater detail. However, strongly typed languages inhibit "clever hacks" that are often required for systems programming. Since database systems are designed to support users who are not computer experts, the benefits of strong typing often outweigh the disadvantages. Nevertheless, many existing systems allow only a small number of types of domains. Newer systems, particularly object-oriented database systems, offer a rich set of domain types that can be extended easily. Object-oriented databases are discussed in Chapters 8 and 9.

The **check** clause in SQL-92 permits domains to be restricted in powerful ways that most programming language type systems do not permit. Specifically, the **check** clause permits the schema designer to specify a predicate that must be satisfied by any value assigned to a variable whose type is the domain. For instance, a **check** clause can ensure that an hourly wage domain allows only values greater than a specified value (such as the minimum wage), as illustrated here:

> **create domain** *hourly-wage* **numeric**(5,2)
>     **constraint** *wage-value-test* **check**(**value** $>=$ 4.00)

The domain *hourly-wage* is declared to be a decimal number with a total of five digits, two of which are placed after the decimal point, and the domain has a constraint that ensures that the hourly wage is greater than 4.00. The clause **constraint** *wage-value-test* is optional, and is used to give the name *wage-value-test* to the constraint. The name is used to indicate which constraint an update violated.

The **check** clause can also be used to restrict a domain to not contain any null values, as illustrated here:

> **create domain** *account-number* **char**(10)
>     **constraint** *account-number-null-test* **check**(**value not null** )

As another example, the domain can be restricted to contain only a specified set of values by using the **in** clause:

> **create domain** *account-type* **char**(10)
>     **constraint** *account-type-test*
>         **check**(**value in** ("Checking", "Saving"))

## 6.2   Referential Integrity

Often, we wish to ensure that a value that appears in one relation for a given set of attributes also appears for a certain set of attributes in another relation. This condition is called *referential integrity*.

### 6.2.1   Basic Concepts

Consider a pair of relations $r(R)$ and $s(S)$, and the natural join $r \bowtie s$. There may be a tuple $t_r$ in $r$ that does not join with any tuple in $s$. That is, there is no $t_s$ in $s$ such that $t_r[R \cap S] = t_s[R \cap S]$. Such tuples are called *dangling* tuples. Depending on the entity set or relationship set being modeled, dangling tuples may or may not be acceptable. In Section 3.5.2, we considered a modified form of join—the outer join—to operate on relations containing dangling tuples. Here, our concern is not with queries, but rather with the matter of when we are willing to permit dangling tuples to exist in the database.

Suppose there is a tuple $t_1$ in the *account* relation with $t_1[branch\text{-}name] =$ "Lunartown," but there is no tuple in the *branch* relation for the Lunartown branch. This situation would be undesirable. We expect the *branch* relation to list all bank branches. Therefore, tuple $t_1$ would refer to an account at a branch that does not exist. Clearly, we would like to have an integrity constraint that prohibits dangling tuples of this sort.

Not all instances of dangling tuples are undesirable, however. Assume that there is a tuple $t_2$ in the *branch* relation with $t_2[branch\text{-}name] =$ "Mokan," but there is no tuple in the *account* relation for the Mokan branch. In this case, a branch exists that has no accounts. Although this situation is not common, it may arise when a branch is opened or is about to close. Thus, we do not want to prohibit this situation.

The distinction between these two examples arises from two facts:

- The attribute *branch-name* in *Account-schema* is a foreign key referencing the primary key of *Branch-schema*.
- The attribute *branch-name* in *Branch-schema* is not a foreign key.

(Recall from Section 3.1.3 that a foreign key is a set of attributes in a relation schema that forms a primary key for another schema.)

In the Lunartown example, tuple $t_1$ in *account* has a value on the foreign key *branch-name* that does not appear in *branch*. In the Mokan-branch example, tuple $t_2$ in *branch* has a value on *branch-name* that does not appear in *account*, but *branch-name* is not a foreign key. Thus, the distinction between our two examples of dangling tuples is the presence of a foreign key.

Let $r_1(R_1)$ and $r_2(R_2)$ be relations with primary keys $K_1$ and $K_2$, respectively. We say that a subset $\alpha$ of $R_2$ is a *foreign key* referencing $K_1$ in relation $r_1$ if it is required that, for every $t_2$ in $r_2$, there must be a tuple $t_1$ in $r_1$ such that $t_1[K_1] = t_2[\alpha]$. Requirements of this form are called *referential integrity constraints*, or *subset dependencies*. The latter term arises because the preceding referential-integrity constraint can be written as $\Pi_\alpha (r_2) \subseteq \Pi_{K_1} (r_1)$. Note that, for a referential-integrity constraint to make sense, either $\alpha$ must be equal to $K_1$, or $\alpha$ and $K_1$ must be compatible sets of attributes.

## 6.2.2    Referential Integrity in the E-R Model

Referential-integrity constraints arise frequently. If we derive our relational-database schema by constructing tables from E-R diagrams, as we saw in Chapter 2, then every relation arising from a relationship set has referential-integrity constraints. Figure 6.1 shows an N-ary relationship set $R$, relating entity sets $E_1$, $E_2$, ..., $E_n$. Let $K_i$ denote the primary key of $E_i$. The attributes of the relation schema for relationship set $R$ include $K_1 \cup K_2 \cup \ldots \cup K_n$. Each $K_i$ in the schema for $R$ is a foreign key that leads to a referential-integrity constraint.

Another source of referential-integrity constraints is weak entity sets. Recall from Chapter 2 that the relation schema for a weak entity set must include the primary key of the entity set on which the weak entity set depends. Thus, the relation schema for each weak entity set includes a foreign key that leads to a referential-integrity constraint.

## 6.2.3    Database Modification

Database modifications can cause violations of referential integrity. We list here the test that we must make for each type of database modification to preserve the following referential-integrity constraint:

$$\Pi_\alpha (r_2) \subseteq \Pi_K (r_1)$$

- Insert. If a tuple $t_2$ is inserted into $r_2$, the system must ensure that there is a tuple $t_1$ in $r_1$ such that $t_1[K] = t_2[\alpha]$. That is,

$$t_2[\alpha] \in \Pi_K (r_1)$$

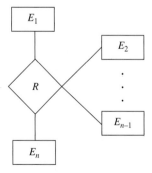

Figure 6.1    An N-ary relationship set.

- Delete. If a tuple $t_1$ is deleted from $r_1$, the system must compute the set of tuples in $r_2$ that reference $t_1$:

$$\sigma_{\alpha \,=\, t_1[K]}\,(r_2)$$

If this set is not empty, either the delete command is rejected as an error, or the tuples that reference $t_1$ must themselves be deleted. The latter solution may lead to cascading deletions, since tuples may reference tuples that reference $t_1$, and so on.

- Update. We must consider two cases for update: updates to the referencing relation $(r_2)$, and updates to the referenced relation $(r_1)$.
  - If a tuple $t_2$ is updated in relation $r_2$, and the update modifies values for the foreign key $\alpha$, then a test similar to the insert case is made. Let $t_2'$ denote the new value of tuple $t_2$. The system must ensure that

$$t_2'[\alpha] \;\in\; \Pi_K\,(r_1)$$

  - If a tuple $t_1$ is updated in $r_1$, and the update modifies values for the primary key $(K)$, then a test similar to the delete case is made. The system must compute

$$\sigma_{\alpha \,=\, t_1[K]}\,(r_2)$$

using the old value of $t_1$ (the value before the update is applied). If this set is not empty, the update is rejected as an error, or the update is cascaded in a manner similar to delete.

## 6.2.4   Referential Integrity in SQL

Primary and candidate keys and foreign keys can be specified as part of the SQL **create table** statement:

- The **primary key** clause of the **create table** statement includes a list of the attributes that constitute the primary key.
- The **unique** clause of the **create table** statement includes a list of the attributes that constitute a candidate key.
- The **foreign key** clause of the **create table** statement includes both a list of the attributes that constitute the foreign key and the name of the relation referenced by the foreign key.

We illustrate primary- and foreign-key declarations using the partial SQL DDL definition of our bank database shown in Figure 6.2. Note that, as in earlier chapters, we do not attempt to model precisely the real world in the bank-database example. In the real world, multiple people may have the same name, so *customer-name* would not be a primary key for *customer*. In the real world, some other attribute, such as the social-security number, or a combination of attributes such as name and address, would be used as a primary key. We use *customer-name* as a primary key to keep our database schema simple and short.

**create table** *customer*
    (*customer-name*    **char**(20) **not null**,
    *customer-street*    **char**(30),
    *customer-city*    **char**(30),
    **primary key** (*customer-name*))

**create table** *branch*
    (*branch-name*    **char**(15) **not null**,
    *branch-city*    **char**(30),
    *assets*    **integer**,
    **primary key** (*branch-name*),
    **check** (*assets* $>= 0$))

**create table** *account*
    (*account-number*    **char**(10) **not null**,
    *branch-name*    **char**(15),
    *balance*    **integer**,
    **primary key** (*account-number*),
    **foreign key** (*branch-name*) **references** *branch*,
    **check** (*balance* $>= 0$))

**create table** *depositor*
    (*customer-name*    **char**(20) **not null**,
    *account-number*    **char**(10) **not null**,
    **primary key** (*customer-name*, *account-number*),
    **foreign key** (*customer-name*) **references** *customer*,
    **foreign key** (*account-number*) **references** *account*)

Figure 6.2    SQL data definition for part of the bank database.

We can use the following short form to declare that a single column is a foreign key:

    *branch-name*        **char**(15) **references** *branch*

SQL also supports a version of the foreign-key clause where a list of attributes of the referenced relation can be specified explicitly, and these attributes are used instead of the primary key; the specified list of attributes must be declared as a candidate key of the referenced relation.

When a referential-integrity constraint is violated, the normal procedure is to reject the action that caused the violation. However, a **foreign key** clause in SQL-92 can specify that, if a delete or update action on the referenced relation violates the constraint, then, instead of rejecting the action, steps are to be taken to change the tuple in the referencing relation to restore the constraint. Consider the following definition of an integrity constraint on the relation *account*:

> **create table** *account*
> ( ...
>    **foreign key** (*branch-name*) **references** *branch*
>            **on delete cascade**
>            **on update cascade**,
>
> ... )

Due to the clause **on delete cascade** associated with the foreign-key declaration, if a delete of a tuple in *branch* results in the preceding referential-integrity constraint being violated, the delete is not rejected. Instead, the delete "cascades" to the *account* relation, deleting the tuple that refers to the branch that was deleted. Similarly, an update to a field referenced by the constraint is not rejected if it violates the constraint; instead, the field *branch-name* in the referencing tuples in *account* are updated to the new value as well. SQL-92 also allows the **foreign key** clause to specify actions other than cascade, such as setting the referencing field (here, *branch-name*) to null, or to a default value, if the constraint is violated.

    If there is a chain of foreign-key dependencies across multiple relations, a deletion or update at one end of the chain can propagate across the entire chain. An interesting case where the **foreign key** constraint on a relation references the same relation is considered in Exercise 6.4. If a cascading update or delete causes a constraint violation that cannot be handled by a further cascading operation, the system aborts the transaction. As a result, all the changes caused by the transaction and its cascading actions are undone.

    The semantics of the keys in SQL is complicated by the fact that SQL allows null values. The following rules, some of which are arbitrary, are used to deal with null values:

- All attributes of the primary key are implicitly declared to be **not null**.

- Attributes of a **unique** declaration (that is, attributes of a candidate key) are allowed to be null, provided that they have not otherwise been declared to be nonnull. The uniqueness constraint on a relation is violated only if two tuples in the relation have the same values for all the attributes in a **unique** constraint, and all the values are nonnull. Thus, any number of tuples can be equal on all columns declared to be unique without violating the constraint, provided that at least one of the columns has a null value. The treatment of nulls here is the same as that of the **unique** construct defined in Section 4.6.4.

- Attributes of foreign keys are allowed to be null, provided that they have not otherwise been declared to be nonnull. If all the columns of a foreign key are nonnull in a given tuple, the usual definition of foreign-key constraints is used for that tuple. If any of the foreign-key columns is null, the tuple is defined automatically to satisfy the constraint. This definition is arbitrary and may not always be the right choice, so SQL also provides constructs that allow you to change the behavior with null values; we do not discuss the constructs here.

Given the complexity and arbitrary nature of the way constraints in SQL behave with null values, it is best to ensure that all columns of **unique** and **foreign key** specifications are declared to be nonnull.

# 6.3   Assertions

An *assertion* is a predicate expressing a condition that we wish the database always to satisfy. Domain constraints and referential-integrity constraints are special forms of assertions. We have paid substantial attention to these forms of assertion because they are easily tested and apply to a wide range of database applications. However, there are many constraints that we cannot express using only these special forms. Examples of such constraints include

- The sum of all loan amounts for each branch must be less than the sum of all account balances at the branch.
- Every loan has at least one customer who maintains an account with a minimum balance of $1000.00.

An assertion in SQL-92 takes the form

   **create assertion** <assertion-name> **check** <predicate>

The two constraints mentioned can be written as shown next. Since SQL does not provide a "for all $X$, $P(X)$" construct (where $P$ is a predicate), we are forced to implement the construct using then equivalent "not exists $X$ such that not $P(X)$" construct, which can be written in SQL.

**create assertion** *sum-constraint* **check**
    (**not exists** (**select** * **from** *branch*
        **where** (**select sum**(*amount*) **from** *loan*
            **where** *loan.branch-name* $=$ *branch.branch-name*)
        $>=$ (**select sum**(*amount*) **from** *account*
            **where** *account.branch-name* $=$ *branch.branch-name*)))

**create assertion** *balance-constraint* **check**
    (**not exists** (**select** * **from** *loan*
        **where not exists** ( **select** *
            **from** *borrower, depositor, account*
            **where** *loan.loan-number* $=$ *borrower.loan-number*
                **and** *borrower.customer-name* $=$ *depositor.customer-name*
                **and** *depositor.account-number* $=$ *account.account-number*
                **and** *account.balance* $>=$ 1000)))

When an assertion is created, the system tests it for validity. If the assertion is valid, then any future modification to the database is allowed only if it does not cause that assertion to be violated. This testing may introduce a significant amount of overhead if complex assertions have been made. Hence, assertions should be used with great care. The high overhead of testing and maintaining assertions has led some system developers to omit support for general assertions, or to provide specialized forms of assertions that are easier to test.

## 6.4 Triggers

A *trigger* is a statement that is executed automatically by the system as a side effect of a modification to the database. To design a trigger mechanism, we must meet two requirements:

1. Specify the conditions under which the trigger is to be executed.
2. Specify the actions to be taken when the trigger executes.

Triggers are useful mechanisms for alerting humans, or for performing certain tasks automatically when certain conditions are met. As an illustration, suppose that, instead of allowing negative account balances, the bank deals with overdrafts by setting the account balance to zero, and creating a loan in the amount of the overdraft. This loan is given a loan number identical to the account number of the overdrawn account. For this example, the condition for executing the trigger is an update to the *account* relation that results in a negative *balance* value. Suppose that Jones withdrew some money from an account that resulted in the account balance being negative. Let $t$ denote the account tuple with a negative *balance* value. The actions to be taken are as follows:

- Insert a new tuple $s$ in the *loan* relation with

$$s[branch\text{-}name] = t[branch\text{-}name]$$
$$s[loan\text{-}number] = t[account\text{-}number]$$
$$s[amount] = -t[balance]$$

  (Note that, since $t[balance]$ is negative, we negate $t[balance]$ to get the loan amount—a positive number.)
- Insert a new tuple $u$ in the *borrower* relation with

$$u[customer\text{-}name] = \text{"Jones"}$$
$$u[loan\text{-}number] = t[account\text{-}number]$$

- Set $t[balance]$ to 0.

The SQL-92 standard does not include triggers, although the original System R SQL proposal included a limited trigger feature. Several existing systems have their own nonstandard trigger features. Here, we illustrate how the account-overdraft trigger would be written in the original version of SQL:

> **define trigger** *overdraft* **on update of** *account T*
>    (**if new** *T.balance* < 0
>    **then** (**insert into** *loan* **values**
>                   (*T.branch-name, T.account-number*, − **new** *T.balance*)
>            **insert into** *borrower*
>                   (**select** *customer-name, account-number*
>                    **from** *depositor*
>                    **where** *T.account-number* = *depositor.account-number*)
>            **update** *account S*
>            **set** *S.balance* = 0
>            **where** *S.account-number* = *T.account-number*))

The keyword **new** used before *T.balance* indicates that the value of *T.balance* after the update should be used; if it is omitted, the value before the update is used.

Triggers are sometimes called *rules*, or *active rules*, but should not be confused with Datalog rules (see Section 5.3), which are really view definitions.

## 6.5   Functional Dependencies

This section focuses on a particular kind of constraint called a *functional dependency*. The notion of functional dependency is a generalization of the notion of *key*, as discussed in Chapters 2 and 3. Functional dependencies play an important role in database design, which we study in Chapter 7.

### 6.5.1   Basic Concepts

Functional dependencies are constraints on the set of legal relations. They allow us to express facts about the enterprise that we are modeling with our database.

In Chapter 2, we defined the notion of a *superkey* as follows. Let $R$ be a relation schema. A subset $K$ of $R$ is a *superkey* of $R$ if, in any legal relation $r(R)$, for all pairs $t_1$ and $t_2$ of tuples in $r$ such that $t_1 \neq t_2$, then $t_1[K] \neq t_2[K]$. That is, no two tuples in any legal relation $r(R)$ may have the same value on attribute set $K$.

The notion of functional dependency generalizes the notion of superkey. Let $\alpha \subseteq R$ and $\beta \subseteq R$. The *functional dependency*

$$\alpha \rightarrow \beta$$

holds on $R$ if, in any legal relation $r(R)$, for all pairs of tuples $t_1$ and $t_2$ in $r$ such that $t_1[\alpha] = t_2[\alpha]$, it is also the case that $t_1[\beta] = t_2[\beta]$.

Using the functional-dependency notation, we say that $K$ is a superkey of $R$ if $K \rightarrow R$. That is, $K$ is a superkey if, whenever $t_1[K] = t_2[K]$, it is also the case that $t_1[R] = t_2[R]$ (that is, $t_1 = t_2$).

Functional dependencies allow us to express constraints that we cannot express using superkeys. Consider the schema

> *Loan-info-schema* = (*branch-name, loan-number, customer-name, amount*).

The set of functional dependencies that we expect to hold on this relation schema is

$$loan\text{-}number \rightarrow amount$$
$$loan\text{-}number \rightarrow branch\text{-}name$$

We would not, however, expect the functional dependency

$$loan\text{-}number \rightarrow customer\text{-}name$$

to hold, since, in general, a given loan can be made to more than one customer (for example, to both members of a husband–wife pair).

We shall use functional dependencies in two ways:

1. We use them to specify constraints on the set of legal relations. We shall thus concern ourselves with *only* those relations that satisfy a given set of functional dependencies. If we wish to constrain ourselves to relations on schema $R$ that satisfy a set $F$ of functional dependencies, we say that $F$ *holds* on $R$.

2. We use them to test relations to see whether the latter are legal under a given set of functional dependencies. If a relation $r$ is legal under a set $F$ of functional dependencies, we say that $r$ *satisfies* $F$.

Let us consider the relation $r$ of Figure 6.3, to see which functional dependencies are satisfied. Observe that $A \rightarrow C$ is satisfied. There are two tuples that have an $A$ value of $a_1$. These tuples have the same $C$ value—namely, $c_1$. Similarly, the two tuples with an $A$ value of $a_2$ have the same $C$ value, $c_2$. There are no other pairs of distinct tuples that have the same $A$ value. The functional dependency $C \rightarrow A$ is not satisfied, however. To see that is is not, consider the tuples $t_1 = (a_2, b_3, c_2, d_3)$ and $t_2 = (a_3, b_3, c_2, d_4)$. These two tuples have the same $C$ values, $c_2$, but they have different $A$ values, $a_2$ and $a_3$, respectively. Thus, we have found a pair of tuples $t_1$ and $t_2$ such that $t_1[C] = t_2[C]$, but $t_1[A] \neq t_2[A]$.

Many other functional dependencies are satisfied by $r$, including, for example, the functional dependency $AB \rightarrow D$. Note that we use $AB$ as a shorthand for $\{A,B\}$, to conform with standard practice. Observe that there is no pair of distinct tuples $t_1$ and $t_2$ such that $t_1[AB] = t_2[AB]$. Therefore, if $t_1[AB] = t_2[AB]$, it must be that $t_1 = t_2$ and, thus, $t_1[D] = t_2[D]$. So, $r$ satisfies $AB \rightarrow D$.

| $A$ | $B$ | $C$ | $D$ |
|-----|-----|-----|-----|
| $a_1$ | $b_1$ | $c_1$ | $d_1$ |
| $a_1$ | $b_2$ | $c_1$ | $d_2$ |
| $a_2$ | $b_2$ | $c_2$ | $d_2$ |
| $a_2$ | $b_3$ | $c_2$ | $d_3$ |
| $a_3$ | $b_3$ | $c_2$ | $d_4$ |

Figure 6.3    Sample relation $r$.

| customer-name | customer-street | customer-city |
|---------------|-----------------|---------------|
| Jones         | Main            | Harrison      |
| Smith         | North           | Rye           |
| Hayes         | Main            | Harrison      |
| Curry         | North           | Rye           |
| Lindsay       | Park            | Pittsfield    |
| Turner        | Putnam          | Stamford      |
| Williams      | Nassau          | Princeton     |
| Adams         | Spring          | Pittsfield    |
| Johnson       | Alma            | Palo Alto     |
| Glenn         | Sand Hill       | Woodside      |
| Brooks        | Senator         | Brooklyn      |
| Green         | Walnut          | Stamford      |

Figure 6.4    The *customer* relation.

Some functional dependencies are said to be *trivial* because they are satisfied by all relations. For example, $A \rightarrow A$ is satisfied by all relations involving attribute $A$. Reading the definition of functional-dependency literally, we see that, for all tuples $t_1$ and $t_2$ such that $t_1[A] = t_2[A]$, it is the case that $t_1[A] = t_2[A]$. Similarly, $AB \rightarrow A$ is satisfied by all relations involving attribute $A$. In general, a functional dependency of the form $\alpha \rightarrow \beta$ is trivial if $\beta \subseteq \alpha$.

To distinguish between the concepts of a relation satisfying a dependency and a dependency holding on a schema, we return to the banking example. If we consider the *customer* relation (on *Customer-schema*) as shown in Figure 6.4, we see that *customer-street* $\rightarrow$ *customer-city* is satisfied. However, we believe that, in the real world, two cities can have streets with the same name. Thus, it is possible, at some time, to have an instance of the *customer* relation in which *customer-street* $\rightarrow$ *customer-city* is not satisfied. So, we would not include *customer-street* $\rightarrow$ *customer-city* in the set of functional dependencies that hold on *Customer-schema*.

In the *loan* relation (on *Loan-schema*) of Figure 6.5, we see that *loan-number* $\rightarrow$ *amount* is satisfied. Unlike the case of *customer-city* and *customer-street* in *Customer-schema*, we do believe that the real-world enterprise that we are modeling requires each loan to have only one amount. Therefore, we want to require that *loan-number* $\rightarrow$ *amount* be satisfied by the *loan* relation at all times. In other words, we require that the constraint that *loan-number* $\rightarrow$ *amount* hold on *Loan-schema*.

In the *branch* relation of Figure 6.6, we see that *branch-name* $\rightarrow$ *assets* is satisfied, as is *assets* $\rightarrow$ *branch-name*. We want to require that *branch-name* $\rightarrow$ *assets* hold on *Branch-schema*. However, we do not wish to require that *assets* $\rightarrow$ *branch-name* hold, since it is possible to have several branches that have the same asset value.

Although SQL does not provide a simple way of specifying functional dependencies, we can write queries to test for functional dependencies, as well as

| branch-name | loan-number | amount |
|-------------|-------------|--------|
| Downtown | L-17 | 1000 |
| Redwood | L-23 | 2000 |
| Perryridge | L-15 | 1500 |
| Downtown | L-14 | 1500 |
| Mianus | L-93 | 500 |
| Round Hill | L-11 | 900 |
| Pownal | L-29 | 1200 |
| North Town | L-16 | 1300 |
| Downtown | L-18 | 2000 |
| Perryridge | L-25 | 2500 |
| Brighton | L-10 | 2200 |

Figure 6.5   The *loan* relation.

to create assertions that enforce functional dependencies, as discussed in Exercise 6.19.

In what follows, we assume that, when we design a relational database, we first list those functional dependencies that must always hold. In the banking example, our list of dependencies includes the following:

- On *Branch-schema*:

$$branch\text{-}name \rightarrow branch\text{-}city$$
$$branch\text{-}name \rightarrow assets$$

- On *Customer-schema*:

$$customer\text{-}name \rightarrow customer\text{-}city$$
$$customer\text{-}name \rightarrow customer\text{-}street$$

- On *Loan-schema*:

$$loan\text{-}number \rightarrow amount$$
$$loan\text{-}number \rightarrow branch\text{-}name$$

| branch-name | branch-city | assets |
|-------------|-------------|--------|
| Downtown | Brooklyn | 9000000 |
| Redwood | Palo Alto | 2100000 |
| Perryridge | Horseneck | 1700000 |
| Mianus | Horseneck | 400000 |
| Round Hill | Horseneck | 8000000 |
| Pownal | Bennington | 300000 |
| North Town | Rye | 3700000 |
| Brighton | Brooklyn | 7100000 |

Figure 6.6   The *branch* relation.

- On *Borrower-schema*:

  no functional dependencies

- On *Account-schema*:

  $account\text{-}number \rightarrow branch\text{-}name$
  $account\text{-}number \rightarrow balance$

- On *Depositor-schema*:

  no functional dependencies

## 6.5.2   Closure of a Set of Functional Dependencies

It is not sufficient to consider the given set of functional dependencies. Rather, we need to consider *all* functional dependencies that hold. We shall see that, given a set $F$ of functional dependencies, we can prove that certain other functional dependencies hold. We say that such functional dependencies are *logically implied* by $F$.

Suppose we are given a relation schema $R = (A, B, C, G, H, I)$ and the set of functional dependencies

$$A \rightarrow B$$
$$A \rightarrow C$$
$$CG \rightarrow H$$
$$CG \rightarrow I$$
$$B \rightarrow H$$

The functional dependency

$$A \rightarrow H$$

is logically implied. That is, we can show that, whenever our given set of functional dependencies holds, $A \rightarrow H$ must hold also. Suppose that $t_1$ and $t_2$ are tuples such that

$$t_1[A] = t_2[A]$$

Since we are given that $A \rightarrow B$, it follows from the definition of functional dependency that

$$t_1[B] = t_2[B]$$

Then, since we are given that $B \rightarrow H$, it follows from the definition of functional dependency that

$$t_1[H] = t_2[H]$$

Therefore, we have shown that, whenever $t_1$ and $t_2$ are tuples such that $t_1[A] = t_2[A]$, it must be that $t_1[H] = t_2[H]$. But that is exactly the definition of $A \rightarrow H$.

Let $F$ be a set of functional dependencies. The closure of $F$ is the set of all functional dependencies logically implied by $F$. We denote the *closure* of $F$ by $F^+$. Given $F$, we can compute $F^+$ directly from the formal definition of functional dependency. If $F$ were large, this process would be lengthy and difficult. Such a computation of $F^+$ requires arguments of the type given previously to show that $A \rightarrow H$ is in the closure of our example set of dependencies. There are simpler techniques for reasoning about functional dependencies.

The first technique is based on three *axioms* or rules of inference for functional dependencies. By applying these rules repeatedly, we can find all of $F^+$ given $F$. In the rules that follow, we adopt the convention of using Greek letters ($\alpha$, $\beta$, $\gamma$, ...) for sets of attributes, and uppercase Roman letters from the beginning of the alphabet for individual attributes. We use $\alpha\beta$ to denote $\alpha \cup \beta$.

- **Reflexivity rule**. If $\alpha$ is a set of attributes and $\beta \subseteq \alpha$, then $\alpha \rightarrow \beta$ holds.
- **Augmentation rule**. If $\alpha \rightarrow \beta$ holds and $\gamma$ is a set of attributes, then $\gamma\alpha \rightarrow \gamma\beta$ holds.
- **Transitivity rule**. If $\alpha \rightarrow \beta$ holds and $\beta \rightarrow \gamma$ holds, then $\alpha \rightarrow \gamma$ holds.

These rules are *sound*, because they do not generate any incorrect functional dependencies. The rules are *complete*, because, for a given set $F$ of functional dependencies, they allow us to generate all $F^+$. This collection of rules is called *Armstrong's axioms* in honor of the person who first proposed it.

Although Armstrong's axioms are complete, it is tiresome to use them directly for the computation of $F^+$. To simplify matters further, we list additional rules. It is possible to use Armstrong's axioms to prove that these rules are correct (see Exercises 6.12, 6.13, and 6.14).

- **Union rule**. If $\alpha \rightarrow \beta$ holds and $\alpha \rightarrow \gamma$ holds, then $\alpha \rightarrow \beta\gamma$ holds.
- **Decomposition rule**. If $\alpha \rightarrow \beta\gamma$ holds, then $\alpha \rightarrow \beta$ holds and $\alpha \rightarrow \gamma$ holds.
- **Pseudotransitivity rule**. If $\alpha \rightarrow \beta$ holds and $\gamma\beta \rightarrow \delta$ holds, then $\alpha\gamma \rightarrow \delta$ holds.

Let us apply our rules to the example that we presented earlier of schema $R = (A, B, C, G, H, I)$ and the set $F$ of functional dependencies $\{A \rightarrow B, A \rightarrow C, CG \rightarrow H, CG \rightarrow I, B \rightarrow H\}$. We list several members of $F^+$ here:

- $A \rightarrow H$. Since $A \rightarrow B$ and $B \rightarrow H$ holds, we apply the transitivity rule. Observe that it was much easier to use Armstrong's axioms to show that $A \rightarrow H$ holds than it was to argue directly from the definitions, as we did earlier.
- $CG \rightarrow HI$. Since $CG \rightarrow H$ and $CG \rightarrow I$, the union rule implies that $CG \rightarrow HI$.
- $AG \rightarrow I$. Since $A \rightarrow C$ and $CG \rightarrow I$, the pseudotransitivity rule implies that $AG \rightarrow I$ holds.

### 6.5.3 Closure of Attribute Sets

To test whether a set $\alpha$ is a superkey, we must devise an algorithm for computing the set of attributes functionally determined by $\alpha$. We shall see that such an algorithm is useful also as part of the computation of the closure of a set $F$ of functional dependencies.

Let $\alpha$ be a set of attributes. We call the set of all attributes functionally determined by $\alpha$ under a set $F$ of functional dependencies the *closure* of $\alpha$ under $F$; we denote it by $\alpha^+$. Figure 6.7 shows an algorithm, written in pseudo-Pascal, to compute $\alpha^+$. The input is a set $F$ of functional dependencies and the set $\alpha$ of attributes. The output is stored in the variable *result*.

To illustrate how the algorithm of Figure 6.7 works, we shall use the algorithm to compute $(AG)^+$ with the functional dependencies defined previously. We start with *result* = $AG$. The first time that we execute the **while** loop to test each functional dependency, we find that

- $A \rightarrow B$ causes us to include $B$ in *result*. To see this fact, we observe that $A \rightarrow B$ is in $F$, $A \subseteq result$ (which is $AG$), so $result := result \cup B$.
- $A \rightarrow C$ causes *result* to become $ABCG$.
- $CG \rightarrow H$ causes *result* to become $ABCGH$.
- $CG \rightarrow I$ causes *result* to become $ABCGHI$.

The second time that we execute the **while** loop, no new attributes are added to *result*, and the algorithm terminates.

Let us see why the algorithm of Figure 6.7 is correct. The first step is correct, since $\alpha \rightarrow \alpha$ always holds (by the reflexivity rule). We claim that, for any subset $\beta$ of *result*, $\alpha \rightarrow \beta$. Since we start the **while** loop with $\alpha \rightarrow result$ being true, we can add $\gamma$ to *result* only if $\beta \subseteq result$ and $\beta \rightarrow \gamma$. But then $result \rightarrow \beta$ by the reflexivity rule, so $\alpha \rightarrow \beta$ by transitivity. Another application of transitivity shows that $\alpha \rightarrow \gamma$ (using $\alpha \rightarrow \beta$ and $\beta \rightarrow \gamma$). The union rule implies that $\alpha \rightarrow result \cup \gamma$, so $\alpha$ functionally determines any new result generated in the **while** loop. Thus, any attribute returned by the algorithm is in $\alpha^+$.

It is easy to see that the algorithm finds all $\alpha^+$. If there is an attribute in $\alpha^+$ that is not yet in *result*, then there must be a functional dependency $\beta \rightarrow \gamma$ for which $\beta \subseteq result$, and at least one attribute in $\gamma$ is not in *result*.

It turns out that, in the worst case, this algorithm may take time quadratic in the size of $F$. There is a faster (although slightly more complex) algorithm that runs in time linear in the size of $F$; that algorithm is presented as part of Exercise 6.18.

```
result := α;
while (changes to result) do
        for each functional dependency β → γ in F do
            begin
                if β ⊆ result then result := result ∪ γ;
            end
```

Figure 6.7    An algorithm to compute $\alpha^+$, the closure of $\alpha$ under $F$.

## 6.5.4  Canonical Cover

Suppose that we have a set of functional dependencies $F$ on a relation schema. Whenever an update is performed on the relation, the database system must ensure that all the functional dependencies in $F$ are satisfied in the new database state, and must rollback the update if they are not. We can reduce the effort required to perform the test by simplifying the given set of functional dependencies without changing that set's closure. Any database that satisfies the simplified set of functional dependencies will also satisfy the original set, and vice versa, since the two sets have the same closure. However, the simplified set is easier to test. The simplified set can be constructed as we shall describe in a moment. First, we need some definitions.

An attribute of a functional dependency is *extraneous* if we can remove it without changing the closure of the set of functional dependencies. Formally, extraneous attributes are defined as follows. Consider a set $F$ of functional dependencies and the functional dependency $\alpha \rightarrow \beta$ in $F$.

- Attribute $A$ is extraneous in $\alpha$ if $A \in \alpha$, and $F$ logically implies $(F - \{\alpha \rightarrow \beta\}) \cup \{(\alpha - A) \rightarrow \beta\}$.
- Attribute $A$ is extraneous in $\beta$ if $A \in \beta$, and the set of functional dependencies $(F - \{\alpha \rightarrow \beta\}) \cup \{\alpha \rightarrow (\beta - A)\}$ logically implies $F$.

A *canonical cover* $F_c$ for $F$ is a set of dependencies such that $F$ logically implies all dependencies in $F_c$, and $F_c$ logically implies all dependencies in $F$. Furthermore, $F_c$ must have the following properties:

- No functional dependency in $F_c$ contains an extraneous attribute.
- Each left side of a functional dependency in $F_c$ is unique. That is, there are no two dependencies $\alpha_1 \rightarrow \beta_1$ and $\alpha_2 \rightarrow \beta_2$ in $F_c$ such that $\alpha_1 = \alpha_2$.

A canonical cover for a set of functional dependencies $F$ can be computed as follows:

**repeat**
       Use the union rule to replace any dependencies in $F$ of the form
           $\alpha_1 \rightarrow \beta_1$ and $\alpha_1 \rightarrow \beta_2$ with $\alpha_1 \rightarrow \beta_1 \beta_2$.
       Find a functional dependency $\alpha \rightarrow \beta$ with an extraneous
          attribute either in $\alpha$ or in $\beta$.
       If an extraneous attribute is found, delete it from $\alpha \rightarrow \beta$.
**until** $F$ does not change.

The canonical cover of $F$, $F_c$, can be shown to have the same closure as $F$; hence, testing whether $F_c$ is satisfied is equivalent to testing whether $F$ is satisfied. However, $F_c$ is minimal in a certain sense—it does not contain extraneous attributes, and functional dependencies with the same left side have been combined. It is cheaper to test $F_c$ than it is to test $F$ itself.

Consider the following set $F$ of functional dependencies on schema $(A, B, C)$:

$$A \rightarrow BC$$
$$B \rightarrow C$$
$$A \rightarrow B$$
$$AB \rightarrow C$$

Let us compute the canonical cover for $F$.

- There are two functional dependencies with the same set of attributes on the left side of the arrow:

$$A \rightarrow BC$$
$$A \rightarrow B$$

We combine these functional dependencies into $A \rightarrow BC$.

- $A$ is extraneous in $AB \rightarrow C$ because $F$ logically implies $(F - \{AB \rightarrow C\}) \cup \{B \rightarrow C\}$. This assertion is true because $B \rightarrow C$ is already in our set of functional dependencies.

- $C$ is extraneous in $A \rightarrow BC$, since $A \rightarrow BC$ is logically implied by $A \rightarrow B$ and $B \rightarrow C$.

Thus, our canonical cover is

$$A \rightarrow B$$
$$B \rightarrow C$$

Given a set $F$ of functional dependencies, it may be that an entire functional dependency in the set is extraneous, in the sense that dropping it does not change the closure of $F$. We can show that a canonical cover $F_c$ of $F$ contains no such extraneous functional dependency. Suppose that, to the contrary, there was such an extraneous functional dependency in $F_c$. The right side attributes of the dependency would then be extraneous, which is not possible by the definition of canonical covers.

## 6.6    Summary

Integrity constraints ensure that changes made to the database by authorized users do not result in a loss of data consistency. In earlier chapters, we considered several forms of constraints, including key declarations and the declaration of the form of a relationship (many to many, many to one, one to one). In this chapter, we considered several additional forms of constraints, and discussed mechanisms for ensuring the maintenance of these constraints.

Domain constraints specify the set of possible values that may be associated with an attribute. Such constraints may also prohibit the use of null values for particular attributes.

Referential-integrity constraints ensure that a value that appears in one relation for a given set of attributes also appears for a certain set of attributes in another relation.

Functional dependencies are a generalization of key dependencies. They require that the value for a certain set of attributes determines uniquely the value for another set of attributes. Using the formal definition of functional dependencies, we saw how to determine the set of all functional dependencies logically implied by a given set $F$ of functional dependencies. This set is called the closure of $F$. We also saw a way to reduce the size of a set $F$ of functional dependencies without changing the closure. This set is called a canonical cover $F_c$ for $F$.

Domain constraints, referential-integrity constraints, and functional dependencies are relatively easy to test. Use of more complex constraints may lead to substantial overhead. We saw two ways to express more general constraints. Assertions are declarative expressions that state predicates that we require always to be true. Triggers are procedures to be executed when certain events occur.

## Exercises

**6.1.** Complete the SQL DDL definition of the bank database of Figure 6.2 to include the relations *loan* and *borrower*.

**6.2.** Consider the following relational database:

> *employee (person-name, street, city)*
> *works (person-name, company-name, salary)*
> *company (company-name, city)*
> *manages (person-name, manager-name)*

Give an SQL DDL definition of this database. Identify referential-integrity constraints that should hold, and include them in the DDL definition.

**6.3.** Referential-integrity constraints as defined in this chapter involve exactly two relations. Consider a database that includes the following relations:

> *salaried-worker (name, office, phone, salary)*
> *hourly-worker (name, hourly-wage)*
> *address (name, street, city)*

Suppose that we wish to require that every name that appears in *address* appear in either *salaried-worker* or *hourly-worker*, but not necessarily in both.

(*a*) Propose a syntax for expressing such constraints.

(*b*) Discuss the actions that the system must take to enforce a constraint of this form.

**6.4.** The SQL-92 standard allows a foreign-key dependency to refer to the same relation, as in the following example:

> **create table** *manager*
>   (*employee-name*   **char**(20) **not null**
>   *manager-name*   **char**(20) **not null**,
>   **primary key** *employee-name*,
>   **foreign key** (*manager-name*) **references** *manager*
>                           **on delete cascade** )

Here, *employee-name* is a key to the table *manager*, meaning that each employee has at most one manager. The foreign-key clause requires that every manager also be an employee. Explain exactly what happens when a tuple in the relation *manager* is deleted.

**6.5.** Suppose there are two relations $r$ and $s$, such that the foreign key $B$ of $r$ references the primary key $A$ of $s$. Describe how the trigger mechanism can be used to implement the **on delete cascade** option, when a tuple is deleted from $s$.

**6.6.** Write an assertion for the bank database to ensure that the assets value for the Perryridge branch is equal to the sum of all the amounts lent by the Perryridge branch.

**6.7.** Why are certain functional dependencies called *trivial* functional dependencies?

**6.8.** List all functional dependencies satisfied by the relation of Figure 6.8.

**6.9.** Use the definition of functional dependency to argue that each of Armstrong's axioms (reflexivity, augmentation, and transitivity) is sound.

**6.10.** Explain how functional dependencies can be used to indicate the following:
- A one-to-one relationship set exists between entity sets *student* and *advisor*.
- A many-to-one relationship set exists between entity sets *student* and *advisor*.

**6.11.** Consider the following proposed rule for functional dependencies: If $\alpha \rightarrow \beta$ and $\gamma \rightarrow \beta$, then $\alpha \rightarrow \gamma$. Prove that this rule is *not* sound by showing a relation $r$ that satisfies $\alpha \rightarrow \beta$ and $\gamma \rightarrow \beta$, but does not satisfy $\alpha \rightarrow \gamma$.

**6.12.** Use Armstrong's axioms to prove the soundness of the union rule. (Hint: Use the augmentation rule to show that, if $\alpha \rightarrow \beta$, then $\alpha \rightarrow \alpha\beta$. Apply the augmentation rule again, using $\alpha \rightarrow \gamma$, and then apply the transitivity rule.)

**6.13.** Use Armstrong's axioms to prove the soundness of the decomposition rule.

**6.14.** Use Armstrong's axioms to prove the soundness of the pseudotransitivity rule.

| A | B | C |
|---|---|---|
| $a_1$ | $b_1$ | $c_1$ |
| $a_1$ | $b_1$ | $c_2$ |
| $a_2$ | $b_1$ | $c_1$ |
| $a_2$ | $b_1$ | $c_3$ |

Figure 6.8    Relation of Exercise 6.8.

**6.15.** Compute the closure of the following set $F$ of functional dependencies for relation schema $R = (A, B, C, D, E)$.

$$A \rightarrow BC$$
$$CD \rightarrow E$$
$$B \rightarrow D$$
$$E \rightarrow A$$

List the candidate keys for $R$.

**6.16.** Using the functional dependencies of Exercise 6.15, compute $B^+$.

**6.17.** Using the functional dependencies of Exercise 6.15, compute the canonical cover $F_c$.

**6.18.** Consider the algorithm shown in Figure 6.9 to compute $\alpha^+$. Show that this algorithm is more efficient than is the one presented in Figure 6.7 (Section 6.5.3) and that it computes $\alpha^+$ correctly.

**6.19.** Given the database schema $R(a, b, c)$, and a relation $r$ on the schema $R$, write an SQL query to test whether the functional dependency $b \rightarrow c$ holds on relation $r$. Also write an SQL assertion that enforces the functional dependency. Assume that no null values are present.

## Bibliographical Notes

Discussions concerning integrity constraints in the relational model are offered by Hammer and McLeod [1975], Stonebraker [1975], Eswaran and Chamberlin [1975], Schmid and Swenson [1975], and Codd [1979].

Functional dependencies were originally defined by Codd [1970]. Armstrong's axioms were introduced by Armstrong [1974]. The theory of functional dependencies is discussed in Maier [1983]. Formal aspects of the concept of a legal relation are discussed by Graham et al. [1986]. Application of functional dependencies to semantic data models is discussed in Weddell [1992].

The original SQL proposals for assertions and triggers are discussed in Astrahan et al. [1976], Chamberlin et al. [1976], and Chamberlin et al. [1981]. See the bibliographic notes of Chapter 4 for references to SQL standards.

Discussions concerning efficient maintenance and checking of semantic-integrity assertions is offered by Hammer and Sarin [1978], Badal and Popek [1979], Bernstein et al. [1980b], Hsu and Imielinski [1985], McCune and Henschen [1989], and Chomicki [1992a, 1992b]. Active databases are discussed in McCarthy and Dayal [1989], Gehani and Jagadish [1991], and Gehani et al. [1992].

An alternative to using run-time integrity checking is certifying the correctness of programs that access the database. This approach is discussed by Sheard and Stemple [1989].

```
result := ∅;
/* fdcount is an array whose ith element contains the number
   of attributes on the left side of the ith FD that are
   not yet known to be in α⁺ */
for i := 1 to |F| do
   begin
      let β → γ denote the ith FD;
      fdcount [i] := |β|;
   end
/* appears is an array with one entry for each attribute. The
   entry for attribute A is a list of integers. Each integer
   i on the list indicates that A appears on the left side
   of the ith FD */
for each attribute A do
   begin
      appears [A] := NIL;
      for i := 1 to |F| do
         begin
            let β → γ denote the ith FD;
            if A ∈ β then add i to appears [A];
         end
   end
addin (α);
return (result);

procedure addin (α);
for each attribute A in α do
   begin
      if A ∉ result then
         begin
            result := result ∪ {A};
            for each element i of appears[A] do
               begin
                  fdcount [i] := fdcount [i] − 1;
                  if fdcount [i] := 0 then
                     begin
                        let β → γ denote the ith FD;
                        addin (γ);
                     end
               end
         end
   end
```

Figure 6.9    An algorithm to compute $\alpha^+$.

# CHAPTER
# 7

# RELATIONAL
# DATABASE
# DESIGN

This chapter continues our discussion of design issues in relational databases. In general, the goal of a relational-database design is to generate a set of relation schemas that allows us to store information without unnecessary redundancy, yet also allows us to retrieve information easily. One approach is to design schemas that are in an appropriate *normal form*. To determine whether a relation schema is in one of the normal forms, we need additional information about the real-world enterprise that we are modeling with the database. We have already seen how we can use functional dependencies to express facts about the data. In this chapter, we define normal forms using functional dependencies and using other types of data dependencies.

## 7.1 Pitfalls in Relational-Database Design

Before we begin our discussion of normal forms and data dependencies, let us look at what can go wrong in a bad database design. Among the undesirable properties that a bad design may have are

- Repetition of information
- Inability to represent certain information

We shall discuss these problems using a modified database design for our banking example; in contrast to the relation schema used in Chapters 3 to 6, the information concerning loans is now kept in one single relation, *lending*, which is defined

| branch-name | branch-city | assets | customer-name | loan-number | amount |
|---|---|---|---|---|---|
| Downtown | Brooklyn | 9000000 | Jones | L-17 | 1000 |
| Redwood | Palo Alto | 2100000 | Smith | L-23 | 2000 |
| Perryridge | Horseneck | 1700000 | Hayes | L-15 | 1500 |
| Downtown | Brooklyn | 9000000 | Jackson | L-14 | 1500 |
| Mianus | Horseneck | 400000 | Jones | L-93 | 500 |
| Round Hill | Horseneck | 8000000 | Turner | L-11 | 900 |
| Pownal | Bennington | 300000 | Williams | L-29 | 1200 |
| North Town | Rye | 3700000 | Hayes | L-16 | 1300 |
| Downtown | Brooklyn | 9000000 | Johnson | L-23 | 2000 |
| Perryridge | Horseneck | 1700000 | Glenn | L-25 | 2500 |
| Brighton | Brooklyn | 7100000 | Brooks | L-10 | 2200 |

Figure 7.1    Sample *lending* relation.

over the relation schema

*Lending-schema* = (*branch-name, branch-city, assets, customer-name, loan-number, amount*)

Figure 7.1 shows an instance of the relation *lending* (*Lending-schema*). A tuple *t* in the *lending* relation has the following intuitive meaning:

- *t*[*assets*] is the asset figure for the branch named *t*[*branch-name*].
- *t*[*branch-city*] is the city in which the branch named *t*[*branch-name*] is located.
- *t*[*loan-number*] is the number assigned to a loan made by the branch named *t*[*branch-name*] to the customer named *t*[*customer-name*].
- *t*[*amount*] is the amount of the loan whose number is *t*[*loan-number*].

Suppose that we wish to add a new loan to our database. Say that the loan is made by the Perryridge branch to Adams in the amount of $1500. Let the *loan-number* be L-31. In our design, we need a tuple with values on all the attributes of *Lending-schema*. Thus, we must repeat the asset and city data for the Perryridge branch, and must add the tuple

(Perryridge, Horseneck, 1700000, Adams, L-31, 1500)

to the *lending* relation. In general, the asset and city data for a branch must appear once for each loan made by that branch.

The repetition of information required by the use of our alternative design is undesirable. Repeating information wastes space. Furthermore, it complicates updating the database. Suppose, for example, that the Perryridge branch moves from Horseneck to Newtown. Under our original design, one tuple of the *branch* relation needs to be changed. Under our alternative design, many tuples of the *lending* relation need to be changed. Thus, updates are more costly under the alternative design than under the original design. When we perform the update in the alternative database, we must ensure that *every* tuple pertaining to the Perryridge branch is updated, or else our database will show two cities for the Perryridge branch.

That observation is central to understanding why the alternative design is bad. We know that a bank branch is located in exactly one city. On the other hand, we know that a branch may make many loans. In other words, the functional dependency

$$branch\text{-}name \rightarrow branch\text{-}city$$

holds on *Lending-schema*, but we do not expect the functional dependency *branch-name* → *loan-number* to hold. The fact that a branch is located in a city and the fact that a branch makes a loan are independent, and, as we have seen, these facts are best represented in separate relations. We shall see that we can use functional dependencies to specify formally when a database design is good.

Another problem with the *Lending-schema* design is that we cannot represent directly the information concerning a branch (*branch-name*, *branch-city*, *assets*) unless there exists at least one loan at the branch. The problem is that tuples in the *lending* relation require values for *loan-number*, *amount*, and *customer-name*.

One solution to this problem is to introduce *null values* to handle updates through views. Recall, however, that null values are difficult to handle. If we are not willing to deal with null values, then we can create the branch information only when the first loan application at that branch is made. Worse, we would have to delete this information when all the loans have been paid. Clearly, this situation is undesirable, since, under our original database design, the branch information would be available regardless of whether or not loans are currently maintained in the branch, and without resorting to the use of null values.

## 7.2 Decomposition

The example of Section 7.1 of a bad design suggests that we should *decompose* a relation schema that has many attributes into several schemas with fewer attributes. Careless decomposition, however, may lead to another form of bad design.

Consider an alternative design in which *Lending-schema* is decomposed into the following two schemas:

*Branch-customer-schema* = (*branch-name, branch-city, assets, customer-name*)
*Customer-loan-schema* = (*customer-name, loan-number, amount*)

Using the *lending* relation of Figure 7.1, we construct our new relations *branch-customer* (*Branch-customer*) and *customer-loan* (*Customer-loan-schema*) as follows:

$$branch\text{-}customer = \Pi_{branch\text{-}name,\ branch\text{-}city,\ assets,\ customer\text{-}name}\ (lending)$$
$$customer\text{-}loan = \Pi_{customer\text{-}name,\ loan\text{-}number,\ amount}\ (lending)$$

We show the resulting *branch-customer* and *customer-name* relations in Figures 7.2 and 7.3, respectively.

| branch-name | branch-city | assets | customer-name |
|-------------|-------------|--------|---------------|
| Downtown | Brooklyn | 9000000 | Jones |
| Redwood | Palo Alto | 2100000 | Smith |
| Perryridge | Horseneck | 1700000 | Hayes |
| Downtown | Brooklyn | 9000000 | Jackson |
| Mianus | Horseneck | 400000 | Jones |
| Round Hill | Horseneck | 8000000 | Turner |
| Pownal | Bennington | 300000 | Williams |
| North Town | Rye | 3700000 | Hayes |
| Downtown | Brooklyn | 9000000 | Johnson |
| Perryridge | Horseneck | 1700000 | Glenn |
| Brighton | Brooklyn | 7100000 | Brooks |

Figure 7.2    The relation *branch-customer*.

Of course, there are cases in which we need to reconstruct the *loan* relation. For example, suppose that we wish to find all branches that have loans with amounts less than $1000. No relation in our alternative database contains these data. We need to reconstruct the *lending* relation. It appears that we can do so by writing

$$branch\text{-}customer \bowtie customer\text{-}loan$$

Figure 7.4 shows the result of computing *branch-customer* $\bowtie$ *customer-loan*. When we compare this relation and the *lending* relation with which we started (Figure 7.1), we notice some differences. Although every tuple that appears in *lending* appears in *branch-customer* $\bowtie$ *customer-loan*, there are tuples in *branch-customer* $\bowtie$ *customer-loan* that are not in *lending*. In our example,

| customer-name | loan-number | amount |
|---------------|-------------|--------|
| Jones | L-17 | 1000 |
| Smith | L-23 | 2000 |
| Hayes | L-15 | 1500 |
| Jackson | L-14 | 1500 |
| Jones | L-93 | 500 |
| Turner | L-11 | 900 |
| Williams | L-29 | 1200 |
| Hayes | L-16 | 1300 |
| Johnson | L-23 | 2000 |
| Glenn | L-25 | 2500 |
| Brooks | L-10 | 2200 |

Figure 7.3    The relation *customer-loan*.

| branch-name | branch-city | assets | customer-name | loan-number | amount |
|---|---|---|---|---|---|
| Downtown | Brooklyn | 9000000 | Jones | L-17 | 1000 |
| Downtown | Brooklyn | 9000000 | Jones | L-93 | 500 |
| Redwood | Palo Alto | 2100000 | Smith | L-23 | 2000 |
| Perryridge | Horseneck | 1700000 | Hayes | L-15 | 1500 |
| Perryridge | Horseneck | 1700000 | Hayes | L-16 | 1300 |
| Downtown | Brooklyn | 9000000 | Jackson | L-14 | 1500 |
| Mianus | Horseneck | 400000 | Jones | L-17 | 1000 |
| Mianus | Horseneck | 400000 | Jones | L-93 | 500 |
| Round Hill | Horseneck | 8000000 | Turner | L-11 | 900 |
| Pownal | Bennington | 300000 | Williams | L-29 | 1200 |
| North Town | Rye | 3700000 | Hayes | L-15 | 1500 |
| North Town | Rye | 3700000 | Hayes | L-16 | 1300 |
| Downtown | Brooklyn | 9000000 | Johnson | L-23 | 2000 |
| Perryridge | Horseneck | 1700000 | Glenn | L-25 | 2500 |
| Brighton | Brooklyn | 7100000 | Brooks | L-10 | 2200 |

Figure 7.4   The relation *branch-customer* ⋈ *customer-loan*.

*branch-customer* ⋈ *customer-loan* has the following additional tuples:

> (Downtown, Brooklyn, 9000000, Jones, L-93, 500)
> (Perryridge, Horseneck, 1700000, Hayes, L-16, 1300)
> (Mianus, Horseneck, 400000, Jones, L-17, 1000)
> (North Town, Rye, 3700000, Hayes, L-15, 1500)

Consider the query, "Find all branches that have made a loan in an amount less than \$1000." If we look back at Figure 7.1, we see that the only branches with loan amounts less than \$1000 are Mianus and Round Hill. However, when we apply the expression

$$\Pi_{branch\text{-}name} \ (\sigma_{amount \ < \ 1000} \ (branch\text{-}customer \ \bowtie \ customer\text{-}loan))$$

we obtain *three* branch names: Mianus, Round Hill, and Downtown.

Let us examine this example more closely. If a customer happens to have several loans from different branches, we cannot tell which loan belongs to which branch. Thus, when we join *branch-customer* and *customer-loan*, we obtain not only the tuples we had originally in *lending*, but also several additional tuples. Although we have *more* tuples in *branch-customer* ⋈ *customer-loan*, we actually have *less* information. We are no longer able, in general, to represent in the database information about which customers are borrowers from which branch. Because of this loss of information, we call the decomposition of *Lending-schema* into *Branch-customer-schema* and *customer-loan-schema* a *lossy decomposition*, or a *lossy-join decomposition*. A decomposition that is not a lossy-join decomposition is a *lossless-join decomposition*. It should be clear from our example that a lossy-join decomposition is, in general, a bad database design.

Let us examine the decomposition more closely to see why it is lossy. There is one attribute in common between *Branch-customer-schema* and *Customer-loan-schema*:

$$Branch\text{-}customer\text{-}schema \cap Customer\text{-}loan\text{-}schema = \{customer\text{-}name\}$$

The only way that we can represent a relationship between, for example, *loan-number* and *branch-name* is through *customer-name*. This representation is not adequate because a customer may have several loans, yet these loans are not necessarily obtained from the same branch.

Let us consider another alternative design, in which *Lending-schema* is decomposed into the following two schemas:

*Branch-schema* = (branch-name, branch-city, assets)
*Loan-info-schema* = (branch-name, customer-name, loan-number, amount)

There is one attribute in common between these two schemas:

$$Branch\text{-}loan\text{-}schema \cap Customer\text{-}loan\text{-}schema = \{branch\text{-}name\}$$

Thus, the only way that we can represent a relationship between, for example, *customer-name* and *assets* is through *branch-name*. The difference between this example and the preceding one is that the assets of a branch are the same, regardless of the customer to which we are referring, whereas the lending branch associated with a certain loan amount *does* depend on the customer to which we are referring. For a given *branch-name*, there is exactly one *assets* value and exactly one *branch-city*; whereas a similar statement cannot be made for *customer-name*. That is, the functional dependency

$$branch\text{-}name \rightarrow assets\ branch\text{-}city$$

holds, but *customer-name* does not functionally determine *loan-number*.

The notion of lossless joins is central to much of relational-database design. Therefore, we restate the preceding examples more concisely and more formally. Let $R$ be a relation schema. A set of relation schemas $\{R_1, R_2, \ldots, R_n\}$ is a *decomposition* of $R$ if

$$R = R_1 \cup R_2 \cup \ldots \cup R_n$$

That is, $\{R_1, R_2, \ldots, R_n\}$ is a decomposition of $R$ if, for $i = 1, 2, \ldots, n$, each $R_i$ is a subset of $R$, and every attribute in $R$ appears in at least one $R_i$.

Let $r$ be a relation on schema $R$, and let $r_i = \Pi_{R_i}(r)$ for $i = 1, 2, \ldots, n$. That is, $\{r_1, r_2, \ldots, r_n\}$ is the database that results from decomposing $R$ into $\{R_1, R_2, \ldots, R_n\}$. It is always the case that

$$r \subseteq r_1 \bowtie r_2 \bowtie \ldots \bowtie r_n$$

To see that this assertion is true, consider a tuple $t$ in relation $r$. When we compute the relations $r_1, r_2, \ldots, r_n$, the tuple $t$ gives rise to one tuple $t_i$ in each $r_i$, $i = 1, 2, \ldots, n$. These $n$ tuples combine to regenerate $t$ when we compute

$r_1 \bowtie r_2 \bowtie \ldots \bowtie r_n$. The details are left for you to complete as an exercise. Therefore, every tuple in $r$ appears in $r_1 \bowtie r_2 \bowtie \ldots \bowtie r_n$.

In general, $r \neq r_1 \bowtie r_2 \bowtie \ldots \bowtie r_n$. As an illustration, consider our earlier example, in which

- $n = 2$.
- $R = Lending\text{-}schema$.
- $R_1 = Branch\text{-}customer\text{-}schema$.
- $R_2 = Customer\text{-}loan\text{-}schema$.
- $r =$ the relation shown in Figure 7.1.
- $r_1 =$ the relation shown in Figure 7.2.
- $r_2 =$ the relation shown in Figure 7.3.
- $r_1 \bowtie r_2 =$ the relation shown in Figure 7.4.

Note that the relations in Figures 7.1 and 7.4 are not the same.

To have a lossless-join decomposition, we need to impose constraints on the set of possible relations. We found that the decomposition of *Lending-schema* into *Branch-schema* and *Loan-info-schema* is lossless because the functional dependency

$$branch\text{-}name \rightarrow branch\text{-}city \ assets$$

holds on *Branch-schema*.

Later in this chapter, we shall introduce constraints other than functional dependencies. We say that a relation is *legal* if it satisfies all rules, or constraints, that we impose on our database.

Let $C$ represent a set of constraints on the database. A decomposition $\{R_1, R_2, \ldots, R_n\}$ of a relation schema $R$ is a *lossless-join decomposition* for $R$ if, for all relations $r$ on schema $R$ that are legal under $C$,

$$r = \Pi_{R_1}(r) \bowtie \Pi_{R_2}(r) \bowtie \ldots \bowtie \Pi_{R_n}(r)$$

We shall show how to test whether a decomposition is a lossless-join decomposition in the next few sections. A major part of this chapter is concerned with the questions of how to specify constraints on the database, and how to obtain lossless-join decompositions that avoid the pitfalls represented by the examples of bad database designs that we have seen in this section.

## 7.3    Normalization Using Functional Dependencies

We can use a given set of functional dependencies in designing a relational database in which most of the undesirable properties discussed in Section 7.1 do not occur. When we design such systems, it may become necessary to decompose a relation into several smaller relations. Using functional dependencies, we can define several *normal forms* that represent "good" database designs. There are many normal forms. The ones that we shall cover here are BCNF (Section 7.3.2) and 3NF (Section 7.3.3).

## 7.3.1    Desirable Properties of Decomposition

In this subsection, we shall illustrate our concepts by considering the *Lending-schema* schema of Section 7.1:

*Lending-schema* = (*branch-name, branch-city, assets, customer-name, loan-number, amount*)

The set *F* of functional dependencies that we require to hold on *Lending-schema* are

*branch-name* → *assets branch-city*
*loan-number* → *amount branch-name*

As we discussed in Section 7.1, the *Lending-schema* is an example of a bad database design. Assume that we decompose it to the following three relations:

*Branch-schema* = (*branch-name, assets, branch-city*)
*Loan-schema* = (*branch-name, loan-number, amount*)
*Borrower-schema* = (*customer-name, loan-number*)

We claim that this decomposition has several desirable properties, which we discuss next. Note that these three relation schemas are precisely the ones that we used previously, in Chapters 3 through 5.

### 7.3.1.1    Lossless-Join Decomposition

In Section 7.1, we argued that, when decomposing a relation into a number of smaller relations, it is crucial that the decomposition be lossless. We claim that the decomposition in Section 7.3.1 is indeed lossless. To demonstrate our claim, we must first present a criterion for determining whether a decomposition is lossy.

Let *R* be a relation schema, and let *F* be a set of functional dependencies on *R*. Let $R_1$ and $R_2$ form a decomposition of *R*. This decomposition is a lossless-join decomposition of *R* if at least one of the following functional dependencies are in $F^+$:

- $R_1 \cap R_2 \rightarrow R_1$
- $R_1 \cap R_2 \rightarrow R_2$

We now show that our decomposition of *Lending-schema* is a lossless-join decomposition by showing a sequence of steps that generate the decomposition. We begin by decomposing *Lending-schema* into two schemas:

*Branch-schema* = (*branch-name, branch-city, assets*)
*Loan-info-schema* = (*branch-name, customer-name, loan-number, amount*)

Since *branch-name* → *branch-city assets*, the augmentation rule for functional dependencies (Section 6.5.2) implies that

*branch-name* → *branch-name branch-city assets*

Since *Branch-schema* ∩ *Loan-info-schema* = {*branch-name*}, it follows that our initial decomposition is a lossless-join decomposition.

Next, we decompose *Loan-info-schema* into

$$Loan\text{-}schema = (branch\text{-}name, loan\text{-}number, amount)$$
$$Borrower\text{-}schema = (customer\text{-}name, loan\text{-}number)$$

This step results in a lossless-join decomposition, since *loan-number* is a common attribute and *loan-number* → *amount branch-name*.

## 7.3.1.2  Dependency Preservation

There is another goal in relational-database design: *dependency preservation*. When an update is made to the database, the system should be able to check that the update will not create an illegal relation—that is, one that does not satisfy all the given functional dependencies. If we are to check updates efficiently, we should design relational-database schemas that allow update validation without the computation of joins.

To decide whether joins must be computed, we need to determine what functional dependencies may be tested by checking each relation individually. Let $F$ be a set of functional dependencies on a schema $R$, and let $R_1, R_2, \ldots, R_n$ be a decomposition of $R$. The *restriction* of $F$ to $R_i$ is the set $F_i$ of all functional dependencies in $F^+$ that include *only* attributes of $R_i$. Since all functional dependencies in a restriction involve attributes of only one relation schema, it is possible to test satisfaction of such a dependency by checking only one relation.

The set of restrictions $F_1, F_2, \ldots, F_n$ is the set of dependencies that can be checked efficiently. We now must ask whether testing only the restrictions is sufficient. Let $F' = F_1 \cup F_2 \cup \ldots \cup F_n$. $F'$ is a set of functional dependencies on schema $R$, but, in general, $F' \neq F$. However, even if $F' \neq F$, it may be that $F'^+ = F^+$. If the latter is true, then every dependency in $F$ is logically implied by $F'$, and, if we verify that $F'$ is satisfied, we have verified that $F$ is satisfied. We say that a decomposition having the property $F'^+ = F^+$ is a *dependency-preserving* decomposition. Figure 7.5 shows an algorithm for testing dependency preservation. The input is a set $D = \{R_1, R_2, \ldots, R_n\}$ of decomposed relation schemas, and a set $F$ of functional dependencies.

We can now show that our decomposition of *Lending-schema* is dependency preserving. We consider each member of the set $F$ of functional dependencies that we require to hold on *Lending-schema*, and show that each one can be tested in at least one relation in the decomposition.

- We can test the functional dependency: *branch-name* → *branch-city assets* using *Branch-schema* = (*branch-name, branch-city, assets*).
- We can test the functional dependency: *loan-number* → *amount branch-name* using *Loan-schema* = (*branch-name, loan-number, amount*).

As the preceding example shows, it is often easier not to apply the algorithm of

compute $F^+$;
**for each** schema $R_i$ in $D$ **do**
    **begin**
        $F_i :=$ the restriction of $F^+$ to $R_i$;
    **end**
$F' := \emptyset$
**for each** restriction $F_i$ **do**
    **begin**
        $F' = F' \cup F_i$
    **end**
compute $F'^+$;
**if** ($F'^+ = F^+$) **then** return (true)
                **else** return (false);

Figure 7.5     Testing for dependency preservation.

Figure 7.5 to test dependency preservation, since the first step—computation of $F^+$—takes exponential time.

### 7.3.1.3    Repetition of Information

The decomposition of *Lending-schema* does not suffer from the problem of repetition of information that we discussed in Section 7.1. In *Lending-schema*, it was necessary to repeat the city and assets of a branch for each loan. The decomposition separates branch and loan data into distinct relations, thereby eliminating this redundancy. Similarly, observe that, if a single loan is made to several customers, we must repeat the amount of the loan once for each customer (as well as the city and assets of the branch). In the decomposition, the relation on schema *Borrower-schema* contains the *loan-number*, *customer-name* relationship, and no other schema does. Therefore, we have one tuple for each customer for a loan in only the relation on *Borrower-schema*. In the other relations involving *loan-number* (those on schemas *Loan-schema* and *Borrower-schema*), only one tuple per loan needs to appear.

Clearly, the lack of redundancy exhibited by our decomposition is desirable. The degree to which we can achieve this lack of redundancy is represented by several *normal forms*, which we shall discuss in the remainder of this chapter.

### 7.3.2    Boyce–Codd Normal Form

One of the more desirable normal forms that we can obtain is *Boyce–Codd normal form* (*BCNF*). A relation schema $R$ is in BCNF with respect to a set $F$ of functional dependencies if for all functional dependencies in $F^+$ of the form $\alpha \rightarrow \beta$, where $\alpha \subseteq R$ and $\beta \subseteq R$, at least one of the following holds:

- $\alpha \rightarrow \beta$ is a trivial functional dependency (that is, $\beta \subseteq \alpha$).
- $\alpha$ is a superkey for schema $R$.

A database design is in BCNF if each member of the set of relation schemas that constitutes the design is in BCNF.

As an illustration, let us consider the following relation schemas, and their respective functional dependencies:

- *Customer-schema* = (*customer-name, customer-street, customer-city*)
    *customer-name* → *customer-street customer-city*
- *Branch-schema* = (*branch-name, assets, branch-city*)
    *branch-name* → *assets branch-city*
- *Loan-info-schema* = (*branch-name, customer-name, loan-number, amount*)
    *loan-number* → *amount branch-name*

We claim that *Customer-schema* is in BCNF. We note that a candidate key for the schema is *customer-name*. The only nontrivial functional dependencies that hold on *Customer-schema* have *customer-name* on the left side of the arrow. Since *customer-name* is a candidate key, functional dependencies with *customer-name* on the left side do not violate the definition of BCNF. Similarly, it can be shown easily that the relation schema *Branch-schema* is in BCNF.

The schema, *Loan-info-schema*, however, is *not* in BCNF. First, note that *loan-number* is not a superkey for *Loan-info-schema*, since we *could* have a pair of tuples representing a single loan made to two people—for example,

(Downtown, Mr. Bell, L-44, 1000)
(Downtown, Ms. Bell, L-44, 1000)

Because we did not list functional dependencies that rule out the preceding case, *loan-number* is not a candidate key. However, the functional dependency *loan-number* → *amount* is nontrivial. Therefore, *Loan-info-schema* does not satisfy the definition of BCNF.

We claim that *Loan-info-schema* is not in a desirable form, since it suffers from the problem of *repetition of information* that we described in Section 7.1. We observe that, if there are several customer names associated with a loan, in a relation on *Loan-info-schema*, then we are forced to repeat the branch name and the amount once for each customer. We can eliminate this redundancy by redesigning our database such that all schemas are in BCNF. One approach to this problem is to take the existing non-BCNF design as a starting point, and to decompose those schemas that are not in BCNF. Consider the decomposition of *Loan-info-schema* into two schemas:

Loan-schema = (*branch-name, loan-number, amount*)
Borrower-schema = (*customer-name, loan-number*)

This decomposition is a lossless-join decomposition.

*result* := {*R*};
*done* := false;
compute $F^+$;
**while** (**not** *done*) **do**
    **if** (there is a schema $R_i$ in *result* that is not in BCNF)
      **then begin**
             let $\alpha \rightarrow \beta$ be a nontrivial functional dependency that holds
             on $R_i$ such that $\alpha \rightarrow R_i$ is not in $F^+$, and $\alpha \cap \beta = \emptyset$;
             *result* := (*result* − $R_i$) ∪ ($R_i$ − $\beta$) ∪ ($\alpha, \beta$);
      **end**
    **else** *done* := true;

Figure 7.6     BCNF decomposition algorithm.

To determine whether these schemas are in BCNF, we need to determine what functional dependencies apply to them. In this example, it is easy to see that

$$loan\text{-}number \rightarrow amount\ branch\text{-}name$$

applies to *Loan-schema*, and that only trivial functional dependencies apply to *Borrower-schema*. Although *loan-number* is not a superkey for *Loan-info-schema*, it is a candidate key for *Loan-schema*. Thus, both schemas of our decomposition are in BCNF.

It is now possible to avoid redundancy in the case where there are several customers associated with a loan. There is exactly one tuple for each loan in the relation on *Loan-schema*, and one tuple for each customer of each loan in the relation on *Borrower-schema*. Thus, we do not have to repeat the branch name and the amount once for each customer associated with a loan.

We are now able to state a general method to generate a collection of BCNF schemas. If *R* is not in BCNF, we can decompose *R* into a collection of BCNF schemas $R_1, R_2, \ldots, R_n$ using the algorithm of Figure 7.6, which generates not only a BCNF decomposition, but also a lossless-join decomposition. To see why our algorithm generates only lossless-join decompositions, we note that, when we replace a schema $R_i$ with ($R_i$ − $\beta$) and ($\alpha, \beta$), the dependency $\alpha \rightarrow \beta$ holds, and ($R_i$ − $\beta$) ∩ ($\alpha, \beta$) = $\alpha$.

Let us apply the BCNF decomposition algorithm to the *Lending-schema* schema that we used in Section 7.1 as an example of a poor database design:

*Lending-schema* = (*branch-name, branch-city, assets, customer-name,*
                  *loan-number, amount*)

The set of functional dependencies that we require to hold on *Lending-schema* are

$$branch\text{-}name \rightarrow assets\ branch\text{-}city$$
$$loan\text{-}number \rightarrow amount\ branch\text{-}name$$

A candidate key for this schema is {*loan-number, customer-name*}.

We can apply the algorithm of Figure 7.6 to the *Lending-schema* example as follows:

- The functional dependency

$$branch\text{-}name \rightarrow assets \; branch\text{-}city$$

  holds on *Lending-schema*, but *branch-name* is not a superkey. Thus, *Lending-schema* is not in BCNF. We replace *Lending-schema* by

  *Branch-schema* = (*branch-name, branch-city, assets*)
  *Loan-info-schema* = (*branch-name, customer-name, loan-number, amount*)

- The only nontrivial functional dependencies that hold on *Branch-schema* include *branch-name* on the left side of the arrow. Since *branch-name* is a key for *Branch-schema*, the relation *Branch-schema* is in BCNF.
- The functional dependency

$$loan\text{-}number \rightarrow amount \; branch\text{-}name$$

  holds on *Loan-info-schema*, but *loan-number* is not a key for *Loan-info-schema*. We replace *Loan-info-schema* by

  *Loan-schema* = (*branch-name, loan-number, amount*)
  *Borrower-schema* = (*customer-name, loan-number*)

- *Loan-schema* and *Borrower-schema* are in BCNF.

Thus, the decomposition of *Lending-schema* results in the three relation schemas *Branch-schema*, *Loan-schema*, and *Borrower-schema*, each of which is in BCNF. These relation schemas are the same as those used in Section 7.3.1. We demonstrated in that section that the resulting decomposition is both a lossless-join decomposition and a dependency-preserving decomposition.

Not every BCNF decomposition is dependency preserving. As an illustration, consider the relation schema

*Banker-schema* = (*branch-name, customer-name, banker-name*)

which indicates that a customer has a "personal banker" in a particular branch. The set *F* of functional dependencies that we require to hold on the *Banker-schema* is

$$banker\text{-}name \rightarrow branch\text{-}name$$
$$branch\text{-}name \; customer\text{-}name \rightarrow banker\text{-}name$$

Clearly, *Banker-schema* is not in BCNF since *banker-name* is not a superkey.

If we apply the algorithm of Figure 7.6, we obtain the following BCNF decomposition:

$$Banker\text{-}branch\text{-}schema = (banker\text{-}name,\ branch\text{-}name)$$
$$Customer\text{-}banker\text{-}schema = (customer\text{-}name,\ banker\text{-}name)$$

The decomposed schemas preserve only *banker-name → branch-name* (and trivial dependencies), but the closure of {*banker-name → branch-name*} does not include *customer-name branch-name → banker-name*. The violation of this dependency cannot be detected unless a join is computed.

To see why the decomposition of *Banker-schema* into the schemas *Banker-branch-schema* and *Customer-banker-schema* is not dependency preserving, we apply the algorithm of Figure 7.5. We find that the restrictions $F_1$ and $F_2$ of $F$ to each schema are as follows (for brevity, we show only a canonical cover):

$$F_1 = \{banker\text{-}name \rightarrow branch\text{-}name\}$$
$$F_2 = \emptyset\ (\text{only trivial dependencies hold on } Customer\text{-}banker\text{-}schema)$$

Thus, a canonical cover for the set $F'$ is $F_1$.

It is easy to see that the dependency *customer-name branch-name → banker-name* is not in $F'^+$ even though it *is* in $F^+$. Therefore, $F'^+ \neq F^+$, and the decomposition is not dependency preserving.

The preceding example demonstrates that not every BCNF decomposition is dependency preserving. Moreover, it demonstrates that we cannot always satisfy all three design goals:

1. BCNF
2. Lossless join
3. Dependency preservation

We cannot do so here because every BCNF decomposition of *Banker-schema* must fail to preserve *customer-name branch-name → banker-name*.

### 7.3.3   Third Normal Form

In those cases where we cannot meet all three design criteria, we abandon BCNF and accept a weaker normal form called *third normal form* (*3NF*). We shall see that it is always possible to find a lossless-join, dependency-preserving decomposition that is in 3NF.

BCNF requires that all nontrivial dependencies be of the form $\alpha \rightarrow \beta$, where $\alpha$ is a superkey. 3NF relaxes this constraint slightly by allowing nontrivial functional dependencies whose left side is not a superkey.

A relation schema $R$ is in 3NF with respect to a set $F$ of functional dependencies if, for all functional dependencies in $F^+$ of the form $\alpha \rightarrow \beta$, where $\alpha \subseteq R$ and $\beta \subseteq R$, at least one of the following holds:

- $\alpha \rightarrow \beta$ is a trivial functional dependency.

- $\alpha$ is a superkey for $R$.
- Each attribute $A$ in $\beta - \alpha$ is contained in a candidate key for $R$.

The definition of 3NF allows certain functional dependencies that are not allowed in BCNF. A dependency $\alpha \rightarrow \beta$ that satisfies only the third condition of the 3NF definition is not allowed in BCNF, but is allowed in 3NF. These dependencies are examples of *transitive dependencies* (see Exercise 7.13).

Observe that, if a relation schema is in BCNF, then all functional dependencies are of the form "superkey determines a set of attributes," or the dependency is trivial. Thus, a BCNF schema cannot have *any* transitive dependencies. As a result, every BCNF schema is also in 3NF, and BCNF is therefore a more restrictive constraint than is 3NF.

Let us return to our *Banker-schema* example (Section 7.3.2). We have shown that this relation schema does not have a dependency-preserving, lossless-join decomposition into BCNF. This schema, however, turns out to be in 3NF. To see that is is, we note that {*customer-name, branch-name*} is a candidate key for *Banker-schema*, so the only attribute not contained in a candidate key for *Banker-schema* is *banker-name*. The only nontrivial functional dependencies of the form

$$\alpha \rightarrow \textit{banker-name}$$

include {*customer-name, branch-name*} as part of $\alpha$. Since {*customer-name, branch-name*} is a candidate key, these dependencies do not violate the definition of 3NF.

Figure 7.7 shows an algorithm for finding a dependency-preserving, lossless-join decomposition into 3NF. The set of dependencies $F_c$ used in the algorithm is a canonical cover for $F$, and is therefore in in canonical form (Section 6.5.4). From this, it can be shown that each relation schema $R_i$ is in 3NF; the bibliographic notes provide references to a proof. The algorithm ensures preservation of dependencies by building explicitly a schema for each given dependency. It ensures that the decomposition is a lossless-join decomposition by guaranteeing that at least one schema contains a candidate key for the schema being decomposed. Exercise 7.6 provides some insight into the proof that this suffices to guarantee a lossless join.

To illustrate the algorithm of Figure 7.7, we consider the following extension to the *Banker-schema* introduced in Section 7.3.2:

$$\textit{Banker-info-schema} = (\textit{branch-name, customer-name, banker-name,}$$
$$\textit{office-number})$$

The main difference here is that we include the banker's office number as part of the information. The functional dependencies for this relation schema are

$$\textit{banker-name} \rightarrow \textit{branch-name office-number}$$
$$\textit{customer-name branch-name} \rightarrow \textit{banker-name}$$

The **for** loop in the algorithm causes us to include the following schemas in our decomposition:

let $F_c$ be a canonical cover for $F$;
$i := 0$;
**for each** functional dependency $\alpha \to \beta$ in $F_c$ **do**
  **if** none of the schemas $R_j$, $j = 1, 2, \ldots, i$ contains $\alpha\,\beta$
    **then begin**
              $i := i + 1$;
              $R_i := \alpha\,\beta$;
        **end**
**if** none of the schemas $R_j$, $j = 1, 2, \ldots, i$ contains a candidate key for $R$
    **then begin**
              $i := i + 1$;
              $R_i :=$ any candidate key for $R$;
        **end**
  **return** $(R_1, R_2, \ldots, R_i)$

**Figure 7.7**   Dependency-preserving, lossless-join decomposition into 3NF.

*Banker-office-schema = (banker-name, branch-name, office-number)*
*Banker-schema = (customer-name, branch-name, banker-name)*

Since *Banker-schema* contains a candidate key for *Banker-info-schema*, we are finished with the decomposition process.

## 7.3.4   Comparison of BCNF and 3NF

We have seen two normal forms for relational-database schemas: 3NF and BCNF. There is an advantage to 3NF in that we know that it is always possible to obtain a 3NF design without sacrificing a lossless join or dependency preservation. Nevertheless, there is a disadvantage to 3NF. If we do not eliminate all transitive dependencies, we may have to use null values to represent some of the possible meaningful relationships among data items, and there is the problem of repetition of information.

As an illustration, consider again the *Banker-schema* and its associated functional dependencies. Since *banker-name* → *branch-name*, we may want to represent relationships between values for *banker-name* and values for *branch-name* in our database. If we are to do so, however, either there must be a corresponding value for *customer-name*, or we must use a null value for the attribute *customer-name*.

The other difficulty with the *Banker-schema* is repetition of information. As an illustration, consider an instance of *Banker-schema* shown in Figure 7.8. Notice that the information indicating that Johnson is working at the Perryridge branch is repeated.

If we are forced to choose between BCNF and dependency preservation with 3NF, it is generally preferable to opt for 3NF. If we cannot test for dependency preservation efficiently, we either pay a high penalty in system performance or risk the integrity of the data in our database. Neither of these alternatives is attractive. With such alternatives, the limited amount of redundancy imposed by transitive

| *customer-name* | *banker-name* | *branch-name* |
|:---:|:---:|:---:|
| Jones | Johnson | Perryridge |
| Smith | Johnson | Perryridge |
| Hayes | Johnson | Perryridge |
| Jackson | Johnson | Perryridge |
| Curry | Johnson | Perryridge |
| Turner | Johnson | Perryridge |

Figure 7.8    An instance of *Banker-schema*.

dependencies allowed under 3NF is the lesser evil. Thus, we normally choose to retain dependency preservation and to sacrifice BCNF.

In summary, we repeat that our three design goals for a relational-database design are

1. BCNF
2. Lossless join
3. Dependency preservation

If we cannot achieve all three, we accept

1. 3NF
2. Lossless join
3. Dependency preservation

## 7.4   Normalization Using Multivalued Dependencies

There are relation schemas that are in BCNF that do not seem to be sufficiently normalized, in the sense that they still suffer from the problem of repetition of information. Consider again our banking example. Let us assume that, in an alternative design for the bank database schema, we have the schema

*BC-schema* = (*loan-number, customer-name, customer-street, customer-city*)

The astute reader will recognize this schema as a non-BCNF schema because of the functional dependency

*customer-name* → *customer-street customer-city*

that we asserted earlier, and because *customer-name* is not a key for *BC-schema*. However, let us assume that our bank is attracting wealthy customers who have several addresses (say, a winter home and a summer home). Then, we no longer wish to enforce the functional dependency *customer-name* → *customer-street customer-city*. If we remove this functional dependency, we find *BC-schema* to be in BCNF with respect to our modified set of functional dependencies. Yet, even though *BC-schema* is now in BCNF, we still have the problem of repetition of information that we had earlier.

To deal with this problem, we must define a new form of constraint, called a *multivalued dependency*. As we did for functional dependencies, we shall use multivalued dependencies to define a normal form for relation schemas. This normal form, called *fourth normal form* (*4NF*), is more restrictive than BCNF. We shall see that every 4NF schema is also in BCNF, but there are BCNF schemas that are not in 4NF.

## 7.4.1  Multivalued Dependencies

Functional dependencies rule out certain tuples from being in a relation. If $A \rightarrow B$, then we cannot have two tuples with the same $A$ value but different $B$ values. Multivalued dependencies do not rule out the existence of certain tuples. Instead, they *require* that other tuples of a certain form be present in the relation. For this reason, functional dependencies sometimes are referred to as equality-generating dependencies, and multivalued dependencies are referred to as tuple-generating dependencies.

Let $R$ be a relation schema and let $\alpha \subseteq R$ and $\beta \subseteq R$. The *multivalued dependency*

$$\alpha \twoheadrightarrow \beta$$

holds on $R$ if, in any legal relation $r(R)$, for all pairs of tuples $t_1$ and $t_2$ in $r$ such that $t_1[\alpha] = t_2[\alpha]$, there exist tuples $t_3$ and $t_4$ in $r$ such that

$$t_1[\alpha] = t_2[\alpha] = t_3[\alpha] = t_4[\alpha]$$
$$t_3[\beta] = t_1[\beta]$$
$$t_3[R - \beta] = t_2[R - \beta]$$
$$t_4[\beta] = t_2[\beta]$$
$$t_4[R - \beta] = t_1[R - \beta]$$

This definition is less complicated than it appears to be. In Figure 7.9, we give a tabular picture of $t_1$, $t_2$, $t_3$, and $t_4$. Intuitively, the multivalued dependency $\alpha \twoheadrightarrow \beta$ says that the relationship between $\alpha$ and $\beta$ is independent of the relationship between $\alpha$ and $R - \beta$. If the multivalued dependency $\alpha \twoheadrightarrow \beta$ is satisfied by all relations on schema $R$, then $\alpha \twoheadrightarrow \beta$ is a *trivial* multivalued dependency on schema $R$. Thus, $\alpha \twoheadrightarrow \beta$ is trivial if $\beta \subseteq \alpha$ or $\beta \cup \alpha = R$.

|       | $\alpha$ | $\beta$ | $R - \alpha - \beta$ |
|-------|----------|---------|----------------------|
| $t_1$ | $a_1 \ldots a_i$ | $a_{i+1} \ldots a_j$ | $a_{j+1} \ldots a_n$ |
| $t_2$ | $a_1 \ldots a_i$ | $b_{i+1} \ldots b_j$ | $b_{j+1} \ldots b_n$ |
| $t_3$ | $a_1 \ldots a_i$ | $a_{i+1} \ldots a_j$ | $b_{j+1} \ldots b_n$ |
| $t_4$ | $a_1 \ldots a_i$ | $b_{i+1} \ldots b_j$ | $a_{j+1} \ldots a_n$ |

Figure 7.9    Tabular representation of $\alpha \twoheadrightarrow \beta$.

| loan-number | customer-name | customer-street | customer-city |
|-------------|---------------|-----------------|---------------|
| L-23 | Smith | North | Rye |
| L-23 | Smith | Main | Manchester |
| L-93 | Curry | Lake | Horseneck |

Figure 7.10    Relation *bc*: An example of redundancy in a BCNF relation.

To illustrate the difference between functional and multivalued dependencies, we consider again the *BC-schema*, and the relation *bc* (*BC-schema*) of Figure 7.10. We must repeat the loan number once for each address a customer has, and we must repeat the address for each loan a customer has. This repetition is unnecessary, since the relationship between a customer and his address is independent of the relationship between that customer and a loan. If a customer (say, Smith) has a loan (say, loan number L-23), we want that loan to be associated with all Smith's addresses. Thus, the relation of Figure 7.11 is illegal. To make this relation legal, we need to add the tuples (L-23, Smith, Main, Manchester) and (L-27, Smith, North, Rye) to the *bc* relation of Figure 7.11.

Comparing the preceding example with our definition of multivalued dependency, we see that we want the multivalued dependency

$$customer\text{-}name \twoheadrightarrow customer\text{-}street\ customer\text{-}city$$

to hold. (The multivalued dependency *customer-name* $\twoheadrightarrow$ *loan-number* will do as well. We shall soon see that they are equivalent.)

As was the case for functional dependencies, we shall use multivalued dependencies in two ways:

1. To test relations to determine whether they are legal under a given set of functional and multivalued dependencies

2. To specify constraints on the set of legal relations; we shall thus concern ourselves with *only* those relations that satisfy a given set of functional and multivalued dependencies

Note that, if a relation *r* fails to satisfy a given multivalued dependency, we can construct a relation *r'* that *does* satisfy the multivalued dependency by adding tuples to *r*.

| loan-number | customer-name | customer-street | customer-city |
|-------------|---------------|-----------------|---------------|
| L-23 | Smith | North | Rye |
| L-27 | Smith | Main | Manchester |

Figure 7.11    An illegal *bc* relation.

## 7.4.2   Theory of Multivalued Dependencies

As we did for functional dependencies and 3NF and BCNF, we shall need to determine all the multivalued dependencies that are logically implied by a given set of multivalued dependencies.

   We take the same approach here that we did earlier for functional dependencies. Let $D$ denote a set of functional and multivalued dependencies. The closure $D^+$ of $D$ is the set of all functional and multivalued dependencies logically implied by $D$. As we did for functional dependencies, we can compute $D^+$ from $D$, using the formal definitions of functional dependencies and multivalued dependencies. However, it is usually easier to reason about sets of dependencies using a system of inference rules.

   The following list of inference rules for functional and multivalued dependencies is *sound* and *complete*. Recall that *sound* rules do not generate any dependencies that are not logically implied by $D$, and *complete* rules allow us to generate all dependencies in $D^+$. The first three rules are Armstrong's axioms, which we saw earlier in Chapter 6.

1. **Reflexivity rule**. If $\alpha$ is a set of attributes, and $\beta \subseteq \alpha$, then $\alpha \to \beta$ holds.
2. **Augmentation rule**. If $\alpha \to \beta$ holds, and $\gamma$ is a set of attributes, then $\gamma\alpha \to \gamma\beta$ holds.
3. **Transitivity rule**. If $\alpha \to \beta$ holds, and $\beta \to \gamma$ holds, then $\alpha \to \gamma$ holds.
4. **Complementation rule**. If $\alpha \twoheadrightarrow \beta$ holds, then $\alpha \twoheadrightarrow R - \beta - \alpha$ holds.
5. **Multivalued augmentation rule**. If $\alpha \twoheadrightarrow \beta$ holds, and $\gamma \subseteq R$ and $\delta \subseteq \gamma$, then $\gamma\alpha \twoheadrightarrow \delta\beta$ holds.
6. **Multivalued transitivity rule**. If $\alpha \twoheadrightarrow \beta$ holds, and $\beta \twoheadrightarrow \gamma$ holds, then $\alpha \twoheadrightarrow \gamma - \beta$ holds.
7. **Replication rule**. If $\alpha \to \beta$ holds, then $\alpha \twoheadrightarrow \beta$.
8. **Coalescence rule**. If $\alpha \twoheadrightarrow \beta$ holds, and $\gamma \subseteq \beta$, and there is a $\delta$ such that $\delta \subseteq R$, and $\delta \cap \beta = \emptyset$, and $\delta \to \gamma$, then $\alpha \to \gamma$ holds.

   The bibliographic notes provide references to proofs that the preceding rules are sound and complete. The following examples provide insight into how the formal proofs proceed.

   Let $R = (A, B, C, G, H, I)$ be a relation schema. Suppose that $A \twoheadrightarrow BC$ holds. The definition of multivalued dependencies implies that, if $t_1[A] = t_2[A]$, then there exist tuples $t_3$ and $t_4$ such that

$$t_1[A] = t_2[A] = t_3[A] = t_4[A]$$
$$t_3[BC] = t_1[BC]$$
$$t_3[GHI] = t_2[GHI]$$
$$t_4[GHI] = t_1[GHI]$$
$$t_4[BC] = t_2[BC]$$

The complementation rule states that, if $A \twoheadrightarrow BC$, then $A \twoheadrightarrow GHI$. Observe that $t_3$ and $t_4$ satisfy the definition of $A \twoheadrightarrow GHI$ if we simply change the subscripts.

We can provide similar justification for rules 5 and 6 (see Exercise 7.17) using the definition of multivalued dependencies.

Rule 7, the replication rule, involves functional and multivalued dependencies. Suppose that $A \rightarrow BC$ holds on $R$. If $t_1[A] = t_2[A]$ and $t_1[BC] = t_2[BC]$, then $t_1$ and $t_2$ themselves serve as the tuples $t_3$ and $t_4$ required by the definition of the multivalued dependency $A \twoheadrightarrow BC$.

Rule 8, the coalescence rule, is the most difficult of the eight rules to verify (see Exercise 7.19).

We can simplify the computation of the closure of $D$ by using the following rules, which we can prove using rules 1 to 8 (see Exercise 7.20):

- **Multivalued union rule**. If $\alpha \twoheadrightarrow \beta$ holds, and $\alpha \twoheadrightarrow \gamma$ holds, then $\alpha \twoheadrightarrow \beta\gamma$ holds.
- **Intersection rule**. If $\alpha \twoheadrightarrow \beta$ holds, and $\alpha \twoheadrightarrow \gamma$ holds, then $\alpha \twoheadrightarrow \beta \cap \gamma$ holds.
- **Difference rule**. If $\alpha \twoheadrightarrow \beta$ holds, and $\alpha \twoheadrightarrow \gamma$ holds, then $\alpha \twoheadrightarrow \beta - \gamma$ holds and $\alpha \twoheadrightarrow \gamma - \beta$ holds.

Let us apply our rules to the following example. Let $R = (A, B, C, G, H, I)$ with the following set of dependencies $D$ given:

$$A \twoheadrightarrow B$$
$$B \twoheadrightarrow HI$$
$$CG \rightarrow H$$

We list several members of $D^+$ here:

- $A \twoheadrightarrow CGHI$: Since $A \twoheadrightarrow B$, the complementation rule (rule 4) implies that $A \twoheadrightarrow R - B - A$. $R - B - A = CGHI$, so $A \twoheadrightarrow CGHI$.
- $A \twoheadrightarrow HI$: Since $A \twoheadrightarrow B$ and $B \twoheadrightarrow HI$, the multivalued transitivity rule (rule 6) implies that $A \twoheadrightarrow HI - B$. Since $HI - B = HI$, $A \twoheadrightarrow HI$.
- $B \rightarrow H$: To show this fact, we need to apply the coalescence rule (rule 8). $B \twoheadrightarrow HI$ holds. Since $H \subseteq HI$ and $CG \rightarrow H$ and $CG \cap HI = \emptyset$, we satisfy the statement of the coalescence rule, with $\alpha$ being $B$, $\beta$ being $HI$, $\delta$ being $CG$, and $\gamma$ being $H$. We conclude that $B \rightarrow H$.
- $A \twoheadrightarrow CG$: We already know that $A \twoheadrightarrow CGHI$ and $A \twoheadrightarrow HI$. By the difference rule, $A \twoheadrightarrow CGHI - HI$. Since $CGHI - HI = CG$, $A \twoheadrightarrow CG$.

### 7.4.3    Fourth Normal Form

Let us return to our *BC-schema* example in which the multivalued dependency *customer-name* $\twoheadrightarrow$ *customer-street customer-city* holds, but no nontrivial functional dependencies hold. We saw earlier that, although *BC-schema* is in BCNF, the design is not ideal, since we must repeat a customer's address information for each loan. We shall see that we can use the given multivalued dependency to improve the database design, by decomposing *BC-schema* into a *fourth normal form* (4NF) decomposition.

A relation schema $R$ is in 4NF with respect to a set $D$ of functional and multivalued dependencies if, for all multivalued dependencies in $D^+$ of the form $\alpha \rightarrow\!\!\!\rightarrow \beta$, where $\alpha \subseteq R$ and $\beta \subseteq R$, at least one of the following holds

- $\alpha \rightarrow\!\!\!\rightarrow \beta$ is a trivial multivalued dependency.
- $\alpha$ is a superkey for schema $R$.

A database design is in 4NF if each member of the set of relation schemas that constitutes the design is in 4NF.

Note that the definition of 4NF differs from the definition of BCNF in only the use of multivalued dependencies instead of functional dependencies. Every 4NF schema is in BCNF. To see this fact, we note that, if a schema $R$ is not in BCNF, then there is a nontrivial functional dependency $\alpha \rightarrow \beta$ holding on $R$, where $\alpha$ is not a superkey. Since $\alpha \rightarrow \beta$ implies $\alpha \rightarrow\!\!\!\rightarrow \beta$ (by the replication rule), $R$ cannot be in 4NF.

Let $R$ be a relation schema, and let $R_1, R_2, \ldots, R_n$ be a decomposition of $R$. Recall that, for a set $F$ of functional dependencies, the restriction $F_i$ of $F$ to $R_i$ is all functional dependencies in $F^+$ that include *only* attributes of $R_i$. Now consider a set $D$ of both functional and multivalued dependencies. The *restriction* of $D$ to $R_i$ is the set $D_i$, consisting of

- All functional dependencies in $D^+$ that include only attributes of $R_i$
- All multivalued dependencies of the form

$$\alpha \rightarrow\!\!\!\rightarrow \beta \cap R_i$$

where $\alpha \subseteq R_i$ and $\alpha \rightarrow\!\!\!\rightarrow \beta$ is in $D^+$

The analogy between 4NF and BCNF applies to the algorithm for decomposing a schema into 4NF. Figure 7.12 shows the 4NF decomposition algorithm. It is identical to the BCNF decomposition algorithm of Figure 7.6, except for the use

---

*result* := $\{R\}$;
*done* := false;
*compute* $D^+$; Given schema $R_i$, let $D_i$ denote the restriction of $D^+$ to $R_i$
**while** (**not** *done*) **do**
    **if** (there is a schema $R_i$ in *result* that is not in 4NF w.r.t. $D_i$)
      **then begin**
            let $\alpha \rightarrow\!\!\!\rightarrow \beta$ be a nontrivial multivalued dependency that holds
            on $R_i$ such that $\alpha \rightarrow R_i$ is not in $D_i$, and $\alpha \cap \beta = \emptyset$;
            *result* := (*result* $-$ $R_i$) $\cup$ ($R_i$ $-$ $\beta$) $\cup$ ($\alpha, \beta$);
      **end**
    **else** *done* := true;

Figure 7.12     4NF decomposition algorithm.

of multivalued, instead of functional, dependencies and the use of the restriction of $D^+$ to $R_i$.

If we apply the algorithm of Figure 7.12 to *BC-schema*, we find that *customer-name* $\twoheadrightarrow$ *loan-number* is a nontrivial multivalued dependency, and *customer-name* is not a superkey for *BC-schema*. Following the algorithm, we replace *BC-schema* by two schemas:

> *Borrower-schema* $=$ (*customer-name, loan-number*)
> *Customer-schema* $=$ (*customer-name, customer-street, customer-city*).

This pair of schemas, which is in 4NF, eliminates the problem we encountered earlier with the redundancy of *BC-schema*.

As was the case when we were dealing solely with functional dependencies, we are interested in decompositions that are lossless-join decompositions and that preserve dependencies. The following fact about multivalued dependencies and lossless joins shows that the algorithm of Figure 7.12 generates only lossless-join decompositions:

- Let $R$ be a relation schema, and let $D$ be a set of functional and multivalued dependencies on $R$. Let $R_1$ and $R_2$ form a decomposition of $R$. This decomposition is a lossless-join decomposition of $R$ if and only if at least one of the following multivalued dependencies is in $D^+$:

$$R_1 \cap R_2 \twoheadrightarrow R_1$$
$$R_1 \cap R_2 \twoheadrightarrow R_2$$

Recall that we stated earlier that, if $R_1 \cap R_2 \to R_1$ or $R_1 \cap R_2 \to R_2$, then $R_1$ and $R_2$ are a lossless-join decomposition of $R$. The preceding fact regarding multivalued dependencies is a more general statement about lossless joins. It says that, for *every* lossless-join decomposition of $R$ into two schemas $R_1$ and $R_2$, one of the two dependencies $R_1 \cap R_2 \twoheadrightarrow R_1$ or $R_1 \cap R_2 \twoheadrightarrow R_2$ must hold.

The question of dependency preservation when we have multivalued dependencies is not as simple as it is when we have only functional dependencies. A decomposition of schema $R$ into schemas $R_1, R_2, \ldots, R_n$ is a *dependency-preserving decomposition* with respect to a set $D$ of functional and multivalued dependencies if, for every set of relations $r_1(R_1), r_2(R_2), \ldots, r_n(R_n)$ such that for all $i$, $r_i$ satisfies $D_i$ (the restriction of $D$ to $R_i$), there exists a relation $r(R)$ that satisfies $D$ and for which $r_i = \Pi_{R_i}(r)$ for all $i$.

Let us apply the 4NF decomposition algorithm of Figure 7.12 to our example of $R = (A, B, C, G, H, I)$ with $D = \{A \twoheadrightarrow B, B \twoheadrightarrow HI, CG \to H\}$. We shall then test the resulting decomposition for dependency preservation.

$R$ is not in 4NF. Observe that $A \twoheadrightarrow B$ is not trivial, yet $A$ is not a superkey. Using $A \twoheadrightarrow B$ in the first iteration of the **while** loop, we replace $R$ with two schemas, $(A, B)$ and $(A, C, G, H, I)$. It is easy to see that $(A, B)$ is in 4NF since all multivalued dependencies that hold on $(A, B)$ are trivial. However, the schema $(A, C, G, H, I)$ is not in 4NF. Applying the multivalued dependency $CG \twoheadrightarrow H$ (which follows from the given functional dependency $CG \to H$ by the

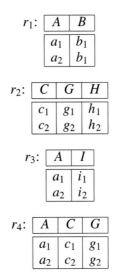

Figure 7.13    Projection of relation $r$ onto a 4NF decomposition of $R$.

replication rule), we replace $(A, C, G, H, I)$ by the two schemas $(C, G, H)$ and $(A, C, G, I)$. Schema $(C, G, H)$ is in 4NF, but schema $(A, C, G, I)$ is not. To see that $(A, C, G, I)$ is not in 4NF, we recall that we showed earlier that $A \twoheadrightarrow HI$ is in $D^+$. Therefore, $A \twoheadrightarrow I$ is in the restriction of $D$ to $(A, C, G, I)$. Thus, in a third iteration of the **while** loop, we replace $(A, C, G, I)$ by two schemas $(A, I)$ and $(A, C, G)$. The algorithm then terminates and the resulting 4NF decomposition is $\{(A, B), (C, G, H), (A, I), (A, C, G)\}$.

This 4NF decomposition is not dependency preserving, since it fails to preserve the multivalued dependency $B \twoheadrightarrow HI$. Consider Figure 7.13, which shows the four relations that may result from the projection of a relation on $(A, B, C, G, H, I)$ onto the four schemas of our decomposition. The restriction of $D$ to $(A, B)$ is $A \twoheadrightarrow B$ and some trivial dependencies. It is easy to see that $r_1$ satisfies $A \twoheadrightarrow B$, because there is no pair of tuples with the same $A$ value. Observe that $r_2$ satisfies *all* functional and multivalued dependencies, since no two tuples in $r_2$ have the same value on any attribute. A similar statement can be made for $r_3$ and $r_4$. Therefore, the decomposed version of our database satisfies all the dependencies in the restriction of $D$. However, there is no relation $r$ on $(A, B, C, G, H, I)$ that satisfies $D$ and decomposes into $r_1, r_2, r_3$, and $r_4$. Figure 7.14 shows the relation $r = r_1 \bowtie r_2 \bowtie r_3 \bowtie r_4$. Relation $r$ does not satisfy $B \twoheadrightarrow HI$. Any relation $s$ containing $r$ and satisfying $B \twoheadrightarrow HI$ must include the tuple $(a_2, b_1, c_2, g_2, h_1, i_1)$. However, $\Pi_{CGH}(s)$ includes a tuple $(c_2, g_2, h_1)$ that is not in $r_2$. Thus, our decomposition fails to detect a violation of $B \twoheadrightarrow HI$.

We have seen that, if we are given a set of multivalued and functional dependencies, it is advantageous to find a database design that meets the three criteria of

| $A$ | $B$ | $C$ | $G$ | $H$ | $I$ |
|-----|-----|-----|-----|-----|-----|
| $a_1$ | $b_1$ | $c_1$ | $g_1$ | $h_1$ | $i_1$ |
| $a_2$ | $b_1$ | $c_2$ | $g_2$ | $h_2$ | $i_2$ |

**Figure 7.14**   A relation $r(R)$ that does not satisfy $B \twoheadrightarrow HI$.

1. 4NF
2. Dependency preservation
3. Lossless join

If all we have are functional dependencies, then the first criterion is just BCNF.

We have seen also that it is not always possible to meet all three of these criteria. We succeeded in finding such a decomposition for the bank example, but failed for the example of schema $R = (A, B, C, G, H, I)$.

When we cannot achieve our three goals, we compromise on 4NF, and accept BCNF or even 3NF, if necessary, to ensure dependency preservation.

## 7.5 Normalization Using Join Dependencies

We have seen that the lossless-join property is one of several properties of a good database design. Indeed, this property is essential: Without it, information is lost. When we restrict the set of legal relations to those satisfying a set of functional and multivalued dependencies, we are able to use these dependencies to show that certain decompositions are lossless-join decompositions.

Because of the importance of the concept of lossless join, it is useful to be able to constrain the set of legal relations over a schema $R$ to those relations for which a given decomposition is a lossless-join decomposition. In this section, we define such a constraint, called a *join dependency*. Just as types of dependency led to other normal forms, join dependencies will lead to a normal form called *project-join normal form (PJNF)*.

### 7.5.1 Join Dependencies

Let $R$ be a relation schema and $R_1, R_2, \ldots, R_n$ be a decomposition of $R$. The join dependency $*(R_1, R_2, \ldots, R_n)$ is used to restrict the set of legal relations to those for which $R_1, R_2, \ldots, R_n$ is a lossless-join decomposition of $R$. Formally, if $R = R_1 \cup R_2 \cup \ldots \cup R_n$, we say that a relation $r(R)$ satisfies the *join dependency* $*(R_1, R_2, \ldots, R_n)$ if

$$r = \Pi_{R_1}(r) \bowtie \Pi_{R_2}(r) \bowtie \ldots \bowtie \Pi_{R_n}(r)$$

A join dependency is *trivial* if one of the $R_i$ is $R$ itself.

Consider the join dependency $*(R_1, R_2)$ on schema $R$. This dependency requires that, for all legal $r(R)$,

$$r = \Pi_{R_1}(r) \bowtie \Pi_{R_2}(r)$$

| | $R_1 - R_2$ | $R_1 \cap R_2$ |
|---|---|---|
| $\Pi_{R_1}(t_1)$ | $a_1 \ \ldots \ a_i$ | $a_{i+1} \ \ldots \ a_j$ |
| $\Pi_{R_1}(t_2)$ | $b_1 \ \ldots \ b_i$ | $a_{i+1} \ \ldots \ a_j$ |

| | $R_1 \cap R_2$ | $R_2 - R_1$ |
|---|---|---|
| $\Pi_{R_2}(t_1)$ | $a_{i+1} \ \ldots \ a_j$ | $a_{j+1} \ \ldots \ a_n$ |
| $\Pi_{R_2}(t_2)$ | $a_{i+1} \ \ldots \ a_j$ | $b_{j+1} \ \ldots \ b_n$ |

Figure 7.15    $\Pi_{R_1}(r)$ and $\Pi_{R_2}(r)$.

Let $r$ contain the two tuples $t_1$ and $t_2$, defined as follows:

$$t_1[R_1 - R_2] = (a_1, a_2, \ldots, a_i) \qquad t_2[R_1 - R_2] = (b_1, b_2, \ldots, b_i)$$
$$t_1[R_1 \cap R_2] = (a_{i+1}, \ldots, a_j) \qquad t_2[R_1 \cap R_2] = (a_{i+1}, \ldots, a_j)$$
$$t_1[R_2 - R_1] = (a_{j+1}, \ldots, a_n) \qquad t_2[R_2 - R_1] = (b_{j+1}, \ldots, b_n)$$

Thus, $t_1[R_1 \cap R_2] = t_2[R_1 \cap R_2]$, but $t_1$ and $t_2$ have different values on all other attributes. Let us compute $\Pi_{R_1}(r) \bowtie \Pi_{R_2}(r)$. Figure 7.15 shows $\Pi_{R_1}(r)$ and $\Pi_{R_2}(r)$. When we compute the join, we get two tuples in addition to $t_1$ and $t_2$, shown by $t_3$ and $t_4$ in Figure 7.16.

If $*(R_1, R_2)$ holds, then, whenever we have tuples $t_1$ and $t_2$, we must also have $t_3$ and $t_4$. Thus, Figure 7.16 shows a tabular representation of the join dependency $*(R_1, R_2)$. Compare Figure 7.16 with Figure 7.9, in which we gave a tabular representation of $\alpha \twoheadrightarrow \beta$. If we let $\alpha = R_1 \cap R_2$ and $\beta = R_1$, then we can see that the two tabular representations in these figures are the same. Indeed, $*(R_1, R_2)$ is just another way of stating $R_1 \cap R_2 \twoheadrightarrow R_1$. Using the complementation and augmentation rules for multivalued dependencies, we can show that $R_1 \cap R_2 \twoheadrightarrow R_1$ implies $R_1 \cap R_2 \twoheadrightarrow R_2$. Thus, $*(R_1, R_2)$ is equivalent to $R_1 \cap R_2 \twoheadrightarrow R_2$. This observation is not surprising in light of the fact we noted earlier that $R_1$ and $R_2$ form a lossless-join decomposition of $R$ if and only if $R_1 \cap R_2 \twoheadrightarrow R_2$ or $R_1 \cap R_2 \twoheadrightarrow R_1$.

Every join dependency of the form $*(R_1, R_2)$ is therefore equivalent to a multivalued dependency. However, there are join dependencies that are not equivalent to any multivalued dependency. The simplest example of such a dependency is on schema $R = (A, B, C)$. The join dependency

$$*((A, B), (B, C), (A, C))$$

| | $R_1 - R_2$ | $R_1 \cap R_2$ | $R_2 - R_1$ |
|---|---|---|---|
| $t_1$ | $a_1 \ \ldots \ a_i$ | $a_{i+1} \ \ldots \ a_j$ | $a_{j+1} \ \ldots \ a_n$ |
| $t_2$ | $b_1 \ \ldots \ b_i$ | $a_{i+1} \ \ldots \ a_j$ | $b_{j+1} \ \ldots \ b_n$ |
| $t_3$ | $a_1 \ \ldots \ a_i$ | $a_{i+1} \ \ldots \ a_j$ | $b_{j+1} \ \ldots \ b_n$ |
| $t_4$ | $b_1 \ \ldots \ b_i$ | $a_{i+1} \ \ldots \ a_j$ | $a_{j+1} \ \ldots \ a_n$ |

Figure 7.16    Tabular representation of $*(R_1, R_2)$.

| A | B | C |
|---|---|---|
| $a_1$ | $b_1$ | $c_2$ |
| $a_2$ | $b_1$ | $c_1$ |
| $a_1$ | $b_2$ | $c_1$ |
| $a_1$ | $b_1$ | $c_1$ |

Figure 7.17   Tabular representation of *$((A, B), (B, C), (A, C))$.

is not equivalent to any collection of multivalued dependencies. Figure 7.17 shows a tabular representation of this join dependency. To see that no set of multivalued dependencies logically implies *$((A, B), (B, C), (A, C))$, we consider Figure 7.17 as a relation $r$ $(A, B, C)$ as shown in Figure 7.18. Relation $r$ satisfies the join dependency *$((A, B), (B, C), (A, C))$, as we can verify by computing

$$\Pi_{AB}(r) \bowtie \Pi_{BC}(r) \bowtie \Pi_{AC}(r)$$

and by showing that the result is exactly $r$. However, $r$ does not satisfy any nontrivial multivalued dependency. To see that it does not, we verify that $r$ fails to satisfy any of $A \twoheadrightarrow B$, $A \twoheadrightarrow C$, $B \twoheadrightarrow A$, $B \twoheadrightarrow C$, $C \twoheadrightarrow A$, or $C \twoheadrightarrow B$.

Just as a multivalued dependency is a way of stating the independence of a pair of relationships, a join dependency is a way of stating that the members of a *set* of relationships are all independent. This notion of independence of relationships is a natural consequence of the way that we generally define a relation. Consider

*Loan-info-schema* = (*branch-name, customer-name, loan-number, amount*)

from our banking example. We can define a relation *loan-info* (*Loan-info-schema*) as the set of all tuples on *Loan-info-schema* such that

- The loan represented by *loan-number* is made by the branch named *branch-name*.
- The loan represented by *loan-number* is made to the customer named *customer-name*.
- The loan represented by *loan-number* is in the amount given by *amount*.

The preceding definition of the *loan-info* relation is a conjunction of three predicates: one on *loan-number* and *branch-name*, one on *loan-number* and *customer-name*, and one on *loan-number* and *amount*. Surprisingly, it can be shown that the

| A | B | C |
|---|---|---|
| $a_1$ | $b_1$ | $c_2$ |
| $a_2$ | $b_1$ | $c_1$ |
| $a_1$ | $b_2$ | $c_1$ |
| $a_1$ | $b_1$ | $c_1$ |

Figure 7.18   Relation $r$ $(A, B, C)$.

preceding intuitive definition of *loan-info* logically implies the join dependency *((*loan-number, branch-name*), (*loan-number, customer-name*), (*loan-number, amount*)).

Thus, join dependencies have an intuitive appeal and correspond to one of our three criteria for a good database design.

For functional and multivalued dependencies, we were able to give a system of inference rules that are sound and complete. Unfortunately, no such set of rules is known for join dependencies. It appears that we must consider more general classes of dependencies than join dependencies to construct a sound and complete set of inference rules. The bibliographic notes contain references to research in this area.

## 7.5.2    Project-Join Normal Form

*Project-join normal form* (*PJNF*) is defined in a manner similar to BCNF and 4NF, except that join dependencies are used. A relation schema $R$ is in PJNF with respect to a set $D$ of functional, multivalued, and join dependencies if, for all join dependencies in $D^+$ of the form $*(R_1, R_2, \ldots, R_n)$, where each $R_i \subseteq R$ and $R = R_1 \cup R_2 \cup \ldots \cup R_n$, at least one of the following holds:

- $*(R_1, R_2, \ldots, R_n)$ is a trivial join dependency.
- Every $R_i$ is a superkey for $R$.

A database design is in PJNF if each member of the set of relation schemas that constitutes the design is in PJNF. PJNF is called *fifth normal form* (*5NF*) in some of the literature on database normalization.

Let us return to our banking example. Given the join dependency *((*loan-number, branch-name*), (*loan-number, customer-name*), (*loan-number, amount*)), *Loan-info-schema* is not in PJNF. To put *Loan-info-schema* into PJNF, we must decompose it into the three schemas specified by the join dependency: (*loan-number, branch-name*), (*loan-number, customer-name*), and (*loan-number, amount*).

Because every multivalued dependency is also a join dependency, it is easy to see that every PJNF schema is also in 4NF. Thus, in general, we may not be able to find a dependency-preserving decomposition into PJNF for a given schema.

## 7.6    Domain-Key Normal Form

The approach we have taken to normalization is to define a form of constraint (functional, multivalued, or join dependency), and then to use that form of constraint to define a normal form. *Domain-key normal form* (*DKNF*) is based on three notions.

1. **Domain declaration**. Let $A$ be an attribute, and let **dom** be a set of values. The domain declaration $A \subseteq$ **dom** requires that the $A$ value of all tuples be values in **dom**.

2. **Key declaration**. Let $R$ be a relation schema with $K \subseteq R$. The key declaration **key** $(K)$ requires that $K$ be a superkey for schema $R$—that is, $K \rightarrow R$. Note that all key declarations are functional dependencies but not all functional dependencies are key declarations.

3. **General constraint**. A *general constraint* is a predicate on the set of all relations on a given schema. The dependencies that we have studied in this chapter are examples of general constraints. In general, a general constraint is a predicate expressed in some agreed-on form, such as first-order logic.

We now give an example of a general constraint that is not a functional, multivalued, or join dependency. Suppose that all accounts whose *account-number* begins with the digit 9 are special high-interest accounts with a minimum balance of $2500. Then, we include as a general constraint, "If the first digit of $t[account-number]$ is 9, then $t[balance] \geq 2500$."

Domain declarations and key declarations are easy to test in a practical database system. General constraints, however, may be extremely costly (in time and space) to test. The purpose of a DKNF database design is to allow us to test the general constraints using only domain and key constraints.

Formally, let **D** be a set of domain constraints and let **K** be a set of key constraints for a relation schema $R$. Let **G** denote the general constraints for $R$. Schema $R$ is in DKNF if $\mathbf{D} \cup \mathbf{K}$ logically imply **G**.

Let us return to the general constraint that we gave on accounts. The constraint implies that our database design is not in DKNF. To create a DKNF design, we need two schemas in place of *Account-schema*:

> *Regular-acct-schema* = (*branch-name, account-number, balance*)
> *Special-acct-schema* = (*branch-name, account-number, balance*)

We retain all the dependencies that we had on *Account-schema* as general constraints. The domain constraints for *Special-acct-schema* require that, for each account,

- The account number begins with 9.
- The balance is greater than 2500.

The domain constraints for *Regular-acct-schema* require that the account number does not begin with 9. The resulting design is in DKNF, although the proof of this fact is beyond the scope of this text.

Let us compare DKNF to the other normal forms that we have studied. Under the other normal forms, we did not take into consideration domain constraints. We assumed (implicitly) that the domain of each attribute was some infinite domain, such as the set of all integers or the set of all character strings. We allowed key constraints (indeed, we allowed functional dependencies). For each normal form, we allowed a restricted form of general constraint (a set of functional, multivalued, or join dependencies). Thus, we can rewrite the definitions of PJNF, 4NF, BCNF, and 3NF in a manner that shows them to be special cases of DKNF.

| branch-name | loan-number |
|-------------|-------------|
| Round Hill  | L-58        |

| loan-number | amount |
|-------------|--------|
|             |        |

| loan-number | customer-name |
|-------------|---------------|
| L-58        | Johnson       |

Figure 7.19     Decomposition in PJNF.

The following is a DKNF-inspired rephrasing of our definition of PJNF. Let $R = (A_1, A_2, \ldots, A_n)$ be a relation schema. Let $\text{dom}(A_i)$ denote the domain of attribute $A_i$, and let all these domains be infinite. Then all domain constraints **D** are of the form $A_i \subseteq \text{dom}(A_i)$. Let the general constraints be a set **G** of functional, multivalued, or join dependencies. If $F$ is the set of functional dependencies in **G**, let the set **K** of key constraints be those nontrivial functional dependencies in $F^+$ of the form $\alpha \to R$. Schema $R$ is in PJNF if and only if it is in DKNF with respect to **D**, **K**, and **G**.

A consequence of DKNF is that all insertion and deletion anomalies are eliminated.

DKNF represents an "ultimate" normal form because it allows arbitrary constraints, rather than dependencies, yet it allows efficient testing of these constraints. Of course, if a schema is not in DKNF, we may be able to achieve DKNF via decomposition, but such decompositions, as we have seen, are not always dependency-preserving decompositions. Thus, although DKNF is a goal of a database designer, it may have to be sacrificed in a practical design.

## 7.7    Alternative Approaches to Database Design

In this section, we reexamine normalization of relation schemas with an emphasis on the effects of normalization on the design of practical database systems.

We have taken the approach of starting with a single relation schema and decomposing it. One of our goals in choosing a decomposition was that the decomposition be a lossless-join decomposition. To consider losslessness, we assumed that it is valid to talk about the join of all the relations of the decomposed database.

Consider the database of Figure 7.19, showing a *loan-info* relation decomposed in PJNF. In Figure 7.19, we represent a situation in which we have not yet determined the amount of loan L-58, but wish to record the remainder of the data on the loan. If we compute the natural join of these relations, we discover that all tuples referring to loan L-58 disappear. In other words, there is no *loan-info* relation corresponding to the relations of Figure 7.19. Tuples that disappear when we compute the join are *dangling tuples* (see Section 6.2.1). Formally, let $r_1(R_1)$, $r_2(R_2), \ldots, r_n(R_n)$ be a set of relations. A tuple $t$ of relation $r_i$ is a dangling tuple if $t$ is not in the relation

$$\Pi_{R_i} \ (r_1 \ \bowtie \ r_2 \ \bowtie \ \ldots \ \bowtie \ r_n)$$

Dangling tuples may occur in practical database applications. They represent incomplete information, as they do in our example, where we wish to store data about a loan that is still in the process of being negotiated. The relation $r_1 \ \bowtie \ r_2 \ \bowtie \ \ldots \ \bowtie \ r_n$ is called a *universal relation*, since it involves all the attributes in the universe defined by $R_1 \ \cup \ R_2 \ \cup \ \ldots \ \cup \ R_n$.

The only way that we can write a universal relation for the example of Figure 7.19 is to include *null values* in the universal relation. We saw in Chapter 3 that null values present serious difficulties. Research regarding null values and universal relations is discussed in the bibliographic notes. Because of the difficulty of managing null values, it may be desirable to view the relations of the decomposed design as representing the database, rather than the universal relation whose schema we decomposed during the normalization process.

Note that we cannot enter all incomplete information into the database of Figure 7.19 without resorting to the use of null values. For example, we cannot enter a loan number unless we know at least one of the following:

- The customer name
- The branch name
- The amount of the loan

Thus, a particular decomposition defines a restricted form of incomplete information that is acceptable in our database.

The normal forms that we have defined generate good database designs from the point of view of representation of incomplete information. Returning again to the example of Figure 7.19, we would not want to allow storage of the following fact: "There is a loan (whose number is unknown) to Jones in the amount of $100." Since

*loan-number* → *customer-name amount*,

the only way that we can relate *customer-name* and *amount* is through *loan-number*. If we do not know the loan number, we cannot distinguish this loan from other loans with unknown numbers.

In other words, we do not want to store data for which the key attributes are unknown. Observe that the normal forms that we have defined do not allow us to store that type of information unless we use null values. Thus, our normal forms allow representation of acceptable incomplete information via dangling tuples, while prohibiting the storage of undesirable incomplete information.

If we allow dangling tuples in our database, we may prefer to take an alternative view of the database-design process. Instead of decomposing a universal relation, we may *synthesize* a collection of normal-form schemas from a given set of attributes. We are interested in the same normal forms, regardless of whether we use decomposition or synthesis. The decomposition approach is better understood and is more widely used. The bibliographic notes provide references to research into the synthesis approach.

Another consequence of our approach to database design is that attribute names must be unique in the universal relation. We cannot use *name* to refer to both *customer-name* and to *branch-name*. It is generally preferable to use unique names, as we have done. Nevertheless, if we defined our relation schemas directly, rather than in terms of a universal relation, we could obtain relations on schemas such as the following for our banking example:

> *branch-loan* (*name, number*)
> *loan-customer* (*number, name*)
> *amt* (*number, amount*)

Observe that, with the preceding relations, expressions such as *branch-loan* ⋈ *loan-customer* are meaningless. Indeed, the expression *branch-loan* ⋈ *loan-customer* finds loans made by branches to customers who have the same name as the name of the branch.

In a language such as SQL, however, there is no natural-join operation, so, in a query involving *branch-loan* and *loan-customer*, we must disambiguate references to *name* by prefixing the relation name. In such environments, the multiple roles for *name* (as branch name and as customer name) are less troublesome and may be simpler to use.

We believe that using the *unique-role assumption*—that each attribute name has a unique meaning in the database—is generally preferable to reusing of the same name in multiple roles. When the unique-role assumption is not made, the database designer must be especially careful when constructing a normalized relational-database design.

## 7.8   Summary

In this chapter, we have presented three criteria for a good database design:

1. PJNF, BCNF, 4NF, or 3NF
2. Lossless join
3. Dependency preservation

We have shown how to achieve these goals, and how to find a good compromise when we cannot achieve all of them.

To represent these criteria, we defined several types of data dependencies:

• Functional dependencies (defined in Chapter 5)
• Multivalued dependencies
• Join dependencies

We studied the properties of these dependencies, with emphasis on what dependencies are logically implied by a set of dependencies.

DKNF is an idealized normal form that may be difficult to achieve in practice. Yet DKNF has desirable properties that should be included to the extent possible in a good database design.

Conspicuous by their absence from our discussion of 3NF, 4NF, and so on, are first and second normal forms. The reason for not discussing *second normal form* (*2NF*) is that this form is of historical interest only. We simply define it, and let you experiment with it in Exercise 7.14. Although we have not mentioned first normal form, we have assumed it since we introduced the relational model in Chapter 3. We say that a relation schema $R$ is in *first normal form* (*1NF*) if the domains of all attributes of $R$ are atomic. A domain is *atomic* if elements of the domain are considered to be indivisible units. We discuss non-atomic domains further in Chapter 8.

In reviewing the issues that we have discussed in this chapter, note that the reason we could define rigorous approaches to relational-database design is that the relational data model rests on a firm mathematical foundation. That is one of the primary advantages of the relational model, as compared with the other data models that we have studied.

## Exercises

**7.1.** Explain what is meant by *repetition of information* and *inability to represent information*. Explain why each of these properties may indicate a bad relational-database design.

**7.2.** Suppose that we decompose the schema $R = (A, B, C, D, E)$ into

$$(A, B, C)$$
$$(A, D, E).$$

Show that this decomposition is a lossless-join decomposition if the following set $F$ of functional dependencies holds:

$$A \rightarrow BC$$
$$CD \rightarrow E$$
$$B \rightarrow D$$
$$E \rightarrow A$$

**7.3.** Show that the following decomposition of the schema $R$ of Exercise 7.2 is not a lossless-join decomposition:

$$(A, B, C)$$
$$(C, D, E).$$

*Hint:* Give an example of a relation $r$ on schema $R$ such that

$$\Pi_{A, B, C} (r) \bowtie \Pi_{C, D, E} (r) \neq r$$

**7.4.** Let $R_1, R_2, \ldots, R_n$ be a decomposition of schema $U$. Let $u(U)$ be a relation, and let $r_i = \Pi_{R_I}(u)$. Show that

$$u \subseteq r_1 \bowtie r_2 \bowtie \ldots \bowtie r_n$$

**7.5.** Show that the decomposition in Exercise 7.2 is not a dependency-preserving decomposition.

**7.6.** Show that it is possible to ensure that a dependency-preserving decomposition into 3NF is a lossless-join decomposition by guaranteeing that at least one schema contains a candidate key for the schema being decomposed. (*Hint*: Show that the join of all the projections onto the schemas of the decomposition cannot have more tuples than the original relation.)

**7.7.** List the three design goals for relational databases, and explain why each is desirable.

**7.8.** Give a lossless-join decomposition into BCNF of the schema $R$ of Exercise 7.2.

**7.9.** Give an example of a relation schema $R'$ and set $F'$ of functional dependencies such that there are at least two distinct lossless-join decompositions of $R'$ into BCNF.

**7.10.** In designing a relational database, why might we choose a non-BCNF design?

**7.11.** Give a lossless-join, dependency-preserving decomposition into 3NF of the schema $R$ of Exercise 7.2.

**7.12.** Show that, if a relation schema is in BCNF, then it is also in 3NF.

**7.13.** Let a *prime* attribute be one that appears in at least one candidate key. Let $\alpha$ and $\beta$ be sets of attributes such that $\alpha \to \beta$ holds, but $\beta \to \alpha$ does not hold. Let $A$ be an attribute that is not in $\alpha$, is not in $\beta$, and for which $\beta \to A$ holds. We say that $A$ is *transitively dependent* on $\alpha$. We can restate our definition of 3NF as follows: A relation schema $R$ is in 3NF with respect to a set $F$ of functional dependencies if there are no nonprime attributes $A$ in $R$ for which $A$ is transitively dependent on a key for $R$.

Show that this new definition is equivalent to the original one.

**7.14.** A functional dependency $\alpha \to \beta$ is called a *partial* dependency if there is a proper subset $\gamma$ of $\alpha$ such that $\gamma \to \beta$. We say that $\beta$ is *partially dependent* on $\alpha$. A relation schema $R$ is in second normal form (*2NF*) if each attribute $A$ in $R$ meets one of the following criteria:
- It appears in a candidate key.
- It is not partially dependent on a candidate key.

Show that every 3NF schema is in 2NF. (*Hint*: Show that every partial dependency is a transitive dependency.)

**7.15.** Given the three goals of relational-database design, is there any reason to design a database schema that is in 2NF, but is in no higher-order normal form? (See Exercise 7.14 for the definition of 2NF.)

**7.16.** List all the nontrivial multivalued dependencies satisfied by the relation of Figure 7.20.

| A | B | C |
|---|---|---|
| $a_1$ | $b_1$ | $c_1$ |
| $a_1$ | $b_1$ | $c_2$ |
| $a_2$ | $b_1$ | $c_1$ |
| $a_2$ | $b_1$ | $c_3$ |

Figure 7.20    Relation of Exercise 7.16.

**7.17.** Use the definition of multivalued dependency (Section 7.4) to argue that each of the following axioms is sound:
  (*a*) The complementation rule
  (*b*) The multivalued augmentation rule
  (*c*) The multivalued transitivity rule

**7.18.** Use the definitions of functional and multivalued dependencies (Sections 6.5 and 7.4) to show the soundness of the replication rule.

**7.19.** Show that the coalescence rule is sound. (*Hint*: Apply the definition of $\alpha \twoheadrightarrow \beta$ to a pair of tuples $t_1$ and $t_2$ such that $t_1[\alpha] = t_2[\alpha]$. Observe that since $\delta \cap \beta = \varnothing$, if two tuples have the same value on $R - \beta$, then they have the same value on $\delta$.)

**7.20.** Use the axioms for functional and multivalued dependencies to show that each of the following rules is sound:
  (*a*) The multivalued union rule
  (*b*) The intersection rule
  (*c*) The difference rule

**7.21.** Let $R = (A, B, C, D, E)$, and let $M$ be the following set of multivalued dependencies

$$A \twoheadrightarrow BC$$
$$B \twoheadrightarrow CD$$
$$E \twoheadrightarrow AD$$

List the nontrivial dependencies in $M^+$.

**7.22.** Give a lossless-join decomposition of schema $R$ in Exercise 7.21 into 4NF.

**7.23.** Give an example of a relation schema $R$ and a set of dependencies such that $R$ is in BCNF, but is not in 4NF.

**7.24.** Explain why 4NF is a normal form more desirable than is BCNF.

**7.25.** Give an example of relation schema $R$ and a set of dependencies such that $R$ is in 4NF, but is not in PJNF.

**7.26.** Explain why PJNF is a normal form more desirable than is 4NF.

**7.27.** Rewrite the definitions of 4NF and BCNF using the notions of domain constraints and general constraints.

**7.28.** Explain why DKNF is a highly desirable normal form, yet is one that is difficult to achieve in practice.

**7.29.** Explain how dangling tuples may arise. Explain problems that they may cause.

# Bibliographical Notes

The first discussion of relational-database design theory appeared in an early paper by Codd [1970]. In that paper, Codd also introduced first, second, and third normal forms.

BCNF was introduced in Codd [1972a]. The desirability of BCNF is discussed in Bernstein and Goodman [1980b]. A polynomial-time algorithm for BCNF decomposition appears in Tsou and Fischer [1982]. Biskup et al. [1979] give the algorithm we used to find a lossless-join dependency-preserving decomposition into 3NF. See Ullman [1988] for a proof that decomposition produced by the algorithm is in 3NF. Fundamental results on the lossless-join property appear in Aho et al. [1979b].

Multivalued dependencies are discussed by Zaniolo [1976]. Beeri et al. [1977] give a set of axioms for multivalued dependencies, and prove that their axioms are sound and complete. Our axiomatization is based on theirs.

The notions of 4NF, PJNF, and DKNF are from Fagin [1977], Fagin [1979], and Fagin [1981], respectively. The synthesis approach to database design is discussed in Bernstein [1976].

Join dependencies were introduced by Rissanen [1979]. Sciore [1982] gives a set of axioms for a class of dependencies that properly includes the join dependencies. In addition to their use in PJNF, join dependencies are central to the definition of universal relation databases. Fagin et al. [1982] introduces the relationship between join dependencies and the definition of a relation as a conjunction of predicates (see Section 7.5.1). This use of join dependencies has led to a large amount of research into *acyclic* database schemas. Intuitively, a schema is acyclic if every pair of attributes is related in a unique way. Formal treatment of acyclic schemas appears in Fagin [1983], and in Beeri et al. [1983].

Additional dependencies are discussed in detail in Maier [1983]. Inclusion dependencies are discussed by Casanova et al. [1984] and Cosmadakis et al. [1990]. Template dependencies are covered by Sadri and Ullman [1982]. Mutual dependencies are examined by Furtado [1978], and by Mendelzon and Maier [1979].

Maier [1983] presents the design theory of relational databases in detail. Ullman [1988], and Abiteboul et al. [1995] present a more theoretic coverage of many of the dependencies and normal forms presented here.

# CHAPTER
# 8

## OBJECT-ORIENTED
## DATABASES

In recent years, several new application areas for database systems have emerged that are limited by restrictions imposed by the relational data model. As a result, several new data models have been proposed to deal with these new application domains. In this chapter, as well as in Chapter 9, we present the basic underlying concepts of these new data models. This chapter concentrates on the *object-oriented model*, which is based on the object-oriented–programming paradigm. This approach to programming was first introduced by the language Simula 67, which was designed for programming of simulations. More recently, the languages C++ and Smalltalk have become the most widely known object-oriented programming languages. In this chapter, we introduce the concepts of object-oriented programming and then consider the use of these concepts in database systems.

## 8.1 New Database Applications

The purpose of database systems is the management of large bodies of information. Early databases developed from file-management systems. These systems evolved first into either network (see Appendix A) or hierarchical (see Appendix B) databases, and later, into relational databases. Among the common features of these "old" applications are the following:

- **Uniformity**. There are large numbers of similarly structured data items, all of which have the same size (in bytes).
- **Record orientation**. The basic data items consist of fixed-length records.

- **Small data items**. Each record is short—records are rarely more than a few hundred bytes long.
- **Atomic fields**. Fields within a record are short and of fixed length. There is no structure within fields. In other words, first normal form holds (see Chapter 7).

In recent years, however, database technology has been applied to applications outside the realm of data processing that, in general, fail to have at least one of the preceding features. These new applications include the following:

- **Computer-aided design (CAD)**. A CAD database stores data pertaining to an engineering design, including the components of the item being designed, the interrelationship of components, and old versions of designs.
- **Computer-aided software engineering (CASE)**. A CASE database stores data required to assist software developers. These data include source code, dependencies among software modules, definitions and uses of variables, and the development history of the software system.
- **Multimedia databases**. A multimedia database contains image, spatial data, audio data, video data, and the like. Databases of this sort arise from the need to store photographs, and geographical data, and from voice-mail systems, graphics applications, and video-on-demand systems.
- **Office information systems (OIS)**. Office automation includes workstation-based tools for document creation and document retrieval, tools for maintaining appointment calendars, and so on. An OIS database must allow queries pertaining to schedules, documents, and contents of documents.
- **Hypertext databases**. Hypertext is text that is enriched with links that point to other documents. The world-wide web is an example of hypertext (or, more accurately, hypermedia, since web documents may be multimedia documents). Hypertext documents may also be structured in specific ways that help index them. Hypertext database must support the ability to retrieve documents based on links, and to query documents based on their structure.

These new applications of databases were not considered in the 1970s, when most current commercial database systems were initially designed. They are now practical owing to the increase in available main memory and disk size, the speedup of central processing units, the lower cost of hardware, and the improved understanding of database management that has developed in recent years.

The relational model and entity-relationship models are not sufficient to model the data requirements of these new applications. Moreover, the modeling requirements of even traditional business applications has grown more complex over time, and it is hard to express some of their requirements in the relational model. For instance, today's business applications often have to deal with image data and hypertext databases.

In this chapter, as well as in Chapter 9, we consider several data-modeling concepts that have been developed to meet the needs of these applications. We shall not discuss the features of all the preceding applications in detail. Rather, we shall use a few of them as examples of those concepts not well illustrated by our bank example. Here, we consider these concepts as they relate to the object-oriented paradigm. In Chapter 9, we consider these concepts as they relate to the object-relational paradigm.

## 8.2   The Object-Oriented Data Model

The object-oriented data model has several aspects, which we study in the following sections.

### 8.2.1   Object Structure

Loosely speaking, an *object* corresponds to an entity in the E-R model. The object-oriented paradigm is based on *encapsulating* data and code related to an object into a single unit. Conceptually, all interactions between an object and the rest of the system are via messages. Thus, the interface between an object and the rest of the system is defined by a set of allowed *messages*.

In general, an object has associated with it

- A set of *variables* that contain the data for the object; variables correspond to attributes in the E-R model

- A set of *messages* to which the object responds; each message may have zero, one, or more *parameters*

- A set of *methods*, each of which is a body of code to implement a message; a method returns a value as the *response* to the message

The term *message* in an object-oriented context does not imply the use of a physical message in a computer network. Rather, it refers to the passing of requests among objects without regard to specific implementation details. The term *invoke a method* is sometimes used to denote the act of sending a message to an object and the execution of the corresponding method.

We can illustrate the motivation for using this approach by considering *employee* entities in a bank database. Suppose the annual salary of an employee is calculated in different ways for different employees. For instance, managers may get a bonus depending on the bank's performance, while tellers may get a bonus depending on how many hours they have worked. We can (conceptually) encapsulate the code for computing the salary with each employee as a method that is executed in response to an *annual-salary* message.

All *employee* objects respond to the *annual-salary* message, but they do so in different ways. By encapsulating within the *employee* object itself the information about how to compute the annual salary, all employee objects present the same interface. Since the only external interface presented by an object is the set of messages to which that object responds, it is possible to modify the definitions of methods and variables without affecting the rest of the system. The ability to modify the definition of an object without affecting the rest of the system is considered to be one of the major advantages of the object-oriented–programming paradigm.

Methods of an object may be classified as either *read-only* or *update*. A read-only method does not affect the values of the variables in an object, whereas an update method may change the values of the variables. The messages to which an object responds can be similarly classified as read-only or update, based on the method that implements the message.

Derived attributes of an entity in the E-R model can be expressed in the object-oriented model as read-only messages. For example, the derived attribute *employment-length* of an *employee* entity can be expressed as an *employment-length* message of an *employee* object. The method implementing the message may determine the employment length by subtracting the *start-date* of the employee from the current date.

Strictly speaking, every attribute of an entity must be expressed as a variable and a pair of messages of the corresponding object in the object-oriented model. The variable is used to store the value of the attribute, one message is used to read the value of the attribute, and the other method is used to update the value. For instance, the attribute *address* of the *employee* entity can be represented by:

- A variable *address*
- A message *get-address* the response to which is the address
- A message *set-address*, which takes a parameter *new-address*, to update the address

However, for simplicity, many object-oriented data models allow variables to be read or updated directly, without having to define messages to read and update them.

## 8.2.2   Object Classes

Usually, there are many similar objects in a database. By *similar*, we mean that they respond to the same messages, use the same methods, and have variables of the same name and type. It would be wasteful to define each such object separately. Therefore, we group similar objects to form a *class*. Each such object is called an *instance* of its class. All objects in a class share a common definition, although they differ in the values assigned to the variables.

The notion of a class in the object-oriented data model corresponds to the notion of an entity-set in the E-R model. Examples of classes in our bank database are employees, customers, accounts, and loans.

We show below the definition of the class *employee*, written in pseudocode. The definition shows the variables and the messages to which the objects of the class respond; the methods for handling the messages are not shown here.

```
class employee {
    /* Variables */
        string name;
        string address;
        date    start-date;
        int     salary;
    /* Messages */
        int     annual-salary();
        string get-name();
        string get-address();
        int     set-address(string new-address);
        int     employment-length();
};
```

In the above definition, each object of the class *employee* contains the variables *name* and *address*, both of which are strings, *start-date*, which is a date, and *salary*, which is an integer. Each object responds to the five messages shown, namely *annual-salary*, *get-name*, *get-address*, *set-address* and *employment-length*. The type name before each message name indicates the type of the response to the message. Also observe that the message *set-address* takes a parameter *new-address*, which specifies the new value of the address.

The concept of classes is similar to the concept of abstract data types. However, there are several additional aspects to the class concept, beyond those of abstract data types. To represent these additional properties, we treat each class as itself being an object. A class object includes

- A set-valued variable whose value is the set of all objects that are instances of the class
- Implementation of a method for the message *new*, which creates a new instance of the class

We return to these features in Section 8.5.2.

## 8.2.3   Inheritance

An object-oriented database schema typically requires a large number of classes. Often, however, several classes are similar. For example, assume that we have an object-oriented database for our bank application. We would expect the class of bank customers to be similar to the class of bank employees, in that both define variables for *name*, *address*, and so on. However, there are variables specific to employees (*salary*, for example) and variables specific to customers (*credit-rating*, for example). It would be desirable to define a representation for the common variables in one place. We can define one only if we combine employees and customers into one class.

To allow the direct representation of similarities among classes, we need to place classes in a specialization hierarchy (the "ISA" relationship) like that defined

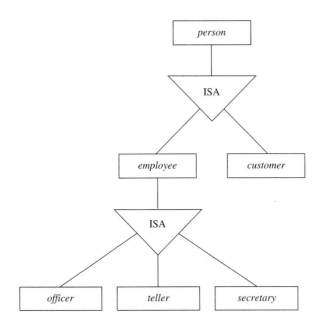

Figure 8.1     Specialization hierarchy for the bank example.

in Chapter 2 for the entity–relationship model. For instance, we say that *employee* is a specialization of *person*, because the set of all employees is a subset of the set of all persons. That is, every employee is a person. Similarly, *customer* is a specialization of *person*.

The concept of a class hierarchy is similar to the concept of specialization in the entity–relationship model. Employees and customers can be represented by classes that are specializations of a *person* class. Variables and methods specific to employees are associated with the *employee* class. Variables and methods specific to customers are associated with the *customer* class. Variables and methods that apply both to employees and to customers are associated with the *person* class.

Figure 8.1 shows an E-R diagram with a specialization hierarchy to repre-sent people involved in the operation of our bank example. Figure 8.2 shows the corresponding class hierarchy. The classes shown in the hierarchy can be defined in pseudocode as shown in Figure 8.3. For brevity, we do not present the methods associated with these classes, although they would be included in a full definition of the bank database.

The keyword **isa** is used to indicate that a class is a specialization of another class. The specializations of a class are called *subclasses*. Thus, for example, *employee* is a subclass of *person*, and *teller* is a subclass of *employee*. Conversely, *employee* is a *superclass* of *teller*, and *person* is a superclass of *employee*.

An object representing an officer contains all the variables of class *officer*; in addition the object representing an officer also contains all the variables of classes *employee* and *person*. This is because every officer is defined to be an employee,

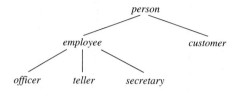

Figure 8.2    Class hierarchy corresponding to Figure 8.1.

and since in turn every employee is defined to be a person, we can infer that every officer is also a person. This property that objects of a class contain variables defined in its superclasses is referred to as the *inheritance* of variables.

Methods are inherited in a manner identical to inheritance of variables. An important benefit of inheritance in object-oriented systems is the notion of *substitutability*: Any method of a class—say, *A* (or a function that takes an object of a class *A* as an argument)—can equally well be invoked with any object belonging to any subclass *B* of *A*. This characteristic leads to code reuse, since the methods and functions do not have to be written again for objects of class *B*. For instance,

```
class person {
    string  name;
    string  address;
};
class customer isa person {
    int     credit-rating;
};
class employee isa person {
    date    start-date;
    int     salary;
};
class officer isa employee {
    int     office-number;
    int     expense-account-number;
};
class teller isa employee {
    int     hours-per-week;
    int     station-number;
};
class secretary isa employee {
    int     hours-per-week;
    string  manager;
};
```

Figure 8.3    Definition of class hierarchy in pseudocode.

if the method *get-name*() is defined for the class *person*, it can be invoked with a *person* object, or with any object belonging to any subclass of *person*, such as *customer* or *officer*.

Earlier, we noted that each class is itself an object, and that that object includes a variable containing the set of all instances of the class. It is easy to determine which objects are associated with classes at the leaves of the hierarchy. For example, we associate with the *customer* class the set of all customers of the bank. For nonleaf classes, however, the issue is more complex. In the hierarchy of Figure 8.2, there are two plausible ways of associating objects with classes:

1. We could associate with the *employee* class all employee objects including those that are instances of *officer*, *teller*, and *secretary*.

2. We could associate with the *employee* class only those employee objects that are instances of neither *officer* nor *teller* nor *secretary*.

Typically, the latter choice is made in object-oriented systems. It is possible to determine the set of all employee objects in this case by taking the union of those objects associated with all subclasses of *employee*. Most object-oriented systems allow the specialization to be partial; that is, they allow objects that belong to a class such as *employee* but that do not belong to any of that class's subclasses.

### 8.2.4    Multiple Inheritance

In most cases, a tree-structured organization of classes is adequate to describe applications. In such cases, all superclasses of a class are ancestors or descendants of one another in the hierarchy. However, there are situations that cannot be represented well in a such tree-structured class hierarchy.

Suppose that we wish to distinguish between full-time and part-time tellers and secretaries in our example of Figure 8.2. Further assume that we require different variables and methods to represent full-time and part-time employees. Thus, each of these employees is classified in two different ways. We could create subclasses: *part-time-teller*, *full-time-teller*, *part-time-secretary* and *full-time-secretary*. The resulting hierarchy shown in Figure 8.4 has a few drawbacks:

- As we noted, there are certain variables and methods specific to full-time employment, and others specific to part-time employment. In Figure 8.4, the variables and methods for full-time employees must be defined twice: once for *full-time-secretary*, and once for *full-time-teller*. A similar redundancy exists for part-time employees. Redundancy of this form is undesirable, since any change to the properties of full- or part-time employees must be made in two places, leading to potential inconsistency. Furthermore, the hierarchy fails to exploit potential code reuse.

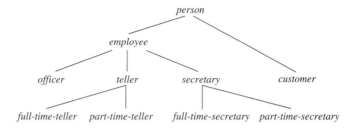

Figure 8.4    Class hierarchy for full- and part-time employees.

- The hierarchy has no means of representing employees who are not officers, tellers or secretaries, unless we expand the hierarchy further to include the classes *full-time-employee* and *part-time-employee*.

If we had several job classifications, instead of the two in our simple example, the limitations of the model would become even more apparent.

The difficulties that we have just observed are dealt with in the object-oriented model by the concept of *multiple inheritance*, which is the ability of a class to inherit variables and methods from multiple superclasses. The class–subclass relationship is represented by a *directed acyclic graph* (*DAG*), in which a class may have more than one superclass. Let us return to our bank example. Using a DAG, we can define properties of full- and part-time employment in one place. As shown in Figure 8.5, we define a class *part-time*, which defines those variables and methods specific to part-time employment, and a class *full-time*, which defines those variables and methods specific to full-time employment. The class *part-time-teller* is a subclass of both *teller* and *part-time*. It inherits from *teller* those variables and methods pertaining to tellers, and from *part-time* those variables and methods pertaining to part-time employment. The redundancy of the hierarchy of Figure 8.4 is eliminated.

Using the DAG of Figure 8.5, we can represent full- and part-time employees who are neither tellers nor secretaries as instances of classes *full-time* and *part-time*, respectively.

When multiple inheritance is used, there is potential ambiguity if the same variable or method can be inherited from more than one superclass. In our bank

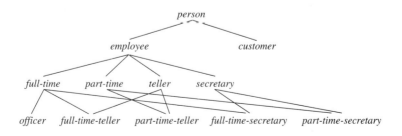

Figure 8.5    Class DAG for the bank example.

example, let us assume that, instead of defining *salary* for class *employee*, we define a variable *pay* for each of *full-time*, *part-time*, *teller*, and *secretary*, as follows:

- *full-time*: *pay* is an integer from 0 to 100,000, containing an annual salary.
- *part-time*: *pay* is an integer from 0 to 20, containing an hourly rate of pay.
- *teller*: *pay* is an integer from 0 to 20,000, containing an annual salary.
- *secretary*: *pay* is an integer from 0 to 25,000, containing an annual salary.

Consider the class *part-time-secretary*. It could inherit the definition of *pay* from either *part-time* or *secretary*. The result is different, depending on the choice made. Among the options chosen by various implementations of the object-oriented model are the following:

- Include both variables, renaming them to *part-time.pay* and *secretary.pay*.
- Choose one or the other, based on the order in which the classes *part-time* and *secretary* were created.
- Force the user to make a choice explicitly in the definition of the class *part-time-secretary*.
- Treat the situation as an error.

No single solution has been accepted as best, and different systems make different choices.

Not all cases of multiple inheritance lead to ambiguity. If, instead of defining *pay*, we retain the definition of variable *salary* in class *employee*, and define it nowhere else, then classes *part-time*, *full-time*, *secretary*, and *teller* all inherit *salary* from *employee*. Since all four of these classes share the same definition of *salary*, no ambiguity results from the inheritance of *salary* by *part-time-secretary*, *full-time-secretary*, and so on.

We can use multiple inheritance to model the concept of "roles." To understand the concept, we consider a university database. The database may have several subclasses of *person*, such as *student*, *teacher*, and *footballPlayer*. An object can belong to several of these categories at once, and each of these categories is called a *role*. We can use multiple inheritance to create subclasses such as *student-teacher*, *student-footballPlayer*, and so on, to model the possibility of an object simultaneously having multiple roles. We discuss data-definition–language issues for multiple inheritance in Chapter 9, where we also present an alternative way of modeling roles.

## 8.2.5  Object Identity

Objects in an object-oriented database usually correspond to an entity in the enterprise being modeled by the database. An entity retains its identity even if some of its properties change over time. Likewise, an object retains its identity even if some or all of the values of variables or definitions of methods change over time. This concept of identity does not apply to tuples of a relational database. In relational systems, the tuples of a relation are distinguished only by the values that they contain.

Object identity is a stronger notion of identity than that typically found in programming languages or in data models not based on object orientation. We illustrate several forms of identity next.

- **Value**. A data value is used for identity. This form of identity is used in relational systems. For instance, the primary key value of a tuple identifies the tuple.

- **Name**. A user-supplied name is used for identity. This form of identity typically is used for files in file systems. Each file is given a name that uniquely identifies the file, regardless of the contents of the file.

- **Built-in**. A notion of identity is built into the data model or programming language, and no user-supplied identifier is required. This form of identity is used in object-oriented systems. Each object is automatically given an identifier by the system when that object is created.

The identity of objects is a conceptual notion; actual systems require a physical mechanism to *identify* objects uniquely. For humans, names along with other information, such as date and place of birth, are often used as identifiers. Object-oriented systems provide a notion of an *object identifier* to identify objects. Object identifiers are *unique*; that is, each object has a single identifier, and no two objects have the same identifier. Object identifiers are not necessarily in a form with which humans are comfortable—they could be long numbers, for example. The ability to store the identifier of an object as a field of another object is more important than is having a name that is easy to remember.

As an example of the use of object identifiers, one of the attributes of a *person* object may be a *spouse* attribute, which is actually the identifier of the *person* object corresponding to the first person's spouse. Thus, the *person* object can store a *reference* to the object representing the person's spouse.

Usually, the identifier is generated automatically by the system. In contrast, in a relational database, the *spouse* field of a *person* relation would typically be a unique identifier (perhaps a social-security number) of the person's spouse, generated external to the database system. There are many situations where having the system generate identifiers automatically is a benefit, since it frees humans from performing that task. However, this ability should be used with care. System-generated identifiers are usually specific to the system, and have to be translated if data are moved to a different database system. System-generated identifiers may be redundant if the entities being modeled already have unique identifiers external to the system. For example, social-security numbers are often used as unique identifiers for people in the United States.

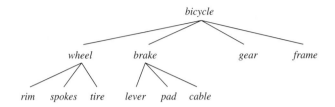

Figure 8.6    Containment hierarchy for bicycle-design database.

## 8.2.6  Object Containment

References between objects can be used to model different real world concepts. One such concept is that of *object containment*. To illustrate containment, we consider the simplified bicycle-design database of Figure 8.6. Each bicycle design contains wheels, a frame, brakes, and gears. Wheels, in turn, contain a rim, a set of spokes, and a tire. Each of the components of the design can be modeled as an object, and the containment of components can be modeled as containment of objects.

Objects that contain other objects are called *complex* or *composite* objects. There can be multiple levels of containment, as shown in Figure 8.6. This situation creates a *containment hierarchy* among objects.

The hierarchy of Figure 8.6 shows the containment relationship among objects in a schematic way by listing class names, rather than individual objects. The links between classes must be interpreted as **is-part-of**, rather than the **is-a** interpretation of links in an inheritance hierarchy.

The variables of the various classes are not shown in the figure. Consider the class *bicycle*. It may include variables such as *brand-name* containing descriptive data about an instance of the class *bicycle*. In addition, class *bicycle* includes variables that contain a reference, or a set of references, to objects from the classes *wheel*, *brake*, *gear*, and *frame*.

Containment is an important concept in object-oriented systems because it allows data to be viewed at different granularities by different users. A wheel designer can focus on instances of class *wheel* without much, if any, concern about the objects of class *gear* or *brake*. A marketing-staff person, attempting to price an entire bicycle, can reference all data pertaining to the bicycle by referencing the appropriate instance of class *bicycle*. The containment hierarchy is used to find all objects contained in a *bicycle* object.

In certain applications, an object may be contained in several objects. In such cases, the containment relationship is represented by a DAG, rather than by a hierarchy.

## 8.3  Object-Oriented Languages

Until now, we have covered the basic concepts of object orientation at an abstract level. To be used in practice in a database system, the concepts have to be expressed in some language. This expression can be done in one of two ways.

1. The concepts of object-orientation are used purely as a design tool, and are encoded into, for example, a relational database. This approach is followed when entity–relationship diagrams are used to model data, and are then manually converted into a set of relations.

2. The concepts of object orientation are incorporated into a language that is used to manipulate the database.

    With this approach, there are several possible languages into which the concepts can be integrated.

    - One choice is to extend a data-manipulation language such as SQL by adding complex types and object-orientation. Systems that provide object-oriented extensions to relational systems are called *object-relational* systems. We describe object-relational systems, and in particular object-oriented extensions to SQL, in Chapter 9.

    - Another choice is to take an existing object-oriented programming language and to extend it to deal with databases. Such languages are called persistent programming languages.

    We study the latter approach in succeeding sections of this chapter. There are different situations in which each approach is better. We discuss their relationship in Chapter 9, after describing object-relational systems.

## 8.4 Persistent Programming Languages

Databases languages differ from traditional programming languages in that they directly manipulate data that are persistent—that is, data that continue to exist even after the program that created it has terminated. A relation in a database and tuples in a relation are examples of persistent data. In contrast, the only persistent data that traditional programming languages directly manipulate are files.

Access to a database is only one component of any real-world application. While a data manipulation language like SQL is quite effective for accessing data, a programming language is required for implementing other components of the application such as user interfaces or communication with other computers. The traditional way of interfacing database to programming languages is by embedding SQL within the programming language.

A *persistent programming language* is a programming language extended with constructs to handle persistent data. Persistent programming languages can be distinguished from languages with embedded SQL in at least two ways:

1. With an embedded language, the type system of the host language usually differs from the type system of the data manipulation language. The programmer is responsible for any type conversions between the host language and the data manipulation language. Requiring the programmer to carry out this task has several drawbacks:

    - The code to convert between objects and tuples operates outside the object-oriented type system, and hence has a higher chance of having undetected errors.

- Conversion between the object-oriented format and the relational format of tuples in the database takes a substantial amount of code. The format translation code, along with the code for loading and unloading data from a database, can form a significant percentage of the total code required for an application.

     In contrast, in a persistent programming language, the query language is fully integrated with the host language, and both share the same type system. Objects can be created and stored in the database without any explicit type or format changes; any format changes required are carried out transparently.

2. The programmer using an embedded query language is responsible for writing explicit code to fetch data from the database into memory. If any updates are performed, the programmer must write code explicitly to store the updated data back in the database.

     In contrast, in a persistent programming language, the programmer can manipulate persistent data without having to write code explicitly to fetch it into memory or store it back to disk.

Persistent versions of programming languages such as Pascal have been proposed in the past. In recent years, persistent versions of object-oriented languages such as C++ or Smalltalk have received much attention. They allow programmers to manipulate data directly from the programming language, without having to go through a data-manipulation language such as SQL. Thereby, they provide tighter integration of the programming languages with the database than, for example, embedded SQL.

There are certain drawbacks to persistent programming languages, however, that we must keep in mind when deciding whether to use them. Since the programming language is typically powerful, it is relatively easy to make programming errors that damage the database. The complexity of the language makes automatic high-level optimization, such as to reduce disk I/O, harder. Support for declarative querying is important for many applications, but persistent programming languages currently do not support declarative querying well.

## 8.4.1   Persistence of Objects

Object-oriented programming languages already have a concept of objects, a type system to define object types, and constructs to create objects. However, these objects are *transient*—they vanish when the program terminates, just as variables in a Pascal or C program vanish when the program terminates. If we wish to turn such a language into a database programming language, the first step is to provide a way to make objects persistent. Several approaches have been proposed.

- **Persistence by class**. The simplest, but least convenient, approach is to declare that a class is persistent. All objects of the class are then persistent objects by default. Objects of nonpersistent classes are all transient.

This approach is not flexible, since it is often useful to have both transient and persistent objects in a single class. In many object-oriented database systems, declaring a class to be persistent is interpreted as saying that objects in the class potentially can be made persistent, rather than that all objects in the class are persistent. Such classes might more appropriately have been called "persistable" classes.

- **Persistence by creation**. In this approach, new syntax is introduced to create persistent objects, by extending the syntax for creating transient objects. Thus, an object is either persistent or transient, depending on how it was created. This approach is followed in several object-oriented database systems.

- **Persistence by marking**. A variant of the preceding approach is to mark objects as persistent after they are created. All objects are created as transient objects, but, if an object is to persist beyond the execution of the program, it must be marked explicitly as persistent before the program terminates. Unlike the previous approach, the decision on persistence or transience is postponed until after the object is created.

- **Persistence by reference**. One or more objects are explicitly declared as (root) persistent objects. All other objects are persistent if (and only if) they are referred to directly, or indirectly, from a root persistent object.

  Thus, all objects referenced from the root persistent objects are persistent. But also, all objects referenced from these objects are persistent, and objects to which they refer are in turn persistent, and so on.

  This scheme has the benefit that it is easy to make entire data structures persistent by merely declaring the root of such structures as persistent. However, the database system has the burden of following chains of references to detect which objects are persistent, and that can be expensive.

## 8.4.2   Object Identity and Pointers

When a persistent object is created, it is assigned a persistent object identifier. In an object-oriented programming language that has not been extended to handle persistence, when an object is created, a transient object identifier is returned. The only difference between the two identifiers is that the transient object identifier is valid only when the program that created it is executing; after that program terminates, the object is deleted, and the identifier is meaningless.

The notion of object identity has an interesting relationship to pointers in programming languages. A simple way to achieve built-in identity is through pointers to physical locations in storage. In particular, in many object-oriented languages such as C++, an object identifier is actually an in-memory pointer.

However, the association of an object with a physical location in storage may change over time. There are several degrees of permanence of identity:

- **Intraprocedure**. Identity persists only during the execution of a single procedure. Examples of intraprogram identity are local variables within procedures.

- **Intraprogram**. Identity persists only during the execution of a single program or query. Examples of intraprogram identity are global variables in programming languages. Main-memory or virtual-memory pointers offer only intraprogram identity.

- **Interprogram**. Identity persists from one program execution to another. Pointers to file-system data on disk offer interprogram identity, but they may change if the way data is stored in the file system is changed.

- **Persistent**. Identity persists not only among program executions, but also among structural reorganizations of the data. It is the persistent form of identity that is required for object-oriented systems.

In persistent extensions of languages such as C++, object identifiers for persistent objects are implemented as "persistent pointers." A *persistent pointer* is a type of pointer that, unlike in-memory pointers, remains valid even after the end of a program execution, and across some forms of data reorganization. A programmer may use a persistent pointer in the same ways that she may use an in-memory pointer in a programming language. Conceptually, we may think of a persistent pointer as a pointer to an object in the database.

### 8.4.3   Storage and Access of Persistent Objects

What does it mean to store an object in a database? Clearly, the data part of an object has to be stored individually for each object. Logically, the code that implements methods of a class should be stored in the database as part of the database schema, along with the type definitions of the classes. However, many implementations simply store the code in files outside the database, to avoid having to integrate system software such as compilers with the database system.

There are several ways to find objects in the database. One approach is to give names to objects, just as we give names to files. This approach works for a relatively small number of objects, but does not scale to millions of objects. A second approach is to expose object identifiers or persistent pointers to the objects, which can be stored externally. Unlike names, these pointers do not have to be mnemonic, and can even be physical pointers pointers into a database.

A third approach is to store collections of objects, and to allow programs to iterate over the collections to find required objects. Collections of objects can themselves be modeled as objects of a *collection type*. Collection types include sets, multisets (that is, sets with possibly many occurrences of a value), lists, and so on. A special case of a collection is a *class extent*, which is the collection of all objects belonging to the class. If a class extent is present for a class, then, whenever an object of the class is created that object is inserted in the class extent automatically, and, whenever an object is deleted, that object is removed from the class extent. Class extents allow classes to be treated like relations in that it is possible to examine all objects in the class, just as we can examine all tuples in a relation.

Most object-oriented database systems support all three ways of accessing persistent objects. All objects have object identifiers. Names are typically given only to class extents and other collection objects, and perhaps to other selected objects, but most objects are not given names. Class extents are usually maintained for all classes that can have persistent objects, but, in many of the implementations, they contain only persistent objects of the class.

# 8.5 Persistent C++ Systems

Several object-oriented databases based on persistent extensions to C++ have appeared in the past few years (see the bibliographic notes). There are differences between them in terms of the system architecture, yet they have many common features in terms of the programming language.

Several of the object-oriented features of the C++ language help in providing a good deal of support for persistence without changing the language itself. For example, we can declare a class called `Persistent_Object` with attributes and methods to support persistence; any other class that should be persistent can be made a subclass of this class, and thereby inherit the support for persistence. The C++ language (like other modern programming languages) also provides the ability to redefine standard function names and operators—such as +, −, the pointer dereference operator ->, and so on—based on the type of the operands on which they are applied. This ability is called *overloading*, and is used to redefine operators to behave in the required manner when they are operating on persistent objects. Examples of the use of such features are presented in the next section.

Providing persistence support via class libraries has the benefit of making minimal changes to C++, and is relatively easy to implement. However, it has the drawback that the programmer has to spend much more time to write a program that handles persistent objects, and it is not easy to specify integrity constraints on the schema, or to provide support for declarative querying. Most of the persistent C++ implementations therefore extend the C++ syntax, at least to some extent.

## 8.5.1 The ODMG C++ Object-Definition Language

The Object Database Management Group (ODMG) has been working on standardizing language extensions to C++ and Smalltalk to support persistence, and on defining class libraries to support persistence. The ODMG standard attempts to extend C++ as little as possible, providing most functionality via class libraries. We describe the ODMG standard using examples. You must have prior knowledge of the C++ programming language to understand the examples fully. (See the bibliographic notes for references to C++ texts.)

There are two parts to the ODMG C++ extension: (1) the *C++ Object Definition Language* (*C++ ODL*), and (2) the *C++ Object Manipulation Language* (*C++ OML*). The C++ ODL extends the C++ type definition syntax.

Figure 8.7 shows a sample of code written in the ODMG C++ ODL. The schema of four classes are defined in the code. Each class is defined as a subclass of `Persistent_Object`, and objects in the class can therefore be made persistent. The classes `Person`, `Branch`, and `Account` are direct subclasses of

```
class Person : public Persistent_Object {
public:
   String name;
   String address;
};

class Customer : public Person {
public:
   Date member_from;
   int customer_id;
   Ref<Branch> home_branch;
   Set<Ref<Account>> accounts inverse Account::owners;
};

class Branch : public Persistent_Object {
public:
   String name;
   String address;
   int assets;
};

class Account : public Persistent_Object {
private:
   int balance;
public:
   int number;
   Set<Ref<Customer>> owners inverse Customer::accounts;
   int find_balance();
   int update_balance(int delta);
};
```

Figure 8.7    Example of ODMG C++ Object Definition Language.

Persistent_Object. The class Customer is a subclass of Person and is therefore indirectly also a subclass of Persistent_Object.

C++ does not support the concept of messages directly. Instead, methods may be directly invoked, and behave like procedure calls. The keyword private indicates that the following attributes or methods are visible to only methods of the class; public indicates that the attributes or methods are visible to other code as well. The use of the keyword public just before the name of a superclass indicates that public attributes or methods inherited from the superclass remain public in the subclass. These features are part of standard C++.

The attribute definitions of type int, String, and Date are in standard C++ syntax; the types String and Date are among the standard types defined by ODMG. Type Ref<Branch> is a *reference*, or persistent pointer, to an object of type Branch. Type Set<Ref<Account>> is a set of persistent pointers to objects of type `Account`. We use the notation **inverse** to specify referential integrity constraints. Consider any `Customer` object. Specifying **inverse** `Account::owners` for the attribute `accounts` says that, for each account object referenced in the `accounts` set of the `Customer` object, the field `owners` of the account object must contain a reference back to the `Customer` object.

The classes `Ref<T>` and `Set<T>` are *template* classes defined in the ODMG standard; they are defined in a type-independent way, and are instantiated to the required types (such as `Ref<Account>`) as desired. The template class `Set<T>` provides functions such as `insert_element` and `delete_element`.

The declaration of class `Account` also illustrates the "encapsulation" features of C++. The attribute `balance` of `Account` is declared to be private, meaning that no function other than methods of the class can read or write it. The class also has two methods: `find_balance()` and `update_balance(int delta)`. These methods can read and write the balance attribute; we shall use them to read and update the balance of the account (we have not presented their code).

The only extension to the C++ syntax in the preceding example is the syntax for declaring inverse relationships to ensure referential integrity. All other functionality added by ODMG is provided by means of class libraries.

Planned extensions to the standard include replacement of `Ref<T>` by the usual C++ notation `T*`, to improve readability. Certain systems, such as Object-Store, provide this enhancement already. To the programmer, pointers to persistent objects appear to be the same as pointers to regular in-memory objects, and that makes programming much easier. This functionality is implemented by means of a translation mechanism called *swizzling*, which converts between persistent pointers and in-memory pointers; swizzling is described in Chapter 10.

## 8.5.2   The ODMG C++ Object Manipulation Language

Figure 8.8 shows an example of code written in the ODMG C++ OML. First, a database is opened, and a transaction is started.

The notion of transactions is covered in detail in Chapter 13. Briefly, a *transaction* is a sequence of steps, demarcated by a call to `begin` a transaction and a call to `commit` or `abort` the transaction. The steps of the transaction are treated as an atomic unit; the database system guarantees that either all the steps are executed successfully, or, if any step cannot be executed for any reason, the effect of already-executed steps is undone in the database. The transaction is said to have *committed* in the first case, and to have *aborted* in the second case.

As the next step, an account and an owner object are created and are initialized as part of the transaction. Finally, the transaction is committed. The class `Persistent_Object` implements several methods, including the persistent version of the C++ memory-allocation operator `new` that is used in the example code. This version of the `new` operator allocates the object in the specified database, rather than in memory. We use the method `insert_element` of the template class `Set<>` to insert customer and account references in the appropriate sets after creating the customer and account objects. If only one of the two inserts was executed, a referential-integrity violation will be detected when the transaction commit occurs, and the transaction will be aborted.

The example code in Figure 8.8 is incomplete in that after the end of the transaction, the identifiers of the customer and account objects are lost, even though the objects are still in the database. We use a persistent set to store the identifiers of persistent `Customer` objects. It is convenient to store the identifier of the set in a global variable associated with the classes `Customer`. The global variable is declared by adding the following line as part of the `Customer` class declaration.

```
static Ref<Set<Ref<Customer>>> all_customers;
```

The persistent set for `Customer` is initially allocated in the database and its identifier stored in the global variable as follows.

```
Customer::all_customers =
        new(bank_db) Set<Ref<Customer>>;
```

When we create a customer object, we insert its identifier in the set of customers by using a statement of the form

```
Customer::all_customers->insert_element(cust);
```

A persistent set for storing identifiers of `Account` objects can be created, and identifiers of account objects stored in it, similarly.

However, the value of the variable `Customer::all_customers`, and thus the identifier of the persistent set, would be lost when the transaction ends.


```
int create_account_owner(String name, String address) {
   Database bank_db_obj;
   Database * bank_db = & bank_db_obj;
   bank_db->open("Bank-DB");
   Transaction Trans;
   Trans.begin();

   Ref<Account> account = new(bank_db) Account;
   Ref<Customer> cust = new(bank_db) Customer;
   cust->name = name;
   cust->address = address;
   cust->accounts.insert_element(account);
   account->owners.insert_element(cust);
   .. Code to initialize customer_id, account number etc.
   Trans.commit();
}
```

**Figure 8.8**    Example of ODMG C++ Object Manipulation Language.

In order to find the set in the database later on, when the set is initially allocated we give its object identifier a name in the database, as follows.

```
bank_db->set_object_name(Customer::all_customers,
                         "All_Customers");
```

When a later transaction starts up, it first opens the database, and then finds the set created earlier and initializes Customer::all_customers as below.

```
Customer::all_customers =
    bank_db->lookup_object("All_Customers");
```

A *constructor* for a class is a special method that is used to initialize objects when they are created, and is called automatically when the new operator is executed. Similarly, a *destructor* for a class is a special method that is called when objects in the class are deleted. By adding the insert_element statement to the constructors of a class, and adding a corresponding delete_element statement to the destructor of the class, a programmer can ensure that the collection Customer::all_customers is maintained correctly. In certain persistent C++ extensions, class extents (that is, collections containing all persistent objects in a class) are created and maintained automatically for every class that can have persistent objects. The programmer then does not have to write code either for creating persistent sets for the class extent, or for inserting or deleting objects from the class extents.

We can iterate over a collection of references using an *iterator*, as shown in Figure 8.9. We create an iterator using the method create_iterator() that

```
int print_customers() {
    Database bank_db_obj;
    Database * bank_db = & bank_db_obj;
    bank_db->open("Bank-DB");
    Transaction Trans;
    Trans.begin();
    Customer::all_customers =
        bank_db->lookup_object("All_Customers");

    Iterator<Ref<Customer>> iter =
        Customer::all_customers.create_iterator();
    Ref<Customer> p;
    while(iter.next(p)) {
        print_cust(p);
    }
    Trans.commit();
}
```

Figure 8.9    Example of use of ODMG C++ iterators.

is provided by the class `Collection` and by that class's subclasses, such as `Set`. We use the method `next()`, provided by the iterator, to step through consecutive elements of the collection of customers. For each customer, the method `print_cust` (which we assume has been defined elsewhere) is called to print out the customer.

## 8.6   Summary

Database applications in such areas as computer-aided design, software engineering, and office information systems do not fit the set of assumptions made for older, data-processing–style applications. The object-oriented data model has been proposed to deal with several of these new type of applications.

The object-oriented data model is an adaptation to database systems of the object-oriented–programming paradigm. It is based on the concept of encapsulating in an object the data, and the code that operates on those data. Similarly structured objects are grouped into classes. The set of classes is structured into sub- and superclasses based on an extension of the ISA concept of the entity–relationship model. Since the value of a data item in an object is also an object, it is possible to represent object containment, resulting in a composite object.

There are two approaches to creating an object-oriented database: We can add the concepts of object orientation to existing database languages, or we can extend existing object-oriented languages to deal with databases by adding concepts such as persistence and collections. Extended relational databases take the former approach. Persistent programming languages follow the latter approach. Persistent extensions to C++ have made significant progress in recent years. Integrating persistence seamlessly and orthogonally with existing language constructs is important for ease of use.

## Exercises

**8.1.** For each of the following application areas, explain why a relational database system would be inadequate. List all specific system components that would need to be modified.

(*a*) Computer-aided design
(*b*) Computer-aided software engineering
(*c*) Multimedia databases
(*d*) Office information systems

**8.2.** How does the concept of an object in the object-oriented model differ from the concept of an entity in the entity–relationship model?

**8.3.** A car-rental company maintains a vehicle database for all vehicles in its current fleet. For all vehicles, it includes the vehicle identification number, license number, manufacturer, model, date of purchase, and color. Special data are included for certain types of vehicles:

- Trucks: cargo capacity
- Sports cars: horsepower, renter age requirement

- Vans: number of passengers
- Off-road vehicles: ground clearance, drivetrain (four- or two-wheel drive)

Construct an object-oriented database schema definition for this database. Use inheritance where appropriate.

**8.4.** Explain why ambiguity potentially exists with multiple inheritance. Illustrate your explanation with an example.

**8.5.** Explain how the concept of object identity in the object-oriented model differs from the concept of tuple equality in the relational model.

**8.6.** Explain the distinction in meaning between edges in a DAG representing inheritance and a DAG representing object containment.

**8.7.** Consider a system that provides persistent objects. Is such a system necessarily a database system? Explain your answer.

**8.8.** Let $O_1$ and $O_2$ be composite objects that contain the same set of objects. Must $O_1$ be identical to $O_2$? Explain your answer.

**8.9.** Why do persistent programming languages allow transient objects? Might it be simpler to use only persistent objects, with unneeded objects deleted at the end of an execution? Explain your answer.

**8.10.** Explain how a persistent pointer is implemented. Contrast this implementation with that of pointers as they exist in general-purpose languages, such as C or Pascal.

**8.11.** If an object is created without any references to it, how can that object be deleted?

# Bibliographical Notes

Applications of database concepts to CAD are discussed in Haskin and Lorie [1982], Kim et al. [1984], Lorie et al. [1985], Ranft et al. [1990], and Bancilhon et al. [1985a, 1985b].

Object-oriented programming is discussed in Goldberg and Robson [1983], Cox [1986], Stefik and Bobrow [1986], and Stroustrup [1988]. Stroustrup [1992] describes the C++ programming language. There are numerous implemented object-oriented database systems, including (in alphabetical order) Cactis (Hudson and King [1989]), E/Exodus, developed at the University of Wisconsin (Carey et al. [1990]), Gemstone (Maier et al. [1986]), Iris, developed at Hewlett-Packard (Fishman et al. [1990]), Jasmine, developed at Fujitsu Labs (Ishikawa et al. [1993]), $O_2$ (Lecluse et al. [1988]), ObjectStore (Lamb et al. [1991]), Ode, developed at Bell Laboratories (Agrawal and Gehani [1989]), Ontos, Open-OODB, Orion (Banerjee et al. [1987a], Kim et al. [1988] and Kim [1990a]), Versant, and others.

Overviews of object-oriented database research include Kim and Lochovsky [1989], Kim [1990b], Zdonik and Maier [1990], and Dittrich [1988]. Object identity is characterized in detail by Khoshafian and Copeland [1990]. Further discussion of object identity appears in Abiteboul and Kanellakis [1989]. The object database standard ODMG-93 is described in detail in Cattell [1994]. Recent advances in object-oriented database systems are discussed in Dogac et al. [1994].

Schema modification in object-oriented databases is more complicated than schema modification in relational databases, since object-oriented databases have complex type systems with inheritance. Schema modification is discussed in Banerjee et al. [1987b] as it pertains to Orion, and in Penney and Stein [1987] as it pertains to Gemstone. Other discussions of schema modification and semantics appear in Skarra and Zdonik [1986].

Goodman [1995] describes the benefits and drawbacks of using an object-oriented databases in a genome database application.

# CHAPTER
# 9

# OBJECT-RELATIONAL
# DATABASES

Persistent programming languages add persistence and other database features to existing programming languages with an existing object-oriented type system. In contrast, *object-relational data models* extend the relational data model by providing a richer type system including object orientation, and add constructs to relational query languages, such as SQL to deal with the added data types. The extended type systems allow attributes of tuples to have complex types. Such extensions attempt to preserve the relational foundations—in particular, the declarative access to data—while extending the modeling power. Object-relational database systems (that is, database systems based on the object-relation model) provide a convenient migration path for users of relational databases who wish to use object-oriented features.

We first present the motivation for the nested relational model, which allows relations that are not in first normal form, and allows direct representation of hierarchical structures. We then show how we can extend the SQL DDL by adding a rich type system and object orientation. Next, we show how we can extend the SQL query language to deal with complex types, including nested relations, and objects. Finally, we discuss differences between persistent programming languages and object-relational systems, and mention criteria for choosing between them.

## 9.1   Nested Relations

In Chapter 7, we defined *first normal form* (1NF), which requires that all attributes have *atomic domains*. A domain is *atomic* if elements of the domain are considered to be indivisible units.

For example, the set of integers is an atomic domain, but the set of all sets of integers is a nonatomic domain. The distinction is that we do not normally consider integers to have subparts, but we consider set of integers to have subparts—namely, the integers constituting the set. If we were to consider each integer to be an ordered list of digits, then the domain of all integers would be considered nonatomic. Thus, the important issue in 1NF is not the domain itself, but rather the way we use domain elements in the database.

We have not drawn attention to the 1NF assumption until now because the assumption of 1NF is a natural one in the bank examples we have considered. However, not all applications are compatible with the 1NF assumption. Rather than viewing the database as a set of records, users of certain applications view the database as a set of objects. These objects may require several records for their representation. We shall see that a simple, easy-to-use interface requires a one-to-one correspondence between the user's intuitive notion of an object and the database system's notion of a data item.

The nested relational model is an extension of the relational model in which domains may be either atomic or relation valued. Thus, the value of a tuple on an attribute may be a relation, and relations may be stored within relations. A complex object thus can be represented by a single tuple of a nested relation. If we view a tuple of a nested relation as a data item, we have a one-to-one correspondence between data items and objects in the user's view of the database.

We illustrate nested relations by an example drawn from office information systems. Consider a document-retrieval system in which we store, for each document, the following information:

- Document title
- Author list
- Date acquired
- Keyword list

We can see that, if we define a relation for the preceding information, several domains will be nonatomic.

- **Authors**. A document may have a set of authors. Nevertheless, we may want to find all documents of which Jones was one of the authors. Thus, we are interested in a subpart of the domain element "set of authors."
- **Keywords**. If we store a set of keywords for a document, we expect to be able to retrieve all documents whose keywords include one or more keywords. Thus, we view the domain of *keyword-list* as nonatomic.
- **Date**. Unlike *keywords* and *authors*, *date* does not have a set-valued domain. However, we may view *date* as consisting of the subfields *day*, *month*, and *year*. This view makes the domain of *date* nonatomic.

Figure 9.1 shows an example document relation, *doc*. The *doc* relation can be represented in 1NF, as shown in Figure 9.2. Since we must have atomic do-

| title | author-list | date | keyword-list |
|---|---|---|---|
| | | (day, month, year) | |
| salesplan | {Smith, Jones} | (1, April, 89) | {profit, strategy} |
| status report | {Jones, Frick} | (17, June, 94) | {profit, personnel} |

Figure 9.1 Non-1NF document relation, *doc*.

mains in 1NF, yet want access to individual authors and to individual keywords, we need one tuple for each (keyword, author) pair. The *date* attribute is replaced in the 1NF version by three attributes: one for each subfield of *date*.

Much of the awkwardness of the *flat-doc* relation in Figure 9.2 is removed if we assume that the following multivalued dependencies hold:

- *title* $\twoheadrightarrow$ *author*
- *title* $\twoheadrightarrow$ *keyword*
- *title* $\rightarrow$ *day month year*

Then, we can decompose the relation into 4NF using the schemas:

- (*title, author*)
- (*title, keyword*)
- (*title, day, month, year*)

Figure 9.3 shows the projection of the relation *flat-doc* of Figure 9.2 onto the preceding decomposition.

Although 1NF can represent our example document database adequately, the non-1NF representation may be an easier-to-understand model, since the typical user of a document-retrieval system thinks of the database in terms of our non-1NF design. The 4NF design would require users to include joins in their queries, thereby complicating interaction with the system. We could define a nonnested relational view that eliminates the need for users to write joins in their query. In

| title | author | day | month | year | keyword |
|---|---|---|---|---|---|
| salesplan | Smith | 1 | April | 89 | profit |
| salesplan | Jones | 1 | April | 89 | profit |
| salesplan | Smith | 1 | April | 89 | strategy |
| salesplan | Jones | 1 | April | 89 | strategy |
| status report | Jones | 17 | June | 94 | profit |
| status report | Frick | 17 | June | 94 | profit |
| status report | Jones | 17 | June | 94 | personnel |
| status report | Frick | 17 | June | 94 | personnel |

Figure 9.2 *flat-doc*, a 1NF version of non-1NF relation *doc*.

| title | author |
|---|---|
| salesplan | Smith |
| salesplan | Jones |
| status report | Jones |
| status report | Frick |

| title | keyword |
|---|---|
| salesplan | profit |
| salesplan | strategy |
| status report | profit |
| status report | personnel |

| title | day | month | year |
|---|---|---|---|
| salesplan | 1 | April | 89 |
| status report | 17 | June | 94 |

Figure 9.3    4NF version of the relation *flat-doc* of Figure 9.2.

such a view, however, we lose the one-to-one correspondence between tuples and documents.

## 9.2   Complex Types and Object Orientation

Nested relations are just one example of extensions to the basic relational model. Other nonatomic data types, such as nested records, have also proved useful. The object-oriented data model has caused a need for features such as inheritance and references to objects. Complex type systems and object orientation enable E-R model concepts, such as identity of entities, multivalued attributes, and generalization and specialization to be represented directly without a complex translation to the relational model.

In this section, we describe extensions to SQL to allow complex types, including nested relations, and object-oriented features. Several such extensions have been proposed, and a standardization effort is under way. Our presentation is based loosely on a preliminary draft of the SQL-3 standard, which is likely to be finalized in a few years. We stress that our presentation does not strictly follow the current draft, and moreover the draft is evolving and changes are likely. Our presentation also incorporates features of other proposed extensions, such as XSQL, and the query language of the Illustra database system. XSQL is a research language that extends SQL with powerful object-oriented features. Illustra is the commercial version of the Postgres database system, developed at the University of California at Berkeley, which was one of the early systems to extend the relational model with object-oriented features. See the bibliographic notes for references to these languages.

## 9.2.1　Structured and Collection Types

Consider the following statements, which define a relation *doc* with the complex attributes described in the previous section.

> **create type** *MyString* **char varying**.
> **create type** *MyDate*
> 　　( *day* **integer**,
> 　　 *month* **char(10)**,
> 　　 *year* **integer**)
> **create type** *Document*
> 　　(*name MyString*,
> 　　 *author-list* **setof**(*MyString*),
> 　　 *date MyDate*,
> 　　 *keyword-list* **setof**(*MyString*))
> **create table** *doc* **of type** *Document*

The first statement defines a type *MyString*, which is a variable-length character string. The next statement defines a type called *MyDate*, which has three components: day, month, and year. The third statement defines a type *Document*, which contains a *name*, an *author-list*, which is a set of authors, a date of type *MyDate*, and a set of keywords. Finally, the table *doc* containing tuples of type *Document* is created. The preceding table definition differs from table definitions in ordinary relational databases, since it allows attributes that are sets, and attributes such as *MyDate* that are structured. These features allow composite attributes and multivalued attributes of E-R diagrams to be represented directly.

An important point to note is that the types created using the preceding statements are recorded in the schema stored in the database. Thus, other statements that access the database can make use of the type definitions. Type definitions in programming languages (including persistent programming languages) typically are not stored in a database, and can be seen only by programs that include a textual file containing the definitions.

We can also create tables directly, without creating an intermediate type for the table. For example, the table *doc* could also be defined as follows:

> **create table** *doc*
> 　　(*name MyString*,
> 　　 *author-list* **setof**(*MyString*),
> 　　 *date MyDate*,
> 　　 *keyword-list* **setof**(*MyString*))

Complex type systems usually support other collection types, such as arrays and multisets (that is, unordered collections, where an element may occur multiple times). The following attribute definitions illustrate the use of such collection types:

> *author-array MyString*[10]
> *print-runs* **multiset(integer)**

Here, *author-array* is an array of author names. As we cannot do from a set of author names, from an array we can determine who is the first author, who is the second author, and so on. The second attribute, *print-runs*, is a multiset of integers, which could represent the number of copies of a document printed in each printing run of the document. Since two printing runs may have the same number of copies, a multiset should be used, rather than a set.

## 9.2.2  Inheritance

Inheritance can be at the level of types, or at the level of tables. Let us first consider inheritance of types. Suppose that we have the following type definition for people:

> **create type** *Person*
> (*name MyString*,
> *social-security* **integer**)

We may want to store extra information in the database about people who are students, and about people who are teachers. Since students and teachers are also people, we can use inheritance to define the student and teacher types as follows:

> **create type** *Student*
> (*degree MyString*,
> *department MyString*)
> **under** *Person*
> **create type** *Teacher*
> (*salary* **integer**,
> *department MyString*)
> **under** *Person*

Both *Student* and *Teacher* inherit the attributes of *Person*—namely, *name* and *social-security*. *Student* and *Teacher* are said to be subtypes of *Person*, and *Person* is a supertype of *Student*, as well as of *Teacher*.

Now suppose that we want to store information about teaching assistants, who are simultaneously students and teachers, perhaps even in different departments. Recall the idea of multiple inheritance, which we studied in Chapter 8. If our type system supports multiple inheritance, we can try to define a type for teaching assistant as follows:

> **create type** *TeachingAssistant*
> **under** *Student, Teacher*

*TeachingAssistant* ought to inherit all the attributes of *Student* and *Teacher*. There is a problem, however, since the attributes *social-security*, *name*, and *department* are present in *Student*, as well as in *Teacher*.

The attributes *social-security* and *name* are actually inherited from a common source, *Person*. So there is no conflict caused by inheriting them from *Student* as well as *Teacher*. However, the attribute *department* is defined separately in *Student* and *Teacher*. In fact, a teaching assistant may be a student of one department and a teacher in another department. To avoid a conflict between the two occurrences of *department*, we can rename them using an **as** clause, as shown in the following definition of the type *TeachingAssistant*:

> **create type** *TeachingAssistant*
> **under** *Student* **with** (*department* **as** *student-dept*),
> *Teacher* **with** (*department* **as** *teacher-dept*)

Inheritance of types should be used with care. A university database may have many subtypes of *Person*, such as *Student*, *Teacher*, *FootballPlayer*, *ForeignCitizen*, and so on. *Student* may itself have subtypes such as *UndergraduateStudent*, *GraduateStudent*, and *PartTimeStudent*. Clearly, a person can belong to several of these categories at once. As mentioned in Chapter 8, each of these categories is sometimes called a *role*.

In most programming languages, an entity must have exactly one *most specific type*; that is, if an entity has more than one type, there must be a single type to which the entity belongs, and that single type must be a subtype of all the types to which the entity belongs. For example, suppose that an entity has the type *Person*, as well as the type *Student*. Then, the most specific type of the entity is *Student*, since *Student* is a subtype of *Person*. However, an entity cannot have the type *Student*, as well as the type *Teacher*, unless it has a type, such as *TeachingAssistant*, that is a subtype of *Teacher*, as well as of *Student*.

For each entity to have exactly one most specific type, we would have to create a subtype for every possible combination of the supertypes. In the preceding example, we would have subtypes such as *ForeignUndergraduateStudent*, *ForeignGraduateStudentFootballPlayer*, and so on. Unfortunately, we would end up with an enormous number of subtypes of *Person*.

A better approach in the context of database systems is to allow an object to have multiple types, without having a most specific type. Object-relational systems can model such a feature by using inheritance at the level of tables, rather than of types, and allowing an entity to exist in more than one table at once. We can rephrase the preceding example of students and teachers as follows. First, we define the *people* table as follows:

> **create table** *people*
> (*name MyString*,
> *social-security* **integer**)

Then, we define the *students* and *teachers* tables as follows:

> **create table** *students*
> (*degree MyString*,
> *department MyString*)
> **under** *people*
> **create table** *teachers*
> (*salary* **integer**,
> *department MyString*)
> **under** *people*

The subtables *students* and *teachers* inherit all the attributes of the table *people*. There is no need to create further subtables, such as *teaching-assistants*, that inherit from both *students* and *teachers*, unless there are attributes specific to entities that are *students* as well as *teachers*.

There are consistency requirements on subtables and supertables. We illustrate them using the same example.

- Each tuple of the supertable *people* can correspond to (that is, have the same values for all inherited attributes as) at most one tuple in each of the tables *students* and *teachers*.

- Each tuple in *students* and *teachers* must have exactly one corresponding tuple (that is, with the same values for all inherited attributes) in *people*.

Without the first condition, we could have two tuples in *students* (or *teachers*) that correspond to the same person. Without the second condition, we could have a tuple in *students* or in *teachers* that does not correspond to any tuple in *people*, or that corresponds to several tuples in *people*. These states cannot correspond to the real world, and are hence erroneous.

Subtables can be stored in an efficient manner without replication of all inherited fields. Inherited attributes other than the primary key of the supertable do not need to be stored, and can be derived by means of a join with the supertable, based on the primary key.

Multiple inheritance is possible with tables, just as it is possible with types. A teaching-assistant entity can simply belong to the table *students*, as well as to the table *teachers*. However, if we want, we can create a table for teaching-assistant entities as follows:

> **create table** *teaching-assistants*
> **under** *students* **with** (*department* **as** *student-dept*),
> *teachers* **with** (*department* **as** *teacher-dept*)

The consistency requirements for subtables ensure that, if an entity is present in the *teaching-assistants* table, it is also present in the *teachers* and in the *students* table.

Inheritance makes schema definition more natural. Without inheritance of tables, the schema designer has to link tables corresponding to subtables explicitly with tables corresponding to supertables via primary keys, and to define constraints between the tables to ensure referential and cardinality constraints. The use of inheritance enables the use of functions defined for supertypes on objects belonging to subtypes, allowing the orderly extension of a database system to incorporate new types.

### 9.2.3   Reference Types

Object-oriented languages provide the ability to refer to objects. An attribute of a type can be a reference to an object of a specified type. For example, references to people are of the type **ref**(*Person*). The author-list field of the type *Document* can be redefined as

*author-list* **setof**(**ref**(*Person*))

which is a set of references to *Person* objects.

Tuples of a table can also have references to them. References to tuples of the table *people* have the type **ref**(*people*). We can implement references to tuples of a table by using the primary key of the table. Alternatively, each tuple of a table may have a tuple identifier as an implicit attribute, and a reference to a tuple is simply the tuple identifier. Subtables implicitly inherit the tuple identifier attribute, just as they inherit other attributes from supertables.

The **ref** notation is used in the Illustra database system. In the preliminary draft of SQL-3 "**ref**(*Person*)" is written as "*Person* **identity**." The identifiers of tuples and objects can be accessed through special attributes **identity** and **oid** (that is, object identifier), respectively. The SQL-3 standard may require that, if we are to allow references to objects of a data type, the data type must be declared to be "**with oid**." Similarly, if we are to allow references to tuples of a table, the table may be required to be declared "**with identity**."

## 9.3  Querying with Complex Types

In this section, we present an extension of the SQL query language to deal with complex types. Let us start with a simple example: Find the name and year of publication of each document. The following query carries out the task:

**select** *name*, *date.year*
**from** *doc*

Notice that the field *year* of the composite attribute *date* is referred to using a dot notation. (A double dot (..) notation has been proposed for SQL-3 , instead of the dot notation.)

### 9.3.1  Relation-Valued Attributes

Our extended SQL allows an expression evaluating to a relation to appear anywhere that a relation name may appear, such as in a **from** clause. The ability to use subexpressions freely makes it possible to take advantage of the structure of nested relations, as the following example shows.

Suppose that we are given a relation *pdoc* with a schema created as follows:

**create table** *pdoc*
( *name MyString*,
*author-list* **setof**(**ref**(*people*)),
*date MyDate*,
*keyword-list* **setof**(*MyString*))

If we want to find all documents that have the word "database" as one of their keywords, we can use the following query:

> **select** *name*
> **from** *pdoc*
> **where** "database" **in** *keyword-list*

Note that we have used the relation-valued attribute *keyword-list* in a position where SQL without nested relations would have required a **select-from-where** subexpression.

Now, suppose that we want a relation containing pairs of the form "document-name, author-name" for each document and each author of the document. We can use the following query:

> **select** *B.name, Y.name*
> **from** *pdoc* **as** *B, B.author-list* **as** *Y*

Since the *author-list* attribute of *pdoc* is a set-valued field, it can be used in a **from** clause where a relation is expected.

Aggregate functions (for example, **min**, **max**, and **count**) take a collection of values as an argument and return a single value as their result. They can be applied to any relation-valued expression. The query, "Find the name, and the number of authors for each document" can be written as

> **select** *name,* **count**(*author-list*)
> **from** *pdoc*

Since *author-list* is a set-valued attribute containing one tuple for each author, a count of the set provides the number of authors.

## 9.3.2   Path Expressions

The dot notation for referring to composite attributes can be used with references. Suppose that we have the table *people* as defined earlier, and a table *phd-student* defined as here:

> **create table** *phd-students*
> (*advisor* **ref**(*people*))
> **under** *people*

Then, we can use the following query to find the names of the advisors of all doctoral students:

> **select** *phd-students.advisor.name*
> **from** *phd-students*

Since *phd-students.advisor* is a reference to tuple in the *people* table, the attribute *name* in the preceding query is the *name* attribute of the tuple from the *people* table. References can be used to hide join operations; in the preceding example, without the use of references, the *advisor* field of *phd-students* would be a foreign key of the table *people*. To find the name of the advisor of a doctoral student, we would require an explicit join of *phd-students* with the *people* relation based on the foreign key. The use of references simplifies the query considerably.

An expression of the form *"students.advisor.name"* is called a *path expression*. In the preceding example, each attribute in the path expression has a single value (a reference in the case of advisor). In general, attributes used in a path expression can be a collection, such as a set or a multiset. If we want to get the names of all authors of documents in the *pdoc* relation, we can write the following query:

> **select** *Y.name*
> **from** *pdoc.author-list* **as** *Y*

The variable *Y* ranges over each author of each document in the *pdoc* relation.

### 9.3.3 Nesting and Unnesting

The transformation of a nested relation into 1NF is called *unnesting*. The *doc* relation has two attributes *author-list* and *keyword-list*, which are nested relations, and two attributes, *name* and *date*, which are not. Suppose that we want to convert the relation into a single flat relation, with no nested relations or structured types as attributes. We can use the following query to carry out the task:

> **select** *name, A* **as** *author, date.day, date.month, date.year,*
>       *K* **as** *keyword*
> **from** *doc* **as** *B, B.author-list* **as** *A, B.keyword-list* **as** *K*

The variable *B* in the from clause is declared to range over *doc*. The variable *A* is declared to range over the authors in *author-list* for that document, and *K* is declared to range over the keywords in the *keyword-list* of the document. Figure 9.1 (in Section 9.1) shows an instance *doc* relation, and Figure 9.2 shows the 1NF relation that is the result of the preceding query.

The reverse process of transforming a 1NF relation into a nested relation is called *nesting*. Nesting can be carried out by an extension of grouping in SQL. In the normal use of grouping in SQL, a temporary multiset relation is (logically) created for each group, and an aggregate function is applied on the temporary relation. By returning the multiset instead of applying the aggregate function, we can create a nested relation. Suppose that we are given a 1NF relation *flat-doc*, as shown in Figure 9.2. The following query nests the relation on the attribute *keyword*:

> **select** *title, author, (day, month, year)* **as** *date,*
>       **set**(*keyword*) **as** *keyword-list*
> **from** *flat-doc*
> **groupby** *title, author, date*

The result of the query on the *doc* relation from Figure 9.2 is shown in Figure 9.4. If we want to nest the author attribute as well, and thereby to convert the 1NF table *flat-doc* in Figure 9.2 back to the nested table *doc* shown in Figure 9.1, we

| title | author | date | keyword-list |
|-------|--------|------|--------------|
| | | (*day, month, year*) | |
| salesplan | Smith | (1, April, 89) | {profit, strategy} |
| salesplan | Jones | (1, April, 89) | {profit, strategy} |
| status report | Jones | (17, June, 94) | {profit, personnel} |
| status report | Frick | (17, June, 94) | {profit, personnel} |

Figure 9.4    A partially nested version of the *flat-doc* relation.

can use the following query:

> **select** *title*, **set**(*author*) **as** *author-list*, (*day, month, year*) **as** *date*,
>         **set**(*keyword*) **as** *keyword-list*
> **from** *flat-doc*
> **groupby** *title, date*

## 9.3.4    Functions

Object-relational systems allow functions to be defined by users. These functions can be defined either in a programming language such as C or C++, or in a data-manipulation language such as SQL. We look at function definitions in our extended SQL first.

Suppose that we want a function that, given a document, returns the count of the number of authors. We can define the function as follows:

> **create function** *author-count*(*one-doc Document*)
>         **returns integer as**
>         **select count**(*author-list*)
>         **from** *one-doc*

Recall that *Document* is a type name. The function is invoked with a single document object, and the **select** statement is executed with a relation *one-doc* containing only a single tuple—namely, the argument of the function. The result of the **select** statement is a single value; strictly speaking, it is a tuple with a single attribute, whose type is converted into a value.

The preceding function can be used in a query that returns the names of all documents that have more than one author:

> **select** *name*
> **from** *doc*
> **where** *author-count*(*doc*) > 1

Note that, in the preceding SQL expression, although *doc* refers to a relation in the **from** clause, it is treated implicitly as a tuple variable in the **where** clause, and can therefore be used as an argument to the *author-count* function.

In general, a select statement can return a collection of values. If the return type of the function is a collection type, the result of the function is the entire collection. If the return type is not a collection type, as is the case in the preceding example, the collection generated by the **select** statement should contain only one tuple, which is returned as the answer. If there is more than one tuple in the result of the **select** statement, the system has two choices: either it can treat this situation as an error, or it can select an arbitrary tuple from the collection and return that tuple as the answer.

Some database systems allow us to define functions using a programming language such as C or C++. Functions defined in this fashion can be more efficient than functions defined using SQL, and computations that cannot be carried out in SQL can be executed by these functions. An example of the use of such functions would be to perform a complex arithmetic computation on the data in a tuple.

Functions defined using a programming language and compiled external to the database system need to be loaded and executed with the database system code. This process carries the risk that a bug in the program can corrupt the database internal structures, and can bypass the access-control functionality of the database system. Certain systems, such as Illustra, that are designed to be extensible typically allow such functions, whereas database systems that emphasize security of data do not.

It may appear that using functions defined in a programming language is not unlike using embedded SQL, in which database queries are included within a general-purpose program. There is, however, an important distinction here. In embedded SQL, the query is passed by the user program to the database system to be run. The results are returned (one tuple at a time) to the program. Therefore, user-written code never needs access to the database itself. The operating system thus can protect the database from access by any user process.

When user-coded functions are employed within queries, either that code must be run by the database system itself, or the data on which the function operates must be copied into a separate data space. The latter imposes an extraordinarily high overhead, whereas the former incurs potential vulnerability in terms of integrity (through bugs in the user code) and in terms of security (through maliciously implanted actions as part of the user code).

# 9.4    Creation of Complex Values and Objects

So far, we have seen how to create complex type definitions and query relations defined using complex types. We now see how to create and update tuples in relations that have complex types.

We can create a tuple of the type defined by the *doc* relation as follows:

("salesplan", **set**("Smith", "Jones"), (1, "April", 89), **set**("profit", "strategy"))

The preceding tuple illustrates several aspects of the creation of complex types. We create the value for the composite attribute *date* by listing the latter's attributes—day, month, and year—within parentheses. We create the set-valued attributes *author-list* and *keyword-list* by enumerating their elements within parentheses following the keyword **set**.

We can use complex values constructed as shown here in a number of ways. If we want to insert the preceding tuple into the relation *doc*, we could execute the statement

**insert into** doc
**values**
("salesplan", **set**("Smith", "Jones"), (1, "April", 89), **set**("profit", "strategy"))

We can also use complex values in queries. For example, anywhere in a query where a set is expected, we can enumerate a set, as illustrated in the following query:

> **select** *name, date*
> **from** *doc*
> **where** *name* **in set**("salesplan", "opportunities", "risks")

The preceding query finds the names and dates of all documents whose name is one of "salesplan", "opportunities", or "risks".

We can create multiset values just like set values, by replacing **set** by **multiset**. A list or array of values can be created just like a tuple values.

To create new objects, we can use *constructor* functions. The constructor function for an object of type $T$ is $T()$; when it is invoked it creates a new uninitialized object of type $T$, fills in its **oid** field, and returns the object. The fields of the object must then be initialized.

We can carry updates of complex relations using the usual SQL **update** clause; such updates are very similar to updates of 1NF relations.

# 9.5   Comparison of Object-Oriented and Object-Relational Databases

We have now studied object-oriented databases built around persistent programming languages, as well as object-relational databases, which are object-oriented databases built on top of the relation model. Database systems of both types are on the market, and a database designer needs to choose the kind of system that is appropriate to the needs of the application.

Persistent extensions to programming languages and object-relational systems have targeted different markets. The declarative nature and limited power (compared to a programming language) of the SQL language provides good protection of data from programming errors, and makes high-level optimizations, such as reducing I/O, relatively easy. (We cover optimization of relational expressions in Chapter 12.) Object-relational systems aim at making data modeling and querying easier by using complex data types. Typical applications include storage and querying of complex data, including multimedia data.

A declarative language such as SQL, however, imposes a significant performance penalty for certain kinds of applications that run primarily in main memory, and that perform a large number of accesses to the database. Persistent programming languages target applications of that form that have high performance requirements. They provide low-overhead access to persistent data, and eliminate the need for data translation if the data are to be manipulated using a programming language. However, they are more susceptible to data corruption due to programming errors, and usually do not have a powerful querying capability. Typical applications include CAD databases.

The strengths of the various kinds of database systems can be summarized as follows:

- **Relational systems**: simple data types, powerful query languages, high protection
- **Persistent programming language based OODBs**: complex data types, integration with programming language, high performance
- **Object-relational systems**: complex data types, powerful query languages, high protection

These descriptions hold in general, but keep in mind that some database systems blur these boundaries. For example, some object-oriented database systems built around a persistent programming language are implemented on top of a relational database system. Such systems may provide lower performance than object-oriented database systems built directly on a storage system, but provide some of the stronger protection guarantees of relational systems.

## 9.6  Summary

Complex types such as nested relations, are useful for modeling complex data in many applications. The relational model is extended beyond 1NF, to allow nonatomic types. Object-relational systems combine complex data based on an extended relational model with object-oriented concepts such as object identity and inheritance. The SQL data-definition and query languages have been extended to deal with complex types and object orientation. We saw a variety of features of the extended data-definition language, as well as the query language, and in particular support for set-valued attributes, inheritance, and object and tuple references.

## Exercises

**9.1.** Consider the database schema

$$Emp = (ename, \textbf{setof}(Children), \textbf{setof}(Skills))$$
$$Children = (name, Birthday)$$
$$Birthday = (day, month, year)$$
$$Skills = (type, \textbf{setof}(Exams))$$
$$Exams = (year, city)$$

Assume that attributes of type **setof**(*Children*), **setof**(*Skills*), and **setof**(*Exams*), have attribute names *ChildrenSet, SkillsSet* and *ExamsSet*, respectively. Write the following queries in the extended SQL for the relation *emp (Emp)*.

(*a*) Find the names of all employees who have a child who has a birthday in March.

(*b*) Find those employees who took an examination for the skill type "typing" in the city "Dayton."

(*c*) List all skill types in the relation *emp*.

**9.2.** Redesign the database of Exercise 9.1 into first normal form and fourth normal form. List any functional or multivalued dependencies that you assume. Also list all referential-integrity constraints that should be present in the first- and fourth-normal-form schemas.

**9.3.** Consider the schemas for the table *people*, and the tables *students* and *teachers*, which were created under *people*, in Section 9.2.2. Give a relational schema in third normal form that represents the same information. Recall the constraints on subtables, and give all constraints that must be imposed on the relational schema so that every database instance of the relational schema can also be represented by an instance of the schema with inheritance.

**9.4.** A car-rental company maintains a vehicle database for all vehicles in its current fleet. For all vehicles, it includes the vehicle identification number, license number, manufacturer, model, date of purchase, and color. Special data are included for certain types of vehicles:
- Trucks: cargo capacity
- Sports cars: horsepower, renter age requirement
- Vans: number of passengers
- Off-road vehicles: ground clearance, drivetrain (four- or two-wheel drive)

Construct an extended SQL schema definition for this database. Use inheritance where appropriate.

**9.5.** Explain the distinction between a type $x$ and a reference type **ref**($x$). Under what circumstances would you choose to use a reference type?

**9.6.** Compare the use of embedded SQL with the use in SQL of functions defined using a general-purpose programming language. Under what circumstances would you use each of these features?

**9.7.** Suppose that you have been hired as a consultant to choose a database system for your client's application. For each of the following applications, state what type of database system (relational, persistent-programming-language–based OODB, object relational; do not specify a commercial product) you would recommend. Justify your recommendation.

(*a*) A computer-aided design system for a manufacturer of airplanes

(*b*) A system to track contributions made to candidates for public office

(*c*) A system to aid managers of highway-construction projects

(*d*) An information system to support the making of movies

# Bibliographical Notes

The nested relational model was introduced in Makinouchi [1977] and Jaeschke and Schek [1982]. Various algebraic query languages are presented in Fischer and Thomas [1983], Zaniolo [1983], Ozsoyoglu et al. [1987], Van Gucht [1987], and Roth et al. [1988]. The management of null values in nested relations is discussed in Roth et al. [1989]. Design and normalization issues are discussed in Ozsoyoglu and Yuan [1987], Roth and Korth [1987], and Mok et al. [1996]. A collection of papers on nested relations appears in Abiteboul et al. [1989]. Sacks-Davis et al. [1995] present an application of the nested relational model to databases containing documents.

Several object-oriented extensions to SQL have been proposed. POSTGRES (Stonebraker and Rowe [1986], Stonebraker [1986a, 1987], and Stonebraker et al. [1987a, 1987b]) was an early implementation of an object-relational system. Illustra is the commercial object-relational system that is the successor of POSTGRES. The Iris database system from Hewlett-Packard (Fishman et al. [1990], and Wilkinson et al. [1990]) provides object-oriented extensions on top of a relational database system. Iris supports a language called Object SQL (OSQL), which is an object-oriented extension of SQL. The $O_2$ query language described in Bancilhon et al. [1989], and in Deux et al. [1991], is an object-oriented extension of SQL implemented in the $O_2$ object-oriented database system. UniSQL is described in [UniSQL 1991]. Triggers in object-oriented database systems are discussed in Gehani and Jagadish [1991], Gehani et al. [1992], and Jagadish and Qian [1992].

XSQL is an object-oriented extension of SQL proposed by Kifer et al. [1992]. Kim [1995] contains a collection of papers on modern database systems, including descriptions of OSQL and ZQL[C++], which integrates declarative querying with C++. Standardization projects for object-oriented extensions to SQL are underway as part of the SQL-3 standard, which is currently being developed. Look up the Web home page of this book (http://www.bell-labs.com/topic/books/db-book) for an update on SQL-3, including differences between SQL-3 and the syntax used in this chapter.

# CHAPTER
# 10

## STORAGE
## AND FILE
## STRUCTURE

In preceding chapters, we have emphasized the higher-level models of a database. At the *conceptual* or *logical* level, we viewed the database, in the relational model, as a collection of tables. The logical model of the database is the correct level for database *users* to focus on. The goal of a database system is to simplify and facilitate access to data. Users of the system should not be burdened unnecessarily with the physical details of the implementation of the system.

In this chapter, as well as in Chapters 11 and 12, we describe various methods for implementing the data models and languages presented in preceding chapters. We start with characteristics of the underlying storage media, such as disk and tape systems. We then define various data structures that will allow fast access to data. We consider several alternative structures, each best suited to a different kind of access to data. The final choice of data structure needs to be made on the basis of the expected use of the system and of the physical characteristics of the specific machine.

## 10.1 Overview of Physical Storage Media

Several types of data storage exist in most computer systems. These storage media are classified by the speed with which data can be accessed, by the cost per unit of data to buy the medium, and by the medium's reliability. Among the media typically available are these:

- **Cache**. The cache is the fastest and most costly form of storage. Cache memory is small; its use is managed by the operating system. We shall not be concerned about managing cache storage in the database system.

- **Main memory**. The storage medium used for data that are available to be operated on is main memory. The general-purpose machine instructions operate on main memory. Although main memory may contain many megabytes of data, it is generally too small (or too expensive) to store the entire database. The contents of main memory are usually lost if a power failure or system crash occurs.

- **Flash memory**. Also known as *electrically erasable programmable read-only memory* (*EEPROM*), flash memory differs from main-memory in that data survive power failure. Reading data from flash memory takes less than 100 nanoseconds (a nanosecond is 0.001 microsecond), which is roughly as fast as is reading data from main memory. However, writing data to flash memory is more complicated—data can be written once, which takes about 4 to 10 microseconds, but cannot be over written directly. To overwrite memory that has been written already, we have to erase an entire bank of memory at once; it is then ready to be written again. A drawback of flash memory is that it can support a only limited number of erase cycles, ranging from 10,000 to 1 million. Flash memory has found popularity as a replacement for magnetic disks for storing small volumes of data (5 to 10 megabytes) in low-cost computer systems, such as computer systems that are embedded in other devices.

- **Magnetic-disk storage**. The primary medium for the long-term on-line storage of data is the magnetic disk. Typically, the entire database is stored on magnetic disk. Data must be moved from disk to main memory to be accessed. After operations are performed, the data that have been modified must be written to disk. Disk storage is referred to as *direct-access* storage, because it is possible to read data on disk in any order (unlike sequential-access storage). Disk storage survives power failures and system crashes. Disk-storage devices themselves may sometimes fail and thus destroy data, but such failures usually occur much less frequently than do system crashes.

- **Optical storage**. The most popular form of optical storage is the *compact-disk read-only memory* (*CD-ROM*). Data are stored optically on a disk, and are read by a laser. The optical disks used in CD-ROM storage cannot be written, but are supplied with data prerecorded, and can be loaded into or removed from a drive. Another version of optical storage is the *write-once, read-many* (*WORM*) disk, which allows data to be written once, but does not allow them to be erased and rewritten; this medium is used for archival storage of data. There are also combined magnetic–optical storage devices that use optical means to read magnetically encoded data, and that allow overwriting of old data.

  Most types of optical storage allow the disks to be removed from the drive and replaced by other disks. *Jukebox* systems contain a few drives and numerous disks that can be loaded into one of the drives automatically (by a robot arm) on demand.

- **Tape storage**. Tape storage is used primarily for backup and archival data. Although magnetic tape is much cheaper than disks, access to data is much slower, because the tape must be accessed sequentially from the beginning. For this reason, tape storage is referred to as *sequential-access* storage. Tapes have a high capacity (5-gigabyte tapes are commonly available), and can be removed from the tape drive, facilitating cheap archival storage. Tape juke-boxes are used to hold exceptionally large collections of data, such as remote-sensing data from satellites, which could include as much as hundreds of terabytes (1 terabyte = $10^{12}$ bytes) in the near future.

The various storage media can be organized in a hierarchy (Figure 10.1) according to their speed and their cost. The higher levels are expensive, but are fast. As we move down the hierarchy, the cost per bit decreases, whereas the access time increases. This tradeoff is reasonable; if a given storage system were both faster and less expensive than another—other properties being the same—then there would be no reason to use the slower, more expensive memory. In fact, many early storage devices, including paper tape and core memories, are relegated to museums now that magnetic tape and semiconductor memory have become faster and cheaper. Magnetic tapes themselves were used to store active data back when disks were expensive and had low storage capacity. Today, almost

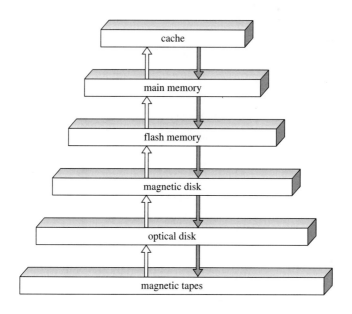

Figure 10.1    Storage-device hierarchy.

all active data are stored on disks, except in rare cases where they are stored on tape or in optical jukeboxes.

The fastest storage media—for example, cache and main memory—are referred to as *primary storage*. The media in the next level in the hierarchy—for example, magnetic disks—are referred to as *secondary storage*, or *on-line storage*. The media in the lowest level in the hierarchy—for example, magnetic tape and optical-disk jukeboxes—are referred to as *tertiary storage*, or *off-line storage*.

In addition to the speed and cost of the various storage systems, there is also the issue of storage volatility. *Volatile storage* loses its contents when the power to the device is removed. In the absence of expensive battery and generator backup systems, data must be written to nonvolatile storage for safekeeping. In the hierarchy shown in Figure 10.1, the storage systems from main memory up are volatile, whereas the storage systems below main memory are nonvolatile. We shall return to this subject in Chapter 15.

## 10.2 Magnetic Disks

Magnetic disks provide the bulk of secondary storage for modern computer systems. The storage capacity of a single disk ranges from 10 megabytes to 10 gigabytes. A typical large commercial database may require hundreds of disks.

### 10.2.1 Physical Characteristics of Disks

Physically, disks are relatively simple (Figure 10.2). Each disk *platter* has a flat circular shape. Its two surfaces are covered with a magnetic material, and infor-

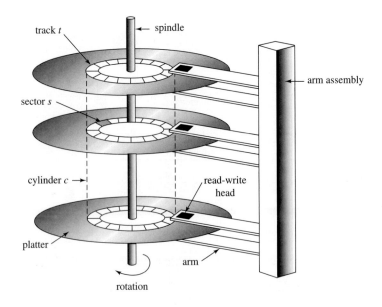

Figure 10.2   Moving-head disk mechanism.

mation is recorded on the surfaces. Platters are made from rigid metal or glass and are covered (usually on both sides) with magnetic recording material. We call such magnetic disks *hard disks*, to distinguish them from *floppy disks*, which are made from flexible material.

When the disk is in use, a drive motor spins it at a constant high speed (usually 60, 90, or 120 revolutions per second). There is a read–write head positioned just above the surface of the platter. The disk surface is logically divided into *tracks*, which are subdivided into *sectors*. A *sector* is the smallest unit of information that can be read from or written to the disk. Depending on the disk type, sectors vary from 32 bytes to 4096 bytes; usually, they are 512 bytes. There are 4 to 32 sectors per track, and from 20 to 1500 tracks per disk surface. The *read–write head* stores information on a sector magnetically as reversals of the direction of magnetization of the magnetic material. There may be hundreds of concentric tracks on a disk surface, containing thousands of sectors.

Each side of a platter of a disk has a read–write head, which is moved across the platter to access different tracks. A disk typically contains many platters, and the read–write heads of all the tracks are mounted on a single assembly called a *disk arm*, and move together. The disk platters mounted on a spindle and the heads mounted on a disk arm are together known as *head–disk assemblies*. Since the heads on all the platters move together, when the head on one platter is on the *i*th track, the heads on all other platters are also on the *i*th track of their respective platters. Hence, the *i*th tracks of all the platters together are called the *i*th *cylinder*.

Disk platters range from 1.8 inches to 14 inches in diameter. Today, 5 1/4- and 3 1/2-inch disks dominate, since they have a lower cost and faster seek times (due to smaller seek distances) than do larger disks, yet they provide high storage capacity.

A *disk controller* interfaces between the computer system and the actual hardware of the disk drive. It accepts high-level commands to read or write a sector, and initiates actions, such as moving the disk arm to the right track and actually reading or writing the data. Disk controllers also attach *checksums* to each sector that is written; the checksum is computed from the data written to the sector. When the sector is read back, the checksum is computed again from the retrieved data and is compared with the stored checksum; if the data are corrupted, with a high probability the newly computed checksum will not match the stored checksum. If such an error occurs, the controller will retry the read several times; if the error continues to occur, the controller will signal a read failure.

Another interesting task performed by disk controllers is *remapping of bad sectors*. If the controller detects that a sector is damaged when the disk is initially formatted, or when an attempt is made to write the sector, it can logically map the sector to a different physical location (allocated from a pool of extra sectors set aside for this purpose). The remapping is noted on disk or in nonvolatile memory, and the write is carried out on the new location.

Figure 10.3 shows how disks are connected to a computer system. Like other storage units, disks are connected to a computer system or to a controller through a high-speed interconnection. The *small computer-system interconnect*

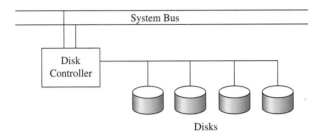

Figure 10.3   Disk subsystem.

(*SCSI*; pronounced "scuzzy") is commonly used to connect disks to personal computers and workstations. Mainframe and server systems usually have a faster and more expensive bus to connect to the disks.

The read–write heads are kept as close as possible to the disk surface to increase the recording density. Often, the head floats or flies only microns from the disk surface, supported by a cushion of air. Because the head floats so close to the surface, platters must be machined carefully to be flat. Head crashes can be a problem. If the head contacts the disk surface (due to a power failure, for example), the head will scrape the recording medium off the disk, destroying the data that had been there. Usually, the head touching the surface causes the removed medium to become airborne and to come between the other heads and their platters, causing more crashes. Under normal circumstances, a head crash results in the entire disk failing and needing to be replaced.

A *fixed-head disk* has a separate head for each track. This arrangement allows the computer to switch from track to track quickly, without having to move the head assembly, but it requires a large number of heads, making the device extremely expensive. Some disk systems have multiple disk arms, allowing more than one track on the same platter to be accessed at a time. Fixed-head disks and multiple arm disks were used in high-performance mainframe systems, but are relatively rare today.

### 10.2.2   Performance Measures of Disks

The main measures of the qualities of a disk are capacity, access time, data-transfer rate, and reliability.

*Access time* is the time from when a read or write request is issued to when data transfer begins. To access (that is, to read or write) data on a given sector of a disk, the arm first must move so that it is positioned over the correct track, and then must wait for the sector to appear under it as the disk rotates. The time for repositioning the arm is called the *seek time*, and it increases with the distance that the arm must move. Typical seek times range from 2 to 30 milliseconds, depending on how far the track is from the initial arm position. Smaller disks tend to have lower seek times since the head has to travel a smaller distance.

The *average seek time* is the average of the seek times, measured over a sequence of (uniformly distributed) random requests, and is about one-third of the worst-case seek time. If the head were positioned at one end (inner or outer) before an access, the average seek time would be one-half of the worst-case seek time; if it were positioned exactly in between the innermost and outermost tracks, the average seek time would be one-fourth of the worst-case seek time. Averaging over all positions of the head, the average seek time is one-third of the worst case.

Once the seek has occurred, the time spent waiting for the sector to be accessed to appear under the head is called the *rotational latency time*. Typical rotational speeds of disks today range from 60 to 120 rotations per second, or, equivalently, 8.35 to 16.7 milliseconds per rotation. On an average, one-half of a rotation of the disk is required for the beginning of the desired sector to appear under the head. Thus, the *average latency time* of the disk is one-half of the time for a full rotation of the disk.

The access time is then the sum of the seek time and the latency, and ranges from 10 to 40 milliseconds. Once the first sector of the data to be accessed has come under the head, data transfer begins. The *data-transfer rate* is the rate at which data can be retrieved from or stored to the disk. Current disk systems support transfer rates from 1 to 5 megabytes per second.

The final commonly used measure of a disk is the *mean time to failure*, which is a measure of the reliability of the disk. The mean time to failure of a disk (or of any other system) is the amount of time that, on average, we can expect the system to run continuously without any failure. The typical mean time to failure of disks today ranges from 30, 000 to 800, 000 hours— about 3.4 to 91 years.

### 10.2.3 Optimization of Disk-Block Access

Requests for disk I/O are generated both by the file system and by the virtual memory manager found in most operating systems. Each request specifies the address on the disk to be referenced; that address is in the form of a *block number*. A *block* is a contiguous sequence of sectors from a single track of one platter. Block sizes range from 512 bytes to several kilobytes. Data are transferred between disk and main memory in units of blocks. The lower levels of the file-system manager convert block addresses into the hardware-level cylinder, surface, and sector number.

Since access to data on disk is several orders of magnitude slower than is access to data in main memory, much attention has been paid to improving the speed of access to blocks on disk. Buffering of blocks in memory to satisfy future requests is discussed in Section 10.5. Here, we discuss several other techniques.

- **Scheduling**. If several blocks from a cylinder need to be transferred from disk to main memory, we may be able to save access time by requesting the blocks in the order in which they will pass under the heads. If the desired blocks are on different cylinders, it is advantageous to request the blocks in an order that minimizes disk-arm movement. *Disk-arm–scheduling* algorithms attempt to order accesses to tracks in a fashion that increases the number of accesses that can be processed. A commonly used algorithm is the *elevator algorithm*, which works in a manner similar to many elevators. Suppose that, initially, the arm is moving from the innermost track toward the outside of the disk. For each track for which there is an access request, it stops at that track, services requests for the track, and then continues moving outward until there are no waiting requests for tracks farther out. At this point, the arm changes direction, and moves toward the inside, again stopping at each track for which there is a request, until it reaches a track where there is no request for tracks farther toward the center. Now, it reverses direction and starts a new cycle. Disk controllers usually perform the task of reordering read requests to improve performance, since they are intimately aware of the organization of blocks on disk, of the rotational position of the disk platters, and of the position of the disk arm.

- **File organization**. To reduce block-access time, we can organize blocks on disk in a way that corresponds closely to the manner in which we expect data to be accessed. For example, if we expect a file to be accessed sequentially, then we should ideally keep all the blocks of the file sequentially on adjacent cylinders. Older operating systems, such as the IBM mainframe operating systems, provided programmers fine control on placement of files, allowing a programmer to reserve a set of cylinders for storing a file. However, this control places a burden on the programmer or system administrator to decide, for example, how many cylinders to allocate for a file, and may require costly reorganization if data are inserted to or deleted from the file.

  Subsequent operating systems, such as Unix and personal-computer operating systems, hide the disk organization from users, and manage the allocation internally. However, over time, a sequential file may become *fragmented*; that is, its blocks become scattered all over the disk. To reduce fragmentation, the system can make a back-up copy of the data on disk and restore the entire disk. The restore operation writes back the blocks of each file contiguously (or nearly so). Some systems (such as MS-DOS) have utilities that scan the disk and then move blocks to decrease the fragmentation. The performance increases realized from these techniques can be large, but the system is generally unusable while these utilities operate.

- **Nonvolatile write buffers**. Since the contents of main memory are lost in a power failure, information about database updates has to be recorded on disk to survive possible system crashes. Hence, the performance of update-intensive database applications, such as transaction-processing systems, is heavily dependent on the speed of disk writes.

  We can use *nonvolatile random-access memory* (*nonvolatile RAM*) to speed up disk writes drastically. The contents of nonvolatile RAM are not lost in power failure. A common way to implement nonvolatile RAM is to use battery-backed-up RAM. The idea is that, when the database system (or the operating system) requests that a block be written to disk, the disk controller writes the block to a nonvolatile RAM buffer, and immediately notifies the operating system that the write completed successfully. The controller writes the data to their destination on disk whenever the disk does not have any other requests, or when the nonvolatile RAM buffer becomes full. When the database system requests a block write, it notices a delay only if the nonvolatile RAM buffer is full. On recovery from a system crash, any pending buffered writes in the nonvolatile RAM are written back to the disk.

The degree to which nonvolatile RAM improves performance is illustrated by the following example. Assume that write requests are received in a random (uniformly distributed) fashion, with the disk being busy on average 90 percent of the time. If we have a nonvolatile RAM buffer of 50 blocks, then, on average, only once per minute will a write find the buffer to be full (and therefore have to wait for a disk write to finish). Thus, in most cases, disk writes can be executed without the database system waiting for a seek or rotational latency. If the disk and the disk controller do not have a nonvolatile RAM write buffer, some operating systems (such as Solaris) can perform write buffering using nonvolatile RAM in the computer system itself.

- **Log disk**. Another approach to reducing write latencies is to use a *log disk*— that is, a disk devoted to writing a sequential log—in much the same way as a nonvolatile RAM buffer. All access to the log disk is sequential, essentially eliminating seek time, and several consecutive blocks can be written at once, making writes to the log disk several times faster than random writes. As before, the data have to be written to their actual location on disk as well, but this write can be done without the database system having to wait for it to complete. After a system crash, the system reads the log disk to find those writes that had not been completed, and carries them out then.

    The *log-based file system* is an extreme version of the log-disk approach. Data are not written back to their original destination on disk; instead, the file system keeps track of where in the log disk the blocks were written most recently, and retrieves them from that location. The log disk itself is compacted periodically, so that old writes that have subsequently been overwritten can be removed. This approach improves write performance, but generates a high degree of fragmentation for files that are updated often. As we noted earlier, such fragmentation increases seek time for sequential reading of files.

# 10.3  RAID

Disk drives have continued to get smaller and cheaper in recent years, so it is now economically feasible to attach a large number of disks to a computer system. Small disks are now mass produced and are relatively inexpensive. Using a large number of cheap small disks to store data may be more cost effective than is using a smaller number of expensive large disks.

Having a large number of disks in a system presents opportunities for improving the rate at which data can be read or written, if the disks are operated in parallel. Furthermore, this setup offers the potential for improving the reliability of data storage, because redundant information can be stored on multiple disks. Thus, failure of one disk does not lead to loss of data. A variety of disk-organization techniques, collectively called *redundant arrays of inexpensive disks* (*RAIDs*), have been proposed to address the performance and reliability issues.

In the past, RAIDs composed of small cheap disks were viewed as a cost-effective alternative to large, expensive disks; today, large disks are used rarely, and RAIDs are used for their higher reliability and higher data transfer rate, rather than for economic reasons. Hence, the I in RAID now stands for *independent*, instead of *inexpensive*.

## 10.3.1   Improvement of Reliability via Redundancy

Let us first consider reliability. The chance that some disk out of a set of $N$ disks will fail is much higher than the chance that a specific single disk will fail. Suppose that the mean time to failure of a single disk is 100,000 hours, or approximately 11.4 years. Further assume that the probability that the disk will fail in a given unit of time does not change with time. (This assumption is not valid in practice, since the probability of failure of a disk is highest late in its life as well as when it is first used, but relatively low in between. We make the assumption for simplicity.) Then, the mean time to failure of some disk in an array of 100 disks will be $100,000/100 = 1000$ hours, or 41.66 days, which is not long at all! If we store only one copy of the data, then each disk failure will result in loss of a significant amount of data (as discussed earlier in Section 10.2.1) and, such a high rate of data loss is unacceptable.

The solution to the problem of reliability is to introduce *redundancy*; that is, we store extra information that is not needed normally, but that can be used in the event of failure of a disk to rebuild the lost information. Thus, even if a disk fails, data are not lost, so the effective mean time to failure is increased, provided that we count only failures that lead to loss of data or to nonavailability of data.

The simplest (but most expensive) approach to introducing redundancy is to duplicate every disk. This technique is called *mirroring* or *shadowing*. A logical disk then consists of two physical disks, and every write is carried out on both disks. If one of the disks fails, the data can be read from the other. Data will be lost only if the second disk fails before the first failed disk is repaired.

The mean time to failure (where failure is the loss of data) of a mirrored disk depends on the mean time to failure of the individual disks, as well as on the *mean time to repair*, which is the time it takes (on an average) to replace a failed disk and to restore the data on it. Suppose that the failures of the two disks are *independent*; that is, there is no connection between the failure of one disk and the failure of the other. Then, if the mean time to failure of a single disk is 100,000 hours, and the mean time to repair is 10 hours, then the *mean time to data loss* of a mirrored disk system is $100000^2/2 * 10 = 500 * 10^6$ hours, or 57,000 years! (We do not go into the derivations here; references in the bibliographic notes provide the details.)

You should be aware that the assumption of independence of disk failures is not valid. Power failures, and natural disasters such as earthquakes, fires, and floods, may result in damage to both disks at the same time. As disks age, the probability of failure increases, increasing the chance that a second disk will fail while the first is being repaired. In spite of all these considerations, however, mirrored-disk systems offer much higher reliability than do single-disk systems. Mirrored-disk systems with mean time to data loss of about 500,000 to 1,000,000 hours, or 55 to 110 years, are available today.

Power failures are a particular source of concern, since they occur far more frequently than do natural disasters. Power failures are not a concern if there is no data transfer to disk in progress when they occur. However, even with mirroring of disks, if writes are in progress to the same block in both disks, and power fails before both blocks are fully written, the two blocks can be in an inconsistent state. The solution to this problem is to write one copy first, then the next, so that one of the two copies is always consistent. Some extra actions are required when we restart after a power failure, to recover from incomplete writes. This matter is examined in Exercise 10.4.

## 10.3.2   Improvement in Performance via Parallelism

Now let us consider the benefit of parallel access to multiple disks. With disk mirroring, the rate at which read requests can be handled is doubled, since read requests can be sent to either disk (as long as both disks in a pair are functional, as is almost always the case). The transfer rate of each read is the same as in a single-disk system, but the number of reads per unit time has doubled.

With multiple disks, we can improve the transfer rate as well (or instead) by striping data across multiple disks. In its simplest form, *data striping* consists of splitting the bits of each byte across multiple disks; such striping is called *bit-level striping*. For example, if we have an array of eight disks, we write bit $i$ of each byte to disk $i$. The array of eight disks can be treated as a single disk with sectors that are eight times the normal size, and, more important, that have eight times the access rate. In such an organization, every disk participates in every access (read or write), so the number of accesses that can be processed per second is about the same as on a single disk, but each access can read eight times as many data in the same time as on a single disk.

Bit-level striping can be generalized to a number of disks that either is a multiple of 8 or divides 8. For example, if we use an array of four disks, bits $i$ and $4 + i$ of each byte go to disk $i$. Further, striping does not need to be at the level of bits of a byte: For example, in *block-level striping*, blocks of a file are striped across multiple disks; with $n$ disks, block $i$ of a file goes to disk $(i \bmod n) + 1$. Other levels of striping, such as bytes of a sector or sectors of a block also are possible.

In summary, there are two main goals of parallelism in a disk system:

1. Load balance multiple small accesses (that is, page accesses), so that the throughput of such accesses increases.
2. Parallelize large accesses so that the response time of large accesses is reduced.

### 10.3.3   RAID Levels

Mirroring provides high reliability, but it is expensive. Striping provides high data-transfer rates, but does not improve reliability. Numerous schemes to provide redundancy at lower cost by using the idea of disk striping combined with "parity" bits (which we describe next) have been proposed. These schemes have different cost–performance tradeoffs, and are classified into levels called *RAID Levels*. We describe the various levels here; Figure 10.4 shows these levels pictorially (in the figure, *P* indicates error-correcting bits, and *C* indicates a second copy of the data). In all cases depicted in the figure, four disks worth of data is stored, and the extra disks are used to store redundant information for failure recovery.

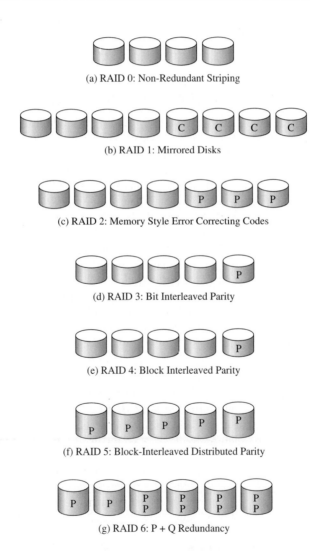

(a) RAID 0: Non-Redundant Striping

(b) RAID 1: Mirrored Disks

(c) RAID 2: Memory Style Error Correcting Codes

(d) RAID 3: Bit Interleaved Parity

(e) RAID 4: Block Interleaved Parity

(f) RAID 5: Block-Interleaved Distributed Parity

(g) RAID 6: P + Q Redundancy

Figure 10.4    RAID levels.

- **RAID level 0** refers to disk arrays with striping at the level of blocks, but without any redundancy (such as mirroring or parity bits). Figure 10.4a shows an array of size 4.

- **RAID level 1** refers to disk mirroring with block striping. Figure 10.4b shows a mirrored organization that holds four disks worth of data.

- **RAID level 2** is also known as memory-style error-correcting-code (ECC) organization. Memory systems have long implemented error detection using parity bits. Each byte in a memory system may have a parity bit associated with it that records whether the numbers of bits in the byte that are set to 1 is even (parity=0) or odd (parity=1). If one of the bits in the byte gets damaged (either a 1 becomes a 0, or a 0 becomes a 1), the parity of the byte changes and thus will not match the stored parity. Similarly, if the stored parity bit gets damaged, it will not match the computed parity. Thus, all 1-bit errors are detected by the memory system. Error-correcting schemes store 2 or more extra bits, and can reconstruct the data if a single bit gets damaged. The idea of error-correcting codes can be used directly in disk arrays via striping of bytes across disks. For example, the first bit of each byte could be stored in disk 1, the second bit in disk 2, and so on until the eighth bit is stored in disk 8, and the error-correction bits are stored in further disks. This scheme is shown pictorially in Figure 10.4, where the disks labeled $P$ store the error-correction bits. If one of the disks fails, the remaining bits of the byte and the associated error-correction bits can be read from other disks, and can be used to reconstruct the damaged data. Figure 10.4c shows an array of size 4; note RAID level 2 requires only three disks' overhead for four disks of data, unlike RAID level 1, which required four disks' overhead.

- **RAID level 3**, or bit-interleaved parity organization, improves on level 2 by noting that, unlike memory systems, disk controllers can detect whether a sector has been read correctly, so a single parity bit can be used for error correction, as well as for detection. The idea is as follows. If one of the sectors gets damaged, we know exactly which sector it is, and, for each bit in the sector, we can figure out whether it is a 1 or a 0 by computing the parity of the corresponding bits from sectors in the other disks. If the parity of the remaining bits is equal to the stored parity, the missing bit is 0; otherwise, it is 1. RAID level 3 is as good as level 2, but is less expensive in the number of extra disks (it has only a one disk overhead), so level 2 is not used in practice. This scheme is shown pictorially in Figure 10.4d.

  RAID level 3 has two benefits over level 1. Only one parity disk is needed for several regular disks, unlike one mirror disk for every disk in level 1, thus reducing the storage overhead. Since reads and writes of a byte are spread out over multiple disks, with $N$-way striping of data, the transfer rate for reading or writing a single block is $N$ times as fast as with a RAID level 1 organization using $N$-way striping. On the other hand, RAID level 3 supports a lower number of I/Os per second, since every disk has to participate in every I/O request.

- **RAID Level 4**, or block-interleaved parity organization, uses block level striping, as in RAID 0, and in addition keeps a parity block on a separate disk for corresponding blocks from $N$ other disks. This scheme is shown pictorially in Figure 10.4e. If one of the disks fails, the parity block can be used with the corresponding blocks from the other disks to restore the blocks of the failed disk.

A block read accesses only one disk, allowing other requests to be processed by the other disks. Thus, the data-transfer rate for each access is slower, but multiple read accesses can proceed in parallel, leading to a higher overall I/O rate. The transfer rates for large reads is high, since all the disks can be read in parallel; large writes also have high transfer rates, since the data and parity can be written in parallel.

Small independent writes, on the other hand, cannot be performed in parallel. A write of a block has to access the disk on which the block is stored, as well as the parity disk, since the parity block has to be updated. Moreover, both the old value of the parity block and the old value of the block being written have to be read for the new parity to be computed. Thus, a single write requires four disk accesses: two to read the two old blocks, and two to write the two blocks.

- **RAID level 5**, or block-interleaved distributed parity, improves on level 4 by partitioning data and parity among all $N + 1$ disks, rather than storing data in $N$ disks and parity in one disk. In level 5, all disks can participate in satisfying read requests, unlike in RAID level 4, where the parity disk cannot participate, so level 5 increases the total number of requests that can be met in a given amount of time. For each block, one of the disks stores the parity, and the others store data. For example, with an array of five disks, the parity for the $n$th block is stored in disk $(n \bmod 5) + 1$; the $n$th blocks of the other four disks store actual data for that block. This setup is denoted pictorially in Figure 10.4f, where the $P$s are distributed across all the disks. Note that a parity block cannot store parity for blocks in the same disk, since then a disk failure would result in loss of data as well as of parity, and hence would not be recoverable. Level 5 subsumes level 4, since it offers better read–write performance at the same cost, so level 4 is not used in practice.

- **RAID Level 6**, also called the P+Q redundancy scheme, is much like RAID level 5, but stores extra redundant information to guard against multiple disk failures. Instead of using parity, error-correcting codes such as the Reed–Solomon codes (see the bibliographic notes) are used. In the scheme shown in Figure 10.4g, 2 bits of redundant data are stored for every 4 bits of data—unlike 1 parity bit in level 5—and the system can tolerate two disk failures.

Finally, we note that numerous improvements have been proposed to the basic RAID schemes described here. As a result, sometimes there is confusion about the exact definitions of the different RAID levels.

### 10.3.4   Choice of the Correct RAID Level

If a disk fails, the time to rebuild its data can be significant, and will vary with the RAID level that is used. Rebuilding is easiest for RAID level 1, since data can be copied from another disk; for the other levels, we need to access all the other disks in the array to rebuild data in a failed disk. The rebuild performance of a RAID system may be an important factor if continuous supply of data is required, as it is in high-performance or interactive database systems. Furthermore, rebuild performance influences the mean time to failure.

Since RAID levels 2 and 4 are subsumed by RAID levels 3 and 5, the choice of RAID levels is restricted to the remaining levels. RAID level 0 is used in high-performance applications where data loss is not critical. RAID level 1 is popular for applications such as storage of log files in a database system, since it offers the best write performance. Due to level 1's high overhead, levels 3 and 5 are often preferred for storing large volumes of data. The difference between levels 3 and 5 is the data-transfer rate versus the overall I/O rate. Level 3 is preferred if a high data-transfer is required; level 5 is preferred if random reads are important, as they are in most database systems. Level 6 is not supported currently by many RAID implementations, but it offers better reliability than level 5.

RAID system designers have to make several other decisions as well. For example, how many disks should there be in an array? How many bits should be protected by each parity bit? If there are more disks in an array, data-transfer rates are higher, but the system would be more expensive. If there are more bits protected by a parity bit, the space overhead due to parity bits is lower, but there is an increased chance that a second disk will fail before the first failed disk is repaired, and that will result in data loss.

### 10.3.5  Extensions

The concepts of RAID have been generalized to other storage devices, including arrays of tapes, and even to the broadcast of data over wireless systems. When applied to arrays of tapes, the RAID structures are able to recover data even if one of the tapes in an array of tapes is damaged. When applied to broadcast of data, a block of data is split into short units and is broadcast along with a parity unit; if one of the units is not received for any reason, it can be reconstructed from the other units.

## 10.4  Tertiary Storage

In a large database system, some of the data may have to reside on tertiary storage. The two most common tertiary storage media are optical disks and magnetic tapes.

### 10.4.1  Optical Disks

CD-ROM has become a popular medium for distributing software, multimedia data such as audio and images, and other electronically published information. CD-ROM has the benefit that the disks can be loaded into or removed from a drive, and the disks have a high storage capacity (about 500 megabytes on a single disk, several hundred times the capacity of a floppy disk). Further, disks are cheap to mass produce, and the drives themselves are cheaper than are magnetic-disk drives.

CD-ROM drives have much longer seek times (250 milliseconds is common) than do magnetic-disk drives; lower rotational speeds (about 400 rpm), leading to a high latency; and lower data-transfer rates (about 150 kilobytes per second). Rotational speeds initially corresponded to the audio CD standards, but drives that spin disks at many times the standard speed are available today, and thereby provide increased data-transfer rates (currently, up to 32 times the standard rate). More recently, a new optical format, *digital video disk* (*DVD*) has become a standard. These disks hold between 4.7 and 17 gigabytes of data.

*Write-once, read-many* (*WORM*) disks can be written by the same drive from which they are read, but differ from magnetic disks in that they can be written only once, and their data cannot be erased; they can be read as many times as desired, however. WORM disks are popular for archival storage of data, since they have a high capacity (about 500 megabytes per disk), have a longer lifetime than magnetic disks, and, like tapes, can be removed from the drive. Moreover, since they cannot be overwritten, they provide an audit trail with which it is hard to tamper. *WORM jukeboxes* are devices that can store a large number of WORM disks, and can load the disks automatically on demand to one of a few WORM drives.

## 10.4.2   Magnetic Tapes

Magnetic tape has long history of use as a secondary-storage medium. Although it is relatively permanent, and can hold large volumes of data, magnetic tape is slow in comparison to magnetic and optical disks. Even more important, magnetic tape is limited to sequential access. Thus, it is unsuitable for providing the random access to meet for most secondary-storage requirements. Tapes are used mainly for backup, for storage of infrequently used information, and as an off-line medium for transferring information from one system to another.

A tape is kept in a spool, and is wound or rewound past a read–write head. Moving to the correct spot on a tape can take minutes rather than milliseconds; once positioned, however, tape drives can write data at densities and speeds approaching those of disk drives. Capacities vary depending on the length and width of the tape, and on the density at which the head can read and write. A tape drive is usually named by its width. Thus, there are 8-millimeter, 1/4-inch, and 1/2-inch (also known as nine-track) tape drives. The 8-millimeter tape drives have the highest density, due to the technology that they use; they currently store 5 gigabytes of data on a 350-foot tape. Tape devices are reliable, but tapes have limits on the number of times that they can be read or written reliably.

Tapes are also used for storage of large volumes of data, such as video or image data that either do not need to be accessible quickly or are so voluminous that magnetic-disk storage would be too expensive. *Tape jukeboxes* hold large numbers of tapes, with a few drives onto which the tapes can be mounted; they are used for storing large volumes of data, ranging up to many terabytes ($10^{12}$ bytes), with access times on the order of seconds to a few minutes. Applications that need such enormous data storage include imaging systems that gather data by remote-sensing satellites.

# 10.5   Storage Access

A database is mapped into a number of different files, which are maintained by the underlying operating system. These files resides permanently on disks, with backups on tapes. Each file is partitioned into fixed-length storage units called *blocks*, which are the units of both storage allocation and data transfer. We shall discuss in Section 10.6 various ways to organize the data logically in files.

A block may contain several data items. The exact set of data items that a block contains is determined by the form of physical data organization being used (see Section 10.6). We shall assume that no data item spans two or more blocks. This assumption is realistic for most data-processing applications, such as our banking example.

A major goal of the database system is to minimize the number of block transfers between the disk and memory. One way to reduce the number of disk accesses is to keep as many blocks as possible in main memory. The goal is to maximize the chance that, when a block is accessed, it is already in main memory, and, thus, no disk access is required.

Since it is not possible to keep all blocks in main memory, we need to manage the allocation of the space available in main memory for the storage of blocks. The *buffer* is that part of main memory available for storage of copies of disk blocks. There is always a copy kept on disk of every block, but the copy on disk may be a version of the block older than the version in the buffer. The subsystem responsible for the allocation of buffer space is called the *buffer manager*.

## 10.5.1   Buffer Manager

Programs in a database system make requests (that is, calls) on the buffer manager when they need a block from disk. If the block is already in the buffer, the requester is passed the address of the block in main memory. If the block is not in the buffer, the buffer manager first allocates space in the buffer for the block, throwing out some other block, if required, to make space for the new block. The block that is thrown out is written back to disk only if it was modified since the most recent time that it was written to the disk. Then, the buffer manager reads in the block from the disk to the buffer, and passes the address of the block in main memory to the requester. The internal actions of the buffer manager are transparent to the programs that issue disk-block requests.

If you are familiar with operating-system concepts, you will note that the buffer manager appears to be nothing more than a virtual-memory manager, like those found in most operating systems. One difference is that the size of the database may be much more than the hardware address space of a machine, so memory addresses are not sufficient to address all disk blocks. Further, to serve the database system well, the buffer manager must use techniques more sophisticated than typical virtual-memory management schemes:

- **Replacement strategy**. When there is no room left in the buffer, a block must be removed from the buffer before a new one can be read in. Typically, operating systems use a least recently used (LRU) scheme, in which the block that was referenced least recently is written back to disk and is removed from the buffer. This simple approach can be improved on for database applications.

- **Pinned blocks**. For the database system to be able to recover from crashes (Chapter 15), it is necessary to restrict those times when a block may be written back to disk. A block that is not allowed to be written back to disk is said to be *pinned*. Although many operating systems do not provide support for pinned blocks, such a feature is essential for the implementation of a database system that is resilient to crashes.

- **Forced output of blocks**. There are situations in which it is necessary to write back the block to disk, even though the buffer space that it occupies is not needed. This write is called the *forced output* of a block. We shall see the reason for requiring forced output in Chapter 15; briefly, main-memory contents and thus buffer contents are lost in a crash, whereas data on disk usually survive a crash.

We discuss buffer-replacement issues next.

## 10.5.2    Buffer-Replacement Policies

The goal of a replacement strategy for blocks in the buffer is the minimization of accesses to the disk. For general-purpose programs, it is not possible to predict accurately which blocks will be referenced. Therefore, operating systems use the past pattern of block references as a predictor of future references. The assumption that is generally made is that blocks that have been referenced recently are likely to be referenced again. Therefore, if a block must be replaced, the least recently referenced block is replaced. This approach is called the *LRU block-replacement scheme*.

LRU is an acceptable replacement scheme in operating systems. However, a database system is able to predict the pattern of future references more accurately than is an operating system. A user request to the database system involves several steps. The database system is often able to determine in advance which blocks will be needed by looking at each of the steps required to perform the user-requested operation. Thus, unlike operating systems, which must rely on the past to predict the future, database systems may have information regarding at least the short-term future.

To illustrate how information about future block access allows us to improve the LRU strategy, we consider the processing of the relational-algebra expression

$$borrower \bowtie customer$$

Assume that the strategy chosen to process this request is given by the pseudocode program shown in Figure 10.5. (We shall study other strategies in Chapter 12.)

Assume that the two relations of this example are stored in separate files. In this example, we can see that, once a tuple of *borrower* has been processed, that tuple is not needed again. Therefore, once processing of an entire block of

**for each** tuple *b* of *borrower* **do**
    **for each** tuple *c* of *customer* **do**
        **if** *b*[*customer-name*] = *c*[*customer-name*]
        **then begin**
                    let *x* be a tuple defined as follows:
                    *x*[*customer-name*] := *b*[*customer-name*]
                    *x*[*loan-number*] := *b*[*loan-number*]
                    *x*[*customer-street*] := *c*[*customer-street*]
                    *x*[*customer-city*] := *c*[*customer-city*]
                    include tuple *x* as part of result of *borrower* ⋈ *customer*
            **end**
    **end**
**end**

Figure 10.5    Procedure for computing join.

*borrower* tuples is completed, that block is no longer needed in main memory, even though it has been used recently. The buffer manager should be instructed to free the space occupied by a *borrower* block as soon as the final tuple has been processed. This buffer-management strategy is called the *toss-immediate* strategy.

Now consider blocks containing *customer* tuples. We need to examine every block of *customer* tuples once for each tuple of the *borrower* relation. When processing of a *customer* block is completed, we know that that block will not be accessed again until all other *customer* blocks have been processed. Thus, the most recently used *customer* block will be the final block to be re-referenced, and the least recently used *customer* block is the block that will be referenced next. This assumption set is the exact opposite of the one that forms the basis for the LRU strategy. Indeed, the optimal strategy for block replacement is the *most recently used (MRU) strategy*. If a *customer* block must be removed from the buffer, the MRU strategy chooses the most recently used block.

For the MRU strategy to work correctly for our example, the system must pin the *customer* block currently being processed. After the final *customer* tuple has been processed, the block is unpinned, and it becomes the most recently used block.

In addition to using knowledge that the system may have about the request being processed, the buffer manager can use statistical information regarding the probability that a request will reference a particular relation. The data dictionary is one of the most frequently accessed parts of the database. Thus, the buffer manager should try not to remove data-dictionary blocks from main memory, unless other factors dictate that it do so. In Chapter 11, we discuss indices for files. Since an index for a file may be accessed more frequently than the file itself, the buffer manager should, in general, not remove index blocks from main memory if alternatives are available.

The ideal database block-replacement strategy needs knowledge of the database operations being performed. No single strategy is known that handles all the possible scenarios well. Indeed, a surprisingly large number of database systems use LRU, despite that strategy's faults. The exercises explore alternative strategies.

The strategy used by the buffer manager for block replacement is influenced by factors other than the time at which the block will be referenced again. If the system is processing requests by several users concurrently, the concurrency-control subsystem (Chapter 14) may need to delay certain requests, to ensure preservation of database consistency. If the buffer manager is given information from the concurrency-control subsystem indicating which requests are being delayed, it can use this information to alter its block-replacement strategy. Specifically, blocks needed by active (nondelayed) requests can be retained in the buffer at the expense of blocks needed by the delayed requests.

The crash-recovery subsystem (Chapter 15) imposes stringent constraints on block replacement. If a block has been modified, the buffer manager is not allowed to write back the new version of the block in the buffer to disk, since that would destroy the old version. Instead, the block manager must seek permission from the crash-recovery subsystem before writing out a block. The crash-recovery subsystem may demand that certain other blocks be force output before it grants permission to the buffer manager to output the block requested. In Chapter 15, we define precisely the interaction between the buffer manager and the crash-recovery subsystem.

## 10.6    File Organization

A *file* is organized logically as a sequence of records. These records are mapped onto disk blocks. Files are provided as a basic construct in operating systems, so we shall assume the existence of an underlying *file system*. We need to consider ways of representing logical data models in terms of files.

Although blocks are of a fixed size determined by the physical properties of the disk and by the operating system, record sizes vary. In a relational database, tuples of distinct relations are generally of different sizes.

One approach to mapping the database to files is to use several files, and to store records of only one fixed length in any given file. An alternative is to structure our files such that we can accommodate multiple lengths for records. Files of fixed-length records are easier to implement than are files of variable-length records. Many of the techniques used for the former can be applied to the variable-length case. Thus, we begin by considering a file of fixed-length records.

### 10.6.1    Fixed-Length Records

As an example, let us consider a file of *account* records for our bank database. Each record of this file is defined as follows:

> **type** *deposit* = **record**
>> *branch-name* : char (22);
>> *account-number* : char(10);
>> *balance* : real;
> **end**

| | | | |
|---|---|---|---|
| record 0 | Perryridge | A-102 | 400 |
| record 1 | Round Hill | A-305 | 350 |
| record 2 | Mianus | A-215 | 700 |
| record 3 | Downtown | A-101 | 500 |
| record 4 | Redwood | A-222 | 700 |
| record 5 | Perryridge | A-201 | 900 |
| record 6 | Brighton | A-217 | 750 |
| record 7 | Downtown | A-110 | 600 |
| record 8 | Perryridge | A-218 | 700 |

Figure 10.6    File containing *account* records.

If we assume that each character occupies 1 byte and that a real occupies 8 bytes, our *account* record is 40 bytes long. A simple approach is to use the first 40 bytes for the first record, the next 40 bytes for the second record, and so on (Figure 10.6). However, there are two problems with this simple approach:

1. It is difficult to delete a record from this structure. The space occupied by the record to be deleted must be filled with some other record of the file, or we must have a way of marking deleted records so that they can be ignored.
2. Unless the block size happens to be a multiple of 40 (which is unlikely), some records will cross block boundaries. That is, part of the record will be stored in one block and part in another. It would thus require two block accesses to read or write such a record.

When a record is deleted, we could move the record that came after it into the space formerly occupied by the deleted record, and so on, until every record following the deleted record has been moved ahead (Figure 10.7). Such an approach requires moving a large number of records. It might be easier simply to move the final record of the file into the space occupied by the deleted record, as shown in Figure 10.8.

It is undesirable to move records to occupy the space freed by a deleted record, since doing so requires additional block accesses. Since insertions tend to be more frequent than deletions, it is acceptable to leave open the space occupied

| | | | |
|---|---|---|---|
| record 0 | Perryridge | A-102 | 400 |
| record 1 | Round Hill | A-305 | 350 |
| record 3 | Downtown | A-101 | 500 |
| record 4 | Redwood | A-222 | 700 |
| record 5 | Perryridge | A-201 | 900 |
| record 6 | Brighton | A-217 | 750 |
| record 7 | Downtown | A-110 | 600 |
| record 8 | Perryridge | A-218 | 700 |

Figure 10.7    File of Figure 10.6, with record 2 deleted and all records moved.

| | | | |
|---|---|---|---|
| record 0 | Perryridge | A-102 | 400 |
| record 1 | Round Hill | A-305 | 350 |
| record 8 | Perryridge | A-218 | 700 |
| record 3 | Downtown | A-101 | 500 |
| record 4 | Redwood | A-222 | 700 |
| record 5 | Perryridge | A-201 | 900 |
| record 6 | Brighton | A-217 | 750 |
| record 7 | Downtown | A-110 | 600 |

Figure 10.8    File of Figure 10.6, with record 2 deleted and final record moved.

by the deleted record, and to wait for a subsequent insertion before reusing the space. A simple marker on a deleted record is not sufficient, since it is hard to find this available space when an insertion is being done. Thus, we need to introduce an additional structure.

At the beginning of the file, we allocate a certain number of bytes as a *file header*. The header will contain a variety of information about the file. For now, all we need to store there is the address of the first record whose contents are deleted. We use this first record to store the address of the second available record, and so on. Intuitively, we can think of these stored addresses as *pointers*, since they point to the location of a record. The deleted records thus form a linked list, which is often referred to as a *free list*. Figure 10.9 shows the file of Figure 10.6 after records 1, 4, and 6 have been deleted.

On insertion of a new record, we use the record pointed to by the header. We change the header pointer to point to the next available record. If no space is available, we add the new record to the end of the file.

The use of pointers requires careful programming. If we move or delete a record, a pointer to which another record contains, that pointer becomes incorrect in the sense that it no longer points to the desired record. Such pointers are called *dangling pointers*; in effect, they point to garbage. To avoid the dangling-pointer problem, we must avoid moving or deleting records that are pointed to by other records. We say that such records are *pinned*.

| | | | | |
|---|---|---|---|---|
| header | | | | |
| record 0 | Perryridge | A-102 | 400 | |
| record 1 | | | | |
| record 2 | Mianus | A-215 | 700 | |
| record 3 | Downtown | A-101 | 500 | |
| record 4 | | | | |
| record 5 | Perryridge | A-201 | 900 | |
| record 6 | | | | |
| record 7 | Downtown | A-110 | 600 | |
| record 8 | Perryridge | A-218 | 700 | |

Figure 10.9    File of Figure 10.6, after deletion of records 1, 4, and 6.

Insertion and deletion for files of fixed-length records are simple to implement, because the space made available by a deleted record is exactly the space needed to insert a record. If we allow records of variable length in a file, this match no longer holds. An inserted record may not fit in the space left free by a deleted record, or it may fill only part of that space.

## 10.6.2  Variable-Length Records

Variable-length records arise in database systems in several ways:

- Storage of multiple record types in a file
- Record types that allow variable lengths for one or more fields
- Record types that allow repeating fields

Different techniques for implementing variable-length records exist. For purposes of illustration, we shall use one example to demonstrate the various implementation techniques. We shall consider a different representation of the *deposit* information stored in the file of Figure 10.6, in which we use one variable-length record for each branch name and for all the account information for that branch. The format of the record is

**type** *account-list* = **record**
                *branch-name* : char (22);
                *account-info* : **array** [1 .. ∞] **of**
                          **record**;
                          *account-number* : char(10);
                          *balance* : real;
                    **end**
      **end**

We define *account-info* as an array with an arbitrary number of elements, so that there is no limit on how large a record can be (up to, of course, the size of the disk!).

### 10.6.2.1  Byte-String Representation

A simple method for implementing variable-length records is to attach a special *end-of-record* (⊥) symbol to the end of each record. We can then store each record as a string of consecutive bytes. Figure 10.10 shows such an organization to represent the file of fixed-length records of Figure 10.6 using variable-length records. An alternative version of the byte-string representation stores the record length at the beginning of each record, instead of using end-of-record symbols.

The byte-string representation as we have discussed it has disadvantages:

- It is not easy to reuse space occupied formerly by a deleted record. Although techniques exist to manage insertion and deletion, they lead to a large number of small fragments of disk storage that are wasted.

| 0 | Perryridge | A-102 | 400 | A-201 | 900 | A-218 | 700 | ⊥ |
| 1 | Round Hill | A-305 | 350 | ⊥ |
| 2 | Mianus | A-215 | 700 | ⊥ |
| 3 | Downtown | A-101 | 500 | A-110 | 600 | ⊥ |
| 4 | Redwood | A-222 | 700 | ⊥ |
| 5 | Brighton | A-217 | 750 | ⊥ |

**Figure 10.10**    Byte-string representation of variable-length records.

- There is no space, in general, for records to grow longer. If a variable-length record becomes longer, it must be moved, and movement is costly if the record is pinned.

Thus, the basic byte-string representation as we described it is not usually used for implementing variable-length records. However, a modified form of the byte-string representation, called the slotted-page structure, is commonly used for organizing records *within* a single block.

The *slotted-page structure* is shown in Figure 10.11. There is a header at the beginning of each block, containing the following information:

1. The number of record entries in the header
2. The end of free space in the block
3. An array whose entries contain the location and size of each record

The actual records are allocated *contiguously* in the block, starting from the end of the block. The free space in the block is contiguous, between the final entry in the header array, and the first record. If a record is inserted, space is allocated for it at the end of free space, and an entry containing its size and location is added to the header.

If a record is deleted, the space that it occupies is freed, and its entry is set to deleted (its size is set to −1, for example). Further, the records in the block before the deleted record are moved, so that the free space created by the deletion gets occupied, and all free space is again between the final entry in the header array and the first record. The end-of-free-space pointer in the header is appropriately

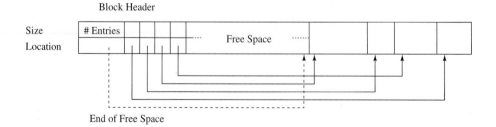

**Figure 10.11**    Slotted-page structure.

updated as well. Records can be grown or shrunk using similar techniques, as long as there is space in the block. The cost of moving the records is not too high, since the size of a block is limited: A typical value is 4 kilobytes.

The slotted-page structure requires that there be no pointers that point directly to records. Instead, pointers must point to the entry in the header that contains the actual location of the record. This level of indirection allows records to be moved to prevent fragmentation of space inside a block, while supporting indirect pointers to the record.

### 10.6.2.2 Fixed-Length Representation

Another way to implement variable-length records efficiently in a file system is to use one or more fixed-length records to represent one variable-length record.

There are two techniques for implementing files of variable-length records using fixed-length records:

1. **Reserved space**. If there is a maximum record length that is never exceeded, we can use fixed-length records of that length. Unused space (for records shorter than the maximum space) is filled with a special null, or end-of-record, symbol.
2. **Pointers**. The variable-length record is represented by a list of fixed-length records, chained together via pointers.

If we choose to apply the reserved-space method to our account example, we need to select a maximum record length. Figure 10.12 shows how the file of Figure 10.6 would be represented if we allowed a maximum of three accounts per branch. A record in this file is of the *account-list* type, but with the array containing exactly three elements. Those branches with fewer than three accounts (for example, Round Hill) have records with null fields. We use the symbol $\perp$ to represent this situation in Figure 10.12. In practice, a particular value that can never represent real data is used (for example, a negative "account number" or a "name" beginning with an "*").

The reserved-space method is useful when most records are of length close to the maximum. Otherwise, a significant amount of space may be wasted. In our bank example, some branches may have many more accounts than others. This situation leads us to consider use of the pointer method. To represent the file

| 0 | Perryridge | A-102 | 400 | A-201 | 900 | A-218 | 700 |
|---|---|---|---|---|---|---|---|
| 1 | Round Hill | A-305 | 350 | $\perp$ | $\perp$ | $\perp$ | $\perp$ |
| 2 | Mianus | A-215 | 700 | $\perp$ | $\perp$ | $\perp$ | $\perp$ |
| 3 | Downtown | A-101 | 500 | A-110 | 600 | $\perp$ | $\perp$ |
| 4 | Redwood | A-222 | 700 | $\perp$ | $\perp$ | $\perp$ | $\perp$ |
| 5 | Brighton | A-217 | 750 | $\perp$ | $\perp$ | $\perp$ | $\perp$ |

Figure 10.12    File of Figure 10.6, using the reserved-space method.

| 0 | Perryridge | A-102 | 400 | |
| 1 | Round Hill | A-305 | 350 | |
| 2 | Mianus | A-215 | 700 | |
| 3 | Downtown | A-101 | 500 | |
| 4 | Redwood | A-222 | 700 | |
| 5 | | A-201 | 900 | |
| 6 | Brighton | A-217 | 750 | |
| 7 | | A-110 | 600 | |
| 8 | | A-218 | 700 | |

Figure 10.13    File of Figure 10.6, using the pointer method.

using the pointer method, we add a pointer field as we did in Figure 10.9. The resulting structure is shown in Figure 10.13.

In effect, the file structures of Figures 10.9 and 10.13 are the same, except that, in Figure 10.9, we used pointers only to chain together deleted records, whereas in Figure 10.13, we chain together all records pertaining to the same branch.

A disadvantage to the structure of Figure 10.13 is that we waste space in all records except the first in a chain. The first record needs to have the *branch-name* value, but subsequent records do not. Nevertheless, we need to include a field for *branch-name* in all records, lest the records not be of fixed length. This wasted space is significant, since we expect, in practice, that each branch has a large number of accounts. To deal with this problem, we allow two kinds of blocks in our file:

1. **Anchor block**, which contains the first record of a chain
2. **Overflow block**, which contains records other than those that are the first record of a chain

Thus, all records *within a block* have the same length, even though not all records in the file have the same length. Figure 10.14 shows this file structure.

## 10.7   Organization of Records in Files

So far, we have studied how records are represented in a file structure. An instance of a relation is a set of records. Given a set of records, the next question is how to organize them in a file. Several of the ways of organizing records in files follow:

- **Heap file organization**. In this organization, any record can be placed anywhere in the file where there is space for the record. There is no ordering of records. Typically, there is a single file for each relation
- **Sequential file organization**. In this organization, records are stored in sequential order, based on the value of the search key of each record. The implementation of this organization is described in Section 10.7.1.

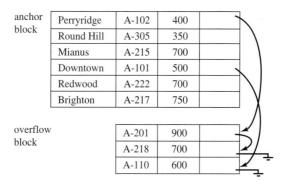

Figure 10.14    Anchor-block and overflow-block structures.

- **Hashing file organization**. In this organization, a hash function is computed on some attribute of each record. The result of the hash function specifies in which block of the file the record should be placed. This organization is described in Chapter 11; it is closely related to the indexing structures described in that chapter.

- **Clustering file organization**. In this organization, records of several different relations can be stored in the same file. Related records of the different relations are stored on the same block, so that one I/O operation fetches related records from all the relations. This organization is described in Section 10.7.2.

## 10.7.1   Sequential File Organization

A *sequential file* is designed for efficient processing of records in sorted order based on some *search key*. To permit fast retrieval of records in search-key order, we chain together records by pointers. The pointer in each record points to the next record in search-key order. Furthermore, to minimize the number of block accesses in sequential file processing, we store records physically in search-key order, or as close to search-key order as possible.

Figure 10.15 shows a sequential file of *account* records taken from our banking example. In that example, the records are stored in search-key order, using *branch-name* as the search key.

The sequential file organization allows records to be read in sorted order; that can be useful for display purposes, as well as for certain query-processing algorithms that we shall study in Chapter 12.

It is difficult, however, to maintain physical sequential order as records are inserted and deleted, since it is costly to move many records as a result of a single insertion or deletion. We can manage deletion using pointer chains, as we saw previously. For insertion, we apply the following rules:

1. Locate the record in the file that comes before the record to be inserted in search-key order.

| Brighton | A-217 | 750 | |
|---|---|---|---|
| Downtown | A-101 | 500 | |
| Downtown | A-110 | 600 | |
| Mianus | A-215 | 700 | |
| Perryridge | A-102 | 400 | |
| Perryridge | A-201 | 900 | |
| Perryridge | A-218 | 700 | |
| Redwood | A-222 | 700 | |
| Round Hill | A-305 | 350 | |

**Figure 10.15    Sequential file for *account* records.**

2. If there is a free record (that is, space left after a deletion) within the same block as this record, insert the new record there. Otherwise, insert the new record in an *overflow block*. In either case, adjust the pointers so as to chain together the records in search-key order.

Figure 10.16 shows the file of Figure 10.15 after the insertion of the record (North Town, A-888, 800). The structure in Figure 10.16 allows fast insertion of new records, but forces sequential file-processing applications to process records in an order that does not match the physical order of the records.

If relatively few records need to be stored in overflow blocks, this approach works well. Eventually, however, the correspondence between search-key order and physical order may be totally lost, in which case sequential processing will become significantly less efficient. At this point, the file should be *reorganized* such that it is once again physically in sequential order. Such reorganizations are costly, and must be done during times when the system load is low. The frequency with which reorganizations are needed depends on the frequency of insertion of new records. In the extreme case in which insertions rarely occur, it is possible

| Brighton | A-217 | 750 | |
|---|---|---|---|
| Downtown | A-101 | 500 | |
| Downtown | A-110 | 600 | |
| Mianus | A-215 | 700 | |
| Perryridge | A-102 | 400 | |
| Perryridge | A-201 | 900 | |
| Perryridge | A-218 | 700 | |
| Redwood | A-222 | 700 | |
| Round Hill | A-305 | 350 | |

| North Town | A-888 | 800 | |
|---|---|---|---|

**Figure 10.16    Sequential file after an insertion.**

always to keep the file in physically sorted order. In such a case, the pointer field shown in Figure 10.15 is not needed.

## 10.7.2   Clustering File Organization

Many relational-database systems store each relation in a separate file, so that they can take full advantage of the file system provided as part of the operating system. Usually, tuples of a relation can be represented as fixed-length records. Thus, relations can be mapped to a simple file structure. This simple implementation of a relational database system is well suited to database systems designed for personal computers. In such systems, the size of the database is small, so little is gained from a sophisticated file structure. Furthermore, in some personal computers, small overall size of the object code for the database system is essential. A simple file structure reduces the amount of code needed to implement the system.

This simple approach to relational-database implementation becomes less satisfactory as the size of the database increases. We have seen that there are performance advantages to be gained from careful assignment of records to blocks, and from careful organization of the blocks themselves. Thus, it is apparent that a more complicated file structure may be beneficial, even if we retain the strategy of storing each relation in a separate file.

However, many large-scale database systems do not rely directly on the underlying operating system for file management. Instead, one large operating-system file is allocated to the database system. All relations are stored in this one file, and the management of this file is left to the database system. To see the advantage of storing many relations in one file, we consider the following SQL query for the bank database:

> **select** *account-number, customer-name, customer-street, customer-city*
> **from** *depositor, customer*
> **where** *depositor.customer-name = customer.customer-name*

This query computes a join of the *depositor* and *customer* relations. Thus, for each tuple of *depositor*, the system must locate the *customer* tuples with the same value for *customer-name*. Ideally, these records will be located with the help of *indices*, which we shall discuss in Chapter 11. Regardless of how these records are located, however, they need to be transferred from disk into main memory. In the worst case, each record will reside on a different block, forcing us to do one block read for each record required by the query.

As a concrete example, consider the *depositor* and *customer* relations of Figures 10.17 and 10.18, respectively. In Figure 10.19, we show a file structure designed for efficient execution of queries involving *depositor* ⋈ *customer*. The *depositor* tuples for each *customer-name* are stored near the *customer* tuple for the corresponding *customer-name*. This structure mixes together tuples of two relations, but allows for efficient processing of the join. When a tuple of the *customer* relation is read, the entire block containing that tuple is copied from disk into main memory. Since the corresponding *depositor* tuples are stored on

| customer-name | account-number |
|:---:|:---:|
| Hayes | A-102 |
| Hayes | A-220 |
| Hayes | A-503 |
| Turner | A-305 |

Figure 10.17    The *depositor* relation.

the disk near the *customer* tuple, the block containing the *customer* tuple contains tuples of the *depositor* relation needed to process the query. If a customer has so many accounts that the *depositor* records do not fit in one block, the remaining records appear on nearby blocks. This file structure, called *clustering*, allows us to read many of the required records using one block read. Thus, we are able to process this particular query more efficiently.

Our use of clustering has enhanced processing of a particular join (*depositor* ⋈ *customer*), but it results in slowing processing of other types of query. For example,

**select** *

**from** *customer*

requires more block accesses than it did in the scheme under which we stored each relation in a separate file. Instead of several *customer* records appearing in one block, each record is located in a distinct block. Indeed, simply finding all the *customer* records is not possible without some additional structure. To locate all tuples of the *customer* relation in the structure of Figure 10.19, we need to chain together all the records of that relation using pointers, as shown in Figure 10.20.

The determination of when clustering is to be used depends on the types of query that the database designer believes to be most frequent. Careful use of clustering can produce significant performance gains in query processing.

## 10.8    Data-Dictionary Storage

So far, we have considered only the representation of the relations themselves. A relational-database system needs to maintain data *about* the relations, such as the schema of the relations. This information is called the *data dictionary*, or *system*

| customer-name | customer-street | customer-city |
|:---:|:---:|:---:|
| Hayes | Main | Brooklyn |
| Turner | Putnam | Stamford |

Figure 10.18    The *customer* relation.

| Hayes | Main | Brooklyn |
|-------|-------|----------|
| Hayes | A-102 | |
| Hayes | A-220 | |
| Hayes | A-503 | |
| Turner | Putnam | Stamford |
| Turner | A-305 | |

Figure 10.19    Clustering file structure.

*catalog*. Among the types of information that the system must store are these:

- Names of the relations
- Names of the attributes of each relation
- Domains and lengths of attributes
- Names of views defined on the database, and definitions of those views
- Integrity constraints (for example, key constraints)

In addition, many systems keep the following data on users of the system:

- Names of authorized users
- Accounting information about users

Further, statistical and descriptive data about relations may be kept on these matters:

- Number of tuples in each relation
- Method of storage used for each relation (for example, clustered or nonclustered)

In Chapter 11, in which we study indices, we shall see a need to store information about each index on each of the relations:

- Name of the index
- Name of the relation being indexed
- Attributes on which the index is defined
- Type of index formed

| Hayes | Main | Brooklyn | |
|-------|-------|----------|---|
| Hayes | A-102 | | |
| Hayes | A-220 | | |
| Hayes | A-503 | | |
| Turner | Putnam | Stamford | |
| Turner | A-305 | | |

Figure 10.20    Clustering file structure with pointer chains.

All this information comprises, in effect, a miniature database. Some database systems store this information using special-purpose data structures and code. It is generally preferable to store the data about the database in the database itself. By using the database to store system data, we simplify the overall structure of the system and allow the full power of the database to be used to permit fast access to system data.

The exact choice of how to represent system data using relations must be made by the system designer. One possible representation follows:

*System-catalog-schema* = (*relation-name, number-of-attributes*)
*Attribute-schema* = (*attribute-name, relation-name, domain-type, position, length*)
*User-schema* = (*user-name, encrypted-password, group*)
*Index-schema* = (*index-name, relation-name, index-type, index-attributes*)
*View-schema* = (*view-name, definition*)

# 10.9    Storage Structures for Object-Oriented Databases

The file-organization techniques described earlier—such as the heap, sequential, hashing and clustering organizations—can also be used for storing objects in an object-oriented databases. However, extra features are needed to support object-oriented database features, such as set-valued fields and persistent pointers.

## 10.9.1    Mapping of Objects to Files

The mapping of objects to files has many similarities to the mapping of tuples to files in a relational system. At the lowest level of data representation, both tuples and the data parts of objects are simply sequences of bytes. We can therefore store object data using the file structures described in earlier sections, with some modifications that we note next.

Objects in object-oriented databases may lack the uniformity of tuples in relational databases. For example, fields of records may be sets, unlike in relational databases, where data are typically required to be (at least) in first normal form. Furthermore, objects may be extremely large. Such objects have to be managed differently from records in a relational system.

We can implement set fields that have a small number of elements using data structures such as linked lists. Set fields that have a larger number of elements can be implemented as B-trees, or as separate relations in the database. Set fields can also be eliminated at the storage level by normalization. The storage system gives the upper levels of the database system the view of a set field, even though the set field has actually been normalized to create a new relation.

Some applications include extremely large objects that are not easily de-composed into smaller components. Such large objects may each be stored in a separate file. We discuss this idea further in Section 10.9.5.

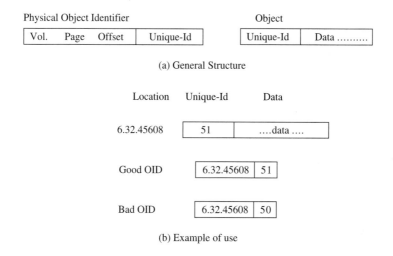

Figure 10.21     Unique identifiers in an OID.

## 10.9.2     Implementation of Object Identifiers

Since objects are identified by object identifiers (OID), an object-storage system needs a mechanism to locate an object given an OID. If the OIDs are *logical*—that is, they do not specify the location of the object—then the storage system must maintain an index that maps OIDs to the actual location of the object. If the OIDs are *physical*—that is, they encode the location of the object—then the object can be found directly. Physical OIDs typically have the following three parts:

**1.** A volume or file identifier.
**2.** A page identifier within the volume or file
**3.** An offset within the page

In addition, physical OIDs may contain a *unique identifier*, which is an integer that distinguishes the OID from the identifiers of other objects that happened to be stored at the same location earlier, and were deleted or moved elsewhere. The unique identifier is also stored with the object, and the identifiers in an OID and the corresponding object should match. If the unique identifier in a physical OID does not match the unique identifier in the object to which that OID points, the system detects that the pointer is a dangling pointer, and signals an error. Figure 10.21 illustrates this scheme.

Such pointer errors occur when physical OIDs corresponding to old objects that have been deleted are used accidentally. If the space occupied by the object had been reallocated, there may be a new object in the location, and it may get incorrectly addressed by the identifier of the old object. If not detected, the use of dangling pointers could result in corruption of a new object stored at the same location. The unique identifier helps to detect such errors, since the unique identifiers of the old physical OID and the new object will not match.

Suppose that an object has to be moved to a new page, perhaps because the size of the object has increased, and the old page has no extra space. Then, the physical OID will point to the old page, which no longer contains the object. Rather than change the OID of the object (which involves changing every object that points to this one), we leave behind a *forwarding address* at the old location. When the database tries to locate the object, it finds the forwarding address instead of the object; it then uses the forwarding address to locate the object.

### 10.9.3 Management of Persistent Pointers

We implement persistent pointers in a persistent programming language using OIDs. In some implementations, persistent pointers are physical OIDs; in others, they are logical OIDs. An important difference between persistent pointers and in-memory pointers is the size of the pointer. In-memory pointers need to be only big enough to address all virtual memory. On current computers, in-memory pointers are 4 bytes long, which is sufficient to address 4 gigabytes of memory. Persistent pointers need to address all the data in a database. Since database systems are often bigger than 4 gigabytes, persistent pointers are typically at least 8 bytes long. Many object-oriented databases also provide unique identifiers in persistent pointers, to catch dangling references. This feature further increases the size of persistent pointers. Thus, persistent pointers are substantially longer than are in-memory pointers.

#### 10.9.3.1 Pointer Swizzling

The action of looking up an object given its identifier is called *dereferencing*. Given an in-memory pointer (as in C++), looking up the object is merely a memory reference. Given a persistent pointer, dereferencing an object has an extra step—we have to find the actual location of the object in memory by looking up the persistent pointer in a table. If the object is not already in memory, it has to be loaded from disk. We can implement the table lookup fairly efficiently using hashing, but the lookup is still slow compared to a pointer dereference, even if the object is already in memory.

*Pointer swizzling* is a way to cut down the cost of locating persistent objects that are already present in memory. The idea is that, when a persistent pointer is first dereferenced, the object is located and is brought into memory if it is not already there. Now an extra step is carried out—an in-memory pointer to the object is stored in place of the persistent pointer. The next time that the *same* persistent pointer is dereferenced, the in-memory location can be read out directly, so the costs of locating the object are avoided. (In the case where persistent objects may be moved from memory back to disk to make space for other persistent objects, an extra step to ensure that the object is still in memory also must be carried out.) Correspondingly, when an object is written out, any persistent pointers that it contained and that were swizzled have to be *deswizzled* and thus converted back to their persistent representation. Pointer swizzling on pointer dereference, as described here, is called *software swizzling*.

Buffer management is more complicated if pointer swizzling is used, since the physical location of an object must not change once that object is brought into the buffer. One way to ensure that it will not change is to pin pages containing swizzled objects in the buffer pool, so that they are never replaced until the program that performed the swizzling was finished. See the bibliographic notes for more complex buffer-management schemes, involving virtual-memory mapping techniques, that remove the requirement of pinning the buffer pages.

### 10.9.3.2   Hardware Swizzling

Having two types of pointers, persistent and transient (in-memory), is rather inconvenient. Programmers have to remember the type of the pointers, and may have to write code twice—once for the persistent pointers and once for the in-memory pointers. It would be more convenient if both persistent and in-memory pointers were of the same type.

A simple way to merge persistent and in-memory pointer types is simply to extend the length of in-memory pointers to the same size as persistent pointers, and to use 1 bit of the identifier to distinguish between persistent and in-memory pointers. However, the storage cost of longer persistent pointers will have to be borne by in-memory pointers as well; hence, this scheme is unpopular.

We shall describe a technique called *hardware swizzling*, which uses the memory-management hardware present in most current computer systems to address this problem.

Hardware swizzling has two major advantages over software swizzling. First, it is able to store persistent pointers in objects in the same amount of space as in-memory pointers require (along with extra storage external to the object). Second, it transparently converts between persistent pointers and in-memory pointers in a clever and efficient way. Software written to deal with in-memory pointers can thereby deal with persistent pointers as well, without any changes.

Hardware swizzling uses the following representation of persistent pointers contained in objects that are on disk. A persistent pointer is conceptually split into two parts: a page identifier in the database, and an offset within the page. The page identifier in a persistent pointer is actually a small indirect pointer which we call the short page identifier. Each page (or other unit of storage) has a translation table that provides a mapping from the short page identifiers to full database page identifiers. The system has to look up the short page identifier in a persistent pointer in the translation table to find the full page identifier.

The translation table, in the worst case, will be only as big as the maximum number of pointers that can be contained in objects in a page; with a page size of 4096, and a pointer size of 4 bytes, the maximum number of pointers is 1024. In practice, the translation table is likely to contain many fewer than the maximum number of elements (1024 in our example), and will not consume excessive space. The short page identifier needs to have only enough bits to identify a row in the table; with a maximum table size of 1024, only 10 bits are required. Hence, a small number of bits is enough to store the short page identifier. Thus, the translation table permits an entire persistent pointer to fit into the same space as an in-memory pointer. Even though only a few bits are needed for the short page

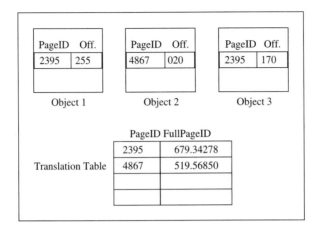

Figure 10.22   Page image before swizzling.

identifier, all the bits of an in-memory pointer, other than the page-offset bits, are used as the short page identifier. This architecture facilitates swizzling, as we shall see.

The persistent-pointer representation scheme is shown in Figure 10.22, where there are three objects in the page, each containing a persistent pointer. The translation table gives the mapping between short page identifiers and the full database page identifiers for each of the short page identifiers in these persistent pointers. The database page identifiers are shown in the format *volume.file.offset*.

Extra information is maintained with each page so that all persistent pointers in the page can be found. The information is updated when an object is created or deleted in the page. The need to locate all persistent pointers in a page will become clear later.

When an in-memory pointer is dereferenced, if the operating system detects that the page in virtual address space that is pointed to does not have storage allocated for it, or has been access protected, then a *segmentation violation* is said to occur. (Many descriptions of hardware swizzling use the term *page fault* instead of *segmentation violation*.) Many operating systems provide a mechanism to specify a function to be called when a segmentation violation occurs, and a mechanism to allocate storage for a page in virtual address space, and to set that pages's access permissions. In most Unix systems, the mmap system call provides this latter functionality, and is used to implement hardware swizzling.

Consider the first time that an in-memory pointer to a page $v$ is dereferenced, when storage has not yet been allocated for the page. As we described, a segmentation violation will occur, and will result in a function call on the database system. The database system first determines what database page was allocated to virtual-memory page $v$; let the full page identifier of the database page be $P$. If there was no database page allocated to $v$, an error is flagged. Otherwise, the database system allocates storage space for page $v$, and loads the database page $P$ into page $v$.

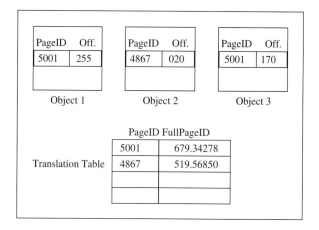

Figure 10.23    Page image after swizzling.

Pointer swizzling is now done for page $P$, as follows. The system locates all persistent pointers contained in objects in page $P$, using the extra information stored in the page. Consider each such pointer; call it $\langle p_i, o_i \rangle$, where $p_i$ is the short page identifier and $o_i$ is the offset within the page. Let $P_i$ be the full page identifier of $p_i$, found in the translation table in page $P$.

If page $P_i$ does not already have a virtual-memory page allocated to it, a free page in virtual address space is now allocated to it. The page $P_i$ will reside at this virtual address location if and when it is brought in. At this point, the page in virtual address space does not have any storage allocated for it, either in memory or on disk; it is merely a range of addresses reserved for the database page.

Let the virtual-memory page allocated (either earlier or in the previous step) for $P_i$ be $v_i$. We update the pointer $\langle p_i, o_i \rangle$ being considered by replacing $p_i$ with $v_i$. Finally, after swizzling all persistent pointers in $P$, the pointer dereference that resulted in the segmentation violation is allowed to continue, and will find the object for which it was looking loaded in memory.

Figure 10.23 shows the state of the page from Figure 10.22 after that page has been brought into memory and the pointers in it have been swizzled. Here, we assume that the page whose database page identifier is 679.34278 has been mapped to page 5001 in memory, whereas the page whose identifier is 519.56850 has been mapped to page 4867 (which is the same as the short page identifier). All the pointers in objects have been updated to reflect the new mapping, and can now be used as in-memory pointers.

At the end of the translation phase for a page, the objects in the page satisfy an important property: All persistent pointers contained in objects in the page have been converted to in-memory pointers. Thus, objects in in-memory pages contain only in-memory pointers. Routines that use these objects do not even need to know about the existence of persistent pointers! For example, existing libraries written for in-memory objects can be used unchanged for persistent objects. That is indeed an important advantage!

Note that, if any memory page $v_i$ as described here has not yet been loaded in virtual memory, then, the first time that any in-memory pointer to it is dereferenced, a segmentation violation will occur. Page $P_i$ is loaded into memory page $v_i$, and pointer swizzling is performed for it, exactly as described for page $P$.

Software swizzling has a deswizzling operation associated with it when a page in memory has to be written back to the database, to convert in-memory pointers back to persistent pointers. Hardware swizzling can even avoid this step— when pointer swizzling is done for the page, the translation table for the page is simply updated, so that the page-identifier part of the swizzled in-memory pointers can be used to look up the table. For example, as shown in Figure 10.23, database page 679.34278 (with short identifier 2395 in the page shown) is mapped to virtual-memory page 5001. At this point, not only is the pointer in object 1 updated from 2395255 to 5001255, but also the short identifier in the table is updated to 5001. Thus, the short identifier 5001 in object 1 and in the table match each other again. Therefore, the page can be written back to disk without any deswizzling.

Several optimizations can be carried out on the basic scheme described here. When swizzling is done for page $P$, for each page $P'$ referred to by any persistent pointer in $P$, the system attempts to allocate $P'$ to the virtual address location indicated by the short page identifier of $P'$ on page $P$. If the page can be allocated as attempted, pointers to it do not need to be updated. In our swizzling example, page 519.56850 with short page identifier 4867 was mapped to virtual-memory page 4867, which is the same as its short page identifier. We can see that the pointer in object 2 to this page did not need to be changed during swizzling. If every page can be allocated to its appropriate location in virtual address space, none of the pointers need to be translated, and the cost of swizzling is reduced significantly.

Hardware swizzling works even if the database is bigger than virtual memory, but only as long as all the pages that a particular process accesses fit into the virtual memory of the process. If they do not, a page that has been brought into virtual memory will have to be replaced, and that replacement is hard, since there may be in-memory pointers to objects in that page. Hardware swizzling can also be used conceptually at the level of sets of pages (often called segments), instead of for a single page, as long as the short page identifier, with the page offset, does not exceed the length of an in-memory pointer.

## 10.9.4    Disk Versus Memory Structure of Objects

The format in which objects are stored in memory may be different from the format in which they are stored on disk in the database. One reason may be the use of software swizzling, where the structures of persistent and in-memory pointers are different. Another reason may be that we want to have the database accessible from different machines, possibly based on different architectures, and from different languages, and from programs compiled under different compilers, all of which result in differences in the in-memory representation.

Consider for example a data-structure definition in a programming language, such as C++. The physical structure (such as sizes and representation of integers) in the object are dependent on the machine on which the program is run.[†] Further, the physical structure may also depend on which compiler is used—in a language as complex as C++, different choices for translation from the high-level description to the physical structure are possible, and each compiler can make its own choice.

The solution to this problem is to make the physical representation of objects in the database independent of the machine and of the compiler. The object can be converted from the disk representation to the form that is required on the specific machine, language, and compiler, when that object is brought into memory. This conversion can be done transparently at the same time that pointers in the object are swizzled, so the programmer does not need to worry about the conversion.

The first step in implementing such a scheme is to define a common language for describing the structure of objects—that is, a data-definition language. Several proposals have been made, one of which is the Object Definition Language (ODL) developed by the Object Database Management Group (ODMG). ODL has mappings defined to C++ and to Smalltalk, so potentially we may manipulate objects in an ODMG-compliant database using either C++ or Smalltalk.

The definition of the structure of each class in the database is stored (logically) in the databases. The code to translate an object in the database to the representation that is manipulated with the programming language (and vice versa) is dependent on the machine as well as on the compiler for the language. We can generate this code automatically, using the stored definition of the class of the object.

An unexpected source of differences between the disk and in-memory representations of data are the hidden-pointers in objects. *Hidden pointers* are transient pointers that are generated by compilers and are stored in objects. These pointers point (indirectly) to tables used to implement certain methods of the object. The tables are typically compiled into executable object code, and the exact location of the tables depends on the executable object code, and hence may be different for different processes. Hence, when an object is accessed by a process, the hidden pointers must be fixed to point to the correct location. The hidden pointers can be initialized at the same time that data-representation conversions are carried out.

## 10.9.5  Large Objects

Objects may also be extremely large; for instance, multimedia objects may occupy several megabytes of space. Exceptionally large data items, such as video sequences, may run into gigabytes, although they are usually split into into multiple objects, each on the order of a few megabytes or fewer. Large objects are

---

[†]For instance, the Motorola 680x0 architectures, the IBM 360 architecture, and the Intel 80386/80486/Pentium architectures all have 4-byte integers. However, they differ in how the bits of an integer are laid out within a word. In earlier-generation personal computers, integers were 2 bytes long; in newer workstation architectures, such as the DEC Alpha, integers can be 8 bytes long.

called *binary large objects* (*blobs*) because they typically contain binary data. In relational systems, record fields that are extremely large are also called *long fields*.

Most relational databases restrict the size of a record to be no larger than the size of a page, to simplify buffer management and free-space management. Large objects and long fields are often stored in a special file (or collection of files) reserved for long-field storage.

A problem with managing large objects is presented by the allocation of buffer pages. Large objects may need to be stored in a contiguous sequence of bytes when they are brought into memory; in that case, if an object is bigger than a page, contiguous pages of the buffer pool must be allocated to store it, which makes buffer management more difficult.

We often modify large objects by updating part of the object, or by inserting or deleting parts of the object, rather than by writing the entire object. If inserts and deletes need to be supported, we can implement large objects using B-tree structures (which we study in Chapter 11). B-tree structures permit us to read the entire object, as well as to insert and delete parts of the object.

For practical reasons, we may manipulate large objects using application programs, rather than doing so within the database:

- **Text data**. Text is usually treated as a byte string manipulated by editors and formatters.

- **Graphical data**. Graphical data may be represented as a bitmap or as a set of lines, boxes, and other geometric objects. Although some graphical data often are managed within the database system itself, special application software is used for many cases. An example of the latter is a VLSI design.

- **Audio and video data**. Audio and video data are typically a digitized, compressed representation created and displayed by separate application software. Modification of data is usually performed with special-purpose editing software, outside the database system.

The most widely used method for updating such data is the *checkout/checkin* method. A user or an application *checks out* a copy of a long-field object, operates on this copy using special-purpose application programs, and then *checks in* the modified copy. The notions of a *checkout* and a *checkin* correspond roughly to those of a read and a write. In some systems, a checkin may create a new version of the object without deleting the old version.

## 10.10  Summary

Several types of data storage exist in most computer systems. These storage media are classified by the speed with which data can be accessed, by the cost per unit of data to buy the memory, and by their reliability. Among the media typically available are cache, main memory, flash memory, magnetic disks, optical disks, and magnetic tapes.

Reliability of storage media is determined by two factors: whether a power failure or system crash causes data to be lost, and what the likelihood is of physical failure of the storage devise. We can reduce the likelihood of physical failure by retaining multiple copies of data. For disks, mirroring can be used. A more sophisticated set of approaches is based on redundant arrays of inexpensive disks (RAIDs). By striping data across disks, they offer high throughput rates on large accesses; by introducing redundancy across disks, they improve reliability greatly. Several different RAID organizations have been proposed, with differing cost, performance and reliability characteristics. RAID level 1 (mirroring) and RAID level 5 are the most commonly used.

A *file* is organized logically as a sequence of records mapped onto disk blocks. One approach to mapping the database to files is to use several files, and to store records of only one fixed length in any given file. An alternative is to structure files such that they can accommodate multiple lengths for records. There are different techniques for implementing variable-length records, including the slotted-page method, the pointer method, and the reserved-space method.

Since data are transferred between disk storage and main memory in units of a block, it is worthwhile to assign file records to blocks such that a single block contains related records. If we can access several of the records desired using only one block access, we save disk accesses. Since disk accesses are usually the bottleneck in the performance of a database system, careful assignment of records to blocks can pay significant performance dividends.

One way to reduce the number of disk accesses is to keep as many blocks as possible in main memory. Since it is not possible to keep all blocks in main memory, we need to manage the allocation of the space available in main memory for the storage of blocks. The *buffer* is that part of main memory available for storage of copies of disk blocks. The subsystem responsible for the allocation of buffer space is called the *buffer manager*.

Storage systems for object-oriented databases are somewhat different from storage systems for relational databases: They must deal with large objects, for example, and must support persistent pointers. There are schemes to detect dangling persistent pointers, and software- and hardware-based swizzling schemes for efficient dereferencing of persistent pointers. The hardware-based schemes use the virtual-memory-management support implemented in hardware, and made accessible to user programs by many current-generation operating systems.

# Exercises

**10.1.** List the physical storage media available on the computers you use routinely. Give the speed with which data can be accessed on each medium.

**10.2.** How does the remapping of bad sectors by disk controllers affect data-retrieval rates?

**10.3.** Consider the following data and parity-block arrangement on four disks:

| Disk 1 | Disk 2 | Disk 3 | Disk 4 |
|--------|--------|--------|--------|
| $B_1$  | $B_2$  | $B_3$  | $B_4$  |
| $P_1$  | $B_5$  | $B_6$  | $B_7$  |
| $B_8$  | $P_2$  | $B_9$  | $B_{10}$ |
| $\vdots$ | $\vdots$ | $\vdots$ | $\vdots$ |

The $B_i$s represent data blocks; the $P_i$s represent parity blocks. Parity block $P_i$ is the parity block for data blocks $B_{4i-3}$ to $B_{4i}$. What, if any, problem might this arrangement present?

**10.4.** A power failure that occurs while a disk block is being written could result in the block being only partially written. Assume that partially written blocks can be detected. An atomic block write is one where either the disk block is fully written or nothing is written (i.e., there are no partial writes). Suggest schemes for getting the effect of atomic block writes with the following RAID schemes. Your schemes should involve work on recovery from failure.

(*a*) RAID level 1 (mirroring)
(*b*) RAID level 5 (block interleaved, distributed parity)

**10.5.** RAID systems typically allow you to replace failed disks without stopping access to the system. Thus, the data in the failed disk must be rebuilt and written to the replacement disk while the system is in operation. With which of the RAID levels is the amount of interference between the rebuild and on-going disk accesses least? Explain your answer.

**10.6.** Give an example of a relational-algebra expression and a query-processing strategy in each of the following situations:

(*a*) MRU is preferable to LRU.
(*b*) LRU is preferable to MRU.

**10.7.** Define the term *pinned record*.

**10.8.** Consider the deletion of record 5 from the file of Figure 10.8. Compare the relative merits of the following techniques for implementing the deletion:

(*a*) Move record 6 to the space occupied by record 5, and move record 7 to the space occupied by record 6.
(*b*) Move record 7 to the space occupied by record 5.
(*c*) Mark record 5 as deleted, and move no records.

**10.9.** Show the structure of the file of Figure 10.9 after each of the following steps:

(*a*) Insert (Brighton, A-323, 1600).
(*b*) Delete record 2.
(*c*) Insert (Brighton, A-626, 2000).

**10.10.** Give an example of a database application in which the reserved-space method of representing variable-length records is preferable to the pointer method. Explain your answer.

**10.11.** Give an example of a database application in which the pointer method of representing variable-length records is preferable to the reserved-space method. Explain your answer.

**10.12.** Show the structure of the file of Figure 10.12 after each of the following steps:
(*a*) Insert (Mianus, A-101, 2800).
(*b*) Insert (Brighton, A-323, 1600).
(*c*) Delete (Perryridge, A-102, 400).

**10.13.** What happens if you attempt to insert the record

(Perryridge, A-929, 3000)

into the file of Figure 10.12?

**10.14.** Show the structure of the file of Figure 10.13 after each of the following steps:
(*a*) Insert (Mianus, A-101, 2800).
(*b*) Insert (Brighton, A-323, 1600).
(*c*) Delete (Perryridge, A-102, 400).

**10.15.** Explain why the allocation of records to blocks affects database-system performance significantly. If a block becomes empty as a result of deletions, for what purposes should the block be reused? Explain your answer.

**10.16.** If possible, determine the buffer-management strategy used by the operating system running on your local computer system. Discuss how useful this strategy would be for the implementation of database systems.

**10.17.** In the sequential file organization, why is an overflow *block* used even if there is, at the moment, only one overflow record?

**10.18.** List two advantages and two disadvantages of each of the following strategies for storing a relational database:
(*a*) Store each relation in one file.
(*b*) Store multiple relations (perhaps even the entire database) in one file.

**10.19.** Consider a relational database with two relations:

*course* (*course-name, room, instructor*)
*enrollment* (*course-name, student-name, grade*)

Define instances of these relations for three courses, each of which enrolls five students. Give a file structure of these relations that uses clustering.

**10.20.** Explain why a physical OID must contain more information than a pointer to a physical storage location.

**10.21.** If physical OIDs are used, is it possible to relocate an object? If so, explain what actions must be taken by the system to relocate an object correctly. If not, explain why relocation is not possible.

**10.22.** Define the term *dangling pointer*. Describe how the unique-id scheme helps in detecting dangling pointers in an object-oriented database.

**10.23.** Consider the example on page 330, which shows that there is no need for deswizzling if hardware swizzling is used. Explain why, in that example, it is safe to change the short identifier of page 679.34278 from 2395 to 5001. Can some other page already have short identifier 5001? If one could, how can you handle that situation?

# Bibliographical Notes

Cache memories, including associative memory, are described and analyzed by Smith [1982]. This paper also includes an extensive bibliography on the subject. Patterson and Hennessy [1995] discuss the hardware aspects of translation lookaside buffers, caches, and memory-management units.

Discussions concerning magnetic-disk technology are presented by Freedman [1983], and by Harker et al. [1981]. Optical disks are covered by Kenville [1982], Fujitani [1984], O'Leary and Kitts [1985], Gait [1988], and Olsen and Kenley [1989]. Ruemmler and Wilkes [1994] present an excellent survey of magnetic-disk technology. Wiederhold [1983], Bohl [1981], Trivedi et al. [1980] and ElMasri and Navathe [1994] discuss the physical properties of disks. Discussions of floppy disks are offered by Pechura and Schoeffler [1983] and Sarisky [1983]. Flash memory is discussed by Dippert and Levy [1993].

Ammon et al. [1985] discuss a high-speed, large-capacity, jukebox optical-disk system. An example of an application of optical storage is given in Christodoulakis and Faloutsos [1986]. General discussions concerning mass-storage technology are offered by Chi [1982], and by Hoagland [1985].

Alternative disk organizations that provide a high degree of fault tolerance include those developed by Gray et al. [1990], and by Bitton and Gray [1988]. Disk striping was described by Salem and Garcia-Molina [1986]. Discussions of redundant arrays of inexpensive disks (RAID) were presented by Patterson et al. [1988] and by Chen and Patterson [1990]. Chen et al. [1994] presents an excellent survey of RAID principles and implementation. Reed-Solomon codes are covered in Pless [1989].

Disk-system architectures for high-performance computing are discussed by Katz et al. [1989]. Nelson and Cheng [1992] compare the performance of IPI and SCSI disks and controllers in a real system. The Loge project [English and Stepanov 1992] experimented with adding intelligence to the disk controller. The log-based file system, which makes disk access sequential, is described in Rosenblum and Ousterhout [1991].

In systems that support mobile computing, data may be broadcast repeatedly. The broadcast medium can be viewed as a level of the storage hierarchy — as a broadcast disk with high latency. These issues are discussed in Acharya et al. [1995]. Caching and buffer management for mobile computing is discussed in Barbará and Imielinski [1994]. Further discussion of storage issues in mobile computing appears in Douglis et al. [1994].

Basic data structures are discussed in Knuth [1973], Aho et al. [1983], and Horowitz and Sahni [1976]. Textbook discussions of file organization and access methods for database systems include those of Teorey and Fry [1982], Smith and Barnes [1987], and Ullman [1988].

There are several papers describing the storage structure of specific database systems. Astrahan et al. [1976] discuss System R. Chamberlin et al. [1981] review System R in retrospect. Stonebraker et al. [1976] describe the implementation of Ingres. The *Oracle 7 Concepts Manual* (Oracle [1992]) describes the storage organization of the Oracle 7 database system. The structure of the Wisconsin Storage System (WiSS) is described in Chou et al. [1985]. A software tool for the physical design of relational database is described by Finkelstein et al. [1988].

Buffer management is discussed in most operating system texts, including in Silberschatz and Galvin [1994]. Stonebraker [1981] discusses the relationship between database-system buffer managers and operating-system buffer managers. Chou and DeWitt [1985] present algorithms for buffer management in database systems, and describe a performance evaluation.

Descriptions and performance comparisons of different swizzling techniques are given in Wilson [1990], Moss [1990], and White and DeWitt [1992]. White and DeWitt [1994] describe the virtual-memory-mapped buffer-management scheme used in the ObjectStore OODB system and in the QuickStore storage manager. Using this scheme, we can map disk pages to a fixed virtual-memory address, even if they are not pinned in the buffer. The Exodus object storage manager is described in Carey et al. [1986]. Biliris and Orenstein [1993] provide a survey of storage systems for object-oriented databases. Jagadish et al. [1994] describe a storage manager for main-memory databases.

# CHAPTER
# 11

## INDEXING AND HASHING

Many queries reference only a small proportion of the records in a file. For example, the query "Find all accounts at the Perryridge branch" references only a fraction of the account records. It is inefficient for the system to have to read every record and to check the *branch-name* field for the name "Perryridge." Ideally, the system should be able to locate these records directly. To allow these forms of access, we design additional structures that we associate with files.

## 11.1  Basic Concepts

An index for a file in the system works in much the same way as a catalog for a book in a library. If we are looking for a book by a particular author, we look in the author catalog, and a card in the catalog tells us where to find the book. To assist us in searching the catalog, the library keeps cards in alphabetic order, so we do not have to check every card to find the one we want.

In real-world databases, indices of the type just described may be too large to be handled efficiently. Instead, more sophisticated indexing techniques may be used. We shall discuss several of these techniques subsequently. There are two basic kinds of indices:

- **Ordered indices**. Such indices are based on a sorted ordering of the values.
- **Hash indices**. Such indices are based on the values being distributed uniformly across a range of buckets. The bucket to which a value is assigned is determined by a function, called a *hash function*.

We shall consider several techniques for both ordered indexing and hashing. No one technique is the best. Rather, each technique is best suited to particular database applications. Each technique must be evaluated on the basis of these factors:

- **Access types**: The types of access that are supported efficiently. These types could include finding records with a specified attribute value, or finding records whose attribute values fall in a specified range.
- **Access time**: The time it takes to find a particular data item, or set of items, using the technique in question.
- **Insertion time**: The time it takes to insert a new data item. This value includes the time it takes to find the correct place to insert the new data item, as well as the time it takes to update the index structure.
- **Deletion time**: The time it takes to delete a data item. This value includes the time it takes to find the item to be deleted, as well as the time it takes to update the index structure.
- **Space overhead**: The additional space occupied by an index structure. Provided that the amount of additional space is moderate, it is usually worthwhile to sacrifice the space to achieve improved performance.

We often want to have more than one index for a file. Returning to the library example, we note that most libraries maintain several card catalogs: for author, for subject, and for title. The attribute or set of attributes used to look up records in a file is called a *search key*. Note that this definition of *key* differs from that used in *primary key*, *candidate key*, and *superkey*. This duplicate meaning for *key* is (unfortunately) well established in practice. Using our notion of a search key, we see that, if there are several indices on a file, there are several search keys.

## 11.2   Ordered Indices

To gain fast random access to records in a file, we can use an index structure. Each index structure is associated with a particular search key. Just like a library catalog, an index stores the values of the search keys in sorted order, and associates with each search key the records that contain that search key.

The records in the indexed file may themselves be stored in some sorted order, just like books in a library are stored sorted by some attribute such as the Dewey decimal number. A file may have several indices, on different search keys. If the file containing the records is sequentially ordered, the index whose search key specifies the sequential order of the file is the *primary index*. (The term *primary index* is sometimes used to mean an index on a primary key. However, such usage is nonstandard and should be avoided). Primary indices are also called *clustering indices*. The search key of a primary index is usually the primary key, although that is not necessarily so. Indices whose search key specifies an order different from the sequential order of the file are called *secondary indices*, or *nonclustering* indices.

| | | | |
|---|---|---|---|
| Brighton | A-217 | 750 | |
| Downtown | A-101 | 500 | |
| Downtown | A-110 | 600 | |
| Mianus | A-215 | 700 | |
| Perryridge | A-102 | 400 | |
| Perryridge | A-201 | 900 | |
| Perryridge | A-218 | 700 | |
| Redwood | A-222 | 700 | |
| Round Hill | A-305 | 350 | |

Figure 11.1    Sequential file for *account* records.

## 11.2.1 Primary Index

In this section, we assume that all files are ordered sequentially on some search key. Such files, with a primary index on the search key, are called *index-sequential files*. They represent one of the oldest index schemes used in database systems. They are designed for applications that require both sequential processing of the entire file and random access to individual records.

Figure 11.1 shows a sequential file of *account* records taken from our banking example. In the example of Figure 11.1, the records are stored in search-key order, with *branch-name* used as the search key.

### 11.2.1.1 Dense and Sparse Indices

There are two types of ordered indices that we can use:

- **Dense index**. An *index record* (or *index entry*) appears for every search-key value in the file. The index record contains the search-key value and a pointer to the first data record with that search-key value. (Some authors use the term *dense index* to mean an index where an index record appears for every *record* in the file.)

- **Sparse index**. An index record is created for only some of the values. As is true in dense indices, each index record contains a search-key value and a pointer to the first data record with that search-key value. To locate a record, we find the index entry with the largest search-key value that is less than or equal to the search-key value for which we are looking. We start at the record pointed to by that index entry, and follow the pointers in the file until we find the desired record.

Figures 11.2 and 11.3 show dense and sparse indices, respectively, for the *account* file. Suppose that we are looking up records for the Perryridge branch. Using the dense index of Figure 11.2, we follow the pointer directly to the first Perryridge record. We process this record, and follow the pointer in that record to locate the next record in search-key (*branch-name*) order. We continue processing records until we encounter a record for a branch other than Perryridge.

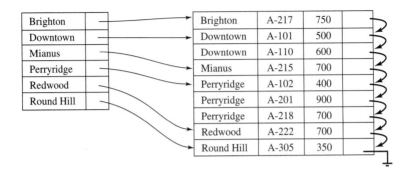

Figure 11.2    Dense index.

If we are using the sparse index (Figure 11.3), we do not find an index entry for "Perryridge." Since the last entry (in alphabetic order) before "Perryridge" is "Mianus," we follow that pointer. We then read the *account* file in sequential order until we find the first Perryridge record, and begin processing at that point.

As we have seen, it is generally faster to locate a record if we have a dense index rather than a sparse index. However, sparse indices have advantages over dense indices in that they require less space and they impose less maintenance overhead for insertions and deletions.

There is a tradeoff that the system designer must make between access time and space overhead. Although the decision regarding this tradeoff is dependent on the specific application, a good compromise is to have a sparse index with one index entry per block. The reason this design is a good tradeoff is that the dominant cost in processing a database request is the time that it takes to bring a block from disk into main memory. Once we have brought in the block, the time to scan the entire block is negligible. Using this sparse index, we locate the block containing the record that we are seeking. Thus, unless the record is on an overflow block (see Section 10.7.1), we minimize block accesses while keeping the size of the index (and thus, our space overhead) as small as possible.

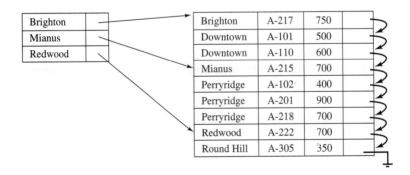

Figure 11.3    Sparse index.

For the preceding technique to be fully general, we must consider the case where records for one search-key value occupy several blocks. It is easy to modify our scheme to handle this situation.

### 11.2.1.2 Multilevel Indices

Even if we use a sparse index, the index itself may become too large for efficient processing. It is not unreasonable, in practice, to have a file with 100,000 records, with 10 records stored in each block. If we have one index record per block, the index has 10,000 records. Index records are smaller than data records, so let us assume that 100 index records fit on a block. Thus, our index occupies 100 blocks. Such large indices are stored as sequential files on disk.

If an index is sufficiently small to be kept in main memory, search time to find an entry is low. However, if the index is so large that it must be kept on disk, a search for an entry requires several disk block reads. Binary search can be used on the index file to locate an entry, but the search still has a large cost. If the index occupies $b$ blocks, binary search requires as many as $\lceil \log_2(b) \rceil$ blocks to be read. ($\lceil x \rceil$ denotes the least integer that is greater than or equal to $x$; that is, we round upward.) For our 100-block index, binary search requires seven block reads. On a disk system where a block read takes 30 milliseconds, the search will take 210 milliseconds, which is long. Note that, if overflow blocks have been used, binary search will not be possible. In that case, a sequential search is typically used, and that requires $b$ block reads, which will take even longer. Thus, the process of searching a large index may be costly.

To deal with this problem, we treat the index just as we would treat any other sequential file, and we construct a sparse index on the primary index, as shown in Figure 11.4. To locate a record, we first use binary search on the outer index to find the record for the largest search-key value less than or equal to the one that we desire. The pointer points to a block of the inner index. We scan this block until we find the record that has the largest search-key value less than or equal to the one that we desire. The pointer in this record points to the block of the file that contains the record for which we are looking.

Using the two levels of indexing, we have read only one index block, rather than the seven we read with binary search, if we assume that the outer index is already in main memory. If our file is extremely large, even the outer index may grow too large to fit in main memory. In such a case, we can create yet another level of index. Indeed, we can repeat this process as many times as necessary. Indices with two or more levels are called *multilevel* indices. Searching for records using a multilevel index requires significantly fewer I/O operations than does searching for records using binary search. Each level of index could correspond to a unit of physical storage. Thus, we may have indices at the track, cylinder, and disk levels.

Multilevel indices are closely related to tree structures, such as the binary trees used for in-memory indexing. We shall examine the relationship later, in Section 11.3.

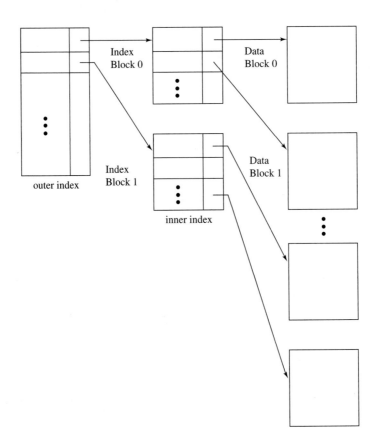

Figure 11.4    Two-level sparse index.

### 11.2.1.3  Index Update

Regardless of what form of index is used, every index must be updated whenever a record is either inserted into or deleted from the file. We describe algorithms for updating single-level indices next.

- **Deletion**. To delete a record, we first look up the record to be deleted. If the deleted record was the only record with its particular search-key value, then the search-key value is deleted from the index. For dense indices, deletion of a search-key value is similar to deletion of a record from a file. For sparse indices, we delete a key value by replacing its entry (if one exists) in the index with the next search-key value (in search-key order). If the next search-key value already has an index entry, the entry is deleted instead of being replaced.

- **Insertion**. First, we perform a lookup using the search-key value that appears in the record to be inserted. If the index is dense, and the search-key value does not appear in the index, the latter is inserted in the index. If the index is sparse and stores an entry for each block, no change needs to be made to the index unless a new block is created. In this case, the first search-key value (in search-key order) appearing in the new block is inserted into the index.

Insertion and deletion algorithms for multilevel indices are a simple extension of the scheme just described. On deletion or insertion, the lowest-level index is updated as described. As far as the second level is concerned, the lowest-level index is merely a file containing records—thus, if there is any change in the lowest-level index, the second-level index is updated as described. The same technique applies to further levels of the index, if there are any.

## 11.2.2   Secondary Indices

A secondary index on a candidate key looks just like a dense primary index, except that the records pointed to by successive values in the index are not stored sequentially. In general, however, secondary indices may be structured differently from primary indices. If the search key of a primary index is not a candidate key, it suffices if the index points to the first record with a particular value for the search key, since the other records can be fetched by a sequential scan of the file.

However, if the search key of a secondary index is not a candidate key, it is not enough to point to just the first record with each search-key value. The remaining records with the same search-key value could be anywhere in the file, since the records are ordered by the search key of the primary index, rather than by the search key of the secondary index. Therefore, a secondary index must contain pointers to all the records. We can use an extra level of indirection to implement secondary indices on search keys that are not candidate keys. The pointers in such a secondary index do not point directly to the file. Instead, each points to a bucket that contains pointers to the file. Figure 11.5 shows the structure of a secondary

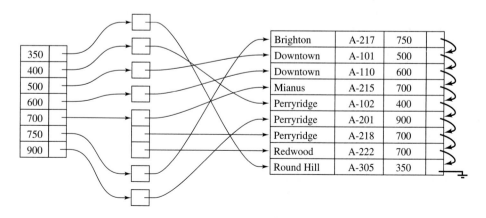

Figure 11.5    Secondary index on *account* file, on non-candidate key *balance*.

index that uses an extra level of indirection on the *account* file, on the search key *balance*.

A *sequential scan* in primary index order is efficient because records in the file are stored physically in the same order as the index order. However, we cannot (except in rare special cases) store a file physically ordered both by the search key of the primary index, and the search key of a secondary index. Because secondary-key order and physical-key order differ, if we attempt to scan the file sequentially in secondary-key order, the reading of each record is likely to require the reading of a new block from disk.

A sparse primary index may store only some of the search-key values, since it is always possible to find records with intermediate search-key values by a sequential access to a part of the file, as described earlier. If a secondary index stores only some of the search-key values, records with intermediate search-key values may be anywhere in the file and, in general, we cannot find them without searching the entire file. Secondary indices must therefore be dense, with an index entry for every search-key value, and a pointer to every record in the file.

The procedure described earlier for deletion and insertion can be applied to a file with multiple indices. Whenever the file is modified, *every* index must be updated.

Secondary indices improve the performance of queries that use keys other than the search key of the primary index. However, they impose a significant overhead on modification of the database. The designer of a database decides which secondary indices are desirable on the basis of an estimate of the relative frequency of queries and modifications.

## 11.3   $B^+$-Tree Index Files

The main disadvantage of the index-sequential file organization is that performance degrades as the file grows, both for index lookups and for sequential scans through the data. Although this degradation can be remedied by reorganization of the file, frequent performance of such reorganizations is undesirable.

The $B^+$-*tree index structure* is the most widely used of several index structures that maintain their efficiency despite insertion and deletion of data. A $B^+$-tree index takes the form of a *balanced* tree in which every path from the root of the tree to a leaf of the tree is of the same length. Each nonleaf node in the tree has between $\lceil n/2 \rceil$ and $n$ children, where $n$ is fixed for a particular tree.

We shall see that the $B^+$-tree structure imposes performance overhead on insertion and deletion, and adds space overhead. This performance overhead is acceptable even for files with a high frequency of modification, since the cost of file reorganization is avoided. Furthermore, since nodes may be as much as half empty (if they have the minimum number of children), there is some wasted space. This space overhead, too, is acceptable given the performance benefits of the $B^+$-tree structure.

| $P_1$ | $K_1$ | $P_2$ | $\cdots$ | $P_{n-1}$ | $K_{n-1}$ | $P_n$ |
|---|---|---|---|---|---|---|

**Figure 11.6    Typical node of a B⁺-tree.**

## 11.3.1    Structure of a B⁺-Tree

A B⁺-tree index is a multilevel index, but it has a structure that differs from that of the multilevel index-sequential file. A typical node of a B⁺-tree is shown in Figure 11.6. It contains up to $n - 1$ search-key values $K_1$, $K_2$, ..., $K_{n-1}$, and $n$ pointers $P_1$, $P_2$, ..., $P_n$. The search-key values within a node are kept in sorted order; thus, if $i < j$, then $K_i < K_j$.

We consider first the structure of the leaf nodes. For $i = 1, 2, \ldots, n - 1$, pointer $P_i$ points to either a file record with search-key value $K_i$ or to a bucket of pointers, each of which points to a file record with search-key value $K_i$. The bucket structure is used only if the search key does not form a primary key, and if the file is not sorted in the search-key value order. Pointer $P_n$ has a special purpose that we shall discuss shortly.

Figure 11.7 shows one leaf node of a B⁺-tree for the *account* file, in which we have chosen $n$ to be 3, and the search key is *branch-name*. Note that, since the account file is ordered by *branch-name*, the pointers in the leaf node point directly to the file.

Now that we have seen the structure of a leaf node, let us consider how search-key values are assigned to particular nodes. Each leaf can hold up to $n - 1$ values. We allow leaf nodes to contain as few as $\lceil (n-1)/2 \rceil$ values. The ranges of values in each leaf do not overlap. Thus, if $L_i$ and $L_j$ are leaf nodes and $i < j$, then every search-key value in $L_i$ is less than every search-key value in $L_j$. If the B⁺-tree index is to be a dense index, every search-key value must appear in some leaf node.

Now we can explain the use of the pointer $P_n$. Since there is a linear order on the leaves based on the search-key values that they contain, we use $P_n$ to chain together the leaf nodes in search-key order. This ordering allows for efficient sequential processing of the file.

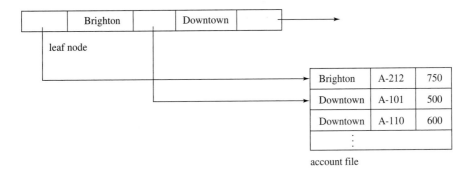

**Figure 11.7    A leaf node for *account* B⁺-tree index ($n = 3$).**

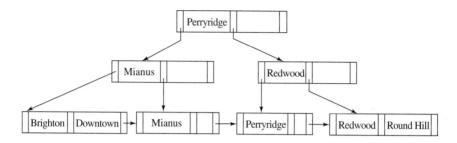

Figure 11.8    B$^+$-tree for *account* file ($n = 3$).

The nonleaf nodes of the B$^+$-tree form a multilevel (sparse) index on the leaf nodes. The structure of nonleaf nodes is the same as that for leaf nodes, except that all pointers are pointers to tree nodes. A nonleaf node may hold up to $n$ pointers, and *must* hold at least $\lceil n/2 \rceil$ pointers. The number of pointers in a node is called the *fanout* of the node.

Let us consider a node containing $m$ pointers. For $i = 2, 3, \ldots, m - 1$, pointer $P_i$ points to the subtree that contains search-key values less than $K_i$ and greater than or equal to $K_{i-1}$. Pointer $P_m$ points to the part of the subtree that contains those key values greater than or equal to $K_{m-1}$, and pointer $P_1$ points to the part of the subtree that contains those search-key values less than $K_1$.

Unlike other nonleaf nodes, the root node can hold fewer than $\lceil n/2 \rceil$ pointers; however, it must hold at least two pointers, unless the tree consists of only one node. It is always possible to construct a B$^+$-tree, for any $n$, that satisfies the preceding requirements. Figure 11.8 shows a complete B$^+$-tree for the *account* file ($n = 3$). For simplicity, we have omitted both the pointers to the file itself and the null pointers. As an example of a B$^+$-tree for which the root must have less than $\lceil n/2 \rceil$ values, Figure 11.9 shows a B$^+$-tree for the *account* file with $n = 5$.

The examples that we have given of B$^+$-trees have all been balanced. That is, the length of every path from the root to a leaf node is the same. This property is a requirement for a B$^+$-tree. Indeed, the "B" in B$^+$-tree stands for "balanced." It is the balance property of B$^+$-trees that ensures good performance for lookup, insertion, and deletion.

## 11.3.2   Queries on B$^+$-Trees

Let us consider how we process queries using a B$^+$-tree. Suppose that we wish to find all records with a search-key value of $k$. First, we examine the root node,

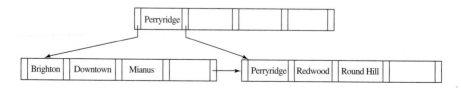

Figure 11.9    B$^+$-tree for *account* file with $n = 5$.

looking for the smallest search-key value greater than $k$. Suppose that we find that this search-key value is $K_i$. We then follow pointer $P_i$ to another node. If we find no such value, then $k \geq K_{m-1}$, where $m$ is the number of pointers in the node. In this case we follow $P_m$ to another node. In the node we reached above, again we look for the smallest search-key value greater than $k$, and once again follow the corresponding pointer as above. Eventually, we reach a leaf node. At the leaf node, if we find search-key value $K_i$ equals $k$, then pointer $P_i$ directs us to the desired record or bucket. If the value $k$ is not found in the leaf node, no record with key value $k$ exists.

Thus, in the processing of a query, a path is traversed in the tree from the root to some leaf node. If there are $K$ search-key values in the file, the path is no longer than $\lceil \log_{\lceil n/2 \rceil}(K) \rceil$.

In practice, only a few nodes need to be accessed, Typically, a node is made to be the same size as a disk block, which is typically 4 kilobytes. With a search-key size of 12 bytes, and a disk-pointer size of 8 bytes, $n$ is around 200. Even with a more conservative estimate of 32 bytes for the search-key size, $n$ is around 100. With $n = 100$, if we have 1 million search-key values in the file, a lookup requires only $\lceil \log_{50}(1,000,000) \rceil = 4$ nodes to be accessed. Thus, at most four blocks need to be read from disk for the lookup. The root node of the tree is usually heavily accessed and is likely to be in the buffer, so typically only three or fewer blocks need to be read from disk.

An important difference between B$^+$-tree structures and in-memory tree structures, such as binary trees, is the size of a node, and as a result, the height of the tree. In a binary tree, each node is small, and has at most two pointers. In a B$^+$-tree, each node is large—typically a disk block—and a node can have a large number of pointers. Thus, B$^+$-trees tend to be fat and short unlike thin and tall binary trees. In a balanced binary tree, the path for a lookup can be of length $\lceil \log_2(K) \rceil$, where $K$ is the number of search-key values. With $K = 1,000,000$ as in the previous example, a balanced binary tree requires around 20 node accesses. If each node were on a different disk block, 20 block reads would be required to process a lookup, in contrast to the four block reads for the B$^+$-tree.

### 11.3.3    Updates on B$^+$-Trees

Insertion and deletion are more complicated than lookup, since it may be necessary to *split* a node that becomes too large as the result of an insertion, or to *combine* nodes if a node becomes too small (fewer than $\lceil n/2 \rceil$ pointers). Furthermore, when a node is split or a pair of nodes is combined, we must ensure that balance is preserved. To introduce the idea behind insertion and deletion in a B$^+$-tree, we shall assume temporarily that nodes never become too large or too small. Under this assumption, insertion and deletion are performed as defined next.

- **Insertion.** Using the same technique as for lookup, we find the leaf node in which the search-key value would appear. If the search-key value already appears in the leaf node, we add the new record to the file and, if necessary, a pointer to the bucket. If the search-key value does not appear, we insert the value in the leaf node, and position it such that the search keys are still in

Figure 11.10    Split of leaf node on insertion of "Clearview."

order. We then insert the new record in the file and, if necessary, create a new bucket with the appropriate pointer.

- **Deletion**. Using the same technique as for lookup, we find the record to be deleted, and remove it from the file. The search-key value is removed from the leaf node if there is no bucket associated with that search-key value or if the bucket becomes empty as a result of the deletion.

We now consider an example in which a node must be split. Assume that we wish to insert a record with a *branch-name* value of "Clearview" into the B⁺-tree of Figure 11.8. Using the algorithm for lookup, we find that "Clearview" should appear in the node containing "Brighton" and "Downtown." There is no room to insert the search-key value "Clearview." Therefore, the node is *split* into two nodes. Figure 11.10 shows the two leaf nodes that result from inserting "Clearview" and splitting the node containing "Brighton" and "Downtown." In general, we take the $n$ search-key values (the $n - 1$ values in the leaf node plus the value being inserted), and put the first $\lceil n/2 \rceil$ in the existing node and the remaining values in a new node.

Having split a leaf node, we must insert the new leaf node into the B⁺-tree structure. In our example, the new node has "Downtown" as its smallest search-key value. We need to insert this search-key value into the parent of the leaf node that was split. The B⁺-tree of Figure 11.11 shows the result of the insertion. The search-key value "Downtown" was inserted into the parent. It was possible to perform this insertion because there was room for an added search-key value. If there were no room, the parent would have had to be split. In the worst case, all nodes along the path to the root must be split. If the root itself is split, the entire tree becomes deeper.

The general technique for insertion into a B⁺-tree is to determine the leaf node *l* into which insertion must occur. If a split results, insert the new node into

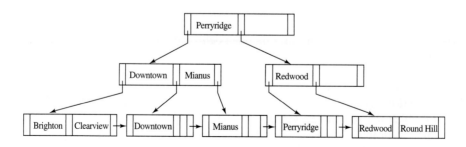

Figure 11.11    Insertion of "Clearview" into the B⁺-tree of Figure 11.8.

the parent of node $l$. If this insertion causes a split, proceed recursively until either an insertion does not cause a split or a new root is created.

Figure 11.12 outlines the insertion algorithm in pseudocode. In the pseudocode $L.K_i$ and $L.P_i$ denote the $i$th value and the $i$th pointer in node $L$, respectively. The pseudocode also makes use of the function $parent(L)$ to find the parent of a node $L$. We can compute a list of nodes in the path from the root to the leaf while initially finding the leaf node, and can use it later to find the parent of any node in the path efficiently. The pseudocode refers to inserting an entry $(V, P)$ into a node. In the case of leaf nodes, the pointer to an entry actually precedes the key value, so the leaf node actually stores $P$ preceding $V$. For internal nodes, $P$ is stored just after $V$.

We now consider deletions that cause tree nodes to contain too few pointers. First, let us delete "Downtown" from the B$^+$-tree of Figure 11.11. We locate the entry for "Downtown" using our lookup algorithm. When we delete the entry for "Downtown" from its leaf node, the leaf becomes empty. Since, in our example, $n = 3$ and $0 < \lceil (n-1)/2 \rceil$, this node must be eliminated from the B$^+$-tree. To delete a leaf node, we must delete the pointer to it from its parent. In our example, this deletion leaves the parent node, which formerly contained three pointers, with only two pointers. Since $2 \geq \lceil n/2 \rceil$, the node is still sufficiently large, and the deletion operation is complete. The resulting B$^+$-tree is shown in Figure 11.13.

When a deletion is made to a parent of a leaf node, the parent node itself may become too small. That is exactly what happens if we delete "Perryridge" from the B$^+$-tree of Figure 11.13. Deletion of the Perryridge entry causes a leaf node to become empty. When we delete the pointer to this node in the latter's parent, the parent is left with only one pointer. Since $n = 3$, $\lceil n/2 \rceil = 2$, and thus only one pointer is too few. However, since the parent node contains useful information, we cannot simply delete it. Instead, we look at the sibling node (the nonleaf node containing the one search key, Mianus). This sibling node has room to accommodate the information contained in our now-too-small node, so we coalesce these nodes, such that the sibling node now contains the keys "Mianus" and "Redwood." The other node (the node containing only the search key "Redwood") now contains redundant information and can be deleted from its parent (which happens to be the root in our example). Figure 11.14 shows the result. Notice that the root has only one child pointer after the deletion, so it is deleted and its sole child becomes the root. So the depth of the B$^+$-tree has been decreased by 1.

It is not always possible to coalesce nodes. As an illustration, let us delete "Perryridge" from the B$^+$-tree of Figure 11.11. In this example, the "Downtown" entry is still part of the tree. Once again, the leaf node containing "Perryridge" becomes empty. The parent of the leaf node becomes too small (only one pointer). However, in this example, the sibling node already contains the maximum number of pointers: three. Thus, it cannot accommodate an additional pointer. The solution in this case is to *redistribute* the pointers such that each sibling has two pointers. The result is shown in Figure 11.15. Note that the redistribution of values necessitates a change of a search-key value in the parent of the two siblings.

**procedure** insert(*value V*, *pointer P*)
    find the leaf node $L$ that should contain value $V$
    insert_entry($L$, $V$, $P$)
**end procedure**

**procedure** insert_entry(*node L*, *value V*, *pointer P*)
    **if** ($L$ has space for ($V$, $P$))
        **then** insert ($V$, $P$) in $L$
        **else begin** /* Split $L$ */
            Create node $L'$
            **if** ($L$ is a leaf) **then begin**
                Let $V'$ be the value such that $\lceil n/2 \rceil$ of the values
                    $L.K_1, \ldots, L.K_{n-1}$, $V$ are less than $V'$
                Let $m$ be the lowest value such $L.K_m \geq V'$
                move $L.P_m, L.K_m, \ldots, L.P_{n-1}, L.K_{n-1}$ to $L'$
                **if** ($V < V'$) **then** insert ($P$, $V$) in $L$
                **else** insert ($P$, $V$) in $L'$
            **end**
            **else begin**
                Let $V'$ be the value such that $\lceil n/2 \rceil$ of the values
                    $L.K_1, \ldots, L.K_{n-1}$, $V$ are greater than or equal to $V'$
                Let $m$ be the lowest value such $L.K_m \geq V'$
                add $Nil, L.K_m, \ldots, L.P_{n-1}, L.K_{n-1}, L.P_n$ to $L'$
                delete $L.K_m, \ldots, L.P_{n-1}, L.K_{n-1}, L.P_n$ from $L$
                **if** ($V < V'$) **then** insert ($V$, $P$) in $L$
                **else** insert ($V$, $P$) in $L'$
                delete ($Nil$, $V'$) from $L'$
            **end**
            **if** ($L$ is not the root of the tree)
                **then** insert_entry(*parent*($L$), $V'$, $L'$);
                **else begin**
                    create a new node $R$ with child nodes $L$ and $L'$ and
                      the single value $V'$
                  make $R$ the root of the tree
                **end**
            **if** ($L$) is a leaf node **then begin** /* Fix next child pointers */
                set $L'.P_n = L.P_n$;
                set $L.P_n = L'$
            **end**
        **end**
**end procedure**

Figure 11.12    Insertion of entry in a $B^+$-tree.

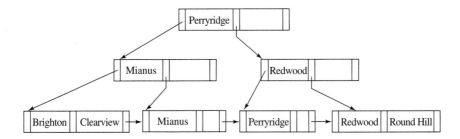

Figure 11.13    Deletion of "Downtown" from the B⁺-tree of Figure 11.11.

In general, to delete a value in a B⁺-tree, we perform a lookup on the value and delete it. If the node is too small, we delete it from its parent. This deletion results in recursive application of the deletion algorithm until the root is reached, a parent remains adequately full after deletion, or redistribution is applied.

Figure 11.16 outlines pseudocode for deletion from a B⁺-tree. The procedure swap_variables($L, L'$) merely swaps the values of the (pointer) variables $L$ and $L'$; this swap has no effect on the tree itself. The pseudocode uses the condition "too few pointers/values." For nonleaf nodes, this criterion means less than $\lceil n/2 \rceil$ pointers; for leaf nodes, it means less than $\lceil (n-1)/2 \rceil$ values. The pseudocode performs redistribution by borrowing a single entry from an adjacent node. We can also do redistribution by repartitioning entries equally between the two nodes. The pseudocode refers to deleting an entry $(V, P)$ from a node. In the case of leaf nodes, the pointer to an entry actually precedes the key value, so the pointer $P$ precedes the key value $V$. For internal nodes, $P$ follows the key value $V$.

Although insertion and deletion operations on B⁺-trees are complicated, they require relatively few operations. It can be shown that the number of operations needed for a worst-case insertion or deletion is proportional to $\log_{\lceil n/2 \rceil}(K)$, where $n$ is the maximum number of pointers in a node, and $K$ is the number of search key values. In other words, the cost of insertion and deletion operations is proportional to the height of the B⁺-tree, and is therefore low. It is the speed of operation on B⁺-trees that makes them a frequently used index structure in database implementations.

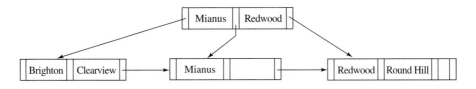

Figure 11.14    Deletion of "Perryridge" from the B⁺-tree of Figure 11.13.

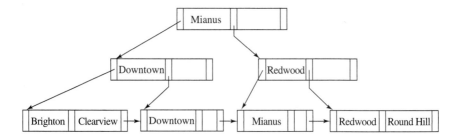

Figure 11.15   Deletion of "Perryridge" from the B$^+$-tree of Figure 11.11.

## 11.3.4   B$^+$-Tree File Organization

As mentioned earlier, the drawback of index-sequential file organization is the degradation of performance as the file grows. We solve the degradation of index lookups by using B$^+$-tree indices on the file. We solve the degradation problem for storing the actual records by using the leaf level of the B$^+$-tree to organize the blocks containing the actual records. In such structures, the B$^+$-tree structure is used not only as an index, but also as an organizer for records into a file.

In a *B$^+$-tree file organization*, the leaf nodes of the tree store records, instead of storing pointers to records. Figure 11.17 shows an example of a B$^+$-tree file organization. Since records are usually larger than pointers, the maximum number of records that can be stored in a leaf node is less than the number of pointers in a nonleaf node. However, the leaf nodes are still required to be at least half full.

Insertion and deletion from a B$^+$-tree file organization are handled in the same way as insertion and deletion of entries in a B$^+$-tree index. When a record with a given key value $v$ is inserted, we locate the block that should contain the record by searching the B$^+$-tree for the largest key in the tree that is $\leq v$. If the block located has enough free space for the record, the record is stored in the block. Otherwise, as in B$^+$-tree insertion, the block is split in two, and the records in it are redistributed (in the B$^+$-tree–key order) to create space for the new record. The split propagates up the B$^+$-tree in the normal fashion. When a record is deleted, it is first removed from the block containing it. If a block $B$ becomes less than half full as a result, the records in $B$ are redistributed with the records in an adjacent block $B'$. Assuming fixed-sized records, each block will hold at least one-half as many records as the maximum that it can hold. The nonleaf nodes of the B$^+$-tree are then updated in the usual fashion.

When a B$^+$-tree is used for file organization, space utilization is particularly important, since the space occupied by the records is likely to be much more than the space occupied by keys and pointers. We can improve the utilization of space in a B$^+$-tree by involving more sibling nodes in redistribution during splits and merges. The technique is applicable to both leaf nodes and internal nodes, and works as follows.

During insertion, if a node is full we attempt to redistribute some of its entries to one of the adjacent nodes, to make space for a new entry. If this attempt

**procedure** delete(*value V, pointer P*)
    find the leaf node $L$ that contains $(V, P)$
    delete_entry($L$, $V$, $P$)
**end procedure**
**procedure** delete_entry(*node L, value V, pointer P*)
    delete $(V, P)$ from $L$
    **if** ($L$ is the root **and** $L$ has only one remaining child)
    **then** make the child of $L$ the new root of the tree and delete $L$
    **else if** ($L$ has too few values/pointers) **then begin**
        Let $L'$ be the previous or next child of *parent*($L$)
        Let $V'$ be the value between pointers $L$ and $L'$ in *parent*($L$)
        **if** (entries in $L$ and $L'$ can fit in a single node)
            **then begin** /* Coalesce nodes */
                **if** ($L$ is a predecessor of $L'$) **then** swap_variables($L, L'$)
                **if** ($L$ is not a leaf)
                    **then** append $V'$ and all pointers and values in $L$ to $L'$
                    **else** append all $(K_i, P_i)$ pairs in $L$ to $L'$; set $L'.P_n = L.P_n$
                delete_entry(*parent*($L$), $V'$, $L$); delete node $L$
            **end**
            **else begin** /* Redistribution: borrow an entry from $L'$ */
                **if** ($L'$ is a predecessor of $L$) **then begin**
                    **if** ($L$ is a non-leaf node) **then begin**
                      let $m$ be such that $L'.P_m$ is the last pointer in $L'$
                      remove $(L'.K_{m-1}, L'.P_m)$ from $L'$
                      insert $(L'.P_m, V')$ as the first pointer and value in $L$,
                          by shifting other pointers and values right
                      replace $V'$ in *parent*($L$) by $L'.K_{m-1}$
                  **end**
                  **else begin**
                    let $m$ be such that $(L'.P_m, L'.K_m)$ is the last pointer/value
                      pair in $L'$
                    remove $(L'.P_m, L'.K_m)$ from $L'$
                    insert $(L'.P_m, L'.K_m)$ as the first pointer and value in $L$,
                        by shifting other pointers and values right
                    replace $V'$ in *parent*($L$) by $L'.K_m$
                **end**
                **end**
                **else** ... symmetric to the **then** case ...
            **end**
        **end**
**end procedure**

Figure 11.16     Deletion of entry from a B$^+$-tree.

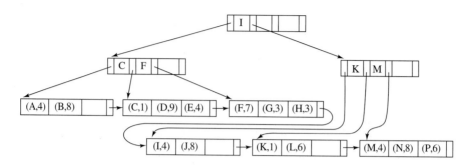

Figure 11.17 B$^+$-tree file organization.

fails because the adjacent nodes are themselves full, we split the node, and split the entries evenly among one of the adjacent nodes and the two nodes that we obtained by splitting the original node. Since the three nodes together contain one more record than can fit in two nodes, each node will be about two thirds full. More precisely, each node will have at least $\lfloor 2n/3 \rfloor$ entries, where $n$ is the maximum number of entries that the node can hold.

During deletion of a record, if the occupancy of a node falls below $\lfloor 2n/3 \rfloor$, we attempt to borrow an entry from one of the sibling nodes. If both sibling nodes have $\lfloor 2n/3 \rfloor$ records, instead of borrowing an entry, we redistribute the entries in the node and in the two siblings evenly between two of the nodes, and we delete the third node. We can use this approach because the total number of entries is $3\lfloor 2n/3 \rfloor - 1$, which is less than $2n$. With three adjacent nodes used for redistribution, each node can be guaranteed to have $\lfloor 3n/4 \rfloor$ entries. In general, if $m$ nodes ($m - 1$ siblings) are involved in redistribution, each node can be guaranteed to contain at least $\lfloor (m - 1)n/m \rfloor$ entries. However, the cost of update becomes higher as more sibling nodes are involved in the redistribution.

## 11.4 B-Tree Index Files

*B-tree indices* are similar to B$^+$-tree indices. The primary distinction between the two approaches is that a B-tree eliminates the redundant storage of search-key values. In the B$^+$-tree of Figure 11.11, the search keys "Downtown," "Mianus," "Redwood," and "Perryridge" appear twice. Every search-key value appears in some leaf node; several are repeated in nonleaf nodes.

A B-tree allows search-key values to appear only once. Figure 11.18 shows a B-tree that represents the same search keys as does the B$^+$-tree of Figure 11.11. Since search keys are not repeated in the B-tree, we may be able to store the index using fewer tree nodes than in the corresponding B$^+$-tree index. However, since search keys that appear in nonleaf nodes appear nowhere else in the B-tree, we are forced to include an additional pointer field for each search key in a nonleaf node. These additional pointers point to either file records or buckets for the associated search key.

A generalized B-tree leaf node appears in Figure 11.19a; a nonleaf node appears in Figure 11.19b. Leaf nodes are the same as in B$^+$-trees. In nonleaf

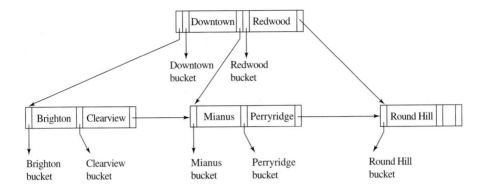

Figure 11.18    B-tree equivalent of B$^+$-tree in Figure 11.11.

nodes, the pointers $P_i$ are the tree pointers that we used also for B$^+$-trees, while the pointers $B_i$ are bucket or file-record pointers. In the generalized B-tree nodes in the figure, there are $n - 1$ keys in the leaf node, but there are $m - 1$ keys in the nonleaf node. This discrepancy occurs because nonleaf nodes must include pointers $B_i$, thus reducing the number of search keys that can be held in these nodes. Clearly, $m < n$, but the exact relationship between $m$ and $n$ depends on the relative size of search keys and pointers.

The number of nodes accessed in a lookup in a B-tree depends on where the search key is located. A lookup on a B$^+$-tree requires traversal of a path from the root of the tree to some leaf node. In contrast, it is sometimes possible to find the desired value in a B-tree before reaching a leaf node. However, roughly $n$ times as many keys are stored in the leaf level of a B-tree as in the nonleaf levels, and, since $n$ is typically large, the benefit of finding certain values early is relatively small. Moreover, the fact that fewer search keys appear in a nonleaf B-tree node, as compared to in B$^+$-trees, implies that a B-tree has a smaller fanout and therefore may have depth greater than that of the corresponding B$^+$-tree. Thus, lookup in a B-tree is faster for some search keys but slower for others, although, in general, lookup time is still proportional to the logarithm of the number of search keys.

Deletion in a B-tree is more complicated. In a B$^+$-tree, the deleted entry always appears in a leaf. In a B-tree, the deleted entry may appear in a nonleaf node. The proper value must be selected as a replacement from the subtree of

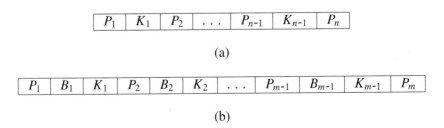

Figure 11.19    Typical nodes of a B-tree. (a) Leaf node. (b) Nonleaf node.

the node containing the deleted entry. Specifically, if search key $K_i$ is deleted, the smallest search key appearing in the subtree of pointer $P_{i+1}$ must be moved to the field formerly occupied by $K_i$. Further actions need to be taken if the leaf node now has too few entries. In contrast, insertion in a B-tree is only slightly more complicated than is insertion in a B$^+$-tree.

The space advantages of B-trees are marginal for large indices, and usually do not outweigh the disadvantages that we have noted. Thus, the structural simplicity of a B$^+$-tree is preferred by many database system implementors. Details of the insertion and deletion algorithms for B-trees are explored in the exercises.

# 11.5   Static Hashing

One disadvantage of sequential file organization is that we must access an index structure to locate data, or must use binary search, and that results in more I/O operations. File organizations based on the technique of *hashing* allow us to avoid accessing an index structure. Hashing also provides a way of constructing indices. We study file organizations and indices based on hashing in the following sections.

## 11.5.1   Hash File Organization

In a hash file organization, we obtain the address of the disk block containing a desired record directly by computing a function on the search-key value of the record. In our description of hashing, we shall use the term *bucket* to denote a unit of storage that can store one or more records. A bucket is typically a disk block, but could be chosen to be smaller or larger than a disk block.

Formally, let $K$ denote the set of all search-key values, and let $B$ denote the set of all bucket addresses. A *hash function h* is a function from $K$ to $B$. Let $h$ denote a hash function.

To insert a record with search key $K_i$, we compute $h(K_i)$, which gives the address of the bucket for that record. Assume for now that there is space in the bucket to store the record. Then, the record is stored in that bucket.

To perform a lookup on a search-key value $K_i$, we simply compute $h(K_i)$, then search the bucket with that address. Suppose that two search keys, $K_5$ and $K_7$, have the same hash value; that is, $h(K_5) = h(K_7)$. If we perform a lookup on $K_5$, the bucket $h(K_5)$ contains records with search-key values $K_5$ and records with search-key values $K_7$. Thus, we have to check the search-key value of every record in the bucket to verify that the record is one that we want.

Deletion is equally straightforward. If the search-key value of the record to be deleted is $K_i$, we compute $h(K_i)$, then search the corresponding bucket for that record, and delete the record from the bucket.

### 11.5.1.1   Hash Functions

The worst possible hash function maps all search-key values to the same bucket. This function is undesirable because all the records have to be kept in the same bucket. A lookup has to examine every such record to find the one desired. An ideal hash function distributes the stored keys uniformly across all the buckets, so that every bucket has the same number of records.

Since we do not know at design time precisely which search-key values will be stored in the file, we want to choose a hash function that assigns search-key values to buckets such that the following hold:

- The distribution is uniform. That is, each bucket is assigned the same number of search-key values from the set of *all* possible search-key values.
- The distribution is random. That is, in the average case, each bucket will have nearly the same number of values assigned to it, regardless of the actual distribution of search-key values. More precisely, the hash value will not be correlated to any externally visible ordering on the search-key values, such as alphabetic ordering or ordering by the length of the search keys; the hash function will appear to be random.

As an illustration of these principles, let us choose a hash function for the *account* file using the search key *branch-name*. The hash function that we choose must have the desirable properties not only on the example *account* file that we have been using, but also on an *account* file of realistic size for a large bank with many branches.

Assume that we decide to have 26 buckets, and we define a hash function that maps names beginning with the *i*th letter of the alphabet to the *i*th bucket. This hash function has the virtue of simplicity, but it fails to provide a uniform distribution, since we expect more branch names to begin with such letters as "B" and "R" than "Q" and "X," for example.

Now suppose that we want a hash function on the search key *balance*. Suppose that the minimum balance is 1 and the maximum balance is 100,000, and we use a hash function that divides the values into 10 ranges, 1–10,000, 10,001–20,000 and so on. The distribution of search-key values is uniform (since each bucket has the same number of different *balance* values), but is not random. But records with balances between 1 and 10,000 are far more common than are records with balances between 90,001 and 100,000. As a result, the distribution of records is not uniform—some buckets receive more records than others do. If the function has a random distribution, even if there are such correlations in the search keys, the randomness of the distribution will make it likely that all buckets will have roughly the same number of records.

Typical hash functions perform computation on the internal binary machine representation of characters in the search key. A simple hash function of this type first computes the sum of the binary representations of the characters of a key, then returns the sum modulo the number of buckets. Figure 11.20 shows the application of such a scheme, using 10 buckets, to the *account* file, under the assumption that the *i*th letter in the alphabet is represented by the integer *i*.

Hash functions require careful design. A bad hash function may result in lookup taking time proportional to the number of search keys in the file. A well-designed function gives an average-case lookup time that is a (small) constant, independent of the number of search keys in the file.

Bucket 0

| | | |
|---|---|---|
| | | |
| | | |

Bucket 5

| Perryridge | A-102 | 400 |
|---|---|---|
| Perryridge | A-201 | 900 |
| Perryridge | A-218 | 700 |
| | | |

Bucket 1

| | | |
|---|---|---|
| | | |
| | | |

Bucket 6

| | | |
|---|---|---|
| | | |
| | | |

Bucket 2

| | | |
|---|---|---|
| | | |
| | | |

Bucket 7

| Mianus | A-215 | 700 |
|---|---|---|
| | | |
| | | |

Bucket 3

| Brighton | A-217 | 750 |
|---|---|---|
| Round Hill | A-305 | 350 |
| | | |

Bucket 8

| Downtown | A-101 | 500 |
|---|---|---|
| Downtown | A-110 | 600 |
| | | |

Bucket 4

| Redwood | A-222 | 700 |
|---|---|---|
| | | |
| | | |

Bucket 9

| | | |
|---|---|---|
| | | |

**Figure 11.20**    Hash organization of *account* file, using *branch-name* as the key.

### 11.5.1.2    Handling of Bucket Overflows

So far, we have assumed that, when a record is inserted, the bucket to which it is mapped has space to store the record. If the bucket does not have enough space, a *bucket overflow* is said to occur. Bucket overflow can occur for several reasons:

- **Insufficient buckets**. The number of buckets, which we denote $n_B$, must be chosen such that $n_B > n_r/f_r$, where $n_r$ denotes the total number of records that will be stored, and $f_r$ denotes the number of records that will fit in a bucket. This designation, of course, is under the assumption that the total number of records is known when the hash function is chosen.

- **Skew**. Some buckets are assigned more records than are others, so a bucket may overflow even when other buckets still have space. This situation is called bucket *skew*. Skew can occur for two reasons:

   **1.** Multiple records may have the same search key.

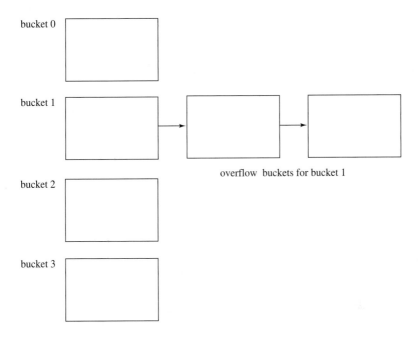

Figure 11.21    Overflow chaining in a hash structure.

2. The chosen hash function may result in nonuniform distribution of search keys.

So that the probability of bucket overflow is reduced, the number of buckets is chosen to be $(n_r/f_r) * (1 + d)$, where $d$ is a fudge factor, typically around 0.2. Some space is wasted: About 20 percent of the space in the buckets will be empty. But the benefit is that the probability of overflow is reduced.

Despite allocation of a few more buckets than required, bucket overflow can still occur. We handle bucket overflow using *overflow buckets*. If a record must be inserted into a bucket $b$, and $b$ is already full, an overflow bucket is provided for $b$, and the record is inserted into the overflow bucket. If the overflow bucket is also full, another overflow bucket is provided, and so on. All the overflow buckets of a given bucket are chained together in a linked list, as shown in Figure 11.21. Overflow handling using such a linked list is called *overflow chaining*.

We must change the lookup algorithm slightly to handle overflow chaining. As before, the hash function is used on the search key to identify a bucket $b$. We must examine all the records in bucket $b$ to see whether they match the search key, as before. In addition, if bucket $b$ has overflow buckets, the records in all the overflow buckets of $b$ must also be examined.

The form of hash structure that we have just described is sometimes referred to as *closed hashing*. Under an alternative approach, called *open hashing*, the set of buckets is fixed, and there are no overflow chains. Instead, if a bucket is full, records are inserted in some other bucket in the initial set of buckets $B$. One policy is to use the next bucket (in cyclic order) that has space; this policy is called *linear probing*. Other policies, such as computing further hash functions, are also used. Open hashing is used in the construction of symbol tables for compilers and assemblers, but closed hashing is preferred for database systems. The reason is that deletion under open hashing is troublesome. Typically, compilers and assemblers perform only lookup and insertion operations on their symbol tables. However, in a database system, it is important to be able to handle deletion as well as insertion. Thus, open hashing is of only minor importance in database implementation.

An important drawback to the form of hashing that we have described is that the hash function must be chosen when we implement the system, and it cannot be changed easily thereafter if the file being indexed grows or shrinks. Since the function $h$ maps search-key values to a fixed set $B$ of bucket addresses, we waste space if $B$ is made large to handle future growth of the file. If $B$ is too small, the buckets contain records of many different search-key values, and bucket overflows can occur. As the file grows, performance suffers. We study later, in Section 11.6, how the number of buckets and the hash function can be changed dynamically.

## 11.5.2   Hash Indices

Hashing can be used not only for file organization, but also for index-structure creation. A *hash index* organizes the search keys, with their associated pointers, into a hash file structure. We construct a hash index as follows. We apply a hash function on a search key to identify a bucket, and store the key and its associated pointers in the bucket (or in overflow buckets). Figure 11.22 shows a secondary hash index on the *account* file, for the search key *account-number*. The hash function used computes the sum of the digits of the account number modulo 7. The hash index has seven buckets, each of size 2 (realistic indices would, of course, have much larger bucket sizes). One of the buckets has three keys mapped to it, so it has an overflow bucket. In this example, *account-number* is a primary key for *account*, so each search-key has only one associated pointer. In general, multiple pointers can be associated with each key.

We use the term *hash index* to denote hash file structures as well as secondary hash indices. Strictly speaking, hash indices are only secondary index structures. A hash index is never needed as a primary index structure, since, if a file itself is organized using hashing, there is no need for a separate hash index structure on it. However, since hash file organization provides the same direct access to records that is provided by indexing, we pretend that a file organized by hashing also has a virtual primary hash index on it.

# 11.6   Dynamic Hashing

As we have seen, the need to fix the set $B$ of bucket addresses presents a serious problem with the static hashing technique of the previous section. Most databases grow larger over time. If we are to use static hashing for such a database, we have

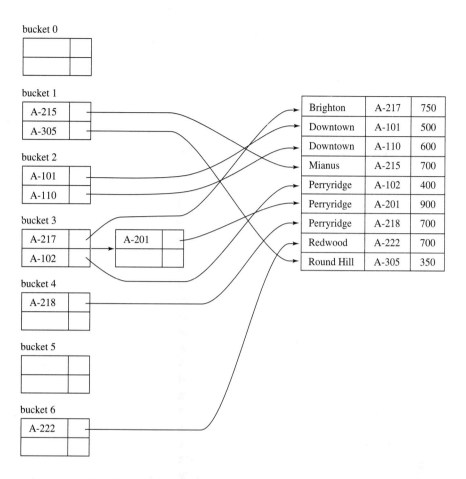

**Figure 11.22**    Hash index on search key *account-number* of *account* file.

three classes of options:

1. Choose a hash function based on the current file size. This option will result in performance degradation as the database grows.

2. Choose a hash function based on the anticipated size of the file at some point in the future. Although performance degradation is avoided, a significant amount of space may be wasted initially.

3. Periodically reorganize the hash structure in response to file growth. Such a reorganization involves choosing a new hash function, recomputing the hash function on every record in the file, and generating new bucket assignments. This reorganization is a massive, time-consuming operation. Furthermore, it is necessary to forbid access to the file during reorganization.

Several *dynamic hashing techniques* allow the hash function to be modified dynamically to accommodate the growth or shrinkage of the database. We describe

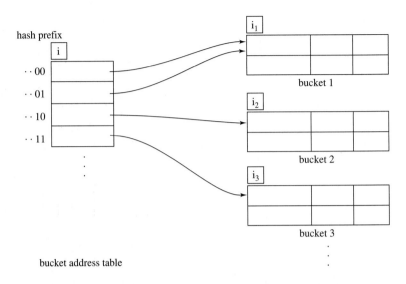

Figure 11.23   General extendable hash structure.

one form of dynamic hashing, called *extendable hashing*. The bibliographic notes
provide references to other forms of dynamic hashing.

Extendable hashing copes with changes in database size by splitting and
coalescing buckets as the database grows and shrinks. As a result, space efficiency
is retained. Moreover, since the reorganization is performed on only one bucket at
a time, the resulting performance overhead is acceptably low.

With extendable hashing, we choose a hash function $h$ with the desirable
properties of uniformity and randomness. However, this hash function generates
values over a relatively large range—namely, $b$-bit binary integers. A typical value
for $b$ is 32.

We do not create a bucket for each hash value. Indeed, $2^{32}$ is over 4 billion,
and that many buckets is unreasonable for all but the largest databases. Instead,
we create buckets on demand, as records are inserted into the file. We do not use
the entire $b$ bits of the hash value initially. At any point, we use $i$ bits, where
$0 \le i \le b$. These $i$ bits are used as an offset into an additional table of bucket
addresses. The value of $i$ grows and shrinks with the size of the database.

Figure 11.23 shows a general extendable hash structure. The $i$ appearing
above the bucket address table in the figure indicates that $i$ bits of the hash value
$h(K)$ are required to determine the correct bucket for $K$. This number will, of
course, change as the file grows. Although $i$ bits are required to find the correct
entry in the bucket address table, several consecutive table entries may point to
the same bucket. All such entries will have a common hash prefix, but the length
of this prefix may be less than $i$. Therefore, we associate with each bucket an
integer giving the length of the common hash prefix. In Figure 11.23 the integer
associated with bucket $j$ is shown as $i_j$. The number of bucket-address-table entries
that point to bucket $j$ is

$$2^{(i-i_j)}$$

To locate the bucket containing search-key value $K_l$, we take the first $i$ high-order bits of $h(K_l)$, look at the corresponding table entry for this bit string, and follow the bucket pointer in the table entry.

To insert a record with search-key value $K_l$, we follow the same procedure for lookup as before, ending up in some bucket—say, $j$. If there is room in the bucket, we insert the record in the bucket. If, on the other hand, the bucket is full, we must split the bucket and redistribute the current records, plus the new one. To split the bucket, we must first determine from the hash value whether we need to increase the number of bits that we use.

- If $i = i_j$, only one entry in the bucket address table points to bucket $j$. Therefore, we need to increase the size of the bucket address table so that we can include pointers to the two buckets that result from splitting bucket $j$. We do so by considering an additional bit of the hash value. We increment the value of $i$ by 1, thus doubling the size of the bucket address table. Each entry is replaced by two entries, both of which contain the same pointer as the original entry. Now two entries in the bucket address table point to bucket $j$. We allocate a new bucket (bucket $z$), and set the second entry to point to the new bucket. We set $i_j$ and $i_z$ to $i$. Next, each record in bucket $j$ is rehashed and, depending on the first $i$ bits (remember we have added 1 to $i$), is either kept in bucket $j$ or allocated to the newly created bucket.

    We now reattempt the insertion of the new record. Usually, the attempt will succeed. However, if all the records in bucket $j$, as well as the new record, have the same hash-value prefix, it will be necessary to split a bucket again, since all the records in bucket $j$ and the new record are assigned to the same bucket. If the hash function has been chosen carefully, it is unlikely that a single insertion will require that a bucket be split more than once, unless there are a large number of records with the same search key. If all the records in bucket $j$ have the same search-key value, no amount of splitting will help. In such cases, overflow buckets are used to store the records, as in static hashing.

- If $i > i_j$, then more than one entry in the bucket address table points to bucket $j$. Thus, we can split bucket $j$ without increasing the size of the bucket address table. Observe that all the entries that point to bucket $j$ correspond to hash prefixes that have the same value on the leftmost $i_j$ bits. We allocate a new bucket (bucket $z$), and set $i_j$ and $i_z$ to the value that results from adding 1 to the original $i_j$ value. Next, we need to adjust the entries in the bucket address table that previously pointed to bucket $j$. (Note that with the new value for $i_j$, not all the entries correspond to hash prefixes that have the same value on the leftmost $i_j$ bits.) We leave the first half of the entries as they were (pointing to bucket $j$), and set all the remaining entries to point to the newly created bucket (bucket $z$). Next, as in the case we saw previously, each record in bucket $j$ is rehashed, and is allocated either to bucket $j$ or to the newly created bucket $z$.

    The insert is then reattempted. In the unlikely case that it again fails, we apply one of the two cases, $i = i_j$ or $i > i_j$, as appropriate.

| Brighton | A-217 | 750 |
|----------|-------|-----|
| Downtown | A-101 | 500 |
| Downtown | A-110 | 600 |
| Mianus | A-215 | 700 |
| Perryridge | A-102 | 400 |
| Perryridge | A-201 | 900 |
| Perryridge | A-218 | 700 |
| Redwood | A-222 | 700 |
| Round Hill | A-305 | 350 |

Figure 11.24    Sample *account* file.

Note that, in both cases, we need to recompute the hash function on only the records in bucket $j$.

To delete a record with search-key value $K_l$, we follow the same procedure for lookup as before, ending up in some bucket—say, $j$. We remove both the search key from the bucket and the record from the file. The bucket too is removed if it becomes empty. Note that, at this point, several buckets can be coalesced, and the size of the bucket address table can be cut in half. The procedure for deciding on when and how to coalesce buckets is left to your to do as an exercise.

We illustrate the operation of insertion using our example *account* file (Figure 11.24). The 32-bit hash values on *branch-name* are shown in Figure 11.25. We assume that, initially, the file is empty, as shown in Figure 11.26. We insert the records one by one. To illustrate all the features of extendable hashing using a small structure, we shall make the unrealistic assumption that a bucket can hold only two records.

Let us insert the record (Brighton, A-217, 750). The bucket address table contains a pointer to the one bucket, and the record is inserted. Next, let us insert the record (Downtown, A-101, 500). This record also is placed in the one bucket of our structure.

When we attempt to insert the next record (Downtown, A-110, 600), we find that the bucket is full. Since $i = i_0$, we need to increase the number of bits that

| *branch-name* | h(*branch-name*) |
|---------------|------------------|
| Brighton | 0010 1101 1111 1011 0010 1100 0011 0000 |
| Downtown | 1010 0011 1010 0000 1100 0110 1001 1111 |
| Mianus | 1100 0111 1110 1101 1011 1111 0011 1010 |
| Perryridge | 1111 0001 0010 0100 1001 0011 0110 1101 |
| Redwood | 0011 0101 1010 0110 1100 1001 1110 1011 |
| Round Hill | 1101 1000 0011 1111 1001 1100 0000 0001 |

Figure 11.25    Hash function for *branch-name*.

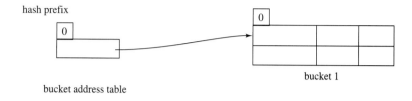

hash prefix

bucket address table

bucket 1

Figure 11.26    Initial extendable hash structure.

we use from the hash value. We now use 1 bit, allowing us $2^1 = 2$ buckets. This increase in the number of bits necessitates doubling the size of the bucket address table to two entries. We split the bucket, placing in the new bucket those records whose search key has a hash value beginning with 1, and leaving in the original bucket the other records. Figure 11.27 shows the state of our structure after the split.

Next, we insert (Mianus, A-215, 700). Since the first bit of $h$(Mianus) is 1, we must insert this record into the bucket pointed to by the "1" entry in the bucket address table. Once again, we find the bucket full and $i = i_1$. We increase the number of bits that we use from the hash to 2. This increase in the number of bits necessitates doubling the size of the bucket address table to four entries, as shown in Figure 11.28. Since the bucket of Figure 11.27 for hash prefix 0 was not split, the two entries of the bucket address table of 00 and 01 both point to this bucket.

For each record in the bucket of Figure 11.27 for hash prefix 1 (the bucket being split), we examine the first 2 bits of the hash value to determine which bucket of the new structure should hold it.

Next, we insert (Perryridge, A-102, 400), which goes in the same bucket as Mianus. The following insertion, of (Perryridge, A-201, 900), results in a bucket overflow, leading to an increase in the number of bits, and a doubling of the size of the bucket address table. The insertion of the third Perryridge record, (Perryridge, A-218, 700), leads to another overflow. However, this overflow cannot be handled

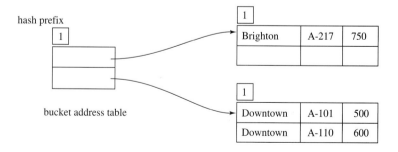

hash prefix

bucket address table

Figure 11.27    Hash structure after three insertions.

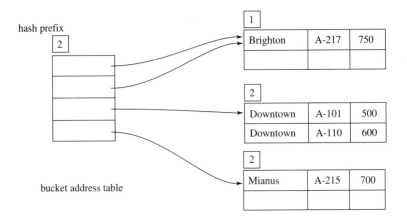

Figure 11.28   Hash structure after four insertions.

by increasing the number of bits, since there are three records with exactly the same hash value. Hence an overflow bucket is used, as shown in Figure 11.29.

We continue in this manner until we have inserted all the *account* records of Figure 11.24. The resulting structure is shown in Figure 11.30.

Let us now examine the advantages and disadvantages of extendable hashing, as compared with the other schemes that we have discussed. The main advantage of extendable hashing is that performance does not degrade as the file grows. Furthermore, there is minimal space overhead. Although the bucket address table incurs additional overhead, it contains one pointer for each hash value for the cur-

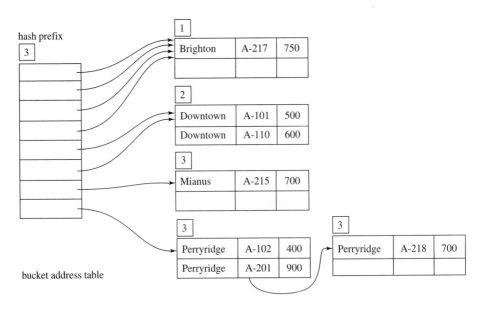

Figure 11.29   Hash structure after seven insertions.

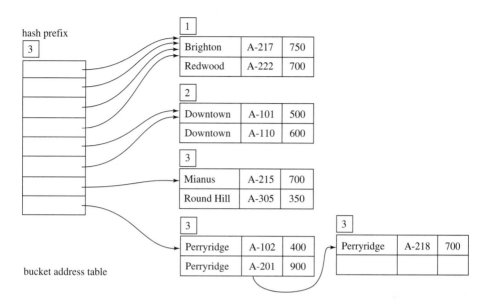

Figure 11.30    Extendable hash structure for the *account* file.

rent prefix length. This table is thus small. The main space saving of extendable hashing over other forms of hashing is that no buckets need to be reserved for future growth; rather, buckets can be allocated dynamically.

A disadvantage of extendable hashing is that lookup involves an additional level of indirection, since we must access the bucket address table before accessing the bucket itself. This extra reference has only a minor effect on performance. Although the hash structures that we discussed earlier do not have this extra level of indirection, they lose their minor performance advantage as they become full.

Thus, extendable hashing appears to be a highly attractive technique, provided that we are willing to accept the added complexity involved in its implementation. More detailed descriptions of the implementation of extendable hashing are referenced in the bibliographic notes. The bibliographic notes also provide references to another form of dynamic hashing called *linear hashing*, which avoids the extra level of indirection associated with extendable hashing, at the possible cost of more overflow buckets.

## 11.7    Comparison of Ordered Indexing and Hashing

We have seen several ordered-indexing schemes and several hashing schemes. We can organize files of records as ordered files, using index-sequential organization, or using B$^+$-tree organizations. Alternatively, we can organize the files using hashing. Finally, we can organize them as heap files, where the records are not ordered in any particular way.

Each scheme has advantages in certain situations. A database-system implementor could provide many schemes, leaving the final decision of which schemes to use to the database designer. However, such an approach requires the implementor to write more code, adding both to the cost of the system and to the space that the system occupies. Thus, most database systems use only a few or just one form of ordered indexing or hashing.

To make a wise choice, the implementor or the database designer must consider the following issues:

- Is the cost of periodic reorganization of the index or hash organization acceptable?
- What is the relative frequency of insertion and deletion?
- Is it desirable to optimize average access time at the expense of increasing the worst-case access time?
- What types of queries are users likely to pose?

We have already examined the first three of these issues, first in our review of the relative merits of specific indexing techniques, and again in our discussion of hashing techniques. The fourth issue, the expected type of query, is critical to the choice of ordered indexing or hashing.

If most queries are of the form

> **select** $A_1, A_2, ..., A_n$
> **from** $r$
> **where** $A_i = c$

then, to process this query, the system will perform a lookup on an ordered index or a hash structure for attribute $A_i$, for value $c$. For queries of this form, a hashing scheme is preferable. An ordered-index lookup requires time proportional to the log of the number of values in $r$ for $A_i$. In a hash structure, however, the average lookup time is a constant independent of the size of the database. The only advantage to an index over a hash structure for this form of query is that the worst-case lookup time is proportional to the log of the number of values in $r$ for $A_i$. By contrast, if hashing is used, the worst-case lookup time is proportional to the number of values in $r$ for $A_i$. However, the worst-case lookup time is unlikely to occur with hashing, and hashing is preferable in this case.

Ordered-index techniques are preferable to hashing in cases where a range of values is specified in the query. Such a query takes the following form:

> **select** $A_1, A_2, ..., A_n$
> **from** $r$
> **where** $A_i \leq c_2$ **and** $A_i \geq c_1$

In other words, the preceding query finds all records with $A_i$ values between $c_1$ and $c_2$.

Let us consider how we process this query using an ordered index. First, we perform a lookup on value $c_1$. Once we have found the bucket for value $c_1$, we follow the pointer chain in the index to read the next bucket in order, and we continue in this manner until we reach $c_2$.

If, instead of an ordered index, we have a hash structure, we can perform a lookup on $c_1$ and can locate the corresponding bucket—but it is not easy, in general, to determine the next bucket that must be examined. The difficulty arises because a good hash function assigns values randomly to buckets. Thus, there is no simple notion of "next bucket in sorted order." The reason we cannot chain buckets together in sorted order on $A_i$ is that each bucket is assigned many search-key values. Since values are scattered randomly by the hash function, the values in the specified range are likely to be scattered across many or all of the buckets. Therefore, we have to read all the buckets to find the required search keys.

Typically, ordered indexing is used unless it is known in advance that range queries will be infrequent, in which case hashing is used. Hash organizations are particularly useful for temporary files created during query processing, if lookups based on a key value are required, but no range queries will be performed.

## 11.8   Index Definition in SQL

The SQL standard does not provide any way for the database user or administrator to control what indices are created and maintained in the database system. Indices are not required for correctness, since they are redundant data structures. However, indices are important for efficient processing of transactions, including both update transactions and queries. Indices are also important for efficient enforcement of integrity constraints. For example, typical implementations enforce a key declaration (Chapter 6) by creating an index with the declared key as the search key of the index.

In principle, a database system can decide automatically what indices to create. However, due to the space cost of indices, as well as to the effect of indices on update processing, it is not easy to make the right choices automatically on what indices to maintain. Therefore, most SQL implementations provide the programmer control over creation and removal of indices via data-definition-language commands. We illustrate the syntax of these commands next. Although the syntax that we show is not part of the SQL-92 standard, it is widely used and supported by many database systems.

An index is created by the **create index** command, which takes the form

> **create index** <index-name> **on** <relation-name> (<attribute-list>)

The *attribute-list* is the list of attributes of the relations that form the search key for the index.

To define an index name *b-index* on the *branch* relation with *branch-name* as the search key, we write

> **create index** *b-index* **on** *branch* (*branch-name*)

If we wish to declare that the search key is a candidate key, we add the attribute **unique** to the index definition. Thus, the command

> **create unique index** *b-index* **on** *branch* (*branch-name*)

declares *branch-name* to be a candidate key for *branch*. If, at the time the **create unique index** command is entered, *branch-name* is not a candidate key, an error message will be displayed, and the attempt to create the index will fail. If the index-creation attempt succeeds, any subsequent attempt to insert a tuple that violates the key declaration will fail. Note that the **unique** feature is redundant if the **unique** declaration of the SQL standard is supported by the database system.

The index name specified for an index is required so that it is possible to drop indices. The **drop index** command takes the form:

**drop index** <index-name>

# 11.9   Multiple-Key Access

Until now, we have assumed implicitly that only one index (or hash table) is used to process a query on a relation. However, for certain types of queries, it is advantageous to use multiple indices if they exist.

Assume that the *account* file has two indices: one for *branch-name* and one for *balance*. Consider the following query: "Find all account numbers at the Perryridge branch with balances equal to $1000." We write

> **select** *loan-number*
> **from** *account*
> **where** *branch-name* = "Perryridge" **and** *balance* = 1000

There are three strategies possible for processing this query:

1. Use the index on *branch-name* to find all records pertaining to the Perryridge branch. Examine each such record to see whether *balance* = 1000.
2. Use the index on *balance* to find all records pertaining to accounts with balances of $1000. Examine each such record to see whether *branch-name* = "Perryridge."
3. Use the index on *branch-name* to find *pointers* to all records pertaining to the Perryridge branch. Also, use the index on *balance* to find pointers to all records pertaining to accounts with a balance of $1000. Take the intersection of these two sets of pointers. Those pointers that are in the intersection point to records pertaining to both Perryridge and accounts with a balance of $1000.

The third strategy is the only one of the three that takes advantage of the existence of multiple indices. However, even this strategy may be a poor choice if all of the following hold:

- There are many records pertaining to the Perryridge branch.
- There are many records pertaining to accounts with a balance of $1000.
- There are only a few records pertaining to *both* the Perryridge branch and accounts with a balance of $1000.

If these conditions hold, we must scan a large number of pointers to produce a small result.

A more efficient strategy for this case is to create and use an index on a search key (*branch-name, balance*)—that is, the search key consisting of the branch name concatenated with the account balance. The structure of the index is the same as that of any other index, the only difference being that the search key is not a single attribute, but rather is a list of attributes. The search key can be represented as a tuple of values, of the form $(a_1, \ldots, a_n)$, where the indexed attributes are $A_1, \ldots, A_n$. The ordering of search-key values is the *lexicographic ordering*. For example, for the case of two attribute search keys, $(a_1, a_2) < (b_1, b_2)$ if either $a_1 < b_1$, or $a_1 = b_1$ and $a_2 < b_2$. Lexicographic ordering is basically the same as alphabetic ordering of words.

The use of an ordered-index structure on multiple attributes has a few shortcomings. As an illustration, consider the query

> **select** *loan-number*
> **from** *account*
> **where** *branch-name* < "Perryridge" **and** *balance* = 1000

We can answer this query using an ordered index on the search key (*branch-name, balance*) as follows: For each value of *branch-name* that is less than "Perryridge" in alphabetic order, records with a *balance* value of 1000 are located. However, each record is likely to be in a different disk block, due to the ordering of records in the file, leading to many I/O operations.

The difference between this query and the previous one is that the condition on *branch-name* is a comparison condition, rather than an equality condition.

To speed the processing of general multiple search-key queries (which can involve one or more comparison operations), we can use several special structures. We shall consider two such structures: the *grid file* and *partitioned hashing*. There is another structure, called the *R-tree*, which can be used for this purpose. Since it is a comparatively complex structure, we postpone its description to Chapter 21.

## 11.9.1 Grid Files

Figure 11.31 shows part of a grid file for the search keys *branch-name* and *balance* on the *account* file. The two-dimensional array in the figure is called the *grid array*, and the one-dimensional arrays are called *linear scales*. The grid file has a single grid array, and one linear scale for each search-key attribute.

Search keys are mapped to cells in a manner described next. Each cell in the grid array has a pointer to a bucket that contains the search-key values and pointers to records. Only some of the buckets and pointers from the cells are shown in the figure. So that space is conserved, multiple elements of the array can point to the same bucket. The dotted boxes in the figure indicate which cells point to the same bucket.

Suppose that we want to insert in the grid-file index a record whose search-key value is ("Brighton", 500000). To find the cell to which the key is mapped, we independently locate the row and column to which the cell belongs.

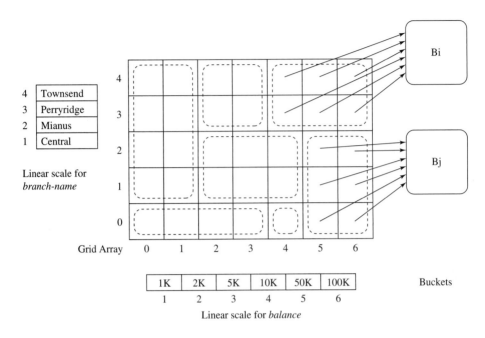

**Figure 11.31** Grid file on keys *branch-name* and *balance* of the *account* file.

We first use the linear scales on *branch-name* to locate the row of the cell to which the search key maps. To do so, we search the array to find the least element that is greater than "Brighton". In this case, it is the first element, so the search key maps to the row marked 0. If it were the $i$th element, the search key would map to row $i - 1$. If the search key is greater than or equal to all elements in the linear scale, it maps to the final row. Next, we use the linear scale on *balance* to find out similarly to which column the search key maps. In this case, the balance 500,000 maps to column 6.

Thus, the search-key value ("Brighton", 500000) maps to the cell in row 0, column 6. Similarly, ("Downtown", 60000) would map to the cell in row 1 column 5. Both cells point to the same bucket (as indicated by the dotted box), so, in both cases, the search-key values and the pointer to the record are stored in the bucket labeled $B_j$ in the figure.

To perform a lookup to answer our example query, with the search condition of

$$branch\text{-}name < \text{``Perryridge''} \textbf{ and } balance = 1000$$

we find all rows that can contain branch names less than "Perryridge", using the linear scale on *branch-name*. In this case, these rows are 0, 1, and 2. Rows 3 and beyond contain branch names greater than or equal to "Perryridge". Similarly, we find that only column 1 can contain a *balance* value of 1000. In this case, only column 1 satisfies this condition. Thus, only the cells in column 1, rows 0, 1, and 2 can contain entries that satisfy the search condition.

We therefore look up all entries in the buckets pointed to from these three cells. In this case, there are only two buckets, since two of the cells point to the same bucket, as indicated by the dotted boxes in the figure. The buckets may contain some search keys that do not satisfy the required condition, so each search key in the buckets must be tested again to see whether it satisfies the search condition. We have to examine only a small number of buckets, however, to answer this query.

The linear scales must be chosen such that the records are uniformly distributed across the cells. If the bucket—call it $A$—becomes full and an entry has to be inserted in it, an extra bucket $B$ is allocated. If more than one cell points to $A$, the cell pointers are changed such that some point to $A$ and others to $B$. The entries in the bucket $A$ and the new entry are then redistributed between $A$ and $B$ based on to which cells they map. If only one cell points to bucket $A$, $B$ becomes an overflow bucket for $A$. To improve performance in such a situation, we must reorganize the grid file, with an expanded grid array and expanded linear scales. The process is much like the expansion of the bucket address table in extensible hashing, and is left for you to do as an exercise.

It is conceptually simple to extend the grid-file approach to any number of search keys. If we want our structure to be used for queries on $n$ keys, we construct an $n$-dimensional grid array with $n$ linear scales.

The grid structure is suitable also for queries involving one search key. Consider this query:

> **select** *
> **from** *account*
> **where** *branch-name* = "Perryridge"

The linear scale on *branch-name* tells us that only cells in row 3 can satisfy this condition. Since there is no condition on *balance*, we examine all buckets pointed to by cells in row 3 to find entries pertaining to Perryridge. Thus, we can use a grid-file index on two search keys to answer queries on either search key by itself, as well as to answer queries on both search keys. Thus, a single grid-file index can serve the role of three separate indices. If each index were maintained separately, the three together would occupy more space, and the cost of updating them would be high.

Grid files provide a significant decrease in processing time for multiple-key queries. However, they impose a space overhead (the grid directory can become large), as well as a performance overhead on record insertion and deletion. Further, it is hard to choose partitioning ranges for the keys such that the distribution of records is uniform. If insertions to the file are frequent, reorganization will have to be carried out periodically, and that can have a high cost.

## 11.9.2  Partitioned Hashing

*Partitioned hashing* is an extension of hashing that allows indexing on multiple attributes. A partitioned hash structure allows queries on individual attributes, as well as queries that involve multiple attributes, although it does not support range

| *search-key value* | *hash value* |
|---|---|
| (Main, Harrison) | 101 111 |
| (North, Rye) | 110 101 |
| (Main, Brooklyn) | 101 001 |
| (North, Princeton) | 110 000 |
| (Park, Palo Alto) | 010 010 |
| (Putnam, Stamford) | 011 001 |
| (Nassau, Princeton) | 011 000 |
| (Spring, Brooklyn) | 001 001 |
| (Alma, Palo Alto) | 110 010 |

Figure 11.32    Partitioned hash function for key (*customer-street, customer-city*).

queries. Suppose that we wish to construct a structure suitable for queries on the *customer* file involving *customer-name*, *customer-street*, and *customer-city*. We construct a hash structure for the key (*customer-street, customer-city*). The only difference between the structure that we shall create and those we saw earlier is that we impose an additional constraint on the hash function $h$. Hash values are split into two parts. The first part depends on only the *customer-street* value; the second part depends on only the *customer-city* value. The hash function is called *partitioned* because the hash values are split into segments that depend on each element of the key.

Figure 11.32 shows a sample hash function in which the first 3 bits depend on *customer-street*, and the final 3 bits depend on *customer-city*. Thus, the hash values for (Main, Harrison) and (Main, Brooklyn) agree on the first 3 bits, and the hash values for (Park, Palo Alto) and (Alma, Palo Alto) agree on the last 3 bits.

We can use the partitioned hash function of Figure 11.32 to answer the query, "Find the names of all customers who live on Main Street in Brooklyn." We simply compute $h$(Main, Brooklyn), and access the hash structure. The same hash structure is suitable for a query involving only one of the two search keys. To find all records pertaining to the customers who live in Brooklyn, we compute *part* of the partitioned hash. Since we have only the *customer-city* value, we are able to compute only the last 3 bits of the hash. For the value "Brooklyn," these 3 bits are 001. We access the hash structure, then scan those buckets for which the last 3 bits of the hash value are 001. In the example of Figure 11.32, we access the buckets for hash values 101 001, 011 001, and 001 001.

Partitioned hashing extends to an arbitrary number of attributes. There are several improvements that we can make in partitioned hashing if we know how frequently a user will specify each attribute in a query. The bibliographic notes reference these techniques. Using partitioned hashing is similar to using grid files, with two differences. First, hash partitioning is used on the key values, instead of range partitioning. Second, there is no directory; instead, the hash value directly gives a bucket address.

Several other hybrid techniques for processing multiple-key queries exist. Such techniques may be useful in applications where the system implementor knows that most queries will be of a restricted form. Again, references to some of the more interesting techniques appear in the bibliographic notes.

## 11.10   Summary

Many queries reference only a small proportion of the records in a file. To reduce the overhead in searching for these records, we can construct *indices* for the files that store the database.

Index-sequential files are one of the oldest index schemes used in database systems. They are designed for applications that require both sequential processing of the entire file and random access to individual records. To permit fast retrieval of records in search-key order, we chain together records by pointers. To allow fast random access, we use an index structure. There are two types of indices that we can use: dense indices and sparse indices.

In a standard index-sequential file, only one index is maintained. If several indices on different search keys are used, the index whose search key specifies the sequential order of the file is the *primary index*. The other indices are called *secondary indices*. Secondary indices improve the performance of queries that use search keys other than the primary one. However, they impose an overhead on modification of the database.

The primary disadvantage of the index-sequential file organization is that performance degrades as the file grows. To overcome this deficiency, we can use a $B^+$-*tree index*. A $B^+$-tree index takes the form of a *balanced* tree, in which every path from the root of the tree to a leaf of the tree is of the same length. Lookup in this scheme is straightforward and efficient. Insertion and deletion, however, are more complicated. Nevertheless, the number of operations required for insertion and deletion on $B^+$-trees is proportional to the logarithm to the base $N$ of the size of the database, where each nonleaf node stores $N$ pointers. Thus, $B^+$-trees are shorter than other balanced binary-tree structures such as AVL trees, and therefore require fewer disk accesses to locate records. We can use $B^+$-trees for indexing a file containing records, as well as to organize records into a file.

B-tree indices are similar to $B^+$-tree indices. The primary advantage of a B-tree is that the B-tree eliminates the redundant storage of search-key values. The major disadvantages are overall complexity and reduced fanout for a given node size. $B^+$-tree indices are almost universally preferred over B-tree indices in practice.

Sequential file organizations require an index structure to locate data. File organizations based on hashing, by contrast, allow us to find the address of a data item directly by computing a function on the search-key value of the desired record. Since we do not know at design time precisely which search-key values will be stored in the file, a good hash function to choose is one that assigns search-key values to buckets such that the distribution is both uniform and random.

*Static hashing* uses hash functions in which the set of bucket addresses is fixed. Such hash functions cannot easily accommodate databases that grow significantly larger over time. There are several *dynamic hashing techniques* that allow the hash function to be modified. One example is *extendable hashing*, which copes with changes in database size by splitting and coalescing buckets as the database grows and shrinks.

We can also use hashing to create secondary indices; such indices are called *hash indices*. For notational convenience, hash file organizations are assumed to have an implicit hash index on the search key used for hashing.

Ordered indices such as B$^+$-trees and hash indices can be used for indexing based on equality conditions involving multiple attributes. Indexing techniques such as the grid file and partitioned hashing handle the general case of indexing with multiple attributes.

# Exercises

**11.1.** When is it preferable to use a dense index rather than a sparse index? Explain your answer.

**11.2.** Since indices speed query processing, why might they not be kept on several search keys? List as many reasons as possible.

**11.3.** What is the difference between a primary index and a secondary index?

**11.4.** Is it possible in general to have two primary indices on the same relation for different search keys? Explain your answer.

**11.5.** Construct a B$^+$-tree for the following set of key values:

$$(2, 3, 5, 7, 11, 17, 19, 23, 29, 31)$$

Assume that the tree is initially empty and values are added in ascending order. Construct B$^+$-trees for the cases where the number of pointers that will fit in one node is as follows:
  (*a*) four
  (*b*) six
  (*c*) eight

**11.6.** For each B$^+$-tree of Exercise 11.5, show the steps involved in the following queries:
  (*a*) Find records with a search-key value of 11.
  (*b*) Find records with a search-key value between 7 and 17, inclusive.

**11.7.** For each B$^+$-tree of Exercise 11.5, show the form of the tree after each of the following series of operations:
  (*a*) Insert 9.
  (*b*) Insert 10.
  (*c*) Insert 8.
  (*d*) Delete 23.
  (*e*) Delete 19.

**11.8.** Consider the modified redistribution scheme for B$^+$-trees described in page 354. What is the expected height of the tree as a function of *n*?

**11.9.** Repeat Exercise 11.5 for a B-tree.

**11.10.** Explain the distinction between closed and open hashing. Discuss the relative merits of each technique in database applications.

**11.11.** What are the causes of bucket overflow in a hash file organization? What can be done to reduce the occurrence of bucket overflows?

**11.12.** Suppose that we are using extendable hashing on a file that contains records with the following search-key values:

$$2, 3, 5, 7, 11, 17, 19, 23, 29, 31.$$

Show the extendable hash structure for this file if the hash function is $h(x) = x \bmod 8$ and buckets can hold three records.

**11.13.** Show how the extendable hash structure of Exercise 11.12 changes as the result of each of the following steps:
(a) Delete 11.
(b) Delete 31.
(c) Insert 1.
(d) Insert 15.

**11.14.** Why is a hash structure not the best choice for a search key on which range queries are likely?

**11.15.** Consider a grid file in which we wish to avoid overflow buckets for performance reasons. In cases where an overflow bucket would be needed, we instead reorganize the grid file. Present an algorithm for such a reorganization.

# Bibliographical Notes

Discussions concerning the basic data structures used in indexing and hashing can be found in Cormen et al. [1990]. B-tree indices were first introduced in Bayer [1972] and Bayer and McCreight [1972], B$^+$-trees are discussed in Comer [1979], Bayer and Unterauer [1977], and Knuth [1973]. Bayer and Schkolnick [1977] and Shasha and Goodman [1988] analyze the problem of managing a B-tree index for a file updated concurrently by several processes. Other discussions of concurrency control within B-trees and similar data structures include those of Lehman and Yao [1981], Kung and Lehman [1980], and Ford and Calhoun [1984]. Gray and Reuter [1993] provide a good description of issues in the implementation of B$^+$-trees.

Several alternative tree and treelike search structures have been proposed. Tries are trees whose structure is based on the "digits" of keys (for example, a dictionary thumb index, which has one entry for each letter). Such trees may not be balanced in the sense that B$^+$-trees are. Tries are discussed by Ramesh et al. [1989], Orestein [1982], Litwin [1981], and Fredkin [1960]. Related work includes the digital B-trees of Lomet [1981].

Knuth [1973] analyzes a large number of different hashing techniques. Several dynamic hashing schemes exist. Extendable hashing was introduced by Fagin et al. [1979]. Linear hashing was introduced by Litwin [1978, 1980]; a performance analysis of that scheme was presented by Larson [1982]. Concurrency with linear hashing is examined by Ellis [1987]. A variant of linear hashing is presented by Larson [1988]. Another scheme, called dynamic hashing, was proposed by Larson [1978]. An alternative given by Ramakrishna and Larson [1989] allows retrieval in a single disk access at the price of a high overhead for a small fraction of database modifications.

The grid file structure appears in Nievergelt et al. [1984], and in Hinrichs [1985]. Partitioned hash functions have been applied to several index structures. Partial-match retrieval uses a partitioned hash function to limit the number of buckets to be searched when a multiple-key query is processed; see Rivest [1976], Burkhard [1976, 1979], and Ullman [1988]. King et al. [1983] use a combination of extendable hashing and partitioned hash functions in an index structure designed for multiple-key queries that include subset queries (as in keyword-based retrieval). Optimal choice of partitioning for a partitioned hash function is discussed in Bolour [1979], and in Aho and Ullman [1979].

# CHAPTER
# 12

## QUERY PROCESSING

*Query processing* refers to the range of activities involved in extracting data from a database. These activities include translation of queries expressed in high-level database languages into expressions that can be implemented at the physical level of the file system, a variety of query-optimizing transformations, and actual evaluation of queries.

The cost of processing a query is usually dominated by disk access, which is slow compared to memory access. There are usually many possible strategies for processing a given query, especially if the query is complex. The difference between a good strategy and a bad strategy, in terms of the number of disk accesses required, is often substantial, and may be several orders of magnitude. Hence, it is worthwhile for the system to spend a substantial amount of time on the selection of a good strategy for processing a query, even if the query is executed only once.

## 12.1 Overview

The steps involved in processing a query are illustrated in Figure 12.1. The basic steps are

1. Parsing and translation
2. Optimization
3. Evaluation

Before query processing can begin, the system must translate the query into a usable form. A language such as SQL is suitable for human use, but is ill-suited

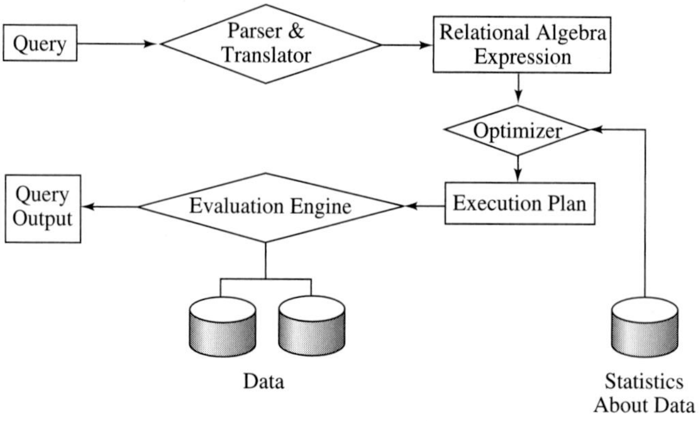

Figure 12.1    Steps in query processing.

to be the system's internal representation of a query. A more useful internal representation is one based on the extended relational algebra.

Thus, the first action the system must take in query processing is to translate a given query into its internal form. This translation process is similar to the work performed by the parser of a compiler. In generating the internal form of the query, the parser checks the syntax of the user's query, verifies that the relation names appearing in the query are names of relations in the database, and so on. A parse-tree representation of the query is constructed, which is then translated into a relational-algebra expression. If the query was expressed in terms of a view, the translation phase also replaces all uses of the view by the relational-algebra expression that defines the view.[†] Parsing is covered in most compiler texts (see the bibliographic notes), and is outside the scope of this book.

In the network and hierarchical models (discussed in Appendices A and B), query optimization is left, for the most part, to the application programmer. That choice is made because the data-manipulation–language statements of these two models are usually embedded in a host programming language, and it is not easy to transform a network or hierarchical query into an equivalent one without knowledge of the entire application program. In contrast, relational-query languages are either declarative or algebraic. Declarative languages permit users to specify what a query should generate without saying how the system should do the generating. Algebraic languages allow for algebraic transformation of users' queries. Based on the query specification, it is relatively easy for an optimizer to generate a variety of equivalent plans for a query, and to choose the least expensive one.

---

[†]For materialized views, the expression defining the view has already been evaluated and stored. Therefore, the stored relation can be used, instead of uses of the view being replaced by the expression defining the view. Recursive views are handled differently, via a fixpoint procedure, as discussed in Section 5.3.6.

In this chapter, we assume the relational model. We shall see that the algebraic basis provided by this model is of considerable help in query optimization. Given a query, there is generally a variety of methods for computing the answer. For example, we have seen that, in SQL, a query could be expressed in several different ways. Each SQL query can itself be translated into a relational-algebra expression in one of several ways. Furthermore, the relational-algebra representation of a query specifies only partially how to evaluate a query; there are usually several ways to evaluate relational-algebra expressions. As an illustration, consider the query

> **select** *balance*
> **from** *account*
> **where** *balance* < 2500

This query can be translated into either of the following relational-algebra expressions:

- $\sigma_{balance<2500} (\Pi_{balance} (account))$
- $\Pi_{balance} (\sigma_{balance<2500} (account))$

Further, we can execute each relational-algebra operation using one of several different algorithms. For example, to implement the preceding selection, we can search every tuple in *account* to find tuples with balance less than 2500. If a $B^+$-tree index is available on the attribute *balance*, we can use the index instead to locate the tuples.

To specify fully how to evaluate a query, we need not only to provide the relational-algebra expression, but also to annotate it with instructions specifying how to evaluate each operation. Annotations may state the algorithm to be used for a specific operation, or the particular index or indices to use. A relational-algebra operation annotated with instructions on how to evaluate it is called an *evaluation primitive*. Several primitives may be grouped together into a *pipeline*, in which each of the primitives starts working on its input tuples even as they are being generated by another primitive. A sequence of primitive operations that can be used to evaluate a query is a *query-execution plan* or *query-evaluation plan*. Figure 12.2 illustrates an evaluation plan for our example query, in which a particular index (denoted in the figure as "index 1") is specified for the selection operation. The *query-execution engine* takes a query-evaluation plan, executes that plan, and returns the answers to the query.

The different evaluation plans for a given query can have different costs. We do not expect users to write their queries in a way that suggests the most

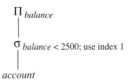

Figure 12.2    A query-evaluation plan.

efficient evaluation plan. Rather, it is the responsibility of the system to construct a query-evaluation plan that minimizes the cost of query evaluation. As we explained, the most relevant performance measure is usually the number of disk accesses.

*Query optimization* is the process of selecting the most efficient query-evaluation plan for a query. One aspect of optimization occurs at the relational-algebra level. An attempt is made to find an expression that is equivalent to the given expression, but that is more efficient to execute. We shall discuss equivalent expressions in greater detail in Section 12.9. The other aspect involves the selection of a detailed strategy for processing the query, such as choosing the algorithm to use for executing an operation, choosing the specific indices to use, and so on.

To choose among different query-evaluation plans, the optimizer has to *estimate* the cost of each evaluation plan. Computing the precise cost of evaluation of a plan is usually not possible without actually evaluating the plan. Instead, optimizers make use of statistical information about the relations, such as relation sizes and index depths, to make a good estimate of the cost of a plan.

Consider the preceding example of a selection applied to the *account* relation. The optimizer estimates the cost of the different evaluation plans. If an index is available on attribute *balance* of *account*, then the evaluation plan shown in Figure 12.2, in which the selection is done using the index, is likely to have the lowest cost, and, thus, to be chosen.

Once the query plan is chosen, the query is evaluated with that plan, and the result of the query is output.

The sequence of steps already described for processing a query is representative; not all databases exactly follow those steps. For instance, instead of using the relational-algebra representation, several databases use an annotated parse-tree representation based on the structure of the given SQL query. However, the concepts that we describe here form the basis of query processing in databases.

In Section 12.2, we construct a cost model that allows us to estimate the cost of various operations. Using this cost measure, we address the optimal evaluation of individual operations in Sections 12.3 through 12.7. In Section 12.8, we examine the efficiencies that we can achieve by combining multiple operations into one pipelined operation. These tools allow us to determine the approximate cost of evaluating a given relational-algebra expression optimally. Finally, in Sections 12.9 and 12.10, we show equivalences among relational-algebra expressions. We can use these equivalences to replace a relational-algebra expression constructed from a user's query with an equivalent expression whose estimated cost of evaluation is lower.

## 12.2    Catalog Information for Cost Estimation

The strategy that we choose for query evaluation depends on the estimated cost of the strategy. Query optimizers make use of of statistical information stored in the DBMS catalog to estimate the cost of a plan. The relevant catalog information about relations includes

- $n_r$ is the number of tuples in the relation $r$.
- $b_r$ is the number of blocks containing tuples of relation $r$.
- $s_r$ is the size of a tuple of relation $r$ in bytes.
- $f_r$ is the blocking factor of relation $r$—that is, the number of tuples of relation $r$ that fit into one block.
- $V(A, r)$ is the number of distinct values that appear in the relation $r$ for attribute $A$. This value is the same as the size of $\Pi_A(r)$. If $A$ is a key for relation $r$, $V(A, r)$ is $n_r$.
- $SC(A, r)$ is the selection cardinality of attribute $A$ of relation $r$. Given a relation $r$ and an attribute $A$ of the relation, $SC(A, r)$ is the average number of records that satisfy an equality condition on attribute $A$, given that at least one record satisfies the equality condition. For example, $SC(A, r) = 1$ if $A$ is a key attribute of $r$; for a nonkey attribute, we estimate that the $V(A, r)$ distinct values are distributed evenly among the tuples, yielding $SC(A, r) = (n_r / V(A, r))$.

The last two statistics, $V(A, r)$ and $SC(A, r)$, can also be maintained for sets of attributes if desired, instead of just for individual attributes. Thus, given a set of attributes $\mathcal{A}$, $V(\mathcal{A}, r)$ is the size of $\Pi_A(r)$.

If we assume that the tuples of relation $r$ are stored together physically in a file, the following equation holds:

$$b_r = \left\lceil \frac{n_r}{f_r} \right\rceil$$

In addition to catalog information about relations, the following catalog information about indices is also used:

- $f_i$ is the average fan-out of internal nodes of index $i$, for tree-structured indices such as B$^+$-trees.
- $HT_i$ is the number of levels in index $i$—that is, the height of index $i$. For a balanced tree index (such as a B$^+$-tree) on attribute $A$ of relation $r$, $HT_i = \lceil \log_{f_i}(V(A, r)) \rceil$. For a hash index, $HT_i$ is 1.
- $LB_i$ is the number of lowest-level index blocks in index $i$—that is, the number of blocks at the leaf level of the index. For a hash index, $LB_i$ is simply the number of blocks, other than directory blocks, in the index.

We use the statistical variables to estimate the size of the result and the cost for various operations and algorithms, as we shall see in the following sections. We refer to the cost estimate of algorithm $A$ as $E_A$.

If we wish to maintain accurate statistics, then, every time a relation is modified, we must also update the statistics. This update incurs a substantial amount of overhead. Therefore, most systems do not update the statistics on every modification. Instead, the updates are done during periods of light system load.

As a result, the statistics used for choosing a query-processing strategy may not be completely accurate. However, if not too many updates occur in the intervals between the updates of the statistics, the statistics will be sufficiently accurate to provide a good estimation of the relative costs of the different plans.

The statistical information noted here is simplified. Real-world optimizers often maintain further statistical information to improve the accuracy of their cost estimates of evaluation plans.

## 12.3    Measures of Query Cost

The cost of query evaluation can be measured in terms of a number of different resources, including disk accesses, CPU time to execute a query, and, in a distributed or parallel database system, the cost of communication (which we discuss later, in Chapters 17 and 18). The response time for a query-evaluation plan (that is, the clock time required to execute the plan), assuming no other activity is going on on the computer, would account for all these costs, and could be used as a good measure of the cost of the plan.

In large database systems, however, disk accesses (which we measure as the number of transfers of blocks from disk) are usually the most important cost, since disk accesses are slow compared to in-memory operations. Moreover, CPU speeds have been improving much faster than have disk speeds. Thus, it is likely that the time spent in disk activity will continue to dominate the total time to execute a query. Finally, estimating the CPU time is relatively hard, compared to estimating the disk-access cost. Therefore, the disk-access cost is considered a reasonable measure of the cost of a query-evaluation plan.

To simplify our computation of disk-access cost, we assume that all transfers of blocks have the same cost. This assumption ignores the variance arising from rotational latency (waiting for the desired data to spin under the read–write head) and seek time (the time that it takes to move the head over the desired track or cylinder). Although these factors are significant, they are difficult to estimate in a shared system. Therefore, we simply use the *number of block transfers* from disk as a measure of the actual cost.

We also ignore the cost of writing the final result of an operation back to disk. Whatever the query-evaluation plan used, this cost does not change; hence, ignoring it does not affect the choice of a plan.

The costs of all the algorithms that we consider depend significantly on the size of the buffer in main memory. In the best case, all data can be read into the buffers, and the disk does not need to be accessed again. In the worst case, we assume that the buffer can hold only a few blocks of data—approximately one block per relation. When presenting cost estimates, we generally assume the worst case.

## 12.4    Selection Operation

In query processing, the *file scan* is the lowest-level operator to access data. File scans are search algorithms that locate and retrieve records that fulfill a selection condition. In relational systems, file scan allows an entire relation to be read in those cases where the relation is stored in a single, dedicated file.

### 12.4.1  Basic Algorithms

Consider a selection operation on a relation whose tuples are stored together in one file. Two scan algorithms to implement the selection operation are as follows:

- **A1** (*linear search*). In a linear search, each file block is scanned, and all records[†] are tested to see whether they satisfy the selection condition. Since all blocks have to be read, $E_{A1} = b_r$. (Recall that $E_{A1}$ denotes the estimated cost of algorithm $A1$.) For a selection on a key attribute, we assume that one-half of the blocks will be searched before the record is found, at which point the scan can terminate. The estimate in this case is $E_{A1} = (b_r/2)$.

   Although it may be inefficient in many cases, the linear search algorithm can be applied to any file, regardless of the ordering of the file or of the availability of indices.

- **A2** (*binary search*). If the file is ordered on an attribute, and the selection condition is an equality comparison on the attribute, we can use a binary search to locate records that satisfy the selection. The binary search is performed on the blocks of the file, giving the following estimate for the file blocks to be scanned:

$$E_{A2} = \lceil \log_2(b_r) \rceil + \left\lceil \frac{SC(A, r)}{f_r} \right\rceil - 1$$

The first term, $\lceil \log_2(b_r) \rceil$, accounts for the cost of locating the first tuple by a binary search on the blocks. The total number of records that will satisfy the selection is $SC(A, r)$, and these records will occupy $\lceil SC(A, r)/f_r \rceil$ blocks,[‡] of which one has already been retrieved, giving the preceding estimate.

   If the equality condition is on a key attribute, then $SC(A, r) = 1$, and the estimate reduces to $E_{A2} = \lceil \log_2(b_r) \rceil$.

   The cost estimates for binary search are based on the assumption that the blocks of a relation are stored contiguously on disk. Otherwise, the cost of looking up the file-access structures (which may be on disk) to locate the physical address of a block in a file must be added to the estimates. The cost estimates also depend on the size of the result of the selection.

   If we assume uniform distribution of values (that is, each value appears with equal probability), then the query $\sigma_{A=a}(r)$ is estimated to have

$$SC(A, r) = \frac{n_r}{V(A, r)}$$

---

[†]We are assuming that the file contains a relation, so each record corresponds to exactly one tuple.
[‡]This formula is based on the (often-valid) assumption that the set of records for a given value start at a block boundary. If this assumption does not hold, one additional block access is required in the worst case.

tuples, assuming that the value $a$ appears in attribute $A$ of some record of $r$. The assumption that the value $a$ in the selection appears in some record is generally true, and cost estimates often make it implicitly. However, it is often not realistic to assume that each value appears with equal probability. The *branch-name* attribute in the *account* relation is an example where the assumption is not valid. There is one tuple in the *account* relation for each account. It is reasonable to expect that the large branches have more accounts than smaller branches. Therefore, certain *branch-name* values appear with greater probability than do others. Despite the fact that the uniform-distribution assumption is often not correct, it is a reasonable approximation of reality in many cases, and it helps us to keep our presentation relatively simple.

As an illustration of this use of the cost estimates, suppose that we have the following statistical information about the *account* relation:

- $f_{account} = 20$     (that is, 20 tuples of *account* fit in one block).
- $V(branch\text{-}name, account) = 50$     (that is, there are 50 different branches).
- $V(balance, account) = 500$     (that is, there are 500 different *balance* values).
- $n_{account} = 10000$     (that is, the *account* relation has 10, 000 tuples).

Consider the query

$$\sigma_{branch\text{-}name=\text{``Perryridge''}}(account)$$

Since the relation has 10, 000 tuples, and each block holds 20 tuples, the number of blocks is $b_{account} = 500$. A simple file scan on *account* therefore takes 500 block accesses.

Suppose that *account* is sorted on *branch-name*. Since $V(branch\text{-}name, account)$ is 50, we expect that $10000/50 = 200$ tuples of the *account* relation pertain to the Perryridge branch. These tuples would fit in $200/20 = 10$ blocks. A binary search to find the first record would take $\lceil log_2(500) \rceil = 9$ block accesses. Thus, the total cost would be $9 + 10 - 1 = 18$ block accesses.

## 12.4.2   Selections Using Indices

Index structures are referred to as *access paths*, since they provide a path through which data can be located and accessed. In Chapter 11, we pointed out that it is efficient to read the records of a file in an order corresponding closely to physical order. Recall that a *primary index* is an index that allows the records of a file to be read in an order that corresponds to the physical order in the file. An index that is not a primary index is called a *secondary index*.

Search algorithms that use an index are referred to as *index scans*. Ordered indices, such as B$^+$-trees, also permit access to tuples in a sorted order, which is useful for implementing range queries. Although indices can provide fast, direct, and ordered access, their use imposes the overhead of access to those blocks containing the index. We need to take into account these block accesses when we estimate the cost of a strategy that involves the use of indices. We use the selection predicate to guide us in the choice of the index to use in processing the query.

- **A3** (*primary index, equality on key*). For an equality comparison on a key attribute with a primary index, we can use the index to retrieve a single record that satisfies the corresponding equality condition. To retrieve a single record, we need to retrieve one block more than the number of index levels ($HT_i$); the cost is $E_{A3} = HT_i + 1$.
- **A4** (*primary index, equality on nonkey*). We can retrieve multiple records by using a primary index when the selection condition specifies an equality comparison on a nonkey attribute, $A$. $SC(A, r)$ records will satisfy an equality condition, and $\lceil SC(A, r)/f_r \rceil$ file blocks will be accessed; hence,

$$E_{A4} = HT_i + \left\lceil \frac{SC(A, r)}{f_r} \right\rceil$$

- **A5** (*secondary index, equality*). Selections specifying an equality condition can use a secondary index. This strategy can retrieve a single record if the indexing field is a key; multiple records can be retrieved if the indexing field is not a key. For an equality condition on attribute $A$, $SC(A, r)$ records satisfy the condition. Given that the index is a secondary index, we assume the worst-case scenario that each matching record resides on a different block, yielding $E_{A5} = HT_i + SC(A, r)$, or, for a key indexing attribute, $E_{A5} = HT_i + 1$.

We assume the same statistical information about *account* as used in the earlier example. We also suppose that the following indices exist on *account*:

- A primary, B$^+$-tree index for attribute *branch-name*
- A secondary, B$^+$-tree index for attribute *balance*†

As mentioned earlier, we make the simplifying assumption that values are distributed uniformly.
Consider the query

$$\sigma_{branch\text{-}name=\text{``Perryridge''}}(account)$$

Since $V(branch\text{-}name, account) = 50$, we expect that $10000/50 = 200$ tuples of the *account* relation pertain to the Perryridge branch. Suppose that we use the index on *branch-name*. Since the index is a clustering index, $200/20 = 10$ block reads are required to read the *account* tuples. In addition, several index blocks must be read. Assume that the B$^+$-tree index stores 20 pointers per node. Since

---

†In practice, it is unlikely that an index would be maintained on *balance*, since balances change frequently. However, the example is useful here to illustrate the relative costs of various access plans.

there are 50 different branch names, the $B^+$-tree index must have between three and five leaf nodes. With this number of leaf nodes, the entire tree has a depth of 2, so two index blocks must be read. Thus, the preceding strategy requires 12 total block reads.

## 12.4.3   Selections Involving Comparisons

Consider a selection of the form $\sigma_{A \le v}(r)$. In the absence of any further information about the comparison, we assume that approximately one-half of the records will satisfy the comparison condition; hence, the result has $n_r/2$ tuples.

   If the actual value used in the comparison $(v)$ is available at the time of cost estimation, a more accurate estimate can be made. The lowest and highest values $(min(A, r)$ and $max(A, r))$ for the attribute can be stored in the catalog. Assuming that values are uniformly distributed, we can estimate the number of records that will satisfy the condition $A \le v$ as 0 if $v < min(A, r)$, as $n_r$ if $v \ge max(A, r)$, and $n_r \cdot \frac{v - min(A,r)}{max(A,r) - min(A,r)}$ otherwise.

   We can implement selections involving comparisons either using a linear or binary search, or using indices in one of the following ways:

- **A6** (*primary index, comparison*). A primary ordered index (for example, a primary $B^+$-tree index) can be used when the selection condition is a comparison. For comparison conditions of the form $A > v$ or $A \ge v$, the primary index can be used to direct the retrieval of tuples, as follows. For $A \ge v$, we look up the value $v$ in the index to find the first tuple in the file that has a value of $A = v$. A file scan starting from that tuple up to the end of the file returns all tuples that satisfy the condition. For $A > v$, the file scan starts with the first tuple such that $A > v$.

   For comparisons of the form $A < v$ or $A \le v$, an index lookup is not required. For $A < v$, we use a simple file scan starting from the beginning of the file, and continuing up to (but not including) the first tuple with attribute $A = v$. The case of $A \le v$ is similar, except that the scan continues up to (but not including) the first tuple with attribute $A > v$. In either case, the index is not useful.

   We assume that approximately one-half of the records will satisfy one of the conditions. Under this assumption, retrieval using the index has the following cost:

$$E_{A6} = HT_i + \frac{b_r}{2}$$

   If the actual value used in the comparison is available at the time of cost estimation, a more accurate estimate can be made. Let the estimated number of values that satisfy the condition (as described earlier) be $c$. Then,

$$E_{A6} = HT_i + \left\lceil \frac{c}{f_r} \right\rceil$$

- **A7** (*secondary index, comparison*). We can use a secondary ordered index to guide retrieval for comparison conditions involving $<, \le, \ge$, or $>$. The lowest-level index blocks are scanned, either from the smallest value up to $v$ (for $<$ and $\leq$), or from $v$ up to the maximum value (for $>$ and $\geq$). For these comparisons, if we assume that at least one-half of the records satisfy the condition, then one-half of the lowest-level index blocks are accessed and, via the index, one-half of the file records are accessed. Furthermore, a path must be traversed in the index from the root block to the first leaf block to be used. Thus, the cost estimate is the following:

$$E_{A7} = HT_i + \frac{LB_i}{2} + \frac{n_r}{2}.$$

As we can with nonequality comparisons on clustering indices, we can get a more accurate estimate if we know the actual value used in the comparison at the time of cost estimation.

In Tandem's Non-Stop SQL System, $B^+$-trees are used both for primary data storage and as secondary access paths. The primary indices are clustering indices, whereas the secondary ones are not. Rather than pointers to records' physical location, the secondary indices contains keys to search the primary $B^+$-tree. The cost formulae described previously for secondary indices will have to be modified slightly if such indices are used.

Although the preceding algorithms show that indices are helpful in processing selections with comparisons, they are not always so useful. As an illustration, consider the query

$$\sigma_{balance < 1200}(account)$$

Suppose that the statistical information about the relations is the same as that used earlier. If we have no information about the minimum and maximum balances in the *account* relation, we assume that one-half of the tuples satisfy the selection.

If we use the index for *balance*, we estimate the number of block accesses as follows. Let us assume that 20 pointers fit into one node of the $B^+$-tree index for *balance*. Since there are 500 different balance values, and each leaf node of the tree must be at least half-full, the tree has between 25 and 50 leaf nodes. The index for *balance* thus has a depth of 3, and three block accesses are required to read the first index block. In the worst case, there are 50 leaf nodes, one-half of which must be accessed. This accessing leads to 24 more block reads. Finally, for each tuple that we locate in the index, we have to retrieve that tuple from the relation. We estimate that 5000 tuples (one-half of the 10,000 tuples) satisfy the condition. Since the index is nonclustering, in the worst case each of these tuple accesses will require a separate block access. Thus, we get a total of 5027 block accesses.

In contrast, a simple file scan will take only $10000/20 = 500$ block accesses. In this case, it is clearly not wise to use the index, and we should use the file scan instead.

## 12.4.4   Implementation of Complex Selections

So far, we have considered only simple selection conditions of the form $A \ op \ B$, where $op$ is an equality or comparison operation. We now consider more complex selection predicates.

- **Conjunction:** A *conjunctive selection* is a selection of the form

$$\sigma_{\theta_1 \wedge \theta_2 \wedge \ldots \wedge \theta_n}(r)$$

We can estimate the result size of such a selection as follows. For each $\theta_i$, we estimate the size of the selection $\sigma_{\theta_i}(r)$, denoted by $s_i$, as described previously. Thus, the probability that a tuple in the relation satisfies selection condition $\theta_i$ is $s_i/n_r$.

The preceding probability is called the *selectivity* of the selection $\sigma_{\theta_i}(r)$. Assuming that the conditions are *independent* of each other, the probability that a tuple satisfies all the conditions is simply the product of all these probabilities. Thus, we estimate the size of the full selection as

$$n_r * \frac{s_1 * s_2 * \ldots * s_n}{n_r^n}$$

- **Disjunction:** A *disjunctive selection* is a selection of the form

$$\sigma_{\theta_1 \vee \theta_2 \vee \ldots \vee \theta_n}(r)$$

A disjunctive condition is satisfied by the union of all records satisfying the individual, simple conditions $\theta_i$.

As before, let $s_i/n_r$ denote the probability that a tuple satisfies condition $\theta_i$. The probability that the tuple will satisfy the disjunction is then 1 minus the probability that it will satisfy *none* of the conditions, or

$$1 - (1 - \frac{s_1}{n_r}) * (1 - \frac{s_2}{n_r}) * \ldots * (1 - \frac{s_n}{n_r})$$

Multiplying this value by $n_r$ gives us the number of tuples that satisfy the selection.

- **Negation:** The result of a selection $\sigma_{\neg\theta}(r)$ is simply the tuples of $r$ that are not in $\sigma_\theta(r)$. We already know how to estimate the size of $\sigma_\theta(r)$. The size of $\sigma_{\neg\theta}(r)$ is therefore estimated to be

$$size(r) - size(\sigma_\theta(r))$$

We can implement a selection operation involving either a conjunction or a disjunction of simple conditions using one of the following algorithms:

- **A8** (*conjunctive selection using one index*). We first determine whether an access path is available for an attribute in one of the simple conditions. If one is, one of the selection algorithms A2 through A7 can retrieve records satisfying that condition. We complete the operation by testing, in the memory buffer, whether or not each retrieved record satisfies the remaining simple conditions.

To reduce the cost, we select a $\theta_i$ and one of algorithms A1 through A7, such that the combination results in the least cost for $\sigma_{\theta_i}(r)$. Of the remaining conditions, the ones that select the smallest number of records should be tested first. Thereby, records that fail to satisfy the conjunction are eliminated after applying fewer tests on them, thus reducing the CPU cost.

- **A9** (*conjunctive selection using composite index*). An appropriate *composite index* (that is, an index on multiple attributes) may be available for some conjunctive selections. If the selection specifies an equality condition on two or more attributes, and a composite index exists on these combined attribute fields, then the index can be searched directly. The type of index determines which of algorithms *A3*, *A4*, or *A5* will be used.

- **A10** (*conjunctive selection by intersection of identifiers*). Another alternative for implementing conjunctive selection operations involves the use of record pointers or record identifiers. This algorithm requires indices with record pointers, on the fields involved in the individual conditions. Each index is scanned for pointers to tuples that satisfy an individual condition. The intersection of all the retrieved pointers is the set of pointers to tuples that satisfy the conjunctive condition. We then use the pointers to retrieve the actual records. If indices are not available on all the individual conditions, then the retrieved records are tested against the remaining conditions.

- **A11** (*disjunctive selection by union of identifiers*). If access paths are available on all the conditions of a disjunctive selection, each index is scanned for pointers to tuples that satisfy the individual condition. The union of all the retrieved pointers yields the set of pointers to all tuples that satisfy the disjunctive condition. We then use the pointers to retrieve the actual records.

    However, if even one of the conditions does not have an access path, we will have to perform a linear scan of the relation to find tuples that satisfy the condition. Therefore, if there is even one such condition in the disjunct, the most efficient access method is a linear scan, with the disjunctive condition tested on each tuple during the scan.

The implementation of selections with negation conditions is left to you as an exercise (Exercise 12.15). Also left to you as an exercise are conditions that combine conjunctions and disjunctions (Exercise 12.16).

To illustrate the preceding algorithms, we suppose that we have the query

> **select** *account-number*
> **from** *account*
> **where** *branch-name* = "Perryridge" **and** *balance* = 1200

We assume that the statistical information about the *account* relation is the same as that in the earlier example.

If we use the index on *branch-name*, we will have a total of 12 block reads, as discussed in the previous section. If we use the index for *balance*, we estimate the number of block accesses as follows. Since $V(balance, account) = 500$, we expect that $10000/500 = 20$ tuples of the *account* relation will have a balance of $1200. However, since the index for *balance* is nonclustering, we anticipate that one block read will be required for each tuple. Thus, 20 block reads are required just to read the *account* tuples.

Let us assume that 20 pointers fit into one node of the $B^+$-tree index for *balance*. Since there are 500 different balance values, the tree has between 25 and 50 leaf nodes. So, as was the case for the $B^+$-tree index on *branch-name*, the index for *balance* has a depth of 2, and two block accesses are required to read the necessary index blocks. Therefore, this strategy requires a total of 22 block reads.

Thus, we conclude that it is preferable to use the index for *branch-name*. Observe that, if both indices were nonclustering, we would prefer to use the index on *balance*, since we would expect only 10 tuples to have *balance* = 1200, versus 200 tuples with *branch-name* = "Perryridge". Without the clustering property, our first strategy could require as many as 200 block accesses to read the data, since, in the worst case, each tuple is on a different block. We add these 200 accesses to the 2 index block accesses, for a total of 202 block reads. However, because of the clustering property of the *branch-name* index, it is actually less expensive in this example to use the *branch-name* index.

Another way in which we could use the indices to process our example query is by using intersection of identifiers. We use the index for *balance* to retrieve pointers to records with *balance* = 1200, rather than retrieving the records themselves. Let $S_1$ denote this set of pointers. Similarly, we use the index for *branch-name* to retrieve pointers to records with *branch-name* = "Perryridge". Let $S_2$ denote this set of pointers. Then, $S_1 \cap S_2$ is a set of pointers to records with *branch-name* = "Perryridge" and *balance* = 1200.

This technique requires both indices to be accessed. Both indices have a height of 2, and, for each index, the number of pointers retrieved, estimated earlier as 20 and 200, will fit into a single leaf page. Thus, we read a total of four index blocks to retrieve the two sets of pointers. The intersection of the two sets of pointers can be computed with no further disk I/O. We estimate the number of blocks that must be read from the *account* file by estimating the number of pointers in $S_1 \cap S_2$.

Since $V(branch-name, account) = 50$ and $V(balance, account) = 500$, we estimate that one tuple in $50 * 500$ or one in $25,000$ has both *branch-name* = "Perryridge" and *balance* = 1200. This estimate is based on an assumption of uniform distribution (which we made earlier), and on an added assumption that the distribution of branch names and balances are independent. Based on these assumptions, out of $10,000$ tuples in *account*, we conservatively estimate that $S_1 \cap S_2$ will contain one pointer. Thus, only one block of *account* needs to be read. The total estimated cost of this strategy is five block reads.

## 12.5  Sorting

Sorting of data plays an important role in database systems for two reasons. First, SQL queries can specify that the output be sorted. Second, and equally important for query processing, several of the relational operations, such as joins, can be implemented efficiently if the input relations are first sorted. Thus, we discuss sorting prior to discussing the join operation in Section 12.6.

We can accomplish sorting by building an index on the sort key, and then using that index to read the relation in sorted order. However, such a process orders the relation only *logically*, through an index, rather than *physically*. Hence, the reading of tuples in the sorted order may lead to a disk access for each tuple. For this reason, it may be desirable to order the tuples physically.

The problem of sorting has been studied extensively, both for the case where the relation fits entirely in main memory, and for the case where the relation is bigger than memory. In the first case, standard sorting techniques such as quicksort can be used. Here, we discuss how to handle the second case.

Sorting of relations that do not fit in memory is called *external sorting*. The most commonly used technique for external sorting is the *external sort–merge* algorithm. We describe the external sort–merge algorithm next. Let $M$ denote the number of page frames in the main-memory buffer (the number of disk blocks whose contents can be buffered in main memory).

1. In the first stage, a number of sorted *runs* are created.

> $i = 0$;
> **repeat**
> > read $M$ blocks of the relation, or the rest of the relation,
> > > whichever is smaller;
> > sort the in-memory part of the relation;
> > write the sorted data to run file $R_i$;
> > $i = i + 1$;
> **until** the end of the relation

2. In the second stage, the runs are *merged*. Suppose, for now, that the total number of runs, $N$, is less than $M$, so that we can allocate one page frame to each run and have space left to hold one page of output. The merge stage operates as follows:

> read one block of each of the $N$ files $R_i$ into a buffer page in memory;
> **repeat**
> > choose the first tuple (in sort order) among all buffer pages;
> > write the tuple to the output, and delete it from the buffer page;
> > **if** the buffer page of any run $R_i$ is empty **and not** end-of-file($R_i$)
> > > **then** read the next block of $R_i$ into the buffer page;
> > **until** all buffer pages are empty

The output of the merge stage is the sorted relation. The output file is buffered to reduce the number of disk write operations. The preceding merge operation is a generalization of the two-way merge used by the standard in-memory sort–merge algorithm; it merges $N$ runs, so it is called an *n-way merge*.

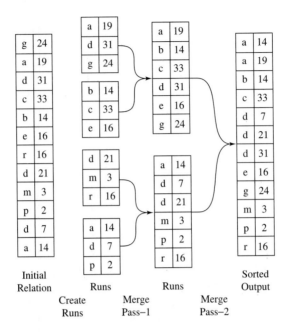

Figure 12.3     External sorting using sort–merge.

In general, if the relation is much larger than memory, there may be $M$ or more runs generated in the first stage, and it is not possible to allocate a page frame for each run during the merge stage. In this case, the merge operation is done in multiple passes. Since there is enough memory for $M - 1$ input buffer pages, each merge can take $M - 1$ runs as input.

The initial *pass* functions as follows. The first $M - 1$ runs are merged (as described previously) to get a single run for the next pass. Then, the next $M - 1$ runs are similarly merged, and so on, until all the initial runs have been processed. At this point, the number of runs has been reduced by a factor of $M - 1$. If this reduced number of runs is still greater than or equal to $M$, another pass is made, with the runs created by the first pass as input. Each pass reduces the number of runs by a factor of $M - 1$. These passes are repeated as many times as required, until the number of runs is less than $M$; a final pass then generates the sorted output.

Figure 12.3 illustrates the steps of the external sort–merge of an example relation. For illustration purposes, we assume that only one tuple fits in a block ($f_r = 1$), and we assume that memory holds at most three page frames. During the merge stage, two page frames are used for input and one for output.

Let us compute how many block transfers are required for the external sort merge. In the first stage, every block of the relation is read and is written out again, giving a total of $2b_r$ disk accesses. The initial number of runs is $\lceil b_r/M \rceil$. Since the number of runs is decreased by a factor of $M - 1$ in each merge pass, the total number of merge passes required is given by $\lceil \log_{M-1}(b_r/M) \rceil$. Each of these passes reads every block of the relation once and writes it out once, with two exceptions. First, the final pass can produce the sorted output without writing its result to disk. Second, there may be runs that are not read in or written out during a pass—for example, if there are $M$ runs to be merged in a pass, $M-1$ are read in and merged, and one run is not accessed during the pass. Ignoring the (relatively small) savings due to the latter effect, the total number of disk accesses for external sorting of the relation is

$$b_r(2\lceil \log_{M-1}(b_r/M)\rceil + 1)$$

Applying this equation to the example in Figure 12.3, we get a total of $12*(4+1) = 60$ block transfers, as you can verify from the figure. Note that this value does not include the cost of writing out the final result.

## 12.6   Join Operation

In this section, we first show how to estimate the size of the result of a join. We then study several algorithms for computing the join of relations, and analyze their respective costs. We use the word *equi-join* to refer to a join of the form $r \bowtie_{r.A=s.B} s$, where $A$ and $B$ are attributes or sets of attributes of relations $r$ and $s$ respectively.

We use as a running example the expression

$$depositor \bowtie customer$$

We assume the following catalog information about the two relations:

- $n_{customer} = 10,000$.
- $f_{customer} = 25$, which implies that $b_{customer} = 10000/25 = 400$.
- $n_{depositor} = 5000$.
- $f_{depositor} = 50$, which implies that $b_{depositor} = 5000/50 = 100$.
- $V(\text{customer-name}, depositor) = 2500$, which implies that, on average, each customer has two accounts.

We also assume that *customer-name* in *depositor* is a foreign key on *customer*.

### 12.6.1   Estimation of the Size of Joins

The Cartesian product $r \times s$ contains $n_r * n_s$ tuples. Each tuple of $r \times s$ occupies $s_r + s_s$ bytes, from which we can calculate the size of the Cartesian product.

Estimation of the size of a natural join is somewhat more complicated than is estimation of the size of a selection or of a Cartesian product. Let $r(R)$ and $s(S)$ be relations.

- If $R \cap S = \emptyset$—that is, the relations have no attribute in common—then $r \bowtie s$ is the same as $r \times s$, and we can use our estimation technique for Cartesian products.

- If $R \cap S$ is a key for $R$, then we know that a tuple of $s$ will join with at most one tuple from $r$. Therefore, the number of tuples in $r \bowtie s$ is no greater than the number of tuples in $s$. If $R \cap S$ forms a foreign key of $S$, referencing $R$, the number of tuples in $r \bowtie s$ is exactly the same as the number of tuples in $s$. The case where $R \cap S$ is a key for $S$ is symmetric to the case just described.

     In our example of *depositor* $\bowtie$ *customer*, *customer-name* in *depositor* is a foreign key referencing *customer*; hence, the size of the result is exactly $n_{depositor}$, which is 5000.

- The most difficult case to consider is when $R \cap S$ is a key for neither $R$ nor $S$. In this case, we assume, as we did for selections, that each value appears with equal probability. Consider a tuple $t$ of $r$, and assume $R \cap S = \{A\}$. We estimate that tuple $t$ produces

$$\frac{n_s}{V(A, s)}$$

tuples in $r \bowtie s$, since this number is the average number of tuples in $s$ with a given value for the attributes $A$. Considering all the tuples in $r$, we estimate that there are

$$\frac{n_r * n_s}{V(A, s)}$$

tuples in $r \bowtie s$. Observe that, if we reverse the roles of $r$ and $s$ in the preceding estimate, we obtain an estimate of

$$\frac{n_r * n_s}{V(A, r)}$$

tuples in $r \bowtie s$. These two estimates differ if $V(A, r) \neq V(A, s)$. If this situation occurs, there are likely to be dangling tuples that do not participate in the join. Thus, the lower of the two estimates is probably the more accurate one.

     The preceding estimate of join size may be too high if the $V(A, r)$ values for attribute $A$ in $r$ have few values in common with the $V(A, s)$ values for attribute $A$ in $s$. However, this situation is unlikely to happen in the real world, since dangling tuples either do not exist, or constitute only a small fraction of the tuples, in most real-world relations. More important, the preceding estimate depends on the assumption that each value appears with equal probability. More sophisticated techniques for size estimation have to be used if this assumption does not hold.

     Let us now compute the size estimates for *depositor* $\bowtie$ *customer* without using information about foreign keys. Since $V(customer\text{-}name, depositor) = 2500$, and $V(customer\text{-}name, customer) = 10000$, the two estimates we get are $5000 * 10000/2500 = 20,000$ and $5000 * 10000/10000 = 5000$, and we choose the lower one. In this case, the lower of these estimates is the same as that which we computed earlier using information about foreign keys.

## 12.6.2  Nested-Loop Join

The procedure in Figure 12.4 shows a simple algorithm to compute the theta join, $r \bowtie_{\theta} s$, of two relations $r$ and $s$. This algorithm is called the *nested-loop join* algorithm, since it basically consists of a pair of nested **for** loops. As shown in the procedure, $r$ is called the *outer* relation and $s$ the *inner* relation of the join, since the loop for $r$ encloses the loop for $s$. The algorithm uses the notation $t_r \cdot t_s$, where $t_r$ and $t_s$ are tuples; $t_r \cdot t_s$ denotes the tuple constructed by concatenating the attribute values of tuples $t_r$ and $t_s$.

Like the linear file-scan algorithm for selection, the nested-loop join algorithm requires no indices, and it can be used regardless of what the join condition is. Extending the algorithm to compute the natural join is straightforward, since the natural join can be expressed as a theta join followed by elimination of repeated attributes by a projection. The only change required is an extra step of deleting repeated attributes from the tuple $t_r \cdot t_s$, before adding it to the result.

The nested-loop join algorithm is expensive, since it examines every pair of tuples in the two relations. Consider the cost of the nested-loop join algorithm. The number of pairs of tuples to be considered is $n_r * n_s$. For each record in $r$, we have to perform a complete scan on $s$. In the worst case, the buffer can hold only one block of each relation, and a total of $n_r * b_s + b_r$ block accesses will be required. In the best case, there is enough space for both relations to fit in memory, so each block will have to be read only once; hence, only $b_r + b_s$ block accesses will be required.

If the smaller relation fits entirely in main memory, it is beneficial to use that relation as the inner relation. This format speeds query processing significantly, since it is necessary to read the inner-loop relation only once. Therefore, if $s$ is small enough to fit in main memory, our strategy requires only a total $b_r + b_s$ accesses—the same cost as that for the case where both relations fit in memory.

Now consider the natural join of *depositor* and *customer*. Let us assume, for now, that we have no indices whatsoever on either relation, and that we are not willing to create any index. We can use the nested loops to compute the join; let us assume that *depositor* is the outer relation, and *customer* is the inner relation, in the join. We will have to examine $5000 * 10000 = 50 * 10^6$ pairs of tuples. In the worst case, the number of block accesses is $5000 * 400 + 100 = 2,000,100$. In the best-case scenario, however, we can read both relations only once, and perform the computation. This computation requires at most $100 + 400 = 500$ block accesses— a significant improvement over the worst-case scenario. If we had used *customer*

> **for each** tuple $t_r$ **in** $r$ **do begin**
>     **for each** tuple $t_s$ **in** $s$ **do begin**
>         test pair $(t_r, t_s)$ to see if they satisfy the join condition $\theta$
>         if they do, add $t_r \cdot t_s$ to the result.
>     **end**
> **end**

Figure 12.4   Nested-loop join.

```
for each block B_r of r do begin
    for each block B_s of s do begin
        for each tuple t_r in B_r do begin
            for each tuple t_s in B_s do begin
                test pair (t_r, t_s) to see if they satisfy the join condition
                if they do, add t_r · t_s to the result.
            end
        end
    end
end
```

Figure 12.5    Block nested-loop join.

as the relation for the outer loop and *depositor* for the inner loop, the worst-case cost of our final strategy would have been lower: $10000 * 100 + 400 = 1,000,400$.

### 12.6.3    Block Nested-Loop Join

If the buffer is too small to hold both relations entirely in memory, we can still obtain a major saving in block accesses if we process the relations on a per-block basis, rather than on a per-tuple basis. The procedure of Figure 12.5 shows a variant of the nested-loop join, where every block of the inner relation is paired with every block of the outer relation. Within each pair of blocks, every tuple in one block is paired with every tuple in the other block, to generate all pairs of tuples. As before, all pairs of tuples that satisfy the join condition are added to the result.

The primary difference in cost between the block nested-loop join and the basic nested-loop join is that, in the worst case, each block in the inner relation $s$ is read only once for each *block* in the outer relation, instead of once for each *tuple* in the outer relation. Thus, in the worst case, there will be a total of $b_r * b_s + b_r$ block accesses. Clearly, it is most efficient to use the smaller relation as the outer relation. In the best case, there will be $b_r + b_s$ block accesses.

Let us return to our example of computing *depositor* ⋈ *customer*, using the block nested-loop join algorithm. In the worst case we have to read each block of *customer* once for each block of *depositor*. Thus, in the worst case, a total of $100 * 400 + 100 = 40,100$ block accesses are required. This cost is a significant improvement over the $5000 * 400 + 100 = 2,000,100$ block accesses needed in the worst case for the basic nested-loop join. The number of block accesses in the best case remains the same—namely, $100 + 400 = 500$.

The performance of the nested-loop and block nested-loop procedures can be further improved:

- If the join attributes in a natural join or an equi-join form a key on the inner relation, then the inner loop can terminate as soon as the first match is found.
- In the block nested-loop algorithm, instead of using disk blocks as the blocking unit for the outer relation, we can use the biggest size that can fit in memory, while leaving enough space for the buffers of the inner relation and

the output. This change reduces the number of times that the inner relation is scanned.

- We can scan the inner loop alternately forward and backward. This scanning method orders the requests for disk blocks such that the data remaining in the buffer from the previous scan can be reused, thus reducing the number of disk accesses needed.
- If an index is available on the inner loop's join attribute, more efficient index lookups can replace file scans. This optimization is described in Section 12.6.4.

## 12.6.4 Indexed Nested-Loop Join

In a nested-loop join (Figure 12.4), if an index (either permanent or temporary) is available on the inner loop's join attribute, index lookups can replace file scans. For each tuple $t_r$ in the outer relation $r$, the index is used to look up tuples in $s$ that will satisfy the join condition with tuple $t_r$.

The preceding join method is called an *indexed nested-loop join*; it can be used with existing indices, as well as with temporary indices created for the sole purpose of evaluating the join.

Looking up tuples in $s$ that will satisfy the join conditions with a given tuple $t_r$ is essentially a selection on $s$. For example, consider *depositor* $\bowtie$ *customer*. Suppose that we have a *depositor* tuple with *customer-name* "John". Then, the relevant tuples in $s$ are those that satisfy the selection "*customer-name* $=$ John".

The cost of index nested-loops join can be computed as follows. For each tuple in the outer relation $r$, a lookup is performed on the index for $s$, and the relevant tuples are retrieved. In the worst case, there is space in the buffer for only one page of $r$ and one page of the index. Then, $b_r$ disk accesses are needed to read relation $r$, and, for each tuple in $r$, we perform an index lookup on $s$. Then, the cost of the join can be computed as $b_r + n_r * c$, where $c$ is the cost of a single selection on $s$ using the join condition. We have already seen how to compute the cost of a single selection on a relation using indices of various types, which computation gives us the value of $c$. The cost formula indicates that, if indices are available on both relations $r$ and $s$, it is generally most efficient to use the one with fewer tuples as the outer relation.

For example, consider an index nested-loop join of *depositor* $\bowtie$ *customer*, with *depositor* as the outer relation. Suppose also that *customer* has a primary B$^+$-tree index on the join attribute *customer-name*, which contains 20 entries in each index node. Since *customer* has 10,000 tuples, the height of the tree is 4, and one more access is needed to find the actual data. Since $n_{depositor}$ is 5000, the total cost is $100 + 5000 * 5 = 25, 100$ disk accesses. This cost is lower than the 40, 100 accesses needed for a block nested-loop join.

## 12.6.5 Merge–Join

The *merge–join* algorithm (also called the *sort–merge-join* algorithm) can be used to compute natural joins and equi-joins. Let $r(R)$ and $s(S)$ be the relations whose natural join is to be computed, and let $R \cap S$ denote their common attributes.

$pr$ := address of first tuple of $r$;
$ps$ := address of first tuple of $s$;
**while** ($ps \neq$ null **and** $pr \neq$ null) **do**
   **begin**
      $t_s$ := tuple to which $ps$ points;
      $S_s := \{t_s\}$;
      set $ps$ to point to next tuple of $s$;
      $done := false$;
      **while** (**not** $done$ **and** $ps \neq$ null) **do**
         **begin**
            $t_s'$ := tuple to which $ps$ points;
            **if** ($t_s'[JoinAttrs] = t_s[JoinAttrs]$)
               **then begin**
                  $S_s := S_s \cup \{t_s'\}$;
                  set $ps$ to point to next tuple of s;
               **end**
            **else** $done := true$;
         **end**
      $t_r$ := tuple to which $pr$ points;
      **while** ($pr \neq$ null **and** $t_r[JoinAttrs] < t_s[JoinAttrs]$) **do**
         **begin**
            set $pr$ to point to next tuple of $r$;
            $t_r$ := tuple to which $pr$ points;
         **end**
      **while** ($pr \neq$ null **and** $t_r[JoinAttrs] = t_s[JoinAttrs]$) **do**
         **begin**
            **for each** $t_s$ **in** $S_s$ **do**
               **begin**
                  add $t_s \bowtie t_r$ to result ;
               **end**
            set $pr$ to point to next tuple of $r$;
            $t_r$ := tuple to which $pr$ points;
         **end**
   **end**.

Figure 12.6    Merge-join.

Suppose that both relations are sorted on the attributes $R \cap S$. Then, their join can be computed by a process much like the merge stage in the merge–sort algorithm.

The merge–join algorithm is shown in Figure 12.6. In the algorithm, *Join-Attrs* refers to the attributes in $R \cap S$, and $t_r \bowtie t_s$, where $t_r$ and $t_s$ are tuples that have the same values for *JoinAttrs*, denotes the concatenation of the attributes of the tuples, followed by projecting out repeated attributes. The merge–join algorithm associates one pointer with each relation. These pointers point initially to the first tuple of the respective relations. As the algorithm proceeds, the pointers move through the relation. A group of tuples of one relation with the same value

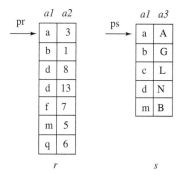

Figure 12.7    Sorted relations for merge–join.

on the join attributes is read into $S_s$. The algorithm shown in Figure 12.6 *requires* that every set of tuples $S_s$ fit in main memory; we shall look at extensions of the algorithm to avoid this assumption later in this section. Then, the corresponding tuples (if any) of the other relation are read in, and are processed as they are read.

Figure 12.7 shows two relations that are sorted on their join attribute $a1$. It is instructive to go through the steps of the merge–join algorithm on the relations shown in the figure.

Since the relations are in sorted order, tuples with the same value on the join attributes are in consecutive order. Thereby, each tuple in the sorted order needs to be read only once, and, as a result, each block is also read only once. Since only a single pass is made through both files, the merge–join method is efficient; the number of block accesses is equal to the sum of the number of blocks in both files, $b_r + b_s$.

If either of the input relations $r$ and $s$ is not sorted on the join attributes, they can be sorted first, and then the merge–join algorithm can be used. The merge–join algorithm can also be easily extended from natural joins to the more general case of equi-joins.

Suppose the merge–join scheme is applied to our example of *depositor* ⋈ *customer*. The join attribute here is *customer-name*. Suppose that the relations are already sorted on the join attribute *customer-name*. In this case, the merge–join takes a total of $400 + 100 = 500$ block accesses. Suppose the relations are not sorted, and the memory size is the worst case of three blocks. Sorting *customer* takes $400*(2\lceil log_2(400/3)\rceil + 1)$, or 6800, block transfers, with 400 more transfers to write out the result. Similarly, sorting *depositor* takes $100*(2\lceil log_2(100/3)\rceil + 1)$, or 1300, transfers, with 100 more transfers to write it out. Thus, the total cost is 9100 block transfers if the relations are not sorted.

As mentioned earlier, the merge–join algorithm of Figure 12.6 requires that the set $S_s$ of all tuples with the same value for the join attributes must fit in main memory. This requirement can usually be met, even if the relation $s$ is large. If it cannot be met, a block nested-loop join must be performed between $S_s$ and the tuples in $r$ with the same values for the join attributes. The overall cost of the merge–join increases as a result.

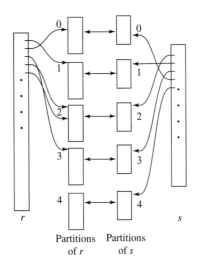

Figure 12.8    Hash partitioning of relations.

It is also possible to perform a variation of the merge–join operation on unsorted tuples, if secondary indices exist on both join attributes. The records are scanned through the indices, resulting in their being retrieved in sorted order. This variation presents a significant drawback, however, since records may be scattered throughout the file blocks. Hence, each tuple access could involve accessing a disk block, and that is costly.

To avoid this cost, we can use a hybrid merge–join technique, which combines indices with merge–join. Suppose that one of the relations is sorted; the other is unsorted, but has a secondary $B^+$-tree index on the join attributes. The *hybrid merge–join algorithm* merges the sorted relation with the leaf entries of the secondary $B^+$-tree index. The result file contains tuples from the sorted relation and addresses for tuples of the unsorted relation. The result file is then sorted on the addresses of tuples of the unsorted relation, allowing efficient retrieval of the corresponding tuples, in physical storage order, to complete the join. Extensions of the technique to handle two unsorted relations are left as an exercise for you.

### 12.6.6   Hash–Join

Like the merge–join algorithm, the hash–join algorithm can be used to implement natural joins and equi-joins. In the hash–join algorithm, a hash function $h$ is used to partition tuples of both relations. The basic idea is to partition the tuples of each of the relations into sets that have the same hash value on the join attributes.

We assume that

- $h$ is a hash function mapping *JoinAttrs* values to $\{0, 1, \dots, max\}$, where *JoinAttrs* denotes the common attributes of $r$ and $s$ used in the natural join.
- $H_{r_0}, H_{r_1}, \dots, H_{r_{max}}$ denote partitions of $r$ tuples, each initially empty. Each tuple $t_r \in r$ is put in partition $H_{r_i}$, where $i = h(t_r[\textit{JoinAttrs}])$.

```
/* Partition s */
for each tuple t_s in s do begin
    i := h(t_s[JoinAttrs]);
    H_{s_i} := H_{s_i} ∪ {t_s};
end
/* Partition r */
for each tuple t_r in r do begin
    i := h(t_r[JoinAttrs]);
    H_{r_i} := H_{r_i} ∪ {t_r};
end
/* Perform join on each partition */
for i := 0 to max do begin
    read H_{s_i} and build an in-memory hash index on it
    for each tuple t_r in H_{r_i} do begin
        probe the hash index on H_{s_i} to locate all tuples t_s
            such that t_s[JoinAttrs] = t_r[JoinAttrs]
        for each matching tuple t_s in H_{s_i} do begin
            add t_r ⋈ t_s to the result
        end
    end
end
```

**Figure 12.9**    Hash–join.

- $H_{s_0}$, $H_{s_1}$, ..., $H_{s_{max}}$ denote partitions of $s$ tuples, each initially empty. Each tuple $t_s \in s$ is put in partition $H_{s_i}$, where $i = h(t_s[JoinAttrs])$.

The hash function $h$ should have the "goodness" properties of randomness and uniformity that we discussed in Chapter 11. The partitioning of the relations is shown pictorially in Figure 12.8.

The idea behind the hash-join algorithm is as follows. Suppose that an $r$ tuple and an $s$ tuple satisfy the join condition; then, they will have the same value for the join attributes. If that value is hashed to some value $i$, the $r$ tuple has to be in $H_{r_i}$ and the $s$ tuple in $H_{s_i}$. Therefore, $r$ tuples in $H_{r_i}$ need only to be compared with $s$ tuples in $H_{s_i}$; they do not need to be compared with $s$ tuples in any other partition.

For example, if $d$ is a tuple in *depositor*, $c$ a tuple in *customer*, and $h$ a hash function on the *customer-name* attributes of the tuples, then $d$ and $c$ must be tested only if $h(c) = h(d)$. If $h(c) \neq h(d)$, then $c$ and $d$ must have different values for *customer-name*. However, if $h(c) = h(d)$, we must test $c$ and $d$ to see whether the values in their join attributes are the same, since it is possible that $c$ and $d$ have different *customer-name*s that have the same hash value.

Figure 12.9 shows the details of the hash–join algorithm to compute the natural join of relations $r$ and $s$. As in the merge-join algorithm, $t_r \bowtie t_s$ denotes the concatenation of the attributes of tuples $t_r$ and $t_s$, followed by projecting out repeated attributes. After the partitioning of the relations, the rest of the hash–join code performs a separate indexed nested-loop join on each of the partition pairs $i$, for $i = 0 \ldots max$. To do so, it first *builds* a hash index on each $H_{s_i}$, and then *probes* (that is, looks up $H_{s_i}$) with tuples from $H_{r_i}$. The relation $s$ is the *build input*, and $r$ is the *probe input*.

The hash index on $H_{s_i}$ is built in memory, so there is no need to access the disk to retrieve the tuples. The hash function used to build this hash index is different from the hash function $h$ used earlier, but is still applied to only the join attributes. In the course of the indexed nested-loop join, the system uses this hash index to retrieve records that will match records in the probe input.

The build and probe phases require only a single pass through both the build and probe inputs. It is straightforward to extend the hash–join algorithm to compute general equi-joins.

The value *max* must be chosen to be large enough such that, for each $i$, the tuples in the partition $H_{s_i}$ of the build relation, along with the hash index on the partition, will fit in memory. It is not necessary for the partitions of the probe relation to fit in memory. Clearly, it is best to use the smaller input relation as the build relation. If the size of the build relation is $b_s$ blocks, then, for each of the *max* partitions to be of size less than or equal to $M$, *max* must be at least $\lceil b_s / M \rceil$. More precisely stated, we have to account for the extra space occupied by the hash index on the partition as well, so *max* should be correspondingly larger. For simplicity, we sometimes ignore the space requirement of the hash index in our analysis.

### 12.6.6.1   Recursive Partitioning

If the value of *max* is greater than or equal to the number of page frames of memory, partitioning of the relations cannot be done in one pass, since there will not be enough buffer pages. Instead, partitioning has to be done by repeated passes. In one pass, the input can be split into at most as many partitions as there are page frames available for use as output buffers. Each bucket generated by one pass is separately read in and partitioned again in the next pass, to create smaller partitions. The hash function used in a pass is, of course, different from the one used in the previous pass. This splitting of the input is repeated until each partition of the build input fits in memory. Such partitioning is called *recursive partitioning*.

A relation does not need recursive partitioning if $M > max + 1$, or equivalently $M > (b_s / M) + 1$, which simplifies (approximately) to $M > \sqrt{b_s}$. For example, consider a memory size of 12 megabytes, divided into 4-kilobyte blocks; it would contain a total of 3000 blocks. We can use a memory of this size to partition relations of size 9 million blocks, which is 36 gigabytes. Similarly, a relation of size 1 gigabyte requires $\sqrt{250,000}$ blocks, or about 2 megabytes.

### 12.6.6.2   Handling of Overflows

*Hash-table overflow* occurs in partition $i$ of the build relation $s$ if the hash index on $H_{s_i}$ is larger than main memory. Hash-table overflow can occur if there are many tuples in the build relation with the same values for the join attributes, or if the hash function does not have the property of randomness and uniformity. In either case, some of the partitions will have more tuples than the average, whereas others will have fewer; partitioning is then said to be *skewed*.

We can handle a small amount of skew by increasing the number of partitions such that the expected size of each partition (including the hash index on the partition) is somewhat less than the size of memory. The number of partitions is therefore increased by a small value called the *fudge factor*, which is usually about 20 percent of the number of hash partitions computed as described earlier.

Even if we are conservative on the sizes of the partitions, by using a fudge factor, overflows can still occur. Hash-table overflows can be handled by either *resolution* or *avoidance*. Overflow resolution is performed during the build phase, if a hash-index overflow is detected. Overflow resolution is done as follows. If $H_{s_i}$, for any $i$, is found to be too large, we further partition it into smaller partitions using a different hash function. Similarly, we also partition $H_{r_i}$ using the new hash function, and only tuples in the matching partitions need to be joined.

In contrast, overflow avoidance performs the partitioning carefully, such that overflows never occur during the build phase. We implement overflow avoidance by partitioning the build relation $s$ initially into many small partitions, and then combining some partitions such that each combined partition fits in memory. The probe relation $r$ must be partitioned in the same way as the combined partitions on $s$, but the sizes of $H_{r_i}$ do not matter.

If a large number of tuples in $s$ have the same value for the join attributes, the resolution and avoidance techniques may fail on some partitions. In that case, instead of creating an in-memory hash index and using a nested-loop join to join the partitions, we can use other join techniques, such as block nested-loop join, on those partitions.

### 12.6.6.3 Cost of Hash–Join

We now consider the cost of a hash–join. Our analysis assumes that there is no hash-table overflow. First, consider the case where recursive partitioning is not required. The partitioning of the two relations $r$ and $s$ calls for a complete reading of both relations, and a subsequent writing back of them. This operation requires $2(b_r + b_s)$ block accesses. The build and probe phases read each of the partitions once, calling for a further $b_r + b_s$ accesses. The number of blocks occupied by partitions could be slightly more than $b_r + b_s$, due to partially filled blocks. Accessing such partially filled blocks can add an overhead of at most $2 * max$ for each of the relations, since each of the $max$ partitions could have a partially filled block that has to be written and read back. Thus, the cost estimate for a hash–join is

$$3(b_r + b_s) + 4 * max$$

The overhead $4 * max$ is quite small compared to $b_r + b_s$, and can be ignored.

Now consider the case where recursive partitioning is required. Each pass reduces the size of each of the partitions by an expected factor of $M - 1$; this size reduction is repeated until each partition is of size at most $M$ blocks. The expected number of passes required for partitioning $s$ is therefore $\lceil log_{M-1}(b_s) - 1 \rceil$. Since, in each pass, every block of $s$ is read in and written out, the total block transfers for partitioning of $s$ is $2b_s \lceil log_{M-1}(b_s) - 1 \rceil$. The number of passes for partitioning of $r$ is the same as the number of passes for partitioning of $s$, giving the following cost estimate for the join:

$$2(b_r + b_s)\lceil log_{M-1}(b_s) - 1 \rceil + b_r + b_s$$

Consider, for example, the join *customer* $\bowtie$ *depositor*. With a memory size of 20 blocks, *depositor* can be partitioned into five partitions, each of size 20 blocks, which size will fit into memory. Only one pass is required for the partitioning. The relation *customer* is similarly partitioned into five partitions, each of size 80. Ignoring the cost of writing partially filled blocks, the cost is $3(100 + 400) = 1500$ block transfers.

The hash–join can be improved if the main memory size is large. When the entire build input can be kept in main memory, *max* can be set to 0; then, the hash–join algorithm executes quickly, without partitioning the relations into temporary files, regardless of the probe input's size. The cost estimate goes down to $b_r + b_s$.

### 12.6.6.4  Hybrid Hash–Join

The *hybrid hash–join* algorithm performs another optimization; it is useful when memory sizes are relatively large, but not all the build relation fits in memory. The partitioning phase of the hash–join algorithm needs one block of memory as a buffer for each partition that is created, and one block of memory as an input buffer. Hence, a total of $max + 1$ blocks of memory are needed for the partitioning the two relations. If memory is larger than $max + 1$, we can use the rest of memory ($M - max - 1$ blocks) to buffer the first partition of the build input (that is, $H_{s_0}$), so that it will not need to be written out and read back in. Further, the hash function is designed such that the hash index on $H_{s_0}$ fits in $M - max - 1$ blocks, so that, at the end of partitioning of $s$, $H_{s_0}$ is completely in memory and a hash index can be built on $H_{s_0}$.

When $r$ is partitioned, tuples in $H_{r_0}$ are again not written to disk; instead, as they are generated, the system uses them to probe the memory-resident hash index on $H_{s_0}$, and to generate output tuples of the join. After being used for probing, the tuples can be discarded, so the partition $H_{r_0}$ does not occupy any memory space. Thus, a write and a read access have been saved for each block of both $H_{r_0}$ and $H_{s_0}$. Tuples in the other partitions are written out as usual, and are joined later. The savings of hybrid hash–join can be significant if the build input is only slightly bigger than memory.

If the size of the build relation is $b_s$, *max* is approximately equal to $b_s/M$. Thus, hybrid hash–join is most useful if $M \gg b_s/M$, or $M \gg \sqrt{b_s}$, where the notation $\gg$ denotes *much larger than*. For example, suppose the block size is 4 kilobytes, and the build relation is of size 1 gigabyte. Then, the hybrid hash–join algorithm is useful if the size of memory is significantly more than 2 megabytes; memory sizes of 50 to 100 megabytes or more are common on computers today.

Consider the join *customer* $\bowtie$ *depositor* again. With a memory size of 25 blocks, *depositor* can be partitioned into five partitions, each of size 20 blocks, and the first of the partitions of the build relation can be kept in memory. It occupies 20 blocks of memory; one block is used for input, and one block each is used for buffering the other four partitions. The relation *customer* is similarly partitioned into five partitions each of size 80, the first of which is used right away for probing, instead of being written out and read back in. Ignoring the cost of writing partially filled blocks, the cost is $3(80 + 320) + 20 + 80 = 1300$ block transfers, instead of 1500 block transfers without the hybrid hashing optimization.

## 12.6.7   Complex Joins

Nested-loop and block nested-loop joins can be used regardless of the join conditions. The other join techniques are more efficient than are the nested-loop join and its variants, but can handle only simple join conditions, such as natural joins or equi-joins. We can implement joins with complex join conditions, such as conjunctions and disjunctions, using the efficient join techniques, by applying the techniques developed in Section 12.4.4 for handling complex selections.

Consider the following join with a conjunctive condition:

$$r \bowtie_{\theta_1 \wedge \theta_2 \wedge \ldots \wedge \theta_n} s$$

One or more of the join techniques described earlier may be applicable for joins on the individual conditions $r \bowtie_{\theta_1} s$, $r \bowtie_{\theta_2} s$, $r \bowtie_{\theta_3} s$, and so on. We can compute the overall join by first computing the result of one of these simpler joins $r \bowtie_{\theta_i} s$; each pair of tuples in the intermediate result is composed of one tuple from $r$ and one from $s$. The result of the complete join consists of those tuples in the intermediate result that satisfy the remaining conditions

$$\theta_1 \wedge \ldots \wedge \theta_{i-1} \wedge \theta_{i+1} \wedge \ldots \wedge \theta_n$$

These conditions can be tested as tuples in $r \bowtie_{\theta_i} s$ are being generated.

A join whose condition is disjunctive can be computed as follows. Consider

$$r \bowtie_{\theta_1 \vee \theta_2 \vee \ldots \vee \theta_n} s$$

The join can be computed as the union of the records in individual joins $r \bowtie_{\theta_i} s$:

$$(r \bowtie_{\theta_1} s) \cup (r \bowtie_{\theta_2} s) \cup \ldots \cup (r \bowtie_{\theta_n} s)$$

Algorithms for computing the union of relations are described in Section 12.7.

Let us now consider a join involving three relations:

$$account \bowtie depositor \bowtie customer$$

Not only do we have a choice of strategy for join processing; we also have a choice of which join to compute first. There are many possible strategies to consider. We describe a few here and leave another as an exercise for you (Exercise 12.4).

- **Strategy 1**. Compute the join *depositor* ⋈ *customer* using one of the techniques that we presented. Using this intermediate result, compute

$$account \bowtie (depositor \bowtie customer)$$

- **Strategy 2**. Proceed as in strategy 1, but compute *account* ⋈ *depositor* first, and then join the result with *customer*. The joins can be computed in other orders as well.

- **Strategy 3**. Instead of performing two joins, perform the pair of joins at once. The technique involves first building two indices:
  - On *account* for *account-number*
  - On *customer* for *customer-name*

  Next, consider each tuple *t* in *depositor*. For each *t*, look up the corresponding tuples in *customer* and the corresponding tuples in *account*. Thus, each tuple of *depositor* is examined exactly once.

Strategy 3 represents a form that we have not considered before. It does not correspond directly to a relational-algebra operation. Instead, it combines two operations into one special-purpose operation. With this strategy, it is often possible to perform a join of three relations more efficiently than we can by using two joins of two relations. The relative costs depend on the way in which the relations are stored, the distribution of values within columns, and the presence of indices. Exercise 12.5 provides an opportunity to compute these costs.

## 12.7    Other Operations

Other relational operations and extended relational operations—such as duplicate elimination, projection, set operations, outer join, and aggregation—can be implemented as outlined in Sections 12.7.1 through 12.7.5.

### 12.7.1    Duplicate Elimination

We can implement duplicate elimination easily using sorting. Identical tuples will appear adjacent to each other during sorting, and all but one copy can be removed. With external sort–merge, duplicates found while a run is being created can be removed before the run is written to disk, thereby reducing the number of block transfers. The remaining duplicates can be eliminated during merging, and the final sorted run will have no duplicates. The worst-case cost estimate for duplicate elimination is the same as the worst-case cost estimate for sorting of the relation.

We can also implement duplicate elimination using hashing, in a manner similar to the hash–join algorithm. First, the relation is partitioned based on a hash function on the whole tuple. Then, each partition is read in, and an in-memory hash index is constructed. While the hash index is being constructed, a tuple is inserted only if it is not already present. Otherwise, it is discarded. After all tuples in the partition have been processed, the tuples in the hash index are written to the result. The cost estimate is the same as the cost of processing (partitioning and reading each partition) of the build relation in a hash–join.

Because of the relatively high cost of duplicate elimination, commercial query languages require an explicit request by the user to remove duplicates; otherwise, the duplicates are retained.

## 12.7.2  Projection

We can implement projection easily by performing projection on each tuple, which gives a relation that could have duplicate records, and then removing duplicate records. Duplicate elimination can be done as described in Section 12.7.1. If the attributes in the projection list include a key of the relation, no duplicates will exist; hence, duplicate elimination is not required. Generalized projection (which was discussed in Section 3.5.1) can be implemented in the same way as projection. The size of a projection of the form $\Pi_A(r)$ is estimated as $V(A, r)$, since projection eliminates duplicates.

## 12.7.3  Set Operations

We can implement the *union, intersection*, and *set-difference operations* by first sorting both relations, and then scanning once through each of the sorted relations to produce the result. In $r \cup s$, when a concurrent scan of both relations reveals the same tuple in both files, only one of the tuples is retained. The result of $r \cap s$ will contain only those tuples that appear in both relations. We implement *set difference*, $r - s$, similarly, by retaining tuples in $r$ only if they are absent in $s$.

For all these operations, only one scan of the two input relations is required, so the cost is $b_r + b_s$. If the relations are not sorted initially, the cost of sorting has to be included. Any sort order can be used in evaluation of set operations, provided that both inputs have that same sort order.

Hashing provides another way to implement these set operations. The first step in each case is to partition the two relations using the same hash function, and thereby to create the partitions $H_{r_0}, \ldots, H_{r_{max}}$, and $H_{s_0}, \ldots, H_{s_{max}}$. The following is then done on each partition $i = 0 \ldots max$.

- $r \cup s$
    1. Build an in-memory hash index on $H_{r_i}$.
    2. Add the tuples in $H_{s_i}$ to the hash index only if they are not already present.
    3. Add the tuples in the hash index to the result.
- $r \cap s$
    1. Build an in-memory hash index on $H_{r_i}$.
    2. For each tuple in $H_{s_i}$, probe the hash index, and output the tuple to the result only if it is already present in the hash index.
- $r - s$
    1. Build an in-memory hash index on $H_{r_i}$.
    2. For each tuple in $H_{s_i}$, probe the hash index, and, if the tuple is present in the hash index, delete it from the hash index.
    3. Add the tuples remaining in the hash index to the result.

## 12.7.4    Outer Join

Recall the *outer-join operations*, which were described in Section 3.5.2. For example, the natural left outer join *customer* $⋈$ *depositor* contains the join of *customer* and *depositor*, and, in addition, for each *customer* tuple $t$ that has no matching tuple in *depositor* (that is, where *customer-name* is not in *depositor*), the following tuple $t_1$ is added to the result. For all attributes in the schema of *customer*, tuple $t_1$ has the same values as tuple $t$. The remaining attributes (from the schema of *depositor*) of tuple $t_1$ contain the value null.

We can implement the outer-join operations using one of two strategies. The first strategy is to compute the corresponding join, and then to add further tuples to the join result to get the outer-join result. Consider the left outer-join operation and two relations: $r(R)$ and $s(S)$. To evaluate $r ⟕_\theta s$, we first compute $r ⋈_\theta s$, and save that result as temporary relation $q_1$. Next, we compute $r - \Pi_R(q_1)$, which gives tuples in $r$ that did not participate in the join. We can use any of the algorithms for computing the joins, projection, and set difference described earlier to compute the outer joins. We pad each of these tuples with null values for attributes from $s$, and add it to $q_1$ to get the result of the outer join.

The right outer-join operation $r ⟖_\theta s$ is equivalent to $s ⟕_\theta r$, and can therefore be implemented in a symmetric fashion to the left outer join. We can implement the full outer-join operation $r ⟗_\theta s$ by computing the join $r ⋈ s$, and then adding the extra tuples of both the left and right outer-join operations, as before.

The second strategy for implementing outer joins is to modify the join algorithms. It is easy to extend the nested-loop join algorithms to compute the left outer join: Tuples in the outer relation that do not match any tuple in the inner relation are written to the output after being padded with null values. However, it is hard to extend the nested-loop join to compute the full outer join.

Natural outer joins and outer joins with an equi-join condition can be computed by extensions of the merge–join and hash–join algorithms. Merge–join can be extended to compute the full outer join as follows. When the merge of the two relations is being done, tuples in either relation that did not match any tuple in the other relation can be padded with nulls and written to the output. Similarly, we can extend merge–join to compute the left and right outer joins by writing out nonmatching tuples (padded with nulls) from only one of the relations. Since the relations are sorted, it is easy to detect whether or not a tuple matches any tuples from the other relation. For example, when a merge–join of *customer* and *depositor* is done, the tuples are read in sorted order of *customer-name*, and it is easy to check, for each tuple, whether there is a matching tuple in the other.

The cost estimates for implementing outer joins using the merge–join algorithm are the same as are those for the corresponding join. The only difference lies in size of the result, and therefore in the block transfers for writing it out, which we did not count in our earlier cost estimates.

The extension of the hash–join algorithm to compute outer joins is left for you to do as an exercise (Exercise 12.17).

### 12.7.5    Aggregation

Recall the aggregation operator $\mathcal{G}$, discussed in Section 3.5.3. For example, the operation

$$_{branch\text{-}name}\mathcal{G}_{\mathbf{sum}(balance)}(account)$$

groups *account* tuples by branch, and computes the total balance of all the accounts at each branch.

The aggregation operation can be implemented in a manner similar to duplicate elimination. We use either sorting or hashing, just as we did for duplicate elimination, but based on the grouping attributes (*branch-name* in the preceding example). However, instead of eliminating tuples with the same value for the grouping attribute, we gather them into groups, and apply the aggregation operations on each group to get the result.

The size of $_A\mathcal{G}_F(r)$ is simply $V(A, r)$, since there is one tuple in $_A\mathcal{G}_F(r)$ for each distinct value of $A$. The cost estimate for implementing the aggregation operation is the same as the cost of duplicate elimination, for aggregate functions such as **min**, **max**, **sum**, **count**, and **avg**.

Instead of gathering all the tuples in a group and then applying the aggregation operations, we can implement the aggregation operations **sum**, **min**, **max**, **count**, and **avg** on the fly as the groups are being constructed. For the case of **sum**, **min**, and **max**, when two tuples in the same group are found, they are replaced by a single tuple containing the **sum**, **min**, or **max**, respectively, of the columns being aggregated. For the **count** operation, a running count is maintained for each group for which a tuple has been found. Finally, we implement the **avg** operation by computing the sum and the count values on the fly, and finally dividing the sum by the count to get the average.

If $V(A, r)$ tuples of the result will fit in memory, both the sort-based and the hashing-based implementations do not need to write any tuples to disk. As the tuples are read in, they can be inserted in a sorted tree structure or in a hash index. When we use on the fly aggregation techniques, only one tuple needs to be stored for each of the $V(A, r)$ groups. Hence, the sorted tree-structure or hash index will fit in memory, and the aggregation can be processed with just $b_r$ block transfers, instead of with the $3b_r$ transfers that would be required otherwise.

## 12.8    Evaluation of Expressions

So far, we have studied how individual relational operations are carried out. Now we consider how to evaluate an expression containing multiple operations. The obvious way to evaluate an expression is simply to evaluate one operation at a time, in an appropriate order. The result of each evaluation is *materialized* in a temporary relation for subsequent use. A disadvantage to this approach is the need to construct the temporary relations, which (unless they are small) must be written to disk. An alternative approach is to evaluate several operations simultaneously in a *pipeline*, with the results of one operation passed on to the next, without the need to store a temporary relation.

In Sections 12.8.1 and 12.8.2, we consider both the *materialization* approach and the *pipelining* approach. We shall see that the costs of these approaches can differ substantially, but also that there are cases where only the materialization approach is feasible.

## 12.8.1   Materialization

It is easiest to understand intuitively how to evaluate an expression by looking at a pictorial representation of the expression in an *operator tree*. Consider the expression

$$\Pi_{customer\text{-}name} \left(\sigma_{balance<2500} \left(account\right) \bowtie customer\right)$$

shown in Figure 12.10.

If we apply the materialization approach, we start from the lowest-level operations in the expression (at the bottom of the tree). In our example, there is only one such operation; the selection operation on *account*. The inputs to the lowest-level operations are relations in the database. We execute these operations using the algorithms that we studied earlier, and we store the results in temporary relations. We can use these temporary relations to execute the operations at the next level up in the tree, where the inputs now are either temporary relations or relations stored in the database. In our example, the inputs to the join are the *customer* relation and the temporary relation created by the selection on *account*. The join can now be evaluated, creating another temporary relation.

By repeating the process, we will eventually evaluate the operation at the root of the tree, giving the final result of the expression. In our example, we get the final result by executing the the projection operation at the root of the tree, using as input the temporary relation created by the join.

Evaluation as just described is called *materialized evaluation*, since the results of each intermediate operation are created (materialized) and then are used for evaluation of the next-level operations.

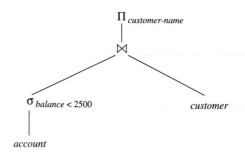

Figure 12.10   Pictorial representation of an expression.

The cost of a materialized evaluation is not simply the sum of the costs of the operations involved. When we computed the cost estimates of algorithms, we ignored the cost of writing the result of the operation to disk. To compute the cost of evaluating an expression as done here, we have to add the costs of all the operations, as well as the cost of writing the intermediate results to disk. We assume that the records of the result accumulate in a buffer, and, when the buffer is full, they are written to disk. The cost of writing out the result can be estimated as $n_r/f_r$, where $n_r$ is the estimated number of tuples in the result relation, and $f_r$ is the blocking factor of the result relation. Double buffering (using two buffers, with one continuing execution of the algorithm while the other is being written out) allows the algorithm to execute more quickly by performing CPU activity in parallel with I/O activity.

## 12.8.2 Pipelining

We can improve query-evaluation efficiency by reducing the number of temporary files that are produced. We achieve this reduction by combining several relational operations into a *pipeline* of operations, in which the results of one operation are passed along to the next operation in the pipeline. Combining operations into a pipeline eliminates the cost of reading and writing temporary relations.

For example, consider a join on a pair of relations followed by a projection $(\Pi_{a1,a2}(r \bowtie s))$. If materialization were applied, evaluation would involve creating a temporary relation to hold the result of the join, and then reading back in the result to perform the projection. These operations can be combined as follows. When the join operation generates a tuple of its result, that tuple is passed immediately to the project operation for processing. By combining the join and the projection, we avoid creating the intermediate result, and instead create the final result directly.

### 12.8.2.1 Implementation of Pipelining

We can implement a pipeline by constructing a single, complex operation that combines the operations that constitute the pipeline. Although this approach may be feasible for various frequently occurring situations, it is desirable in general to reuse the code for individual operations in the construction of a pipeline. Therefore, each operation in the pipeline is modeled as a separate process or thread within the system, which takes a stream of tuples from its pipelined inputs, and generates a stream of tuples for its output. For each pair of adjacent operations in the pipeline, a buffer is created to hold tuples being passed from one operation to the next.

In the example of Figure 12.10, all three operations can be placed in a pipeline, in which the results of the selection are passed to the join as they are generated. In turn, the results of the join are passed to the projection as they are generated. The memory requirements are low, since results of an operation are not stored for long. However, as a result of pipelining, the inputs to the operations are not available all at once for processing.

Pipelines can be executed in one of two ways:

1. Demand driven
2. Producer driven

In a *demand-driven* pipeline, the system makes repeated requests for tuples from the operation at the top of the pipeline. Each time that an operation receives a request for tuples, it computes the next tuple (or tuples) to be returned, and then returns that tuple. If the inputs of the operation are not pipelined, the next tuple(s) to be returned can be computed from the input relations, while we keep track of what has been returned so far. If some of its inputs are pipelined, the operation also makes requests for tuples from its pipelined inputs. Using the tuples received from its pipelined inputs, the operation computes tuples for its output, and passes them up to its parent.

In a *producer-driven* pipeline, operations do not wait for requests to produce tuples, but instead generate the tuples *eagerly*. Each operation at the bottom of a pipeline continually generates output tuples, and puts them in its output buffer, until the buffer is full. An operation at any other level of a pipeline generates output tuples when it gets input tuples from lower down in the pipeline, until its output buffer is full. Once the operation uses a tuple from a pipelined input, it removes the tuple from its input buffer. In either case, once the output buffer is full, the operation waits until tuples are removed from the buffer by its parent operation, so the buffer has space for more tuples. At this point, the operation generates more tuples, until the buffer is full again. This process is repeated by an operation until all the output tuples have been generated.

It is necessary for the system to switch between operations only when an output buffer is full, or an input buffer is empty and more input tuples are needed to generate any more output tuples. In a parallel-processing system, operations in a pipeline may be run concurrently on distinct processors (see Chapter 17).

Using producer-driven pipelining can be thought of as *pushing* data up an operation tree from below, whereas using demand-driven pipelining can be thought of as *pulling* data up an operation tree from the top. Each operation in a demand-driven pipeline can be implemented as an *iterator*, which provides the following functions: *open, next,* and *close*. After a call to *open*, each call to *next* returns the next output tuple of the operation. The implementation of the operation in turn calls *next* on its inputs, to get its input tuples when required. The function *close* tells an iterator that no more tuples are required. The iterator maintains the *state* of its execution in between calls, so that successive *next* requests receive successive result tuples. Details of the implementation of an iterator are left for you to complete in Exercise 12.18. Demand-driven pipelining is used more commonly than producer-driven pipelining, because it is easier to implement.

## 12.8.2.2   Evaluation Algorithms for Pipelining

Consider a join operation whose left-hand–side input is pipelined. Since it is pipelined, the input is not available all at once for processing by the join operation. This unavailability limits the choice of join algorithm to be used. Merge–join, for example, cannot be used if the inputs are not sorted, since it is not possible to sort a relation until all the tuples are available – thus, in effect, turning pipelining into materialization. However, indexed nested-loop join can be used: As tuples are received for the left-hand side of the join, they can be used to index the right-hand–side relation, and to generate tuples in the join result. This example illustrates that choices regarding the algorithm used for an operation and choices regarding pipelining are not independent.

The restrictions on the evaluation algorithms that can be used is a limiting factor for pipelining. As a result, despite the apparent advantages of pipelining, there are cases where materialization achieves lower overall cost. Suppose that the join of $r$ and $s$ is required, and input $r$ is pipelined. If indexed nested-loop join is used to support pipelining, one access to disk may be needed for every tuple in the pipelined input relation. The cost of this technique is $n_r * HT_i$, where $HT_i$ is the height of the index on $s$. With materialization, the cost of writing out $r$ would be $b_r$. With a join technique such as hash–join, it may be possible to perform the join with a cost of about $3(b_r + b_s)$. If $n_r$ is substantially more than $4b_r + 3b_s$, materialization would be cheaper.

The effective use of pipelining requires the use of evaluation algorithms that can generate output tuples even as tuples are received for the inputs to the operation. We can distinguish between two cases:

1. Only one of the inputs to a join is pipelined.
2. Both inputs to the join are pipelined.

If only one of the inputs to a join is pipelined, indexed nested-loop join is a natural choice. If the pipelined input tuples are sorted on the join attributes, and the join condition is an equi-join, merge–join can also be used. Hybrid hash–join can be used, with the pipelined input as the probe relation. However, tuples that are not in the first partition will be output only after the entire pipelined input relation is received. Hybrid hash–join is useful if the nonpipelined input fits entirely in memory, or if at least most of that input fits in memory.

If both inputs are pipelined, the choice of join algorithms is more restricted. If both inputs are sorted on the join attribute, and the join condition is an equi-join, merge–join can be used. Another alternative is the *pipelined-join* technique, shown in Figure 12.11. The algorithm assumes that the input tuples for both input relations, $r$ and $s$, are pipelined. Tuples made available for both relations are queued for processing in a single queue. Special queue entries, called $End_r$ and $End_s$, which serve as end-of-file markers, are inserted in the queue after all tuples from $r$ and $s$ (respectively) have been generated. For efficient evaluation, appropriate indices should be built on the relations $r$ and $s$. As tuples are added to $r$ and $s$, the indices must be kept up to date.

$done_r$ := false;
$done_s$ := false;
$r$ := $\emptyset$;
$s$ := $\emptyset$;
result := $\emptyset$;
**while not** $done_r$ **or not** $done_s$ **do**
   **begin**
      **if** queue is empty, **then** wait until queue is not empty;
      $t$ := top entry in queue;
      **if** $t = End_r$ **then** $done_r$ := true
         **else if** $t = End_s$ **then** $done_s$ := true
            **else if** $t$ is from input $r$ **then**
               **begin**
                  $r$ := $r \cup \{t\}$;
                  result := result $\cup$ ($\{t\} \bowtie s$);
               **end**
               **else** /* $t$ is from input $s$ */
                  **begin**
                     $s$ := $s \cup \{t\}$;
                     result := result $\cup$ ($r \bowtie \{t\}$);
                  **end**
**end**

Figure 12.11    Pipelined join algorithm.

# 12.9    Transformation of Relational Expressions

So far, we have studied algorithms to evaluate extended relational-algebra operations, and have estimated their costs. As we mentioned earlier, a query can be expressed in several different ways, with different costs of evaluation. In this section, rather than taking the relational expression as given, we consider alternative, equivalent expressions.

## 12.9.1    Equivalence of Expressions

Consider the relational-algebra expression for the query "Find the names of all customers who have an account at any branch located in Brooklyn."

$$\Pi_{customer\text{-}name} \left(\sigma_{branch-city = \text{"Brooklyn"}} \left(branch \bowtie \left(account \bowtie depositor\right)\right)\right)$$

This expression constructs a large intermediate relation, $branch \bowtie account \bowtie depositor$. However, we are interested in only a few tuples of this relation (those pertaining to branches located in Brooklyn), and in only one of the six attributes of this relation. Since we are concerned with only those tuples in the *branch* relation that pertain to branches located in Brooklyn, we do not need to consider

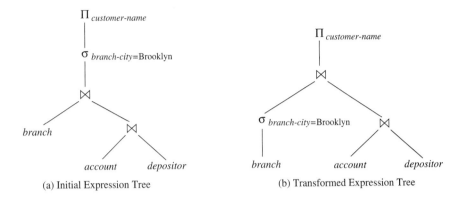

Figure 12.12    Equivalent expressions.

those tuples that do not have *branch-city* = "Brooklyn." By reducing the number of tuples of the *branch* relation that we need to access, we reduce the size of the intermediate result. Our query is now represented by the relational-algebra expression

$$\Pi_{customer\text{-}name} \left( \left( \sigma_{branch\text{-}city \, = \, \text{"Brooklyn"}} (branch) \right) \bowtie (account \bowtie depositor) \right)$$

which is equivalent to our original algebra expression, but which generates smaller intermediate relations. The initial and transformed expressions are shown pictorially in Figure 12.12.

Given a relational-algebra expression, it is the job of the query optimizer to come up with a query-evaluation plan that computes the same result as the given expression, and is the least costly way of generating the result (or, at least, is not much costlier than the least costly way).

To find the least costly query-evaluation plan, the optimizer needs to generate alternative plans that produce the same result as the given expression, and to choose the least costly one. Generation of query-evaluation plans involves two steps: (1) generating expressions that are logically equivalent to the given expression, and (2) annotating the resultant expressions in alternative ways to generate alternative query plans. The two steps are interleaved in the query optimizer— some expressions are generated and annotated, then further expressions are generated and annotated, and so on.

To implement the first step, the query optimizer must generate expressions equivalent to a given expression. It does so by means of *equivalence rules* that specify how to transform an expression into a logically equivalent one. We describe these rules next. In Section 12.10, we describe how to choose a query-evaluation plan. We can choose one based on the *estimated* cost of the plans. Since the cost is an estimate, the selected plan is not necessarily the least costly plan; however, as long as the estimates are good, the plan is likely to be the least costly one, or not much more costly than that one. Such optimization is called *cost-based optimization*, and is described in Section 12.10.2.

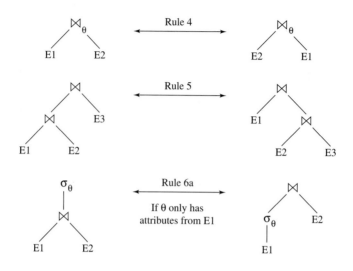

Figure 12.13    Pictorial representation of equivalences.

## 12.9.2    Equivalence Rules

An *equivalence rule* says that expressions of two forms are equivalent: We can transform either to the other while preserving equivalence. By *preserve equivalence* we mean that relations generated by the two expressions have the same set of attributes and contain the same set of tuples, although their attributes may be ordered differently. Equivalence rules are used by the optimizer to transform expressions into other logically equivalent expressions.

We now list a number of general equivalence rules on relational-algebra expressions. Some of the equivalences listed are also illustrated in Figure 12.13. We use $\theta, \theta_1, \theta_2$, and so on to denote predicates, $L_1, L_2, L_3$, and so on to denote lists of attributes, and $E, E_1, E_2$, and so on to denote relational-algebra expressions. A relation name $r$ is simply a special case of a relational-algebra expression, and can be used wherever $E$ appears.

1. Conjunctive selection operations can be deconstructed into a sequence of individual selections. This transformation is referred to as a cascade of $\sigma$.

$$\sigma_{\theta_1 \wedge \theta_2}(E) = \sigma_{\theta_1}(\sigma_{\theta_2}(E))$$

2. Selection operations are commutative.

$$\sigma_{\theta_1}(\sigma_{\theta_2}(E)) = \sigma_{\theta_2}(\sigma_{\theta_1}(E))$$

3. Only the final operations in a sequence of projection operations is needed, the others can be omitted. This transformation can also be referred to as a cascade of $\Pi$.

$$\Pi_{L_1}(\Pi_{L_2}(\dots(\Pi_{L_n}(E))\dots)) = \Pi_{L_1}(E)$$

4. Selections can be combined with Cartesian products and theta joins.
   a. $\sigma_\theta(E_1 \times E_2) = E_1 \bowtie_\theta E_2$
      This expression is just the definition of the theta join.
   b. $\sigma_{\theta_1}(E_1 \bowtie_{\theta_2} E_2) = E_1 \bowtie_{\theta_1 \wedge \theta_2} E_2$
5. Theta-join operations are commutative.

$$E_1 \bowtie_\theta E_2 = E_2 \bowtie_\theta E_1$$

Recall that the natural-join operator is simply a special case of the theta-join operator; hence, natural joins are also commutative.

6. a. Natural-join operations are associative.

$$(E_1 \bowtie E_2) \bowtie E_3 = E_1 \bowtie (E_2 \bowtie E_3)$$

   b. Theta joins are associative in the following manner:

$$(E_1 \bowtie_{\theta_1} E_2) \bowtie_{\theta_2 \wedge \theta_3} E_3 = E_1 \bowtie_{\theta_1 \wedge \theta_3} (E_2 \bowtie_{\theta_2} E_3)$$

   where $\theta_2$ involves attributes from only $E_2$ and $E_3$. Any of these conditions may be empty; hence, it follows that the Cartesian product ($\times$) operation is also associative. The commutativity and associativity of join operations are important for join reordering in query optimization.

7. The selection operation distributes over the theta join operation under the following two conditions:
   a. It distributes when all the attributes in selection condition $\theta_0$ involve only the attributes of one of the expressions ($E_1$) being joined.

$$\sigma_{\theta_0}(E_1 \bowtie_\theta E_2) = (\sigma_{\theta_0}(E_1)) \bowtie_\theta E_2$$

   b. It distributes when selection condition $\theta_1$ involves only the attributes of $E_1$ and $\theta_2$ involves only the attributes of $E_2$.

$$\sigma_{\theta_1 \wedge \theta_2}(E_1 \bowtie_\theta E_2) = (\sigma_{\theta_1}(E_1)) \bowtie_\theta (\sigma_{\theta_2}(E_2))$$

8. The projection operation distributes over the theta join operation.
   a. Let $L_1$ and $L_2$ be attributes of $E_1$ and $E_2$, respectively. Suppose that the join condition $\theta$ involves only attributes in $L_1 \cup L_2$. Then,

$$\Pi_{L_1 \cup L_2}(E_1 \bowtie_\theta E_2) = (\Pi_{L_1}(E_1)) \bowtie_\theta (\Pi_{L_2}(E_2))$$

   b. Consider a join $E_1 \bowtie_\theta E_2$. Let $L_1$ and $L_2$ be sets of attributes from $E_1$ and $E_2$, respectively. Let $L_3$ be attributes of $E_1$ that are involved in join condition $\theta$, but are not in $L_1 \cup L_2$, and let $L_4$ be attributes of $E_2$ that are involved in join condition $\theta$, but are not in $L_1 \cup L_2$. Then,

$$\Pi_{L_1 \cup L_2}(E_1 \bowtie_\theta E_2) = \Pi_{L_1 \cup L_2}((\Pi_{L_1 \cup L_3}(E_1)) \bowtie_\theta (\Pi_{L_2 \cup L_4}(E_2)))$$

9. The set operations union and intersection are commutative.

$$E_1 \cup E_2 = E_2 \cup E_1$$

$$E_1 \cap E_2 = E_2 \cap E_1$$

Set difference is not commutative.

10. Set union and intersection are associative.

$$(E_1 \cup E_2) \cup E_3 = E_1 \cup (E_2 \cup E_3)$$

$$(E_1 \cap E_2) \cap E_3 = E_1 \cap (E_2 \cap E_3)$$

11. The selection operation distributes over the union, intersection, and set-difference operations.

$$\sigma_P(E_1 - E_2) = \sigma_P(E_1) - \sigma_P(E_2)$$

Similarly, the preceding equivalence, with $-$ replaced with either one of $\cup$ or $\cap$, also holds. Further,

$$\sigma_P(E_1 - E_2) = \sigma_P(E_1) - E_2$$

The preceding equivalence, with $-$ replaced by $\cap$, also holds, but does not hold if $-$ is replaced by $\cup$.

12. The projection operation distributes over the union operation.

$$\Pi_L(E_1 \cup E_2) = (\Pi_L(E_1)) \cup (\Pi_L(E_2))$$

The preceding list is only a partial list of equivalences. More equivalences involving extended relational operators, such as the outer join and aggregation, are discussed in the exercises.

## 12.9.3   Examples of Transformations

We now illustrate the use of the equivalence rules. We use our bank example with the relation schemas:

> *Branch-schema = (branch-name, branch-city, assets)*
> *Account-schema = (branch-name, account-number, balance)*
> *Depositor-schema = (customer-name, account-number)*

The relations *branch*, *account*, and *depositor* are instances of these schemas.

In our earlier example, the expression

$$\Pi_{customer\text{-}name}(\sigma_{branch\text{-}city = \text{``Brooklyn''}}(branch \bowtie (account \bowtie depositor)))$$

was transformed into the following expression,

$$\Pi_{customer\text{-}name}((\sigma_{branch\text{-}city = \text{``Brooklyn''}}(branch)) \bowtie (account \bowtie depositor))$$

which is equivalent to our original algebra expression, but generates smaller intermediate relations. We can carry out this transformation using rule 7.a. Remember that the rule merely says that the two expressions are equivalent; it does not say that one is better than the other.

Multiple equivalence rules can be used, one after the other, on a query or on parts of the query. As an illustration, suppose that we modify our original query to restrict attention to customers who have a balance over \$1000. The new relational-algebra query is

$$\Pi_{customer\text{-}name} \, (\sigma_{branch\text{-}city\,=\,\text{``Brooklyn''}\,\wedge\,balance\,>1000}$$
$$(branch \bowtie (account \bowtie depositor)))$$

We cannot apply the selection predicate directly to the *branch* relation, since the predicate involves attributes of both the *branch* and *account* relation. However, we can first apply rule 6.a (associativity of natural join) to transform the join *branch* $\bowtie$ (*account* $\bowtie$ *depositor*) into (*branch* $\bowtie$ *account*) $\bowtie$ *depositor*:

$$\Pi_{customer\text{-}name} \, (\sigma_{branch\text{-}city\,=\,\text{``Brooklyn''}\,\wedge\,balance\,>1000}$$
$$((branch \bowtie account) \bowtie depositor))$$

Then, using rule 7.a, we can rewrite our query as

$$\Pi_{customer\text{-}name} \, ((\sigma_{branch\text{-}city\,=\,\text{``Brooklyn''}\,\wedge\,balance\,>1000}$$
$$(branch \bowtie account)) \bowtie depositor)$$

Let us examine the selection subexpression within this expression. Using rule 1, we can break the selection into two selections, to get the following subexpression:

$$\sigma_{branch\text{-}city\,=\,\text{``Brooklyn''}} \, (\sigma_{balance\,>\,1000} \, (branch \bowtie account))$$

Both of the preceding expressions select tuples with *branch-city* = "Brooklyn" and *balance* > 1000. However, the latter form of the expression provides a new opportunity to apply the "perform selections early" rule, resulting in the subexpression

$$\sigma_{branch\text{-}city\,=\,\text{``Brooklyn''}} \, (branch) \bowtie \sigma_{balance\,>1000} \, (account)$$

The initial expression and the final expression after all the preceding transformations are shown pictorially in Figure 12.14. We could equally well have used rule 7.b to get the final expression directly, without using rule 1 to break the selection into two selections. In fact, rule 7.b can itself be derived from rules 1 and 7.a

A set of equivalence rules is said to be *minimal* if no rule can be derived from any combination of the others. The preceding example illustrates that the set of equivalence rules in Section 12.9.2 is not minimal.

Now consider the following form of our example query:

$$\Pi_{customer\text{-}name} \, ((\sigma_{branch\text{-}city\,=\,\text{``Brooklyn''}} \, (branch) \bowtie account) \bowtie depositor)$$

When we compute the subexpression

$$(\sigma_{branch\text{-}city\,=\,\text{``Brooklyn''}} \, (branch) \bowtie account)$$

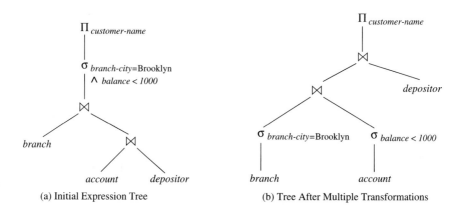

$\Pi_{customer\text{-}name}$

$\sigma_{branch\text{-}city=Brooklyn \atop \wedge\ balance < 1000}$

branch

account    depositor

(a) Initial Expression Tree

$\Pi_{customer\text{-}name}$

depositor

$\sigma_{branch\text{-}city=Brooklyn}$    $\sigma_{balance < 1000}$

branch                    account

(b) Tree After Multiple Transformations

**Figure 12.14    Multiple transformations.**

we obtain a relation whose schema is

*(branch-name, branch-city, assets, account-number, balance)*

We can eliminate several attributes from the schema, by pushing projections using equivalence rules 8.a and 8.b. The only attributes that we must retain are those that either appear in the result of the query or are needed to process subsequent operations. By eliminating unneeded attributes, we reduce the number of columns of the intermediate result. Thus, the size of the intermediate result is reduced. In our example, the only attribute we need from the join of *branch* and *account* is *account-number*. Therefore, we can modify the expression to

$$\Pi_{customer\text{-}name} \left( \left( \Pi_{account\text{-}number} \left( (\sigma_{branch\text{-}city=\text{``Brooklyn''}} (branch)) \bowtie account \right) \right) \bowtie depositor \right)$$

The projection $\Pi_{account\text{-}number}$ reduces the size of the intermediate join results.

### 12.9.4    Join Ordering

A good ordering of join operations is important for reducing the size of temporary results; hence, most query optimizers pay a lot of attention to the join order. As mentioned in Chapter 3 and in equivalence rule 6.a, the natural-join operation is associative. Thus, for all relations $r_1$, $r_2$, and $r_3$,

$$(r_1 \bowtie r_2) \bowtie r_3 = r_1 \bowtie (r_2 \bowtie r_3)$$

Although these expressions are equivalent, the costs of computing them may differ. Consider again the expression

$$\Pi_{customer\text{-}name} ((\sigma_{branch\text{-}city=\text{``Brooklyn''}} (branch)) \bowtie account \bowtie depositor)$$

We could choose to compute *account* $\bowtie$ *depositor* first, and then to join the result with

$$\sigma_{branch\text{-}city=\text{``Brooklyn''}} (branch)$$

However, *account* ⋈ *depositor* is likely to be a large relation, since it contains one tuple for every account. In contrast,

$$\sigma_{branch\text{-}city=\text{"Brooklyn"}} \, (branch) \bowtie account$$

is probably a small relation. To see that it is, we note that, since the bank has a large number of widely distributed branches, it is likely that only a small fraction of the bank's customers have accounts in branches located in Brooklyn. Thus, the preceding expression results in one tuple for each account held by a resident of Brooklyn. Therefore, the temporary relation that we must store is smaller than it would have been had we computed *account* ⋈ *depositor* first.

There are other options to consider for evaluating our query. We do not care about the order in which attributes appear in a join, since it is easy to change the order before displaying the result. Thus, for all relations $r_1$ and $r_2$,

$$r_1 \bowtie r_2 = r_2 \bowtie r_1$$

That is, natural join is commutative (equivalence rule 5).

Using the associativity and commutativity of the natural join (Rules 5 and 6), we can consider rewriting our relational-algebra expression as

$$\Pi_{customer\text{-}name} \, (((\sigma_{branch\text{-}city=\text{"Brooklyn"}} \, (branch)) \bowtie depositor) \bowtie account)$$

That is, we could compute

$$(\sigma_{branch\text{-}city=\text{"Brooklyn"}} \, (branch)) \bowtie depositor$$

first, and, after that, join the result with *account*. Note, however, that there are no attributes in common between *Branch-schema* and *Depositor-schema*, so the join is just a Cartesian product. If there are *b* branches in Brooklyn and *d* tuples in the *depositor* relation, this Cartesian product generates $b * d$ tuples, one for every possible pair of depositor tuple and branches (without regard for whether the account in *depositor* is maintained at the branch). Thus, it appears that this Cartesian product will produce a large temporary relation. As a result, we would reject this strategy. However, if the user had entered the preceding expression, we could use the associativity and commutativity of the natural join to transform this expression to the more efficient expression that we used earlier.

## 12.9.5  Enumeration of Equivalent Expressions

Query optimizers use equivalence rules to generate systematically expressions equivalent to the given query expression. Conceptually, the process is carried out as follows. Given an expression, if any subexpression matches one side of an equivalence rule, a new expression is generated, where the subexpression is transformed to match the other side of the rule. This process continues until no more new expressions can be generated.

The preceding process is costly both in space and in time. The space requirement is reduced as follows. If we generate an expression $E_1$ from an expression

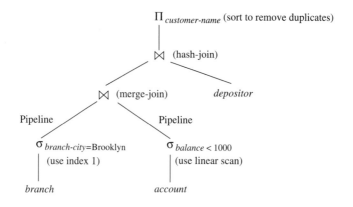

Figure 12.15    An evaluation plan.

$E_2$ using an equivalence rule, then $E_1$ and $E_2$ are similar in structure, and have subexpressions that are identical. Expression-representation techniques that allow both expressions to point to shared subexpressions can reduce the space requirement significantly, and are used in many query optimizers.

Moreover, it is not always necessary to generate every expression that can be generated using the equivalence rules. If cost estimates of evaluation are taken into account, an optimizer may be able to avoid examining some of the expressions, as we shall see in Section 12.10. We can reduce the time required for optimization using techniques such as the ones just described.

## 12.10    Choice of Evaluation Plans

Generation of expressions is only part of the query-optimization process. Each operation in the expression can be implemented with different algorithms. An evaluation plan defines exactly what algorithm is used for each operation, and how the execution of the operations is coordinated. Figure 12.15 illustrates one possible evaluation plan for the expression from Figure 12.14. As we have seen, several different algorithms can be used for each relational operation, giving rise to alternative evaluation plans. Further, decisions about pipelining have to be made. In the figure, the edges from the selection operations to the merge–join operation are marked as pipelined; pipelining is feasible if the selection operations generate their output sorted on the join attributes. They would do so if the indices on *branch* and *account* store records with equal values for the index attributes sorted by *branch-name*.

### 12.10.1    Interaction of Evaluation Techniques

One way to choose an evaluation plan for a query expression is simply to choose for each operation the cheapest algorithm for evaluating it. We can choose any ordering of the operations consistent with operations lower in the tree being executed before operations higher in the tree.

However, choosing the cheapest algorithm for each operation independently is not necessarily a good idea. Although a merge–join at a given level may be costlier than a hash–join, it may provide a sorted output that makes evaluating a later operation (such as duplicate elimination, intersection, or another merge–join) cheaper. Similarly, a nested-loop join with indexing may provide opportunities for pipelining the results to the next operation, and thus may be useful even if it is not the cheapest way of performing the join. To choose the best overall algorithm, we must consider even nonoptimal algorithms for individual operations.

Thus, in addition to considering alternative expressions for a query, we must also consider alternative algorithms for each operation in an expression. We can use rules much like the equivalence rules to define what are the possible algorithms for each operation, including whether or not to pipeline that operation with another expression. We can use these rules to evaluate systematically all the query-evaluation plans for a given expression.

Given an evaluation plan, we can use the techniques discussed earlier in the chapter to estimate its cost. That still leaves the problem of choosing the best evaluation plan for a query. There are two broad approaches: the first searches all the plans, and chooses the best plan in a cost-based fashion. The second uses heuristics to choose a plan. We discuss these approaches next. Practical query optimizers incorporate elements of both approaches.

## 12.10.2   Cost-Based Optimization

A cost-based optimizer generates a range of query-evaluation plans from the given query by using the equivalence rules, and chooses the one with the least cost. For a complex query, the number of different query plans that are equivalent to a given plan can be large. As an illustration, consider the expression

$$r_1 \bowtie r_2 \bowtie \ldots \bowtie r_n$$

where the joins are expressed without any ordering. With $n = 3$, there are 12 different join orderings:

| | | | |
|---|---|---|---|
| $r_1 \bowtie (r_2 \bowtie r_3)$ | $r_1 \bowtie (r_3 \bowtie r_2)$ | $(r_2 \bowtie r_3) \bowtie r_1$ | $(r_3 \bowtie r_2) \bowtie r_1$ |
| $r_2 \bowtie (r_1 \bowtie r_3)$ | $r_2 \bowtie (r_3 \bowtie r_1)$ | $(r_1 \bowtie r_3) \bowtie r_2$ | $(r_3 \bowtie r_1) \bowtie r_2$ |
| $r_3 \bowtie (r_1 \bowtie r_2)$ | $r_3 \bowtie (r_2 \bowtie r_1)$ | $(r_1 \bowtie r_2) \bowtie r_3$ | $(r_2 \bowtie r_1) \bowtie r_3$ |

In general, with $n$ relations, there are $(2(n-1))!/(n-1)!$ different join orders. (We leave the computation of this expression for you to do in Exercise 12.23.) For joins involving small numbers of relations, this number is acceptable; for example, with $n = 5$, the number is 1680. However, as $n$ increases, this number rises quickly. With $n = 7$, the number is 665280; with $n = 10$, the number is greater than 176 billion!

Luckily, it is not necessary to generate all the expressions equivalent to a given expression. For example, suppose that we want to find the best join order for the form:

$$(r_1 \bowtie r_2 \bowtie r_3) \bowtie r_4 \bowtie r_5$$

which represents all join orders where $r_1, r_2$, and $r_3$ are joined first (in some order), and the result is joined (in some order) with $r_4$ and $r_5$. There are 12 different join orders for computing $r_1 \bowtie r_2 \bowtie r_3$, and 12 orders for computing the join of this result with $r_4$ and $r_5$. Thus, there appear to be 144 join orders to examine. However, once we have found the best join order for the subset of relations $\{r_1, r_2, r_3\}$, we can use that order for further joins with $r_4$ and $r_5$, and can ignore all costlier join orders of $r_1 \bowtie r_2 \bowtie r_3$. Thus, instead of 144 choices to examine, we need to examine only $12 + 12$ choices. Using this idea, we can develop a dynamic-programming algorithm for finding optimal join orders, which approach greatly reduces the number of expressions examined. The algorithm computes the best join order for each subset of the given set of $n$ relations. (See Exercise 12.24.)

Actually, the order in which tuples are generated by the join of $r_1 \bowtie r_2 \bowtie r_3$ is also important for finding the best overall join order, since it can affect the cost of further joins (for instance, if merge–join is used). A particular sort order of the tuples is said to be an *interesting sort order* if it could be useful for a later operation. For instance, generating the result of $r_1 \bowtie r_2 \bowtie r_3$ sorted on the attributes common with $r_4$ or $r_5$ may be useful, but generating it sorted on the attributes common to only $r_1$ and $r_2$ is not useful. Using merge–join when computing $r_1 \bowtie r_2 \bowtie r_3$ may be costlier than using some other join technique, but may provide an output sorted in an interesting order.

Hence, it is not sufficient to find the best join order for each subset of the set of $n$ given relations. Instead, we have to find the best join order for each subset, for each interesting sort order of the join result for that subset. The number of subsets of $n$ relations is $2^n$. The number of interesting sort orders is generally not large. Thus, about $2^n$ join expressions need to be stored. The dynamic-programming algorithm for finding the best join order can be easily extended to handle sort orders, and has a time cost of around $3^n$. (See Exercise 12.25.)

With $n = 10$, this number is around 59000, which is much better than the 176 billion different join orders. More important, the storage required is much less than before, since we need to store only one join order for each interesting order of each of 1024 subsets of $r_1, \ldots, r_{10}$. Although both numbers still increase rapidly with $n$, commonly occurring joins usually have less than 10 relations, and can be handled easily.

We can use several techniques to reduce further the cost of searching through a large number of plans. For instance, when examining the plans for an expression, we can terminate after we examine only a part of the expression, if we determine that the cheapest plan for that part is already costlier than the cheapest evaluation plan for a full expression examined earlier. Similarly, suppose that we determine that the cheapest way of evaluating a subexpression is costlier than the cheapest evaluation plan for a full expression examined earlier. Then, no full expression involving that subexpression needs to be examined. We can further reduce the number of evaluation plans that need to be considered fully by first making a heuristic guess of a good plan, and estimating that plan's cost. Then, only a few competing plans will require a full analysis of cost. These optimizations can reduce the overhead of query optimization significantly.

## 12.10.3   Heuristic Optimization

A drawback of cost-based optimization is the cost of optimization itself. Although the cost of query processing can be reduced by clever optimizations, cost-based optimization is still expensive. Hence, many systems use *heuristics* to reduce the number of choices that must be made in a cost-based fashion. Some systems even choose to use only heuristics, and do not used cost-based optimization at all.

An example of a heuristic rule is the following rule for transforming relational-algebra queries:

- Perform selection operations as early as possible.

A heuristic optimizer would use this rule without finding out whether the cost is reduced by this transformation. In the first transformation example in Section 12.9, the selection operation was pushed into a join.

We say that the preceding rule is a heuristic because it usually, but not always, helps to reduce the cost. For an example of where it can result in an increase in cost, consider an expression $\sigma_\theta(r \bowtie s)$, where the condition $\theta$ refers to only attributes in $s$. The selection can certainly be performed before the join. However, if $r$ is extremely small compared to $s$, and if there is an index on the join attributes of $s$, but no index on the attributes used by $\theta$, then it is probably a bad idea to perform the selection early. Performing the selection early—that is, directly on $s$—would require doing a scan of all tuples in $s$. It is probably cheaper, in this case, to compute the join using the index, and then to reject tuples that fail the selection.

The projection operation, like the selection operation, reduces the size of relations. Thus, whenever we need to generate a temporary relation, it is advantageous to apply immediately any projections that are possible. This advantage suggests a companion to the "perform selections early" heuristic that we stated earlier:

- Perform projections early.

It is usually better to perform selections earlier than projections, since selections have the potential to reduce the sizes of relations greatly, and selections enable the use of indices to access tuples. An example similar to the one used for the selection heuristic should convince you that this heuristic does not always reduce the cost.

Drawing on the equivalences discussed in Section 12.9.2, a heuristic optimization algorithm will reorder the components of an initial query tree to achieve improved query execution. We now present an overview of the steps in a typical heuristic optimization algorithm. You can understand the heuristics by visualizing a query expression as a tree, as illustrated earlier.

1. **Deconstruct conjunctive selections into a sequence of single selection operations. Based on equivalence rule 1, this step facilitates moving selection operations down the query tree.**
2. **Move selection operations down the query tree for the earliest possible execution. This step uses the commutativity and distributivity properties of the selection operation noted in equivalence rules 2, 7.a, 7.b, and 11.**

For instance, $\sigma_\theta(r \bowtie s)$ is transformed into either $\sigma_\theta(r) \bowtie s$ or $r \bowtie \sigma_\theta(s)$ whenever possible. Performing value-based selections as early as possible reduces the cost of sorting and merging intermediate results. The degree of reordering permitted for a particular selection is determined by the attributes involved in that selection condition.

3. Determine which selection operations and join operations will produce the smallest relations—that is, will produce the relations with the least number of tuples. Using associativity of the $\bowtie$ operation, rearrange the tree such that the leaf-node relations with these restrictive selections are executed first.

   This step considers the selectivity of a selection or join condition. Recall that the most restrictive selection—that is, the condition with the smallest selectivity—retrieves the fewest records. This step relies on the associativity of binary operations given in equivalence rule 6.

4. Replace with join operations Cartesian product operations that are followed by a selection condition (rule 4.a). As demonstrated in Section 12.9.4, the Cartesian product operation is often expensive to implement. In $r_1 \times r_2$, not only does the result include a record for each combination of records from $r_1$ and $r_2$, but also the result attributes include all the attributes of $r_1$ and $r_2$. Therefore, it is advisable to avoid using the Cartesian product operation.

5. Deconstruct and move as far down the tree as possible lists of projection attributes, creating new projections where needed. This step draws on the properties of the projection operation given in equivalence rules 3, 8.a, 8.b, and 12.

6. Identify those subtrees whose operations can be pipelined, and execute them using pipelining.

In summary, the heuristics listed here reorder an initial query-tree representation such that the operations that reduce the size of intermediate results are applied first; early selection reduces the number of tuples, and early projection reduces the number of attributes. The heuristic transformations also restructure the tree such that the most restrictive selection and join operations are performed before other similar operations.

Heuristic optimization further maps the heuristically transformed query expression into alternative sequences of operations to produce a set of candidate evaluation plans. An evaluation plan includes not only the relational operations to be performed, but also the indices to be used, the order in which tuples are to be accessed, and the order in which the operations are to be performed. The *access-plan–selection* phase of a heuristic optimizer chooses the most efficient strategy for each operation.

## 12.10.4    Structure of Query Optimizers

So far, we have described the two basic approaches to choosing an evaluation plan. Most practical query optimizers combine elements of both approaches. Certain query optimizers, such as the System R optimizer, do not consider all join orders,

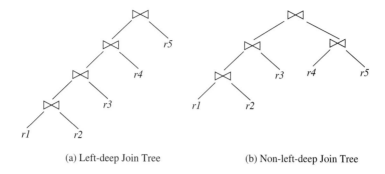

(a) Left-deep Join Tree          (b) Non-left-deep Join Tree

Figure 12.16   Left-deep join trees.

but rather restrict the search to particular kinds of join orders. The System R optimizer considers only those join orders where the right operand of each join is one of the initial relations $r_1, \ldots, r_n$. Such join orders are called *left-deep join orders*. Left-deep join orders are particularly convenient for pipelined evaluation, since the right operand is a stored relation, and thus only one input to each join is pipelined.

Figure 12.16 illustrates the difference between left-deep join trees and non–left-deep join trees. The time it takes to consider all left-deep join orders is $O(n!)$, which is much less than the time to consider all join orders. With the use of some optimizations, the System R optimizer can find the best join order in time approximately $O(2^n)$. Contrast this cost with the $3^n$ time required to find the best overall join order. The System R optimizer uses heuristics to push selections and projections down the query tree.

The cost estimate that we presented for scans using secondary indices assumed that every tuple access results in an I/O operation. The estimate is likely to be accurate with small buffers; with large buffers, however, the page containing the tuple may already be in the buffer. The Sybase optimizer incorporates a better cost-estimation technique for such scans: It takes into account the probability that the page containing the tuple is in the buffer.

Query optimization approaches that integrate heuristic selection and the generation of alternative access plans have been adopted in several systems. The approach used in System R and in its successor, the Starburst project, consists of a hierarchical procedure based on the nested-block concept of SQL. The cost-based optimization techniques described here are used for each block of the query separately. Ingres uses heuristic decomposition to reduce a query to a set of subqueries containing no more than two relations. Detailed access plans are then generated for each of these subqueries.

The Oracle7 optimizer has two components: one is based on heuristic rules, and the other is cost based.[†] The heuristic approach works roughly as we shall describe. For an $n$-way join, it considers $n$ evaluation plans constructed as follows.

---

[†]The details that we describe apply to the Oracle7 release of December 1992. Later versions may follow other optimization techniques.

Each plan uses a left-deep join order, starting with a different one of the $n$ relations. The heuristic constructs the join order for each of the $n$ evaluation plans by repeatedly selecting the "best" relation to join next, based on a ranking of the available access paths. Either nested-loop or sort–merge join is chosen for each of the joins, based on the available access paths. Finally, one of the $n$ evaluation plans is chosen in a heuristic manner, based on minimizing the number of nested-loop joins that do not have an index available on the inner relation, and on the number of sort–merge joins.

The intricacies of SQL introduce a good deal of complexity into query optimizers. In particular, it is hard to translate subqueries in SQL into relational algebra. Many optimizers, such as System R and Starburst, attempt to rewrite SQL queries to transform subqueries into joins where possible. Where the transformation is not possible, the subqueries are kept as separate expressions, and are optimized separately. The chosen evaluation plans are then combined via special evaluation algorithms. Similarly, for compound SQL queries (using the $\cup$, $\cap$, or $-$ operation), each component is optimized separately, and the evaluation plans are combined to form the overall evaluation plan.

Even with the use of heuristics, cost-based query optimization imposes a substantial overhead on query processing. However, the added cost of cost-based query optimization is usually more than offset by the saving at query-execution time, which is dominated by slow disk accesses. The difference in execution time between a good plan and a bad one may be huge, making query optimization essential. The achieved saving is magnified in those applications that run on a regular basis, where the query can be optimized once, and the selected query plan can be used on each run. Therefore, most commercial systems include relatively sophisticated optimizers. The bibliographic notes give references to descriptions of the query optimizers of actual database systems.

## 12.11 Summary

The first action that the system must perform on a query is to translate the query into its internal form, which (for relational database systems) is usually based on the relational algebra. In the process of generating the internal form of the query, the parser checks the syntax of the user's query, verifies that the relation names appearing in the query are names of relations in the database, and so on. If the query was expressed in terms of a view, the parser replaces all references to the view name with the relational-algebra expression to compute the view.

Given a query, there is generally a variety of methods for computing the answer. It is the responsibility of the system to transform the query as entered by the user into an equivalent query that can be computed more efficiently. This *optimizing* or, more accurately, improving of the strategy for processing a query is called *query optimization*.

The evaluation of complex queries involves many accesses to disk. Since the transfer of data from disk is slow relative to the speed of main memory and the CPU of the computer system, it is worthwhile to allocate a considerable amount of processing to choose a method that minimizes disk accesses.

The strategy that we choose for evaluating an operation depends on the size of each relation and on the distribution of values within columns. So that they can choose a strategy based on reliable information, database systems may store statistics for each relation $r$. These statistics include

- The number of tuples in the relation $r$
- The size of a record (tuple) of relation $r$ in bytes
- The number of distinct values that appear in the relation $r$ for a particular attribute

These statistics allow us to estimate the sizes of the results of various operations, as well as the cost of executing the operations. Statistical information about relations is particularly useful when several indices are available to assist in the processing of a query. The presence of these structures has a significant influence on the choice of a query-processing strategy.

We can process queries involving simple selections by performing a linear scan, by doing a binary search, or by making use of indices. We can handle complex selections by computing unions and intersections of the results of simple selections. We can sort relations larger than memory using the external merge–sort algorithm. Queries involving a natural join may be processed in several ways, depending on the availability of indices and the form of physical storage used for the relations. If the join result is almost as large as the Cartesian product of the two relations, a *block nested-loop* join strategy may be advantageous. If indices are available, the *indexed nested-loop* join can be used. If the relations are sorted, a *merge–join* may be desirable. It may be advantageous to sort a relation prior to join computation (so as to allow use of the merge–join strategy). It may also be advantageous to compute a temporary index for the sole purpose of allowing a more efficient join strategy to be used. The *hash–join* algorithm partitions the relations into several pieces, such that each piece of one of the relations fits in memory. The partitioning is carried out with a hash function on the join attributes, so that corresponding pairs of partitions can be joined independently. Hashing and sorting are dual, in the sense that many operations such as duplicate elimination, aggregation, joins, and outer joins can be implemented via either hashing or sorting.

Each relational-algebra expression represents a particular sequence of operations. The first step in selecting a query-processing strategy is to find a relational-algebra expression that is equivalent to the given expression and is estimated to cost less to execute. There are a number of equivalence rules that we can use to transform an expression into an equivalent one. We use these rules to generate systematically all expressions equivalent to the given query, and we choose the cheapest expression. Alternative evaluation plans for each expression can be generated by similar rules, and the cheapest plan across all expressions can be chosen. Several optimization techniques are available to reduce the number of alternative expressions and plans that need to be generated.

We use heuristics to reduce the number of plans considered, and thereby to reduce the cost of optimization. Heuristic rules for transforming relational-algebra queries include "perform selection operations as early as possible," "perform projections early," and "avoid Cartesian products."

## Exercises

**12.1.** At what point during query processing does optimization occur?

**12.2.** Why is it not desirable to force users to make an explicit choice of a query-processing strategy? Are there cases in which it *is* desirable for users to be aware of the costs of competing query-processing strategies? Explain your answer.

**12.3.** Consider the following SQL query for our bank database:

> **select** *T.branch-name*
> **from** *branch T, branch S*
> **where** *T.assets > S.assets* **and** *S.branch-city* = "Brooklyn"

Write an efficient relational-algebra expression that is equivalent to this query. Justify your choice.

**12.4.** Consider the relations $r_1(A, B, C)$, $r_2(C, D, E)$, and $r_3(E, F)$, with primary keys $A$, $C$, and $E$, respectively. Assume that $r_1$ has 1000 tuples, $r_2$ has 1500 tuples, and $r_3$ has 750 tuples. Estimate the size of $r_1 \bowtie r_2 \bowtie r_3$, and give an efficient strategy for computing the join.

**12.5.** Consider the relations $r_1(A, B, C)$, $r_2(C, D, E)$, and $r_3(E, F)$ of Exercise 12.4. Assume that there are no primary keys, except the entire schema. Let $V(C, r_1)$ be 900, $V(C, r_2)$ be 1100, $V(E, r_2)$ be 50, and $V(E, r_3)$ be 100. Assume that $r_1$ has 1000 tuples, $r_2$ has 1500 tuples, and $r_3$ has 750 tuples. Estimate the size of $r_1 \bowtie r_2 \bowtie r_3$, and give an efficient strategy for computing the join.

**12.6.** Clustering indices may allow faster access to data than is afforded by a nonclustering index. When must we create a nonclustering index, despite the advantages of a clustering index? Explain your answer.

**12.7.** What are the advantages and disadvantages of hash indices relative to $B^+$-tree indices? How might the type of index available influence the choice of a query-processing strategy?

**12.8.** Assume (for simplicity in this exercise) that only one tuple fits in a block and memory holds at most 3 page frames. Show the runs created on each pass of the sort-merge algorithm, when applied to sort the following tuples on the first attribute: (kangaroo, 17), (wallaby, 21), (emu, 1), (wombat,13), (platypus, 3), (lion, 8), (warthog, 4), (zebra, 11), (meerkat, 6), (hyena, 9), (hornbill, 2), (baboon, 12).

**12.9.** Let relations $r_1(A, B, C)$ and $r_2(C, D, E)$ have the following properties: $r_1$ has 20,000 tuples, $r_2$ has 45,000 tuples, 25 tuples of $r_1$ fit on one block, and 30 tuples of $r_2$ fit on one block. Estimate the number of block accesses required, using each of the following join strategies for $r_1 \bowtie r_2$:

(a) Nested-loop join

(b) Block nested-loop join

(c) Merge–join

(d) Hash–join

**12.10.** Design a variant of the hybrid merge–join algorithm for the case where both relations are not physically sorted, but both have a sorted secondary index on the join attributes.

**12.11.** The indexed nested-loop join algorithm described in Section 12.6.4 can be inefficient if the index is a secondary index, and there are multiple tuples with the same value for the join attributes. Why is it inefficient? Describe a way, using sorting, to reduce the cost of retrieving tuples of the inner relation. Under what conditions would this algorithm be more efficient than hybrid merge–join?

**12.12.** Estimate the number of block accesses required by your solution to Exercise 12.10 for $r_1 \bowtie r_2$, where $r_1$ and $r_2$ are as defined in Exercise 12.9.

**12.13.** Consider relations $r_1$ and $r_2$ of Exercise 12.9, with a relation $r_3(E, F)$. Assume that $r_3$ has 30,000 tuples, and that 40 tuples of $r_3$ fit on one block. Estimate the costs of the three strategies of Section 12.6.7 for computing $r_1 \bowtie r_2 \bowtie r_3$.

**12.14.** Let $r$ and $s$ be relations with no indices, and assume that the relations are not sorted. Assuming infinite memory, what is the lowest cost way (in terms of I/O operations) to compute $r \bowtie s$? What is the amount of memory required for this algorithm?

**12.15.** Suppose that a $B^+$-tree index on *branch-city* is available on relation *branch*, and that no other index is available. What would be the best way to handle the following selections that involve negation?

(a) $\sigma_{\neg(branch\text{-}city<\text{"Brooklyn"})}(branch)$

(b) $\sigma_{\neg(branch\text{-}city=\text{"Brooklyn"})}(branch)$

(c) $\sigma_{\neg(branch\text{-}city<\text{"Brooklyn"} \,\vee\, assets<5000)}(branch)$

**12.16.** Suppose that a $B^+$-tree index on *(branch-name, branch-city)* is available on relation *branch*. What would be the best way to handle the following selection?

$$\sigma_{(branch\text{-}city<\text{"Brooklyn"}) \,\wedge\, (assets<5000)\wedge(branch\text{-}name=\text{"Downtown"})}(branch)$$

**12.17.** The hash–join algorithm as described in Section 12.6.6 computes the natural join of two relations. Describe how to extend the hash–join algorithm to compute the natural left outer join, the natural right outer join and the natural full outer join. (Hint: Keep extra information with each tuple in the hash index, to detect whether any tuple in the probe relation matches the tuple in the hash index.) Try out your algorithm on the *customer* and *depositor* relations.

**12.18.** Write pseudocode for an iterator that implements indexed nested-loop join, where the outer relation is pipelined. Use the standard iterator functions in your pseudocode. Show what state information the iterator must maintain between calls.

**12.19.** Show that the following equivalences hold. Explain how you can apply then to improve the efficiency of certain queries:

(a) $E_1 \bowtie_\theta (E_2 - E_3) = (E_1 \bowtie_\theta E_2 - E_1 \bowtie_\theta E_3)$.

(b) $\sigma_\theta(\ _A\mathcal{G}_F(E)) = \ _A\mathcal{G}_F(\sigma_\theta(E))$, where $\theta$ uses only attributes from $A$.

(c) $\sigma_\theta(E_1 \bowtie E_2) = \sigma_\theta(E_1) \bowtie E_2$ where $\theta$ uses only attributes from $E_1$.

**12.20.** Show how to derive the following equivalences by a sequence of transformations using the equivalence rules in Section 12.9.2.

(a) $\sigma_{\theta_1 \wedge \theta_2 \wedge \theta_3}(E) = \sigma_{\theta_1}(\sigma_{\theta_2}(\sigma_{\theta_3}(E)))$

(b) $\sigma_{\theta_1 \wedge \theta_2}(E_1 \bowtie_{\theta_3} E_2) = \sigma_{\theta_1}(E_1 \bowtie_{\theta_3} (\sigma_{\theta_2}(E_2)))$, where $\theta_2$ involves only attributes from $E_2$

**12.21.** For each of the following pairs of expressions, give instances of relations that show the expressions are not equivalent.

(a) $\Pi_A(R - S)$ and $\Pi_A(R) - \Pi_A(S)$

(b) $\sigma_{B<4}(\ _A\mathcal{G}_{max(B)}(R))$ and $\ _A\mathcal{G}_{max(B)}(\sigma_{B<4}(R))$

(c) In the preceding expressions, if both occurrences of *max* were replaced by *min* would the expressions be equivalent?

(d) $(R \bowtie S) \bowtie T$ and $R \bowtie (S \bowtie T)$

In other words, the natural left outer join is not associative. (Hint: Assume that the schemas of the three relations are $R(a, b1)$, $S(a, b2)$, and $T(a, b3)$, respectively.)

(e) $\sigma_\theta(E_1 \bowtie E_2)$ and $E_1 \bowtie \sigma_\theta(E_2)$, where $\theta$ uses only attributes from $E_2$

**12.22.** The SQL language allows relations with duplicates (Chapter 4).

(a) Define versions of the basic relational-algebra operations $\sigma$, $\Pi$, $\times$, $\bowtie$, $-$, $\cup$, and $\cap$ that work on relations with duplicates, in a way consistent with SQL.

(b) Check which of the equivalence rules 1 through 7.b hold for the multiset version of the relational-algebra defined in part a.

**12.23.** Show that, with $n$ relations, there are $(2(n-1))!/(n-1)!$ different join orders.

**12.24.** Describe a dynamic-programming algorithm for finding the most efficient join order for the join of $n$ relations. Assume that there is only one interesting sort order. (Hint: Show how to derive the lowest cost join order (and its cost) for a set of $n$ relations, given the lowest cost join order (and its cost) for each subset of the $n$ relations.)

**12.25.** Show that the lowest cost join order can be computed in time $O(3^n)$. Assume that you can store and look up information about a set of relations (such as the optimal join order for the set, and the cost of that join order) in constant time. (If you find this exercise difficult, at least show the looser time bound of $O(2^{2n})$.)

**12.26.** Show that, if only left-deep join trees are considered, as in the System R optimizer, the time taken to find the most efficient join order is around $2^n$. Assume that there is only one interesting sort order.

**12.27.** A set of equivalence rules is said to be *complete* if, whenever two expressions are equivalent, one can be derived from the other by a sequence of uses of the equivalence rules. Is the set of equivalence rules that we considered in Section 12.9.2 complete? Hint: Consider the equivalence $\sigma_{3=5}(r) = \{\ \}$.

# Bibliographical Notes

A query processor must parse statements in the query language, and must translate them into an internal form. Parsing of query languages differs little from parsing of traditional programming languages. Most compiler texts, including Aho et al. [1986] and Tremblay and Sorenson [1985], cover the main parsing techniques. These two texts also present optimization from a programming-languages point of view.

Knuth [1973] presents an excellent description of external sorting algorithms, including an optimization that can create initial runs that are (on the average) twice the size of memory. Based on performance studies conducted in the mid-1970s, database systems used only nested-loop join and merge–join. These studies, which were related to the development of System R, determined that either the nested-loop join or merge–join nearly always provided the optimal join method [Blasgen and Eswaran 1976]; hence, these two were the only join algorithms implemented in System R.

The System R study, however, did not include an analysis of hash–join algorithms. Today, hash–joins are considered to be highly efficient. Hash–join algorithms were initially developed for parallel database systems. Experimental systems using hash–join methods were developed in the mid-1980s; notable among these systems are the Grace database machine (Kitsuregawa et al. [1983], Fushimi et al. [1986]) and the Gamma database machine (DeWitt et al. [1986, 1990]). Hash–join techniques are described in Kitsuregawa et al. [1983], and extensions including hybrid hash–join are described in Shapiro [1986]. More recent results by Zeller and Gray [1990] and Davison and Graefe [1994] describe hash–join techniques that can adapt to the available memory, which is important in systems where multiple queries may be running at a time.

Query processing in main memory database is covered by DeWitt et al. [1984], and Whang and Krishnamurthy [1990]. Kim [1982, 1984] describes join strategies and the optimal use of available main memory. Processing of queries using outer joins is described in Rosenthal and Reiner [1984], Galindo-Legaria and Rosenthal [1992] and Galindo-Legaria [1994]. Klug [1982] discusses optimization of relational-algebra expressions with aggregate functions. Theoretical results on the complexity of the computation of relational-algebra operations appear in Gotlieb [1975], Pecherer [1975], and Blasgen and Eswaran [1976]. A comparison of various query-evaluation algorithms is given by Yao [1979b]. Additional discussions are presented in Kim et al. [1985].

Graefe [1993] presents an excellent survey of query-evaluation techniques. An earlier survey of query-processing techniques appears in Jarke and Koch [1984].

The seminal work of Selinger et al. [1979] describes access-path selection in the System R optimizer, which was one of the earliest relational-query optimizers. Wong and Youssefi [1976] describe a technique called *decomposition*, which is used in the Ingres query optimizer. Query processing in Starburst is described in Haas et al. [1989]. Query optimization in Oracle is briefly outlined in Oracle [1992].

Graefe and McKenna [1993] describe the extensibility and search-efficiency features of Volcano, a rule-based query optimizer. Exhaustive searching of all query plans is impractical for optimization of joins involving many relations, and techniques based on randomized searching, which do not examine all alternatives, have been proposed. Ioannidis and Wong [1987], Swami and Gupta [1988], and Ioannidis and Kang [1990] present results in this area. Parametric query-optimization techniques have been proposed by Ioannidis et al. [1992], to handle query processing when relation sizes change frequently. A set of plans—one for each of several different sizes of relations—is computed, and is stored by the optimizer, at compile time. One of these plans is chosen at run time, based on the actual relation sizes, avoiding the cost of full optimization at run time. Nonuniform distributions of values causes problems for estimation of query size and cost. Cost-estimation techniques that use histograms of value distributions have been proposed to tackle the problem. Ioannidis and Christodoulakis [1993], Ioannidis and Poosala [1995], and Poosala et al. [1996] present results in this area.

The SQL language poses several challenges for query optimization, including the presence of duplicates and nulls, and the semantics of nested subqueries. Extension of relational algebra to duplicates is described in Dayal et al. [1982]; optimization of nested subqueries is discussed in Kim [1982], Ganski and Wong [1987], and Dayal [1987]. Chaudhuri and Shim [1994] describe techniques for optimization of queries that use aggregation.

Sellis [1988] describes multiquery optimization, which is the problem of optimizing the execution of several queries as a group. If an entire group of queries is consider ed, it is possible to discover *common subexpressions* that can be evaluated once for the entire group. Finkelstein [1982] and Hall [1976] consider optimization of a group of queries and the use of common subexpressions.

Query optimization can make use of semantic information, such as functional dependencies and other integrity constraints. Semantic-query optimization in relational databases is covered by King [1981]. Malley and Zdonick [1986] present a knowledge-based approach to query optimization. Chakravarthy et al. [1990] use integrity constraints to assist in query optimization.

Query processing for object-oriented databases is discussed in Maier and Stein [1986], Beech [1988], Bertino and Kim [1989], Cluet et al. [1989], Kim [1989], and Kim et al. [1989].

When queries are generated through views, more relations often are joined than is necessary for computation of the query. A collection of techniques for join minimization has been grouped under the name *tableau optimization*. The notion of a tableau was introduced by Aho et al. [1979a, 1979c], and was further extended by Sagiv and Yannakakis [1981]. Ullman [1988] and Maier [1983] provide a textbook coverage of tableaux.

# CHAPTER
# 13

# TRANSACTIONS

Often, a collection of several operations on the database is considered to be a single unit from the point of view of the database user. For example, a transfer of funds from a checking account to a savings account is a single operation when viewed from the customer's standpoint; within the database system, however, it comprises several operations. Clearly, it is essential that all these operations occur, or that, in case of a failure, none occur. It would be unacceptable if the checking account were debited, but the savings account were not credited.

Collections of operations that form a single logical unit of work are called *transactions*. A database system must ensure proper execution of transactions despite failures—either the entire transaction executes, or none of it does. Furthermore, it must manage concurrent execution of transactions in a way that avoids the introduction of inconsistency. Returning to our funds-transfer example, a transaction computing the customer's total money might see the checking-account balance before it is debited by the funds-transfer transaction, but see the savings balance after it is credited. As a result, it would obtain an incorrect result.

This chapter provides an introduction to the basic concepts of transaction processing. Details on concurrent transaction processing and recovery from failures are covered in Chapters 14 and 15, respectively. Further topics in transaction processing are discussed in Chapter 20.

## 13.1 Transaction Concept

A *transaction* is a *unit* of program execution that accesses and possibly updates various data items. A transaction usually results from the execution of a user program written in a high-level data-manipulation language or programming language (for example, SQL, COBOL, C, or Pascal), and is delimited by statements (or function calls) of the form **begin transaction** and **end transaction**. The transaction consists of all operations executed between the begin and end of the transaction.

To ensure integrity of the data, we require that the database system maintains the following properties of the transactions:

- **Atomicity.** Either all operations of the transaction are reflected properly in the database, or none are.
- **Consistency.** Execution of a transaction in isolation (that is, with no other transaction executing concurrently) preserves the consistency of the database.
- **Isolation.** Even though multiple transactions may execute concurrently, the system guarantees that, for every pair of transactions $T_i$ and $T_j$, it appears to $T_i$ that either $T_j$ finished execution before $T_i$ started, or $T_j$ started execution after $T_i$ finished. Thus, each transaction is unaware of other transactions executing concurrently in the system.
- **Durability.** After a transaction completes successfully, the changes it has made to the database persist, even if there are system failures.

These properties are often called the ACID properties; the acronym is derived from the first letter of each of the four properties.

To gain a better understanding of ACID properties and the need for these properties, let us consider a simplified banking system consisting of several accounts and a set of transactions that access and update those accounts. For the time being, we assume that the database permanently resides on disk, but that some portion of it is temporarily residing in main memory.

Access to the database is accomplished by the following two operations:

- **read**($X$), which transfers the data item $X$ from the database to a local buffer belonging to the transaction that executed the **read** operation.
- **write**($X$), which transfers the data item $X$ from the the local buffer of the transaction that executed the **write** back to the database.

In a real database system, the **write** operation does not necessarily result in the immediate update of the data on the disk; the **write** operation may be temporarily stored in memory and executed on the disk later. For now, however, we shall assume that the **write** operation updates the database immediately. We shall return to this subject in Chapter 15.

Let $T_i$ be a transaction that transfers \$50 from account $A$ to account $B$. This transaction can be defined as

$$T_i: \textbf{read}(A);$$
$$A := A - 50;$$
$$\textbf{write}(A);$$
$$\textbf{read}(B);$$
$$B := B + 50;$$
$$\textbf{write}(B).$$

Let us now consider each of the ACID requirements. (For ease of presentation, we consider them in an order different from the order A-C-I-D).

- **Consistency**: The consistency requirement here is that the sum of $A$ and $B$ be unchanged by the execution of the transaction. Without the consistency requirement, money could be created or destroyed by the transaction! It can be verified easily that, if the database is consistent before an execution of the transaction, the database remains consistent after the execution of the transaction.

    Ensuring consistency for an individual transaction is the responsibility of the application programmer who codes the transaction. This task may be facilitated by automatic testing of integrity constraints, as we discussed in Chapter 6.

- **Atomicity**: Suppose that, just prior to the execution of transaction $T_i$ the values of accounts $A$ and $B$ are \$1000 and \$2000, respectively. Now suppose that, during the execution of transaction $T_i$, a failure has occurred that prevented $T_i$ from completing its execution successfully. Examples of such failures include power failures, hardware failures, and software errors. Further, suppose that the failure happened after the **write**($A$) operation was executed, but before the **write**($B$) operation was executed. In this case, the value of accounts $A$ and $B$ reflected in the database are \$950 and \$2000. We have destroyed \$50 as a result of this failure. In particular, we note that the sum $A + B$ is no longer preserved.

    Thus, as the result of the failure, the state of the system no longer reflects a real state of the world that the database is supposed to capture. We term such a state an *inconsistent* state. We must ensure that such inconsistencies are not visible in a database system. Note, however, that the system must at some point be in an inconsistent state. Even if transaction $T_i$ is executed to completion, there exists a point at which the value of account $A$ is \$950 and the value of account $B$ is \$2000, which is clearly an inconsistent state. This state, however, is eventually replaced by the consistent state where the value of account $A$ is \$950, and the value of account $B$ is \$2050. Thus, if the transaction never started or was guaranteed to complete, such an inconsistent state would not be visible except during the execution of the transaction. That is the reason for the atomicity requirement: If the atomicity property is provided, all actions of the transaction are reflected in the database, or none are.

    The basic idea behind ensuring atomicity is as follows. The database system keeps track (on disk) of the old values of any data on which a transaction performs a write, and, if the transaction does not complete its execution, the old values are restored to make it appear as though the transaction never executed. We discuss these ideas further in Section 13.2. Ensuring atomicity is the responsibility of the database system itself; specifically, it is handled by a component called the *transaction-management component*, which we describe in detail in Chapter 15.

- **Durability:** Once the execution of the transaction completes successfully, and the user who initiated the transaction has been notified that the transfer of funds has taken place, it must be the case that no system failure will result in a loss of data corresponding to this transfer of funds.

  The durability property guarantees that, once a transaction completes successfully, all the updates that it carried out on the database persist, even if there is a system failure after the transaction completes execution.

  We assume for now that a failure of the computer system may result in loss of data in main memory, but data written to disk are never lost. We can guarantee durability by ensuring that either

  1. The updates carried out by the transaction have been written to disk before the transaction completes.
  2. Information about the updates carried out by the transaction and written to disk is sufficient to enable the database to reconstruct the updates when the database system is restarted after the failure.

  Ensuring durability is the responsibility of a component of the database system called the *recovery-management component*. The transaction-management component and the recovery-management component are closely related, and we describe their implementation in Chapter 15.

- **Isolation:** Even if the consistency and atomicity properties are ensured for each transaction, if several transactions are executed concurrently, their operations may interleave in some undesirable way, resulting in an inconsistent state.

  For example, as we saw earlier, the database is temporarily inconsistent while the transaction to transfer funds from $A$ to $B$ is executing, with the deducted total written to $A$ and the increased total yet to be written to $B$. If a second concurrently running transaction reads $A$ and $B$ at this intermediate point and computes $A + B$, it will observe an inconsistent value. Furthermore, if this second transaction then performs updates on $A$ and $B$ based on the inconsistent values that it read, the database may be left in an inconsistent state even after both transactions have completed.

  A solution to the problem of concurrently executing transactions is to execute transactions serially—that is, one after the other. However, concurrent execution of transactions provides significant performance benefits, as we shall see in Section 13.4. Other solutions have therefore been developed; they allow multiple transactions to execute concurrently.

  We discuss the problems caused by concurrently executing transactions in Section 13.4. The isolation property of a transaction ensures that the concurrent execution of transactions results in a system state that is equivalent to a state that could have been obtained had these transactions executed one at a time in some order. We shall discuss the principles of isolation further in Section 13.5. Ensuring the isolation property is the responsibility of a component of the database system called the *concurrency-control component*, which we discuss later, in Chapter 14.

# 13.2   Transaction State

In the absence of failures, all transactions complete successfully. However, as we noted earlier, a transaction may not always complete its execution successfully. Such a transaction is termed *aborted*. If we are to ensure the atomicity property, an aborted transaction must have no effect on the state of the database. Thus, any changes that the aborted transaction made to the database must be undone. Once the changes caused by an aborted transaction have been undone, we say that the transaction has been *rolled back*. It is part of the responsibility of the recovery scheme to manage transaction aborts.

A transaction that completes its execution successfully is said to be *committed*. A committed transaction that has performed updates transforms the database into a new consistent state, which must persist even if there is a system failure.

Once a transaction has committed, we cannot undo its effects by aborting it. The only way to undo the effects of a committed transaction is to execute a *compensating transaction*; however, it is not always possible to create such a compensating transaction. Therefore, the responsibility of writing and executing a compensating transaction is left to the user, and is not handled by the database system. Chapter 20 includes a discussion of compensating transactions.

We need to be more precise about what we mean by *successful completion* of a transaction. We therefore establish a simple abstract transaction model. A transaction must be in one of the following states:

- **Active**, the initial state; the transaction stays in this state while it is executing
- **Partially committed**, after the final statement has been executed
- **Failed**, after the discovery that normal execution can no longer proceed
- **Aborted**, after the transaction has been rolled back and the database has been restored to its state prior to the start of the transaction
- **Committed**, after successful completion

The state diagram corresponding to a transaction is shown in Figure 13.1. We say that a transaction has committed only if it has entered the committed state. Similarly, we say that a transaction has aborted only if it has entered the aborted state. A transaction is said to have *terminated* if has either committed or aborted.

A transaction starts in the active state. When it finishes its final statement, it enters the partially committed state. At this point, the transaction has completed its execution, but it is still possible that it may have to be aborted, since the actual output may still be temporarily residing in main memory, and thus a hardware failure may preclude its successful completion.

The database system then writes out enough information to disk that, even in the event of a failure, the updates performed by the transaction can be recreated when the system restarts after the failure. When the last of this information is written out, the transaction enters the committed state.

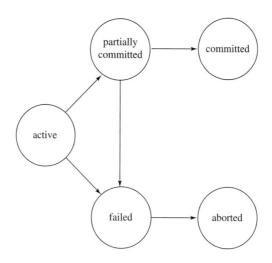

Figure 13.1   State diagram of a transaction.

As mentioned earlier, we assume for now that failures do not result in loss of data on disk. Techniques to deal with loss of data on disk are discussed in Chapter 15.

A transaction enters the failed state after the system determines that the transaction can no longer proceed with its normal execution (for example, because of hardware or logical errors). Such a transaction must be rolled back. Then, it enters the aborted state. At this point, the system has two options:

- It can **restart the transaction**, but only if the transaction was aborted as a result of some hardware or software error that was not created through the internal logic of the transaction. A restarted transaction is considered to be a new transaction.

- It can **kill the transaction**. It usually does so because of some internal logical error that can be corrected only by rewriting of the application program, or because the input was bad, or because the desired data were not found in the database.

We must be cautious when dealing with *observable external writes*, such as writes to a terminal or printer. Once such a write has occurred, it cannot be erased, since it may have been seen external to the database system. Most systems allow such writes to take place only after the transaction has entered the committed state. One way to implement such a scheme is for the database system to store any value associated with such external writes temporarily in nonvolatile storage, and to perform the actual writes only after the transaction enters the committed state. If the system should fail after the transaction has entered the committed state, but before it could complete the external writes, the database system will carry out the external writes (using the data in nonvolatile storage) when the system is restarted.

For certain applications, it may be desirable to allow active transactions to display data to users, particularly for long-duration transactions that run for minutes or hours. Unfortunately, we cannot allow such output of observable data unless we are willing to compromise transaction atomicity. Most current transaction systems ensure atomicity and, therefore, forbid this form of interaction with users. In Chapter 20, we discuss alternative transaction models that support long-duration, interactive transactions.

## 13.3  Implementation of Atomicity and Durability

The recovery-management component of a database system implements the support for atomicity and durability. We first consider a simple, but extremely inefficient, scheme. This scheme assumes that only one transaction is active at a time, and is based on making copies of the database, called *shadow* copies. The scheme assumes that the database is simply a file on disk. A pointer called db_pointer is maintained on disk; it points to the current copy of the database.

In the shadow-database scheme, a transaction that wants to update the database first creates a complete copy of the database. All updates are done on the new database copy, leaving the original copy, called the *shadow copy*, untouched. If at any point the transaction has to be aborted, the new copy is merely deleted. The old copy of the database has not been affected.

If the transaction completes, it is committed as follows. First, the operating system is asked to make sure that all pages of the new copy of the database have been written out to disk. On Unix systems, the flush command is used for this purpose. After the flush has completed, the pointer db_pointer is updated to point to the new copy of the database; the new copy then becomes the current copy of the database. The old copy of the database is then deleted. The scheme is depicted pictorially in Figure 13.2, where the database state before and after the update are shown.

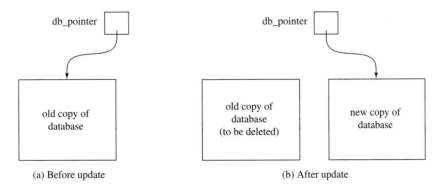

Figure 13.2   Shadow-copy technique for atomicity and durability.

The transaction is said to have been *committed* at the point where the updated db_pointer is written to disk. We now consider how transaction and system failures are handled by this technique. First, consider transaction failure. If the transaction fails at any time before db_pointer is updated, the old contents of the database are not affected. We can abort the transaction by deleting simply the new copy of the database. Once the transaction has been committed, all the updates that it performed are in the database pointed to by db_pointer. Thus, either all updates of the transaction are reflected, or none of the effects are reflected, regardless of transaction failure.

Now consider the issue of system failure. Suppose that the system fails at any time before the updated db_pointer is written to disk. Then, when the system restarts, it will read db_pointer, and will thus see the original contents of the database, and none of the effects of the transaction will be visible on the database. Next, suppose that the system fails after db_pointer has been updated on disk. Before the pointer is updated, all updated pages of the new copy of the database were written to disk. As mentioned earlier, we assume that, once a file is written to disk, its contents will not be damaged even if there is a system failure. Therefore, when the system restarts, it will read db_pointer, and will thus see the contents of the database *after* all the updates performed by the transaction.

The implementation actually depends on the write to db_pointer being atomic; that is, either all its bytes are written or none of its bytes are written. If some of the bytes of the pointer were updated by the write, but others were not, the pointer is meaningless, and neither old nor new versions of the database may be found when the system restarts. Luckily, disk systems provide atomic updates to entire blocks, or at least to a disk sector. In other words, the disk system guarantees that it will update db_pointer atomically.

Thus, the atomicity and durability properties of transactions are ensured by the shadow-copy implementation of the recovery-management component.

As a simple example of a transaction outside the database domain, consider a text-editing session. An entire editing session can be modeled as a transaction. The actions executed by the transaction are reading and updating the file. Saving the file at the end of editing corresponds to a commit of the editing transaction; quitting the editor session without saving the file corresponds to an abort of the editing transaction.

Many text editors use essentially the implementation just described, to ensure that an editing session is transactional. A new file is used to store the updated file. At the end of the editing session, if the updated file is to be saved, a file *rename* command is used to rename the new file to have the actual file name. The rename is assumed to be implemented as an atomic operation by the underlying file system, and deletes the old file as well.

Unfortunately, this implementation is extremely inefficient in the context of large databases, since executing a single transaction requires copying the *entire* database. Furthermore, the implementation does not allow transactions to execute concurrently with one another. There are practical ways of implementing atomicity and durability that are much less expensive and more powerful. We study these recovery techniques in Chapter 15.

# 13.4   Concurrent Executions

Transaction-processing systems usually allow multiple transactions to run concurrently. Allowing multiple transactions to update data concurrently causes several complications with consistency of the data, as we saw earlier. Ensuring consistency in spite of concurrent execution of transactions requires extra work; it is far easier to insist that transactions run *serially*—that is, one at a time, each starting only after the previous one has completed. However, there are two good reasons for allowing concurrency.

- A transaction consists of multiple steps. Some involve I/O activity; others involve CPU activity. The CPU and the disks in a computer system can operate in parallel. Therefore, I/O activity can be done in parallel with processing at the CPU. The parallelism of the CPU and the I/O system can therefore be exploited to run multiple transactions in parallel. While a read or write on behalf of one transaction is in progress on one disk, another transaction can be running in the CPU, while another disk may be executing a read or write on behalf of a third transaction. Thereby, there is an increase in the *throughput* of the system—that is, in the number of transactions that can be executed in a given amount of time. Correspondingly, the processor and disk *utilization* also increase; in other words, the processor and disk spend less time idle, or not performing any useful work.

- There may be a mix of transactions running on a system, some short and some long. If transactions are run serially, a short transaction may have to wait for a preceding long transaction to complete, which can lead to unpredictable delays in running a transaction. If the transactions are operating on different parts of the database, it is better to let them run concurrently, sharing the CPU cycles and disk accesses among them. Concurrent execution reduces the unpredictable delays in running transactions. Moreover, it also reduces the *average response time*: the average time for a transaction to be completed after it has been submitted.

The motivation for using concurrent execution in a database is essentially the same as the motivation for using *multiprogramming* in an operating system.

When several transactions run concurrently, database consistency can be destroyed despite the correctness of each individual transaction. In this section, we present the concept of schedules to help identify those executions that are guaranteed to ensure consistency.

The database system must control the interaction among the concurrent transactions to prevent them from destroying the consistency of the database. It does so through a variety of mechanisms called *concurrency-control* schemes. We study concurrency-control schemes in Chapter 14; for now, we focus on the concept of correct concurrent execution.

Consider again the simplified banking system of Section 13.1, which has several accounts, and a set of transactions that access and update those accounts. Let $T_1$ and $T_2$ be two transactions that transfer funds from one account to another.

Transaction $T_1$ transfers \$50 from account $A$ to account $B$ and is defined as

$$
\begin{aligned}
T_1: \ &\textbf{read}(A); \\
&A := A - 50; \\
&\textbf{write}(A); \\
&\textbf{read}(B); \\
&B := B + 50; \\
&\textbf{write}(B).
\end{aligned}
$$

Transaction $T_2$ transfers 10 percent of the balance from account $A$ to account $B$, and is defined as

$$
\begin{aligned}
T_2: \ &\textbf{read}(A); \\
&temp := A * 0.1; \\
&A := A - temp; \\
&\textbf{write}(A); \\
&\textbf{read}(B); \\
&B := B + temp; \\
&\textbf{write}(B).
\end{aligned}
$$

Let the current values of accounts $A$ and $B$ be \$1000 and \$2000, respectively. Suppose that the two transactions are executed one at a time in the order $T_1$ followed by $T_2$. This execution sequence is represented in Figure 13.3. In the figure, the sequence of instruction steps is in chronological order from top to bottom, with instructions of $T_1$ appearing in the left column, and instructions of $T_2$ appearing in the right column. The final values of accounts $A$ and $B$, after the execution in Figure 13.3 takes place, are \$855 and \$2145, respectively. Thus, the total amount of money in accounts $A$ and $B$—that is, the sum $A + B$—is preserved after the execution of both transactions.

| $T_1$ | $T_2$ |
|---|---|
| **read**($A$) | |
| $A := A - 50$ | |
| **write**($A$) | |
| **read**($B$) | |
| $B := B + 50$ | |
| **write**($B$) | |
| | **read**($A$) |
| | $temp := A * 0.1;$ |
| | $A := A - temp$ |
| | **write**($A$) |
| | **read**($B$) |
| | $B := B + temp$ |
| | **write**($B$) |

Figure 13.3   Schedule 1 — a serial schedule in which $T_1$ is followed by $T_2$.

| $T_1$ | $T_2$ |
|---|---|
| | **read**($A$) |
| | $temp := A * 0.1;$ |
| | $A := A - temp$ |
| | **write**($A$) |
| | **read**($B$) |
| | $B := B + temp$ |
| | **write**($B$) |
| **read**($A$) | |
| $A := A - 50$ | |
| **write**($A$) | |
| **read**($B$) | |
| $B := B + 50$ | |
| **write**($B$) | |

Figure 13.4    Schedule 2—a serial schedule in which $T_2$ is followed by $T_1$.

Similarly, if the transactions are executed one at a time in the order $T_2$ followed by $T_1$, then the corresponding execution sequence is that of Figure 13.4. Again, as expected, the sum $A + B$ is preserved, and the final values of accounts $A$ and $B$ are \$850 and \$2150, respectively.

The execution sequences just described are called *schedules*. They represent the chronological order in which instructions are executed in the system. Clearly, a schedule for a set of transactions must consist of all instructions of those transactions, and must preserve the order in which the instructions appear in each individual transaction. For example, in transaction $T_1$, the instruction **write**($A$) must appear before the instruction **read**($B$), in any valid schedule. In the following discussion, we shall refer to the first execution sequence ($T_1$ followed by $T_2$) as schedule 1, and to the second execution sequence ($T_2$ followed by $T_1$) as schedule 2.

These schedules are *serial*. Each serial schedule consists of a sequence of instructions from various transactions, where the instructions belonging to one single transaction appear together in that schedule. Thus, for a set of $n$ transactions, there exist $n!$ different valid serial schedules.

When several transactions are executed concurrently, the corresponding schedule no longer needs to be serial. If two transactions are running concurrently, the operating system may execute one transaction for a little while, then perform a context switch, execute the second transaction for some time, and then switch back to the first transaction for some time, and so on. With multiple transactions, the CPU time is shared among all the transactions.

Several execution sequences are possible, since the various instructions from both transactions may now be interleaved. In general, it is not possible to predict exactly how many instructions of a transaction will be executed before the CPU switches to another transaction. Thus, the number of possible schedules for a set of $n$ transactions is much larger than $n!$.

| $T_1$ | $T_2$ |
|---|---|
| **read**($A$) | |
| $A := A - 50$ | |
| **write**($A$) | |
| | **read**($A$) |
| | $temp := A * 0.1;$ |
| | $A := A - temp$ |
| | **write**($A$) |
| **read**($B$) | |
| $B := B + 50$ | |
| **write**($B$) | |
| | **read**($B$) |
| | $B := B + temp$ |
| | **write**($B$) |

Figure 13.5    Schedule 3—a concurrent schedule equivalent to schedule 1.

Returning to our previous example, suppose that the two transactions are executed concurrently. One possible schedule is shown in Figure 13.5. After this execution takes place, we arrive at the same state as the one in which the transactions are executed serially in the order $T_1$ followed by $T_2$. The sum $A + B$ is indeed preserved.

Not all concurrent executions result in a correct state. To illustrate, consider the schedule of Figure 13.6. After the execution of this schedule, we arrive at a state where the final values of accounts $A$ and $B$ are \$950 and \$2100, respectively. This final state is an *inconsistent state*, since we have gained \$50 in the process of

| $T_1$ | $T_2$ |
|---|---|
| **read**($A$) | |
| $A := A - 50$ | |
| | **read**($A$) |
| | $temp := A * 0.1;$ |
| | $A := A - temp$ |
| | **write**($A$) |
| | **read**($B$) |
| **write**($A$) | |
| **read**($B$) | |
| $B := B + 50$ | |
| **write**($B$) | |
| | $B := B + temp$ |
| | **write**($B$) |

Figure 13.6    Schedule 4—a concurrent schedule.

the concurrent execution. Indeed, the sum $A + B$ is not preserved by the execution of the two transactions.

If control of concurrent execution is left entirely to the operating system, many possible schedules, including ones that leave the database in an inconsistent state, such as the one just described, are possible. It is the job of the database system to ensure that any schedule that gets executed will leave the database in a consistent state. The component of the database system that carries out this task is called the *concurrency-control* component.

We can ensure consistency of the database under concurrent execution by making sure that any schedule that executed has the same effect as a schedule that could have occurred without any concurrent execution. That is, the schedule should, in some sense, be equivalent to a serial schedule. We examine this idea in Section 13.5.

## 13.5   Serializability

The database system must control concurrent execution of transactions, to ensure that the database state remains consistent. Before we examine how the database system can carry out this task, we must first understand which schedules will ensure consistency, and which schedules will not.

Since transactions are programs, it is computationally difficult to determine what are the exact operations that a transaction performs, and how operations of various transactions interact. For this reason, we shall not interpret the type of operations that a transaction can perform on a data item. Instead, we consider only two operations: **read** and **write**. We thus assume that, between a **read**($Q$) instruction and a **write**($Q$) instruction on a data item $Q$, a transaction may perform an arbitrary sequence of operations on the copy of $Q$ that is residing in the local buffer of the transaction. Thus, the only significant operations of a transaction, from a scheduling point of view, are its **read** and **write** instructions. We shall therefore usually show only **read** and **write** instructions in schedules, as we do in the representation of schedule 3 that is shown in Figure 13.7.

In this section, we discuss different forms of schedule equivalence; they lead to the notions of *conflict serializability* and *view serializability*.

| $T_1$ | $T_2$ |
|---|---|
| **read**($A$) | |
| **write**($A$) | |
| | **read**($A$) |
| | **write**($A$) |
| **read**($B$) | |
| **write**($B$) | |
| | **read**($B$) |
| | **write**($B$) |

Figure 13.7   Schedule 3—showing only the **read** and **write** instructions.

## 13.5.1  Conflict Serializability

Let us consider a schedule $S$ in which there are two consecutive instructions $I_i$ and $I_j$, of transactions $T_i$ and $T_j$, respectively $(i \neq j)$. If $I_i$ and $I_j$ refer to different data items, then we can swap $I_i$ and $I_j$ without affecting the results of any instruction in the schedule. However, if $I_i$ and $I_j$ refer to the same data item $Q$, then the order of the two steps may matter. Since we are dealing with only **read** and **write** instructions, there are four cases that we need to consider:

1. $I_i$ = **read**($Q$), $I_j$ = **read**($Q$). The order of $I_i$ and $I_j$ does not matter, since the same value of $Q$ is read by $T_i$ and $T_j$, regardless of the order.

2. $I_i$ = **read**($Q$), $I_j$ = **write**($Q$). If $I_i$ comes before $I_j$, then $T_i$ does not read the value of $Q$ that is written by $T_j$ in instruction $I_j$. If $I_j$ comes before $I_i$, then $T_i$ reads the value of $Q$ that is written by $T_j$. Thus, the order of $I_i$ and $I_j$ matters.

3. $I_i$ = **write**($Q$), $I_j$ = **read**($Q$). The order of $I_i$ and $I_j$ matters for reasons similar to those of the previous case.

4. $I_i$ = **write**($Q$), $I_j$ = **write**($Q$). Since both instructions are **write** operations, the order of these instructions does not affect either $T_i$ or $T_j$. However, the value obtained by the next **read**($Q$) instruction of $S$ is affected, since the result of only the latter of the two **write** instructions is preserved in the database. If there is no other **write**($Q$) instruction after $I_i$ and $I_j$ in $S$, then the order of $I_i$ and $I_j$ directly affects the final value of $Q$ in the database state that results from schedule $S$.

Thus, only in the case where both $I_i$ and $I_j$ are **read** instructions does the relative order of their execution not matter.

We say that $I_i$ and $I_j$ *conflict* if they are operations by different transactions on the same data item, and at least one of these instructions is a **write** operation.

To illustrate the concept of conflicting instructions, we consider schedule 3, as shown in Figure 13.7. The **write**($A$) instruction of $T_1$ conflicts with the **read**($A$) instruction of $T_2$. However, the **write**($A$) instruction of $T_2$ does not conflict with the **read**($B$) instruction of $T_1$, because the two instructions access different data items.

Let $I_i$ and $I_j$ be consecutive instructions of a schedule $S$. If $I_i$ and $I_j$ are instructions of different transactions and $I_i$ and $I_j$ do not conflict, then we can swap the order of $I_i$ and $I_j$ to produce a new schedule $S'$. We expect $S$ to be equivalent to $S'$, since all instructions appear in the same order in both schedules except for $I_i$ and $I_j$, whose order does not matter.

Since the **write**($A$) instruction of $T_2$ in schedule 3 of Figure 13.7 does not conflict with the **read**($B$) instruction of $T_1$, we can swap these instructions to generate an equivalent schedule, schedule 5, as shown in Figure 13.8. Regardless of the initial system state, schedules 3 and 5 both produce the same final system state.

$$
\begin{array}{c|c}
T_1 & T_2 \\
\hline
\textbf{read}(A) & \\
\textbf{write}(A) & \\
 & \textbf{read}(A) \\
\textbf{read}(B) & \\
 & \textbf{write}(A) \\
\textbf{write}(B) & \\
 & \textbf{read}(B) \\
 & \textbf{write}(B) \\
\end{array}
$$

Figure 13.8    Schedule 5—schedule 3 after swapping of a pair of instructions.

Let us continue to swap nonconflicting instructions as follows:

- Swap the **read**(B) instruction of $T_1$ with the **read**(A) instruction of $T_2$.
- Swap the **write**(B) instruction of $T_1$ with the **write**(A) instruction of $T_2$.
- Swap the **write**(B) instruction of $T_1$ with the **read**(A) instruction of $T_2$.

The final result of these swaps, as shown in schedule 6 of Figure 13.9, is a serial schedule. Thus, we have shown that schedule 3 is equivalent to a serial schedule. This equivalence implies that, regardless of the initial system state, schedule 3 will produce the same final state as will some serial schedule.

If a schedule $S$ can be transformed into a schedule $S'$ by a series of swaps of nonconflicting instructions, we say that $S$ and $S'$ are *conflict equivalent*.

Returning to our previous examples, we note that schedule 1 is not conflict equivalent to schedule 2. However, schedule 1 is conflict equivalent to schedule 3, because the **read**(B) and **write**(B) instruction of $T_1$ can be swapped with the **read**(A) and **write**(A) instruction of $T_2$.

The concept of conflict equivalence leads to the concept of conflict serializability. We say that a schedule $S$ is *conflict serializable* if it is conflict equivalent to a serial schedule. Thus, schedule 3 is conflict serializable, since it is conflict equivalent to the serial schedule 1.

$$
\begin{array}{c|c}
T_1 & T_2 \\
\hline
\textbf{read}(A) & \\
\textbf{write}(A) & \\
\textbf{read}(B) & \\
\textbf{write}(B) & \\
 & \textbf{read}(A) \\
 & \textbf{write}(A) \\
 & \textbf{read}(B) \\
 & \textbf{write}(B) \\
\end{array}
$$

Figure 13.9    Schedule 6—a serial schedule that is equivalent to schedule 3.

| $T_3$ | $T_4$ |
|---|---|
| **read**($Q$) | |
| | **write**($Q$) |
| **write**($Q$) | |

Figure 13.10    Schedule 7.

Finally, consider schedule 7 of Figure 13.10; it consists of only the significant operations (that is, the **read** and **write**) of transactions $T_3$ and $T_4$. This schedule is not conflict serializable, since it is not equivalent to either the serial schedule $<T_3,T_4>$ or the serial schedule $<T_4,T_3>$.

It is possible to have two schedules that produce the same outcome, but that are not conflict equivalent. For example, consider transaction $T_5$, which transfers $10 from account $B$ to account $A$. Let schedule 8 be as defined in Figure 13.11. We claim that schedule 8 is not conflict equivalent to the serial schedule $<T_1,T_5>$, since, in schedule 8, the **write**($B$) instruction of $T_5$ conflicts with the **read**($B$) instruction of $T_1$. Thus, we cannot move all the instructions of $T_1$ before those of $T_5$ by swapping consecutive nonconflicting instructions. However, the final values of accounts $A$ and $B$ after the execution of either schedule 8 or the serial schedule $<T_1,T_5>$ are the same—namely, $960 and $2040, respectively.

We can see from this example that there are less stringent definitions of schedule equivalence than there are of conflict equivalence. For the system to determine that schedule 8 produces the same outcome as the serial schedule $<T_1,T_5>$, it must analyze the computation performed by $T_1$ and $T_5$, rather than just the **read** and **write** operations. In general, such analysis is hard to implement and is computationally expensive. However, there are other definitions of schedule equivalence

| $T_1$ | $T_5$ |
|---|---|
| **read**($A$) | |
| $A := A - 50$ | |
| **write**($A$) | |
| | **read**($B$) |
| | $B := B - 10$ |
| | **write**($B$) |
| **read**($B$) | |
| $B := B + 50$ | |
| **write**($B$) | |
| | **read**($A$) |
| | $A := A + 10$ |
| | **write**($A$) |

Figure 13.11    Schedule 8.

based purely on the **read** and **write** operations. We will consider one such definition in the next section.

## 13.5.2  View Serializability

In this section, we consider a form of equivalence that is less stringent than conflict equivalence, but that, like conflict equivalence, is based on only the **read** and **write** operations of transactions.

Consider two schedules $S$ and $S'$, where the same set of transactions participates in both schedules. The schedules $S$ and $S'$ are said to be *view equivalent* if the following three conditions are met:

1. For each data item $Q$, if transaction $T_i$ reads the initial value of $Q$ in schedule $S$, then transaction $T_i$ must, in schedule $S'$, also read the initial value of $Q$.

2. For each data item $Q$, if transaction $T_i$ executes **read**($Q$) in schedule $S$, and that value was produced by transaction $T_j$ (if any), then transaction $T_i$ must, in schedule $S'$, also read the value of $Q$ that was produced by transaction $T_j$.

3. For each data item $Q$, the transaction (if any) that performs the final **write**($Q$) operation in schedule $S$ must perform the final **write**($Q$) operation in schedule $S'$.

Conditions 1 and 2 ensure that each transaction reads the same values in both schedules and, therefore, performs the same computation. Condition 3, coupled with conditions 1 and 2, ensures that both schedules result in the same final system state.

Returning to our previous examples, we note that schedule 1 is not view equivalent to schedule 2, since, in schedule 1, the value of account $A$ read by transaction $T_2$ was produced by $T_1$, whereas this case does not hold in schedule 2. However, schedule 1 is view equivalent to schedule 3, because the values of account $A$ and $B$ read by transaction $T_2$ were produced by $T_1$ in both schedules.

The concept of view equivalence leads to the concept of view serializability. We say that a schedule $S$ is *view serializable* if it is view equivalent to a serial schedule.

As an illustration, suppose that we augment schedule 7 with transaction $T_6$, and obtain schedule 9, as depicted in Figure 13.12. schedule 9 is view serializable. Indeed, it is view equivalent to the serial schedule $<T_3, T_4, T_6>$, since the one **read**($Q$) instruction reads the initial value of $Q$ in both schedules, and $T_6$ performs the final write of $Q$ in both schedules.

Every conflict-serializable schedule is view serializable, but there are view-serializable schedules that are not conflict serializable. Indeed, schedule 9 is not conflict serializable, since every pair of consecutive instructions conflicts, and, thus, no swapping of instructions is possible.

Observe that, in schedule 9, transactions $T_4$ and $T_6$ perform **write**($Q$) operations without having performed a **read**($Q$) operation. Writes of this sort are called *blind writes*. Blind writes appear in any view-serializable schedule that is not conflict serializable.

| $T_3$ | $T_4$ | $T_6$ |
|---|---|---|
| **read**($Q$) | | |
| | **write**($Q$) | |
| **write**($Q$) | | |
| | | **write**($Q$) |

**Figure 13.12    Schedule 9—a view-serializable schedule.**

## 13.6    Recoverability

So far, we have studied what schedules are acceptable from the viewpoint of consistency of the database, assuming implicitly that there are no transaction failures. We now address the effect of transaction failures during concurrent execution.

If a transaction $T_i$ fails, for whatever reason, we need to undo the effect of this transaction to ensure the atomicity property of the transaction. In a system that allows concurrent execution, it is necessary also to ensure that any transaction $T_j$ that is dependent on $T_i$ (that is, $T_j$ has read data written by $T_i$) is also aborted. To achieve this surety, we need to place restrictions on the type of schedules permitted in the system.

In the following two subsections, we address the issue of what schedules are acceptable from the viewpoint described. As mentioned earlier, we describe in Chapter 14 how to ensure that only such acceptable schedules are generated.

### 13.6.1    Recoverable Schedules

Consider schedule 11, shown in Figure 13.13, in which $T_9$ is a transaction that performs only one instruction: **read**($A$). Suppose that the system allows $T_9$ to commit immediately after executing the **read**($A$) instruction. Thus, $T_9$ commits before $T_8$ does. Now suppose that $T_8$ fails before it commits. Since $T_9$ has read the value of data item $A$ written by $T_8$, we must abort $T_9$ to ensure transaction atomicity. However, $T_9$ has already committed and cannot be aborted. Thus, we have a situation where it is impossible to recover correctly from the failure of $T_8$.

Schedule 11, with the commit happening immediately after the **read**($A$) instruction, is an example of a *nonrecoverable* schedule, which should be not allowed. Most database system require that all schedules be *recoverable*. A recov-

| $T_8$ | $T_9$ |
|---|---|
| **read**($A$) | |
| **write**($A$) | |
| | **read**($A$) |
| **read**($B$) | |

**Figure 13.13    Schedule 11.**

| $T_{10}$ | $T_{11}$ | $T_{12}$ |
|---|---|---|
| **read**($A$) | | |
| **read**($B$) | | |
| **write**($A$) | | |
| | **read**($A$) | |
| | **write**($A$) | |
| | | **read**($A$) |

Figure 13.14    Schedule 12.

erable schedule is one where, for each pair of transactions $T_i$ and $T_j$ such that $T_j$ reads a data items previously written by $T_i$, the commit operation of $T_i$ appears before the commit operation of $T_j$.

### 13.6.2  Cascadeless Schedules

Even if a schedule is recoverable, to recover correctly from the failure of a transaction $T_i$, we may have to roll back several transactions. Such situations occur if transactions have read data written by $T_i$. As an illustration, consider the partial schedule of Figure 13.14. Transaction $T_{10}$, writes a value of $A$ that is read by transaction $T_{11}$. Transaction $T_{11}$ writes a value of $A$ that is read by transaction $T_{12}$. Suppose that, at this point, $T_{10}$ fails. $T_{10}$ must be rolled back. Since $T_{11}$ is dependent on $T_{10}$, $T_{11}$ must be rolled back. Since $T_{12}$ is dependent on $T_{11}$, $T_{12}$ must be rolled back. This phenomenon, in which a single transaction failure leads to a series of transaction rollbacks, is called *cascading rollback*.

Cascading rollback is undesirable, since it leads to the undoing of a significant amount of work. It is desirable to restrict the schedules to those where cascading rollbacks cannot occur. Such schedules are called *cascadeless* schedules. A cascadeless schedule is one where, for each pair of transactions $T_i$ and $T_j$ such that $T_j$ reads a data item previously written by $T_i$, the commit operation of $T_i$ appears before the read operation of $T_j$. It is easy to verify that every cascadeless schedule is also recoverable.

## 13.7  Implementation of Isolation

So far, we have seen what properties a schedule must have if it is to leave the database in a consistent state, and to allow transaction failures to be handled in a safe manner. Specifically, schedules that are conflict or view serializable and cascadeless satisfy these requirements.

There are various *concurrency-control* schemes that we can use to ensure that, even when multiple transactions are executed concurrently, only acceptable schedules are generated, regardless of how the operating-system time-shares resources (such as CPU time) among the transactions.

As a trivial example of a concurrency-control scheme, consider this scheme: A transaction acquires a *lock* on the entire database before it starts, and releases the lock after it has committed. While a transaction holds a lock, no other transaction is allowed to acquire the lock, and all must therefore wait for the lock to be released. As a result of the locking policy, only one transaction can execute at a time. Therefore, only serial schedules are generated. These are trivially serializable, and it is easy to verify that they are cascadeless as well.

A concurrency-control scheme such as this one leads to poor performance, since it forces transactions to wait for preceding transactions to finish before they can start. In other words, it provides a poor degree of concurrency. As explained in Section 13.4, concurrent execution has several performance benefits.

The goal of concurrency-control schemes is to provide a high degree of concurrency, while ensuring that all schedules that can be generated are conflict or view serializable, and are cascadeless.

We study a number of concurrency-control schemes in Chapter 14. The schemes have different tradeoff in terms of the amount of concurrency they allow and the amount of overhead that they incur. Some of them allow only conflict-serializable schedules to be generated; others allow view-serializable schedules that are not conflict-serializable to be generated.

## 13.8    Transaction Definition in SQL

A data-manipulation language must include a construct for specifying the set of actions that constitute a transaction.

The SQL standard specifies that a transaction begins implicitly. Transactions are ended by one of the following SQL statements:

- **Commit work** commits the current transaction and begins a new one.
- **Rollback work** causes the current transaction to abort.

The keyword **work** is optional in both the statements. If a program terminates without either of these commands, the updates are either committed or rolled back—which of the two happens is not specified by the standard, and is implementation dependent.

The standard also specifies that the system must ensure both serializability and freedom from cascading rollback. The definition of *serializability* used by the standard is that a schedule must have the *same effect* as would a serial schedule. Thus, conflict and view serializability are both acceptable.

The SQL-92 standard also allows a transaction to specify that it may be executed in a manner that causes it to become nonserializable with respect to other transactions. For instance, a transaction may operate at the level of **read uncommitted**, which permits the transaction to read records even if they have not been committed. Such features are provided for long transactions whose results do not need to be precise. For instance, approximate information is usually sufficient for statistics used for query optimization. If these transactions were to execute in a serializable fashion, they could interfere with other transactions, causing the others execution to be delayed.

The levels of consistency specified by SQL-92 are as follows:

- **Serializable** is the default.
- **Repeatable read** allows only committed records to be read, and further requires that, between two reads of a record by a transaction, no other transaction is allowed to update the record. However, the transaction may not be serializable with respect to other transactions. For instance, when it is searching for records satisfying some conditions, a transaction may find some of the records inserted by a committed transaction, but may not find others.
- **Read committed** allows only committed records to be read, but does not require even repeatable reads. For instance, between two reads of a record by the transaction, the records may have been updated by other committed transactions.
- **Read uncommitted** allows even uncommitted records to be read. It is the lowest level of consistency allowed by SQL-92.

# 13.9    Testing for Serializability

When designing concurrency control schemes, we must show that schedules generated by the scheme are serializable. To do that, we must first understand how to determine, given a particular schedule $S$, whether the schedule is serializable. In this section, we shall present methods for determining conflict and view serializability. We will show that there exists a simple and efficient algorithm to determine conflict serializability. However, there is no efficient algorithm for determining view serializability.

## 13.9.1    Test for Conflict Serializability

Let $S$ be a schedule. We construct a directed graph, called a *precedence graph*, from $S$. This graph consists of a pair $G = (V,E)$, where $V$ is a set of vertices, and $E$ is a set of edges. The set of vertices consists of all the transactions participating in the schedule. The set of edges consists of all edges $T_i \rightarrow T_j$ for which one of the following three conditions hold

1. $T_i$ executes **write**($Q$) before $T_j$ executes **read**($Q$).
2. $T_i$ executes **read**($Q$) before $T_j$ executes **write**($Q$).
3. $T_i$ executes **write**($Q$) before $T_j$ executes **write**($Q$).

If an edge $T_i \rightarrow T_j$ exists in the precedence graph, then, in any serial schedule $S'$ equivalent to $S$, $T_i$ must appear before $T_j$.

For example, the precedence graph for schedule 1 is shown in Figure 13.15a. It contains the single edge $T_1 \rightarrow T_2$, since all the instructions of $T_1$ are executed before the first instruction of $T_2$ is executed. Similarly, Figure 13.15b shows the precedence graph for schedule 2 with the single edge $T_2 \rightarrow T_1$, since all the instructions of $T_2$ are executed before the first instruction of $T_1$ is executed.

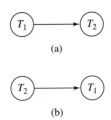

(a)

(b)

Figure 13.15    Precedence graph for (a) schedule 1 and (b) schedule 2.

The precedence graph for schedule 4 is depicted in Figure 13.16. It contains the edge $T_1 \rightarrow T_2$, because $T_1$ executes **read**(A) before $T_2$ executes **write**(A). It also contains the edge $T_2 \rightarrow T_1$, because $T_2$ executes **read**(B) before $T_1$ executes **write**(B).

If the precedence graph for $S$ has a cycle, then schedule $S$ is not conflict serializable. If the graph contains no cycles, then the schedule $S$ is conflict serializable. The serializability order can be obtained through *topological sorting*, which determines a linear order consistent with the partial order of the precedence graph. There are, in general, several possible linear orders that can be obtained through a topological sorting. For example, the graph of Figure 13.17a has two acceptable linear orderings, as illustrated in Figures 13.17b and 13.17c.

Thus, to test for conflict serializability, we need to construct the precedence graph and to invoke a cycle-detection algorithm. Cycle-detection algorithms can be found in standard textbooks on algorithms. Cycle-detection algorithms, such as those based on depth-first search, require on the order of $n^2$ operations, where $n$ is the number of vertices in the graph (that is, the number of transactions). Thus, we have a practical scheme for determining conflict serializability.

Returning to our previous examples, note that the precedence graphs for schedules 1 and 2 (Figure 13.15) indeed do not contain cycles. The precedence graph for schedule 4 (Figure 13.16), on the other hand, contains a cycle, indicating that this schedule is not conflict serializable.

### 13.9.2    Test for View Serializability

We can modify the precedence-graph test for conflict serializability to test for view serializability, as we show next. However, the resultant test is expensive in CPU time. In fact, testing for view serializability is computationally an expensive problem, as we shall see later.

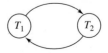

Figure 13.16    Precedence graph for schedule 4.

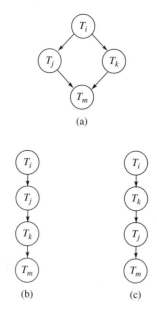

(a)

(b)                    (c)

Figure 13.17    Illustration of topological sorting.

In the case of testing for conflict serializability, we know that, if two transactions, $T_i$ and $T_j$, access a data item $Q$, and at least one of these transactions writes $Q$, then either the edge, $T_i \rightarrow T_j$ or the edge $T_j \rightarrow T_i$ is inserted in the precedence graph. This situation, however, is no longer the case when we are testing for view serializability. As we shall see shortly, this difference is the cause of our inability to come up with an efficient algorithm for such a test.

Consider schedule 9, which we saw earlier in Figure 13.12. If we follow the rule in the conflict-serializability test for forming the precedence graph, we get the graph of Figure 13.18. This graph contains a cycle, indicating that schedule 9 is not conflict serializable. However, as we saw earlier, schedule 9 is view serializable, since it is view equivalent to the serial schedule $<T_3, T_4, T_6>$. The edge $T_4 \rightarrow T_3$ should *not* have been inserted in the graph, since the values of item $Q$ produced by $T_3$ and $T_4$ were never used by any other transaction, and $T_6$ produced

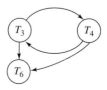

Figure 13.18    Precedence graph for schedule 9.

a new final value of $Q$. The **write**$(Q)$ instructions of $T_3$ and $T_4$ are called *useless writes*.

What we have pointed out is that we cannot simply use the precedence-graph scheme of Section 13.9.1 to test for view serializability. We need to develop a scheme for deciding whether an edge needs to be inserted in a precedence graph.

Let $S$ be a schedule. Suppose that transaction $T_j$ reads the value of data item $Q$ written by $T_i$. Clearly, if $S$ is view serializable, then, in any serial schedule $S'$ that is equivalent to $S$, $T_i$ must precede $T_j$. Suppose now that, in schedule $S$, transaction $T_k$ executed a **write**$(Q)$. Then, in schedule $S'$, $T_k$ must either precede $T_i$ or follow $T_j$. It cannot appear between $T_i$ and $T_j$, because otherwise $T_j$ would not read the value of $Q$ written by $T_i$ and thus $S$ would not be view equivalent to $S'$.

These constraints cannot be expressed in terms of the simple precedence-graph model previously discussed. The difficulty occurs because we know that, in the preceding example, one of the pair of edges $T_k \rightarrow T_i$, $T_j \rightarrow T_k$ must be inserted in the graph, but we have not yet formed the rule for determining the appropriate choice.

To form it, we need to extend the precedence graph to include labeled edges. We term such a graph a *labeled precedence graph*. As before, the nodes of the graph are the transactions participating in the schedule. The rules for inserting labeled edges are described next.

Let $S$ be a schedule consisting of transactions $\{T_1, T_2, \ldots, T_n\}$. Let $T_b$ and $T_f$ be two dummy transactions such that $T_b$ issues **write**$(Q)$ for each $Q$ accessed in $S$, and $T_f$ issues **read**$(Q)$ for each $Q$ accessed in $S$. We construct a new schedule $S'$ from $S$ by inserting $T_b$ at the beginning of $S$, and appending $T_f$ to the end of $S$. We construct the labeled precedence graph for schedule $S'$ as follows:

1. Add an edge $T_i \overset{0}{\rightarrow} T_j$, if transaction $T_j$ reads the value of data item $Q$ written by transaction $T_i$.

2. Remove all the edges incident on useless transactions. A transaction $T_i$ is *useless* if there exists no path, in the precedence graph, from $T_i$ to transaction $T_f$.

3. For each data item $Q$ such that $T_j$ reads the value of $Q$ written by $T_i$, and $T_k$ executes **write**$(Q)$ and $T_k \neq T_b$, do the following:

    a. If $T_i = T_b$ and $T_j \neq T_f$, then insert the edge $T_j \overset{0}{\rightarrow} T_k$ in the labeled precedence graph.

    b. If $T_i \neq T_b$ and $T_j = T_f$, then insert the edge $T_k \overset{0}{\rightarrow} T_i$ in the labeled precedence graph.

    c. If $T_i \neq T_b$ and $T_j \neq T_f$, then insert the pair of edges $T_k \overset{p}{\rightarrow} T_i$, and $T_j \overset{p}{\rightarrow} T_k$ in the labeled precedence graph where $p$ is a unique integer larger than 0 that has not been used earlier for labeling edges.

Rule 3c reflects that, if $T_i$ writes a data item that $T_j$ reads, then a transaction $T_k$ that writes the same data item must come before $T_i$ or after $T_j$. Rules 3a and 3b are special cases that result from the fact that $T_b$ and $T_f$ are necessarily the first and final transactions, respectively. When we apply rule 3c, we are *not* requiring $T_k$ to be *both* before $T_i$ *and* after $T_j$. Rather, we have a choice of where $T_k$ may appear in an equivalent serial ordering.

As an illustration, consider again schedule 7 (Figure 13.10). The graph constructed in steps 1 and 2 is depicted in Figure 13.19a. It contains the edge $T_b \xrightarrow{0} T_3$, since $T_3$ reads the value of $Q$ written by $T_b$. It contains the edge $T_3 \xrightarrow{0} T_f$, since $T_3$ was the final transaction that wrote $Q$ and, thus, $T_f$ read that value. The final graph corresponding to schedule 7 is depicted in Figure 13.19b. It contains the edge $T_3 \xrightarrow{0} T_4$ as a result of step 3a. It contains the edge $T_4 \xrightarrow{0} T_3$ as a result of step 3b.

Consider now schedule 9 (Figure 13.12). The graph constructed in steps 1 and 2 is depicted in Figure 13.20a. The final graph is shown in Figure 13.20b. It contains the edges $T_3 \xrightarrow{0} T_4$ and $T_3 \xrightarrow{0} T_6$ as a result of step 3a. It contains the edges $T_3 \xrightarrow{0} T_6$ (already in the graph) and $T_4 \xrightarrow{0} T_6$ as a result of step 3b.

Finally, consider schedule 10 of Figure 13.21. Schedule 10 is view serializable, since it is view equivalent to the serial schedule $<T_3,T_4,T_7>$. The corresponding labeled precedence graph, constructed in steps 1 and 2, is depicted in Figure 13.22a. The final graph is depicted in Figure 13.22b. The edges $T_3 \xrightarrow{0} T_4$ and $T_3 \xrightarrow{0} T_7$ were inserted as a result of rule 3a. The pair of edges $T_3 \xrightarrow{1} T_4$ and $T_7 \xrightarrow{1} T_3$ was inserted as the result of a *single* application of rule 3c.

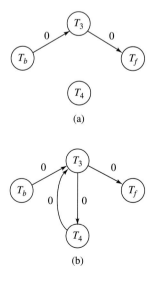

(a)

(b)

Figure 13.19    Labeled precedence graph of schedule 7.

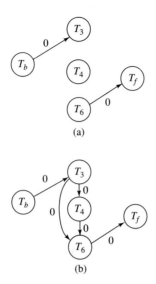

Figure 13.20     Labeled precedence graph of schedule 9.

The graphs depicted in Figures 13.19b and 13.22b contain the following minimal cycles, respectively:

- $T_3 \xrightarrow{0} T_4 \xrightarrow{0} T_3$
- $T_3 \xrightarrow{0} T_7 \xrightarrow{1} T_3$

The graph in Figure 13.20b, on the other hand, contains no cycles.

If the graph contains no cycle, the corresponding schedule is view serializable. Indeed, the graph of Figure 13.20b contains no cycle, and its corresponding schedule 9 is view serializable. However, if the graph contains a cycle, that condition does *not* necessarily imply that the corresponding schedule is not view serializable. For instance, the graph of Figure 13.19b contains a cycle, and its corresponding schedule 7 is not view serializable. The graph of Figure 13.22b, on the other hand, contains a cycle, but its corresponding schedule 10 is view serializable.

How, then, do we determine whether a schedule is view serializable? The answer lies in an appropriate interpretation of the precedence graph. Suppose

| $T_3$ | $T_4$ | $T_7$ |
|---|---|---|
| **read**($Q$) | | |
| | **write**($Q$) | |
| | | **read**($Q$) |
| **write**($Q$) | | |
| | | **write**($Q$) |

Figure 13.21     Schedule 10.

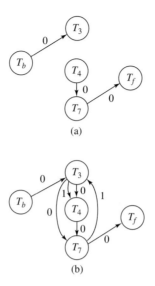

Figure 13.22    Labeled precedence graph of schedule 10.

that there are $n$ distinct edge pairs. That is, we applied rule 3c $n$ times in the construction of the precedence graph. Then, there exist $2^n$ different graphs, where each graph contains only one edge from each pair. If any one of these graphs is acyclic, then the corresponding schedule is view serializable. The serializability order is determined by the removal of the dummy transactions $T_b$ and $T_f$, and by the topological sorting of the remaining acyclic graph.

Return to the graph of Figure 13.22b. Since there is exactly one distinct pair, there are two different graphs that need to be considered. The two graphs are depicted in Figure 13.23. Since the graph of Figure 13.23a is acyclic, we know that the corresponding schedule 10 is view serializable.

The algorithm just described requires exhaustive testing of all possible distinct graphs. It has been shown that the problem of testing for an acyclic graph in this set falls in the class of *NP*-complete problems (see the bibliographic notes for references to discussion of the theory of *NP*-complete problems). Any algorithm for an *NP*-complete problem will almost certainly take time that is exponential in the size of the problem.

In fact, it has been shown that the problem of testing for view serializability is itself *NP*-complete. Thus, almost certainly there exists no efficient algorithm to test for view serializability. However, concurrency-control schemes can still use *sufficient conditions* for view serializability. That is, if the sufficient conditions are satisfied, the schedule is view serializable, but there may be view-serializable schedules that do not satisfy the sufficient conditions.

# 13.10   Summary

A *transaction* is a *unit* of program execution that accesses and possibly updates various data items. Understanding the concept of a transaction is critical for un-

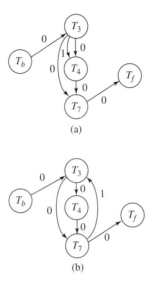

Figure 13.23    Two distinct precedence graphs.

derstanding and implementing updates of data in a database, such that concurrent executions and failures of various forms do not result in the database becoming inconsistent. Transactions are required to have the ACID properties: atomicity, consistency, isolation and durability.

Atomicity ensures that either all the effects of a transaction are reflected in the database, or none are; a failure cannot leave the database in a state where a transaction is partially executed. Consistency ensures that, if the database is initially consistent, the execution of the transaction (by itself) leaves the database in a consistent state. Isolation ensures that concurrently executing transactions are isolated from one another, such that each has the impression that no other transaction is executing concurrently with it. Durability ensures that, once a transaction has been committed, that transaction's updates do not get lost, even if there is a system failure.

When several transactions execute concurrently in the database, the consistency of data may no longer be preserved. It is therefore necessary for the system to control the interaction among the concurrent transactions. Since a transaction is a unit that preserves consistency, a serial execution of transactions guarantees that consistency is preserved. We therefore require that any schedule produced by concurrent processing of a set of transactions will have an effect equivalent to a schedule produced when these transactions are run serially in some order. A system that guarantees this property is said to ensure *serializability*. There are several different notions of equivalence leading to the concepts of *conflict serializability* and *view serializability*.

Serializability of schedules generated by concurrently executing transactions can be ensured through one of a variety of mechanisms called *concurrency-control* schemes. The concurrency-control–management component of the database is responsible for handling the concurrency-control schemes. The recovery-management component of a database is responsible for ensuring the atomicity and durability properties of transactions.

We can test a given schedule for conflict serializability by constructing a *precedence graph* for the schedule, and by searching for absence of cycles in the graph. The time taken for the test is of the order of $n^2$, where $n$ is the number of transactions. We can test for view serializability in order $2^n$ time by constructing a *labeled precedence graph* and searching over all possible distinct labeled graphs for a graph without a cycle.

## Exercises

**13.1.** List the ACID properties. Explain the usefulness of each.

**13.2.** Suppose that there is a database system that never fails. Is a recovery manager required for this system?

**13.3.** Consider a file system such as the one on your favorite operating system. Are the issues of atomicity and durability relevant to the following? Explain your answer.

(*a*) A user of the file system

(*b*) An implementor of the file system

**13.4.** Database-system implementors have paid much more attention to the ACID properties than have file-system implementors. Why does that make sense?

**13.5.** During its execution, a transaction passes through several states, until it finally commits or aborts. List all possible sequences of states through which a transaction may pass. Explain why each state transition may occur.

**13.6.** Explain the distinction between the terms *serial schedule* and *serializable schedule*.

**13.7.** Consider the following two transactions:

$$T_1: \textbf{read}(A);$$
$$\textbf{read}(B);$$
$$\textbf{if } A = 0 \textbf{ then } B := B + 1;$$
$$\textbf{write}(B).$$
$$T_2: \textbf{read }(B);$$
$$\textbf{read }(A);$$
$$\textbf{if } B = 0 \textbf{ then } A := A + 1;$$
$$\textbf{write}(A).$$

Let the consistency requirement be $A = 0 \lor B = 0$, with $A = B = 0$ the initial values.

(*a*) Show that every serial execution involving these two transactions preserves the consistency of the database.

(*b*) Show a concurrent execution of $T_1$ and $T_2$ that produces a nonserializable schedule.

(*c*) Is there a concurrent execution of $T_1$ and $T_2$ that produces a serializable schedule?

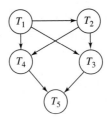

Figure 13.24    Precedence graph.

**13.8.** Since every conflict-serializable schedule is view serializable, why do we emphasize conflict serializability rather than view serializability?

**13.9.** Consider the precedence graph of Figure 13.24. Is the corresponding schedule conflict serializable? Explain your answer.

**13.10.** Consider the labeled precedence graph of Figure 13.25. Is the corresponding schedule view serializable? Explain your answer.

**13.11.** What is a recoverable schedule? Why is recoverability of schedules desirable? Are there any circumstances under which it would be desirable to allow nonrecoverable schedules? Explain your answer.

**13.12.** What is a cascadeless schedule? Why is cascadelessness of schedules desirable? Are there any circumstances under which it would be desirable to allow noncascadeless schedules? Explain your answer.

## Bibliographical Notes

Textbook discussions of concurrency control and recovery are given by Bernstein et al. [1987] and Papadimitriou [1986]. A comprehensive survey paper on implementation issues in concurrency control and recovery is presented by Gray [1978]. Gray and Reuter [1993] provide extensive textbook coverage of transaction-processing concepts and techniques, including concurrency control and recovery issues. Lynch et al. [1994] provide extensive textbook coverage of atomic transactions.

The concept of serializability was formulated by Eswaran et al. [1976] in connection to their work on concurrency control for System R. The results con-

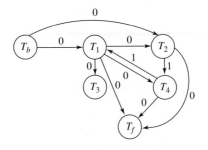

Figure 13.25    Labeled precedence graph.

cerning serializability testing are from Papadimitriou et al. [1977], and Papadimitriou [1979]. Cycle-detection algorithms can be found in standard algorithm textbooks, such as Cormen et al. [1990], and Aho et al. [1983].

Papadimitriou [1979] shows that testing for view serializability is NP-complete. (The theory of NP-completeness is presented in Aho et al. [1974], and in Garey and Johnson [1979].)

References covering specific aspects of transaction processing are cited in Chapters 14, 15, and 20.

# CHAPTER
# 14

## CONCURRENCY CONTROL

We saw in Chapter 13 that one of the fundamental properties of a transaction is isolation. When several transactions execute concurrently in the database, the isolation property may no longer be preserved. It is necessary for the system to control the interaction among the concurrent transactions; this control is achieved through one of a variety of mechanisms called *concurrency-control* schemes.

The concurrency-control schemes that we discuss in this chapter are all based on the serializability property. That is, all the schemes presented here ensure that the schedules are serializable. In Chapter 20, we discuss concurrency control schemes that admit nonserializable schedules. In this chapter, we consider the management of concurrently executing transactions, and we ignore failures. In Chapter 15, we shall see how the system can recover from failures.

## 14.1 Lock-Based Protocols

One way to ensure serializability is to require that access to data items be done in a mutually exclusive manner; that is, while one transaction is accessing a data item, no other transaction can modify that data item. The most common method used to implement this requirement is to allow a transaction to access a data item only if it is currently holding a lock on that item.

### 14.1.1 Locks

There are various modes in which a data item may be locked. In this section, we restrict our attention to two modes:

1. **Shared**. If a transaction $T_i$ has obtained a shared-mode lock (denoted by S) on item $Q$, then $T_i$ can read, but cannot write, $Q$.

2. **Exclusive**. If a transaction $T_i$ has obtained an exclusive-mode lock (denoted by X) on item $Q$, then $T_i$ can both read and write $Q$.

We require that every transaction *request* a lock in an appropriate mode on data item $Q$, depending on the types of operations that it will perform on $Q$. The request is made to the concurrency-control manager. The transaction can proceed with the operation only after the concurrency-control manager *grants* the lock to the transaction.

Given a set of lock modes, we can define a *compatibility function* on them as follows. Let $A$ and $B$ represent arbitrary lock modes. Suppose that a transaction $T_i$ requests a lock of mode $A$ on item $Q$ on which transaction $T_j$ ($T_i \neq T_j$) currently holds a lock of mode $B$. If transaction $T_i$ can be granted a lock on $Q$ immediately, in spite of the presence of the mode $B$ lock, then we say mode $A$ is *compatible* with mode $B$. Such a function can be represented conveniently by a matrix. The compatibility relation between the two modes of locking used in this section is given by the matrix **comp** of Figure 14.1. An element **comp**$(A,B)$ of the matrix has the value *true* if and only if mode $A$ is compatible with mode $B$.

Note that shared mode is compatible with shared mode, but not with exclusive mode. At any time, several shared-mode locks can be held simultaneously (by different transactions) on a particular data item. A subsequent exclusive-mode lock request has to wait until the currently held shared-mode locks are released.

A transaction requests a shared lock on data item $Q$ by executing the **lock-S($Q$)** instruction. Similarly, an exclusive lock is requested through the **lock-X($Q$)** instruction. A data item $Q$ can be unlocked via the **unlock($Q$)** instruction.

To access a data item, transaction $T_i$ must first lock that item. If the data item is already locked by another transaction in an incompatible mode, the concurrency-control manager will not grant the lock until all incompatible locks held by other transactions have been released. Thus, $T_i$ is made to *wait* until all incompatible locks held by other transactions have been released.

Transaction $T_i$ may unlock a data item that it had locked at some earlier point. Note that a transaction must hold a lock on a data item as long as it accesses that item. Moreover, for a transaction to unlock a data item immediately after its final access of that data item is not always desirable, since serializability may not be ensured.

|   | S | X |
|---|---|---|
| S | true | false |
| X | false | false |

Figure 14.1    Lock-compatibility matrix **comp**.

As an illustration, consider again the simplified banking system that we introduced in Chapter 13. Let $A$ and $B$ be two accounts that are accessed by transactions $T_1$ and $T_2$. Transaction $T_1$ transfers \$50 from account $B$ to account $A$, and is defined as

$$T_1: \textbf{lock-X}(B);$$
$$\textbf{read}(B);$$
$$B := B - 50;$$
$$\textbf{write}(B);$$
$$\textbf{unlock}(B);$$
$$\textbf{lock-X}(A);$$
$$\textbf{read}(A);$$
$$A := A + 50;$$
$$\textbf{write}(A);$$
$$\textbf{unlock}(A).$$

Transaction $T_2$ displays the total amount of money in accounts $A$ and $B$—that is, the sum $A + B$—and is defined as

$$T_2: \textbf{lock-S}(A);$$
$$\textbf{read}(A);$$
$$\textbf{unlock}(A);$$
$$\textbf{lock-S}(B);$$
$$\textbf{read}(B);$$
$$\textbf{unlock}(B);$$
$$\textbf{display}(A + B).$$

Suppose that the values of accounts $A$ and $B$ are \$100 and \$200, respectively. If these two transactions are executed serially, either in the order $T_1$, $T_2$ or the order $T_2$, $T_1$, then transaction $T_2$ will display the value \$300. If, however, these transactions are executed concurrently, then schedule 1, as shown in Figure 14.2, is possible. In this case, transaction $T_2$ displays \$250, which is incorrect. The reason for this mistake is that the transaction $T_1$ unlocked data item $B$ too early, as a result of which $T_2$ saw an inconsistent state.

The schedule shows the actions executed by the transactions, as well as the points when the locks are granted by the concurrency-control manager. The transaction making a lock request cannot execute its next action until the lock is granted by the concurrency-control manager; hence, the lock must be granted in the interval of time between the lock-request operation and the following action of the transaction. Exactly when within this interval the lock is granted is not important; the lock can be safely assumed to be granted just before the following action of the transaction. Hence, we shall drop the column depicting the actions of the concurrency-control manager from all schedules depicted in the rest of the chapter. We let you infer when locks are granted.

Suppose now that unlocking is delayed to the end of the transaction. Transaction $T_3$ corresponds to $T_1$ with unlocking delayed, and is defined as

$$T_3: \textbf{lock-X}(B);$$
$$\textbf{read}(B);$$
$$B := B - 50;$$
$$\textbf{write}(B);$$
$$\textbf{lock-X}(A);$$
$$\textbf{read}(A);$$
$$A := A + 50;$$
$$\textbf{write}(A);$$
$$\textbf{unlock}(B);$$
$$\textbf{unlock}(A).$$

Transaction $T_4$ corresponds to $T_2$ with unlocking delayed, and is defined as

$$T_4: \textbf{lock-S}(A);$$
$$\textbf{read}(A);$$
$$\textbf{lock-S}(B);$$
$$\textbf{read}(B);$$
$$\textbf{display}(A + B);$$
$$\textbf{unlock}(A);$$
$$\textbf{unlock}(B).$$

| $T_1$ | $T_2$ | concurrency-control manager |
|-------|-------|------------------------------|
| **lock-X**($B$) | | |
| | | **grant-X**($B,T_1$) |
| **read**($B$) | | |
| $B := B - 50$ | | |
| **write**($B$) | | |
| **unlock**($B$) | | |
| | **lock-S**($A$) | |
| | | **grant-S**($A,T_2$) |
| | **read**($A$) | |
| | **unlock**($A$) | |
| | **lock-S**($B$) | |
| | | **grant-S**($B,T_2$) |
| | **read**($B$) | |
| | **unlock**($B$) | |
| | **display**($A + B$) | |
| **lock-X**($A$) | | |
| | | **grant-X**($A,T_2$) |
| **read**($A$) | | |
| $A := A + 50$ | | |
| **write**($A$) | | |
| **unlock**($A$) | | |

Figure 14.2    Schedule 1.

| $T_3$ | $T_4$ |
|---|---|
| **lock-X**($B$) | |
| **read**($B$) | |
| $B := B - 50$ | |
| **write**($B$) | |
| | **lock-S**($A$) |
| | **read**($A$) |
| | **lock-S**($B$) |
| **lock-X**($A$) | |

Figure 14.3    Schedule 2.

You should verify that the sequence of reads and writes in schedule 1, which lead to an incorrect total of $250 being displayed, is no longer possible with $T_3$ and $T_4$. Other schedules are possible. $T_4$ will not print out an inconsistent result in any of them; we shall see why later.

Unfortunately, the use of locking can lead to an undesirable situation. Consider the partial schedule of Figure 14.3 for $T_3$ and $T_4$. Since $T_3$ is holding an exclusive-mode lock on $B$ and $T_4$ is requesting a shared-mode lock on $B$, $T_4$ is waiting for $T_3$ to unlock $B$. Similarly, since $T_4$ is holding a shared-mode lock on $A$ and $T_3$ is requesting an exclusive-mode lock on $A$, $T_3$ is waiting for $T_4$ to unlock $A$. Thus, we have arrived at a state where neither of these transactions can ever proceed with its normal execution. This situation is called *deadlock*. When deadlock occurs, the system must roll back one of the two transactions. Once a transaction has been rolled back, the data items that were locked by that transaction are unlocked. These data items are then available to the other transaction, which can continue with its execution. We shall return to the issue of deadlock handling in Section 14.6.

If we do not use locking, or unlock data items as soon as possible after reading or writing them, we may get inconsistent states. On the other hand, if we do not unlock a data item before requesting a lock on another data item, deadlocks may occur. There are ways to avoid deadlock in some situations, as we shall see in Section 14.1.4. However, in general, deadlocks are a necessary evil associated with locking, if we want to avoid inconsistent states. Deadlocks are definitely preferable to inconsistent states, since they can be handled by rolling back of transactions, whereas inconsistent states may lead to real-world problems that cannot be handled by the database system.

We shall require that each transaction in the system follow a set of rules, called a *locking protocol*, indicating when a transaction may lock and unlock each of the data items. Locking protocols restrict the number of possible schedules. The set of all such schedules is a proper subset of all possible serializable schedules. We shall present several locking protocols that allow only conflict-serializable schedules. Before doing so, we need a few definitions.

Let $\{T_0, T_1, ..., T_n\}$ be a set of transactions participating in a schedule $S$. We say that $T_i$ *precedes* $T_j$ in $S$, written $T_i \rightarrow T_j$, if there exists a data item $Q$ such that $T_i$ has held lock mode $A$ on $Q$, and $T_j$ has held lock mode $B$ on $Q$ later, and **comp**($A,B$) = false. If $T_i \rightarrow T_j$, then that precedence implies that in any equivalent serial schedule, $T_i$ must appear before $T_j$. Observe that this graph is similar to the precedence graph that we used in Section 13.9.1 to test for conflict serializability. Conflicts between instructions correspond to noncompatibility of lock modes.

We say that a schedule $S$ is *legal* under a given locking protocol if $S$ is a possible schedule for a set of transactions following the rules of the locking protocol. We say that a locking protocol *ensures conflict serializability* if and only if, for all legal schedules, the associated $\rightarrow$ relation is acyclic.

## 14.1.2   Granting of Locks

When a transaction requests a lock on a data item in a particular mode, and no other transaction has a lock on the same data item in a conflicting mode, the lock can be granted. However, care must be taken to avoid the following scenario. Suppose a transaction $T_2$ has a shared-mode lock on a data item, and another transaction $T_1$ requests an exclusive-mode lock on the data item. Clearly, $T_1$ has to wait for $T_2$ to release the shared-mode lock. Meanwhile, a transaction $T_3$ may request a shared-mode lock on the same data item. The lock request is compatible with the lock granted to $T_2$, so $T_3$ may be granted the shared-mode lock. At this point $T_2$ may release the lock, but still $T_1$ has to wait for $T_3$ to finish. But again, there may be a new transaction $T_4$ that requests a shared-mode lock on the same data item, and is granted the lock before $T_3$ releases it. In fact, it is possible that there is a sequence of transactions that each requests a shared-mode lock on the data item, and each transaction releases the lock a short while after it is granted, but $T_1$ never gets the exclusive-mode lock on the data item. The transaction $T_1$ may never make progress, and is said to be *starved*.

We can avoid starvation of transactions by granting locks as follows. When a transaction $T_i$ requests a lock on a data item $Q$ in a particular mode $M$, the lock is granted provided that

1. There is no other other transaction holding a lock on $Q$ in a mode that conflicts with $M$.

2. There is no other transaction that is waiting for a lock on $Q$, and that made its lock request before $T_i$.

## 14.1.3   The Two-Phase Locking Protocol

One protocol that ensures serializability is the *two-phase locking protocol*. This protocol requires that each transaction issue lock and unlock requests in two phases:

1. **Growing phase**. A transaction may obtain locks, but may not release any lock.

2. **Shrinking phase**. A transaction may release locks, but may not obtain any new locks.

Initially, a transaction is in the growing phase. The transaction acquires locks as needed. Once the transaction releases a lock, it enters the shrinking phase, and it can issue no more lock requests.

For example, transactions $T_3$ and $T_4$ (see page 474) are two phase. On the other hand, transactions $T_1$ and $T_2$ (see page 473) are not two phase. Note that the unlock instructions do not need to appear at the end of the transaction. For example, in the case of transaction $T_3$, we could move the **unlock**($B$) instruction to just after the **lock-X**($A$) instruction, and still retain the two-phase locking property.

We can show that the two-phase locking protocol ensures conflict serializability. Consider any transaction. The point in the schedule where the transaction has obtained its final lock (the end of its growing phase) is called the *lock point* of the transaction. Now, transactions can be ordered according to their lock points— this ordering is, in fact, a serializability ordering for the transactions. We leave the proof as an exercise for you to do (see Exercise 14.1).

Two-phase locking does *not* ensure freedom from deadlock. Observe that transactions $T_3$ and $T_4$ are two-phase, but, in schedule 2 (Figure 14.3), they are deadlocked.

Recall from Section 13.6.2 that, in addition to their being serializable, it is desirable that schedules be cascadeless. Cascading rollback may occur under two-phase locking. As an illustration, consider the partial schedule of Figure 14.4. Each transaction observes the two-phase locking protocol, but the failure of $T_5$ after the **read**($A$) step of $T_7$ leads to cascading rollback of $T_6$ and $T_7$.

Cascading rollbacks can be avoided by a modification of two-phase locking called the *strict two-phase locking* protocol. The strict two-phase locking protocol, requires, that in addition to locking being two-phase, all exclusive-mode locks taken by a transaction must be held until that transaction commits. This

| $T_5$ | $T_6$ | $T_7$ |
|---|---|---|
| **lock-X**($A$) | | |
| **read**($A$) | | |
| **lock-S**($B$) | | |
| **read**($B$) | | |
| **write**($A$) | | |
| **unlock**($A$) | | |
| | **lock-X**($A$) | |
| | **read**($A$) | |
| | **write**($A$) | |
| | **unlock**($A$) | |
| | | **lock-S**($A$) |
| | | **read**($A$) |

Figure 14.4    Partial schedule under two-phase locking.

requirement ensures that any data written by an uncommitted transaction are locked in exclusive mode until the transaction commits, preventing any other transaction from reading the data.

Another variant of two-phase locking is the *rigorous two-phase* locking protocol, which requires all locks to be held until the transaction commits. It can be easily verified that, with rigorous two-phase locking, transactions can be serialized in the order in which they commit. Most database systems implement either strict or rigorous two-phase locking.

Consider the following two transactions for which we have shown only some of the significant **read** and **write** operations. Transaction $T_8$ is defined as

$$T_8: \textbf{read}(a_1);$$
$$\textbf{read}(a_2);$$
$$\ldots$$
$$\textbf{read}(a_n);$$
$$\textbf{write}(a_1).$$

Transaction $T_9$ is defined as

$$T_9: \textbf{read}(a_1);$$
$$\textbf{read}(a_2);$$
$$\textbf{display}(a_1 + a_2).$$

If we employ the two-phase locking protocol, then $T_8$ must lock $a_1$ in exclusive mode. Therefore, any concurrent execution of both transactions amounts to a serial execution. Notice, however, that $T_8$ needs an exclusive lock on $a_1$ only at the end of its execution, when it writes $a_1$. Thus, if $T_8$ could initially lock $a_1$ in shared mode, and then could later change the lock to exclusive mode, we could get more concurrency, since $T_8$ and $T_9$ could access $a_1$ and $a_2$ simultaneously.

This observation leads us to a refinement of the basic two-phase locking protocol, in which lock *conversions* are allowed. We shall provide a mechanism for upgrading a shared lock to an exclusive lock, and downgrading an exclusive lock to a shared lock. We denote conversion from shared to exclusive modes by **upgrade**, and from exclusive to shared by **downgrade**. Lock conversion cannot be allowed to occur arbitrarily. Rather, upgrading can take place in only the growing phase, whereas downgrading can take place in only the shrinking phase.

Returning to our example, transactions $T_8$ and $T_9$ can run concurrently under the refined two-phase locking protocol, as shown in the incomplete schedule of Figure 14.5, where only some of the locking instructions are shown.

Note that a transaction attempting to upgrade a lock on an item $Q$ may be forced to wait. This enforced wait occurs if $Q$ is currently locked by *another* transaction in shared mode.

Just like the basic two-phase locking protocol, two-phase locking with lock conversion generates only conflict-serializable schedules, and transactions can be serialized by their lock points. Further, if exclusive locks are held until the end of the transaction, the schedules are cascadeless.

| $T_8$ | $T_9$ |
|---|---|
| **lock-S**($a_1$) | |
| | **lock-S**($a_1$) |
| **lock-S**($a_2$) | |
| | **lock-S**($a_2$) |
| **lock-S**($a_3$) | |
| **lock-S**($a_4$) | |
| | **unlock**($a_1$) |
| | **unlock**($a_2$) |
| **lock-S**($a_n$) | |
| **upgrade**($a_1$) | |

Figure 14.5    Incomplete schedule with a lock conversion.

We now describe a simple but widely used scheme that automatically generates the appropriate lock and unlock instructions for a transaction. When a transaction $T_i$ issues a **read**($Q$) operation, the system issues a **lock-S**($Q$) instruction followed by the **read**($Q$) instruction. When $T_i$ issues a **write**($Q$) operation, the system checks to see whether $T_i$ already holds a shared lock on $Q$. If it does, then the system issues an **upgrade**($Q$) instruction, followed by the **write**($Q$) instruction. Otherwise, the system issues a **lock-X**($Q$) instruction, followed by the **write**($Q$) instruction. All locks obtained by a transaction are unlocked after that transaction commits or aborts.

For a set of transactions, there may be conflict-serializable schedules that cannot be obtained through the two-phase locking protocol. However, to obtain conflict-serializable schedules through non-two-phase locking protocols, we need either to have additional information about the transactions or to impose some structure or ordering on the set of data items in the database. In the absence of such information, two-phase locking is necessary for conflict serializability—if $T_i$ is a non–two-phase transaction, it is always possible to find another transaction $T_j$ that is two-phase such that there is a schedule possible for $T_i$ and $T_j$ that is not conflict serializable.

Strict two-phase locking and rigorous two-phase locking (with lock conversions) are used extensively in commercial database systems.

## 14.1.4    Graph-Based Protocols

As we pointed out, in the absence of information concerning the manner in which data items are accessed, the two-phase locking protocol is both necessary and sufficient for ensuring serializability. Thus, if we wish to develop protocols that are not two-phase, we need additional information on how each transaction will access the database. There are various models that differ in the amount of such information provided. The simplest model requires that we have prior knowledge about the order in which the database items will be accessed. Given such information, it is possible to construct locking protocols that are not two-phase, but that, nevertheless, ensure conflict serializability.

To acquire such prior knowledge, we impose a partial ordering $\rightarrow$ on the set $\mathbf{D} = \{d_1, d_2, ..., d_h\}$ of all data items. If $d_i \rightarrow d_j$, then any transaction accessing both $d_i$ and $d_j$ must access $d_i$ before accessing $d_j$. This partial ordering may be the result of either the logical or the physical organization of the data, or it may be imposed solely for the purpose of concurrency control.

The partial ordering implies that the set $\mathbf{D}$ may now be viewed as a directed acyclic graph, called a *database graph*. In this section, for the sake of simplicity, we will restrict our attention to only those graphs that are rooted trees. We will present a simple protocol, called the *tree protocol*, which is restricted to employ only *exclusive* locks. References to other, more complex, graph-based locking protocols are provided in the bibliographic notes.

In the tree protocol, the only lock instruction allowed is **lock-X**. Each transaction $T_i$ can lock a data item at most once, and must observe the following rules:

1. The first lock by $T_i$ may be on any data item.
2. Subsequently, a data item $Q$ can be locked by $T_i$ only if the parent of $Q$ is currently locked by $T_i$.
3. Data items may be unlocked at any time.
4. A data item that has been locked and unlocked by $T_i$ cannot subsequently be relocked by $T_i$.

As we stated earlier, all schedules that are legal under the tree protocol are conflict serializable.

To illustrate this protocol, consider the database graph of Figure 14.6. The following four transactions follow the tree protocol on this graph. We have shown

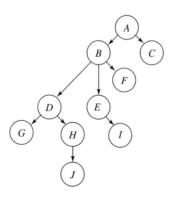

Figure 14.6   Tree structured database graph.

only the lock and unlock instructions:

$T_{10}$: **lock-X**($B$); **lock-X**($E$); **lock-X**($D$); **unlock**($B$); **unlock**($E$); **lock-X**($G$); **unlock**($D$); **unlock**($G$).

$T_{11}$: **lock-X**($D$); **lock-X**($H$); **unlock**($D$); **unlock**($H$).

$T_{12}$: **lock-X**($B$); **lock-X**($E$); **unlock**($E$); **unlock**($B$).

$T_{13}$: **lock-X**($D$); **lock-X**($H$); **unlock**($D$); **unlock**($H$).

One possible schedule in which these four transactions participated is depicted in Figure 14.7. Note that, during its execution, transaction $T_{10}$ holds locks on two *disjoint* subtrees.

Observe that the schedule of Figure 14.7 is conflict serializable. It can be shown not only that the tree protocol ensures conflict serializability, but also that this protocol ensures freedom from deadlock.

The tree-locking protocol has an advantage over the two-phase locking protocol in that unlocking may occur earlier. Earlier unlocking may lead to shorter waiting times, and to an increase in concurrency. In addition, since the protocol is deadlock-free, no rollbacks are required. However, the protocol has the disadvantage that, in some cases, a transaction may have to lock data items that it does not access. For example, a transaction that needs to access data items $A$ and $J$ in the database graph of Figure 14.6 must lock not only $A$ and $J$, but also data items $B$, $D$, and $H$. This additional locking results in increased locking overhead,

| $T_{10}$ | $T_{11}$ | $T_{12}$ | $T_{13}$ |
|---|---|---|---|
| **lock-X**($B$) | | | |
| | **lock-X**($D$) | | |
| | **lock-X**($H$) | | |
| | **unlock**($D$) | | |
| **lock-X**($E$) | | | |
| **lock-X**($D$) | | | |
| **unlock**($B$) | | | |
| **unlock**($E$) | | | |
| | | **lock-X**($B$) | |
| | | **lock-X**($E$) | |
| | **unlock**($H$) | | |
| **lock-X**($G$) | | | |
| **unlock**($D$) | | | |
| | | | **lock-X**($D$) |
| | | | **lock-X**($H$) |
| | | | **unlock**($D$) |
| | | | **unlock**($H$) |
| | | **unlock**($E$) | |
| | | **unlock**($B$) | |
| **unlock**($G$) | | | |

**Figure 14.7**    Serializable schedule under the tree protocol.

the possibility of additional waiting time, and a potential decrease in concurrency. Further, without prior knowledge of what data items will need to be locked, transactions will have to lock the root of the tree, and that can reduce concurrency greatly.

For a set of transactions, there may be conflict-serializable schedules that cannot be obtained through the tree protocol. Indeed, there are schedules possible under the two-phase locking protocol that are not possible under the tree protocol, and vice versa. Examples of such schedules are explored in the exercises.

## 14.2   Timestamp-Based Protocols

In the locking protocols that we have described thus far, the order between every pair of conflicting transactions is determined at execution time by the first lock that they both request that involves incompatible modes. Another method for determining the serializability order is to select an ordering among transactions in advance. The most common method for doing so is to use a *timestamp-ordering* scheme.

### 14.2.1   Timestamps

With each transaction $T_i$ in the system, we associate a unique fixed timestamp, denoted by $TS(T_i)$. This timestamp is assigned by the database system before the transaction $T_i$ starts execution. If a transaction $T_i$ has been assigned timestamp $TS(T_i)$, and a new transaction $T_j$ enters the system, then $TS(T_i) < TS(T_j)$. There are two simple methods for implementing this scheme:

1. Use the value of the *system clock* as the timestamp; that is, a transaction's timestamp is equal to the value of the clock when the transaction enters the system.

2. Use a *logical counter* that is incremented after a new timestamp has been assigned; that is, a transaction's timestamp is equal to the value of the counter when the transaction enters the system.

The timestamps of the transactions determine the serializability order. Thus, if $TS(T_i) < TS(T_j)$, then the system must ensure that the produced schedule is equivalent to a serial schedule in which transaction $T_i$ appears before transaction $T_j$.

To implement this scheme, we associate with each data item $Q$ two timestamp values:

- **W-timestamp**($Q$) denotes the largest timestamp of any transaction that executed **write**($Q$) successfully.
- **R-timestamp**($Q$) denotes the largest timestamp of any transaction that executed **read**($Q$) successfully.

These timestamps are updated whenever a new **read**($Q$) or **write**($Q$) instruction is executed.

## 14.2.2   The Timestamp-Ordering Protocol

The *timestamp-ordering protocol* ensures that any conflicting **read** and **write** operations are executed in timestamp order. This protocol operates as follows:

1. Suppose that transaction $T_i$ issues **read**($Q$).
    a. If TS($T_i$) < W-timestamp($Q$), then $T_i$ needs to read a value of $Q$ that was already overwritten. Hence, the **read** operation is rejected, and $T_i$ is rolled back.
    b. If TS($T_i$) ≥ W-timestamp($Q$), then the **read** operation is executed, and R-timestamp($Q$) is set to the maximum of R-timestamp($Q$) and TS($T_i$).
2. Suppose that transaction $T_i$ issues **write**($Q$).
    a. If TS($T_i$) < R-timestamp($Q$), then the value of $Q$ that $T_i$ is producing was needed previously, and the system assumed that that value would never be produced. Hence, the **write** operation is rejected, and $T_i$ is rolled back.
    b. If TS($T_i$) < W-timestamp($Q$), then $T_i$ is attempting to write an obsolete value of $Q$. Hence, this **write** operation is rejected, and $T_i$ is rolled back.
    c. Otherwise, the **write** operation is executed, and W-timestamp($Q$) is set to TS($T_i$).

A transaction $T_i$, that is rolled back by the concurrency-control scheme as result of either a **read** or **write** operation being issued, is assigned a new timestamp and is restarted.

To illustrate this protocol, we consider transactions $T_{14}$ and $T_{15}$. Transaction $T_{14}$ displays the contents of accounts $A$ and $B$, and is defined as

$$T_{14}: \quad \textbf{read}(B);$$
$$\textbf{read}(A);$$
$$\textbf{display}(A + B).$$

Transaction $T_{15}$ transfers $50 from account $A$ to account $B$, and then displays the contents of both:

$$T_{15}: \quad \textbf{read}(B);$$
$$B := B - 50;$$
$$\textbf{write}(B);$$
$$\textbf{read}(A);$$
$$A := A + 50;$$
$$\textbf{write}(A);$$
$$\textbf{display}(A + B).$$

In presenting schedules under the timestamp protocol, we shall assume that a transaction is assigned a timestamp immediately before its first instruction. Thus, in schedule 3 of Figure 14.8, TS($T_{14}$) < TS($T_{15}$), and the schedule is possible under the timestamp protocol.

We note that the preceding execution can also be produced by the two-phase locking protocol. There are, however, schedules that are possible under the two-

| $T_{14}$ | $T_{15}$ |
|---|---|
| **read**($B$) | |
| | **read**($B$) |
| | $B := B - 50$ |
| | **write**($B$) |
| **read**($A$) | |
| | **read**($A$) |
| **display**($A + B$) | |
| | $A := A + 50$ |
| | **write**($A$) |
| | **display**($A + B$) |

Figure 14.8    Schedule 3.

phase locking protocol, but are not possible under the timestamp protocol, and vice versa (see Exercise 14.20).

The timestamp-ordering protocol ensures conflict serializability. This assertion follows from the fact that conflicting operations are processed in timestamp order. The protocol ensures freedom from deadlock, since no transaction ever waits. The protocol can generate schedules that are not recoverable. However, it can be extended to make the schedules recoverable and cascadeless, either by performing writes only at the end of the transaction, or by using a limited form of locking (see Exercise 14.23).

### 14.2.3   Thomas' Write Rule

We now present a modification to the timestamp-ordering protocol that allows greater potential concurrency than does the protocol of Section 14.2.2. Let us consider schedule 4 of Figure 14.9, and apply the timestamp-ordering protocol. Since $T_{16}$ starts before $T_{17}$, we shall assume that TS($T_{16}$) < TS($T_{17}$). The **read**($Q$) operation of $T_{16}$ succeeds, as does the **write**($Q$) operation of $T_{17}$. When $T_{16}$ attempts its **write**($Q$) operation, we find that TS($T_{16}$) < W-timestamp($Q$), since W-timestamp($Q$) = TS($T_{17}$). Thus, the **write**($Q$) by $T_{16}$ is rejected and transaction $T_{16}$ must be rolled back.

Although the rollback of $T_{16}$ is required by the timestamp-ordering protocol, it is unnecessary. Since $T_{17}$ has already written $Q$, the value that $T_{16}$ is attempting to write is one that will never need to be read. Any transaction $T_i$ with TS($T_i$) < TS($T_{17}$) that attempts a **read**($Q$) will be rolled back, since TS($T_i$) < W-timestamp($Q$). Any transaction $T_j$ with TS($T_j$) > TS($T_{17}$) must read the value of $Q$ written by $T_{17}$, rather than the value written by $T_{16}$.

| $T_{16}$ | $T_{17}$ |
|---|---|
| **read**($Q$) | |
| | **write**($Q$) |
| **write**($Q$) | |

Figure 14.9    Schedule 4.

This observation leads to a modified version of the timestamp-ordering protocol in which obsolete **write** operations can be ignored under certain circumstances. The protocol rules for **read** operations remain unchanged. The protocol rules for **write** operations, however, are slightly different from the timestamp-ordering protocol of Section 14.2.2.

Suppose that transaction $T_i$ issues **write**($Q$).

1. If $TS(T_i) <$ R-timestamp($Q$), then the value of $Q$ that $T_i$ is producing was previously needed, and it was assumed that the value would never be produced. Hence, the **write** operation is rejected, and $T_i$ is rolled back.

2. If $TS(T_i) <$ W-timestamp($Q$), then $T_i$ is attempting to write an obsolete value of $Q$. Hence, this **write** operation can be ignored.

3. Otherwise, the **write** operation is executed, and W-timestamp($Q$) is set to $TS(T_i)$.

The difference between the preceding rules and those of Section 14.2.2 lies in the second rule. The timestamp-ordering protocol requires that $T_i$ be rolled back if $T_i$ issues **write**($Q$) and $TS(T_i) <$ W-timestamp($Q$). However, here, in those cases where $TS(T_i) \geq$ R-timestamp($Q$), we ignore the obsolete **write**. This modification to the timestamp-ordering protocol is called *Thomas' write rule*.

Thomas' write rule makes use of view serializability by, in effect, deleting obsolete **write** operations from the transactions that issue them. This modification of transactions makes it possible to generate serializable schedules that would not be possible under the other protocols presented in this chapter. For example, schedule 4 of Figure 14.9 is not conflict serializable and, thus, is not possible under any of two-phase locking, the tree protocol, or the timestamp-ordering protocol. Under Thomas' write rule, the **write**($Q$) operation of $T_{16}$ would be ignored. The result is a schedule that is view equivalent to the serial schedule $<T_{16},T_{17}>$.

# 14.3   Validation-Based Protocols

In cases where the majority of transactions are read-only transactions, the rate of conflicts among transactions may be low. Thus, many of these transactions, if executed without the supervision of a concurrency-control scheme, would nevertheless leave the system in a consistent state. A concurrency control scheme imposes overhead of code execution and possible delay of transactions. It may be desirable to use an alternative scheme that imposes less overhead. A difficulty in reducing the overhead is that we do not know in advance which transactions will be involved in a conflict. To gain that knowledge, we need a scheme for *monitoring* the system.

We assume that each transaction $T_i$ executes in two or three different phases in its lifetime, depending on whether it is a read-only or an update transaction. The phases are, in order, as follows:

1. **Read phase**. During this phase, the execution of transaction $T_i$ takes place. The values of the various data items are read, and are stored in variables

local to $T_i$. All **write** operations are performed on temporary local variables, without updates of the actual database.

2. **Validation phase**. Transaction $T_i$ performs a validation test to determine whether it can copy to the database the temporary local variables that hold the results of **write** operations without causing a violation of serializability.

3. **Write phase**. If transaction $T_i$ succeeds in validation (step 2), then the actual updates are applied to the database. Otherwise, $T_i$ is rolled back.

Each transaction must go through the three phases in the order shown. However, all three phases of concurrently executing transactions can be interleaved.

The read and write phases are self-explanatory. The only phase that needs further discussion is the validation phase. To perform the validation test, we need to know when the various phases of transactions $T_i$ took place. We shall, therefore, associate three different timestamps with transaction $T_i$:

1. **Start**($T_i$), the time when $T_i$ started its execution

2. **Validation**($T_i$), the time when $T_i$ finished its read phase and started its validation phase

3. **Finish**($T_i$), the time when $T_i$ finished its write phase

We determine the serializability order by the timestamp-ordering technique using the value of the timestamp Validation($T_i$). Thus, the value $TS(T_i) = $ Validation($T_i$) and, if $TS(T_j) < TS(T_k)$, then any produced schedule must be equivalent to a serial schedule in which transaction $T_j$ appears before transaction $T_k$. The reason we have chosen Validation($T_i$), rather than Start($T_i$), as the timestamp of transaction $T_i$ is that we can expect faster response time provided that conflict rates among transactions are indeed low.

The validation test for transaction $T_j$ requires that, for all transactions $T_i$ with $TS(T_i) < TS(T_j)$, one of the following two conditions must hold:

1. Finish($T_i$) < Start($T_j$). Since $T_i$ completes its execution before $T_j$ started, the serializability order is indeed maintained.

2. The set of data items written by $T_i$ does not intersect with the set of data items read by $T_j$, and $T_i$ completes its write phase before $T_j$ starts its validation phase (Start($T_j$) < Finish($T_i$) < Validation($T_j$)). This condition ensures that the writes of $T_i$ and $T_j$ do not overlap. Since the writes of $T_i$ do not affect the read of $T_j$, and since $T_j$ cannot affect the read of $T_i$, the serializability order is indeed maintained.

As an illustration, consider again transactions $T_{14}$ and $T_{15}$. Suppose that $TS(T_{14}) < TS(T_{15})$. Then, the validation phase succeeds in producing schedule 5, which is depicted in Figure 14.10. Note that the writes to the actual variables are performed only after the validation phase of $T_{15}$. Thus, $T_{14}$ reads the old values of $B$ and $A$, and this schedule is serializable.

| $T_{14}$ | $T_{15}$ |
|---|---|
| **read**($B$) | |
| | **read**($B$) |
| | $B := B - 50$ |
| | **read**($A$) |
| | $A := A + 50$ |
| **read**($A$) | |
| ⟨ *validate* ⟩ | |
| **display**($A + B$) | |
| | ⟨ *validate* ⟩ |
| | **write**($B$) |
| | **write**($A$) |

Figure 14.10    Schedule 5, a schedule produced using validation.

The validation scheme automatically guards against cascading rollbacks, since the actual writes take place only after the transaction issuing the write has committed.

## 14.4  Multiple Granularity

In the concurrency control schemes described thus far, we have used each individual data item as the unit on which synchronization is performed.

There are circumstances, however, where it would be advantageous to group several data items, and to treat them as one individual synchronization unit. For example, if a transaction $T_i$ needs to access the entire database, and a locking protocol is used, then $T_i$ must lock each item in the database. Clearly, executing these locks is time consuming. It would be better if $T_i$ could issue a *single* lock request to lock the entire database. On the other hand, if transaction $T_j$ needs to access only a few data items, it should not be required to lock the entire database, since otherwise concurrency is lost.

What is needed is a mechanism to allow the system to define multiple levels of *granularity*. We can make one by allowing data items to be of various sizes and defining a hierarchy of data granularities, where the small granularities are nested within larger ones. Such a hierarchy can be represented graphically as a tree. Note that the tree that we describe here is significantly different from that used by the tree protocol (Section 14.1.4). A nonleaf node of the multiple-granularity tree represents the data associated with its descendants. In the tree protocol, each node is an independent data item.

As an illustration, consider the tree of Figure 14.11, which consists of four levels of nodes. The highest level represents the entire database. Below it are nodes of type *area*; the database consists of exactly these areas. Each area in turn has nodes of type *file* as its children. Each area contains exactly those files that are its child nodes. No file is in more than one area. Finally, each file has nodes of

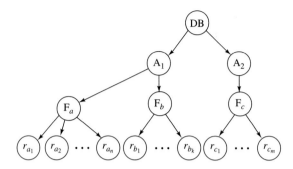

Figure 14.11     Granularity hierarchy.

type *record*. As before, the file consists of exactly those records that are its child nodes, and no record can be present in more than one file.

Each node in the tree can be locked individually. As we did in the two-phase locking protocol, we shall use *shared* and *exclusive* lock modes. When a transaction locks a node, in either *shared* or *exclusive* mode, the transaction also has locked all the descendants of that node in the same lock mode. For example, if transaction $T_i$ locks *explicitly* file $F_c$ of Figure 14.11, in exclusive mode, then it has locked *implicitly* in exclusive mode all the records belonging to that file. It does not need to lock the individual records of $F_c$ *explicitly*.

Suppose that transaction $T_j$ wishes to lock record $r_{b_6}$ of file $F_b$. Since $T_i$ has locked $F_b$ explicitly, it follows that $r_{b_6}$ is also locked (implicitly). But, when $T_j$ issues a lock request for $r_{b_6}$, $r_{b_6}$ is not explicitly locked! How does the system determine whether $T_j$ can lock $r_{b_6}$? $T_j$ must traverse the tree from the root to record $r_{b_6}$. If any node in that path is locked in an incompatible mode, then $T_j$ must be delayed.

Suppose now that transaction $T_k$ wishes to lock the entire database. To do so, it simply must lock the root of the hierarchy. Note, however, that $T_k$ should not succeed in locking the root node, since $T_i$ is currently holding a lock on part of the tree (specifically, on file $F_b$). But how does the system determine if the root node can be locked? One possibility is for it to search the entire tree. This solution, however, defeats the whole purpose of the multiple-granularity locking scheme. A more efficient way to gain this knowledge is to introduce a new class of lock modes, called *intention* lock modes. If a node is locked in an intention mode, explicit locking is being done at a lower level of the tree (that is, at a finer granularity). Intention locks are put on all the ancestors of a node before that node is locked explicitly. Thus, a transaction does not need to search the entire tree to determine whether it can lock a node successfully. A transaction wishing to lock a node—say, $Q$—must traverse a path in the tree from the root to $Q$. While traversing the tree, the transaction locks the various nodes in an intention mode.

There is an intention mode associated with *shared* mode, and there is one with *exclusive* mode. If a node is locked in *intention-shared* (IS) mode, explicit locking is being done at a lower level of the tree, but with only shared-mode

|     | IS    | IX    | S     | SIX   | X     |
|-----|-------|-------|-------|-------|-------|
| IS  | true  | true  | true  | true  | false |
| IX  | true  | true  | false | false | false |
| S   | true  | false | true  | false | false |
| SIX | true  | false | false | false | false |
| X   | false | false | false | false | false |

Figure 14.12    Compatibility matrix.

locks. Similarly, if a node is locked in *intention-exclusive* (IX) mode, then explicit locking is being done at a lower level, with exclusive-mode or shared-mode locks. Finally, if a node is locked in *shared and intention-exclusive* (SIX) mode, the subtree rooted by that node is locked explicitly in shared mode, and that explicit locking is being done at a lower level with exclusive-mode locks. The compatibility function for these lock modes is presented in Figure 14.12.

The multiple-granularity locking protocol that follows ensures serializability. Each transaction $T_i$ can lock a node $Q$, using the following rules:

1. The lock-compatibility function of Figure 14.12 must be observed.
2. The root of the tree must be locked first, and can be locked in any mode.
3. A node $Q$ can be locked by $T_i$ in S or IS mode only if the parent of $Q$ is currently locked by $T_i$ in either IX or IS mode.
4. A node $Q$ can be locked by $T_i$ in X, SIX, or IX mode only if the parent of $Q$ is currently locked by $T_i$ in either IX or SIX mode.
5. $T_i$ can lock a node only if it has not previously unlocked any node (that is, $T_i$ is two-phase).
6. $T_i$ can unlock a node $Q$ only if none of the children of $Q$ are currently locked by $T_i$.

Observe that the multiple-granularity protocol requires that locks be acquired in top-down (root-to-leaf) order, whereas locks must be released in bottom-up (leaf-to-root) order.

As an illustration of the protocol, consider the tree of Figure 14.11 and the following transactions:

- Suppose that transaction $T_{18}$ reads record $r_{a_2}$ in file $F_a$. Then, $T_{18}$ needs to lock the database, area $A_1$, and $F_a$ in IS mode (and in that order), and finally to lock $r_{a_2}$ in S mode.
- Suppose that transaction $T_{19}$ modifies record $r_{a_9}$ in file $F_a$. Then, $T_{19}$ needs to lock the database, area $A_1$, and file $F_a$ in IX mode, and finally to lock $r_{a_9}$ in X mode.
- Suppose that transaction $T_{20}$ reads all the records in file $F_a$. Then, $T_{20}$ needs to lock the database and area $A_1$ (in that order) in IS mode, and finally to lock $F_a$ in S mode.

- Suppose that transaction $T_{21}$ reads the entire database. It can do so after locking the database in S mode.

We note that transactions $T_{18}$, $T_{20}$, and $T_{21}$ can access the database concurrently. Transaction $T_{19}$ can execute concurrently with $T_{18}$, but not with either $T_{20}$ or $T_{21}$.

This protocol enhances concurrency and reduces lock overhead. It is particularly useful in applications that include a mix of

- Short transactions that access only a few data items
- Long transactions that produce reports from an entire file or set of files

There is a similar locking protocol that is applicable to database systems in which data granularities are organized in the form of a directed acyclic graph. See the bibliographic notes for additional references. Deadlock is possible in the protocol that we have, as it is in the two-phase locking protocol. There are techniques to reduce deadlock frequency in the multiple-granularity protocol, and also to eliminate deadlock entirely. These techniques are referenced in the bibliographic notes.

# 14.5   Multiversion Schemes

The concurrency-control schemes discussed thus far ensure serializability by either delaying an operation or aborting the transaction that issued the operation. For example, a **read** operation may be delayed because the appropriate value has not been written yet; or it may be rejected (that is, the issuing transaction must be aborted) because the value that it was supposed to read has already been overwritten. These difficulties could be avoided if old copies of each data item were kept in a system.

In *multiversion* database systems, each **write**($Q$) operation creates a new version of $Q$. When a **read**($Q$) operation is issued, the system selects one of the versions of $Q$ to be read. The concurrency-control scheme must ensure that the selection of the version to be read is done in a manner that ensures serializability. It is also crucial, for performance reasons, that a transaction be able to determine easily and quickly which version of the data item should be read.

## 14.5.1   Multiversion Timestamp Ordering

The most common technique used among multiversion schemes is timestamping. With each transaction $T_i$ in the system, we associate a unique static timestamp, denoted by $TS(T_i)$. This timestamp is assigned before the transaction starts execution, as described in Section 14.2.

With each data item $Q$, a sequence of versions $<Q_1, Q_2, ..., Q_m>$ is associated. Each version $Q_k$ contains three data fields:

- **Content** is the value of version $Q_k$.

- **W-timestamp**($Q_k$) is the timestamp of the transaction that created version $Q_k$.
- **R-timestamp**($Q_k$) is the largest timestamp of any transaction that successfully read version $Q_k$.

A transaction—say, $T_i$—creates a new version $Q_k$ of data item $Q$ by issuing a **write**($Q$) operation. The content field of the version holds the value written by $T_i$. The W-timestamp and R-timestamp are initialized to TS($T_i$). The R-timestamp value is updated whenever a transaction $T_j$ reads the content of $Q_k$, and R-timestamp($Q_k$) < TS($T_j$).

The multiversion timestamp scheme presented next ensures serializability. The scheme operates as follows. Suppose that transaction $T_i$ issues a **read**($Q$) or **write**($Q$) operation. Let $Q_k$ denote the version of $Q$ whose write timestamp is the largest write timestamp less than or equal to TS($T_i$).

1. If transaction $T_i$ issues a **read**($Q$), then the value returned is the content of version $Q_k$.
2. If transaction $T_i$ issues a **write**($Q$), and if TS($T_i$) < R-timestamp($Q_k$), then transaction $T_i$ is rolled back. Otherwise, if TS($T_i$) = W-timestamp($Q_k$), the contents of $Q_k$ are overwritten, otherwise a new version of $Q$ is created.

The justification for rule 1 is clear. A transaction reads the most recent version that comes before it in time. The second rule forces a transaction to abort if it is "too late" in doing a write. More precisely, if $T_i$ attempts to write a version that some other transaction would have read, then we cannot allow that write to succeed.

Versions that are no longer needed are removed based on the following rule. Suppose that there are two versions, $Q_k$ and $Q_j$, of a data item, and that both versions have a W-timestamp less than the timestamp of the oldest transaction in the system. Then, the older of the two versions $Q_k$ and $Q_j$ will not be used again, and can be deleted.

The multiversion timestamp-ordering scheme has the desirable property that a read request never fails and is never made to wait. In typical database systems, where reading is a more frequent operation than is writing, this advantage may be of major practical significance.

The scheme, however, suffers from two undesirable properties. First, the reading of a data item also requires the updating of the R-timestamp field, resulting in two potential disk accesses, rather than one. Second, the conflicts between transactions are resolved through rollbacks, rather than through waits. This alternative may be expensive. An algorithm to alleviate this problem is described in Section 14.5.2.

## 14.5.2   Multiversion Two-Phase Locking

The multiversion two-phase locking protocol attempts to combine the advantages of multiversion concurrency control with the advantages of two-phase locking.

This protocol differentiates between read-only transactions and update transactions. *Update transactions* perform rigorous two-phase locking; that is, they hold all locks up to the end of the transaction. Thus, they can be serialized according to their commit order. Each version of a data item has a single timestamp. The timestamp in this case is not a real clock-based timestamp, but rather is a counter, which we will call the **ts_counter**, that is incremented during commit processing.

We assign a timestamp to read-only transactions by reading the current value of **ts_counter** before they start execution; they follow the multiversion timestamp-ordering protocol for performing reads. Thus, when a read-only transaction $T_i$ issues a **read**($Q$), the value returned is the contents of the version whose timestamp is the largest timestamp less than $TS(T_i)$.

When an update transaction reads an item, it gets a shared lock on the item, and reads the latest version of that item. When an update transaction wants to write an item, it first gets an exclusive lock on the item, and then creates a new version of the data item. The write is performed on the new version, and the timestamp of the new version is initially set to a value $\infty$, which value is greater than that of any possible timestamp.

When the update transaction $T_i$ completes its actions, it carries out commit processing as follows: First, $T_i$ sets the timestamp on every version it has created to 1 more than the value of **ts_counter**; then, $T_i$ increments **ts_counter** by 1. Only one update transaction is allowed to perform commit processing at a time.

As a result, read-only transactions that start after $T_i$ increments **ts_counter** will see the values updated by $T_i$, whereas those that start before $T_i$ increments the **ts_counter** will see the value before the updates by $T_i$. In either case, read-only transaction never need to wait for locks.

Versions are deleted in a manner similar to that of multiversion timestamp ordering. Suppose there are two versions, $Q_k$ and $Q_j$, of a data item, and that both versions have a timestamp less than the timestamp of the oldest read-only transaction in the system. Then, the older of the two versions $Q_k$ and $Q_j$ will not be used again and can be deleted.

Multiversion two-phase locking or variations of it are used in some commercial database systems.

## 14.6  Deadlock Handling

A system is in a deadlock state if there exists a set of transactions such that every transaction in the set is waiting for another transaction in the set. More precisely, there exists a set of waiting transactions $\{T_0, T_1, ..., T_n\}$ such that $T_0$ is waiting for a data item that is held by $T_1$, and $T_1$ is waiting for a data item that is held by $T_2$, and ..., and $T_{n-1}$ is waiting for a data item that is held by $T_n$, and $T_n$ is waiting for a data item that is held by $T_0$. None of the transactions can make progress in such a situation. The only remedy to this undesirable situation is for the system to invoke some drastic action, such as rolling back some of the transactions involved in the deadlock.

There are two principal methods for dealing with the deadlock problem. We can use a *deadlock-prevention* protocol to ensure that the system will *never* enter a deadlock state. Alternatively, we can allow the system to enter a deadlock state, and then try to recover using a *deadlock-detection and deadlock-recovery* scheme. As we shall see, both methods may result in transaction rollback. Prevention is commonly used if the probability that the system would enter a deadlock state is relatively high; otherwise, detection and recovery are more efficient.

Note that a detection and recovery scheme requires overhead that includes not only the run-time cost of maintaining the necessary information and of executing the detection algorithm, but also the potential losses inherent in recovery from a deadlock.

## 14.6.1   Deadlock Prevention

There are two approaches to deadlock prevention. One approach ensures that no cyclic waits can occur by ordering the requests for locks, or requiring all locks to be acquired together. The other approach is closer to deadlock recovery, and performs transaction rollback instead of waiting for a lock, whenever the wait could potentially result in a deadlock.

The simplest scheme under the first approach requires that each transaction locks all its data items before it begins execution. Moreover, either all are locked in one step or none are locked. There are two main disadvantages to this protocol. First, it is often hard to predict, before the transaction begins, what data items need to be locked. Second, *data-item utilization* may be very low, since many of the data items may be locked but unused for a long time.

Another scheme for preventing deadlocks is to impose a partial ordering of all data items, and to require that a transaction lock a data item only in the order specified by the partial order. We have seen one such scheme in the tree protocol.

The second approach for preventing deadlocks is to use preemption and transaction rollbacks. In preemption, when a transaction $T_2$ requests a lock that is held by a transaction $T_1$, the lock granted to $T_1$ may be *preempted* by rolling back of $T_1$, and granting of the lock to $T_2$. To control the preemption, we assign a unique timestamp to each transaction. The system uses these timestamps only to decide whether a transaction should wait or roll back. Locking is still used for concurrency control. If a transaction is rolled back, it retains its *old* timestamp when restarted. Two different deadlock-prevention schemes using timestamps have been proposed:

1. The **wait–die** scheme is based on a nonpreemptive technique. When transaction $T_i$ requests a data item currently held by $T_j$, $T_i$ is allowed to wait only if it has a timestamp smaller than that of $T_j$ (that is, $T_i$ is older than $T_j$). Otherwise, $T_i$ is rolled back (dies). For example, suppose that transactions $T_{22}$, $T_{23}$, and $T_{24}$ have timestamps 5, 10, and 15, respectively. If $T_{22}$ requests a data item held by $T_{23}$, then $T_{22}$ will wait. If $T_{24}$ requests a data item held by $T_{23}$, then $T_{24}$ will be rolled back.

2. The **wound–wait** scheme is based on a preemptive technique and is a counterpart to the *wait–die* scheme. When transaction $T_i$ requests a data item currently held by $T_j$, $T_i$ is allowed to wait only if it has a timestamp

larger than that of $T_j$ (that is, $T_i$ is younger than $T_j$). Otherwise, $T_j$ is rolled back ($T_j$ is *wounded* by $T_i$). Returning to our previous example, with transactions $T_{22}$, $T_{23}$, and $T_{24}$, if $T_{22}$ requests a data item held by $T_{23}$, then the data item will be preempted from $T_{23}$, and $T_{23}$ will be rolled back. If $T_{24}$ requests a data item held by $T_{23}$, then $T_{24}$ will wait.

Whenever transactions are rolled back, it is important to ensure that there is no *starvation*—that is, no transaction gets rolled back repeatedly and is never allowed to make progress.

Both the wound–wait and the wait–die schemes avoid starvation: At any time, there is a transaction with the smallest timestamp. This transaction *cannot* be required to roll back in either scheme. Since timestamps always increase, and since transactions are *not* assigned new timestamps when they are rolled back, a transaction that is rolled back will eventually have the smallest timestamp. Thus, it will not be rolled back again.

There are, however, significant differences in the way that the two schemes operate.

- In the *wait–die* scheme, an older transaction must wait for a younger one to release its data item. Thus, the older the transaction gets, the more it tends to wait. By contrast, in the *wound–wait* scheme, an older transaction never waits for a younger transaction.

- In the *wait–die* scheme, if a transaction $T_i$ dies and is rolled back because it requested a data item held by transaction $T_j$, then $T_i$ may reissue the same sequence of requests when it is restarted. If the data item is still held by $T_j$, then $T_i$ will die again. Thus, $T_i$ may die several times before acquiring the needed data item. Contrast this series of events with what happens in the *wound–wait* scheme. Transaction $T_i$ is wounded and rolled back because $T_j$ requested a data item that it holds. When $T_i$ is restarted and requests the data item now being held by $T_j$, $T_i$ waits. Thus, there may be fewer rollbacks in the *wound–wait* scheme.

The major problem with both of these schemes is that unnecessary rollbacks may occur.

### 14.6.2 Timeout-Based Schemes

Another simple approach to deadlock handling is based on *lock timeouts*. In this approach, a transaction that has requested a lock waits for at most a specified amount of time. If the lock has not been granted within that time, the transaction is said to time out, and it rolls itself back and restarts. If there was in fact a deadlock, one or more transactions involved in the deadlock will time out and roll back, allowing the others to proceed. This scheme falls somewhere between deadlock prevention, where a deadlock will never occur, and deadlock detection and recovery, which is discussed in Section 14.6.3.

The timeout scheme is particularly easy to implement, and works well if transactions are short, and if long waits are likely to be due to deadlocks. However, in general it is hard to decide how long a transaction must wait before timing out. Too long a wait results in unnecessary delays once a deadlock has occurred. Too short a wait results in transaction rollback even when there is no deadlock, leading to wasted resources. Starvation is also a possibility with this scheme. Hence, the timeout-based scheme has limited applicability.

### 14.6.3  Deadlock Detection and Recovery

If a system does not employ some protocol that ensures deadlock freedom, then a detection and recovery scheme must be used. An algorithm that examines the state of the system is invoked periodically to determine whether a deadlock has occurred. If one has, then the system must attempt to recover from the deadlock. To do so, the system must

- Maintain information about the current allocation of data items to transactions, as well as any outstanding data item requests.
- Provide an algorithm that uses this information to determine whether the system has entered a deadlock state.
- Recover from the deadlock when the detection algorithm determines that a deadlock exists.

In this section, we elaborate on these issues.

#### 14.6.3.1  Deadlock Detection

Deadlocks can be described precisely in terms of a directed graph called a *wait-for graph*. This graph consists of a pair $G = (V,E)$, where $V$ is a set of vertices and $E$ is a set of edges. The set of vertices consists of all the transactions in the system. Each element in the set $E$ of edges is an ordered pair $T_i \rightarrow T_j$. If $T_i \rightarrow T_j$ is in $E$, then there is a directed edge from transaction $T_i$ to $T_j$, implying that transaction $T_i$ is waiting for transaction $T_j$ to release a data item that it needs.

When transaction $T_i$ requests a data item currently being held by transaction $T_j$, then the edge $T_i \rightarrow T_j$ is inserted in the wait-for graph. This edge is removed only when transaction $T_j$ is no longer holding a data item needed by transaction $T_i$.

A deadlock exists in the system if and only if the wait-for graph contains a cycle. Each transaction involved in the cycle is said to be deadlocked. To detect deadlocks, the system needs to maintain the wait-for graph, and periodically to invoke an algorithm that searches for a cycle in the graph.

To illustrate these concepts, consider the wait-for graph in Figure 14.13, which depicts the following situation:

- Transaction $T_{25}$ is waiting for transactions $T_{26}$ and $T_{27}$.
- Transaction $T_{27}$ is waiting for transaction $T_{26}$.

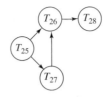

Figure 14.13    Wait-for graph with no cycle.

- Transaction $T_{26}$ is waiting for transaction $T_{28}$.

Since the graph has no cycle, the system is not in a deadlock state.

Suppose now that transaction $T_{28}$ is requesting an item held by $T_{27}$. The edge $T_{28} \rightarrow T_{27}$ is added to the wait-for graph, resulting in a new system state as depicted in Figure 14.14. This time, the graph contains the cycle

$$T_{26} \rightarrow T_{28} \rightarrow T_{27} \rightarrow T_{26}$$

implying that transactions $T_{26}$, $T_{27}$, and $T_{28}$ are all deadlocked.

Consequently, the question arises: When should we invoke the detection algorithm? The answer depends on two factors:

**1.** How often does a deadlock occur?
**2.** How many transactions will be affected by the deadlock?

If deadlocks occur frequently, then the detection algorithm should be invoked more frequently than usual. Data items allocated to deadlocked transactions will be unavailable to other transactions until the deadlock can be broken. In addition, the number of cycles in the graph may also grow. In the worst case, we would invoke the detection algorithm every time a request for allocation could not be granted immediately.

### 14.6.3.2    Recovery from Deadlock

When a detection algorithm determines that a deadlock exists, the system must *recover* from the deadlock. The most common solution is to roll back one or more transactions to break the deadlock. Three actions need to be taken:

**1. Selection of a victim**. Given a set of deadlocked transactions, we must determine which transaction (or transactions) to roll back to break the

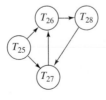

Figure 14.14    Wait-for graph with a cycle.

deadlock. We should roll back those transactions that will incur the minimum cost. Unfortunately, the term *minimum cost* is not a precise one. Many factors may determine the cost of a rollback, including

    **a.** How long the transaction has computed, and how much longer the transaction will compute before it completes its designated task.

    **b.** How many data items the transaction has used.

    **c.** How many more data items the transaction needs for it to complete.

    **d.** How many transactions will be involved in the rollback.

2. **Rollback**. Once we have decided that a particular transaction must be rolled back, we must determine how far this transaction should be rolled back. The simplest solution is a total rollback: Abort the transaction and then restart it. However, it is more effective to roll back the transaction only as far as necessary to break the deadlock. But this method requires the system to maintain additional information about the state of all the running transactions. See the bibliographic notes section for relevant references.

3. **Starvation**. In a system where the selection of victims is based primarily on cost factors, it may happen that the same transaction is always picked as a victim. As a result, this transaction never completes its designated task. This situation is called *starvation*. We must ensure that transaction can be picked as a victim only a (small) finite number of times. The most common solution is to include the number of rollbacks in the cost factor.

## 14.7   Insert and Delete Operations

Until now, we have restricted our attention to **read** and **write** operations. This restriction limits transactions to data items already in the database. Some transactions require not only access to existing data items, but also the ability to create new data items. Others require the ability to delete data items. To examine how such transactions affect concurrency control, we introduce the following additional operations:

- **delete**($Q$) deletes data item $Q$ from the database.
- **insert**($Q$) inserts a new data item $Q$ into the database and assigns $Q$ an initial value.

An attempt by a transaction $T_i$ to perform a **read**($Q$) operation after $Q$ has been deleted results in a logical error in $T_i$. Likewise, an attempt by a transaction $T_i$ to perform a **read**($Q$) operation before $Q$ has been inserted results in a logical error in $T_i$. It is also a logical error to attempt to delete a nonexistent data item.

### 14.7.1   Deletion

To understand how the presence of **delete** instructions affects concurrency control, we must decide when a **delete** instruction conflicts with another instruction. Let $I_i$ and $I_j$ be instructions of $T_i$ and $T_j$, respectively, that appear in schedule $S$ in consecutive order. Let $I_i = $ **delete**$(Q)$. We consider several instructions $I_j$

- $I_j = $ **read**$(Q)$. $I_i$ and $I_j$ conflict. If $I_i$ comes before $I_j$, $T_j$ will have a logical error. If $I_j$ comes before $I_i$, $T_j$ can execute the **read** operation successfully.
- $I_j = $ **write**$(Q)$. $I_i$ and $I_j$ conflict. If $I_i$ comes before $I_j$, $T_j$ will have a logical error. If $I_j$ comes before $I_i$, $T_j$ can execute the **write** operation successfully.
- $I_j = $ **delete**$(Q)$. $I_i$ and $I_j$ conflict. If $I_i$ comes before $I_j$, $T_i$ will have a logical error. If $I_j$ comes before $I_i$, $T_i$ will have a logical error.
- $I_j = $ **insert**$(Q)$. $I_i$ and $I_j$ conflict. Suppose that data item $Q$ did not exist prior to the execution of $I_i$ and $I_j$. Then, if $I_i$ comes before $I_j$, a logical error results for $T_i$. If $I_j$ comes before $I_i$, then no logical error results. Likewise, if $Q$ existed prior to the execution of $I_i$ and $I_j$, then a logical error results if $I_j$ comes before $I_i$, but not otherwise.

We can conclude that, if two-phase locking is used, an exclusive lock is required on a data item before that item can be deleted. Under the timestamp-ordering protocol, a test similar to that for a **write** must be performed. Suppose that transaction $T_i$ issues **delete**$(Q)$.

- If TS$(T_i) < $ R-timestamp$(Q)$, then the value of $Q$ that $T_i$ was to delete has already been read by a transaction $T_j$ with TS$(T_j) > $ TS$(T_i)$. Hence, the **delete** operation is rejected, and $T_i$ is rolled back.
- If TS$(T_i) < $ W-timestamp$(Q)$, then a transaction $T_j$ with TS$(T_j) > $ TS$(T_i)$ has written $Q$. Hence, this **delete** operation is rejected, and $T_i$ is rolled back.
- Otherwise, the **delete** is executed.

### 14.7.2   Insertion

We have already seen that an **insert**$(Q)$ operation conflicts with a **delete**$(Q)$ operation. Similarly, **insert**$(Q)$ conflicts with a **read**$(Q)$ operation or a **write**$(Q)$ operation. No **read** or **write** can be performed on a data item before the latter exists.

Since an **insert**$(Q)$ assigns a value to data item $Q$, an **insert** is treated similarly to a **write** for concurrency-control purposes:

- Under the two-phase locking protocol, if $T_i$ performs an **insert**$(Q)$ operation, $T_i$ is given an exclusive lock on the newly created data item $Q$.
- Under the timestamp-ordering protocol, if $T_i$ performs an **insert**$(Q)$ operation, the values R-timestamp$(Q)$ and W-timestamp$(Q)$ are set to TS$(T_i)$.

### 14.7.3   The Phantom Phenomenon

Consider a transaction $T_{29}$, that executes the following SQL query on the bank database:

> **select sum**(*balance*)
> **from** *account*
> **where** *branch-name* = "Perryridge"

Transaction $T_{29}$ requires access to all tuples of the *account* relation pertaining to the Perryridge branch.

Let $T_{30}$ be a transaction which executes the following SQL insertion:

> **insert into** *account*
> **values** ("Perryridge", A-201, 900)

Let $S$ be a schedule involving $T_{29}$ and $T_{30}$. We expect there to be potential for a conflict for the following reasons:

- If $T_{29}$ uses the tuple newly inserted by $T_{30}$ in computing **sum**(*balance*), then $T_{29}$ read a value written by $T_{30}$. Thus, in a serial schedule equivalent to $S$, $T_{30}$ must come before $T_{29}$.
- If $T_{29}$ does not use the tuple newly inserted by $T_{30}$ in computing **sum**(*balance*), then in a serial schedule equivalent to $S$, $T_{29}$ must come before $T_{30}$.

The second of these two cases is curious. $T_{29}$ and $T_{30}$ do not access any tuple in common, yet they conflict with each other! In effect, $T_{29}$ and $T_{30}$ conflict on a phantom tuple. Thus, the phenomenon we have just described is called the *phantom phenomenon*. If concurrency control is performed at the tuple granularity, this conflict would go undetected.

To prevent the phantom phenomenon, we allow $T_{29}$ to prevent other transactions from creating new tuples in the *account* relation with *branch-name* = "Perryridge."

To find all *account* tuples with *branch-name* = "Perryridge", $T_{29}$ must search either the whole *account* relation, or at least an index on the relation. Up to now, we have assumed implicitly that the only data items accessed by a transaction are tuples. However, $T_{29}$ is an example of a transaction that reads information about what tuples are in a relation, and $T_{30}$ is an example of a transaction that updates that information. Clearly, it is not sufficient merely to lock the tuples that are accessed; locking also is required for the information about what tuples are in the relation.

The simplest solution to this problem is to associate a data item with the relation itself. Transactions, such as $T_{29}$, that read the information about what tuples are in a relation would then have to lock the data item corresponding to the *account* relation in shared mode. Transactions, such as $T_{30}$, which update the information about what tuples are in a relation would have to lock the data item in exclusive mode. Thus, $T_{29}$ and $T_{30}$ would conflict on a real data item, rather than on a phantom.

Do not confuse the locking of an entire relation, as in multiple granularity locking, with the locking of the data item corresponding to the relation. By locking the data item, a transaction only prevents other transactions from updating information about what tuples are in the relation. Locking is still required on tuples. A transactions that directly accesses a tuple can be granted a lock on the tuples even when another transaction has an exclusive lock on the data item corresponding to the relation itself.

The major disadvantage of locking a data item corresponding to the relation is the low degree of concurrency— two transactions that insert different tuples into a relation are prevented from executing concurrently.

A better solution is the *index-locking* technique. Any transaction that inserts a tuple into a relation must insert information into every index maintained on the relation. We eliminate the phantom phenomenon by imposing a locking protocol for indices. For simplicity we shall only consider $B^+$-tree indices.

As we saw in Chapter 11, every search-key value is associated with an index leaf node. A query will usually use one or more indices to access a relation. An insert must insert the new tuple in all indices on the relation. In our example, we assume that there is an index on *account* for *branch-name*. Then, $T_{30}$ must modify the leaf containing the key Perryridge. If $T_{29}$ reads the same leaf node to locate all tuples pertaining to the Perryridge branch, then $T_{29}$ and $T_{30}$ conflict on that leaf node.

The index-locking protocol takes advantage of the availability of indices on a relation, by turning instances of the phantom phenomenon into conflicts on locks on index leaf nodes. The protocol operates as follows:

- Every relation must have at least one index.
- Tuples of a relation can be accessed only after first finding them through one or more of the indices on the relation.
- A transaction $T_i$ that performs a lookup (whether a range lookup or a point lookup) must acquire a shared lock all the index leaf nodes that it accesses.
- A transaction $T_i$ may not insert, delete or update a tuple $t_i$ in a relation $r$ without updating all indices on $r$. The transaction must obtain exclusive locks on all index leaf nodes which are affected by the insertion, deletion or update. For insertion and deletion, the leaf nodes affected are those that contain (after insertion) or contained (before deletion) the search-key value of the tuple. For updates, the leaf nodes affected are those that (before the modification) contained the old value of the search-key, and nodes that (after the modification) contain the new value of the search-key.
- The rules of the two-phase locking protocol must be observed.

Variants of the index-locking technique exist for eliminating the phantom phenomenon under the other concurrency-control protocols presented in this chapter.

## 14.8   Concurrency in Index Structures

It is possible to treat access to index structures like any other database structure, and to apply the concurrency-control techniques discussed earlier. However, since indices are accessed frequently, they will become point of great lock contention, leading to a low degree of concurrency. Luckily, indices do not have to be treated like other database structures, since they provide the high-level abstraction of mapping search keys to tuples in the database. It is perfectly acceptable for a transaction to look up an index twice, and to find that the structure of the index has changed in-between, as long as the index lookup returns the correct set of tuples. Thus, it is acceptable to have nonserializable concurrent access to an index, as long as the accuracy of the index is maintained.

We show a technique for managing concurrent access to $B^+$-trees. The bibliographic notes reference other techniques for $B^+$-trees, as well as techniques for other index structures.

The technique that we present for $B^+$-trees is based on locking, but neither two-phase locking nor the tree protocol is employed. The algorithms for lookup, insertion, and deletion are those used in Chapter 11, with only minor modifications. We require that every node (rather than just the leaves) maintain a pointer to its right sibling. Trees meeting this requirement are called *B-link trees*. This pointer is required because a lookup that occurs while a node is being split may have to search not only that node but also that node's right sibling (if one exists). We shall illustrate this technique with an example after we present the modified procedures.

- **Lookup**. Each node of the $B^+$-tree must be locked in shared mode before it is accessed. This lock is released before any lock on any other node in the $B^+$-tree is requested. If a split occurs concurrently with a lookup, the desired search-key value may no longer appear within the range of values represented by a node accessed during lookup. In such a case, the search-key value is represented by a sibling node, which the system locates by following the pointer to the right sibling. However, locking of leaf nodes is performed following the two-phase locking protocol, as described in Section 14.7.3, to avoid the phantom phenomenon.

- **Insertion and deletion**. The system follows the rules for lookup to locate the leaf node into which the insertion or deletion is to be made. The shared-mode lock on this node is upgraded to exclusive mode, and the insertion or deletion is performed. Locking of leaf nodes affected by insertion or deletion is performed following the two-phase locking protocol, as described in Section 14.7.3, to avoid the phantom phenomenon.

- **Split**. If a node is split, a new node is created according to the algorithm of Section 11.3. The right-sibling pointers of both the original node and the new node are set. Following this, the exclusive lock on the original node is released, and an exclusive lock is requested on the parent, so that a pointer to the new node can be inserted.

- **Coalescence**. If a node has too few search-key values after a deletion, the node with which it will be coalesced must be locked in exclusive mode. Once these two nodes have been coalesced, an exclusive lock is requested on the parent so that the deleted node can be removed. At this point, the lock on the coalesced node is released. Unless the parent node must be coalesced also, its lock is released.

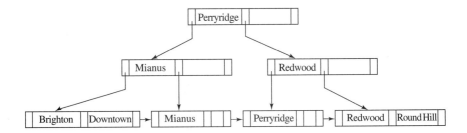

Figure 14.15    B$^+$-tree for *account* file with $n = 3$.

It is important to observe that an insertion or deletion may lock a node, unlock it, and subsequently relock it. Furthermore, a lookup that runs concurrently with a split or coalescence operation may find that the desired search key has been moved to the right-sibling node by the split or coalescence operation.

As an illustration, consider the B$^+$-tree in Figure 14.15. Assume that there are two concurrent operations on this B$^+$-tree:

**1.** Insert "Clearview"

**2.** Lookup "Downtown"

Let us assume that the insertion operation begins first. It does a lookup on "Clearview," and finds that the node into which "Clearview" should be inserted is full. It therefore converts its shared lock on the node to exclusive mode, and creates a new node. The original node now contains the search-key values "Brighton" and "Clearview." The new node contains the search-key value "Downtown."

Now assume that a context switch occurs that results in control passing to the lookup operation. This lookup operation accesses the root, and follows the pointer to the left child of the root. It then accesses that node, and obtains a pointer to the left child. This left-child node originally contained the search-key values "Brighton" and "Downtown." Since this node is currently locked by the insertion operation in exclusive mode, the lookup operation must wait. Note that, at this point, the lookup operation holds no locks at all!

The insertion operation now unlocks the leaf node and relocks its parent, this time in exclusive mode. It completes the insertion, leaving the B$^+$-tree as shown in Figure 14.16. The lookup operation proceeds. However, it is holding a pointer to an incorrect leaf node. It therefore follows the right-sibling pointer to locate the next node. If this node, too, turns out to be incorrect, that node's right-sibling pointer is followed. It can be shown that, if a lookup holds a pointer to an incorrect node, then, by following right sibling pointers, the lookup must eventually reach the correct node.

Lookup and insertion operations cannot lead to deadlock. Coalescing of nodes during deletion can cause inconsistencies, since a lookup may have read a pointer to a deleted node from its parent, before the parent node was updated, and may then try to access the deleted node. The lookup would then have to restart from the root. Leaving nodes uncoalesced avoids such inconsistencies. This solution results in nodes that contain too few search-key values and that violate

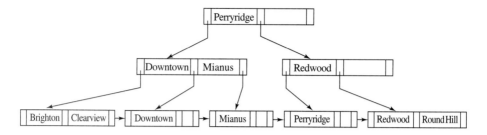

Figure 14.16    Insertion of "Clearview" into the B$^+$-tree of Figure 14.15.

some properties of B$^+$-trees. In most databases, however, insertions are more frequent than deletions, so it is likely that nodes that have too few search-key values will gain additional values relatively quickly.

## 14.9   Summary

When several transactions execute concurrently in the database, the consistency of data may no longer be preserved. It is necessary for the system to control the interaction among the concurrent transactions, and this control is achieved through one of a variety of mechanisms called *concurrency-control* schemes.

To ensure serializability, we can use various concurrency-control schemes. All these schemes either delay an operation or abort the transaction that issued the operation. The most common ones are locking protocols, timestamp-ordering schemes, validation techniques, and multiversion schemes.

A locking protocol is a set of rules, the members of which state when a transaction may lock and unlock each of the data items in the database. The *two-phase* locking protocol allows a transaction to lock a new data item only if that transaction has not yet unlocked any data item. The protocol ensures serializability, but not deadlock freedom. In the absence of information concerning the manner in which data items are accessed, the two-phase locking protocol is both necessary and sufficient for ensuring serializability.

A timestamp-ordering scheme ensures serializability by selecting an ordering in advance between every pair of transactions. A unique fixed timestamp is associated with each transaction in the system. The timestamps of the transactions determine the serializability order. Thus, if the timestamp of transaction $T_i$ is smaller than the timestamp of transaction $T_j$, then the scheme ensures that the produced schedule is equivalent to a serial schedule in which transaction $T_i$ appears before transaction $T_j$. It does so by rolling back a transaction whenever such an order is violated.

A validation scheme is an appropriate concurrency-control method in cases where the majority of transactions are read-only transactions, and thus the rate of conflicts among these transactions is low. A unique fixed timestamp is associated with each transaction in the system. The serializability order is determined by the timestamp of the transaction. A transaction in this scheme is never delayed. It must, however, pass a validation test, to complete. If it does not pass the validation test, it is rolled back to its initial state.

There are circumstances where it would be advantageous to group several data items, and to treat them as one aggregate data item for purposes of working, resulting in multiple levels of *granularity*. We allow data items of various sizes, and define a hierarchy of data items, where the small items are nested within larger ones. Such a hierarchy can be represented graphically as a tree. Locks are acquired in root-to-leaf order; they are released in leaf-to-root order. The protocol ensures serializability, but not freedom from deadlock.

A multiversion concurrency-control scheme is based on the creation of a new version of a data item for each transaction that writes that item. When a read operation is issued, the system selects one of the versions to be read. The concurrency-control scheme ensures that the version to be read is selected in a manner that ensures serializability, by using timestamps. A read operation always succeeds. In multiversion timestamp ordering, a write operation may result in the rollback of the transaction. In multiversion two-phase locking, write operations may result in a lock wait or, possibly, in deadlock.

Various locking protocols do not guard against deadlocks. One way to prevent deadlock is to use preemption and transaction rollbacks. To control the preemption, we assign a unique timestamp to each transaction. These timestamps are used to decide whether a transaction should wait or roll back. If a transaction is rolled back, it retains its *old* timestamp when restarted. The wait–die and wound–wait schemes are two preemptive schemes. Another method for dealing with deadlock is to use a deadlock detection and recovery scheme. To do so, a wait-for graph is constructed. A system is in a deadlock state if and only if the wait-for graph contains a cycle. When a detection algorithm determines that a deadlock exists, the system must recover from the deadlock. It does so by rolling back one or more transactions to break the deadlock.

A **delete** operation may be performed only if the transaction deleting the tuple has an exclusive lock on the tuple to be deleted. A transaction that inserts a new tuple into the database is given an X-mode lock on the tuple. Insertions can lead to the phantom phenomenon, in which an insertion conflicts with a query even though the two transactions may access no tuple in common. The index-locking technique solves this problem by requiring locks on certain index buckets. These locks ensure that all conflicting transactions conflict on a real data item, rather than on a phantom.

Special concurrency-control techniques can be developed for special data structures. Often, special techniques are applied in $B^+$-trees to allow greater concurrency. These techniques allow nonserializable access to the $B^+$-tree, but they ensure that the $B^+$-tree structure is correct, and ensure that accesses to the database itself are serializable.

# Exercises

**14.1.** Show that the two-phase locking protocol ensures conflict serializability, and that transactions can be serialized according to their lock points.

**14.2.** Consider the following two transactions:

$$T_{31}:\ \textbf{read}(A);$$
$$\textbf{read}(B);$$
$$\textbf{if } A\ =\ 0 \textbf{ then } B := B + 1;$$
$$\textbf{write}(B).$$
$$T_{32}:\ \textbf{read } (B);$$
$$\textbf{read } (A);$$
$$\textbf{if } B\ =\ 0 \textbf{ then } A := A + 1;$$
$$\textbf{write}(A).$$

Add lock and unlock instructions to transactions $T_{31}$ and $T_{32}$, so that they observe the two-phase locking protocol. Can the execution of these transactions result in a deadlock?

**14.3.** What benefit is provided by strict two-phase locking? What disadvantages result?

**14.4.** What benefit is provided by rigorous two-phase locking? How does it compare with other forms of two-phase locking?

**14.5.** The concurrency-control manager of a database system must decide whether to grant a lock request or to cause the requesting transaction to wait. Design a space-efficient data structure that allows the concurrency-control manager to make this decision quickly.

**14.6.** Most implementations of database systems use strict two-phase locking. Suggest three reasons for the popularity of this protocol.

**14.7.** Consider the following extension to the tree-locking protocol, which allows both shared and exclusive locks:
- A transaction can be either a read-only transaction, in which case it can request only shared locks, or an update transaction, in which case it can request only exclusive locks.
- Each transaction must follow the rules of the tree protocol. Read-only transactions may lock any data item first, whereas update transactions must lock the root first.

Show that the protocol ensures serializability and deadlock freedom.

**14.8.** Consider a database organized in the form of a rooted tree. Suppose that we insert a dummy vertex between each pair of vertices. Show that, if we follow the tree protocol on the new tree, we get better concurrency than if we follow the tree protocol on the original tree.

**14.9.** Consider the following graph-based locking protocol, which allows only exclusive lock modes, and which operates on data graphs that are in the form of a rooted directed acyclic graph.
- A transaction can lock any vertex first.
- To lock any other vertex, the transaction must be holding a lock on the majority of the parents of that vertex.

Show that the protocol ensures serializability and deadlock freedom.

**14.10.** Show by example that there are schedules possible under the tree protocol that are not possible under the two-phase locking protocol, and vice versa.

**14.11.** Consider the following graph-based locking protocol that allows only exclusive lock modes, and that operates on data graphs that are in the form of a rooted directed acyclic graph.

- A transaction can lock any vertex first.
- To lock any other vertex, the transaction must have visited all the parents of that vertex, and must be holding a lock on one of the parents of the vertex.

Show that the protocol ensures serializability and deadlock freedom.

**14.12.** Consider a variant of the tree protocol called the *forest* protocol. The database is organized as a forest of rooted trees. Each transaction $T_i$ must follow the following rules:

- The first lock in each tree may be on any data item.
- The second, and all subsequent, locks in a tree may be requested only if the parent of the requested node is currently locked.
- Data items may be unlocked at any time.
- A data item may not be relocked by $T_i$ after it has been unlocked by $T_i$.

Show that the forest protocol does *not* ensure serializability.

**14.13.** Consider a database system that includes an atomic **increment** operation, in addition to the **read** and **write** operations. Let $V$ be the value of data item $X$. The operation

$$\textbf{increment}(X) \text{ by } C$$

sets the value of $X$ to $V + C$ in an atomic step. The value of $X$ is not available to the transaction unless the latter executes a **read**($X$). Figure 14.17 shows a lock-compatibility matrix for three lock modes: share mode, exclusive mode, and incrementation mode.

(a) Show that, if all transactions lock the data that they access in the corresponding mode, then two-phase locking ensures serializability.

(b) Show that the inclusion of **increment** mode locks allows for increased concurrency. (Hint: Consider check-clearing transactions in our bank example.)

**14.14.** In timestamp ordering, **W-timestamp**($Q$) denotes the largest timestamp of any transaction that executed **write**($Q$) successfully. Suppose that, instead, we defined it to be the timestamp of the most recent transaction to execute

|   | S | X | I |
|---|---|---|---|
| S | true | false | false |
| X | false | false | false |
| I | false | false | true |

Figure 14.17    Lock-compatibility matrix.

write($Q$) successfully. Would this change in wording make any difference? Explain your answer.

**14.15.** When a transaction is rolled back under timestamp ordering, it is assigned a new timestamp. Why can it not simply keep its old timestamp?

**14.16.** In multiple-granularity locking, what is the difference between implicit and explicit locking?

**14.17.** Although SIX mode is useful in multiple-granularity locking, an exclusive and intend-shared (XIS) mode is of no use. Why is it useless?

**14.18.** Use of multiple-granularity locking may require more or fewer locks than an equivalent system with a single lock granularity. Provide examples of both situations, and compare the relative amount of concurrency allowed.

**14.19.** Consider the validation-based concurrency-control scheme of Section 14.3. Show that by choosing Validation($T_i$), rather than Start($T_i$), as the timestamp of transaction $T_i$, we can expect better response time provided that conflict rates among transactions are indeed low.

**14.20.** Show that there are schedules that are possible under the two-phase locking protocol, but are not possible under the timestamp protocol, and vice versa.

**14.21.** For each of the following protocols, describe aspects of practical applications that would lead you to suggest using the protocol, and aspects that would suggest not using the protocol:

- Two-phase locking
- Two-phase locking with multiple granularity locking
- The tree protocol
- Timestamp ordering
- Validation
- Multiversion timestamp ordering
- Multiversion two-phase locking

**14.22.** For each of the timestamp-based protocols, check whether it is cascadeless, and whether it is recoverable.

**14.23.** Under a modified version of the timestamp protocol, we require that a commit bit be tested to see whether a **read** request must wait. Explain how the commit bit can prevent cascading abort. Why is this test not necessary for **write** requests?

**14.24.** Under what conditions is it less expensive to avoid deadlock than to allow deadlocks to occur and then to detect them?

**14.25.** If deadlock is avoided, is starvation still possible? Explain your answer.

**14.26.** Explain the phantom phenomenon. Why may this phenomenon lead to an incorrect concurrent execution despite the use of the two-phase locking protocol?

**14.27.** Devise a timestamp-based protocol that avoids the phantom phenomenon.

**14.28.** Suppose that we use the tree protocol of Section 14.1.4 to manage concurrent access to a B$^+$-tree. Since a split may occur on an insert that affects the root, it appears that an insert operation cannot release any locks until it has completed the entire operation. Under what circumstances is it possible to release a lock earlier?

**14.29.** Locking is not done explicitly in persistent programming languages. Rather, objects (or the corresponding pages) must be locked when the objects are accessed. Most modern operating systems allow the user to set access protections (no-access, read, write) on pages, and memory access that violate the access protections result in a protection violation (see the Unix `mprotect` command, for example). Describe how the access-protection mechanism can be used for page-level locking in a persistent programming language. (Hint: The technique is somewhat similar to that used for hardware swizzling in Section 10.9.3.2).

# Bibliographical Notes

The two-phase locking protocol was introduced by Eswaran et al. [1976]. The tree-locking protocol is from Silberschatz and Kedem [1980]. Other non–two-phase locking protocols that operate on more general graphs were developed by Yannakakis et al. [1979], Kedem and Silberschatz [1983], and Buckley and Silberschatz [1985]. General discussions concerning locking protocols are offered by Lien and Weinberger [1978], Yannakakis et al. [1979], Yannakakis [1981], and Papadimitriou [1982]. Korth [1983] explores various lock modes that can be obtained from the basic shared and exclusive lock modes. Various algorithms for concurrent access to dynamic search trees were developed by Bayer and Schkolnick [1977], Ellis [1980a, 1980b], Lehman and Yao [1981], and Manber and Ladner [1984]. Exercise 14.7 is from Kedem and Silberschatz [1983]. Exercise 14.8 is from Buckley and Silberschatz [1984]. Exercise 14.9 is from Kedem and Silberschatz [1979]. Exercise 14.11 is from Yannakakis et al. [1979]. Exercise 14.13 is from Korth [1983].

The timestamp-based concurrency-control scheme is from Reed [1983]. An exposition of various timestamp-based concurrency-control algorithms is presented by Bernstein and Goodman [1980a]. A timestamp algorithm that does not require any rollback to ensure serializability is presented by Buckley and Silberschatz [1983]. The validation concurrency-control scheme is from Kung and Robinson [1981]. A single-site and distributed validation concurrency-control scheme is presented by Bassiouni [1988].

The locking protocol for multiple-granularity data items is from Gray et al. [1975]. A detailed description is presented by Gray et al. [1976]. The effects of locking granularity are discussed by Ries and Stonebraker [1977]. Korth [1983] formalizes multiple-granularity locking for an arbitrary collection of lock modes (allowing for more semantics than simply read and write). This approach includes a class of lock modes called *update* modes to deal with lock conversion. Carey [1983] extends the multiple-granularity idea to timestamp-based concurrency control. An extension of the protocol to ensure deadlock freedom is presented by Korth [1982]. Multiple-granularity locking for object-oriented database systems is discussed in Lee and Liou [1996].

Discussions concerning multiversion concurrency control are offered by Bernstein et al. [1983]. A multiversion tree-locking algorithm appears in Silberschatz [1982]. Multiversion timestamp order was introduced in Reed [1978, 1983]. Lai and Wilkinson [1984] describes a multiversion two-phase locking certifier.

Dijkstra [1965] was one of the first and most influential contributors in the deadlock area. Holt [1971, 1972] was the first to formalize the notion of deadlocks in terms of a graph model similar to the one presented in this chapter. The timestamp deadlock-detection algorithm is from Rosenkrantz et al. [1978]. An analysis of the probability of waiting and deadlock is presented by Gray et al. [1981b]. Theoretical results concerning deadlocks and serializability are presented by Fussell et al. [1981], and by Yannakakis [1981].

Cycle-detection algorithms can be found in standard algorithm textbooks, such as Cormen et al. [1990], and Aho et al. [1983].

Concurrency in $B^+$-trees was studied by Bayer and Schkolnick [1977] and Johnson and Shasha [1993]. The technique presented in Section 14.8 is based on Kung and Lehman [1980], and on Lehman and Yao [1981]. Related work includes Kwong and Wood [1982], Manber and Ladner [1984], and Ford and Calhoun [1984]. Shasha and Goodman [1988] present a good characterization of concurrency protocols for index structures. Ellis [1987] presents a concurrency-control technique for linear hashing. B-link trees are discussed in Lomet and Salzberg [1992]. Concurrency-control algorithms for other index structures appear in Ellis [1980a, 1980b].

A comprehensive survey paper on concurrency control and recovery is presented by Gray [1978]. Textbook discussions are offered by Date [1983a], Bernstein et al. [1987], Papadimitriou [1986], and Gray and Reuter [1993]. Transaction-processing in object-oriented database systems is discussed in Garza and Kim [1988]. Transaction processing in design and software-engineering applications is discussed in Korth et al. [1988], Kaiser [1990], and Weikum [1991]. Theoretical aspects of multi-level transactions are presented in Lynch et al. [1988], and Weihl and Liskov [1990].

The ARIES transaction manager, developed at the IBM Almaden Research Center has had significant influence on transaction management. It is discussed in a series of papers including Mohan [1990a, 1990b], Mohan et al. [1991, 1992], and Mohan and Narang [1994, 1995].

A computer system, like any other device, is subject to failure. There is a variety of causes of such failure, including disk crash, power failure, software error, a fire in the machine room, or even sabotage. In each of these cases, information may be lost. Therefore, the database system must take actions in advance to ensure that the atomicity and durability properties of transactions, introduced in Chapter 13, are preserved, in spite of such failures. An integral part of a database system is a recovery scheme that is responsible for the restoration of the database to a consistent state that existed prior to the occurrence of the failure.

## 15.1  Failure Classification

There are various types of failure that may occur in a system, each of which needs to be dealt with in a different manner. The simplest type of failure to deal with is one that does not result in the loss of information in the system. The failures that are more difficult to deal with are those that result in loss of information. In this chapter, we shall consider only the following types of failure:

- **Transaction Failure.** There are two types of errors that may cause a transaction to fail:
  - **Logical error**. The transaction can no longer continue with its normal execution, owing to some internal condition, such as bad input, data not found, overflow, or resource limit exceeded.
  - **System error**. The system has entered an undesirable state (for example, deadlock), as a result of which a transaction cannot continue with its normal execution. The transaction, however, can be reexecuted at a later time.

- **System crash**. There is a hardware malfunction, or a bug in the database software or the operating system, that causes the loss of the content of volatile storage, and brings transaction processing to a halt. The content of nonvolatile storage remains intact, and is not corrupted.

  The assumption that hardware errors and bugs in the software bring the system to a halt, but do not corrupt the nonvolatile storage contents, is known as the *fail-stop* assumption. Well-designed systems have numerous internal checks, at the hardware and the software level, which bring the system to a halt when there is an error. Hence, the fail-stop assumption is a reasonable one.

- **Disk failure**. A disk block loses its content as a result of either a head crash or failure during a data transfer operation. Copies of the data on other disks, or archival backups on tertiary media, such as tapes, are used to recover from the failure.

To determine how the system should recover from failures, we need to identify the failure modes of those devices used for storing data. Next, we must consider how these failure modes affect the contents of the database. We can then propose algorithms to ensure database consistency and transaction atomicity despite failures. These algorithms are known as recovery algorithms, although they have two parts:

1. Actions taken during normal transaction processing to ensure that enough information exists to allow recovery from failures.
2. Actions taken following a failure to recover the database contents to a state that ensures database consistency, transaction atomicity, and durability.

## 15.2   Storage Structure

As we saw in Chapter 10, the various data items in the database may be stored and accessed in a number of different storage media. To understand how to ensure the atomicity and durability properties of a transaction, we must gain a better understanding of these storage media and their access methods.

### 15.2.1   Storage Types

There are various types of storage media; they are distinguished by their relative speed, capacity, and resilience to failure.

- **Volatile storage**. Information residing in volatile storage does not usually survive system crashes. Examples of such storage are main memory and cache memory. Access to volatile storage is extremely fast, both because of the speed of the memory access itself, and because it is possible to access any data item in volatile storage directly.

- **Nonvolatile storage**. Information residing in nonvolatile storage survives system crashes. Examples of such storage are disk and magnetic tapes. Disks are used for online storage, whereas tapes are used for archival storage. Both, however, are subject to failure (for example, head crash), which may result in loss of information. At the current state of technology, nonvolatile storage is slower than volatile storage by several orders of magnitude. This distinction is the result of disk and tape devices being electromechanical, rather than based entirely on chips, as is volatile storage. In database systems, disks are used for most nonvolatile storage. Other nonvolatile media are normally used only for backup data.

- **Stable storage**. Information residing in stable storage is *never* lost (*never* should be taken with a grain of salt, since theoretically *never* cannot be guaranteed — for example, it is possible, although extremely unlikely, that a black hole may envelop the earth and permanently destroy all data!). Although stable storage is theoretically impossible to obtain, it can be closely approximated by techniques that make data loss extremely unlikely. Stable-storage implementation is discussed in Section 15.2.2.

The distinctions among the various storage types are often less clear in practice than in our presentation. Certain systems provide battery backup, so that some main memory can survive system crashes and power failures. Alternative forms of nonvolatile storage, such as optical media, provide an even higher degree of reliability than do disks.

## 15.2.2  Stable-Storage Implementation

To implement stable storage, we need to replicate the needed information in several nonvolatile storage media (usually disk) with independent failure modes, and to update the information in a controlled manner to ensure that failure during data transfer does not damage the needed information.

Recall (from Chapter 10) that RAID systems guarantee that the failure of a single disk (even during data transfer) will not result in loss of data. The simplest and fastest form of RAID is the mirrored disk, which keeps two copies of each block, on separate disks. Other forms of RAID offer lower costs, but at the expense of lower performance.

RAID systems, however, cannot guard against data loss due to disasters such as fires or flooding. Many systems store archival backups of tapes off-site to guard against such disasters. However, since tapes cannot be carried off-site continually, updates since the most recent time that tapes were carried off-site could be lost in such a disaster. More secure systems keep a copy of each block of stable storage at a remote site, writing it out over a computer network, in addition to storing the block on a local disk system. Since the blocks are output to a remote system as and when they are output to local storage, once an output operation is complete, the output is not lost, even in the event of a disaster such as a fire or flood.

In the remainder of this section, we discuss how storage media can be protected from failure during data transfer. Block transfer between memory and disk storage can result in

- **Successful completion**. The transferred information arrived safely at its destination.
- **Partial failure**. A failure occurred in the midst of transfer, and the destination block has incorrect information.
- **Total failure**. The failure occurred sufficiently early during the transfer that the destination block remains intact.

We require that, if a data-transfer failure occurs, the system detects it and invokes a recovery procedure to restore the block to a consistent state. To do so, the system must maintain two physical blocks for each logical database block; in the case of mirrored disks, both blocks are at the same location; in the case of remote backup, one of the blocks is local, whereas the other is at a remote site. An output operation is executed as follows:

1. Write the information onto the first physical block.
2. When the first write completes successfully, write the same information onto the second physical block.
3. The output is completed only after the second write completes successfully.

During recovery, each pair of physical blocks is examined. If both are the same and no detectable error exists, then no further actions are necessary. (Recall that errors in a disk block, such as a partial write to the block, are detected by storing a checksum with each block.) If an error is detected in one block, then we replace its content with the content of the other block. If both blocks contain no detectable error, but they differ in content, then we replace the content of the first block with the value of the second. This recovery procedure ensures that a write to stable storage either succeeds completely (that is, updates all copies) or results in no change.

The requirement of comparing every corresponding pair of blocks during recovery is expensive to meet. We can reduce the cost greatly by keeping track of block writes that are in progress, using a small amount of nonvolatile RAM. On recovery, only blocks for which writes were in progress need to be compared.

The protocols for writing out a block to a remote site are similar to the protocols for writing blocks to a mirrored disk system, which we examined in Chapter 10, and particularly in Exercise 10.4.

We can extend this procedure easily to allow the use of an arbitrarily large number of copies of each block of stable storage. Although a large number of copies reduces the probability of a failure to even lower than with two copies, it is usually reasonable to simulate stable storage with only two copies.

## 15.2.3  Data Access

As we saw in Chapter 10, the database system resides permanently on nonvolatile storage (usually disks), and is partitioned into fixed-length storage units called

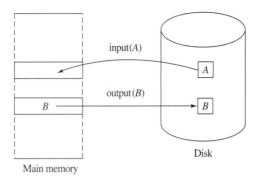

Figure 15.1    Block storage operations.

*blocks*. Blocks are the units of data transfer to and from disk, and may contain several data items. We shall assume that no data item spans two or more blocks. This assumption is realistic for most data-processing applications, such as our banking example.

Transactions input information from the disk to main memory, and then output the information back onto the disk. The input and output operations are done in block units. The blocks residing on the disk are referred to as *physical blocks*; the blocks residing temporarily in main memory are referred to as *buffer blocks*. The area of memory where blocks reside temporarily is called the *disk buffer*.

Block movements between disk and main memory are initiated through the following two operations:

1. **input**($B$) transfers the physical block $B$ to main memory.
2. **output**($B$) transfers the buffer block $B$ to the disk, and replaces the appropriate physical block there.

This scheme is illustrated in Figure 15.1.

Each transaction $T_i$ has a private work area in which copies of all the data items accessed and updated by $T_i$ are kept. This work area is created when the transaction is initiated; it is removed when the transaction either commits or aborts. Each data item $X$ kept in the work area of transaction $T_i$ is denoted by $x_i$. Transaction $T_i$ interacts with the database system by transferring data to and from its work area to the system buffer. We transfer data using the following two operations:

1. **read**($X$) assigns the value of data item $X$ to the local variable $x_i$. This operation is executed as follows:
   a. If the block $B_X$ on which $X$ resides is not in main memory, then issue **input**($B_X$).
   b. Assign to $x_i$ the value of $X$ from the buffer block.

**2. write**(X) assigns the value of local variable $x_i$ to data item X in the buffer block. This operation is executed as follows:

    **a.** If block $B_X$ on which X resides is not in main memory, then issue **input**($B_X$).

    **b.** Assign the value of $x_i$ to X in buffer $B_X$.

Note that both operations may require the transfer of a block from disk to main memory. They do not, however, specifically require the transfer of a block from main memory to disk.

A buffer block is eventually written out to the disk either because the buffer manager needs the memory space for other purposes or because the database system wishes to reflect the change to B on the disk. We shall say that the database system *force-outputs* buffer B if it issues an **output**(B).

When a transaction needs to access a data item X for the first time, it must execute **read**(X). All updates to X are then performed on $x_i$. After the transaction accesses X for the final time, it must execute **write**(X) to reflect the change to X in the database itself.

The **output**($B_X$) operation for the buffer block $B_X$ on which X resides does not need to take effect immediately after **write**(X) is executed, since the block $B_X$ may contain other data items that are still being accessed. Thus, the actual output takes place later. Notice that, if the system crashes after the **write**(X) operation was executed but before **output**($B_X$) was executed, the new value of X is never written to disk and, thus, is lost.

## 15.3    Recovery and Atomicity

Consider again our simplified banking system and transaction $T_i$ that transfers $50 from account A to account B, with initial values of A and B being $1000 and $2000, respectively. Suppose that a system crash has occurred during the execution of $T_i$, after **output**($B_A$) has taken place, but before **output**($B_B$) was executed, where $B_A$ and $B_B$ denote the buffer blocks on which A and B reside. Since the memory contents were lost, we do not know the fate of the transaction; thus, we could invoke one of two possible recovery procedures.

- **Reexecute** $T_i$. This procedure will result in the value of A becoming $900, rather than $950. Thus, the system enters an inconsistent state.
- **Do not reexecute** $T_i$. The current system state is values of $950 and $2000 for A and B, respectively. Thus, the system enters an inconsistent state.

In either case, the database is left in an inconsistent state, and thus this simple recovery scheme does not work. The reason for this difficulty is that we have modified the database without having assurance that the transaction will indeed commit. Our goal is to perform either all or no database modifications made by $T_i$. However, if $T_i$ performed multiple database modifications, several output operations may be required, and a failure may occur after some of these modifications have been made, but before all of them are made.

To achieve our goal of atomicity, we must first output information describing the modifications to stable storage, without modifying the database itself. As we shall see, this procedure will allow us to output all the modifications made by a committed transaction, despite failures. There are two ways to perform such outputs; we study them in Sections 15.4 and 15.5. In these two sections, we shall assume that *transactions are executed serially*; that is, only a single transaction is active at a time. We shall describe how to handle concurrently executing transactions later, in Section 15.6.

## 15.4 Log-Based Recovery

The most widely used structure for recording database modifications is the *log*. The log is a sequence of *log records*, and maintains a record of all the update activities in the database. There are several types of log records. An *update log record* describes a single database write, and has the following fields:

- **Transaction identifier** is the unique identifier of the transaction that performed the **write** operation.
- **Data-item identifier** is the unique identifier of the data item written. Typically, it is the location on disk of the data item.
- **Old value** is the value of the data item prior to the write.
- **New value** is the value that the data item will have after the write.

Other special log records exist to record significant events during transaction processing, such as the start of a transaction and the commit or abort of a transaction. We denote the various types of log records as follows:

- $<T_i$ **start**$>$. Transaction $T_i$ has started.
- $<T_i, \; X_j, \; V_1, \; V_2>$. Transaction $T_i$ has performed a write on data item $X_j$. $X_j$ had value $V_1$ before the write, and will have value $V_2$ after the write.
- $<T_i$ **commit**$>$. Transaction $T_i$ has committed.
- $<T_i$ **abort**$>$. Transaction $T_i$ has aborted.

Whenever a transaction performs a write, it is essential that the log record for that write be created before the database is modified. Once a log record exists, we can output the modification to the database if that is desirable. Also, we have the ability to *undo* a modification that has already been output to the database. We undo it by using the old-value field in log records.

For log records to be useful for recovery from system and disk failures, the log must reside in stable storage. For now, we assume that every log record is written to the end of the log on stable storage as soon as it is created. In Section 15.7, we shall see when it is safe to relax this requirement so as to reduce the overhead imposed by logging. In Sections 15.4.1 and 15.4.2, we shall introduce two techniques for using the log to ensure transaction atomicity despite failures. Observe that the log contains a complete record of all database activity. As a result, the volume of data stored in the log may become unreasonably large. In Section 15.4.3, we shall show when it is safe to erase log information.

## 15.4.1  Deferred Database Modification

The deferred-modification technique ensures transaction atomicity by recording all database modifications in the log, but deferring the execution of all **write** operations of a transaction until the transaction partially commits. Recall that a transaction is said to be partially committed once the final action of the transaction has been executed. The version of the deferred-modification technique that we describe in this section assumes that transactions are executed serially.

When a transaction partially commits, the information on the log associated with the transaction is used in executing the deferred writes. If the system crashes before the transaction completes its execution, or if the transaction aborts, then the information on the log is simply ignored.

The execution of transaction $T_i$ proceeds as follows. Before $T_i$ starts its execution, a record $<T_i$ **start**$>$ is written to the log. A **write**(X) operation by $T_i$ results in the writing of a new record to the log. Finally, when $T_i$ partially commits, a record $<T_i$ **commit**$>$ is written to the log.

When transaction $T_i$ partially commits, the records associated with it in the log are used in executing the deferred writes. Since a failure may occur while this updating is taking place, we must ensure that, prior to the start of these updates, all the log records are written out to stable storage. Once they have been written, the actual updating takes place, and the transaction enters the committed state.

Observe that only the new value of the data item is required by the deferred-modification technique. Thus, we can simplify the general update-log record structure that we saw in the previous section, by omitting the old-value field.

To illustrate, let us reconsider our simplified banking system. Let $T_0$ be a transaction that transfers $50 from account A to account B. This transaction is defined as follows:

$$T_0:\ \textbf{read}(A)$$
$$A := A - 50$$
$$\textbf{write}(A)$$
$$\textbf{read}(B)$$
$$B := B + 50$$
$$\textbf{write}(B)$$

Let $T_1$ be a transaction that withdraws $100 from account C. This transaction is defined as

$$T_1:\ \textbf{read}(C)$$
$$C := C - 100$$
$$\textbf{write}(C)$$

Suppose that these transactions are executed serially, in the order $T_0$ followed by $T_1$, and that the values of accounts A, B, and C before the execution took place were $1000, $2000, and $700, respectively. The portion of the log containing the relevant information on these two transactions is presented in Figure 15.2.

$$<T_0 \text{ start}>$$
$$<T_0, \ A, \ 950>$$
$$<T_0, \ B, \ 2050>$$
$$<T_0 \text{ commit}>$$
$$<T_1 \text{ start}>$$
$$<T_1, \ C, \ 600>$$
$$<T_1 \text{ commit}>$$

Figure 15.2     Portion of the database log corresponding to $T_0$ and $T_1$.

There are various orders in which the actual outputs can take place to both the database system and the log as a result of the execution of $T_0$ and $T_1$. One such order is presented in Figure 15.3. Note that the value of $A$ is changed in the database only after the record $<T_0, \ A, \ 950>$ has been placed in the log.

Using the log, the system can handle any failure that results in the loss of information on volatile storage. The recovery scheme uses the following recovery procedure:

- **redo**($T_i$) sets the value of all data items updated by transaction $T_i$ to the new values.

The set of data items updated by $T_i$ and their respective new values can be found in the log.

The **redo** operation must be *idempotent*; that is, executing it several times must be equivalent to executing it once. This characteristic is required of we are to guarantee correct behavior even if a failure occurs during the recovery process.

After a failure has occurred, the recovery subsystem consults the log to determine which transactions need to be redone. Transaction $T_i$ needs to be redone if and only if the log contains both the record $<T_i \text{ start}>$ and the record $<T_i \text{ commit}>$. Thus, if the system crashes after the transaction completes its execution, the information in the log is used in restoring the system to a previous consistent state after the transaction had completed.

As an illustration, let us return to our banking example with transactions $T_0$ and $T_1$ executed one after the other in the order $T_0$ followed by $T_1$. Figure 15.2

| **Log** | **Database** |
|---|---|
| $<T_0 \text{ start}>$ | |
| $<T_0, \ A, \ 950>$ | |
| $<T_0, \ B, \ 2050>$ | |
| $<T_0 \text{ commit}>$ | |
| | $A = 950$ |
| | $B = 2050$ |
| $<T_1 \text{ start}>$ | |
| $<T_1, \ C, \ 600>$ | |
| $<T_1 \text{ commit}>$ | |
| | $C = 600$ |

Figure 15.3     State of the log and database corresponding to $T_0$ and $T_1$.

shows the log that results from the complete execution of $T_0$ and $T_1$. Let us suppose that the system crashes before the completion of the transactions, so that we can see how the recovery technique restores the database to a consistent state. Assume that the crash occurs just after the log record for the step

**write(B)**

of transaction $T_0$ has been written to stable storage. The log at the time of the crash is as shown in Figure 15.4a. When the system comes back up, no redo actions need to be taken, since no commit record appears in the log. The values of accounts $A$ and $B$ remain $1000 and $2000, respectively. The log records of the incomplete transaction $T_0$ can be deleted from the log.

Now, let us assume the crash comes just after the log record for the step

**write(C)**

of transaction $T_1$ has been written to stable storage. In this case, the log at the time of the crash is as shown in Figure 15.4b. When the system comes back up, the operation **redo($T_0$)** is performed, since the record

**<$T_0$ commit>**

appears in the log on the disk. After this operation is executed, the values of accounts $A$ and $B$ are $950 and $2050, respectively. The value of account $C$ remains $700. As before, the log records of the incomplete transaction $T_1$ can be deleted from the log.

Lastly, assume that a crash occurs just after the log record

**<$T_1$ commit>**

is written to stable storage. The log at the time of this crash is as shown in Figure 15.4c. When the system comes back up, two commit records are in the log: one for $T_0$ and one for $T_1$. Therefore, the operations **redo($T_0$)** and **redo($T_1$)** must be performed, in the order in which their commit records appear in the log. After these operations are executed, the values of accounts $A$, $B$, and $C$ are $950, $2050, and $600, respectively.

Finally, let us consider a case in which a second system crash occurs during recovery from the first crash. Some changes may have been made to the database as a result of the **redo** operations, but all changes may not have been made. When the system comes up after the second crash, recovery proceeds exactly as in the

| | | |
|---|---|---|
| <$T_0$ **start**> | <$T_0$ **start**> | <$T_0$ **start**> |
| <$T_0$, A, 950> | <$T_0$, A, 950> | <$T_0$, A, 950> |
| <$T_0$, B, 2050> | <$T_0$, B, 2050> | <$T_0$, B, 2050> |
| | <$T_0$ **commit**> | <$T_0$ **commit**> |
| | <$T_1$ **start**> | <$T_1$ **start**> |
| | <$T_1$, C, 600> | <$T_1$, C, 600> |
| | | <$T_1$ **commit**> |
| (a) | (b) | (c) |

Figure 15.4    The same log as that in Figure 15.3, shown at three different times.

preceding examples. For each commit record

$$<T_i \text{ commit}>$$

found in the log, the operation **redo**($T_i$) is performed. In other words, the recovery actions are restarted from the beginning. Since **redo** writes values to the database independent of the values currently in the database, the result of a successful second attempt at **redo** is the same as though **redo** had succeeded the first time.

## 15.4.2 Immediate Database Modification

The immediate-update technique allows database modifications to be output to the database while the transaction is still in the active state. Data modifications written by active transactions are called *uncommitted modifications*. In the event of a crash or a transaction failure, the system must use the old-value field of the log records described in Section 15.4 to restore the modified data items to the value they had prior to the start of the transaction. This restoration is accomplished through the **undo** operation described next.

Before a transaction $T_i$ starts its execution, the record $<T_i$ **start**$>$ is written to the log. During its execution, any **write**($X$) operation by $T_i$ is *preceded* by the writing of the appropriate new update record to the log. When $T_i$ partially commits, the record $<T_i$ **commit**$>$ is written to the log.

Since the information in the log is used in reconstructing the state of the database, we cannot allow the actual update to the database to take place before the corresponding log record is written out to stable storage. We therefore require that, prior to execution of an **output**($B$) operation, the log records corresponding to $B$ be written onto stable storage. We shall return to this issue in Section 15.7.

As an illustration, let us reconsider our simplified banking system, with transactions $T_0$ and $T_1$ executed one after the other in the order $T_0$ followed by $T_1$. The portion of the log containing the relevant information concerning these two transactions is presented in Figure 15.5.

One possible order in which the actual outputs took place to both the database system and the log as a result of the execution of $T_0$ and $T_1$ is described in Figure 15.6. Notice that this order could not be obtained in the deferred-modification technique of Section 15.4.1.

Using the log, the system can handle any failure that does not result in the loss of information on nonvolatile storage. The recovery scheme uses two recovery

$$<T_0 \text{ start}>$$
$$<T_0, \ A, \ 1000, \ 950>$$
$$<T_0, \ B, \ 2000, \ 2050>$$
$$<T_0 \text{ commit}>$$
$$<T_1 \text{ start}>$$
$$<T_1, \ C, \ 700, \ 600>$$
$$<T_1 \text{ commit}>$$

Figure 15.5    Portion of the system log corresponding to $T_0$ and $T_1$.

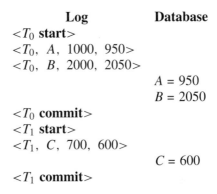

**Log**                    **Database**
$<T_0$ **start**$>$
$<T_0,\ A,\ 1000,\ 950>$
$<T_0,\ B,\ 2000,\ 2050>$
                                   $A = 950$
                                   $B = 2050$
$<T_0$ **commit**$>$
$<T_1$ **start**$>$
$<T_1,\ C,\ 700,\ 600>$
                                   $C = 600$
$<T_1$ **commit**$>$

**Figure 15.6**   State of system log and database corresponding to $T_0$ and $T_1$.

procedures:

- **undo**$(T_i)$ restores the value of all data items updated by transaction $T_i$ to the old values.
- **redo**$(T_i)$ sets the value of all data items updated by transaction $T_i$ to the new values.

The set of data items updated by $T_i$ and their respective old and new values can be found in the log.

The **undo** and **redo** operations must be idempotent to guarantee correct behavior even if a failure occurs during the recovery process.

After a failure has occurred, the recovery scheme consults the log to determine which transactions need to be redone, and which need to be undone. This classification of transactions is accomplished as follows:

- Transaction $T_i$ needs to be undone if the log contains the record $<T_i$ **start**$>$, but does not contain the record $<T_i$ **commit**$>$.
- Transaction $T_i$ needs to be redone if the log contains both the record $<T_i$ **start**$>$ and the record $<T_i$ **commit**$>$.

As an illustration, let us return to our banking example, with transaction $T_0$ and $T_1$ executed one after the other in the order $T_0$ followed by $T_1$. Let us suppose that the system crashes before the completion of the transactions. We shall consider three cases. The state of the logs for each of these cases is shown in Figure 15.7.

First, let us assume that the crash occurs just after the log record for the step

$$\textbf{write}(B)$$

of transaction $T_0$ has been written to stable storage (Figure 15.7a). When the system comes back up, it finds the record $<T_0$ **start**$>$ in the log, but no corresponding $<T_0$ **commit**$>$ record. Thus, transaction $T_0$ must be undone, so an

| $<T_0$ **start**$>$ | $<T_0$ **start**$>$ | $<T_0$ **start**$>$ |
|---|---|---|
| $<T_0,\ A,\ 1000,\ 950>$ | $<T_0,\ A,\ 1000,\ 950>$ | $<T_0,\ A,\ 1000,\ 950>$ |
| $<T_0,\ B,\ 2000,\ 2050>$ | $<T_0,\ B,\ 2000,\ 2050>$ | $<T_0,\ B,\ 2000,\ 2050>$ |
| | $<T_0$ **commit**$>$ | $<T_0$ **commit**$>$ |
| | $<T_1$ **start**$>$ | $<T_1$ **start**$>$ |
| | $<T_1,\ C,\ 700,\ 600>$ | $<T_1,\ C,\ 700,\ 600>$ |
| | | $<T_1$ **commit**$>$ |
| (a) | (b) | (c) |

Figure 15.7    The same log, shown at three different times.

**undo**$(T_0)$ is performed. As a result, the values in accounts $A$ and $B$ (on the disk) are restored to \$1000 and \$2000, respectively.

Next, let us assume that the crash comes just after the log record for the step

$$\textbf{write}(C)$$

of transaction $T_1$ has been written to stable storage (Figure 15.7b). When the system comes back up, two recovery actions need to be taken. The operation **undo**$(T_1)$ must be performed, since the record $<T_1$ **start**$>$ appears in the log, but there is no record $<T_1$ **commit**$>$. The operation **redo**$(T_0)$ must be performed, since the log contains both the record $<T_0$ **start**$>$ and the record $<T_0$ **commit**$>$. At the end of the entire recovery procedure, the values of accounts $A$, $B$, and $C$ are \$950, \$2050, and \$700, respectively. Note that the **undo**$(T_1)$ operation is performed before the **redo**$(T_0)$. In this example, the same outcome would result if the order were reversed. However, the order of doing **undo** operations first, and then **redo** operations, is important for the recovery algorithm that we shall see in Section 15.6.

Finally, let us assume that the crash occurs just after the log record

$$<T_1\ \textbf{commit}>$$

has been written to stable storage (Figure 15.7c). When the system comes back up, both $T_0$ and $T_1$ need to be redone, since the records $<T_0$ **start**$>$ and $<T_0$ **commit**$>$ appear in the log as do the records $<T_1$ **start**$>$ and $<T_1$ **commit**$>$. After the recovery procedures **redo**$(T_0)$ and **redo**$(T_1)$ are performed, the values in accounts $A$, $B$, and $C$ are \$950, \$2050, and \$600, respectively.

## 15.4.3   Checkpoints

When a system failure occurs, we must consult the log to determine those transactions that need to be redone and those that need to be undone. In principle, we need to search the entire log to determine this information. There are two major difficulties with this approach:

1. The search process is time-consuming.
2. Most of the transactions that, according to our algorithm, need to be redone have already written their updates into the database. Although redoing them will cause no harm, it will nevertheless cause recovery to take longer.

To reduce these types of overhead, we introduce *checkpoints*. During execution, the system maintains the log, using one of the two techniques described in Sections 15.4.1 and 15.4.2. In addition, the system periodically performs checkpoints, which require the following sequence of actions to take place:

1. Output onto stable storage all log records currently residing in main memory.
2. Output to the disk all modified buffer blocks.
3. Output onto stable storage a log record <**checkpoint**>.

Transactions are not allowed to perform any update actions, such as writing to a buffer block or writing a log record, while a checkpoint is in progress.

The presence of a <**checkpoint**> record in the log allows the system to streamline its recovery procedure. Consider a transaction $T_i$ that committed prior to the checkpoint. For such a transaction, the <$T_i$ **commit**> record appears in the log before the <**checkpoint**> record. Any database modifications made by $T_i$ must have been written to the database either prior to the checkpoint or as part of the checkpoint itself. Thus, at recovery time, there is no need to perform a **redo** operation on $T_i$.

This observation allows us to refine our previous recovery schemes. (We continue to assume that transactions are run serially.) After a failure has occurred, the recovery scheme examines the log to determine the most recent transaction $T_i$ that started executing before the most recent checkpoint took place. It can find such a transaction by searching the log backward, from the end of the log, until it finds the first <**checkpoint**> record (since we are searching backward, the record found is the final <**checkpoint**> record in the log); then it continues the search backward until it finds the next <$T_i$ **start**> record. This record identifies a transaction $T_i$.

Once transaction $T_i$ has been identified, the **redo** and **undo** operations need to be applied to only transaction $T_i$ and all transactions $T_j$ that started executing after transaction $T_i$. Let us denote these transactions by the set $T$. The remainder (earlier part) of the log can be ignored, and can be erased whenever desired. The exact recovery operations to be performed depend on whether the immediate-modification technique or the deferred-modification technique is being used. The recovery operations that are required if the immediate-modification technique is employed are as follows:

- For all transactions $T_k$ in $T$ that have no <$T_k$ **commit**> record in the log, execute **undo**($T_k$).
- For all transactions $T_k$ in $T$ such that the record <$T_k$ **commit**> appears in the log, execute **redo**($T_k$).

Obviously, the **undo** operation does not need to be applied when the deferred-modification technique is being employed.

As an illustration, consider the set of transactions $\{T_0, T_1, ..., T_{100}\}$ executed in the order of the subscripts. Suppose that the most recent checkpoint took place during the execution of transaction $T_{67}$. Thus, only transactions $T_{67}, T_{68}, ..., T_{100}$

need to be considered during the recovery scheme. Each of them needs to be redone if it has committed; otherwise, it needs to be undone.

In Section 15.6.3, we consider an extension of the checkpoint technique for concurrent transaction processing.

## 15.5 Shadow Paging

An alternative to log-based crash-recovery techniques is *shadow paging*. The shadow-paging technique is essentially an improvement on the shadow-copy technique that we saw in Section 13.3. Under certain circumstances, shadow paging may require fewer disk accesses than do the log-based methods discussed previously. There are, however, disadvantages to the shadow-paging approach, as we shall see. For example, it is hard to extend shadow paging to allow multiple transactions to execute concurrently.

As before, the database is partitioned into some number of fixed-length blocks, which are referred to as *pages*. The term *page* is borrowed from operating systems, since we are using a paging scheme for memory management. Let us assume that there are $n$ pages, numbered 1 through $n$. (In practice, $n$ may be in the hundreds of thousands.) These pages do not need not to be stored in any particular order on disk (there are many reasons why they do not, as we saw in Chapter 10). However, there must be a way to find the $i$th page of the database for any given $i$. We use a *page table*, as shown in Figure 15.8, for this purpose. The page table has $n$ entries — one for each database page. Each entry contains a pointer to a page on disk. The first entry contains a pointer to the first page of the database, the second entry points to the second page, and so on. The example in Figure 15.8 shows that the logical order of database pages does not need to correspond to the physical order in which the pages are placed on disk.

The key idea behind the shadow-paging technique is to maintain *two* page tables during the life of a transaction: the *current* page table and the *shadow* page table. When the transaction starts, both page tables are identical. The shadow page table is never changed over the duration of the transaction. The current page table may be changed when a transaction performs a **write** operation. All **input** and **output** operations use the current page table to locate database pages on disk.

Suppose that the transaction $T_j$ performs a **write**($X$) operation, and that $X$ resides on the $i$th page. The **write** operation is executed as follows:

1. If the $i$th page (that is, the page on which $X$ resides) is not already in main memory, then issue **input**($X$).
2. If this is the write first performed on the $i$th page by this transaction, then modify the current page table as follows:
   a. Find an unused page on disk. Typically, the database system has access to a list of unused (free) pages, as we saw in Chapter 10.
   b. Delete the page found in step 2a from the list of free page frames; copy the contents of the $i$th page to the page found in step 2a.
   c. Modify the current page table such that the $i$th entry points to the page found in step 2a.
3. Assign the value of $x_j$ to $X$ in the buffer page.

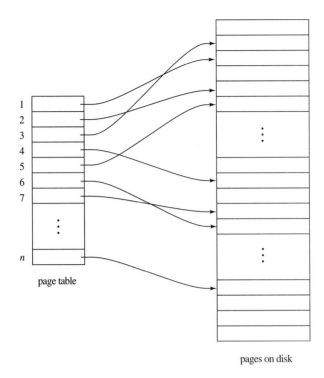

Figure 15.8   Sample page table.

Let us compare the preceding action for a **write** operation with that de-scribed in Section 15.2.3 The only difference is that we have added a new step. Steps 1 and 3 above correspond to steps 1 and 2 in Section 15.2.3. The added step, step 2, manipulates the current page table. Figure 15.9 shows the shadow and current page tables for a transaction performing a write to the fourth page of a database consisting of 10 pages.

Intuitively, the shadow-page approach to recovery is to store the shadow page table in nonvolatile storage, so that the state of the database prior to the execution of the transaction can be recovered in the event of a crash, or trans-action abort. When the transaction commits, the current page table is written to nonvolatile storage. The current page table then becomes the new shadow page table, and the next transaction is allowed to begin execution. It is important that the shadow page table be stored in nonvolatile storage, since it provides the only means of locating database pages. The current page table may be kept in main memory (volatile storage). We do not care whether the current page table is lost in a crash, since the system recovers using the shadow page table.

Successful recovery requires that we find the shadow page table on disk after a crash. A simple way of finding it is to choose one fixed location in stable storage that contains the disk address of the shadow page table. When the system comes back up after a crash, we copy the shadow page table into main memory, and use it for subsequent transaction processing. Because of our definition of the

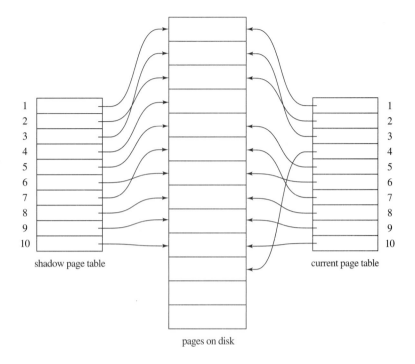

1
2
3
4
5
6
7
8
9
10

shadow page table

1
2
3
4
5
6
7
8
9
10

current page table

pages on disk

Figure 15.9    Shadow and current page tables.

**write** operation, we are guaranteed that the shadow page table will point to the database pages corresponding to the state of the database prior to any transaction that was active at the time of the crash. Thus, aborts are automatic. Unlike our log-based schemes, no **undo** operations need to be invoked.

To commit a transaction, we must do the following:

1. Ensure that all buffer pages in main memory that have been changed by the transaction are output to disk. (Note that these output operations will not change database pages pointed to by some entry in the shadow page table.)

2. Output the current page table to disk. Note that we must not overwrite the shadow page table, since we may need it for recovery from a crash.

3. Output the disk address of the current page table to the fixed location in stable storage containing the address of the shadow page table. This action overwrites the address of the old shadow page table. Therefore, the current page table has become the shadow page table, and the transaction is committed.

If a crash occurs prior to the completion of step 3, we revert to the state just prior to the execution of the transaction. If the crash occurs after the completion of step 3, the effects of the transaction will be preserved; no **redo** operations need to be invoked.

Shadow paging offers several advantages over log-based techniques. The overhead of log-record output is eliminated, and recovery from crashes is significantly faster (since no **undo** or **redo** operations are needed). However, there are drawbacks to the shadow-page technique:

- **Commit overhead**. The commit of a single transaction using shadow paging requires multiple blocks to be output — the actual data blocks, the current page table, and the disk address of the current page table. Log-based schemes need to output only the log records, which, for typical small transactions, fit within one block.
- **Data fragmentation**. In Chapter 10, we considered strategies to keep related database pages close physically on the disk. This locality allows for faster data transfer. Shadow paging causes database pages to change location when they are updated. As a result, either we lose the locality property of the pages or we must resort to more complex, higher-overhead schemes for physical storage management. (See the bibliographic notes for references.)
- **Garbage collection**. Each time that a transaction commits, the database pages containing the old version of data changed by the transaction become inaccessible. In Figure 15.9, the page pointed to by the fourth entry of the shadow page table will become inaccessible once the transaction of that example commits. Such pages are considered *garbage*, since they are not part of free space and do not contain usable information. Garbage may be created also as a side effect of crashes. Periodically, it is necessary to find all the garbage pages, and to add them to the list of free pages. This process, called *garbage collection*, imposes additional overhead and complexity on the system. There are several standard algorithms for garbage collection. (See the bibliographic notes for references.)

In addition to the drawbacks of shadow paging, that we have just mentioned, shadow paging is more difficult than logging to adapt to systems that allow several transactions to execute concurrently. In such systems, some logging is typically required, even if shadow paging is used. The System R prototype, for example, used a combination of shadow paging and a logging scheme similar to that presented in Section 15.4.2. It is relatively easy to extend the log-based recovery schemes to allow concurrent transactions, as we shall see in Section 15.6. For these reasons, shadow paging is not widely used.

## 15.6   Recovery with Concurrent Transactions

Until now, we considered recovery in an environment where only a single transaction at a time is executing. We now discuss how we can modify and extend the log-based recovery scheme to deal with multiple concurrent transactions. Regardless of the number of concurrent transactions, the system has a single disk buffer and a single log. The buffer blocks are shared by all transactions. We allow immediate updates, and permit a buffer block to have data items updated by one or more transactions.

### 15.6.1 Interaction with Concurrency Control

The recovery scheme depends greatly on the concurrency-control scheme that is used. To roll back a failed transaction, we must undo the updates performed by the transaction. Suppose that a transaction $T_0$ has to be rolled back, and a data item $Q$ that was updated by $T_0$ has to be restored to its old value. Using the log-based schemes for recovery, we restore the value using the undo information in a log record. Suppose now that a second transaction $T_1$ has performed yet another update on $Q$ *before* $T_0$ is rolled back. Then, the update performed by $T_1$ will be lost if $T_0$ is rolled back.

Therefore, we require that, if a transaction $T$ has updated a data item $Q$, no other transaction may update the same data item until $T$ has committed or been rolled back. We can ensure this requirement easily by using strict two-phase locking — that is, two-phase locking with exclusive locks held until the end of the transaction.

### 15.6.2 Transaction Rollback

We roll back a failed transaction, $T_i$, using the log. The log is scanned backward; for every log record of the form $<T_i, \ X_j, \ V_1, \ V_2>$ found in the log, the data item $X_j$ is restored to its old value $V_1$. The scanning of the log terminates when the log record $<T_i,$ **start**$>$ is found.

Scanning the log backward is important, since a transaction may have updated a data item more than once. As an illustration, consider the pair of log records

$$<T_i, \ A, \ 10, \ 20>$$
$$<T_i, \ A, \ 20, \ 30>$$

The log records represent a modification of data item $A$ by $T_i$, followed by another modification of $A$ by $T_i$. Scanning the log backward sets $A$ correctly to 10. If the log were scanned in the forward direction, $A$ would be set to 20, which value is incorrect.

If strict two-phase locking is used for concurrency control, locks held by a transaction $T$ may be released only after the transaction has been rolled back as described. Once transaction $T$ (that is being rolled back) has updated a data item, no other transaction could have updated the same data item, due to the concurrency-control requirements mentioned previously. Therefore, restoring the old value of the data item will not erase the effects of any other transaction.

### 15.6.3 Checkpoints

In Section 15.4.3, we used checkpoints to reduce the number of log records that must be scanned when the system recovers from a crash. Since we assumed no concurrency, it was necessary to consider only the following transactions during recovery:

- Those transactions that started after the most recent checkpoint
- The one transaction, if any, that was active at the time of the most recent checkpoint

The situation is more complex when transactions can execute concurrently, since several transactions may have been active at the time of the most recent checkpoint.

In a concurrent transaction-processing system, we require that the checkpoint log record be of the form <**checkpoint** $L$>, where $L$ is a list of transactions active at the time of the checkpoint. Again, we assume that transactions do not perform updates either on the buffer blocks or on the log, while the checkpoint is in progress.

The requirement that transactions must not perform any updates to buffer blocks or to the log during checkpointing can be bothersome, since transaction processing will have to halt while a checkpoint is in progress. A *fuzzy checkpoint* is a checkpoint where transactions are allowed to perform updates even while buffer blocks are being written out. The bibliographic notes provide references to extensions of the recovery techniques to allow checkpoints to be fuzzy. Fuzzy checkpointing schemes are described in Section 15.9.5.

## 15.6.4    Restart Recovery

When the system recovers from a crash, it constructs two lists: The *undo-list* consists of transactions to be undone, and the *redo-list* consists of transactions to be redone.

These two lists are constructed on recovery as follows. Initially, they are both empty. We scan the log backward, examining each record, until the first <**checkpoint**> record is found:

- For each record found of the form <$T_i$ **commit**>, we add $T_i$ to *redo-list*.
- For each record found of the form <$T_i$ **start**>, if $T_i$ is not in *redo-list*, then we add $T_i$ to *undo-list*.

When all the appropriate log records have been examined, we check the list $L$ in the checkpoint record. For each transaction $T_i$ in $L$, if $T_i$ is not in *redo-list* then we add $T_i$ to the *undo-list*.

Once the redo-list and undo-list have have been constructed, the recovery proceeds as follows:

1. Rescan the log from the most recent record backward, and perform an **undo** for each log record that belongs transaction $T_i$ on the *undo-list*. Log records of transactions on the *redo-list* are ignored in this phase. The scan stops when the <$T_i$ **start**> records have been found for every transaction $T_i$ in the *undo-list*.

**2.** Locate the most recent <**checkpoint** $L$> record on the log. Notice that this step may involve scanning the log forward, if the checkpoint record was passed in step 1.

**3.** Scan the log forward from the most recent <**checkpoint** $L$> record, and perform **redo** for each log record that belongs to a transaction $T_i$ that is on the *redo-list*. Ignore log records of transactions on the *undo-list* in this phase.

It is important in step 1 to process the log backward, to ensure that the resulting state of the database is correct.

After all transactions on the *undo-list* have been undone, those transactions on the *redo-list* are redone. It is important, in this case, to process the log forward. When the recovery process has completed, transaction processing resumes.

It is important to undo the transaction in the *undo-list* before redoing transactions in the *redo-list*, using the preceding algorithm. Otherwise, the following problem may occur. Suppose that data item $A$ initially has the value 10. Suppose that a transaction $T_i$ updated data item $A$ to 20 and aborted; transaction rollback would restore $A$ to the value 10. Suppose that another transaction $T_j$ then updated data item $A$ to 30 and committed, following which the system crashed. The state of the log at the time of the crash is

$$<T_i, \ A, \ 10, \ 20>$$
$$<T_j, \ A, \ 10, \ 30>$$
$$<T_j \ \textbf{commit}>$$

If the redo pass is performed first, $A$ will be set to 30; then, in the undo pass, $A$ will be set to 10, which is wrong. The final value of $Q$ should be 30, which we can ensure by performing undo before performing redo.

## 15.7    Buffer Management

In this section, we consider several subtle details that are essential to the implementation of a crash-recovery scheme that ensures data consistency and imposes a minimal amount of overhead on interactions with the database.

### 15.7.1    Log-Record Buffering

Earlier, we assumed that every log record is output to stable storage at the time it is created. This assumption imposes a high overhead on system execution for the following reasons. Typically, output to stable storage is in units of blocks. In most cases, a log record is much smaller than a block. Thus, the output of each log record translates to a much larger output at the physical level. Furthermore, as we saw in Section 15.2.2, the output of a block to stable storage may involve several output operations at the physical level.

The cost of performing the output of a block to stable storage is sufficiently high that it is desirable to output multiple log records at once. To do so, we write log records to a log buffer in main memory, where they stay temporarily until they are output to stable storage. Multiple log records can be gathered in the log buffer, and output to stable storage in a single output operation. The order of log records in the stable storage must be exactly the same as the order in which they were written to the log buffer.

Due to the use of log buffering, a log record may reside in only main memory (volatile storage) for a considerable time before it is output to stable storage. Since such log records are lost if the system crashes, we must impose additional requirements on the recovery techniques to ensure transaction atomicity:

- Transaction $T_i$ enters the commit state after the $<T_i$ **commit**$>$ log record has been output to stable storage.
- Before the $<T_i$ **commit**$>$ log record can be output to stable storage, all log records pertaining to transaction $T_i$ must have been output to stable storage.
- Before a block of data in main memory can be output to the database (in nonvolatile storage), all log records pertaining to data in that block must have been output to stable storage.

    The latter rule is called the *write-ahead logging* (WAL) rule. (Strictly speaking, the WAL rule requires only that the undo information in the log have been output to stable storage, and permits the redo information to be written later. The difference is relevant in systems where undo and redo information is stored in separate log records.)

Writing the buffered log to disk is sometimes referred to as a *log force*. The preceding rules state situations in which certain log records *must* have been output to stable storage. There is no problem resulting from the output of log records *earlier* than necessary. Thus, when the system finds it necessary to output a log record to stable storage, it outputs an entire block of log records, if there are enough log records in main memory to fill a block. If there are insufficient log records to fill the block, all log records in main memory are combined into a partially full block, and are output to stable storage.

## 15.7.2   Database Buffering

In Section 15.2, we described the use of a two-level storage hierarchy. The database is stored in nonvolatile storage (disk), and blocks of data are brought into main memory as needed. Since main memory is typically much smaller than the entire database, it may be necessary to overwrite a block $B_1$ in main memory when another block $B_2$ needs to be brought into memory. If $B_1$ has been modified, $B_1$ must be output prior to the input of $B_2$. As discussed in Section 10.5.1 in Chapter 10, this storage hierarchy is the standard operating system concept of *virtual memory*.

The rules for the output of log records limit the freedom of the system to output blocks of data. If the input of block $B_2$ causes block $B_1$ to be chosen for output, all log records pertaining to data in $B_1$ must be output to stable storage before $B_1$ is output. Thus, the sequence of actions by the system would be as follows:

- Output log records to stable storage until all log records pertaining to block $B_1$ have been output.
- Output block $B_1$ to disk.
- Input block $B_2$ from disk to main memory.

It is important that no writes to the block $B_1$ be in progress while the preceding sequence of actions is carried out. We can ensure that they are not by using a special means of locking, as follows. Before a transaction performs a write on a data item, it must acquire an exclusive lock on the block in which the data item resides. The lock can be released immediately after the update has been performed. Before a block is output, the system obtains an exclusive lock on the block, to ensure that no transaction is updating the block. The lock is released once the block output has completed. Locks that are held for a short duration are often called *latches*. Latches are treated as distinct from locks used by the concurrency-control system. As a result, they may be released without regard to any locking protocol, such as two-phase locking, required by the concurrency-control system.

To illustrate the need for the preceding sequence of actions, we consider our banking example with transactions $T_0$ and $T_1$. Suppose that the state of the log is

$$<T_0 \text{ start}>$$
$$<T_0, \ A, \ 1000, \ 950>$$

and that transaction $T_0$ issues a **read**($B$). Assume that the block on which $B$ resides is not in main memory, and that main memory is full. Suppose that the block on which $A$ resides is chosen to be output to disk. If the system outputs this block to disk and then a crash occurs, the values in the database for accounts $A$, $B$, and $C$ are \$950, \$2000, and \$700, respectively. This database state is inconsistent. However, due to the preceding requirements, the log record

$$<T_0, \ A, \ 1000, \ 950>$$

must be output to stable storage prior to output of the block on which $A$ resides. The system can use the log record during recovery to bring the database back to a consistent state.

### 15.7.3   Operating System Role in Buffer Management

We can manage the database buffer using one of two approaches:

1. The database system reserves part of main memory to serve as a buffer that it, rather than the operating system, manages. The database system manages data-block transfer in accordance with the requirements that we discussed.

   This approach has the drawback of limiting flexibility in the use of main memory. The buffer must be kept small enough that other applications have sufficient main memory available for their needs. However, even when the other applications are not running, the database will not be able to make use of all the available memory. Likewise, nondatabase applications may not use that part of main memory reserved for the database buffer, even if some of the pages in the database buffer are not being used.

2. The database system implements its buffer within the virtual memory provided by the operating system. Since the operating system knows about the memory requirements of all processes in the system, ideally it should be in charge of deciding what buffer blocks must be force-output to disk, and when. But, to ensure the write-ahead logging requirements that we discussed, the operating system should not write out the database buffer pages itself, but instead should request the database system to force-output the buffer blocks. The database system in turn would force-output the buffer blocks to the database, after writing relevant log records to stable storage.

   Unfortunately, almost all current-generation operating systems retain complete control of virtual memory. The operating system reserves space on disk for storing virtual-memory pages that are not currently in main memory; this space is called *swap space*. If the operating system decides to output a block $B_x$, that block is output to the swap space on disk, and there is no way for the database system to get control of the output of buffer blocks.

   Therefore, if the database buffer is in virtual memory, transfers between database files and the buffer in virtual memory must be managed by the database system, which enforces the write-ahead logging requirements that we discussed.

   This approach may result in extra output of data to disk. If a block $B_x$ is output by the operating system, that block is not output to the database. Instead, it is output to the swap space for the operating system's virtual memory. When the database system needs to output $B_x$, the operating system may need first to input $B_x$ from its swap space. Thus, instead of a single output of $B_x$, there may be two outputs of $B_x$ (one by the operating system, and one by the database system) and one extra input of $B_x$.

Although both approaches suffer from some drawbacks, one or the other must be chosen unless the operating system is designed to support the requirements of database logging. Only a few current operating systems, such as the Mach operating system, support these requirements.

## 15.8 Failure with Loss of Nonvolatile Storage

Until now, we have considered only the case where a failure results in the loss of information residing in volatile storage while the content of the nonvolatile storage remains intact. Although failures in which the content of nonvolatile storage is lost are rare, we nevertheless need to be prepared to deal with this type of failure. In this section, we discuss only disk storage. Our discussions apply as well to other nonvolatile storage types.

The basic scheme is to *dump* the entire content of the database to stable storage periodically — say, once per day. For example, we may dump the database to one or more magnetic tapes. If a failure occurs that results in the loss of physical database blocks, the most recent dump is used in restoring the database to a previous consistent state. Once this restoration has been accomplished, the system uses the log to bring the database system to the most recent consistent state.

More precisely, no transaction may be active during the dump procedure, and a procedure similar to checkpointing must take place:

1. Output all log records currently residing in main memory onto stable storage.
2. Output all buffer blocks onto the disk.
3. Copy the contents of the database to stable storage.
4. Output a log record <**dump**> onto the stable storage.

Steps 1, 2, and 4 correspond to the three steps used for checkpoints in Section 15.4.3.

To recover from the loss of nonvolatile storage, we restore the database to disk using the most recent dump. Then, the log is consulted, and all the transactions that have committed since the most recent dump occurred are redone. Notice that no **undo** operations need to be executed.

A dump of the database contents is also referred to as an *archival dump*, since we can archive the dumps and use them later to examine old states of the database. Dumps of a database and checkpointing of buffers are similar.

The simple dump procedure described here is costly for the following two reasons. First, the entire database must be be copied to stable storage, resulting in considerable data transfer. Second, since transaction processing is halted during the dump procedure, CPU cycles are wasted. *Fuzzy dump* schemes have been developed, which allow transactions to be active while the dump is in progress. They are similar to fuzzy checkpointing schemes; see the bibliographic notes for more details.

# 15.9 Advanced Recovery Techniques

The recovery techniques described in Section 15.6 require that, once a transaction updates a data item, no other transaction may update the same data item until the first commits or is rolled back. We ensure the condition by using strict two-phase locking. Although strict two-phase locking is acceptable for records in relations, as discussed in Section 14.8, it causes a significant decrease in concurrency when applied to certain specialized structures, such as $B^+$-tree index pages.

To increase concurrency, we can use the $B^+$-tree concurrency-control algorithm described in Section 14.8 to allow locks to be released early, in a non–two-phase manner. As a result, however, the recovery techniques from Section 15.6 will become inapplicable. Several alternative recovery techniques, applicable even with early lock release, have been proposed. We describe one such recovery technique in this section.

## 15.9.1 Logical Undo Logging

For actions where locks are released early, we cannot perform the undo actions by simply writing back the old value of the data items. Consider a transaction $T$ that inserts an entry into a $B^+$-tree, and, following the $B^+$-tree concurrency-control protocol, releases some locks after the insertion operation completes, but before the transaction commits. After the locks are released, other transactions may perform further insertions or deletions, thereby causing further changes to the $B^+$-tree pages.

Even though the operation releases some locks early, it must retain enough locks to ensure that no other transaction is allowed to execute any conflicting operation (such as reading the inserted value, or deleting the inserted value). For this reason, the $B^+$-tree concurrency-control protocol that we studied earlier holds locks on the leaf level of the $B^+$-tree until the end of the transaction.

Now let us consider how to perform transaction rollback. If the old values of the internal $B^+$-tree nodes (before the insertion operation was executed) are written back during transaction rollback, some of the updates performed by later insertion or deletion operations executed by other transactions could be lost. Instead, the insertion operation has to be undone *logically* — that is, by execution of a delete operation.

Therefore, when the insertion action completes, before it releases any locks, it writes a log record $<T_i, O_j,$ **operation-end**, $U>$, where the $U$ denotes undo information, and $O_j$ denotes a unique identifier for (the instance of) the operation. For example, if the operation inserted an entry in a $B^+$-tree, the undo information $U$ would indicate that a deletion operation is to be performed, and would identify the $B^+$-tree and what to delete from the tree. Such logging of information about operations is called *logical logging*. In contrast, logging of old-value and new-value information is called *physical logging*, and the corresponding log records are called *physical log records*.

The insertion and deletion operations are examples of a class of operations that requires logical undo operations since it releases locks early; we call such operations *logical operations*. Before a logical operation begins, it writes a log record $<T_i, O_j,$ **operation-begin**$>$, where $O_j$ is the unique identifier for the operation. While the operation is being executed, logging is done in the normal fashion for all updates performed by the operation. Thus, the usual old-value and new-value information is written out for each update. When the operation finishes, an **operation-end** log record is written as described earlier.

## 15.9.2 Transaction Rollback

Let us first consider transaction rollback during normal operation (that is, not during recovery from system failure). The log is scanned backward, and we use log records belonging to the transaction to restore the old values of data items. Unlike before, we write out special redo-only log records of the form $<T_i, X_j, V>$ containing the value $V$ being restored to data item $X_j$ during the rollback. These log records are sometimes called compensation log records. Whenever a log record $<T_i, O_j,$ **operation-end**, $U>$ is found, special actions are taken:

1. We roll back the operation by using the undo information $U$ in the log record. The updates performed during the rollback of the operation are logged just like updates performed when the operation was first executed. But instead of generating a log record $< T_i, O_j,$ **operation-end**, $U >$, a log record $< T_i, O_j,$ **operation-abort**$>$ is generated.

2. When the backward scan of the log continues, we skip all log records of the transaction until we find the log record $<T_i, O_j,$ **operation-begin**$>$. After the **operation-begin** log record is found, log records of the transaction are processed in the normal manner again.

If a record $< T_i, O_j,$ **operation-abort**$>$ is found, all preceding records are skipped till we find the record $< T_i, O_j,$ **operation-begin**$>$. These preceding log records must be skipped to prevent multiple rollback of the same operation, in case there had been a crash during an earlier rollback, and the transaction had already been partly rolled back. When the transaction $T_i$ has been rolled back, a record $<T_i$ **abort**$>$ is added to the log.

If failures occur while a logical operation is in progress, the **operation-end** log record for the operation will not be found when the transaction is rolled back. However, for every update performed by the operation, undo information — in the form of the old value in the physical log records — is available in the log. The physical log records will be used to roll back the incomplete operation. Observe that skipping over physical log records when the **operation-end** log record is found during rollback ensures that the old values in the physical log record are not used for rollback, once the operation completes.

If locking is used for concurrency control, locks held by a transaction $T$ may be released only after the transaction has been rolled back as described.

### 15.9.3   Checkpoints

Checkpointing is performed as described in Section 15.6. Updates to the database are temporarily suspended, and the following actions are carried out:

1. Output to stable storage all log records currently residing in main memory.
2. Output to the disk all modified buffer blocks.
3. Output onto stable storage a log record $<$**checkpoint** $L>$, where $L$ is a list of all active transactions.

### 15.9.4   Restart Recovery

Recovery actions, when the database system is restarted after a failure, are carried out in two phases:

1. In the *redo phase*, we replay updates of *all* transactions by scanning the log forward from the last checkpoint. The log records that are replayed include log records for transactions that were rolled back before system crash, and those that had not committed when the system

crash occurred. The log records replayed include the usual log records of the form $<T_i,\ X_j,\ V_1,\ V_2>$ and the special log records of the form $<T_i,\ X_j,\ V_2>$; the value $V_2$ is written to data item $X_j$ in either case. This phase also determines all transactions that are either in the transaction list in the checkpoint record, or started later, but did not have either a $<T_i$ **abort**$>$ or a $<T_i$ **commit**$>$ record in the log. All these transactions have to be rolled back, and their transaction identifiers are put in an *undo-list*.

2. In the *undo phase*, we roll back all transactions in the *undo-list*. We perform rollback by scanning the log backward from the end. Whenever a log record belonging to a transaction in the *undo-list* is found, undo actions are performed in exactly the same manner as though the log record were found during the rollback of a failed transaction. Thus, log records of a transaction preceding an **operation-end** record, but after the corresponding **operation-begin** record, are ignored.

   When a $<T_i$ **start**$>$ log record is found for a transaction $T_i$ in *undo-list*, a $<T_i$ **abort**$>$ log record is written out to the log. Scanning of the log stops when $<T_i$ **start**$>$ log records have been found for all transactions in the *undo-list*.

The redo phase of restart recovery replays every physical log record since the most recent checkpoint record. In other words, this phase of restart recovery repeats all the update actions that were executed after the checkpoint, and whose log records reached the stable log. The actions include actions of incomplete transactions and the actions carried out to roll failed transactions back. The actions are repeated in the same order in which they were carried out; hence, this process is called *repeating history*. Repeating history simplifies recovery schemes greatly.

## 15.9.5  Fuzzy Checkpointing

The checkpointing technique described in Section 15.6.3 requires that all updates to the database be temporarily suspended while the checkpoint is in progress. It is possible to modify the technique to permit updates to start once the **checkpoint** record has been written, but before the modified buffer blocks are written to disk. The checkpoint thus generated is a *fuzzy checkpoint*.

The idea is as follows. Instead of scanning backward in the log to find a checkpoint record, we store the location in log of the last checkpoint record in a fixed position **last_checkpoint** on disk. However, this information is not updated when the **checkpoint** record is written. Instead, before the **checkpoint** record is written, a list of all modified buffer blocks is created. The **last_checkpoint** information is updated only after all buffer blocks in the list of modified buffer blocks have been output to disk. Buffer blocks must not be updated while being output to disk, and write-ahead log protocol must be followed so that (undo) log records pertaining to the block are on stable storage before the block is output. Note that, in our scheme, logical logging is used only for undo purposes, whereas physical logging is used for redo and undo purposes. There are recovery schemes that use logical logging for redo purposes. However, such schemes cannot be used with fuzzy checkpointing, and are therefore not widely used.

## 15.10    Summary

A computer system, like any other mechanical or electrical device, is subject to failure. There is a variety of causes of such failure, including disk crash, power failure, and software errors. In each of these cases, information concerning the database system is lost. In addition to system failures, transactions may also fail for various reasons, such as violation of integrity constraints or deadlocks. An integral part of a database system is a recovery scheme that is responsible for the detection of failures and for the restoration of the database to a state that existed prior to the occurrence of the failure.

The various types of storage in a computer are volatile storage, nonvolatile storage, and stable storage. Data in volatile storage, such as in RAM, are lost when the computer crashes. Data in nonvolatile storage, such as disk, are not lost when the computer crashes, but may occasionally be lost due to failures such as disk crashes. Data in stable storage are never lost. Stable storage that must be accessible online is approximated with mirrored disks, or other forms of RAID, which provide redundant data storage. Offline, or archival, stable storage may consist of multiple tape copies of data stored in a physically secure location.

In case of failure, the state of the database system may no longer be consistent; that is, it may not reflect a state of the world that the database is supposed to capture. To preserve consistency, we require that each transaction be atomic. It is the responsibility of the recovery scheme to ensure the atomicity property. There are basically two different schemes for ensuring atomicity.

- **Log-based**. All updates are recorded on the log, which must be kept in stable storage. In the deferred-modifications scheme, during the execution of a transaction, all the **write** operations are deferred until the transaction partially commits, at which time the information on the log associated with the transaction is used in executing the deferred writes. In the immediate-modifications scheme, all updates are applied directly to the database. If a crash occurs, the information in the log is used in restoring the state of the system to a previous consistent state. To reduce the overhead of searching the log and redoing transactions, we can use the checkpointing technique.

- **Shadow paging**. Two page tables are maintained during the life of a transaction: the current page table and the shadow page table. When the transaction starts, both page tables are identical. The shadow page table is never changed during the duration of the transaction. The current page table may be changed when a transaction performs a **write** operation. All **input** and **output** operations use the current page table to locate database pages on disk. When the transaction partially commits, the shadow page table is discarded, and the current table becomes the new page table. If the transaction aborts, the current page table is simply discarded.

If multiple transactions are allowed to execute concurrently, the shadow-paging technique is not applicable, but the log-based technique can be used. No transaction can be allowed to update a data item that has already been updated by an incomplete transaction. We can use strict two-phase locking to ensure this condition.

Transaction processing is based on a storage model in which main memory holds a log buffer, a database buffer, and a system buffer. The system buffer holds pages of system object code and local work areas of transactions.

Efficient implementation of a recovery scheme requires that the number of writes to the database and to stable storage be minimized. Log records may be kept in volatile log buffer initially, but must be written to stable storage when one of the following conditions occurs:

- Before the $<T_i$ **commit**$>$ log record may be output to stable storage, all log records pertaining to transaction $T_i$ must have been output to stable storage.
- Before a block of data in main memory is output to the database (in non-volatile storage), all log records pertaining to data in that block must have been output to stable storage.

To recover from failures that result in the loss of nonvolatile storage, we must dump the entire contents of the database onto stable storage periodically — say, once per day. If a failure occurs that results in the loss of physical database blocks, we use the most recent dump in restoring the database to a previous consistent state. Once this restoration has been accomplished, we use the log to bring the database system to the most recent consistent state.

Advanced recovery techniques have been developed to support high-concurrency locking techniques, such as those used for $B^+$-tree concurrency control. These techniques are based on logical (operation) undo, and follow the principle of repeating history. When recovering from system failure, we perform a redo pass using the log, followed by an undo pass on the log to roll back incomplete transactions.

## Exercises

**15.1.** Explain the difference between the three storage types — volatile, non-volatile, and stable — in terms of I/O cost.

**15.2.** Stable storage cannot be implemented.
  (*a*) Explain why it cannot be.
  (*b*) Explain how database systems deal with this problem

**15.3.** Compare the deferred- and immediate-modification versions of the log-based recovery schemes, in terms of ease of implementation and overhead cost.

**15.4.** Assume that immediate modification is used in a system. Show, by an example, how an inconsistent database state could result if log records for a transaction are not output to stable storage prior to data updated by the transaction being written to disk.

**15.5.** Explain the purpose of the checkpoint mechanism. How often should check-points be performed? How does the frequency of checkpoints affect

- System performance when no failure occurs
- The time it takes to recover from a system crash
- The time it takes to recover from a disk crash

**15.6.** When the system recovers from a crash (see Section 15.6.4), it constructs an undo-list and a redo-list. Explain why log records for transactions on the undo-list must be processed in reverse order, while those log records for transactions on the redo-list are processed in a forward direction.

**15.7.** Compare the shadow-paging recovery scheme with the log-based recovery schemes in terms of ease of implementation and overhead cost.

**15.8.** Consider a database consisting of 10 consecutive disk blocks (block 1, block 2, ..., block 10). Show the buffer state and a possible physical ordering of the blocks after the following updates, assuming that shadow paging is used, that the buffer in main memory can hold only three blocks, and that a least recently used (LRU) strategy is used for buffer management.

> **read** block 3
> **read** block 7
> **read** block 5
> **read** block 3
> **read** block 1
> **modify** block 1
> **read** block 10
> **modify** block 5

**15.9.** Explain how the buffer manager may cause the database to become inconsistent if some log records pertaining to a block are not output to stable storage before the block is output to disk.

**15.10.** Explain the recovery procedure that needs to take place after a disk crash.

**15.11.** Explain the benefits of logical logging. Give examples of one situation where logical logging is preferable to physical logging and one situation where physical logging is preferable to logical logging.

**15.12.** Explain the reasons why recovery of interactive transactions is more difficult to deal with than is recovery of batch transactions. Is there a simple way to deal with this difficulty? (Hint: Consider an automatic teller machine transaction in which cash is withdrawn.)

**15.13.** Logging of updates is not done explicitly in persistent programming languages. Describe how page access protections provided by modern operating systems can be used to create before- and after-images of pages that are updated. Hint: See Exercise 14.29.

## Bibliographical Notes

Two early papers that present initial theoretical work in the area of recovery are Davies [1973] and Bjork [1973]. Chandy et al. [1975], which describes analytic models for rollback and recovery strategies in database systems, is another early work in this area.

Most of the recovery mechanisms introduced in this chapter are based on those used in System R. An overview of the recovery scheme of that system is presented by Gray et al. [1981a]. The shadow-paging mechanism of System R is described by Lorie [1977]. A fast transaction-oriented logging scheme is presented by Reuter [1980].

Tutorial and survey papers on various recovery techniques for database systems are presented by Gray [1978], Lindsay et al. [1980], and Verhofstad [1978]. The concepts of fuzzy checkpointing and fuzzy dumps are described in Lindsay et al. [1980]. A comprehensive presentation of the principles of recovery is offered by Haerder and Reuter [1983]. Basic textbook discussions are offered by Date [1983a], and Bernstein et al. [1987]. Gray and Reuter [1993] is an excellent textbook source of information about recovery, including interesting implementation and historical details.

The state of the art in recovery methods is best illustrated by the ARIES recovery method, described in Mohan et al. [1992], Mohan and Narang [1995], and by Mohan [1990b]. The recovery technique described in Section 15.9 is loosely based on the ARIES recovery method. Specialized recovery techniques for index structures are described in Mohan and Levine [1992], and in Mohan [1993]; Mohan and Narang [1994] describe recovery techniques for client–server architectures.

Remote backup for disaster recovery (loss of an entire computing facility by, for example, fire, flood, or earthquake) is considered in Polyzois and Garcia-Molina [1994] and King et al. [1991].

Operating-system issues for database management are discussed in Stonebraker [1981], Traiger [1982, 1983], and Haskin et al. [1988]. References pertaining to long-duration transactions and related recovery issues are listed in Chapter 20.

# CHAPTER 16

# DATABASE SYSTEM ARCHITECTURES

The architecture of a database system is greatly influenced by the underlying computer system on which the database system runs. Aspects of computer architecture—such as networking, parallelism, and distribution—are reflected in the architecture of the database system.

- Networking of computers allows some tasks to be executed on a server system, and some tasks to be executed on client systems. This division of work has led to the development of *client–server* database systems.

- Parallel processing within a computer system allows database-system activities to be speeded up, allowing faster response to transactions, as well as more transactions per second. Queries can be processed in a manner that exploits the parallelism offered by the underlying computer system. The need for parallel query processing has lead to the development of *parallel* database systems.

- Distributing data across sites or departments in an organization allows those data to reside where they are generated or most needed, but still to be accessible from other sites and from other departments. Keeping multiple copies of the database across different sites also allows large organizations to continue their database operations even when one site is affected by a natural disaster, such as flood, fire, or earthquake. *Distributed* database systems have been developed to handle geographically or administratively distributed data spread across multiple database systems.

We study the architecture of database systems in this chapter, starting with the traditional centralized systems, and covering client–server, parallel, and distributed database systems.

## 16.1    Centralized Systems

Centralized database systems are those that run on a single computer system and do not interact with other computer systems. Such systems span a range from single-user database systems running on personal computers to high-performance database systems running on mainframe systems.

A modern, general-purpose computer system consists of one to a few CPUs and a number of device controllers that are connected through a common bus that provides access to shared memory (Figure 16.1). The CPUs have local cache memories that store local copies of parts of the memory, to speed up access to data. Each device controller is in charge of a specific type of device (for example, a disk drive, an audio device, or a video display). The CPU and the device controllers can execute concurrently, competing for memory access. Cache memory reduces the contention for memory access, since it reduces the number of times that the CPU needs to access the shared memory.

We distinguish two ways in which computers are used: as single-user systems and as multiuser systems. Personal computers and workstations fall into the first category. A typical *single user system* is a desktop unit used by a single person, has only one CPU and one or two hard disks, and has an operating system

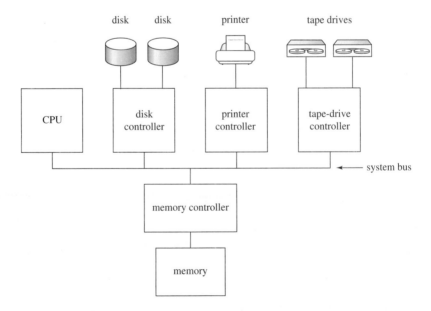

Figure 16.1    A centralized computer system.

that may support only one user. A typical *multiuser system*, on the other hand, has more disks and more memory, may have multiple CPUs, and has a multiuser operating system. It serves a large number of users who are connected to the system via terminals. Such systems are often called *server* systems.

Database systems designed for single-user systems, such as personal computers, typically do not provide many of the facilities that a multiuser database provides. In particular, they do not support concurrency control, which is not required when only a single user can generate updates. The crash-recovery facilities in such systems are either absent or primitive—for example, simply making a backup of the database before any update. Many such systems do not support SQL, and provide a simpler query language, such as a variant of QBE.

Although general-purpose computer systems today have multiple processors, they have *coarse-granularity* parallelism, with only a few processors (about two to four, typically), all sharing main memory. Databases running on such machines typically do not attempt to partition a single query among the processors; instead, each query is run on a single processor, allowing multiple queries to run concurrently. Thus, such systems support a higher throughput; that is, they allow a greater number of transactions to run per second, although individual transactions do not run any faster.

Databases designed for single-processor machines already provide multitasking, allowing multiple processes to run on the same processor in a time-shared manner, giving a view to the user of multiple processes running in parallel. Thus, coarse-granularity parallel machines logically appear to be identical to single-processor machines, and database systems designed for time-shared machines can be easily adapted to run on them.

In contrast, *fine-granularity* parallel machines have a large number of processors, and database systems running on such machines attempt to parallelize single tasks (queries, for example) submitted by users. We study the architecture of parallel database systems in Section 16.3.

## 16.2   Client–Server Systems

As personal computers have become faster, more powerful, and cheaper, there has been a shift away from the centralized system architecture. Terminals connected to centralized systems are now being supplanted by personal computers. Correspondingly, user-interface functionality that used to be handled directly by the centralized systems is increasingly being handled by the personal computers. As a result, centralized systems today act as *server systems* that satisfy requests generated by *client systems*. The general structure of a client–server system is depicted in Figure 16.2.

Database functionality can be broadly divided into two parts—the front-end and the back-end—as shown in Figure 16.3. The back-end manages access structures, query evaluation and optimization, concurrency control, and recovery. The front-end of a database system consists of tools such as *forms, report writers,*

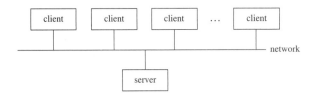

Figure 16.2    General structure of a client–server system.

and graphical user-interface facilities. The interface between the front-end and the back-end is through SQL, or through an application program.

Server systems can be broadly categorized as transaction servers and data servers.

- *Transaction-server* systems, also called *query-server* systems, provide an interface to which clients can send requests to perform an action, in response to which they execute the action and send back results to the client. Users may specify requests in SQL, or through an application program interface, using a *remote-procedure-call* mechanism.

- *Data-server systems* allow clients to interact with the servers by making requests to read or update data, in units such as files or pages. For example, file servers provide a file-system interface where clients can create, update, read, and delete files. Data servers for database systems offer much more functionality; they support units of data—such as pages, tuples, or objects—that are smaller than a file. They provide indexing facilities for data, and provide transaction facilities so that the data are never left in an inconsistent state if a client machine or process fails.

We shall elaborate on the transaction-server and data-server architectures in Sections 16.2.1 and 16.2.2.

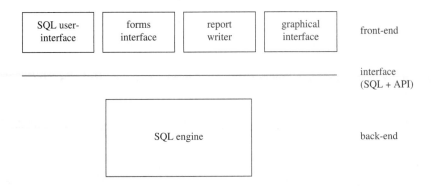

Figure 16.3    Front-end and back-end functionality.

## 16.2.1   Transaction Servers

In centralized systems, the front-end and the back-end are both executed within a single system. However, the transaction-server architecture follows the functional division between the front-end and the back-end. Due to the greater processing requirements of graphical user-interface code, and the increasing power of personal computers, front-end functionality is supported on personal computers. The personal computers act as *clients* of the server systems, which store large volumes of data and support the back-end functionality. Clients ship transactions to the server systems where those transactions are executed, and results are shipped back to clients that are in charge of displaying the data.

Standards such as *Open Database Connectivity* (ODBC), have been developed for interfacing of clients with servers. ODBC is an application program interface that allows clients to generate SQL statements that are sent to a server, where the statements are executed. Any client that uses the ODBC interface can connect to any server that provides the interface. In earlier-generation database systems, the lack of such standards necessitated that the front-end and the back-end be provided by the same software vendor.

With the growth of interface standards, the front-end tools and the back-end server are increasingly provided by different vendors. Gupta SQL and Power-Builder are examples of front-end systems that are independent of the back-end servers. Further, certain application programs, such as spreadsheets and statistical-analysis packages, use the client–server interface directly to access data from a back-end server. In effect, they provide front-ends specialized for particular tasks.

Client–server interfaces other than ODBC are also used in some transaction-processing systems. They are defined by an application programming interface, using which clients make *transactional remote procedure calls* on the server. These calls appear like ordinary procedure calls to the programmer, but all the remote procedure calls from a client are enclosed in a single transaction at the server end. Thus, if the transaction aborts, the server can undo the effects of the individual remote procedure calls.

The fact that individual small machines are now cheaper to buy and maintain has resulted in an industry-wide trend toward *down-sizing*. Many companies are replacing their mainframes with networks of workstations or personal computers connected to back-end server machines. The advantages include better functionality for the cost, more flexibility in locating resources and expanding facilities, better user interfaces, and easier maintenance.

## 16.2.2   Data Servers

Data-server systems are used in local-area networks, where there is a high-speed connection between the clients and the server, the client machines are comparable in processing power to the server machine, and the tasks to be executed are compute intensive. In such an environment, it makes sense to ship data to client machines, to perform all processing at the client machine (which may take a while), and then to ship the data back to the server machine. Note that this architecture requires full back-end functionality (see Figure 16.3) at the clients. Data-server architectures have been particularly popular in object-oriented database systems.

Interesting issues arise in such an architecture, since the time cost of communication between the client and the server is high compared to that of a local memory reference (milliseconds, versus less than 100 nanoseconds).

- **Page shipping versus item shipping**. The unit of communication for data can be coarse granularity, such as a page, or fine-granularity, such as a tuple (or an object, in the context of object-oriented database systems). We use the term *item* to refer to both tuples and objects.

  If the unit of communication is a single item, the overhead of message passing is high compared to the number of data transmitted. Instead, when an item is requested, it makes sense also to send back other items that are likely to be used in the near future. Fetching items even before they are requested is called *prefetching*. Page shipping can be considered a form of prefetching if multiple items reside on a page, since all the items in the page are shipped when a process desires to access a single item in the page.

- **Locking**. Locks are usually granted by the server for the data items that it ships to the client machines. A disadvantage of page shipping is that client machines may be granted locks of too coarse a granularity— a lock on a page implicitly locks all items contained in the page. Even if the client is not accessing some items in the page, it has implicitly acquired locks on all prefetched items. Other client machines that require locks on those items may be blocked unnecessarily. Techniques for *lock deescalation* have been proposed, where the server can request its clients to transfer back locks on prefetched items. If the client machine does not need a prefetched item, it can transfer locks on the item back to the server, and the locks can then be allocated to other clients.

- **Data caching**. Data that are shipped to a client on behalf of a transaction can be *cached* at the client, even after the transaction completes, if sufficient storage space is available. Successive transactions at the same client may be able to make use of the cached data. However, cache coherency is an issue: Even if a transaction finds cached data, it must make sure that those data are up to date, since they may have been updated by a different client after they were cached. Thus, a message must still be exchanged with the server to check validity of the data, and to acquire a lock on the data.

- **Lock caching**. If the use of data is mostly partitioned among the clients, with clients rarely requesting data that are also requested by other clients, locks can also be cached at the client machine. Suppose that a data item is found in the cache, and that the lock required for an access to the data item is also found in the cache. Then, the access can proceed without any communication with the server. However, the server must keep track of cached locks; if a client requests a lock from the server, the server must *call back* all conflicting locks on the data item from any other client machines that have cached the locks. The task becomes more complicated when machine failures are taken into account. This technique differs from lock deescalation in that lock caching is done across transactions; otherwise, the two techniques are similar.

The bibliographic references provide more information about client–server database systems.

# 16.3   Parallel Systems

Parallel systems improve processing and I/O speeds by using multiple CPUs and disks in parallel. Parallel machines are becoming increasingly common, making the study of parallel database systems correspondingly more important. The driving force behind parallel database systems has been the demands of applications that have to query extremely large databases (of the order of terabytes—that is, $10^{12}$ bytes) or that have to process an extremely large number of transactions per second (of the order of thousands of transactions per second). Centralized and client–server database systems are not powerful enough to handle such applications.

In parallel processing, many operations are performed simultaneously, as opposed to in serial processing, in which the computational steps are performed sequentially. A *coarse-grain* parallel machine consists of a small number of powerful processors; a *massively parallel* or *fine-grain* machine uses thousands of smaller processors. Most high-end machines today offer some degree of coarse-grain parallelism: Two or four processor machines are common. Massively parallel computers can be distinguished from the coarse-grain parallel machines by the much larger degree of parallelism that they support. Parallel computers with hundreds of CPUs and disks are available commercially.

There are two main measures of performance of a database system. The first is *throughput*: the number of tasks that can be completed in a given time interval. The second is *response time*: the amount of time it takes to complete a single task from the time it is submitted. A system that processes a large number of small transactions can improve throughput by processing many transactions in parallel. A system that processes large transactions can improve response time as well as throughput by performing subtasks of each transaction in parallel.

## 16.3.1   Speedup and Scaleup

Two important issues in studying parallelism are speedup and scaleup. *Speedup* refers to running a given task in less time by increasing the degree of parallelism. *Scaleup* refers to handling larger tasks by increasing the degree of parallelism.

Consider a database application running on a parallel system with a certain number of processors and disks. Now suppose that we increase the size of the system by increasing the number or processors, disks, and other components of the system. The goal is to process the task in time inversely proportional to the number of processors and disks allocated. Suppose that the execution time of a task on the larger machine is $T_L$, and that the execution time of the same task on the smaller machine is $T_S$. The speedup due to parallelism is defined as $T_S/T_L$.

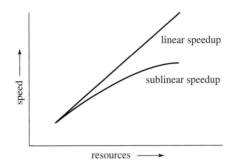

Figure 16.4    Speedup with increasing resources.

The parallel system is said to demonstrate *linear speedup* if the speedup is $N$ when the larger system has $N$ times the resources (CPU, disk, and so on) of the smaller system. If the speedup is less than $N$, the system is said to demonstrate *sublinear speedup*. Figure 16.4 illustrates linear and sublinear speedup.

Scaleup relates to the ability to process larger tasks in the same amount of time by providing more resources. Let $Q$ be a task, and let $Q_N$ be a task that is $N$ times bigger than $Q$. Suppose that the execution time of task $Q$ on a given machine $M_S$ is $T_S$, and the execution time of task $Q_N$ on a parallel machine $M_L$, which is $N$ times larger than $M_S$, is $T_L$. The scaleup is then defined as $T_S/T_L$. The parallel system $M_L$ is said to demonstrate *linear scaleup* on task $Q$ if $T_L = T_S$. If $T_L > T_S$, the system is said to demonstrate *sublinear scaleup*. Figure 16.5 illustrates linear and sublinear scaleups. There are two kinds of scaleup that are relevant in parallel database systems, depending on how the size of the task is measured:

- In *batch scaleup*, the size of the database increases, and the tasks are large jobs whose runtime depends on the size of the database. An example of such a task is a scan of a relation whose size is proportional to the size of the database. Thus, the size of the database is the measure of the size

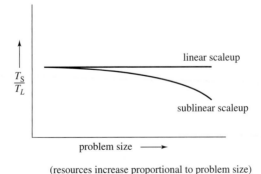

Figure 16.5    Scaleup with increasing problem size.

of the problem. Batch scaleup also applies in scientific applications, such as executing a query at an $N$-times finer resolution or performing an $N$-times longer simulation.

- In *transaction scaleup*, the rate at which transactions are submitted to the database increases and the size of the database increases proportional to the transaction rate. This kind of scaleup is what is relevant in transaction-processing systems where the transactions are small updates—for example, a deposit or withdrawal from an account—and transaction rates grow as more accounts are created. Such transaction processing is especially well adapted for parallel execution, since transactions can run concurrently and independently on separate processors, and each transaction takes roughly the same amount of time, even if the database grows.

Scaleup is usually the more important metric for measuring efficiency of parallel database systems. The goal of parallelism in database systems is usually to make sure that the database system can continue to perform at an acceptable speed, even as the size of the database and the number of transactions increases. Increasing the capacity of the system by increasing the parallelism provides a smoother path for growth for a company than does replacing a centralized system by a faster machine (even assuming that such a machine exists). However, we must also look at absolute performance numbers when using scaleup measures; a machine that scales up linearly may perform worse than a machine that scales less than linearly, simply because the latter machine is much faster to start off with.

A number of factors work against efficient parallel operation and can diminish both speedup and scaleup.

- **Startup costs**. There is a startup cost associated with initiating a single process. In a parallel operation consisting of thousands of processes, the *startup time* may overshadow the actual processing time, affecting speedup adversely.

- **Interference**. Since processes executing in a parallel system often access shared resources, a slowdown may result from the *interference* of each new process as it competes with existing processes for commonly held resources, such as a system bus, or shared disks, or even locks. Both speedup and scaleup are affected by this phenomenon.

- **Skew**. By breaking down a single task into a number of parallel steps, we reduce the size of the average step. Nonetheless, the service time for the single slowest step will determine the service time for the task as a whole. It is often difficult to divide a task into exactly equal-sized parts, and the way that the sizes are distributed is therefore *skewed*. For example, if a task of size 100 is divided into 10 parts, and the division is skewed, there may be some tasks of size less than 10 and some tasks of size more than 10; if even one task happens to be of size 20, the speedup obtained by running the tasks in parallel is only five, instead of ten, as we would have hoped.

## 16.3.2 Interconnection Networks

Parallel systems consist of a set of components (processors, memory and disks) that can communicate with each other via an *interconnection network*. Examples of interconnection networks include:

- **Bus**. All the system components can send data on and receive data from a single communication bus. The bus could be an ethernet, or a parallel interconnect. Bus architectures work well for small numbers of processors. However, they do not scale well with increasing parallelism since the bus can handle communication from only one component at a time.

- **Mesh**. The components are arranged as nodes in a grid, and each component is connected to all its adjacent components in the grid. In a two-dimensional mesh each node is connected to four adjacent nodes, while in a three-dimensional mesh each node is connected to six adjacent nodes. Nodes that are not directly connected can communicate with one another by routing messages via a sequence of intermediate nodes that are directly connected to one another. The number of communication links grows as the number of components grows, and the communication capacity of a mesh therefore scales better with increasing parallelism.

- **Hypercube**. The components are numbered in binary, and a component is connected to another if the binary representations of their numbers differ in exactly one bit. Thus, each of the $n$ components is connected to $log(n)$ other components. It can be verified that in a hypercube interconnection a message from a component can reach any other component by going via at most $log(n)$ links. In contrast, in a mesh a component may be $2(\sqrt{n} - 1)$ links away from some of the other components (or $\sqrt{n}$ links away, if the mesh interconnection wraps around at the edges of the grid). Thus communication delays in a hypercube are significantly lower than in a mesh.

## 16.3.3 Parallel Database Architectures

There are several architectural models for parallel machines. Among the most prominent ones are those shown in Figure 16.6 (in the figure, M denotes memory, P denotes a processor, and disks are shown as cylinders):

- **Shared memory**. All the processors share a common memory. This model is depicted in Figure 16.6a.

- **Shared disk**. All the processors share a common disk. This model is depicted in Figure 16.6b. Shared-disk systems are sometimes called as *clusters*.

- **Shared nothing**. The processors share neither a common memory nor common disk. This model is depicted in Figure 16.6c.

- **Hierarchical**. This model is depicted in Figure 16.6d; it is a hybrid of the preceding architectures.

In Sections 16.3.3.1 through 16.3.3.4, we elaborate on each of these models.

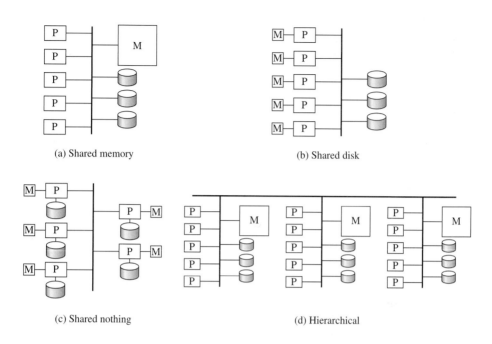

Figure 16.6   Parallel database architectures.

### 16.3.3.1   Shared Memory

In a shared-memory architecture, the processors and disks have access to a common memory, typically via a bus or through an interconnection network. The benefit of shared memory is extremely efficient communication between processors—data in shared memory can be accessed by any processor without being moved with software. A processor can send messages to other processors much faster by using memory writes, (which usually take less than a microsecond) than by sending a message through a communication mechanism. The downside of shared-memory machines is that the architecture is not scalable beyond 32 or 64 processors, since the bus or the interconnection network becomes a bottleneck (since it is shared by all processors). Adding more processors does not help after a point, since the processors will spend most of their time waiting for their turn on the bus to access memory. Shared-memory architectures usually have large memory caches at each processor, so that referencing of the shared memory is avoided whenever possible. However, at least some of the data will not be in the cache, and accesses will have to go to the shared memory. Consequently, shared-memory machines are not capable of scaling up beyond a point; current shared-memory machines cannot support more than 64 processors.

### 16.3.3.2   Shared Disk

In the shared-disk model, all processors can access all disks directly via an interconnection network, but the processors have private memories. There are two benefits for a shared-disk architecture over a shared-memory architecture. First, since each processor has its own memory, the memory bus is not a bottleneck. Second, this architecture offers a cheap way to provide a degree of *fault tolerance*: If a processor (or its memory) fails, the other processors can take over its tasks, since the database is resident on disks that are accessible from all processors. We can make the disk subsystem itself fault-tolerant by using a RAID architecture, as described in Chapter 10. The shared-disk architecture has found acceptance in many applications; systems built around this architecture are often called *clusters*.

The main problem with a shared-disk system is again scalability. Although the memory bus is no longer a bottleneck, the interconnection to the disk subsystem is now a bottleneck; it is particularly so in a situation where the database makes a large number of accesses to disks. As compared to shared-memory systems, shared-disk systems can scale to a somewhat larger number of processors, but communication across processors is slower (up to a few milliseconds in the absence of special purpose hardware for communication), since it has to go through a communication network.

DEC clusters running Rdb were one of the early commercial users of the shared-disk database architecture. (Rdb is now owned by Oracle, and is called Oracle Rdb.)

### 16.3.3.3   Shared Nothing

In a shared-nothing system, each node of the machine consists of a processor, memory, and one or more disks. The processors at one node may communicate with another processor at another node using a high-speed interconnection network. A node functions as the server for the data on the disk or disks that the node owns. Since local disk references are serviced by local disks at each processor, the shared-nothing model overcomes the disadvantage of requiring all I/O to go through a single interconnection network; only queries, accesses to nonlocal disks, and result relations are passed through the network. Moreover, the interconnection networks for shared-nothing systems are usually designed to be scalable, so that their transmission capacity increases as more nodes are added. Consequently, shared-nothing architectures are more scalable and can easily support a large number of processors. The main drawback of shared-nothing systems are the costs of communication and of nonlocal disk access, which are higher than in a shared-memory or shared-disk architecture since sending data involves software interaction at both ends.

The Teradata database machine was among the earliest commercial systems to use the shared-nothing database architecture. The Grace and the Gamma research prototypes were also built on shared-nothing architectures.

### 16.3.3.4   Hierarchical

The hierarchical architecture combines the characteristics of shared-memory, shared-disk, and shared-nothing architectures. At the top level, the system consists of nodes that are connected by an interconnection network, and do not share disks or memory with one another. Thus, the top level is a shared-nothing architecture. Each node of the system could actually be a shared-memory system with a few processors. Alternatively, each node could be a shared-disk system, and each of the systems sharing a set of disks could be a shared-memory system. Thus, a system could be built as a hierarchy, with shared-memory architecture with a few processors at the base, and a shared-nothing architecture at the top, with possibly a shared-disk architecture in the middle. Figure 16.6d illustrates a hierarchical architecture with shared-memory nodes connected together in a shared-nothing architecture. Commercial parallel database systems today run on several of these architectures.

Attempts to reduce the complexity of programming such systems have resulted in *distributed virtual-memory* architectures, where logically there is a single shared memory, but physically there are multiple disjoint memory systems; the virtual-memory–mapping hardware coupled with extra software supports a single virtual-memory area view of these disjoint memories.

## 16.4   Distributed Systems

In a distributed database system, the database is stored on several computers. The computers in a distributed system communicate with one another through various communication media, such as high-speed networks or telephone lines. They do not share main memory or disks. The computers in a distributed system may vary in size and function, ranging from workstations up to mainframe systems.

The computers in a distributed system are referred to by a number of different names, such as *sites* or *nodes*, depending on the context in which they are mentioned. We mainly use the term *site*, to emphasize the physical distribution of these systems. The general structure of a distributed system is shown in Figure 16.7.

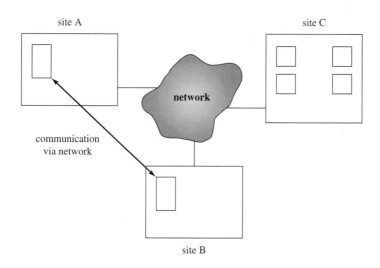

Figure 16.7   A distributed system.

The main differences between shared-nothing parallel databases and distributed databases are that distributed database are typically geographically separated, are separately administered, and have a slower interconnection. Another major difference is that, in a distributed system, we differentiate between *local* and *global* transactions. A local transaction is one that accesses data in the *single* site at which the transaction was initiated. A global transaction, on the other hand, is one which either accesses data in a site different from the one at which the transaction was initiated, or accesses data in several different sites.

## 16.4.1   Illustrative Example

Consider a banking system consisting of four branches located in four different cities. Each branch has its own computer, with a database consisting of all the accounts maintained at that branch. Each such installation is thus a site. There also exists one single site that maintains information about all the branches of the bank. Each branch maintains (among others) a relation *account*(*Account-schema*), where

$$Account\text{-}schema = (branch\text{-}name, account\text{-}number, balance)$$

The site containing information about the four branches maintains the relation *branch*(*Branch-schema*), where

$$Branch\text{-}schema = (branch\text{-}name, branch\text{-}city, assets)$$

There are other relations maintained at the various sites; we ignore them for the purpose of our example.

To illustrate the difference between the two types of transactions, we consider the transaction to add \$50 to account number A-177 located at the Valleyview branch. If the transaction was initiated at the Valleyview branch, then it is considered local; otherwise, it is considered global. A transaction to transfer \$50 from account A-177 to account A-305, which is located at the Hillside branch, is a global transaction, since accounts in two different sites are accessed as a result of its execution.

What makes this configuration a distributed database system are these facts:

- The various sites are aware of one another.
- The sites share a common global schema, although some relations may be stored at only some sites.
- Each site provides an environment for executing both local and global transactions.
- Each site runs the same distributed database-management software.

If different sites run different database-management software, it is difficult to manage global transactions. Such systems are called *multidatabase systems* or *heterogeneous distributed database systems*. We discuss these systems in Section 18.9, where we show how to achieve a degree of global control despite the heterogeneity of the component systems.

## 16.4.2   Tradeoffs

There are several reasons for building distributed database systems, including sharing of data, autonomy, and availability.

- **Sharing data.** The major advantage in building a distributed database system is the provision of an environment where users at one site may be able to access the data residing at other sites. For instance, in the distributed banking-system example from Section 16.4.1, it is possible for a user in one branch to access data in another branch. Without this capability, a user wishing to transfer funds from one branch to another would have to resort to some external mechanism that would couple existing systems.

- **Autonomy.** The primary advantage of sharing data by means of data distribution is that each site is able to retain a degree of control over data that are stored locally. In a centralized system, the database administrator of the central site controls the database. In a distributed system, there is a global database administrator responsible for the entire system. A part of these responsibilities is delegated to the local database administrator for each site. Depending up the design of the distributed database system, each administrator may have a different degree of *local autonomy*. The possibility of local autonomy is often a major advantage of distributed databases.

- **Availability.** If one site fails in a distributed system, the remaining sites may be able to continue operating. In particular, if data items are replicated in several sites, a transaction needing a particular data item may find that item in any of several sites. Thus, the failure of a site does not necessarily imply the shutdown of the system.

  The failure of one site must be detected by the system, and appropriate action may be needed to recover from the failure. The system must no longer use the services of the failed site. Finally, when the failed site recovers or is repaired, mechanisms must be available to integrate it smoothly back into the system.

  Although recovery from failure is more complex in distributed systems than in centralized systems, the ability of most of the system to continue to operate despite the failure of one site results in increased availability. Availability is crucial for database systems used for real-time applications. Loss of access to data by, for example, an airline may result in the loss of potential ticket buyers to competitors.

The primary disadvantage of distributed database systems is the added complexity required to ensure proper coordination among the sites. This increased complexity takes various forms:

- **Software-development cost**. It is more difficult to implement a distributed database system; thus, it is more costly.

- **Greater potential for bugs**. Since the sites that constitute the distributed system operate in parallel, it is harder to ensure the correctness of algorithms, especially operation during failures of part of the system, and recovery from failures. The potential exists for extremely subtle bugs.

- **Increased processing overhead**. The exchange of messages and the additional computation required to achieve intersite coordination are a form of overhead that does not arise in centralized systems.

In choosing the design for a database system, the designer must balance the advantages against the disadvantages of distribution of data. There are several approaches to distributed database design, ranging from fully distributed designs to ones that include a large degree of centralization. We study them in Chapter 18.

# 16.5   Network Types

Distributed databases and client–server systems are built around communication networks. There are basically two types of networks: *local-area networks* and *wide-area networks*. The main difference between the two is the way in which they are distributed geographically. Local-area networks are composed of processors that are distributed over small geographical areas, such as a single building or a number of adjacent buildings. Wide-area networks, on the other hand, are composed of a number of autonomous processors that are distributed over a large geographical area (such as the United States, or the entire world). These differences imply major variations in the speed and reliability of the communication network, and are reflected in the distributed operating-system design.

## 16.5.1   Local-Area Networks

Local-area networks (LANs) emerged in the early 1970s, as a way for computers to communicate and to share data with one another. People recognized that, for many enterprises, numerous small computers, each with its own self-contained applications, are more economical than a single large system. Because each small computer is likely to need access to a full complement of peripheral devices (such as disks and printers), and because some form of data sharing is likely to occur in a single enterprise, it was a natural step to connect these small systems into a network.

LANs are usually designed to cover a small geographical area (such as a single building, or a few adjacent buildings) and are generally used in an office environment. All the sites in such systems are close to one another, so the communication links tend to have a higher speed and lower error rate than do their counterparts in wide-area networks. The most common links in a local-area network are twisted pair, baseband coaxial cable, broadband coaxial cable, and fiber optics. Communication speeds range from 1 megabyte per second, for networks such as Appletalk and IBM's slow token ring, to 1 gigabit per second for experimental optical networks. Ten megabits per second is most common, and is the speed of the standard Ethernet. The optical-fiber–based FDDI network and Fast Ethernet run at 100 megabits per second. Networks based on a protocol called

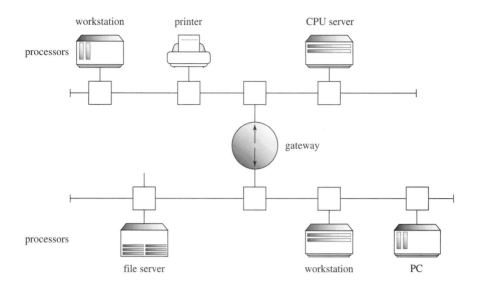

Figure 16.8    Local-area network.

*asynchronous transfer mode* (*ATM*) can run at even higher speeds, such as 144 megabits per second, and are growing in popularity.

A typical LAN may consist of a number of different workstations, one or more server systems, various shared peripheral devices (such as laser printers or magnetic-tape units), and one or more gateways (specialized processors) that provide access to other networks (Figure 16.8). An Ethernet scheme is commonly used to construct LANs.

## 16.5.2    Wide-Area Networks

Wide-area networks (WANs) emerged in the late 1960s, mainly as an academic research project to provide efficient communication among sites, allowing hardware and software to be shared conveniently and economically by a wide community of users. Systems that allowed remote terminals to be connected to a central computer via telephone lines were developed in the early 1960s, but they were not true WANs. The first WAN to be designed and developed was the *Arpanet*. Work on the Arpanet began in 1968. The Arpanet has grown from a four-site experimental network to a worldwide network of networks, the Internet, comprising millions of computer systems. Typical links in a WAN are telephone circuits, which are carried on fiber-optic lines and (sometimes) satellite channels.

As an example, let us consider the Internet network, which connects computers across the globe. The system provides an ability for hosts at geographically separated sites to communicate with one another. The host computers typically differ from one another in type, speed, word length, operating system, and so on. Hosts are generally on LANs, which are connected to regional networks. The regional networks are interlinked with routers to form the worldwide network. Connections between networks frequently use a telephone-system service called

T1, which provides a transfer rate of 1.544 megabits per second, or T3, which provides a transfer rate of 44.736 megabits per second. Messages sent on the network are routed by systems called *routers*, which control the path each message takes through the network. This routing may be either dynamic, to increase communication efficiency, or static, to reduce security risks or to allow communication charges to be computed more easily.

Other WANs in operation use standard telephone lines as their primary means of communication. *Modems* are the devices that accept digital data from the computer side and convert those data to the analog signals that the telephone system uses. A modem at the destination site converts the analog signal back to digital, and the destination receives the data. Modem speeds range from 2400 bits per second up to about 32 kilobits per second. Phone systems that support the *Integrated Services Digital Network* (ISDN) standard permit data to be transmitted from point–to–point at higher rates, with 128 kilobits per second being a typical speed.

The UNIX network, UUCP, allows systems to communicate with one another at limited (and, usually, predetermined) times, via modems, to exchange messages. The messages are then routed to other nearby systems and, in this way, either are propagated to all hosts on the network (public messages) or are transferred to their destination (private messages).

WANs can be classified into two types:

- In **discontinuous connection** WANs, such as those based on UUCP, hosts are connected to the network only part of the time.
- In **continuous connection** WANs, such as the Internet, hosts are connected to the network at all times.

The design of distributed database systems is influenced strongly by the type of underlying WAN. True distributed database systems can run on only those networks that are connected continuously—at least during the hours when the distributed database is operational.

Networks that are not continuously connected typically do not allow transactions across sites, but may keep local copies of remote data, and refresh the copies periodically (every night, for instance). For applications where consistency is not critical, such as sharing of documents, groupware systems such as Lotus Notes allow updates of remote data to be made locally, and the updates are then propagated back to the remote site periodically. There is a potential for conflicting updates at different sites, which have to be detected and resolved. A mechanism for detecting conflicting updates is described later, in Section 21.7.4; the resolution mechanism for conflicting updates is, however, application dependent.

## 16.6   Summary

Centralized database systems run entirely on a single computer. All database systems were initially centralized. With the growth of personal computers and local-area networking, the database front-end functionality has been moved increasingly to clients, and the back-end functionality is provided by server systems. Client–server interface protocols have helped the growth of client–server database systems. Servers can be either transaction servers or data servers.

Parallel database systems consist of multiple processors and multiple disks connected by a fast interconnection network. Speedup measures how much we can increase processing speed by increasing parallelism, for a single transaction. Scaleup measures how well we can handle an increased number of transactions by increasing parallelism. Parallel database architectures include the shared-memory, shared-disk, shared-nothing, and hierarchical architectures. These architectures have different tradeoffs on scalability versus communication speed.

A distributed database is a collection of partially independent databases that share a common schema, and coordinate processing of transactions that access nonlocal data. The processors communicate with one another through a communication network that handles routing and connection strategies.

Principally, there are two types of communication networks: local-area networks and wide-area networks. Local-area networks are composed of processors that are distributed over small geographical areas, such as a single building or a few adjacent buildings. Wide-area networks are composed of processors distributed over a large geographical area. Computers in a wide-area network may be connected to one another continuously or only periodically, such as once per day or a few times per day.

# Exercises

**16.1.** Why is it relatively easy to port a database from a single processor machine to a multi-processor machine if individual queries need not be parallelized?

**16.2.** Transaction server architectures are popular for client-server relational databases, where transactions are short. On the other hand, data server architectures are popular for client-server object-oriented database systems, where transactions are expected to be relatively long. Give two reasons why data servers may be popular for object-oriented databases but not for relational databases.

**16.3.** In typical client-server systems the server machine is much more powerful than the clients, that is, its processor is faster, it may have multiple processors, and it has more memory and disk capacity. Consider instead a scenario where client and server machines have exactly the same power. Would it make sense to build a client-server system in such a scenario? Why? Which scenario would be better suited to a data-server architecture?

**16.4.** Consider an object-oriented database system based on a client-server architecture, with the server acting as a data server.

   (*a*) What is the effect of the speed of the interconnection between the client and the server on the choice between object and page shipping?

   (*b*) If page shipping is used, the cache of data at the client can be organized either as an object cache or a page cache. The page cache stores data in units of a page, while the object cache stores data in units of objects. Assume objects are smaller than a page. Describe one benefit of an object cache over a page cache.

**16.5.** What is lock de-escalation, and under what conditions is it required? Why is it not required if the unit of data shipping is an item?

**16.6.** Suppose you were in charge of the database operations of a company whose main job is to process transactions. Suppose the company is growing rapidly each year, and has outgrown its current computer system. When you are choosing a new parallel computer, what measure is most relevant—speedup, batch scale-up, or transaction scale-up? Why?

**16.7.** Suppose a transaction is written in C with embedded SQL, and about 80 percent of the time is spent in the SQL code, with the remaining 20 percent spent in C code. How much speedup can one hope to attain if parallelism is used only for the SQL code? Explain.

**16.8.** What are the factors that can work against linear scale-up in a transaction processing system? Which of the factors are likely to be the most important in each of the following architectures: shared memory, shared disk, and shared nothing?

**16.9.** Consider a bank which has a collection of sites, each running a database system. Suppose the only way the databases interact is by electronic transfer of money between one another. Would such a system qualify as a distributed database? Why?

**16.10.** Consider a network based on dial-up phone lines, where sites communicate periodically, such as every night. Such networks are often configured with a server site and multiple client sites. The client sites connect only to the server, and exchange data with other clients by storing data at the server and retrieving data stored at the server by other clients. What is the advantage of such an architecture over one where a site can exchange data with another site only by first dialing it up?

## Bibliographical Notes

The textbooks of Patterson and Hennessy [1995] and Stone [1993] provide a good introduction to the area of computer architecture.

Gray and Reuter [1993] provides a textbook description of transaction processing, including the architecture of client-server and distributed systems. Geiger [1995] and Signore et al. [1995] describe the ODBC standard for client-server connectivity. North [1995] describes the use of a variety of tools for client-server database access.

Carey et al. [1991] and Franklin et al. [1993] describe data-caching techniques for client-server database systems. Biliris and Orenstein [1994] survey object storage management systems, including client-server related issues. Franklin et al. [1992] and Mohan and Narang [1994] describe recovery techniques for client-server systems.

A survey of parallel computer architectures is presented by Duncan [1990]. General discussions concerning multiprocessing are given by Jones and Schwarz

[1980]. Multiprocessor hardware is discussed by Satyanarayanan [1980]. Performance of multiprocessor systems is presented by Agrawal et al. [1986] and Bhuyan et al. [1989]. Dubois and Thakkar [1992] is a collection of papers on scalable shared-memory architectures.

DeWitt and Gray [1992] describe parallel database systems, including their architecture and performance measures. Ceri and Pelagatti [1984] and Bell and Grimson [1992] provide textbook coverage of distributed database systems. Further references pertaining to parallel and distributed database systems appear in the bibliographic notes of Chapters 17 and 18, respectively.

Comer [1995] and Thomas [1996] describe the computer networking and the Internet. Tanenbaum [1996] and Halsall [1992] provided general overviews of computer networks. Fortier [1989] presented a detailed discussion of networking hardware and software. Discussions concerning ATM Networks and switches are offered by Prycker [1993]. The general state of networks is described by Quarterman [1990].

# CHAPTER
# 17

# PARALLEL
# DATABASES

In this chapter, we discuss fundamental algorithms used in parallel database systems that are based on the relational data model. In particular, we focus on the placement of data on multiple disks and the parallel evaluation of relational operations, which have been instrumental in the success of parallel databases.

## 17.1   Introduction

In the past decade, parallel database systems have advanced from being nearly written off by even some of their staunchest advocates, to being successfully marketed by companies such as Teradata, Tandem, and Oracle. Fueling this transition are the following trends:

- The transaction requirements of organizations have grown with increasing use of computers.
- Organizations are using increasingly large volumes of transaction processing data—such as data about what items people buy, or when people make telephone calls—to plan their activities and pricing. Queries used for such purposes are called *decision-support* queries, and the data requirements for such queries may run into terabytes. Single-processor systems are not capable of handling such large volumes of data at the required rates.
- Commercial parallel database systems, such as the Teradata DBC series of computers, and research systems, such as Grace and Gamma, have clearly demonstrated the feasibility of parallel database queries. In fact, the set-oriented nature of database queries naturally lends itself to parallelization.

- With microprocessors having become cheap, parallel machines have become common and relatively inexpensive.

As we discussed in Chapter 16, parallelism is used to provide speedup, where queries are executed faster because more resources, such as processors and disks, are provided. Parallelism is also used to provide scaleup, where increasing workloads are handled without increased response time, via an increase in the degree of parallelism.

We outlined in Chapter 16 the different architectures for parallel database systems: shared-memory, shared-disk, shared-nothing, and hierarchical architectures. Briefly, in shared-memory architectures, all processors share a common memory and disks; in shared-disk architectures, processors have independent memories, but share disks; in shared-nothing architectures, processors share neither memory nor disks; and hierarchical architectures have nodes that share neither memory nor disks with each other, but internally each node has a shared-memory or a shared-disk architecture.

## 17.2   I/O Parallelism

In it simplest form, *I/O parallelism* refers to reducing the time required to retrieve relations from disk by partitioning the relations on multiple disks. The most common form of data partitioning in a parallel database environment is *horizontal partitioning*. In horizontal partitioning, the tuples of a relation are divided (or declustered) among many disks, such that each tuple resides on one disk. Several partitioning strategies have been proposed.

### 17.2.1   Partitioning Techniques

We present three basic data-partitioning strategies. We assume that there are $n$ disks, $D_0, D_1, \ldots, D_{n-1}$, across which the data are to be partitioned.

- *Round-robin.* The relation is scanned in any order and the $i$th tuple is sent to disk numbered $D_{i \bmod n}$. The round-robin scheme ensures an even distribution of tuples across disks; that is, each disk has approximately the same number of tuples as do the others.
- *Hash partitioning.* In this declustering strategy, one or more attributes from the given relation's schema are designated as the partitioning attributes. A hash function is chosen whose range is $\{0, 1, \ldots, n - 1\}$. Each tuple of the original relation is hashed on the partitioning attributes. If the hash function returns $i$, then the tuple is placed on disk $D_i$.
- *Range partitioning.* This strategy distributes contiguous attribute-value ranges to each disk. A partitioning attribute, $A$, is chosen, as is a *partitioning vector*. Let $[v_0, v_1, \ldots, v_{n-2}]$ denote the partitioning vector, such that, if $i < j$, then $v_i < v_j$. The relation is partitioned as follows. Consider a tuple $t$ such that $t[A] = x$. If $x < v_0$, then $t$ is placed on disk $D_0$. If $x \geq v_{n-2}$, then $t$ is placed on disk $D_{n-1}$. If $v_i \leq x < v_{i+1}$, then $t$ is placed on disk $D_{i+1}$.

## 17.2.2  Comparison of Partitioning Techniques

Once a relation has been partitioned among several disks, we can retrieve it in parallel using all the disks. Similarly, when a relation is being partitioned, it can be written to multiple disks in parallel. Thus, the transfer rates for reading or writing an entire relation are much faster with I/O parallelism than without it. However, reading an entire relation, or *scanning a relation*, is only one kind of access to data. Access to data can be classified as follows:

1. Scanning the entire relation
2. Locating a tuple associatively, (for example, *employee-name* = "Campbell"); these queries, called *point* queries, seek tuples that have a specified value for a specific attribute
3. Locating all tuples such that the value of a given attribute lies within a specified range (for example, $10000 < salary < 20000$); these queries are called *range* queries

The different partitioning techniques support these types of access at different levels of efficiency:

- *Round-robin.* The scheme is ideally suited for applications that wish to read the entire relation sequentially for each query. However, with this scheme, both point queries and range queries are complicated to process, since each of the $n$ disks must be used for the search.
- *Hash partitioning.* This scheme is best suited for point queries based on the partitioning attribute. For example, if a relation is partitioned on the *telephone-number* attribute, then we can answer the query "Find the record of the employee with *telephone-number* = 555-3333" by applying the partitioning hash function to 555-3333 and then searching that disk. Directing a query to a single disk saves the startup cost of initiating a query on multiple disks, and leaves the other disks free to process other queries.

   Hash partitioning is also useful for sequential scans of the entire relation. If the hash function is a good randomizing function, and the partitioning attributes form a key of the relation, then the number of tuples in each of the disks is approximately the same, without much variance. Hence, the time taken to scan the relation is approximately $1/n$ of the time required to scan the relation in a single disk system.

   The scheme, however, is not well suited for point queries on nonpartitioning attributes. Hash-based partitioning is also not well suited for answering range queries, since, typically, hash functions do not preserve proximity within a range. Therefore, all the disks need to be scanned for range queries to be answered.
- *Range partitioning.* This scheme is well-suited for point and range queries on the partitioning attribute. For point queries, we can consult the partitioning vector to locate the disk where the tuple resides. For range queries, we consult the partitioning vector to find the range of disks on which the tuples may

reside. In both cases, the search is narrowed to exactly those disks that might have any tuples of interest.

This feature is both an advantage and a disadvantage. The advantage is that, if there are only a few tuples in the queried range, then the query is typically sent to one disk, as opposed to all the disks. Since other disks can be used to answer other queries, range partitioning results in higher throughput while maintaining good response time. On the other hand, if there are many tuples in the queried range (as there are when the queried range is a larger fraction of the domain of the relation), many tuples have to be retrieved from a few disks, resulting in an I/O bottleneck (hot spot) at those disks. In this example of *execution skew*, all processing occurs in one—or only a few—partitions. In contrast, hash partitioning and round-robin partitioning would engage all the disks for such queries, giving a faster response time for approximately the same throughput.

The type of partitioning also affects other relational operations, such as joins, as we shall see in Section 17.5. Thus, the choice of partitioning technique also depends on the operations that need to be executed. In general, hash partitioning or range partitioning are preferred to round-robin partitioning.

In a system with many disks, the number of disks across which to partition a relation can be chosen as follows. If a relation contains only a few tuples that will fit into a single disk block, then it is better to assign the relation to a single disk. Large relations are preferably partitioned across all the available disks. If a relation consists of $m$ disk blocks and there are $n$ disks available in the system, then the relation should be allocated **min**$(m, n)$ disks.

### 17.2.3   Handling of Skew

The distribution of tuples when a relation is partitioned (except for round-robin) may be skewed, with a high percentage of tuples placed in some partitions and fewer tuples in other partitions. The ways that skew may appear are classified as follows:

• Attribute-value skew
• Partition skew

*Attribute-value skew* refers to the fact that some values appear in the partitioning attributes of many tuples. All the tuples with the same value for the partitioning attribute end up in the same partition, resulting in skew. *Partition skew* refers to the fact that there may be load imbalance in the partitioning, even when there is no attribute skew.

Attribute-value skew can result in skewed partitioning regardless of whether range partitioning or hash partitioning is used. If the partition vector is not chosen carefully, range partitioning may result in partition skew. Partition skew is less likely with hash partitioning, if a good hash function is chosen.

As we noted in Section 16.3.1, even a small skew can result in a significant decrease in performance. Skew becomes an increasing problem with a higher degree of parallelism. For example, if a relation of 1000 tuples is divided into 10 parts, and the division is skewed, then there may be some partitions of size less than 100 and some partitions of size more than 100; if even one partition happens to be of size 200, the speedup that we would obtain by accessing the partitions in parallel is only five, instead of the ten for which we would have hoped. If the same relation has to be partitioned into 100 parts, a partition will have 10 tuples on an average. If even one partition has 40 tuples (which is possible, given the large number of partitions) the speedup that we would obtain by accessing them in parallel would be 25, rather than 100. Thus, we see that the loss of speedup due to skew increases with parallelism.

If the partitioning attributes form a key for the relation, a good range-partitioning vector can be constructed by means of sorting, as follows. The relation is first sorted on the partitioning attributes. The relation is then scanned in sorted order. After every $1/n$ of the relation has been read, the value of the partitioning attribute of the next tuple is added to the partition vector. Here, $n$ denotes the number of partitions to be constructed. The disadvantage of this method is the extra I/O overhead incurred in doing the initial sort.

## 17.3 Interquery Parallelism

In *interquery parallelism*, different queries or transactions execute in parallel with one another. Transaction throughput can be increased by this form of parallelism. However, the response times of individual transactions are no faster than they would be if the transactions were run run in isolation. Thus, the primary use of interquery parallelism is to scale up a transaction-processing system to support a larger number of transactions per second.

Interquery parallelism is the easiest form of parallelism to support in a database system—particularly in a shared-memory parallel system. Database systems designed for single-processor systems can be used with few or no changes on a shared-memory parallel architecture, since even sequential database systems support concurrent processing. Transactions that would have operated in a time-shared concurrent manner on a sequential machine operate in parallel in the shared-memory parallel architecture.

Supporting interquery parallelism is more complicated in a shared-disk or shared-nothing architecture. Processors have to perform some tasks, such as locking and logging, in a coordinated fashion, and that requires that they pass messages to each other. A parallel database system must also ensure that two processors do not update the same data independently at the same time. Further, when a processor accesses or updates data, the database system must ensure that the processor has the latest version of the data in its buffer pool. The latter problem is known as the *cache-coherency* problem.

Various protocols have been developed to guarantee cache coherency; often, cache-coherency protocols are integrated with concurrency-control protocols so that their overhead is reduced. One such protocol for a shared-disk system is as follows:

1. Before any read or write access to a page, a transaction locks the page in shared or exclusive mode, as appropriate. Immediately after the transaction obtains either a shared or exclusive lock on a page, it also reads the most recent copy of the page from the shared disk.
2. Before a transaction releases an exclusive lock on a page, it flushes the page to the shared disk; then, it releases the lock.

The preceding protocol ensures that, when a transaction sets a shared or exclusive lock on a page, it gets the correct copy of the page.

More complex protocols have been developed to avoid the repeated reading and writing to disk required by the preceding protocol. With such protocols, pages are not written to disk when exclusive locks are released. When a shared or exclusive lock is obtained, if the most recent version of a page is in the buffer pool of some processor, the page is obtained from there. The protocols have to be designed to handle concurrent requests. The shared-disk protocols can be extended to shared-nothing architectures as follows. Each page has a *home* processor $P_i$, and is stored on disk $D_i$. When other processors want to read or write the page, they send requests to the home processor $P_i$ of the page, since they cannot directly communicate with the disk. The other actions are the same as in the shared-disk protocols.

The Oracle 7 and Oracle Rdb systems are examples of shared-disk parallel database systems that support interquery parallelism.

## 17.4   Intraquery Parallelism

*Intraquery parallelism* refers to the execution of a single query in parallel on multiple processors and disks. Using intraquery parallelism is important for speeding up long-running queries. Interquery parallelism docs not help in this task, since each query is run sequentially.

To illustrate the parallel evaluation of a query, we consider a query that requires a relation to be sorted. Suppose that the relation has been partitioned across multiple disks by range partitioning on some attribute, and the sort is requested on the partitioning attribute. The sort operation can be implemented as follows: each partition is sorted in parallel, and the sorted partitions are concatenated to get the final sorted relation.

Thus, we can parallelize a query by parallelizing individual operations. There is another source of parallelism in evaluating a query: The *operator tree* for a query can contain multiple operations. We can parallelize the evaluation of the operator tree by evaluating in parallel some of the operations that do not depend on one another. Further, as mentioned in Chapter 12, we may be able to pipeline the output of one operation to another operation. The two operations can be executed in parallel on separate processors, one generating output that is consumed by the other, even as it is generated.

In summary, the execution of a single query can be parallelized in two ways:

- *Intraoperation parallelism.* We can speed up processing of a query by parallelizing the execution of each individual operation, such as sort, select, project, and join. We consider intra-operation parallelism in Section 17.5.
- *Interoperation parallelism.* We can speed up processing of a query by executing in parallel the different operations in a query expression. We consider this form of parallelism in Section 17.6.

The two forms of parallelism are complementary, and can be used simultaneously on a query. Since the number of operations in a typical query is small, compared to the number of tuples processed by each operation, the first form of parallelism can scale better with increasing parallelism. However, with the relatively small number of processors in typical parallel systems today, both forms of parallelism are important.

In the following discussion on parallelization of queries, we assume that the queries are *read only*. The choice of algorithms for parallelizing query evaluation depends on the machine architecture. Rather than presenting algorithms for each architecture separately, we use a shared-nothing architecture model in our description. Thus, we explicitly describe when data have to be transferred from one processor to another. We can simulate this model easily using the other architectures, since transfer of data can be done via shared-memory in a shared-memory architecture, and via shared disks in a shared-disk architecture. Hence, algorithms for shared-nothing architectures can be used on the other architectures too. We mention occasionally how the algorithms can be further optimized for shared-memory or shared-disk systems.

To simplify the presentation of the algorithms, we assume that there are $n$ processors, $P_0, \ldots, P_{n-1}$, and $n$ disks $D_0, \ldots, D_{n-1}$, where disk $D_i$ is associated with processor $P_i$. A real system may have multiple disks per processor. It is not hard to extend the algorithms to allow multiple disks per processor: We simply allow $D_i$ to be a set of disks. However, for simplicity of presentation, we assume here that $D_i$ is a single disk.

## 17.5   Intraoperation Parallelism

Since relational operations work on relations containing large sets of tuples, we can parallelize the operations by executing them in parallel on different subsets of the relations. Since the number of tuples in a relation can be large, the degree of parallelism is potentially enormous. Thus, intraoperation parallelism is natural in a database system. We shall study parallel versions of some common relational operations in Sections 17.5.1 through 17.5.3.

### 17.5.1   Parallel Sort

Suppose that we wish to sort a relation that resides on $n$ disks $D_0, D_1, \ldots, D_{n-1}$. If the relation has been range partitioned on the attributes on which it is to be sorted, then, as we noted in Section 17.2.2, we can sort each partition separately, and can concatenate the results to get the full sorted relation. Since the tuples are partitioned on $n$ disks, the time required for reading the entire relation is reduced due to parallel access.

If the relation has been partitioned in any other way, we can sort it in one of two ways:

1. We can range partition it on the sort attributes, and then sort each partition separately

2. We can use a parallel version of the external sort–merge algorithm

### 17.5.1.1   Range-Partitioning Sort

When we sort by range partitioning the relation, it is not necessary to range partition the relation on the same processors or disks as those on which that relation is stored. Suppose that we choose processors $P_0, \ldots, P_m$, where $m < n$ to sort the relation. There are two steps involved in this operation:

1. We redistribute the relation using a range-partition strategy, such that all tuples that lie within the $i$th range are sent to processor $P_i$, which stores the relation temporarily on disk $D_i$. This step requires disk I/O and communication overhead.

2. Each of the processors sorts its partition of the relation locally, without interaction with the other processors. Each processor executes the same operation—namely, sorting—on a different data set. (Execution of the same operation in parallel on different sets of data is called *data parallelism*.)

   The final merge operation is trivial, because the range partitioning in the first phase ensures that, for $1 \leq i < j \leq m$, the key values in processor $P_i$ are all less than the key values in $P_j$.

As we noted earlier in Section 17.2.3, we must do range partitioning using a load-balanced partition vector, so that each partition will have approximately the same number of tuples.

### 17.5.1.2   Parallel External Sort–Merge

Using *parallel external sort–merge* is an alternative to range partitioning. Suppose that the relation has already been partitioned among disks $D_0, \ldots, D_{n-1}$ (it does not matter how the relation has been partitioned). Parallel external sort–merge then works as follows:

1. Each processor $P_i$ locally sorts the data on disk $D_i$.

2. The sorted runs on each processor are then merged to get the final sorted output.

The merging of the sorted runs in step 2 can be parallelized as follows:

1. The sorted partitions at each processor $P_i$ are range partitioned (using the same partition vector) across the processors $P_0, \ldots, P_{m-1}$. The tuples are sent in sorted order, so that each processor receives the tuples in sorted streams.
2. Each processor $P_i$ performs a merge on the streams as they are received, to get a single sorted run.
3. The sorted runs on processors $P_0, \ldots, P_{m-1}$ are concatenated to get the final result.

Some machines, such as the Teradata DBC series machines, use specialized hardware to perform merging. The Y-net interconnection network in the Teradata DBC machines can merge output from multiple processors to give a single sorted output.

## 17.5.2　Parallel Join

The join operation requires that we test pairs of tuples to see whether they satisfy the join condition; if they do, the pair is added to the join output. Parallel join algorithms attempt to split over several processors the pairs to be tested. Each processor then computes part of the join locally. Then, we collect the results from each processor to produce the final result.

### 17.5.2.1　Partitioned Join

For certain kinds of joins, such as equi-joins and natural joins, it is possible to *partition* the two input relations across the processors, and to compute the join locally at each processor. Suppose that we are using $n$ processors, and that the relations to be joined are $r$ and $s$. Then, the relations are each partitioned into $n$ partitions, denoted $r_0, r_1, \ldots, r_{n-1}$ and $s_0, s_1, \ldots, s_{n-1}$. The partitions $r_i$ and $s_i$ are sent to processor $P_i$, where their join is computed locally.

The preceding technique works correctly only if the join is an equi-join (for example, $r \bowtie_{r.A=s.B} s$), and, if we partition $r$ and $s$ using the same partitioning function on their join attributes. The idea of partitioning is exactly the same as the idea behind the partitioning step of hash–join. However, there are two different ways of partitioning $r$ and $s$:

- Range partitioning on the join attributes
- Hash partitioning on the join attributes

In either case, the same partitioning function must be used for both relations. For range partitioning, the same partition vector must be used for both relations. For hash-partitioning, this means that the same hash function must be used on both relations. Figure 17.1 depicts the partitioning used in a partitioned parallel join.

Once the relations are partitioned, we can use any join technique locally at each processor $P_i$ to compute the join of $r_i$ and $s_i$. For example, hash–join,

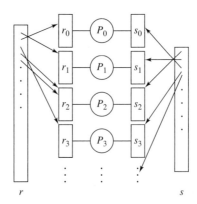

Figure 17.1    Partitioned parallel join.

merge–join, or nested-loop join could be used. Thus, we can use partitioning to parallelize any join technique.

If one or both of the relations $r$ and $s$ are already partitioned on the join attributes (via either hash partitioning or range partitioning), the work needed for partitioning is reduced greatly. If the relations are not partitioned, or are partitioned on attributes other than the join attributes, then the tuples need to be repartitioned. Each processor $P_i$ reads in the tuples on disk $D_i$, computes for each tuple $t$ the partition $j$ to which $t$ belongs, and sends tuple $t$ to processor $P_j$. Processor $P_j$ stores the tuples on disk $D_j$.

We can optimize the join algorithm used locally at each processor to reduce I/O by not writing some of the tuples to disk, but instead buffering them in memory. We describe such optimizations in Section 17.5.2.3.

Skew presents a special problem when range partitioning is used, since a partition vector that splits one relation of the join into equal-sized partitions may split the other relations into partitions of widely varying size. The partition vector should be such that $| r_i | + | s_i |$ (that is, the sum of the sizes of $r_i$ and $s_i$) is roughly equal over all the $i = 0, 1, \ldots, n - 1$. With a good hash function, hash partitioning is likely to have a smaller skew, except when there are many tuples with the same values for the join attributes.

### 17.5.2.2  Fragment-and-Replicate Join

Partitioning is not applicable to all types of joins. For instance, if the join condition is an inequality, such as $r \bowtie_{r.a < s.b} s$, it is possible that all tuples in $r$ join with some tuple in $s$ (and vice versa). Thus, there may be no nontrivial means of partitioning $r$ and $s$ such that tuples in partition $r_i$ join with only tuples in partition $s_i$.

We can parallelize such joins using a technique called *fragment and replicate*. We first consider a special case of fragment and replicate—*asymmetric fragment-and-replicate*—which works as follows.

1. One of the relations—say, $r$—is partitioned. Any partitioning technique can be used on $r$, including round-robin partitioning.

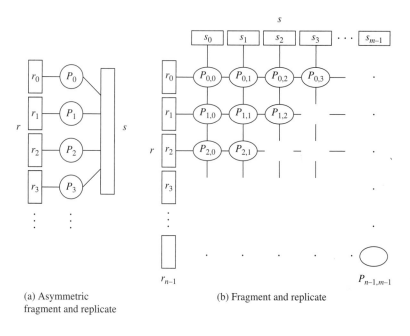

(a) Asymmetric
fragment and replicate

(b) Fragment and replicate

Figure 17.2    Fragment-and-replicate schemes.

2. The other relation, $s$, is replicated across all the processors.

3. Processor $P_i$ then locally computes the join of $r_i$ with all of $s$, using any join technique.

The asymmetric fragment-and-replicate scheme is shown in Figure 17.2a. If $r$ is already stored by partitioning, there is no need to partition it further in step 1. All that is required is to replicate $s$ across all processors.

The general case of fragment and replicate is shown in Figure 17.2b; it works as follows. Relation $r$ is partitioned into $n$ partitions, $r_0, r_1, \ldots, r_{n-1}$, and $s$ is partitioned into $m$ partitions, $s_0, s_1, \ldots, s_{m-1}$. As before, any partitioning technique may be used on $r$ and on $s$. The values of $m$ and $n$ do not need to be equal, but they must be chosen such that there are at least $m * n$ processors. Asymmetric fragment and replicate is simply a special case of general fragment and replicate, where $m = 1$. Fragment and replicate reduces the sizes of the relations at each processor, as compared to asymmetric fragment and replicate.

Let us label the processors as $P_{0,0}, P_{0,1}, \ldots, P_{0,m-1}, P_{1,0}, \ldots, P_{n-1,m-1}$. Processor $P_{i,j}$ computes the join of $r_i$ with $s_j$. To do so, $r_i$ is replicated to processors $P_{i,0}, P_{i,1}, \ldots, P_{i,m-1}$ (which form a row in Figure 17.2b), and $s_i$ is replicated to processors $P_{0,i}, P_{1,i}, \ldots, P_{n-1,i}$ (which form a column in Figure 17.2b). Any join technique can be used at each processor $P_{i,j}$.

Fragment and replicate works with any join condition, since every tuple in $r$ can be tested with every tuple in $s$. Thus, it can be used where partitioning cannot be.

Fragment and replicate usually has a higher cost than does partitioning, when both relations are of roughly the same size, since at least one of the relations has to be replicated. However, if one of the relations—say, $s$—is small, it may be cheaper to replicate $s$ across all processors, rather than to repartition $r$ and $s$ on the join attributes. In such a case, asymmetric fragment and replicate is preferable, even though partitioning could be used.

### 17.5.2.3   Partitioned Parallel Hash–Join

In this section, we show how the partitioned hash–join of Section 12.6 can be parallelized.

Suppose that we have $n$ processors, $P_0$, $P_1$, ..., $P_{n-1}$, and two relations $r$ and $s$, such that the relations $r$ and $s$ are partitioned across multiple disks. Recall from Section 12.6 that the smaller relation is chosen as the build relation. If the size of $s$ is less than that of $r$, the parallel hash–join algorithm proceeds as follows.

1. Choose a hash function—say, $h_1$—that takes the join attribute value of each tuple in $r$ and $s$ and maps the tuple to one of the $n$ processors. Let $r_i$ denote the tuples of relation $r$ that are mapped to processor $P_i$; similarly, let $s_i$ denote the tuples of relation $s$ that are mapped to processor $P_i$. Each processor $P_i$ reads the tuples of $s$ that are on its disk $D_i$, and sends each tuple to the appropriate processor based on hash function $h_1$.

2. As the tuples of $s_i$ are received at the destination processor $P_i$, they are further partitioned using another hash function, $h_2$, which the processor uses to compute the hash–join locally. The partitioning at this stage is exactly the same as in the partitioning phase of the sequential hash–join algorithm. Each processor $P_i$ executes this step independently from the other processors.

3. Once the tuples of $s$ have been distributed, the system redistributes the larger relation $r$ across the $m$ processors using the hash function $h_1$, in the same way as before. As each tuple is received, the destination processor repartitions it using the function $h_2$, just as the probe relation is partitioned in the sequential hash–join algorithm.

4. Each processor $P_i$ executes the build and probe phases of the hash–join algorithm on the local partitions $r_i$ and $s_i$ of $r$ and $s$ to produce a partition of the final result of the hash–join.

The hash–join performed at each processor is independent of that performed at other processors, and receiving the tuples of $r_i$ and $s_i$ is similar to reading them from disk. Therefore, any of the optimizations of the hash–join described in Chapter 12 can be applied as well to the parallel case. In particular, we can use the hybrid hash–join algorithm to cache some of the incoming tuples in memory, and thus to avoid the costs of writing them and of reading them back in.

### 17.5.2.4   Parallel Nested-Loop Join

To illustrate the use of fragment-and-replicate based parallelization, we consider the case where the relation $s$ is much smaller than relation $r$. Suppose also that relation $r$ is stored by partitioning; the attribute on which it is partitioned is irrelevant. Finally, suppose that there is an index on a join attribute of relation $r$ at each of the partitions of relation $r$.

We use asymmetric fragment and replicate, with relation $s$ being replicated, and with the existing partitioning of relation $r$. Each processor $P_j$ where a partition of relation $s$ is stored reads the tuples of relation $s$ stored in $D_j$, and replicates the tuples to every other processor $P_i$. At the end of this phase, relation $s$ is replicated at all sites that store tuples of relation $r$.

Now, each processor $P_i$ performs an indexed nested-loop join of relation $s$ with the $i$th partition of relation $r$. We can overlap the indexed nested-loop join with the distribution of tuples of relation $s$, to reduce the costs of writing the tuples of relation $s$ to disk, and of reading them back. However, the replication of relation $s$ must be synchronized with the join so that there is enough space in the in-memory buffers at each processor $P_i$ to hold the tuples of relation $s$ that have been received but that have not yet been used in the join.

### 17.5.3 Other Relational Operations

The evaluation of other relational operations also can be parallelized:

- *Selection.* Let the selection be $\sigma_\theta(r)$. Consider first the case where $\theta$ is of the form $a_i = v$, where $a_i$ is an attribute, and $v$ is a value. If the relation $r$ is partitioned on $a_i$, the selection is performed at a single processor. If $\theta$ is of the form $l \le a_i \le u$—that is, $\theta$ is a range selection—and the relation has been range-partitioned on $a_i$, then the selection is performed at each processor whose partition overlaps with the specified range of values. In all other cases, the selection is performed in parallel at all the processors.

- *Duplicate elimination.* Duplicate elimination can be performed by sorting; either of the parallel sort techniques can be used, with the optimization of eliminating duplicates as soon as they are found during sorting. We can also parallelize duplicate elimination by partitioning the tuples (using either range or hash partitioning) and performing duplicate elimination locally at each processor.

- *Projection.* Projection without duplicate elimination can be performed as tuples are read in from disk in parallel. If duplicate elimination is to be performed, the techniques just described can be used.

- *Aggregation.* Consider an aggregation operation. We can parallelize the operation by partitioning the relation on the grouping attributes, and then computing the aggregate values locally at each processor. Either hash partitioning or range partitioning can be used. If the relation is already partitioned on the grouping attributes, the first step can be skipped.

  We can reduce the cost of transferring tuples during partitioning by partly computing aggregate values before partitioning, at least for the commonly used aggregate functions. Consider an aggregation operation on a relation $r$, using the **sum** aggregate function on attribute $B$, with grouping on attribute $A$. The operation can be performed at each processor $P_i$ on those $r$ tuples stored on disk $D_i$. This computation results in tuples with partial sums at each processor; there is one tuple at $P_i$ for each value for attribute $A$ present in $r$ tuples stored on $D_i$. The result of the local aggregation is partitioned on the grouping attribute $A$, and the aggregation is performed again (on tuples with the partial sums) at each processor $P_i$ to get the final result.

As a result of this optimization, fewer tuples need to be sent to other processors during partitioning. This idea can be extended easily to the **min** and **max** aggregate functions. Extensions to the **count** and **avg** aggregate functions are left for you to do in Exercise 17.8.

The parallelization of other operations is covered in several of the the the exercises.

## 17.5.4   Cost of Parallel Evaluation of Operations

We achieve parallelism by partitioning the I/O among multiple disks, and partitioning the CPU work among multiple processors. If such a split is achieved without any overhead, and if there is no skew in the splitting of work, a parallel operation using $n$ processors will take $1/n$ times as long as will the same operation on a single processor. We already know how to estimate the cost of an operation such as a join or a selection. The time cost of parallel processing would then be $1/n$ of the time cost of sequential processing of the operation.

We must also account for the following costs:

- Startup costs for initiating the operation at multiple processors
- Skew in the distribution of work among the processors, with some processors getting a larger number of tuples than others
- Contention for resources—such as memory, disk, and the communication network—resulting in delays
- Cost of assembling the final result by transmitting partial results from each processor

The time taken by a parallel operation can be estimated as

$$T_{\text{part}} + T_{\text{asm}} + \max(T_0, T_1, \ldots, T_{n-1})$$

where $T_{\text{part}}$ is the time for partitioning the relations, $T_{\text{asm}}$ is the time for assembling the results and $T_i$ the time taken for the operation at processor $P_i$. Assuming that the tuples are distributed without any skew, the number of tuples sent to each processor can be estimated as $1/n$ of the total number of tuples. Ignoring contention, $T_i$, the cost of the operations at each processor $P_i$ can then be estimated via the techniques described in Chapter 12.

The preceding estimate will be an optimistic estimate, since skew is common. Even though breaking down a single query into a number of parallel steps

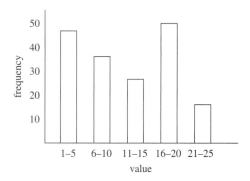

Figure 17.3    Example of histogram.

reduces the size of the average step, it is the time for processing the single slowest step that determines the time taken for processing the query as a whole. A partitioned parallel evaluation, for instance, is only as fast as the slowest of the parallel executions. Thus, performance is greatly affected by any skew in the distribution of the work across processors.

The problem of skew in partitioning is closely related to the problem of partition overflow in sequential hash–joins (Chapter 12). We can use overflow resolution and avoidance techniques developed for hash–joins to handle skew when hash partitioning is used.

One technique to handle skew in joins with range partitioning is to construct and store a frequency table, or *histogram*, of the attribute values for each attribute of each relation. Figure 17.3 shows an example of a histogram for an integer-valued attribute that takes values in the range 1 to 25. We then construct a load-balanced range-partitioning function using histograms on the join attributes of the relations, to make the distribution of tuples more even. Approaches that construct the histogram based on sampling the relations, using only tuples from a randomly chosen subset of the disk blocks of the relation, have also been proposed to reduce the I/O overhead.

# 17.6    Interoperation Parallelism

There are two forms of *interoperation parallelism*: pipelined parallelism, and independent parallelism.

## 17.6.1    Pipelined Parallelism

As we discussed in Chapter 12, pipelining forms an important source of economy of computation for database query processing. Recall that, in pipelining, the output tuples of one operation, $A$, are consumed by a second operation, $B$, even before the first operation has produced the entire set of tuples in its output. The major advantage of pipelined execution in a sequential evaluation is that we can carry out a sequence of such operations without writing any of the intermediate results to disk.

In a parallel system, pipelining is used primarily for the same reason that it is used in a sequential system. However, pipelining can be used as a source of parallelism as well, in the same way that instruction pipelines are used as a source of parallelism in hardware design. In the preceding example, it is possible to run $A$ and $B$ simultaneously on different processors, such that $B$ consumes tuples in parallel with $A$ producing them. This form of parallelism is called *pipelined parallelism*.

Let us consider a join of four relations:

$$r_1 \bowtie r_2 \bowtie r_3 \bowtie r_4$$

We can set up a pipeline that allows the three joins to be computed in parallel. Let processor $P_1$ be assigned the computation of $temp_1 \leftarrow r_1 \bowtie r_2$, and let $P_2$ be assigned the computation of $r_3 \bowtie temp_1$. As $P_1$ computes tuples in $r_1 \bowtie r_2$, it makes these tuples available to processor $P_2$. Thus, $P_2$ has available to it some of the tuples in $r_1 \bowtie r_2$ before $P_1$ has finished its computation. $P_2$ can use those tuples that are available to begin computation of $temp_1 \bowtie r_3$, even before $r_1 \bowtie r_2$ is fully computed by $P_1$. Likewise, as $P_2$ computes tuples in $(r_1 \bowtie r_2) \bowtie r_3$, it makes these tuples available to $P_3$, which computes the join of these tuples with $r_4$.

Pipelined parallelism is useful with a small number of processors, but does not scale up well. First, pipeline chains generally do not attain sufficient length to provide a high degree of parallelism. Second, it is not possible to pipeline relational operators that do not produce output until all inputs have been accessed, such as the set-difference operation. Third, only marginal speedup is obtained for the frequent cases in which one operator's execution cost is much higher than are those of the others. Thus, when the degree of parallelism is high, the importance of pipelining as a source of parallelism is secondary to that of partitioned parallelism. The most important reason for using pipelining is that pipelined executions can avoid writing intermediate results to disk.

## 17.6.2 Independent Parallelism

Operations in a query expression that do not depend on one another can be executed in parallel. This form of parallelism is called *independent parallelism*.

Let us again consider the join $r_1 \bowtie r_2 \bowtie r_3 \bowtie r_4$. Clearly, we can compute $temp_1 \leftarrow r_1 \bowtie r_2$ in parallel with $temp_2 \leftarrow r_3 \bowtie r_4$. When these two computations complete, we compute

$$temp_1 \bowtie temp_2$$

To obtain further parallelism, we can pipeline the tuples in $temp_1$ and $temp_2$ into the computation of $temp_1 \bowtie temp_2$, which is itself carried out via a pipelined join (Section 12.8.2.2).

Like pipelined parallelism, independent parallelism does not provide a high degree of parallelism, and is less useful in a highly parallel system, although it is useful with a lower degree of parallelism.

## 17.6.3  Query Optimization

An important factor in the success of relational technology has been the successful design of query optimizers. Recall that a query optimizer takes a query, and finds the cheapest execution plan among the many possible execution plans that give the same answer.

Query optimizers for parallel query evaluation are more complicated than are query optimizers for sequential query evaluation. First, the cost models are more complicated, since partitioning costs have to be accounted for, and issues such as skew and resource contention must be taken into account. More important is the issue of how to parallelize a query. Suppose that we have somehow chosen an expression (from among those equivalent to the query) to be used for evaluating the query. The expression can be represented by an operator tree, as discussed in Section 12.8.

To evaluate an operator tree in a parallel system, we must make the following decisions:

- How to parallelize each operation, and how many processors to use for it
- What operations to pipeline across different processors, what operations to execute independently in parallel, and what operations to execute sequentially, one after the other

These decisions constitute the task of *scheduling* the execution tree.

Determining the resources of each kind—such as processors, disks, and memory—that should be allocated to each operation in the tree is another aspect of the optimization problem. For instance, it may appear wise to use the maximum amount of parallelism available, but it is a good idea not to execute certain operations in parallel. Operations whose computational requirements are significantly smaller than the communication overhead should be clustered with one of their neighbors. Otherwise, the advantage of parallelism is negated by the overhead of communication.

One concern when pipelining is used is that long pipelines do not lend themselves to good resource utilization. Unless the operations are coarse grained, the final operation of the pipeline may wait for a long time to get inputs, while holding precious resources, such as memory. Hence, long pipelines should be avoided.

The number of parallel evaluation plans from which to choose is much larger than is the number of sequential evaluation plans. Optimizing parallel queries by considering all alternatives is therefore much more expensive than is optimizing sequential queries. Hence, we usually adopt heuristic approaches to reduce the number of parallel execution plans that we consider. We describe two popular heuristics here.

The first heuristic is to consider only evaluation plans that parallelize every operation across all processors, and that do not use any pipelining. This approach is used in the Teradata DBC series machines. Finding the best such execution plan is similar to doing query optimization in a sequential system. The main differences lie in how the partitioning is performed, and in what cost-estimation formula are used.

The second heuristic is to choose the most efficient sequential evaluation plan, and then to parallelize the operations in that evaluation plan.

Yet another dimension of optimization is the design of physical-storage organization to speed up queries. The optimal physical organization differs for different queries. The database administrator must choose a physical organization that is believed to be good for the expected mix of database queries. Thus, the area of parallel query optimization is complex, and is still an area of active research.

## 17.7    Design of Parallel Systems

So far, in this chapter, we have concentrated on parallelization of data storage and of query processing. Since large-scale parallel database systems are used primarily for storing large volumes of data, and for processing decision-support queries on those data, these topics are the most important in a parallel database system. Parallel loading of data from external sources is an important requirement, if we are to handle large volumes of incoming data.

A large parallel database system must also address the following availability issues:

- Resilience to failure of some processors or disks
- On-line reorganization of data and schema changes

We consider these issues here.

With a large number of processors and disks, the probability that at least one processor or disk will malfunction is significantly greater than in a single-processor system with one disk. A poorly designed parallel system will stop functioning if any component (processor or disk) fails. Assuming that the probability of failure of a single processor or disk is small, the probability of failure of the system goes up linearly with the number of processors and disks. If a single processor or disk would fail once every 5 years, a system with 100 processors would have a failure every 18 days.

Therefore, large-scale parallel database systems, such as Tandem and Teradata machines, are designed to operate even if a processor or disk fails. Data are replicated across at least two processors. If a processor fails, the data that it stored can still be accessed from the other processors. The system keeps track of failed processors and distributes the work among functioning processors. Requests for data stored at the failed site are automatically routed to the backup sites that store a replica of the data. If all the data of a processor $A$ are replicated at a single processor $B$, $B$ will have to handle all the requests to $A$ as well as those to itself, and that will result in $B$ becoming a bottleneck. Therefore, the replicas of the data of a processor are partitioned across multiple other processors.

When we are dealing with large volumes of data (ranging in the terabytes), simple operations, such as creating indices, and changes to schema, such as adding a column to a relation, can take a long time — perhaps hours or even days.

Therefore, it is unacceptable for the database system to be unavailable while such operations are in progress. Parallel database systems, such as the Tandem systems, allow such operations to be performed *on-line*.

Consider, for instance, on-line index construction. A system that supports this feature allows insertions, deletions, and updates to be performed on a relation even as an index is being built on the relation. The index-building operation therefore cannot lock the entire relation in shared mode, as it would have done otherwise. Instead, the process keeps track of updates that occur while it is active, and incorporates the changes into the index being constructed.

## 17.8   Summary

Parallel databases have gained significant commercial acceptance in the past 15 years. In I/O parallelism, relations are partitioned among available disks so that retrieval can be made faster. Three commonly used partitioning techniques are round-robin partitioning, hash partitioning, and range partitioning. Skew is a major problem, especially with increasing degrees of parallelism.

In interquery parallelism, we run different queries concurrently to increase throughput. Intraquery parallelism attempts to reduce the cost of running a query. There are two types of intraquery parallelism: intraoperation parallelism and interoperation parallelism.

We use intraoperation parallelism to execute relational operations, such as sorts and joins, in parallel. Intraoperation parallelism is natural for relational operations, since they are set oriented. There are two basic approaches to parallelizing a binary operation such as a join. In partitioned parallelism, the relations are split into several parts, and tuples in $r_i$ are joined with only tuples from $s_i$. In asymmetric fragment and replicate, one of the relations is replicated while the other is partitioned. Unlike partitioned parallelism, fragment and replicate can be used with any join condition. Both parallelization techniques can be used in conjunction with any join technique.

In independent parallelism, different operations that do not depend on one another are executed in parallel. In pipelined parallelism, processors send the results of one operation to another operation as those results are computed, without waiting for the entire operation to finish. Query optimization in parallel databases is significantly more complex than is query optimization in sequential databases.

## Exercises

**17.1.** For each of the three partitioning techniques, namely round-robin, hash-partitioning, and range-partitioning, give an example of a query for which that partitioning technique would provide the fastest response.

**17.2.** When performing a range selection on a range-partitioned attribute, it is possible that only one disk may need to be accessed. Describe the benefits and drawbacks of this property.

**17.3.** What factors could result in skew when a relation is partitioned on one of its attributes using:
  (a) Hash-partitioning
  (b) Range-partitioning
  In each case above, what can be done to reduce the skew?

**17.4.** What form of parallelism (inter-query, inter-operation, or intra-operation) is likely to be the most important for each of the following tasks.
  (a) Increasing the throughput of a system with many small queries.
  (b) Increasing the throughput of a system with a few large queries, when the number of disks and processors is large.

**17.5.** With pipelined parallelism, it is often a good idea to perform several operations in a pipeline on a single processor, even when many processors are available.
  (a) Explain why.
  (b) Would the above arguments hold if the machine used has a shared-memory architecture? Explain why or why not?
  (c) Would the above arguments hold with independent parallelism? (That is, are there cases where even if the operations are not pipelined, and there are many processors available, it is still a good idea to perform several operations on the same processor?)

**17.6.** Give an example of a join that is not a simple equi-join, for which partitioned parallelism can be used. What attributes should be used for partitioning?

**17.7.** Consider join processing using symmetric fragment and replicate with range partitioning. How can you optimize the evaluation if the join condition is of the form $\mid r.A - s.B \mid \; \leq k$, where $k$ is a small constant. Here, $\mid x \mid$ denotes the absolute value of $x$. A join with such a join condition is called a *band join*.

**17.8.** Describe a good way to parallelize each of the following.
  (a) The difference operation.
  (b) Aggregation using the **count** operation.
  (c) Aggregation using the **count distinct** operation.
  (d) Aggregation using the **avg** operation.
  (e) Left outer join, if the join condition involves only equality.
  (f) Left outer join, if the join condition involves comparisons other than equality.
  (g) Full outer join, if the join condition involves comparisons other than equality.

**17.9.** Recall that histograms are used for constructing load balanced range partitions.
  (a) Suppose you have a histogram where values are between 1 and 100, and are partitioned into 10 ranges, $1 - 10, 11 - 20, \ldots, 91 - 100$, with frequencies 15, 5, 20, 10, 10, 5, 5, 20, 5, and 5, respectively. Give a load balanced range partitioning function to divide the values into 5 partitions.

(*b*) Give an algorithm for computing a load-balanced range partition with *p* partitions, given a histogram of frequency distributions containing *n* ranges.

**17.10.** Describe the benefits and drawbacks of using pipelined parallelism.

**17.11.** Some parallel database systems store an extra copy of each data item on disks attached to a different processor, to avoid loss of data if one of the processors fails.

(*a*) Why is it a good idea to partition the copies of the data items of a processor across multiple processors?

(*b*) What are the benefits and drawbacks of using RAID storage instead of storing an extra copy of each data item?

# Bibliographical Notes

Relational database systems began appearing in the marketplace in 1983; now, they dominate it. By the late 1970s and early 1980s, as the relational model gained reasonably sound footing, people recognized that relational operators are highly parallelizable and have good dataflow properties. A commercial system, Teradata, and several research projects, such as GRACE (Kitsuregawa et al. [1983], Fushimi et al. [1986]), GAMMA (DeWitt et al. [1986, 1990]), and Bubba (Boral et al. [1990]), were launched in quick succession. Researchers used these parallel database systems to investigate the practicality of parallel execution of relational operators. Subsequently, in the late 1980s and the 1990s, several more companies—such as Tandem, Oracle, Informix, and Red-Brick—have entered the market. Research projects in the academic world include XPRS (Stonebraker et al. [1989]) and Volcano (Graefe [1990]).

Locking in parallel databases is discussed in Joshi [1991], and in Mohan and Narang [1991, 1992b]. Cache-coherency protocols for parallel database systems are discussed by Dias et al. [1989], Mohan and Narang [1991, 1992], and Rahm [1993]. Carey et al. [1991] discuss caching issues in a client–server system. Parallelism and recovery in database systems are discussed by Bayer et al. [1980].

Graefe [1993] presents an excellent survey of query processing, including parallel processing of queries. Parallel sorting is discussed in DeWitt et al. [1992]. Parallel join algorithms are described by Nakayama et al. [1984], Kitsuregawa et al. [1983], and Richardson et al. [1987], Schneider and DeWitt [1989], Kitsuregawa and Ogawa [ 1990, Lin et al. [1994], and Wilschut et al. [1995], among other works. Parallel join algorithms for shared-memory architectures are described by Tsukuda et al. [1992], Deshpande and Larson [1992], and by Shatdal and Naughton [1993]. Skew handling in parallel joins is described by Walton et al. [1991], Wolf [1991], and DeWitt et al. [1992]. Sampling techniques for parallel databases are described by Seshadri and Naughton [1992] and Ganguly et al. [1996].

Graefe [1990, 1993] advocates a model of parallelization called the *exchange-operator* model, which uses existing implementations of operations, operating on local copies of data, coupled with an exchange operation that moves data around. Our description of parallelization of operations is based loosely on this model.

Parallel query-optimization techniques are described by Lu et al. [1991], Hong and Stonebraker [1991], Ganguly et al. [1992], Lanzelotte et al. [1993], and Hasan and Motwani [1995].

# CHAPTER
# 18

---

# DISTRIBUTED
# DATABASES

In Chapter 16, we discussed the basic structure of distributed systems. Unlike parallel systems, in which the processors are tightly coupled and constitute a single database system, a distributed database system consists of loosely coupled sites that share no physical components. Furthermore, the database systems that run on each site may have a substantial degree of mutual independence.

Each site may participate in the execution of transactions that access data at one site, or several sites. The main difference between centralized and distributed database systems is that, in the former, the data reside in one single location, whereas in the latter, the data reside in several locations. This distribution of data is the cause of many difficulties in transaction processing and query processing. In this chapter, we address these difficulties.

We start with the question of how to store data in a distributed database, in Section 18.1. In Section 18.2, we consider issues of network transparency and of naming of data items. Several techniques have been developed for processing queries in a distributed database; they are examined in Section 18.3.

The next few sections address transaction processing. The basic model and problems caused by different kinds of failures are examined in Section 18.4. Commit protocols designed to provide atomic transaction commit, in spite of these problems, are described in Section 18.5. Recovery issues related to selecting new coordinators when a site designated as a coordinator fails are considered in Section 18.6. Concurrency control in distributed systems is examined in Section 18.7; the issue of handling deadlocks is dealt with in Section 18.8.

In recent years, the need has arisen for accessing and updating data from a variety of preexisting databases, which differ in their hardware and software environments, and in the schemas under which data are stored. A *multidatabase system* is a software layer that enables such a heterogeneous collection of databases to be treated like a homogeneous distributed database. Section 18.9 deals with query-processing and transaction-processing issues related to multidatabase systems.

# 18.1 Distributed Data Storage

Consider a relation $r$ that is to be stored in the database. There are several approaches to storing this relation in the distributed database:

- **Replication**. The system maintains several identical replicas (copies) of the relation. Each replica is stored at a different site, resulting in data replication. The alternative to replication is to store only one copy of relation $r$.
- **Fragmentation**. The relation is partitioned into several fragments. Each fragment is stored at a different site.
- **Replication and fragmentation**. The relation is partitioned into several fragments. The system maintains several replicas of each fragment.

In the following subsections, we elaborate on each of these techniques.

## 18.1.1 Data Replication

If relation $r$ is replicated, a copy of relation $r$ is stored in two or more sites. In the most extreme case, we have *full replication*, in which a copy is stored in every site in the system.

There are a number of advantages and disadvantages to replication.

- **Availability**. If one of the sites containing relation $r$ fails, then the relation $r$ can be found in another site. Thus, the system can continue to process queries involving $r$, despite the failure of one site.
- **Increased parallelism**. In the case where the majority of accesses to the relation $r$ result in only the reading of the relation, then several sites can process queries involving $r$ in parallel. The more replicas of $r$ there are, the greater the chance that the needed data will be found in the site where the transaction is executing. Hence, data replication minimizes movement of data between sites.
- **Increased overhead on update**. The system must ensure that all replicas of a relation $r$ are consistent; otherwise, erroneous computations may result. Thus, whenever $r$ is updated, the update must be propagated to all sites containing replicas. The result is increased overhead. For example, in a banking system, where account information is replicated in various sites, it is necessary to ensure that the balance in a particular account agrees in all sites.

In general, replication enhances the performance of **read** operations and increases the availability of data to read-only transactions. However, update transactions incur greater overhead. Controlling concurrent updates by several transactions to replicated data is more complex than is using the centralized approach to concurrency control that we saw in Chapter 14. We can simplify the management of replicas of relation $r$ by choosing one of them as the *primary copy of r*. For example, in a banking system, an account can be associated with the site in which the account has been opened. Similarly, in an airline-reservation system, a flight can be associated with the site at which the flight originates. We shall examine the options for distributed concurrency control in Section 18.7.

## 18.1.2   Data Fragmentation

If relation $r$ is fragmented, $r$ is divided into a number of *fragments* $r_1, r_2, ..., r_n$. These fragments contain sufficient information to allow reconstruction of the original relation $r$. As we shall see, this reconstruction can take place through the application of either the union operation or a special type of join operation on the various fragments. There are two different schemes for fragmenting a relation: *horizontal* fragmentation and *vertical* fragmentation. Horizontal fragmentation splits the relation by assigning each tuple of $r$ to one or more fragments. Vertical fragmentation splits the relation by decomposing the scheme $R$ of relation $r$ in a special way that we shall discuss. These two schemes can be applied successively to the same relation, resulting in a number of different fragments. Note that some information may appear in several fragments.

We discuss the various ways for fragmenting a relation in Sections 18.1.2.1 to 18.1.2.3. We shall illustrate these approaches by fragmenting the relation *account*, with schema

   *Account-schema* = (*branch-name, account-number, balance*)

The relation *account* (*Account-schema*) is shown in Figure 18.1.

### 18.1.2.1   Horizontal Fragmentation

The relation $r$ is partitioned into a number of subsets, $r_1, r_2, ..., r_n$. Each tuple of relation $r$ must belong to at least one of the fragments, so that the original relation can be reconstructed, if needed.

A fragment can be defined as a *selection* on the global relation $r$. That is, we use a predicate $P_i$ to construct fragment $r_i$ as follows:

$$r_i \;=\; \sigma_{P_i}(r)$$

| branch-name | account-number | balance |
|-------------|----------------|---------|
| Hillside    | A-305          | 500     |
| Hillside    | A-226          | 336     |
| Valleyview  | A-177          | 205     |
| Valleyview  | A-402          | 10000   |
| Hillside    | A-155          | 62      |
| Valleyview  | A-408          | 1123    |
| Valleyview  | A-639          | 750     |

Figure 18.1    Sample *account* relation.

| branch-name | account-number | balance |
|-------------|----------------|---------|
| Hillside | A-305 | 500 |
| Hillside | A-226 | 336 |
| Hillside | A-155 | 62 |

$$account_1$$

| branch-name | account-number | balance |
|-------------|----------------|---------|
| Valleyview | A-177 | 205 |
| Valleyview | A-402 | 10000 |
| Valleyview | A-408 | 1123 |
| Valleyview | A-639 | 750 |

$$account_2$$

**Figure 18.2**    Horizontal fragmentation of relation *account*.

We obtain the reconstruction of the relation $r$ by taking the union of all fragments; that is,

$$r = r_1 \cup r_2 \cup \ldots \cup r_n$$

As an illustration, suppose that the relation $r$ is the *account* relation of Figure 18.1. This relation can be divided into $n$ different fragments, each of which consists of tuples of accounts belonging to a particular branch. If the banking system has only two branches—Hillside and Valleyview—then there are two different fragments:

$$account_1 = \sigma_{branch\text{-}name\ =\ \text{``Hillside''}} (account)$$
$$account_2 = \sigma_{branch\text{-}name\ =\ \text{``Valleyview''}} (account)$$

These two fragments are shown in Figure 18.2. Fragment $account_1$ is stored in the Hillside site. Fragment $account_2$ is stored in the Valleyview site.

In our example, the fragments are disjoint. By changing the selection predicates used to construct the fragments, we can have a particular tuple of $r$ appear in more than one of the $r_i$. This form of data replication is discussed further at the end of this section.

### 18.1.2.2 Vertical Fragmentation

In its simplest form, vertical fragmentation is the same as decomposition (see Chapter 7). Vertical fragmentation of $r(R)$ involves the definition of several subsets of attributes $R_1$, $R_2$, ..., $R_n$ of the schema $R$ such that

$$R = R_1 \cup R_2 \cup \ldots \cup R_n$$

Each fragment $r_i$ of $r$ is defined by

$$r_i = \Pi_{R_i} (r)$$

| branch-name | account-number | customer-name | balance |
|---|---|---|---|
| Hillside | A-305 | Lowman | 500 |
| Hillside | A-226 | Camp | 336 |
| Valleyview | A-177 | Camp | 205 |
| Valleyview | A-402 | Kahn | 10000 |
| Hillside | A-155 | Kahn | 62 |
| Valleyview | A-408 | Kahn | 1123 |
| Valleyview | A-639 | Green | 750 |

Figure 18.3    Sample *deposit* relation.

The fragmentation should be done such that we can reconstruct relation *r* from the fragments by taking the natural join

$$r = r_1 \Join r_2 \Join r_3 \Join \dots \Join r_n$$

One way of ensuring that the relation *r* can be reconstructed is to include the primary-key attributes of *R* in each of the $R_i$. More generally, any superkey can be used. It is often convenient to add a special attribute, called a *tuple-id*, to the schema *R*. The tuple-id value of a tuple is a unique value, used to distinguish the tuple from all other tuples. The tuple-id attribute thus serves as a candidate key for the augmented schema, and is included in each of the $R_i$s. The physical or logical address for a tuple can be used as a tuple-id, since each tuple has a unique address.

To illustrate vertical fragmentation, we consider for our bank database an alternative database design that includes the schema[†]

*Deposit-schema* = (*branch-name, account-number, customer-name, balance*)

Figure 18.3 shows the *deposit* relation for our example. In Figure 18.4, we show the relation *deposit'*: the *deposit* relation of Figure 18.3 with tuple-ids

| branch-name | account-number | customer-name | balance | tuple-id |
|---|---|---|---|---|
| Hillside | A-305 | Lowman | 500 | 1 |
| Hillside | A-226 | Camp | 336 | 2 |
| Valleyview | A-177 | Camp | 205 | 3 |
| Valleyview | A-402 | Kahn | 10000 | 4 |
| Hillside | A-155 | Kahn | 62 | 5 |
| Valleyview | A-408 | Kahn | 1123 | 6 |
| Valleyview | A-639 | Green | 750 | 7 |

Figure 18.4    The *deposit* relation of Figure 18.3 with tuple-ids.

[†]Although the highly normalized database design that we use elsewhere in this text can be vertically fragmented, such fragmentation is not particularly useful. Vertical fragmentation is more meaningful for a schema such as the one we use here.

| branch-name | customer-name | tuple-id |
|:---:|:---:|:---:|
| Hillside | Lowman | 1 |
| Hillside | Camp | 2 |
| Valleyview | Camp | 3 |
| Valleyview | Kahn | 4 |
| Hillside | Kahn | 5 |
| Valleyview | Kahn | 6 |
| Valleyview | Green | 7 |

$deposit_1$

| account-number | balance | tuple-id |
|:---:|:---:|:---:|
| A-305 | 500 | 1 |
| A-226 | 336 | 2 |
| A-177 | 205 | 3 |
| A-402 | 10000 | 4 |
| A-155 | 62 | 5 |
| A-408 | 1123 | 6 |
| A-639 | 750 | 7 |

$deposit_2$

Figure 18.5    Vertical fragmentation of relation *deposit*.

added. Figure 18.5 shows a vertical decomposition of the schema *Deposit-schema* $\cup$ {*tuple-id*} into

Deposit-schema-1 = (branch-name, customer-name, tuple-id)
Deposit-schema-2 = (account-number, balance, tuple-id)

The two relations shown in Figure 18.5 result from computing

$$deposit_1 = \Pi_{Deposit\text{-}schema\text{-}1} (deposit')$$
$$deposit_2 = \Pi_{Deposit\text{-}schema\text{-}2} (deposit')$$

To reconstruct the original *deposit* relation from the fragments, we compute

$$\Pi_{Deposit\text{-}schema} (deposit_1 \bowtie deposit_2)$$

Note that the expression

$$deposit_1 \bowtie deposit_2$$

is a special form of natural join. The join attribute is *tuple-id*. Although the *tuple-id* attribute facilitates the implementation of vertical partitioning, it must not be visible to users, since it is an internal artifact of the implementation, and violates data independence — which is one of the main virtues of the relational model.

### 18.1.2.3  Mixed Fragmentation

The relation $r$ is divided into a number of fragment relations $r_1$, $r_2$, ..., $r_n$. Each fragment is obtained as the result of application of either the horizontal-fragmentation or vertical-fragmentation scheme on relation $r$, or on a fragment of $r$ that was obtained previously.

As an illustration, suppose that the relation $r$ is the *deposit* relation of Figure 18.3. This relation is divided initially into the fragments $deposit_1$ and $deposit_2$, as defined previously. We can now further divide fragment $deposit_1$, using the horizontal-fragmentation scheme, into the following two fragments:

$$deposit_{1a} = \sigma_{branch\text{-}name\ =\ \text{``Hillside''}}\ (deposit_1)$$
$$deposit_{1b} = \sigma_{branch\text{-}name\ =\ \text{``Valleyview''}}\ (deposit_1)$$

Thus, relation $r$ is divided into three fragments: $deposit_{1a}$, $deposit_{1b}$, and $deposit_2$. Each of these fragments may reside in a different site.

### 18.1.3  Data Replication and Fragmentation

The techniques described in Sections 18.1.1 and 18.1.2 for data replication and data fragmentation can be applied successively to the same relation. That is, a fragment can be replicated, replicas of fragments can be fragmented further, and so on. For example, consider a distributed system consisting of sites $S_1$, $S_2$, ..., $S_{10}$. We can fragment *deposit* into $deposit_{1a}$, $deposit_{1b}$, and $deposit_2$, and, for example, store a copy of $deposit_{1a}$ at sites $S_1$, $S_3$, and $S_7$; a copy of $deposit_{1b}$ at sites $S_7$ and $S_{10}$; and a copy of $deposit_2$ at sites $S_2$, $S_8$, and $S_9$.

## 18.2  Network Transparency

In Section 18.1, we saw that a relation $r$ can be stored in a variety of ways in a distributed database system. It is essential that the system minimize the degree to which a user needs to be aware of how a relation is stored. As we shall see, a system can hide the details of the distribution of data in the network. We call this hiding *network transparency*, and define it as the degree to which system users can remain unaware of the details of how and where the data items are stored in a distributed system.

We shall consider the issues of transparency from the points of view of

- Naming of data items
- Replication of data items
- Fragmentation of data items
- Location of fragments and replicas

### 18.2.1  Naming of Data Items

Data items—such as relations, fragments, and replicas — must have unique names. This property is easy to ensure in a centralized database. In a distributed database, however, we must take care to ensure that two sites do not use the same name for distinct data items.

One solution to this problem is to require all names to be registered in a central *name server*. The name server helps to ensure that the same name does not get used for different data items. We can also use the name server to locate a data item, given the name of the item. This approach, however, suffers from two major disadvantages. First, the name server may become a performance bottleneck when data items are located via their names, resulting in poor performance. Second, if the name server crashes, it may not be possible for any site in the distributed system to continue to run.

An alternative approach is to require that each site prefix its own site identifier to any name that it generates. This approach ensures that no two sites generate the same name (since each site has a unique identifier). Furthermore, no central control is required. This solution, however, fails to achieve network transparency, since site identifiers are attached to names. Thus, the *account* relation might be referred to as *site17.account*, rather than as simply *account*.

To overcome this problem, the database system can create a set of alternative names or *aliases* for data items. A user may thus refer to data items by simple names that are translated by the system to complete names. The mapping of aliases to the real names can be stored at each site. With aliases, the user can be unaware of the physical location of a data item. Furthermore, the user will be unaffected if the database administrator decides to move a data item from one site to another.

Each replica of a data item and each fragment of a data item must also have a unique name. It is important that the system be able to determine those replicas that are replicas of the same data item and those fragments that are fragments of the same data item. We adopt the convention of postfixing ".*f1*", ".*f2*", ..., ".*fn*" to fragments of a data item, and ".*r1*", ".*r2*", ..., ".*rn*" to replicas. Thus

$$site17.account.f3.r2$$

refers to replica 2 of fragment 3 of *account*, and tells us that this item was generated by site 17.

It is undesirable to expect users to refer to a specific replica of a data item. Instead, the system should determine which replica to reference on a **read** request, and should update all replicas on a **write** request. We can ensure that it does so by maintaining a catalog table, which the system uses to determine all replicas for the data item.

Similarly, a user should not be required to know how a data item is fragmented. As we observed earlier, vertical fragments may contain *tuple-ids*. Horizontal fragments may involve complicated selection predicates. Therefore, a distributed database system should allow requests to be stated in terms of the unfragmented data items. This requirement presents no major difficulty, since it is always possible to reconstruct the original data item from its fragments. However, it may be inefficient to reconstruct data from fragments. Returning to our horizontal fragmentation of *account*, consider the query

$$\sigma_{branch\text{-}name\,=\,\text{"Hillside"}}\,(account)$$

**if** *name* appears in the alias table
    **then** *expression* := *map* (*name*)
    **else** *expression* := *name*;

**function** *map* (*n*)
    **if** *n* appears in the replica table
        **then** *result* := name of a replica of *n*;
    **if** *n* appears in the fragment table
        **then begin**
            *result* := expression to construct fragment;
            **for each** *n'* **in** *result* **do begin**
                replace *n'* in *result* with *map* (*n'*);
            **end**
        **end**
    **return** *result*;

Figure 18.6    Name-translation algorithm.

We could answer this query using only the $account_1$ fragment. However, fragmentation transparency requires that the user not be aware of the existence of fragments $account_1$ and $account_2$. If we reconstruct *account* prior to processing the query, we obtain the expression

$$\sigma_{branch\text{-}name = \text{"Hillside"}} (account_1 \cup account_2)$$

The optimization of this expression is left to the query optimizer (see Section 18.3).

Figure 18.6 shows the complete translation scheme for a given data-item name. To illustrate the operation of the scheme, we consider a user located in the Hillside branch (site $S_1$). This user uses the alias *local-account* for the local fragment *account.f1* of the *account* relation. When this user references *local-account*, the query-processing subsystem looks up *local-account* in the alias table, and replaces *local-account* with *S1.account.f1*. It is possible that *S1.account.f1* is replicated. If so, the system must consult the replica table in order to choose a replica. This replica could itself be fragmented, requiring examination of the fragmentation table. In most cases, only one or two tables must be consulted. However, the name-translation scheme of Figure 18.6 is sufficiently general to deal with any combination of successive replication and fragmentation of relations.

## 18.2.2    Transparency and Updates

Providing transparency for users that update the database is somewhat more difficult than is providing transparency for readers. The main problems are ensuring that all replicas of a data item are updated, and that all affected fragments are updated.

In its full generality, the update problem for replicated and fragmented data is related to the problem of view maintenance—that is, to the problem of keeping materialized views up-to-date when the database relations are updated (Section 3.7.1). Consider our example of the *account* relation, and the insertion of the tuple

$$(\text{"Valleyview"}, A\text{-}733, 600)$$

If *account* is fragmented horizontally, there is a predicate $P_i$ associated with the $i$th fragment. We apply $P_i$ to the tuple ("Valleyview", A-733, 600) to test whether that tuple must be inserted in the $i$th fragment. Using our example of *account* being fragmented into

$$account_1 = \sigma_{branch\text{-}name = \text{"Hillside"}} (account)$$
$$account_2 = \sigma_{branch\text{-}name = \text{"Valleyview"}} (account)$$

the tuple would be inserted into $account_2$.

Now consider a vertical fragmentation of deposit into $deposit_1$ and $deposit_2$. The tuple ("Valleyview", A-733, "Jones", 600) must be split into two fragments: one to be inserted into $deposit_1$, and one to be inserted into $deposit_2$.

If an update is made to a replicated relation, the update must be applied to all replicas. This requirement presents a problem if there is concurrent access to the relation, since it is possible that one replica will be updated earlier than another. We consider this problem in Section 18.7.

# 18.3    Distributed Query Processing

In Chapter 12, we saw that there is a variety of methods for computing the answer to a query. We examined several techniques for choosing a strategy for processing a query that minimize the amount of time that it takes to compute the answer. For centralized systems, the primary criterion for measuring the cost of a particular strategy is the number of disk accesses. In a distributed system, we must take into account several other matters, including

- The cost of data transmission over the network
- The potential gain in performance from having several sites process parts of the query in parallel

The relative cost of data transfer over the network and data transfer to and from disk varies widely depending on the type of network and on the speed of the disks. Thus, in general, we cannot focus solely on disk costs or on network costs. Rather, we must find a good tradeoff between the two.

## 18.3.1    Query Transformation

Let us consider an extremely simple query: "Find all the tuples in the *account* relation." Although the query is simple — indeed, trivial—processing of this query is not trivial, since the *account* relation may be fragmented, replicated, or both, as we saw in Section 18.1. If the *account* relation is replicated, we have a choice of replica to make. If no replicas are fragmented, we choose the replica for which the transmission cost is lowest. However, if a replica is fragmented, the choice is not so easy to make, since we need to compute several joins or unions to reconstruct the *account* relation. In this case, the number of strategies for our simple example may be large. Query optimization by exhaustive enumeration of all alternative strategies may not be practical in such situations.

Fragmentation transparency implies that a user may write a query such as

$$\sigma_{branch\text{-}name\,=\,\text{"Hillside"}}\,(account)$$

Since *account* is defined as

$$account_1 \;\cup\; account_2$$

the expression that results from the name translation scheme is

$$\sigma_{branch\text{-}name\,=\,\text{"Hillside"}}\,(account_1 \;\cup\; account_2)$$

Using the query-optimization techniques of Chapter 12, we can simplify the preceding expression automatically. The result is the expression

$$\sigma_{branch\text{-}name\,=\,\text{"Hillside"}}\,(account_1) \;\cup\; \sigma_{branch\text{-}name\,=\,\text{"Hillside"}}\,(account_2)$$

which includes two subexpressions. The first involves only $account_1$, and thus can be evaluated at the Hillside site. The second involves only $account_2$, and thus can be evaluated at the Valleyview site.

There is a further optimization that can be made in evaluating

$$\sigma_{branch\text{-}name\,=\,\text{"Hillside"}}\,(account_1)$$

Since $account_1$ has only tuples pertaining to the Hillside branch, we can eliminate the selection operation. In evaluating

$$\sigma_{branch\text{-}name\,=\,\text{"Hillside"}}\,(account_2)$$

we can apply the definition of the $account_2$ fragment to obtain

$$\sigma_{branch\text{-}name\,=\,\text{"Hillside"}}\,(\sigma_{branch\text{-}name\,=\,\text{"Valleyview"}}\,(account))$$

This expression is the empty set, regardless of the contents of the *account* relation.

Thus, our final strategy is for the Hillside site to return $account_1$ as the result of the query.

## 18.3.2 Simple Join Processing

As we saw in Chapter 12, a major aspect of the selection of a query-processing strategy is choosing a join strategy. Consider the following relational-algebra expression:

$$account \bowtie depositor \bowtie branch$$

Assume that the three relations are neither replicated nor fragmented, and that *account* is stored at site $S_1$, *depositor* at $S_2$, and *branch* at $S_3$. Let $S_I$ denote the site at which the query was issued. The system needs to produce the result at site $S_I$. Among the possible strategies for processing this query are the following:

- Ship copies of all three relations to site $S_I$. Using the techniques of Chapter 12, choose a strategy for processing the entire query locally at site $S_I$.
- Ship a copy of the *account* relation to site $S_2$, and compute $temp_1 = account \bowtie depositor$ at $S_2$. Ship $temp_1$ from $S_2$ to $S_3$, and compute $temp_2 = temp_1 \bowtie branch$ at $S_3$. Ship the result $temp_2$ to $S_I$.
- Devise strategies similar to the previous one, with the roles of $S_1$, $S_2$, $S_3$ exchanged.

No one strategy is always the best one. Among the factors that must be considered are the volume of data being shipped, the cost of transmitting a block of data between a pair of sites, and the relative speed of processing at each site. Consider the first two strategies listed. If we ship all three relations to $S_I$, and indices exist on these relations, we may need to recreate these indices at $S_I$. This recreation of indices entails extra processing overhead and extra disk accesses. However, the second strategy has the disadvantage that a potentially large relation (*customer* $\bowtie$ *account*) must be shipped from $S_2$ to $S_3$. This relation repeats the address data for a customer once for each account that the customer has. Thus, the second strategy may result in extra network transmission, as compared with the first strategy.

### 18.3.3  Semijoin Strategy

Suppose that we wish to evaluate the expression $r_1 \bowtie r_2$, where $r_1$ and $r_2$ are stored at sites $S_1$ and $S_2$, respectively. Let the schemas of $r_1$ and $r_2$ be $R_1$ and $R_2$. Suppose that we wish to obtain the result at $S_1$. If there are many tuples of $r_2$ that do not join with any tuple of $r_1$, then shipping $r_2$ to $S_1$ entails shipping tuples that fail to contribute to the result. It is desirable to remove such tuples before shipping data to $S_1$, particularly if network costs are high.

A strategy can be implemented as follows:

**1.** Compute $temp_1 \leftarrow \Pi_{R_1 \cap R_2} (r_1)$ at $S_1$.
**2.** Ship $temp_1$ from $S_1$ to $S_2$.
**3.** Compute $temp_2 \leftarrow r_2 \bowtie temp_1$ at $S_2$.
**4.** Ship $temp_2$ from $S_2$ to $S_1$.
**5.** Compute $r_1 \bowtie temp_2$ at $S_1$. The resulting relation is the same as $r_1 \bowtie r_2$.

Before considering the efficiency of this strategy, let us verify that the strategy computes the correct answer. In step 3, $temp_2$ has the result of $r_2 \bowtie \Pi_{R_1 \cap R_2} (r_1)$. In step 5, we compute

$$r_1 \bowtie r_2 \bowtie \Pi_{R_1 \cap R_2} (r_1)$$

Since join is associative and commutative, we can rewrite this expression as

$$(r_1 \bowtie \Pi_{R_1 \cap R_2} (r_1)) \bowtie r_2$$

Since $r_1 \bowtie \Pi_{(R_1 \cap R_2)} (r_1) = r_1$, the expression is, indeed, equal to $r_1 \bowtie r_2$.

This strategy is particularly advantageous when relatively few tuples of $r_2$ contribute to the join. This situation is likely to occur if $r_1$ is the result of a relational-algebra expression involving selection. In such a case, $temp_2$ may have significantly fewer tuples than $r_2$. The cost savings of the strategy result from having to ship only $temp_2$, rather than all of $r_2$, to $S_1$. Additional cost is incurred in shipping $temp_1$ to $S_2$. If a sufficiently small fraction of tuples in $r_2$ contribute to the join, the overhead of shipping $temp_1$ will be dominated by the savings of shipping only a fraction of the tuples in $r_2$.

This strategy is called a *semijoin strategy*, after the semijoin operator of the relational algebra, denoted $\ltimes$. The semijoin of $r_1$ with $r_2$, denoted $r_1 \ltimes r_2$, is

$$\Pi_{R_1}(r_1 \bowtie r_2)$$

Thus, $r_1 \ltimes r_2$ selects those tuples of $r_1$ that contributed to $r_1 \bowtie r_2$. In step 3, $temp_2 = r_2 \ltimes r_1$.

For joins of several relations, this strategy can be extended to a series of semijoin steps. A substantial body of theory has been developed regarding the use of semijoins for query optimization. Some of this theory is referenced in the bibliographic notes.

### 18.3.4   Join Strategies that Exploit Parallelism

Implementing intraoperation parallelism by redistributing tuples is generally not considered viable in a distributed system, due to the small degree of parallelism and the high cost of communication. However, interoperation parallelism, including pipelined parallelism and independent parallelism (Section 17.6), can be useful in a distributed system.

For example, consider a join of four relations:

$$r_1 \bowtie r_2 \bowtie r_3 \bowtie r_4$$

where relation $r_i$ is stored at site $S_i$. Assume that the result must be presented at site $S_1$. There are many possible strategies for parallel evaluation; for example, any of the strategies described in Section 17.6 may be used. In one such strategy, $r_1$ is shipped to $S_2$, and $r_1 \bowtie r_2$ computed at $S_2$. At the same time, $r_3$ is shipped to $S_4$, and $r_3 \bowtie r_4$ computed at $S_4$. Site $S_2$ can ship tuples of $(r_1 \bowtie r_2)$ to $S_1$ as they are produced, rather than waiting for the entire join to be computed. Similarly, $S_4$ can ship tuples of $(r_3 \bowtie r_4)$ to $S_1$. Once tuples of $(r_1 \bowtie r_2)$ and $(r_3 \bowtie r_4)$ arrive at $S_1$, the computation of $(r_1 \bowtie r_2) \bowtie (r_3 \bowtie r_4)$ can begin, with the pipelined join technique of Section 12.8.2.2. Thus, computation of the final join result at $S_1$ can be done in parallel with the computation of $(r_1 \bowtie r_2)$ at $S_2$, and with the computation of $(r_3 \bowtie r_4)$ at $S_4$.

## 18.4   Distributed Transaction Model

Access to the various data items in a distributed system is usually accomplished through transactions, which must preserve the ACID properties (Section 13.1). There are two types of transaction that we need to consider. The *local* transactions are those that access and update data in only one local database; the *global* transactions are those that access and update data in several local databases. Ensuring the ACID properties of the local transactions can be done in a manner similar to that discussed in Chapters 13, 14, and 15. However, in the case of global transactions, this task is much more complicated, since several sites may be participating in execution. The failure of one of these sites, or the failure of a communication link connecting these sites, may result in erroneous computations.

## 18.4.1    System Structure

Each site has its own *local transaction manager*, whose function is to ensure the ACID properties of those transactions that execute at that site. The various transaction managers cooperate to execute global transactions. To understand how such a manager can be implemented, we define an abstract model of a transaction system. Each site of the system contains two subsystems:

- The **transaction manager** manages the execution of those transactions (or subtransactions) that access data stored in a local site. Note that each such transaction may be either a local transaction (that is, a transaction that executes at only that site) or part of a global transaction (that is, a transaction that executes at several sites).

- The **transaction coordinator** coordinates the execution of the various transactions (both local and global) initiated at that site.

The overall system architecture is depicted in Figure 18.7.

The structure of a transaction manager is similar in many respects to the structure used in the centralized-system case. Each transaction manager is responsible for

- Maintaining a log for recovery purposes
- Participating in an appropriate concurrency-control scheme to coordinate the concurrent execution of the transactions executing at that site

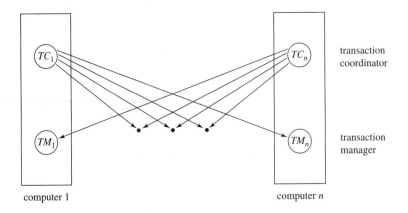

**Figure 18.7    System architecture.**

As we shall see, we need to modify both the recovery and concurrency schemes to accommodate the distribution of transactions.

The transaction coordinator subsystem is not needed in the centralized environment, since a transaction accesses data at only a single site. A transaction coordinator, as its name implies, is responsible for coordinating the execution of all the transactions initiated at that site. For each such transaction, the coordinator is responsible for

- Starting the execution of the transaction
- Breaking the transaction into a number of subtransactions, and distributing these subtransactions to the appropriate sites for execution
- Coordinating the termination of the transaction, which may result in the transaction being committed at all sites or aborted at all sites

## 18.4.2   System Failure Modes

A distributed system may suffer from the same types of failure that a centralized system does (for example, software errors, hardware errors, or disk crashes). There are, however, additional types of failure with which we need to deal in a distributed environment. The basic failure types are

- Failure of a site
- Loss of messages
- Failure of a communication link
- Network partition

The loss or corruption of messages is always a possibility in a distributed system. The system uses transmission-control protocols, such as TCP/IP, to handle such errors. Information about such protocols may be found in standard textbooks on networking (see the bibliographic notes).

To understand the effect of failures of communication links, and of network partition, we must first understand how sites in a distributed system are interconnected. The sites in the system can be connected physically in a variety of ways. Some of the most common configurations are depicted in Figure 18.8.

Each configuration has advantages and disadvantages. The configurations can be compared with one another, based on the following criteria:

- **Installation cost**. The cost of physically linking the sites in the system
- **Communication cost**. The cost in time and money to send a message from site $A$ to site $B$
- **Availability**. The degree to which data can be accessed despite the failure of some links or sites

The various topologies are depicted in Figure 18.8 as graphs whose nodes correspond to sites. An edge from node $A$ to node $B$ corresponds to a direct

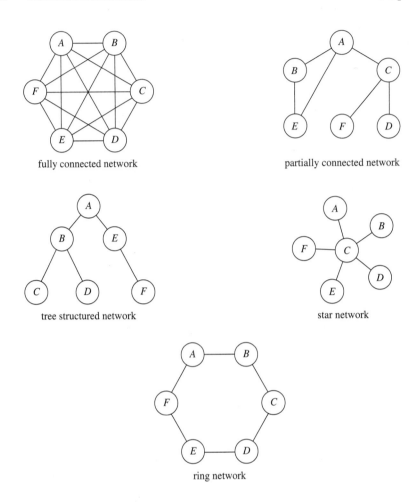

Figure 18.8   Network topology.

communication link between the two sites. In a fully connected network, each site is directly connected to every other site. However, the number of links grows as the square of the number of sites, resulting in a huge installation cost. Therefore, fully connected networks are impractical in any large system.

In a *partially connected network*, direct links exist between some—but not all—pairs of sites. Hence, the installation cost of such a configuration is lower than that of the fully connected network. However, if two sites A and B are not directly connected, messages from one to the other must be *routed* through a sequence of communication links. This requirement results in a higher communication cost.

If a communication link fails, messages that would have been transmitted across the link must be rerouted. In some cases, it is possible to find another route through the network, so that the messages are able to reach their destination. In other cases, a failure may result in there being no connection between some pairs of sites. A system is *partitioned* if it has been split into two (or more) subsystems, called *partitions*, that lack any connection between them. Note that, under this definition, a subsystem may consist of a single node.

The different partially connected network types shown in Figure 18.8 have different failure characteristics and installation and communication costs. Installation and communication costs are relatively low for a tree-structured network. However, the failure of a single link in a tree-structured network can result in the network becoming partitioned. In a ring network, at least two links must fail for partition to occur. Thus, the ring network has a higher degree of availability than does a tree structured network. However, the communication cost is high, since a message may have to cross a large number of links. In a star network, the failure of a single link results in a network partition, but one of the partitions has only a single site. Such a partition can be treated as a single-site failure. The star network also has a low communication cost, since each site is at most two links away from every other site. However, the failure of the central site results in every site in the system becoming disconnected.

### 18.4.3   Robustness

For a distributed system to be robust, it must *detect* failures, *reconfigure* the system so that computation may continue, and *recover* when a processor or a link is repaired.

The different types of failures are handled in different ways. Message loss is handled by retransmission. Repeated retransmission of a message across a link, without receipt of an acknowledgment, is usually a symptom of a link failure. The network usually attempts to find an alternative route for the message. Failure to find such a route is usually a symptom of network partition.

It is generally not possible, however, to differentiate clearly between site failure and network partition. The system can usually detect that a failure has occurred, but it may not be able to identify the type of failure. For example, suppose that site $S_1$ is not able to communicate with $S_2$. It could be that $S_2$ has failed. However, another possibility is that the link between $S_1$ and $S_2$ has failed, resulting in network partition.

Suppose that site $S_1$ has discovered that a failure has occurred. It must then initiate a procedure that will allow the system to reconfigure, and to continue with the normal mode of operation.

- If replicated data are stored at the failed site, the catalog should be updated so that queries do not reference the copy at the failed site.
- If transactions were active at the failed site at the time of the failure, these transactions should be aborted. It is desirable to abort such transactions promptly, since they may hold locks on data at sites that are still active.
- If the failed site is a central server for some subsystem, an *election* must be held to determine the new server (see Section 18.6.2). Examples of central servers include a name server, a concurrency coordinator, or a global deadlock detector.

Since it is, in general, not possible to distinguish between network link failures and site failures, any reconfiguration scheme must be designed to work correctly in case of a partitioning of the network. In particular, the following situations must be avoided:

- Two or more central servers are elected in distinct partitions.
- More than one partition updates a replicated data item.

Reintegration of a repaired site or link into the system also requires care. When a failed site recovers, it must initiate a procedure to update its system tables to reflect changes made while it was down. If the site had replicas of any data items, it must obtain the current values of these data items and ensure that it receives all future updates. Reintegration of a site is more complicated than it may seem to be at first glance, since there may be updates to the data items processed during the time that the site is recovering. An easy solution is temporarily to halt the entire system while the failed site rejoins it. In most applications, however, such a temporary halt is unacceptably disruptive. Techniques have been developed to allow failed sites to reintegrate while allowing concurrent updates to data items. If a failed link recovers, two or more partitions can be rejoined. Since a partitioning of the network limits the allowable operations by some or all sites, it is desirable to inform all sites promptly of the recovery of the link. See the bibliographic notes for more information on recovery in distributed systems.

## 18.5   Commit Protocols

If we are to ensure atomicity, all the sites in which a transaction $T$ executed must agree on the final outcome of the execution. $T$ must either commit at all sites, or it must abort at all sites. To ensure this property, the transaction coordinator of $T$ must execute a *commit protocol*.

Among the simplest and most widely used commit protocols is the *two-phase commit* protocol (2PC), which is described in Section 18.5.1. An alternative is the *three-phase commit* protocol (3PC), which avoids certain disadvantages of the 2PC protocol but adds to complexity and overhead. The 3PC protocol is described in Section 18.5.2.

### 18.5.1   Two-Phase Commit

Let $T$ be a transaction initiated at site $S_i$, and let the transaction coordinator at $S_i$ be $C_i$.

#### 18.5.1.1   The Commit Protocol

When $T$ completes its execution—that is, when all the sites at which $T$ has executed inform $C_i$ that $T$ has completed—$C_i$ starts the 2PC protocol.

- **Phase 1**. $C_i$ adds the record <**prepare** $T$> to the log, and forces the log onto stable storage. It then sends a **prepare** $T$ message to all sites at which

*T* executed. On receiving such a message, the transaction manager at that site determines whether it is willing to commit its portion of *T*. If the answer is no, it adds a record <**no** *T*> to the log, and then responds by sending an **abort** *T* message to $C_i$. If the answer is yes, it adds a record <**ready** *T*> to the log, and forces the log (with all the log records corresponding to *T*) onto stable storage. The transaction manager then replies with a **ready** *T* message to $C_i$.

- **Phase 2**. When $C_i$ receives responses to the **prepare** *T* message from all the sites, or when a prespecified interval of time has elapsed since the **prepare** *T* message was sent out, $C_i$ can determine whether the transaction *T* can be committed or aborted. Transaction *T* can be committed if $C_i$ received a **ready** *T* message from all the participating sites. Otherwise, transaction *T* must be aborted. Depending on the verdict, either a record <**commit** *T*> or a record <**abort** *T*> is added to the log and the log is forced onto stable storage. At this point, the fate of the transaction has been sealed. Following this point, the coordinator sends either a **commit** *T* or an **abort** *T* message to all participating sites. When a site receives that message, it records the message in the log.

A site at which *T* executed can unconditionally abort *T* at any time prior to its sending the message **ready** *T* to the coordinator. The **ready** *T* message is, in effect, a promise by a site to follow the coordinator's order to commit *T* or to abort *T*. The only means by which a site can make such a promise is if the needed information is stored in stable storage. Otherwise, if the site crashes after sending **ready** *T*, it may be unable to make good on its promise.

Since unanimity is required to commit a transaction, the fate of *T* is sealed as soon as at least one site responds **abort** *T*. Since the coordinator site $S_i$ is one of the sites at which *T* executed, the coordinator can decide unilaterally to abort *T*. The final verdict regarding *T* is determined at the time that the coordinator writes that verdict (commit or abort) to the log and forces that verdict to stable storage. In some implementations of the 2PC protocol, a site sends an **acknowledge** *T* message to the coordinator at the end of the second phase of the protocol. When the coordinator receives the **acknowledge** *T* message from all the sites, it adds the record <**complete** *T*> to the log.

### 18.5.1.2   Handling of Failures

We now examine in detail how the 2PC protocol responds to various types of failures.

- **Failure of a participating site**. If the coordinator $C_i$ detects that a site has failed, it takes the following actions. If the site fails before responding with a **ready** *T* message to $C_i$, it is assumed to have responded with an **abort** *T* message. If the site fails after the coordinator has received the **ready** *T* message from the site, the rest of the commit protocol is executed in the normal fashion, ignoring the failure of the site.

  When a participating site $S_k$ recovers from a failure, it must examine its log to determine the fate of those transactions that were in the midst of execution when the failure occurred. Let $T$ be one such transaction. We consider each of the possible cases:

- The log contains a <**commit** $T$> record. In this case, the site executes **redo**($T$).
- The log contains an <**abort** $T$> record. In this case, the site executes **undo**($T$).
- The log contains a <**ready** $T$> record. In this case, the site must consult $C_i$ to determine the fate of $T$. If $C_i$ is up, it notifies $S_k$ regarding whether $T$ committed or aborted. In the former case, it executes **redo**($T$); in the latter case, it executes **undo**($T$). If $C_i$ is down, $S_k$ must try to find the fate of $T$ from other sites. It does so by sending a **query-status** $T$ message to all the sites in the system. On receiving such a message, a site must consult its log to determine whether $T$ has executed there, and if $T$ has, whether $T$ committed or aborted. It then notifies $S_k$ about this outcome. If no site has the appropriate information (that is, whether $T$ committed or aborted), then $S_k$ can neither abort nor commit $T$. The decision concerning $T$ is postponed until $S_k$ can obtain the needed information. Thus, $S_k$ must periodically resend the **query-status** message to the other sites. It continues to do so until a site recovers that contains the needed information. Note that the site at which $C_i$ resides always has the needed information.
- The log contains no control records (**abort, commit, ready**) concerning $T$. Thus, we know that $S_k$ failed before responding to the **prepare** $T$ message from $C_i$. Since the failure of $S_k$ precludes the sending of such a response, by our algorithm $C_i$ must abort $T$. Hence, $S_k$ must execute **undo**($T$).

- **Failure of the coordinator**. If the coordinator fails in the midst of the execution of the commit protocol for transaction $T$, then the participating sites must decide the fate of $T$. We shall see that, in certain cases, the participating sites cannot decide whether to commit or abort $T$, and therefore these sites must wait for the recovery of the failed coordinator.
  - If an active site contains a <**commit** $T$> record in its log, then $T$ must be committed.
  - If an active site contains an <**abort** $T$> record in its log, then $T$ must be aborted.
  - If some active site does *not* contain a <**ready** $T$> record in its log, then the failed coordinator $C_i$ cannot have decided to commit $T$, because a site that does not have a <**ready** $T$> record in its log cannot have sent a **ready** $T$ message to $C_i$. However, the coordinator may have decided to abort $T$, but not to commit $T$. Rather than wait for $C_i$ to recover, it is preferable to abort $T$.
  - If none of the preceding cases holds, then all active sites must have a <**ready** $T$> record in their logs, but no additional control records (such as <**abort** $T$> or <**commit** $T$>). Since the coordinator has failed, it is impossible to determine whether a decision has been made, and if one has, what that decision is, until the coordinator recovers. Thus, the active sites must wait for $C_i$ to recover. Since the fate of $T$ remains in doubt, $T$ may

continue to hold system resources. For example, if locking is used, $T$ may hold locks on data at active sites. Such a situation is undesirable, because it may be hours or days before $C_i$ is again active. During this time, other transactions may be forced to wait for $T$. As a result, data items may be unavailable not only on the failed site ($C_i$), but on active sites as well. This situation is called the *blocking* problem, because $T$ is blocked pending the recovery of site $C_i$.

- **Network partition**. When a network partitions, two possibilities exist:
    1. The coordinator and all its participants remain in one partition. In this case, the failure has no effect on the commit protocol.
    2. The coordinator and its participants belong to several partitions. From the viewpoint of the sites in one of the partitions, it appears that the sites in other partitions have failed. Sites that are not in the partition containing the coordinator simply execute the protocol to deal with failure of the coordinator. The coordinator and the sites that are in the same partition as the coordinator follow the usual commit protocol, assuming that the sites in the other partitions have failed.

Thus, the major disadvantage of the 2PC protocol is that coordinator failure may result in blocking, where a decision either to commit or to abort $T$ may have to be postponed until $C_i$ recovers.

### 18.5.1.3   Recovery and Concurrency Control

When a failed site restarts, we can perform recovery using, for example, the recovery algorithm described in Section 15.9. To deal with distributed commit protocols (such as 2PC and 3PC), the recovery procedure must treat *in-doubt* transactions specially; in-doubt transactions are transactions for which a <**ready** $T$> log record is found, but neither a <**commit** $T$> log record, nor an <**abort** $T$> log record, is found. The recovering site must determine the commit–abort status of such transactions by contacting other sites, as described in Section 18.5.1.2.

If recovery is done as just described, however, normal transaction processing at the site cannot begin until all in-doubt transactions have been committed or rolled back. Finding the status of in-doubt transactions can be slow, since multiple sites may have to be contacted. Further, if the coordinator has failed, and no other site has information about the commit–abort status of an incomplete transaction, recovery potentially could become blocked if 2PC is used. As a result, the site performing restart recovery may remain unusable for a long period.

To circumvent this problem, recovery algorithms typically provide support for noting lock information in the log. (We are assuming here that locking is used for concurrency control.) Instead of a <**ready** $T$> log record being written, a <**ready** $T, L$> log record is written out, where $L$ is a list of all locks held by the transaction $T$ when the log record is written. At recovery time, after performance of local recovery actions, for every in-doubt transaction $T$, all the locks noted in the <**ready** $T, L$> log record (read from the log) are reacquired.

After lock reacquisition is complete for all in-doubt transactions, transaction processing can start at the site, even before the commit–abort status of the in-doubt transactions is determined. The commit or rollback of in-doubt transactions is performed concurrently with the execution of new transactions. Thus, site recovery is faster, and never gets blocked. Note that new transactions that have a lock conflict with any in-doubt transactions will be unable to make progress until the conflicting in-doubt transactions have been committed or rolled back.

## 18.5.2    Three-Phase Commit

The 3PC protocol is designed to avoid the possibility of blocking in a restricted case of possible failures. The version of the 3PC protocol that we describe requires that

- No network partition can occur.
- At most $K$ participating sites can fail while the 3PC protocol is being executed for a transaction. $K$ is a parameter indicating the resiliency of the protocol to site failures.
- At any point, at least $K + 1$ sites must be up.

The protocol achieves the nonblocking property by adding an extra phase in which a preliminary decision is reached regarding the fate of $T$. The information made available to the participating sites as a result of this preliminary decision allows a decision to be made despite the failure of the coordinator.

### 18.5.2.1    The Commit Protocol

As before, let $T$ be a transaction initiated at site $S_i$, and let the transaction coordinator at $S_i$ be $C_i$.

- **Phase 1**. This phase is identical to phase 1 of the 2PC protocol.
- **Phase 2**. If $C_i$ receives an **abort** $T$ message from a participating site, or if $C_i$ receives no response within a prespecified interval from a participating site, then $C_i$ decides to abort $T$. The abort decision is implemented in the same way as is the 2PC protocol. If $C_i$ receives a **ready** $T$ message from every participating site, $C_i$ makes the preliminary decision to *precommit T*. Precommit differs from commit in that $T$ may still be aborted eventually. The precommit decision allows the coordinator to inform each participating site that all participating sites are ready. $C_i$ adds a record <**precommit** $T$> to the log and forces the log onto stable storage. Then, $C_i$ sends a **precommit** $T$ message to all participating sites. When a site receives a message from the coordinator (either **abort** $T$ or **precommit** $T$), it records that message in its log, forces this information to stable storage, and sends a message **acknowledge** $T$ to the coordinator.
- **Phase 3**. This phase is executed only if the decision in phase 2 was to precommit. After the **precommit** $T$ messages are sent to all participating sites, the coordinator must wait until it receives at least $K$ **acknowledge** $T$ messages. Then, the coordinator reaches a commit decision. It adds a <**commit** $T$>

record to its log, and forces the log to stable storage. Then, $C_i$ sends a **commit** $T$ message to all participating sites. When a site receives that message, it records the information in its log.

Just as in the 2PC protocol, a site at which $T$ executed can unconditionally abort $T$ at any time prior to sending the message **ready** $T$ to the coordinator. The **ready** $T$ message is, in effect, a promise by a site to follow the coordinator's order to commit $T$ or to abort $T$. In contrast to the 2PC protocol, in which the coordinator can unconditionally abort $T$ at any time prior to sending the message **commit** $T$, the **precommit** $T$ message in the 3PC protocol is a promise by the coordinator to follow the participant's order to commit $T$.

Since phase 3 always leads to a commit decision, it may seem to be of little use. The role of the third phase becomes apparent when we look at how the 3PC protocol handles failures.

In some implementations of the 3PC protocol, a site sends a message **ack** $T$ to the coordinator upon receipt of the **commit** $T$ message. (Note the use of **ack** to distinguish this term from the **acknowledge** messages that were used in phase 2.) When the coordinator receives the **ack** $T$ message from all sites, it adds the record <**complete** $T$> to the log.

### 18.5.2.2 Handling of Failures

We now examine in detail how the 3PC protocol responds to various types of failures.

- **Failure of a participating site**. If the coordinator $C_i$ detects that a site has failed, the actions that it takes are similar to the actions taken in 2PC. If the site fails before responding with a **ready** $T$ message to $C_i$, it is assumed to have responded with an **abort** $T$ message. Otherwise, the rest of the commit protocol is executed in the normal fashion, ignoring the failure of the site.

   When a participating site $S_j$ recovers from a failure, it must examine its log to determine the fate of those transactions that were in the midst of execution when the failure occurred. Let $T$ be one such transaction. We consider each of the possible cases:
   ○ The log contains a <**commit** $T$> record. In this case, the site executes **redo**($T$).
   ○ The log contains an <**abort** $T$> record. In this case, the site executes **undo**($T$).
   ○ The log contains a <**ready** $T$> record, but no <**abort** $T$> or <**precommit** $T$> record. In this case, the site attempts to consult $C_i$ to determine the fate of $T$. If $C_i$ responds with a message that $T$ aborted, the site executes **undo**($T$). If $C_i$ responds with a message **precommit** $T$, the site (as in phase 2) records this information in its log, and resumes the protocol by sending an **acknowledge** $T$ message to the coordinator. If $C_i$ responds with a message that $T$ committed, the site executes **redo**($T$). In the event that $C_i$ fails to respond within a prespecified interval, the site executes a coordinator failure protocol (see next list entry).

○ The log contains a <**precommit** $T$> record, but no <**abort** $T$> or <**commit** $T$> record. As before, the site consults $C_i$. If $C_i$ responds that $T$ aborted or committed, the site executes **undo**($T$) or **redo**($T$), respectively. If $C_i$ responds that $T$ is still in the precommit state, the site resumes the protocol at this point. If $C_i$ fails to respond within a prescribed interval, the site finds the new coordinator (waiting for one to be selected, if required) and consults the new coordinator as before.

- **Failure of the coordinator**. When a participating site fails to receive a response from the coordinator, for whatever reason, it executes the *coordinator-failure protocol*. This protocol results in the selection of a new coordinator. When the failed coordinator recovers, it does so in the role of a participating site. It no longer acts as coordinator; rather, it must determine the decision that has been reached by the new coordinator.

### 18.5.2.3   Coordinator-Failure Protocol

The coordinator-failure protocol is triggered by a participating site that fails to receive a response from the coordinator within a prespecified interval. Since we assume no network partition, the only possible cause for this situation is the failure of the coordinator.

1. The active participating sites select a new coordinator using an election protocol (see Section 18.6).
2. The new coordinator, $C_{new}$, sends a message to each participating site requesting the local status of $T$.
3. Each participating site, including $C_{new}$, determines the local status of $T$:
   - **Committed**. The log contains a <**commit** $T$> record.
   - **Aborted**. The log contains an <**abort** $T$> record.
   - **Ready**. The log contains a <**ready** $T$> record, but contains no <**abort** $T$> or <**precommit** $T$> record.
   - **Precommitted**. The log contains a <**precommit** $T$> record, but contains no <**abort** $T$> or <**commit** $T$> record.
   - **Not ready**. The log contains neither a <**ready** $T$> nor an <**abort** $T$> record.

   Each participating site sends its local status to $C_{new}$.
4. Depending on the responses received, $C_{new}$ decides either to commit or abort $T$, or to restart the 3PC protocol:
   - If at least one site has local status = **committed**, then $C_{new}$ commits $T$.
   - If at least one site has local status = **aborted**, then $C_{new}$ aborts $T$. (Note that it is not possible for some site to have local status = **committed** while another has local status = **aborted**.)
   - If no site has local status = **aborted**, and no site has local status = **committed**, but at least one site has local status = **precommitted**, then $C_{new}$ resumes the 3PC protocol by sending new **precommit** messages.
   - Otherwise, $C_{new}$ aborts $T$.

The coordinator-failure protocol allows the new coordinator to obtain knowledge about the state of the failed coordinator, $C_i$.

If any active site has a <**commit** $T$> in its log, then $C_i$ must have decided to commit $T$. If an active site responds saying it has <**precommit** $T$> in its log, then $C_i$ must have reached a preliminary decision to precommit $T$, and that means that all sites, including any that may have failed, have reached **ready** states. Further, the transaction could not have been aborted, since any earlier coordinator (which later failed) would have found the active site in precommit state, and resumed the 3PC protocol to commit the transaction. It is therefore safe to commit $T$. However, $C_{\text{new}}$ does not commit $T$ unilaterally; doing so would create the same blocking problem, if $C_{\text{new}}$ fails, as in 2PC. It is for this reason that phase 3 is resumed by $C_{\text{new}}$.

Consider the case where no active site has received a precommit message from $C_i$. We must consider three possibilities:

1. $C_i$ had decided to commit $T$ prior to $C_i$ failing.
2. $C_i$ had decided to abort $T$ prior to $C_i$ failing.
3. $C_i$ had not yet decided the fate of $T$.

We shall show that the first of these alternatives is not possible, and that, therefore, it is safe to abort $T$.

Suppose that $C_i$ had decided to commit $T$. Then, at least $K$ sites must have decided to precommit $T$ and have sent acknowledge messages to $C_i$. Since $C_i$ has failed, and we assume that at most $K$ sites (including the coordinator) fail while the 3PC protocol is executed for a transaction, at least one of the $K$ sites that sent the acknowledge message must be active. Hence at least one active site would inform $C_{\text{new}}$ that it has received a precommit message. Thus, if no active site had received a precommit message, a commit decision certainly could not have been reached by $C_i$. Therefore, it is indeed safe to abort $T$. It is possible that $C_i$ had not decided to abort $T$, so it may still be possible to commit $T$. However, detecting that $C_i$ had not decided to abort $T$ would require waiting for $C_i$ (or for some other failed site that had received a precommit message) to recover. Hence, the protocol aborts $T$ if no active site has received a precommit message.

In the preceding discussion, if more than $K$ sites could fail while the 3PC protocol is executed for a transaction, it may not be possible for the surviving participants to determine the action taken by $C_i$ prior to failing; this situation would force blocking to occur until $C_i$ recovers. Although a large value for $K$ is best from this standpoint, it forces a coordinator to wait for more responses before deciding to commit—thus delaying routine (failure-free) processing. Further, if fewer than $K$ participants (in addition to the coordinator) are active, it may not be possible for the coordinator to complete the commit protocol, resulting in blocking. Thus, the choice of a value for $K$ is crucial, as it determines the degree to which the protocol avoids blocking.

Our assumption of no network partitions is crucial to our discussion. As mentioned earlier, it is, in general, impossible to differentiate between network failure and site failure. Thus, network partitioning could lead to the election of two new coordinators (each of which believes that all sites in partitions other than its own have failed). The decisions of the two coordinators may not agree, resulting in the transaction being committed in some sites while being aborted in others.

### 18.5.3  Comparison of Protocols

The 2PC protocol is widely used, despite its potential for blocking. The probability of blocking occurring in practice is usually sufficiently low that the extra cost of the 3PC protocol is not justified. The vulnerability of 3PC to link failures is another practical issue. This disadvantage can be overcome by network-level protocols, but that solution adds overhead.

We can streamline both protocols to reduce the number of messages sent, and to reduce the number of times that records must be forced to stable storage. The 3PC protocol can be extended to allow more than $K$ failures, provided that not more than $K$ sites fail before the new coordinator makes a commit decision. The bibliographic notes contain references to several such techniques.

## 18.6  Coordinator Selection

Several of the algorithms that we have presented require the use of a coordinator. If the coordinator fails because of a failure of the site at which it resides, the system can continue execution only by restarting a new coordinator on another site. It can do so by maintaining a backup to the coordinator that is ready to assume responsibility if the coordinator fails. Or, it can choose the new coordinator after the coordinator has failed. The algorithms that determine where a new copy of the coordinator should be restarted are called *election* algorithms.

### 18.6.1  Backup Coordinators

A *backup coordinator* is a site that, in addition to other tasks, maintains enough information locally to allow it to assume the role of coordinator with minimal disruption to the distributed system. All messages directed to the coordinator are received by both the coordinator and its backup. The backup coordinator executes the same algorithms and maintains the same internal state information (such as, for a concurrency coordinator, the lock table) as does the actual coordinator. The only difference in function between the coordinator and its backup is that the backup does not take any action that affects other sites. Such actions are left to the actual coordinator.

In the event that the backup coordinator detects the failure of the actual coordinator, it assumes the role of coordinator. Since the backup has all the information available to it that the failed coordinator had, processing can continue without interruption.

The prime advantage to the backup approach is the ability to continue processing immediately. If a backup were not ready to assume the coordinator's responsibility, a newly appointed coordinator would have to seek information from all sites in the system so that it could execute the coordination tasks. Frequently, the only source of some of the requisite information is the failed coordinator. In this case, it may be necessary to abort several (or all) active transactions, and to restart them under the control of the new coordinator.

Thus, the backup-coordinator approach avoids a substantial amount of delay while the distributed system recovers from a coordinator failure. The disadvantage is the overhead of duplicate execution of the coordinator's tasks. Furthermore, a coordinator and its backup need to communicate regularly to ensure that their activities are synchronized.

In short, the backup-coordinator approach incurs overhead during normal processing to allow fast recovery from a coordinator failure. In Section 18.6.2, we consider a lower-overhead recovery scheme that requires somewhat more effort to recover from a failure.

### 18.6.2 Election Algorithms

Election algorithms require that a unique identification number be associated with each active site in the system. For ease of notation, we shall assume that the identification number of site $S_i$ is $i$. Also, to simplify our discussion, we assume that the coordinator always resides at the site with the largest identification number. The goal of an election algorithm is to choose a site for the new coordinator. Hence, when a coordinator fails, the algorithm must elect the active site that has the largest identification number. This number must be sent to each active site in the system. In addition, the algorithm must provide a mechanism by which a site recovering from a crash can identify the current coordinator.

The various election algorithms usually differ in terms of the network configuration. In this section, we present one of these algorithms: the *bully* algorithm.

Suppose that site $S_i$ sends a request that is not answered by the coordinator within a prespecified time interval $T$. In this situation, it is assumed that the coordinator has failed, and $S_i$ tries to elect itself as the site for the new coordinator.

Site $S_i$ sends an election message to every site that has a higher identification number. Site $S_i$ then waits, for a time interval $T$, for an answer from any one of these sites. If it receives no response within time $T$, it assumes that all sites with numbers greater than $i$ have failed, and it elects itself as the site for the new coordinator and sends a message to inform all active sites with identification numbers lower than $i$ that it is the site at which the new coordinator resides.

If $S_i$ does receive an answer, it begins a time interval $T'$, to receive a message informing it that a site with a higher identification number has been elected. (Some other site is electing itself coordinator, and should report the results within time $T'$.) If no message is received within $T'$, then the site with a higher number is assumed to have failed, and site $S_i$ restarts the algorithm.

After a failed site recovers, it immediately begins execution of the same algorithm. If there are no active sites with higher numbers, the recovered site forces all sites with lower numbers to let it become the coordinator site, even if there is a currently active coordinator with a lower number. It is for this reason that the algorithm is termed the *bully* algorithm.

## 18.7 Concurrency Control

In this section, we show how some of the concurrency-control schemes discussed earlier can be modified such that they can be used in a distributed environment.

We assume that each site participates in the execution of a commit protocol to ensure global transaction atomicity.

## 18.7.1   Locking Protocols

The various locking protocols described in Chapter 14 can be used in a distributed environment. The only change that needs to be incorporated is in the way the lock manager is implemented. We present several possible schemes that are applicable to an environment where data can be replicated in several sites. As in Chapter 14, we shall assume the existence of the *shared* and *exclusive* lock modes.

### 18.7.1.1   Single-Lock-Manager Approach

The system maintains a *single* lock manager that resides in a *single* chosen site— say, $S_i$. All lock and unlock requests are made at site $S_i$. When a transaction needs to lock a data item, it sends a lock request to $S_i$. The lock manager determines whether the lock can be granted immediately. If the lock can be granted, the lock manager sends a message to that effect to the site at which the lock request was initiated. Otherwise, the request is delayed until it can be granted, at which time a message is sent to the site at which the lock request was initiated. The transaction can read the data item from *any* one of the sites at which a replica of the data item resides. In the case of a write, all the sites where a replica of the data item resides must be involved in the writing.

The scheme has the following advantages:

- **Simple implementation**. This scheme requires two messages for handling lock requests, and one message for handling unlock requests.
- **Simple deadlock handling**. Since all lock and unlock requests are made at one site, the deadlock-handling algorithms discussed in Chapter 14 can be applied directly to this environment.

The disadvantages of the scheme include the following:

- **Bottleneck**. The site $S_i$ becomes a bottleneck, since all requests must be processed there.
- **Vulnerability**. If the site $S_i$ fails, the concurrency controller is lost. Either processing must stop, or a recovery scheme must be used so that a new site can take over lock management from $S_i$, as described in Section 18.6.

### 18.7.1.2   Multiple Coordinators

A compromise between the advantages and disadvantages just noted can be achieved through a *multiple-coordinator approach*, in which the lock-manager function is distributed over several sites.

Each lock manager administers the lock and unlock requests for a subset of the data items. Each lock manager resides in a different site. This approach reduces the degree to which the coordinator is a bottleneck, but it complicates deadlock handling, since the lock and unlock requests are not made at a single site.

### 18.7.1.3 Majority Protocol

In a majority protocol, each site maintains a local lock manager whose function is to administer the lock and unlock requests for those data items that are stored in that site. When a transaction wishes to lock data item $Q$, which is not replicated and resides at site $S_i$, a message is sent to the lock manager at site $S_i$ requesting a lock (in a particular lock mode). If data item $Q$ is locked in an incompatible mode, then the request is delayed until it can be granted. Once it has determined that the lock request can be granted, the lock manager sends a message back to the initiator indicating that it has granted the lock request. The scheme has the advantage of simple implementation. It requires two message transfers for handling lock requests, and one message transfer for handling unlock requests. However, deadlock handling is more complex. Since the lock and unlock requests are no longer made at a single site, the various deadlock-handling algorithms discussed in Chapter 14 must be modified, as we shall discuss in Section 18.8.

If data item $Q$ is replicated in $n$ different sites, then a lock-request message must be sent to more than one-half of the $n$ sites in which $Q$ is stored. Each lock manager determines whether the lock can be granted immediately (as far as it is concerned). As before, the response is delayed until the request can be granted. The transaction does not operate on $Q$ until it has successfully obtained a lock on a majority of the replicas of $Q$.

This scheme deals with replicated data in a decentralized manner, thus avoiding the drawbacks of central control. However, when there is replication of data, it suffers from the following disadvantages:

- **Implementation**. The majority protocol is more complicated to implement than are the previous schemes. It requires $2(n/2 + 1)$ messages for handling lock requests, and $(n/2 + 1)$ messages for handling unlock requests.
- **Deadlock handling**. Since the lock and unlock requests are not made at one site, the deadlock-handling algorithms must be modified (see Section 18.8). In addition, it is possible for a deadlock to occur even if only one data item is being locked. As an illustration, consider a system with four sites and full replication. Suppose that transactions $T_1$ and $T_2$ wish to lock data item $Q$ in exclusive mode. Transaction $T_1$ may succeed in locking $Q$ at sites $S_1$ and $S_3$, while transaction $T_2$ may succeed in locking $Q$ at sites $S_2$ and $S_4$. Each then must wait to acquire the third lock; hence, a deadlock has occurred. Luckily, we can avoid such deadlocks with relative ease, by requiring all sites to request locks on the replicas of a data item in the same predetermined order.

### 18.7.1.4 Biased Protocol

The *biased protocol* is based on a model similar to that of the majority protocol. The difference is that requests for shared locks are given more favorable treatment than requests for exclusive locks. The system maintains a lock manager at each site. Each manager manages the locks for all the data items stored at that site. *Shared* and *exclusive* locks are handled differently.

- **Shared locks**. When a transaction needs to lock data item $Q$, it simply requests a lock on $Q$ from the lock manager at one site that contains a replica of $Q$.
- **Exclusive locks**. When a transaction needs to lock data item $Q$, it requests a lock on $Q$ from the lock manager at all sites that contain a replica of $Q$.

As before, the response to the request is delayed until it can be granted.

The biased scheme has the advantage of imposing less overhead on **read** operations than does the majority protocol. This savings is especially significant in common cases in which the frequency of **read** is much greater than the frequency of **write**. However, the additional overhead on writes is a disadvantage. Furthermore, the biased protocol shares the majority protocol's disadvantage of complexity in handling deadlock.

### 18.7.1.5  Primary Copy

In the case of data replication, we can choose one of the replicas as the primary copy. Thus, for each data item $Q$, the primary copy of $Q$ must reside in precisely one site, which we call the *primary site of Q*.

When a transaction needs to lock a data item $Q$, it requests a lock at the primary site of $Q$. As before, the response to the request is delayed until it can be granted.

Thus, the primary copy enables concurrency control for replicated data to be handled in a manner similar to that for unreplicated data. This similarity allows for a simple implementation. However, if the primary site of $Q$ fails, $Q$ is inaccessible, even though other sites containing a replica may be accessible.

## 18.7.2  Timestamping

The principal idea behind the timestamping scheme discussed in Section 14.2 is that each transaction is given a *unique* timestamp that the system uses in deciding the serialization order. Our first task, then, in generalizing the centralized scheme to a distributed scheme is to develop a scheme for generating unique timestamps. Then, our previous protocols can be applied directly to the nonreplicated environment.

There are two primary methods for generating unique timestamps, one centralized and one distributed. In the centralized scheme, a single site is chosen for distributing the timestamps. The site can use a logical counter or its own local clock for this purpose.

In the distributed scheme, each site generates a unique local timestamp using either a logical counter or the local clock. We obtain the unique global timestamp by concatenating the unique local timestamp with the site identifier, which also must be unique (Figure 18.9). The order of concatenation is important! We use the site identifier in the least significant position to ensure that the global timestamps

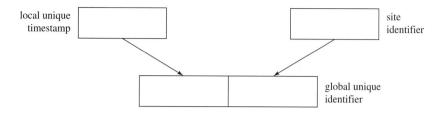

Figure 18.9    Generation of unique timestamps.

generated in one site are not always greater than those generated in another site. Compare this technique for generating unique timestamps with the one that we presented earlier for generating unique names.

We may still have a problem if one site generates local timestamps at a rate faster than that of the other sites. In such a case, the fast site's logical counter will be larger than that of other sites. Therefore, all timestamps generated by the fast site will be larger than those generated by other sites. What we need is a mechanism to ensure that local timestamps are generated fairly across the system. We define within each site $S_i$ a *logical clock* ($LC_i$), which generates the unique local timestamp. The logical clock can be implemented as a counter that is incremented after a new local timestamp is generated. To ensure that the various logical clocks are synchronized, we require that a site $S_i$ advance its logical clock whenever a transaction $T_i$ with timestamp $<x,y>$ visits that site and $x$ is greater than the current value of $LC_i$. In this case, site $S_i$ advances its logical clock to the value $x + 1$.

If the system clock is used to generate timestamps, then timestamps are assigned fairly, provided that no site has a system clock that runs fast or slow. Since clocks may not be perfectly accurate, a technique similar to that used for logical clocks must be used to ensure that no clock gets far ahead of or behind another clock.

## 18.8    Deadlock Handling

The deadlock-prevention and deadlock-detection algorithms presented in Chapter 14 can be used in a distributed system, provided that modifications are made. For example, we can use the tree protocol by defining a *global* tree among the system data items. Similarly, the timestamp-ordering approach could be directly applied to a distributed environment, as we saw in Section 18.7.2.

Deadlock prevention may result in unnecessary waiting and rollback. Furthermore, certain deadlock-prevention techniques may require more sites to be involved in the execution of a transaction than would otherwise be the case.

If we allow deadlocks to occur and rely on deadlock detection, the main problem in a distributed system is deciding how to maintain the wait-for graph. Common techniques for dealing with this issue require that each site keep a *local* wait-for graph. The nodes of the graph correspond to all the transactions (local as well as nonlocal) that are currently either holding or requesting any of the items local to that site. For example, Figure 18.10 depicts a system consisting of two

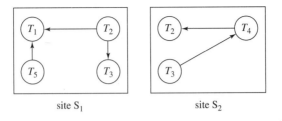

Figure 18.10    Local wait-for graphs.

sites, each maintaining its local wait-for graph. Note that transactions $T_2$ and $T_3$ appear in both graphs, indicating that the transactions have requested items at both sites.

These local wait-for graphs are constructed in the usual manner for local transactions and data items. When a transaction $T_i$ on site $S_1$ needs a resource in site $S_2$, a request message is sent by $T_i$ to site $S_2$. If the resource is held by transaction $T_j$, an edge $T_i \rightarrow T_j$ is inserted in the local wait-for graph of site $S_2$.

Clearly, if any local wait-for graph has a cycle, deadlock has occurred. On the other hand, the fact that there are no cycles in any of the local wait-for graphs does not mean that there are no deadlocks. To illustrate this problem, we consider the local wait-for graphs of Figure 18.10. Each wait-for graph is acyclic; nevertheless, a deadlock exists in the system because the *union* of the local wait-for graphs contains a cycle. This graph is shown in Figure 18.11.

Several common schemes for organizing the wait-for graph in a distributed system are described in Sections 18.8.1 and 18.8.2.

## 18.8.1    Centralized Approach

In the *centralized approach*, a global wait-for graph (union of all the local graphs) is constructed and maintained in a *single* site: the deadlock-detection coordinator. Since there is communication delay in the system, we must distinguish between two types of wait-for graphs. The *real* graph describes the real but unknown state of the system at any instance in time, as would be seen by an omniscient observer. The *constructed* graph is an approximation generated by the controller during the execution of the controller's algorithm. Obviously, the constructed graph must be generated such that, whenever the detection algorithm is invoked, the reported results are correct in the sense that, if a deadlock exists, it is reported promptly, and if the system reports a deadlock, it is indeed in a deadlock state.

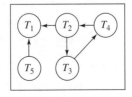

Figure 18.11    Global wait-for graph for Figure 18.10.

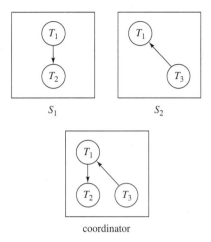

Figure 18.12    False cycles in the global wait-for graph.

The global wait-for graph can be constructed under these conditions:

- Whenever a new edge is inserted in or removed from one of the local wait-for graphs.
- Periodically, when a number of changes have occurred in a local wait-for graph.
- Whenever the coordinator needs to invoke the cycle-detection algorithm.

When the deadlock-detection algorithm is invoked, the coordinator searches its global graph. If a cycle is found, a victim is selected to be rolled back. The coordinator must notify all the sites that a particular transaction has been selected as victim. The sites, in turn, roll back the victim transaction.

We note that this scheme may produce unnecessary rollbacks, as a result of one of the following:

- *False cycles* may exist in the global wait-for graph. As an illustration, consider a snapshot of the system represented by the local wait-for graphs of Figure 18.12. Suppose that $T_2$ releases the resource that it is holding in site $S_1$, resulting in the deletion of the edge $T_1 \rightarrow T_2$ in $S_1$. Transaction $T_2$ then requests a resource held by $T_3$ at site $S_2$, resulting in the addition of the edge $T_2 \rightarrow T_3$ in $S_2$. If the **insert** $T_2 \rightarrow T_3$ message from $S_2$ arrives before the **remove** $T_1 \rightarrow T_2$ message from $S_1$, the coordinator may discover the false cycle $T_1 \rightarrow T_2 \rightarrow T_3$ after the **insert** (but before the **remove**). Deadlock recovery may be initiated, although no deadlock has occurred.

  Note that the preceding example could not occur under two-phase locking. Indeed, the likelihood of false cycles is usually sufficiently low that false cycles do not cause a serious performance problem.

- Unnecessary rollbacks may also result when a *deadlock* has indeed occurred and a victim has been picked, while one of the transactions was aborted for

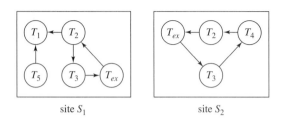

Figure 18.13    Local wait-for graphs.

reasons unrelated to the deadlock. For example, suppose that site $S_1$ in Figure 18.10 decides to abort $T_2$. At the same time, the coordinator has discovered a cycle, and has picked $T_3$ as a victim. Both $T_2$ and $T_3$ are now rolled back, although only $T_2$ needed to be rolled back.

## 18.8.2    Fully Distributed Approach

In the *fully distributed* deadlock-detection algorithm, all controllers share equally the responsibility for detecting deadlock. In this scheme, every site constructs a wait-for graph that represents a part of the total graph, depending on the dynamic behavior of the system. The idea is that, if a deadlock exists, a cycle will appear in (at least) one of the partial graphs. We present one such algorithm that involves construction of partial graphs in every site.

We assume that a transaction runs at a single site, and makes requests to other sites for accessing non-local data. Locks are obtained at the site containing the data. Each site maintains its own local wait-for graph for locks on local data; thus site $S_k$ would have an edge $T_i \rightarrow T_j$ if $T_i$ is waiting on a lock held by $T_j$. Note that $T_i$ and $T_j$ may be non-local transactions. In addition, the local wait-for graph has one additional node $T_{ex}$. An arc $T_i \rightarrow T_{ex}$ exists in the graph at site $S_k$ if either (a) $T_i$ is executing at site $S_k$, and is waiting for a reply to a request made on another site, or (b) $T_i$ is non-local to site $S_k$, and a lock has been granted to $T_i$ at $S_k$. Similarly, an arc $T_{ex} \rightarrow T_i$ exists in the graph at a site $S_k$ if either (a) $T_i$ is non-local to site $S_k$, and is waiting on a lock for data at site $S_k$, or (b) $T_i$ is local to site $S_k$, and has accessed data from an external site.

As an illustration, consider the two local wait-for graphs of Figure 18.10. The addition of the node $T_{ex}$ in both graphs results in the local wait-for graphs shown in Figure 18.13.

If a local wait-for graph contains a cycle that does not involve node $T_{ex}$, then the system is in a deadlock state. However, the existence of a cycle involving $T_{ex}$ implies that there is a *possibility* of a deadlock. To ascertain whether a deadlock really exists, we must invoke a distributed deadlock detection algorithm.

Suppose that site $S_i$ contains in its local wait-for graph a cycle involving node $T_{ex}$. This cycle must be of the form

$$T_{ex} \rightarrow T_{k_1} \rightarrow T_{k_2} \rightarrow \dots \rightarrow T_{k_n} \rightarrow T_{ex}$$

which indicates that transaction $T_{k_n}$ in $S_i$ is waiting to acquire a data item in some other site — say, $S_j$. On discovering this cycle, site $S_i$ sends to site $S_j$ a deadlock-detection message containing information about that cycle.

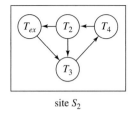

site $S_2$

**Figure 18.14**    Local wait-for graph.

When site $S_j$ receives this deadlock-detection message, it updates its local wait-for graph with the new information that it has obtained. Next, it searches the newly constructed wait-for graph for a cycle not involving $T_{ex}$. If one exists, a deadlock is found, and an appropriate recovery scheme is invoked. If a cycle involving $T_{ex}$ is discovered, then $S_j$ transmits a deadlock-detection message to the appropriate site — say, $S_k$. Site $S_k$, in return, repeats the previous procedure. Thus, after a finite number of rounds, if a deadlock exists, it is discovered; if no deadlock exists, the deadlock-detection computation halts.

As an illustration, consider the local wait-for graphs of Figure 18.13. Suppose that site $S_1$ discovers the cycle

$$T_{ex} \rightarrow T_2 \rightarrow T_3 \rightarrow T_{ex}$$

Since $T_3$ is waiting to acquire a data item in site $S_2$, a deadlock-detection message describing that cycle is transmitted from site $S_1$ to site $S_2$. When site $S_2$ receives this message, it updates its local wait-for graph, obtaining the wait-for graph of Figure 18.14. This graph contains the cycle

$$T_2 \rightarrow T_3 \rightarrow T_4 \rightarrow T_2$$

which does not include node $T_{ex}$. Therefore, the system is in a deadlock state, and an appropriate recovery scheme must be invoked.

Note that the outcome would be the same if site $S_2$ discovered the cycle first in its local wait-for graph, and sent the deadlock-detection message to site $S_1$. In the worst case, both sites discover the cycle at about the same time, and two deadlock-detection messages are sent: one by $S_1$ to $S_2$, and another by $S_2$ to $S_1$. This unnecessary message transfer adds to overhead in updating the two local wait-for graphs and searching for cycles in both graphs.

To reduce message traffic, we assign to each transaction $T_i$ a unique identifier, which we denote by $ID(T_i)$. When site $S_k$ discovers that its local wait-for graph contains a cycle involving node $T_{ex}$ of the form

$$T_{ex} \rightarrow T_{K_1} \rightarrow T_{K_2} \rightarrow \ldots \rightarrow T_{K_n} \rightarrow T_{ex}$$

it will send a deadlock-detection message to another site only if

$$ID(T_{K_n}) < ID(T_{K_1})$$

Otherwise, site $S_k$ continues its normal execution, leaving the burden of initiating the deadlock-detection algorithm to some other site.

Consider again the wait-for graphs maintained at sites $S_1$ and $S_2$ in Figure 18.13. Suppose that

$$ID(T_1) \; < \; ID(T_2) \; < \; ID(T_3) \; < \; ID(T_4)$$

Assume that both sites discover these local cycles at about the same time. The cycle in site $S_1$ is of the form

$$T_{ex} \; \rightarrow \; T_2 \; \rightarrow \; T_3 \; \rightarrow \; T_{ex}$$

Since $ID(T_3) > ID(T_2)$, site $S_1$ does not send a deadlock-detection message to site $S_2$.

The cycle in site $S_2$ is of the form

$$T_{ex} \; \rightarrow \; T_3 \; \rightarrow \; T_4 \; \rightarrow \; T_2 \; \rightarrow \; T_{ex}$$

Since $ID(T_2) < ID(T_3)$, site $S_2$ does send a deadlock-detection message to site $S_1$. On receiving the message, $S_1$ updates its local wait-for graph, searches for a cycle in the graph, and discovers that the system is in a deadlock state.

## 18.9 Multidatabase Systems

In recent years, new database applications have been developed that require data from a variety of preexisting databases located in a heterogeneous collection of hardware and software environments. Manipulation of information located in a heterogeneous database requires an additional software layer on top of existing database systems. This software layer is called a *multidatabase system*. The local database systems may employ different logical models and data-definition and data-manipulation languages, and may differ in their concurrency-control and transaction-management mechanisms. A multidatabase system creates the illusion of logical database integration without requiring physical database integration.

Full integration of existing systems into a *homogeneous* distributed database–the kind of distributed environment we have considered up to this point–is often difficult or impossible:

1. **Technical difficulties.** The investment in application programs based on existing database systems may be huge, and the cost of converting these applications may be prohibitive.

2. **Organizational difficulties.** Even if integration is *technically* possible, it may not be *politically* possible, due to the existing database systems belonging to different corporations or organizations.

In the second case, it is important for a multidatabase system to allow the local database systems to retain a high degree of *autonomy* over the local database and transactions running against that data.

For these reasons, multidatabase systems offer significant advantages that outweigh their overhead. In this section, we provide an overview of the challenges faced in constructing a multidatabase environment from the standpoints of data definition and transaction management.

## 18.9.1   Unified View of Data

Each local DBMS may use a different data model. That is, some may employ modern data models, such as the relational model, whereas others may employ older data models, such as the network model (see Appendix A) or the hierarchical model (see Appendix B).

Since the multidatabase system is supposed to provide the illusion of a single, integrated database system, a common data model must be used. The natural choice is the relational model, with SQL as the common query language. Indeed, there are several systems available today that allow SQL queries to a nonrelational DBMS.

Another difficulty is the provision of a common conceptual schema. Each local DBMS provides its own conceptual schema. The multidatabase system must integrate these separate schemas into one common schema. Schema integration is a complicated task, mainly due to the semantic heterogeneity.

Schema integration is not simply straightforward translation between data-definition languages. The same attribute names may appear in different local DBMSs but with different meanings. The data types used in one system may not be supported by other systems, and translation between types may not be simple. Even for identical data types, problems may arise due to the physical representation of data. One system may use ASCII, another EBCDIC. Floating-point representations may differ. Integers may be represented in *big-endian* or *little-endian* form. At the semantic level, an integer value for length may be inches in one system and millimeters in another, thus creating an awkward situation in which equality of integers is only an approximate notion (as is always the case for floating-point numbers). The same name may appear in different languages in different systems. For example, a system based in the United States may refer to the city "Cologne," whereas one in Germany refers to it as "Köln".

All these seemingly minor distinctions must be properly recorded in the common global conceptual schema. Translation functions must be provided. Indices must be annotated for system-dependent behavior (for example, the sort order of nonalphanumeric characters is not the same in ASCII as in EBCDIC). As we noted earlier, the alternative of converting each database to a common format may not be feasible without obsoleting existing application programs.

Under these circumstances, query processing is complex. Query optimization at the global level is difficult. The usual solution is to rely on only local-level optimization.

## 18.9.2   Transaction Management

A multidatabase system supports two types of transactions:

1. **Local transactions**. These transactions are executed by each local DBMS, outside of the multidatabase system's control.
2. **Global transactions**. These transactions are executed under the multidatabase system's control.

The multidatabase system is aware of the fact that local transactions may run at the local sites, but it is not aware of what specific transactions are being executed, or of what data they may access.

Ensuring the local autonomy of each DBMS requires making no changes to the local DBMS software. A DBMS at one site thus is not able to communicate directly with a DBMS at any other sites to synchronize the execution of a global transaction active at several sites.

Since the multidatabase system has no control over the execution of local transactions, each local DBMS must use a concurrency-control scheme (for example, two-phase locking or timestamping) to ensure that its schedule is serializable. In addition, in case of locking, the local DBMS must be able to guard against the possibility of local deadlocks.

The guarantee of local serializability is not sufficient to ensure global serializability. As an illustration, consider two global transactions $T_1$ and $T_2$, each of which accesses and updates two data items, $A$ and $B$, located at sites $S_1$ and $S_2$, respectively. Suppose that the local schedules are serializable. It is still possible to have a situation where, at site $S_1$, $T_2$ follows $T_1$, whereas, at $S_2$, $T_1$ follows $T_2$, resulting in a nonserializable global schedule. Indeed, even if there is no concurrency among global transactions (that is, a global transaction is submitted only after the previous one commits or aborts), local serializability is not sufficient to ensure global serializability (see Exercise 18.20).

There are many protocols for ensuring consistency despite concurrent execution of global and local transactions in multidatabase systems. Some are based on imposing sufficient conditions to ensure global serializability. Others ensure only a form of consistency weaker than serializability, but achieve this consistency by less restrictive means. We consider one of the latter schemes: *two-level serializability*. Section 20.4 describes further approaches to consistency without serializability; other approaches are cited in the bibliographic notes.

### 18.9.2.1    Two-Level Serializability

Two-level serializability (2LSR) ensures serializability at two levels of the system:

- Each local DBMS ensures local serializability among its local transactions, including those that are part of a global transaction.
- The multidatabase system ensures serializability among the global transactions alone — *ignoring the orderings induced by local transactions*.

Each of these serializability levels is simple to enforce. Local systems already offer guarantees of serializability; thus, the first requirement is easy to achieve. The second requirement applies to only a projection of the global schedule in which local transactions do not appear. Thus, the MBDS can ensure the second requirement using standard concurrency-control techniques (the precise choice of technique does not matter).

The two requirements of 2LSR are not sufficient to ensure global serializability. However, under the 2LSR-based approach, we adopt a requirement weaker than serializability, called *strong correctness*:

1. Preservation of consistency as specified by a set of consistency constraints
2. Guarantee that the set of data items read by each transaction is consistent

It can be shown that certain restrictions on transaction behavior, combined with 2LSR, are sufficient to ensure strong correctness (although not necessarily to ensure serializability). We list several of these restrictions.

In each of the protocols, we distinguish between *local* and *global* data. Local data items belong to a particular site and are under the sole control of that site. Note that there cannot be any consistency constraints between local data items at distinct sites. Global data items belong to the multidatabase system, and, though they may be stored at a local site, are under the control of the multidatabase system.

The *global-read protocol* allows global transactions to read, but not to update, local data items, while disallowing all access to global data by local transactions. The global-read protocol ensures strong correctness if all the following hold:

1. Local transactions access only local data items.
2. Global transactions may access global data items, and may read local data items (although they must not write local data items).
3. There are no consistency constraints between local and global data items.

The *local-read protocol* grants local transactions read access to global data, but disallows all access to local data by global transactions. In this protocol, we need to introduce the notion of a *value dependency*. A transaction has a value dependency if the value that it writes to a data item at one site depends on a value that it read for a data item on another site.

The local-read protocol ensures strong correctness if all the following hold:

1. Local transactions may access local data items, and may read global data items stored at the site (although they must not write global data items).
2. Global transactions access only global data items.
3. No transaction may have a value dependency.

The *global-read–write/local-read protocol* is the most generous in terms of data access of the protocols that we have considered. It allows global transactions to read and write local data, and allows local transactions to read global data. However, it imposes both the value-dependency condition of the local-read protocol, and the condition from the global-read protocol that there be no consistency constraints between local and global data.

The global-read–write/local-read protocol ensures strong correctness if all of the following hold:

1. Local transactions may access local data items, and may read global data items stored at the site (although they must not write global data items).

**2.** Global transactions may access global data items as well as local data items (that is, they may read and write all data).

**3.** There are no consistency constraints between local and global data items.

**4.** No transaction may have a value dependency.

### 18.9.2.2   Ensuring Global Serializability

Early multidatabase systems restricted global transactions to be read only. They thus avoided the possibility of global transactions introducing inconsistency to the data, but were not sufficiently restrictive to ensure global serializability. We leave it to the reader to demonstrate that it is indeed possible to get such global schedules, and to develop a scheme to ensure global serializability (Exercise 18.21).

There are a number of general schemes to ensure global serializability in an environment where update as well read-only transactions can execute. Several of these schemes are based on the idea of a *ticket*. A special data item called a ticket is created in each local DBMS. Every global transaction that accesses data at a site must write the ticket at that site. This requirement ensures that global transactions conflict directly at every site they visit. Furthermore, the global transaction manager can control the order in which global transactions are serialized, by controlling the order in which the tickets are accessed. References to such schemes appear in the bibliographic notes.

If we want to ensure global serializability in an environment where no direct local conflicts are generated in each site, some assumptions must be made about the schedules allowed by the local DBMSs. For example, if the local schedules are such that the commit order and serialization order are always identical, we can ensure serializability by controlling only the order in which transactions commit.

The problem with schemes that ensure global serializability is that they may restrict concurrency unduly. They are particularly likely to do so because most transactions submit SQL statements to the underlying DBMS, rather than submitting individual **read**, **write**, **commit**, and **abort** steps. Although it is still possible to ensure global serializability under this assumption, the level of concurrency may be such that other schemes, such as the two-level serializability technique discussed previously, are attractive alternatives.

## 18.10   Summary

A distributed database system consists of a collection of sites, each of which maintains a local database system. Each site is able to process local transactions: those transactions that access data in only that single site. In addition, a site may participate in the execution of global transactions; those transactions that access data in several sites. The execution of global transactions requires communication among the sites.

There are several reasons for building distributed database systems, including sharing of data, reliability and availability, and speedup of query processing. However, along with these advantages come several disadvantages, including higher software-development cost, greater potential for bugs, and increased processing overhead. The primary disadvantage of distributed database systems is the added complexity required to ensure proper coordination among the sites.

There are several issues involved in storing a relation in the distributed database, including replication and fragmentation. It is essential that the system minimize the degree to which a user needs to be aware of how a relation is stored.

A distributed system may suffer from the same types of failure that can afflict a centralized system. There are, however, additional failures with which we need to deal in a distributed environment, including the failure of a site, the failure of a link, loss of a message, and network partition. Each of these problems needs to be considered in the design of a distributed recovery scheme. If the system is to be robust, therefore, it must detect any of these failures, reconfigure itself such that computation may continue, and recover when a processor or a link is repaired.

If we are to ensure atomicity, all the sites in which a transaction $T$ executed must agree on the final outcome of the execution. $T$ either commits at all sites or aborts at all sites. To ensure this property, the transaction coordinator of $T$ must execute a commit protocol. The most widely used commit protocol is the two-phase commit protocol.

The two-phase commit protocol may lead to blocking: a situation in which the fate of a transaction cannot be determined until a failed site (the coordinator) recovers. To avoid blocking, we can use the three-phase commit protocol.

The various concurrency-control schemes that can be used in a centralized system can be modified for use in a distributed environment. In the case of locking protocols, the only change that needs to be incorporated is in the way that the lock manager is implemented. There is a variety of different approaches here. One or more central coordinators may be used. If, instead, a distributed approach is taken, replicated data must be treated specially. Protocols for handling replicated data include the majority, biased, and primary-copy protocols. In the case of timestamping and validation schemes, the only needed change is to develop a mechanism for generating unique global timestamps. We can develop one by either concatenating a local timestamp with the site identification or advancing local clocks whenever a message arrives with a larger timestamp.

The primary method for dealing with deadlocks in a distributed environment is deadlock detection. The main problem is deciding how to maintain the wait-for graph. Different methods for organizing the wait-for graph include a centralized approach, a hierarchical approach, and a fully distributed approach.

Some of the distributed algorithms require the use of a coordinator. If the coordinator fails owing to the failure of the site at which it resides, the system can continue execution only by restarting a new copy of the coordinator on some other site. It can do so by maintaining a backup to the coordinator that is ready to assume responsibility if the coordinator fails. Another approach is to choose the new coordinator after the coordinator has failed. The algorithms that determine where a new copy of the coordinator should be restarted are called election algorithms.

A multidatabase system provides an environment in which new database applications can access data from a variety of preexisting databases located in various heterogeneous hardware and software environments. The local database systems may employ different logical models and data-definition and data-manipulation languages, and may differ in their concurrency-control and transaction-management mechanisms. A multidatabase system creates the illusion of logical database integration, without requiring physical database integration.

## Exercises

**18.1.** Discuss the relative advantages of centralized and distributed databases.

**18.2.** Explain how the following differ: fragmentation transparency, replication transparency, and location transparency.

**18.3.** How might a distributed database designed for a local-area network differ from one designed for a wide-area network?

**18.4.** When is it useful to have replication or fragmentation of data? Explain your answer.

**18.5.** Explain the notions of transparency and autonomy. Why are these notions desirable from a human-factors standpoint?

**18.6.** Consider a relation that is fragmented horizontally by *plant-number*:

*employee (name, address, salary, plant-number)*

Assume that each fragment has two replicas: one stored at the New York site, and one stored locally at the plant site. Describe a good processing strategy for the following queries entered at the San Jose site.
(*a*) Find all employees at the Boca plant.
(*b*) Find the average salary of all employees.
(*c*) Find the highest-paid employee at each of the following sites: Toronto, Edmonton, Vancouver, Montreal.
(*d*) Find the lowest-paid employee in the company.

**18.7.** Consider the relations

*employee (name, address, salary, plant-number)*
*machine (machine-number, type, plant-number)*

Assume that the *employee* relation is fragmented horizontally by *plant-number*, and that each fragment is stored locally at its corresponding plant site. Assume that the *machine* relation is stored in its entirety at the Armonk site. Describe a good strategy for processing each of the following queries.
(*a*) Find all employees at the plant that contains machine number 1130.
(*b*) Find all employees at plants that contain machines whose type is "milling machine."
(*c*) Find all machines at the Almaden plant.
(*d*) Find employee ⋈ machine.

**18.8.** For each of the strategies of Exercise 18.7, state how your choice of a strategy depends on:
(*a*) The site at which the query was entered
(*b*) The site at which the result is desired

**18.9.** Compute $r \bowtie s$ for the following relations:

| $r$ | $A$ | $B$ | $C$ |
|---|---|---|---|
| | 1 | 2 | 3 |
| | 4 | 5 | 6 |
| | 1 | 2 | 4 |
| | 5 | 3 | 2 |
| | 8 | 9 | 7 |

| $s$ | $C$ | $D$ | $E$ |
|---|---|---|---|
| | 3 | 4 | 5 |
| | 3 | 6 | 8 |
| | 2 | 3 | 2 |
| | 1 | 4 | 1 |
| | 1 | 2 | 3 |

**18.10.** Is $r_i \bowtie r_j$ necessarily equal to $r_j \bowtie r_i$? Under what conditions does $r_i \bowtie r_j = r_j \bowtie r_i$ hold?

**18.11.** To build a robust distributed system, you must know what kinds of failures can occur.
   (a) List possible types of failure in a distributed system.
   (b) Which items in your list from part a are also applicable to a centralized system?

**18.12.** Consider a failure that occurs during 2PC for a transaction. For each possible failure that you listed in Exercise 18.11a, explain how 2PC ensures transaction atomicity despite the failure.

**18.13.** Repeat Exercise 18.12 for 3PC.

**18.14.** List those types of failure that 3PC cannot handle. Describe how failures of these types could be handled by lower-level protocols.

**18.15.** Consider a distributed deadlock-detection algorithm in which the sites are organized in a hierarchy. Each site checks for deadlocks local to the site, and for global deadlocks that involve descendant sites in the hierarchy. Give a detailed description of this algorithm. Argue that the algorithm detects all deadlocks. Compare the relative merits of this hierarchical scheme with those of the centralized scheme and of the fully distributed scheme.

**18.16.** Consider a distributed system with two sites, $A$ and $B$. Can site $A$ distinguish among the following?
   • $B$ goes down.
   • The link between $A$ and $B$ goes down.
   • $B$ is extremely overloaded and response time is 100 times longer than normal.
   What implications does your answer have for recovery in distributed systems?

**18.17.** If we apply a distributed version of the multiple-granularity protocol of Chapter 14 to a distributed database, the site responsible for the root of the DAG may become a bottleneck. Suppose we modify that protocol as follows:
   • Only intention-mode locks are allowed on the root.
   • All transactions are given all possible intention-mode locks on the root automatically.

Show that these modifications alleviate this problem without allowing any nonserializable schedules.

**18.18.** Discuss the advantages and disadvantages of the two methods that we presented in Section 18.7.2 for generating globally unique timestamps.

**18.19.** Consider the following deadlock-detection algorithm. When transaction $T_i$, at site $S_1$, requests a resource from $T_j$, at site $S_3$, a request message with timestamp $n$ is sent. The edge $(T_i, T_j, n)$ is inserted in the local wait-for of $S_1$. The edge $(T_i, T_j, n)$ is inserted in the local wait-for graph of $S_3$ only if $T_j$ has received the request message and cannot immediately grant the requested resource. A request from $T_i$ to $T_j$ in the same site is handled in the usual manner; no timestamps are associated with the edge $(T_i, T_j)$. A central coordinator invokes the detection algorithm by sending an initiating message to each site in the system.

On receiving this message, a site sends its local wait-for graph to the coordinator. Note that such a graph contains all the local information that the site has about the state of the real graph. The wait-for graph reflects an instantaneous state of the site, but it is not synchronized with respect to any other site.

When the controller has received a reply from each site, it constructs a graph as follows:

- The graph contains a vertex for every transaction in the system.
- The graph has an edge $(T_i, T_j)$ if and only if
  - There is an edge $(T_i, T_j)$ in one of the wait-for graphs.
  - An edge $(T_i, T_j, n)$ (for some $n$) appears in more than one wait-for graph.

Show that, if there is a cycle in the constructed graph, then the system is in a deadlock state, and that, if there is no cycle in the constructed graph, then the system was not in a deadlock state when the execution of the algorithm began.

**18.20.** Consider a multidatabase system in which it is guaranteed that at most one global transaction is active at any time, and every local site ensures local serializability.

(a) Suggest ways in which the multidatabase system can ensure that there is at most one active global transaction at any time.

(b) Show by example that it is possible for a nonserializable global schedule to result despite the assumptions.

**18.21.** Consider a multidatabase system in which every local site ensures local serializability, and all global transactions are read-only.

(a) Show by example that nonserializable executions may result in such a system.

(b) Show how you could use ticket scheme to ensure global serializability.

# Bibliographical Notes

Computer networks are discussed in Tanenbaum [1996] and Halsall [1992]. A survey paper discussing major issues concerning distributed database systems has been written by Rothnie and Goodman [1977]. Textbook discussions are offered by Bray [1982], Date [1983], Ceri and Pelagatti [1984], and Ozsu and Valduriez [1991].

Distributed query processing is discussed in Wong [1977], Epstein et al. [1978], Hevner and Yao [1979], Epstein and Stonebraker [1980], Apers et al. [1983], Ceri and Pelagatti [1983], and Wong [1983]. Selinger and Adiba [1980], and Daniels et al. [1982], discuss the approach to distributed query processing taken by R* (a distributed version of System R). Mackert and Lohman [1986] provide a performance evaluation of query-processing algorithms in R*. The performance results also serve to validate the cost model used in the R* query optimizer. Theoretical results concerning semijoins are presented by Bernstein and Chiu [1981], Chiu and Ho [1980], Bernstein and Goodman [1981b], and Kambayashi et al. [1982].

The implementation of the transaction concept in a distributed database are presented by Gray [1981], Traiger et al. [1982], Spector and Schwarz [1983], and Eppinger et al. [1991]. The 2PC protocol was developed by Lampson and Sturgis [1976], and by Gray [1978]. The three-phase commit protocol is from Skeen [1981]. Mohan and Lindsay [1983] discuss two modified versions of 2PC, called *presume commit* and *presume abort*, that reduce the overhead of 2PC by defining default assumptions regarding the fate of transactions.

The bully algorithm presented in Section 18.6.2 is from Garcia-Molina [1982]. Distributed clock synchronization is discussed in Lamport [1978].

Papers covering distributed concurrency control are offered by Rosenkrantz et al. [1978], Bernstein et al. [1978, 1980a], Menasce et al. [1980], Bernstein and Goodman [1980a, 1981a, 1982], and Garcia-Molina and Wiederhold [1982]. The transaction manager of R* is described in Mohan et al. [1986].

Concurrency control for replicated data that is based on the concept of voting is presented by Gifford [1979] and Thomas [1979]. Validation techniques for distributed concurrency-control schemes are described by Schlageter [1981], Ceri and Owicki [1983], and Bassiouni [1988]. Discussions concerning semantic-based transaction-management techniques are offered by Garcia-Molina [1983], and by Kumar and Stonebraker [1988]. Recently, the problem of concurrent update to replicated data has re-emerged as an important research issue in the context of data warehouses. Problems in this environment are discussed in Gray et al. [1996].

Attar et al. [1984] discuss the use of transactions in distributed recovery in database systems with replicated data. A survey of techniques for recovery in distributed database systems is presented by Kohler [1981].

Distributed deadlock-detection algorithms are presented by Gray [1978], Rosenkrantz et al. [1978], Menasce and Muntz [1979], Gligor and Shattuck [1980], Chandy and Misra [1982], and Chandy et al. [1983]. Knapp [1987] surveys the distributed deadlock-detection literature. The algorithm presented in

Section 18.8.2 comes from Obermark [1982]. Exercise 18.19 is from Stuart et al. [1984].

Transaction processing in multidatabase systems is discussed in Breitbart [1990], Breitbart et al. [1991, 1992], Soparkar et al. [1991], and Mehrotra et al. [1992a, 1992b]. The ticket scheme is presented in Georgakopoulos et al. [1994]. 2LSR is introduced in Mehrotra et al. [1991]. An earlier approach, called *quasi-serializability*, is presented in Du and Elmagarmid [1989].

In earlier chapters, we covered the basic principles of database design and implementation. In this and subsequent chapters, we briefly cover a number of special topics in the area of database systems. In Chapter 20, we discuss advanced transaction processing schemes. In Chapter 21, we consider new applications of database systems, and the challenges that they pose to database system design. The bibliographic notes at the end of these chapters provide references for each topic; they can serve as a starting point for detailed study.

## 19.1 Security and Integrity

The data stored in the database need to be protected from unauthorized access, malicious destruction or alteration, and accidental introduction of inconsistency. In Chapter 6, we saw how integrity constraints can be specified. In Chapter 7, we saw how databases can be designed to facilitate checking of integrity constraints. In Chapters 13, 14, and 15, we saw how to preserve integrity despite failures, crashes, and potential anomalies from concurrent processing. In Chapters 17 and 18, we saw how to preserve integrity in parallel and distributed systems. Until now, we have considered only how to prevent the accidental loss of data integrity. In this section, we examine the ways in which data may be misused or intentionally made inconsistent. We then present mechanisms to guard against such occurrences.

### 19.1.1 Security and Integrity Violations

Misuse of the database can be categorized as being either intentional (malicious) or accidental. Accidental loss of data consistency may result from

- Crashes during transaction processing

- Anomalies caused by concurrent access to the database
- Anomalies caused by the distribution of data over several computers
- Logical errors that violate the assumption that transactions preserve the database consistency constraints

It is easier to protect against accidental loss of data consistency than to protect against malicious access to the database. Among the forms of malicious access are the following:

- Unauthorized reading of data (theft of information)
- Unauthorized modification of data
- Unauthorized destruction of data

Absolute protection of the database from malicious abuse is not possible, but the cost to the perpetrator can be made sufficiently high to deter most if not all attempts to access the database without proper authority. Database *security* usually refers to protection from malicious access, whereas *integrity* refers to the avoidance of accidental loss of consistency. In practice, the dividing line between security and integrity is not always clear. We shall use the term *security* to refer to both *security* and *integrity* in cases where the distinction between these concepts is not essential.

To protect the database, we must take security measures at several levels:

- **Physical**. The site or sites containing the computer systems must be physically secured against armed or surreptitious entry by intruders.
- **Human**. Users must be authorized carefully to reduce the chance of any such user giving access to an intruder in exchange for a bribe or other favors.
- **Operating system**. No matter how secure the database system is, weakness in operating-system security may serve as a means of unauthorized access to the database.
- **Network**. Since almost all database systems allow remote access through terminals or networks, software-level security within the network software is as important as physical security, both on the Internet and in networks private to an enterprise.
- **Database system**. Some database-system users may be authorized to access only a limited portion of the database. Other users may be allowed to issue queries, but may be forbidden to modify the data. It is the responsibility of the database system to ensure that these authorization restrictions are not violated.

Security at all these levels must be maintained if database security is to be ensured. A weakness at a low level of security (physical or human) allows circumvention of strict high-level (database) security measures.

It is worthwhile in many applications to devote considerable effort to preserving the integrity and security of the database. Large databases containing payroll or other financial data are inviting targets to thieves. Databases that contain data pertaining to corporate operations may be of interest to unscrupulous competitors. Furthermore, loss of such data, whether via accident or fraud, can seriously impair the ability of the corporation to function.

In the remainder of this section, we shall address security at the database-system level. Security at the physical and human levels, although important, is far beyond the scope of this text. Security within the operating system is implemented at several levels, ranging from passwords for access to the system to the isolation of concurrent processes running within the system. The file system also provides some degree of protection. The bibliographic notes reference coverage of these topics in operating-system texts. Finally, network-level security has gained widespread recognition as the Internet has evolved from an academic research platform to the basis of international electronic commerce. The bibliographic notes list textbook coverage of the basic principles of network security. We shall present our discussion of security in terms of the relational data model, although the concepts of this chapter are equally applicable to all data models.

## 19.1.2   Authorization

A user may have several forms of authorization on parts of the database. Among them are the following:

- **Read authorization** allows reading, but not modification, of data.
- **Insert authorization** allows insertion of new data, but not modification of existing data.
- **Update authorization** allows modification, but not deletion, of data.
- **Delete authorization** allows deletion of data.

A user may be assigned all, none, or a combination of these types of authorization.

In addition to these forms of authorization for access to data, a user may be granted authorization to modify the database schema:

- **Index authorization** allows the creation and deletion of indices.
- **Resource authorization** allows the creation of new relations.
- **Alteration authorization** allows the addition or deletion of attributes in a relation.
- **Drop authorization** allows the deletion of relations.

The **drop** and **delete** authorization differ in that **delete** authorization allows deletion of tuples only. If a user deletes all tuples of a relation, the relation still exists, but it is empty. If a relation is dropped, it no longer exists.

The ability to create new relations is regulated through **resource** authorization. A user with **resource** authorization who creates a new relation is given all privileges on that relation automatically.

**Index** authorization may appear unnecessary, since the creation or deletion of an index does not alter data in relations. Rather, indices are a structure for performance enhancements. However, indices also consume space, and all database modifications are required to update indices. If **index** authorization were granted to all users, those who performed updates would be tempted to delete indices, whereas those who issued queries would be tempted to create numerous indices. To allow the *database administrator* to regulate the use of system resources, it is necessary to treat index creation as a privilege.

The ultimate form of authority is that given to the database administrator. The database administrator may authorize new users, restructure the database, and so on. This form of authorization is analogous to that provided to a *superuser* or operator for an operating system.

### 19.1.3  Authorization and Views

In Chapter 3, we introduced the concept of *views* as a means of providing a user with a personalized model of the database. A view can hide data that a user does not need to see. The ability of views to hide data serves both to simplify usage of the system and to enhance security. System usage is simplified because the user is allowed to restrict attention to the data of interest. Although a user may be denied direct access to a relation, the user may be allowed to access part of that relation through a view. Thus, a combination of relational-level security and view-level security can be used to limit a user's access to precisely the data that user needs.

In our banking example, consider a clerk who needs to know the names of all customers who have a loan at each branch. This clerk is not authorized to see information regarding specific loans that the customer may have. Thus, the clerk must be denied direct access to the *loan* relation. But, if she is to have access to the information needed, the clerk must be granted access to the view *cust-loan*, which consists of only the names of customers and the branches at which they have a loan at. This view can be defined in SQL as follows:

> **create view** *cust-loan* **as**
>   (**select** *branch-name, customer-name*
>   **from** *borrower, loan*
>   **where** *borrower.loan-number = loan.loan-number*)

Suppose that the clerk issues the following SQL query:

> **select** *
> **from** *cust-loan*

Clearly, the clerk is authorized to see the result of this query. However, when the query is translated by the query processor into a query on the actual relations in the database, we obtain a query on *borrower* and *loan*. Thus, authorization must be checked on the clerk's query before query processing begins.

Creation of a view does not require **resource** authorization. A user who creates a view does not necessarily receive all privileges on that view. Such a user receives only those privileges that provide no additional authorization beyond those that he already had. For example, a user cannot be given **update** authorization on a view without having **update** authorization on the relations used to define the view. If a user creates a view on which no authorization can be granted, the view creation request is denied. In our example using *cust-loan* view, the creator of the view must have **read** authorization on both the *borrower* and *loan* relations.

## 19.1.4   Granting of Privileges

A user who has been granted some form of authorization may be allowed to pass on this authorization to other users. However, we must be careful how authorization may be passed among users, to ensure that such authorization can be revoked at some future time.

Consider, as an example, the granting of update authorization on the *loan* relation of the bank database. Assume that, initially, the database administrator grants update authorization on *loan* to users $U_1$, $U_2$, and $U_3$, who may in turn pass on this authorization to other users. The passing of authorization from one user to another can be represented by an *authorization graph*. The nodes of this graph are the users. An edge $U_i \rightarrow U_j$ is included in the graph if user $U_i$ grants update authorization on *loan* to $U_j$. The root of the graph is the database administrator. A sample graph appears in Figure 19.1. Observe that user $U_5$ is granted authorization by both $U_1$ and $U_2$; $U_4$ is granted authorization by only $U_1$.

A user has an authorization *if and only if* there is a path from the root of the authorization graph (namely, the node representing the database administrator) down to the node representing the user.

Suppose that the database administrator decides to revoke the authorization of user $U_1$. Since $U_4$ has been granted authorization from $U_1$, that authorization should be revoked as well. However, $U_5$ was granted authorization by both $U_1$ and $U_2$. Since the database administrator did not revoke **update** authorization on *loan* from $U_2$, $U_5$ retains **update** authorization on *loan*. If $U_2$ eventually revokes authorization from $U_5$, then $U_5$ loses the authorization.

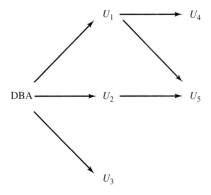

Figure 19.1   Authorization-grant graph.

A pair of devious users might attempt to defeat the rules for revocation of authorization by granting authorization to each other, as shown in Figure 19.2a. If the database administrator revokes authorization from $U_2$, $U_2$ retains authorization through $U_3$, as shown in Figure 19.2b. If authorization is revoked subsequently from $U_3$, $U_3$ appears to retain authorization through $U_2$, as shown in Figure 19.2c. However, when the database administrator revokes authorization from $U_3$, the edges from $U_3$ to $U_2$ and from $U_2$ to $U_3$ are no longer part of a path starting with the database administrator. We require that all edges in an authorization graph be part of some path originating with the database administrator. These edges are deleted; the resulting authorization graph is as shown in Figure 19.3.

## 19.1.5   Security Specification in SQL

The SQL data-definition language includes commands to grant and revoke privileges. The SQL standard includes **delete**, **insert**, **select**, and **update** privileges. The **select** privilege corresponds to the **read** privilege. SQL also includes a **references** privilege that restricts a user's ability to declare foreign keys when creating relations. If the relation to be created includes a foreign key that references attributes of another relation, the user must have been granted **references** privilege on those attributes. The reason that the **references** privilege is a useful feature is somewhat subtle, and is explained later in this section.

The **grant** statement is used to confer authorization. The basic form of this statement is as follows:

**grant** <privilege list> **on** <relation name or view name> **to** <user list>

The *privilege list* allows the granting of several privileges in one command. The following **grant** statement grants users $U_1$, $U_2$, and $U_3$ **select** authorization on the *branch* relation:

**grant select on** *branch* **to** $U_1$, $U_2$, $U_3$

The **update** authorization may be given either on all attributes of the relation or on only some. If **update** authorization is included in a **grant** statement, the list of attributes on which update authorization is to be granted optionally appears in parentheses immediately after the **update** keyword. If the list of attributes is omitted, the update privilege is granted on all attributes of the relation. The following **grant** statement gives users $U_1$, $U_2$, and $U_3$ update authorization on the *amount* attribute of the *loan* relation:

**grant update** (*amount*) **on** *loan* **to** $U_1$, $U_2$, $U_3$

In SQL-92, the **insert** privilege may also specify a list of attributes; any inserts to the relation must specify only these attributes, and each of the remaining attributes is either given default values (if a default is defined for the attribute) or set to null. The SQL **references** privilege is granted on specific attributes in a manner similar to that shown for the **update** privilege. The following **grant** statement allows user $U_1$ to create relations that reference the key *branch-name* of the *branch*

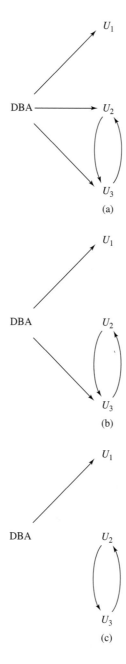

Figure 19.2    Attempt to defeat authorization revocation.

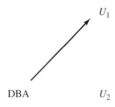

Figure 19.3    Authorization graph.

relation as a foreign key:

$$\textbf{grant references } (\textit{branch-name}) \textbf{ on } \textit{branch} \textbf{ to } U_1$$

Initially, it may appear that there is no reason ever to prevent users from creating foreign keys referencing another relation. However, recall from Chapter 6 that foreign-key constraints restrict deletion and update operations on the referenced relation. In the preceding example, if $U_1$ creates a foreign key in a relation $r$ referencing the *branch-name* attribute of the *branch* relation, and then inserts a tuple into $r$ pertaining to the Perryridge branch, it is no longer possible to delete the Perryridge branch from the *branch* relation without also modifying relation $r$. Thus, the definition of a foreign key by $U_1$ restricts future activity by other users; therefore, there is a need for the **references** privilege.

The privilege **all privileges** can be used as a short form for all the allowable privileges. Similarly, the user name **public** refers to all current and future users of the system. SQL-92 also includes a **usage** privilege that authorizes a user to use a specified domain (recall that a domain corresponds to the programming-language notion of a type, and may be user defined).

By default, a user who is granted a privilege in SQL is not authorized to grant that privilege to another user. If we wish to grant a privilege and to allow the recipient to pass the privilege on to other users, we append the **with grant option** clause to the appropriate **grant** command. For example, if we wish to allow $U_1$ the **select** privilege on *branch* and allow $U_1$ to grant this privilege to others, we write

$$\textbf{grant select on } \textit{branch} \textbf{ to } U_1 \textbf{ with grant option}$$

To revoke an authorization, we use the **revoke** statement. It takes a form almost identical to that of **grant**:

**revoke** <privilege list> **on** <relation name or view name>
**from** <user list> [**restrict** | **cascade**]

Thus, to revoke the privileges that we granted previously, we write

> **revoke select on** *branch* **from** $U_1$, $U_2$, $U_3$ **cascade**
> **revoke update** (*amount*) **on** *loan* **from** $U_1$, $U_2$, $U_3$
> **revoke references** (*branch-name*) **on** *branch* **from** $U_1$

As we saw in Section 19.1.4, the revocation of a privilege from a user may cause other users also to lose that privilege. This behavior is called *cascading of the revoke*. The **revoke** statement may also specify **restrict**:

> **revoke select on** *branch* **from** $U_1$, $U_2$, $U_3$ **restrict**

In this case, an error is returned if there are any cascading revokes, and the revoke action is not carried out. The following **revoke** statement revokes only the grant option, rather than the actual **select** privilege.

> **revoke grant option for select on** *branch* **from** $U_1$

The SQL-92 standard specifies a primitive authorization mechanism for the database schema: Only the owner of the schema can carry out any modification to the schema. Thus, schema modifications—such as creating or deleting relations, adding or dropping attributes of relations, and adding or dropping indices—may be executed by only the owner of the schema. Several database implementations have more powerful authorization mechanisms for database schemas, similar to those discussed earlier, but these mechanisms are nonstandard.

## 19.1.6 Encryption

The various provisions that a database system may make for authorization may not provide sufficient protection for highly sensitive data. In such cases, data may be *encrypted*. It is not possible for encrypted data to be read unless the reader knows how to decipher (*decrypt*) them.

There is a vast number of techniques for the encryption of data. Simple encryption techniques may not provide adequate security, since it may be easy for an unauthorized user to break the code. As an example of a weak encryption technique, consider the substitution of each character with the next character in the alphabet. Thus,

Perryridge

becomes

Qfsszsjehf

If an unauthorized user sees only "Qfsszsjehf," she probably has insufficient information to break the code. However, if the intruder sees a large number of encrypted branch names, she could use statistical data regarding the relative frequency of characters (for example, *e* is more common than *f*) to guess what substitution is being made.

A good encryption technique has the following properties:

- It is relatively simple for authorized users to encrypt and decrypt data.
- The encryption scheme depends not on the secrecy of the algorithm, but rather on a parameter of the algorithm called the *encryption key*.
- It is extremely difficult for an intruder to determine the encryption key.

One approach, the *Data Encryption Standard* (DES), does both a substitution of characters and a rearrangement of their order on the basis of an encryption key. For this scheme to work, the authorized users must be provided with the encryption key via a secure mechanism. This requirement is a major weakness, since the scheme is no more secure than the security of the mechanism by which the encryption key is transmitted.

*Public-key encryption* is an alternative scheme that avoids some of the problems that we face with the DES. It is based on two keys; a *public key* and a *private key*. Each user $U_i$ has a public key $E_i$ and a private key $D_i$. All public keys are published: They can be seen by anyone. Each private key is known to only the one user to whom the key belongs. If user $U_1$ wants to store encrypted data, $U_1$ encrypts them using public key $E_1$. Decryption requires the private key $D_1$.

Because the encryption key for each user is public, it is possible to exchange information securely using this scheme. If user $U_1$ wants to share data with $U_2$, $U_1$ encrypts the data using $E_2$, the public key of $U_2$. Since only user $U_2$ knows how to decrypt the data, information is transferred securely.

For public-key encryption to work, there must be a scheme for encryption that can be made public without making it easy for people to figure out the scheme for decryption. In other words, it must be hard to deduce the private key, given the public key. Such a scheme does exist and is based on the following:

- There is an efficient algorithm for testing whether or not a number is prime.
- No efficient algorithm is known for finding the prime factors of a number.

For purposes of this scheme, data are treated as a collection of integers. We create a public key by computing the product of two large prime numbers: $P_1$ and $P_2$. The private key consists of the pair $(P_1, P_2)$, and the decryption algorithm cannot be used successfully if only the product $P_1 P_2$ is known. Since all that is published is the product $P_1 P_2$, an unauthorized user would need to be able to factor $P_1 P_2$ to steal data. By choosing $P_1$ and $P_2$ to be sufficiently large (over 100 digits), we can make the cost of factoring $P_1 P_2$ prohibitively high (on the order of years of computation time, on even the fastest computers).

The details of public-key encryption and the mathematical justification of this technique's properties are referenced in the bibliographic notes.

Although public-key encryption using the scheme described is secure, it is also computationally expensive. A hybrid scheme used for secure communication is as follows: DES keys are exchanged via a public-key–encryption scheme, and DES encryption is used on the data transmitted subsequently.

Another interesting application of cryptography is in *digital signatures*, which play the electronic role of physical signatures used to verify authenticity of data. One scheme for digital signatures uses public-key encryption in reverse: The private key is used to encode data, and the encoded data can be made public. Anyone can decode them using the public key, but no one could have generated the encoded data without having the private key. Thus, we can verify that the data were indeed created by the person who claims to have created them.

### 19.1.7 Statistical Databases

Suppose that, in our banking example, the bank wants to grant an outsider access to its database under the condition that only statistical studies (averages, medians, and so on) are made on the data, and that information about individual customers is not divulged. In this section, we examine the difficulty of ensuring the privacy of individuals while allowing use of data for statistical purposes.

One possible approach is to give the outsider access to only those views that provide relevant aggregate data, such as sum and count. One weakness in such a statistical database is unusual cases. For example, suppose that a user asks for the total bank-account balances for all customers living in Smalltown. If only one customer happens to live in Smalltown, the system has divulged information about an individual. Of course, a security breach has occurred only if the user knows that only one customer lives in Smalltown. However, that information is easily determined by the statistical query "Find the number of customers living in Smalltown."

A simple way to deal with potential security breaches like that just described is for the system to reject any query that involves fewer than some predetermined number of individuals. Suppose that this predetermined number is $n$. A malicious user who has an account with the bank can find an individual's balance in two queries. Suppose that the user wants to find the account balance of Rollo. The user chooses $n - 1$ customers and issues two queries to compute:

- $x$, the total balances for the malicious user and the $n - 1$ customers
- $y$, the total balances for Rollo and the $n - 1$ customers

Rollo's total balance is

$$y - x + \text{the malicious user's balance}$$

The critical flaw that was exploited in this example is that the two queries referred to many of the same data items. The number of data items that the two queries have in common is called their *intersection*.

Thus, in addition to requiring that a query reference data pertaining to at least $n$ individuals, we may require that no two queries have an intersection larger than $m$. By adjusting $n$ and $m$, we can increase the difficulty a user will face in determining data about an individual, but we cannot upgrade it to an impossibility.

These two restrictions do not preclude the possibility of some extremely clever query that divulges individual data. However, if, in addition, all queries are restricted to computing sums, counts, or averages, and if a malicious user knows only the data value for himself, then we can show that it will take at least $1 + (n - 2)/m$ queries for the malicious user to determine data about another individual. The proof of this assertion is beyond the scope of this text; it is referenced in the bibliographic notes. This fact is, nonetheless, only partially reassuring. We can limit a user to fewer than $1 + (n - 2)/m$ queries, but a conspiracy of two malicious users can result in data being divulged.

Another approach to security is *data pollution*, or the random falsification of data provided in response to a query. This falsification must be done such that the statistical significance of the response is not destroyed. A similar technique involves random modification of the query itself. For both of these techniques, the goals involve a tradeoff between accuracy and security.

Regardless of the approach taken to security of statistical data, it is possible for a malicious user to determine individual data values. However, good techniques can make the expense, in terms of cost and time, sufficiently high that it serves as a deterrent.

# 19.2    Standardization

*Standards* define the interface of a software system; for example, standards define the syntax and semantics of a programming language, or the functions in an application-program interface, or even a data model (such as the object-oriented–database standards). Today, database systems are complex, and are often made up of multiple independently created parts that need to interact. For example, client programs may be created independently of back-end systems, but the two must be able to interact with each other. A company that has multiple heterogeneous database systems may need to exchange data between the databases. Given such a scenario, standards play an important role.

*Formal standards* are developed by a standards organization, or by industry groups, through a public process. Dominant products sometimes become *de facto standards*, in that they become generally accepted as standards without any formal process of recognition. Some formal standards, like many aspects of the SQL-92 standard, are *anticipatory standards* that lead the marketplace; they define features that vendors then implement in products. In other cases, the standards, or parts of the standards, are *reactionary standards*, in that they attempt to standardize features that some vendors have already implemented, and that may even have become de facto standards. SQL-89 was in many ways reactionary, since it standardized features, such as integrity checking, that were already present in the IBM SAA SQL standard, and in other databases.

Formal standards committees are typically composed of representatives of the vendors, and members from user groups and standards organizations such as the International Standards Organization (ISO) or the American National Standards Institute (ANSI), or professional bodies, such as the Institute for Electrical and Electronic Engineers (IEEE). Formal standards committees meet periodically, and members present proposals for features to be added to or modified in the standard. After a (usually extended) period of discussion, modifications to the proposal, and public review, members vote on whether to accept or reject a feature.

Some time after a standard has been defined and implemented, its shortcomings become clear, and new requirements become apparent. The process of updating the standard then begins, and a new version of the standard is typically released after a few years. This cycle typically repeats every few years, until eventually (perhaps many years later) the standard becomes technologically irrelevant, or loses its user base.

The DBTG CODASYL standard for network databases, formulated by the Database Task Group, was one of the early formal standards in the area of databases. IBM database products used to establish de facto standards, since IBM commanded much of the database market. With the growth of relational databases came a number of new entrants in the database business; hence, the need for formal standards arose.

Since SQL is the most widely used query language, much work has been done on standardizing it. ANSI and ISO, with the various database vendors, have played a leading role in this work. The SQL-86 standard was the initial version. The IBM Systems Application Architecture (SAA) standard for SQL was released in 1987. As people identified the need for more features, updated versions of the formal SQL standard were developed, called SQL-89 and SQL-92. The next version of the SQL standard, currently called SQL-3, is under development, and will add a variety of object-oriented features to SQL.

Today, database systems are often organized as a front-end client that provides a graphical user interface, and a back-end database server. So that users will have maximum flexibility in choosing front-ends and back-ends, standards for client-server interconnectivity have evolved. In the personal-computer end of the market, the most commonly used standard for client–server interconnection is the *Open DataBase Connectivity* (*ODBC*) standard for client–server application-program interfaces (APIs) defined by Microsoft.

ODBC is based on the SQL *Call-Level Interface* (CLI) standards developed by the *X/Open* industry consortium and the SQL Access Group, but has several extensions. Figure 19.4 schematically illustrates the role of the ODBC standard. ODBC basically defines an API that client programs can use to connect to database systems and to issue SQL commands. Clients, such as graphical user interfaces,

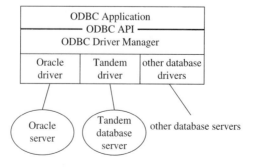

Figure 19.4    ODBC architecture

statistics packages, or spreadsheets, can make use of the same ODBC API to connect to any database server that supports ODBC. Each database system provides a driver that is controlled by the ODBC driver manager at the client end, and is responsible for connecting to and communicating with the server, as well as for doing any data and query format translations that may be required.

The ODBC API defines a CLI, an SQL syntax definition, and rules about permissible sequences of CLI calls. The standard also defines conformance levels for the CLI and the SQL syntax. For example, the core level of the CLI has commands to connect to a database, to prepare and execute SQL statements, to get back results or status values, and to manage transactions. The next level of conformance (level 1) requires support for catalog information retrieval and some other features over and above the core-level CLI; level 2 requires further features, such as ability to send and retrieve arrays of parameter values, and to retrieve more detailed catalog information.

ODBC allows a client to connect simultaneously to multiple data sources and to switch among them, but transactions on each are independent; ODBC does not support two-phase commit.

A distributed system provides a more general environment than that provided by a client–server system. The X/Open consortium has also developed the *X/Open XA* standards for interoperation of databases. These standards define transaction-management primitives (such as transaction begin, commit, abort, and prepare-to-commit) that compliant databases should provide; a transaction manager can invoke these primitives, to implement distributed transactions using two-phase commit. The XA standards are independent of the data model and of the specific interfaces between clients and databases to exchange data. Thus, we can use the XA protocols to implement a distributed transaction system where a single transaction can access relational as well as object-oriented databases, yet the transaction manager ensures global consistency via two-phase commit.

Standards in the area of object-oriented databases have so far been driven primarily by OODB vendors. The Object Database Management Group (ODMG), is a group formed by OODB vendors to standardize the data model and language interfaces to OODBs. The C++ language interface specified by ODMG was discussed in Chapter 8. The ODMG has also specified a Smalltalk interface.

The *Object Management Group* (*OMG*) is a consortium of companies, formed with the objective of developing a standard architecture for distributed software applications based on the object-oriented model. OMG brought out the *Object Management Architecture* (OMA) reference model. The *Object Request Broker* (*ORB*) is a component of the OMA architecture that provides message dispatch to distributed objects transparently, so the physical location of the object is not important. The *Common Object Request Broker Architecture* (*CORBA*) provides a detailed specification of the ORB, and includes an *Interface Description Language* (*IDL*) which is used to define the data types used for data interchange. The IDL helps to support data conversion when data are shipped between systems with different data representations. IDL is essentially an object-oriented data-definition language, and people are working to create a unified version of IDL and the ODMG object-definition language (ODL).

The bibliographic notes at the end of the chapter provide references to detailed descriptions of the standards mentioned in this section.

## 19.3 Performance Benchmarks

As database servers become more standardized, the differentiating factor among the products of different vendors is those products' performance. Performance benchmarks are suites of tasks that are used to quantify the performance of software systems.

### 19.3.1 Suites of Tasks

Since most software systems, such as databases, are complex, there is a good deal of variation in their implementation by different vendors. As a result, there is a significant amount of variation in their performance on different tasks. One system may be the most efficient on a particular task; another may be the most efficient on a different task. Hence, a single task is usually insufficient to quantify the performance of the system. Instead, the performance of a system is measured by a suite of tasks, called a *performance benchmark*.

Combining the performance numbers from multiple tasks must be done with care. Suppose that we have two tasks, $T_1$ and $T_2$, and that we measure the throughput of a system as the number of transactions of each type that run in a given amount of time—say, 1 second. Suppose that system $A$ runs $T_1$ at 99 transactions per second, and that $T_2$ runs at 1 transaction per second. Similarly, let system $B$ run both $T_1$ and $T_2$ at 50 transactions per second. Suppose also that a workload has an equal mixture of the two types of transactions.

If we took the average of the two pairs of numbers (that is, 99 and 1, versus 50 and 50), it might appear that the two systems have equal performance. However, it is *wrong* to take the averages in this fashion—if we ran 50 transactions of each type, system $A$ would take about 50.5 seconds to finish, whereas system $B$ would finish in just 2 seconds!

The preceding example shows that a simple measure of performance is misleading if there is more than one type of transaction. The right way to average out the numbers is to take the *time to completion* for the workload, rather than the average *throughput* for each transaction type. We can then compute system performance accurately in transactions per second for a specified workload. Thus, system $A$ takes 50.5/100, which is 0.505 seconds per transaction, whereas system $B$ takes 0.02 seconds per transaction, on an average. In terms of throughput, system $A$ runs at an average of 1.98 transactions per second, whereas system $B$ runs at 50 transactions per second. Assuming that transactions of all the types are equally likely, the correct way to average out the throughputs on different transaction types is to take the *harmonic mean* of the throughputs. The harmonic mean of $n$ throughputs $t_1, \ldots, t_n$ is defined as

$$\frac{n}{(\frac{1}{t_1} + \frac{1}{t_2} + \ldots + \frac{1}{t_n})}.$$

For our example, the harmonic mean for the throughputs in system $A$ is 1.98. For system $B$, it is 50. Thus, system $B$ is approximately 25 times faster than system $A$ on a workload consisting of an equal mixture of the two example types of transactions.

### 19.3.2   Database-Application Classes

Online transaction processing (OLTP) and decision support (including online analytical processing (OLAP)) are two broad classes of applications handled by database systems. These two classes of tasks have different requirements. High concurrency and clever techniques to speed up commit processing are required for supporting a high rate of update transactions. On the other hand, good query-evaluation algorithms and query optimization are required for decision support. The architecture of some database systems has been tuned to transaction processing; that of others, such as the Teradata DBC series of parallel database systems, has been tuned to decision support. Other vendors try to strike a balance between the two tasks.

Applications typically have a mixture of transaction-processing and decision-support requirements. Hence, which database system is best for an application depends on what mix of the two requirements the application has.

Suppose that we have throughput numbers for the two classes of applications separately, and the application at hand has a mix of transactions in the two classes. We must be careful even about taking the harmonic mean of the throughput numbers, due to *interference* between the transactions. For example, a long-running decision-support transaction may acquire a number of locks, which may prevent all progress of update transactions. The harmonic mean of throughputs should be used only if the transactions do not interfere with one another.

### 19.3.3   The TPC Benchmarks

The *Transaction Processing Performance Council* (TPC), is an organization that has defined a series of benchmark standards for database systems.

The first in the series was the TPC-A benchmark, which was defined in 1989. The TPC-A benchmark measures performance in update-intensive database environments typical in *on-line transaction processing* (*OLTP*) applications. Such environments have multiple on-line terminal sessions, have significant disk I/O, and require transaction integrity. This benchmark simulates a typical bank application, using a single type of transaction that models cash withdrawal and deposit at a bank teller. The transaction updates several relations—such as the bank balance, the teller's balance, and the customers balance—and adds a record to an audit trail relation. Moreover, the benchmark also incorporates communication with terminals, to model the end-to-end performance of the system realistically.

The TPC benchmarks are defined in great detail. They define the set of relations, and the sizes of the tuples. The benchmarks define the number of tuples in the relations not as a fixed number, but rather as a multiple of the number of claimed transactions per second, to reflect that a larger rate of transaction execution is likely to be correlated with a larger number of accounts. The performance metric used is throughput, expressed as *transactions per second* (*TPS*). When its performance is measured, the system must provide a response time within certain bounds, so that a high throughput cannot be obtained at the cost of very long response times. Further, for business applications, cost is of great importance. Hence, the TPC benchmark also measures performance in terms of *price per TPS*. A large system may have a high number of transactions per second, but may be expensive (that is, have a high price per TPS). Moreover, a company cannot claim TPC benchmark numbers for its systems *without* an external audit that ensures that the system faithfully follows the definition of the benchmark, including full support for the ACID properties of transactions.

The TPC-B benchmark was designed to test the core performance of the database system, along with the operating system on which the system runs. It removes the parts of the TPC-A benchmark that deal with users, communication, or terminals, to focus on the back-end database server. The TPC-B benchmark is relatively less widely used.

The TPC-C benchmark was designed to model a more complex system than that modeled by the TPC-A benchmark. The TPC-C benchmark concentrates on the main activities in an order-entry environment, such as entering and delivering orders, recording payments, checking status of orders, and monitoring levels of stock.

The TPC-D benchmark was designed to test the performance of database systems on decision-support queries. Decision-support systems are becoming increasingly important today. The TPC-A, TPC-B, and TPC-C benchmarks measure performance on transaction-processing workloads, and should not be used as a measure of performance on decision-support queries. The "D" in TPC-D can be understood as standing for decision support. The benchmark consists of a set of 17 queries modeling decision-support systems; the queries must be implemented in SQL. Some of the queries make use of complex SQL features, such as aggregation.

### 19.3.4   The OODB Benchmarks

The nature of applications in an OODB is different from that of typical transaction-processing applications. Therefore, a different set of benchmarks has been proposed for OODBs. The Object Operations benchmark, version 1, popularly known as the OO1 benchmark, was an early proposal. The OO7 benchmark is widely used today. This benchmark follows a philosophy different from that of the TPC benchmarks. The TPC benchmarks provide one or two numbers (in terms of average transactions per second, and transactions per second per dollar); the OO7 benchmark provides a set of numbers, containing a separate benchmark number for each of several different kinds of operations. The reason for this approach is that it is not yet clear what is the *typical* OODB transaction. It is clear that such a transaction will carry out certain operations, such as traversing a set of connected objects, or retrieving all objects in a class, but it is not clear exactly what mix of these operations will be used. Hence, the benchmark provides separate numbers for each class of operations; the numbers can be combined in an appropriate way, depending on the specific application.

## 19.4    Performance Tuning

Tuning the performance of a system involves adjusting various parameters and design choices to improve its performance for a specific application. Various aspects of a database-system design—ranging from high-level aspects such as the schema and transaction design, to database parameters such as buffer sizes, down to hardware issues such as number of disks—affect the performance of an application. Each of these aspects can be adjusted such that performance is improved.

### 19.4.1    Location of Bottlenecks

The performance of most systems (at least before they are tuned) is limited primarily by the performance of one or a few components, which are called *bottlenecks*. For instance, a program may spend 80 percent of its time in a small loop deep in the code, and the remaining 20 percent of the time distributed across the rest of the code; the small loop then is a bottleneck. Improving the performance of a component that is not a bottleneck does little to improve the overall speed of the system; in the preceding example, improving the speed of the rest of the code cannot lead to more than a 20 percent improvement overall, whereas improving the speed of the bottleneck loop could result in an improvement of nearly 80 percent overall, in the best case.

Hence, when tuning a system, we must first try to discover what are the bottlenecks, and then to eliminate the bottlenecks by improving the performance of the components causing the bottlenecks. When one bottleneck is removed, it may turn out that another component becomes the bottleneck. In a well-balanced system, no single component is the bottleneck. If the system contains bottlenecks, components that are not part of the bottleneck are underutilized, and could perhaps have been replaced by cheaper components with lower performance.

For simple programs, the time spent in each region of the code determines the overall execution time. However, database systems are much more complex, and can be modeled as *queueing systems*. A transaction requests various services from the database system, starting from entry to a server process, disk reads during execution, CPU cycles, and locks for concurrency control. Each of these services has a queue associated with it, and small transactions may spend most of their time waiting in queues—especially in disk I/O queues—rather than executing code. Figure 19.5 illustrates some of the queues in a database system.

As a result of the numerous queues in the database, bottlenecks in a database system typically show up in the form of long queues for a particular service, or, equivalently, in high utilizations for a particular service. If requests are spaced exactly uniformly, and the time to service a request is less than or equal to the time when the next request arrives, then each request will find the resource idle

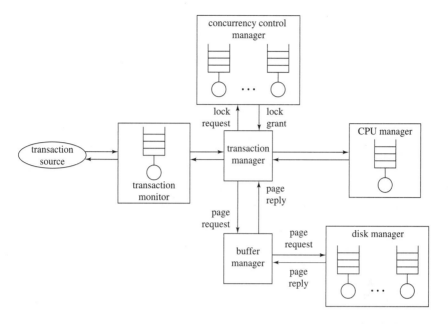

Figure 19.5    Queues in a database system

and can therefore start execution immediately without waiting. Unfortunately, the arrival of requests in a database system is never so uniform, and is instead random.

If a resource, such as a disk, has a low utilization, then, when a request is made, the resource is likely to be idle, in which case the waiting time for the request will be 0. Assuming uniformly randomly distributed arrivals, the length of the queue (and correspondingly the waiting time) go up exponentially with utilization; as utilization approaches 100 percent, the queue length increases sharply, resulting in excessively long waiting times. The utilization of a resource should be kept low enough that queue length is short. As a rule of the thumb, utilizations of around 70 percent are considered to be good, and utilizations above 90 percent are considered excessive, since they will result in significant delays. To learn more about the theory of queueing systems, generally referred to as *queueing theory*, you can consult the references cited in the bibliographic notes.

### 19.4.2   Tunable Parameters

Database administrators can tune a database system at three levels. The lowest level is at the hardware level. Options for tuning systems at this level include adding disks or using a RAID system if disk I/O is a bottleneck, adding more memory if the disk buffer size is a bottleneck, or moving to a faster processor if CPU use is a bottleneck.

The second level consists of the database-system parameters, such as buffer size and checkpointing intervals. The exact set of database-system parameters that can be tuned depends on the specific database system. Most database-system manuals provide information on what database-system parameters can be adjusted, and how you should choose values for the parameters. Well-designed database systems perform as much tuning as possible automatically, freeing the user or database administrator from the burden. For instance, many database systems have a buffer of fixed size, and the buffer size can be tuned. If the system automatically adjusts the buffer size by observing indicators such as page-fault rates, then the user will not have to worry about tuning the buffer size.

The third level is the higher-level design, including the schema and transactions. You can tune the design of the schema, the indices that are created, and the transactions that are executed, to improve performance. Tuning at this level is comparatively system independent. In the rest of this section, we discuss performance tuning of the higher-level design.

The three levels of tuning interact with one another; we must consider them together when tuning a system. For example, tuning at a higher level may result in the hardware bottleneck changing from the disk system to the CPU, or vice versa.

## 19.4.3 Tuning of the Schema

Within the constraints of the normal form adopted, it is possible to partition relations vertically. For example, consider the *account* relation, with the schema

*account (branch-name, account-number, balance)*

for which *account-number* is a key. Within the constraints of the normal forms (BCNF and third normal forms), we can partition the *account* relation into two relations as follows:

*account-branch (account-number, branch-name)*
*account-balance (account-number, balance)*

The two representations are logically equivalent, since *account-number* is a key, but they have different performance characteristics.

If most accesses to account information look at only the *account-number* and *balance*, then they can be run against the *account-balance* relation, and access is likely to be somewhat faster, since the *branch-name* attribute is not fetched. For the same reason, more tuples of *account-balance* will fit in the buffer than corresponding tuples of *account*, again leading to faster performance. This effect would be particularly marked if the *branch-name* attribute were large. Hence, a schema consisting of *account-branch* and *account-balance* would be preferable to a schema consisting of the *account* relation in this case.

On the other hand, if most accesses to account information require both *balance* and *branch-name*, using the *account* relation would be preferable, since the cost of the join of *account-balance* and *account-branch* would be avoided. Also, the storage overhead would be lower, since there would be only one relation, and the attribute *account-number* would not be replicated.

Another trick used to improve performance is to store a denormalized relation, such as a join of *account* and *depositor*, where the information about branch-names and balances is repeated for every account holder. More effort has to be expended to make sure the relation is consistent whenever an update is carried out. However, a query that fetches the names of the customers and the associated balances will be speeded up, since the join of *account* and *depositor* will have been precomputed. If such a query is executed frequently, and has to be performed as efficiently as possible, use of the denormalized relation could be beneficial. Another approach supported by some databases is to cluster records that would match in the join, on the same disk page, so that the join can be computed efficiently.

## 19.4.4   Tuning of Indices

We can tune the indices in a system to improve performance. If queries are the bottleneck, we can often speed them up by creating appropriate indices on relations. If updates are the bottleneck, there may be too many indices, which have to be updated when the relations are updated. Removing indices may speed up updates.

The choice of the type of index also is important. Some database systems support different kinds of indices, such as hash indices and B-tree indices. If range queries are common, B-tree indices are preferable to hash indices. Whether or not to make an index a clustered index is another tunable parameter. Only one index on a relation can be made clustered; generally, the one that benefits the most number of queries and updates should be made clustered.

## 19.4.5   Tuning of Transactions

Both read-only and update transactions can be tuned. In the past, optimizers on many database systems were not particularly good, so how a query was written would have a big influence on how it was executed, and therefore on the performance. Today, optimizers are advanced, and can transform even badly written queries and execute them efficiently. However, optimizers have limits on what they can do. Most systems provide a mechanism to find out the exact execution plan for a query, and to use it to tune the query.

In embedded SQL, if a query is executed frequently with different values for a parameter, it may help to combine the calls into a more set-oriented query that is executed only once. The costs of communication of SQL queries can be high in client–server systems, so combining the embedded SQL calls is particularly helpful in such systems. For example, consider a program that steps through each department specified in a list, invoking an embedded SQL query to find the total expenses of the department using the **group by** construct on a relation *expenses(date, employee, department, amount)*. If the *expenses* relation does not have a clustered index on *department*, each such query will result in a scan of the relation. Instead, we can use a single embedded SQL query to find total expenses of every department, and to store the total in a temporary relation; the query can be evaluated with a single scan. The relevant departments can then be looked up in this (presumably much smaller) temporary relation.

Another technique used widely in client–server systems to reduce the cost of communication and SQL compilation is to use stored procedures, where queries are stored at the server in the form of procedures, which may be precompiled. Clients can invoke these stored procedures, rather than communicate entire queries.

Concurrent execution of different types of transactions can sometimes lead to poor performance due to contention on locks. Consider, for example, a banking database. During the day, numerous small update transactions are executed almost continuously. Suppose that a large query that computes statistics on branches is run at the same time. If the query performs a scan on a relation, it may block out all updates on the relation while it runs, and that can have a disastrous effect on the performance of the system. Such large queries are best executed when updates are few or nonexistent, such as late at night.

Long update transactions can cause performance problems with system logs, and with the time taken to recover from system crashes. If the transactions performs many updates, the system log may get full even before the transaction completes, in which case the transaction will have to be rolled back. If an update transaction runs for a long time (even with few updates), it may block deletion of old parts of the log, if the logging system is not well designed. Again, this blocking could lead to the log getting filled up.

To avoid such problems, many database systems impose strict limits on the number of updates that a single transaction can carry out. Even if the system does not impose such limits, it is often helpful to break up a large update transaction into a set of smaller update transactions where possible. For example, a transaction that gives a raise to every employee in a large corporation could be split up into a series of small transactions, each of which updates a small range of employee-ids. Such transactions are called *mini-batch* transactions. However, mini-batch transactions must be used with care. First, if there are concurrent updates on the set of employees, the result of the set of smaller transactions may not be equivalent to that of the single large transaction. Second, if there is a failure, the salaries of some of the employees would have been increased by committed transactions, but salaries of other employees would not. To avoid this problem, as soon as the system recovers from failure, we must execute the transactions remaining in the batch.

## 19.4.6    Performance Simulation

To test the performance of a database system even before it is installed, we can create a performance-simulation model of the database system. Each service shown in Figure 19.5, such as the CPU, each disk, the buffer, and the concurrency control is modeled in the simulation. Instead of modeling details of a service, the simulation model may capture only some aspects of each service, such as the *service time*—that is, the time taken to finish processing a request once processing has begun. Thus, the simulation can model a disk access based on just the average disk access time.

Since requests for a service generally have to wait their turn, each service has an associated queue in the simulation model. A transaction consists of a series of requests. The requests are queued up as they arrive, and are serviced according to the policy for that service, such as first come first served. The models for services such as CPU and the disks conceptually operate in parallel, to account for the fact that these subsystems operate in parallel in a real system.

Once the simulation model for transaction processing is built, a number of experiments can be run on it. Experiments with simulated transactions arriving at different rates are used to find how the system would behave under various load conditions. Other experiments could vary the service times for each service to find out how sensitive the performance is to each of them. System parameters can be varied, so that performance tuning can be don on the simulation model.

## 19.5   Time in Databases

A database models the state of some aspect of the real world outside itself. Typically, databases model only one state—the current state—of the real world, and do not store information about past states, except perhaps as audit trails. When the state of the real world changes, the database gets updated, and information about the old state gets lost. However, in many applications, it is important to store and retrieve information about past states. For example, a patient database must store information about the medical history of a patient. A factory monitoring system may store information about current and past readings of sensors in the factory, for analysis. Databases that store information about states of the real world across time are called *temporal databases*.

When considering the issue of time in database systems, we must distinguish between time as measured by the system and time as observed in the real world. The *valid time* for a fact is the set of time intervals during which the fact is true in the real world. The *transaction time* for a fact is the time interval during which the fact is current within the database system. This latter time is based on the transaction serialization order and is generated automatically by the system. Note that valid-time intervals, being a real-world concept, cannot be generated automatically and must be provided to the system.

A *temporal relation* is one where each tuple has an associated time when it is true; the time may be either valid time or transaction time. Of course, both valid time and transaction time can be stored, in which case the relation is said to be a *bitemporal relation*. Figure 19.6 shows an example of a temporal relation. To simplify the representation, each tuple has only one time interval associated with it; thus, a tuple is represented once for every disjoint time interval in which it is true. Intervals are shown here as a pair of attributes *from* and *to*; an actual implementation would have a structured type, perhaps called *Interval*, that contains both fields. Note that some of the tuples have a "*" in the *to* time column; these asterisks indicate that the tuple is true until the value in the *to* time column is changed; thus, the tuple is true at the current time. Although times are shown in textual form, they can be stored in a more compact form, such as in the number

| branch-name | account-number | balance | from | | to | |
|---|---|---|---|---|---|---|
| Downtown | A-101 | 500 | 94/1/1 | 9:00 | 94/1/24 | 11:30 |
| Downtown | A-101 | 100 | 94/1/24 | 11:30 | * | |
| Mianus | A-215 | 700 | 95/6/2 | 15:30 | 95/8/8 | 10:00 |
| Mianus | A-215 | 900 | 95/8/8 | 10:00 | 95/9/5 | 8:00 |
| Mianus | A-215 | 700 | 95/9/5 | 8:00 | * | |
| Brighton | A-217 | 750 | 94/7/5 | 11:00 | 95/5/1 | 16:00 |

Figure 19.6    A temporal *account* relation.

of seconds since some fixed time on a fixed date, which can be translated back to the normal textual form.

### 19.5.1    Time Specification in SQL-92

The SQL-92 standard defines the types **date**, **time**, and **timestamp**. The type **date** contains four digits for the year (1–9999), two digits for the month (1–12), and two digits for the date (1–31). The type **time** contains two digits for the hour, two digits for the minute, and two digits for the second, plus optional fractional digits. The seconds field can go beyond 60, to allow for leap seconds that are added during some years to correct for small variations in the speed of rotation of the earth. The type **timestamp** contains the fields of **date** and **time**, with six fractional digits for the seconds field. The SQL-92 times are specified in the *Universal Coordinated Time* (*UTC*), which is a standard for specifying time. (The standard abbreviation is UTC, rather than UCT, since it is an abbreviation of "Universal Coordinated Time" written in French as *universel temps coordonné*. SQL-92 also supports two types, **time with time zone**, and **timestamp with time zone** which specify the time as a local time plus the offset of the local time from UTC. For instance, the time could be expressed in terms of U.S. Eastern Standard time, with an offset of −6:00, since U.S. Eastern Standard time is 6 hours behind UTC.

SQL-92 supports a type called **interval** (which more properly ought to have been called *span*), which allows us to refer to a period of time such as "1 day" or "2 days and 5 hours," without specifying a particular time when this period starts. This notion differs from the notion of interval used previously, which is to an interval of time with specific starting and ending times.

### 19.5.2    Temporal Query Languages

A database relation, as we have defined it in this text, is sometimes called a *snapshot relation*, since it reflects the state in a snapshot of the real world. Thus, a snapshot of a temporal relation at a point in time *t* is the set of tuples in the relation that are true at time *t*, with the time-interval attributes projected out. The snapshot operation on a temporal relation gives the snapshot of the relation at a specified time (or the current time, if the time is not specified).

A *temporal selection* is a selection that involves the time attributes; a *temporal projection* is a projection where the tuples in the projection inherit their times from the tuples in the original relation. A *temporal join* is one where the time of a tuple in the result is the intersection of the times of the tuples from which it is derived. If the times do not intersect, the tuple is removed from the result.

The predicates *precedes*, *overlaps*, and *contains*, can be applied on intervals; their meanings should be clear. The *intersect* operation can be applied on two intervals, to give a single (possibly empty) interval. However, the union of two intervals may or may not be a single interval.

Functional dependencies must be used with care in a temporal relation. Although the account number may functionally determine the balance at any given point in time, obviously the balance can change over time. A temporal functional dependency $X \stackrel{\tau}{\to} Y$ holds on a relation schema $R$ if, for all legal instances $r$ of $R$, all snapshots of $r$ satisfy the functional dependency $X \to Y$.

Several proposals have been made for extending query languages such as QUEL and SQL to improve their support of temporal data. The proposal that currently has the widest support is TSQL2, which extends SQL-92. The bibliographic notes provide references on TSQL2.

## 19.6   User Interfaces

User interfaces for databases have progressed a long way from the early days when the only interface to the database was through procedure calls. Today, database systems provide a variety of tools that allow specialized interfaces, for tasks such as order entry and report generation, to be constructed quickly.

User interfaces to a database can be broadly classified in the following categories:

- Line-oriented interfaces
- Forms interfaces
- Report writers
- Graphical user interfaces

Unfortunately, there are no standards for user interfaces, and each database system typically has its own user interface. In this section, we describe the basic concepts, without going into the details of any particular user interface.

Line-oriented interfaces are the most basic user interfaces. For example, interactive SQL systems allow users to type in queries, and display answers to the queries in tabular form. Although line-oriented interfaces are good for ad hoc querying, they are not convenient for repetitive tasks, such as those performed by bank tellers and salespersons.

Forms interfaces are widely used for entering data into databases. Online forms have a visual appearance much like a paper form. A common example of the use of forms is the entry of orders; Figure 19.7 shows an example of such a form. Forms are also useful for retrieving certain kinds of information from a

| **Acme Supply Company Inc.** | | | **Component Order Form** | |

Customer Name: _____    Date: _____

Customer Number: _____    Order No.: _____

Address: _____

Phone Number: _____

| Part Number | Part Description | Unit Price | Quantity | Subtotal |
|---|---|---|---|---|
|  |  |  |  |  |
|  |  |  |  |  |
|  |  |  |  |  |
|  |  |  |  |  |
|  |  |  |  |  |
|  |  |  |  |  |
|  |  |  |  |  |
|  |  | | Total |  |

Figure 19.7    An order-entry form.

database. For example, the order-entry form can also be used for retrieving old orders, when the order number or customer name is provided.

Creating a forms interface using a programming language such as Pascal or C is a tedious task. Most database systems provide forms packages that allow users to create forms in an easy declarative fashion, using form-editor programs. Users can define the type, size, and format of each field in a form using the form editor. System actions can be associated with user actions, such as hitting a function key on the keyboard, or typing the enter key in a specified field. For instance, the execution of a transaction to register a filled-in order may be associated with typing the enter key in a field labeled *Submit*. As another example, the action associated with entering a value for the customer-id field may retrieve customer information from a database, and may automatically fill in values for other fields, such as customer name and address.

We can perform simple error checks by defining constraints on the fields in the form. For example, a constraint on the item-number field may check that the item number typed in by the user corresponds to an actual item in the database. Although such constraints can be checked when the transaction is executed, de-tecting errors early allows the forms system to indicate which field in the form has the error. Forms packages also provide features such as menus that indicate the valid values that can be entered in a field. The ability to control such features

**Acme Supply Company Inc.**
**Quarterly Sales Report**

`Period:`   Jan. 1 to March 31, 1996

| Region | Category | Sales | Subtotal |
|---|---|---|---|
| North | Computer Hardware | 1,000,000 | |
| | Computer Software | 500,000 | |
| | All categories | | 1,500,000 |
| South | Computer Hardware | 200,000 | |
| | Computer Software | 400,000 | |
| | All categories | | 600,000 |

`Total Sales`   2,100,000

Figure 19.8    A formatted report.

declaratively reduces the effort greatly, as compared to creating a form directly using a programming language.

Report writers are another form of user interface supported by many database systems. People often query databases to detect trends—examples of such queries include include finding the total sales in the past month, and comparing the total sales in the past month with the sales in the corresponding month in the previous year. The output of such queries needs to be properly formatted in the form of a report that can be given to managers. Moreover, such reports need to be generated regularly—for example, at the end of each month. Report-writer packages provide a clean way to combine text formatting for creating reports, with database querying to generate the data that goes into the report.

We specify report formats using the text-formatting facilities provided by the report writer. Variables can be used to store parameters such as the month and the year, and fields in the report can be defined with these variables. Tables, graphs, bar charts, or other graphics can be defined via queries on the database. The query definitions can make use of the parameter values stored in the variables. Once we have defined a report structure using a report-writer facility, we can store it, and can execute it at any time to generate a report. Report-writer systems provide a variety of facilities for structuring tabular output, such as defining table and column headers, displaying subtotals for each group in a table, automatically splitting long tables into multiple pages, and displaying subtotals at the end of each page.

Figure 19.8 shows an example of a formatted report. The data in the report can be generated by aggregation on information about orders.

The collections of application-development tools provided by database systems, such as forms packages and report writers, are often referred to as *fourth-generation languages* (4GLs). The name emphasizes that these tools offer a programming paradigm different from the imperative programming paradigm offered by third-generation programming languages, such as Pascal and C.

In recent years, personal computers that support graphical user interfaces have replaced terminals in many data-entry applications. Graphical user interfaces support interaction based on the point-and-click paradigm, using features such as menus and icons. Forms systems can be thought of a primitive type of graphical user interfaces. Graphical interfaces also provide an excellent means of displaying data, by using bar charts, pie charts, graphs, and other such devices. Numerous tools have been developed to simplify the creation of graphical interfaces to databases. Power Builder, Gupta SQL, and the user interface of the Microsoft Access database system are examples of such tools.

The most recent addition to the family of graphical user interfaces to databases has been the World Wide Web, often called simple the Web. (See Chapter 21 for more information about the World Wide Web.) Within a short period of the development of the Web standards, numerous vendors have announced Web interfaces to their databases. Web interfaces to databases are based primarily on the graphical-forms facilities provided by the *Hypertext Markup Language* (*HTML*). The Web is an area of intense development, and new graphical user interface facilities are likely to emerge on the Web.

## 19.7    Active Databases

Early-generation database systems stored data passively, and performed only actions explicitly requested by a user transaction. In contrast, an active database system not only stores data, but also carries out actions in response to events, such as changes in the data. *Active rules* specify when to carry out actions, and what actions to carry out.

The *event–condition–action* model for active rules is widely used. The general form of rules in this model is as follows:

> **on** *event*
> **if** *condition*
> **then** *action*

Changes to the database—such as insertions, deletions, and updates to tuples—are modeled as *events*. In an object-oriented database, an event could be an action, such as creating or deleting an object, or the execution of a method on the object. Other examples of events are temporal events, such as "at 11:59 P.M. on 31 December, 1999", or "at 12:00 A.M. every weekday."

When an event occurs, one or more rules may be *triggered*. The event is called the *triggering event* of the rules. Once a rule is triggered, the *conditions* of the rule are checked. Examples of conditions to check include whether inventory levels have fallen below a minimum, or whether the update has left the database in an inconsistent state.

If the conditions are satisfied, the *actions* of the rule are executed. Examples of actions are the ordering of fresh stock if the inventory level has fallen below a minimum, or rollback of the transaction (if the update would make the database inconsistent).

Active rules can be used for diverse purposes. An example application is *alerting*, where the rules monitor the system and notify the administrator or user if an unusual event has occurred. Active rules also can be used for checking integrity constraints. Another example of the use of active rules is in maintenance of derived data, such as indices and materialized views. If a view has been materialized (that is, computed and stored), it needs to be updated in response to changes to the database relations on which it is defined. The actions needed for keeping the view up to date can be encoded as active rules.

Suppose that we want to enforce a constraint that, when an employee record is inserted into the *employee* relation, the salary of the employee must be less than the salary of the employee's manager. The following rule can be used to enforce the constraint:

> **define trigger** *employee-sal*
> **on insert** *employee*
> **if** *employee.salary* >
>     (**select** *E.salary* **from** *employee* **as** *E*
>       **where** *E.name* = *employee.manager*)
> **then** *abort*

The **define trigger** clause serves to give a name to the trigger. As an alternative to aborting the transaction, the rule designer could have specified some other action, such as reducing the employee's salary to that of the manager.

The syntax for active rules is not yet standardized, and may differ across systems. The trigger facility described in Chapter 6 is an example of an active-rule facility.

Rules are typically stored in the database, just like regular data, so that they are persistent and are accessible to all database operations. Once a rule is entered into the database, the database system takes on the responsibility of executing the action whenever the specified event occurs and the corresponding condition is satisfied.

If the database system does not support triggers, some applications can manage with *polling*. That is, a process periodically queries (polls) the database to see whether any event of interest has occurred, and then carries out necessary condition checks and actions. However, detecting that an event—such as insertion or deletion—has occurred can be expensive if proper support is not available from the database, since a large relation may have to be scanned each time. Further, since the transaction that performed the update could have committed before polling occurs, actions such as aborting the transaction cannot be implemented. Hence, polling is not practical for many applications. The use of active rules avoids the problems of polling.

When you are designing a collection of active rules, there are several points that you should keep in mind:

- **Termination**. The execution of the actions of a rule may cause the occurrence of some new events. These events may, in turn, trigger other rules. These in turn could potentially trigger others, leading to possible chains of triggering.

If a rule occurs twice in a chain, there is a potential for the execution of the rule to (indirectly) trigger itself. In such a case, there is a possibility that an infinite chain of triggering could occur, and the triggering of rules might never terminate. Note that the presence of a rule twice in a chain does not necessarily imply that an infinite loop will occur, since the rule may have been triggered on updates of different tuples. The designer of a rule system must ensure that no update on an consistent state of the database can result in an infinite chain of rule triggering.

- **Priority**. If several rules are triggered by the same event, they have to be executed in some order. Rule systems usually provide a means of specifying a priority value for each rule. If multiple rules are triggered, they are executed in the order of their priority value. Some systems allow multiple rules to have the same priority value. If several rules with the same priority are triggered, the system makes a nondeterministic (that is, arbitrary) choice of the order of execution of those rules.

- **Event-execution binding**. The event-execution binding specifies when a rule gets executed. For instance, if the binding is specified as *immediate*, the rule gets executed as soon as the triggering event (such as insertion or deletion of a tuple) occurs. The rule execution is treated as part of the transaction that performed the update. If the binding is specified as *deferred*, the rule gets executed at the end of the transaction that performed the update, as part of the same transaction. If the binding is specified as *decoupled*, the rule gets executed in a separate transaction, after the transaction that performed the update has committed. Decoupled binding requires support from the recovery system to ensure that the actions will get executed eventually, even if there are intervening system failures after the triggering transaction commits. Some rule systems provide more powerful means for specifying when rules are to be executed, allowing, for example, a choice between *before* or *after* the triggering event.

- **Error handling**. If the execution of a rule results in a run-time error, error recovery must be initiated. As long as the event-execution binding is either immediate or deferred, the rule execution is part of the transaction that performed the update. In a well-designed rule system, such an error probably reflects an error in the transaction, rather than in the rule itself. Error recovery could then just roll back the transaction.

  Error recovery is much harder if the event-execution binding is decoupled. In this case, when the error is detected, it is too late to roll back the transaction. Not executing the rule could result in some forms of inconsistency in the database. Thus, it is not clear, in general, exactly how to deal with an error in a decoupled rule execution. Manual intervention may be needed to deal with the error. It is therefore important to design the rule system such that run-time errors do not occur during the execution of decoupled rules.

# 19.8   Summary

The data stored in the database need to be protected from unauthorized access, malicious destruction or alteration, and accidental introduction of inconsistency. It is easier to protect against accidental loss of data consistency than to protect against malicious access to the database. Absolute protection of the database from malicious abuse is not possible, but the cost to the perpetrator can be made sufficiently high to deter most, if not all, attempts to access the database without proper authority.

A user may have several forms of authorization on parts of the database. Authorization is a means by which the database system can be protected against malicious or unauthorized access. A user who has been granted some form of authority may be allowed to pass on this authority to other users. However, we must be careful about how authorization can be passed among users if we are to ensure that such authorization can be revoked at some future time.

The various authorization provisions in a database system may not provide sufficient protection for highly sensitive data. In such cases, data can be *encrypted*. Only a reader who knows how to decipher (*decrypt*) the encrypted data can read them.

It is difficult to ensure the privacy of individuals while allowing use of data for statistical purposes. A simple way to deal with potential security breaches is for the system to reject any query that involves fewer than some predetermined number of individuals. Another approach to security is data pollution, or the random falsification of data provided in response to a query. A similar technique involves random modification of the query itself. For both of these techniques, the goals involve a tradeoff between accuracy and security. Regardless of the approach taken to security of statistical data, it is possible for a malicious user to determine individual data values. However, good techniques can make the expense in terms of cost and time sufficiently high that it becomes a deterrent.

Standards are important in database systems, due to the latter's complexity and the need for interoperation. Formal standards exist for SQL. De-facto standards, such as ODBC, and standards adopted by industry groups, such as CORBA, have played an important role in the growth of client–server database systems. Standards for object-oriented databases, such as ODMG, are being developed by industry groups.

Performance benchmarks play an important role in comparisons of database systems, especially as systems become more standards compliant. The TPC benchmark suites are widely used, and the different TPC benchmarks are useful for comparing the performance of databases under different workloads. Tuning of the database-system parameters, as well as the higher-level database design—such as the schema, indices and transactions—is important for achieving good performance. Tuning is best done by identifying bottlenecks, and eliminating them.

Time plays an important role in database systems. Databases are models of the real world. Whereas most databases model the state of the real world at a point in time (at the current time), temporal databases model the states of the real world across time. Facts in temporal relations have associated times when they are valid, which can be represented as a union of intervals. Temporal query languages have been proposed to simplify modeling of time, as well as time-related queries.

There are several types of user interfaces to databases, ranging from command-line interfaces to graphical user interfaces. Form interfaces are widely used for data entry and for some types of packaged queries. Forms packages help programmers to construct forms in a simple declarative manner. Report writers are used for generating reports based on data in the database. They combine text formatting with data retrieval from the database. Languages for defining forms and report-writer languages constitute what are known as fourth-generation languages (4GLs).

Active databases support the specification and execution of rules in the database. In the event–condition–action model, rules are triggered by events; the database system checks the conditions of rules that have been triggered; and, if the conditions are satisfied, the database system executes the actions specified by the rules. Rules are used for a variety of purposes such as for alerting users to unusual activity, for reordering stock, or for enforcing integrity constraints. We must be careful to ensure that the rule set will terminate, if the action of a rule can cause an event that (directly or indirectly) triggers the same rule.

## Exercises

**19.1.** Make a list of security concerns for a bank. For each item on your list, state whether this concern relates to physical security, human security, operating-system security, or database security.

**19.2.** Using the relations of our sample bank database, write an SQL expression to define the following views:

   (*a*) A view containing the account numbers and customer names (but not the balances) for all accounts at the Deer Park branch.

   (*b*) A view containing the names and addresses of all customers who have an account with the bank, but do not have a loan.

   (*c*) A view containing the name and average account balance of every customer of the Rock Ridge branch.

**19.3.** For each of the views that you defined in Exercise 19.2, explain how updates would be performed (if they should be allowed at all). *Hint*: See the discussion of views in Chapter 3.

**19.4.** In Chapter 3, we described the use of views to simplify access to the database by users who need to see only part of the database. In this chapter, we described the use of views as a security mechanism. Do these two purposes for views ever conflict? Explain your answer.

**19.5.** What is the purpose of having separate categories for index authorization and resource authorization?

**19.6.** Database systems that store each relation in a separate operating-system file may use the operating system's security and authorization scheme, rather than defining a special scheme themselves. Discuss an advantage and a disadvantage of such an approach.

**19.7.** What are two advantages of encrypting data stored in the database?

**19.8.** How does data encryption affect the index schemes of Chapter 11? In particular, how might it affect schemes that attempt to store data in sorted order?

**19.9.** Suppose that the bank of our running example maintains a statistical database containing the average balances of all customers. The schema for this relation is (*customer-name, customer-city, avg-balance*). Assume that, for security reasons, the following restrictions are imposed on queries against this data:
  • Every query must involve at least 10 customers.
  • The intersection of any pair of queries, that is, the number of customers involved in both queries in the pair, may be at most 5.
Construct a series of queries to find the average balance of a customer. *Hint*: This can be done in fewer than seven queries.

**19.10.** Perhaps the most important data items in any database system are the passwords that control access to the database. Suggest a scheme for the secure storage of passwords. Be sure that your scheme allows the system to test passwords supplied by users who are attempting to log into the system.

**19.11.** List some benefits and drawbacks of an anticipatory standard as compared to a reactionary standard.

**19.12.** Suppose a system runs three types of transactions. Transactions of type A run at the rate of 50 per second, transactions of type B run at 100 per second, and transactions of type C run at 200 per second. Suppose the mix of transactions has 25 percent of type A, 25 percent of type B, and 50 percent of type C.
  (*a*) What is the average transaction throughput of the system, assuming there is no interference between the transactions.
  (*b*) What factors may result in interference between the transactions of different types, leading to the calculated throughput being incorrect?

**19.13.** List some of the features of the TPC benchmarks that help make them realistic and dependable measures.

**19.14.** (*a*) What are the three broad levels at which a database system can be tuned to improve performance?
  (*b*) Give two examples of how tuning can be done, for each of the levels.

**19.15.** What is the motivation for splitting a long transaction into a series of small one? What problems could arise as a result, and how can these problems be averted?

**19.16.** What are the two types of time, and how are they different. Why does it make sense to have both types of time associated with a tuple?

**19.17.** Will functional dependencies be preserved if a relation is converted to a temporal relation by adding a time attribute? How is the problem handled in a temporal database?

**19.18.** Consider a view *branch-cust* defined as follows:

> **create view** *branch-cust* **as**
>   **select** *branch-name, customer-name*
>   **from** *depositor, account*
>   **where** *depositor.account-number = account.account-number*

Suppose that the view is *materialized*, that is, the view is computed and stored. Write active rules to *maintain* the view, that is, to keep it up to date on insertions to and deletions from *depositor* or *account*. Do not bother about updates.

# Bibliographical Notes

Security aspects of computer systems in general are discussed in Bell and La-Padula [1976], and by the U.S. Department of Defense [1985]. Security aspects of SQL are discussed in detail in ANSI [1992], and are summarized in Date and Darwen [1993] and in Melton and Simon [1993]. Stonebraker and Wong [1974] discuss the Ingres approach to security, which involves modification of users' queries so as to ensure that users do not access data for which authorization has not been granted. Denning and Denning [1979] survey database security. Database systems that can produce incorrect answers when necessary for security mainte-nance are discussed in Winslett et al. [1994] and Tendick and Matloff [1994].

Work on security in relational databases includes that of Lunt et al. [1990], Stachour and Thuraisingham [1990], Jajodia and Sandhu [1990], Kogan and Jajo-dia [1990], and Qian and Lunt [1996]. Rabitti et al. [1988,1991] and Thomas and Sandhu [1996] discuss security in object-oriented databases. Lunt [1995] provides an overview of issues in authorization.

Operating-system security issues are discussed in most operating-system texts, including Silberschatz and Galvin [1994].

Chin and Ozsoyoglu [1981] discuss the design of statistical databases. Sev-eral papers provide mathematical analysis of the number of queries required to break privacy in a database under a variety of assumptions. Among these are Kam and Ullman [1977], Chin [1978], DeMillo et al. [1978], Dobkin et al. [1979], Yao [1979a], Denning [1980], and Leiss [1982b].

Another aspect of security that has been studied from a mathematical stand-point is data encryption. The Data Encryption Standard is presented by the U.S. Dept. of Commerce [1977]. Public-key encryption is discussed by Rivest et al. [1978]. Other discussions on cryptography include Diffie and Hellman [1979], Lempel [1979], Simmons [1979], Davies [1980], Fernandez et al. [1981], Den-ning [1982], Leiss [1982a], and Akl [1983].

The American National Standard SQL-86 is described in ANSI [1986]. The IBM Systems Application Architecture definition of SQL is defined by IBM [1987]. The standards for SQL-89 and SQL-92 are available as ANSI [1989] and ANSI [1992] respectively. The SQL-3 standardization effort is currently in progress; look up the Web home page of this book (see preface) for recent developments. The X/Open SQL call-level interface is defined in X/Open [1993]; the ODBC API is described in Microsoft [1992]. The X/Open XA interface is defined in X/Open [1991]. The ODMG-93 standard is defined in Catell [1994].

An early proposal for a database-system benchmark (the Wisconsin benchmark) was made by Bitton et al. [1983]. The TPC A, B and C benchmarks are described in Gray [1993]. An online version of all the TPC benchmarks descriptions, as well as benchmark results, is available on the World Wide Web at the URL http://www.tpc.org; the site also contains up-to-date information about new benchmarks such as TPC-E, a proposed extension of TPC-C. The OO1 benchmark for OODBs is described in Catell and Skeen [1992]; the OO7 benchmark is described in Carey et al. [1993]. In contrast to the TPC benchmarks, the OODB benchmarks were designed by individuals, rather than by a council.

Kleinrock's two volumes [1975, 1976] are popular textbooks on queueing theory. Shasha [1992] provides a good overview of database tuning. O'Neil's textbook [1994] describes performance measurement and tuning. Brown et al. [1994] describe an approach to automated tuning.

The incorporation of time into the relational data model is discussed in Snodgrass and Ahn [1985], Clifford and Tansel [1985], Gadia [1986, 1988], Snodgrass [1987], Tansel et al. [1993], Snodgrass et al. [1994], and Tuzhilin and Clifford [1990]. Stam and Snodgrass [1988] and Soo [1991] provide surveys on temporal data management. Jensen et al. [1994] presents a glossary of temporal-database concepts, aimed at unifying the terminology. Snodgrass et al. [1994] present the TSQL2 proposal. Tansel et al. [1993] is a collection of articles on different aspects of temporal databases. Chomicki [1995] presents techniques for managing temporal integrity constraints. A concept of completeness for temporal query languages analogous to relational completeness (equivalence to the relational algebra) is given in Clifford et al. [1994].

The user interfaces of commercial database systems—in particular, their forms and report-writer interfaces—are described in the respective user manuals. Nguyen and Srinivasan [1996] describe the World Wide Web interface to the IBM DB2 database system.

The trigger subsystem of System R is described by Eswaran and Chamberlin [1975]. McCarthy and Dayal [1989] discuss the architecture of an active database system based on the event–condition–action formalism. Widom and Finkelstein [1990] describe the architecture of a rule system based on set-oriented rules; the implementation of the rule system on the Starburst extensible database system is presented in Widom et al. [1991]. Consider an execution mechanism that allows a nondeterministic choice of which rule to execute next. A rule system is said to be *confluent* if, regardless of the rule chosen, the final state is the same. Issues of termination, nondeterminism, and confluence of rule systems are discussed in Aiken et al. [1995]. Modularity as a means to manage large rule bases in considered in Baralis et al. [1996].

# CHAPTER 20

# ADVANCED TRANSACTION PROCESSING

In Chapters 13, 14, and 15, we introduced the concept of a transaction, which is a program unit that accesses—and possibly updates—various data items, and whose execution ensures the preservation of the ACID properties. We discussed in those chapters a variety of schemes for ensuring the ACID properties in an environment where failure can occur, and where the transactions may run concurrently. In this chapter, we go beyond the basic schemes discussed previously, and cover more advanced transaction-processing concepts, including remote backup systems, transaction-processing monitors, high-performance transaction systems, long-duration transactions, nested transactions, real-time transaction systems, and transaction systems that ensure a level of consistency weaker than serializability.

## 20.1 Remote Backup Systems

Traditional transaction-processing systems are centralized or client–server systems. Such systems are vulnerable to environmental disasters such as fire, flooding, or earthquakes. Increasingly, there is a need for transaction-processing systems that offer high availability, and that can function in spite of environmental disasters.

We can achieve *high availability* by using a distributed database where the data are replicated, and transactions update all copies of the data. Two-phase commit can be used for synchronization of the sites. If a site fails, transaction processing can still continue, using other sites. However, actions such as concurrency control, which were earlier performed at a single site, now require synchronization

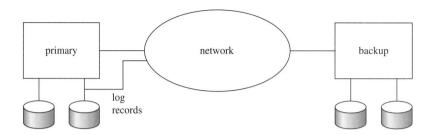

Figure 20.1    Architecture of remote-backup system.

across multiple sites, with the resultant delays. Further, two-phase commit itself is expensive. Hence, transaction throughput suffers under such a scheme.

An alternative is to perform transaction processing at a single site, called the *primary* site, but to have a *remote backup* site, where all the data from the primary site are replicated. The remote backup site is sometimes also called the *secondary* site. The remote site must be kept synchronized with the primary site, as updates are performed at the primary. We achieve synchronization by sending all log records from primary site to the remote backup site. The remote backup site must be physically separated from the primary—for example, we can locate it in a different state—so that a disaster at the primary does not damage the remote backup site. Figure 20.1 shows the architecture of a remote backup system.

When the primary site fails, the remote backup site takes over processing. First, however, it performs recovery, using its (perhaps outdated) copy of the data from the primary, and the log records received from the primary. In effect, the remote backup site is performing recovery actions that would have been performed at the primary site when the latter recovered. Standard recovery algorithms, with minor modifications, can be used for recovery at the remote backup site. Once recovery has been performed, the remote backup site starts processing transactions.

Availability is greatly increased over a single-site system, since the system can recover even if all data at the primary site are lost. The performance of a remote backup system is better than the performance of a distributed system with two-phase commit.

Several issues for you to address when you are designing a remote backup system follow:

- **Detection of failure.** As it is in failure-handling protocols for distributed system, it is important for the remote backup system to detect when the primary has failed. Failure of communication lines can fool the remote backup into believing that the primary has failed. To avoid this problem, we maintain several communication links with independent modes of failure between the primary and the remote backup. For example, in addition to the network connection, there may be a separate modem connection over a telephone line, with services provided by different telecommunication companies. These connections may be backed up via manual intervention by operators, who can communicate over the telephone system.

- **Transfer of control.** When the primary fails, the backup site takes over processing and becomes the new primary. When the original primary site recovers, it can either play the role of remote backup, or take over the role of primary site again. In either case, the old primary must receive a log of updates carried out by the backup site while the old primary was down.

  The simplest way of transferring control is for the old primary to receive redo logs from the old backup site, and to catch up with the updates by applying them locally. The old primary can then act as a remote backup site. If control must be transferred back, the old backup site can pretend to have failed, resulting in the old primary taking over.

- **Time to recover.** If the log at the remote backup grows large, recovery will take a long time. The remote backup site can periodically process the redo log records that it has received, and can perform a checkpoint, so that earlier parts of the log can be deleted. The delay before the remote backup takes over can be significantly reduced as a result.

  A *hot-spare* configuration can make takeover by the backup site almost instantaneous. In this configuration, the remote backup site continually processes redo log records as they arrive, applying the updates locally. As soon as the failure of the primary is detected, the backup site completes recovery by rolling back incomplete transactions; it is then ready to process new transactions.

- **Time to commit.** So that we ensure that the updates of a committed transaction are durable, a transaction must not be declared committed until its log records have reached the backup site. This delay can result in a longer wait to commit a transaction, and some systems therefore permit lower degrees of durability. The degrees of durability can be classified as follows.

  ○ **One-safe.** A transaction commits as soon as its commit log record is written to stable storage at the primary site.

    The problem with this scheme is that the updates of a committed transaction may not have made it to the backup site, when the backup site takes over processing. Thus, the updates may appear to be lost. When the primary site recovers, the lost updates cannot be merged in directly, since the updates may conflict with later updates performed at the backup site. Thus, human intervention may be required to bring the database to a consistent state.

  ○ **Two-very-safe.** A transaction commits as soon as its commit log record is written to stable storage at the primary and the backup site.

    The problem with this scheme is that transaction processing cannot proceed if either the primary or the backup site is down. Thus, availability is actually less than in the single-site case, although the probability of data loss is much less.

  ○ **Two-safe.** This scheme is the same as two-very-safe if both primary and backup sites are active. If only the primary is active, the transaction is allowed to commit as soon as is commit log record is written to stable storage at the primary site.

This scheme provides better availability than does two-very-safe, while avoiding the problem of lost transactions faced by the one-safe scheme. It results in a slower commit than the one-safe scheme, but the benefits generally outweigh the cost.

Several commercial shared-disk systems provide a level of fault tolerance that is intermediate between centralized and remote backup systems. In these systems, the failure of a CPU does not result in system failure, Instead, other CPUs take over, and they carry out recovery. Recovery actions include rollback of transactions running on the failed CPU, and recovery of locks held by those transactions. Since data are on a shared disk, there is no need for transfer of log records. However, we should safeguard the data from disk failure by using, for example, a RAID disk organization.

## 20.2  Transaction-Processing Monitors

Database systems have traditionally been viewed as monolithic systems. In the real world, however, data are often partitioned across multiple database systems, file systems, and applications, all of which may run on different machines. Users may need to run updates on several of these systems, as part of a single transaction. Thus, the transactional properties for consistency and recovery from failures are essential. The two-phase commit protocol forms a building block for supporting transactions that span multiple databases. However, layers of software, and corresponding software architectures, are needed to coordinate the execution of such tasks. *Transaction-processing* (*TP*) *monitors* are systems that provide such support.

TP monitors were developed in the 1970s and 1980s, initially in response to a need to support a large number of remote terminals (such as airline-reservation terminals) from a single computer. The term *TP monitor* initially stood for *teleprocessing monitor*. These systems have since evolved to provide the core support for distributed transaction processing, and the term *TP monitor* has acquired its current meaning. Commercial TP monitors (in rough order of introduction) include the IMS system and CICS (introduced in the 1970s) from IBM, Pathway from Tandem (1979), ACMS and RTR from Digital Equipment (1981 and 1987), Tuxedo and Top End from NCR (1985 and 1991), and Encina from Transarc (1993).

### 20.2.1  TP-Monitor Architectures

In a typical operating system today, users log in and execute one or more processes. Consider an airline-reservation system with thousands of reservation terminals active at a time, all connected to a central computer. The operating system has considerable memory overhead for each login session, and the memory overhead would be excessive if each user of a terminal had to log in to the computer system. Further, for reasons of security, it is not a good idea to let many remote users have full access to the operating system via login sessions.

Instead of having one login session per terminal, an alternative is to have a server process that communicates with the terminal, and handles authentication

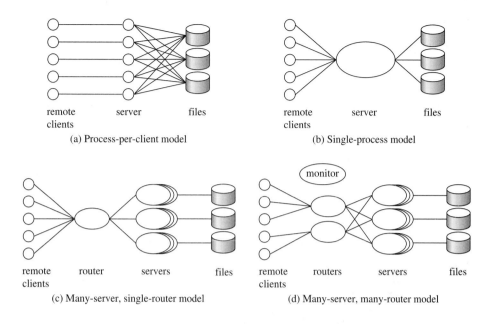

Figure 20.2   TP-monitor architectures.

and executes actions requested by the terminal. This *process-per-client* model is illustrated in Figure 20.2a. This model presents several problems with respect to memory utilization and processing speed:

- Per-process memory requirements are high. Even if memory for program code is shared by all processes, each process consumes memory for local data and open file descriptors, as well as for operating-system overhead, such as page tables to support virtual memory.

- The operating system divides up available CPU time among processes by switching among them; this technique is called *multitasking*. Each *context switch* between one process and the next has considerable CPU overhead; even on today's fast systems, a context switch can take hundreds of microseconds.

With this model, given the limited memory and processor power available in the 1970s and 1980s, it would have been impossible to serve more than tens to hundreds of users at a time without running out of memory and CPU resources.

To avoid these problems, systems such as IBM CICS introduced the concept of a *teleprocessing monitor*. These systems had a single server process to which all remote terminals connect; this model is called the *single-server* model, and is illustrated in Figure 20.2b. Remote terminals send requests to the server process, which then executes those requests. This model is also used in client–server environments, where clients send requests to a single server process. The server process handles tasks, such as user authentication, that would normally be handled by the operating system. To avoid blocking other clients when processing a long request for one client, the server process is *multithreaded*: The server process has a thread of control for each client, and, in effect, implements its own low-overhead multitasking. It executes code on behalf of one client for a while, then saves the internal context and switches to the code for another client. Unlike the overhead of full multitasking, the cost of switching between threads is low (typically only a few microseconds).

Systems based on the single-server model, such as the original version of the IBM CICS TP monitor and file servers such as Novel's NetWare, successfully provided high transaction rates with limited resources. However, they had problems, especially when multiple applications accessed the same database:

- Since all the applications run as a single process, there is no protection among them. A bug in one application can affect all the other applications as well. It would be best to run each application as a separate process.

- Such systems are not suited for parallel or distributed databases, since a server process cannot execute on multiple computers at once. (However, concurrent threads within a process can be supported in a shared-memory multiprocessor system.) Distributed data are becoming increasingly common in large organizations.

One way to solve these problems is to run multiple application-server processes that access a common database, and to let the clients communicate with the application through a single communication process that routes requests. This model is called the *many-server, single-router* model, and is illustrated in Figure 20.2c. This model supports independent server processes for multiple applications; further, each application can have a pool of server processes, any one of which can handle a client session. The request can, for example, be routed to the most lightly loaded server in a pool. As before, each server process can itself be multithreaded, so that it can handle multiple clients concurrently. As a further generalization, the application servers can run on different sites of a parallel or distributed database, and the communication process can handle the coordination among the processes.

A more general architecture has multiple processes, rather than just one, to communicate with clients. The client communication processes interact with one or more router processes, which route their requests to the appropriate server. Later-generation TP monitors therefore have a different architecture, called the *many-server, many-router* model, illustrated in Figure 20.2d. A controller process starts up the other processes, and supervises their functioning. Tandem Pathway is an example of the later-generation TP monitors that use this architecture.

The detailed structure of a TP monitor is shown in Figure 20.3. A TP monitor does more than simply pass messages to application servers. When messages arrive, they have to be queued; thus, there is a *queue manager* for incoming messages. The messages may even be logged on stable storage, so that, once received, they will be processed eventually, regardless of system failures. Authorization and application-server management (e.g., server startup, and routing of messages to servers) are further functions of a TP monitor. TP monitors often provide log-

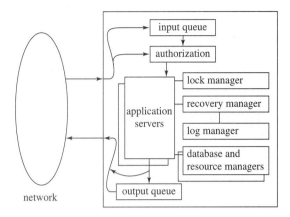

Figure 20.3    TP-monitor components.

ging, recovery, and concurrency-control facilities, allowing application servers to implement the ACID transaction properties directly if required.

Finally, TP monitors also provide durable queueing for outgoing messages. Thus, a server can send a message as part of a transaction; the TP monitor guarantees that the message will be delivered if (and only if) the transaction commits, thereby providing ACID properties not just for the actions within a database, but also for messages sent outside the database.

In addition to these facilities, many TP monitors also provide *presentation facilities* for dumb clients such as terminals; the presentation facilities help to create menu and form interfaces.

## 20.2.2    Application Coordination Using TP monitors

Applications today often have to interact with multiple databases. They may also have to interact with legacy systems,[†] such as special-purpose data-storage systems built directly on file systems. Finally, they may have to communicate with users or other applications at remote sites. Hence, they also have to interact with communication subsystems. It is important to be able to coordinate data accesses, and to implement ACID properties for transactions across such systems.

Modern TP monitors provide support for the construction and administration of such large applications, built up from multiple subsystems such as databases, legacy systems, and communication systems. A TP monitor treats each subsystem as a *resource manager* that provides transactional access to some set of resources. The interface between the TP monitor and the resource manager is defined by a set of transaction primitives, such as *begin_transaction*, *commit_transaction*, *abort_transaction*, and *prepare_to_commit_transaction* (for two-phase commit). Of

---

[†]Legacy systems are older-generation systems that are incompatible with current-generation standards and systems. Such systems may still contain valuable data, and may support critical applications. Porting these applications to a more modern environment is often costly in terms of both time and money. Thus, it is important to support these older-generation, or legacy, systems, and to facilitate their interoperation with newer systems.

course, the resource manager must also provide other services, such as supplying data, to the application.

The resource-manager interface is defined by the X/Open Distributed Transaction Processing standard. Many database systems support the X/Open standards, and can act as resource managers. TP monitors—as well as other products, such as SQL systems, that support the X/Open standards—can connect to the resource managers. In addition, TP monitors provide services, such as persistent queue management and message transport, which act as resource managers supporting transactions. The TP monitor can coordinate transactions among these services and the database systems. For example, when a queued update transaction is executed, an output message is delivered, and the request transaction is removed from the request queue; the TP monitor ensures that, regardless of failures, either all these actions occur, or none occurs.

In client–server systems, clients often interact with servers via a *remote-procedure-call* (*RPC*) mechanism, where a client invokes a procedure call, which is actually executed at the server, with the results sent back to the client. As far as the client code that invokes the RPC is concerned, the call looks like a local procedure-call invocation. TP monitor systems, such as Encina, provide a *transactional RPC* interface to their services. In such an interface, the RPC mechanism provides calls that can be used to enclose a series of RPC calls within a transaction. Thus, updates performed by an RPC are carried out within the scope of the transaction, and can be rolled back if there is any failure.

We can also use TP monitors to administer complex client–server systems consisting of multiple servers and a large number of clients. Each server behaves like a resource manager, and registers with the TP monitor. The TP monitor coordinates activities, such as system checkpoints and shutdowns. It provides security and authentication of clients. It administers server pools by adding servers or removing servers without interruption of the system. Finally, it controls the scope of failures. If a server fails, the TP monitor can detect this failure, abort the transactions in progress, and restart the transactions. If a node fails, the TP monitor can migrate transactions to servers at other nodes, again backing out incomplete transactions. When failed nodes restart, the TP monitor can govern the recovery of the node's resource managers.

Modern database systems support replication of databases; updates performed at a primary site are carried out automatically on the replicas of the site as well. Remote backup systems are an example of such replication. If the primary site fails, one of the secondary sites takes over processing (see Section 20.1). TP monitors can be used to hide database failures in such replicated systems; transaction requests are sent to the TP monitor, which relays the messages to one of the database replicas. If one site fails, the TP monitor can transparently route messages to a backup site, masking the failure of the first site.

# 20.3    High-Performance Transaction Systems

To allow a high rate of transaction processing (hundreds or thousands of transactions per second), we must use high-performance hardware, and must exploit parallelism. These techniques alone, however, are insufficient to obtain high performance in transaction processing, for the following reasons:

- Disk I/O remains a bottleneck—about 10 milliseconds are required for each I/O, and this number has not decreased at a rate comparable to the increase in processor speeds. Disk I/O is often the bottleneck for reads, as well as for transaction commits.

- Transactions running in parallel may attempt to read or write the same data item, resulting in data conflicts that reduce effective parallelism. This problem is exacerbated by long-running transactions.

In Sections 20.3.1 and 20.3.2, we discuss techniques to reduce the influence of these problems.

## 20.3.1   Main-Memory Databases

Usually, the performance of database systems is limited by the speed at which data are read from and written to disk. We can reduce the degree to which a database system is disk bound by increasing the size of the database buffer. Advances in main-memory technology have made it possible for us to construct large main memories at relatively low cost. Today, there are commercial 64-bit systems that can support main memories as large as 14 gigabytes.

The long disk latency (about 10 milliseconds average) increases not only the time to access a data item, but also limits the number of accesses per second. Therefore, for some applications, such as in real-time control, it is necessary to store data in main memory to meet performance requirements. The memory size required for most such systems is not exceptionally large, although there are at least a few applications that require multiple gigabytes of data to be memory resident. As memory sizes grow, more applications can be expected to have data that fit into main memory.

Large main memories allow faster processing of transactions, since data are memory resident. However, there are still disk-related limitations:

- Log records must be written to stable storage before a transaction is committed. The improved performance made possible by a large main memory may result in the logging process becoming a bottleneck. We can reduce commit time by creating a stable log buffer in main memory, using battery backed-up memory (also called *nonvolatile RAM*). The overhead imposed by logging can also be reduced by the *group-commit* technique discussed next, in Section 20.3.2. Throughput (number of transactions per second) is still limited by the data-transfer rate of the log disk.

- Buffer blocks marked as modified by committed transactions still have to be written so that the amount of log that has to be replayed at recovery time is reduced. If the update rate is extremely high, the disk data-transfer rate may become a bottleneck.

- If the system crashes, all of main memory is lost. On recovery, the system has an empty database buffer, and data items must be input from disk when they are accessed. Therefore, even after recovery is complete, it takes some time before the database is fully loaded in main memory and high-speed processing of transactions can resume.

On the other hand, main-memory database provide opportunities for optimizations:

- Since memory is costlier than disk space, internal data structures in main-memory databases have to be designed to reduce space requirements. However, data structures can have pointers crossing multiple pages unlike in disk databases, where the cost of the I/Os to traverse multiple pages would be excessively high. For example, tree structures in main-memory databases can be relatively deep, unlike B$^+$-trees, but should minimize space requirements.
- There is no need to pin buffer pages in memory before data are accessed, since buffer pages will never be replaced.
- Query-processing techniques should be designed to minimize space overhead, so that main memory limits are not exceeded while a query is being evaluated; that situation would result in paging to swap area, and would slow down query processing.
- Once the disk I/O bottleneck is removed, operations such as locking and latching may become bottlenecks. Such bottlenecks must be eliminated by improvements in the implementation of these operations.
- Recovery algorithms can be optimized, since pages rarely need to be written out to make space for other pages.

Additional information on main-memory databases is given in the references provided in the bibliographic notes.

## 20.3.2   Group Commit

The process of committing a transaction $T$ requires the following to be written to stable storage:

- All log records associated with $T$ that have not been output to stable storage
- The <T **commit**> log record

These output operations frequently require the output of blocks that are only partially filled. To ensure that nearly full blocks are output, we use the *group-commit* technique. Instead of attempting to commit $T$ when $T$ completes, the system waits until several transactions have completed. It then commits this group of transactions together. Blocks written to stable storage may contain records of several transactions. By careful choice of group size, the system can ensure that blocks are full when they are written to stable storage. This technique results, on average, in fewer output operations per committed transaction.

Although group commit reduces the overhead imposed by logging, it results in transactions being delayed in committing until a sufficiently large group of transactions is ready to commit. The delay is acceptable in high-performance transaction systems, since it does not take much time for a group of transactions to be ready to commit.

# 20.4   Long-Duration Transactions

The transaction concept was developed initially in the context of data-processing applications, in which most transactions are noninteractive and of short duration. Although the techniques presented here and earlier in Chapters 13, 14, and 15 work well in those applications, serious problems arise when this concept is applied to database systems that involve human interaction. Such transactions have the following key properties:

- **Long duration**. Once there is any human interaction with an active transaction, that transaction becomes a long-duration transaction from the perspective of the computer, since human response time is slow relative to computer speed. Furthermore, in design applications, the human activity being modeled may involve hours, days, or an even longer period. Thus, transactions may be of long duration in human terms, as well as in machine terms.

- **Exposure of uncommitted data**. Data generated and displayed to a user by a long-duration transaction are uncommitted, since the transaction may abort. Thus, users—and, as a result, other transactions—may be forced to read uncommitted data. If several users are cooperating on a design, user transactions may need to exchange data prior to transaction commit.

- **Subtasks**. An interactive transaction may consist of a set of subtasks initiated by the user. The user may wish to abort a subtask without necessarily causing the entire transaction to abort.

- **Recoverability**. It is unacceptable to abort a long-duration interactive transaction because of a system crash. The active transaction must be recovered to a state that existed shortly before the crash so that relatively little human work is lost.

- **Performance**. Good performance in an interactive transaction system is defined as fast response time. This definition is in contrast to that in a noninteractive system, in which high throughput (number of transactions per second) is the goal. Systems with high throughput make efficient use of system resources. However, in the case of interactive transactions, the most costly resource is the user. If the efficiency and satisfaction of the user is to be optimized, response time should be fast (from a human perspective). In those cases where a task takes a long time, response time should be predictable (that is, the variance in response times should be low), so that users can manage their time well.

In Sections 20.4.1 through 20.4.5, we shall see why these five properties are incompatible with the techniques presented thus far, and shall discuss how those techniques can be modified to accommodate long-duration interactive transactions.

## 20.4.1   Nonserializable Executions

The properties that we discussed make it impractical to enforce the requirement used in earlier chapters that only serializable schedules be permitted. Each of the concurrency-control protocols of Chapter 14 has adverse effects on long-duration transactions:

- **Two-phase locking**. When a lock cannot be granted, the transaction requesting the lock is forced to wait for the data item in question to be unlocked. The duration of this wait is proportional to the duration of the transaction holding the lock. If the data item is locked by a short-duration transaction, we expect that the waiting time will be short (except in case of deadlock or extraordinary system load). However, if the data item is locked by a long-duration transaction, the wait will be of long duration. Long waiting times lead to both longer response time and an increased chance of deadlock.

- **Graph-based protocols**. Graph-based protocols allow for locks to be released earlier than under the two-phase locking protocols, and they prevent deadlock. However, they impose an ordering on the data items. Transactions must lock data items in a manner consistent with this ordering. As a result, a transaction may have to lock more data than it needs. Furthermore, a transaction must hold a lock until there is no chance that the lock will be needed again. Thus, long-duration lock waits are likely to occur.

- **Timestamp-based protocols**. Timestamp protocols never require a transaction to wait. However, they do require transactions to abort under certain circumstances. If a long-duration transaction is aborted, a substantial amount of work is lost. For noninteractive transactions, this lost work is a performance issue. For interactive transactions, the issue is also one of user satisfaction. It is highly undesirable for a user to find that several hours' worth of work have been undone.

- **Validation**. Like timestamp-based protocols, validation protocols enforce serializability by means of transaction abort.

Thus, it appears that the enforcement of serializability results in long-duration waits, in abort of long-duration transactions, or in both. There are theoretical results, cited in the bibliographic notes, that substantiate this conclusion.

Further difficulties with the enforcement of serializability arise when we consider recovery issues. We previously discussed the problem of cascading rollback, in which the abort of a transaction may lead to the abort of other transactions. This phenomenon is undesirable, particularly for long-duration transactions. If locking is used, exclusive locks must be held until the end of the transaction, if cascading rollback is to be avoided. This holding of exclusive locks, however, increases the length of transaction waiting time.

Thus, it appears that the enforcement of transaction atomicity must either lead to an increased probability of long-duration waits or create a possibility of cascading rollback.

These considerations are the basis for the alternative concepts of correctness of concurrent executions and transaction recovery that we consider in the remainder of this section.

## 20.4.2   Concurrency Control

The fundamental goal of database concurrency control is to ensure that concurrent execution of transactions does not result in a loss of database consistency. The concept of serializability can be used to achieve this goal, since all serializable schedules preserve consistency of the database. However, not all schedules that preserve consistency of the database are serializable. Let us illustrate this assertion by considering again a bank database consisting of two accounts $A$ and $B$, with the consistency requirement that the sum $A + B$ be preserved. For example, although the schedule of Figure 20.4 is not conflict serializable, it nevertheless preserves the sum of $A + B$. It also illustrates two important points about the concept of correctness without serializability.

- Correctness depends on the specific consistency constraints for the database.
- Correctness depends on the properties of operations performed by each transaction.

It is of prohibitive computational cost to perform an automatic analysis of low-level operations by transactions, and of their potential effect on a fully specified database consistency constraint. However, there are simpler, less costly techniques. One is to use the database consistency constraints as the basis for a split of the database into subdatabases on which concurrency can be managed separately. Another is to treat some operations besides **read** and **write** as fundamental low-level operations, and to extend concurrency control to deal with them.

| $T_1$ | $T_2$ |
|---|---|
| **read**($A$) | |
| $A := A - 50$ | |
| **write**($A$) | |
| | **read**($B$) |
| | $B := B - 10$ |
| | **write**($B$) |
| **read**($B$) | |
| $B := B + 50$ | |
| **write**($B$) | |
| | **read**($A$) |
| | $A := A + 10$ |
| | **write**($A$) |

Figure 20.4   A non–conflict-serializable schedule.

The bibliographic notes reference other techniques for ensuring consistency without requiring serializability. Many of these techniques exploit variants of multiversion concurrency control (see Section 15.6). For older data-processing applications that need only one version, multiversion protocols impose a high space overhead to store the extra versions. Since many of the new database applications require the maintenance of versions of data, concurrency-control techniques that exploit multiple versions are practical.

### 20.4.3   Nested and Multilevel Transactions

A long-duration transaction can be viewed as a collection of related subtasks or subtransactions. By structuring a transaction as a set of subtransactions, we are able to enhance parallelism, since it may be possible to run several subtransactions in parallel. Furthermore, it is possible to deal with failure of a subtransaction (due to abort, system crash, and so on) without having to roll back the entire long-duration transaction.

A nested or multilevel transaction $T$ consists of a set $T = \{t_1, t_2, \ldots, t_n\}$ of subtransactions and a partial order $P$ on $T$. A subtransaction $t_i$ in $T$ may abort without forcing $T$ to abort. Instead, $T$ may either restart $t_i$ or simply choose not to run $t_i$. If $t_i$ commits, this action does not make $t_i$ permanent (unlike the situation in Chapter 15). Instead, $t_i$ *commits to* $T$, and may still abort (or require compensation—see Section 20.4.4) if $T$ aborts. An execution of $T$ must not violate the partial order $P$. That is, if an edge $t_i \rightarrow t_j$ appears in the precedence graph, then $t_j \rightarrow t_i$ must not be in the transitive closure of $P$.

Nesting may be several levels deep, representing a subdivision of a transaction into subtasks, subsubtasks, and so on. At the lowest level of nesting, we have the standard database operations **read** and **write** that we have used previously.

If a subtransaction of $T$ is permitted to release locks on completion, $T$ is called a *multilevel* transaction. When a multilevel transaction represents a long-duration activity, the transaction is sometimes referred to as a *saga*. Alternatively, if locks held by a subtransaction $t_i$ of $T$ are automatically assigned to $T$ on completion of $t_i$, $T$ is called a *nested transaction*.

Although the main practical value of multi-level transactions arises in complex, long-duration transactions, we shall use the simple example of Figure 20.4 to show how nesting can create higher-level operations that may enhance concurrency. We rewrite transaction $T_1$ using subtransactions $T_{1,1}$ and $T_{1,2}$ that perform increment or decrement operations:

- $T_1$ consists of
  - $T_{1,1}$, which subtracts 50 from $A$
  - $T_{1,2}$, which adds 50 to $B$

Similarly, we rewrite transaction $T_2$ using subtransactions $T_{2,1}$ and $T_{2,2}$ that perform increment or decrement operations:

- $T_2$ consists of
  - $T_{2,1}$, which subtracts 10 from $B$
  - $T_{2,2}$, which adds 10 to $A$

No ordering is specified on $T_{1,1}$, $T_{1,2}$, $T_{2,1}$, and $T_{2,2}$. Any execution of these subtransactions will generate a correct result. The schedule of Figure 20.4 corresponds to the schedule $< T_{1,1},\ T_{2,1},\ T_{1,2},\ T_{2,2} >$.

### 20.4.4   Compensating Transactions

To reduce the frequency of long-duration waiting, we arrange for uncommitted updates to be exposed to other concurrently executing transactions. Indeed, multi-level transactions may allow this exposure. However, the exposure of uncommitted data creates the potential for cascading rollbacks. The concept of *compensating transactions* helps us to deal with this problem.

Let transaction $T$ be divided into several subtransactions $t_1, t_2, \ldots, t_n$. After a subtransaction $t_i$ commits, it releases its locks. Now, if the outer-level transaction $T$ has to be aborted, the effect of its subtransactions must be undone. Suppose that subtransactions $t_1, \ldots, t_k$ have committed, and that $t_{k+1}$ was executing when the decision to abort is made. We can undo the effects of $t_{k+1}$ by aborting that subtransaction. However, it is not possible to abort subtransactions $t_1, \ldots, t_k$, since they have committed already.

Instead, we execute a new subtransaction $ct_i$, called a *compensating transaction* to undo the effect of a subtransaction $t_i$. Each subtransaction $t_i$ is required to have a compensating transaction $ct_i$. The compensating transactions must be executed in the inverse order $ct_k, \ldots, ct_1$. We give several examples of compensation here:

- Consider the schedule of Figure 20.4, which we have shown to be correct, although not conflict serializable. Each subtransaction releases its locks once it completes. Suppose that $T_2$ fails just prior to termination, after $T_{2,2}$ has released its locks. We then run a compensating transaction for $T_{2,2}$ that subtracts 10 from $A$ and a compensating transaction for $T_{2,1}$ that adds 10 to $B$.

- Consider a database insert by transaction $T_i$ that, as a side effect, causes a $B^+$-tree index to be updated. The insert operation may have modified several nodes of the $B^+$-tree index. Other transactions may have read these nodes in accessing data other than the record inserted by $T_i$. As discussed in Section 15.9, we can undo the insertion by deleting the record inserted by $T_i$. The result is a correct, consistent $B^+$-tree, but is not necessarily one with exactly the same structure as the one we had before $T_i$ started. Thus, deletion is a compensating action for insertion.

- Consider a long-duration transaction $T_i$ representing a travel reservation. Transaction $T$ has three subtransactions: $T_{i,1}$, which makes airline reservations; $T_{i,2}$, which reserves rental cars; and $T_{i,3}$, which reserves a hotel room. Suppose that the hotel cancels the reservation. Instead of undoing all of $T_i$, we compensate for the failure of $T_{i,3}$ by deleting the old hotel reservation and making a new one.

If the system crashes in the middle of executing an outer-level transaction, its subtransactions must be rolled back when it recovers. The techniques described in Section15.9 can be used for this purpose.

Compensation for the failure of a transaction requires use of semantics of the failed transaction. For certain operations, such as incrementation or insertion into a $B^+$-tree, the corresponding compensation is easily defined. For more complex transactions, the application programmers may have to define the correct form of compensation at the time that the transaction is coded. For complex interactive transactions, it may be necessary for the system to interact with the user to determine the proper form of compensation.

## 20.4.5   Implementation Issues

The transaction concepts discussed in this section create serious difficulties for implementation. We present a few of them here, and discuss how we can address these problems.

Long-duration transactions must survive system crashes. We can ensure that they will by performing a **redo** on committed subtransactions, and by performing either an **undo** or compensation for any short-duration subtransactions that were active at the time of the crash. However, these actions solve only part of the problem. In typical database systems, such internal system data as lock tables and transactions timestamps are kept in volatile storage. For a long-duration transaction to be resumed after a crash, these data must be restored. Therefore, it is necessary to log not only changes to the database, but also changes to internal system data pertaining to long-duration transactions.

Logging of updates is made more complex by the types of data items that may exist in the database. A data item may be a CAD design, text of a document, or another form of composite design. Such data items are physically large. Thus, storing both the old and new values of the data item in a log record is undesirable.

There are two approaches to reducing the overhead of ensuring the recoverability of large data items:

- **Operation logging**. Only the operation performed on the data item and the data-item name are stored in the log. Operation logging is also called *logical logging*. For each operation, an inverse operation must exist. We perform **undo** using the inverse operation, and **redo** using the operation itself. Recovery through operation logging is more difficult, since **redo** and **undo** are not idempotent. Further, using logical logging for an operation that updates multiple pages is greatly complicated by the fact that some, but not all, of the updated pages may have been written to the disk, so it is hard to apply either the **redo** or the **undo** of the operation on the disk image during recovery.

- **Logging and shadow paging**. Logging is used for modifications to small data items, but large data items are made recoverable via a shadow-page technique (see Section 15.5). When we use shadowing, only those pages that are actually modified need to be stored in duplicate.

Regardless of the technique used, the complexities introduced by long-duration transactions and large data items complicate the recovery process. Thus, it is desirable to allow certain noncritical data to be exempt from logging, and to rely instead on offline backups and human intervention.

## 20.5   Real-Time Transaction Systems

The constraints that we have considered thus far pertain to the values stored in the database. In certain applications, the constraints include *deadlines* by which a task must be completed. Examples of such applications include plant management, traffic control, and scheduling. When deadlines are included, correctness of an execution is no longer solely an issue of database consistency. Rather, we are concerned with how many deadlines are missed, and by how much time they are missed. Deadlines are characterized as follows:

- **Hard**. The task has zero value if it is completed after the deadline.
- **Soft**. The task has diminishing value if it is completed after the deadline, with the value approaching zero as the degree of lateness increases.

Systems with deadlines are called *real-time* systems.

Transaction management in real-time systems must take deadlines into account. If the concurrency-control protocol determines that a transaction $T_i$ must wait, it may cause $T_i$ to miss the deadline. In such cases, it may be preferable to preempt the transaction holding the lock, and to allow $T_i$ to proceed. Preemption must be used with care, however, because the time lost by the preempted transaction (due to rollback and restart) may cause the transaction to miss its deadline. Unfortunately, it is difficult to determine whether rollback or waiting is preferable in a given situation.

A major difficulty in supporting real-time constraints arises from the variance in transaction execution time. In the best case, all data accesses reference data in the database buffer. In the worst case, each access causes a buffer page to be written to disk (preceded by the requisite log records), followed by the reading from disk of the page containing the data to be accessed. Because the two or more disk accesses required in the worst case take several orders of magnitude more time than the main-memory references required in the best case, transaction execution time can be estimated only very poorly if data are resident on disk. Hence, main-memory databases are often used if real-time constraints have to be met. However, even if data are resident in main memory, variances in execution time arise from lock waits, transaction aborts, and so on.

In high-performance transaction systems (see Section 20.3), speed is the critical issue. In real-time systems, deadlines, rather than absolute speed, are the most important issue. Designing a real-time system involves ensuring that there is enough processing power exists to meet deadlines without requiring excessive hardware resources. Achieving this objective, despite the variance in execution time resulting from transaction management, remains a challenging problem. The bibliographic notes provide references to research in the area of real-time databases.

# 20.6  Weak Levels of Consistency

In Chapter 14, the concept of serializability was presented, and protocols were defined to ensure that only serializable schedules are possible. Serializability is a useful concept because it allows programmers to ignore issues related to concurrency when they code transactions. If every transaction has the property that it maintains database consistency if executed alone, then serializability ensures that concurrent executions maintain consistency. However, the protocols required to ensure serializability may allow too little concurrency for certain applications. In these cases, weaker levels of consistency are used. The use of weaker levels of consistency places additional burdens on programmers for ensuring database correctness.

## 20.6.1  Degree-Two Consistency

The purpose of *degree-two consistency* is to avoid cascading aborts without necessarily ensuring serializability. The locking protocol for degree-two consistency uses the same two lock modes as we used for the two-phase locking protocol: shared (S) and exclusive (X). A transaction must hold the appropriate lock mode when it accesses a data item.

In contrast to the situation in two-phase locking, S-locks may be released at any time, and locks may be acquired at any time. Exclusive locks cannot be released until the transaction either commits or aborts. Serializability is not ensured by this protocol. Indeed, a transaction may read the same data item twice and obtain different results. In Figure 20.5, $T_3$ reads the value of $Q$ before and after that value is written by $T_4$.

The potential for inconsistency due to non-serializable schedules under degree-two consistency makes this approach undesirable for many applications.

## 20.6.2  Cursor Stability

*Cursor stability* is a form of degree-two consistency designed for programs written in general-purpose, record-oriented languages such as Pascal, C, Cobol, PL/I, or Fortran. Such programs often iterate over the tuples of a relation. Rather than locking the entire relation, cursor stability ensures that

- The tuple that is currently being processed by the iteration is locked in shared mode.
- Any modified tuples are locked in exclusive mode until the transaction commits.

| $T_3$ | $T_4$ |
|---|---|
| **lock-S**($Q$) | |
| **read**($Q$) | |
| **unlock**($Q$) | |
| | **lock-X**($Q$) |
| | **read**($Q$) |
| | **write**($Q$) |
| | **unlock**($Q$) |
| **lock-S**($Q$) | |
| **read**($Q$) | |
| **unlock**($Q$) | |

Figure 20.5   Nonserializable schedule with degree-two consistency.

These rules ensure that degree-two consistency is obtained. Two-phase locking is not required. Serializability is not guaranteed. Cursor stability is used in practice on heavily accessed relations as a means of increasing concurrency and improving system performance. Applications that use cursor stability must be coded in a way that ensures database consistency despite the possibility of nonserializable schedules. Thus, the use of cursor stability is limited to specialized situations with simple consistency constraints.

## 20.7   Transactional Workflows

A *workflow* is an activity involving the coordinated execution of multiple tasks performed by different processing entities. A *task* defines some work to be done and can be specified in a number of ways, including a textual description in a file or an electronic-mail message, a form, a message, or a computer program. A *processing entity* that performs the tasks may be a person or a software system (for example, a mailer, an application program, or a database-management system).

Figure 20.6 shows examples of such workflows. A simple example of a workflow is in an electronic-mail system. The delivery of a single mail message

| Workflow application | Typical tasks | Typical processing entities |
|---|---|---|
| electronic-mail routing | electronic-mail message | mailers |
| loan processing | form processing | humans, application software |
| purchase-order processing | form processing | humans, application software, DBMSs |

Figure 20.6   Examples of workflows.

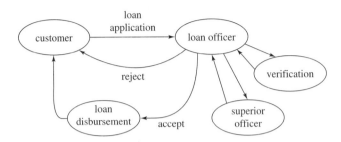

Figure 20.7     Workflow in loan processing.

may involve several mailer systems that receive and forward the mail message, until the message reaches its destination, where it is stored. Each mailer performs a task—namely, forwarding the mail to the next mailer—and the tasks of multiple mailers may be required to route mail from source to destination. Other terms used in the database and related literature to refer to workflows include *task flow* and *multisystem applications*. Tasks are also sometimes called *steps*.

In general, workflows may involve one or more humans. For instance, consider the processing of a loan. The relevant workflow is shown in Figure 20.7. The person who wants a loan fills out a form, which is then checked by a loan officer. An employee who processes loan applications verifies the data in the form using sources such as credit-reference bureaus. When all the required information has been collected, the loan officer may decide to approve the loan; that decision may then have to be approved by one or more superior officers, after which the loan can be made. Each human here performs a task; in a bank that has not automated the task of loan processing, the coordination of the tasks is typically carried out via passing of the loan application, with attached notes and other information, from one employee to the next. Other examples of workflows include processing of expense vouchers, of purchase orders, and of credit-card transactions.

Today, all the information related to a workflow is more than likely to be stored in a digital form on one or more computers, and, with the growth of networking, information can be easily transferred from one computer to another. Hence, it is feasible for organizations to automate their workflows. For example, to automate the tasks involved in loan processing, we can store the loan application and associated information in a database. The workflow itself then involves handing of charge from one human to the next, and possibly even to programs that can automatically fetch the required information. Humans can coordinate their activities using means such as electronic mail.

We have to address two problems, in general, to automate a workflow. The first is the *specification* of a workflow: detailing the tasks that must be carried out, and defining the execution requirements. The second problem is the *execution* of workflows, which we must do while providing the safeguards of traditional database systems related to computation correctness, data integrity and durability.

For example, it is not acceptable for a loan application or a voucher to be lost, or to be processed multiple times, because of a system crash. The idea behind transactional workflows is to use and extend the concepts of transactions to the context of workflows.

Both problems are complicated by the fact that many organizations use multiple independently managed information-processing systems that, in most cases, were developed separately to automate different functions. Workflow activities may require interactions among several such systems, each performing a task, as well as interactions with humans.

A number of workflow systems have been developed in recent years. Here, we study properties of workflow systems at a relatively abstract level, without going into the details of any particular system.

## 20.7.1 Workflow Specification

The idea of a workflow can be traced to the job-control language (JCL) of batch operating systems, which allowed the user to specify a job as a collection of steps. Each step was an invocation of a program, and the steps were executed in sequence. Some steps could be executed conditionally—for example, only if the previous step was successful, or if that step failed. Thus, a JCL specification can be thought of as an example of a workflow specification.

Internal aspects of a task do not need to be modeled for the purpose of workflow management. In an abstract view of a task, a task may use parameters stored in its input variables, may retrieve and update data in the local system, may store its results in its output variables, and may be queried about its execution state. At any time during the execution, the *state of a workflow* consists of the collection of states of the workflow's constituent tasks, and the states (values) of all variables in the workflow specification.

The coordination of tasks can be specified either statically or dynamically. In a static specification, the tasks and dependencies among them are defined before the execution of the workflow begins. For instance, the tasks in an expense-voucher workflow may consist of the approvals of the voucher by a secretary, a manager, and an accountant, in that order, and finally by the delivery of a check. The dependencies among the tasks may be simple—each task has to be completed before the next begins.

A generalization of this strategy is to have a precondition for execution of each task in the workflow, so that all possible tasks in a workflow and their dependencies are known in advance, but only those tasks whose preconditions are satisfied are executed. The preconditions can be defined through dependencies such as the following:

- *Execution states* of other tasks—for example, "task $t_i$ cannot start until task $t_j$ has ended," or "task $t_i$ must abort if task $t_j$ has committed"
- *Output values* of other tasks—for example, "task $t_i$ can start if task $t_j$ returns a value greater than 25," or "the manager-approval task can start if the secretary-approval task returns a value of OK"

- *External variables* modified by external events—for example, "task $t_i$ cannot be started before 9 AM GMT," or "task $t_i$ must be started within 24 hours of the completion of task $t_j$"

We can combine the dependencies using the regular logical connectors (**or, and, not**) to form complex scheduling preconditions.

An example of dynamic scheduling of tasks is an electronic-mail routing system. The next task to be scheduled for a given mail message depends on what the destination address of the message is, and on which intermediate routers are functioning.

## 20.7.2    Failure-Atomicity Requirements of a Workflow

Based on the semantics of a workflow, the workflow designer may specify the *failure-atomicity* requirements of the workflow. The traditional notion of failure atomicity would require that a failure of any task results in the failure of the workflow. However, a workflow can, in many cases, survive the failure of one of its tasks—for example, by executing a functionally equivalent task at another site. Therefore, we should allow the designer to define failure-atomicity requirements of a workflow. The system must guarantee that every execution of a workflow will terminate in a state that satisfies the failure-atomicity requirements defined by the designer. We call those states *acceptable termination states* of a workflow. All other execution states of a workflow constitute a set of *nonacceptable termination states*, in which the failure-atomicity requirements may be violated.

An acceptable termination state can be designated as committed or aborted. A *committed acceptable termination state* is an execution state in which the objectives of a workflow have been achieved. In contrast, an *aborted acceptable termination state* is a valid termination state in which a workflow has failed to achieve its objectives. If an aborted acceptable termination state has been reached, all undesirable effects of the partial execution of the workflow must be undone in accordance with that workflow's failure-atomicity requirements.

A workflow must reach an acceptable termination state *even in the presence of system failures*. Thus, if a workflow was in a nonacceptable termination state at the time of failure, during system recovery it must be brought to an acceptable termination state (whether aborted or committed).

For example, in the loan-processing workflow, in the final state, either the loan applicant is told that a loan cannot be made, or the loan is disbursed. In case of failures such as a long failure of the verification system, the loan application could be returned to the loan applicant with a suitable explanation; this outcome would constitute an aborted acceptable termination. A committed acceptable termination would be either the acceptance or the rejection of the loan.

In general, a task can commit and release its resources before the workflow reaches a termination state. However, if the multitask transaction later aborts, its failure atomicity may require that we undo the effects of already completed tasks (for example, committed subtransactions) by executing compensating tasks (as subtransactions). The semantics of compensation requires that a compensating transaction eventually completes its execution successfully, possibly after a number of resubmissions.

In an expense-voucher–processing workflow, for example, a department-budget balance may be reduced based on an initial approval of a voucher by the manager. If the voucher is later rejected, whether due to failure or for other reasons, the budget may have to be restored by a compensating transaction.

### 20.7.3   Execution of Workflows

The execution of the tasks may be controlled by a human coordinator or by a software system called a *workflow-management system*. A workflow-management system consists of a scheduler, task agents, and a mechanism to query the state of the workflow system. A task agent controls the execution of a task by a processing entity. A scheduler is a program that processes workflows by submitting various tasks for execution, monitoring various events, and evaluating conditions related to intertask dependencies. A scheduler may submit a task for execution (to a task agent), or may request that a previously submitted task be aborted. In the case of multidatabase transactions, the tasks are subtransactions, and the processing entities are local DBMSs. In accordance with the workflow specifications, the scheduler enforces the scheduling dependencies and is responsible for ensuring that tasks reach acceptable termination states.

There are three architectural approaches to the development of a workflow-management system. A centralized approach has a single scheduler that schedules the tasks for all concurrently executing workflows. The partially distributed approach is to have one (instance of) a scheduler for each workflow. When the issues of concurrent execution can be separated from the scheduling function, the latter option is a natural choice. A fully distributed approach has no scheduler, but the task agents coordinate their execution by communicating with one another to satisfy task dependencies and other workflow execution requirements.

The simplest workflow-execution systems follow the fully distributed approach just described, and are based on electronic mail. Each site has a task agent that executes tasks received over electronic mail. Execution may also involve presenting electronic mail to humans, who have then to carry out some action. When a task is completed at a site, and needs to be processed at another site, the task agent dispatches an electronic-mail message to the next site. The message contains all relevant information about the task to be performed. Such electronic-mail–based workflow systems are particularly useful in networks that may be disconnected for part of the time, such as dial-up networks.

The centralized approach is used in workflow systems where the data are stored in a central database. The scheduler notifies various agents, such as humans or computer programs, that a task has to be carried out, and keeps track of task completion. It is easier to keep track of the state of a workflow with a centralized approach than it is with a fully distributed approach.

The scheduler must guarantee that a workflow will terminate in one of the specified acceptable termination states. Ideally, before attempting to execute a workflow, the scheduler should examine that workflow to check whether the workflow may terminate in a nonacceptable state. If the scheduler cannot guarantee that a workflow will terminate in an acceptable state, it should reject such specifications without attempting to execute the workflow. As an example, let us consider a workflow consisting of two tasks represented by subtransactions $S_1$ and $S_2$, with the failure-atomicity requirements indicating that either both or neither of the subtransactions should be committed. If $S_1$ and $S_2$ do not provide prepared-to-commit states (for a two-phase commit), and further do not have compensating transactions, then it is possible to reach a state where one subtransaction is committed and the other aborted, and there is no way to bring both to the same state. Therefore, such a workflow specification is *unsafe*, and should be rejected.

Safety checks such as the one just described may be impossible or impractical to implement in the scheduler; it then becomes the responsibility of the person designing the workflow specification to ensure that the workflows are safe.

### 20.7.4   Recovery of a Workflow

The objective of failure recovery in workflow management is to enforce the failure atomicity of workflows. The recovery procedures must make sure that, if a failure occurs in any of the workflow-processing components (including the scheduler), the workflow will eventually reach an acceptable termination state (whether aborted or committed). For example, the scheduler could continue processing after failure and recovery, as though nothing happened, thus providing forward recoverability. Otherwise, the scheduler could abort the whole workflow (that is, reach one of the global abort states). In either case, some subtransactions may need to be committed or even submitted for execution (for example, compensating subtransactions).

We assume that the processing entities involved in the workflow have their own local recovery systems and handle their local failures. To recover the execution-environment context, the failure-recovery routines need to restore the state information of the scheduler at the time of failure, including the information about the execution states of each task. Therefore, the appropriate status information must be logged on stable storage.

We also need to consider the contents of the message queues. When one agent hands off a task to another, the handoff should be carried out exactly once: if the handoff happens twice a task may get executed twice; if the handoff does not occur, the task may get lost.

If a persistent message mechanism is used, the messages are stored in stable storage and are not lost in case of failure. The persistent message system is then responsible for making sure that messages get delivered eventually, even in the presence of system failures. Persistent message support may be provided by a transaction-processing monitor, or may be provided directly by the operating system, as it is in the mailboxes provided by the DEC VMS operating system. Before an agent commits, it writes to the persistent message queue whatever messages need to be sent out. The message system at the receiving end must also log requests in stable storage so that it can detect multiple receipts of a request.

## 20.8  Summary

Remote backup systems provide a high degree of availability, allowing transaction processing to continue even if the primary site is destroyed by a fire, flood, or earthquake. Transaction processing is faster than in a replicated distributed system.

Transaction-processing monitors were initially developed as multithreaded servers that could service large numbers of terminals from a single process. They have since evolved, and today they provide the infrastructure for building and administering complex transaction-processing systems that have a large number of clients and multiple servers. They provide services such as presentation facilities to simplify the writing of user-interface applications, persistent queueing of client requests and server responses, routing of client messages to servers, and coordination of two-phase commit when transactions access multiple servers.

Large main memories are exploited in certain systems to achieve high system throughput. In such systems, logging is a bottleneck. Under the group-commit concept, the number of outputs to stable storage can be reduced, thus releasing this bottleneck.

The efficient management of long-duration interactive transactions is more complex, because of the long-duration waits, and because of the possibility of aborts. Since the concurrency-control techniques used in Chapter 14 use waits, aborts, or both, alternative techniques must be considered. These techniques must ensure correctness without requiring serializability. A long-duration transaction is represented as a nested transaction with atomic database operations at the lowest level. If a transaction fails, only active short-duration transactions abort. Active long-duration transactions resume once any short-duration transactions have recovered. We can do recovery using the **undo** mechanism discussed in Chapter 15. However, it is often possible to use a compensating transaction, instead of an **undo**. A compensating transaction corrects, or compensates for, the failure of a transaction, without causing cascading rollback.

In systems with real-time constraints, correctness of execution involves not only database consistency but also deadline satisfaction. The wide variance of execution times for read and write operations complicates the transaction-management problem for time-constrained systems.

We can sometimes use alternative notions of consistency that do not ensure serializability, to improve performance. Cursor stability and degree-two consistency ensure that no transaction can read data written by an uncommitted transaction. However, nonserializable executions are possible.

Workflows are activities that involve the coordinated execution of multiple tasks performed by different processing entities. They exist not just in computer applications, but also in almost all organizational activities. With the growth of networks, and the existence of multiple autonomous database systems, workflows provide a convenient way of carrying out tasks that involve multiple systems. Although the usual ACID transactional requirements are too strong or are unimplementable for such workflow applications, workflows must satisfy a limited set of transactional properties that guarantee that a process is not left in an inconsistent state.

## Exercises

**20.1.** Explain the difference between a system crash and a "disaster."

**20.2.** Explain the difference between data replication in a distributed system and the maintenance of a remote backup site.

**20.3.** For each of the following requirements, identify the best choice of degree of durability:

(*a*) Data loss must be avoided but some loss of availability may be tolerated.

(*b*) Transaction commit must be accomplished quickly, even at the cost of loss of some committed transactions in a disaster.

(*c*) A high degree of availability and durability is required, but a longer running time for the transaction commit protocol is acceptable.

**20.4.** Explain how a TP monitor manages memory and processor resources more effectively than a typical operating system.

**20.5.** If the entire database fits in main memory, do we still need a database system to manage the data? Explain your answer.

**20.6.** Consider a main-memory database system recovering from a system crash. Explain the relative merits of

- Loading the entire database back into main memory before resuming transaction processing.
- Loading data as it is requested by transactions.

**20.7.** In the group-commit technique, how many transactions should be part of a group? Explain your answer.

**20.8.** Let $T_1$ and $T_2$ be transactions that each modify two data items. Assume that 100 log records fit on one block. How many block writes are required if $T_1$ and $T_2$ are committed separately? How many are required if $T_1$ and $T_2$ are committed as a group?

**20.9.** Explain why it may be impractical to require serializability for long-duration transactions.

**20.10.** Discuss the modifications that need to be made in each of the recovery schemes covered in Chapter 15 if we allow nested transactions. Also, explain any differences that result if we allow multilevel transactions.

**20.11.** What is the purpose of compensating transactions? Present two examples of their use.

**20.12.** Is a high-performance transaction system necessarily a real-time system? Why or why not?

**20.13.** In a database system using write-ahead logging, what is the worst-case number of disk accesses required to read a data item? Explain why this presents a problem to designers of real-time database systems.

**20.14.** Explain the reason for the use of degree-two consistency. What disadvantages does this approach have?

**20.15.** Workflow systems require concurrency and recovery management as do database systems. List 3 reasons why we cannot simply apply a relational DBMS using 2PL, WAL, and 2PC

# Bibliographical Notes

Gray and Edwards [1995] provide an overview of TP monitor architectures; Gray and Reuter [1993] provide a detailed (and excellent) textbook description of transaction-processing systems, including chapters on TP monitors. Our description of TP monitors is modeled on these two sources. X/Open [1991] defines the X/Open XA interface. Transaction processing in Tuxedo is described in Huffman [1993]. Wipfler [1987] is one of several texts on application development using CICS.

There has been much work on high-performance transaction systems. Garcia-Molina and Salem [1992] provide an overview of main-memory databases. Jagadish et al. [1993] describe a recovery algorithm designed for main-memory databases. A storage manager for main-memory databases is described in Jagadish et al. [1994]. Degree-two consistency was introduced in Gray et al. [1975].

Nested and multilevel transactions are presented by Lynch [1983], Moss [1982, 1985], Lynch and Merritt [1986], Fekete et al. [1990a, 1990b], Korth and Speegle [1994], and Pu et al. [1988]. Several extended-transaction models have been defined including sagas (Garcia-Molina and Salem [1987]), ACTA (Chrysanthis and Ramamritham [1994]), the ConTract model (Wächter and Reuter [1992]), ARIES (Mohan et al. [1992]), and the NT/PV model (Korth and Speegle [1994]). Splitting transaction to achieve higher performance is addressed in Shasha et al. [1995]. A model for concurrency in nested transactions systems is presented in Beeri et al. [1989]. Relaxation of serializability is discussed in Garcia-Molina [1983], and in Sha et al. [1988]. Recovery in nested transaction systems is discussed by Moss [1987], Haerder and Rothermel [1987], and Rothermel and Mohan [1989]. Multilevel transaction management is discussed in Weikum [1991]. Gray [1981], Skarra and Zdonik [1989], and Korth and Speegle [1988, 1990] discuss long-duration transactions. Transaction processing for long-duration transactions is considered by Weikum and Schek [1984], Haerder and Rothermel [1987], Weikum et al. [1990], and Korth et al. [1990a]. Salem et al. [1994] present an extension of 2PL for long-duration transactions by allowing the early release of locks under certain circumstances.

Transaction processing in real-time databases is discussed by Abbot and Garcia-Molina [1992], and by Dayal et al. [1990]. Barclay et al. [1982] describe a real-time database system used in a telecommunications switching system. Complexity and correctness issues in real-time databases are addressed by Korth et al. [1990b], and Soparkar et al. [1995]. Concurrency control and scheduling in real-time databases are discussed by Haritsa et al. [1990], Hong et al. [1993], and Pang et al. [1995]. Ozsoyoglu and Snodgrass [1995] is a survey of research in real-time and temporal databases.

Security considerations in transaction processing are addressed by Smith et al. [1996].

The levels of consistency – or isolation – offered in SQL-92 are explained and critiqued in Berenson et al. [1995].

Our description of workflows follows the model of Rusinkiewicz and Sheth [1995], who discuss the specification and execution of transactional workflows. Reuter [1989] presents ConTracts, a method for grouping transactions into multitransaction activities. Some issues related to workflows were addressed in the work on long-running activities by Dayal et al. [1990, 1991]. They propose event–condition–action rules as a technique for specifying workflows. Jin et al. [1993] describe workflow issues in telecommunication applications. A reference model for workflows, proposed by the Workflow Management Coalition, is presented in Hollinsworth [1994].

# CHAPTER
# 21

# NEW
# APPLICATIONS

Relational databases have been in use for over two decades. A large portion of the applications of relational databases have been in the commercial world, supporting such tasks as transaction processing for banks and stock exchanges, sales and reservations for a variety of businesses, and inventory and payroll for almost all companies. We study several new applications, which have become increasingly important in recent years.

- **Decision-support systems**. As the online availability of data has grown, businesses have begun to exploit the available data to make better decisions about their activities, such as what items to stock and how best to target customers to increase sales. We can extract much information for decision support by using simple SQL queries. Recently, however, people have felt the need for better decision support based on data analysis and data mining, or knowledge discovery, using data from a variety of sources. Section 21.1 presents an overview of decision-support systems. Data analysis is described in Section 21.2; data mining in described in Section 21.3; data warehousing is described in Section 21.4.
- **Spatial databases**. Spatial databases include geographic databases, which store maps and associated information, and computer-aided–design databases, which store information such as integrated-circuit or building designs. Applications of spatial data initially stored data as files in a file system, as did early-generation business applications. But as the complexity and volume of the data, and the number of users, have grown, ad hoc approaches to storing and retrieving data in a file system have proved insufficient for the needs of

applications that use spatial data. Spatial-data applications require facilities offered by a database system—in particular, the ability to store and query large amounts of data efficiently. Some applications may also require other database features, such as atomic updates to parts of the stored data, durability, and concurrency control. In Section 21.5, we study the extensions needed to traditional database systems to support spatial data.

- **Multimedia databases**. In Section 21.6, we study the features required in database systems that store data such as image, video, and audio data. The main distinguishing feature of video and audio data is that the display of the data requires retrieval at a steady, predetermined rate; hence, such data are called *continuous-media* data.

- **Mobile databases**. In Section 21.7, we study the database requirements of the new generation of mobile computing systems, such as notebook computers and palmtop computing devices, which are connected to base stations via wireless digital communications networks. Such computers need to be able to operate while disconnected from the network, unlike the distributed database systems discussed in Chapter 18. They also have limited storage capacity, and thus require special techniques for memory management.

- **Information retrieval**. In parallel with the field of database systems, the field of information systems has seen large growth in the last few decades. Information systems have much in common with database systems—in particular, the storage and retrieval of data on secondary storage. However, the emphasis in the field of information systems has been different from that in database systems, concentrating on issues such as querying based on keywords; the relevance of documents to the query; and the analysis, classification and indexing of documents. In Section 21.8, we study issues that arise in information-retrieval systems.

- **Distributed information retrieval**. In recent years computer networking has grown enormously, and today tens of millions of computers are connected on the global *internet*. Many of the users (people as well as organizations) have information stored on these computers that they would like to share with the rest of the world. Distributed information systems deal with the problem of how to present a uniform interface to the information, and how to allow a user to locate information in which she is interested from amidst the vast amount of information that is available on the internet. We discuss issues and challenges in distributed information systems in Section 21.9.

## 21.1    Decision-Support Systems

Database applications can be broadly classified into transaction processing and decision support (Section 19.3.2). Transaction-processing systems are widely used today, and companies have accumulated a vast amount of information generated by these systems.

For example, company databases often contain enormous quantities of information about customers and transactions. The size of the information storage required may range into gigabytes, or even terabytes for large retail chains. Transaction information for a retailer may include the name or identifier (such as credit-card number) of the customer, the items purchased, the price paid, and the dates on which the purchases were made. Information about the items purchased may include the type of item, the manufacturer, the model number, the color, and the size. Customer information may include credit history, annual income, residence, age, and even educational background.

Such large databases can be treasure troves of information for making business decisions, such as what items to stock, or what discounts to offer. For instance, a retail company may notice a sudden spurt in purchases of flannel shirts in the Pacific Northwest, may realize that there is a trend, and may start stocking a larger number of such shirts in shops in that area. As another example, a car company may find, on querying its database, that most of its small sports cars are bought by young women whose annual incomes are above $50,000. The company may then target its marketing to attract more such women to buy its small sports cars, and may avoid wasting money trying to attract other categories of people to buy those cars. In both cases, the company has identified patterns in customer behavior, and has used the patterns to make business decisions.

The storage and retrieval of data for decision support raises several issues:

- Although many decision support queries can be written in SQL, others either cannot be expressed in SQL or cannot be expressed easily in SQL. Several SQL extensions have therefore been proposed. In Section 21.2, we study a few such extensions that simplify the task of generating summary data.

- Database query languages are not suited to the performance of detailed *statistical analyses* of data. There are several packages, such as S++, that help in statistical analysis. Such packages have been interfaced with databases, to allow large volumes of data to be stored in the database and retrieved efficiently for analysis. The field of statistical analysis is a large discipline on its own, and we shall not discuss it here; see the references in the bibliographic notes for more information.

- Knowledge-discovery techniques, developed by the artificial-intelligence community, attempt to discover automatically statistical rules and patterns from data. The field of *data mining* combines ideas about knowledge discovery with efficient implementation techniques that enable them to be used on extremely large databases. Data mining is discussed in Section 21.3.

- Large companies have diverse sources of data that they need to use for making business decisions. The sources may store the data under different schemas. For performance reasons (as well as for reasons of organization control), the data sources usually will not permit other parts of the company to retrieve data on demand.

    To execute queries efficiently on such diverse data, companies have started building *data warehouses*. Data warehouses gather data from multiple sources under a unified schema, at a single site. Thus, they provide the user a single uniform interface to data. We study issues in building and maintaining a data warehouse in Section 21.4.

## 21.2   Data Analysis

Although complex statistical analysis is best left to statistics packages, databases should support simple, commonly used, forms of data analysis. Since the data stored in databases are usually large in volume, they need to be summarized in some fashion if we are to derive information that humans can use. Aggregate functions are commonly used for this task.

The SQL aggregation functionality is limited, so several extensions have been implemented by different databases. For instance, although SQL defines only a few aggregate functions, many database systems provide a richer set of functions, including variance, median, and so on. Some systems also allow users to add new aggregate functions.

Histograms are frequently used in data analysis. A histogram partitions the values taken by an attribute into ranges, and computes an aggregate, such as sum, over the values in each range. For example, a histogram on salaries values might count the number of people whose salaries fall in each of the ranges 0 to 20000, 20001 to 40000, 40001 to 60000, and above 60000. Using SQL to construct such a histogram efficiently would be cumbersome. We leave it as an exercise for you to verify our claim. Extensions to the SQL syntax that allow functions to be used in the **groupby** clause have been proposed to simplify the task. For instance, the $N\_tile$ function supported on the Red Brick database system divides values into percentiles. Consider the following query:

> **select** *percentile*, **avg**(*balance*)
> **from** *account*
> **groupby** $N\_tile(balance, 10)$ **as** *percentile*

Here, $N\_tile(balance, 10)$ divides the values for *balance* into 10 consecutive ranges, with an equal number of values in each range; duplicates are not eliminated. Thus, the first range would have the bottom 10 percent of the values, and the tenth range would have the top 10 percent of the values. The rest of the query performs a groupby based on these ranges, and returns the average balance for each range.

Statistical analysis often requires aggregation on multiple attributes. Consider an application where a shop wants to find out what kinds of clothes are popular. Let us suppose that clothes are classified based on color and size, and that we have a relation *sales* with the schema *Sales(color, size, number)*. To analyze the sales by color (light versus dark) and size (small, medium, large), a manager may want to see data laid out as shown in the table in Figure 21.1.

The table in Figure 21.1 is an example of a *cross-tabulation (cross-tab)*. Many report writers provide support for such tables. In this case, the data are two-dimensional, since they are based on two attributes: *size* and *color*. In general, the data can be represented as a multidimensional array, with a value for each element of the array. Such data are called *multidimensional* data.

|        | Small | Medium | Large | Total |
|--------|-------|--------|-------|-------|
| Light  | 8     | 35     | 10    | 53    |
| Dark   | 20    | 10     | 5     | 35    |
| Total  | 28    | 45     | 15    | 88    |

Figure 21.1    Cross tabulation of *sales* by *size* and *color*.

The data in a cross-tabulation cannot be generated by a single SQL query, since totals are taken at several different levels. Moreover, we can see easily that a cross-tabulation is not the same as a relational table. We can represent the data in relational form by introducing a special value **all** to represent subtotals, as shown in Figure 21.2.

Consider the tuples (Light, **all**, 53) and (Dark, **all**, 35). We have obtained these tuples by eliminating individual tuples with different values for *size*, and by replacing the value of *number* by an aggregate—namely, sum. The value **all** can be thought of as representing the set of values for *size*. Moving from finer-granularity data to a coarser granularity by means of aggregation is called doing a *rollup*. In our example, we have rolled up the attribute *size*. The opposite operation—that of moving from coarser-granularity data to finer-granularity data—is called *drill down*. Clearly, finer-granularity data cannot be generated from coarse-granularity data; they must be generated either from the original data, or from yet-more-fine–granularity summary data.

The number of different ways in which the tuples can be grouped for aggregation can be large, as you can verify easily from the table in Figure 21.2. In fact, for a table with $n$ dimensions, rollup can be performed on each of the $2^n$ subsets of the $n$ dimensions. Consider a three-dimensional version of the *sales* relation, with attributes *size*, *color*, and *price* as the three dimensions. Figure 21.3 shows the subsets of attributes of the relation as corners of a three-dimensional cube;

| Color | Size   | Number |
|-------|--------|--------|
| Light | Small  | 8      |
| Light | Medium | 35     |
| Light | Large  | 10     |
| Light | **all**    | 53     |
| Dark  | Small  | 20     |
| Dark  | Medium | 10     |
| Dark  | Large  | 5      |
| Dark  | **all**    | 35     |
| **all**   | Small  | 28     |
| **all**   | Medium | 45     |
| **all**   | Large  | 15     |
| **all**   | **all**    | 88     |

Figure 21.2    Relational representation of the data in Figure 21.1.

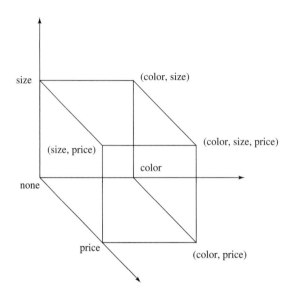

Figure 21.3    Three-dimensional data cube.

rollup can be performed on each of these subsets of attributes. In general, the subsets of attributes of an $n$-dimensional relation can be visualized as the corners of a corresponding $n$-dimensional cube.

Although we can generate tables such as the one in Figure 21.2 using SQL, doing so is cumbersome. The query involves the use of the **union** operation, and can be long; we leave it to you as an exercise to generate the rows containing **all** from a table containing the other rows.

There have been proposals to extend the SQL syntax with a **cube** operator. For instance, the following extended SQL query would generate the table shown in Figure 21.2:

> **select** *color, size,* **sum**(*number*)
> **from** *sales*
> **groupby** *color, size* **with cube**

## 21.3    Data Mining

The term *data mining* refers loosely to finding relevant information, or "discovering knowledge," from a large volume of data. Like knowledge discovery in artificial intelligence, data mining attempts to discover statistical rules and patterns automatically from data. However, data mining differs from machine learning in that it deals with large volumes of data, stored primarily on disk.

Knowledge discovered from a database can be represented by a set of *rules*. The following is an example of a rule, stated informally: "Young women with annual incomes greater than $50,000 are the most likely people to buy small sports cars."

We first describe the structure of rules used to represent knowledge, in Section 21.3.1. We then consider several classes of data-mining applications, to explain the need for data mining, in Section 21.3.2. We can discover rules from database using one of two models:

- In the first model, the user is involved directly in the process of knowledge discovery. This model is discussed in Section 21.3.3.
- In the second model, the system is responsible for automatically discovering knowledge from the database, by detecting patterns and correlations in the data. This model is covered in more detail in Section 21.3.4.

Knowledge-discovery systems may have elements of both models, with the system discovering some rules automatically, and the user guiding the process of rule discovery.

## 21.3.1 Knowledge Representation Using Rules

Rules provide a common framework in which to express various types of knowledge. Rules are of the general form

$$\forall \overline{X} antecedent \Rightarrow consequent$$

where $\overline{X}$ is a list of one or more variables with associated ranges. Let the database contain a relation *buys* that specifies what was bought in each transaction. The following is an example of a rule:

$$\forall transactions \ T, \ buys(T, bread) \Rightarrow buys(T, milk)$$

Here, $T$ is a variables whose range is the set of all transactions. The rule says that, if there is a tuple $(t_i, bread)$ in the relation *buys*, there must also be a tuple $(t_i, milk)$ in the relation *buys*.

The range of a variable defines a set of values that the variable can take. The cross-product of the ranges of the variables in the rule forms the *population*. Many data-mining systems restrict a rule to have a single variable.

Rules have an associated *support*, as well as an associated *confidence*.

- *Support* is a measure of what fraction of the population satisfies the both the antecedent and the consequent of the rule.

    For instance, if 0.001 percent of all transactions include the purchase of milk and bread, the support for the rule

$$\forall transactions \ T, \ buys(T, bread) \Rightarrow buys(T, milk)$$

is low. The rule may not even be statistically significant—perhaps there was only a single transaction that purchased both bread and milk. Businesses are often not interested in rules that have low support, since the latter involve few customers, and are not worth bothering about. On the other hand, if 50 percent of all transactions involve the purchase of milk and bread, then support is relatively high, and the rule is worth attention. Exactly what minimum degree of support is considered desirable depends on the application.

- *Confidence* is a measure of how often the consequent is true when the antecedent is true. For instance, the rule

$$\forall \ transactions \ \ T, \ buys(T, bread) \Rightarrow buys(T, milk)$$

has a confidence of 80 percent if 80 percent of the transactions that include the purchase of bread also include the purchase of milk. A rule with a low confidence is not meaningful. In business applications, rules usually have confidences significantly less than 100 percent, whereas in other domains, such as in physics, rules may have high confidences.

## 21.3.2  Classes of Data-Mining Problems

Two important classes of problems in data mining are *classification* and *association rules*.

Classification involves finding rules that partition the given data into disjoint groups. For instance, suppose that a credit-card company wants to decide whether or not to give a credit card to an applicant. The company has a variety of information about the person—such as her age, educational background, annual income, current debts, and housing location—which it can use for making a decision.

Some of this information could be relevant to the credit worthiness of the applicant, whereas some may not be. To make the decision, the company assigns a credit-worthiness level of excellent, good, average, or bad to each of a sample set of *current* customers. The assignment of credit worthiness is based on the customer's payment history. Then, the company attempts to find rules that classify its current customers into excellent, good, average, or bad, based on the information about the person, other than the actual payment history (which is unavailable for new customers). Let us consider just two attributes: education level (highest degree earned) and income. The rules may be of the following form:

$$\forall person \ \ P, \ P.degree = Masters \ \textbf{and} \ P.income \geq 75000$$
$$\Rightarrow P.credit = excellent$$
$$\forall \ person \ \ P, \ P.degree = Bachelors \ \textbf{or}$$
$$(P.income \geq 25000 \ \textbf{and} \ P.income < 75000) \ \Rightarrow P.credit = good$$

Similar rules would also be present for the other credit worthiness levels (average and bad).

Other important uses of classification include making loan approvals, setting insurance premiums, deciding whether or not to stock a particular item in a shop based on statistical information about customers, and so on.

Retail shops are often interested in *associations* between different items that people buy. For instance, someone who buys bread is quite likely also to buy milk — an association represented by the rule that we saw earlier:

$$\forall\ transactions\ \ T,\ \ buys(T, bread) \Rightarrow buys(T, milk)$$

with an associated confidence level and support.

Association information can be used in several ways. A shop may decide to place bread close to milk, to help shoppers finish their task faster. Or the shop may place them at opposite ends of a row, and place other associated items inbetween to tempt people to buy those items as well, as the shoppers walk from one end of the row to the other. A shop that offers discounts on one associated item may not offer a discount on the other, since the customer will probably buy the other anyway.

Another important class of data-mining applications is sequence correlations. Time-series data, such as stock prices on a sequence of days, form an example of sequence data. Stock-market analysts want to find correlations among stock-market price sequences. An example of such a correlation is the following rule: "Whenever bond rates go up, the stock prices go down within 2 days." Discovering such correlations between sequences can help us to make intelligent investment decisions.

## 21.3.3   User-Guided Data Mining

In the user-guided model for data mining, the user has primary responsibility for discovering rules, and the database system plays a supporting rule. Typically, the user makes up a hypothesis, and runs tests on the database to verify or refute that hypothesis. For instance, a user may have a hypothesis that people who hold master's degrees are the most likely to have an excellent credit rating, and may use the database to verify his hypothesis. The data may indicate that people who hold master's degrees are more likely than others to have an excellent credit rating.

The user may then come up with a new hypothesis, or may refine the existing hypothesis, and may verify it against the database. Thus, there may be several iterations, involving successive refinement of the hypothesis, as the user tests more refined versions.

For instance, since people who hold master's degrees have been detected to be slightly more likely to have an excellent credit rating than others, perhaps a subclass of such people are even more likely to have an excellent credit rating. The user may come up with a hypothesis that customers who hold master's degrees *and* who earn \$75,000 or more per year are likely to have an excellent credit rating. The confidence and support for the rule can be derived from the database. Now, the confidence may be high (close to 1), and the user may stop at this point, having derived a rule of the form

$$\forall\ people\ P,\ \ P.degree = Masters\ \textbf{and}\ C.income \geq 75,000$$
$$\Rightarrow\ \ C.credit = excellent$$

with the appropriate confidence and support levels.

*Data-visualization* systems help users to examine large volumes of data, and to detect patterns visually. Visual displays of data—such as maps, charts, and other graphical representations—allow data to be presented compactly to users. A single graphical screen can encode as much information as can a far larger number of text screens.

For example, if the user wants to find out whether production problems at plants are correlated to the location of the plants, the problem locations can be encoded in a special color—say, red—on a map. The user can then quickly discover locations in which problems are occurring. The user may then form hypotheses about why problems are occurring in those locations, and may verify the hypotheses quantitatively against the database.

As another example, information about values can be encoded as a color, and can be displayed with as little as one pixel of screen area. To detect associations between pairs of items, we can use a two-dimensional pixel matrix, with each row and each column representing an item. The percentage of transactions that buy both items can be encoded by the color intensity of the pixel. Items with high association will show up as bright pixels in the screen — easy to detect against the darker background.

## 21.3.4   Automatic Discovery of Rules

Work on automatic discovery of rules has been influenced strongly by work in the artificial-intelligence community on machine learning. The main differences lie in the volume of data handled in databases, and in the need to access disk. Specialized data-mining algorithms have been developed to handle large volumes of disk-resident data efficiently.

The manner in which rules are discovered depends on the class of data-mining application. We illustrate rule discovery using two application classes: classification and associations.

### 21.3.4.1   Discovery of Classification Rules

The process of discovery of classification rules starts from a sample of data, called a *training set*. For each tuple in the training set, the grouping is already known. For instance, the training set for a credit-card application may be the existing customers, with their credit worthiness determined from their payment history. The actual data, or population, may consist of all people, including those who are not existing customers.

The example from Section 21.3.3 of finding which class of people have an excellent credit rating illustrates not only how a human would discover rules, but also hints at how a data-mining system can discover rules.

The data-mining system starts first with antecedents consisting of only a simple condition on a single attribute. The possible conditions on the degree attribute are $P.degree = None$, $P.degree = Bachelors$, $P.degree = Masters$, and $P.degree = Doctorate$, if these are the only possible degrees. For attributes whose value is numeric, the data-mining system divides up the possible values into intervals; the salary-attribute value could be divided into intervals 0 to 25,000,

25,000 to 50,000, 50,000 to 75,000, and over 75,000. Thus, if we consider any attribute, the conditions based on that attribute partition the set of tuples into disjoint groups.

If, for any attribute, all or most of the tuples in each group have the same classification value (the credit worthiness, in our example), a set of rules based on that attribute can be output, and data mining stops. More likely, this situation will not hold. Rules based on the *degree* attribute or the *income* attribute alone will not be sufficient to classify the data properly.

In this case, one of the attributes is chosen—usually, the one that best partitions the data. The data are divided into groups based on the conditions on this attribute, and then classification is done separately, based on the other attributes, for each group. Suppose that *degree* is chosen as the attribute on which to partition. Consider the partition corresponding to *Masters*. The partitioning at the next level would be made on one of the other attributes; in our example, we use the attribute *income*. The rules in the group for *Masters* would have a condition of the form *degree = Masters*, in addition to the condition on *income*, in their antecedent. The other partitions, with *degree = None* and so on, would be separately classified in the same manner.

This method generates a *classification tree* from the top down. Part of the classification tree for our problem is shown in Figure 21.4. Each node of the tree partitions the data into groups based on one attribute. The construction of a path in the tree stops when either the attribute has properly classified the data, or all attributes have been considered. In our example, within each partition based on degree, the partitions defined by *income* adequately classify the tuples. Tree construction stops at this level for each partition based on degree. In general, different branches of the tree could grow to different levels.

Numerous improvements on the basic technique have been developed. The number of rules generated can be reduced by means of merging rules together—

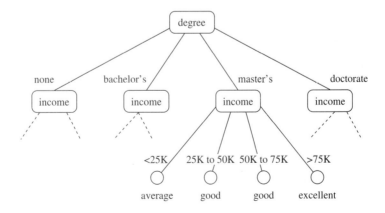

Figure 21.4    Classification tree.

for instance, if adjacent intervals belong to the same classification group. The I/O cost can be reduced by techniques that grow multiple branches of a tree with a single scan of the tuples. See the bibliographic notes for more information.

### 21.3.4.2   Discovery of Association Rules

Consider our earlier example of an association rule:

$$\forall \ transactions \ \ T, \ buys(T, bread) \Rightarrow buys(T, milk)$$

We can derive rules such as this one efficiently by associating a bitmap with each transaction, with one bit per item of interest in the shop. This approach is reasonable if the number of items of interest is not large. Even if the initial set of items is large, users will typically want only those rules that have strong support, which will involve only items purchased in a significant percentage of the transactions. Thus, the set of relevant items can be deduced quickly, and is likely to be small.

Now, to discover association rules of the form

$$\forall \ transactions \ \ T, \ buys(T, i_1) \ \textbf{and} \ \ldots \ \textbf{and} \ buys(T, i_n) \Rightarrow buys(T, i_0)$$

we must consider all subsets of the set of relevant items, and, for each set, must check whether there is a sufficient number of transactions in which all the items in the set are purchased.

If the number of such sets is small, a single pass over the transactions suffices to detect the level of support for all the sets. A count is maintained for each set, initially set to 0. When a transaction is fetched, the count is incremented for each set of items, all of whose bits are set in the transaction's bitmap. Those sets with a sufficiently high count at the end of the pass correspond to items that have a high degree of association.

If the number of sets is high, the cost of processing each transaction becomes correspondingly large. Techniques have been developed that use multiple passes on the database, considering only some sets in each pass. Once a set is eliminated because it occurs in too small a fraction of the transactions, none of its supersets needs to be considered.

## 21.4   Data Warehousing

Large companies have presences at numerous sites, each of which may generate a large volume of data. For instance, large retail chains have shops at hundreds or thousands of sites, whereas insurance companies may have data from thousands of local branches. Further, large organizations have a complex internal organization structure, due to which different data are present in different locations, or on different operational systems, and under different schemas. For instance, manufacturing-problem data and customer-complaints data may be stored on different database systems. Corporate decision makers require access to information

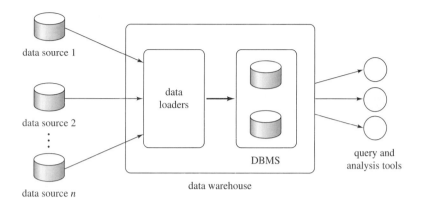

Figure 21.5    Data-warehouse architecture.

from all such sources. Setting up queries on individual sources is both cumbersome and inefficient. Moreover, the sources of data may store only current data, whereas decision makers may need access to past data as well; for instance, information about how purchase patterns have changed in the past year could be of great importance. Data warehouses provide a solution to these problems.

A *data warehouse* is a repository (or archive) of information gathered from multiple sources, stored under a unified schema, at a single site. Once gathered, the data are stored for a long time, permitting access to historical data. Thus, data warehouses provide the user a single consolidated interface to data, making decision-support queries easier to write. Moreover, by accessing information for decision support from a data warehouse, the decision maker ensures that on-line transaction-processing systems are not affected by the decision-support workload.

Figure 21.5 shows the architecture of a typical data warehouse, and illustrates the gathering of data, the storage of data, and the querying and data-analysis support. Among the issues to be addressed in building a warehouse are the following:

- **When and how to gather data.** In a source-driven architecture for gathering data, the data sources transmit new information, either continually, as transaction processing takes place, or periodically, such as each night. In a destination-driven architecture, the data warehouse periodically sends requests for new data to the sources.

  Unless updates at the sources are replicated at the warehouse via two-phase commit, the warehouse will never be quite up to date with the sources. Two-phase commit is usually far too expensive to be an option, so data warehouses typically have slightly out-of-date data. That, however, is usually not a problem for decision-support systems.

- **What schema to use.** Data sources that have been constructed independently are likely to have different schemas. In fact, they may even use different data models. Part of the task of a warehouse is to perform schema integration, and to convert data to the integrated schema before they are stored. As a result, the data stored in the warehouse are not just a copy of the data at the sources. Instead, they can be thought of as a stored view (or materialized view) of the data at the sources.

- **How to propagate updates**. Updates on relations at the data sources must be propagated to the data warehouse. If the relations at the data warehouse are exactly the same as those at the data source, the propagation is straightforward. If they are not, the problem of propagating updates is basically the *view-maintenance* problem, which was discussed briefly in Section 3.7.1.

- **What data to summarize.** The raw data generated by a transaction-processing system may be too large to store on-line. However, we can answer many queries by maintaining just summary data obtained by aggregation on a relation, rather than maintaining the entire relation. For example, instead of storing data about every sale of clothing, we can store total sales of clothing by category.

    Suppose that a relation $r$ has been replaced by a summary relation $s$. Users may still be permitted to pose queries as though the relation $r$ were available on-line. If the query requires only summary data, it may be possible to transform it into an equivalent one using $s$ instead. This transformation can be done as follows. The stored summary relation $s$ is defined as a view on the original relation. However, $s$ is a materialized view, rather than a view computed on demand. The query optimizer must then decide whether it can replace uses of $r$ in the given query by $s$, with some other associated changes, based on analysis of the given query and the view definition of $s$. See the bibliographic notes for more information.

## 21.5   Spatial and Geographic Databases

Spatial databases store information related to spatial locations, and provide support for efficient querying and indexing based on spatial locations. For example, suppose that we want to store a set of polygons in a database, and to query the database to find all polygons that intersect a given polygon. We cannot use standard index structures, such as B-trees or hash indices, to answer such a query efficiently. A spatial database would use special-purpose index structures, such as R-trees (which we study later) for the task.

    Two types of spatial databases are particularly important:

- *Design databases*, or computer-aided-design (CAD) databases, are spatial databases used to store design information about how objects—such as buildings, cars, or aircraft—are constructed. Other important examples of computer-aided–design databases are integrated-circuit and electronic-device layouts.

- *Geographic databases* are spatial databases used to store geographic information, such as maps. Geographic databases are often called *geographic information systems*.

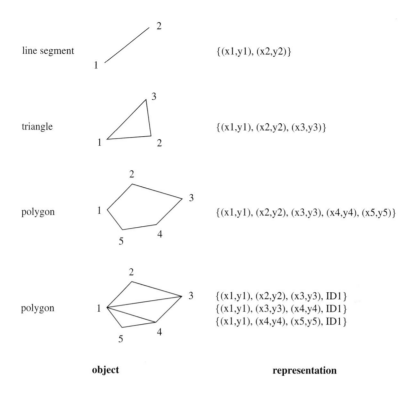

Figure 21.6    Representation of geometric constructs.

## 21.5.1    Representation of Geometric Information

Figure 21.6 illustrates how various geometric constructs can be represented in a database, in a normalized fashion. We stress here that geometric information can be represented in several different ways, only some of which we describe.

A line segment can be represented by the coordinates of its endpoints. We can approximately represent an arbitrary curve by partitioning it into a sequence of segments. To allow the use of fixed-size tuples, we can give the curve an identifier, and can represent each segment as a separate tuple that also carries with it the identifier of the curve. This representation is useful for two-dimensional features such as roads; here, the width of the road is small enough relative to the size of the full map that it can be considered two dimensional. For a map database, the two coordinates of a point would be its latitude and longitude.

We can represent a polygon by listing its vertices in order, as shown in Figure 21.6. The list of vertices actually specifies the boundary of a polygonal region. For simplicity, we consider only *closed polygons*—that is, polygons where the starting vertex in the list is the same as the ending vertex in the list. The interior of the boundary forms the polygonal region.

In an alternative representation, a closed polygon can be divided into a set of triangles, as shown in Figure 21.6. This process is called *triangulation*, and any closed polygon can be triangulated. In a manner similar to the representation of curves, the complex polygon is given an identifier, and each of the triangles into which it is divided carries the identifier of the polygon. Complex two-dimensional features bounded by curves, such as circles, can be approximated by polygons.

The triangulated representation is designed to be stored in a first-normal-form relational format. Non–first-normal-form representations, such as ones representing a polygon by a list of vertices or edges, are also used in practice, where supported by the underlying database. Such list-based representations are often convenient for query processing.

The representation of points and line segments in three-dimensional space is similar to their representation in two-dimensional space, with the only difference that points have an extra $z$ component. Similarly, the representation of planar figures—such as triangles, rectangles, and other polygons—does not change much when we move to three dimensions. Tetrahedrons and cuboids can be represented similar to triangles and rectangles. We can represent arbitrary polyhedra by dividing them into tetrahedrons, like triangulating polygons. We can also represent them by listing their faces, each of which is itself a polygon, along with an indication of which side of the face is inside the polyhedron.

## 21.5.2   Design Databases

Computer-aided design (CAD) has been in use for many years now. CAD systems traditionally stored data in memory during editing or other processing, and wrote the data back to a file at the end of a session of editing. The drawbacks of such a scheme include the cost (programming complexity, as well as time cost) of transforming data from one form to another, and the need to read in an entire file even if only parts of it are required. For large designs, such as the design of a large-scale integrated circuit, or the design of an entire airplane, it may be impossible to hold the complete design in memory. Designers of object-oriented databases were motivated in large part by the database requirements of CAD systems. Components of the design are represented as objects, and the connections between the objects indicate how the design is structured.

The objects stored in a design database are generally geometric objects. Simple two-dimensional geometric objects include points, lines, triangles, rectangles, and, in general, polygons. Complex two-dimensional objects can be formed from simple objects by means of union, intersection, and difference operations. Similarly, complex three-dimensional objects may be formed from simpler objects such as spheres, cylinders, and cuboids, by union, intersection, and difference operations, as illustrated in Figure 21.7. Three-dimensional surfaces may also be represented by *wireframe* models, which essentially model the surface as a set of simpler objects, such as line segments, triangles, and rectangles.

Design databases also store nonspatial information about objects, such as the material from which the objects are constructed. We can usually model such

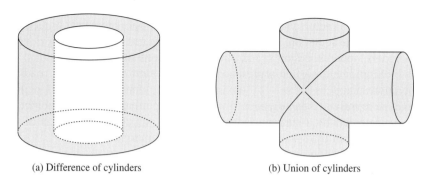

(a) Difference of cylinders　　　　　　　　　　(b) Union of cylinders

Figure 21.7　Complex three-dimensional objects.

information using standard data-modeling techniques. We concern ourselves here with only the spatial aspects.

Various spatial operations must be performed on the design. For instance, the task may be to retrieve that part of the design that corresponds to a particular region of interest. Spatial-index structures, discussed in Section 21.5.5, are useful for such tasks. Such spatial-index structures are multidimensional, dealing with two- and three-dimensional data, rather than dealing with just the simple one-dimensional ordering provided by the $B^+$-trees.

Spatial-integrity constraints, such as "two pipes should not be in the same location," are important in design databases. Such errors often occur if the design is performed manually, and are detected only when a prototype is being constructed. As a result, these errors can be expensive to fix. Database support for spatial-integrity constraints helps people to avoid design errors, thereby keeping the design consistent. Implementing such integrity checks again depends on the availability of efficient multidimensional index structures.

## 21.5.3　Geographic Data

Geographic data are spatial in nature, but differ from design data in certain ways. Maps and satellite images are typical examples of geographic data. Maps may provide not only location information—such as boundaries, rivers and roads—but also much more detailed information associated with locations, such as elevation, soil type, land usage, and annual rainfall.

Geographic data can be categorized into two types:

- **Raster data**. Such data consist of bit maps or pixel maps, in two or more dimensions. A typical example of a two-dimensional raster image is a satellite image of cloud cover, where each pixel stores the cloud visibility in a particular area. Such data can be three-dimensional—for example, the temperature at different altitudes at different regions, again measured with the help of a satellite. Time could form another dimension—for example, the surface temperature measurements at different points in time. Design databases generally do not store raster data.

- **Vector data**. Vector data are constructed from basic geometric objects, such as points, line segments, triangles, and other polygons in two dimensions, and cylinders, spheres, cuboids, and other polyhedrons in three dimensions.

  Map data are often represented in vector format. Rivers and roads may be represented as unions of multiple line segments. States and countries may be represented as polygons. Topological information, such as height, may be represented by a surface divided into polygons covering regions of equal height, with a height value associated with each polygon.

### 21.5.3.1    Representation of Geographical Data

Geographical features, such as states and large lakes, are represented as complex polygons. Some features, such as rivers, may be represented either as complex curves or as complex polygons, depending on whether their width is relevant.

Geographic information related to regions, such as annual rainfall, can be represented as an array—that is, in raster form. For space efficiency, the array can be stored in a compressed form. In Section 21.5.5, we study an alternative representation of such arrays using a data structure called a *quadtree*.

As described earlier, we can represent region information in vector form, using polygons, where each polygon is a region within which the array value is the same. The vector representation is more compact than the raster representation in some applications. It is also more accurate for some tasks, such as depicting roads, where dividing the region into pixels (which may be fairly large) leads to a loss of precision in location information. However, the vector representation is unsuitable for applications where the data are intrinsically raster based, such as satellite images.

### 21.5.3.2    Applications of Geographic Data

Geographic databases have a variety of uses, including vehicle-navigation systems; distribution-network information for public-service utilities such as telephone, electric-power and water-supply systems; and land-usage information for ecologists and planners.

Vehicle-navigation systems store information about roads and services for the use of drivers. Such information includes the layout of roads, speed limits on roads, road conditions, connections between roads, and one-way restrictions. At the simplest level, these systems can be used to generate on-line maps for humans. An important benefit of on-line maps is that it is easy to scale the map to the desired size—that is, to zoom in and out to locate relevant features. With this additional information about roads, the maps can be used for automatic trip planning. Users can query on-line information about services to locate, for example, hotels, gas stations, or restaurants with desired offerings and price ranges.

Vehicle-navigation systems are typically mobile, and are mounted on the dashboard of a vehicle. A useful addition to a mobile geographic information system is a *Global Positioning System (GPS)* unit, which uses information broadcast from GPS satellites to find the current location with an accuracy of tens of meters.

With such a system, a driver can never[†] get lost—the GPS unit finds the location in terms of {latitude, longitude, elevation} and the geographic database can be queried to find where and on which road the vehicle is currently located.

Geographic databases used for public-utility information are becoming increasingly important as the network of buried cables and pipes grows. Due to a lack of detailed maps, work carried out by one utility may damage the cables of another utility, resulting in large-scale disruption of service. Geographic databases, coupled with location-finding systems, promise the hope of avoiding such disasters in the future.

So far, we have explained why people use spatial databases. In the rest of the section, we shall study technical details, such as representation and indexing of spatial information.

### 21.5.4  Spatial Queries

There are a number of types of queries that involve spatial locations.

- *Nearness queries* request objects that lie near a specified location. A query to find all restaurants that lie within a given distance of a given point is an example of a nearness query. The *nearest-neighbor query* requests the object that is nearest to a specified point. For example, we may want to find the nearest gasoline station. Note that this query does not have to specify a limit on the distance, and hence we can ask it even if we have no idea how far the nearest gasoline station lies.

- *Region queries* deal with spatial regions. Such a query can ask for objects that lie partially or fully inside a specified region. A query to find all retail shops within the geographic boundaries of a given town is an example.

- Queries may also request **intersections** and **unions** of regions. For example, given region information, such as annual rainfall and population density, a query may request all regions with a low annual rainfall as well as a high population density.

Queries that compute intersections of regions can be thought of as computing the *spatial join* of two spatial relations—one representing rainfall and the other representing population density—with the location playing the role of join attribute. In general, given two relations, each containing spatial objects, the spatial join of the two relations generates either pairs of objects that intersect, or the intersection regions of such pairs.

Several join algorithms have been developed that compute efficiently spatial joins on vector data. Although nested-loop join and indexed nested-loop join (with spatial indices) can be used, hash joins and sort–merge joins cannot be used on spatial data. Join techniques based on coordinated traversal of spatial index

---

[†]Well, hardly ever!

structures on the two relations have also been proposed. See the bibliographic notes for more information.

In general, queries on spatial data may have a combination of spatial and nonspatial requirements. For instance, we may want to find the nearest restaurant that has vegetarian selections, and that charges less than $10 for a meal.

Since spatial data are inherently graphical, we typically query them using a graphical query language. Results of such queries are also displayed graphically, rather than in tables. The user can invoke various operations on the interface, such as choosing an area to be viewed (for example, by pointing and clicking on suburbs west of Manhattan), zooming in and out, choosing what to display based on selection conditions (for example, houses with more than three bedrooms), overlay of multiple maps (for example, houses with more than three bedrooms overlayed on a map showing areas with low crime rates), and so on. The graphical interface constitutes the front-end. Extensions of SQL have been proposed as a back-end, allowing relational databases to store and retrieve spatial information, and also allowing queries to mix spatial and nonspatial conditions. Extensions include allowing abstract data types, such as lines, polygons, and bit maps, and allowing spatial conditions, such as *contains* or *overlaps*.

## 21.5.5 Indexing of Spatial Data

Indices are required for efficient access to spatial data. Traditional index structures, such as hash indices and B-trees, are not suitable, since they only deal with one-dimensional data, whereas spatial data are typically of two or more dimensions.

### 21.5.5.1 k-d Trees

To understand how to index spatial data consisting of two or more dimensions, we consider first the indexing of points in one-dimensional data. Tree structures, such as binary trees and B-trees, operate by successively dividing space into smaller parts. For instance, each internal node of a binary tree partitions a one-dimensional interval in two. Points that lie in the left partition go into the left subtree; points that lie in the right partition go into the right subtree. In a balanced binary tree, the partition is chosen such that approximately one-half of the points stored in the subtree fall in each partition. Similarly, each level of a B-tree splits a one-dimensional interval into multiple parts.

We can use that intuition to create tree structures for two-dimensional space, as well as in higher-dimensional spaces. A tree structure called a *k-d tree* was one of the early structures used for indexing in multiple dimensions. Each level of a k-d tree partitions the space into two. The partitioning is done along one dimension at the node at the top level of the tree, along another dimension in nodes at the next level, and so on, cycling through the dimensions. The partitioning is done such that, at each node, approximately one-half of the points stored in the subtree fall on one side, and one-half fall on the other. Partitioning stops when a node has less than a given maximum number of points. Figure 21.8 shows a set of points in two-dimensional space, and a k-d tree representation of the set of points. Each line corresponds to a node in the tree, and the maximum number of points in a

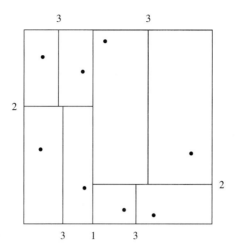

Figure 21.8 Division of space by a k-d tree.

leaf node has been set at 1. Each line in the figure (other than the outside box) corresponds to a node in the k-d tree. The numbering of the lines in the figure indicates the level of the tree at which the corresponding node appears.

The *k-d-B tree* extends the k-d tree to allow multiple child nodes for each internal node, just as a B-tree extends a binary tree, to reduce the height of the tree. k-d-B trees are better suited for secondary storage than are k-d trees.

### 21.5.5.2 Quadtrees

An alternative representation for two-dimensional data is a *quadtree*. An example of the division of space by a quadtree is shown in Figure 21.9. The set of points is the same as that used in Figure 21.8. Each node of a quadtree is associated with a rectangular region of space. The top node is associated with the entire target space.

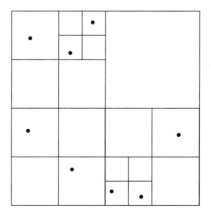

Figure 21.9 Division of space by a quadtree.

Each nonleaf node in a quadtree divides its region into four equal-sized quadrants, and correspondingly each such node has four child nodes corresponding to the four quadrants. Leaf nodes have between zero and some fixed maximum number of points. Correspondingly, if the region corresponding to a node has more than the maximum number of points, child nodes are created for that node. In the example shown in Figure 21.9, the maximum number of points in a leaf node is set to 1.

The type of quadtree described is called a *PR quadtree*, to indicate it stores points, and that space is divided based on regions, rather than on the actual set of points stored. We can use *region quadtrees* to store array (raster) information. A node in a region quadtree is a leaf node if all the array values in the region that it covers are the same. Otherwise, it is subdivided further into four children of equal area, and is therefore an internal node. Each node in the region quadtree corresponds to a subarray of values. The subarrays corresponding to leaves either contain just a single array element, or have multiple array elements, all of which have the same value.

Indexing of line segments and polygons presents new problems. There are extensions of k-d trees and quadtrees for this task. However, a line segment or polygon may cross a partitioning line. If it does, it has to be split and represented in each of the subtrees in which its pieces occur. Multiple occurrences of a line segment or polygon can result in inefficiencies in storage, as well as inefficiencies in querying.

### 21.5.5.3   R-Trees

A storage structure called an *R-tree* is useful for indexing of rectangles and other polygons. An R-tree is a balanced tree structure, much like a B-tree; however, instead of a range of values, a rectangular *bounding box* is associated with each tree node. Polygons are stored in only leaf nodes. The bounding box of a leaf node is the smallest rectangle (parallel to the axes) that contains all objects stored in the leaf node. The bounding box of internal nodes is similarly the smallest rectangle (parallel to the axes) that contains the bounding boxes of its child nodes.

Figure 21.10 shows an example of a set of rectangles (drawn with a solid line) and the bounding boxes (drawn with a dashed line) of the nodes of an R-tree for the set of rectangles. The R-tree itself is shown on the right. Note that the bounding boxes are shown with extra space inside them, to make them stand out pictorially. In reality, the boxes would be smaller, and each side would touch at least some of the objects or bounding boxes from one level down.

The bounding box associated with sibling nodes may overlap, unlike with k-d trees and quadtrees, where the ranges do not overlap. A search for polygons containing a point therefore has to follow *all* child nodes whose associated bounding boxes contain the point; as a result, multiple paths may have to be searched. Similarly, a query to find all polygons that intersect a given polygon has to go down every node where the associated rectangle intersects the polygon.

When we insert a polygon into an R-tree, we select a leaf node to hold the polygon. If the node is already full, node splitting is performed (and propagated

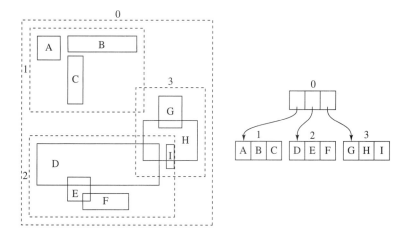

Figure 21.10    An R-tree.

upward if required) in a manner similar to $B^+$-tree insertion. The insertion algorithm ensures that the tree remains balanced, and the bounding boxes of leaf as well as internal nodes, remain consistent. There are multiple ways in which to split a node that is overfull; see the bibliographic references for more details on R-trees, as well as on variants of R-trees, called $R^*$-trees or $R^+$-trees.

The storage efficiency of R-trees is better than that of k-d trees or quadtrees, since a polygon is stored only once, and we can ensure easily that each node is at least half full. However, querying may be slower, since multiple paths have to be searched. Spatial joins are simpler using quadtrees than using R-trees, since all quadtrees on a region are partitioned in the same manner. However, because of their better storage efficiency, and their similarity to B-trees, R-trees and their variants have proved popular in database systems that support spatial data.

## 21.6   Multimedia Databases

Recently, there has been much interest in databases that store multimedia data, such as images, audio, and video. Today, multimedia data typically are stored outside the database, in file systems. When the number of multimedia objects is relatively small, features provided by databases are usually not important.

Database functionality becomes important when the number of multimedia objects stored is large. Issues such as transactional updates, querying facilities, and indexing then become important. Multimedia objects often have descriptive attributes, such as those indicating when they were created, who created them, and to what category they belong. One approach to building a database for such multimedia objects is to use databases for storing the descriptive attributes, and for keeping track of the files in which the multimedia objects are stored.

However, storing multimedia outside the database makes it harder to provide database functionality, such as indexing on the basis of actual multimedia data content. It can also lead to inconsistencies, such a file that is noted in the database, but whose contents are missing, or vice versa. It is therefore desirable to store the data themselves in the database.

Several issues have to be addressed if multimedia data are to be stored in a database.

- The database must support large objects, since multimedia data such as videos can occupy up to a few gigabytes of storage. Many relational systems do not support such large objects, although object-storage systems such as Exodus do provide support for large objects.
- Similarity-based retrieval is needed in many multimedia database applications. For example, in a database that stores fingerprint images, a query fingerprint image is provided, and fingerprints in the database that are similar to the query fingerprint must be retrieved. Index structures such as $B^+$-trees and R-trees cannot be used for this purpose; special index structures need to be created. We discuss similarity-based retrieval in Section 21.6.1
- The retrieval of some types of data, such as audio and video, has the requirement that data delivery must proceed at a guaranteed steady rate. Such data are sometimes called *isochronous data*, or *continuous-media data*. For example, if audio data are not supplied in time, there will be gaps in the sound. If the data are supplied too fast, system buffers may overflow, resulting in loss of data. We discuss continuous-media data in Section 21.6.2.

## 21.6.1   Similarity-Based Retrieval

In many multimedia applications, data are described only approximately in the database. We noted previously the example of fingerprint data. Other examples follow:

- **Pictorial data.** Two pictures or images that are slightly different as represented in the database may be considered the same by a user. For instance, a database may store trademark designs. When a new trademark is to be registered, the system may need first to identify all similar trademarks that were registered previously.
- **Audio data.** Speech-based user interfaces are being developed that allow the user to give a command or identify a data item by speaking. The input from the user must then be tested for similarity to those commands or data items stored in the system.
- **Handwritten data.** Handwritten input can be used to identify a handwritten data item or command stored in the database. Here again, similarity testing is required.

The notion of similarity is often subjective and user specific. However, similarity testing is often more successful than speech or handwriting recognition, because the input can be compared to data already in the system and, thus, the set of choices available to the system is limited.

Several algorithms for finding the best matches to a given input using similarity testing exist. Some systems, including a dial-by-name, voice-activated telephone system, have been deployed commercially. Details of these algorithms are beyond the scope of this text; see the bibliographic notes for references.

## 21.6.2   Continuous-Media Data

The most important types of continuous-media data are video and audio data (for example, a database of movies). Continuous-media systems are characterized by their high data volumes and real-time information-delivery requirements:

- Data must be delivered sufficiently fast that no gaps in the audio or video result.
- Data must be delivered at a rate that does not cause overflow of system buffers.
- Synchronization among distinct data streams must be maintained. This need arises, for example, when the video of a person speaking must show lips moving synchronously with the audio of the person speaking.

### 21.6.2.1   Multimedia Data Formats

Because of the large number of bytes required to represent multimedia data, it is essential that the latter be stored and transmitted in compressed form. For image data, the most widely used format is JPEG, named after the standards body that created it, the Joint Picture Experts Group. We can store video data by encoding each frame of video using JPEG format, but such an encoding is wasteful, since successive frames of a video are often nearly the same. The Motion Picture Experts Group (MPEG) has developed standards for encoding video and audio data that use commonalities among a sequence of frames to achieve a greater degree of compression. The MPEG-1 standard stores a minute of 30-frame-per-second video and audio in approximately 12.5 megabytes (as compared with approximately 75 megabytes for video using only JPEG). However, MPEG-1 encoding introduces some loss of video quality, to a level roughly comparable to that of VHS video tape. The MPEG-2 standard is designed for digital broadcast systems and digital video disks (DVD); it introduces only a negligible loss of video quality. MPEG-2 compresses 1 minute of video and audio to approximately 17 megabytes.

### 21.6.2.2   Video Servers

Video-on-demand servers are being developed by many vendors. Current systems are based on file systems, because existing database systems do not meet the need that these applications have for real-time response. The basic architecture of a video-on-demand system consists of the following:

- **Video server.** Multimedia data are stored on several disks (usually in a RAID configuration). Systems containing a large volume of data may use tertiary storage for less frequently accessed data.

- **Terminals.** People view multimedia data through various devices collectively referred to as *terminals*. Examples of such devices include personal computers or televisions attached to a small, inexpensive computer called a *set-top box*.
- **Network.** Transmission of multimedia data from a server to multiple terminals requires a high-capacity network. Asynchronous-transfer-mode (ATM) networks are used frequently for this purpose.

We envision that video-on-demand service eventually will become ubiquitous, in the way that cable and broadcast television are currently. At present, the main applications of video-server technology are in offices (for training, viewing recorded talks and presentations, and the like), in hotels, and in video-production facilities.

## 21.7    Mobility and Personal Databases

Large-scale, commercial databases have traditionally been stored in central computing facilities. In the case of distributed database applications, there has usually been strong central database and network administration. Two technology trends have combined to create applications in which this assumption of central control and administration is not entirely correct:

1. The increasingly widespread use of personal computers, and, more important, of laptop or "notebook" computers
2. The development of a relatively low-cost wireless digital communication infrastructure, based on wireless local-area networks, cellular digital packet networks, and other technologies

Mobile computing has proved useful in many applications. Many business travelers use laptop computers to enable them to work and to access data en route. Delivery services use mobile computers to assist in package tracking. Emergency-response services use mobile computers at the scene of disasters, medical emergencies, and the like to access information and to enter data pertaining to the situation. New applications of mobile computers continue to emerge.

Wireless computing creates a situation where machines no longer have fixed locations and network addresses. This complicates query processing, since it becomes difficult to determine the optimal location at which to materialize the result of a query. In some cases, the location of the user is a parameter of the query. An example is a traveler's information system that provides data on hotels, roadside services, and the like to motorists. Queries about services that are ahead on the current route must be processed based on knowledge of the user's location, direction of motion, and speed.

Energy (battery power) is a scarce resource for mobile computers. This limitation influences many aspects of system design. Among the more interesting consequences of the need for energy efficiency is the use of scheduled data broadcasts to reduce the need for mobile systems to transmit queries.

Increasing amounts of data may reside on machines administered by users, rather than by database administrators. Furthermore, these machines may, at times, be disconnected from the network. In many cases, there is a conflict between the user's need to continue to work while disconnected and the need for global data consistency.

In Sections 21.7.1 through 21.7.4, we discuss techniques in use and under development to deal with the problems of mobility and personal computing.

## 21.7.1 A Model of Mobile Computing

The mobile-computing environment consists of mobile computers, referred to as *mobile hosts*, and a wired network of computers. Mobile hosts communicate with the wired network via computers referred to as *mobile support stations*. Each mobile support station manages those mobile hosts within its *cell*—that is, the geographical area that it covers. Mobile hosts may move between cells, thus necessitating a *handoff* of control from one mobile support station to another. Since mobile hosts may, at times, be powered down, a host may leave one cell and rematerialize later at some distant cell. Therefore, moves between cells are not necessarily between adjacent cells. Within a small area, such as a building, mobile hosts may be connected by a wireless local-area network that provides lower-cost connectivity than would a wide-area cellular network, and that reduces the overhead of handoffs.

It is possible for mobile hosts to communicate directly without the intervention of a mobile support station. However, such communication can occur between only nearby hosts.

The size and power limitations of many mobile computers have led to alternative memory hierarchies. Instead of, or in addition to, disk storage, flash memory, which we discussed in Section 10, may be included. If the mobile host includes a hard disk, the disk may be allowed to spin down when it is not in use, to save energy.

## 21.7.2 Routing and Query Processing

A consequence of the mobile-computing model is that the route between a pair of hosts may change over time if one of the two hosts is mobile. This simple fact has a dramatic effect at the network level, since location-based network addresses are no longer constants within the system. These networking issues are beyond the scope of this text.

Another consequence of the mobile-computing model directly affects database query processing. As we saw in Chapter 18, we must consider communication costs when we choose a distributed query-processing strategy. Mobility results in dynamically changing communication costs, thus complicating the optimization process. Furthermore, there are competing notions of cost to consider:

- **User time** is a highly valuable commodity in many business applications

- **Connection time** is the unit by which monetary charges are assigned in some cellular systems
- **Number of bytes, or packets, transferred** is the unit by which charges are computed in digital cellular systems
- **Time-of-day based charges** vary based on whether communication occurs during peak or off-peak periods
- **Energy** is limited. Often, battery power is a scarce resource whose use must be optimized. A basic principle of radio communication is that it requires less energy to receive than to transmit radio signals. Thus, transmission and reception of data impose different power demands on the mobile host.

## 21.7.3  Broadcast Data

It is often desirable for frequently requested data to be broadcast in a continuous cycle by mobile support stations, rather than transmitted to mobile hosts on demand. A typical application of broadcast data is stock-market price information. There are two reasons for using broadcast data. First, the mobile host avoids the energy cost for transmitting data requests. Second, the broadcast data can be received by a large number of mobile hosts at once, at no extra cost. Thus, the available transmission bandwidth is utilized more effectively.

Mobile hosts can then receive data when those data are transmitted, rather than consuming energy by transmitting a request. The mobile host may have local nonvolatile storage available to cache the broadcast data when those data are received, for possible later use. Given a query, the mobile host may optimize energy costs by determining whether it can process that query using only cached data. If the cached data are insufficient, there are two options: Wait for the data to be broadcast, or transmit a request for data. To make this decision, the mobile host must know when the relevant data will be broadcast.

Broadcast data may be transmitted according to a fixed schedule or a changeable schedule. In the former case, the mobile host uses the known fixed schedule to determine when the relevant data will be transmitted. In the latter case, the broadcast schedule must itself be broadcast at a well-known radio frequency and at well-known time intervals.

In effect, the broadcast medium can be modeled as a disk with a high latency. Requests for data can be thought of as being serviced when the requested data are broadcast. The transmission schedules behave like indices on the disk. The use of broadcast data as part of a mobile-information-system environment is under study. The bibliographic notes list recent research papers in this area.

## 21.7.4  Disconnectivity and Consistency

Since wireless communication may be paid for on the basis of connection time, there is an incentive for certain mobile hosts to be disconnected for substantial periods. During these periods of disconnection, the mobile host may remain in operation. The user of the mobile host may issue queries and updates on data that reside or are cached locally. This situation creates several problems, among which the most noteworthy are the following:

- **Recoverability:** Updates entered on a disconnected machine may be lost if the mobile host experiences a catastrophic failure. Since the mobile host represents a single point of failure, stable storage cannot be simulated well.
- **Consistency:** Locally cached data may become out of date, but the mobile host cannot discover this situation until it is reconnected. Likewise, updates occurring in the mobile host cannot be propagated until reconnection occurs. We explored this problem in Chapter 18, where we discussed network partitioning, and we elaborate on it here.

In wired distributed systems, partitioning is considered to be a failure mode; in mobile computing, partitioning via disconnection is part of the normal mode of operation. It is therefore necessary to allow data access to proceed despite partitioning, even at the risk of some loss of consistency.

For data updated by only the mobile host, it is a simple matter to propagate those updates when the mobile host reconnects. However, if the mobile host caches read-only copies of data that may be updated by other computers, the cached data may become inconsistent. When the mobile host is connected, it can be sent *invalidation reports* that inform it of out-of-date cache entries. However, when the mobile host is disconnected, it may miss an invalidation report. A simple solution to this problem is to invalidate the entire cache on reconnection, but such an extreme solution is highly costly. Several caching schemes are cited in the bibliographic notes.

If updates can occur at both the mobile host and elsewhere, detecting conflicting updates is more difficult. Version-numbering–based schemes have been developed to allow updates of shared files from disconnected hosts. These schemes do not guarantee that the updates will be consistent. Rather, they guarantee that, if two hosts independently update the same version of a document, the clash will be detected eventually, when the hosts exchange information either directly or through a common host. The basic idea is for each host $i$ to store, with its copy of each document $d$, a *version vector*—that is, a set of version numbers $\{V_{d,i,j}\}$, with one entry for each other host $j$ on which the document could potentially be updated. When a host $i$ updates a document $d$, it increments the version number $V_{d,i,i}$.

Whenever two hosts $i$ and $j$ connect with each other, they exchange updated documents, so that both obtain new versions of the documents. However, before exchanging documents, the hosts have to discover whether the copies are consistent:

1. If the version vectors are the same on both hosts—that is, for each $k$, $V_{d,i,k} = V_{d,j,k}$—then the copies of document $d$ are identical.
2. If, for each $k$, $V_{d,i,k} \leq V_{d,j,k}$, and the version vectors are not identical, then the copy of document $d$ at host $i$ is older than the one at host $j$. That is, the copy of document $d$ at host $j$ was obtained by one or more modifications of the copy of the document at host $i$. Host $i$ replaces its

copy of $d$, as well as its copy of the version vector for $d$, with the copies from host $j$.

3. If there is a pair of hosts $k$ and $l$ such that $V_{d,i,k} < V_{d,j,k}$ and $V_{d,i,l} > V_{d,j,l}$, then the copies are *inconsistent*; that is, the copy of $d$ at $i$ contains updates performed by host $k$ that have not been propagated to host $j$, and, similarly, the copy of $d$ at $j$ contains updates performed by host $l$ that have not been propagated to host $i$. Then, the copies of $d$ are inconsistent, since two or more updates have been performed on $d$ independently. Manual intervention may be required to merge the updates.

The preceding version-vector scheme was initially designed to deal with failures in distributed file systems. The scheme gained importance because mobile computers often store copies of files that are also present on server systems, in effect resulting in a distributed file system that is often disconnected. Another application of the scheme has been in groupware systems, where hosts are connected periodically, rather than continuously, and must exchange updated documents. The version-vector scheme also has applications in replicated databases.

The version-vector scheme, however, fails to address the most difficult and most important issue arising from updates to shared data—the reconciliation of inconsistent copies of data. Many applications can perform reconciliation automatically by executing in each computer those operations that had performed updates on remote computers during the period of disconnection. This solutions works if update operations commute—that is, they generate the same result, regardless of the order in which they are executed. Alternative techniques may be available in certain applications; in the worst case, however, it must be left to the users to resolve the inconsistencies. Dealing with such inconsistency automatically, and assisting users in resolving inconsistencies that cannot be handled automatically, remains an area of research.

Another weakness is that the version-vector scheme requires substantial communication between a reconnecting mobile host and that host's mobile support station. Consistency checks can be delayed until the data are needed, although this delay may increase the overall inconsistency of the database.

The potential for disconnection and the cost of wireless communication limit the practicality of transaction-processing techniques discussed in Chapter 18 for distributed systems. Often, it is preferable to let users prepare transactions on mobile hosts, but to require that, instead of executing the transactions locally, they submit transactions to a server for execution. Transactions than span more than one computer and that include a mobile host face long-term blocking during transaction commit, unless disconnectivity is rare or predictable.

## 21.8  Information-Retrieval Systems

The field of *information retrieval* has developed in parallel with the field of databases. The traditional model used in this field is as follows. Information is organized into documents, and it is assumed that there is a large number of documents. The process of information retrieval consists of locating relevant documents, based on user input, such as keywords or example documents.

Typical examples of information-retrieval systems are online library catalogs, and online document-management systems such as those that store newspaper articles. The data in such systems are organized as a collection of *documents*; a newspaper article or a catalog entry (in a library catalog) are examples of documents. A user of such a system may want to retrieve a particular document or a particular class of documents. The intended documents are typically described by a set of *keywords*—for example, the keywords "database system" may be used to locate books on database systems, and the keywords "stock" and "scandal" may be used to locate articles about stock-market scandals. Documents have associated with them a set of keywords, and documents whose keywords contain those supplied by the user are retrieved.

There are several differences between this model and the models used in traditional database systems.

- Database systems deal with several operations that are not addressed in information-retrieval systems. For instance, database systems deal with updates, with the associated transactional requirements of concurrency control and durability. These matters are viewed as less important in information systems. Similarly, database systems deal with structured information organized with relatively complex data models (such as the relational model or object-oriented data models), whereas information-retrieval systems traditionally have used a much simpler model, where the information in the database is organized simply as a collection of unstructured documents.

- Information-retrieval systems deal with several issues that have not been addressed adequately in database systems. For instance, the field of information retrieval has dealt with the problems of managing unstructured documents, such as approximate searching using keywords, and of retrieving documents based on the degree of relevance of the documents to the query.

## 21.8.1   Queries

Keyword-based information retrieval is common not only in information systems that store text data, but also in systems that store other kinds of data, such as multimedia data (audio or video clips, or still-picture images). Descriptive keywords can be created for multimedia data. A movie may have associated with it keywords such as its title, director, actors, type, and so on.

Information-retrieval systems based on keywords often allow queries to use expressions formed out of the keywords. A user could ask for all documents that contain the keywords "motorcycle *and* maintenance," or documents that contain the keywords "computer *or* micro-processor," or even documents that contain the keyword "computer *but not* database."

Consider the problem of locating catalog entries for books about motorcycle maintenance using the keywords "motorcycle" and "maintenance." Suppose that the keywords for each catalog entry are the words in the title and the names of the authors. The catalog entry of a book called *Motorcycle Repair* would not be retrieved, since the word "maintenance" does not occur in its title.

We can solve that problem by making use of *synonyms*. Each word can have a set of synonyms defined, and the occurrence of a word can be replaced by the *or* of all its synonyms (including the word itself). Thus, the query "motorcycle *and* repair" can be replaced by "motorcycle *and* (repair *or* maintenance)." This query would find the desired catalog entry.

Another important issue in information retrieval is the degree of *relevance* of a document. Suppose that in addition to the title and authors, a list of topics covered in the book is created, and is used as a portion of the keywords in the catalog. There may be a number of books on car racing that include sections on cars and motorcycles, as well as a section on maintenance. The keywords "motorcycle" and "maintenance" would be associated with the catalog entry, and all these books would be retrieved in response to the query on motorcycle maintenance, in addition to the books on motorcycle maintenance. However, these other books are only of marginal relevance to the query. A book where the keywords "motorcycle" and "maintenance" occur close to each other is more likely to be relevant than one where they occur far apart. Some information-retrieval systems permit queries to specify that the two words should occur one after another in the text, or within the same sentence. In general, documents where the specified keywords occur close to one another is more likely to be relevant than one where they appear far apart. Documents that contain all the specified keywords can then be given a score of likely relevance based on the nearness of the keywords, and can be sorted in order of relevance when presented to the user. If the list is long, the system is free to present only the most relevant few documents.

Certain information-retrieval systems permit *similarity-based retrieval*. Here, the user can give the system a document $A$, and ask the system to retrieve documents that are "similar" to $A$. The similarity of two documents may be defined, for example, based on common keywords. If the set of documents similar to $A$ is large, the system may present the user a few of the documents, allow him to choose the most relevant few, and start a new search based on similarity to $A$ *and* to the chosen documents.

## 21.8.2  Indexing of Documents

An effective index structure is important for efficient processing of queries in an information-retrieval system. This system can locate documents that contain a specified keyword using an *inverted index*, which maps each keyword $K_i$ to the set $S_i$ of (identifiers of) the documents that contain $K_i$. To support relevance ranking based on proximity of keywords, such an index may provide not just identifiers of documents, but also a list of locations in the document where the keyword appears. Since such indices must be stored on disk, the index organization also attempts to minimize the number of I/O operations to retrieve the set of documents that contain a keyword. Thus, the system may attempt to keep the set of documents for a keyword in consecutive disk pages.

Each keyword may be contained in a large number of documents; hence, a compact representation is critical to keep space usage of the index low. Thus, the sets of documents for a keyword are maintained in a compressed form. So that storage space is saved, the index is sometimes stored such that the retrieval is approximate; a few relevant documents may not be retrieved (called a *false drop*), or a few irrelevant documents may be retrieved (called a *false positive*). A good index structure will not have *any* false drops, but may permit a few false positives; the system can filter them away later by looking at the keywords that they actually contain.

Two metrics are used to measure how well an information-retrieval system is able to answer queries. The first, *precision*, measures what percentage of the retrieved documents are actually relevant to the query. The second, *recall*, measures what percentage of the documents relevant to the query were retrieved.

The *and* operation finds documents that contain all of a specified set of keywords $K_1, K_2, \ldots, K_n$. We implement the *and* operation by first retrieving the sets of document identifiers $S_1, S_2, \ldots, S_n$ of all documents that contain the respective keywords. The intersection, $S_1 \cap S_2 \cap \ldots \cap S_n$, of the sets gives the document identifiers of the desired set of documents. The *or* operation gives the set of all documents that contain at least one of the keywords $K_1, K_2, \ldots, K_n$; We implement the *or* operation by computing the union, $S_1 \cup S_2 \cup \ldots \cup S_n$, of the sets. The *but not* operation finds documents that do not contain a specified keyword $K_i$. Given a set of document identifiers $S$, we can eliminate documents that contain the specified keyword $K_i$ by taking the difference $S - S_i$, where $S_i$ is the set of identifiers of documents that contain the keyword $K_i$.

A *full-text index* on a document uses every word in the document as a keyword; such an index can be used on short documents. However, almost all text documents contain words such as "and," "or," "a," and so on, and hence these words are useless for indexing purposes. Information-retrieval systems define a set of words called *stop words*, containing one-hundred or so of the most common words, and remove this set from the document when indexing; such words are not allowed as keywords in queries either.

### 21.8.3  Browsing and Hypertext

Information systems were initially conceived primarily as catalog systems, such as library catalogs. The actual documents were stored outside the system. However, as disk capacities have increased greatly and more documents are created and stored online, information-retrieval systems are now being used to store the actual documents as well. Therefore, current-generation information systems allow the user to view documents that are stored online.

A typical library user may use a catalog to locate a book for which she is looking. When she retrieves the book from the shelf, however, she is likely to *browse* through other books that are located nearby. Libraries organize books such that related books are kept close together. Hence, a book that is physically near the desired book may be of interest as well, making it worthwhile for users to browse through such books.

To keep related books close together, libraries use a *classification hierarchy*. Books on science are classified together. Within this set of books, there is a finer classification, with computer-science books organized together, mathematics

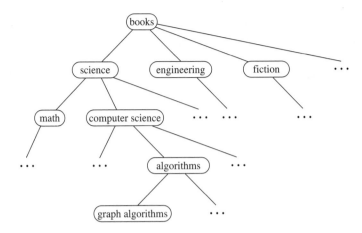

Figure 21.11   A classification hierarchy for a library system.

books organized together, and so on. Since there is a relation between mathematics and computer science, relevant sets of books are stored close to each other physically. At yet another level in the classification hierarchy, computer-science books are broken down into subareas, such as operating systems, languages, or algorithms. Figure 21.11 illustrates a classification hierarchy that may be used by a library. Because books can be kept at only one place, each book in a library is classified into exactly one spot in the classification hierarchy.

In an information-retrieval system, there is no great need to store related documents close together—the speed of disk access is high enough that disk-arm movement is typically not a major performance issue in such systems. However, such systems need to *organize documents logically* so as to permit browsing. Thus, such a system could use a classification hierarchy similar to one that libraries use, and, when a particular document is displayed, it can display a brief description of books that are close in the hierarchy.

In an information-retrieval system, there is no need to keep a document in a single spot in the hierarchy. A book that talks of mathematics for computer scientists could be classified under mathematics as well as under computer science. All that is stored at each spot is an identifier of the document (that is, a pointer to the document), and it is easy to fetch the contents of the document by using the identifier.

As a result of this flexibility, not only can a book be classified under two locations, but also a subarea in the classification hierarchy can itself occur under two areas. The class of "graph algorithm" books can appear both under mathematics and under computer science. Thus, the classification hierarchy is now a directed acyclic graph (DAG), as shown in Figure 21.12. A graph-algorithm book may appear in a single location in the DAG, but can be reached via multiple paths.

In response to a query, the information-retrieval system can not only display related documents, but also even display related classes in the classification hierarchy. The user can then look at all books (or subclasses) within that class.

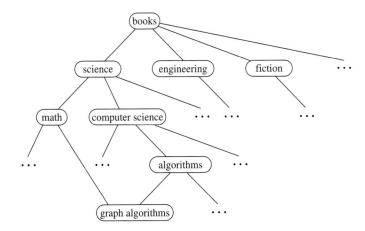

**Figure 21.12**   A classification DAG for a library information-retrieval system.

A typical document, such as a textbook or a research paper, has a list of references to other documents that provide related information. The references provide the name of the document, the authors, the publisher; the system uses these keywords to locate the document. However, if the document is already in the system, the user can provide an identifier of the document with the reference, avoiding the need for a query using keywords.

*Hypertext* systems are based on this idea of storing identifiers of other documents; they provide a powerful facility where the user can easily switch from the first document to the others. Typically, she does so using a point-and-click interface, where a simple mouse click on the display screen on top of the referred document retrieves and displays the document. *Hypertext* systems also permit references to specific locations within the or other documents. A click on such a link takes the user to the desired position within the document. Hypertext systems provide an extremely convenient way of browsing documents.

An early hypertext system was HyperCard, introduced on the Apple Macintosh computer systems. *Hypermedia* systems provide not only text, but also other media, such as images, videos, audio clips, and so on. The popular *online encyclopedias* today provide such facilities, as well as keyword-based retrieval. Unlike traditional encyclopedias, which provide only text and images, these systems include audio and video segments. We shall use the word *hypertext* to refer to hypermedia systems as well.

Today, *distributed hypertext* systems even permit references to documents stored at other sites in a distributed system. We study the most popular such system, the World Wide Web, in Section 21.10.

## 21.9  Distributed Information Systems

One of the most important developments in the field of computer science in recent years has been the rise of long-distance computer networks, in particular the global Internet. It is now easy for a person located in one area (say, India) to connect to a computer based in a distant geographic area (say, the United States), and to retrieve information stored on the distant computer. The initial uses of long-distance computer networks were mainly to send electronic mail, to post news on electronic bulletin boards, to transfer data files (ftp), and to connect to remote computers (remote login or telnet).

People soon realized that computer networks could be used to access a wealth of useful information—for example, directories of people, and on-line versions of documents such as research papers. There was also a wealth of other information that could potentially be stored online, but what was missing was a convenient, standardized way of accessing the data, along with standardized graphical user interfaces. Several distributed information systems have been developed to fill this gap, and have seen significant success.

The most widespread distributed information system today is the *World Wide Web*. Since this system is one of much interest, we discuss it in detail in Section 21.10.

The Internet *Gopher* from the University of Minnesota, and the *Wide Area Information System*, were two of the early distributed information systems, that predated the World Wide Web. They represent two distinct approaches to organizing and retrieving information in a distributed system.

A Gopher system consists of servers and clients. A Gopher server organizes data into directories, much like a classification hierarchy. The Gopher client initially communicates with a server, and displays the top-level directory of the server hierarchy as a menu, as illustrated in Figure 21.13. The user can then choose an item in the menu, which can be another directory in the hierarchy, or a document, or a link to a directory on another server. If the chosen item is a directory in the hierarchy, the data in the directory are displayed as a menu. If the chosen item is a document, the document is displayed. If the chosen item is a link to a directory on

```
             Internet Gopher Information Client 2.0 p18

         University of XYZ Computer Science Department Gopher

   -->  1.   WELCOME
        2.   Information About Gopher/
        3.   About the University of XYZ CS Department
        4.   University of XYZ Campus Information/
        5.   Search Gopher Titles at the Univ. of Minnesota <?>
        6.   University of Minnesota Gopher (Gopher Central)/
        7.   Libraries/
        8.   Phone Books/
        9.   Other Gopher and Information Servers/
        10. Internet file server (ftp) sites/


Press ? for Help, q to Quit, u to go up a menu      Page: 1/1
```

Figure 21.13    A sample Gopher client display.

another Gopher server, the client connects to the new Gopher server and displays the directory as a menu. Thus, the Gopher system allows a seamless connection to remote servers. Logically, there is no difference between a local and a remote server.

The model of information retrieval in a Gopher system is based on browsing and navigating a directory hierarchy. However, an item in a Gopher directory may be a link to other kinds of servers, such as index servers, which can provide keyword-based indexing capabilities. Figure 21.13 illustrates typical topics stored on a Gopher server. The figure also illustrates menu items corresponding to documents, corresponding to index servers (with a " <?>" suffix), and corresponding to directories (with a " /" suffix)

The Wide Area Information System (WAIS) follows a different approach to information retrieval. The basic model in WAIS is the indexing of information by server systems. Each server stores information on one or more subjects, and supports a powerful keyword-based indexing mechanism on its local data. In addition, each server maintains a directory, or description, of other servers. The directory is a summary of what kind of information is stored at the server, and how to access that information. If a query is presented at a WAIS server, the server uses its directory information to tell the user what other servers may have relevant information. It is infeasible to run a query at every WAIS server in the Internet, since there is an enormous number of such servers. The directory provides a means of narrowing down the search, as well as a means of freeing the user from remembering which servers may contain relevant information for a query.

## 21.10   The World Wide Web

The *World Wide Web* (*WWW*, or *Web*) is a distributed information system based on hypertext. Documents stored under the Web can be of one of several types. The most common type are hypertext documents formatted according to the HyperText Markup Language (HTML), which itself is based on the Standard Generalized Markup Language (SGML). HTML documents contain text, font specifications, and other formatting instructions. Links to other documents (whether local or remote) can be associated with regions of the text. Images can also be referenced with appropriate formatting instructions (such as a link to an image file).

The user of a Web system sees formatted text along with images, rather than the raw text with formatting instructions. Formatted text with images is visually much more appealing than is plain text. Further, the displayed document is a hypertext document; with an appropriate browser, the user can click on a region that has a link associated with it, and the document pointed to by the link will be displayed. Thus, the hypertext interface to the Web forms a powerful and visually attractive browsing interface. More recently, Web browsers have begun to support a programming language called *Java*, which allows documents to contain programs that are executed at the user's site. Thus, documents can now be *active*, rather than just passive.

In Sections 21.10.1 through 21.10.5, we study the basic technology underlying the Web, and examine how the Web is likely to influence database systems.

## 21.10.1   Uniform Resource Locators

Recall that a hypertext system must be able to store pointers to documents. In the Web, the functionality of pointers is provided by *Uniform Resource Locators* (URLs). The following is an example of an URL:

> http://www.bell-labs.com/topic/book/db-book

The first part of the URL indicates how the document is to be accessed: "http" indicates that the document is to be accessed using the HyperText Transfer Protocol, which is a protocol for transferring HTML documents. The second part gives the unique name of a machine on the Internet. The rest of the URL is the path name of the file on the machine.

Thus, URLs provide a globally unique name for each document that can be accessed from a Web system. Since URLs are human readable, a human can use them directly to access a desired document, instead of navigating down a path from a predefined location. Since they allow the use of an Internet machine name, they are global in scope, and people can use them to create links across machines.

Unlike in the Gopher system, where what is displayed is either a document or a directory, a HTML document display is simultaneously a document and a directory. Another important difference is that, since URLs are human readable, and can specify a file in the system, it is easy for anyone on a machine connected to the Internet to create a document that other users can then access using the Web. Gopher systems tend to be set up and controlled by system administrators. The Web is much more open: Any user can create documents on the Web, and can give the URL to anyone else. In fact, as a result, the Web is almost anarchic—there is no central authority governing anything on the Web. Many Internet users today have *home pages* on the Web; such pages often contain information about users' personal and work lives.

The fact that a URL can specify how to access a document is also of importance. In addition to supporting http, Web clients support other protocols for transferring documents, such as the widely used file transfer protocol (ftp). The Web client even provides a hypertext-based front-end to the ftp services.

## 21.10.2   Web Servers

HTTP provides powerful features, beyond the simple transfer of documents, such as encryption for security. The document name in a URL may identify an executable program that, when run, generates a HTML document. When a HTTP server receives a request for such a document, it executes the program, and sends back the HTML document that is generated. Further, the Web client can pass extra arguments with the name of the document; they are then passed as arguments when the program is executed. Thus, the generated document can depend on the arguments that were passed in.

As a result of these features, a Web server can easily act as a front-end server for a variety of information services. To install a new service on the Web, a person needs only to create and install an executable program that provides the service. The language supported by the Web, HTML, is used to implement the graphical user interface to the information service.

## 21.10.3   Display Languages

Today's computer systems not only provide a simple character-based interface, but also support graphics, multiple fonts, color, and so on, which options can greatly enhance the quality of displayed information. However, there is a variety of standards for graphical displays, and different kinds of computers have different interfaces. It is hard to write a program that can support multiple display interfaces directly. Page-description languages, such as PostScript, and standard text-formatting languages, such as nroff or TEX/LATEX, provide standardized interfaces, but have a large set of features, making them slow and thus unsuitable for interactive use.

Text-markup languages, such as the Standard Generalized Markup Language (SGML), were developed to fill a void between plain text and page-description or text-formatting languages. The markup languages provide simple formatting commands, such as paragraph separators and numbered or itemized lists, as well as a degree of control over displayed fonts. Thus, they provide a standard output interface for programs.

Text-markup languages are particularly important for general-purpose distributed information systems, since the information to be displayed ought to be formatted in a pleasing manner, rather than being merely plain text. An alternative way to implement such formatting would be for each information service to run a special-purpose program at the client site—which solution is obviously inconvenient for a user who wants to access many information services.

### 21.10.3.1   HyperText Markup Language

SGML provides a grammar for specifying document formats based on standard markup annotations. HTML is a general-purpose hypertext display language, based on SGML. It specifies a document format that allows text-formatting commands, as well as hypertext-link commands and image-display commands. Figure 21.14 shows an example of the source of a HTML document. Figure 21.15 shows the displayed image corresponding to the same document.

HTML also provides limited input features. For example, an HTML document can specify that a form should be displayed. The HTML display program (that is, the Web client) allows the user to fill in entries in the form. Menus and other graphical input facilities are also provided, and let the user select a menu item, move a slider bar to select a value in a range, point to and click on a location in an image (such as a map), and so on. When the user has finished entering values, she can press a "submit" button.

At this point, values entered by the user are collected, and the Web client sends a request for the document, with the values entered by the user as arguments.

```
<title>WWW Home Page</title>
<img src="lucent_logo.gif"> <img src="iitb-logo.gif">
<hr>
<h3> <a href=
    "http://www.bell-labs.com/topic/books/db-book">
    Database System Concepts:   Home Page </a>
</h3>
<h3> Information Services </h3>
<dl>
    <dd> <a href="http://www.altavista.digital.com">
            The Altavista Information
            Gathering Service</a>
    <dd> <a href=
            "http://www.informatik.uni-trier.de/~ley/db">
            Database and Logic Programming
            Bibliography</a>
    <dd> <a href="http://cs.indiana.edu/cstr/search">
            Indiana University's Unified
            CS Tech. Report Service</a>
    <dd> <a href="http://www.ncstrl.org">
            Networked Computer Science
            Tech. Report Library</a>
</dl>
```

Figure 21.14    A portion of an HTML source text.

This document is an executable program, and the Web server invokes the program with the specified arguments. As described earlier, the program generates an HTML document, which is then sent back to be displayed

The actual layout of the screen, and the specific forms to be filled and menu items to be chosen, are all under the control of the HTML document. Thus, HTML provides a graphical user interface that can run on almost any computer. However, there is no continuous connection between the client and the server; the server keeps no history of its interaction with the client, and all state information has to be stored at the client and sent to the server with each communication. In spite of these limitations (which may well be removed in the future), HTML it is likely to prove of increasing importance to distributed information systems in the future.

### 21.10.3.2   Java

A more recent development has been the release of the Java language, which allows documents to be *active*, carrying out activities such as animation by executing programs at the local site, rather than just presenting passive text and graphics. The Java language, developed by Sun, is an interpreted language that resembles C++. The Java language also provides standardized libraries of graphical

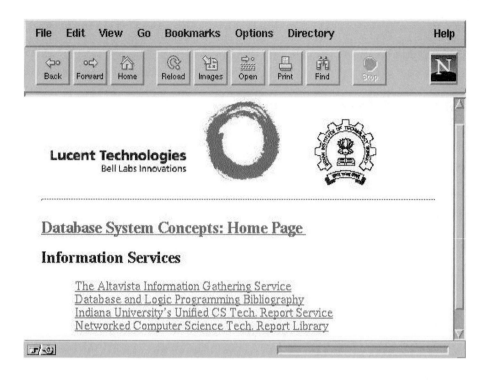

Figure 21.15    Display of HTML source from Figure 21.14.

user-interface functions. When a Java program is compiled, instead of generating machine code, the compiler generates byte code, which can be executed on an interpreter. Java interpreters have been written for practically every platform (combination of hardware and operating system), and hence the same Java program can run on practically any platform.

As a result of the uniformity of the Java environment, Java programs can be stored at server sites just like HTML documents, and can be downloaded and executed by any client site, regardless of the client platform. Thus, Java provides a convenient way of distributing (small) programs. The primary use of such programs is flexible interaction with the user, beyond the limited interaction power provided by HTML and HTML forms. Further, executing programs at the client site speeds up interaction greatly, compared to every interaction being sent to a server site for processing.

With the power of downloading and executing programs at the click of a button comes the danger of downloaded programs causing damage, such as deleting files, at the client site. Unlike system programs, downloaded programs have no authority, such as a vendor, which has checked them for absence of malicious behavior. Therefore, it is important that Java programs be allowed only those facilities that can cause no permanent damage, such as displaying data on the screen, and that they not be allowed to make system calls directly. Hence, Java interpreters have a security system built in. The security system ensures that the Java code does not make any system calls directly. The user is notified about potentially dangerous actions, such as file writes, and has the option to abort the program or to continue execution.

## 21.10.4    Web Interfaces to Databases

Interfacing of databases to the World Wide Web is important for two reasons. First, with the growth of electronic commerce on the Web, databases used for transaction processing must be linked with the Web. The HTML forms interface is convenient for transaction processing. The user can fill in details in an order form, and can click a submit button to send a message to the server containing the information that he has filled in. A program corresponding to the order form is executed, in turn executing a transaction on a database at the server site. The results of the transaction can be formatted into HTML and displayed to the user.

The second reason for interfacing databases to the Web is that fixed HTML sources for display to users have limitations:

- The use of fixed Web documents does not allow the display to be tailored to the user. For instance, a company may want to display promotional material tailored to the interests of the user.

- When the company data are updated, the Web documents become outdated if they are not updated simultaneously. The problem becomes more acute if multiple Web documents replicate important data, and all must be updated.

We can fix these problems by generating Web documents dynamically. When a document is requested, a program can be executed at the server site, which runs queries on the database, and generates a document based on the query results. The Web document displayed can be tailored to the user, based on user information stored in the database. Data in Web documents can also be defined by queries on a database, so that, whenever relevant data in the database are updated, the Web documents will be up-dated too.

Translating variables defined in HTML forms to SQL can involve making format conversions. Translating tables and other data generated by a database query into HTML can be even more tedious, since the programmer has to know about details such as field formats and sizes, and the number of tuples generated. Web interfaces to databases simplify these tasks. These interfaces are similar to report writers (see Section 19.6); in fact, the main difference is that, instead of generating formatted text, they generate HTML documents. The programmer can define a HTML document in a macro language with embedded SQL queries. Variables defined in HTML forms can be used directly in the embedded SQL queries. When the document is requested, a macro processor executes the SQL queries, and generates the actual HTML document that is sent to the user. The HTML document written in the macro language may have two parts — a forms-input interface, and a result-display interface. Interaction then occurs in two phases. In the first, the forms part of the HTML document is generated and is sent back to the client. When the client submits the form, the result part of the document is generated and is sent back.

## 21.10.5 Locating of Information on the Web

The Web provides a convenient way to get to, and to interact with, information sources across the Internet. However, a persistent problem facing the Web is the explosion of stored information, with little guidance to help the user to locate what is interesting.

One simple way in which users can find out about interesting information is simply to ask friends! In fact, that is how most information about interesting Web sites gets propagated even today. A second way, which is slightly more sophisticated, but is perhaps less useful, is for a user to note in her home page a list of the most interesting Web sites that she has seen. Other people can follow these links to locate interesting sites. Neither of these techniques is a particularly efficient means for locating information.

Let us step back and look at the world of tourism—visiting a place physically has similarities to visiting a place on the Web, to retrieve a document or to use an information service. Whereas time and money are constraints for tourism, time is usually the only constraint for visiting places on the Web. How do you decide what geographic places to visit? One source of information is friends who have traveled. Guide books tell you about places to visit. Libraries, with their classification of books, help you to browse related guide books easily. Finally, a library catalog lets you locate specific books.

There are rough counterparts to each of these sources on the Web. There are Web sites that provide information about other Web sites in a fashion similar to a guide book. Some of these sites even act as online shopping malls, collecting at one site services that let you shop for various goods via the Web. Some sites maintain a classification hierarchy of information about sites on the Web. You can follow the hierarchy to find desired Web sites.

The equivalent of the library catalog is the hardest information source to implement on the Web. In a library, every book that is purchased goes through the librarian, who adds an entry to the catalog. No such librarian exists on the Web. Who is to find what Web sites exist, and what they contain? A similar problem also exists for other information systems, such as the Gopher.

Distributed information-gathering systems perform the task of finding out what information exists on the Web. Whereas WAIS systems send queries to remote systems when users ask for information, distributed information-gathering systems periodically fetch information from remote systems, and create an index locally. The systems thus combines at one site information from multiple sources. Client programs can access the distributed information-gathering system and can pose queries, which the system answers using its locally stored index. Due to disk-space limitations, the documents typically are not stored within the information-gathering system; instead, pointers to the remotely located documents are returned as answers to a query.

An early example of such a system was the Computer Science Technical Report Index, which collects information about computer-science technical reports stored on-line at various ftp sites. A more ambitious system of this kind is the Archie system, which automatically follows Gopher links to locate information, and creates a centralized index of information found from various sites.

Various information-gathering systems, generically called *Web crawlers*, have been developed for locating and gathering information on the Web. They recursively follow hypertext links present in known documents to find other documents. The documents are retrieved, and information found in the document is added to a combined index; again, the document is not stored. These services run a daemon process in the background to find new sites by following links, obtain updated information from known sites, and discard sites that no longer exist, so that the information in the index is kept reasonably up to date.

With the explosive growth of the Web today, the workload of Web crawlers becomes progressively heavier, as more sites need to be indexed. Further, with a huge number of sites, a query may generate a correspondingly huge number of answers, and good techniques for distinguishing relevant sites from irrelevant sites will be required. However, Web crawlers have the significant advantage that no central authority is required for registering documents, so it is easy for users to create new documents and to have people locate the documents via an index. Indexing of data on the Web is an area of ongoing research.

Finding documents based on keywords is a simplistic form of query processing, compared to the query functionality provided by database systems. The problem with supporting more complex queries is that data on the Web typically are in the form of unstructured text, unlike the highly structured data stored in relational databases. *Semistructured data* are data that are mostly unstructured and have only some degree of structure. For instance, documents that are tagged with values for some or all of the attributes *author:*, *title:*, *subject:* and *keywords:* could be considered semistructured data. Query processing using semistructured data is another topic of ongoing research.

# 21.11   Summary

Decision-support systems are gaining in importance, as companies realize the value of the on-line data collected by their on-line transaction-processing systems. Proposed extensions to SQL, such as the **cube** operation, help to support generation of summary data. Data mining seeks to discover knowledge automatically, in the form of statistical rules and patterns from large databases. Data-visualization systems help humans to discover such knowledge visually. A data warehouse is a repository (or archive) of information gathered from multiple sources, stored under a unified schema, at a single site. Once gathered, the data are stored for a long period, permitting access to historical data for decision-support purposes.

Spatial databases are finding increasing use today to store computer-aided–design data as well as geographic data. Design data are stored primarily as vector data; geographic data consist of a combination of vector and raster data. Spatial-integrity constraints are important for design data. Vector data can be encoded as first-normal-form data, or can be stored using non–first-normal-form structures, such as lists. Special-purpose index structures are particularly important for accessing spatial data, and for processing spatial queries. R-trees are a two-dimensional extension of B-trees; with variants such as R+-trees and R*-trees, they have proved popular in spatial databases. Index structures that partition space in a regular fashion, such as quadtrees, help in processing spatial join queries.

Multimedia databases are growing in importance. Issues such as similarity-based retrieval and delivery of data at guaranteed rates are topics of current research.

Mobile computing systems have become common, leading to interest in database systems that can run on such systems. Query processing in such systems may involve lookups on server databases. The query cost model must include the cost of communication, including monetary cost and battery-power cost, which is relatively high for mobile systems. Broadcast is much cheaper per recipient than is point-to-point communication, and broadcast of data such as stock-market data helps mobile systems to pick up data inexpensively. Disconnected operation, use of broadcast data, and caching of data are three important issues being addressed in mobile computing.

Information-retrieval systems use a simpler data model than do database systems, but provide more powerful querying capabilities within the restricted model. Queries attempt to locate documents that are of interest by specifying, for example, sets of keywords. The query that a user has in mind usually cannot be stated precisely; hence, information-retrieval systems order answers based on potential relevance.

Distributed information systems that run on the Internet have seen explosive growth in recent years. The World Wide Web system supports browsing such information using the hypertext paradigm. Tools that integrate HTML with SQL ease the task of creating HTML front-ends to databases. Distributed information-gathering systems help people to find information on the Web.

# Exercises

**21.1.** Consider the *balance* attribute of the *account* relation. Write an SQL query to compute a histogram of *balance* values, dividing the range 0 to the maximum account balance present, into three equal ranges.

**21.2.** Consider the *sales* relation from Section 21.2. Write an SQL query to compute the cube operation on the relation, giving the relation shown in Figure 21.2. Do not use the **with cube** construct.

**21.3.** Suppose there are two classification rules, one which says that people with salaries between 10,000 and 20,000 have a credit rating of *good*, and another which says that people with salaries between 20,000 and 30,000 have a credit rating of *good*. Under what conditions can the rules be replaced, without any loss of information, by a single rule that says people with salaries between 10, 000 and 30, 000 have a credit rating of *good*.

**21.4.** Suppose half of all the transactions in a clothes shop purchase jeans, and one third of all transactions in the shop purchase t-shirts. Suppose also that half of the transactions that purchase jeans also purchase t-shirts. Write down all the (non-trivial) association rules you can deduce from the above information, giving support and confidence of each rule.

**21.5.** Consider the problem of finding *frequent item-sets*, that is, sets of items that are frequently purchased together. The *support* of an item-set is the number of transactions that purchase every item in the item-set. An item-set is a frequent item-set if its support is greater than $k$, for some pre-defined $k$.

    (*a*) Describe how to find the support for a given collection of item-sets using a single scan of the data. Assume that the item-sets and associated information, such as counts, will fit in memory.

    (*b*) Suppose an item-set has support less than $j$. Show that no superset of this item-set can have support greater than or equal to $j$.

    (*c*) Due to memory limitations, it is possible to find the support for only a small number of item-sets (as many as will fit in memory) in one scan of the data. Devise an algorithm for reducing the number of scans of the data (and thereby, the I/O required) for finding frequent item-sets, by finding support for as few item-sets as possible.

**21.6.** Describe benefits and drawbacks of a source-driven architecture for gathering of data at a data-warehouse, as compared to a destination-driven architecture.

**21.7.** Suppose you have a relation containing the x,y coordinates and names of restaurants. Suppose also that the only queries that will be asked are of the following form: the query specifies a point, and asks if there is a restaurant exactly at that point. Which type of index would be preferable: R-tree or B-tree? Why?

**21.8.** Consider two-dimensional vector data where the data items do not overlap. Is it possible to convert such vector data to raster data? If so, what are the drawbacks of storing raster data obtained by such conversion, instead of the original vector data?

**21.9.** Suppose you have a spatial database that supports region queries (with circular regions) but not nearest-neighbor queries. Describe an algorithm to find the nearest neighbor by making use of multiple region queries?

**21.10.** Suppose you want to store line segments in an R-tree. If a line segment is not parallel to the axes, the bounding box for it can be large, containing a large empty area.

    • Describe the performance effect of having large bounding boxes, on queries that ask for line segments intersecting a given region.

    • Briefly describe a technique to improve performance for such queries and give an example of its benefit.

      Hint: you can divide segments into smaller pieces.

**21.11.** What problems can occur in a continuous-media system if data is delivered either too slowly or too fast?

**21.12.** Describe how the ideas behind the RAID organization (Section 10.3) can be used in a broadcast-data environment, where there may occasionally be noise that prevents reception of part of the data being transmitted.

**21.13.** List 3 main features of mobile computing over wireless networks that are distinct from traditional distributed systems.

**21.14.** List 3 factors that need to be considered in query optimization for mobile computing that are not considered in traditional query optimizers.

**21.15.** Define a model of broadcast data in which the broadcast medium is a virtual disk. Describe how seek time, latency, and data-transfer rate for this virtual disk differ from the corresponding values for a typical hard disk.

**21.16.** Consider a database of documents in which all documents are kept in a central database. Copies of some documents are kept on mobile computers. Suppose that mobile computer A updates a copy of document 1 while it is disconnected, and, at the same time, mobile computer B updates a copy of document 2 while it is disconnected. Show how the version-vector scheme can ensure proper updating of the central database and mobile computers when a mobile computer re-connects.

**21.17.** Give an example to show that the version-vector scheme does not ensure serializability. (Hint: Use the example from Exercise 21.16, with the assumption that documents 1 and 2 are available on both mobile computers A and B, and take into account the possibility that a document may be read without being updated.)

**21.18.** What is the difference between a false positive and a false drop? If it is essential that no relevant information be missed by an information retrieval query, is it acceptable to have either false positives or false drops? Why?

**21.19.** Suppose you want to find documents that contain at least $k$ of a given set of $n$ keywords. Suppose also you have a keyword index that gives you a (sorted) list of identifiers of documents that contain a specified keyword. Give an efficient algorithm to find the desired set of documents.

**21.20.** Give three main features of HTML that have lead to its enormous success.

**21.21.** Describe the main feature provided by Java that HTML lacks, and some of the benefits of this feature.

**21.22.** Describe some benefits of dynamic generation of Web pages from data stored in a database.

**21.23.** Describe three distinct ways a user can find information on the Web.

## Bibliographical Notes

Gray et al. [1995] describe the data-cube operator. Harinarayan et al. [1996] describe techniques for efficient lazy implementation of the data-cube operator, to generate required aggregates on demand.

Fayyad et al. [1995] present an extensive collection of articles on knowledge discovery and data mining. Agrawal et al. [1993] provide an early overview of data mining in databases. Agrawal et al. [1992] describe data-mining techniques for classification; Ng and Han [1994] describe data-mining techniques based on spatial clustering. Srikant and Agrawal [1996] present techniques for deducing quantitative association rules.

Poe [1995] and Mattison [1996] provide textbook coverage of data warehousing. Zhuge et al. [1995] describe view maintenance in a data-warehousing environment. Larson and Yang [1985] and Dar et al. [1996] describe how to use materialized relations to answer queries.

There has been a great deal of work on spatial index structures, and Samet [1995b] provides a recent overview of the field. Samet [1990] provides a textbook coverage of spatial data structures. An early description of the quad tree is provided by Finkel and Bentley [1974]; Samet [1990, 1995b] describes numerous variants of quad trees. Bentley [1975] describes the k-d tree, and Robinson [1981] describes the k-d-B tree. The R-tree was originally presented in Guttman [1984]. Extensions of the R-tree are presented by Sellis et al. [1987], who describe the $R^+$ tree; Beckmann et al. [1990], who describe the $R^*$ tree; and Kamel and Faloutsos [1992], who describe a parallel version of the R-tree.

Brinkhoff et al. [1993] discuss an implementation of spatial joins using R-trees. Lo and Ravishankar [1996], and Patel and DeWitt [1996] present partitioning-based methods for computation of spatial joins. Samet and Aref [1995] provide an overview of spatial data models, spatial operations, and the integration of spatial and nonspatial data. Indexing of handwritten documents is discussed in Aref et al. [1995a, 1995b], and Lopresti and Tomkins [1993]. Joins of approximate data are discussed in Barbará et al. [1992]. Evangelidis et al. [1995] present a technique for concurrent access to indices on spatial data.

Samet [1995a] describes research issues in multimedia database. Indexing of multimedia data is discussed in Faloutsos and Lin [1995]. Video servers are discussed in Anderson et al. [1992], Rangan et al. [1992], Özden et al. [1994], Freedman and DeWitt [1995], and Özden et al. [1996a]. Fault tolerance is discussed in Berson et al. [1995] and Özden et al. [1996b]. Reason et al. [1996] suggest alternative compression schemes for video transmission over wireless networks. Disk storage management techniques for video data are described in Chen et al. [1995], Chervenak et al. [1995], Özden et al. [1995a], and Özden et al. [1995b].

Information management in systems that include mobile computers is studied in Alonso and Korth [1993] and Imielinski and Badrinath [1994]. Imielinski and Korth [1996] present an introduction to mobile computing and a collection of research papers on the subject. Indexing of data broadcast over wireless media is considered in Imielinski et al. [1995]. Caching of data in mobile environments is discussed in Barbará and Imielinski [1994] and Acharya et al. [1995]. Disk management in mobile computers is addressed in Douglis et al. [1994].

The version-vector scheme for detecting inconsistency in distributed file systems is described by Popek et al. [1981], and by Parker et al. [1983].

Salton's book [1989] is a good textbook source for material on information-retrieval systems. Other work on text databases includes Gravano et al. [1994] and Tomasic et al. [1994]. There are numerous books about the Internet, which include material on the distributed information systems described in this chapter. Krol [1994] presents a description of some distributed information systems, along with a directory of sources of information on the Internet. Most of the popular distributed information systems are available free of charge on the Internet; the most effective way to learn more about these systems is to use them. Nguyen and Srinivasan [1996] describe an interface between HTML and SQL, based on embedding SQL queries in HTML documents. There are several distributed information-gathering and indexing systems on the Web, one of the more popular of which is the Digital Altavista system at the URL http://www.altavista.digital.com. The Yahoo system, at the URL http://www.yahoo.com, provides an extensive classification hierarchy for Web sites.

# NETWORK MODEL

In the relational model, the data and the relationships among data are represented by a collection of tables. The network model differs from the relational model in that data are represented by collections of *records*, and relationships among data are represented by *links*.

## A.1 Basic Concepts

A network database consists of a collection of records connected to one another through links. A record is in many respects similar to an entity in the entity–relationship (E-R) model. Each record is a collection of fields (attributes), each of which contains only one data value. A link is an association between precisely two records. Thus, a link can be viewed as a restricted (binary) form of relationship in the sense of the E-R model.

As an illustration, consider a database representing a *customer-account* relationship in a banking system. There are two record types, *customer* and *account*. As we saw earlier, we can define the *customer* record type, using Pascal-like notation, as follows:

> **type** *customer* = **record**
> > *customer-name*: string;
> > *customer-street*: string;
> > *customer-city*: string;
> **end**

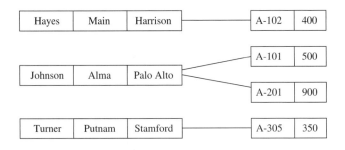

**Figure A.1    Sample database.**

The *account* record type can be defined as follows:

**type** *account* = **record**
                           *account-number*: string;
                           *balance*: integer;
          **end**

The sample database in Figure A.1 shows that Hayes has account A-102, Johnson has accounts A-101 and A-201, and Turner has account A-305.

## A.2    Data-Structure Diagrams

A *data-structure diagram* is a schema representing the design of a network database. Such a diagram consists of two basic components: boxes, which correspond to record types, and lines, which correspond to links. A data-structure diagram serves the same purpose as an E-R diagram; namely, it specifies the overall logical structure of the database. E-R diagrams can be translated into corresponding data-structure diagrams.

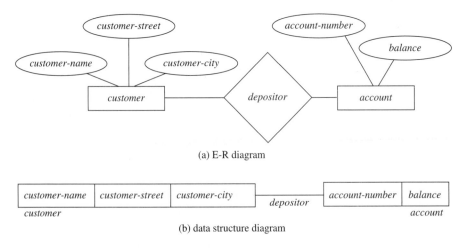

**Figure A.2    E-R diagram and its corresponding data-structure diagram.**

To illustrate, consider the E-R diagram of Figure A.2a, consisting of two entity sets, *customer* and *account*, related through a binary, many-to-many relationship *depositor*, with no descriptive attributes. This diagram specifies that a customer may have several accounts, and that an account may belong to several different customers. The corresponding data-structure diagram is illustrated in Figure A.2b. The record type *customer* corresponds to the entity set *customer*. It includes three fields—*customer-name*, *customer-street*, and *customer-city*—as defined above. Similarly, *account* is the record type corresponding to the entity set *account*. It includes the two fields *account-number* and *balance*. Finally, the relationship *depositor* has been replaced with the link *depositor*. If the relationship *depositor* were one to many from *customer* to *account*, then the link *depositor* would have an arrow pointing to *customer* record type. Similarly, if the relationship *depositor* were one to one, then the link *depositor* would have two arrows: one pointing to *account* record type, and one pointing to *customer* record type.

Consider the E-R diagram of Figure A.3a, which consists of three entity sets—*account*, *customer*, and *branch*—related through the general relationship *CAB* with no descriptive attribute. This diagram specifies that a customer may

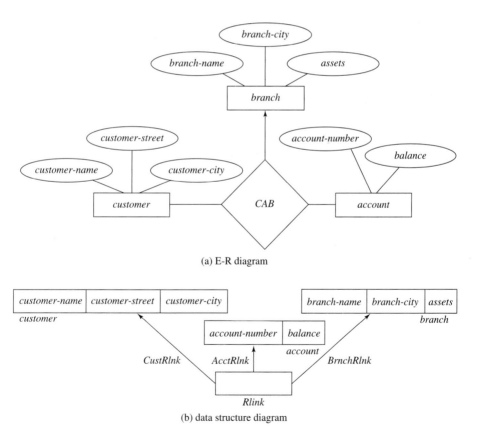

(a) E-R diagram

(b) data structure diagram

Figure A.3   E-R diagram and its corresponding data-structure diagram.

have several accounts, each located in a specific bank branch, and that an account may belong to several different customers.

Since a link can connect precisely two different record types, we need to connect these three record types through a new record type that is linked to each of them directly.

To transform the E-R diagram of Figure A.3a to a network data-structure diagram, we must create a new record type *Rlink* that may either have no fields or have a single field containing a unique identifier. This identifier is supplied by the system, and is not used directly by the application program. This new type of record is sometimes referred to as a *dummy* (or *link* or *junction*) record type. We must also create three many-to-one links, *CustRlnk*, *AcctRlnk*, and *BrncRlnk*, as depicted in Figure A.3b. If the relationship *CAB* had any descriptive attributes, they would become fields of the record type *Rlink*.

## A.3    The DBTG CODASYL Model

The first database-standard specification, called the CODASYL DBTG 1971 report, was written in the late 1960s by the Database Task Group. In the DBTG model, only many-to-one links can be used. One-to-one links are represented as many-to-one links. Many-to-many links are disallowed to simplify the implementation.

If the *depositor* relationship is many to many, then our transformation algorithm must be refined as follows. Consider the relationship shown in (Figure A.4a). To transform the relationship, we must create a new dummy record type, *Rlink*, that may either have no fields or have a single field containing an externally

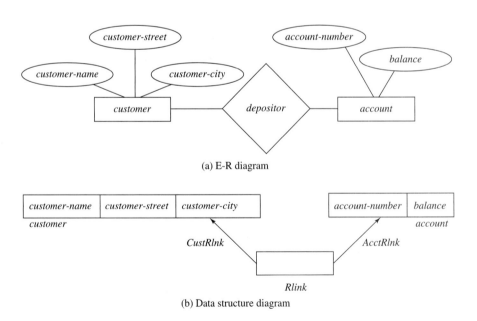

(a) E-R diagram

(b) Data structure diagram

Figure A.4    E-R diagram and its corresponding data-structure diagram.

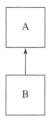

Figure A.5    DBTG-set.

defined unique identifier, and two many-to-one links *CustRlnk* and *AcctRlnk* as depicted in Figure A.4b.

Given that only many-to-one links can be used in the DBTG model, a data-structure diagram consisting of two record types that are linked together has the general form of Figure A.5. This structure is referred to in the DBTG model as a *DBTG set*. The name of the set is usually chosen to be the same as the name of the link connecting the two record types.

In each such DBTG set, the record type *A* is designated as the *owner* (or *parent*) of the set, and the record type *B* is designated as the *member* (or *child*) of the set. Each DBTG set can have any number of *set occurrences*—that is, actual instances of linked records. For example, in Figure A.6, we have three set occurrences corresponding to the DBTG set of Figure A.5.

Since many-to-many links are disallowed, each set occurrence has precisely one owner, and has zero or more member records. In addition, no member record of a set can participate in more than one occurrence of the set at any point. A member record, however, can participate simultaneously in several set occurrences of *different* DBTG sets.

The data-manipulation language of the DBTG proposal consists of commands that are embedded in a host language. The commands enable the programmer to select records from the database based on the value of a specified field, and to iterate over the selected records by repeated commands to get the next record. The programmer is also provided with commands find the owner of a set in which a record participates, and to iterate over the members of the set. And of course, there are commands to update the database.

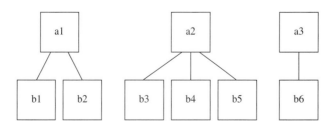

Figure A.6    Three set occurrences.

## A.4    Implementation Techniques

Links are implemented in the DBTG model by adding *pointer fields* to records that are associated via a link. To illustrate the implementation, suppose the *depositor* relationship is many-to-one from *account* to *customer*. An *account* record can be associated with only one *customer* record. Thus, we need only one pointer in the *account* record to represent the *depositor* relationship. However, a *customer* record can be associated with many *account* records. Rather than using multiple pointers in the *customer* record, we can use a *ring structure* to represent the entire occurrence of the DBTG set *depositor*. In a ring structure, the records of both the owner and member types for a set occurrence are organized into a circular list. There is one circular list for each set occurrence (that is, for each record of the owner type).

Figure A.7 shows the ring structure for the example of Figure A.1. Let us examine the DBTG-set occurrence owned by the "Johnson" record. There are two member-type (*account*) records. Rather than containing one pointer to each member record, the owner (Johnson) record contains a pointer to only the first member record (account A-101). This member record contains a pointer to the next member record (account A-201). Since the record for account A-201 is the final member record, it contains a pointer to the owner record.

It is significantly harder to implement many-to-many links using pointers. Hence the DBTG model restricted links to be many-to-one. The implementation strategy for the DBTG model also provided the basis for the DBTG data retrieval facility.

## A.5    Discussion

It is clear from the preceding discussion that the network model is closely tied to the implementation. As we saw earlier, the database designer has to create artificial record types even to implement simple many-to-many relationships. Unlike in the

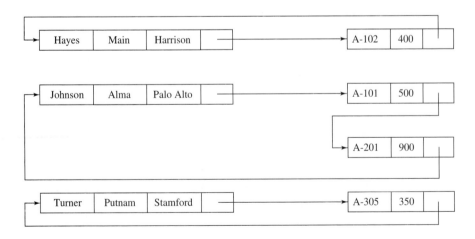

Figure A.7    Ring structure for instance of Figure A.1.

relational model, where querying can be done in a simple, declarative, manner, querying is significantly more complicated. The programmer is forced to think in terms of links, and how to traverse them to get at needed information; data-manipulation in the network model is hence said to be *navigational*.

Thus, the network model significantly increases the burden on the programmer, for database design as well as for data manipulation, as compared to the relational model. It held up against the relational model for many years since the implementations of the relational model were initially rather inefficient. Today, there are excellent implementations of the relational model, and the network model has therefore been losing importance. Hence it is no longer covered in detail in this book.

However, a detailed description of the network model is available on the Web for the benefit of those who wish to study it, at the URL:

```
http://www.bell-labs.com/topic/books/db-book
```

or via anonymous FTP from `ftp.research.bell-labs.com` in the sub-directory `dist/db-book`

# HIERARCHICAL MODEL

In the network model, the data are represented by collections of *records*, and relationships between data are represented by *links*. This structure holds for the hierarchical model as well. The only difference is that, in the hierarchical model, records are organized as collections of trees, rather than as arbitrary graphs.

## B.1 Basic Concepts

A hierarchical database consists of a collection of *records* that are connected to each other through *links*. A record is similar to a record in the network model. Each record is a collection of fields (attributes), each of which contains only one data value. A link is an association between precisely two records. Thus, a link here is similar to a link in the network model.

Consider a database that represents a *customer-account* relationship in a banking system. There are two record types: *customer* and *account*. The *customer* record type can be defined in the same manner as in Appendix A. It consists of three fields: *customer-name*, *customer-street*, and *customer-city*. Similarly, the *account* record consists of two fields: *account-number* and *balance*.

A sample database appears in Figure B.1. It shows that customer Hayes has account A-305, customer Johnson has accounts A-101 and A-201, and customer Turner has account A-305.

Note that the set of all customer and account records is organized in the form of a rooted tree, where the root of the tree is a dummy node. As we shall see, a hierarchical database is a collection of such rooted trees, and hence forms a forest. We shall refer to each such rooted tree as a *database tree*.

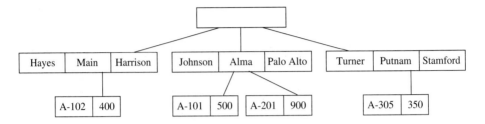

Figure B.1    Sample database.

## B.2    Tree-Structure Diagrams

A *tree-structure diagram* is the schema for a hierarchical database. Such a diagram consists of two basic components: *boxes*, which correspond to record types, and *lines*, which correspond to links. A tree-structure diagram serves the same purpose as does an (E-R) diagram; namely, it specifies the overall logical structure of the database. A tree-structure diagram is similar to a data-structure diagram in the network model. The main difference is that, in the former, record types are organized in the form of a *rooted tree*, whereas in the latter, record types are organized in the form of an arbitrary graph. There can be no cycles in the underlying graph of a tree-structure diagram. However, we can still transform E-R diagrams into corresponding tree-structure diagrams.

To illustrate, consider the E-R diagram of Figure B.2a; it consists of the two entity sets *customer* and *account* related through a binary, one-to-many relationship *depositor*, with no descriptive attributes. This diagram specifies that

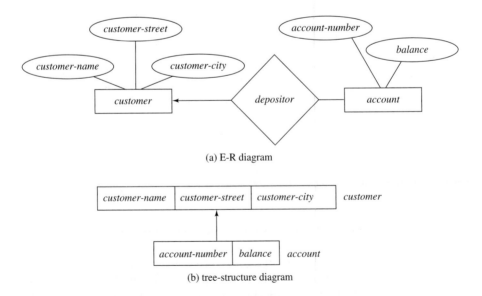

(a) E-R diagram

(b) tree-structure diagram

Figure B.2    E-R diagram and its corresponding tree-structure diagram.

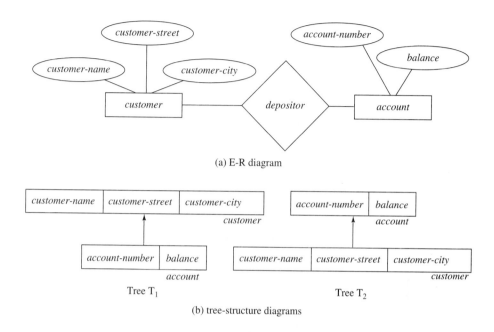

(a) E-R diagram

(b) tree-structure diagrams

**Figure B.3**  E-R diagram and its corresponding tree-structure diagrams.

a customer can have several accounts, but an account can belong to only one customer. The corresponding tree-structure diagram is depicted in Figure B.2b. The record type *customer* corresponds to the entity set *customer*. It includes three fields: *customer-name*, *customer-street*, and *customer-city*. Similarly, *account* is the record type corresponding to the entity set *account*. It includes two fields: *account-number* and *balance*. Finally, the relationship *depositor* has been replaced with the link *depositor*, with an arrow pointing to *customer* record type.

An instance of a database corresponding to the described schema may thus contain a number of *customer* records linked to a number of *account* records, as shown in Figure B.1. Since the relationship is one to many from *customer* to *account*, a customer can have more than one account, as does Johnson, who has both accounts A-101 and A-201. An account, however, cannot belong to more than one customer; none do in the sample database.

If the relationship *depositor* is many to many (see Figure B.3a), then the transformation from an E-R diagram to a tree-structure diagram is more complicated. Only one-to-many and one-to-one relationships can be directly represented in the hierarchical model.

To transform the E-R diagram of Figure B.3a to a tree-structure diagram, we do the following:

1. Create two separate tree-structure diagrams, $T_1$ and $T_2$, each of which has the *customer* and *account* record types. In tree $T_1$, *customer* is the root; in tree $T_2$, *account* is the root.

**2.** Create the following two links:

- *depositor*, a many-to-one link from *account* record type to *customer* record type, in $T_1$
- *account-customer*, a many-to-one link from *customer* record type to *account* record type, in $T_2$

The resulting tree-structure diagram is depicted in Figure B.3b.

    The database schema is represented as a collection of tree-structure diagrams. For each such diagram, there exists one *single* instance of a database tree. The root of this tree is a dummy node. The children of that node are instances of the appropriate record type. Each such child instance may, in turn, have several instances of various record types, as specified in the corresponding tree-structure diagram.

    A sample database corresponding to the tree-structure diagram of Figure B.3b is shown in Figure B.4. There are two database trees. The first tree (Figure B.4a) corresponds to the tree-structure diagram $T_1$; the second tree (Figure B.4b) corresponds to the tree-structure diagram $T_2$. As we can see, all *customer* and *account*

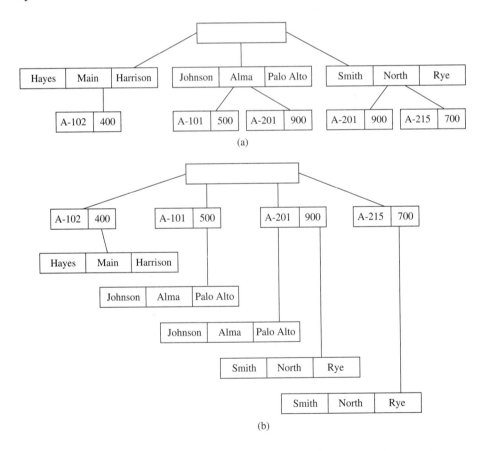

Figure B.4    Sample database corresponding to diagram of Figure B.3b.

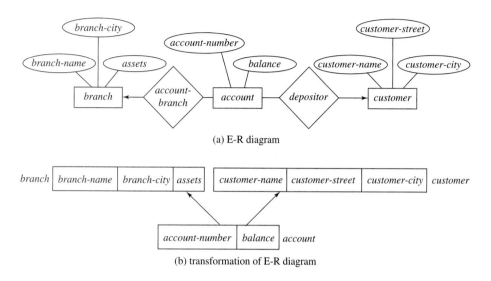

(a) E-R diagram

branch | branch-name | branch-city | assets | customer-name | customer-street | customer-city | customer

account-number | balance | account

(b) transformation of E-R diagram

Figure B.5     E-R diagram and its transformation.

records are replicated in both database trees. In addition, *account* record A-201 appears twice in the first tree, whereas *customer* records Johnson and Smith appear twice in the second tree.

Consider the E-R diagram of Figure B.5a. By applying the transformation algorithm described earlier the relationships *account-branch* and *depositor*, we obtain the diagram of Figure B.5b. This diagram is not a rooted tree, since the only possible root can be the record type *account*, but this record type has many-to-one relationships with both its children, and that violates our definition of a rooted tree. To transform this diagram into one that is in the form of a rooted tree, we replicate the *account* record type, and create two separate trees, as shown in Figure B.6. Note that each such tree is indeed a rooted tree. Thus, in general, we can split such a diagram into several diagrams, each of which is a rooted tree.

## B.3  Implementation Techniques

Record replication has two major drawbacks:

1. Data inconsistency may result when updating takes place.
2. Waste of space is unavoidable.

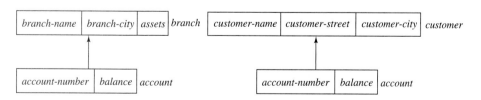

branch-name | branch-city | assets | branch     customer-name | customer-street | customer-city | customer

account-number | balance | account         account-number | balance | account

Figure B.6     Tree-structure diagram corresponding to Figure B.5a.

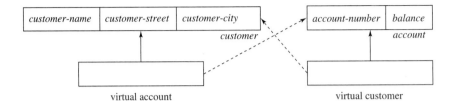

Figure B.7    Tree-structure diagram with virtual records.

The solution is to introduce the concept of a *virtual record* Such a record contains no data value; it does contain a logical pointer to a particular physical record. When a record is to be replicated in several database trees, we keep a single copy of that record in one of the trees, and replace every other record with a virtual record containing a pointer to that physical record.

As an example, consider the E-R diagram of Figure B.3a and its corresponding tree-structure diagram, which comprises two separate trees, each consisting of both *customer* and *account* record types (Figure B.3b).

To eliminate data replication, we create two virtual record types: *virtual-customer* and *virtual-account*. We then replace record type *account* with record type *virtual-account* in the first tree, and replace record type *customer* with record type *virtual-customer* in the second tree. We also add a dashed line from *virtual-customer* record to *customer* record, and a dashed line from *virtual-account* record to *account* record, to specify the association between a virtual record and its corresponding physical record. The resulting tree-structure diagram is depicted in Figure B.7.

An instance of a tree-structure diagram can be implemented using *leftmost-child* and *next-sibling* pointers. A record has only two pointers. The leftmost-child pointer points to one child. The next-sibling pointer points to another child of the same parent. Figure B.8 shows this structure for the database tree of Figure B.1. Under this structure, every record has exactly two pointers. Thus, fixed-length records retain their fixed length when we add the necessary pointers.

# B.4    The IMS Database System

The hierarchical model is significant primarily because of the importance of IBM's IMS database system. The IBM Information Management System (IMS) is one of the oldest and most widely used database systems. Since IMS databases have historically been among the largest, the IMS developers were among the first to deal with such issues as concurrency, recovery, integrity, and efficient query processing.

The need for high-performance transaction processing led to the introduction of the *IMS Fast Path*. Fast Path uses an alternative physical data organization designed to allow the most active parts of the database to reside in main memory, and is a forerunner of work in main-memory database systems.

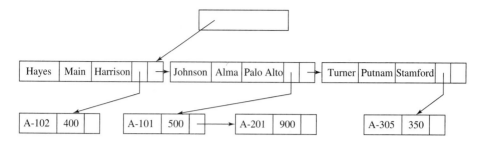

Figure B.8    Implementation with leftmost child and next-sibling pointers.

The data-manipulation language for hierarchical databases consists of commands that are embedded in a host language. It is similar in flavor to the data-manipulation language for network databases, although there are differences in the facilities provided. The data-manipulation language of the IMS database system is called DL/I.

## B.5    Discussion

The hierarchical model suffers from the same shortfalls as the network model. The complexity of the tree-structure diagrams, and the restrictions to many-to-one links makes the design of databases a rather complex task. Further, the lack of declarative querying facilities, and the need for navigation of pointers to access needed information make querying rather complex.

Like the network model, the hierarchical model held up against the relational model for many years since the implementations of the hierarchical model, such as IMS were superior to implementations of the relational model. Today, there are excellent implementations of the relational model, and the hierarchical model has therefore lost its importance. Hence it is no longer covered in detail in this book.

However, a detailed description of the hierarchical model is available on the Web for the benefit of those who wish to study it, at the URL:

```
http://www.bell-labs.com/topic/books/db-book
```

or via anonymous FTP from `ftp.research.bell-labs.com` in the subdirectory `dist/db-book`.

# BIBLIOGRAPHY

[**Abbott and Garcia-Molina 1992**]  R. Abbott and H. Garcia-Molina, "Scheduling Real-Time Transactions: A Performance Evaluation," *ACM Transactions on Database Systems*, Volume 17, Number 3 (September 1992), pages 513–560.

[**Abiteboul and Kanellakis 1989**]  S. Abiteboul and P. Kanellakis, "Object Identity as a Query Language Primitive," *Proceedings of the ACM SIGMOD International Conference on the Management of Data* (1989), pages 159–173.

[**Abiteboul et al. 1989**]  S. Abiteboul, P. C. Fischer, and H. J. Schek (Editors), *Nested Relations and Complex Objects in Databases*, Lecture Notes in Computer Science 361, Springer-Verlag (1989).

[**Abiteboul et al. 1995**]  S. Abiteboul, R. Hull, and V. Vianu, *Foundations of Databases*, Addison-Wesley, Reading, MA (1995).

[**Acharya et al. 1995**]  S. Acharya, R. Alonso, M. Franklin, and S. Zdonik, "Broadcast Disks: Data Management for Asymmetric Communication Environments," *Proceedings of the ACM SIGMOD International Conference on Management of Data* (1995), pages 19–210. Also appears in [**Imielinski and Korth 1996**], Chapter 12.

[**Agrawal and Gehani 1989**]  R. Agrawal and N. Gehani, "Ode (Object Database and Environment): The Language and the Data Model," *Proceedings of the ACM SIGMOD International Conference on Management of Data* (May 1989), pages 36–45.

[**Agrawal et al. 1986**]  D. P. Agrawal, V. K. Janakiram, and G. C. Pathak, "Evaluating the Performance of Multicomputer Configurations," *Communications of the ACM*, Volume 29, Number 5 (May 1986), pages 23–37.

[**Agrawal et al. 1992**]  R. Agrawal, S. P. Ghosh, T. Imielinski, B. R. Iyer, and A. N. Swami, "An Interval Classifier for Database Mining Applications," *Proceedings of the International Conference on Very Large Data Bases* (1992), pages 560–573.

[**Agrawal et al. 1993**]  R. Agrawal, T. Imielinski and A. N. Swami, "Database Mining: A Performance Perspective," *IEEE Transactions on Knowledge and Data Engineering*, Volume 5, Number 6 (1993), pages 914–925.

[**Aho and Ullman 1979**]  A. V. Aho and J. D. Ullman, "Optimal Partial Match Retrieval When Fields Are Independently Specified," *ACM Transactions on Database Systems*, Volume 4, Number 2 (June 1979), pages 168–179.

[**Aho et al. 1974**]  A. V. Aho, J. E. Hopcroft, and J. D. Ullman, *The Design and Analysis of Computer Algorithms*, Addison-Wesley, Reading, MA (1974).

[**Aho et al. 1979a**]  A. V. Aho, Y. Sagiv, and J. D. Ullman, "Equivalences among Relational Expressions," *SIAM Journal of Computing*, Volume 8, Number 2 (June 1979), pages 218–246.

[**Aho et al. 1979b**]  A. V. Aho, C. Beeri, and J. D. Ullman, "The Theory of Joins in Relational Databases," *ACM Transactions on Database Systems*, Volume 4, Number 3 (September 1979), pages 297–314.

[**Aho et al. 1979c**]  A. V. Aho, Y. Sagiv, and J. D. Ullman, "Efficient Optimization of a Class of Relational Expressions," *ACM Transactions on Database Systems*, Volume 4, Number 4 (December 1979), pages 435–454.

[**Aho et al. 1983**]  A. V. Aho, J. E. Hopcroft, and J. D. Ullman, *Data Structures and Algorithms*, Addison-Wesley, Reading, MA (1983).

[**Aho et al. 1986**]  A. V. Aho, R. Sethi, and J. D. Ullman, *Compilers: Principles, Techniques, and Tools*, Addison-Wesley, Reading, MA (1986).

[**Aiken et al. 1995**]  A. Aiken, J. Hellerstein, and J. Widom, "Static Analysis Techniques for Predicting the Behavior of Active Database Rules," *ACM Transactions on Database Systems*, Volume 20, Number 1 (March 1995), pages 3–41.

[**Akl 1983**]  S. Akl, "Digital Signatures, A Tutorial Survey," *IEEE Computer*, Volume 16, Number 2 (February 1983), pages 15–24.

[**Alonso and Korth 1993**]  R. Alonso and H. F. Korth, "Database System Issues in Nomadic Computing," *Proceedings of the ACM SIGMOD International Conference on Management of Data* (1993), pages 388–392.

[**Ammon et al. 1985**]  G. J. Ammon, J. A. Calabria, and D. T. Thomas, "A High-Speed, Large-Capacity, 'Jukebox' Optical Disk System," *IEEE Computer*, Volume 18, Number 7 (July 1985), pages 36–48.

[**Anderson et al. 1992**]  D. P. Anderson, Y. Osawa, and R. Govidan, "A File System for Continuous Media," *ACM Transactions on Computer Systems*, Volume 10, Number 4 (November 1992), pages 311–337.

[**ANSI 1975**]  "Study Group on Data Base Management Systems: Interim Report," *FDT*, Volume 7, Number 2, ACM, New York, NY (1975).

[**ANSI 1986**]  "American National Standard for Information Systems: Database Language SQL," *FDT*, ANSI X3,135–1986, American National Standards Institute, New York (1986).

[**ANSI 1989**]  "Database Language SQL With Integrity Enhancement," ANSI X3,135–1989, American National Standards Institute, New York (1989). Also available as ISO/IEC Document 9075:1989.

[**ANSI 1992**]  "Database Language SQL," ANSI X3,135–1992, American National Standards Institute, New York (1992). Also available as ISO/IEC Document 9075:1992.

[**Apers et al. 1983**] P. M. G. Apers, A. R. Hevner, and S. B. Yao, "Optimization Algorithms for Distributed Queries," *IEEE Transactions on Software Engineering*, Volume SE-9, Number 1 (January 1983), pages 57–68.

[**Apt and Pugin 1987**] K. R. Apt and J.-M. Pugin, "Maintenance of Stratified Database Viewed as a Belief Revision System," *Proceedings of the ACM SIGACT-SIGMOD Symposium on the Principles of Database Systems* (1987), pages 136–145.

[**Aref et al. 1995a**] W. Aref, D. Barbará, and P. Vallabhaneni, "The Handwritten Trie: Indexing Electronic Ink," *Proceedings of the ACM SIGMOD International Conference on Management of Data* (1995), pages 151–162.

[**Aref et al. 1995b**] W. Aref, D. Barbará, D. Lopresti, and A. Tomkins, "Ink as a First-Class Multimedia Object," in [**Jajodia and Subramanian 1995**]a30.

[**Armstrong 1974**] W. W. Armstrong, "Dependency Structures of Data Base Relationships," *Proceedings of the 1974 IFIP Congress* (1974), pages 580–583.

[**Astrahan et al. 1976**] M. M. Astrahan, M. W. Blasgen, D. D. Chamberlin, K. P. Eswaran, J. N. Gray, P. P. Griffiths, W. F. King, R. A. Lorie, P. R. McJones, J. W. Mehl, G. R. Putzolu, I. L. Traiger, B. W. Wade, and V. Watson, "System R, A Relational Approach to Data Base Management," *ACM Transactions on Database Systems*, Volume 1, Number 2 (June 1976), pages 97–137.

[**Astrahan et al. 1979**] M. M. Astrahan, M. W. Blasgen, D. D. Chamberlin, J. N. Gray, W. F. King, B. G. Lindsay, R. A. Lorie, J. W. Mehl, T. G. Price, G. R. Putzolu, M. Schkolnick, P. G. Selinger, D. R. Slutz, H. R. Strong, P. Tiberio, I. L. Traiger, B. W. Wade, and R. A. Yost, "System R: A Relational Database Management System," *IEEE Computer*, Volume 12, Number 5 (May 1979), pages 43–48.

[**Attar et al. 1984**] R. Attar, P. A. Bernstein, and N. Goodman, "Site Initialization, Recovery, and Backup in a Distributed Database System," *IEEE Transactions on Software Engineering*, Volume SE-10, Number 6 (November 1984), pages 645–650.

[**Atzeni and De Antonellis 1993**] P. Atzeni and V. De Antonellis, *Relational Database Theory*, Benjamin Cummings, Menlo Park, CA (1993).

[**Bachman 1969**] C. W. Bachman, "Data Structure Diagrams," *Journal of ACM SIGBDP* Volume 1, Number 2 (March 1969), pages 4–10

[**Bachman and Williams 1964**] C. W. Bachman and S. S. Williams, "A General Purpose Programming System for Random Access Memories," *Proceedings of the Fall Joint Computer Conference*, Volume 26, AFIPS Press (1964), pages 411–422.

[**Badal and Popek 1979**] D. S. Badal and G. Popek, "Cost and Performance Analysis of Semantic Integrity Validation Methods," *Proceedings of the ACM SIGMOD International Conference on Management of Data* (1979), pages 109–115.

[**Bancilhon and Buneman 1990**] F. Bancilhon and P. Buneman, *Advances in Database Programming Languages,* ACM Press, New York, NY (1990).

[**Bancilhon and Ramakrishnan 1986**] F. Bancilhon and R. Ramakrishnan, "An Amateur's Introduction to Recursive Query-Processing Strategies," *Proceedings of the ACM SIGMOD International Conference on Management of Data* (1986), pages 16–52.

[**Bancilhon and Spyratos 1981**] F. Bancilhon and N. Spyratos "Update Semantics and Relational Views," *ACM Transactions on Database Systems,* Volume 6, Number 4 (December 1981), pages 557–575.

[**Bancilhon et al. 1985a**] F. Bancilhon, W. Kim, and H. F. Korth, "A Model of CAD Transactions," *Proceedings of the International Conference on Very Large Data Bases* (1985), pages 25–31.

[**Bancilhon et al. 1985b**] F. Bancilhon, W. Kim, and H. F. Korth, "Transactions and Concurrency Control in CAD Databases," *Proceedings of the IEEE International Conference on Computer Design: VLSI in Computers* (1985).

[**Bancilhon et al. 1989**] F. Bancilhon, S. Cluet, and C. Delobel, "A Query Language for the $O_2$ Object-Oriented Database," *Proceedings of the Second Workshop on Database Programming Languages* (1989).

[**Banerjee et al. 1987a**] J. Banerjee, H. T. Chou, J. F. Garza, W. Kim, D. Woelk, N. Ballou, and H. J. Kim, "Data Model Issues for Object-Oriented Applications," *ACM Transactions on Office Information Systems* (January 1987).

[**Banerjee et al. 1987b**] J. Banerjee, W. Kim, H. J. Kim, and H. F. Korth, "Semantics and Implementation of Schema Evolution in Object-Oriented Databases," *Proceedings of the ACM SIGMOD International Conference on Management of Data* (1987), pages 311–322.

[**Baralis et al. 1996**] E. Baralis, S. Ceri, and S. Paroboschi, "Modularization Techniques for Active Rules Design," *ACM Transactions on Database Systems*, Volume 21, Number 1 (March 1996), pages 1–29.

[**Barbará and Imielinski 1994**] D. Barbará and T. Imielinski, "Sleepers and Workaholics: Caching Strategies in Mobile Environments," *Proceedings of the ACM SIGMOD International Conference on Management of Data* (1994), pages 1–12.

[**Barbará et al. 1992**] D. Barbará, H. Garcia-Molina, and D. Porter, "The Management of Probabilistic Data," *IEEE Transactions on Knowledge and Data Engineering,* Volume 4, Number 5 (October 1992), pages 487–502.

[**Barclay et al. 1982**] D. K. Barclay, E. R. Byrne, and F. K. Ng, "A Real-Time Database Management System for No.5 ESS," *Bell System Technical Journal*, Volume 61, Number 9 (November 1982), pages 2423–2437.

[**Barsalou et al. 1991**] T. Barsalou, N. Siambela, A. Keller, and G. Wiederhold, "Updating Relational Databases Through Object-Based Views," *Proceedings of the ACM SIGMOD International Conference on the Management of Data* (1991).

[**Bassiouni 1988**] M. Bassiouni, "Single-site and Distributed Optimistic Protocols for Concurrency Control," *IEEE Transactions on Software Engineering*, Volume SE-14, Number 8 (August 1988), pages 1071–1080.

[**Batini et al. 1992**] C. Batini, S. Ceri, and S. Navathe, *Database Design: An Entity-Relationship Approach*, Benjamin Cummings, Redwood City, CA (1992).

[**Batini et al. 1986**] C. Batini, M. Lenzerini, and S. Navathe, "A Comparative Analysis of Methodologies for Database Schema Integration," *ACM Computing Surveys,* Volume 18, Number 4 (1986), pages 323–364.

[**Batory and Gotlieb 1982**] D. S. Batory and C. C. Gotlieb, "A Unifying Model of Physical Databases," *ACM Transactions on Database Systems*, Volume 7, Number 4 (December 1982), pages 509–539.

[**Bayer 1972**] R. Bayer, "Symmetric Binary B-trees: Data Structure and Maintenance Algorithms," *Acta Informatica*, Volume 1, Number 4 (1972), pages 290–306.

[**Bayer and McCreight 1972**] R. Bayer and E. M. McCreight, "Organization and Maintenance of Large Ordered Indices," *Acta Informatica*, Volume 1, Number 3 (1972), pages 173–189.

[**Bayer and Schkolnick 1977**] R. Bayer and M. Schkolnick, "Concurrency of Operating on B-trees," *Acta Informatica*, Volume 9, Number 1 (1977), pages 1–21.

[**Bayer and Unterauer 1977**] R. Bayer and K. Unterauer, "Prefix B-trees," *ACM Transactions on Database Systems*, Volume 2, Number 1 (March 1977), pages 11–26.

[**Bayer et al. 1978**] R. Bayer, R. M. Graham, and G. Seegmuller (Editors), *Operating Systems: An Advanced Course*, Springer-Verlag, Berlin, Germany (1978).

[**Bayer et al. 1980**] R. Bayer, H. Heller, and A. Reiser, "Parallelism and Recovery in Database Systems," *ACM Transactions on Database Systems*, Volume 5, Number 2 (June 1980), pages 139–156.

[**Beckmann et al. 1990**] , N. Beckmann, H. P. Kriegel, R. Schneider, and B. Seeger, "The R*-tree: An Efficient and Robust Access Method for Points and Rectangles," *Proceedings of the ACM SIGMOD International Conference on Management of Data* (May 1990), pages 322–331.

[**Beech 1988**] D. Beech, "OSQL: A Language for Migrating from SQL to Object Databases," *Proceedings of the International Conference on Extending Database Technology* (March 1988).

[**Beeri and Ramakrishnan 1991**] C. Beeri and R. Ramakrishnan, "On the Power of Magic," *Journal of Logic Programming*, Volume 10, Numbers 3 and 4 (1991), pages 255–300.

[**Beeri et al. 1977**] C. Beeri, R. Fagin, and J. H. Howard, "A Complete Axiomatization for Functional and Multivalued Dependencies," *Proceedings of the ACM SIGMOD International Conference on Management of Data* (1977), pages 47–61.

[**Beeri et al. 1983**] C. Beeri, R. Fagin, D. Maier, and M. Yannakakis, "On the Desirability of Acyclic Database Schemes," *Journal of the ACM*, Volume 30, Number 3 (July 1983), pages 479–513.

[**Beeri et al. 1989**] C. Beeri, P. A. Bernstein, and N. Goodman, "A Model for Concurrency in Nested Transactions Systems," *Journal of the ACM*, Volume 36, Number 2 (April 1989).

[**Bell and Grimson 1992**] D. Bell and J. Grimson, *Distributed Database Systems*, Addison-Wesley, Reading, MA (1992).

[**Bell and LaPadula 1976**] D. E. Bell and L. J. LaPadula, "Secure Computer Systems: Unified Exposition and Multics Interpretation," Mitre Corporation, Bedford, MA (1976).

[**Benneworth et al. 1981**] R. L. Benneworth, C. D. Bishop, C. J. M. Turnbull, W. D. Holman, and F. M. Monette, "The Implementation of GERM, an Entity-Relationship Data Base Management System," *Proceedings of the International Conference on Very Large Data Bases* (1981), pages 478–484.

[**Bentley 1975**] J. L. Bentley, "Multidimensional Binary Search Trees Used for Associative Searching," *Communications of the ACM*, Volume 18, Number 9 (September 1975), pages 509–517.

[**Berenson et al. 1995**] H. Berenson, P. Bernstein, J. Gray, J. Melton, E. O'Neil, and P. O'Neil, "A Critique of ANSI SQL Isolation Levels," *Proceedings of the ACM SIGMOD International Conference on Management of Data* (1995), pages 1–10.

[**Bernstein 1976**]  P. A. Bernstein, "Synthesizing Third Normal Form Relations from Functional Dependencies," *ACM Transactions on Database Systems*, Volume 1, Number 4 (December 1976), pages 277–298.

[**Bernstein and Chiu 1981**]  P. A. Bernstein and D. W. Chiu, "Using Semijoins to Solve Relational Queries," *Journal of the ACM*, Volume 28, Number 1 (January 1981), pages 25–40.

[**Bernstein and Goodman 1980a**]  P. A. Bernstein and N. Goodman, "Timestamp-based Algorithms for Concurrency Control in Distributed Database Systems," *Proceedings of the International Conference on Very Large Data Bases* (1980), pages 285–300.

[**Bernstein and Goodman 1980b**]  P. A. Bernstein and N. Goodman, "What Does Boyce-Codd Normal Form Do?," *Proceedings of the International Conference of Very Large Data Bases* (1980), pages 245–259.

[**Bernstein and Goodman 1981a**]  P. A. Bernstein and N. Goodman, "Concurrency Control in Distributed Database Systems," *ACM Computing Surveys*, Volume 13, Number 2 (June 1981), pages 185–221.

[**Bernstein and Goodman 1981b**]  P. A. Bernstein and N. Goodman, "The Power of Natural Semijoins," *SIAM Journal of Computing*, Volume 10, Number 4 (December 1981), pages 751–771.

[**Bernstein and Goodman 1982**]  P. A. Bernstein and N. Goodman, "A Sophisticate's Introduction to Distributed Database Concurrency Control," *Proceedings of the International Conference on Very Large Data Bases* (1982), pages 62–76.

[**Bernstein et al. 1978**]  P. A. Bernstein, N. Goodman, J. B. Rothnie, Jr., and C. H. Papadimitriou, "Analysis of Serializability of SDD-1: A System of Distributed Databases (the Fully Redundant Case)," *IEEE Transactions on Software Engineering*, Volume SE-4, Number 3 (May 1978), pages 154–168.

[**Bernstein et al. 1980a**]  P. A. Bernstein, D. W. Shipman, and J. B. Rothnie, Jr., "Concurrency Control in a System for Distributed Databases (SDD-1)," *ACM Transactions on Database Systems*, Volume 5, Number 1 (March 1980), pages 18–51.

[**Bernstein et al. 1980b**]  P. A. Bernstein, B. Blaustein, and E. Clarke, "Fast Maintenance of Semantic Integrity Assertions Using Redundant Aggregate Data," *Proceedings of the International Conference on Very Large Data Bases* (1980).

[**Bernstein et al. 1983**]  P. A. Bernstein, N. Goodman, and M. Y. Lai, " Analyzing Concurrency Control when User and System Operations Differ," *IEEE Transactions on Software Engineering*, Volume SE-9 Number 3 (May 1983), pages 233–239.

[**Bernstein et al. 1987**]  A. Bernstein, V. Hadzilacos, and N. Goodman, *Concurrency Control and Recovery in Database Systems*, Addison-Wesley, Reading, MA (1987).

[**Berson et al. 1995**]  S. Berson, L. Golubchik, and R. R. Muntz, "Fault Tolerant Design of Multimedia Servers," *Proceedings of the ACM SIGMOD International Conference on Management of Data* (1995), pages 364–375.

[**Bertino and Kim 1989**]  E. Bertino and W. Kim, "Indexing Techniques for Queries on Nested Objects," *IEEE Transactions on Knowledge and Data Engineering* (October 1989).

[**Bhuyan et al. 1989**]  L. N. Bhuyan, Q. Yang, and D. P. Agrawal, "Performance of Multiprocessor Interconnection Networks," *IEEE Computer*, Volume 22, Number 2 (February 1989), pages 25–37.

[**Biliris and Orenstein 1994**] A. Biliris and J. Orenstein, "Object Storage Management Architectures," in [**Dogac et al. 1994**], pages 185–200.

[**Biskup et al. 1979**] J. Biskup, U. Dayal, and P. A. Bernstein, "Synthesizing Independent Database Schemas," *Proceedings of the ACM SIGMOD International Conference on Management of Data* (1979), pages 143–152.

[**Bitton and Gray 1988**] D. Bitton and J. N. Gray, "Disk Shadowing," *Proceedings of the International Conference on Very Large Data Bases* (1988), pages 331–338.

[**Bitton et al. 1983**] D. Bitton, D. J. DeWitt, and C. Turbyfill, "Benchmarking Database Systems: A Systematic Approach," *Proceedings of the International Conference on Very Large Data Bases* (1983).

[**Bjork 1973**] L. A. Bjork, "Recovery Scenario for a DB/DC System," *Proceedings of the ACM Annual Conference* (1973), pages 142–146.

[**Bjorner and Lovengren 1982**] D. Bjorner and H. Lovengren, "Formalization of Database Systems and a Formal Definition of IMS," *Proceedings of the International Conference on Very Large Data Bases* (1982), pages 334–347.

[**Blakeley et al. 1986**] J. A. Blakeley, P. Larson, and F. W. Tompa, "Efficiently Updating Materialized Views," *Proceedings of the ACM SIGMOD International Conference on Management of Data* (1986), pages 61–71.

[**Blakeley et al. 1989**] J. Blakeley, N. Coburn, and P. Larson, "Updating Derived Relations: Detecting Irrelevant and Autonomously Computable Updates," *ACM Transactions on Database Systems*, Volume 14, Number 3 (1989), pages 369–400.

[**Blasgen and Eswaran 1976**] M. W. Blasgen and K. P. Eswaran, "On the Evaluation of Queries in a Relational Database System," *IBM Systems Journal*, Volume 16 (1976), pages 363–377.

[**Bohl 1981**] M. Bohl, *Introduction to IBM Direct Access Storage Devices*, Science Research Associates, Chicago, IL (1981).

[**Bolour 1979**] A. Bolour, "Optimal Retrieval Algorithms for Small Region Queries," *Journal of the ACM*, Volume 26, Number 2 (April 1979), pages 721–741.

[**Boral et al. 1990**] H. Boral, W. Alexander, L. Clay, G. Copeland, S. Danforth, M. Franklin, B. Hart, M. Smith, and P. Valduriez, "Prototyping Bubba, a Highly Parallel Database System," *IEEE Transactions on Knowledge and Data Engineering* Volume 2, Number 1 (March 1990).

[**Boyce et al. 1975**] R. Boyce, D. D. Chamberlin, W. F. King, and M. Hammer, "Specifying Queries as Relational Expressions," *Communications of the ACM*, Volume 18, Number 11 (November 1975), pages 621–628.

[**Bracchi and Nijssen 1979**] G. Bracchi and G. M. Nijssen (Editors), *Data Base Architecture*, North Holland, Amsterdam, The Netherlands (1979).

[**Bradley 1978**] J. Bradley, "An Extended Owner-Coupled Set Data Model and Predicate Calculus for Database Management," *ACM Transactions on Database Systems*, Volume 3, Number 4 (December 1978), pages 385–416.

[**Bray 1982**] O. H. Bray, *Distributed Database Management Systems*, Lexington Books (1982).

[**Brinkhoff et al. 1993**] T. Brinkhoff, H-P. Kriegel, and B. Seeger, "Efficient Processing of Spatial Joins Using R-trees," *Proceedings of the ACM SIGMOD International Conference on Management of Data* (May 1993), pages 237–246.

[**Brown et al. 1994**] K. P. Brown, M. Mehta, M. Carey, and M. Livny, "Towards Automated Performance Tuning for Complex Overloads," *Proceedings of the International Conference on Very Large Data Bases* (September 1994).

[**Buckley and Silberschatz 1983**] G. Buckley and A. Silberschatz, "Obtaining Progressive Protocols for a Simple Multiversion Database Model," *Proceedings of the International Conference on Very Large Data Bases* (1983), pages 74–81.

[**Buckley and Silberschatz 1984**] G. Buckley and A. Silberschatz, "Concurrency Control in Graph Protocols by Using Edge Locks," *Proceedings of the ACM SIGACT-SIGMOD Symposium on the Principles of Database Systems* (1984), pages 45–50.

[**Buckley and Silberschatz 1985**] G. Buckley and A. Silberschatz, "Beyond Two-Phase Locking," *Journal of the ACM*, Volume 32, Number 2 (April 1985), pages 314–326.

[**Buneman and Frankel 1979**] P. Buneman and R. Frankel, "FQL: A Functional Query Language," *Proceedings of the ACM SIGMOD International Conference on the Management of Data* (1979), pages 52–58.

[**Burkhard 1976**] W. A. Burkhard, "Hashing and Trie Algorithms for Partial Match Retrieval," *ACM Transactions on Database Systems*, Volume 1, Number 2 (June 1976), pages 175–187.

[**Burkhard 1979**] W. A. Burkhard, "Partial-match Hash Coding: Benefits of Redundancy," *ACM Transactions on Database Systems*, Volume 4, Number 2 (June 1979), pages 228–239.

[**Campbell et al. 1985**] D. Campbell, D. Embley, and B. Czejdo, "A Relationally Complete Query Language for the Entity-Relationship Model," *Proceedings of the International Conference on Entity-Relationship Approach* (1985).

[**Cannan and Otten 1993**] S. Cannan and G. Otten, *SQL—The Standard Handbook*, McGraw-Hill International, Maidenhead, UK (1993).

[**Carey 1983**] M. J. Carey, "Granularity Hierarchies in Concurrency Control," *Proceedings of the ACM SIGACT-SIGMOD Symposium on the Principles of Database Systems* (1983), pages 156–165.

[**Carey et al. 1986**] M. J. Carey, D. DeWitt, J. Richardson, and E. Shekita, "Object and File Management in the EXODUS Extensible Database System," *Proceedings of the International Conference on Very Large Data Bases* (1986), pages 91–100.

[**Carey et al. 1990**] M. J. Carey, D. DeWitt, G. Graefe, D. Haight, J. Richardson, D. Schuh, E. Shekita, and S. Vandenberg, "The EXODUS Extensible DBMS Project: An Overview," in [**Zdonik and Maier 1990**], pages 474–499.

[**Carey et al. 1991**] M. Carey, M. Franklin, M. Livny, and E. Shekita, "Data Caching Tradeoffs in Client-Server DBMS Architectures," *Proceedings of the ACM SIGMOD International Conference on the Management of Data* (May 1991).

[**Carey et al. 1993**] M. J. Carey, D. DeWitt, and J. Naughton, "The OO7 Benchmark," *Proceedings of the ACM SIGMOD International Conference on Management of Data* (May 1993).

[**Casanova et al. 1984**] M. A. Casanova, R. Fagin, and C. Papadimitriou, "Inclusion Dependencies and Their Interaction with Functional Dependencies," *Journal of Computer and System Sciences*, Volume 28, Number 1 (January 1984), pages 29–59.

[**Cattell 1994**] R. Cattell (Editor), *The Object Database Standard: ODMG – 93*, Release 1.1, Morgan Kaufmann, San Francisco, CA (1994).

[**Cattell and Skeen 1992**] R. Cattell and J. Skeen, "Object Operations Benchmark," *ACM Transactions on Database Systems,* Volume 17, Number 1 (March 1992).

[**Ceri and Owicki 1983**] S. Ceri and S. Owicki, "On the Use of Optimistic Methods for Concurrency Control in Distributed Databases," *Proceedings of the Sixth Berkeley Workshop on Distributed Data Management and Computer Networks* (1983).

[**Ceri and Pelagatti 1983**] S. Ceri and G. Pelagatti, "Correctness of Query Execution Strategies in Distributed Databases," *ACM Transactions on Database Systems*, Volume 8, Number 4 (December 1983), pages 577–607.

[**Ceri and Pelagatti 1984**] S. Ceri and G. Pelagatti, *Distributed Databases: Principles and Systems*, McGraw-Hill, NY (1984).

[**Chakravarthy et al. 1990**] U. S. Chakravarthy, J. Grant, and J. Minker, "Logic-Based Approach to Semantic Query Optimization," *ACM Transactions on Database Systems,* Volume 15, Number 2 (June 1990), pages 162–207.

[**Chamberlin and Boyce 1974**] D. D. Chamberlin and R. F. Boyce, "SEQUEL: A Structured English Query Language," *Proceedings of the ACM SIGMOD Workshop on Data Description, Access, and Control* (1974), pages 249–264.

[**Chamberlin et al. 1976**] D. D. Chamberlin, M. M. Astrahan, K. P. Eswaran, P. P. Griffiths, R. A. Lorie, J. W. Mehl, P. Reisner, and B. W. Wade, "SEQUEL 2: A Unified Approach to Data Definition, Manipulation, and Control," *IBM Journal of Research and Development*, Volume 20, Number 6 (November 1976), pages 560–575.

[**Chamberlin et al. 1981**] D. D. Chamberlin, M. M. Astrahan, M. W. Blasgen, J. N. Gray, W. F. King, B. G. Lindsay, R. A. Lorie, J. W. Mehl, T. G. Price, P. G. Selinger, M. Schkolnick, D. R. Slutz, I. L. Traiger, B. W. Wade, and R. A. Yost, "A History and Evaluation of System R," *Communications of the ACM*, Volume 24, Number 10 (October 1981), pages 632–646.

[**Chandra and Harel 1982**] A. K. Chandra and D. Harel, "Structure and Complexity of Relational Queries," *Journal of Computer and System Sciences*, Volume 15, Number (January 1982), pages 99–128.

[**Chandy and Misra 1982**] K. M. Chandy and J. Misra, "A Distributed Algorithm for Detecting Resource Deadlocks in Distributed Systems," *Proceedings of the ACM SIGACT-SIGOPS Symposium on the Principles of Distributed Computing* (1982), pages 157–164.

[**Chandy et al. 1975**] K. M. Chandy, J. C. Browne, C. W. Dissley, and W. R. Uhrig, "Analytic Models for Rollback and Recovery Strategies in Database Systems," *IEEE Transactions on Software Engineering*, Volume SE-1, Number 1 (March 1975), pages 100–110.

[**Chandy et al. 1983**] K. M. Chandy, L. M. Haas, and J. Misra, " Distributed Deadlock Detection," *ACM Transactions on Computer Systems*, Volume 1, Number 2 (May 1983), pages 144–156.

[**Chaudhuri and Shim 1994**] S. Chaudhuri and K. Shim, "Including Group-By in Query Optimization," *Proceedings of the International Conference on Very Large Data Bases* (1994).

[**Chen 1976**] P. P. Chen, "The Entity-Relationship Model: Toward a Unified View of Data," *ACM Transactions on Database Systems*, Volume 1, Number 1 (January 1976), pages 9–36.

[**Chen and Patterson 1990**] P. Chen and D. Patterson, "Maximizing Performance in a Striped Disk Array," *Proceedings of the Seventeenth Annual International Symposium on Computer Architecture* (May 1990).

[**Chen et al. 1994**] P. M. Chen, E. K. Lee, G. A. Gibson, R. H. Katz, and D. A. Patterson, "RAID: High-Performance, Reliable Secondary Storage," *ACM Computing Surveys*, Volume 26, Number 2 (June 1994).

[**Chen et al. 1995**] M.-S. Chen, H.-I. Hsiao, C.-S. Li, and P. S. Yu, "Using Rotational Mirrored Declustering for Replica Placement in a Disk Array Based Video Server," *Proceedings of the Third ACM International Multimedia Conference and Exhibition* (1995), pages 121–130.

[**Chervenak et al. 1995**] A. L. Chervenak, D. A. Patterson, and R. H. Katz, "Choosing the Best Storage System for Video Service," *Proceedings of the Third ACM International Multimedia Conference and Exhibition* (1995), pages 109–120.

[**Chi 1982**] C. S. Chi, "Advances in Computer Mass Storage Technology," *IEEE Computer*, Volume 15, Number 5 (May 1982), pages 60–74.

[**Chin 1978**] F. Y. Chin, "Security in Statistical Databases for Queries with Small Counts," *ACM Transactions on Database Systems*, Volume 3, Number 1 (January 1978), pages 92–104.

[**Chin and Ozsoyoglu 1981**] F. Y. Chin and G. Ozsoyoglu, "Statistical Database Design," *ACM Transactions on Database Design*, Volume 6, Number 1 (January 1981), pages 113–139.

[**Chiu and Ho 1980**] D. M. Chiu and Y. C. Ho, "A Methodology for Interpreting Tree Queries into Optimal Semi-join Expressions," *Proceedings of the ACM SIGMOD International Conference on the Management of Data* (1980), pages 169–178.

[**Chomicki 1992a**] J. Chomicki, "History-less checking of Dynamic Integrity Constraints," *Proceedings of the International Conference on Data Engineering* (1992).

[**Chomicki 1992b**] J. Chomicki, "Real-Time Integrity Constraints," *Proceedings of the ACM SIGACT-SIGMOD-SIGART Symposium on the Principles of Database Systems* (1992).

[**Chomicki 1995**] J. Chomicki, "Efficient Checking of Temporal Integrity Constraints Using Bounded History Encoding," *ACM Transactions on Database Systems*, Volume 20, Number 2 (June 1995), pages 149–186.

[**Chou et al. 1985**] H-T. Chou, D. J. Dewitt, R. H. Katz, A. C. Klug, "The Wisconsin Storage System Software," *Software—Practice and Experience*, Volume 15, Number 10 (October 1985), pages 943–962.

[**Chou and DeWitt 1985**] H. T. Chou and D. J. Dewitt, "An Evaluation of Buffer Management Strategies for Relational Database Systems," *Proceedings of the International Conference on Very Large Data Bases* (1985), pages 127–141.

[**Christodoulakis and Faloutsos 1986**] S. Christodoulakis and C. Faloutsos, "Design and Performance Considerations for an Optical Disk-Based Multimedia Object Server," *IEEE Computer*, Volume 19, Number 12 (December 1986), pages 45–56.

[**Chrysanthis and Ramamritham 1994**] P. Chrysanthis and K.Ramamritham, "Synthesis of Extended Transaction Models Using ACTA," *ACM Transactions on Database Systems*, Volume 19, Number 3 (September 1994) pages 450–491.

[**Clemons 1978**] E. K. Clemons, "An External Schema Facility to Support Data Base Update," in [**Schneiderman 1978**], pages 371–398.

[**Clemons 1979**] E. K. Clemons, "An External Schema Facility for CODASYL 1978," *Proceedings of the International Conference on Very Large Data Bases* (1979), pages 119–128.

[**Clifford and Tansel 1985**] J. Clifford and A. Tansel, "On an Algebra for Historical Relational Databases: Two Views," *Proceedings of the ACM SIGMOD International Conference on Management of Data* (1985), pages 247–267.

[**Clifford et al. 1994**] J. Clifford, A. Croker, and A. Tuzhilin, "On Completeness of Historical Relational Query Languages," *ACM Transactions on Database Systems*, Volume 19, Number 1 (March 1994), pages 64–116.

[**Cluet et al. 1989**] S. Cluet, C. Delobel, C. Lecluse, and P. Richard, "Reloop: An Algebra-Based Query Language for an Object-Oriented Database System," *Proceedings of the International Conference on Deductive and Object-Oriented Databases* (December 1989).

[**CODASYL 1971**] "CODASYL Data Base Task Group April 71 Report," ACM, New York, NY (1971).

[**CODASYL 1978**] *CODASYL Data Description Language Journal of Development*, Material Data Management Branch, Department of Supply and Services, Ottawa, Ontario (1978).

[**Codd 1970**] E. F. Codd, "A Relational Model for Large Shared Data Banks," *Communications of the ACM*, Volume 13, Number 6 (June 1970), pages 377–387.

[**Codd 1972a**] E. F. Codd, "Further Normalization of the Data Base Relational Model," in [**Rustin 1972**], pages 33–64.

[**Codd 1972b**] E. F. Codd, "Relational Completeness of Data Base Sublanguages," in [**Rustin 1972**], pages 65–98.

[**Codd 1979**] E. F. Codd, "Extending the Database Relational Model to Capture More Meaning," *ACM Transactions on Database Systems*, Volume 4, Number 4 (December 1979), pages 397–434.

[**Codd 1982**] E. F. Codd, "The 1981 ACM Turing Award Lecture: Relational Database: A Practical Foundation for Productivity," *Communications of the ACM*, Volume 25, Number 2 (February 1982), pages 109–117.

[**Codd 1990**] E. F. Codd, *The Relational Model for Database Management: Version 2*, Addison-Wesley, Reading, MA (1990).

[**Comer 1979**] D. Comer, "The Ubiquitous B-tree," *ACM Computing Surveys*, Volume 11, Number 2 (June 1979), pages 121–137.

[**Comer 1995**] D. Comer, *The Internet Book: Everything You Need to Know about Computer Networking*, Prentice-Hall, Englewood Cliffs, NJ (1995).

[**Cormen et al. 1990**] T. Cormen, C. Leiserson, and R. Rivest, *An Introduction to Algorithms*, McGraw-Hill, New York, NY (1990).

[**Corrigan and Gurry 1993**] P. Corrigan and M. Gurry, *ORACLE Performance Tuning*, O'Reilly and Associates, Inc. (1993).

[**Cosmadakis and Papadimitriou 1984**] S. S. Cosmadakis and C. H. Papadimitriou, "Updates of Relational Views," *Journal of the ACM*, Volume 31, Number 4 (October 1984), pages 742–760.

[**Cosmadakis et al. 1990**] S. Cosmadakis, P. Kanellakis, and M. Vardi, "Polynomial-Time Implication Problems for Unary Inclusion Dependencies," *Journal of the ACM,* Volume 37, Number 1 (January 1990), pages 15–46.

[**Cox 1986**] B. J. Cox, *Object-Oriented Programming: An Evolutionary Approach*, Addison-Wesley, Reading, MA (1986).

[**Dahl and Bubenko 1982**] R. Dahl and J. Bubenko, "IDBD: An Interactive Design Tool for CODASYL DBTG Type Databases," *Proceedings of the International Conference on Very Large Data Bases* (1982), pages 108–121.

[**Daniels et al. 1982**] D. Daniels, P. G. Selinger, L. M. Haas, B. G. Lindsay, C. Mohan, A. Walker, and P. F. Wilms, "An Introduction to Distributed Query Compilation in R*," in [**Schneider 1982**].

[**Dar et al. 1996**] S. Dar, H. V. Jagadish, A. Levy, and D. Srivastava, "Answering Queries with Aggregation Using Views," *Proceedings of the International Conference on Very Large Data Bases* (1996).

[**Date 1983a**] C. J. Date, *An Introduction to Database Systems*, Volume II, Addison-Wesley, Reading, MA (1983).

[**Date 1983b**] C. J. Date, "The Outer Join," *IOCOD-2*, John Wiley and Sons, New York, NY (1993), pages 76–106.

[**Date 1986**] C. J. Date, *Relational Databases: Selected Writings,* Addison-Wesley, Reading, MA (1986).

[**Date 1987**] C. J. Date, *A Guide to Ingres*, Addison-Wesley, Reading, MA (1987).

[**Date 1990**] C. J. Date, *Relational Database Writings, 1985-1989*, Addison-Wesley, Reading, MA (1990).

[**Date 1993**] C. J. Date, "How SQL Missed the Boat," *Database Programming and Design* Volume 6, Number 9 (September 1993).

[**Date 1995**] C. J. Date, *An Introduction to Database Systems*, Sixth Edition, Addison-Wesley, Reading, MA (1995).

[**Date and Darwen 1993**] C. J. Date and G. Darwen, *A Guide to the SQL Standard*, Third Edition, Addison-Wesley, Reading, MA (1993).

[**Date and White 1989**] C. J. Date and C. J. White, *A Guide to SQL/DS*, Addison-Wesley, Reading, MA (1989).

[**Date and White 1993**] C. J. Date and C. J. White, *A Guide to DB2*, Fourth Edition, Addison-Wesley, Reading, MA (1993).

[**Davies 1980**] D. W. Davies, "Protection," in *Distributed Systems: An Advanced Course*, Springer-Verlag, Berlin, Germany (1980), pages 211–245.

[**Davies 1973**] C. T. Davies, Jr., "Recovery Semantics for a DB/DC System," *Proceedings of the ACM Annual Conference* (1973), pages 136–141.

[**Davis et al. 1983**] C. Davis, S. Jajodia, P. A. Ng, and R. Yeh (Editors), *Entity-Relationship Approach to Software Engineering*, North Holland, Amsterdam, The Netherlands (1983).

[**Davison and Graefe 1994**] D. L. Davison and G. Graefe, "Memory-Contention Responsive Hash Joins," *Proceedings of the International Conference on Very Large Data Bases* (September 1994).

[**Dayal 1987**] U. Dayal, "Of Nests and Trees: A Unified Approach to Processing Queries that Contain Nested Subqueries, Aggregates and Quantifiers," *Proceedings of the International Conference on Very Large Data Bases* (1987), pages 197–208.

[**Dayal and Bernstein 1978**] U. Dayal and P. A. Bernstein, "The Updatability of Relational Views," *Proceedings of the International Conference on Very Large Data Bases* (1978), pages 368–377.

[**Dayal and Bernstein 1982**] U. Dayal and P. A. Bernstein, "On the Correct Translation of Update Operations on Relational Views," *ACM Transactions on Database Systems*, Volume 3, Number 3 (September 1982), pages 381–416.

[**Dayal et al. 1982**] U. Dayal, N. Goodman, and R. H. Katz, "An Extended Relational Algebra with Control over Duplicate Elimination," *Proceedings of the ACM SIGACT-SIGMOD Symposium on Principles of Database Systems* (1982).

[**Dayal et al. 1990**] U. Dayal, M. Hsu, and R. Ladin, "Organizing Long-Running Activities with Triggers and Transactions," *Proceedings of the ACM SIGMOD International Conference on the Management of Data* (1990), pages 204–215.

[**Dayal et al. 1991**] U. Dayal, M. Hsu, and R. Ladin, "A Transactional Model for Long-Running Activities," *Proceedings of the International Conference on Very Large Data Bases* (September 1991), pages 113–122.

[**DeMillo et al. 1978**] R. A. DeMillo, D. P. Dobkin, A. K. Jones, and R. J. Lipton, *Foundations of Secure Computation*, Academic Press, New York, NY (1978).

[**Denning 1980**] D. E. Denning, "Secure Statistical Databases with Random Sample Queries," *ACM Transactions on Database Systems*, Volume 5, Number 3 (September 1980), pages 291–315.

[**Denning 1982**] P. J. Denning, *Cryptography and Data Security*, Addison-Wesley, Reading, MA (1982).

[**Denning and Denning 1979**] D. E. Denning and P. J. Denning, "Data Security," *ACM Computing Surveys*, Volume 11, Number 3 (September 1979), pages 227–250.

[**Deshpande and Larson 1992**] V. Deshpande and P. A. Larson, "The Design and Implementation of a Parallel Join Algorithm for Nested Relations on Shared-Memory Multiprocessors," *Proceedings of the International Conference on Data Engineering* (1992), page 68.

[**Derr et al. 1993**] M. A. Derr, S. Morishita, and G. Phipps, "Design and Implementation of the Glue-Nail Database System," *Proceedings of the ACM SIGMOD International Conference on Management of Data* (1993), pages 147–156.

[**Deux et al. 1991**] O. Deux et al., "The $O_2$ System," *Communications of the ACM*, Volume 34, Number 10 (October 1991), pages 34–49.

[**DeWitt and Gray 1992**] D. DeWitt and J. Gray, "Parallel Database Systems: The Future of High Performance Database Systems," *Communications of the ACM*, Volume 35, Number 6 (June 1992), pages 85–98.

[**DeWitt et al. 1984**] D. DeWitt, R. Katz, F. Olken, L. Shapiro, M. Stonebraker, and D. Wood, "Implementation Techniques for Main Memory Databases," *Proceedings of the ACM SIGMOD International Conference on Management of Data* (1984), pages 1–8.

[**DeWitt et al. 1986**] D. DeWitt, R. Gerber, G. Graefe, M. Heytens, K. Kumar, and M. Muralikrishna, "GAMMA — A High Performance Dataflow Database Machine," *Proceedings of the International Conference on Very Large Data Bases* (1986).

**[DeWitt et al. 1990]** D. DeWitt et al., "The Gamma Database Machine Project," *IEEE Transactions on Knowledge and Data Engineering* Volume 2, Number 1 (March 1990).

**[DeWitt et al. 1992]** D. DeWitt, J. Naughton, D. Schneider, and S. Seshadri, "Practical Skew Handling in Parallel Joins," *Proceedings of the International Conference on Very Large Data Bases* (1992).

**[Dias et al. 1989]** D. Dias, B. Iyer, J. Robinson, and P. Yu, "Integrated Concurrency-Coherency Controls for Multisystem Data Sharing," *IEEE Transactions on Software Engineering*, Volume 15, Number 4 (April 1989), pages 437–448.

**[Di Battista and Lenzerini 1989]** G. Di Battista and M. Lenzerini "A Deductive Method for Entity-Relationship Modeling," *Proceedings of the International Conference on Very Large Data Bases* (1989), pages 13–22.

**[Diffie and Hellman 1979]** W. Diffie and M. E. Hellman, "Privacy and Authentication," *Proceedings of the IEEE*, Volume 67, Number 3 (March 1979), pages 397–427.

**[Dijkstra 1965]** E. W. Dijkstra, "Cooperating Sequential Processes," Technical Report EWD-123, Technological University, Eindhoven, The Netherlands (1965); reprinted in **[Genuys 1968]**, pages 43–112.

**[Dippert and Levy 1993]** B. Dippert and M. Levy, *Designing with FLASH Memory*, Annabooks 1993.

**[Dittrich 1988]** K. Dittrich (Editor), *Advances in Object-Oriented Database Systems*, Lecture Notes in Computer Science 334, Springer-Verlag (1988).

**[Dobkin et al. 1979]** D. Dobkin, A. K. Jones, and R. J. Lipton, "Secure Databases: Protection Against User Inference," *ACM Transactions on Database Systems*, Volume 4, Number 1 (March 1979), pages 97–106.

**[Dodd 1969]** G. G. Dodd, "APL-A Language for Associative Data Handling in PL/I," *Proceedings of the Fall Joint Computer Conference* (1969), pages 667–684.

**[Dogac et al. 1994]** A. Dogac, M. T. Ozsu, A. Biliris, and T. Selis (Editors), *Advances in Object-Oriented Database Systems*, Computer and Systems Sciences, NATO ASI Series F, Volume 130, Springer-Verlag (1994).

**[Douglis et al. 1994]** F. Douglis, R. Cáceres, B. Marsh, F. Kaashoek, K. Li, and J. Tauber, "Storage Alternatives for Mobile Computers," *Proceedings of the Symposium on Operating Systems Design and Implementation* (1994), pages 25–37. An updated version appears as [Douglis et al. 1996]a214.

**[Douglis et al. 1996]** F. Douglis, R. Cáceres, M. F. Kaashoek, P. Krishnan, K. Li, B. Marsh, and J. Tauber, "Storage Alternatives for Mobile Computers," in [Imielinski and Korth 1996]a216, Chapter 18.

**[Du and Elmagarmid 1989]** W. Du and A. Elmagarmid, "Quasi Serializability: A Correctness Criterion for Global Database Consistency in InterBase," *Proceedings of the International Conference on Very Large Data Bases* (1989), pages 347–356.

**[Dubois and Thakkar 1992]** M. Dubois and S. Thakkar (Editors), *Scalable Shared Memory Multiprocessors*, Kluwer Academic Publishers, Boston, MA (1992).

**[Duncan 1990]** R. Duncan, "A Survey of Parallel Computer Architectures," *IEEE Computer*, Volume 23, Number 2 (February 1990), pages 5–16.

**[Ellis 1980a]** C. S. Ellis, "Concurrent Search and Insertion in 2–3 Trees," *Acta Informatica*, Volume 14 (1980), pages 63–86.

**[Ellis 1980b]** C. S. Ellis, "Concurrent Search and Insertion in AVL Trees," *IEEE Transactions on Computers*, Volume C-29, Number 3 (September 1980), pages 811–817.

**[Ellis 1987]** C. S. Ellis, "Concurrency in Linear Hashing," *ACM Transactions on Database Systems*, Volume 12, Number 2 (June 1987), pages 195–217.

**[Elmasri and Larson 1985]** R. Elmasri and J. Larson, "A Graphical Query Facility for E-R Databases," *Proceedings of the International Conference on Entity-Relationship Approach* (1985).

**[Elmasri and Navathe 1994]** R. Elmasri and S. B. Navathe, *Fundamentals of Database Systems*, Second Edition, Benjamin Cummings, Redwood City, CA (1994).

**[Elmasri and Wiederhold 1981]** R. Elmasri and G. Wiederhold, "GORDAS: A Formal High-Level Query Language for the Entity-Relationship Model," *Proceedings of the International Conference on Entity-Relationship Approach* (1981).

**[English and Stepanov 1992]** R. M. English and A. A. Stepanov, "Loge: A Self-Organizing Disk Controller," *Proceedings of the Winter 1992 USENIX Conference*, San Francisco, CA (January 1992), pages 238–252.

**[Eppinger et al. 1991]** J. L Eppinger, L. B. Mummert and A. Z. Spector, *Camelot and Avalon: A Distributed Transaction Facility*, Morgan Kaufmann Publishers, Inc. (1991).

**[Epstein and Stonebraker 1980]** R. Epstein and M. R. Stonebraker, "Analysis of Distributed Database Processing Strategies," *Proceedings of the International Conference on Very Large Data Bases* (1980), pages 92–110.

**[Epstein et al. 1978]** R. Epstein, M. R. Stonebraker, and E. Wong, "Distributed Query Processing in a Relational Database System," *Proceedings of the ACM SIGMOD International Conference on Management of Data* (1978), pages 169–180.

**[Escobar-Molano et al. 1993]** M. Escobar-Molano, R. Hull, and D. Jacobs, "Safety and Translation of Calculus Queries with Scalar Functions," *Proceedings of the ACM SIGACT-SIGMOD-SIGART Symposium on the Principles of Database Systems* (1993), pages 253–264.

**[Eswaran and Chamberlin 1975]** K. P. Eswaran and D. D. Chamberlin, "Functional Specifications of a Subsystem for Database Integrity," *Proceedings of the International Conference on Very Large Data Bases* (1975), pages 48–68.

**[Eswaran et al. 1976]** K. P. Eswaran, J. N. Gray, R. A. Lorie, and I. L. Traiger, "The Notions of Consistency and Predicate Locks in a Database System," *Communications of the ACM*, Volume 19, Number 11 (November 1976), pages 624–633.

**[Evangelidis et al. 1995]** G. Evangelidis, D. Lomet and B. Salzberg, "The hB-Pi Tree: A Modified hB-tree Supporting Concurrency, Recovery and Node Consolidation," *Proceedings of the International Conference on Very Large Data Bases* (1995), pages 551–561.

**[Fagin 1977]** R. Fagin, "Multivalued Dependencies and a New Normal Form for Relational Databases," *ACM Transactions on Database Systems*, Volume 2, Number 3 (September 1977), pages 262–278.

[**Fagin 1979**]  R. Fagin, "Normal Forms and Relational Database Operators," *Proceedings of the ACM SIGMOD International Conference on Management of Data* (1979), pages 153–160.

[**Fagin 1981**]  R. Fagin, "A Normal Form for Relational Databases That Is Based on Domains and Keys," *ACM Transactions on Database Systems*, Volume 6, Number 3 (September 1981), pages 387–415.

[**Fagin 1983**]  R. Fagin, "Types of Acyclicity of Hypergraphs and Relational Database Schemes," *Journal of the ACM*, Volume 30, Number 3 (July 1983), pages 514–550.

[**Fagin et al. 1979**]  R. Fagin, J. Nievergelt, N. Pippenger, and H. R. Strong, "Extendible Hashing — A Fast Access Method for Dynamic Files," *ACM Transactions on Database Systems*, Volume 4, Number 3 (September 1979), pages 315–344.

[**Fagin et al. 1982**]  R. Fagin, A. O. Mendelzon, and J. D. Ullman, "A Simplified Universal Relation Assumption and Its Properties," *ACM Transactions on Database Systems*, Volume 7, Number 3 (September 1982), pages 343–360.

[**Faloutsos and Lin 1995**]  C. Faloutsos and K.-I. Lin, "Fast Map: A Fast Algorithm for Indexing, Data-Mining and Visualization of Traditional and Multimedia Datasets," *Proceedings of the ACM SIGMOD International Conference on Management of Data* (1995), pages 163–174.

[**Fayyad et al. 1995**]  U. Fayyad, G. Piatetsky-Shapiro, P. Smyth, and R. Uthurusamy, *Advances in Knowledge Discovery and Data Mining*, MIT Press, Cambridge, MA (1995).

[**Fekete et al. 1990a**]  A. Fekete, N. Lynch, and W. Weihl, "A Serialization Graph Construction for Nested Transactions," *Proceedings of the ACM SIGACT-SIGMOD-SIGART Symposium on the Principles of Database Systems* (1990), pages 94–108.

[**Fekete et al. 1990b**]  A. Fekete, N. Lynch, M. Merritt, and W. Weihl, "Commutativity-Based Locking for Nested Transactions," *Journal of Computer and System Sciences* (August 1990), pages 65–156.

[**Fernandez et al. 1981**]  E. Fernandez, R. Summers, and C. Wood, *Database Security and Integrity*, Addison-Wesley, Reading, MA (1981).

[**Finkel and Bentley 1974**]  R. A. Finkel and J. L. Bentley, "Quad Trees: A Data Structure for Retrieval on Composite Keys," *Acta Informatica*, Volume 4 (1974), pages 1–9.

[**Finkelstein 1982**]  S. Finkelstein, "Common Expression Analysis in Database Applications," *Proceedings of the ACM SIGMOD International Conference on Management of Data* (1982), pages 235–245.

[**Finkelstein et al. 1988**]  S. Finkelstein, M. Schkolnick, and P. Tiberio, "Physical Database Design for Relational Databases," *ACM Transactions on Database Systems*, Volume 13, Number 1 (March 1988), pages 53–90.

[**Fischer and Thomas 1983**]  P. C. Fischer and S. Thomas, "Operators for Non-First-Normal-Form Relations," *Proceedings of the International Computer Software Applications Conference* (1983), pages 464–475.

[**Fishman et al. 1990**]  D. Fishman, D. Beech, H. Cate, E. Chow, T. Connors, J. Davis, N. Derrett, C. Hoch, W. Kent, P. Lyngbaek, B. Mahbod, M. Neimat, T. Ryan, and M. Shan, "IRIS: An Object-Oriented Database Management System," in [**Zdonik and Maier 1990**], pages 216–226.

[**Ford and Calhoun 1984**] R. Ford and J. Calhoun, "Concurrency Control Mechanism and the Serializability of Concurrent Tree Algorithms," *Proceedings of the ACM SIGACT-SIGMOD Symposium on the Principles of Database Systems* (1984), pages 51–60.

[**Fortier 1989**] P. J. Fortier, *Handbook of LAN Technology,* McGraw Hill, New York, NY (1989).

[**Franklin et al. 1992**] M. J. Franklin, M. J. Zwilling, C. K. Tan, M. J. Carey, and D. J. DeWitt, "Crash Recovery in Client-Server EXODUS," *Proceedings of the ACM SIGMOD International Conference on Management of Data* (June 1992), pages 165–174.

[**Franklin et al. 1993**] M. J. Franklin, M. Carey, and M. Livny, "Local Disk Caching for Client-Server Database Systems," *Proceedings of the International Conference on Very Large Data Bases* (August 1993).

[**Fredkin 1960**] E. Fredkin, "Trie Memory," *Communications of the ACM*, Volume 4, Number 2 (September 1960), pages 490–499.

[**Freedman 1983**] D. H. Freedman, "Searching for Denser Disks," *Infosystems* (September 1983).

[**Freedman and DeWitt 1995**] C. S. Freedman and D. J. DeWitt, "The SPIFFI Scalable Video-on-Demand Server," *Proceedings of the ACM SIGMOD International Conference on Management of Data* (1995), pages 352–363.

[**Fry and Sibley 1976**] J. Fry and E. Sibley, "Evolution of Data-Base Management Systems," *ACM Computing Surveys*, Volume 8, Number 1 (March 1976), pages 7–42.

[**Fujitani 1984**] L. Fujitani, "Laser Optical Disk: The Coming Revolution in On-Line Storage," *Communications of the ACM,* Volume 27, Number 6 (June 1984), pages 546–554.

[**Furtado 1978**] A. L. Furtado, "Formal Aspects of the Relational Model," *Information Systems,* Volume 3, Number 2 (1978), pages 131–140.

[**Fushimi et al. 1986**] S. Fushimi, M. Kitsuregawa, and H. Tanaka, "An Overview of the Systems Software of a Parallel Relational Database Machine: GRACE," *Proceedings of the International Conference on Very Large Databases* (August 1986).

[**Fussell et al. 1981**] D. S. Fussell, Z. Kedem, and A. Silberschatz, "Deadlock Removal Using Partial Rollback in Database Systems," *Proceedings of the ACM SIGMOD International Conference on the Management of Data* (1981), pages 65–73.

[**Gadia 1986**] S. K. Gadia, "Weak Temporal Relations," *Proceedings of the ACM SIGACT-SIGMOD Symposium on the Principles of Database Systems* (1986), pages 70–77.

[**Gadia 1988**] S. K. Gadia, "A Homogeneous Relational Model and Query Language for Temporal Databases," *ACM Transactions on Database Systems*, Volume 13, Number 4 (December 1988), pages 418–448.

[**Gait 1988**] J. Gait, "The Optical File Cabinet: A Random-Access File System for Write-Once Optical Disks," *IEEE Computer*, Volume 21, Number 6 (June 1988).

[**Galindo-Legaria 1994**] C. Galindo-Legaria, "Outerjoins as Disjunctions," *Proceedings of the ACM SIGMOD International Conference on Management of Data* (1994).

[**Galindo-Legaria and Rosenthal 1992**] C. Galindo-Legaria and A. Rosenthal, "How to Extend a Conventional Optimizer to Handle One- and Two-Sided Outerjoin," *Proceedings of the International Conference on Data Engineering* (1992), pages 402–409.

**[Gallaire and Minker 1978]** H. Gallaire and J. Minker (Editors), *Logic and Databases*, Plenum Press, New York, NY (1978).

**[Gallaire et al. 1984]** H. Gallaire, J. Minker, and J. M. Nicolas, "Logic and Databases: A Deductive Approach," *ACM Computing Surveys*, Volume 16, Number 2 (June 1984), pages 154–185.

**[Ganguly et al. 1992]** S. Ganguly, W. Hasan and R. Krishnamurthy, "Query Optimization for Parallel Execution," *Proceedings of the ACM SIGMOD International Conference on Management of Data* (1992).

**[Ganguly et al. 1996]** S. Ganguly, P. Gibbons, Y. Matias, and A. Silberschatz, "A Sampling Algorithm for Estimating Join Size," *Proceedings of the ACM SIGMOD International Conference on Management of Data* (May 1996).

**[Ganski and Wong 1987]** R. A. Ganski and H. K. T. Wong, "Optimization of Nested SQL Queries Revisited," *Proceedings of the ACM SIGMOD International Conference on Management of Data* (May 1987).

**[Garcia-Molina 1982]** H. Garcia-Molina, "Elections in Distributed Computing Systems," *IEEE Transactions on Computers*, Volume C-31, Number 1 (January 1982), pages 48–59.

**[Garcia-Molina 1983]** H. Garcia-Molina, "Using Semantic Knowledge for Transaction Processing in a Distributed Database," *ACM Transactions on Database Systems*, Volume 8, Number 2 (June 1983), pages 186–213.

**[Garcia-Molina and Salem 1992]** H. Garcia-Molina and K. Salem, "Main Memory Database Systems: An Overview," *IEEE Transactions on Knowledge and Data Engineering*, Volume 4, Number 6 (December 1992), pages 509–516.

**[Garcia-Molina and Wiederhold 1982]** H. Garcia-Molina and G. Wiederhold, "Read-only Transactions in a Distributed Database," *ACM Transactions on Database Systems*, Volume 7, Number 2 (June 1982), pages 209–234.

**[Gardarin and Valduriez 1989]** G. Gardarin and P. Valduriez, *Relational Databases and Knowledge Bases,* Addison-Wesley, Reading, MA (1989).

**[Garey and Johnson 1979]** M. R. Garey and D. S. Johnson, *Computers and Intractability: A Guide to the Theory of NP-Completeness*, Freeman, New York, NY (1979).

**[Garza and Kim 1988]** J. Garza and W. Kim, "Transaction Management in an Object-Oriented Database System," *Proceedings of the ACM SIGMOD International Conference on the Management of Data* (1988), pages 37–45.

**[Gehani and Jagadish 1991]** N. Gehani and H. Jagadish, "Ode as an Active Database: Constraints and Triggers," *Proceedings of the International Conference on Very Large Data Bases* (1991).

**[Gehani et al. 1992]** N. Gehani, H. Jagadish, and O. Shmueli, "Composite Event Specification in Active Databases: Model and Implementation," *Proceedings of the International Conference on Very Large Data Bases* (1992).

**[Geiger 1995]** K. Geiger, *Inside ODBC*, Microsoft Press, Redmond, WA (1995).

**[Genuys 1968]** F. Genuys (Editor), *Programming Languages*, Academic Press, London, England (1968).

**[Georgakopoulos et al. 1994]** D. Georgakopoulos, M. Rusinkiewicz, and A. Seth, "Using Tickets to Enforce the Serializability of Multidatabase Transactions," *IEEE Transactions on Knowledge and Data Engineering,* Volume 6, Number 1 (February 1994), pages 166–180.

[**Gerritsen 1975**] R. Gerritsen, "A Preliminary System for the Design of DBTG Data Structures," *Communications of the ACM*, Volume 18, Number 10 (October 1975) pages 551–557.

[**Gifford 1979**] D. K. Gifford, "Weighted Voting for Replicated Data," *Proceedings of the ACM SIGOPS Symposium on Operating Systems Principles* (1979), pages 150–162.

[**Gligor and Shattuck 1980**] V. D. Gligor and S. H. Shattuck, "On Deadlock Detection in Distributed Systems," *IEEE Transactions on Software Engineering*, Volume SE-6, Number 5 (September 1980), pages 435–439.

[**Gogolla and Hohenstein 1991**] M. Gogolla and U. Hohenstein, "Towards a Semantic view of an Extended Entity-Relationship Model," *ACM Transactions on Database Systems*, Volume 16, Number 3 (September 1991), pages 369–416.

[**Goldberg and Robson 1983**] A. Goldberg and D. Robson, *Smalltalk-80: The Language and Its Implementation*, Addison-Wesley, Reading, MA (1983).

[**Goodman 1995**] N. Goodman, "An Object-Oriented DBMS War Story: Developing a Genome Mapping Database in C++," in [**Kim 1995**], pages 216–237.

[**Gotlieb 1975**] L. R. Gotlieb, "Computing Joins of Relations," *Proceedings of the ACM SIGMOD International Conference on the Management of Data* (1975), pages 55–63.

[**Graefe 1990**] G. Graefe, "Encapsulation of Parallelism in the Volcano Query Processing System," *Proceedings of the ACM SIGMOD International Conference on Management of Data* (1990), pages 102–111.

[**Graefe 1993**] G. Graefe, "Query Evaluation Techniques for Large Databases," *ACM Computing Surveys*, Volume 25, Number 2 (June 1993), pages 73–170.

[**Graefe and McKenna 1993**] G. Graefe and W. McKenna, "The Volcano Optimizer Generator," *Proceedings of the International Conference on Data Engineering* (1993), pages 209–218.

[**Graham et al. 1986**] M. H. Graham, A. O. Mendelzon, and M. Y. Vardi, "Notions of Dependency Satisfaction," *Journal of the ACM*, Volume 33, Number 1 (January 1986), pages 105–129.

[**Gravano et al. 1994**] L. Gravano, H. Garcia-Molina, and A. Tomasic, "The Effectiveness of GIOSS for the Test Database Discovery Problem," *Proceedings of the ACM SIGMOD International Conference on Management of Data* (1994), pages 126–137.

[**Gray 1978**] J. Gray, "Notes on Data Base Operating System," in [**Bayer et al. 1978**], pages 393–481.

[**Gray 1981**] J. Gray, "The Transaction Concept: Virtues and Limitations," *Proceedings of the International Conference on Very Large Data Bases* (1981), pages 144–154.

[**Gray 1991**] J. Gray, *The Benchmark Handbook for Database and Transaction Processing Systems,* Second Edition, Morgan-Kaufmann, San Mateo, CA (1991).

[**Gray and Edwards 1995**] J. Gray and J. Edwards, "Scale Up with TP Monitors," *Byte*, Volume 20, Number 4 (April 1995), pages 123–130.

[**Gray and Reuter 1993**] J. Gray and A. Reuter, *Transaction Processing: Concepts and Techniques*, Morgan Kaufmann, San Mateo, CA (1993).

[**Gray et al. 1975**] J. Gray, R. A. Lorie, and G. R. Putzolu, "Granularity of Locks and Degrees of Consistency in a Shared Data Base," *Proceedings of the International Conference on Very Large Data Bases* (1975), pages 428–451.

[**Gray et al. 1976**] J. Gray, R. A. Lorie, G. R. Putzolu, and I. L. Traiger, "Granularity of Locks and Degrees of Consistency in a Shared Data Base," in [**Nijssen 1976**], pages 365–395.

[**Gray et al. 1981a**] J. Gray, P. R. McJones, and M. Blasgen, "The Recovery Manager of the System R Database Manager," *ACM Computing Surveys*, Volume 13, Number 2 (June 1981), pages 223–242.

[**Gray et al. 1981b**] J. Gray, P. Homan, H. F. Korth, and R. Obermarck, "A Straw Man Analysis of the Probability of Waiting and Deadlock," Research Report RJ3066, IBM Research Laboratory, San Jose, CA (1981).

[**Gray et al. 1990**] J. Gray, B. Horst, and M. Walker, "Parity Striping of Disc Arrays: Low-Cost Reliable Storage with Acceptable Throughput," *Proceedings of the International Conference on Very Large Data Bases* (1990), pages 148–161.

[**Gray et al. 1995**] J. Gray, A. Bosworth, A. Layman, and H. Pirahesh, "Data Cube: A Relational Aggregation Operator Generalizing Group-By, Cross-Tab and Sub-Totals," Technical Report MSR-TR-95-22, Microsoft Research (November 1995).

[**Gray et al. 1996**] J. Gray, P. Helland, and P. O'Neil, "The Dangers of Replication and a Solution," *Proceedings of the ACM SIGMOD International Conference on Management of Data* (1996), pages 173–182.

[**Griffin and Libkin 1995**] T. Griffin and L. Libkin, "Incremental Maintenance of Views with Duplicates," *Proceedings of the ACM SIGMOD International Conference on Management of Data* (1995).

[**Gupta and Mumick 1995**] A. Gupta and I. S. Mumick, "Maintenance of Materialized Views: Problems, Techniques and Applications," *IEEE Data Engineering Bulletin*, Volume 18, Number 2 (June 1995).

[**Guttman 1984**] A. Guttman, "R-Trees: A Dynamic Index Structure for Spatial Searching," *Proceedings of the ACM SIGMOD International Conference on Management of Data* (1984), pages 47–57.

[**Haas et al. 1989**] L. M. Haas, J. C. Freytag, G. M. Lohman, and H. Pirahesh, "Extensible Query Processing in Starburst," *Proceedings of the ACM SIGMOD International Conference on Management of Data* (1989), pages 377–388.

[**Haerder and Reuter 1983**] T. Haerder and A. Reuter, "Principles of Transaction-Oriented Database Recovery," *ACM Computing Surveys*, Volume 15, Number 4 (December 1983), pages 287–318.

[**Haerder and Rothermel 1987**] T. Haerder and K. Rothermel, "Concepts for Transaction Recovery in Nested Transactions," *Proceedings of the ACM SIGMOD International Conference on Management of Data* (1987), pages 239–248.

[**Hall 1976**] P. A. V. Hall, "Optimization of a Single Relational Expression in a Relational Database System," *IBM Journal of Research and Development*, Volume 20, Number 3 (1976), pages 244–257.

[**Halsall 1992**] F. Halsall, *Data Communications, Computer Networks, and Open Systems*, Addison-Wesley, Reading, MA (1992).

[**Hammer and McLeod 1975**] M. Hammer and D. McLeod, "Semantic Integrity in a Relational Data Base System," *Proceedings of the International Conference on Very Large Data Bases* (1975), pages 25–47.

[**Hammer and McLeod 1981**] M. Hammer and D. McLeod, "Database Description with SDM: A Semantic Data Model," *ACM Transactions on Database Systems*, Volume 6, Number 3 (September 1980), pages 351–386.

[**Hammer and Sarin 1978**] M. Hammer and S. Sarin, "Efficient Monitoring of Database Assertions," *Proceedings of the ACM SIGMOD International Conference on Management of Data* (1978).

[**Harinarayan et al. 1996**] V. Harinarayan, J. D. Ullman, and A. Rajaraman, "Implementing Data Cubes Efficiently," *Proceedings of the ACM SIGMOD International Conference on the Management of Data* (1996).

[**Haritsa et al. 1990**] J. Haritsa, M. Carey, and M. Livny, "On Being Optimistic about Real-Time Constraints," *Proceedings of the ACM SIGACT-SIGMOD Symposium on Principles of Database Systems* (April 1990).

[**Harker et al. 1981**] J. M. Harker, D. W. Brede, R. E. Pattison, G. R. Santana, and L. G. Taft, "A Quarter Century of Disk File Innovation," *IBM Journal of Research and Development,* Volume 25, Number 5 (September 1981), pages 677–689.

[**Hasan and Motwani 1995**] W. Hasan and R. Motwani, "Coloring Away Communication in Parallel Query Optimization," *Proceedings of the International Conference on Very Large Data Bases* (1995).

[**Haskin and Lorie 1982**] R. Haskin and R. A. Lorie, "On Extending the Functions of a Relational Database System," *Proceedings of the ACM SIGMOD International Conference on the Management of Data* (1982), pages 207–212.

[**Haskin et al. 1988**] R. Haskin, Y. Malachi, W. Sawdon, and G. Chan, "Recovery Management in Quicksilver," *ACM Transactions on Computer Systems*, Volume 6, Number 1 (January 1988), pages 82–108.

[**Hevner and Yao 1979**] A. R. Hevner and S. B. Yao, "Query Processing in Distributed Database Systems," *IEEE Transactions on Software Engineering*, Volume SE-5, Number 3 (May 1979), pages 177–187.

[**Hinrichs 1985**] K. H. Hinrichs, "The Grid File System: Implementation and Case Studies of Applications," Ph.D. thesis, Swiss Federal Institute of Technology, Zurich, Switzerland (1985).

[**Hoagland 1985**] A. S. Hoagland, "Information Storage Technology — A Look at the Future," *IEEE Computer*, Volume 18, Number 7 (July 1985), pages 60–68.

[**Hollinsworth 1994**] D. Hollinsworth, "The Workflow Reference Model," *Workflow Management Coalition,* Number TC00-1003 (December 1994).

[**Holt 1971**] R. C. Holt, "Comments on Prevention of System Deadlocks," *Communications of the ACM*, Volume 14, Number 1 (January 1971), pages 36–38.

[**Holt 1972**] R. C. Holt, "Some Deadlock Properties of Computer Systems," *ACM Computing Surveys*, Volume 4, Number 3 (September 1972), pages 179–196.

[**Hong and Stonebraker 1991**] W. Hong and M. Stonebraker, "Optimization of Parallel Query Execution Plans in XPRS," *Proceedings of the International Symposium on Parallel and Distributed Information Systems* (1991), pages 218–225.

[**Hong et al. 1993**] D. Hong, T. Johnson, S. Chakravarthy, "Real-Time Transaction Scheduling: A Cost Conscious Approach," *Proceedings of the ACM SIGMOD International Conference on Management of Data* (April 1993).

[**Horowitz and Sahni 1976**] E. Horowitz and S. Sahni, *Fundamentals of Data Structures*, Computer Science Press, Rockville, MD (1976).

[**Hsu and Imielinski 1985**] A. Hsu and T. Imielinski, "Integrity Checking for Multiple Updates," *Proceedings of the ACM SIGMOD International Conference on Management of Data* (1985), pages 152–168.

[**Hudson and King 1989**] S. E. Hudson and R. King, "Cactis: A Self-Adaptive, Concurrent Implementation of an Object-Oriented Database Management System," *ACM Transactions on Database Systems*, Volume 14, Number 3 (September 1989), pages 291–321.

[**Huffman 1993**] A. Huffman, "Transaction Processing with TUXEDO," *Proceedings of the International Symposium on Parallel and Distributed Information Systems* (1993).

[**Hull and King 1987**] R. Hull and R. King, "Semantic Database Modeling: Survey, Applications and Research Issues," *ACM Computing Surveys*, Volume 19, Number 3 (September 1987), pages 201–260.

[**IBM 1978a**] IBM Corporation, *Information Management System/Virtual Storage General Information*, IBM Form Number GH20–1260, SH20–9025, SH20–9026, SH20–9027.

[**IBM 1978b**] IBM Corporation, *Query-by Example Terminal Users Guide*, IBM Form Number SH20–20780 (1978).

[**IBM 1987**] IBM Corporation, *Systems Application Architecture: Common Programming Interface, Database Reference*, IBM Form Number SC26–4348–0 (1987).

[**Imielinski and Badrinath 1994**] T. Imielinski and B. R. Badrinath, "Mobile Computing — Solutions and Challenges," *Communications of the ACM*, Volume 37, Number 10 (October 1994).

[**Imielinski and Korth 1996**] T. Imielinski and H. F. Korth (Editors), *Mobile Computing*, Kluwer Academic Publishers (1996).

[**Imielinski et al. 1995**] T. Imielinski, S. Viswanathan, and B. R. Badrinath, "Energy Efficient Indexing on the Air," *Proceedings of the ACM SIGMOD International Conference on Management of Data* (1995), pages 25–36.

[**Ioannidis and Christodoulakis 1993**] Y. Ioannidis and S. Christodoulakis, "Optimal Histograms for Limiting Worst-Case Error Propagation in the Size of Join Results," *ACM Transactions on Database Systems*, Volume 18, Number 4 (December 1993), pages 709–748.

[**Ioannidis and Kang 1990**] Y. Ioannidis and Y. Kang, "Randomized Algorithms for Optimizing Large Join Queries," *Proceedings of the ACM SIGMOD International Conference on Management of Data* (1990), pages 312–321.

[**Ioannidis and Poosala 1995**] Y. E. Ioannidis and V. Poosala, "Balancing Histogram Optimality and Practicality for Query Result Size Estimation," *Proceedings of the ACM SIGMOD International Conference on Management of Data* (1995), pages 233–244.

[**Ioannidis and Wong 1987**] Y. E. Ioannidis and E. Wong, "Query Optimization by Simulated Annealing," *Proceedings of the ACM SIGMOD International Conference on Management of Data* (1987), pages 9–22.

[**Ioannidis et al. 1992**] Y. E. Ioannidis, R. T. Ng, K. Shim, and T. K. Sellis, "Parametric Query Optimization," *Proceedings of the International Conference on Very Large Data Bases* (1992), pages 103–114.

[**Ishikawa et al. 1993**] H. Ishikawa, F. Suzuki, F. Kozakura, A. Makinouchi, M. Miyag-ishima, Y. Izumida, M. Aoshima, and Y. Yamana, "The Model, Language, and Implementation of an Object-Oriented Multimedia Knowledge Base Management System," *ACM Transactions on Database Systems*, Volume 18, Number 1 (March 1993), pages 1–50.

[**Jaeschke and Schek 1982**] G. Jaeschke and H. J. Schek, "Remarks on the Algebra of Non First Normal Form Relations," *Proceedings of the ACM SIGACT-SIGMOD Symposium on Principles of Database Systems* (1982), pages 124–138.

[**Jagadish and Qian 1992**] H. V. Jagadish and X. Qian, "Integrity Maintenance in an Object-Oriented Database," *Proceedings of the International Conference on Very Large Data Bases* (1992).

[**Jagadish et al. 1993**] H. V. Jagadish, A. Silberschatz, and S. Sudarshan, "Recovering from Main-Memory Lapses," *Proceedings of the International Conference on Very Large Data Bases* (August 1993).

[**Jagadish et al. 1994**] H. Jagadish, D. Lieuwen, R. Rastogi, A. Silberschatz, and S. Sudarshan, "Dali: A High Performance Main Memory Storage Manager," *International Conference on Very Large Databases* (September 1994).

[**Jajodia and Sandhu 1990**] S. Jajodia and R. Sandhu, "Polyinstantiation Integrity in Multilevel Relations," *Proceedings of the IEEE Symposium on Research in Security and Privacy* (1990), pages 104–115.

[**Jajodia and Subramanian 1995**] S. Jajodia and V. S. Subramanian (Editors), *Multimedia Database Systems: Issues and Research Directions*, Springer-Verlag (1995).

[**Jarke and Koch 1984**] M. Jarke and J. Koch, "Query Optimization in Database Systems," *ACM Computing Surveys*, Volume 16, Number 2 (June 1984), pages 111–152.

[**Jensen et al. 1994**] C. S. Jensen and others, "A Consensus Glossary of Temporal Database Concepts," *ACM SIGMOD Record,* Volume 23, Number 1 (March 1994), pages 52–64.

[**Jin et al. 1993**] W. Jin, L. Ness, M. Rusinkiewicz, and A. Sheth, "Concurrency Control and Recovery of Multidatabase Work Flows in Telecommunication Applications," *Proceedings of the ACM SIGMOD International Conference on Management of Data* (May 1993).

[**Johnson and Shasha 1993**] T. Johnson and D. Shasha, "The Performance of Concurrent B-Tree Algorithms," *ACM Transactions on Database Systems*, Volume 18, Number 1 (March 1993).

[**Jones and Schwarz 1980**] A. K. Jones and P. Schwarz, "Experience Using Multiprocessor Systems — A Status Report," *Computing Surveys,* Volume 12, Number 2 (June 1980), pages 121–165.

[**Joshi 1991**] A. Joshi, "Adaptive Locking Strategies in a Multi-Node Shared Data Model Environment," *Proceedings of the International Conference on Very Large Data Bases* (1991).

[**Kaiser 1990**] G. Kaiser, "A Flexible Transaction Model for Software Engineering," *Proceedings of the International Conference on Data Engineering* (1990).

[**Kam and Ullman 1977**] J. B. Kam and J. D. Ullman, "A Model of Statistical Databases and Their Security," *ACM Transactions on Database Systems*, Volume 2, Number 1 (January 1977), pages 1–10.

[**Kambayashi et al. 1982**] Y. Kambayashi, M. Yoshikawa, and S. Yajima, "Query Processing for Distributed Databases Using Generalized Semi-joins," *Proceedings of the ACM SIGMOD International Conference on the Management of Data* (1982), pages 151–160.

[**Kamel and Faloutsos 1992**] I. Kamel, and C. Faloutsos, "Parallel R-Trees," *Proceedings of the ACM SIGMOD International Conference on Management of Data* (June 1992).

[**Katz and Wong 1982**] R. H. Katz and E. Wong, "Decompiling CODASYL DML into Relational Queries," *ACM Transactions on Database Systems*, Volume 7, Number 1 (March 1982), pages 1–23.

[**Katz et al. 1989**] R. H. Katz, G. A. Gibson, and D. A. Patterson, "Disk System Architectures for High Performance Computing," *Proceedings of the IEEE*, Volume 77, Number 12 (December 1989).

[**Kedem and Silberschatz 1979**] Z. M. Kedem and A. Silberschatz, "Controlling Concurrency Using Locking Protocols," *Proceedings of the Annual IEEE Symposium on Foundations of Computer Science* (1979), pages 275–285.

[**Kedem and Silberschatz 1983**] Z. M. Kedem and A. Silberschatz, "Locking Protocols: From Exclusive to Shared Locks," *Journal of the ACM*, Volume 30, Number 4 (October 1983), pages 787–804.

[**Keller 1985**] A. M. Keller, "Updating Relational Databases Through Views," Ph.D. thesis, Department of Computer Science, Stanford University, Stanford, CA (1985).

[**Kenville 1982**] R. F. Kenville, "Optical Disk Data Storage," *IEEE Computer*, Volume 15, Number 7 (July 1982), pages 21–26.

[**Khoshafian and Copeland 1990**] S. Khoshafian and G. P. Copeland, "Object Identity," in [**Zdonik and Maier 1990**], pages 37–46.

[**Kifer et al. 1992**] M. Kifer, W. Kim, and Y. Sagiv, "Querying Object Oriented Databases," *Proceedings of the ACM SIGMOD International Conference on the Management of Data* (1992), pages 393–402.

[**Kim 1982**] W. Kim, "On Optimizing an SQL-like Nested Query," *ACM Transactions on Database Systems*, Volume 3, Number 3 (September 1982), pages 443–469.

[**Kim 1984**] W. Kim, "Query Optimization for Relational Database Systems," in [**Unger et al. 1984**].

[**Kim 1989**] W. Kim, "A Model of Queries for Object-Oriented Databases," *Proceedings of the International Conference on Very Large Data Bases* (1989).

[**Kim 1990a**] W. Kim, "Architectural Issues in Object-Oriented Databases," *Journal of Object-Oriented Programming* (March/April 1990).

[**Kim 1990b**] W. Kim, *Introduction to Object-Oriented Databases*, MIT Press, Cambridge, MA (1990).

[**Kim 1995**] W. Kim (Editor), *Modern Database Systems,* ACM Press/Addison Wesley (1995).

[**Kim and Lochovsky 1989**] W. Kim and F. Lochovsky (Editors), *Object-Oriented Concepts, Databases, and Applications*, Addison-Wesley, Reading, MA (1989).

[**Kim et al. 1984**] W. Kim, R. Lorie, D. McNabb, and W. Plouffe, "Transaction Mechanism for Engineering Design Databases," *Proceedings of the International Conference on Very Large Data Bases*, (August 1984), pages 355-362.

[**Kim et al. 1985**]  W. Kim, D. S. Reiner, and D. S. Batory (Editors), *Query Processing in Database Systems*, Springer-Verlag, Berlin, Germany (1985).

[**Kim et al. 1988**]  W. Kim, N. Ballou, J. Banerjee, H. T. Chou, J. F. Garza, and D. Woelk, "Integrating an Object-Oriented Programming System with a Database System," *Proceedings of the International Conference on Object-Oriented Programming Systems, Languages, and Applications* (1988).

[**Kim et al. 1989**]  W. Kim, K. C. Kim, and A. Dale, "Indexing Techniques for Object-Oriented Databases," in [**Kim and Lochovsky 1989**], pages 371–394.

[**King 1981**]  J. J. King, "QUIST: A System for Semantic Query Optimization in Relational Data Bases," *Proceedings of the International Conference on Very Large Data Bases* (1981), pages 510–517.

[**King et al. 1983**]  R. P. King, H. F. Korth, and B. E. Willner, " Design of a Document Filing and Retrieval Service," *Proceedings of the ACM SIGMOD-SIGBDB Database Week* (1983).

[**King et al. 1991**]  R. P. King, N. Halim, H. Garcia-Molina, and C. Polyzois, "Management of a Remote Backup Copy for Disaster Recovery," *ACM Transactions on Database Systems*, Volume 16, Number 2 (June 1991), pages 338–368.

[**Kitsuregawa and Ogawa 1990**]  M. Kitsuregawa and Y Ogawa, "Bucket Spreading Parallel Hash: A New, Robust, Parallel Hash Join Method for Skew in the Super Database Computer," *Proceedings of the International Conference on Very Large Data Bases* (1990), pages 210–221.

[**Kitsuregawa et al. 1983**]  M. Kitsuregawa, H. Tanaka, and T. MotoOka, "Application of Hash to a Database Machine and its Architecture," *New Generation Computing*, Number 1 (1983), pages 62–74.

[**Kleinrock 1975**]  L. Kleinrock, *Queuing Systems, Volume 1: Theory,* John Wiley and Sons Publishers, New York, NY (1975).

[**Kleinrock 1976**]  L. Kleinrock, *Queuing Systems, Volume 2: Computer Applications,* John Wiley and Sons Publishers, New York, NY (1976).

[**Klug 1982**]  A. Klug, "Equivalence of Relational Algebra and Relational Calculus Query Languages Having Aggregate Functions," *Journal of the ACM*, Volume 29, Number 3 (July 1982), pages 699–717.

[**Knapp 1987**]  E. Knapp, "Deadlock Detection in Distributed Databases," *ACM Computing Surveys,* Volume 19, Number 4 (December 1987).

[**Knuth 1973**]  D. E. Knuth, *The Art of Computer Programming, Volume 3: Sorting and Searching*, Addison-Wesley, Reading, MA (1973).

[**Koch and Loney 1995**]  G. Koch and K. Loney, *Oracle: The Complete Reference*, Third Edition, Osborne, McGraw-Hill, Oracle (1995).

[**Kogan and Jajodia 1990**]  B. Kogan and S. Jajodia, "Concurrency Control in Multilevel-secure Databases Using Replicated Architecture," *Proceedings of the ACM SIGMOD International Conference on the Management of Data* (1990), pages 153–162.

[**Kohler 1981**]  W. H. Kohler, "A Survey of Techniques for Synchronization and Recovery in Decentralized Computer Systems," *ACM Computing Surveys*, Volume 13, Number 2 (June 1981), pages 149–183.

[**Korth 1982**]  H. F. Korth, " Deadlock Freedom Using Edge Locks," *ACM Transactions on Database Systems*, Volume 7, Number 4 (December 1982), pages 632–652.

[**Korth 1983**] H. F. Korth, "Locking Primitives in a Database System," *Journal of the ACM*, Volume 30, Number 1 (January 1983), pages 55–79.

[**Korth and Speegle 1988**] H. F. Korth and G. Speegle, "Formal Model of Correctness Without Serializability," *Proceedings of the ACM SIGMOD International Conference on Management of Data* (1988), pages 379–386.

[**Korth and Speegle 1990**] H. F. Korth and G. Speegle, "Long Duration Transactions in Software Design Projects," *Proceedings of the International Conference on Data Engineering* (1990), pages 568–575.

[**Korth and Speegle 1994**] H. F. Korth and G. Speegle, "Formal Aspects of Concurrency Control in Long Duration Transaction Systems Using the NT/PV Model," *ACM Transactions on Database Systems*, Volume 19, Number 3 (September 1994), pages 492–535.

[**Korth et al. 1988**] H. F. Korth, W. Kim, and F. Bancilhon, "On Long Duration CAD Transactions," *Information Science*, Volume 46 (October 1988), pages 73–107.

[**Korth et al. 1990a**] H. F. Korth, E. Levy, and A. Silberschatz, "A Formal Approach to Recovery by Compensating Transactions," *Proceedings of the International Conference on Very Large Data Bases* (1990), pages 95–106.

[**Korth et al. 1990b**] H. F. Korth, N. Soparkar, and A. Silberschatz, "Triggered Real-Time Databases with Consistency Constraints," *Proceedings of the International Conference on Very Large Data Bases* (1990), pages 71–82.

[**Krol 1994**] E. Krol, *The Whole Internet: Users Guide and Catalog,* Second Edition, O'Reilly & Associates, Sebastopol, CA (1994).

[**Kumar and Stonebraker 1988**] A. Kumar and M. Stonebraker, "Semantics Based Transaction Management Techniques for Replicated Data," *Proceedings of the ACM SIGMOD International Conference on Management of Data* (1988), pages 117–125.

[**Kung and Lehman 1980**] H. T. Kung and P. L. Lehman, "Concurrent Manipulation of Binary Search Trees," *ACM Transactions on Database Systems*, Volume 5, Number 3 (September 1980), pages 339–353.

[**Kung and Robinson 1981**] H. T. Kung and J. T. Robinson, " Optimistic Concurrency Control," *ACM Transactions on Database Systems*, Volume 6, Number 2 (June 1981), pages 312–326.

[**Kwong and Wood 1982**] Y. S. Kwong and D. Wood, "Method for Concurrency in B+-trees," *IEEE Transactions on Software Engineering*, Volume SE-8, Number 3 (March 1982), pages 211–223.

[**Lai and Wilkinson 1984**] M. Y. Lai and W. K. Wilkinson "Distributed Transaction Management in JASMIN," *Proceedings of the International Conference on Very Large Data Bases* (1984), pages 466–472.

[**Lamb et al. 1991**] C. Lamb, G. Landis, J. Orenstein, and D. Weinreb, "The ObjectStore Database System," *Communications of the ACM*, Volume 34, Number 10 (October 1991), pages 51–63.

[**Lamport 1978**] L. Lamport, "Time, Clocks, and the Ordering of Events in a Distributed System," *Communications of the ACM*, Volume 21, Number 7 (July 1978), pages 558–565.

[**Lampson and Sturgis 1976**] B. Lampson and H. Sturgis "Crash Recovery in a Distributed Data Storage System," Technical Report, Computer Science Laboratory, Xerox, Palo Alto Research Center, Palo Alto, CA (1976).

[**Langerak 1990**] R. Langerak, "View Updates in Relational Databases with an Independent Scheme," *ACM Transactions on Database Systems,* Volume 15, Number 1 (March 1990), pages 40–66.

[**Lanzelotte et al. 1993**] R. Lanzelotte, P. Valduriez, and M. Zat, "On the Effectiveness of Optimization Search Strategies for Parallel Execution Spaces," *Proceedings of the International Conference on Very Large Data Bases* (1993).

[**Larson 1978**] P. Larson, "Dynamic Hashing," *BIT,* 18 (1978).

[**Larson 1982**] P. Larson, "Performance Analysis of Linear Hashing with Partial Expansions," *ACM Transactions on Database Systems,* Volume 7, Number 4 (December 1982), pages 566–587.

[**Larson 1988**] P. Larson, "Linear Hashing with Separators — A Dynamic Hashing Scheme Achieving One-Access Retrieval," *ACM Transactions on Database Systems,* Volume 19, Number 3 (September 1988), pages 366–388.

[**Larson and Yang 1985**] P. Larson and H. Z. Yang, "Computing Queries from Derived Relations," *Proceedings of the International Conference on Very Large Data Bases* (1985), pages 259–269.

[**Lecluse et al. 1988**] C. Lecluse, P. Richard, and F. Velez, "O2: An Object-Oriented Data Model," *Proceedings of the ACM International Conference on the Management of Data* (1988), pages 424–433.

[**Lee and Liou 1996**] S. Y. Lee and R. L. Liou, "A Multi-Granularity Locking Model for Concurrency Control in Object-Oriented Database Systems," *IEEE Transactions on Knowledge and Data Engineering,* Volume 8, Number 1 (February 1996), pages 144–156.

[**Leiss 1982a**] E. Leiss, *Principles of Data Security*, Plenum Press, New York, NY (1982).

[**Leiss 1982b**] E. Leiss, "Randomizing: A Practical Method for Protecting Statistical Databases Against Compromise," *Proceedings of the International Conference on Very Large Data Bases* (1982), pages 189–196.

[**Lehman and Yao 1981**] P. L. Lehman and S. B. Yao, "Efficient Locking for Concurrent Operations on B-trees," *ACM Transactions on Database Systems,* Volume 6, Number 4 (December 1981), pages 650–670.

[**Lempel 1979**] A. Lempel, "Cryptography in Transition," *ACM Computing Surveys,* Volume 11, Number 4 (December 1979), pages 286–303.

[**Lenzerini and Santucci 1983**] M. Lenzerini and C. Santucci, "Cardinality Constraints in the Entity Relationship Model," in [**Davis et al. 1983**].

[**Lien and Weinberger 1978**] Y. E. Lien and P. J. Weinberger, "Consistency, Concurrency and Crash Recovery," *Proceedings of the ACM SIGMOD International Conference on Management of Data* (1978), pages 9–14.

[**Lin et al. 1994**] E. T. Lin, E. R. Omiecinski, and S. Yalamanchili, "Large Join Optimization on a Hypercube Multiprocessor," *IEEE Transactions on Knowledge and Data Engineering,* Volume 6, Number 2 (April 1994), pages 304-315.

[**Lindsay et al. 1980**] B. G. Lindsay, P. G. Selinger, C. Galtieri, J. N. Gray, R. A. Lorie, T. G. Price, G. R. Putzolu, I. L. Traiger, and B. W. Wade, "Notes on Distributed

Databases," in [*Distributed Data Bases*, Draffen and Poole [Ed.]431 Cambridge University Press, Cambridge, England (1980)]a431, pages 247–284.

[**Litwin 1978**] W. Litwin, "Virtual Hashing: A Dynamically Changing Hashing," *Proceedings of the International Conference on Very Large Data Bases* (1978), pages 517–523.

[**Litwin 1980**] W. Litwin, "Linear Hashing: A New Tool for File and Table Addressing," *Proceedings of the International Conference on Very Large Data Bases* (1980), pages 212–223.

[**Litwin 1981**] W. Litwin, "Trie Hashing," *Proceedings of the ACM SIGMOD International Conference on Management of Data* (1981), pages 19–29.

[**Lo and Ravishankar 1996**] M.-L. Lo and C. V. Ravishankar, "Spatial Hash-Joins," *Proceedings of the ACM SIGMOD International Conference on the Management of Data* (1996).

[**Lomet 1981**] D. G. Lomet, "Digital B-trees," *Proceedings of the International Conference on Very Large Data Bases* (1981), pages 333–344.

[**Lomet and Salzberg 1992**] D. Lomet and B. Salzberg, "Access Method Concurrency with Recovery," *Proceedings of the ACM SIGMOD International Conference on Management of Data* (1992), pages 351–360. A new version will appear in *The VLDB Journal* (1997).

[**Lopresti and Tomkins 1993**] D. P. Lopresti and A. Tomkins, "Approximate Matching of Hand Drawn Pictograms," *Proceedings of the INTERCHI 93 Conference* (1993).

[**Lorie 1977**] R. A. Lorie, "Physical Integrity in a Large Segmented Database," *ACM Transactions on Database Systems*, Volume 2, Number 1 (March 1977), pages 91–104.

[**Lorie et al. 1985**] R. Lorie, W. Kim, D. McNabb, W. Plouffe, and A. Meier, "Supporting Complex Objects in a Relational System for Engineering Databases," in [**Kim et al. 1985**], pages 145–155.

[**Lu et al. 1991**] H. Lu, M. Shan, and K. Tan, "Optimization of Multi-Way Join Queries for Parallel Execution," *Proceedings of the International Conference on Very Large Data Bases* (1991), pages 549–560.

[**Lunt 1995**] T. F. Lunt, "Authorization in Object-Oriented Databases," in [**Kim 1995**], pages 130–145.

[**Lunt et al. 1990**] T. F. Lunt, D. E. Denning, R. R. Schell, M. Heckman, and W. R. Shockley, "The SeaView Security Model," *IEEE Transactions on Software Engineering,* Volume SE-16, Number 6 (June 1990), pages 593–607.

[**Lynch 1983**] N. A. Lynch, "Multilevel Atomicity–A New Correctness Criterion for Database Concurrency Control," *ACM Transactions on Database Systems*, Volume 8, Number 4 (December 1983), pages 484–502.

[**Lynch and Merritt 1986**] N. A. Lynch and M. Merritt, "Introduction to the Theory of Nested Transactions," *Proceedings of the International Conference on Database Theory* (1986).

[**Lynch et al. 1988**] N. A. Lynch, M. Merritt, W. Weihl, and A. Fekete, "A Theory of Atomic Transactions," *Proceedings of the International Conference on Database Theory* (1988), pages 41–71.

[**Lynch et al. 1994**] N. A. Lynch, M. Merritt, W. Weihl, and A. Fekete, *Atomic Transactions*, Morgan Kaufmann Publishers, Inc., San Mateo, CA (1994).

[**Lyngbaek and Vianu 1987**] P. Lyngbaek and V. Vianu, "Mapping a Semantic Database Model to the Relational Model," *Proceedings of the ACM SIGMOD International Conference on the Management of Data* (1987), pages 132–142.

[**Mackert and Lohman 1986**] L. F. Mackert, G. M. Lohman, "R* Optimizer Validation and Performance Evaluation for Distributed Queries," *Proceedings of the International Conference on Very Large Data Bases* (August 1986).

[**Maier 1983**] D. Maier, *The Theory of Relational Databases*, Computer Science Press, Rockville, MD (1983).

[**Maier and Stein 1986**] D. Maier and J. Stein, "Indexing in an Object-Oriented DBMS," *Proceedings of the International Workshop on Object-Oriented Database Systems* (1986).

[**Maier et al. 1986**] D. Maier, J. Stein, A. Otis, and A. Purdy, "Development of an Object-Oriented DBMS," *Proceedings of the International Conference on Object-Oriented Programming Systems, Languages, and Applications* (1986), pages 472–482.

[**Makinouchi 1977**] A. Makinouchi, "A Consideration of Normal Form on Not-necessarily Normalized Relations in the Relational Data Model," *Proceedings of the International Conference on Very Large Data Bases* (1977), pages 447–453.

[**Malamud 1989**] C. Malamud, *Ingres: Tools for Building an Information Architecture*, Van Nostrand Reinhold (1989).

[**Malley and Zdonick 1986**] C. Malley and S. Zdonick, "A Knowledge-Based Approach to Query Optimization," *Proceedings of the International Conference on Expert Database Systems* (1986), pages 329–344.

[**Manber and Ladner 1984**] U. Manber and R. E. Ladner, "Concurrency Control in a Dynamic Search Structure," *ACM Transactions on Database Systems*, Volume 9, Number 3 (September 1984), pages 439–455.

[**March et al. 1981**] S. T. March, D. G. Severance, and M. Wilens, "Frame Memory: A Storage Architecture to Support Rapid Design and Implementation of Efficient Databases," *ACM Transactions on Database Systems*, Volume 6, Number 3 (September 1981), pages 441–463.

[**Markowitz and Raz 1983**] V. Markowitz and Y. Raz, "ERROL: An Entity-Relationship, Role Oriented, Query Language," in [**Davis et al. 1983**].

[**Markowitz and Shoshani 1992**] V. M. Markowitz and A. Shoshani, "Represented Extended Entity-Relationship Structures in Relational Databases," *ACM Transactions on Database Systems*, Volume 17 (1992), pages 385–422.

[**Martin et al. 1989**] J. Martin, K. K. Chapman, and J. Leben, *DB2: Concepts, Design, and Programming*, Prentice-Hall, Englewood Cliffs, NJ (1989).

[**Mattison 1996**] R. Mattison, *Data Warehousing: Strategies, Technologies, and Techniques*, McGraw-Hill, New York, NY (1996).

[**McCarthy and Dayal 1989**] D. McCarthy and U. Dayal, "The Architecture of an Active Database Management System," *Proceedings of the ACM SIGMOD International Conference on Management of Data* (1989), pages 215–224.

[**McCune and Henschen 1989**] W. W. McCune and L. J. Henschen, "Maintaining State Constraints in Relational Databases: A Proof Theoretic Basis," *Journal of the ACM*, Volume 36, Number 1 (January 1989), pages 46–68.

[McGee 1977] W. C. McGee, "The Information Management System IMS/VS Part I: General Structure and Operation," *IBM Systems Journal*, Volume 16, Number 2 (June 1977), pages 84–168.

[Mehrotra et al. 1991] S. Mehrotra, R. Rastogi, H. F. Korth, and A. Silberschatz, "Non-Serializable Executions in Heterogeneous Distributed Database Systems," *Proceedings of the First International Conference on Parallel and Distributed Information Systems* (December 1991).

[Mehrotra et al. 1992a] S. Mehrotra, R. Rastogi, H. F. Korth, A. Silberschatz, and Y. Breitbart, "The Concurrency Control Problem in Multidatabases: Characteristics and Solutions," *Proceedings of the ACM SIGMOD International Conference on Management of Data* (1992).

[Mehrotra et al. 1992b] S. Mehrotra, R. Rastogi, Y. Breitbart, H. F. Korth, and A. Silberschatz, "Ensuring Transaction Atomicity in Multidatabase Systems," *ACM SIGACT-SIGMOD Symposium on the Principles of Database Systems* (1992).

[Melton 1993] J. Melton (Editor), *ISO/ANSI Working Draft: Database Language SQL (SQL3)*, X3H2-93-091/ISO DBL YOK-003.

[Melton 1996] J. Melton, "An SQL-3 Snapshot," *Proceedings of the International Conference on Data Engineering* (1996), pages 666–672.

[Melton and Simon 1993] J. Melton and A. R. Simon, *Understanding The New SQL: A Complete Guide*, Morgan Kaufmann, San Francisco, CA (1993).

[Menasce and Muntz 1979] D. A. Menasce and R. R. Muntz, "Locking and Deadlock Detection in Distributed Databases," *IEEE Transactions on Software Engineering*, Volume SE-5, Number 3 (May 1979), pages 195–202.

[Menasce et al. 1980] D. A. Menasce, G. Popek, and R. Muntz, "A Locking Protocol for Resource Coordination in Distributed Databases," *ACM Transactions on Database Systems*, Volume 5, Number 2 (June 1980), pages 103–138.

[Mendelzon and Maier 1979] A. O. Mendelzon and D. Maier, "Generalized Mutual Dependencies and the Decomposition of Database Relations," *Proceedings of the International Conference on Very Large Data Bases* (1979), pages 75–82.

[Meng et al. 1995] W. Meng, C. Yu, and W. Kim, "A Theory of Translation from Relational to Hierarchical Queues," *IEEE Transactions on Knowledge and Data Engineering*, Volume 7, Number 2 (April 1995), pages 228–245.

[Microsoft 1992] *ODBC Programmer's Reference*, Microsoft Press (1992).

[Minker 1988] J. Minker, *Foundations of Deductive Databases and Logic Programming*, Morgan-Kaufmann, San Mateo, CA (1988).

[Mohan 1990a] C. Mohan, "ARIES/KVL: A Key-Value Locking Method for Concurrency Control of Multiaction Transactions Operations on B-Tree indexes," *Proceedings of the International Conference on Very Large Data Bases* (1990), pages 392–405.

[Mohan 1990b] C. Mohan, "Commit-LSN: A Novel and Simple Method for Reducing Locking and Latching in Transaction Processing Systems," *Proceedings of the International Conference on Very Large Data Bases* (1990), pages 406–418.

[Mohan 1993] C. Mohan, "IBM's Relational Database Products: Features and Technologies," *Proceedings of the ACM SIGMOD International Conference on Management of Data* (1993).

[**Mohan and Levine 1992**] C. Mohan and F. Levine, "ARIES/IM: An Efficient and High-Concurrency Index Management Method Using Write-Ahead Logging," *Proceedings of the ACM SIGMOD International Conference on Management of Data* (1992).

[**Mohan and Lindsay 1983**] C. Mohan and B. Lindsay, "Efficient Commit Protocols for the Tree of Processes Model of Distributed Transactions," *Proceedings of the Second ACM SIGACT-SIGOPS Symposium on the Principles of Distributed Computing* (1983).

[**Mohan and Narang 1991**] C. Mohan and I. Narang, "Recovery and Coherency-Control Protocols for Fast Intersystem Page Transfer and Fine-Granularity Locking in a Shared Disks Transaction Environment," *Proceedings of the International Conference on Very Large Data Bases* (September 1991).

[**Mohan and Narang 1992**] C. Mohan and I. Narang, "Efficient Locking and Caching of Data in the Multisystem Shared Disks Transaction Environment," *Proceedings of the International Conference on Extending Database Technology* (1992).

[**Mohan and Narang 1994**] C. Mohan and I. Narang, "ARIES/CSA: A Method for Database Recovery in Client-Server Architectures," *Proceedings of the ACM SIGMOD International Conference on Management of Data* (May 1994), pages 55–66.

[**Mohan et al. 1986**] C. Mohan, B. Lindsay, and R. Obermarck, "Transaction Management in the R\* Distributed Database Management System," *ACM Transactions on Database Systems,* Volume 11, Number 4 (December 1986), pages 378–396.

[**Mohan et al. 1991**] C. Mohan, D. Haderle, B. Lindsay, H. Pirahesh, and P. Schwarz, "ARIES: A Transaction Recovery Method Supporting Fine-Granularity Locking and Partial Rollback Using Write-Ahead Logging," *ACM Transactions on Database Systems* (1991).

[**Mohan et al. 1992**] C. Mohan, "ARIES: A Transaction Recovery Method Supporting Fine-Granularity Locking and Partial Rollbacks Using Write-Ahead Logging," *ACM Transactions on Database Systems*, Volume 17, Number 1 (March 1992).

[**Mok et al. 1996**] W. Y. Mok, Y.-K. Ng, and D. W. Embley, "A Normal Form for Precisely Characterizing Redundancy in Nested Relations," *ACM Transactions on Database Systems*, Volume 21, Number 1 (March 1996), pages 77–106.

[**Moss 1982**] J. E. B. Moss, "Nested Transactions and Reliable Distributed Computing," *Proceedings of the Symposium on Reliability in Distributed Software and Database Systems* (1982).

[**Moss 1985**] J. E. B. Moss, *Nested Transactions: An Approach to Reliable Distributed Computing,* MIT Press, Cambridge, MA (1985).

[**Moss 1987**] J. E. B. Moss, "Log-Based Recovery for Nested Transactions," *Proceedings of the International Conference on Very Large Data Bases* (1987), pages 427–432.

[**Moss 1990**] J. E. B. Moss, "Working with Objects: To Swizzle or Not to Swizzle," Technical Report COINS TR 90-38, Computer and Information Science, University of Massachusetts, Amherst (1990).

[**MRI 1974**] MRI Systems Corporation, "System 2000 Reference Manual," Document UMN-1 (1974).

[**MRI 1979**] MRI Systems Corporation, "Language Specification Manual: The DEFINE Language," Document LSM-DEF-10 (1979).

[**Mumick et al. 1996**] I. S. Mumick, S. Finkelstein, H. Pirahesh, and R. Ramakrishnan, "Magic Conditions," *ACM Transactions on Database Systems*, Volume 21, Number 1 (March 1996), pages 107–155.

[**Nakayama et al. 1984**] T. Nakayama, M. Hirakawa, and T. Ichikawa, "Architecture and Algorithm for Parallel Execution of a Join Operation," *Proceedings of the International Conference on Data Engineering* (1984).

[**Naqvi and Tsur 1988**] S. Naqvi and S. Tsur, *A Logic Language for Data and Knowledge Bases*, Computer Science Press, Rockville, MD (1988).

[**Nelson and Cheng 1992**] B. Nelson and Y. Cheng, "How and Why SCSI is better than IPI for NFS," *Proceedings of the Winter 1992 USENIX Conference,* San Francisco, CA, (January 1992), pages 253–270.

[**Ng and Han 1994**] R. T. Ng and J. Han, "Efficient and Effective Clustering Methods for Spatial Data Mining," *Proceedings of the International Conference on Very Large Data Bases* (1994).

[**Nguyen and Srinivasan 1996**] T. Nguyen and V. Srinivasan, "Accessing Relational Databases from the World Wide Web," *Proceedings of the ACM SIGMOD International Conference on the Management of Data* (1996).

[**Nievergelt et al. 1984**] J. Nievergelt, H. Hinterberger, and K. C. Sevcik, "The Grid File: An Adaptable Symmetric Multikey File Structure," *ACM Transactions on Database Systems*, Volume 9, Number 1 (March 1984), pages 38–71.

[**Nijssen 1976**] G. M. Nijssen (Editor), *Modeling in Data Base Management Systems*, North Holland, Amsterdam, The Netherlands (1976).

[**North 1995**] K. North, *Windows Multi-DBMS Programming: Using C++, Visual Basic, ODBC, OLE2, and Tools for DBMS Projects*, John Wiley and Sons, New York, NY (1995).

[**Obermarck 1980**] R. Obermarck "IMS/VS Program Isolation Feature," Research Report RJ2879, IBM Research Laboratory, San Jose, CA (1980).

[**Obermarck 1982**] R. Obermarck, "Distributed Deadlock Detection Algorithm," *ACM Transactions on Database Systems*, Volume 7, Number 2 (June 1982), pages 187–208.

[**O'Leary and Kitts 1985**] B. T. O'Leary and D. L. Kitts, "Optical Device for a Mass Storage System," *IEEE Computer*, Volume 18, Number 7 (July 1985).

[**Olsen and Kenley 1989**] R. P. Olsen and G. Kenley, "Virtual Optical Disks Solve the On-Line Storage Crunch," *Computer Design,* Volume 28, Number 1 (January 1989), pages 93–96.

[**O'Neil 1994**] P. O'Neil, *Database: Principles, Programming, Performance*, Morgan Kaufmann Publishers, Inc. (1994).

[**Oracle 1992**] Oracle Corporation, *Oracle 7 Concepts Manual,* Redwood Shores, Ca (1992).

[**Orestein 1982**] J.A. Orestein, "Multidimensional Tries Used for Associative Searching," *Information Processing Letters*, Volume 14, Number 4 (June 1982), pages 150–157.

[**Ozden et al. 1994**] B. Özden, A. Biliris, R. Rastogi, and A. Silberschatz, "A Low-cost Storage Server for a Movie on Demand Database," *International Conference on Very Large Databases* (September 1994).

[**Ozden et al. 1995a**] B. Özden, R. Rastogi, and A. Silberschatz, "A Framework for the Storage and Retrieval of Continuous Media Data," *IEEE International Conference on Multimedia Computing and Systems* (May 1995).

[**Ozden et al. 1995b**] B. Özden, R. Rastogi, and A. Silberschatz, "Research Issues in Multimedia Storage Servers," *ACM Computing Surveys*, Volume 27, Number 4 (December 1995), pages 617–620.

[**Ozden et al. 1996a**] B. Özden, R. Rastogi, and A. Silberschatz, "On the Design of a Low-Cost Video-on-Demand Storage System," *Multimedia Systems Journal*, Volume 4, Number 1 (February 1996), pages 40–54.

[**Ozden et al. 1996b**] B. Özden, R. Rastogi, P. Shenoy, and A. Silberschatz, "Fault-Tolerant Architectures for Continuous Media Servers," *ACM-SIGMOD International Conference on Management of Data* (May 1996).

[**Ozsoyoglu and Snodgrass 1995**] G. Ozsoyoglu and R. Snodgrass, "Temporal and Real-Time Databases: A Survey," *IEEE Transactions on Knowledge and Data Engineering*, Volume 7, Number 4 (August 1995), pages 513–532.

[**Ozsoyoglu and Yuan 1987**] G. Ozsoyoglu and L. Yuan, "Reduced MVDs and Minimal Covers," *ACM Transactions on Database Systems*, Volume 12, Number 3 (September 1987), pages 377–394.

[**Ozsoyoglu et al. 1987**] G. Ozsoyoglu, Z. M. Ozsoyoglu, and V. Matos, "Extending Relational Algebra and Relational Calculus with Set-Valued Attributes and Aggregate Functions," *ACM Transactions on Database Systems*, Volume 12, Number 4 (December 1987), pages 566–592.

[**Ozsu and Valduriez 1991**] T. Ozsu and P. Valduriez, *Principles of Distributed Database Systems*, Prentice-Hall, Englewood Cliffs, NJ (1991).

[**Pang et al. 1995**] H.-H. Pang, M. J. Carey, and M. Livny, "Multiclass Scheduling in Real-Time Database Systems," *IEEE Transactions on Knowledge and Data Engineering*, Volume 7, Number 4 (August 1995), pages 533-551.

[**Papadimitriou 1979**] C. H. Papadimitriou, "The Serializability of Concurrent Database Updates," *Journal of the ACM*, Volume 26, Number 4 (October 1979), pages 631–653.

[**Papadimitriou 1982**] C. H. Papadimitriou, "A Theorem in Database Concurrency Control," *Journal of the ACM*, Volume 29, Number 5 (October 1982), pages 998–1006.

[**Papadimitriou 1986**] C. H. Papadimitriou, *The Theory of Database Concurrency Control*, Computer Science Press, Rockville, MD (1986).

[**Papadimitriou et al. 1977**] C. H. Papadimitriou, P. A. Bernstein, and J. B. Rothnie, "Some Computational Problems Related to Database Concurrency Control," *Proceedings of the Conference on Theoretical Computer Science* (1977), pages 275–282.

[**Parent and Spaccapietra 1985**] C. Parent and S. Spaccapietra, "An Algebra for a General Entity-Relationship Model," *IEEE Transactions on Software Engineering*, Volume SE-11, Number 7 (July 1985), pages 634–643.

[**Parker et al. 1983**] D. S. Parker, G. J. Popek, G. Rudisin, A. Stoughton, B. J. Walker, E. Walton, J.M. Chow, D. Edwards, S. Kiser, and C. Kline, "Detection of Mutual

Inconsistency in Distributed Systems," *IEEE Transactions on Software Engineering*, Volume 9, Number 3 (May 1983), pages 240–246.

**[Patel and DeWitt 1996]** J. Patel and D. J. DeWitt, "Partition Based Spatial-Merge Join," *Proceedings of the ACM SIGMOD International Conference on the Management of Data* (1996).

**[Patterson and Hennessy 1995]** D. A. Patterson and J. L. Hennessy, *Computer Architecture: A Quantitative Approach*, Second Edition, Morgan Kaufmann Publishers, Inc., San Mateo, CA (1995).

**[Patterson et al. 1988]** D. A. Patterson, G. Gibson, and R. H. Katz, "A Case for Redundant Arrays of Inexpensive Disks (RAID)," *Proceedings of the ACM SIGMOD International Conference on the Management of Data* (1988), pages 109–116.

**[Pecherer 1975]** R. M. Pecherer, "Efficient Evaluation of Expressions in a Relational Algebra," *Proceedings of the ACM Pacific Conference* (1975), pages 17–18.

**[Pechura and Schoeffler 1983]** M. A. Pechura and J. D. Schoeffler, "Estimating File Access Time of Floppy Disks," *Communications of the ACM*, Volume 26, Number 10 (October 1983), pages 754–763.

**[Peckham and Maryanski 1988]** J. Peckham and F. Maryanski, "Semantic Data Models," *Computing Surveys*, Volume 20, Number 3 (September 1988), pages 153–189.

**[Penney and Stein 1987]** J. Penney and J. Stein, "Class Modification in the GemStone Object-Oriented DBMS," *Proceedings of the International Conference on Object-Oriented Programming Systems, Languages, and Applications* (1987).

**[Pless 1989]** V. Pless, *Introduction to the Theory of Error-Correcting Codes*, Second Edition, John Wiley and Sons, New York, NY (1989).

**[Poe 1995]** V. Poe, *Building a Data Warehouse for Decision Support*, Prentice-Hall, Englewood Cliffs, NJ (1995).

**[Polyzois and Garcia-Molina 1994]** C. Polyzois and H. Garcia-Molina, "Evaluation of Remote Backup Algorithms for Transaction-Processing Systems," *ACM Transactions on Database Systems*, Volume 19, Number 3 (September 1994), pages 423–449.

**[Poosala et al. 1996]** V. Poosala, Y. E. Ioannidis, P. J. Haas, and E. J. Shekita, "Improved Histograms for Selectivity Estimation of Range Predicates," *Proceedings of the ACM SIGMOD International Conference on Management of Data* (1996), pages 294–305.

**[Popek at al. 1981]** G. J. Popek, B. J. Walker, J. M. Chow, D. Edwards, C. Kline, G. Rudisin, and G. Thiel, "LOCUS: A Network Transparent, High Reliability Distributed System," *Proceedings of the Eighth Symposium on Operating System Principles*, (1981), pages 169–177.

**[Prycker 1993]** M. de Prycker, *Asynchronous Transfer Mode: Solution for Broadband ISDN*, Second Edition, Ellis Horwood (1993).

**[Pu et al. 1988]** C. Pu, G. Kaiser, and N. Hutchinson, "Split-transactions for Open-Ended Activities," *Proceedings of the International Conference on Very Large Data Bases* (1988), pages 26–37.

**[Qian and Lunt 1996]** X. Qian and T. F. Lunt, "A MAC Policy Framework for Multilevel Relational Databases," *IEEE Transactions on Knowledge and Data Engineering*, Volume 8, Number 1 (February 1996), pages 3–15.

**[Quarterman 1990]** J. S. Quarterman, *The Matrix: Computer Networks and Conferencing Systems Worldwide*, Digital Press, Bedford, MA (1990).

[**Rabitti et al. 1988**] F. Rabitti, D. Woelk, and W. Kim, "A Model of Authorization for Object-Oriented and Semantic Databases," *Proceedings of the International Conference on Extending Database Technology* (1988), pages 231–250.

[**Rabitti et al. 1991**] F. Rabitti, E. Bertino, W. Kim, and D. Woelk, "A Model of Authorization for Next-Generation Database Systems," *ACM Transactions on Database Systems,* Volume 16, Number 1 (March 1991), pages 88–131.

[**Rahm 1993**] E. Rahm, "Empirical Performance Evaluation of Concurrency and Coherency Control Protocols for Database Sharing Systems," *ACM Transactions on Database Systems*, Volume 18, Number 2 (June 1993).

[**Ramakrishna and Larson 1989**] M. V. Ramakrishna and P. Larson, "File Organization Using Composite Perfect Hashing," *ACM Transactions on Database Systems,* Volume 14, Number 2 (June 1989), pages 231–263.

[**Ramakrishnan and Ullman 1995**] R. Ramakrishnan and J. D. Ullman, "A Survey of Deductive Database Systems," *Journal of Logic Programming,* Volume 23, Number 2 (1995), pages 125–149.

[**Ramakrishnan et al. 1992a**] R. Ramakrishnan, D. Srivastava, and S. Sudarshan, "CORAL: Control, Relations, and Logic," *Proceedings of the International Conference on Very Large Data Bases* (1992), pages 238–250.

[**Ramakrishnan et al. 1992b**] R. Ramakrishnan, D. Srivastava, and S. Sudarshan, "Efficient Bottom-up Evaluation of Logic Programs," in [**Vandewalle 1992**].

[**Ramakrishnan et al. 1992c**] R. Ramakrishnan, D. Srivastava, and S. Sudarshan, "Controlling the Search in Bottom-up Evaluation," *Joint International Conference and Symposium on Logic Programming* (1992), pages 273–287.

[**Ramakrishnan et al. 1993**] R. Ramakrishnan, D. Srivastava, S. Sudarshan, and P. Sheshadri, "Implementation of the CORAL Deductive Database System," *Proceedings of the ACM SIGMOD International Conference on Management of Data* (1993), pages 167–176.

[**Ramesh et al. 1989**] R. Ramesh, A. J. G. Babu, and J. P. Kincaid, "Index Optimization: Theory and Experimental Results," *ACM Transactions on Database Systems,* Volume 14, Number 1 (March 1989), pages 41–74.

[**Ranft et al. 1990**] M. Ranft, S. Rehm, and K. Dittrich, "How to Share Work on Shared Objects in Design Databases," *Proceedings of the International Conference on Data Engineering* (1990).

[**Rangan et al. 1992**] P. V. Rangan, H. M. Vin, and S. Ramanathan, "Designing an On-Demand Multimedia Service," *IEEE Communications Magazine*, Volume 1, Number 1 (July 1992), pages 56–64.

[**Reason et al. 1996**] J. M. Reason, L. C. Yun, A. Y. Lao, and D. G. Messerschmitt, "Asynchronous Video: Coordinated Video Coding and Transport for Heterogeneous Networks with Wireless Access," in [**Imielinski and Korth 1996**], Chapter 10.

[**Reed 1978**] D. Reed, "Naming and Synchronization in a Decentralized Computer System," Ph.D. thesis, Department of Electrical Engineering, MIT, Cambridge, MA (1978).

[**Reed 1983**] D. Reed, "Implementing Atomic Actions on Decentralized Data," *ACM Transactions on Computer Systems*, Volume 1, Number 1 (February 1983), pages 3–23.

[**Reuter 1980**] A. Reuter, "A Fast Transaction-Oriented Logging Scheme for UNDO Recovery," *IEEE Transactions on Software Engineering*, Volume SE-6, Number 4 (July 1980), pages 348–356.

[**Reuter 1989**] A. Reuter, "ConTracts: A Means for Extending Control Beyond Transaction Boundaries," *Proceedings of the 3rd International Workshop on High Performance Transaction Systems* (September 1989).

[**Richardson et al. 1987**] J. Richardson, H. Lu, and K. Mikkilineni, "Design and Evaluation of Parallel Pipelined Join Algorithms," *Proceedings of the ACM SIGMOD International Conference on Management of Data* (1987).

[**Ries and Stonebraker 1977**] D. R. Ries and M. Stonebraker, "Effects of Locking Granularity in a Database Management System," *ACM Transactions on Database Systems*, Volume 2, Number 3 (September 1977), pages 233–246.

[**Rissanen 1979**] J. Rissanen, "Theory of Joins for Relational Databases - A Tutorial Survey," *Proceedings of the Symposium on Mathematical Foundations of Computer Science*, Springer-Verlag, Berlin, Germany (1979), pages 537–551.

[**Rivest 1976**] R. L Rivest, "Partial Match Retrieval Via the Method of Superimposed Codes," *SIAM Journal of Computing*, Volume 5, Number 1 (1976), pages 19–50.

[**Rivest et al. 1978**] R. L. Rivest, A. Shamir, and L. Adelman, "On Digital Signatures and Public Key Cryptosystems," *Communications of the ACM*, Volume 21, Number 2 (February 1978), pages 120–126.

[**Robinson 1981**] J. Robinson. "The k-d-B Tree: A Search Structure for Large Multidimensional Indexes," *Proceedings of the ACM SIGMOD International Conference on Management of Data* (1981), pages 10–18.

[**Rosenblum and Ousterhout 1991**] M. Rosenblum and J. K. Ousterhout, "The Design and Implementation of a Log-Structured File System," *Proceedings of the 13th ACM Symposium on Operating Systems Principles* (October 1991), pages 1–15.

[**Rosenkrantz et al. 1978**] D. J. Rosenkrantz, R. E. Stearns, and P. M. Lewis II, "System Level Concurrency Control For Distributed Data Base Systems," *ACM Transactions on Database Systems*, Volume 3, Number 2 (March 1978), pages 178–198.

[**Rosenthal and Reiner 1984**] A. Rosenthal and D. Reiner, "Extending the Algebraic Framework of Query Processing to Handle Outerjoins," *Proceedings of the International Conference on Very Large Databases* (August 1984), pages 334–343.

[**Ross 1990**] K. A. Ross, "Modular Stratification and Magic Sets for DATALOG Programs with Negation," *ACM SIGACT-SIGMOD Symposium on the Principles of Database Systems* (April 1990).

[**Roth and Korth 1987**] M. A. Roth and H. F. Korth, "The Design of ¬1NF Relational Databases into Nested Normal Form," *Proceedings of the ACM SIGMOD International Conference on Management of Data* (1987), pages 143–159.

[**Roth et al. 1988**] M. A. Roth, H. F. Korth, and A. Silberschatz, "Extended Algebra and Calculus for Nested Relational Databases," *ACM Transactions on Database Systems*, Volume 13, Number 4 (December 1988), pages 389–417.

[**Roth et al. 1989**] M. A. Roth, H. F. Korth, and A. Silberschatz, "Null Values in Nested Relational Databases," *Acta Informatica*, Volume 26 (1989), pages 615–642.

[**Rothermel and Mohan 1989**] K. Rothermel and C. Mohan, "ARIES/NT: A Recovery Method Based on Write-Ahead Logging for Nested Transactions," *Proceedings of the International Conference on Very Large Data Bases* (August 1989), pages 337–346.

[**Rothnie and Goodman 1977**] J. B. Rothnie, Jr. and N. Goodman, "A Survey of Research and Development in Distributed Database Management," *Proceedings of the International Conference on Very Large Data Bases* (1977), pages 48–62.

[**Roussopoulos and Mylopoulos 1975**] N. Roussopoulos and J. Mylopoulos, "Using Semantic Networks for Data Base Management," *Proceedings of the International Conference on Very Large Data Bases* (1975), pages 144–172.

[**Ruemmler and Wilkes 1994**] C. Ruemmler and J. Wilkes, "An Introduction to Disk Drive Modeling," *IEEE Computer*, Volume 27, Number 3 (March 1994), pages 17–27.

[**Rusinkiewicz and Sheth 1995**] M. Rusinkiewicz and A. Sheth, "Specification and Execution of Transactional Workflows," in [**Kim 1995**], pages 592–620.

[**Rustin 1972**] R. Rustin (Editor), *Data Base Systems*, Prentice-Hall, Englewood Cliffs, NJ (1972).

[**Sacks-Davis et al. 1995**] R. Sacks-Davis, A. Kent, K. Ramamohanarao, J. Thom, and J. Zobel, "Atlas: A Nested Relational Database System for Text Applications," *IEEE Transactions on Knowledge and Data Engineering,* Volume 7, Number 3 (June 1995), pages 454–470.

[**Sadri and Ullman 1982**] F. Sadri and J. Ullman, "Template Dependencies: A Large Class of Dependencies in Relational Databases and Its Complete Axiomatization," *Journal of the ACM*, Volume 29, Number 2 (April 1982), pages 363–372.

[**Sagiv and Yannakakis 1981**] Y.Sagiv and M. Yannakakis, "Equivalence among Relational Expressions with the Union and Difference Operators," *Journal of the ACM*, Volume 27, Number 4 (November 1981).

[**Salem and Garcia-Molina 1986**] K. Salem and H. Garcia-Molina, "Disk Striping," *Proceedings of the International Conference on Data Engineering* (1986), pages 336–342.

[**Salem et al. 1994**] K. Salem, H. Garcia-Molina, and J. Sands, "Altruistic Locking," *ACM Transactions on Database Systems*, Volume 19, Number 1 (March 1994), pages 117–165.

[**Salton 1989**] G. Salton, *Automatic Text Processing,* Addison Wesley, Reading, MA (1989).

[**Samet 1990**] H. Samet, *The Design and Analysis of Spatial Data Structures,* Addison Wesley, Reading, MA (1990).

[**Samet 1995a**] H. Samet, "General Research Issues in Multimedia Database Systems," *ACM Computing Surveys*, Volume 27, Number 4 (1995), pages 630–632.

[**Samet 1995b**] H. Samet, "Spatial Data Structures," in [**Kim 1995**], pages 361–385.

[**Samet and Aref 1995**] H. Samet and W. Aref, "Spatial Data Models and Query Processing," in [**Kim 1995**], pages 338–360.

[**Sarisky 1983**] L. Sarisky, "Will Removable Hard Disks Replace the Floppy?," *Byte* (March 1983), pages 110–117.

[**Satyanarayanan 1980**] M. Satyanarayanan, *Multiprocessors: A Comparative Study,* Prentice-Hall, Englewood Cliffs, NJ (1980).

[**Schenk 1974**] K. L. Schenk, "Implementational Aspects of the CODASYL DBTG Proposal," *Proceedings of the IFIP Working Conference on Data Base Management Systems* (1974).

[**Schlageter 1981**] G. Schlageter, "Optimistic Methods for Concurrency Control in Distributed Database Systems," *Proceedings of the International Conference on Very Large Data Bases* (1981), pages 125–130.

[**Schmid and Swenson 1975**] H. A. Schmid and J. R. Swenson, "On the Semantics of the Relational Model," *Proceedings of the ACM SIGMOD International Conference on the Management of Data* (1975), pages 211-223.

[**Schneider 1982**] H. J. Schneider, "Distributed Data Bases," *Proceedings of the International Symposium on Distributed Databases* (1982).

[**Schneider and DeWitt 1989**] D. Schneider and D. DeWitt, "A Performance Evaluation of Four Parallel Join Algorithms in a Shared-Nothing Multiprocessor Environment," *Proceedings of the ACM SIGMOD International Conference on the Management of Data* (1989).

[**Schneiderman 1978**] B. Schneiderman (Editor), *Database: Improving Usability and Responsiveness*, Academic Press, New York, NY (1978).

[**Sciore 1982**] E. Sciore, "A Complete Axiomatization for Full Join Dependencies," *Journal of the ACM*, Volume 29, Number 2 (April 1982), pages 373–393.

[**Selinger and Adiba 1980**] P. G. Selinger and M. E. Adiba, "Access Path Selection in Distributed Database Management Systems," Research Report RJ2338, IBM Research Laboratory, San Jose, CA (1980).

[**Selinger et al. 1979**] P. G. Selinger, M. M. Astrahan, D. D. Chamberlin, R. A. Lorie, and T. G. Price, "Access Path Selection in a Relational Database System," *Proceedings of the ACM SIGMOD International Conference on the Management of Data* (1979), pages 23–34.

[**Sellis 1988**] T. K. Sellis, "Multiple Query Optimization," *ACM Transactions on Database Systems*, Volume 13, Number 1 (March 1988), pages 23–52.

[**Sellis et al. 1987**] T. K. Sellis, N. Roussopoulos, and C. Faloutsos, "The $R^+$-Tree: A Dynamic Index for Multi-Dimensional Objects," *Proceedings of the International Conference on Very Large Data Bases* (1987), pages 507–518.

[**Seshadri and Naughton 1992**] S. Seshadri and J. Naughton, "Sampling Issues in Parallel Database Systems," *Proceedings of the International Conference on Extending Database Technology* (1992).

[**Sha et al. 1988**] L. Sha, J. Lehoczky, and D. Jensen, "Modular Concurrency Control and Failure Recovery," *IEEE Transactions on Computing*, Volume 37, Number 2 (February 1988), pages 146–159.

[**Shapiro 1986**] L. D. Shapiro, "Join Processing in Database Systems with Large Main Memories," *ACM Transactions on Database Systems*, Volume 11, Number 3 (September 1986), pages 239–264.

[**Shasha 1992**] D. Shasha, *Database Tuning: A Principled Approach,* Prentice-Hall, Englewood Cliffs, NJ (1992).

[**Shasha and Goodman 1988**] D. Shasha and N. Goodman, "Concurrent Search Structure Algorithms," *ACM Transactions on Database Systems*, Volume 13, Number 1 (March 1988), pages 53–90.

[**Shasha et al. 1995**] D. Shasha, F. Llirabat, E. Simon, and P. Valduriez, "Transaction Chopping: Algorithms and Performance Studies," *ACM Transactions on Database Systems*, Volume 20, Number 3 (September 1995), pages 325–363.

[**Shatdal and Naughton 1993**] A. Shatdal and J. Naughton, "Using Shared Virtual Memory for Parallel Join Processing," *Proceedings of the ACM SIGMOD International Conference on the Management of Data* (1993).

[**Sheard and Stemple 1989**] T. Sheard and D. Stemple, "Automatic Verification of Database Transaction Safety," *ACM Transactions on Database Systems*, Volume 14, Number 3 (September 1989), pages 322–368.

[**Shipman 1981**] D. Shipman, "The Functional Data Model and the Data Language DAPLEX," *ACM Transactions on Database Systems*, Volume 6, Number 1 (March 1981), pages 140–173.

[**Sibley 1976**] E. Sibley, "The Development of Database Technology," *ACM Computing Surveys*, Volume 8, Number 1 (March 1976), pages 1–5.

[**Sibley and Kerschberg 1977**] E. Sibley and L. Kerschberg, "Data Architecture and Data Model Considerations," *Proceedings of the AFIPS National Computer Conference* (1977).

[**Signore et al. 1995**] R. Signore, J. Creamer, M. O. Stegman, *The ODBC Solution: Open Database Connectivity in Distributed Environments*, McGraw-Hill, New York, NY (1995).

[**Silberschatz 1982**] A. Silberschatz, "A Multi-Version Concurrency Control Scheme With No Rollbacks," *ACM SIGACT-SIGOPS Symposium on Principles of Distributed Computing* (1982), pages 216–223.

[**Silberschatz and Galvin 1994**] A. Silberschatz and P. Galvin, *Operating System Concepts,* Fourth Edition, Addison Wesley, Reading, MA (1994).

[**Silberschatz and Kedem 1980**] A. Silberschatz and Z. Kedem, "Consistency in Hierarchical Database Systems," *Journal of the ACM*, Volume 27, Number 1 (January 1980), pages 72–80.

[**Silberschatz et al. 1990**] A. Silberschatz, M. R. Stonebraker, and J. D. Ullman (Editors), "Database Systems: Achievements and Opportunities," *ACM SIGMOD Record,* Volume 19, Number 4 (1990).

[**Silberschatz et al. 1996**] A. Silberschatz, M. Stonebraker, and J. Ullman, "Database Research: Achievements and Opportunities into the 21st Century," Technical Report CS-TR-96-1563, Department of Computer Science, Stanford University, Stanford, CA (1996).

[**Simmons 1979**] G. J. Simmons, "Symmetric and Asymmetric Encryption," *ACM Computing Surveys*, Volume 11, Number 4 (December 1979), pages 304–330.

[**Skarra and Zdonik 1986**] A. Skarra and S. Zdonik, "The Management of Changing Types in an Object-Oriented Database," *Proceedings of the International Conference on Object-Oriented Programming Systems, Languages, and Applications* (1986).

[**Skarra and Zdonik 1989**] A. Skarra and S. Zdonik, "Concurrency Control in Object-Oriented Databases," in [**Kim and Lochovsky 1989**], pages 395–421.

[**Skeen 1981**] D. Skeen, "Non-blocking Commit Protocols," *Proceedings of the ACM SIGMOD International Conference on the Management of Data* (1981), pages 133–142.

**[Smith 1982]** A. J. Smith, "Cache Memories," *ACM Computing Surveys,* Volume 14, Number 3 (September 1982), pages 473–530

**[Smith and Barnes 1987]** P. Smith and G. Barnes, *Files and Databases: An Introduction,* Addison Wesley, Reading, MA (1987).

**[Smith and Smith 1977]** J. M. Smith and D. C. P. Smith, "Database Abstractions: Aggregation and Generalization," *ACM Transactions on Database Systems,* Volume 2, Number 2 (March 1977), pages 105–133.

**[Smith et al. 1996]** K. P. Smith, B. T. Blaustein, S. Jajodia, L. Notargiacomo, "Correctness Criteria for Multilevel Secure Transactions," *IEEE Transactions on Knowledge and Data Engineering,* Volume 8, Number 1 (February 1996), pages 32–45.

**[Snodgrass 1987]** R. Snodgrass, "The Temporal Query Language TQuel," *ACM Transactions on Database Systems,* Volume 12, Number 2 (March 1987), pages 247–298.

**[Snodgrass and Ahn 1985]** R. Snodgrass and I. Ahn, "A Taxonomy of Time in Databases," *Proceedings of the ACM SIGMOD International Conference on the Management of Data* (1985), pages 236–246.

**[Snodgrass et al. 1994]** R. Snodgrass and others, "TSQL2 Language Specification," *ACM SIGMOD Record,* Volume 23, Number 1 (March 1994), pages 65–86.

**[Soo 1991]** M. Soo, "Bibliography on Temporal Databases," *ACM SIGMOD Record,* Volume 20, Number 1 (1991) pages 14–23.

**[Soparkar et al. 1991]** N. Soparkar, H. F. Korth, and A. Silberschatz, "Failure-Resilient Transaction Management in Multidatabases," *IEEE Computer,* Volume 24, Number 12 (December 1991), pages 28–36.

**[Soparkar et al. 1995]** N. Soparkar, H. F. Korth, and A. Silberschatz, "Databases with Deadline and Contingency Constraints," *IEEE Transactions on Knowledge and Data Engineering,* Volume 7, Number 4 (August 1995), pages 552–565.

**[Spector and Schwarz 1983]** A. Z. Spector and P. M. Schwarz, "Transactions: A Construct for Reliable Distributed Computing," *ACM SIGOPS Operating Systems Review,* Volume 17, Number 2 (1983), pages 18–35.

**[Srikant and Agrawal 1996]** R. Srikant and R. Agrawal, "Mining Quantitative Association Rules in Large Relational Tables," *Proceedings of the ACM SIGMOD International Conference on the Management of Data* (1996).

**[Srivastava et al. 1995]** D. Srivastava, S. Sudarshan, R. Ramakrishnan, and J. Naughton, "Space Optimization in Deductive Databases," *ACM Transactions on Database Systems,* Volume 20, Number 4 (December 1995), pages 472–516.

**[Stachour and Thuraisingham 1990]** P. D. Stachour and B. Thuraisingham, "Design of LDV: A Multilevel Secure Relational Database Management System," *IEEE Transactions on Knowledge and Data Engineering,* Volume 2, Number 2 (June 1990), pages 190–209

**[Stam and Snodgrass 1988]** R. Stam and R. Snodgrass, "A Bibliography on Temporal Databases," *Database Engineering,* Volume 7, Number 4 (December 1988), pages 231–239.

**[Stefik and Bobrow 1986]** M. Stefik and D. G. Bobrow, "Object-Oriented Programming: Themes and Variations," *The AI Magazine* (January 1986), pages 40–62.

**[Stone 1993]** H. S. Stone, *High-Performance Computer Architecture,* Third Edition, Addison Wesley, Reading, MA (1993).

[**Stonebraker 1975**] M. Stonebraker, "Implementation of Integrity Constraints and Views by Query Modification," *Proceedings of the ACM SIGMOD International Conference on the Management of Data* (1975), pages 65–78.

[**Stonebraker 1980**] M. Stonebraker, "Retrospection on a Database System," *ACM Transactions on Database Systems*, Volume 5, Number 2 (March 1980), pages 225–240. Also in [**Stonebraker 1986b**], pages 46–62.

[**Stonebraker 1981**] M. Stonebraker, "Operating System Support for Database Management," *Communications of the ACM*, Volume 24, Number 7 (July 1981), pages 412–418. Also in [**Stonebraker 1986b**], pages 172–182.

[**Stonebraker 1986a**] M. Stonebraker, "Inclusion of New Types in Relational Database Systems," *Proceedings of the International Conference on Data Engineering* (1986), pages 262–269.

[**Stonebraker 1986b**] M. Stonebraker (Editor), *The Ingres Papers*, Addison Wesley, Reading, MA (1986).

[**Stonebraker 1987**] M. Stonebraker, "The Design of the POSTGRES Storage System," *Proceedings of the International Conference on Very Large Data Bases* (1987).

[**Stonebraker 1994**] M. Stonebraker (Editor), *Readings in Database Systems*, Second Edition, Morgan Kaufmann Publishers, Inc., San Mateo, CA (1994).

[**Stonebraker and Rowe 1986**] M. Stonebraker and L. Rowe, "The Design of POSTGRES," *Proceedings of the ACM SIGMOD International Conference on the Management of Data* (1986).

[**Stonebraker and Wong 1974**] M. Stonebraker and E. Wong, "Access Control in a Relational Database Management System by Query Modification," *Proceedings of the ACM National Conference* (1974), pages 180–187.

[**Stonebraker et al. 1976**] M. Stonebraker, E. Wong, P. Kreps, and G. D. Held, "The Design and Implementation of INGRES," *ACM Transactions on Database Systems*, Volume 1, Number 3 (September 1976), pages 189–222. Also in [**Stonebraker 1986b**], pages 1–45.

[**Stonebraker et al. 1987a**] M. Stonebraker, J. Anton, and E. Hanson, "Extending a Database System with Procedures," *ACM Transactions on Database Systems*, Volume 12, Number 3 (September 1987), pages 350–376.

[**Stonebraker et al. 1987b**] M. Stonebraker, E. Hanson, and C. H. Hong, "The Design of the POSTGRES Rule System," *Proceedings of the International Conference on Data Engineering* (1987), pages 356–374.

[**Stonebraker et al. 1989**] M. Stonebraker, P. Aoki, and M. Seltzer, "Parallelism in XPRS," *Proceedings of the ACM SIGMOD International Conference on the Management of Data* (1989).

[**Stroustrup 1988**] B. Stroustrup, "What Is Object-Oriented Programming?," *IEEE Software* (May 1988), pages 10–20.

[**Stroustrup 1992**] B. Stroustrup, *The C++ Programming Language*, Second Edition, Addison-Wesley, Reading, MA (1992).

[**Stuart et al. 1984**] D. G. Stuart, G. Buckley, and A. Silberschatz, "A Centralized Deadlock Detection Algorithm," Technical Report, Department of Computer Sciences, University of Texas, Austin, TX (1984).

[**Swami and Gupta 1988**]  A. Swami and A. Gupta, "Optimization of Large Join Queries," *Proceedings of the ACM SIGMOD International Conference on Management of Data* (1988), pages 8–17.

[**Tanenbaum 1996**]  A. S. Tanenbaum, *Computer Networks*, Third Edition, Prentice-Hall, Englewood Cliffs, NJ (1996).

[**Tansel et al. 1993**]  A. Tansel, J. Clifford, S. Gadia, S. Jajodia, A. Segev, and R. Snodgrass, *Temporal Databases: Theory, Design and Implementation,* Benjamin Cummings, Redwood City, CA (1993).

[**Taylor and Frank 1976**]  R. W. Taylor and R. L. Frank, "CODASYL Data Base Management Systems," *ACM Computing Surveys*, Volume 8, Number 1 (March 1976), pages 67–103

[**Tendick and Matloff 1994**]  P. Tendick and N. Matloff, "A Modified Random Perturbation Method for Database Security," *ACM Transactions on Database Systems*, Volume 19, Number 1 (March 1994), pages 47–63.

[**Teorey and Fry 1982**]  T. J. Teorey and J. P. Fry, *Design of Database Structures*, Prentice-Hall, Englewood Cliffs, NJ (1982).

[**Teorey et al. 1986**]  T. J. Teorey, D. Yang, and J. P. Fry, "A Logical Design Methodology for Relational Databases Using the Extended Entity-Relationship Model," *ACM Computing Surveys*, Volume 18, Number 2 (June 1986), pages 197–222.

[**Thomas 1979**]  R. H. Thomas, "A Majority Consensus Approach to Concurrency Control," *ACM Transactions on Database Systems*, Volume 4, Number 2 (June 1979), pages 180–219.

[**Thomas 1996**]  S. A. Thomas, *IPng and the TCP/IP Protocols: Implementing the Next Generation Internet*, John Wiley and Sons, New York, NY (1996).

[**Thomas and Sandhu 1996**]  R. K. Thomas and R. S. Sandhu, "A Trusted Subject Architecture for Multilevel Secure Object-Oriented Databases," *IEEE Transactions on Knowledge and Data Engineering,* Volume 8, Number 1 (February 1996), pages 16–31.

[**Todd 1976**]  S. J. P. Todd, "The Peterlee Relational Test Vehicle - A System Overview," *IBM Systems Journal*, Volume 15, Number 4 (1976), pages 285–308.

[**Tomasic et al. 1994**]  A. Tomasic, H. Garcia-Molina, and K. Shoens, "Incremental Updates of Inverted Lists for Text Document Retrieval," *Proceedings of the ACM SIGMOD International Conference on Management of Data* (1994), pages 289–300.

[**Traiger 1982**]  I. L. Traiger, "Virtual Memory for Database Systems," *ACM SIGOPS Operating Systems Review*, Volume 16, Number 4 (1982), pages 26–48.

[**Traiger 1983**]  I. L. Traiger, "Trends in Systems Aspects of Database Management," Research Report RJ3845, IBM Research Laboratory, San Jose, CA (1983).

[**Traiger et al. 1982**]  I. L. Traiger, J. N. Gray, C. A. Galtieri, and B. G. Lindsay, "Transactions and Consistency in Distributed Database Management Systems," *ACM Transactions on Database Systems*, Volume 7, Number 3 (September 1982), pages 323–342.

[**Tremblay and Sorenson 1985**]  J.-P. Tremblay and P. G. Sorenson, *The Theory and Practice of Compiler Writing*, McGraw-Hill, New York, NY (1985).

[**Trivedi et al. 1980**]  K. S. Trivedi, R. A. Wagner, and T. M. Sigmon, "Optimal Selection of CPU Speed, Device Capacities and File Assignment," *Journal of the ACM*, Volume 7, Number 3 (July 1980), pages 457–473.

[**Tsichritzis and Lochovsky 1976**] D. C. Tsichritzis and F. H. Lochovsky, "Hierarchical Data-base Management: A Survey," *ACM Computing Surveys*, Volume 8, Number 1 (March 1976), pages 67–103.

[**Tsou and Fischer 1982**] D.-M. Tsou and P. Fischer, "Decomposition of a Relation Scheme into Boyce-Codd Normal Form," *ACM SIGACT News*, Volume 14, Number 3 (1982), pages 23–29.

[**Tsukuda et al. 1992**] S. Tsukuda, M. Nakano, M. Kitsuregawa, and M. Takagi, "Parallel Hash Join on Shared-Everything Multiprocessor," *Proceedings of the Eighth International Conference on Data Engineering* (1992).

[**Tsur and Zaniolo 1986**] S. Tsur and C. Zaniolo, "LDL: A Logic-Based Data-Language," *Proceedings of the International Conference on Very Large Data Bases* (1986), pages 33–41.

[**Tuzhilin and Clifford 1990**] A. Tuzhilin and J. Clifford, "A Temporal Relational Algebra as a Basis for Temporal Relational Completeness," *Proceedings of the International Conference on Very Large Data Bases* (1990), pages 13–23.

[**UniSQL 1991**] UniSQL Inc., *UniSQL/X Database Management System User's Manual: Release 1.2*, (1991).

[**U.S. Dept. of Commerce 1977**] United States Department of Commerce, *Data Encryption Standard*, National Bureau of Standards Federal Information Processing Standards Publication 46 (1977).

[**U.S. Dept. of Commerce 1992**] United States Department of Commerce, *Database Language SQL*, National Bureau of Standards Federal Information Processing Standards Publication 127-2 (1992).

[**U.S. Dept. of Defense 1985**] United States Department of Defense, "Department of Defense Trusted Computer System Evaluation Criteria," National Computer Security Center (1985).

[**Ullman 1988**] J. D. Ullman, *Principles of Database and Knowledge-base Systems*, Volume I, Computer Science Press, Rockville, MD (1988).

[**Ullman 1989**] J. D. Ullman, *Principles of Database and Knowledge-base Systems*, Volume II, Computer Science Press, Rockville, MD (1989).

[**Unger et al. 1984**] E. A. Unger, P. S. Fisher, and J. Slonim (Editors), *Advances in Data Base Management*, Volume 2, John Wiley and Sons, New York, NY (1984).

[**Valduriez and Gardarin 1989**] P. Valduriez and G. Gardarin, *Analysis and Comparison of Relational Database Systems*, Addison Wesley, Reading, MA (1989).

[**Vandewalle 1992**] J. Vandewalle (Editor), *The State of the Art in Computer Systems and Software Engineering*, Kluwer Academic Publishers (1992).

[**Van Gucht 1987**] D. Van Gucht, "On the Expressive Power of the Extended Relational Algebra for the Unnormalized Relational Model," *Proceedings of the ACM SIGACT-SIGMOD-SIGART Symposium on Principles of Database Systems* (1987), pages 302–312.

[**Verhofstad 1978**] J. S. M. Verhofstad, "Recovery Techniques for Database Systems," *ACM Computing Surveys*, Volume 10, Number 2 (June 1978), pages 167–195.

[**Wächter and Reuter 1992**] H. Wächter and A. Reuter, "The ConTract Model," in *Database Transaction Models for Advanced Applications*, Morgan Kaufmann Publishers, Inc. (1992).

[**Walton et al. 1991**] C. Walton, A. Dale, and R. Jenevein, "A Taxonomy and Performance Model of Data Skew Effects in Parallel Joins," *Proceedings of the International Conference on Very Large Data Bases* (1991).

[**Weddell 1992**] G. Weddell, "Reasoning About Functional Dependencies Generalized for Semantic Data Models," *ACM Transactions on Database Systems*, Volume 17, Number 1 (March 1992).

[**Weihl and Liskov 1990**] W. Weihl and B. Liskov, "Implementation of Resilient, Atomic Data Types," in [**Zdonik and Maier 1990**], pages 332–344.

[**Weikum 1991**] G. Weikum, "Principles and Realization Strategies of Multilevel Transaction Management," *ACM Transactions on Database Systems,* Volume 16, Number 1 (March 1991).

[**Weikum and Schek 1984**] G. Weikum and H. J. Schek, "Architectural Issues of Transaction Management in Multi-Level Systems," *Proceedings of the International Conference on Very Large Data Bases* (1984), pages 454–465.

[**Weikum et al. 1990**] G. Weikum, C. Hasse, P. Broessler, and P. Muth, "Multi-Level Recovery," *Proceedings of the ACM SIGACT-SIGMOD-SIGART Symposium on Principles of Database Systems* (1990), pages 109–123.

[**Weldon 1981**] J. Weldon, *Data Base Administration*, Plenum Press, New York, NY (1981).

[**Whang and Krishnamurthy 1990**] K. Whang and R. Krishnamurthy, "Query Optimization in a Memory-Resident Domain Relational Calculus Database System," *ACM Transactions on Database Systems,* Volume 15, Number 1 (March 1990), pages 67–95.

[**Whang et al. 1982**] K. Whang, G. Wiederhold, and D. Sagalowicz, "Physical Design of Network Model Databases Using the Property of Separability," *Proceedings of the International Conference on Very Large Data Bases* (1982), pages 98–107.

[**White and DeWitt 1992**] S. J. White and D. J. DeWitt, "A Performance Study of Alternative Object Faulting and Pointer Swizzling Strategies," *Proceedings of the International Conference on Very Large Data Bases* (1992).

[**White and DeWitt 1994**] S. J. White and D. J. DeWitt, "QuickStore: A High Performance Mapped Object Store," *Proceedings of the ACM SIGMOD International Conference on the Management of Data* (1994).

[**Widom and Finkelstein 1990**] J. Widom and S. Finkelstein, "Set-Oriented Production Rules in Relational Database Systems," *Proceedings of the ACM SIGMOD International Conference on Management of Data* (1990).

[**Widom et al. 1991**] J. Widom, R. Cochrane, and B. Lindsay, "Implementing Set-Oriented Production Rules as an Extension to Starburst," *Proceedings of the International Conference on Very Large Data Bases* (1991).

[**Wiederhold 1983**] G. Wiederhold, *Database Design*, Second Edition, McGraw-Hill, New York, NY (1983).

[**Wilkinson et al. 1990**] K. Wilkinson, P. Lyngbaek, and W. Hasan, "The Iris Architecture and Implementation," *IEEE Transactions on Knowledge and Data Engineering* (March 1990), pages 63–75.

[**Wilson 1990**] P. R. Wilson, "Pointer Swizzling at Page Fault Time: Efficiently Supporting Huge Address Spaces on Standard Hardware," Technical Report UIC-EECS-90-6, University of Illinois at Chicago (December 1990).

[**Wilschut et al. 1995**] A. N. Wilschut, J. Flokstra, and P. M. Apers, "Parallel Evaluation of Multi-Join Queues," *Proceedings of the ACM SIGMOD International Conference on Management of Data* (1995), pages 115–126.

[**Winslett et al. 1994**] M. Winslett, K. Smith, and X. Qian, "Formal Query Languages for Secure Relational Databases," *ACM Transactions on Database Systems*, Volume 19, Number 4 (December 1994), pages 626–662.

[**Wipfler 1987**] A. J. Wipfler, *CICS: Application Development and Programming*, Macmillan Publishing, New York, NY (1987).

[**Wolf 1991**] J. Wolf, "An Effective Algorithm for Parallelizing Hash Joins in the Presence of Data Skew," *Proceedings of the Seventh International Conference on Data Engineering* (1991).

[**Wong 1977**] E. Wong, "Retrieving Dispersed Data from SDD-1: A System for Distributed Databases," *Proceedings of the Berkeley Workshop on Distributed Data Management and Computer Networks* (1977), pages 217–235.

[**Wong 1983**] E. Wong, "Dynamic Rematerialization-Processing Distributed Queries Using Redundant Data," *IEEE Transactions on Software Engineering*, Volume SE-9, Number 3 (May 1983), pages 228–232.

[**Wong and Mylopoulos 1977**] H. K. T. Wong and J. Mylopoulos, "Two Views of Data Semantics: A Survey of Data Models in Artificial Intelligence and Database Management," *INFOR*, Volume 15 (1977), pages 344–383.

[**Wong and Youssefi 1976**] E. Wong and K. Youssefi, "Decomposition-A Strategy for Query Processing," *ACM Transactions on Database Systems*, Volume 1, Number 3 (September 1976), pages 223–241.

[**X/Open 1991**] *X/Open Snapshot: X/Open DTP: XA Interface*, X/Open Company, Ltd. (1991).

[**X/Open 1992**] *Structured Query Language (SQL): CAE specification C201* (September 1992).

[**X/Open 1993**] *X/Open Data Management: SQL Call Level Interface (CLI)*, X/Open Company, Ltd. (1993).

[**Yannakakis 1981**] M. Yannakakis, "Issues of Correctness in Database Concurrency Control by Locking," *Proceedings of the ACM Symposium on the Theory of Computing* (1981), pages 363–367.

[**Yannakakis et al. 1979**] M. Yannakakis, C. H. Papadimitriou, and H. T. Kung, "Locking Protocols: Safety and Freedom from Deadlock," *Proceedings of the IEEE Symposium on the Foundations of Computer Science* (1979), pages 286–297.

[**Yao 1979a**] A. C. Yao, "A Note on a Conjecture of Kam and Ullman Concerning Statistical Databases," *Information Processing Letters* (1979).

[**Yao 1979b**] S. Yao, "Optimization of Query Evaluation Algorithms," *ACM Transactions on Database Systems*, Volume 4, Number 2 (June 1979), pages 133–155

[**Zaniolo 1976**] C. Zaniolo, "Analysis and Design of Relational Schemata for Database Systems," Ph.D. thesis, Department of Computer Science, University of California, Los Angeles, CA (1976).

[**Zaniolo 1979a**]  C. Zaniolo, "Design of Relational Views over Network Schemas," *Proceedings of the ACM SIGMOD International Conference on the Management of Data* (1979), pages 179–190.

[**Zaniolo 1979b**]  C. Zaniolo, "Multimodel External Schemas for CODASYL Data Base Management Systems," in [**Bracchi and Nijssen 1979**], pages 157–176.

[**Zaniolo 1983**]  C. Zaniolo, "The Database Language GEM," *Proceedings of the ACM SIGMOD International Conference on the Management of Data* (1983), pages 207–218.

[**Zdonik and Maier 1990**]  S. Zdonik and D. Maier, *Readings in Object-Oriented Database Systems*, Morgan Kaufmann Publishers, Inc., San Mateo, CA (1990).

[**Zeller and Gray 1990**]  H. Zeller and J. Gray, "An Adaptive Hash Join Algorithm for Multiuser Environments," *Proceedings of the International Conference on Very Large Data Bases* (1990), pages 186–197.

[**Zhang and Mendelzon 1983**]  Z. Q. Zhang and A. O. Mendelzon, "A Graphical Query Language for Entity-Relationship Databases," in [**Davis et al. 1983**], pages 441–448.

[**Zhuge et al. 1995**]  Y. Zhuge, H. Garcia-Molina, J. Hammer, and J. Widom, "View Maintenance in a Warehousing Environment," *Proceedings of the ACM SIGMOD International Conference on the Management of Data* (1995), pages 316–327.

[**Zloof 1977**]  M. M. Zloof, "Query-by-Example: A Data Base Language," *IBM Systems Journal*, Volume 16, Number 4 (1977), pages 324–343.

# INDEX